Chambers Student Guide

CAREERS IN THE LAW

2014

Introduction

Published by Chambers and Partners Publishing
(a division of Orbach & Chambers Ltd)
39-41 Parker Street, London, WC2B 5PQ
Tel: (020) 7606 8844 Fax: (020) 7831 5662
email: info@ChambersandPartners.co.uk
www.ChambersandPartners.com

Our thanks to the many students, trainees,
pupils, solicitors, barristers and graduate recruitment personnel who
assisted us in our research. Also to the researchers of Chambers UK 2013
from which all firm rankings are drawn.
Copyright © 2013 Michael Chambers and
Orbach & Chambers Ltd

ISBN: 978-0-85514-317-6

Publisher: Michael Chambers
Editor: Antony Cooke
Deputy Editors: Sam Morris, Sara Veale
Contributing editor: Rich Simmons
Writers: Alice Saville, Anna Winter, Ben McCarthy, Elizabeth Sands,
Francesca Wright, Haleema Mansoor, Jack Watkins, James Pulford,
Natalie Stanton, Paul Rance, Phil Roe, Rich Simmons
A-Z Co-ordinator: Tom Hewitt
Production: Jasper John, John Osborne
Business Development Manager: Brad D. Sirott
Business Development Team: Bianca Maio,
Catriona Howie, Liz Brennan, Neil Murphy, Richard Ramsay
Proofreaders: John Bradley, Nicholas Widdows,
Sally McGonigal

So you want to be a lawyer...

Welcome to the 2014 edition of the *Chambers Student Guide* to careers in the law. We've written this book to give you the information, tools and confidence to help you made a sound career decision.

This guide is the only publication to offer these four key ingredients.

- The True Picture: an insight into the training schemes at 115 law firms, based on in-depth interviews with thousands of trainees. The trainees were selected by us, not by their law firms, and they spoke to us freely and frankly under the protection of anonymity.
- Chambers Reports: a look at life inside 29 barristers' chambers. These reports were written after visits to each of the sets and interviews with pupils, barristers and clerks.
- Law school reviews: compiled after feedback from students who have completed courses at each of the schools, plus interviews with course directors.
- Additional online advice and information in key areas, including details of the recruitment process at all our featured firms with tips from recruiters and trainees and in-depth interviews with managing partners and training partners detailing their firms' strategies for the future.

Chambers and Partners publishes guides to the legal professions around the world. You will benefit enormously from using our *Chambers UK* guide to refine your search for a law firm or chambers to train with. The best performing firms and sets in over 65 areas of practice are identified by way of league tables in *Chambers UK*, and you can get all this information online, for free, by visiting www.chambersandpartners.com.

All the guides we publish have one thing in common: they are independent. In a market flooded with publications for law students we take great pride in this fact. No one's money influences what we say about them.

This book could be the most useful thing you read this year, so get stuck in, and we wish you great success for your future career.

The *Student Guide* team
October 2013

Introduction

Contents

This guide, if used properly, can greatly ease the process of pursuing a career in the law

Use this book in conjunction with www.chambersandpartners.com to find your perfect traineeship or pupillage

Our Editorial Team

Antony Cooke
Student Editor. Graduated from Durham University in Russian & French. Taught English at St. Petersburg State University. Previously worked at Michelin, and at PricewaterhouseCoopers as an audit associate in Investment Management. Fluent in Russian and French.

Sam Morris
Deputy Editor. Graduated from the University of Leiden, The Netherlands with a First in Political Science in 2008 and from the London School of Economics with an MSc in Comparative Politics in 2009. Has worked for the Dutch Ministry of Foreign Affairs. Speaks Dutch and German.

Sara Veale
Deputy Editor. Graduated Magna Cum Laude from the University of North Carolina at Charlotte with degrees in English and Dance, and recently completed an MA in English at University College London. She is a published poet and currently freelances as a literary critic.

Paul Rance
Senior Researcher. Graduated from Exeter University with a First in English Literature, and also spent a year abroad at the University of Toronto to read Canadian literature. He completed his MA in English at UCL in 2010.

Alice Saville
Graduated from Oxford University with a First in English, then completed an MA in Medieval and Renaissance Studies at UCL. She also writes theatre criticism and features for several arts publications.

Anna Winter
Graduated with a BA in English Literature from Balliol College, Oxford. Took journalism qualifications following internships at The Observer and The New Statesman magazine.

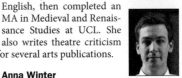

Ben McCarthy
Graduated from the University of Reading with a First in History, and also presented a paper at the International Children of War Conference in 2011. Currently writes for a film review site in his spare time.

Francesca Wright
Read Classics at University College London. Recently completed GDL and LPC at the College of Law.

Jack Watkins
Graduated with a BA Honours degree in History from the University of Sheffield in 2010.

James Pulford
Graduated from the University of Manchester in 2012 with a BA in English Literature and an MA in Creative Writing. Also writes fiction, drama and criticism.

Phil Roe
Deputy Editor of Chambers Associate. Joined Chambers & Partners in 2007 from a global executive search firm, where he advised Private Equity clients. Has written extensively for both Chambers Associate and the Chambers Student Guide. Graduated with an MA in English from Oxford University, and is a theatre critic for London-based newspapers in his free time.

Becoming a Lawyer

Law fair strategies:

Depending on which approach you take, you'll get very different things out of your law fair experience. What sort of law fair attendee are you?

1. The magpie: You're passive and blend into the crowd. The most you'll get out of the day is a few pens, plastic bags and chocolate bars.

2. The weight-lifter: You pick up all the literature you can. You'll have sore arms and a mountain of material to plough through at a later date... if you ever get round to it.

3. The explorer: You have a rough idea where you want to work and which areas you'd like to specialise in. This is your chance to scout around, have a chat, and hone in on those firms that really take your fancy.

4. The interrogator: You've done your research, and have pinpointed which firms you're interested in. Now's your chance to get the inside scoop on the things that matter to you. What pro bono work can trainees do? Are there any diversity initiatives at the firm? If you're lucky, you might even make some contacts you can mention on the dreaded application form.

Calendar of events 2013

Law Fairs

October 2013

16	City University; University of Kent
23	University of Cambridge
24	University of Nottingham; University of York
28	Queen Mary
29	De Montfort University
30	SOAS
31	University of Hull

November 2013

5	Cardiff University; Northumbria University; London School of Economics; University of Leicester
6	University of Salford; Queen's University, Belfast; University of Northampton; University of Sussex & University of Brighton; University of Reading; University of Portsmouth; University of Bristol
7	University of East Anglia; University of Leeds; University of Bristol; London School of Economics
9	University of Oxford
11	UCL; Newcastle University
12	UCL; University of Warwick
13	University of Bradford; University of Liverpool; University of Exeter
14	University of Essex
19	University of Manchester
20	University of Birmingham; University of Sheffield & Sheffield Hallam; Lancaster University
21	University of Central Lancashire; University of Southampton
22	King's College, London
23	King's College, London
24	King's College, London
26	University of Durham
27	University of Durham

Vacation Scheme Deadlines

October 2013

31	Allen & Overy (winter – graduates and finalists)
	Jones Day (winter)
	Norton Rose Fulbright (winter)

November 2013

3	Stephenson Harwood (winter)
15	Cleary Gottlieb Steen & Hamilton (winter)

December 2013

31	Bird & Bird
	Jones Day (spring)

"Don't be afraid to let loose with your questions at law fairs, particularly when you're talking to representatives from a firm you're interested in. The answers can reveal a lot about a firm's culture and what's expected of its employees."

Trainee

January 2014

6	Freshfields Bruckhaus Deringer
12	Skadden
14	Allen & Overy (summer – penultimate year under-graduates)
15	Kirkland & Ellis
	Mishcon de Reya
	Nabarro
28	Cleary Gottlieb Steen & Hamilton (spring and summer)
31	Addleshaw Goddard
	Bond Dickinson (Easter and summer)
	Clyde & Co
	CMS Cameron McKenna
	Covington & Burling
	David Polk & Wardwell
	Dechert
	Edwards Wildman Palmer
	Eversheds
	Farrer & Co
	Gateley
	Hill Dickinson
	Irwin Mitchell
	Jones Day (summer)
	Kennedys
	Lawrence Graham
	Macfarlanes
	Maclay Murray & Spens
	Mills & Reeve
	Morgan Lewis & Bockius
	Muckle
	Norton Rose Fulbright (summer)
	Olswang
	O'Melveny & Myers
	PwC Legal
	RPC
	SJ Berwin (Easter and summer)
	Squire Sanders
	Stephenson Harwood (spring and summer)
	Stevens & Bolton
	Sullivan & Cromwell
	Taylor Wessing
	Travers Smith
	Walker Morris
	Watson, Farley & Williams
	White & Case
	Withers
	Wragge & Co

Vacation Scheme Deadlines

Feburary 2014

31	Capsticks Holman Fenwick Willan
24	SGH Martineau
28	Penningtons Vinson & Elkins Ward Hadaway Wedlake Bell

Feburary 2014

31	Capsticks Holman Fenwick Willan

March 2014

31	Ashfords Lester Aldridge

April 2014

28	Foot Anstey

"Make sure anything you put in your application can be substantiated. It's awful to catch people out."

Trainee

Training Contract Deadlines

January 2014

14	Allen & Overy (non-law)
15	Herbert Smith Freehills (for finalists/graduates) Nabarro
31	Bristows (February interviews)

March 2014

31	Ashfords (for vac scheme and training contract) Dentons (non-law) Simmons & Simmons (for non-law finalists/graduates)

April 2014

30	Hogan Lovells (non-law)

May 2014

31	B P Collins (for 2015) Kingsley Napley (for 2015)

June 2014

1	Foot Anstey
27	Orrick, Herrington & Sutcliffe
30	Boodle Hatfield (graduates and non-law) Brabners Davenport Lyons Lester Aldridge Veale Wasbrough Vizards Winckworth Sherwood

July 2014

1	Gordons Michelmores
13	Freeth Cartwright
15	Mishcon de Reya
31	Addleshaw Goddard (for September 2016 and March 2017) Ashurst Bingham McCutchen Berwin Leighton Paisner (for 2016 and 2017) Bircham Dyson Bell Bird & Bird Bond Dickinson Boodle Hatfield (law) BPE Solicitors Bristows (August interviews) Charles Russell Cleary Gottlieb Clyde & Co CMS Cameron McKenna Covington & Burling Curtis, Mallet-Prevost, Davis Polk & Wardwell Dechert Dentons (law) DLA Piper DWF Edwards Wildman Palmer Eversheds Farrer & Co Forbes Gateley Gordons Government Legal Service Harbottle & Lewis Herbert Smith Freehills (penultimate year students) Hill Dickinson Hogan Lovells (law) Holman Fenwick Willan Irwin Mitchell K&L Gates Kennedys (for 2015) Kirkland & Ellis Latham & Watkins Lawrence Graham Macfarlanes Mayer Brown	McDermott Will & Emery (for 2015) Memery Crystal Mills & Reeve Morgan Lewis & Bockius Muckle Norton Rose Fulbright Olswang Osborne Clarke Paul Hastings Penningtons PwC Legal Reed Smith (for 2016 and 2017) RPC SGH Martineau Shearman & Sterling Sheridans Shoosmiths Simmons & Simmons (law) SJ Berwin Skadden Speechly Bircham Squire Sanders Stephenson Harwood Stevens & Bolton Sullivan & Cromwell Thomas Cooper TLT Travers Smith Trethowans Vinson & Elkins Walker Morris Ward Hadaway Watson, Farley & Williams Wedlake Bell Weil, Gotshal & Manges White & Case Wilsons Withers Wragge & Co

Training Contract Deadlines

August 2014

1	Trowers & Hamlins
11	Capsticks
31	Hewitsons Maclay Murray & Spens (London office)

"Proofread your application over and over. Just a single typo could mean you don't get invited to an interview."

Trainee

What kind of lawyer do you want to be?

Let's start with one of the most basic questions – do you want to be a barrister or a solicitor?

Barrister

Ask a solicitor about the key difference between the two sides of the profession and they'll probably tell you it comes down to one thing: ego. At first glance the role of a barrister certainly looks a lot cooler than that of a solicitor. You know the deal – it's all about striding into courtrooms, robes flowing, tense moments waiting for missing witnesses and razor-sharp cross-examinations. Glamorous? It's downright sexy! The truth, of course, is that there's a great deal more to it than looking good in a wig…

Essentially barristers do three things:

- Appear in court to represent others
- Give specialised legal advice in person or in writing
- Draft court documents

The proportion of time spent on each depends on the type of law the barrister practises. Criminal barristers are in court most of the time, often with only an hour or two's notice of the details of their cases. By contrast, commercial barristers spend most of their time in chambers, writing tricky opinions and advising in conference on complicated legal points.

Barristers must display the skill and clarity to make complex or arcane legal arguments accessible to lay clients, juries and the judiciary. Their style of argument must be clear and persuasive, both in court and on paper. It has been some time since barristers have had exclusive rights of audience in the courts, though. Solicitors can train to become accredited advocates in even the higher courts. This encroachment hasn't been an utter disaster for the Bar, although solicitor advocates are handling a lot more of the most straightforward cases. When it comes to more complicated and lengthy matters, barristers are usually still briefed to do the advocacy, not least because this is often the most cost-effective way of managing a case. As a point of interest, solicitor advocates do not wear the wig and gown and are referred to as 'my friend' rather than 'my learned friend'.

Solicitors value barristers' detailed knowledge of the litigation process and their ability to assess and advise on the merits and demerits of a case. A solicitor will pay good money for 'counsel's opinion'. Certainly, in the area of commercial law a barrister must understand the client's perspective and use their legal knowledge to develop solutions that make business or common sense as well as legal sense. If you think a career as a barrister will allow you to rise above the rigours and scraping of modern-day capitalism, think again.

Of the UK's 15,600 or so barristers, over 12,700 are self-employed. This is why you hear the expression 'the independent Bar'. The remainder are employed by companies, public bodies or law firms, and they make up 'the employed Bar'. To prevent independence from turning into isolation, barristers, like badgers, work in groups called 'sets', sharing premises and professional managers, etc. Barristers do not work for their sets, just at their premises, and as 'tenants' they contribute to the upkeep of their chambers. A percentage of their earnings also goes to pay their clerks and administrators. Unlike employed barristers and solicitors, those at the independent Bar get no sickness pay, holiday pay, maternity leave or monthly salary. What they do get is a good accountant. To enter practice, LLB grads need to complete the Bar Professional Training Course (BPTC) before starting a much sought-after year of 'pupillage'. Non-law grads need to first complete the Graduate Diploma in Law (GDL) before taking the BPTC. After the pupillage, hopefully, the set you're with will then take you on as a tenant, though you may have to look elsewhere. Once tenancy is established, you're home free (well, except for the gruelling schedule, high pressure, concerns over how much you'll earn, dedicated wig maintenance…).

The competition to become a barrister is truly fierce. The main difficulty is that there are many more aspiring barristers than can possibly achieve a career at the Bar. If you want to know more, take a look at the final section of this book, where we provide details on the recruitment process, practice areas, terminology and the difficulties that aspiring barristers may encounter. The **Chambers Reports** give invaluable insight into the lives of pupils and junior barristers at some of the best sets. The Bar's professional body is the Bar Council, and it is regulated by the Bar Standards Board.

Solicitor

Most lawyers qualify as solicitors: in fact, there are almost eight times as many solicitors as barristers in the UK. Their role is to provide legal services directly to lay clients, who could be individuals, companies (private or public) or other bodies. In short, clients come to solicitors for guidance on how to deal with their business or personal proposals and problems. These could be anything from drafting a will to defending a murder charge or buying a multibillion-pound business. The solicitor advises on the steps needed to proceed and then manages the case or the deal for the client until its conclusion. They will bring in a barrister if and when a second opinion or specialist advocacy is needed. The solicitor's role is much more like that of a project manager than the barrister's. According to the Law Society, there are 128,800 solicitors in England and Wales, with practising certificates issued annually by the Solicitors Regulation Authority (SRA). Over 87,800 of them are in 'private practice' in solicitors' firms, and of those 44,000 are employed in London. Many thousands work in-house for companies, charities or public authorities.

After an undergraduate degree, law school beckons. Law grads need to take the Legal Practice Course (LPC). Non-law grads must first complete the Graduate Diploma in Law (GDL) before being eligible for the LPC. Next comes the practical training. The most common way of qualifying is by undertaking a two-year training contract with a firm of solicitors, law centre, in-house legal team or public body. Much of the rest of this book deals with the nature of training contracts at different firms and how to procure one. The SRA's website gives all the fine detail you could wish for as to the requirements for training. Upon satisfactory completion of their training contract and the mandatory Professional Skills Course (PSC), a person can be admitted to the roll of those eligible to practise as a solicitor and apply for a practising certificate. They are then fully qualified.

Where people often trip up is not being fully aware of when they should apply for a training contract. Most big employers recruit two years in advance. If you are studying law and you want to work in a commercial firm, the crucial time for research and applications is early on during your penultimate year at uni. If you are a non-law student intending to proceed straight to a GDL 'conversion course' before going to a commercial firm, you'll have to juggle exams and career considerations in your final year. Smaller firms and high-street practices often recruit closer to the start date, and often after a trial period of working as a paralegal.

Larger commercial firms more often than not cover the cost of their future trainees' law school fees and other basic expenses. However, for students hoping to practise in smaller firms financial assistance is far from likely, and this can make law school a costly and uncertain endeavour.

Needless to say, your choice of firm will shape the path of your career. A firm's clients, its work and its reputation will determine not only the experience you gain but probably also your future marketability as a lawyer. At Chambers and Partners, we've made it our business to know who does what, how well they do it and what it might be like working at a particular firm. Our parent publication *Chambers UK* will also be an incredibly useful resource for you. Its league tables show which firms command greatest respect from clients and other professionals in different areas of practice right across the country. You can search the entire thing for free at www.chambersandpartners.com and use it to help create a shortlist of firms to apply to.

In the **True Picture** section of this guide we've profiled 115 firms in England and Wales. Our goal is to help you understand what kind of firm might suit you and the kind of work you can expect to undertake when you get there. It is the product of many hundreds of interviews with trainees and we think you'll really benefit from making it your regular bedtime reading or favourite bookmark on your smartphone. We've also interviewed recruiters, training partners and managing partners to give you the lowdown on firms' business models, plans for the future and recruitment strategies. You should also read through the **Solicitors' Practice Areas** section of this guide to gain an understanding of what's involved in different fields of practice.

Different types of law firm

There are nearly 11,000 private practice firms in England and Wales. All offer a very different experience. The following will help you drill down.

London: magic circle

The membership of this club traditionally extends to Allen & Overy, Clifford Chance, Freshfields Bruckhaus Deringer, Linklaters, and Slaughter and May. To those for whom bigger is better (bigger deals, bigger money, bigger staff numbers), this is the place to be. Corporate and finance work dominates these firms, as do international big-bucks business clients. By organising their training on a massive scale, these firms can offer seemingly unlimited office facilities, great perks, overseas postings and excellent formal training sessions. Although these five giants top many lists, not least for revenue and partner profits, consider carefully whether they'd top yours. Training in a magic circle firm is CV gold but not suited to everyone. One factor to consider is the requirement to work really long hours to keep profits fat and international clients happy. A great camaraderie develops among trainees, but be prepared to not see your other friends too often…

London: large commercial

The top ten City of London firms (including the magic circle) offer roughly 800 traineeships between them each year, representing approximately 16% of all new training contracts registered with the SRA. In terms of day-to-day trainee experiences, there's not such a huge difference between the magic circle and the so-called 'silver circle' firms such as Ashurst, Herbert Smith and a few others. Training contracts at these chasing-pack firms are strongly flavoured with corporate and finance deals and, again, international work. The salaries match those paid by the magic circle, which is only fair given that many of the lawyers work equally hard. Many of these firms have recently enlarged further thanks to mergers with large US, Canadian and Australian firms: Norton Rose Fulbright (formerly Norton Rose) and Hogan Lovells (formerly Lovells) are just two examples.

London: American firms

Since the 1970s, there has been a steady stream of US firms crossing the Atlantic to take their place in the UK market. Currently around 40 of them offer training contracts to would-be UK solicitors, with new schemes popping up all the time. We'd suggest staying eagle-eyed if you've a thing for stars and stripes. At the risk of overgeneralising, these firms are characterised by international work (usually corporate or finance-led), small offices, more intimate training programmes and very long hours. On the other hand they usually give trainees a good amount of responsibility. Famously, many of them pay phenomenally high salaries. Lawyers at the hotshot US firms frequently work opposite magic circle lawyers on deals; indeed many of them were previously magic circle and top-ten firm partners or associates. We've also noticed that since these firms' training contracts are often small, many don't look much further than Oxbridge and London for their trainees: they can afford to be selective.

As we've already mentioned, UK and US firms are increasingly merging with each other, and with Aussie and Canadian firms, further blurring the definition of which are 'American' and which are not. Some firms are quite happy to be labelled as American; others prefer to be described as 'international'. Look at their websites to get an idea of which term to use.

London: mid-sized commercial

Just like their bigger cousins, these firms are mostly dedicated to business law and business clients. Generally, they don't require trainees to spend quite so many hours in the office; however, some of the most successful mid-sizers – eg Macfarlanes and Travers Smith – give the big boys a run for their money in terms of profitability. Generally, the size of deals and cases in these firms means trainees can do much more than just administrative tasks. The atmosphere is a bit more intimate than at the giants of the City, with the greater likelihood of working for partners directly and, arguably, more scope to stand out within the trainee group. You shouldn't expect such an international emphasis to all the work.

London: smaller commercial

For those who don't mind taking home a slightly more modest pay cheque in exchange for better hours, these firms are a great choice. After all, money isn't everything. There are dozens of small commercial firms dotted around London: Wedlake Bell and Boodle Hatfield are just two examples. Usually these firms will be 'full-service', although some may have developed on the back of one or two particularly strong practice areas or via a reputation in certain industries. Real estate is commonly a big deal at these firms. Along with commercial work, a good number offer private client services to wealthier people. At firms like these you usually get great exposure to partners and there's less risk of losing contact with the outside world.

Niche firms

London is awash with firms specialising in areas as diverse as aviation, media, insurance, shipping, family, intellectual property, sport… you name it, there's a firm for it. Niche firms have also sprouted in areas of the country with high demand for a particular service. How about marine law in Plymouth? If you are absolutely certain that you want to specialise in a particular field – especially if you have already worked in a relevant industry – a niche firm is an excellent choice. You need to be able to back up your passion with hard evidence of your commitment, however. Many of these firms also cover other practice areas, but if any try to woo you by talking at length about their other areas of work, ask some searching questions.

Regional firms

Many of you will agree that there is more to life than the Big Smoke. There are some very fine regional firms acting for top-notch clients on cases and deals the City firms would snap up in a heartbeat. There is also international work going on outside the capital. The race for training contracts in the biggest of these firms is just as competitive as in the City. Some regional firms are even more discerning than their London counterparts in that applicants may have to demonstrate a long-term commitment to living in the area. Understandable, as they hardly want to shell out for training only to see their qualifiers flit off to the capital. Smaller regional firms tend to focus on the needs of regional clients and would therefore suit anyone who wants to become an integral part of their local business community. Salaries are lower outside London, in some cases significantly so, but so is the cost of living. There's a perception that working outside London means a chummier atmosphere and more time for the gym/pub/ family, but do bear in mind that the biggest and most ambitious regional players will expect hours that aren't so dissimilar to firms with an EC postcode.

National and multi-site firms

Multi-site firms are necessarily massive operations, some of them with office networks spanning the length and breadth of the country and overseas. To give you just two examples, Eversheds has nine branches in England and Wales plus many overseas; DLA Piper has six in England and many more overseas. These firms attract students who want to do bigger-ticket work outside London – a sometimes unwelcome consequence of which is doing London levels of work for a lower salary. Some of the multi-site firms allow trainees to stay in one office, whereas others expect them to move around. Make sure you know the firm's policy or you could end up having a long-distance relationship with friends, family and your significant other while you move to a new town for a few months or are saddled with a punishing commute. The work on offer is mostly commercial, although some private client experience may be available.

General practice/small firms

If you're put off by the corporate jargon, City-slicking lifestyle and big-business attitude of some of the firms in this guide, then the small firm might be just what you're after. If you want to grow up fast as a lawyer and see how the law actually affects individuals and the community in which you practise, then a high-street firm may be the best option for you. We provide a lot more information on training at this type of outfit on our website.

Larger firms may take up to half a dozen or so trainees a year; the smallest will recruit on an occasional basis. It is in this part of the profession where salaries are the lowest. The SRA's minimum required salary for trainees is to be scrapped as of 1 August 2014. From that date, employers will only have to adhere to the national minimum wage, currently £6.31 per hour. Many high-street firms depend on legal aid funding and anyone thinking of entering this sector should be aware of the dramatic cuts being made to public funding of legal services. We discuss this in considerable detail on our website.

What is a training contract?

Basically, a training contract is the step between your academic life and your life as a qualified solicitor.

Most training contracts are taken on a full-time basis and last two years. Part-time options are much rarer. The part-time-study training contract lasts between three and four years, allowing you to learn while you earn, balancing the LPC and/or GDL with part-time training at a firm. The part-time training contract is an option for those who have already completed their LPC. It involves working a minimum of two-and-a-half days per week for up to four years.

Training contracts must comply with SRA guidelines. The most important of these are:

- It's a *training* contract, not an *employment* contract. This means it is nearly impossible for you to be sacked. For a training contract to be terminated there must be mutual agreement between the firm and trainee, a cancellation clause (like failing the GDL or LPC), or a formal application to the SRA when issues cannot be resolved internally. Instances of trainees being fired are extremely rare.
- Trainees must gain practical experience in at least three areas of English law and develop skills in both contentious and non-contentious areas. Some firms send trainees on litigation courses that fulfil the contentious requirement without them having to do a full contentious seat. Firms can also arrange secondments for trainees to gain contentious experience.
- Trainees must complete the Professional Skills Course. The firm has to allow trainees paid study-leave to attend these courses and has to pay the course fees.

The norm is to spend time in four departments over the two years (six months in each). Each stint is called a seat. At some firms you'll find yourself doing six four-month seats or some other more bespoke arrangement. At very small firms it's likely that your training won't be as structured. Sometimes trainees repeat a seat, especially during six-seat schemes. Typically, repeat seats are in either the firm's largest department or the department in which you hope to qualify.

Besides the SRA's contentious/non-contentious requirement, some firms may require that you do a seat in one or more particular departments over the course of your training. For the other seats, firms usually ask you to identify your preferred departments and try to best accommodate your wishes. However, seat allocation isn't always a simple task and you might not get what you want. It usually depends on the needs of departments and trainee seniority.

You will be allocated a supervisor in each seat who will be responsible for giving you assignments and (hopefully) helping out with any questions you have. Supervisors are typically mid-level to senior associates/assistants or partners. Usually you will share an office with your supervisor or sit near them in an open-plan setting. You may also have the opportunity to spend a seat (or part of one) seconded to one of your firm's clients or one of its overseas offices. Appraisals are important and most firms will arrange a formal meeting between trainee and supervisor/HR at the end of each seat and probably also midway through.

What the experience entails:
- Long hours are almost a given; however, they are more likely when you work at a large, international or corporate/finance-focused firm. They are less likely at litigation-led firms and smaller domestic advisory or boutique firms.
- There is a hierarchical structure to law firms, and while this is felt more strongly at some firms than others, trainees should be prepared to start at the bottom. Salaries usually follow the hierarchy too, rising with seniority rather than being based on performance.
- Trainee groups tend to be close-knit and most firms provide some sort of budget for trainee socialising. Larger firms with larger intakes of trainees tend to have more active social scenes.
- You're not guaranteed a job at the end of it. If you've done well, the firm will retain you on qualification, finding you a job in a department that you've come to love… or in a department that needs new junior lawyers. The firm that trained you is not obligated to keep you. Our research shows that about 78.5% of qualifying trainees stayed at their firms in 2013; the rest either elected to look elsewhere or were forced to. You should regard your training contract as a two-year job interview.

One training partner put it perfectly when he said: *"Trainees should view the training contract as an opportunity to be a sponge and soak up all the right ways to be the lawyer they want to be. A degree of open-mindedness about your career is imperative."*

Trends affecting the recruitment market

The employment market is tough – no question. Here are the main issues you should be aware of.

It's the economy, stupid

As the 2008 financial crisis recedes into the annals of history, its lasting effects on the UK and world economy are becoming ever clearer. What caused the crash could fill several books (and indeed does, with tomes like Too Big to Fail and The Ascent of Money making excellent reading). Suffice to say, that if you harbour ambitions of being a commercial lawyer you will need to be able to speak with confidence about the crash and its consequences – this remains a common topic of discussion in job interviews.

The recession has had a big impact on law firms. A decline in property transactions hit real estate lawyers; a squeeze on credit was bad news for those in banking; fewer business transactions meant less work for M&A lawyers. At the same time, bankruptcy and insolvency lawyers picked up more instructions as businesses went bust, and litigators battled it out as investors and businesses squabbled over financial contracts. Many firms rebalanced their practice areas and made hundreds of redundancies, cutting the fat in areas where lawyers were idle.

More innovative businesses and law firms have realised that they can't just sit around and wait for the economy to get better. Firms are aware that their future success depends on prudent and efficient handling of finances and gaining work by offering better quality services than competitors at home and abroad.

Trainee recruitment

Law firms have been tightening their belt-buckles and trying to do more with less. This has meant a squeeze on recruitment, with a significant drop in the number of training contracts on offer. 4,869 were registered in 2011/12, nearly a quarter less than there were in 2007/08. The trend for cuts has been felt up and down the market from the high street to the City. Between them the five magic circle firms told us this year that they were looking to recruit 455 graduates; that figure was 575 in 2008.

Many now believe that the demand for junior lawyers will never return to pre-crash levels. With tighter budgets, clients are demanding greater value for money. They are no longer willing to pay for a junior lawyer to sit in a room photocopying if a temp can do the same for a tenth of the price. New technology is also hitting demand for trainees. Many functions can be performed by legal software and globalisation means that firms can easily outsource low-level tasks to countries like India and South Africa. Many top City firms are already doing this.

That's the bad news. Now for the good: the world will always need lawyers and good graduates will always have a chance of making it in the profession. English law is increasingly popular overseas for doing business deals and resolving disputes (especially in the BRIC countries and the Middle East). For a structured career path that almost guarantees a solid lifetime income, the law is right up there with accounting and consultancy. We certainly wouldn't want to encourage anyone to try to become a lawyer just because they think it's an easy way of getting a cushy job. It isn't.

Our point is: if you have a passion for the law and the right skills, then there's no need for doom and gloom. At the same time, the days when students could waltz into a top job by being bright, young and perky are over – forever. Applicants for training contracts are expected to know the firms they are applying to inside out, and have a stash of solid life experiences under their belts as evidence of a skill set. Today's applicants have access to more information about the law than ever before – but this also means they are expected to know more. We live in an information age, which means that not having information will put you at a distinct disadvantage.

Law firm mergers

You'll often hear law firm managing partners and market observers talking about 'consolidation' in the market. What they really mean is that there are fewer law firms about. Some have gone into administration: many high-street outfits have ceased operations in the past few years, and some major law firms too – Halliwells, Dewey & LeBoeuf, Cobbetts – have gone the way of the dodo. These three big casualties were all victim of financial mismanagement exposed by worsening market conditions. There are still firms out there in financial difficulty, with costs rising and profits plummeting. In June 2013, the SRA went so far as to announce that it was closely monitoring the finances of 30 top-200 firms as they were at risk of failure.

For the moment, however, law firm mergers are a much bigger trend than firm failures. A fifth of firms profiled in the 2009 Student Guide have undergone a major merger since then, and many others are considering the option. Mergers happen for all manner of reasons. Some are genuine attempts to expand a firm's business across the UK or around the world. A merger can boost internal client referrals and offer economies of scale by sharing overheads. 'Strength in numbers' is the mantra. Other mergers are attempts to shore up the financial or market position of struggling firms or are little more than bail-outs. International and transatlantic mergers are common – quite a few Brits have paired up with US or even Australian outfits. On 1st November 2013 SJ Berwin will become the first to merge with an Asia-Pacific firm, King & Wood Mallesons. Elsewhere in the market, CMS, Orrick and Mayer Brown have made no secret of their merger ambitions. So you should be aware that if you apply to a midsize City firm or small English outfit, after a merger you may eventually end up working for a big American beast.

Trainees' contracts are honoured when firms merge. And, for the moment, many merged entities appear to be continuing to recruit similar numbers to their legacy halves. Even in the case of firm failures, rival outfits where large numbers of out-of-work lawyers been taken on have subsequently increased their trainee intakes or even instituted entirely new schemes. However, it's not at all clear that this trend will hold and merged firms remain likely to cut recruitment in future as they pursue further economies of scale.

Public spending cuts

A knock-on effect from the recession, sweeping government spending cuts have been hitting the country hard. (Unless you have been living in a cave for the past three years you should know all about this, and it's another issue which forms a common topic of conversation in job interviews.) The cuts have been affecting law firms in various ways. First, firms which rely heavily on public funding – sectors like healthcare, housing, local government, transport, education, infrastructure, charities – have found themselves in a spot of bother. A good example is Bevan Brittan, which has seen revenues fall by a fifth in the past five years, and cut its trainee intake in half. Firms like this are branching out to do more private sector work.

Meanwhile, the public funding of litigation through legal aid is facing severe cuts, with the Ministry of Justice aiming to trim the legal aid budget by a quarter.

Combined with other funding changes, this is squeezing lawyers' fees in areas like crime, housing, family, employment and personal injury. While larger commercial firms practising in these areas are not affected, the cuts will doubtless affect recruitment at smaller firms. For more on this topic, take a look at the Solicitor's Practice Areas sections for each area mentioned above, or read our online feature on How legal aid works.

Legal education

After a delay of six months, the Legal Education and Training Review was finally published in June 2013. While encouraging more emphasis on ethics, commercial awareness and professionalism in law school, the review did not recommend any wholesale reshaping of legal education. Some observers criticised the report for not urging the profession to introduce greater changes, calling it a 'missed opportunity'. Still, some firms are finding creative ways of offering alternative ways into the profession or a leg-up to those seeking more work experience. These include legal apprenticeships (launched by DWF, Shoosmiths and Addleshaw Goddard among others) and Plexus Law's graduate pathways programme. The role of paralegals and qualified legal executives is also expected to become more important in future.

As legal education is expensive and job prospects are uncertain, the Law Society has seen fit to issue a health warning to students: 'You should not view qualifying as a solicitor to be an easy process... Competition is fierce and it has been made more so by the recession.' We couldn't agree more. Be warned that the biggest LPC providers like BPP and the University of Law are profit-making businesses and have a vested interest in more graduates studying with them. So you should consider your options very carefully before parting with any hard-earned cash to pay for law school. A large number of the trainees we speak to secured their training contracts before starting law school, and all other things being equal this is the course we would advise you to follow. Starting law school without a training contract or pupillage lined up will always be a calculated gamble.

The Legal Services Act

The Legal Services Act 2007 has now largely come into force. In a nutshell, the Act aims to liberalise and regulate the market for legal services. First, it makes it possible for non-solicitors to become partners in law firms, forming so-called multidisciplinary partnerships or MDPs. Second, under alternative business structure (ABS) lawyers are now able to team up with other professionals to offer a range of services to clients. The idea is still pretty new, but in the near future a commercial firm could handle a business' accounts and its contracts disputes, while a high-street firm might advise an individual on securing a mortgage as well as all the conveyancing. ABSs will also allow firms to seek external investment. National firm Irwin Mitchell is one of the most innovative players here, having gained five ABS licenses in late 2012.

ABSs also open the door to firms being floated on the stock market. In 2007, Australia's Slater & Gordon became the world's first publicly listed firm, and in 2012 it entered the UK market by acquiring Russell Jones & Walker. Some observers thought that liberalisation of the market would lead to an influx of private equity cash into the profession. But, for the moment, neither firms nor investors are keen on this idea, partly because of the financial requirements it would place on firms and partners.

Ultimately, the Legal Services Act aims to make legal services as easily accessible as your local supermarket – quite literally. In the not-so-distant future it may be possible to write your will at a bank or buy divorce services alongside your groceries. 'Tesco law' – regarded only a few years ago as comical and dangerous by some – is now here. Co-op Legal Services was the first business to win an ABS license in the UK. It employs 500 staff and offers services including fixed-fee family advice. Trainees are being recruited too; it's just a few at the moment, but in 2012 The Co-op stated an ambition of recruiting 100 trainees and having 3,000 staff within five years.

Pay and prospects

Despite the profession being under pressure in various ways, lawyer salaries at commercial firms remain generous. Previously, the SRA set a minimum salary for trainees that was well above minimum wage, but from 1 August 2014 this is being scrapped and firms will only be obliged to pay the national minimum wage (currently £6.31 per hour). Advocates of this change say it will allow small firms to employ more trainees, while detractors have suggested it will mean trainees can be exploited as low-paid lackeys.

The good news is that none of this will affect the top of the market. Salaries at the biggest firms both in and outside London are as robust as ever, and at some they are even on the up. Several of the magic circle firms have recently announced increases in trainee pay. According to figures provided to us by the SRA in summer 2013, average trainee salary in central London is £34,787. The lowest average salary is in Wales, where it's £17,943.

If you do manage to win a training contract you should be well placed for the future. The number of trainees who stay with the firm they trained with varies from employer to employer, but on average the firms covered in this guide retained 78.5% of their trainees upon qualification. There was a noticeable dip in retention in 2009 and 2010, but over the past three years the figure has hovered around the 80% mark. You can go to our website for further analysis and retention stats for every firm we've covered in the True Picture since 2000.

Some other career options

There are a number of different roles and organisations to look at other than becoming a solicitor or barrister in private practice. Here are a few of the main ones.

Working in-house for a company

According to the Law Society, 14,255 solicitors work directly for corporations, many of which fall into the financial services, manufacturing, retail, construction, media, transport and telecoms sectors. As an in-house lawyer, your day-to-day role depends on the work the business in question conducts, but the experience is nonetheless likely to be broad. One day you might be handling an employment issue, the next drafting a commercial contract or advising on a potential M&A transaction.

Most in-house lawyers begin their career working for a law firm and switch to an in-house role some time after qualification. Many agree that training in private practice provides a good foundation for the business know-how and commercial acumen necessary for working in-house.

The number of training contracts offered in-house is much smaller than that of private practice, and unfortunately there's no centralised system that gathers all commercial in-house opportunities. As such, it can take a good deal of effort to track one down. The reality is that around 500 companies have permission to offer training contracts, but most recruit on an ad-hoc basis, taking newbies as and when they're needed. Your best bet is to target the organisations and sectors in which you have the most knowledge and/or experience and check their online recruitment info regularly.

Check out our website for more ideas as well as a list of organisations registered to offer training contracts.

Law Centres

Law Centres are not-for-profit legal practices with local management committees and a remit to 'help people to stay in their homes, keep their families together and get into employment or education.' Advice and representation is provided without charge to the public, with funding coming from local authorities, the Legal Services Commission and some major charities like the Big Lottery Fund. However, according to one Law Centre volunteer, *"the criteria of eligibility is becoming stricter with every passing year. The cuts to legal aid are affecting those who most need our help."* Law Centres' horizons tend to be broader than those of Citizens Advice Bureaux, and they tend to take on cases with a wider social impact, including community care, all types of discrimination, education, employment, housing, immigration, asylum and public law matters. Legal problems handled may vary from one Centre to another, but all who work in the sector are considered social welfare law specialists.

The network of Law Centres in the UK now numbers over 50 and most employ several lawyers. If you're attracted to the idea of colleagues with shared ideals and a social conscience, it's worth investigating a career in the sector. Routes to a Law Centre position are as varied as the work each handles: newly qualified solicitors with relevant experience in private practice are taken on, as are those who have worked as paralegals for non-profit agencies and gained supervisor-level status. As a newly qualified solicitor your salary at a Law Centre will roughly match private practice on the high street or local authority salary scales – that's £24,000 to £30,000 (or more in London). However, Law Centres tend to lose their competitive edge when seeking to appoint more experienced lawyers. Let's just say such organisations tend to attract those who feel there is more to being enriched than being rich. Law Centres regularly take on volunteers and are an excellent way of both giving back to the community and gaining valuable experience.

Government Legal Service

The GLS ostensibly has only one client – the Queen. In practice, however, 'clients' include policymakers and managers within various government departments, while lawyers act as full-time litigators and solicitors who draft new legislation and advise ministers how best to legally put policy into practice. Despite ongoing government budget cuts, the GLS is still currently recruiting. Before you apply, it's important to consider whether you'll be happy working at the interface of law and politics and dealing with matters that directly impact UK society. If this sounds appealing, read our True Picture and Chambers Reports features on the GLS.

Local government

Local government lawyers advise elected council members and senior officers on a wide variety of topics, including commercial/contracts, conveyancing/property, employment issues, information management, administrative law and governance. Additional work depends on the type of local authority involved and can include litigation/prosecution, social care, children, consumer protection, environmental, highways and planning, education and housing matters, to name but a few. Lawyers tend to maintain broad practices in the smaller authorities, while those in larger ones usually specialise in a single area like housing, planning, highways, education or social services. Duties include keeping councils on the straight and narrow, making sure they don't spend their money unlawfully and advising councillors on the legal implications of their actions. The typical salary for a local authority solicitor is between £29,700 and £39,900, though some senior solicitors can earn more than £40,000.

Be prepared to wade through the bureaucratic bog and at times be driven to distraction by the slow machinations of local government. Still, the benefits of a government training contract – variety in your day-to-day work, flexible hours and a sense of serving the community – generally outweigh the downsides.

Crown Prosecution Service

The Crown Prosecution Service is the government department responsible for bringing prosecutions against people who have been charged with a criminal offence in England and Wales. The CPS handles all stages of the process, from advising the police on the possibility of prosecution, right through to the delivery of advocacy in the courtroom.

The CPS employs over 2,700 lawyers to handle more than 1.2 million cases in the Magistrates' and Crown Courts. Its prosecutors review and prosecute criminal cases following investigation by the police, and also advise the police on matters of criminal law and evidence in order to combat the problem of failed prosecutions. Specifically, lawyers advise the police on appropriate charges for certain crimes, and generally split their time between preparing cases in the office and prosecuting in the Magistrates' Court. A special band of lawyers entitled Crown Advocates prosecute Crown Court cases including murder, rape and robbery.

The CPS's training programme, which we've covered quite comprehensively in the past, was put on hold in 2011 in line with government cutbacks; however, as of spring 2012 it has reopened to those who have completed the LPC or BPTC. The Legal Trainee Scheme 2013 offered ten pupillages or training contracts. For more information visit www.cps.gov.uk/careers/.

The armed forces

Unsurprisingly, the army always needs lawyers, and in typical army no-nonsense fashion, it knows how to sell the position: 'No billing, no timesheets, no rat race – a job to be proud of,' declares the website. Fully qualified barristers and solicitors with a good understanding of army activities and preferably some work experience under their belt can join the Army Legal Services (ALS) and expect to see all sorts of work, from court-martial to international cases. You should be physically fit and aged between 24 and 32. Legal Officers can expect to get involved in the three main areas of the ALS's work – prosecution, general advisory and operational law. Major Hannah Giles at the ALS told us: *"You'll need leadership skills, integrity, courage, a practical mind, determination and the ability to work under pressure."*

Recruitment goes as follows: once or twice a year, up to nine suitable candidates are called for interview before attending the Army Officer Selection Board at Westbury, in Wiltshire. Successful applicants are then offered a Short Service Commission in ALS, which lasts four years, including an 18-month initial probational period. Six months of training will lead on to your first legal appointment, either at home or in Germany or Cyprus. Lawyers and other professionally qualified officers are commissioned as Captains, with a starting salary of £37,915. Further international opportunities occasionally arise in Afghanistan, Kenya, the USA and Canada. NATO and the UN are also worth bearing in mind as future job prospects. See http://www.army.mod.uk/agc/31483.aspx for more details on the ALS.

The Royal Air Force also employs barristers and solicitors to deal with criminal cases and prosecutions, both at home and abroad. The Air Force's legal department is small, but the work is juicy – areas of law covered include Air Force law, the law of armed conflict, new legislation plus the host of civil issues that affect RAF personnel. A linear career path can see you rise to the position of Squadron Leader after four years and Wing Commander after a further six. Previous legal officers have found themselves providing advice to people in Iraq, the Falklands, Kosovo and Germany. The starting salary is £37,915 after training, and recruitment is done according to needs rather than annually. Applicants must be aged between 21 and 34. Visit the RAF website to learn more: www.raf.mod.uk/careers/jobs/legalofficer.cfm

The Navy doesn't have such a clear recruitment path, though we've been told that qualified lawyers should sign up as a Logistics Officer in the first instance. From there officers are streamed depending on their skills, so there's a good chance you'll be considered for legal work if there are vacancies.

The police

Only Sherlock Holmes can operate for and outside of the law and get away with it. All other members of the police force are as accountable as everyone else and therefore need good legal representation when their own conduct is called into question. This is where police lawyers step in. As well as the aforementioned civil actions, they might find themselves working in corporate governance, employment law and discrimination, personal injury and neighbourhood safety matters (for example, issuing AS-BOs or Sexual Offences Protection Orders). There are also a small number of 'duty lawyer' roles in police stations across the country.

We were told by Alpa Patel, head of professional support at the Metropolitan Police, that the Met's in-house legal department plans to *"undertake recruitment campaigns for qualified lawyers according to needs of the service and the levels of work coming in."* In other words, because of cuts to public spending in recent years the Met no longer has an annual recruitment drive. Unfortunately, it's a similar story across the rest of the country for qualified lawyers seeking a career with the police. It's worth bearing in mind that there are occasionally opportunities in areas like forensics, operational policing and criminal justice units, and you don't necessarily have to be a qualified solicitor to get in there. Check online with your local police force for information about any vacancies.

Legal executive

Becoming a qualified lawyer doesn't mean you have to start your career with a training contract. You can still become an advocate, partner in a law firm or even a judge through the CILEx route. The Chartered Institute of Legal Executives (CILEx) has helped over 95,000 members secure a successful career in law in the last 25 years alone. There are currently over 20,000 Chartered Legal Executive lawyers and trainees across England and Wales, all of whom are independently regulated.

Taking the Chartered Legal Executive route means aspiring lawyers can earn as they learn and gain valuable practical experience in one fell swoop. Once their CILEx studies and qualifying employment are complete, they can call themselves qualified lawyers straight away without having to undertake an LPC or wait for an elusive training contract. CILEx members are employed across the full spectrum of legal services, from private practice to government departments, and within the in-house legal teams of major companies. Around 60% of students are funded by their employer.

For those with no prior legal training, the CILEx Level 3 Professional Diploma in Law and Practice is the first stage of the academic training. The second stage of the CILEx route is the Level 6 Professional Higher Diploma in Law and Practice, which is assessed at honours degree level. For those with a qualifying law degree obtained within the last seven years, CILEx offers the Graduate Fast-Track Diploma. The qualification can help you become a Chartered Legal Executive lawyer instead of becoming a solicitor or barrister through the LPC or BPTC. CILEx has seen a 30% rise in fast-track students.

While being a Chartered Legal Executive can be a rewarding career in its own right, don't forget CILEx can provide a useful route to qualifying as a solicitor. Most people can seek exemptions from much of the GDL (having already covered its core subjects) and, more crucially, they're also usually exempt from the two-year training contract, provided they are already a qualified Chartered Legal Executive before completing their LPC.

Paralegal

Traditionally, a stint paralegaling could fill space after law school or before commencing a training contract, offering a broad taste of the legal experience. With fewer training contracts on offer, however, a job as a paralegal can act a feasible longer-term option.

Legal employers tend to view any time spent paralegaling favourably as it demonstrates a commitment to the profession and enables candidates to gain industry insight and experience. *"A major factor in getting my training contract was the fact that I could talk about my responsibilities as a paralegal: attending court, going to client meetings, drafting documents. I was able to show enthusiasm for the legal process and demonstrate that I would be a committed and enthusiastic future trainee,"* said one former paralegal. What's more, the job remains a valuable position in its own right. It's a good idea to take into account factors such as a firm's size and number of trainees when making applications – a smaller trainee intake often means you'll get to see much better quality work.

It's not just wannabe solicitors who should consider a stint paralegaling, either; some recruitment agencies now specialise in putting pre-qualification barristers in paralegal positions.

The term 'paralegal' is quite generic and the job duties that paralegals encounter can vary drastically: some are given their own files to run, while others end up with dull document management tasks for months on end. At the end of the day experiences depend on the firm.

Legal secretary

"Being a legal secretary is a good way to get your foot in the door," explained one of our lawyer contacts. This particular source would know – it's exactly how they started their career. For anyone unsure of whether they want the full-bore pressure of working as a solicitor, this route could be perfect. *"A major pro is that you're work-*

ing in law without the more intense responsibility of being a lawyer." It's also a smart way to spend a few years if you're struggling to get your finances back on track and can't yet contemplate law school.

According to the Institute of Legal Secretaries and PAs (ILSPA), taking a legal secretarial role is suitable for anyone with an interest in law or a background in administrative work. That said, it's important to know that the market is pretty full right now – many firms are reducing their support staff to reduce costs, and there's a lot of competition for jobs.

People can take on legal secretarial positions at any stage of life, be it instead of university, after a degree or as a complete career change. Whenever you take this step, you'll need to be certain that you have the right qualities and temperament: you need to work well under pressure and have a lot of patience as well as be detail-oriented, organised and articulate. You must also get to know your boss quickly and be able to think for them.

Her Majesty's Courts and Tribunals Service

HMCTS is an agency of the Ministry of Justice, responsible for running the civil, family and criminal courts and tribunals in England and Wales. Its 21,000 employees look after the management of properties and court buildings, and deal with the timetabling, management and proceeding of hearings. You can find a link to all MoJ jobs at www.justice.gov.uk/jobs/hmcts.

Many HMCTS jobs are administrative in nature; however, the Service also recruits Judicial Assistants (JAs), who are assigned to work for a senior Court of Appeal judge for up to 12 months. Duties include legal research, advice and providing assistance in drafting judgements. There are usually ten positions available at any one time. Applicants need at least a 2:1 and must have completed or be about to complete pupillage or a training contract. Positions are advertised in *The Times* and the *Law Gazette*, as well as on the MoJ's website.

Long-term careers are available for administrative officers, bailiffs, ushers and court clerks. Magistrates' Court clerks (also known as legal advisers) are qualified solicitors or barristers who provide legal advice to lay magistrates and district judges. Unfortunately, public sector cuts and Magistrates' Court closures have led to a hiring freeze for trainee legal advisers.

The Law Commission

Many laws are the product of centuries of precedent; others arise from little more than political expediency. Constant reform is needed to ensure that the law is fit for pur-

pose in the modern age. However, the government is not always best placed to see where reforms could be made. The Law Commission, an advisory non-departmental public body sponsored by the Ministry of Justice, was set up by Parliament in 1965 to review the laws of England and Wales and propose reform where necessary.

The Commission is engaged in about 20 projects at any one time. Among topics it set out to examine in its most recent reform programme were: the confusing and outdated laws surrounding the defence of insanity and automatism (which covers acts performed when the defendant is unconscious – for example, crimes committed during night terrors); repealing obsolete laws relating to British India; and looking at how the law on contempt of court should change in the internet age, as jurors increasingly commit contempt online.

It's not just a case of repealing laws that are clearly archaic; it's equally important not to accidentally remove the legal basis for someone's rights. Researchers for the Commission analyse many different areas of law, identifying defects in the current system and examining foreign law models to see how they deal with similar problems. They also help draft consultation papers, instructions to Parliamentary Counsel and final reports.

The Commission takes on 10-12 researchers annually on year-long contracts. These researchers are normally law graduates and postgraduates who *"tend to leave in order to qualify as lawyers – its a good jumping-off point for a legal career.*" The Commission also recruits qualified lawyers throughout the year. The job of research assistant involves some fascinating (and less fascinating) subjects and is intellectually challenging on the whole.

Candidates should have a First or a high 2:1, along with a keen interest in current affairs and the workings of the law. The job suits those with an analytical mind and a hatred of waffle. They must also love research, because there's a lot of it – be it devising questionnaires and analysing the responses, studying statistics or examining court files.

To find out just which proposed reforms have been implemented and rejected, read the Law Commission annual report at http://lawcommission.justice.gov.uk/docs/lcar12-13_web.pdf

Keep up to speed with the Law Commission's recruitment needs at www.lawcom.gov.uk. December is usually the month when they start looking for people.

Legal Aid Agency (formerly Legal Services Commission)

The Legal Aid Agency was formed in April 2013 to replace the Legal Services Commission (LSC), which in turn replaced the Legal Aid Board in 2000. It was created as part of the reforms to legal aid funding introduced by the Legal Aid, Sentencing and Punishment of Offenders Act (LASPO) – which became law in May 2012 – and is an executive body of the Ministry of Justice, giving ministers closer control over the government's legal aid budget.

The LAA now shares headquarters with the Ministry of Justice in Westminster and has a further 12 offices across England and Wales. These branches manage the distribution of public funds for both civil legal services and criminal defence services. The new agency aims to save £17m by 2015 by reducing the financial irregularities that dogged the old LSC and sharing administrative resources with the Ministry of Justice. Further savings are likely to be achieved via redundancies, details of which have yet to be announced.

LASPO is set to introduce fee cuts, which should save a further £160m a year, as well as scope and eligibility changes, which are set to save up to £240m by 2014-15. The LAA will oversee a new competitive tendering process and plans to introduce a new online system for law firms applying for payments. The work of the LAA is essentially divided into the Community Legal Service (CLS) and the Criminal Defence Service (CDS).

The role of the CLS is to ensure people can get information and advice about their legal rights and help with enforcing them. This tends to fall into the areas of family breakdown, debt, housing, immigration, welfare benefits, community care, clinical negligence and public law. Caseworkers assess the merits of applications for legal funding and means test applicants. The CLS works with legal aid solicitors, the Citizens Advice Bureau, Law Centres, local authority services and other organisations. Recent reforms have seen the CLS working with local authorities to create Community Legal Advice Centres in a bid to provide a more integrated service in relation to social welfare law.

The CDS manages the supply of legal advice to those under police investigation or facing criminal charges using local solicitors accredited by the service. It also performs an audit role in relation to authorised providers of criminal legal advice. Part of the CDS's work is the Public Defender Service (PDS). Its four offices, set up in 2001, advise members of the public 24/7 in what the LSC believes to be a more cost-effective and efficient way. They are located in Cheltenham, Darlington, Pontypridd and Swansea.

The LAA is currently in transition, and it's as yet unclear what redundancies will be made. We're unable to comment on possible recruitment opportunities for the future, but students can keep up to date at www.legalservices. gov.uk.

Patent attorney

Over 2,000 patent attorneys are registered in the UK, usually in private practice firms, large companies and government departments. Their job is to obtain, protect and enforce intellectual property rights for their owners. It typically takes four or five years to become a UK Chartered Patent Attorney and/or a European Patent Attorney. All candidates must have a scientific or technical background (usually a related degree) and the aptitude for learning the relevant law. Attention to detail, good drafting skills and a very logical, analytical mind are crucial.

Candidates who wish to become a patent attorney typically find a post with a patent attorney firm or in industry, then sit both foundation and advanced examinations, which are run by the Chartered Institute of Patent Attorneys. Once qualified, there's the opportunity to obtain a further qualification that entitles the successful candidate to conduct litigation in the High Court, although all patent attorneys have the right to conduct litigation and appear as advocate in the specialist Patents County Court. In order to become a European Patent Attorney, candidates must complete another set of examinations. The website for the Chartered Institute of Patent Attorneys (CIPA), www.cipa.org.uk, has a useful careers section and job vacancy listings.

Trade mark attorney

A trade mark is a form of intellectual property used to distinguish a manufacturer or trader's particular brand from its competitors. It can be anything from a logo or picture to a colour – in 2012 Cadbury successful trade marked the distinctive purple hue that's made its packaging famous. Trade mark attorneys provide advice on the suitability of words or logos as trade marks, on the action needed to safeguard a protected trade mark and on how to deal with infringements by another parties. *"It's quite a pedantic job,"* commented one insider, *"and requires you to pay a lot of attention as you're constantly dealing and playing with words."*

There are about 570 fully qualified trade mark attorneys in the UK, all registered with the Institute of Trade Mark Attorneys (ITMA). Most work for large companies or at firms of patent and trade mark attorneys. In 2012, 51 individuals qualified into the profession. To become a trade mark attorney you must complete two training courses and a period in practice. A degree isn't a prerequisite to qualification, although it can offer exemption from some coursework and is sometimes viewed as desirable by some employers. There's no central admissions procedure, so students need to approach firms or in-house trade mark departments directly. Check out www.itma.org.uk for more information.

Compliance officer or analyst

Banks and other financial services companies occasionally recruit law and non-law grads into their compliance units, which take on the vital role of advising senior management on how to comply with the laws, regulations and rules that govern the sector. Due to the proliferation of financial regulation, the importance of compliance departments has grown enormously so that in larger banks they're often equivalent in size to in-house legal teams.

The role of a compliance officer or analyst requires astute advice, clear guidance, reliable professional judgement and the ability to work in a team. Attention to detail and a determination to see the consistent application of compliance policies and practices are essential.

A minimum 2:1 degree is standard for successful applicants, and salaries are typically comparable with other graduate trainees in the City. With some compliance teams numbering more than 100, there's plenty of scope for career development. Several banks run a two-year compliance analyst training scheme, over the course of which a trainee will gain a broad base of business knowledge and technical experience.

Barristers' clerk

Barristers' clerks should not be confused with any other type of clerk, as their role is very different. They help provide all the admin services a barristers' chambers needs by: liaising and organising meetings with solicitors (and the CPS); negotiating and collecting fees; allocating cases and planning their duration; administering databases, timetables, finances and diaries; and marketing their set's members. The most brilliant barristers aren't always the best at selling themselves, and so a good team of clerks can be a godsend in this respect.

The traditional image of a barristers' clerk is that of a Cockney barrow boy – think Michael Caine in a suit – with a wide tie-knot, wheeling around a trolley of legal briefs just like his father did before him. As with most professions, clerking these days is now more mixed, with plenty of women and people from other backgrounds, though there are still many burly, earthy types. Certain forward-thinking sets have retitled their clerks as 'practice managers', but it's essentially the same job under a different name.

Clerks are usually school leavers and the minimum academic requirement is four GCSEs at C or above. Some clerks also have A-levels and degrees, but it's personality coupled with legal, business or court administration experience that matter most.

Policy and regulatory

So you did a law degree because you eventually wanted to end up writing the law of the land yourself? Unfortunately, the harsh truth is that the winter of discontent is well and truly upon us when it comes to recruitment into the (quasi-)public sector and the policy/regulatory world. That's not to say that all organisations have frozen recruiting altogether (though many have), but the onus is on you to dig a little deeper.

If you're prepared to be dynamic, the policy route remains a fascinating and rewarding career path. But how to make that first step? Knowing people who can champion your cause and offer you work experience here and there doesn't hurt. We suggest you start networking early. Internships with think tanks, charities, NGOs and international organisations are a must. Otherwise, it's a question of researching which government departments and regulators might interest you and contacting them directly to ask about recruitment.

For ideas try typing 'policy' into the Guardian Jobs website search engine every so often, as well as checking regularly on the websites of organisations such as the Judicial Appointments Commission and Queen's Council Appointments. The Law Society, Solicitors Regulatory Authority, Bar Council and Bar Standards Board websites are all worth looking at for vacancies, as are various industry ombudsmen (check out www.ombudsmanassociation.org). The Financial Conduct Authority also runs a graduate training scheme: see fcacareers.org.uk/graduate-programme for details.

How suitable are you and what do recruiters want?

So you've got a degree? No biggie. So will everyone else. Now is time to make sure your CV and experience square with what recruiters demand and build your self-confidence to improve your prospects.

The road to a training contract or pupillage is smoother for some than others, but before starting to apply you will need to make sure your CV and experiences square with what recruiters demand. A structured approach to gaining the right experiences and a healthy dose of self-confidence can improve anyone's prospects.

Did we mention that competition for training contracts and pupillages is fierce? To win yourself one you will need not just an excellent academic record, but a stash of experiences to prove you have the ability to dive into the professional world with greater confidence than your rivals. Applying directly out of university with one or two interesting extra-curricular experiences under your belt works for some. However, our research has shown that an increasing number of those entering the profession made an effort to gain substantive life experience before starting to make applications. It's no bad thing if you've already taken several steps up the career ladder by the time you start a traineeship or pupillage.

How impressive is your degree?

Having a law degree is no reason to assume entitlement. From the top sets at the Bar to the little-known solicitors' firms on the high street, non-law graduates are just as able to secure training positions as their LLB peers. In the few cases where employers prefer law grads they will specify this, so unless you hear differently, conversion route applicants may proceed with confidence. Many recruiters tell us just how highly they regard staff with language skills and scientific or technical degrees, particularly where their clients' businesses will benefit, and humanities degrees require many of the research, analytical or communication skills needed by lawyers.

It's a fact of life that many solicitors' firms and barristers' chambers subscribe to the idea of a pecking order of universities; at some the bias is undeniably evident. If you worry that your university isn't one of the best regarded then you should make sure you get the best degree result possible and work on enriching your CV in other ways.

As obvious as it may sound, working for good results throughout your degree is crucial. Be aware that you may already be applying for training contracts and vacation schemes in your second year, so if most of your first year marks are thirds or 2:2s, you'll not get far.

Most firms and sets in this guide require recruits to have at least a 2:1. If you get a First that will definitely impress (at least on paper); if you wind up with a 2:2, you're going to have a tough time. Many recruiters will tell you that they take exceptional circumstances into account, but these circumstances do truly need to be exceptional – ie the star student who suffered a serious accident as finals loomed. Confirmation of this by means of a letter from your tutor (or, better still, a doctor's note) might assist. In addition, you will need something pretty awesome to overcome that 2:2 – a year or more in a great job, a further degree or impressive voluntary work might cut it. Of course, none of these is a guaranteed fix. *"If you have average or less than average grades, you're really going to struggle,"* one recruiter told us. *"I sometimes feel that no one warns students about that early enough."* A Desmond is less likely to get you anywhere in a professional career, so work your socks off at university.

Extra-curricular activities

Addicted to Buzzfeed or obsessed with online cat pictures? Get over it. To succeed in your aim of becoming a lawyer, you will need to devote a large chunk of your free time at university and thereafter to undertaking worthwhile, constructive pursuits. Take advantage of the practically unlimited opportunities on offer. Almost every university has a wide range of societies, meeting groups and sports clubs. Better still: set up your own event, society, club or business or social venture. Being able to show you are entrepreneurial and can achieve concrete results working on projects is increasingly important to recruiters. But you cannot undertake these pursuits just as CV fodder. Do something you are genuinely interested in. Recruiters are always telling us they want to see that individuals have a passion for the things they have done.

Some kind of legal experience, whether it's organising events for your university law society or shadowing your aunt's neighbour's lawyer friend, is crucial since you need to convince prospective employers that you're serious about the profession. You can acquire experience later on through open days and vacation schemes, but it's never too early to start, not least because vac schemes and open days are now devilishly hard to get onto. Non-legal extra-curriculars can be just as useful to show that you play well with others. It also gives you something to write about when an application form says: 'Discuss a time when you worked with a group to achieve a common goal.'

Relevant work experience is vital to almost every successful job application, so search hard for suitable positions. Many universities run law-specific career seminars in association with solicitors' firms or barristers' chambers. Be savvy, go along and find out as much as you can by talking to trainee solicitors and recruiters. Networking is a key tactic you should be employing. Our website has further advice on **The niceties and no-nos of networking**.

Researching firms

When you apply, research should be your watchword. Demonstrating your understanding of what a firm is about and what the work will entail, and being able to explain honestly and realistically why you want to do it, are among the most important things to get across when you make an application. Adopting a scattergun approach works for some, but simply sending the same covering letter to 50 firms will get you nowhere. Recruiters can tell very easily which applicants have a genuine interest in their firm and which have put in minimal effort. On our website, you can find a feature on **How to research firms properly**.

Commercial awareness

If you want to become a commercial lawyer you'll need this thing they call commercial awareness. Try and gain a sense of what's going on in the business world. The key issue to be aware of is how the current economic climate is affecting the way businesses and other organisations operate. Big topics of the day are: the Eurozone crisis and weak economies' constant need for bailouts; the rise of the BRIC and MENA economies; the basic issues involved in UK public spending cuts; efforts to boost the British economy and strengthen business; and the greater emphasis placed on regulation in the financial services sector. Why not follow the news on a specific industry which you're interested in? Energy, technology and the media are particularly vibrant sectors at the moment.

Read the *Financial Times, The Economist* or any newspaper's business section. Not only will it help you follow the news, but it will get you up to speed on all the relevant business jargon. BBC Radio 4's *Today* programme also puts out a good daily business podcast. The *Student Guide*'s a Facebook page often links to stories that will broaden your knowledge of the business world and private client law.

It's also important to understand the role of a lawyer as a service provider. Lawyers must be able to relate to their clients and know something about their businesses. If the firms you apply to have certain specialisms or target certain industry sectors, then find out about those sectors.

Students looking to go into criminal law should be aware of recent legislation and current issues. Future family lawyers should be able to discuss the major cases that have hit the headlines. Anyone interested in administrative and public law issues will have a full-time job keeping up to date with all the various developments in that field; Radio 4's *Law in Action* podcasts should be a real help. Hopeful crime, family and human rights lawyers should also be aware of the ways in which legal aid cuts are hitting these practices.

Travel

International travel in a gap year can broaden your horizons and teach you new organisational and problem-solving skills. Overseas experience is usually only valued by employers if you've spent time working, perhaps undertaking a project for a charity or in business. If you don't want to travel, don't worry: you can stand out in other ways. Above all, be original (as much as it's possible) in the experiences you pursue.

Mature candidates

Many employers now welcome mature applicants, and some – often smaller niche or regional outfits – actively seek out those with previous career experience. With age comes wisdom and probably an impressive set of transferable skills and industry knowledge. We've chatted with successful barristers and solicitors who've done everything from secretarial work, professional football, radio DJing, forensic science, physiotherapy and music production to accountancy, consultancy, piloting, policing and soldiering.

Diversity

Women and ethnic minorities are increasingly present at the young end of the profession. Out of all the trainees registered in 2011/12, 60.3% were women and 22.7% were drawn from minority ethnic groups. More women than men have been entering the profession for over a decade now, although disappointingly these groups are still very much underrepresented at the senior end. You can find more information about diversity and diversity affinity groups on our website as well as diversity statistics for firms in the True Picture.

Coming from overseas

If you're a non-Brit and you want to become a lawyer in the UK, your best bet is study here and then follow the standard route to qualification. Some people do join the profession after completing studies overseas, but the recognition of foreign degrees and qualifications is a complex and sketchy business. A specific programme called the Qualified Lawyer Transfer Scheme exists for those who are already practising lawyers overseas and are moving to the UK. We devote more attention to **Qualifying from overseas** on our website. If you hold an EU passport or have a pre-existing right to live and work in the UK, you can proceed with optimism. However, London firms which recruit non-EU candidates have recently expressed concern at the more restrictive approach to issuing visas adopted by the Home Office in the past few years. In all cases, excellent written and spoken English is essential, and you will need a convincing reason why you want to work in the UK.

And finally...

What with studying hard, following the business and professional news, helping out at the CAB, captaining your rugby team, debating, acting as student law society president and attending careers events, you'll hardly have time for a pint. Your years at university are supposed to be fun, but don't waste valuable time that could be spent CV building.

"Being interested in and up-to-date on commercial issues is important, otherwise recruiters will never believe that you will be able to convey genuine expertise to clients."

Trainee

How to make successful applications

We can't emphasise this more strongly: bulk applications rarely end well. Here are some tips on how to proceed.

Law firms are not homogeneous; each of them offers something unique. The applications you send off should be just as unique. Whenever we ask trainees for their words of wisdom on this subject, we often get an answer like this (a Pinsent Masons trainee, in this case): *"It's so important to know the ins and outs of the firm you're applying to. If you're submitting an application that could easily be for just about any firm out there, then you'll get found out very quickly."* Recruiters think along the same lines. Take DWF's training principal Carl Graham for example: *"What I've found with many unsuccessful candidates is that they err towards rehearsed answers. Not knowing your subject really well can be your downfall."*

None of this means that you should be putting all your eggs in one basket and merely targeting one or two firms. Given that the market's so competitive today, it makes sense to identify several firms that suit you best – no matter how many that may be – and then take it from there. But you stand a much better chance of success if you've tailored each and every application to the firm in question. In addition, some informal contact or networking with the firms you apply to can help you on your way.

Do your research

If you do manage to secure a training contract at a firm, bear in mind that you're likely to be there for a minimum of two years. In other words: it's a big decision to make. As such, it's essential for you to find out which firms best match your personality and interests. Some can have pretty gruelling working hours attached to them, for example; others allow you to get home for the 6pm showing of The Big Bang Theory. Of equal importance is pinpointing the areas of law you're interested in and coupling that with the firms specialised in those areas. If you have an interest in a certain industry sector – healthcare, education, retail – it's worth taking that into account and looking at firms with the appropriate focus. As for useful resources, here are a few for you to cherish:

- The Student Guide. The **True Picture**, the **Chambers Reports**, the **Solicitors' Practice Areas**, **Practice Areas at the Bar** and the **comparison charts** are all designed to help you work out which employer and area of law is right for you. On our website, we provide a 'How to get a training contract at...' article for each firm in the True Picture detailing its application and selection process.
- Our parent publication *Chambers UK* identifies and ranks all the best firms in over 70 areas of practice. It can be read online for free at www.chambersandpartners.com.
- The legal press. *The Lawyer*, *Legal Week* and *The Law Gazette* as well as legal gossip websites can all be of value. Things to look out for include information on firms' business strategies as well as case and deals highlights.
- Law firms' websites. Study them vigorously! On top of laying out the key facts, they'll give a valuable insight into what that firm essentially stands for and how it sees itself. A firm's recruitment pages will also list its minimum requirements. Check your qualifications and abilities match up. The **Applications and selections** table on page **489** should help with this, as well as the **law firm profiles** at the back of this book.
- Industry journals and the local press. Find out more about the sectors a firm works in or its involvement in the local community. Read the national and international business press too, to build up your commercial awareness.

Get organised

- Law firm recruitment is a veritable fest of deadlines. Be aware of them, put them in your diary. The deadline calendars is this book will help you.
- Application forms take far, far longer to complete than you'd expect, especially when they're done well.
- Some barristers' chambers use the Pupillage Gateway, some don't. Make sure you know which is which. Check their websites The **Bar** section of this guide discusses the Pupillage Gateway in more detail.

- Increasingly firms are digitising the application process and only accepting full applications from those who perform well enough in online tests – often verbal and numerical reasoning. There are books and websites with sample tests and helpful hints on how to perform well.

Some firms still require a formal CV, but many now ask you to fill out relevant background information on an application form or online. Nonetheless, much of the advice below still applies.

Tighten up your CV

- Chronological gaps can easily tarnish your CV, no matter how much work experience you gained. If you've taken time off, put it down and be prepared to explain why.
- Content is more crucial than style. Don't waste time with photos or unusual fonts. Saying that, bullet points can make things more eye-catching.
- Don't just say what you did at uni – mention sports teams, work experience and volunteering, and be prepared to talk about the skills this gave you, or how this tested you.
- Mistakes can be damning. Recruiters are constantly telling us that basic spelling and grammar errors still occur. Such mistakes provide an easy and legitimate reason to put your application straight in the bin. Check spelling thoroughly and get a friend to read over your CV and applications.
- A CV should not be a brochure – keep the page count to one or two – move onto a third if you've won Nobel Prizes. Recruiters have to read countless numbers of them, so avoid flowery language and non-pertinent information. Part of a lawyer's skill set is effective communication. A third page signals a waffler and a weak communicator.
- Every point needs some evidence behind it. Putting down that you're fascinated by a particular area of law isn't enough; you're going to have to prove your passion with examples. Speak to lawyers whenever you can – it all helps to show that you understand the reality of practice. As Allen & Overy's graduate recruitment partner Richard Hough suggests: *"Nothing replaces face-to-face interaction, however you can achieve it."*
- You can use any kind of work to prove you have commercial awareness. Even if you worked in a pub you can still talk about being aware of costs, budget.

Nail that application form

- Answer questions directly – no cutting and pasting or repetition.
- Don't use glossy terms or jargon. Be clear and be concise.

- If a word limit is indicated, stick too it. It usually indicates how much detail you should go into. If you fall short, don't worry: it's better to be clear and concise than just to waffle on for no reason.
- Keep copies of everything you send out. Before an interview or assessment day you will need to remind yourself of what you wrote. Recruiters will most likely use your application as a basis for their questioning.

Don't undersell yourself

- Prizes, professional qualifications, impressive A levels, vac schemes – these things are obvious essentials on any CV.
- Experiences should demonstrate as many of the following as you can muster: teamwork; problem-solving skills; judgement; decision-making; leadership; dedication; the ability to thrive outside your comfort zone; a commercial outlook; and commitment to becoming a lawyer.
- Explain what you learned from your experiences rather than just listing them.
- If you can demonstrate that you're a real grafter who paid their way through uni, then do so.
- It won't always be appropriate to list all your part-time employment so you might need to group some jobs into a more general category. Unless the list is extensive, indicate the key aspects of your role in each position.
- If you studied a musical instrument to a high level then say so. It shows you can commit to something and work diligently to achieve it. The same goes for other pastimes or pursuits.
- Sports are good application fodder. Again, the commitment factor will come through, and if it's a team sport you play then what better confirmation is there of your being a team player?
- Were you ever selected – or, better still, elected – to a position of responsibility? To be chosen by your peers as a student representative, for example, suggests that people admire you and have confidence in your abilities.
- If you are still at university, or have very recently graduated, then mentioning things from your later school days is still permissible. If it has been some time since you left uni then you need to find some more recent examples.

There's no room for error

You may think you're the ideal candidate, but any mistakes on your applications, no matter how minuscule, will almost certainly cost you. Recruiters want people who are likely to be a roaring success and not make mistakes. A final word goes to Jones Day's recruitment partner David Smith: *"We're not looking for people who will do the job of a trainee and NQ, but won't be able to go any further than that. In a nutshell, we're looking for the partners of the future."*

How to succeed at interviews and assessment days

Interviews and assessment days are to be celebrated, not dreaded. You'll send out dozens of application forms and get blanked by many firms. So when you do get an interview, give it your all.

Interviews

Well done on bagging an interview. That may have been hard work, but it's no guarantee that you've got the job. Now it's time to ratchet things up another notch. Turn on the charm, stand up straight, dress smartly and be thorough with your homework.

Before any interview:

Read and think about your application form. Interviewers will pick up on what you wrote and question you on it. A lot of the time, they'll discuss your application form as an icebreaker. It's your chance to speak about things that interest you and to build up rapport. Chat, be expansive, maybe even flash the pearly whites. If you fibbed on your application form, this is when you'll be found out, so don't lie.

Research the firm. A stock question is 'Why this firm?' Recruiters tell us this is where many people trip up. Make sure you've got something good, innovative and non-generic to say. Read the True Picture reports and find out about the firm's strengths, its history and what is being said about it in the legal press. Ideally you will find a topic or two that can be developed into a reason why you and the firm are a perfect match.

Research the people who are interviewing you, if possible. Know your enemy. Practice areas, precedent-setting cases they've won, previous firms they've worked at, their favourite sport – all of this is gold and firm websites often contain such details. Don't quote it all back at them though… that's creepy.

Have a finger on the pulse of legal news and current affairs. The Lawyer, Legal Week, Solicitors Journal and Law Gazette are all very good, as is Thursday's Law supplement in The Times. And have you signed up to the Student Guide's Facebook page? Be ready to see the connections between law and the real world of politics, society and business.

Practise answers, but not too much. It's not hard to guess what sort of questions you're going to get; something along the lines of 'Why do you want to be a lawyer?' is a bona fide cert. It is wise to rehearse a little to collect your thoughts, but you've got to be ready to deviate from the script. Speaking off the cuff makes you sound more interesting and often a classic question will be slightly altered and you need to be ready to adapt. Almost no firm will directly ask questions about black-letter law, although some do favour enquiries about lawyerly ethics or client confidentiality, which are designed to be appropriate for graduates of all fields.

Think about what skills you can offer. Increasingly, interviewers are asking competency-based questions. Common examples include 'give an example of a time you successfully achieved a set goal'; 'tell me about how you've dealt with a difficult person in a team'; and 'what do you think constitutes excellent client or customer service?'. Before an interview think about how the skills you've acquired in your work and life experiences can benefit the law firm your interviewing with.

Expect the unexpected. Some firms are known for asking quirky questions: 'If you were a biscuit what type of biscuit would you be?' or 'If I put your iPod on shuffle what track would be likely to come up?' are just two examples. Ideally, your answer should say something about your personality or at least show that you're quick-witted. Interviewers may also challenge your views or hit you with an unexpected question. If you encounter this, the best strategy is usually to stand your ground and explain the reasoning behind what you've said.

The default setting when going into an interview is to want to be liked, but remember that the interview is a crucial opportunity for you to figure out whether you like the firm back. You should have a couple of questions prepared to ask the firm. There are so many things you might ask so do pick something that isn't already covered in the firm's own literature. You could find out what your interviewers like about the firm or ask them about when they trained. You could ask them what the firm is doing in reaction to a major development in the legal or business world. Be confident and use this opportunity to improve the rapport with your interviewers.

The usual interview tips apply:

- Arrive early. Have a contact number ready in case some cruel act of divine vengeance makes you late.
- Dress appropriately.
- Be polite to everyone, including receptionists and support staff.
- Shake hands firmly (but avoid the 'bone crusher' handshake) and make eye contact. Smile non-menacingly.
- Speak to everyone on the panel, ensuring you make eye contact with all present.
- Don't fidget or sit awkwardly. Don't allow your body to tense.
- Do mock interviews beforehand and get feedback from whoever tests you. Even family members and friends can be surprisingly good at this if you explain what sort of questions you want them to ask. They may identify an annoying verbal tic. Do what you can to eradicate any rogue erms and umms.
- Listen carefully to questions so you can establish what it is the interviewer seeks. Don't just shoehorn in pre-packaged answers. *"Recruiters really don't like it if people are too polished and give standard answers,"* a trainee told us.
- Finally, be yourself. The interview process is *"about showing your personality, showing yourself as you are normally,"* one graduate recruiter told us. *"There's nothing worse than seeing someone trying to be what they think we want them to be."*

Assessment days   Even though you might have an LPC distinction, a first, 5 A*s at A level, 29 GCSEs and a gold star from Mrs Haslem's nursery class, many firms will want to see you in action and test you out with their own assessments. In their arsenal, firms have written and negotiation exercises, personality profiling, research tasks, group tasks, in-tray exercises and presentations. Often, an assessment day will also include an interview. Different firms prefer different methods. On our website we detail the hoops you'll need to leap through at each of our profiled firms. *"I felt the assessments were pitched at testing social confidence and whether you are a friendly person,"* recalled one trainee at a City firm. Most group tasks and exercises are serious in tone: examples include mock client meetings, an e-mail inbox full of correspondence to deal with, or a feedback session with a partner and an associate. Advertising pitches to faux-clients and pretend mini-transactions are also common, but be warned that firms frequently change the make-up of their assessment days. A (decreasing) number use more unusual methods: over the years we've heard of scenarios where groups of candidates were asked to build Lego towers, determine the allocations of eggs to different parts if a country, and debate who should be allowed to leave a (hypothetical) cave first. Remember: however out-of-the-ordinary an assessment, it is still aimed at testing business skills, and your attitude should at all times remain professional and aimed at showcasing your competencies. Recruiters are especially keen to see whether you can work in a team. Be careful not to dominate group tasks too much or fade into the background. Don't relax too much if there's a social event as these are often just as important when it comes to making a good impression. Some firms have lunches where you sit round with three or four partners and a handful of other applicants and make small talk. Who will your prospective supervisor want to hire? The girl who kept her eyes on the plate for the entire meal and whispered unintelligible answers to every question? The chap who drank too much and spent most of the meal calling him 'buddy'? Or the nice young man who made some pertinent observations on the Eurozone crisis and showed an interest in his kite-surfing hobby? Similarly, a drink with the firm's trainees is an opportunity to strike up a rapport with them, not to start making comments about how your vac scheme at Ashurst was soooo much better. Either as part of the assessment day or application process, you may be asked to complete one or more psychometric tests. Some look at verbal or numerical skills, while others test your judgement when confronted by certain scenarios. You can find examples of these types of tests online (start on Wikipedia), or ask your careers service. Verbal and numerical reasoning tests usually consist of multiple-choice questions with right and wrong answers. Accuracy, intellectual rigour, efficiency and mental agility are imperative. Personality and situational judgement tests aim to find out whether you are a leader or a follower, a planner or impulsive, etc. In theory, there are no correct answers, but before you expose your soul to recruiters, it is worth thinking about why they have set this test and what they are looking for: profiling yourself as an indecisive, emotionally fragile control freak isn't going to help you.

And finally...

The sad fact is that for many people it could take a while to succeed. Don't let rejection bring you down: ask recruiters why you didn't make the cut and learn from it.

Managing job offers

After all the hard work involved in securing a training contract offer, you'll need to know what to do when you actually land one.

The Solicitors Regulation Authority publishes a 'voluntary code to good practice in the recruitment of trainee solicitors' at www.sra.org.uk/documents/students/training-contract/voluntarycode.pdf.

Read through these guidelines if at any stage you are in doubt as to what you should do. They address the conduct of both recruiters and students. Law firms are not obliged to follow these guidelines, though most will.

On offers, the guidelines say:

- If you're still an undergrad, a training contract offer should not be made before 1 September in your final undergraduate year. If you've impressed a firm during a vacation scheme or period of work experience, it must wait until this date before making you an offer.
- At an interview, you will be told if there is a further stage to the selection process. You should also be told within two weeks of reaching the end of the process whether or not you have been successful.
- Offers should be made in writing. If you receive an offer by phone you don't need to say yes or no: you can ask the firm to send a formal offer in writing for you to consider.

On deadlines, the guidelines say:

- No deadline should expire earlier than four weeks from the date of an offer. If you need more time to mull over an offer, firms are supposed to consider your request 'sympathetically', provided you have a good reason. No definition of 'good reason' is given in the guidelines.
- If a firm is going to pay your law school fees it should set out the terms and conditions of the arrangement in the training contract offer letter. A firm's willingness to provide financial assistance should not affect the time limit for accepting the contract.
- If you feel you need more time, you will have to enter into diplomatic discussions with the law firm, telling them how much longer you need. Ask for written confirmation of any extension to the deadline so both parties are clear what has been decided.

You may want to hang on to an offer from one firm while you pursue applications with others. This is okay, but you must bear in mind the following:

- You should not hold more than two (as yet unaccepted or declined) offers at any one time.
- Students are supposed to respond promptly to a firm that's made an offer, either by accepting or rejecting it. The word 'promptly' is not defined in the code.
- Because offers can and will be made with time limits for acceptance, do guard against allowing a deadline to elapse. The stupidity tax you may otherwise pay doesn't bear thinking about.
- Once you have accepted your preferred offer in writing, you must then confirm to everyone else that you are withdrawing your application. This is only fair to busy recruiters and other applicants who may suffer if you clog up a shortlist.

The guidelines are silent on the issue of what happens if a student changes their mind after accepting an offer. It's a rare firm that will be particularly sympathetic to a post-acceptance withdrawal but, on occasions, these things do happen. We can give no general advice on this subject, as each individual case will have its own merits. What we can say is that the smooth running of the whole trainee recruitment market relies on most parties playing by the above 'rules'. So what if a law firm puts pressure on you to accept an offer earlier than the guidelines say they should? Again, there is no simple answer as the SRA's code of conduct is voluntary. If this situation arises you will have to enter into delicate negotiations with the law firm. You could also discuss the problem with your university or college careers adviser and ask if they can recommend a course of action.

Pro bono and volunteering

Deriving from the Latin pro bono publico, meaning 'for the public good', the idea of providing free legal advice has been ingrained in the legal profession for centuries.

The past decade has seen the rise of structured pro bono programmes at law firms, sets of chambers, law schools and universities. Bringing these all together, ProBonoUK. net was started in 2003 and is the most comprehensive resource on pro bono activities in the UK. 2013's National Pro Bono week runs from 4th to 9th November.

Why participate?

The legal aid bill is being cut thick and fast. On top of £350m already removed from the scheme's £2.2bn annual budget, Justice Secretary Chris Grayling has announced a further £220m cut to criminal legal aid. The government has estimated that around 600,000 people will lose access to legal advice as a result, and former Labour legal aid minister Lord Bach has estimated that the cuts will remove 86% of funding which law centres receive to provide advice and 'legal help'. Birmingham Law Centre was forced to close in summer 2013 and it's feared that other centres will go the same way.

As a result of paid jobs going, involvement in some form of pro bono or volunteering work is becoming increasingly important, not just because there are people out there who need your help, but because pro bono experience can really help boost your CV. Experience suggests that those who have been most active have found it much easier to land job interviews. Being able to demonstrative proactive involvement in a cause and achieving real results for those in need will help get your application to the front of the queue. Practising lawyers can – and perhaps ought to – continue to help their communities by providing free legal advice via organisations like LawWorks.

Law schools make a particular effort to introduce students to pro bono. As Jessica Austen, joint director of pro bono at BPP, told us: *"Being involved in pro bono can make a huge difference to student engagement with the courses they are undertaking. They can see the law they are studying come to life in a practical sense and realise the impact their participation can have on the community around them. This is particularly true now, given access to justice is so much more challenging following the legal aid cuts. Pro bono projects give students the chance to improve their organisational and interpersonal skills as well as making a worthwhile contribution to those un-*able to afford to pay for legal assistance."* Many firms now have formal pro bono relationships with organisations such as community legal advice centres. Arguably the increased scope and visibility of pro bono work is in part due to the greater importance placed on pro bono activities by the influx of US law firms into the UK market. Certainly more home-grown law firms now recognise the business case for doing this kind of work, not least because of the PR benefits of telling the world what caring organisations they are.

Real life

Getting involved couldn't be easier when you're at law school as most now offer extensive programmes. Cardiff Law School has the Innocence Project, for example, which deals with long-term prisoners who maintain their innocence and have exhausted the initial appeals process. Kaplan Law School has developed a close relationship with Amicus, and sponsors students to attend training sessions which allows them to assist with defence counsel representations for those facing execution in the US. At the other end of the pro bono spectrum, BPP works in conjunction with the charity Own It to provide free IP advice to the creative industries, while the University of Westminster's LPC course has a clinical law elective, during which students work on a pro bono basis for the CAB and submit a project at the end of the elective. And as if you needed a greater incentive than a warm glow in the pit of your belly, there are various national prizes on offer for students who excel in this field, including the Law Society's annual Junior Lawyers Division Pro Bono Award. At University level, student pro bono opportunities have been more limited, largely because it's too risky for inexperienced undergrads to provide real-life legal advice. This is changing as undergraduates are receiving more support. You can go to www.studentprobono.net for a comprehensive list of opportunities at each institution.

If you hope to go to the Bar or become a solicitor specialising in any contentious area of law then you should seriously consider becoming a ratified member of The Free Representation Unit (FRU), a charity founded in 1972 to provide legal advice, case preparation and advocacy for people who aren't able to claim legal aid.

Vacation schemes

Pack your bags for a holiday placement... but don't forget to bring your common sense cap.

Still at uni and unsure if you really want to be a lawyer? If so, then giving up a week or two of your hard-earned holiday during Christmas, Easter or the summer to sample law firm life is a small price to pay. As one training partner told us, vacations schemes are a great opportunity to test the waters, *"a chance to gain an insight into life as a lawyer, get feedback on your work and grow from the experience."* And as a trainee recalled of their vac scheme at a City firm: *"It given you a very good picture of what life as a trainee will be like."*

But be under no illusions: you will also be on trial, because in this ever-more competitive market most firms (and some more than others) treat the vac scheme almost as a pre-screening exercise when it comes to handing out training contracts. The prime example of a firm that relies heavily on vac schemes is City firm Nabarro, which now takes almost all of its trainees from people it sees on its three-week placement. Another is US giant Skadden, which informs us: *"We do accept applications from those who haven't done vacation schemes with us, but we really only look at those if something has gone wrong with our placement and it hasn't thrown up enough quality candidates."*

This stance is not (yet) the prevailing recruiting model, and many firms who offer vacation schemes recruit just as many trainees who haven't done one with them as those who have. But the message is clear: whichever vac scheme you end up doing you'll be assessed, no matter how informally, and you should plan and act accordingly.

How do you get on one?

Our table of vac schemes over the page will tell you exactly what places are available with the firms covered by this guide and when to apply. Timing your application is important; certain schemes are targeted at penultimate-year law grads or final-year non-law grads, which can leave other students frustrated. Suffice to say, law undergrads need to start thinking about their application campaign during the summer after their first year at university. The application deadlines for the majority of vac schemes come in January and February, but some firms run schemes in the Christmas and Easter holidays and the deadlines for applying to those can be as early as October. Don't miss out! You'll generally find full details of ex-

actly how to make your application on firms' recruitment websites.

What do firms look for when recruiting for the vac scheme? *"Same as the training contract really,"* one tells us: *"Strong academics and an interest in our practice areas."* As competition for training contracts gets more intense, it's no surprise that competition for vac scheme places is equally so. Obvious conclusion: you'll need to put as much effort into vac scheme applications as you do into training contract applications. For some tips on how to do this refer to our feature on how to make successful applications. On our website we have also detailed advice on the application procedures for each of the firms covered in the **True Picture**. The strongest applicants always manage to secure a clutch of offers, but don't despair if you can't secure a place – it doesn't necessarily mean you'll never get a training contract. Try and build your CV up in other ways – say with voluntary work or other legal or commercial experience – and then have another stab at vac scheme applications.

Even if you navigate the vac scheme obstacle course perfectly, don't get complacent. You'll still need to prepare well for a training contract interview.

What will I get to do?

At some firms, vac schemes are structured down to the minute with talks about the firm and its training contract, followed by tasks and social engagements. At others, vac schemers may be tied to a trainee or qualified solicitor and what they do will depend on that individual. Elsewhere, panhandling for work and knocking on doors to find assignments will be the name of the game. The best vac schemes get students involved in ongoing cases and deals and puts them in the heat of the action – or at least let's them feel that way. *"You are expected to contribute to real work,"* recalled one ex-vac schemer. *"I remember doing some very serious assignments – although looking back I probably thought they were more serious than they actually were."* For detailed information on each firm's vacation scheme, go to our website.

What should I look out for?

When on a vac scheme, become an anthropologist. Observe your environment and its inhabitants; figure out the social structures, the hierarchies, the shared values that bond people (if indeed there are any). Watch how the trainees fit in with all of this. Eavesdrop. You've got to be on your guard, though, because people will be conscious you're there, and some of our sources did end up concluding: *"It can be an artificial exercise – you see what they want you to see."* Your aim is to peer beyond the mask at the living, breathing, sweating entity behind it.

Try also to get a feel for how different departments work by reading as much as you can. A starting point would be our **Solicitors' Practice Areas**. It'll help you figure out what sort of work might suit you best and will enable you to ask intelligent questions of your supervisors. Intelligent questions pave the road to success, so lay as many down as possible without becoming annoying.

How will I be assessed?

"The vacation scheme is a great way of meeting prospective trainees and giving them a real taster of what life is like here," one recruiter explains. But don't forget that, on the other hand, *"it's a good way of meeting the candidates and seeing them in action."* Vac schemers are often given research to do as a way of evaluating their abilities; expect to be given some specifics to look into before reporting back to solicitors with your findings. You might be asked to shadow someone, helping them out with their workload. This is an excellent opportunity for you to find more out about the firm while proving yourself at the same time. You might even get to go to client meetings or visit court. Last, but certainly not least, are the mini-assessment tasks designed to test your ability to present, argue and work as a team. *"Don't be over-assertive, but don't fade into the background either. Remember to ask other people what their opinions are – you have to look like a team player."* Some assessments we heard about involved advertising pitches to faux potential clients, mock mini-transactions and business advice scenarios.

How should I act?

"Those who are successful have the drive, imagination and confidence to see the scheme for the learning opportunity it really is rather than just an assessment centre in which they are competing with other students,*"* one training partner at a larger outfit advises. *"Students become part of the firm when they arrive; many make friendships. And the firm will always make room for excellent candidates it sees on the scheme, whatever the numbers."*

While you're busy watching everyone else, don't forget that they're watching you, watching them, watching you. This recruitment lark is a delicate dance, so attune yourself to the characters around you and follow their lead. More than anything else, people will be trying to see if you 'share the firm's core values'. Ultimately, 'professionalism' should be your watchword. This is a job interview, even when you're eating lunch in the canteen. Don't be late for work. Switch off your mobile phone when in the office. Don't bitch or send stupid e-mails. Thinking about browsing Facebook in a slack moment? Why take the risk?

Okay, so don't be an idiot. That much is obvious. But how can you impress? As one recruiter says, it's all about *"marketing yourself well."* Does that sound a little intimidating? It's really not. After all, you marketed yourself well on paper when you sent your application form in, now you are just doing it in person. Asking well-timed questions and showing an interest is an easy way of doing this. Just remember, *"seeking out work and raising your profile without pestering people is a fine line to walk."* A trainee confirmed that you have to strike the right balance, telling us that on the last vac scheme he was involved with *"there were a couple of people who were just a bit too enthusiastic!"*

Coming for a quick drink? Bankers, lawyers, doctors and even priests all know how effective alcohol can be when it comes to greasing the wheels. But the trick is to drink the right amount or none at all. Even when firms take vac schemers out to snazzy clubs, recruiters' mental notepads will still be out. So gauge the situation: is the firm boozy or abstemious?

At the end of the day, a law firm is just like any other office workplace and you'll find all sorts of characters. You'll also find variety within any group of vac schemers. *"You get the quiet ones, the loud ones, the ones who say inappropriate things, the ones who're always smiling."* Obviously, you're being assessed on how good a lawyer you're likely to be, but don't underestimate how far having a normal, attractive personality will get you.

Vacation Schemes

Firm name	Vacancies	Duration	Remuneration	Deadline
Addleshaw Goddard	70	1-2 weeks	Not known	31 January 2014
Allen & Overy	60 – winter (final year undergraduates & graduates); summer (penultimate year undergraduates)	Not known	Not known	31 October 2013 (winter); 14 January 2014 (summer)
Ashfords	Yes	Not known	Not known	31 March 2014
Ashurst	Spring (final year law & non-law, & grads); summer (penult-year law)	2-3 weeks	£275 p.w.	Not known
Bates Wells & Braithwaite	12	2 weeks	£300	March 2014
Bird & Bird	34	3 weeks	Not known	31 December 2013
Bond Dickinson	Easter & summer	Not known	Not known	31 January 2014
Boodle Hatfield	6 – summer	2 weeks	Not known	Not known
BP Collins	Yes	1-2 weeks	Not known	31 March 2014
Bristows	Winter, spring & summer	Not known	Not known	Not known
Capsticks	Summer	2 weeks	Not known	14 February 2014
Cleary Gottlieb	35 (5 in winter, 10 in spring & 20 in summer)	Not known	Not known	15 November 2013 (winter); 28 January 2014 (spring and summer)
Clyde & Co	Easter and summer	2 weeks	Not known	31 January 2014
CMS	60 – spring & summer	2 weeks	£250 p.w.	31 January 2014
Covington & Burling	24 – summer	3 weeks	£300 p.w.	31 January 2014
Davenport Lyons	Summer	Not known	£250 p.w.	Not known
Davis Polk & Wardwell	16-20 – Summer	2 weeks	Not known	31 January 2014
Dechert	Summer + spring open days	2 weeks	Not known	31 January 2014
Dentons	Summer (law & non-law students) + winter open days (non-law)	1 week	Not known	Not known
DLA Piper	130	2 weeks	Not known	Not known
DWF	Summer	1 week	Not known	Not known
Edwards Wildman Palmer	8 – summer + winter, easter & summer open days	2 weeks	Not known	31 January 2014
Eversheds	Summer	2 weeks	Not known	31 January 2014
Farrer & Co	30 – easter & summer	2 weeks	£275 p.w.	31 January 2014
Foot Anstey	Summer	Not known	Not known	28 April 2014
Forbes	Summer	2 weeks	Not known	Not known
Freshfields Bruckhaus Deringer	Yes (aimed at penult-year under-grads)	Not known	Not known	6 January 2014
Gateley	Summer	2 weeks	Not known	31 January 2014
Government Legal Service	10-15 – summer	Not known	Not known	Not known
Herbert Smith Freehills	Winter, spring & summer	Not known	Not known	Not known
Hewitsons	Yes	Not known	Not known	Not known
Hill Dickinson	c. 60	Not known	Not known	31 January 2014
Holman Fenwick Willan	Up to 30 – spring & summer	1-2 weeks	Not known	14 February 2014
Irwin Mitchell	Summer	Not known	Not known	31 January 2014
Jones Day	64 – winter, spring, & summer	2 weeks	£400 p.w.	31 October 2013 (winter); 31 December 2013 (spring); 31 January 2014 (summer)
K&L Gates	Yes	Not known	Not known	Not known
Kennedys	Summer	Not known	Not known	31 January 2014

Vacation Schemes

Firm name	Vacancies	Duration	Remuneration	Deadline
Kirkland & Ellis	c. 20	2 weeks	£350 p.w.	15 January 2014
Latham & Watkins	Easter & summer	2 weeks	£350 p.w.	31 December 2013 (easter); 31 January 2014 (summer)
Lawrence Graham	10 – summer	2 weeks	£350 p.w.	31 January 2014
Lester Aldridge	Summer	2 weeks	Not known	31 March 2014
Linklaters	Summer (penult-year undergrads) + work experience	Not known	Not known	Not known
Macfarlanes	55	2 weeks	£300 p.w.	31 January 2014
Maclay Murray & Spens	Summer	3 weeks	Not known	31 January 2014
Mayer Brown	Spring & summer	2-3 weeks	Not known	Not known
Memery Crystal	Open days	1 day	Not known	Not known
Michelmores	July	1 week	Not known	28 February 2014
Mills & Reeve	Summer	2 weeks	Not known	31 January 2014
Mishcon de Reya	30 – easter & summer	2 weeks	Not known	15 January 2014
Morgan Lewis	20 – spring	Not known	Not known	31 January 2014
Muckle	Summer	Not known	Not known	31 January 2014
Nabarro LLP	60 – summer	3 weeks	Not known	15 January 2014
Norton Rose Fulbright	Winter (final year undergrads & grads) & summer (penult-year undergrads) + open days	Not known	Not known	31 October 2013 (winter); 31 January 2014 (summer)
Olswang	20 – spring & summer	Not known	£275 p.w.	31 January 2014
O'Melveny & Myers	Summer	Not known	Not known	31 January 2014
Orrick	Open days	Not known	Not known	Not known
Osborne Clarke	Summer	2 weeks	Not known	Not known
Penningtons Solicitors	Summer + open days	Not known	Not known	28 February 2014
Pinsent Masons	c. 100 – summer	2 weeks	Not known	Not known
PwC Legal	Summer	3 weeks	Paid	31 January 2014
Reed Smith	Up to 20 – summer	2 weeks	Not known	Not known
RPC	Yes	Not known	Not known	31 January 2014
SGH Martineau	Yes	2 days	Not known	24 February 2014
Shoosmiths	Yes	Not known	Not known	Not known
Simmons & Simmons	Winter (final year & grads non-law); spring (first year law & penult-year non-law); summer (penult-year law, final year non-law & grads) + open days	3 weeks	Not known	Not known
SJ Berwin	Easter and summer	Not known	Not known	31 January 2014
Skadden Arps	Easter & summer (penult-year law & non-law)	2 weeks	Paid	12 January 2014
Slaughter and May	Easter & summer (penult-year law & non-law) + open days	Not known	Not known	Not known
Speechly Bircham	Summer	3 weeks	Not known	Not known
Squire Sanders (Hammonds)	40 – summer	2 weeks	£215-230 p.w.	31 January 2014
Stephenson Harwood	40 – winter, spring & summer + open days	1-2 weeks	£260 p.w.	3 November 2013 (winter); 31 January 2014 (spring & summer)
Stevens & Bolton	Summer	1 week	Not known	31 January 2014

Vacation Schemes

Firm name	Vacancies	Duration	Remuneration	Deadline
Sullivan & Cromwell	Summer (penult-year law & final non-law)	2 weeks	£500 p.w.	31 January 2014
Taylor Wessing	40 – summer	2 weeks	£250 p.w.	31 January 2014
TLT	Easter & summer	1 week	Not known	31 January 2014
Travers Smith	60 (15 in winter & 45 in summer)	2 weeks	£275	31 January 2014 (summer)
Trowers & Hamlins	Summer	2 weeks	Not known	Not known
Veale Wasbrough Vizards	Summer	1 week	Unpaid	Not known
Vinson & Elkins	Summer	Not known	Not known	28 February 2014
Walker Morris	48	1 week	£175 p.w.	31 January 2014
Ward Hadaway	Spring & summer	1 week	Not known	28 February 2014
Watson, Farley & Williams	Yes	2 weeks	Not known	31 January 2014
Wedlake Bell	8 – Summer	3 weeks	Not known	End of February 2014
Weil, Gotshal & Manges	Up to 30 – spring & summer	2 weeks	Paid	Not known
White & Case	75 (15 in spring & 60 in summer)	2 weeks	£350 p.w.	31 January 2014
Wilsons	Summer	1 week	Not known	Not known
Winckworth Sherwood	Summer	Not known	Not known	Not known
Withers	Easter & summer	2 weeks	Not known	31 January 2014
Wragge & Co	Yes	Not known	Not known	31 January 2014

Solicitors' Timetable

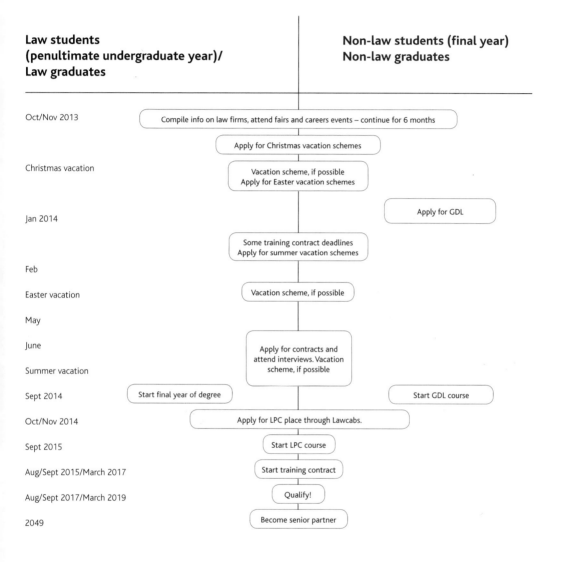

Law students (penultimate undergraduate year)/ Law graduates		Non-law students (final year) Non-law graduates
Oct/Nov 2013	Compile info on law firms, attend fairs and careers events – continue for 6 months	
	Apply for Christmas vacation schemes	
Christmas vacation	Vacation scheme, if possible Apply for Easter vacation schemes	
Jan 2014		Apply for GDL
	Some training contract deadlines Apply for summer vacation schemes	
Feb		
Easter vacation	Vacation scheme, if possible	
May		
June	Apply for contracts and attend interviews. Vacation scheme, if possible	
Summer vacation		
Sept 2014	Start final year of degree	Start GDL course
Oct/Nov 2014	Apply for LPC place through Lawcabs.	
Sept 2015	Start LPC course	
Aug/Sept 2015/March 2017	Start training contract	
Aug/Sept 2017/March 2019	Qualify!	
2049	Become senior partner	

Notes

1   It is important to check application closing dates for each firm as these will vary.
2   Some firms will only accept applications for vacation schemes from penultimate-year students, whether law or non-law. See A-Z pages for further information.
3   Some firms require very early applications from non-law graduates. See A-Z pages for further information.
4   The timetable refers primarily to those firms that recruit two years in advance. Smaller firms often recruit just one year in advance or for immediate vacancies.
5   This timetable assumes students will progress straight through from university to law school and a training contract. This is not necessarily the most appropriate or achievable course of action for all students.

Barristers' Timetable

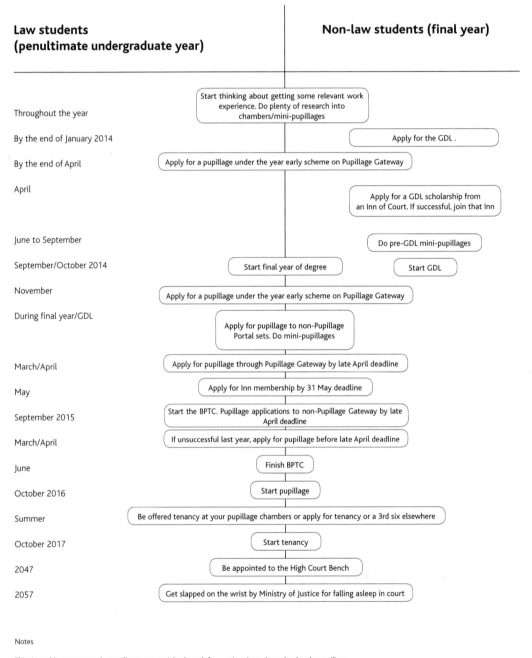

Law students
(penultimate undergraduate year)

Non-law students (final year)

Throughout the year	Start thinking about getting some relevant work experience. Do plenty of research into chambers/mini-pupillages
By the end of January 2014	Apply for the GDL .
By the end of April	Apply for a pupillage under the year early scheme on Pupillage Gateway
April	Apply for a GDL scholarship from an Inn of Court. If successful, join that Inn
June to September	Do pre-GDL mini-pupillages
September/October 2014	Start final year of degree / Start GDL
November	Apply for a pupillage under the year early scheme on Pupillage Gateway
During final year/GDL	Apply for pupillage to non-Pupillage Portal sets. Do mini-pupillages
March/April	Apply for pupillage through Pupillage Gateway by late April deadline
May	Apply for Inn membership by 31 May deadline
September 2015	Start the BPTC. Pupillage applications to non-Pupillage Gateway by late April deadline
March/April	If unsuccessful last year, apply for pupillage before late April deadline
June	Finish BPTC
October 2016	Start pupillage
Summer	Be offered tenancy at your pupillage chambers or apply for tenancy or a 3rd six elsewhere
October 2017	Start tenancy
2047	Be appointed to the High Court Bench
2057	Get slapped on the wrist by Ministry of Justice for falling asleep in court

Notes

This timetable assumes students will progress straight through from university to law school and a pupillage.
This is not necessarily the most appropriate or achievable course of action for students.

The Graduate Diploma in Law (GDL)

Whether you chose to spend your undergrad years exploring the ritual ceremonies of Amazonians, immersing yourself in Chaucer and Langland, or grappling with some insoluble questions existentielles, you can still come to the law via a one-year conversion course known as the Graduate Diploma in Law (GDL).

NB: The course is also referred to as the CPE (Common Professional Exam) or PgDL (Postgraduate Diploma in Law).

Because skills like textual analysis, research, logical argument, and written and oral presentation can be acquired in a whole range of disciplines, from English lit to zoology, legal employers tend not to make a distinction between applicants with an LLB and those who take the GDL route.

The GDL is essentially a crash law degree, designed to bring you up to the required standard in seven core legal subjects that would typically be taught in the first two years of an LLB. So that's two years of study crammed into one – not exactly a walk in the park. Taken full-time it lasts a minimum of 36 weeks and can demand up to 45 hours of lectures, tutorials and personal study each week. It is possible to take the course part-time over two years, and you will find that course providers offer a surprisingly wide range of flexible study options, from distance learning to weekends or evening-only classes.

The standard requirement for admission is a degree from a university in the UK or Republic of Ireland. It is possible for non-graduates to get onto a course if they've shown the requisite drive and determination, and have exceptional ability in some other field. Such candidates – and those with a degree from an overseas university – must obtain a Certificate of Academic Standing from the Bar Standards Board or Solicitors Regulation Authority before enrolling on the GDL.

Assessments tend to be by written exams taken at the end of the academic year. These will make up the bulk of your final grade, so make sure you are adequately prepared. Most GDL providers offer their students the opportunity to take mock exams throughout the year, and while these are generally optional, it's probably a good idea to get as many as you can under your belt. If nothing else, they will give you an indication of your progress and the chance to receive feedback from tutors. Other assessments and essays completed during the year can count for up to 30% of your final grade, so do not underestimate their importance, and coursework does allow for a degree of flexibility, meaning that students can write about areas that aren't necessarily explored in depth on the course, such as immigration or copyright law. Depending on the institution, there will be more or less emphasis on academic essays, written problem questions or practical preparation for classroom debates.

Because the institutions that offer the GDL vary in perceived quality, their approach and the composition of their student bodies, it is well worth doing your research before you apply. City University and Nottingham are renowned for offering more academic courses, thought to be ideally suited to students headed to the Bar. In London, BPP and the University of Law, for example, are packed with plenty of City types and place special emphasis on helping you gain practical legal skills.

Be aware that an increasing number of City firms are appointing a particular law school as their preferred provider. If you have your heart set on doing your training contract with a particular law firm, do your research and find out whether they have a preferred provider before you apply to the schools.

There's a huge amount to take in so you need to be disciplined. Try and work out a study timetable early on, and stick to it. Don't count on being able to catch up, as time will fly by. You're there to learn a set curriculum, not to think outside the box. That said, it is important that you gain an overall understanding of how the law works, so avoid studying each subject in isolation. Probably the best use of your creativity is to come up with amusing ways of remembering case names. Attend classes! Particularly if you have already secured a training contract before starting the GDL, as some law schools will report on attendance, if asked by your future employer.

Contract

As a practising civil lawyer, you will apply your knowledge of contract law on a daily basis because it underpins nearly every single legal relationship. You'll start by studying the rules that determine when an agreement becomes legally binding and enforceable, and which formalities are required to create a contract. You'll then move on to study what terms are permissible and find out what happens when you omit to read the small print. You'll hear about the doctrine of misrepresentation, mistake and duress, and you'll find out what your remedy is when an art dealer has neglected to tell you the Jackson Pollock you've just bought is actually the product of his son's finger painting. Armed with your knowledge of the Sale of Goods Act, you may be tempted to bring any number of small claims against the high-street retailers whose products fall apart the minute you get them home.

Tort

Broadly defined, the law of tort is concerned with remedying wrongs committed by one individual against another via the civil rather than the criminal courts. Beyond this very sensible definition hides one of the most intellectually challenging and stimulating courses on the GDL. The law of negligence is the big subject in tort, and you will devote the best part of the year to getting your head around it and applying it to specific situations such as clinical negligence. The course will also cover wrongs ranging from defamation to private nuisance. This is the field which fuels the so-called compensation culture and gives 'ambulance-chasing' lawyers a bad name. While studying tort you will hear about the fate of victims of gruesome work or road traffic accidents, and catastrophic events such as the Hillsborough disaster. But you will also come across downright comical stories, including snails in bottles of ginger beer or a case of compensation for scratchy underwear.

Public law

Public law, as it is generically referred to, is a course that includes the study of constitutional law, human rights and administrative law (the order may vary depending on where you study). If you have no interest in politics (shame on you), you may find the whole subject a little obscure, but with over ten years since the passing of the Human Rights Act, and with several constitutional reforms in the works, now is arguably the best of times to study this fascinating subject. The course will normally kick off with an analysis of the UK's constitutional arrangements. This part is largely academic and will cover the doctrines of Parliamentary sovereignty, the Rule of Law, the Royal Prerogative and Responsible Government. Those with politics degrees should be able to hit the ground running. You're also likely to enjoy the constitutional bit of the subject if you're a history or philosophy

buff. If you do not fit the description, why not Google 'Dicey' and see where that takes you.

You'll also be taught about the Human Rights Act, with particular emphasis being given to the concepts of freedom of speech, the right to privacy, the right to a fair trial and the nitty-gritty of exactly how much force the police can use when they throw you in the back of their van. After the academic bit is over, a large chunk of the rest of the course is devoted to judicial review, the process by which individuals with sufficient standing can challenge the decisions of public authorities. Those who don't enjoy the theoretical feel of constitutional law should appreciate the more practical nature of judicial review.

Crime

Whether it is through reading crime novels, watching *Law and Order* or simply perusing newspaper headlines, you are in contact with criminal activity on a daily basis, and you could be forgiven for thinking that the law begins and ends at crime. Studying criminal law will allow you to discover the reality behind the storylines. The syllabus will take you through assault, battery, sexual offences, criminal damage, theft, fraud and homicide. Also covered are the liability of accomplices, attempted offences and the defences available to those accused of committing criminal acts.

Whether your interest is in policy or the gruesome things that people do to one another, the crime course should provide plenty to engage and surprise. Overall, the subject follows a logical pattern and doesn't hide many difficult philosophical concepts. You will find out early on that you always need to identify the actus reus (the guilty act) and the mens rea (the guilty mind) in order to establish an offence. Follow this structure religiously and you can't go wrong. By the end of the course you'll also be in a better position to explain why killing someone is not necessarily unlawful, or why you could be guilty of theft without actually making off with somebody else's property.

Equity and trusts

This course will provide you with an introduction to the fundamental principles of equity, an intriguing area of law which calls upon the idea of conscience to remedy injustices brought about by the application of black letter law. Also on the agenda is the concept of trust, which is the legal arrangement whereby one person holds property for the benefit of another.

One preconception about the subject is that it is the preserve of those who have their heart set on Chancery work at the Bar or wish to practise in the private wealth sector. While this is partially true, equity and trusts form a particularly dynamic area of law, and you'll not only learn about the creation of gifts and trusts in the family

The GDL Providers

Aberystwyth University (ft)

Aston University (ft/pt)

Birmingham City University (ft/pt)

Bournemouth University (ft/pt)

BPP Law School, Birmingham (ft/pt)

BPP Law School, Bristol (ft/pt)

BPP Law School, Cambridge (ft/pt)

BPP Law School, Leeds (ft/pt)

BPP Law School, Liverpool (ft/pt)

BPP Law School, London (ft/pt)

BPP Law School, Manchester

University of Bradford (ft/pt)

University of Brighton (ft/pt)

Brunel University (ft/pt)

Cardiff University (ft/pt)

University of Central Lancashire (ft/pt)

City Law School (ft)

De Montfort University (ft/pt)

University of East Anglia (ft)

University of Hertfordshire (ft/pt)

University of Huddersfield (ft/pt)

Kaplan Law School (ft)

Keele University (ft/pt)

Kingston University (ft/pt)

University of Law, Bristol (ft/pt)

University of Law, Chester (ft/pt)

University of Law, Guildford (ft/pt)

University of Law, London (ft/pt)

University of Law, Manchester (ft/pt)

University of Law, York (ft/pt)

Leeds Metropolitan University (ft/pt)

University of Lincoln (ft)

Liverpool John Moores University (ft/pt)

London Metropolitan University (ft/pt)

London South Bank University (ft/pt)

Manchester Metropolitan University (ft/pt)

Middlesex University (ft/pt)

Northumbria University (ft/pt)

Nottingham Trent University (ft/pt)

Oxford Brookes University (ft/pt)

University of Plymouth (ft)

University of Sheffield (ft)

University of South Wales (ft/pt)

Staffordshire University (ft/pt)

Swansea University (ft)

University of Sussex (ft)

University of the West of England (ft/pt)

University of Westminster (ft/pt)

University of Winchester (ft/pt)

University of Wolverhampton (ft/pt)

context, you'll also see that the concept has many uses in the commercial and financial worlds, particularly where tax evasion or the tracing of misappropriated funds are concerned. The topic is mostly precedent-based, meaning that you'll have to memorise a huge number of cases. On the bright side, these can be amusing and memorable. You'll hear about adulterous husbands trying to set up secret trusts for their mistresses and illegitimate children, or wealthy eccentrics attempting to set up a pension for a beloved pet. Be aware that the concept of equity pervades the GDL course, so what you've learned here will also be relevant to your land law and contract modules. Past students report that there's a mathematical side to this module, and that the complex nature of some of the concepts promotes a different way of thinking.

Land law

This module will teach you everything you need to know about the ownership of land, starting with the startling realisation that all of it ultimately belongs to Her Majesty the Queen. Many students may find the subject off-putting to begin with because it uses archaic, mind-numbing jargon and calls on concepts such as overreaching, flying freeholds or overriding interests, which defy any sense of logic. Give it some time and everything will start to fall into place. You'll find the topic has practical implications for your everyday life, including tips on how to handle a dispute with your landlord or how to arrange your first mortgage. The course will also take you through the basics of conveyancing and how to acquire interests in land such as easements or covenants, before going through the detail of how those interests operate.

The subject is formalistic and particularly statute-heavy. In addition to remembering loads of cases, you will be required to memorise countless statutory provisions on the creation and registration of interests in land. Don't wait to familiarise yourself with the most important sections of the Law of Property Act: start creating flowcharts and checklists early on and you will laugh your way through the exam. As with most topics on the GDL, you will need to gain a good overall understanding of land law to be able to deal with specific matters, so don't bet on revising selected subjects for the exam. There can be important overlap between them, particularly with equity and trusts.

EU

Whether the *Daily Mail* likes it or not, EU law now affects our lives in many ways. This course should help dispel a few misconceptions about the British membership of the European Union – it touches on far more than the way in which EU bureaucrats regulate the shape and size of bananas. You'll learn that the European Court of Justice (ECJ) is effectively the highest court of appeal for all the member states, and that EU law plays a central role in the creation of new rights against discrimination on grounds of age, disability, race, religion or sexual orientation, for example. Students become familiar with the institutional framework, foundations and underlying principles of the European Union before going on to explore certain areas of substantive EU law. Big subjects include the free movement of goods and workers, competition law and the freedom of establishment, as well as the incorporation of the European Convention on Human Rights into our national law. For Euro-philes, this course will provide a fascinating mix of politics, history, economics and comparative jurisprudence, but its case law contains some of the longest and most tongue-twisting names you're likely to see.

How to apply

In addition to the seven core subjects, certain GDL providers, particularly those with a City slant, also offer optional classes designed to ease your passage into the corporate world. These may include additional lectures or seminars on company law, intellectual property and international law. Most also organise mooting competitions and pro bono work. These should give you an early opportunity to try your counselling and advocacy skills and find out if a legal career is really for you, particularly if you're headed for the Bar. A number of providers have degree-awarding powers allowing you to upgrade your qualification to an LLB, either upon successful completion of your GDL and LPC or after a summer course following the GDL. Unlike the GDL, the LLB gives you an internationally recognised accreditation.

All GDL applications are made online through the Central Applications Board (www.lawcabs.ac.uk). Remember, there's an application fee and it's worth getting your application in as early as possible if you have your heart set on a particular institution, particularly as Lawcabs need your referee to respond to them before your application is passed on to the schools you're interested in. Many law schools now offer January as well as September starts for their GDL programmes, and so the application timetable has been reformed to accommodate this. Replacing the old process involving first and second round offers, law schools will now recruit GDL students on a rolling basis.

The application form for courses beginning in 2014 will be available from early October 2013, and commencing early November these applications will be sent to law schools who may then make offers to students. The later you apply the more flexible you may have to be about where you study. Applications for part-time courses should be made directly to the providers. If you intend to do an LPC or BPTC at a popular institution you might stand a better chance if you choose it for your GDL, as many providers guarantee places to their GDL graduates. Our website has a table detailing all the GDL providers, their stated fees and loads of other useful information.

The Legal Practice Course (LPC)

Before starting your glorious career as a solicitor, you'll need to jump through the unavoidable hoop that is the LPC. Just don't let all of those flexible and alluring study options distract from the underlying truth that the LPC is intense, costly, and not a guaranteed pass to a training contract.

LETR of recommendation

After two years of unparalleled excitement and anticipation (well, possibly) the Legal Education Training Review (LETR) report was finally delivered to the Review Executive in June 2013. Launched back in 2011 in response to the *"unprecedented degree of change"* currently being experienced in the legal services sector – especially since the Legal Services Act was passed in 2007 – the joint project between the SRA, the Bar Standards Board and ILEX Professional Standards (IPS) was described as *"the most fundamental review of legal education in 30 years,"* and one that would see a *"big shake-up of the legal profession."* The reality, though, was far less enthralling. Essentially the report recommended a few tweaks to the system already in place. A snapshot of the main findings are:

- There is *"considerable dissatisfaction"* from students paying in pursuit of a career *"they're never likely to achieve."* Not only have undergrad tuition fees trebled since 2010, but the already high cost of legal training continues to rise.
- However, the idea of aptitude testing was rejected by the LETR on *"diversity grounds."* Rather, a focus on opening up alternative, cheaper ways to becoming a lawyer is being encouraged.
- Noting a *"lack of variety of models of vocational training for solicitors and barristers,"* the report calls for further development of apprenticeships, greater integration of vocational and workplace training, and new *"work-based learning pathways through the training contract."*
- Due to the growing gap between the number of LPC students and the number of training contracts, providers are urged to take on smaller cohorts.

The numbers game

Yes, the final outcome of the LETR may be underwhelming (especially considering the length of time it took to complete) but whether the current system needed a massive overhaul was already a contentious point. The course leaders we spoke with certainly felt the LPC still had an important part to play in training the next generation of lawyers. *"I do think the LPC is underrated in PR terms,"* said one. *"It's a highly relevant course and highly regarded within firms, so I don't see an immediate need to totally change it."* However, they did acknowledge that the current education system has one key failing: *"The problem isn't the course itself – it works very well. What doesn't work well is matching the number of LPC grads with the number of available jobs."* According to The Law Society, the number of new training contracts registered between July 2011 and July 2012 totalled a dismal 4,869 (a 10.5% drop on the previous year). However, the number registered between July 2010 and July 2011 was 5,441, an 11.6% rebound from 2009-10. The number of training contracts is going through a classic peaks and troughs experience as the market right-sizes itself while the country lurches its way out of recession.

Despite the heady numbers of training contracts available in 2011, there were still far too many aspiring lawyers for everyone to get one. With the number of contracts declining again in 2012, this disparity has only widened. Despite the struggles of the National College of Legal Training (NCLT) and Oxford Brookes, who both ceased their LPC provision for 2013 in response to dwindling application numbers, other providers have signalled that enrolments for September 2013 are either matching or seeing an increase on last year's totals. Some even posted record numbers, and with the University of Law relocating its York branch to Leeds in September 2014, the number of students it can accommodate will increase further. You don't need to be the next Einstein to figure out that not everyone who completes the LPC will get a training contract – as the SRA gently points out: *"If you are planning to apply for a training contract, you need to know that the number of employers able to offer training contracts may*

Law School

be dictated by economic factors and can be significantly lower than the number of LPC graduates."

The SRA claims that it has no power to cap the number of places that institutions are validated for, so effectively institutions can continue to invite people to the party, even though the dance floor is already full. Course providers have told us that increasingly *"firms [especially smaller outfits] are very keen to take on LPC graduates as paralegals and not offer training contracts,"* as trainees are more expensive and smaller firms are not willing to take the risk. *"For a small firm, taking on a trainee is an onerous burden and a risk because if it's the wrong decision, then you're saddled with an ineffective person for a long period of time."* In some cases, paralegalling does lead to a training contract; however the shape of the legal world is changing, with increased cost pressures on firms and non-lawyers taking on more responsibility.

Law schools are very proactive when it comes to delivering careers advice to their LPC students, but it is really up to the individual to take a long, hard objective look at their prospects of securing a training contract after the course. The Bar Standards Board has introduced a compulsory aptitude test for the BPTC (the vocational course all prospective barristers must pass before being called to the Bar). The aim of the test (called the BCAT) is to assess applicants' chances of securing a pupillage before spending one year and many thousands of pounds on a qualification they may never use. While many feel this is the way forward for the LPC, the LETR rejected the proposal – as we mentioned above – and earlier attempts to do so by Kaplan Law School were thwarted by the SRA. Most providers aren't exactly enthralled by the idea anyway: *"An aptitude test for what? The market is so broad, and there's quite a bit of difference between someone who wants to be a back-room tax lawyer and someone who wants to be a corporate high-flyer. If you introduce an aptitude test then you can be sure as hell that people will be hot-housed for it. Where would the diversity be?"*

Third time's the charm

The LPC3 was rolled out at law schools in 2009 and 2010, with feedback suggesting that both course providers and students appreciate the increased flexibility of the course and the freedom to 'tailor' the LPC towards a specific area of legal practice. Several providers have re-engineered the compulsory subjects to reflect the interests and future destinations of their students, whether they be more corporate, commercial or high-street in nature. LPC programmes are now constantly updated and rejigged, in order to keep up to date with the developments in the legal sector. For example, the University of Law has put together an 'international LPC' (something its good rival BPP is also contemplating replicating), reflecting the increasingly global outlook of many City firms. Add to this the many 'knowledge modules' that have been woven into

the LPC to bolster students' business acumen, as well as an ever increasing list of other options, and you can see the freedom of the LPC3 in full swing. Theoretically at least, the option is there to build your very own bespoke LPC. Pretty much anything goes so long as the LPC is completed within five years.

Another trend in recent years has been law school expansion. The two big course providers – BPP and UoL, who collectively dominate the market – have opened up new centres up and down the country from Bristol to Liverpool. More schools outside the major city centres are to be welcomed, as they allow students the less-expensive option of studying from home and they generally cost less than their City counterparts. However, having BPP or UoL open up in your city can be detrimental, as Anglia Ruskin found out when BPP set up camp in Cambridge: the former was forced to cancel its part-time course due to lack of student interest. The NCLT probably won't be thanking either provider for setting up shop in Bristol recently either. Will we see much more expansion from the UoL and BPP? A source at UoL said last year that *"we now have a centre in every region, so I'm comfortable in saying that we wouldn't want to expand any further."* However, when the news came through in March 2013 that Oxford Brookes was ceasing its LPC provision, UoL stepped into the void and will now deliver its course on the university's campus in 2013/14. Both providers are keeping their ears to the ground in relation to international expansion, too. UoL has already tapped into the Singapore market, while BPP is also looking at potential overseas opportunities through the US education company Apollo, which it became a part of in 2009.

My money on my mind

Wherever you choose to do it, the LPC is an expensive affair. Unless you've been hooked up by a generous commercial law firm that's sponsoring you, it's time to dig deep. While some providers have frozen their 2013 fees, most have inevitably risen and will continue to do so year by year. The University of Glamorgan was incorporated into the new University of South Wales this year and its full-time fees spiked from £7,150 to £9,000. That still puts them on par with most other providers but at the top end you could be shelling out a whopping £14,000. And that's before you factor in living expenses. For a comprehensive comparison of course fees look at the LPC Providers Table on our website. For advice on how to fund your trip to law school, see page 92.

Law schools are a business: they sell the LPC to prospective solicitors for around £10k and welcome in as many people as they can without compromising on quality. The Law Society and the SRA caution against stumbling into the LPC without considering future job prospects, but claim not to have the power to restrict the number of LPC places. A 2:2 degree will pretty much guarantee you a place on a course, but finding a firm that will want to train you afterwards is an entirely different proposition. When faced with a 2:2 candidate, firms usually expect a pretty good reason for the grade (ie valid extenuating circumstances), some outstanding features on your CV or, if you're a more 'mature' candidate, a strong first career under your belt, which show that your degree results are historic and not a true reflection of your abilities. Some law schools, like Kaplan and Nottingham, take an *"ethical approach"* by asking for a 2:1 in most cases, while others are less prescriptive, earning them some fierce criticism from former students: *"They are taking the piss with how many people they are taking on who are not good enough to get training contracts. It's not fair."* One such provider does assure us that students with a 2:2 receive *"specialist advice – we always say that they must be alive to the fact that they need to demonstrate something over and above. It's not impossible, but they must also be prepared to struggle more to get a vac scheme, and seriously consider paralegal work."*

The nuts and bolts of the LPC

It's important to remember that the LPC is not an academic course – it's vocational. Treat it like the first year of your professional life. The LPC requires good time management, organisation and preparation, and even though some providers have open-book exams, it's far from advisable to be sitting at your desk with an exam paper in front of you searching furiously through the textbooks at your side. Keep on top of things as the course progresses, and perhaps even think about sharing the revision workload with classmates. Many students complain that the *"learn, apply, regurgitate, pass"* approach of the LPC isn't as stimulating as an undergraduate degree. However, the course isn't designed to be stimulating; it's meant to get you ready to start a training contract. With classes on semicolons and spelling, it can feel like you're back at school, but you'll pick up plenty of tricks and tips along the way, including:

- How to conduct an interview (usually a strong handshake accompanied by the offer of a beverage);
- How to sign off a letter – not 'lots of love' or 'peace', as a rule;
- How to minimise tax exposure – it's about avoidance, not evasion;
- How many directors it takes to make a board meeting – this isn't a bad joke;
- When litigation documents must be served on the other side – you will curse the day bank holidays were invented;
- Whether you or your landlord is responsible when the roof leaks; and
- Why it's never a good idea to dabble with clients' money.

Make the right choice

When and how: Timetables can vary wildly between providers, and while some course providers have taken advantage of the freedoms afforded by LPC3 to condense teaching into three or even two days, either mornings or afternoons, others still require attendance four days a week alongside a sizeable chunk of self-study. Term dates and even the length of the whole course can vary substantially. Students can opt to spend anywhere between seven months and five years studying for the qualification. Think realistically about what timetable structure will fit most easily into your life. Also think about whether or not you will need a job during the course because, while all providers are reluctant to acknowledge that students will be able to fit in a part-time job, they are increasingly aware that this may be unavoidable, so the majority offer the choice of studying part-time.

Meanwhile, the use of online learning is becoming even more pervasive. BPP, for example, has rolled out an entirely distance learning-based LPC, a 'blended' approach that makes physical attendance entirely unnecessary (well, almost; the SRA dictates there most be a minimum of ten hours face-to-face interaction). Students at Birmingham City University can access work from virtual law firm 'BCU Solicitors', while UoL has replaced the passive lecture format with i-tutorials. Some students thrive on electronic learning methods, and part-time students in particular appreciate being able to fit the work around their already busy lives. However, working from home does require a degree of dedication and self-discipline, so think carefully about what mode of teaching will suit you best before you sign up. Can you actually focus in pyjamas?

Assessments: The vast majority of providers examine their students using open-book exams and written assessments. A notable minority, including BPP, have stuck with the closed-book approach. Although it's easy to feel drawn to the open-book approach, the timeframes are such that you have very little time to trawl through books in the exams.

Facilities: For every provider at which students must search plaintively for a quiet study corner, there is another where they can spread out in blessed peace in their own 'office'. Take the LPC at a university and you'll belong to a proper law faculty surrounded by chilled-out undergrads and deep-thinking postgrads; elsewhere, leather sofas and acres of plate glass might make you think you've strayed into the offices of a City firm. Given the importance of IT to the LPC, you should consider whether the institution offers endless vistas of the latest flat screens or a few dusty computers in a basement.

Atmosphere and direction: A large institution may appeal to students keen to chug anonymously through the system. Conversely, the intimacy of fewer students and easily accessible tutors may tip the scales in favour of a smaller provider. Some places are known to attract very corporate types destined to be City high-flyers; others cultivate the talents of those headed for regional practice. Still others purport to attract a broad a mix of students, so the commercially minded can mingle with future high-street practitioners. These distinctions are likely to become increasingly pronounced with the variety of courses ushered in by the LPC3, so do consider which flavour you're after.

Money and location: Fees vary and so do the providers' policies on the inclusion of the cost of textbooks and Law Society membership, etc. Even if you have sponsorship, living expenses still need to be taken into account. The cost of living in London can be an especially nasty shock. Plenty of students find that tight finances restrict their choice of provider. Although it might seem reprehensible to some, living with the parents will obviously save you a packet. If you're desperate to strike out on your own (or you haven't lived with The Olds for some time), then it's worth considering what you like or don't like about your university or GDL provider and whether you want to prolong your undergraduate experience or escape it. When weighing up providers in large cities, find out whether the campus is in the city centre or out on a ring road.

Extra qualifications: A current trend among providers is the offer of a top-up LLM, with students using their LPC credits to count towards a Masters in legal practice. Students at UoL can top up their LPC with an LLM in either Professional Legal Practice or International Legal Practice, while BPP now offers all its students a new MA

programme ('LPC with business'). A handful of providers also have degree-awarding powers, which means you can turn your GDL and LPC into an LLB.

Social mix and social life: Student-y cities such as Nottingham and Bristol are always a lot of fun, but the bright lights of the capital may be irresistible. Experience tells us that compared to those in other cities, many students in London tend to slink off the moment classes end rather than socialise into the evening.

Making applications

The Central Applications Board administers all applications for full-time LPCs. The application timetable has been overhauled in response to the fact that several course providers have introduced January and February start dates. LPC admissions will now be processed on a rolling basis with the application form available from early October 2013. Beginning early November 2013 applications will be sent to law schools week by week and the course providers may make offers to students immediately. Obviously the later the application the less secure a place, but it should be remembered that almost every school will have more validated places than enrolled students on its both full-time and part-time courses. Some of the most popular institutions must be placed first on the LawCabs application form – see the LPC Providers Table on our website – but students can apply for up to three. Check also whether your university, GDL provider or future law firm has any agreement or relationship with a provider. Applications for part-time courses should be made directly to the individual provider.

LPC Provider Reports

See our website for a comprehensive table detailing all the providers – compare their fees, student numbers, available subjects and other helpful info. Read the reports below for extra background plus feedback from past students and course leaders...

Aberystwyth University

Number of places: 65 FT
Fees (2013/14): £10,000 (10% discount for alumni)
Pro: surfers' paradise
Con: the weather

Aber's Department of Law and Criminology moved to the university's Llanbadarn campus in September 2013 as part of a £5m re-investment project. LPC students can take advantage of brand new mock courtrooms, dedicated pro bono rooms and state-of-the-art IT facilities. Aberystwyth is also running a GDL course for the first time this year.

Candidates who name Aber as their first-choice provider and get in are guaranteed accommodation at the school. Though there's no strict timetable, students can typically expect six to eight hours of lectures on a Monday, while on Tuesdays, Wednesdays and Thursdays there are one or two workshops of two hours duration. Friday is left free for other activities, and the chance to sit with a local district judge is organised by the school.

Aberystwyth provides over 400 hours of face-to-face teaching throughout the course. *"We have a small intake on our LPC so we get to know our students very well,"* a representative told us. Teaching is conducted through a combination of large and small group sessions. The school runs seven electives at Stage Two, with a good mix of commercial and private client offerings.

Students get an employability and professional development tutor who advises on applications and other aspects of job hunting. The school runs a number of work placements during the autumn reading week and at Easter, and lucky students can join the staff at local firms, the local county council, the Welsh Government or bigger, commercially focused firms in Cardiff. The majority of grads go on to high-street firms, but they have followed a range of career paths over the years. *"Some have gone on to the likes of Clifford Chance or Eversheds, and others have gone to local authorities across England and Wales."*

Students are able to get involved with the Innocence Project if they're looking to try their hand at some pro bono work, while the school has a number of other relationships with local charities. A tie-up with the local courts is also currently being investigated. For students looking for a further boost to their education, a top-up LLM in legal practice is available to those who submit a 20,000 word dissertation after the conclusion of the course.

Anglia Ruskin University

Number of places: 80 FT (Chelmsford), 60 FTE (Cambridge)
Fees (2013/14): £8,375
Pro: choice of campuses
Con: no part-time option

Anglia Ruskin runs a full-time LPC at both its Cambridge and Chelmsford campuses. At Chelmsford the course is taught over four days a week, while in Cambridge the full-time equivalent (FTE) is delivered over two fixed days – Tuesday and Thursday. This gives students the ability to study around other commitments, including employment or training opportunities. Most large group sessions are delivered by i-lecture, allowing students to view them remotely. Workshops usually include 16 to 20 students. All the supporting learning tools are available through the Virtual Learning Environment, which can be accessed off-campus. This includes the i-lectures, all workshop materials and access to ARU's online library.

ARU offers specialist non-assessed training throughout Stage One. Topics include: careers and professional development; billing; file management and commercial awareness; and negotiation skills. Mock courtrooms are on both campuses.

ARU has strong links with practitioners throughout the Eastern region and beyond – most of the student body are from the area and go on to practise at local firms. Regional practitioners are involved in developing the LPC to ensure its curriculum is current and appropriate. Local solicitors also visit frequently to provide careers guidance and sometimes offer opportunities to interview for a training contract, and the school recently developed a link with the Essex Legal Services Board which should enhance opportunities for LPC grads with local authorities in Essex.

Birmingham City University

Number of places: 60 FT, 40 PT
Fees (2013/14): £8,500
Pro: small intake
Con: no advanced criminal lit elective

The small intake means small teaching groups and a great staff-to-student ratio. The law school is upping sticks in 2015 to Millennium Point, as the whole university embarks on a move to the city centre. *"It will give students better access to the amenities in Birmingham and provide us with some great new facilities,"* a BCU source tells us.

Full-time students are on-site for the first three days of the week, while Thursday and Friday are kept free to allow for other activities. Electives are timetabled over one or two days, and part-time students are expected in on Tuesday and Thursday evenings. Although BCU students *"usually go on to high-street firms,"* the school aims to offer a broad coverage to suit any career path. The range of electives on offer reflects this, and there is a number of commercial and private client avenues students can pursue. The school has decided to stop running its advanced criminal litigation option, while welfare and immigration is now just known as immigration. *"Employability is the big agenda"* at BCU, and so mentoring schemes are in place which see members of practice – or other professionals for those looking at differing careers – paired up with students. Career talks by guest presenters occur frequently throughout the duration of the course.

BCU offers a wide range of pro bono opportunities, like work with CABs, the local council, benefits advice agencies, employment law advice agencies or centres that deal with human rights cases. Our source says: *"If students have a particular need or desire in relation to pro bono we can usually accommodate that."*

BCU's fees are some of the lowest in the country and a loyalty discount of 10% is available to its former undergrads, while a repayment schedule plan has also been introduced for students this year. From September 2013 the school will offer a top-up LLM for the first time.

Bournemouth University

Number of places: 85 FTE
Fees (2013/14): £11,000
Pro: golden sandy beaches
Con: weever fish

"I was very impressed with Bournemouth," one former student told us. *"The quality of the course was pretty high, the teaching was hands-on and the facilities were very good as the business school is an entirely new building."* The Department of Law resides in Bournemouth's new business centre on the Lansdowne Campus and LPC students can access dedicated law libraries, extensive online legal research materials, as well as innovative, state-of-the-art teaching facilities such as multimedia 'technopods' – hi-tech booths with space for eight people.

BU has delivered the LPC since 1994 and offers a broadly based course, combining the knowledge of core areas of legal practice together with necessary skills – including employability – and a good range of electives that cover both high-street and more commercially-based lines of work. Like at most schools, the LPC is taught through a mixture of lectures and small group sessions. There's a focus on face-to-face learning and teaching, as BU puts an emphasis on interaction between students and staff to help mimic the experience of a life in practice. However, the university does utilise online learning and specific lectures, such as accounts, are uploaded onto the internet to allow students access for revision or preparation purposes. A part-time study option is available, and those on this route will study units in the same classes as the full-time students, but only for two or three days each week.

The teaching staff is active in the local legal community, either as practising lawyers, or as members and chairs of local law societies. Local firms and organisations donate prizes to students on the law courses at BU, including the Dorset Magistrates' Association prize for Advocacy specifically for the LPC.

LPC students who went to unis in Southampton, Portsmouth or Winchester get 10% off.

BPP Law School

Number of places: Lots (see below)
Fees (2013/14): £13,950 + £126 (London)
Pro: great links with big firms
Con: expensive

"Our philosophy is to make sure that our students are work-ready," our contact at BPP informs us. *"We take feedback from law firms very seriously and we make sure the course will equip our students properly for when they become solicitors."* As such, BPP has launched a new programme which means students can study for a unique MA (LPC with Business). In addition to the standard LPC, two additional business modules and a 'business intelligence project' are undertaken to equip students with an understanding of the environments in which clients and law firms operate. *"It has proved very popular and our exclusive clients really like the idea, as commercial awareness is commonly lacking in a student's education."*

To further help their cohort gain a competitive edge, BPP offers all LPC students the chance to study the 'Law Firm as a Business' module, which further covers key skills relating to business and commercial awareness and the practicalities of being a trainee. BPP also rolled out an international trade elective this year for students in September 2013. This reflects the needs of the bigger firms that BPP serves: *"All of the modules we deliver have an international flavour to them anyway. A lot of the larger City law firms have international clients so their trainees need a background to what's going in other jurisdictions."*

Part of the reason BPP takes such a keen interest in firm feedback is that, like rivals University of Law and Kaplan, it has exclusive partnerships with a number of leading firms to teach their future trainees. Slaughter and May, Freshfields, Skadden and Travers Smith are just some of those on board. BPP offers a 'fast-track', seven-month LPC for some of these partner firms that sees students undertake two additional hours of face-to-face teaching and three extra hours of self-study each week. This route is only available at the Leeds, London (Holborn) and Birmingham centres. Perhaps unsurprisingly the focus of the LPC at BPP is on commercial and City practice, but with *"one of the broadest selection of electives on offer"* there's something for anyone with more humble ambitions. In fact, there is an optional 'high-street extra' module which gives students the chance to focus in more depth on areas relevant to high-street practice. Students can also undertake a non-assessed 'fourth elective' that can be completed entirely online, with all lectures and other materials accessible remotely.

For those not undertaking the 'fast-track' LPC there is a wealth of other study routes available. Full-timers can opt to attend classes in the morning or afternoons and over four, three or even two days. Part-timers have just as much flexibility and can choose to attend every Saturday, a full weekend every three or four weeks, or evening sessions. It's probably best to check the website though, as the availability tends to vary between the different centres. In addition, a 'blended learning' programme is in place which allows students to study the majority of the course remotely, with only a minimum of ten hours face-to-face teaching required.

Students at the larger BPP branches – London, Manchester and Leeds – can decide to either attend live lectures or watch them online along with students from BPP's smaller outposts. Additional teaching is conducted through two-hour, small group sessions. All teaching materials can be found online at a later date, allowing you to consolidate your learning or revise wherever necessary. Teachers are all qualified solicitors or barristers and they also draft the course content to keep it up-to-date and relevant to the modern legal profession.

BPP believes in offering a high level of pastoral support and each student is assigned a dedicated personal tutor, while you can also sign up for one-to-one mentoring with local practitioners. From the moment you accept your place on the LPC you can access the careers service, which offers advice on applications, CVs, covering letters and how to prepare for interviews or assessments centres, as well as running mock interview sessions. BPP also offers its cohorts a careers guarantee: if you don't find legal employment within six months of completing the LPC you can study another qualification at the school for no additional fee.

A diverse range of pro bono projects enables students to put their skills and knowledge into practice for real clients, under the supervision of qualified lawyers. A Human Rights Unit, Employment Law Telephone Advice Line, legal translation service and various regional projects are all in place to help students gain some practical experience and boost their CV. An LLM in Advanced Legal Practice can also be obtained after the course has been completed.

Although BPP remains one of the most expensive providers, the blow to the pocket may be softened by interest-free payment plans, a raft of scholarships that can applied for, and even a 'Law Loan' worth up to £25,000 in co-operation with Investec Bank. As we went to press – and a full eight months after its initial application – BPP's bid for full university status was confirmed as successful.

BPP Law School, Birmingham

Number of places: 150 FTE
Pro: parking discounts
Con: relatively new on the scene

BPP's Birmingham centre offers the 'fast-track' LPC as well as the year-long full-time course and 18-month, Saturday taught, part-time route. The law school here is relatively new on the scene, re-launching in brand-new premises as recently as 2010. Situated in the middle of Birmingham's central business district, BPP has excellent links with the city's major firms and organisations. The location allows students easy access to a variety of public transport and is close to many of the main shopping areas, including The Bullring.

The learning centre holds classrooms equipped with audio-visual technology, while a student lounge has a TV area, PCs and quiet study zones. There's free WiFi too. The teaching team has all worked in or qualified for practice. Careers advisers and pro bono opportunities are available. Students driving into Birmingham for the course can get discounts on parking nearby.

BPP Law School, Bristol

Number of places: 80 FTE
Pro: renowned party city
Con: renowned party city

BPP Bristol is in Queen Square, a large, open green space set against a backdrop of Georgian town houses in Bristol's city centre. Located in one of the main business districts of Bristol, you will find many law, accountancy and other professional service firms nearby, as well as a wealth of cafés, shops and restaurants. After a short stroll you can also stumble across the waterfront and the railway station.

BPP Bristol was founded in 1991, but until 2010 it was only teaching the professional accountancy course. However, with Bristol the major legal hub of the South West, BPP aimed to cash in on a market that was being dominated by rivals UoL and BILP. The centre boasts state-of-the-art technology in its classrooms, and its virtual learning environment allows students to access all their lectures, or seek additional support, online. Students appreciated the personal touch here: *"There was a lot of small group work – about six or seven people in each seminar – which was great as it made it much easier to interact."* A careers service is on hand to offer support, while pro bono opportunities are also easily accessible.

BPP Law School, Cambridge

Number of places: 80 FTE
Pro: dreaming spires
Con: dodging the bicycles and tourists

BPP's school sits plum in the centre of the city and opened in 2011, giving the LPC course at Anglia Ruskin a bit of healthy competition. Cambridge offers either the full-time or 18-month study routes. Like all the BPP centres, Cambridge comes equipped with a raft of jazzy new facilities. Classrooms are not only kitted out with the latest audio-visual technology to aid the learning process, they're also all fully air-conditioned to aid the cooling process. The South East of England is known for having the warmest climate in the UK, after all. The student lounge is ideal for a bit of R&R after classes, while for those looking to do some extra study there's a raft of computers available, or free WiFi if you prefer to bring your own from home. Perhaps unsurprisingly for a city renowned for its love of cycling, there's plenty of bike racks just outside the school.

BPP Law School, Leeds

Number of places: 374 FTE
Pro: helpful careers service
Con: the football team (actually there were no big cons, but read/watch *The Damned United* anyway)

The Leeds Whitehall Quay study centre is in the heart of the city, just a short stroll away from the train station and main shopping areas. BPP Leeds has mock courtrooms, top-end tech facilities and comfy common rooms. Students can improve their prospects in the profession by volunteering in projects organised by the school's Pro Bono Centre – human rights work and the Legal Advice Clinic being just some examples. Former students were full of praise for the course here: *"I thought BPP was very good in general but what was particularly strong was the careers service on offer – there was a lot of help and advice to hand at all times,"* said one. Another added: *"I thought the facilities were very good – the library especially – and there are a lot of electronic resources. All the lectures were placed online, but you also feel very connected to the teachers as we were taught in very small groups. The campus is right near the train station as well, so it was great for commuting."*

BPP Law School, Liverpool

Number of places: 80 FTE
Pro: free Fairtrade tea and coffee
Con: high fees

BPP's Liverpool branch is known as one of the leading finance trainers in Merseyside and the surrounding areas. Even though it has only been running the LPC since 2011, it has built a burgeoning reputation for its provision of legal training. Based in Merchants' Court in central Liverpool, BPP sits in the heart of the legal district, next to the crown and youth courts and a variety of major chambers and law firms. It is also conveniently located near to car parks, railway and bus stations, and is just a stone's throw from the Liverpool One Shopping Centre. Its facilities are just as modern and impressive as the other BPP sites, and it even offers free Fairtrade tea and coffee.

BPP Law School, London

Number of Holborn places: 1,850 FTE
Number of Waterloo places: 282 FTE
Pro: it's Lahndan, innit?
Con: obscenely expensive city

BPP has two centres in London but most LPC students head to the Holborn branch. This is where a large portion of BPP's partner firms send their future trainees, as Waterloo doesn't offer the 'fast-track' LPC. Waterloo, therefore, is generally the destination for late applicants.

Close to the Inns of Court and Law Society, the Holborn centre is in a thriving legal hub and with Soho, Covent Garden and the West End on your doorstep, you'll never be short of things to do once class is dismissed. Housed in a *"striking building"* that is sure to make a lasting impression, students assured us the facilities are also *"top-notch."* Mock courtrooms help you hone your skills and

Bristol Institute of Legal Practice at UWE

Bristol Institute of Legal Practice, University of the West of England, Coldharbour Lane, Bristol BS16 1QY
Email: bilpinfo@uwe.ac.uk
Website: www.uwe.ac.uk/bilp

Contact
For further information about all of our courses, please contact us via email on bilpinfo@uwe.ac.uk or visit our website www.uwe.ac.uk/bilp.

Law School

Institute Profile

The Bristol Institute of Legal Practice (BILP) at UWE Bristol is a leading provider of professional legal education with an established track record of excellence. We offer flexible study, a choice of timetabling options, superb facilities and are large enough to provide a range and depth of quality provision. Our courses are designed and taught by experienced solicitors/barristers teaching within their own subject areas. The emphasis is on practical learning within a supportive environment and on providing students with the skills/ knowledge to ensure they are 'practice ready'.

Graduate Diploma in Law (GDL/CPE) full and part time

Our GDL enables non-law graduates to progress with confidence to the LPC/BPTC and is supported by a dedicated team of tutors who understand the demands of the GDL. Teaching is not shared with undergraduates. The curriculum is divided into two teaching blocks with assessments after each block.

Legal Practice Course (LPC) full and part time

We are one of very few providers nationally to have consistently achieved the highest possible grading of 'excellent' from our regulator. Students are offered a broad based Stage 1 designed to prepare them for the full variety of practice followed by a selection of 13 elective subjects.

Bar Professional Training Course (BPTC) full and part time

Our BPTC equips students to excel at the Bar and beyond, providing outstanding opportunities in advocacy, research, conference and mediation skills and to assist our students in securing pupillage. There are exceptional links with the local Bar.

University of the West of England
BRISTOL

there's a fantastic amount of e-resources – *"they give you the lectures on DVD, which is useful."* If you're struggling to locate a computer on site, a screen will point you in the direction of some available stations. *"It's a pretty slick outfit,"* said a former student. *"It feels very professional and very different from university. It feels like you're there to get ready for working life. It was incredibly professional, as you'd expect – they charge enough."*

Some felt the course could be tedious and wasn't as engaging as they'd hoped. *"It's a big-old-law-school machine,"* commented one. *"There's quite a factory-like approach. You just had to learn various things and didn't get to use any imagination. You're spoon-fed information and you've just got to remember it."* However, this type of complaint is commonly levelled against the LPC at a whole host of providers.

Despite many attending students having already secured training contracts, a careers service is on hand to offer support and guidance for those who are unsure of what their next step will be. It's important to know that the course here will definitely have a corporate/commercial slant, but even so students can get involved in a variety of pro bono projects, including an environmental law clinic or legal translation services.

Students who ventured to Waterloo weren't disheartened by their time there. One told us: *"I know that most people tend to go to Holborn, but I liked Waterloo. It was a good experience and you met a variety of people, not just your stereotypical City lawyer. There's a wider audience of student."*

BPP Law School, Manchester

Number of places: 411 FTE
Pro: the coolest city in the North
Con: the rainiest city in the North

BPP's Manchester St James branch is in the bustling city centre, conveniently close to the Oxford Road train station and main shopping areas. Students will find classrooms equipped with all the latest audio-visual technology, a large breakout area, and plenty of silent study spaces. A Pro Bono Centre is in place to help students practise skills relevant for the profession, and specialist careers advice can be sought from the careers service or personal tutors. There are also plenty of clubs and societies for students to immerse themselves in if they need a break from study – you can give anything from football to mooting, squash or Iyengar yoga a go. Students said: *"The teaching was really good and I thought the careers service was great in terms of helping people get training contracts and being prepared for interviews."*

Bristol Institute of Legal Practice at UWE

Number of places: 200 FT, 80 PT
Fees (2013/14): £10,300
Pro: *"personal feel"*
Con: campus outside the city centre

The LPC at BILP is designed *"to prepare you for practice – you won't just acquire knowledge to pass the exams, you'll also develop the critical skills and awareness of how legal practice works."* Students said: *"There aren't many other regional options, but you can't go far wrong with UWE. The lectures are great, I found the course leaders engaging and approachable, and the class sizes are quite small so it felt personal."*

The presence of BPP and the University of Law has brought BILP some competition in the South West, but this highly regarded provider was still confident enough to raise its fees for the second year running. Many students have links with the region either through their upbringing or university, *"and many stay in or around Bristol to commence their careers in either a high-street or commercial practice."* A 15% discount is available for returning UWE undergrads.

A full-time timetable requires students to be on-site for two days (either two full days or one full day and two half days). It's at your discretion when you come in provided the schedule allows it. Fridays are always kept free to allow students to pursue other activities or independent study. Part-timers can choose from two study paths: the first is ten two-day teaching sessions (each with five timetabled workshops) which take place on Fridays and Saturdays every three to four weeks; the second option – *"which is rising in popularity"* – sees students attend weekly one-day sessions that typically include two workshops.

Nearly all LPC teaching takes place in practice-based workshops with a maximum of 16 students in each. These two-and-a-half-hour sessions take place in both the morning and afternoon, and the emphasis is on interactive learning through role play, online tests and small group work, as well as regular practice in the key legal skills. Lectures are recorded and available online a few hours after completion. *"It's a great resource, not only if students miss a lecture but also for when they come to revise. It's proven intensely popular on our course."* There are 13 electives on offer at Stage Two, with specialisms including intellectual property and competition, private client, or more commercial and corporate-based offerings. The school keeps a close eye on the electives to *"make sure they are as relevant as possible,"* but aren't anticipating any changes in the near future.

A central tenet of the course is the array of pro bono opportunities available to students – something BILP views as necessary to improve the professional and educational standards of its graduates. BILP has close ties with Streetlaw, the Innocence Project and Community Legal Advice and Representation Service (CLARS), while other initiatives are continually under scrutiny.

Supervising principals are on hand to lend support and guidance, as are careers tutors. Practitioners at local firms (including ex-BILP students) host careers sessions, while a work placement scheme launched in 2011 in connection with the Bristol Law Society gives students a chance to work in-house for local firms such as CMS or Bevan Brittan. *"We've got our roots firmly in the South West and that's where we focus all our efforts from an employability view,"* says a senior BILP source. *"We're glad we've been in business for two decades now and the region is full of our alumni, be it at large or small firms. We can therefore engage with those alumni, and they can help us get our students into the careers they're searching for."*

A talent scholarship worth 100% of the fees can be claimed by one lucky – and talented – individual.

Cardiff Law School

Number of places: 220 FTE
Fees (2013/14): £10,545
Pro: massive student population
Con: Prifddinas Cymru i Fyfyrwyr

A large number of LPC-ers stay in the area after graduation, but *"a lot also go on to London, Birmingham, Bristol, or the other larger legal hubs. We've always liked to keep our courses generalist so they don't lean too far towards either the smaller high-street or larger commercial firms."*

Cardiff runs both full-time and part-time courses. Full-timers have their teaching concentrated on three days a week to allow students time to pursue independent study or work part-time jobs. Part-timers will attend classes every Friday. The school places an emphasis on face-to-face teaching, and small group sessions of around 16 people are evidence of the *"personal nature"* you'll find during the course. *"We've always had extremely good relationships with the students and there's close ties between them and the staff. We pride ourselves on our accessibility both inside and outside of the classroom."* Most lectures are delivered live to full-timers, but others are pre-recorded. All are uploaded onto the internet at a later date. A choice of nine electives catering for both high-street and commercial paths is on offer, as well as an optional course in Welsh advocacy. The housing law elective was recently replaced by personal injury.

Students can take advantage of all the resources the university has to offer, including all the campus libraries, study areas and computers. There's a legal practice library which has practitoners' texts, study spaces and its own raft of computers. The school runs a work placement scheme for students who don't possess a training contract or are light on recent work experience. Around 60 to 70 students will delve into the legal profession and gain valuable knowledge with firms or other organisations during the October reading week. An array of pro bono opportunities to get stuck into includes a tie-up with Welsh legal heavyweight Hugh James, where the civil pro bono unit deals with NHS continuing care cases. In addition, students can help out with the Innocence Project, which supports convicted criminals who maintain their innocence.

Students looking for a CV boost can pursue the top-up LLM after completing the LPC, while from 2014 the school plans to allow exemptions on part of the LPC. Cardiff is also a signatory of the Law Society's Diversity and Access scheme, which offers free tuition to successful candidates.

City Law School, London

Number of places: 420 FTE
Fees (2013/14): £12,500
Pro: close relationship with CASS Business School
Con: no tube stop on the doorstep

"We have high standards, but we provide a supportive learning environment with one-on-one assistance available where necessary," our City source tells us. *"However, we don't spoon-feed students as it doesn't best assist them to prepare for practice."* Although validated for 420 FTE places, City actively recruits only half that number. *"Our course is distinct. Our ethos is that we want to provide a personal touch. It's not a one-size-fits-all course, it's tailored to students as individuals."* The school therefore places an emphasis on face-to-face teaching and small group sessions.

The LPC aims to be as reflective of practice as possible. Teachers come from a variety of practice backgrounds and maintain close links with the profession, while an advisory board of firms is on hand to keep the course current. Students attend classes four days a week and can opt for morning or afternoon sessions, allowing the entire cohort to be brought together for large group sessions at 1pm. City aims to avoid the passive format of traditional lectures, so these sessions will either involve students in research and drafting tasks via networked computers in the lecture theatre, or see them split into smaller groups to allow for greater interaction and engagement. For every large class – made up of the entire cohort – there will be two workshops with a maximum 18 people. Skills sessions are delivered to groups of six to eight people. Quizzes and other tools can be found online to supplement learning, and the school is planning to record more lectures. *"They will be used as a revision tool to aid students. The focus remains on face-to-face, engaged learning."*

Cardiff Law School

Centre for Professional Legal Studies, Cardiff University, Museum Avenue,
Cardiff CF10 3AX
Website: www.law.cardiff.ac.uk/cpls

Contact
GDL: Julie Webb
Tel 029 2087 4941
Email law-gdl@cf.ac.uk
LPC: Kerry Lester
Tel 029 2087 4941
Email law-lpc@cf.ac.uk
BPTC: Lucy Burns
Tel 029 2087 4964
Email law-bptc@cf.ac.uk
LLM in Legal Practice: Julie Webb
Tel 029 2087 4964
Email law-cpls-LLM@cf.ac.uk

Other postgraduate law courses:
The Postgraduate Office
Tel 029 2087 6102
Email law-PG@cardiff.ac.uk

University profile

Cardiff Law School is one of the most successful law schools in the UK and enjoys an international reputation for its teaching and research, being ranked 7th in the UK for research. Cardiff offers opportunities for students to pursue postgraduate study by research leading to the degrees of MPhil and PhD and a broadly based Masters (LLM) programme which is offered in full and part-time mode. Cardiff also has a Pro Bono Scheme which gives students an opportunity to experience the law in action, work alongside volunteer legal professionals and develop transferable skills to add to their CVs.

The Law School is the leading provider of legal training in Wales and is validated to offer the GDL, LPC and BPTC. Students are taught by experienced solicitors and barristers who have been specifically recruited for this purpose. The Law School prides itself on its friendly and supportive teaching environment and its strong links with the legal profession. Placements with solicitors' firms or sets of chambers are available to students pursuing the vocational courses.

Graduate Diploma in Law (full-time or part-time)

The GDL is a one-year (full-time) or two-year (part-time) course for non-law graduates to convert to law. This intensive course covers all of the essential topics of a qualifying law degree. Completion of the GDL allows you to progress to the professional stage of training – the LPC for solicitors and the BPTC for barristers.

Legal Practice Course (full-time or part-time)

Cardiff has delivered its LPC since 1993 and is highly regarded by both students and employers. Cardiff offers the LPC both full-time (3 days a week) and part-time (1 day a week). Through both courses the Law School provides an excellent learning experience which includes a high degree of hands-on teaching. Placements with solicitors' firms are available to some students without training contracts or recent work experience.

Bar Professional Training Course

Cardiff delivers a high-quality and highly regarded BPTC. There is a relatively small student cohort and the course provides a highly supportive learning environment with high levels of individual tutor feedback on all live skills performances. The learning mostly takes place in small groups. There is a focus on the development of Advocacy skills, with two hour classes in groups of six or less almost every week across all three terms. Students are offered two weeks of placements giving them the opportunity to marshall with both a Circuit Judge and a District Judge in addition to undertaking a mini-pupillage.

LLM in Legal Practice

Cardiff offers a one year LLM in Legal Practice which can be taken part-time or by distance learning. The LLM is open to students who have successfully completed the LPC, BPTC or BVC, whether at Cardiff or another recognised institution. Assessment takes the form of a practice-based dissertation.

Facilities

The Law School has dedicated accommodation for the vocational courses which houses a practitioner library, a suite of class rooms with interactive teaching and audio visual equipment and extensive computer facilities. In addition, the main law library contains one of the largest collections of primary and secondary material within the UK. The Law School is housed in its own building at the heart of the campus, itself located in one of the finest civic centres in Britain.

City does its best to give students a head start in the profession, and *"as soon as you accept a place on the course you're entitled to make an appointment with the careers service to get assistance with CVs, covering letters or where best to target applications."* A Training Contact Advisory Service (TCAS) is also available and students can take part in mock interviews through it. The school has continued to develop its mentoring scheme in association with recently qualified solicitors from various firms, which has been *"extremely successful and very well received, and has led to some work experience placements for those involved."* A programme of lectures from practitioners has also been expanded this year and will feature a selection of guest speakers relevant to LPC, BPTC and GDL students. Students can also take advantage of a dedicated lecture programme at the CASS Business School nearby.

Pro bono opportunities include a community employment clinic, Amnesty International, the London Innocence Project and even the possibility of volunteering as a police station adviser. The school is a participant in various client interviewing and mediation competitions, and will take part in new negotiation competitions this year. There is one full scholarship and two worth 50% of the fees up for grabs. In addition, there's a discount for former City University students, and three financial prizes awarded at the end of the LPC to the best-performing students, one of which specifically relates to pro bono. A current *"refurbishment and redecoration"* project will see improvements across the three buildings on the edge of Gray's Inn that comprise the law school.

A good range of electives is on offer and caters for students destined for high-street firms, commercial ones, City heavyweights or the public sector. A media law elective was recently introduced and *"a lot of students chose to do it. The market interest is definitely there."* An LLM in Professional Legal Practice can be secured after the LPC upon the completion of a dissertation.

De Montfort University

Number of places: 80 FT, 80 PT
Fees (2013/14): £8,250
Pro: purpose-built law school
Con: no scholarships currently available

DMU's law school is located in a purpose-built, £35m energy-efficient building, complete with a dedicated LPC library, mock courtrooms and interview rooms. Full-timers are timetabled to be on campus on Mondays and Tuesdays during both stages. There are optional live lectures on a Wednesday during Stage One, but these can also be viewed online. For part-time students teaching is mainly restricted to weekends to make it easier for people to maintain full-time jobs. 'Solicitor development' sessions

are integrated into Stage One and build on the core skills required of future lawyers such as negotiation.

A broad range of commercial and private client electives is on offer at Stage Two, with options such as child law, sports and media law, and personal injury and clinical negligence. Elderly client was recently replaced by a private client option, but generally the electives are *"subject to addition rather than subtraction."* The course is taught by a team of staff who are all qualified solicitors, while the school aims to have around 15 students in each tutorial.

With a potential three days off for full-timers, students can take advantage of the pro bono and careers services available. Work placements are arranged in the not-for-profit sector with charities including Shelter and Reunite, an international child abduction charity. They can also hone their research and presentation skills with the Streetlaw initiative, where students present relevant legal topics to members of the local community. The school also has links with the Citizens' Advice Bureau and Leicester's local council. DMU says that *"the aim is to give every student an opportunity to engage with law on a practical basis, enabling them to develop their knowledge, skills and experience to enhance their employability."* A careers tutor organises a programme of events, including talks from in-house and private practice solicitors: *"Students will meet people from all sorts of legal backgrounds, from local recruitment consultants in Nottingham, to lawyers from Irwin Mitchell and employment tribunal judges."* They can also take part in a mentoring scheme with local solicitors, and some have successfully gone on to secure training contracts with their mentor's organisation.

The student body *"on the full-time course is mostly split between local and regional students, but the part-time course is more diverse, and we get students coming from Canada, Hong Kong, Dubai and the Caribbean – all over the world."* A potential alumni scholarship is in the pipeline, offering £500 for previous DMU and Leicester University students.

University of Hertfordshire

Number of places: 80 FT
Fees (2013/14): £10,200
Pro: courtroom better than Judge Judy's
Con: does anything happen in Hatfield?

The University of Hertfordshire's full-time LPC combines both distance and on-campus learning – roughly a 60/40 split. All lectures and relevant course materials can be accessed via 'StudyNet', the school's bespoke intranet system. This allows students to study and prepare for face-to-face workshops independently at home. Groups of 16 to 20 students are taught on campus on Wednesdays between 9am and 5pm, and then 9am to 7pm at the elective stage. There are 11 electives to choose from and these *"respond to the demands of corporate and commercial law firms, private client relationships, and also branch out to consider alternative methods of dispute resolution."* The programme also affords the chance to obtain specialisms in some of these areas.

The law school upped-sticks to a new £10m building on the university's £120m de Havilland campus in 2011. It houses a Mediation Centre – a central hub for training aspiring mediators in the area – and a mock courtroom that had local barristers purring their approval when they came to visit. Students also have access to the university's 24-hour resources centre and Sports Village.

"If a student comes to us and engages with the course and the opportunities we present, they will meet people, make contacts and secure their training contract." A Law Clinic is available for students, often allowing them to take a leading role on family, employment or consumer protection disputes under the guidance of practitioners. The careers service posts bulletins on available jobs or training contract opportunities, and offers 'surgeries' for students to get general careers advice.

If the LPC is successfully navigated students can go on to study for an LLM, where credit towards a full masters degree can be secured by working through an internship. Academic credit is awarded for the work produced during this placement, along with a portfolio, extended essays, and a series of master classes and reflective exercises. The school is also *"getting into providing short courses in mediation, advocacy and negotiation as add-ons to the LPC."*

Hertfordshire is *"distinguishable because you're not one of a crowd. We have small group sizes and you will receive personal attention. If you come to us we will know who you are."*

University of Huddersfield

Number of places: 80 FT, 35 PT
Fees (2013/14): £8,750
Pro: offers an exempting law degree; amazing train station
Con: heavy snowfalls

Huddersfield is one of a minority of institutions to run an exempting law degree, whereby students combine their LLB studies with the LPC over three or four years rather than studying the professional course separately. This has proved a particularly popular route for students, but a standalone LPC is in operation as well. For this, teaching is condensed onto Mondays and Tuesdays, with the other days left free for work experience, part-time jobs or additional self-study. Part-timers attend one day a week.

The law department can be found in Huddersfield's Business School, which moved into a new building in 2010 following a healthy £17m investment. Not only does the state-of-the art facility feature modern classrooms with excellent IT facilities, dedicated LPC study rooms and a mock law court, its location in landscaped grounds by the restored canal makes it the most environmentally friendly building on campus.

Teaching is conducted through a mixture of large and small group sessions with an emphasis on practical work and interactive, face-to-face learning. The intake of students is deliberately limited to around 40. Small group sessions involve the use of realistic, transaction-based case studies. A selection of eight electives at Stage Two cater for all career aspirations, whether it be with a commercial firm or more general practice.

The University of Huddersfield runs a Partners in Law scheme with firms such as DLA Piper, Walker Morris and Eversheds. Students can benefit from networking, mentoring and training opportunities through this. In addition, a careers liaison counsellor is on hand to offer advice on CVs or applications, there's a series of guest lecturers, and opportunities for work experience placements with local authorities.

Kaplan Law School

Number of places: 300 FT
Fees (2013/14): £13,150
Pro: high graduate to training contract conversion rate
Con: notoriously selective

"It's been a great year," beamed a senior representative at Kaplan. *"We're very happy with the quality of the students we're getting and we also opened a new facilities site near our main school."* Kaplan Law School is based by Borough Market and Southwark Cathedral, and its new site on Borough High Street includes a second library and further IT and study facilities. *"We take student feedback very seriously: they told us they wanted more PCs, so we gave them more PCs."*

Kaplan has only offered the LPC since 2007 and despite being relatively new on the scene it has grown consistently – the addition of new facilities serves as a good indication that it's trying to service ever-increasing numbers. Students feel the size remains appropriate to their needs, though: *"I really like how small and friendly Kaplan is,"* said one. *"It's a good learning environment and feels a little more intimate than other providers I've experienced."* Kaplan's small group sessions generally comprise 16 to 18 students, giving them as much contact with tutors as possible. Although the school is *"going to make more use of the online delivery"* of materials, the focus remains on face-to-face contact, and part of the reason for more e-learning is to free up time for additional small group ses-

Kaplan Law School

Kaplan Law School
Palace House, 3 Cathedral Street, London SE1 9DE
Tel: (020) 7367 6455
Email: admissions@kaplanlawschool.org.uk
Website: www.kaplanlawschool.org.uk

Contact
Apply to GDL & LPC Central
Applications Board
www.lawcabs.ac.uk
BPTC online
www.barprofessionaltraining.org.
uk
Location: London Bridge

College profile

Kaplan Law School offers the most highly regarded Graduate Diploma in Law (GDL), Legal Practice Course (LPC) and Bar Professional Training Course (BPTC) with excellent pass rates and a truly hands on and proactive careers service.

Face-to-face tuition is key; Kaplan's teaching model is based around small groups of no more than 16 on the GDL and 18 on the LPC. This helps student learning, as well as giving tutors more contact time with each student. Our tutors are all qualified lawyers with a proven track record in practice and legal education.

At Kaplan we do not offer places to fill bums on seats. Our strict admissions criteria ensures that all students on the course have a realistic chance of gaining a training contract or pupillage. Our careers service is run by a former graduate recruiter, so we know exactly what law firms and chambers are looking for. Students can make weekly appointments and never need to send off an application until it has been checked. When students get through to the next stage of the application process, they will be given mock interviews bespoke to the firm or chambers they are interviewing at.

GDL: Graduate Diploma in Law (full-time)

Designed for any non-law graduate who intends to become a solicitor or barrister in the UK, with most teaching weeks taking place over three days giving students flexibility to work or make applications. Kaplan's GDL places the academic subjects into a work related context so that students are more prepared for practice. Those considering the Bar can opt into the Bar GDL, featuring additional sessions to get students ready for pupillage applications.

LPC: Legal Practice Course (full-time)

Kaplan offer the Nottingham Law School LPC at our London Bridge campus. Students study core modules and then choose elective subjects to specialise in. Those sponsored by one of our client firms also participate in our Bridge To Practice course, an umbrella programme designed to get students ready for their training contract.

BPTC: Bar Professional Training Course (full-time)

This skills-based course is designed to equip those intent on becoming barristers. Given the competitiveness of gaining pupillage, the course is highly selective and shortlisted applicants attend a selection event. Teaching takes place in groups of either 6 or 12 students with group work and advocacy forming a focal point of the course with students carrying out practical tasks and exercises.

Careers & Open events

Kaplan runs a full programme of careers and open events throughout the year, designed to help you make the decision of whether to pursue law, give you the opportunity to meet people from the profession and in some cases bolster your CV. Alternatively students can visit for a guided tour and the opportunity to sit with our careers service to see how they will work with you.

Kaplan offers a scholarship programme across all courses including one free place for the GDL and LPC.

KAPLAN
LAW SCHOOL

sions. Students are in classes Monday to Thursday, with Fridays traditionally kept free to allow for other activities. Attendance at all classes is compulsory, so you'll need a decent excuse should you fail to show up.

Kaplan – like competitors BPP and UoL – has signed exclusive provision deals with a number of law firms, including the likes of Bird & Bird, Mills & Reeve and Holman Fenwick Willan, to teach their future trainees the LPC. Although the school caters for the commercial foundation these students need, it offers a broad range of subjects for those with differing career routes in mind, and a number of graduates go on to secure positions at high-street firms. A new elective in international trade, shipping and arbitration was introduced in 2012 and has been *"very well received."*

Kaplan's careers department has been expanding and runs lots of event throughout the year. These cover matters such as how to make yourself more employable and how to make a good first impression with recruiters. Visits from firms and practitioners take place on a regular basis and tutors are on hand to offer guidance throughout the duration of the course. A series of 'business breakfasts' have been introduced and will take place once a week to develop commercial awareness. *"We see this as a complete process. We don't just want students to attend classes; we need them to understand what is ahead of them, too."* In 2012, 83% of graduates secured a training contract after completing the LPC.

The school runs a range of pro bono projects that students can get stuck into. They can assist at a Legal Advice Clinic, advising on issues such as employment and housing under the supervision of practitioners. There is also a pro bono scholarship up for grabs, and a student who demonstrates particular dedication can be eligible to receive the course fees in full. There are scholarships worth £3,000 available for those who show exceptional potential in the legal profession, alongside diversity scholarships, too.

Our Kaplan source told us: *"We do look for potential in students and we hope we are ethical in that sense. We are very focused on getting people into employment and not just taking their money."* Thus, although the school will consider applicants with a 2:2, most students will have a 2:1 or higher.

University of Central Lancashire
Number of places: 80 FT, 40 PT
Fees (2013/14): £7,900
Pro: state-of-the-art facilities
Con: Preston

UCLan's law school is based on its Preston campus, with the majority of teaching sessions taking place in the impressive Harris Building, which houses a dedicated moot courtroom – a mock-up of a real courtroom equipped latest audio-visual technology that's especially handy for developing your oral skills. The course is delivered through a series of interactive large and small group sessions, where the focus is on 'student-centred learning'. For some large-group teaching other lecture theatres on campus may be utilised. All small group sessions include between 12 and 16 students, and the teaching rooms for these contain similarly modern equipment to enhance and support the learning experience. LPC students also have exclusive use of dedicated skills development and resources rooms.

Full-time teaching takes place Monday to Thursday from 9am to 5pm. Occasionally classes run on Fridays, but this is usually kept free for self-study. Part-time teaching is normally conducted from 10am to 8pm on Wednesdays. During Stage Two there are no lectures and the timetable is reduced. As part of instilling a professional work ethic and persona, UCLan states that attendance at all sessions is compulsory. Throughout the course a strong emphasis is placed on enhancing students' commercial awareness and personal and professional development so as to leave them well prepared for a life in a competitive market place. Therefore, transferable skills such as teamwork, numeracy, communication, presentation, IT, critical thinking and problem solving are integrated into the teaching programme.

Inevitably this also means that UCLan focuses a lot of attention on careers support. A guest speaker programme supported by alumni and other legal professionals is in place, and an annual careers fair attracts a variety of legal employers to give students an opportunity to discuss work experience, the application process and training contracts. The law school has good links with the profession and firms in the North West contact UCLan directly to advertise training contracts or paralegal positions. There are opportunities to shadow local practitioners, while recent tie-ups with local courts mean time can be spent marshalling judges.

Students have the opportunity to participate in the school's pro bono clinic, which has a busy and varied programme to suit all interests. A number of LPC students are former UCLan undergrads and those who follow this path are eligible for a discount on their fees.

University of Law of England and Wales

Number of places: 4,750 FT, 2,000 PT
Fees 2013/14: £13,905 (London)
Pro: now a fully-fledged university
Con: a legal education juggernaut

It's been another eventful year at the University of Law – perhaps better known by its former incarnation as the College of Law. The new name seems an appropriate point on which to start and came about as a result of being awarded full university status. *"We've had degree awarding powers since 2006 and they were renewed in 2012,"* a senior source told us. *"We have satisfied the university criteria for many years, but we decided to go for full status because it enabled us to become more broadly recognised both in the undergraduate and postgraduate market, nationally and internationally. It equips our students with CV-enhancing qualifications, and the student body was overwhelmingly in favour of having the University of Law on their degrees."*

From 2013 a new LLM LPC is being run by the university, which will see students not only awarded an LPC qualification but also an internationally recognised Master of Laws. For the same price and duration as the previous LPC, students can specialise in either international or national practice and choose between the award of an LLM in International Legal Practice or Professional Legal Practice. CMS is already on board and has appointed UoL to teach its future trainees the LLM in International Legal Practice. *"In the international market place, most lawyers are educated to Masters level, so it seemed wrong that our students were doing a 12-month postgraduate course but not getting the appropriate accreditation. So we've enhanced our LPC to make sure they get a globally recognised and transferable qualification."*

There are eight UoL centres in England: two in London (Bloomsbury and Moorgate), then one each in Birmingham, Bristol, Chester, Guildford, Manchester and York. UoL will also be filling the void left after the Oxford Institute of Legal Practice at Oxford Brookes ceased its LPC provision, and for the time being will be running its own course out of the university. The school has also dipped its toe into the international market for the first time, and a programme in Singapore got underway in March 2013.

Back in Blighty there are a range of study routes: an accelerated seven-month course with January or July start dates; a full-time, one-year course; or an 18 or 24-month part-time study route with day, evening or weekend attendance options. From 2013 a newly titled i-LLM LPC is also available – an internet-based, part-time mode of study which sees students monitored by online tutors. *"It's structured to mimic the full-time course and you'll*

still get the same amount of contact time as you would on that. It's proving to be very popular and the feedback has been amazing."

In addition to the LPC routes available to all students, UoL runs courses specifically designed for students who have already secured training contracts with the likes of Allen & Overy, Clifford Chance and Linklaters. Taught exclusively at the Moorgate branch, this option is based on corporate law modules with firm-specific precedents and materials, while the electives will match the practice areas of the firm. A further number of partner firms – including Ashurst, Baker & McKenzie and Pannone – have opted for the 'LPC+' route, which sees their students mix in with the rest at Stage One before sidling off on their own at the elective stage.

Although students used to select a corporate, commercial and private, or legal aid route at Stage One, this is no longer applicable. *"Based on student feedback we now have a Stage One programme that everybody studies,"* we were informed. *"It was actually at the elective stage that students wanted more choice so now that's where the choice is. We now run 18 electives instead of 13, and the new additions are international to allow for the International LLM."* Alongside the core materials covered during Stage One, a 'business of law' programme has been integrated, covering professional skills topics such as commerciality and client relationships to help students understand crucial details about how law firms actually operate.

Across all full-time study routes, workshops will take up ten hours per week. These are usually spread over four days, but it is *"pretty popular"* for students at all centres to select concentrated timetabling, which allows them to pack it all into two days instead. This face-to-face contact is supported by innovative online learning resources. All lecture-format teaching is delivered via i-tutorials, which students stream directly from ELITE, an online resource page which holds all the course materials. The i-tutorials contain additional learning resources and activities embedded in them to enable an interactive experience alongside traditional textbook study.

UoL has an extensive careers service that covers the breadth of the nation. A team of 20 specialist careers advisers works for the university, and every student at every centre has access to all the same information and opportunities. A database containing up to 3,000 training contract and paralegal vacancies, alongside useful tips on how to successfully navigate applications, is part of a 'virtual learning environment' that can be accessed by every student. There are plenty of careers workshops and the school has created the Future Lawyers Network, an online community with over 12,000 members that provides specialist careers advice and an opportunity to network online. Every centre has *"a thriving legal advice clinic"* and they team up with local advice centres to give support on a variety of pro bono cases. *"We have over 2,000 vacant places a year in various activities, so the vast majority of students who want to get involved in pro bono can be accommodated for."* Relationships with initiatives such as Streetlaw or the National Centre for Domestic Violence are in place, but check the website to see which projects each individual centre offers. There are also many additional mooting or debating activities for those looking to add some padding to their CV.

University of Law, Birmingham

Pro: great pro bono opportunities
Con: *"the format can be slightly chunky"*

Being situated in Birmingham's historic Jewellery Quarter means students are well placed to take advantage of the Second City's best social haunts and shopping districts (when they're not in class, of course). UoL's partnership with The Birmingham Legal Advice Clinic received a LawWorks Award in 2012 in the Best Partnership category, while the school's pro bono centre has also been shortlisted for Birmingham Law Society awards in recent years. The employability service is in regular contact with firms, sets of chambers and other legal employers to give students up-to-date and relevant information regarding legal careers. Guest presenters frequently lead employer-specific talks, skills-based workshops and educational discussions, while there's a mentoring programme to take advantage of as well. Students said of UoL Birmingham: *"There's a really good standard of teaching here so you never felt like you didn't understand anything. Tutors take the time to speak to you, and you can also develop personal friendships with them."*

University of Law, Bristol

Pro: good links with the South West's biggest firms
Con: vibrant uni party scene to distract you

Bristol is UoL's newest centre and sprang into operation in 2010. This allowed it to take a share of the South West market that was previously monopolised by BILP. Students can take advantage of 'practice awareness presentations' held by local practitioners, mentoring schemes, court visits, mooting and negotiation competitions, and a speed networking event in connection with the Bristol Junior Lawyers Division and the University of Bristol Student Law Club. Local practices such as Osborne Clarke, Clarke Willmott, TLT, Burges Salmon and Bond Dickinson have all recently taken part to give students a clearer picture of the variety and complexity of work carried out by firms in Bristol. The school is a ten-minute walk from Temple Meads station and just a 20-minute jaunt from the student-laden Clifton area. *"The teaching was really good. We had sessions on how to lay out a memo or draft a letter, and other little things like that*

you don't really think about before you begin the LPC," a student source informed us.

University of Law, Chester

Pro: the incredible city walls
Con: a bit off the legal beaten track

Set in 14 acres of its own parkland, UoL Chester provides a *"legal oasis in a historical city."* Although a far cry from the buzzy, whirlwind pace of London, the school has good links with firms in the North West and students said *"the location and venue are both really nice; it's just a really relaxed place to be."* There's a variety of pro bono projects available including Streetlaw, Your Day in Court, Crown Court Challenge, Legal Advice Clinics, the Telephone Employment Helpline and domestic violence programmes. An active careers service runs numerous workshops throughout the year and operates a mentoring scheme. Students can also take advantage of a variety of sports teams and social events, including party trips on the River Dee or the Three Peaks Challenge.

University of Law, Guildford

Pro: beautiful(ish) setting
Con: Guildford's social scene

"The Guildford centre is in this beautiful old manor house, set in incredible grounds, but next to these unfortunate 1960s pre-fabricated buildings," a former student informed us. *"We'd go and play croquet on the lawn and enjoy sandwiches, but more importantly it's a friendly law school, with good electronic learning resources and accessible lecturers."* Guildford is a good option for those looking to avoid the real hustle and bustle of London, but who still want easy access to the capital (it's roughly 35 minutes away by train). The careers service offers all the usual guidance, information and events, and also runs a Pre-Interview Peer Support system, whereby if you have an interview or assessment day pending, the careers team will try to put you in contact with a student who successfully secured a training contract with the corresponding firm.

University of Law, London (Bloomsbury & Moorgate)

Pro: big city life
Con: the hit to your bank balance

UoL advertises its Bloomsbury branch with the tagline: 'You can't get more central than here.' Operating from two buildings on Store Street – just off Tottenham Court Road – you will find that Covent Garden, Soho, Oxford Street and many other trendy shopping, dining and boozing destinations are within walking distance. Not only

The University of Law

Braboeuf Manor, Portsmouth Road, Guildford GU3 1HA
Freephone 0800 289997
International (+44) (0)1483 216000
Email: admissions@law.ac.uk
Website: www.law.ac.uk

University profile

At The University of Law you'll get the best possible start to your legal career. We are the world's leading professional law school and, with 8 centres around the UK, we're the first choice for aspiring solicitors or barristers looking for effective legal training. Our innovative courses are designed and taught by lawyers, with a clear focus on building the practical skills, commercial awareness and independent thinking you need to succeed in legal practice. The University of Law is the first choice of many leading law firms and over 30 send their trainees exclusively to us for their GDL and LPC.

Graduate Diploma in Law - full-time/part-time/i-GDL (supported online learning programme)

The University of Law GDL is designed to build knowledge and skills that more than match a law degree – with a clear focus on preparing you for life in practice. Academic training is built around real-life examples and case studies, and you'll be given research assignments that directly reflect the way you'll work as a lawyer. In addition its unique Preparing for Practice module equips you with the professional skills you'll need as a modern lawyer.

LLM Legal Practice Course - full-time/part-time/ i-LLM LPC (supported online learning programme)

When you study your LPC at The University of Law, you can qualify with a Masters. Our LLM in Legal Practice LPC, as well as being your LPC, is also an internationally-recognised Masters qualification with the scope to specialise in international or national legal practice. The cost of the LLM LPC is the same as for a traditional LPC, and if you choose to qualify with a Masters, you need to complete a Professional Practice Dissertation.

We are the only globally-recognised professional law school to offer an LLM LPC with an increased international focus and an unparalleled choice of 18 electives. Graduating with The University of Law LLM LPC, means you will be better prepared and more employable for modern legal services than graduates from any other law school. Your LLM will be recognised globally as the leading qualification in legal services.

Bar Professional Training Course - full-time/part-time

The University of Law BPTC has been designed to resemble practice as closely as possible. Study follows a logical, realistic process from initial instruction to final appeal and learning is based around the seven core skills and three knowledge areas stipulated by the Bar Standards Board. Most of your learning will be in small groups and you'll have plenty of opportunities to put your learning into action through: practitioner evenings, mock trials, court visits, mooting, negotiating and advocacy competitions, and pro bono.

LLM Masters Degree - i-LLM (supported online learning programme with no attendance required)/ full-time attendance

Our LLM in International Legal Practice is a truly professional qualification and reflects cutting-edge approaches to legal practice. We offer a wide choice of flexible, specialist modules to suit your area of interest and enhance your expertise.

Events

We run events of all types, including open days, law fairs, insight days and online webinars. Take a look at what's available on our website: law.ac.uk/events11

Contact
Freephone: 0800 289997
International:
+44 (0)1483 216000
Email: admissions@law.ac.uk
Website:
www.law.ac.uk

GDL & LLM LPC full-time
Apply to: Central Applications Board www.lawcabs.ac.uk

GDL & LLM LPC part-time
Apply to: The University of Law
Contact: admissions@law.ac.uk

BPTC full & part-time
Apply to Bar Standards Board (BSB)
www.barprofessionaltraining.org.uk

LLM Masters Degrees
Apply to: The University of Law
Contact: LLM@law.ac.uk

The University of Law
incorporating The College of Law

this, but all the major legal hubs of the capital are located nearby. The Moorgate centre is based in a *"nice and flashy building with great coffee facilities"* in the heart of London's financial district. The Bloomsbury contingent admitted their own home wasn't quite as impressive, giving off a more *"student-y"* vibe, but did say the central location meant they had a lot more *"fun."*

Students told us that *"Moorgate has more of a corporate focus"* than Bloomsbury and also *"has a greater focus on training contracts."* With a number of magic circle and other leading City firms having specific LPC provision deals with the Moorgate branch to teach their future trainees, this is perhaps understandable. Even so, Bloomsbury has an active careers service and runs mentoring schemes with local practitioners and buddy schemes in connection with former students undertaking a training contract, and hosts numerous other talks and workshops.

A range of parties and balls organised for Bloomsbury and Moorgate students throughout the year includes a freshers' party, 'Holly and Mistletoe' party and an end of year ball. There's also a good chance you'll find at least some of the Bloomsbury cohort next door at The College Arms pub getting some liquid refreshment when classes have finished.

University of Law, Manchester

Pro: *"they were really interested in each individual's development"*
Con: *"the main problem was the IT"*

The UoL centre at Manchester opened its doors in 2009 and is located just a stone's throw from the Piccadilly Gardens and Arndale Shopping Centre. Students were a little dismayed by what they saw as *"astronomical fees"* for the region, but did feel this was compensated for by a *"slick and efficient structure,"* *"brilliant"* teaching and an *"expert"* careers service. *"They speak with a lot of firms in the North West so they always know of any opportunities coming up. They help a lot of people to get jobs that way."* Local law firms are on hand to participate in the school's mentoring scheme, with practitioners providing essential support and guidance to students. UoL also has good links with the judiciary, the Coroners Court and the Employment Tribunal to support the needs of students looking to progress into a range of different legal careers.

University of Law, York

Pro: The Jorvik Viking Centre
Con: it won't exist soon

The beautiful city of York is one of UoL's campus-based locations. The centre is known for its small intakes which creates a strong, collegiate feel among its attendants. The school organises a number of court and prison visits,

while there's mooting and negotiation competitions to get involved in, too. Relationships are in place with a number of Legal Advice Clinics, including Doncaster Women's Centre and Castlegate York, and students can also participate in a number of shadowing schemes that see them shadow and observe duty solicitors, criminal solicitors or even district judges. UoL is a keen participant in the yearly York legal sports day and there's a hearty amount of other social activities to delve into. For students who like a little flutter, the racecourse situated nearby should satisfy any cravings.

From September 2014 UoL is relocating its York branch to Leeds.

Leeds Metropolitan University

Number of places: 105 FT, 45 PT
Fees (2013/14): £7,500
Pro: cheap as chips (as far as law schools go)
Con: Kaiser Chiefs

Leeds Metropolitan's LPC is delivered at Cloth Hall Court, a centre in the heart of the city's legal district decked out with modern lecture theatres and classrooms, a mock courtroom and LPC resource rooms. There are also recording facilities in every classroom for the teaching and assessment of oral skills. A wide range of teaching and learning methods are employed, including lectures, small and large group work, and seminars. Some preparatory materials such as podcasts and videos can be found online, but the school likes the emphasis to be on face-to-face teaching. Full-timers will be on campus four days a week, while the part-time course consists of one day's tuition each week.

Beyond the standard subject matter, LMU's course focuses on employability and other skills – networking, for example – that are essential for a solicitor. A 'Professional and Career Development' programme is in place to help give students an edge in the search for a training contract. In addition, every individual is assigned a professional mentor – a local practitioner who can offer practical support and help provide work-based learning or career opportunities. Local law firms such as Eversheds, DWF and Pinsent Masons also actively engage with school by helping with teaching, leading career development sessions, or judging and providing prizes for a number of legal competitions.

Stage One subjects have an emphasis on litigation, but the six Stage Two electives offer a range of specialisms to cater for differing career paths. The LPC qualification can be used as credit toward an LLM for those looking to bolster their credentials.

Manchester Metropolitan University

Manchester Law School, Manchester Metropolitan University, Sandra Burslem Building, Lower Ormond Street, Manchester M15 6BH
Tel: (0161) 247 3046   Email: law@mmu.ac.uk
Facebook: /manchesterlawschool   Twitter: @mmu_law

College profile

Manchester Law School is one of the largest legal education providers in the UK, with a long history of providing top class training at the centre of the UK's second largest legal hub. As part of Manchester Metropolitan University, Manchester Law School benefits from exceptional facilities, with the additional advantage of being adjoined to the new £75m Business School and Student Hub.

Students gain huge benefits from regular contact with the legal profession due to strong, long-lasting links and the advantage of many staff still being in practice. Outstanding Pro Bono programmes, careers support, mentoring schemes and work experience opportunities make Manchester Law School a popular choice for postgraduate and professional study.

Each year over 1500 students study on a range of undergraduate, postgraduate and professional programmes, including the LLB (Hons), Legal Practice Course (LPC), Bar Professional Training Course (BPTC), Graduate Diploma in Law (GDL) and LLM.

We offer the following postgraduate courses, on a full and part-time basis:

GDL

If you are a non-law graduate looking for a legal career, our GDL is the perfect start. Our new 'Legal Skills and Practice' module will equip you with all the skills you need to train as a solicitor or barrister. We offer high levels of face-to-face teaching, innovative teaching methods and exceptional extra-curricular opportunities.

LPC

Our LPC is the perfect training for aspiring solicitors. You will receive all the vocational training you need for your future career, delivered by our innovative teaching team. You will also benefit from our excellent links to the local legal profession and the opportunity to gain work experience in your chosen elective subjects.

BPTC (full-time only)

We have a long and successful history of training barristers and our BPTC is rigorous, interactive and practical. We have outstanding, lasting links to the local Bar, giving you a great start to your career as well as significantly more advocacy training than the BSB advises. You will also receive the opportunity to obtain an independent professional qualification in mediation at no additional cost.

LLM

Our legal masters programme has been tremendously popular since its inception in 2010 and has two exciting routes. The taught LLM is for those with an LLB/GDL or a degree in social sciences. It allows you to research an area of the law that interests you and provides an excellent addition to your CV. The "top-up" LLM route is for those who already have an LPC/BPTC. It is a streamlined, fast-track way of getting a masters – you only complete one taught module and a research project.

Scholarships are available for the GDL, LPC and BPTC, visit law.mmu.ac.uk/scholarships for details.

For further information on our programmes visit www.law.mmu.ac.uk

Contact

GDL
law@mmu.ac.uk

LPC
lpc@mmu.ac.uk

BPTC
bptc@mmu.ac.uk

LLM
law@mmu.ac.uk

To apply

GDL & LPC full-time
Central Applications Board
www.lawcabs.ac.uk

BPTC
BPTC online
www.barprofessionaltraining.org.uk

Part-time GDL
Directly to Manchester Law School,
www.law.mmu.ac.uk/gdl

Part-time LPC
Directly to Manchester Law School,
www.law.mmu.ac.uk/lpc

LLM
Directly to Manchester Law School,
www.law.mmu.ac.uk/llm

Law School

Liverpool John Moores University (JMU)

Number of places: 72 FT, 72 PT
Fees (2013/14): £8,585
Pro: the new Redmonds Building has its own Starbucks
Con: pro bono opps are less readily available

LPC students at JMU have the luxury of being taught in the new, £38m Redmonds Building which is equipped with a mock courtroom, all the latest IT wizardry and a Starbucks on the ground floor. *"It's fabulous,"* beamed our source. *"It really is bloody lovely."*

Full-timers can expect to be on-site for between 12 and 15 hours each week, with teaching usually concentrated on Monday, Tuesday and Wednesday. However, JMU expects its full-time students to put in 40 hours of work per week, meaning that *"for every hour you're here, you need to do two hours preparation afterwards."* With potentially two days off, students can undertake work experience or other activities, but will be expected to keep on top of their work, too. A part-time day release route was introduced in addition to the evening study path to afford students greater flexibility when it comes to working jobs on the side.

All lectures are face-to-face and interactive, although most of the materials will go online afterwards as an additional learning or revision resource. JMU believes its *"small group sessions are vital, as that is where students will do the majority of their learning."* These contain no more than 20 students and are supplemented by larger group sessions, self-study exercises and individual preparation.

The school is proud to offer its cohorts *"lifetime careers support. We literally mean that; they can come back to us at any point in the future."* The careers service is very active and a dedicated law careers officer hosts sessions on CV writing, psychometric testing and mock interviews. There's also a number of workshops that bring in employers or current trainees to speak to LPC students.

A source told us: *"We've run the LPC in Liverpool since September 1994 and a huge number of local solicitors have graduated from this course. We have good links with our alumni right across the North West."* More than 50 local solicitors are part of the 'Solicitor Mentor Scheme', and local firms have not been shy in recruiting straight from the school in the past. JMU also runs a 'World of Work' programme which is endorsed by a series of FTSE 100 companies and gives students the chance to gain a certificate proving they possess good acumen for the business world.

There is a range of other opportunities on offer and last year some JMU students jetted off to Dubai to partici-
pate in the inaugural Invitational Law Schools Mediation Tournament. Strong individual performances saw the team come in first place overall, and take home the title of 'International Champions'. Chances to get involved with pro bono are also available, although they are usually subject specific. Once the course is completed students can continue their studies to work towards an LLM.

London Metropolitan University

Number of places: 192 FTE
Fees (2013/14): £8,370
Pro: the 'barrister to solicitor' conversion course
Con: not a big transactional focus

With the introduction of the LPC3 in 2010, London Metropolitan reorganised its compulsory subject focus to better reflect the destinations of its graduates. A more pronounced focus was given to litigation, while business law & practice and property law & practice took more of a back seat. *"Most of our students go on to jobs which involve litigation, so we felt that it was more useful for them to have a greater background in that."* Classes are interactive and taught in three-hour blocks to groups of no more than 16. One hour of that is teacher-led while the remaining two hours is student-led. These are supplemented with online tests and revision lectures, the more complex of which are made available online. Full-time students are on campus for two days a week – usually Tuesdays and Thursdays – while part-timers attend either one day a week or two evenings. There are currently ten electives on offer at Stage Two, and while most of these have a litigation focus, there are some commercial offerings too.

To help students' career prospects a professional mentor is designated to provide individual advice and guidance, while there are a number of work placements within solicitor's firms, at court or within not-for-profit organisations on offer as well. A whole week of careers events is held in March and sees the school provide mock interviews, CV surgeries and networking workshops, among many other opportunities. The school also offers pro bono work for those looking to improve their links with the profession and a dedicated pro bono supervisor is on hand to offer guidance and support.

LMU's law school sits within spitting distance of the iconic Gherkin, as well as the renowned hipster hangouts near Liverpool Street and Brick Lane. The state-of-the-art building in the City comes equipped with a mock courtroom, teaching rooms, a resource centre and a common room.

LMU has introduced a 'barrister to solicitor' conversion course off the back of the SRA's decision to allow exemptions on the LPC for those who had already completed the

BPTC, while those looking to secure a Masters in addition to their LPC can pursue a top-up LLM.

Manchester Metropolitan University

Number of places: 168 FT, 72 PT
Fees (2013/14): £9,065
Pro: a broad-based course to suit all tastes
Con: waistlines beware: 'The Curry Mile' is just down the road

Manchester Metropolitan's LPC should appeal to any budding solicitors, no matter which professional route you anticipate taking. *"Our graduates go on to small high-street firms, big national ones, or even take on contracts with local or central government,"* a senior source informed us. *"We haven't got a bespoke LPC that limits the opportunities available to students. Our Stage One subjects are appropriate for those who want to go into private practice or public sector work, while at Stage Two we offer a wide range of electives."*

This year the school increased the number of work placements linked to its elective subjects and also introduced two timetabled employability events into the calendar, with employers and ex-students coming in to talk about current issues, networking, pro bono, placements or other relevant topics. The careers and employability team also provides additional guest speakers, runs CV clinics and organises the practitioner mentoring scheme, which sees students paired up with local solicitors, many of whom are former graduates of the MMU LPC. The school has pro bono relationships with the Manchester Mediation Service, Manchester Citizen's Advice Bureau, Trafford Law Centre, Shelter and Amicus. This year it has also developed a connection with InnerSpace – which supports small and start-up businesses – to give students the chance to work on commercial pro bono projects.

The school itself can be found in a £16m, purpose-built building on Manchester Met's main university campus, next to the new £75m Business School and Student Hub. This gives students access to a wealth of fantastic facilities, including an LPC resources room, specific postgraduate areas in the Business School, a mock courtroom and the university's 750,000-book library. Teaching is largely conducted through workshops – the average group size is about 15 – and supported by online tutorials which are available via Moodle, the school's virtual learning environment. *"We've moved a lot of materials online to provide an interactive delivery of knowledge for students to prepare for workshops. It might involve reading, podcasts, partially drafting documents, or preparing a questionnaire."* All workshop materials are produced in-house by a team of MMU tutors: *"It means they are entirely up-to-date and meet not only the needs of the student, but also the local market. We can build in exercises which tick their requirements alongside the SRAs."* Full-timers have

a two or three-day teaching week, whereas part-timers attend for face-to-face contact one day a week, usually Wednesdays.

Most of the student body hails from the North West, but there's also a healthy contingent from Northern Ireland. Former MMU graduates can take advantage of a 10% discount, while there are also three scholarships up for grabs worth a third of the stated fees. Students can also top up their LPC with an LLM in Legal Practice to give their CV a little extra boost.

Northumbria University Law School

Number of places: 150 FT, 100 PT
Fees (2013/14): £9,400
Pro: free iPads
Con: marauding weekend drinking crowds

Northumbria University has been providing legal education courses in the North East for over 40 years. Its Student Law Office elective gives students the opportunity to undertake live client work through the Student Law Office (SLO). A former attendee said: *"The SLO is hands-down the best thing about the course – and there's a lot of good things about it. It really makes it stand out and gives you experience before most people would ever receive it."* Another added: *"It's like a little legal aid office overseen by qualified lawyers. You have clients coming in and you handle your own cases. It was a superb experience."* Northumbria has also undertaken a research project exploring and evaluating the use of iPads in legal education, meaning students now receive an iPad as part of their enrolment package and are allowed to keep it upon the conclusion of the course. An optional series of lectures covering issues relevant to law firms as businesses, such as marketing, management and career progression, will run during Stage Two. The Law School sits in a new £70m development in central Newcastle, and contains mock courtrooms and teaching facilities.

Both full-time and part-time students can tailor the LPC to their preferred career path. At Stage One they can follow one of two routes: general or commercial practice. The teaching staff come from a range of practice backgrounds, and as such Northumbria can offer a wide range of electives at Stage Two appropriate for either chosen path. Flexible timetabling means full-time students can opt to attend either two or four days a week with one lecture, one workshop and one small group session per subject. The part-time course sees students attend one day a week. Northumbria prides itself on the level of support it can offer and *"puts a premium on face-to-face teaching."* Workshops are taught to groups of around 16 students.

Every student has the opportunity to gain some vital work experience through a placement with a firm or organisation the school has links with – Ward Hadaway, Virgin

Nottingham Law School

Nottingham Law School, Burton Street, Nottingham NG1 4BU
Tel: +44 (0)115 848 4460
Email: nls.enquiries@ntu.ac.uk
Website: www.ntu.ac.uk/nls

Contact
Nottingham Law School
Burton Street
Nottingham Trent University
Nottingham NG1 4BU
Tel: +44 (0)115 848 4460
Email: nls.enquiries@ntu.ac.uk
Website: www.ntu.ac.uk/nls

School profile

One of the largest and most diverse law schools in the UK, we are committed to retaining strong links to practice. We seek to ensure that all our clients, from students to experienced practitioners, receive the best practical legal education and training. You will be taught by a unique mix of qualified lawyers with a proven track record in practice and legal education.

Nottingham Law School has an excellent reputation for graduate employability. Our focus on practical skills, award-winning pro bono scheme and dedicated careers and recruitment service has helped to keep our training contract and pupillage rates consistently high. We also have a number of competitive scholarships for our postgraduate and professional courses.

Graduate Diploma in Law (full time or distance learning)

This conversion course is designed for any non-law graduate who intends to become a solicitor or barrister in the UK. The intensive course effectively covers the seven core subjects of an undergraduate law degree in one go. It is the stepping stone to the LPC or the BPTC and to a legal career thereafter. It is possible for the Law School to award a Graduate LLB degree to students who have achieved the LPC or BPTC after completing the GDL with us.

Legal Practice Course (full or part time)

Our highly regarded Legal Practice Course has received the highest possible rating in every SRA/Law Society assessment. This course has been designed to be challenging and stimulating for students and responsive to the needs of firms, varying from large commercial to smaller high street practices. Our Legal Practice Course is designed to enable you to select pathways that lead to a specific type of practice, or maintain a broad based professional legal education if you are not sure yet what practice you intend to move to. In addition to our broad-based LPC, we offer corporate, commercial and public funding pathways. Nottingham's Legal Practice Course allows you to select your pathway after starting the course, rather than commit to a particular route in advance.

Bar Professional Training Course (full time)

Nottingham Law School designed its BPTC to develop to a high standard a range of core practical skills, and to equip students to succeed in the fast-changing environment of practice at the Bar. Particular emphasis is placed on the skill of advocacy. The BPTC is taught entirely by qualified practitioners, and utilises the same integrated and interactive teaching methods as all of the school's other professional courses. Essentially, students learn by doing. Students are encouraged to realise, through practice and feedback, their full potential.

Masters in Law (LLM)

Our taught masters in Law programme offers a wide range of subject pathways taught by tutors whose research is nationally and internationally recognised.

Subject areas include: Corporate and Insolvency, Health and Ethics, Human Rights and Justice, Intellectual Property, International Trade and Commercial, Sports, and Oil, Gas and Mining Law.

LLM Legal Practice (distance learning)

This new LLM award is for those with professional legal qualifications, for example the BPTC or LPC (or their precursors). Credit points are awarded for these professional qualifications and students can then 'top-up' these points with a dissertation or publishable article to gain this LLM.

NOTTINGHAM
LAW SCHOOL
Nottingham Trent University

Money and Nexus, for example – or they will be assigned a professional mentor who can offer assistance and guidance. There's careers advice on offer from the law school, including a practice interview scheme and other events and presentations throughout the year. In addition, you can benefit from the University Careers and Employment Service, which offers advice on CVs, assessment centres and training contract applications.

Those looking to jazz up their CV at the end of the course can go on to complete an LLM in Advanced Legal Practice. Northumbria also recently established a Dean's Awards Fund of £10,000 for a few lucky LPC students.

Nottingham Law School

Number of places: 650 FT, 100 PT
Fees (2013/14): £11,000
Pro: *"the lecturers are fantastic."*
Con: watch out for the trams

Nottingham Law School's LPC has been designed to allow students to specialise in a particular practice area or keep their options open. On offer are a choice of 'pathways' suitable for those with their eyes on high-street firms, City corporates or the publicly funded sector. At Stage One, students will select between a corporate or general route, with the latter currently inching ahead in the popularity stakes. *"A lot of students who join aren't absolutely certain of the type of lawyer they want to be. Following the broader route means they won't have closed any doors."* These are further enhanced with tailored skills pathways, which teach relevant skills within the context of a student's chosen route. *"The idea is that if you want to be a commercial lawyer, you will practise your skills in sessions focused on commercial scenarios. If you're a generalist there will naturally be more variety in the scenarios."*

Teaching is delivered through both large and small group sessions. A new 'blended' approach – which mixes face-to-face teaching, online group work, video simulations and independent online learning – is also on offer. All lectures are delivered live but also recorded and put online for students to access at a later date. Full-timers tend to be on campus for the first four days of the week, while part-timers can expect a large group session on Friday followed by smaller group sessions at the weekend. During Stage One, full-timers can choose between morning or afternoon teaching, making it easier for those who want to pursue work experience, a paid job, or just *"prefer the chance to undertake solid chunks of self-study."* There are currently nine electives on offer, with students able to pick a trio that will complement their selected pathway at Stage One. The advanced criminal practice elective has been designed to give students as much advocacy experience as possible, while a mediation module is now being offered as an added extra at no additional cost.

Nottingham Law School was redeveloped in 2011 and students have access to mock courtrooms, moot rooms and top-of-the-range teaching facilities. Nottingham Trent University itself is currently undergoing a major expansion programme that will see brand new student accommodation and a new student union built. Law students can take advantage of a dedicated law library and the main university library, both of which are being refurbished and expanded. In a bid to stay aligned with Generation Y all new starters will now be provided with an iPad as part of their teaching package. All course materials can be downloaded onto it and students are allowed to keep it in their possession even once the course is completed.

A dedicated careers team is on hand to assist with students' search for training contracts or paralegal positions. The personnel are specialists in the legal field rather than general careers advisers and offer help with CVs, interviews and applications. Nottingham has good links with local practices and practitioners, and offers a mentoring scheme in conjunction with them, as well as various work experience placements. A professional practice lecture series sees practitioners from the likes of Eversheds, Irwin Mitchell and Gateleys provide guidance on specialist aspects of law, the life of a solicitor and how to secure training contracts. Networking sessions are then commonly run in the aftermath of these. As part of a 'Bridge to Practice' programme, LPC staff will take on the role of partners in a firm and *"stay completely in character to simulate the real experience of working in a law firm to help improve students' commercial awareness."*

Nottingham has consciously expanded its pro bono offering to help prepare students for life in law firm. A purpose-built pro bono centre is located on site and there's a legal advice clinic for students to volunteer in. The school has an employment tribunal representation unit running in connection with the Free Representation Unit – the only one operating outside of London – while students are also given the opportunity to do pro bono work directly with outside bodies such as the Nottingham Citizens Advice Bureau, Nottingham Law Centre, Streetlaw or the Innocence Project.

Nottingham undergraduates are eligible for £1,000 continuation discount, while there are five general and three dedicated scholarships worth £2,000 also available. After completing the LPC you can top-up your credits and gain an additional LLM in Legal Practice at no extra cost.

University of Plymouth

Number of places: 80 FT
Fees (2013/14): £9,000
Pro: work placement scheme
Con: very regionally-focused

Plymouth University took over the running of Exeter University's LPC in 2006 and between them they have taught the next generation of lawyers for almost two decades. *"As we've run the LPC for nearly 20 years now there is a growing number of solicitors in the South West who we have actually taught,"* a senior source disclosed. *"They are very supportive in terms of helping us secure work placements and it allows us to be middle men between students and prospective employers."* Plymouth's close association with local practices and practitioners not only aids students in their legal education, it provides a invaluable opportunity for them to help forge their own careers – the current *"hot topic"* for all those who enlist. The school has actively sought out local solicitors, partners and consultants to supplement the teaching by coming on campus to deliver lectures or to offer advice.

A real draw of the course is Plymouth's work placement scheme. The school's extensive contacts with firms in the South West mean students can take advantage of a one-week placement opportunity during Term One. *"In the current climate it's a big ask for firms to find the space for our students, but the programme ran again this year and proved very successful."* In fact, roughly half of former students have left with a training contract in tow.

Pro bono opportunities are also easily sourced and the school's law clinic continues to help students take their first steps in the profession. Work with the Innocence Project, the South West Employment Rights Centre – *"some of our students were employed in a tribunal relating to that"* – and Plymouth City Council are all on offer, while there is an increasing amount of co-operation with the Junior Lawyers Division.

The full-time LPC sees students follow a *"regular pattern"* of two or three days on campus each week, with the targeted hours of 10am to 4pm stuck to as closely as possible. *"We try to keep a structure in place so people can manage other issues like childcare or travel. Roughly 50% are travelling in from outside Plymouth so it's appreciated by all the students."* Teaching is primarily done through small group sessions of approximately ten people, although this can drop to *"five or six"* when it comes to the elective stage. Technical issues such as professional conduct or solicitors' accounts are still taught via lectures and additional materials can be found through podcasts or the school's intranet service.

There are eight electives on offer at Stage Two and students are free to choose *"whatever combination they like."* The choices available are *"designed primarily to fit*

with the South West market but also reflect the national market," and include commercial law and practice; family law; and private client among others.

There are ten Saltram scholarships available per intake which knock a handsome £2,000 off the stated fees, while former students of either Plymouth or Exeter University are eligible for a 10% discount.

The University of Sheffield

Number of places: 180 FT, 35 PT
Fees (2013/14): £9,950
Pro: one of two Russell Group unis to offer the LPC
Con: Sheffield's steep hills (especially post-libations)

"Being one of only two Russell Group universities to offer the LPC, we do feel Sheffield has more to offer than most," say sources at Sheffield. Given that the School of Law is based in an institution renowned for research, there's a *"strong academic side to the law school, but the importance of professional legal education is widely recognised."*

There are two ways to study the LPC at Sheffield: either full-time, which runs from Monday to Thursday, or part-time, where students are taught on Fridays. Members of the full-time cohort also have the choice, during Stage One at least, of opting to take classes in morning or afternoon sessions, either from 10am until 1pm, or 1.30pm until 4.30pm. *"While some LPC providers will ask students to come in for only two days a week, we have found that to be too intensive, so study sessions are designed to be spread out across the week, helping students to plan and organise their workload."*

Towards the end of Stage One students opt to study elements of the core modules from either a commercial or high-street point of view. Combined with the ten electives on offer at Stage Two – that vary from the general to the commercial – students have more freedom to focus their LPC in a particular direction, should they so choose.

The majority of teaching is delivered via workshops, each taking in around 18 students, and is supplemented by screencasts, as well as various online learning activities such as drag and drop exercises, multiple-choice questions and short-answer quizzes. While many lectures have shifted to online streaming, there are still some for students to attend, but these are *"few and far between."* For those who prefer to remain on campus to work, dedicated postgraduate study spaces are available in the school.

The school currently has a careers adviser who offers one-to-one help with CVs and job applications. Students can also undergo a mock interview with a local solicitor, which is filmed and later watched by the student and the careers adviser who provides feedback on performance.

"They have an excellent reputation for careers advice and helping students acquire a training contract, and that's the main reason I actually chose to do the LPC at Sheffield," says one former student, now a practising solicitor.

Students can bolster their CVs through pro bono work for the Innocence Project and also through a legal advice clinic – the FreeLaw project. Students who volunteer for FreeLaw help charities by researching areas of social welfare law, as well as staffing a drop-in clinic for the local community, with all advice being overseen by a practising solicitor who is also a member of the LPC teaching team.

At the end of the course, students who achieve a commendation or distinction award on the LPC can choose to convert their diploma to an MA in Legal Practice, which involves selecting an area of law and practice, developing a research plan and writing a dissertation. This takes a further six months and can considerably help students boost their academic profile.

Sheffield's LPC prides itself on its quality of teaching and sense of community, with many of its students already being successful Sheffield graduates. With alumni benefiting from a 10% reduction in course fees at present, that community continues to grow. As one former student puts it: *"Sheffield stood out over other providers because the staff-student ratio was quite low so I knew that I'd get one-to-one help if I needed it. Everybody knows who you are because it's a small, friendly course."*

University of South Wales

Number of places: 90 FT, 40 PT
Fees (2013/14): £9,000
Pro: work experience opportunities
Con: fees hike after the merger

The University of Glamorgan merged with the University of Wales, Newport in 2013 to form the brand-spanking new University of South Wales. Despite this change, the LPC has remained much the same (apart from the almost £2,000 fee increase). It is still taught on the university's Treforest campus – a 20 minute train-ride north of Cardiff – in the recently renovated, Grade II-listed Ty Crawshay building, which houses a wide range of facilities, including a mock courtroom, dedicated LPC resource rooms, spacious open-plan social learning areas, meeting rooms and study areas.

Full-time students usually work four days a week between 9am and 5pm, and are taught in one-hour 'briefing sessions', either with the whole cohort together or in smaller 'practice sessions' taken by classes of up to 15 people. Part-time students are taught in the same way, but on one day a week. Emphasis is placed firmly on face-to-face interaction, although extra teaching support materials are available through an online portal called Blackboard, one of the most widely used virtual learning tools in the UK.

Lecturers encourage students to arrange regular individual face-to-face meetings. Key emphasis is also placed on employability, and students can enhance their legal skills in the real world through the university's LPC-specific work placement scheme. It allows students to network with local law firms where they can either work on a weekly basis or for an extended block of time. Past students have secured longer term employment this way and others have joined a variety of commercial firms, high-street practices, the CPS, private practice and government. LPC-focused commercial awareness seminars, careers workshops and talks are also organised. Studying at the University of South Wales provides a realistic career-oriented experience, with courses and facilities designed in consultation with major companies, private and public sector practitioners. The university's MLaw is an example of a course that has been designed and developed in this way. This new programme of study is unique in Wales and emphasis is placed on academic learning alongside providing students with the skills needed to work in an increasingly competitive environment. Furthermore, on completion of the MLaw students will graduate with a Masters-level qualification, while also achieving a Qualifying Law Degree and exemption from the LPC, therefore enabling students to progress directly to a training contract to become solicitors.

Staffordshire University

Number of Places: 150 FTE
Fees (2013/14): £9,500
Pro: multiple study options
Con: blended learning = less classroom learning

If studying the LPC is another component in an already hectic and fully-loaded schedule – perhaps you've got a job or other long-standing commitments – then you could do worse than look at Staffordshire University's offering. There's a whole raft of study routes here. For the full-time course you can choose to attend classes four days a week, cram them into two, or study across a single day and two evenings sessions. There are also three modes of part-time study: you can attend one day a week, rock up for two evening sessions, or do a combination of day and night classes. If all these options aren't enough then fear not; a new 'blended' learning option is also available in both full and part-time formats. This intensive delivery method sees 90% of the course taught online, with additional face to face sessions to enhance learning.

Staffordshire offers much more than great flexibility though. The modern law school building has a law library and legally qualified librarians. There's also a mock courtroom with video facilities, and rooms designated for learning and practice-based workshops. Upon enrol-

Law School

ment, LPC students are allocated to a Practice Office. These equate to hi-tech office bases that students can use for workshops or private study, and come equipped with state-of-the-art computers, printers and a range of e-resources.

Each year the careers department puts on a range of lectures and interactive workshops covering different parts of the job hunt, and these are supplemented by one-to-one advice and mock interviews. The university has well-established legal practice links, and regularly arranges for representatives to impart their wisdom and advice on graduate employment opportunities. A mentoring scheme is also in operation that pairs students with local practitioners to provide an extra insight into the professional world.

A register of all those searching for training contracts is maintained so that when firms approach the school about vacancies it can inform students through the Blackboard careers section. Staffs also pays for its LPC cohort to become members of the Local Junior Lawyers Division (JLD) to provide networking opportunities and help students get a leg-up in the profession.

Students can also participate in a variety of key skills competitions, such as mooting, negotiation and interviewing, while pro bono activity is highly encouraged. You can study for the LLM in Legal Practice at the same time as the LPC by attending a small number of additional lectures and completing a dissertation within four years, or you can simply go for the top-up LLM upon completion of the LPC.

Swansea University

Number of places: 100 FT
Fees (2013/14): £9,400
Pro: beautiful coastal location
Con: monsoons

Swansea University is set in parkland and botanical gardens overlooking Swansea Bay beach. Set on the edge of the Gower Peninsula, there's fantastic scenery to behold should the notoriously wet Welsh weather subside, yet Swansea's city centre is also within easy reach.

The LPC is offered full-time and part-time, and is staffed by a team of professionals with experience of practice. Full-timers attend for four days a week during Stage One (although this can often be crammed into three), while Stage Two sees them on campus three days a week. The part-time course is a new addition this year and is taught for one day and one evening a week across two years. Swansea likes to provide as much face-to-face contact as possible. Both stages are delivered through large introductory and interactive group sessions, and smaller workshops in which real-life professional case studies

and transactions are undertaken. Workshops last roughly four hours and usually take place in the afternoon, while materials from the larger group sessions are placed on the Blackboard site for future use. Stage Two offers a variety of high-street and corporate electives to cater for students with differing career aspirations.

Students at Swansea are encouraged to adopt a professional attitude, become business-focused and treat the course as a dry run of the first year of their training contract. Tutors actually adopt the roles of supervising partners within the firm of Caswell Clyne set up by the course team. Bulletins of job vacancies in the area are posted by LPC staff, and students can take advantage of talks from practitioners and the local Junior Lawyers Division. An established work placement programme helps give students experience of the working world at local courts, with sole practitioners, or within large commercial practices. A unique feature of the programme allows students to engage with firms on a Friday for a number of weeks during Stage Two.

Students can also participate in the Swansea Pro Bono Law Clinic if they need to jazz up their CV. Run by law students under the supervision of qualified local practitioners, the clinic offers invaluable experience of real-life cases. Tie-ups with the CAB and Streetlaw are also available, and the school has good links with the Swansea Law Society.

University of West London

Number of places: 60 FTE
Fees (2013/14): £8,970
Pro: the mini careers module included in the course structure
Con: larger class sizes

The University of West London's law school can be found in the affluent London suburb of Ealing – just a 30-minute tube ride from the capital's bustling centre. The LPC underwent a redesign in 2012 to better reflect the career paths of UWL's graduates. This meant there was a greater concentration on criminal litigation and property law, while the emphasis on business law and practice reduced. Successful students go on to both high-street and commercial firms, and a broad range of elective subjects are on offer to reflect this diversity.

"We're very aware of the pressures on students to make themselves employable and secure a training contract," said our senior source. The school therefore actively engages with students to try and help them stand out from the crowd in a competitive market. A mini careers module is embedded in the course structure and helps give students' CVs, applications and interview skills a touch up before they seek out firms, and this has been expanded over the last year to provide information about how social

media can be used in the search for legal employment. There are also mentoring and work experience schemes in place to help improve students' prospects. *"We had a large firm come in and run a mock application process for legal work experience, giving students the opportunity to test out their CVs and interview skills. A number of students were selected for a week's work experience in September off the back of it."* You can expect regular talks from practitioners, networking evenings and careers advisers who will support students for up to three years after they've completed the course. There's also the chance to gain legal work experience by joining the school's advice clinic – the Community Advice Programme – which runs fortnightly surgeries in co-operation with the Ealing Equality Council. New outreach clinics are currently *"expanding and are very much in demand."*

The course is primarily taught through workshops of about 20 students (this number falls at the elective stage) rather than lectures. Preliminary reading and other course materials can be found through the school's Blackboard site. Full-timers are in classes for two-and-a-half days per week – Tuesday, Thursday and part of Wednesday – while part-timers attend one day a week, with an extra evening tagged on during the second year. At the elective stage the workshops extend in length, meaning students can cram all their teaching into a day and a half if they'd like to.

A lot of the student body progress from undergraduate or GDL courses at the university, although there is a smattering of international students and other universities represented. A 5% early payment discount is available to all, while former UWL students can take advantage of a *"discretionary loyalty discount."* LPC students have free access to CPD legal update courses run by the Professional Development Centre and Middlesex Law Society, while a top-up LLM is also an option.

University of Westminster

Number of places: 120 FT, 64 PT
Fees (2013/14): £10,360
Pro: Central London location
Con: Central London tourists

The University of Westminster's law school is located just off Oxford Street – a big draw for any fashion gurus, entertainment-seekers, or someone looking for an easy commute from the capital's outskirts. Most students are from the UK but recently the school has seen *"more and more overseas candidates applying,"* with special interest coming from Trinidad and Pakistan. Most of the cohort will pay their fees in three instalments throughout the year, but those willing to stump up the full amount before the end of September receive a 1.5% discount.

Full-timers are in classes on Mondays, Tuesdays and Thursdays from 10.30am to 4.30pm during Stage One, but once you've navigated your way to Stage Two this reduces to a day-and-a-half. Part-timers attend two evenings per week. Teaching is conducted through small group sessions of roughly 15 to 18 students in the morning, while there is additional tuition or larger group work in the afternoons. Students can take advantage of both live and online lectures: *"Every subject will have some lectures online, but more technical matters such as business law practice or property law tend to have more than others. On the whole students prefer the live lectures, but a number of part-time students prefer the online lectures – probably because they don't have to hang around so late – so it's important to be able to offer both."* All relevant learning materials are uploaded to the school's Blackboard site.

"The majority of our students will probably end up going to high-street firms, as our private client electives are more popular on the whole than our commercial ones," a source said. However, with eight commercial electives offered alongside six private client options, those with their hearts set on the biggest firms should not feel disadvantaged. Undertaking the clinical elective offers students the chance to do a work placement scheme in connection with the CAB, while those who do the immigration elective will be given the opportunity to complete Level 1 of the Immigration Accreditation Scheme.

The school has a *"very active"* careers service. There are dedicated careers officers who teach on the course and are available to see students one-on-one to go over their CV or offer other job advice. There are careers workshops featuring representatives from local law firms, while a mentoring scheme launched in 2010 sees students pair up with Westminster alumni now working in the profession. *"It could just be going for a cup of coffee or having an informal chat, but one of our students managed to get their CV to a law firm representative and got themselves a training contract."* The pro bono centre sits right next door to the law school and students have access to *"six or seven"* projects each year, including work with the Land Registry Commission or on immigration matters.

Ongoing building work and refurbishment means that the dedicated LPC resource rooms – and the law school in general – will be nice, shiny and modern in time for Christmas 2013. The school is also unique in London and the South East as it runs an exempting degree alongside the LPC, meaning an LLB and LPC can be combined into four years of study.

University of Wolverhampton

Number of places: 60 FT, 30 PT
Fees (2013/14): £9,010
Pro: small class sizes
Con: Wolverhampton

The University of Wolverhampton's LPC runs with the aim of *"promoting access to the profession in the area."* As part of one of the smallest intakes nationwide, students can benefit from a *"personal and supportive atmosphere with a strong open-door policy."* There are only 60 full-time places up for grabs and *"the make-up of the student body is predominately local"* – either those who completed undergraduate degrees at the university or others nearby. Former Wolves alumni can get a hearty 20% off the stated fees.

Each subject includes a one-hour lecture followed by two small group workshops with no more than 15 students in each. Workshops run Monday to Wednesday, with additional skills assessments on Fridays. Students can take advantage of a state-of-the-art courtroom, a specialist resources room based in the library, and access to the media department's recording studios for interview and advocacy training. Part-timers are required on campus two evenings per week.

All lectures are now pre-recorded, allowing students to watch them at their leisure, as long as the relevant material is viewed before the corresponding workshop. *"Part-time students initially had access to them to save them coming in for an extra evening, but then the full-timers wanted to purchase them for revision purposes. It was generally just more popular to offer them in that way, so they're placed in advance onto the intranet system."* The intranet – known as Wolf – also offers additional online study materials and in the week before Christmas students combine into individual 'firms' and are set instructions through the portal. There are currently eight electives available at Stage Two including the ever-popular family, insolvency and employment options, alongside offerings for the more commercially minded, too.

The school has an active careers support network (which was somewhat of a guarantee considering its stated aims about promoting access to the profession). A dedicated careers adviser works across the whole of the law department, while there's also a mentoring scheme in conjunction with local firms. Local practitioners are invited in to give talks and presentations to students throughout the year, including during the LPC foundation week. This programme has been extended to also help final-year undergrads set their career wheels in motion. *"We have presentations focused on careers throughout the year as we're really trying to offer as much as we can and encourage the students to make more use of the opportunity."* Students can also volunteer in a legal advice clinic set up by LPC staff in the local Mander shopping centre.

If you wish to impress would-be employers even further, the LPC can be topped up with an LLM. This is offered to LPC students at massively reduced figure of £700.

Ethnicity and the law

23% of new trainees came from ethnic minority backgrounds in 2011-12

12.6% of all solicitors come from ethnic minority backgrounds; just under half are based in London

9.7% of self-employed barristers hail from ethnic minorities

78.1% of all solicitors are white

7.1% of solicitors are Asian (the biggest single known ethnic minority category)

5.2% of QCs come from an ethnic minority background

Pupil barristers:

79% white

13% ethnic minority

8% undisclosed

BPTC students:

43.7% white

42.4% ethnic minority

13.9% undisclosed

*Figures from the Law Society and Bar Council.

The Bar Professional Training Course (BPTC)

The BPTC is the necessary link between either an LLB or GDL and pupillage for would-be barristers. Nine law schools are authorised by the Bar Standards Board (BSB) to teach the course at locations in London, Bristol, Cardiff, Nottingham, Manchester, Leeds and Newcastle. The full-time course lasts a year; the part-time option is spread over two. Those with the gift of the gab, step up please.

A career at the Bar? You may need your health checked

Unfortunately it's not just LPC students that are finding it increasingly difficult to find employment at the end of a time-consuming and costly course; those chasing a career at the Bar are also facing up to the prospect of being well trained and highly qualified, but with little more than a £15k-sized hole in their pockets to show for it. The current disparity between the legions of BPTC graduates and the relatively miserly amount of available pupillages means the BSB has deemed it necessary to put out a 'health warning' to prospective barristers: *"We need to give a signal to those who aren't up to it that they're wasting their money* [or risk] *gaining an army of enemies,"* says Lady Deech, Chair of the BSB. Strong words, but a quick glance at the recent employment statistics of those called to the Bar would give even the next Dinah Rose something to ponder. The BSB states in its health warning that applicants should 'consider some of the facts and figures concerning a career at the Bar before you commit yourself.' It outlines that approximately 1,700 students take the Bar course each year but typically only around 480 are offered pupillages.

For example, in 2010/11, 1,422 students enrolled on the BPTC (after 3,099 applied), but only 446 first-six pupillage were up for grabs that year. (The Bar Council was unable to provide us with any more recent statistics.) It's important to also bear in mind that the BPTC has a lifespan of five years, so this figure includes graduates from previous years who were unsuccessful in their first, second, third or even fourth attempt. Over 3,000 individuals may be applying for pupillage in any given year, while chambers regularly receive over 100 applications for a single position. The odds are clearly stacked against aspiring barristers, and most students will have to strike the right balance between *"realism and optimism; they know it's tough, but then again you always think that you will be the one to get a pupillage."*

The quest for a pupillage can look almost as daunting as Frodo's ring-destroying adventure when you consider the qualifications of those who do make the cut; the academic records of new tenants are quite simply terrifying. Some 35% hold First-class degrees (less than 5% of new tenants graduated with 2:2s) and a similar percentage attended Oxbridge. Another third will have attended a Russell Group university. Throw into the mix a bountiful array of MAs, PhDs, academic prizes, scholarships and languages and you can see that the competition is fierce. As Lady Deech said: *"If you're tone deaf, don't go to music school; if you have two left feet don't go to ballet school"* – with reference to BPTC students who lack the required command of the English language. The point is, winning arguments over the dinner table and fancying yourself as Atticus Finch or Mark Darcy just isn't going to cut it. You really need to make a cold, hard assessment of whether you can cut it in the profession.

In 2009 and 2010, the BSB piloted an aptitude test for the BPTC as a more proactive way of protecting wide-eyed students, while also looking to ensure the future strength and quality of the Bar. Now all prospective students have to undertake the BCAT and they must achieve a minimum required standard in logic and reasoning questions in order to take up their place on the BPTC. Oh, and they must also shell out a £150 fee to take the test.

The move to give the go-ahead for this test has been a controversial one, with the Law Society flagging up various concerns about the viability of the BCAT, especially since the Legal Education and Training Review rejected proposals for an aptitude test for LPC students on *"diversity grounds."* A homogenisation of the Bar has been predicted by some, but Legal Services Board chief executive Chris Kenny says the validity of these concerns is *"impossible to verify in absolute terms at this stage."* The BSB is therefore undertaking a five-year data gathering and evaluation period, after which a decision will be made about the ongoing use of the BCAT. BPTC providers (apart from Kaplan, which already ran an aptitude test) were on the whole *"unconvinced that aptitude tests tell you much more than a paper application."*

Sources at Nottingham Law School, which runs the exact same course as Kaplan but without a prerequisite aptitude test, said that *"the profile of the students at both institutions is remarkably similar,"* and that exam results demonstrate an equal level of *"those who are competent and those who aren't."* One welcome outcome is that the test is likely to protect certain misguided students from the burden of a heavy debt unnecessarily incurred, but we'll have to wait a few more years before the true worth of an aptitude test is fully known.

2:2 boohoo

A second contention in enlisting quality candidates onto the BPTC arises from course providers. The BSB's minimum requirement for admission onto the courses is a 2:2 at degree level, and a pass on the GDL (where taken). Several providers have chosen to up the ante. Kaplan Law School, for example, now requires all applicants to possess a 2:1, and even those subsequently shortlisted will have to attend an assessment day, where they undertake a written advocacy exercise, an oral advocacy exercise and an interview. As sources there say: *"We need students who can fire on all cylinders."* In fact, most providers will be looking for students with at least a 2:1, and according to recent statistics over 60% of BPTC students across all providers had this qualification or higher. One course leader told us: *"In line with BSB requirements we never outrightly say no to someone with a 2:2, but increasingly we have looked to recruit people with at least a 2:1 and mini-pupillage or practical experience. They have to have a fighting chance."* However, success at the Bar is based on more than impeccable academics and most providers are on the lookout for an applicant's commitment to practice, either through public speaking, such as mooting or debating, or relevant work experience. This is no different for the sets offering pupillage, so if a life at the Bar is the one for you, do everything you can to stand out from the crowd.

The mismatch between BPTC graduates and the number of pupillages is tempered to a certain extent by those individuals who have decided that the Bar is simply not for them, and by the significant number of international students (estimated at between 20 and 25% of all BPTC students) who return home rather than seeking pupillage in England and Wales. This contingent may be set to fall as many course providers, prompted by the BSB, are getting tougher on their entry requirements as concerns English language ability. Currently the BSB requires all students whose first language is not English or Welsh to demonstrate that they have a minimum 7.5 IELTS standard, or equivalent. Over the past few years we've heard rumbling criticisms that some students' English just isn't up to scratch, which causes difficulties in the classroom

for other students practising key skills that rely on rhetorical ability. It seems that law schools are finally reacting, taking steps to ensure applicants possess the required standard of English.

Mad skillz

The BPTC has been designed to ensure that wannabe barristers acquire the skills, knowledge, attitudes and competencies needed for practice. Cue: developing students' advocacy, drafting, opinion writing, conferencing, case analysis and legal research skills. As for knowledge, students are schooled in civil litigation and remedies, criminal litigation and sentencing, evidence, and professional ethics. These core areas, especially ethics, are essential because *"barristers are individuals, and they get thrown to wolves more often. When you're a solicitor you have the protection of the firm around you – barristers have to be equipped with all the knowledge they can get."* In the final term, students select two option subjects in areas they're targeting for practice.

Almost wherever you study the emphasis is very much on face-to-face teaching – usually to groups of about 12, but for all-important skills there's often six students or fewer. Still, many use computers in lectures to make learning more stimulating, while writing skills classes often involve the use of whiteboards. Oral skills classes make increasing use of video-recording equipment in role-plays so students can improve by assessing their own performance as well as that of their peers. The skills acquired are then examined using a variety of assessments in the second and third terms. Written skills are tested through a mix of unseen tests and 'homework', and the BSB recently permitted students at BPP to type their written skills assessment for the first time. Professional actors are commonly drafted in to take part in oral assessments. One area where the BPTC differs most from its predecessor the (Bar Vocational Course) is its focus on alternative dispute resolution (ADR). A new 'Resolution of Disputes Out of Court' module replaced the old negotiation skills course, heralding a broader approach to avoiding litigation.

Though skills assessments will continue to be set and marked by the individual providers, the future of testing knowledge has changed. The BSB now sets standardised and centralised exams for civil litigation, criminal litigation and ethics to ensure confidence in the parity between course providers. The exams consist of a blend of multiple choice questions and short answer questions. The latter are still marked locally by the providers, while the former are centrally marked by a computer. The BSB then samples and moderates the written exam papers.

This was all introduced for the first time in 2012 and the response from both providers and students hasn't been hugely positive. Providers' responses ranged from moderate annoyance to full-on fury: *"I'm upset about it, to the point where I want to run to the BSB with a pitchfork in hand."* Students were also unimpressed, and hundreds signed a petition to the BSB expressing their dissatisfaction. One provider put it thus: *"As long as I can remember exams were set locally; if you did the course at Nottingham, then Nottingham set the exams and marked them. The assessments were aimed at what students could be expected to know based on the teaching at that institution. It's just inevitable when exams are centralised that the questions are going to be one step removed from the providers – the exams may cover things that students haven't come across before."*

While some students have done less well under the new system, others have actually thrived, and providers told us that *"in the end our students ended up doing more or less how they expected they would. Our pass rates are not dissimilar to what they were last year."* The problem, then, seems to be with the stress of having to revise a vaster body of material than ever before...

All systems go

Course directors tell us that the BPTC is *"a very demanding, intensive and rigorous course."* The timetable is described as *"undulating"* – *"intense in parts and boring in others"* – and often the course is *"front-loaded."* But don't use the quieter times to relax. This is your chance to improve your pupillage prospects, as one student advised: *"Organise dining with the Inns, mooting, debating, pro bono, mini-pupillages, marshalling and the like to give your CV a fighting chance of reaching interview stage."* It's essential to look carefully at the extracurricular opportunities offered at each provider and throw yourself into everything you can. Most providers will deliberately keep days free of classes to allow students this opportunity.

How to apply through BPTC online

An application for the BPTC costs £40, and the process is all done online. There is no cap on the number of providers you may apply to, although during the first phase of the process only your top-three choices will look at your application. While many providers will say that it's not vital that you put their institution as a top choice, many popular providers fill their places with first and second-choice applicants alone. Prioritise your favourites if you want to avoid disappointment.

How to pick a provider

The fight for pupillage is a truly testing one, so choose your course provider carefully. Read through prospectus-

es and websites, attend open days, try to speak to current or former students. Read our **BPTC Provider Reports** and consider the following criteria:

Cost: London is clearly going to be pricier than Northumbria, but even in the capital there's variation. If you're an international student, look at the differential in price. Part-timers should note whether fees increase in the second year.

Location: Regional providers may be the best option for those looking for pupillage on the regional circuits, not least because of their stronger links and networking opportunities with the local Bar. London students benefit from proximity to the Inns of Court and easier access to London sets for pupillage interviews. However, compulsory dining and advocacy training courses in the Inns enable regional students to maintain their links with the capital's beating legal heart.

Size: Smaller providers pride themselves on offering a more intimate and collegial environment, and student feedback indicates that this does make a positive difference to the experience. You can also expect a noticeably different feel at the providers that are within universities to those that aren't.

Facilities: Students can tap into a far wider range of support services, sports and social activities by taking the BPTC at a university. Library and IT resources vary from one provider to the next, as does the level of technology used in teaching. Some providers make technology a key feature of the course.

Option subjects: Available option subjects vary. For example, although judicial review and immigration are popular, they're not offered everywhere. Check out our Table of BPTC Providers to see what's on offer at each one. This table also compares fees and offers provider-specific application tips.

Pro Bono: Opportunities range from minimal to superb across the nine providers.

BPTC Provider Reports

Which of the law schools teaching the BPTC will be right for you? All quotes come from course directors or other official sources at the providers.

BPP Law School, London

Number of places: 264 FT, 96 PT
Pro: proximity to the Inns of Court
Con: BPP prices + London living costs = OMG

Legal education heavyweight BPP is never one to sit still and rest on its laurels; some significant recent changes to its BPTC offering over the last year prove this. Firstly, three new options have been introduced for London students: public international criminal law, professional discipline, and advanced commercial litigation. Secondly, the BSB permitted BPP students to type their written skills assessment for the first time after the school came across some nifty new software – *"an important development because hand writing is just not reflective of practice."* And finally, from September 2013 BPP will be running the BPTC from its Manchester centre for the first time.

The London branch is based in Holborn, a central London location ('Midtown', as the council is trying to rebrand the area) that's also home to various Inns of Court and a smattering of barristers' chambers. Full-timers are on-site for four days a week, with either Monday or Friday left free for additional study, pro bono or other extracurriculars. The timetable is *a little bit lighter and more flexible"* in term three, so students will potentially have more days off. Part-timers attend one weekend a month over two years.

The civil and criminal litigation components of the course are taught in one-and-a-half-hour tutorials to groups of 12 students. Rather than interweaving advocacy into these sessions, it's taught separately to groups of four in a dedicated tutorial each week. BPP actually offers around 30% more advocacy than BSB guidelines stipulate. Although professional ethics is generally front-loaded at the start of the course, *"there are also additional small group sessions or tutorials in the run up to exams. In the interim period we treat ethics as a pervasive topic. We will put up ethics podcasts on a weekly basis, and ethical points will always come up in other subjects."* Students receive feedback for every oral skills performance, while for written skills they're given formal written feedback on at least two pieces of work and oral feedback in every small group session.

A minimum of five hours must be committed to pro bono. The school has a Pro Bono Centre, and students can gain valuable work experience with real clients through connections with FRU, Liberty, Streetlaw and projects at the Royal Courts of Justice. If students have their own contacts or causes then they are more than encouraged to pursue them, *"providing it's been approved by a programme leader; we don't want unsupervised students offering advice."*

A *"very active"* careers service helps students in their hunt for a pupillage. A professional careers team gives general advice on CVs, covering letters and applications, while a BPTC-specific careers officer (and course tutor) will organise useful titbits such as mock interviews, panel discussions or commercial awareness workshops. You can also practise your skills through mock trial and mooting events, which are judged by members of the judiciary and practitioners. The final of the annual mooting competition will see the lucky competitors descend on the RCJ.

Although BPP will make conditional offers to candidates holding a 2:2 (in line with BSB guidelines), *"the vast majority of students will come with a 2:1 or higher."* Those who complete the BPTC with BPP can then work towards an LLM in Professional Legal Practice.

BPP Law School, Leeds

Number of places: 48 FT, 48 PT
Pro: mentoring scheme
Con: no mediation competitions this year

The Leeds Whitehall Quay study centre is in the city's heart, a short stroll away from the train station and main shopping areas. It boasts state-of-the art mock court rooms, top-end tech facilities and comfy common rooms. The course is the mirror image of that in London, although with a cohort almost six times smaller than you'll find in the capital it's a closer-knit operation. BPP facilitates relations with members of the local Bar, and students can take advantage of the meet-and-greet sessions and guest speaker programme the school runs. Also, BPP's regional centres run a mentoring scheme that isn't available in London. *"We don't run it in London because the Inns already have very similar schemes and we're just across the road from them."* Students can improve their career prospects by volunteering in projects organised by the school's Pro Bono Centre – human rights work and the Legal Advice Clinic being just some examples. As in London, students who successfully complete the BPTC can go on to pursue an LLM in Professional Legal Practice.

BPP Law School, Manchester

Number of places: 48 FT
Pro: Iyengar yoga
Con: surrounded by hip Manchester distractions

From September 2013, BPP will be running the BPTC from its Manchester centre for the first time. BPP will become only the second provider in the city and will rival Manchester Met for a share of the spoils. The Manchester St James branch is in the bustling city centre, and in close proximity to the Oxford Road train station and main shopping areas. The course structure is exactly the same as it is in London and Leeds, and students will find classrooms equipped with all the latest audio-visual technology, as well as a large breakout area and plenty of silent study spaces. A Pro Bono Centre is in place to help students practise skills they'll need in the profession, and specialist careers advice can be sought from the careers service or personal tutors. There's also plenty of clubs and societies for students to immerse themselves in if they need a break from study – you can give anything from football to mooting, squash or Iyengar yoga a go.

Bristol Institute of Legal Practice at UWE

Number of places: 84 FT, 48 PT
Pro: close ties with the local Bar
Con: campus is outside city centre

UWE's law school is on the Frenchay campus four miles outside Bristol's city centre. Don't be put off by the short commute though, as awaiting you on site is a range of state-of-the-art facilities including postgrad study rooms and a 24-hour chambers library. Throw in the university's law library and dedicated base rooms, and BPTC students can access a wide range of legal resources at any time of day or night. There are also mock courtrooms equipped with the latest recording equipment to allow advocacy sessions to be subsequently analysed.

"Our real selling point is the close ties we have with the local Bar," a senior source from BILP told us. Local practitioners lead advocacy 'masterclasses' to help students perfect their professional style, and also lend their time to host mock pupillage interviews that put BILP's would-

be barristers through their paces. *"Students will get a real grilling, but it's a hugely worthwhile experience."* There are three chambers-sponsored advocacy competitions throughout the year, while a new mooting competition is also set to be established. Although these come with cash prize incentives, the real appeal comes with the chance to show off your skills in front of the local Bar – who knows when a job offer might rear its head?

The school is dropping the available number of full-time places from 120 to 84 *"as a pilot."* This is partly in response to three of its lecturers being set to retire. BILP will *"never say no"* to someone applying off the back of a 2:2, but is ideally looking for applicants with a 2:1 or higher and relevant practical experience. There are no scholarships or bursaries on offer, although there is a 15% discount available for UWE undergrads.

A healthy portion of the student body has affiliations with the South West, although the school has recently seen more and more recruits coming from London or further afield. There's a strong contingent from outside the UK as well, with the likes of Mauritius, the British Virgin Islands, Pakistan, Malaysia and Bangladesh all represented. One of many reasons UWE is a big draw for those beyond Bristol's hinterlands is that the BPTC offers students the chance to become an accredited civil and commercial or workplace mediator of the Bristol ADR group at no additional cost.

Students can expect to be in classes for up to 16 hours a week. This is usually completed within three days but can sometimes spill over into four. An additional 20 hours of independent study is expected each week, while Fridays are kept free *"99.9% of the time"* to allow for pro bono or other commitments. Teaching is led by professional practitioners and is generally undertaken in small group sessions of six to 12 students.

There are currently eight options to choose from, including diverse areas of law like clinical negligence, international trade and family. Environmental law has been replaced with a new commercial option that has proven extremely popular amongst the current intake: *"We limited it to 24 places and 24 people accepted it immediately, so we're intent on continuing with that option next year."*

BILP has a *"very strong"* pro bono unit which is well supported by the local judiciary. For example, students can attend the Civil Justice Centre and offer free legal representation in relation to family law generally, but with a particular focus on domestic violence.

Cardiff Law School

Number of places: 84 FT
Pro: only Russell Group uni to offer the BPTC
Con: no scholarships or bursaries on offer

Throw together the only Russell Group University to offer the BPTC and its campus right in the heart of a bustling capital city and you've got a popular destination for aspiring barristers. Cardiff Law School sees a lot of former Cardiff Uni undergrads enrol, but a *"good number of geographical locations are also represented, including overseas."* Cardiff consistently receives *"more first-choice applications than we have places, so it's hard for us to consider those who put us lower than that."* In other words, if you want to come here, make it obvious. Graduates of the BPTC and LPC are now able to enrol for a top-up LLM in Legal Practice should they want to obtain a Masters qualification after the conclusion of their course.

Classes run Monday through Thursday, with Friday left free to allow students a chance to catch-up or undertake work experience. Cardiff deliberately keeps its intake low to ensure that teaching is limited to small groups. Oral skills are generally taught to groups of six people, but often as few as four. A teacher will observe students in pairs when they practise their oral skills, with verbal and written feedback provided to each student individually. Although the BSB requires a minimum of 12 advocacy sessions during the BPTC course, Cardiff goes above and beyond this, offering over 25 sessions annually. A limited amount of large group sessions concentrate on knowledge-based content, while all the course materials are uploaded onto the school's 'central learning environment' for students to access at a later date. A good range of elective options are on offer to cater for those looking for differing career paths, although those listed are always indicative and never guaranteed.

A unique part of the BPTC at Cardiff is the two-week placement scheme that runs each year. Students are guaranteed to marshall a circuit judge and district judge during the first week, followed by a mini-pupillage or other relevant employment in the second week. There's a standalone careers department within the university should you need any general advice, while people within the law school hold regular careers talks.

Cardiff provides *"a wealth of different pro bono opportunities"* through its 'Law in the Real World' programme that gives students access to real-life cases and better prepares them for the rigours of practice. It is also the only UK law school to run a legal advice clinic in conjunction with the NHS Continuing Care Scheme, while The Cardiff Law School Innocence Project is another example of what's on offer. Students can further enhance their skills by participating in negotiation, advocacy and mediation competitions.

City Law School, London

Number of places: 420 FT, 60 PT
Pro: boasts a 'who's who' of alumni
Con: commonly oversubscribed

City Law School (formerly Inns of Court School of Law) was the founding provider of the Bar course and had a monopoly on it until 1999. As such, many alumni of ICSL have gone on to become judges, Queen's Counsel or distinguished academics. It can even boast that four British Prime Ministers – Tony Blair, Margaret Thatcher, Clement Attlee and Herbert Asquith – and Mahatma Gandhi passed through its doors. The school has built a good reputation both at home and abroad and many international students, especially those from the Commonwealth, will seek training here. As a competitive and challenging course, City expects international students to demonstrate a minimum of 7.5 on the IELTS scale to ensure they can follow classes competently. With the course commonly oversubscribed (and City deliberately recruiting fewer students than it's validated for), it's a good idea to put it as your first-choice destination.

City offers the course both full and part-time. Full-timers will be in classes three days a week, with the remaining two days left free for preparation, professional development or research. City recommends that an additional 20-plus hours of private study should be undertaken weekly. Part-time teaching takes place two evenings per week. In an effort to acclimatise students to the professional world, it's stated that attendance at all classes is mandatory.

The course is designed to replicate the demands and discipline required of life in chambers, and the emphasis is on learning by doing. The programme is written and developed in consultation with practitioners to ensure it imparts the relevant skills and knowledge needed for a career at the modern-day Bar. Course director Stuart Sime even works closely with Oxford University Press to write textbooks that are used across the country. Teaching is conducted by qualified legal professionals, many of whom are directly involved in practice or sit, or have sat, in a part-time judicial capacity. Small group sessions contain up to 12 students, while interactive large group sessions also occur frequently. City has made efforts to improve its provision of online materials, and its 'online learning environment', Moodle, allows instant access to course materials and communication tools from any computer.

Advocacy is a key subject at City. It offers three times as much advocacy training than the BSB requires and is taught in a courtroom setting to groups of six. Students will receive regular feedback during these classes and one-to-one advice can be sought throughout the year. A wide selection of options are available and three of them – FRU, domestic violence and social security –

are pro bono-based, providing the opportunity for some real-life case experience as part of the course. For those looking to get involved with pro bono and add some gloss to their CV without dedicating a whole option to it, City runs a pro bono programme. Partnerships with the FRU, London Innocence Project and the National Centre for Domestic Violence are just some of the initiatives through which students can hone their skills.

Students are free to seek advice from the City University careers team but a dedicated pupillage advisory service is also available for those seeking information or assistance. It offers mock interviews, advocacy exercises or just general guidance on how to best navigate the path to pupillage. A guest speaker programme will see prominent members of the legal community impart their wisdom, while students can also participate in mock trial and mooting competitions.

The school's Future Lawyer Excellence Award gives one full fee and six 50% scholarships to eligible students. In addition, there's a variety of external awards and scholarships available, and former City grads receive a loyalty discount.

Kaplan Law School

Number of places: 120 FT
Pro: good track record for graduates securing pupillages
Con: tough to secure a place

Despite only running the BPTC for the first time in 2010, Kaplan has already made quite a name for itself. It's now validated to offer the course to 120 would-be barristers – double the number it could offer during its first year – and secured its highest-ever enrolment figures this year, too. This is an impressive feat even before you consider Kaplan's robust selection process. The school requires its students to hold a minimum of a 2:1, and even those who do, have to navigate their way through a 'selection event' before they can bank on enrolling. *"When we feel that candidates meet our initial requirements – we look at qualifications, but also their commitment to a career at the Bar and any relevant extracurriculars – we will then invite them to the selection event."* Prospective students have to contend with three separate tasks at this stage: a piece of advocacy work, a written examination and an interview with a barrister. *"The results of those feed into who we make an offer to."*

The course itself mirrors that offered at Nottingham Law School (with whom Kaplan is affiliated) and consists of three civil briefs and four criminal. Teaching is conducted over four days each week, and there are no more than 12 students in classes for written skills, and no more than six in oral skills lessons. There are six elective options on offer: advanced crime, advanced civil, commercial, family,

employment, and landlord and tenant. The former four are *"the most popular."*

The school is a big advocate of mooting and mock trial competitions, and students have enjoyed *"a really high degree of success"* at small local events and on the international stage. A new venture last year saw some students participate in mock trials at the Old Bailey, where baby constables and judges were involved to add to the sense of authenticity. *"We're hoping that project will be expanded and regularly included in our programme."* A Master or Mistress of Moots scholarship worth 50% of the fees is awarded to a person who can demonstrate a proven track record in organising and leading successful student activity in mooting, debating or advocacy, while a further ten advocacy scholarships worth £2,000 are available.

Kaplan's campus can be found on the South Bank of The Thames, not far from London Bridge tube station. The South Bank is home to attractions such as The London Eye, Tate Modern and the National Theatre, while Borough Market is also on the school's doorstep. Considering the wealth of trendy bars and restaurants nearby, and that London's legal and financial hub is just over the river, Kaplan really is in an ideal location for students. Kaplan comes kitted out with nice new classrooms, breakout areas and mock courtrooms. A secondary professional resource centre has recently opened on Borough High Street, complete with new PCs and a quiet study area which BPTC students have sole use of.

As soon as students accept a place on the course they have access to Kaplan's careers advice service, which runs appointments three days a week. It also puts on a careers event at least once a week, and these have included guest speakers, mock interviews and CV surgeries in the past. There is also a range of pro bono programmes students can immerse themselves in, including the FRU or volunteering at the Kaplan Legal Advice Centre. The school is also looking to develop an outreach programme with prisons, while plans to forge relationships with domestic violence and family law initiatives are at *"an embryonic stage."*

Kaplan has a strong track record of finding its students pupillages and 55% of the class of 2012 secured one upon graduation. *"We expect that number will continue to rise, too,"* a source told us.

Manchester Metropolitan University

Number of places: 108 FT
Pro: over double the amount of required advocacy sessions
Con: not recruiting sufficient numbers to run a part-time course

With Manchester Metropolitan's law school located in a £16m purpose-built building adjoining the new £75m Business School and Student Hub, BPTC students will have access to wealth of fabulous facilities. These include dedicated resource areas and base rooms, as well as a mock courtroom fully kitted out with DVD-recording technology. Students can also access specific postgraduate areas in the Business School and the university's 750,000-book library.

The full-time course is taught across four days. Students are initially split into nine 'mini-chambers' of no more than 12 people, and then further divided into groups of six to practise oral skills. These chambers are then rotated at the elective stage. Students alternate weekly between civil and criminal litigation, and teaching focuses on knowledge at the beginning of the week before building up to the relevant skill – advocacy, for example – at the end. The school employs a variety of e-learning methods, such as podcasts, to aid teaching, while some of the lectures can also be found online. Man Met prides itself on the experience of its teaching staff and counts Deputy District Judges, pupil supervisors, tribunal chairs and a number of people still in practice among its ranks.

Although the BSB requires only 12 advocacy sessions throughout the BPTC, Man Met goes *"over and above"* this and offers *"a minimum of 24 sessions."* Students can even take advantage of additional advocacy sessions delivered by practitioners. One big change at Man Met has seen the law school now offer anyone who studies the BPTC the chance to add an independent professional qualification in mediation at no extra cost.

A dedicated careers adviser is on hand to offer students guidance on finding a pupillage or another route into the profession, while a practitioner from the Northern circuit is assigned to act as mentor to each 'mini-chamber'. In addition, students can take advantage of the university's careers service, which is quick to advertise any job vacancies that arise. At the start of the academic year, BPTC students enjoy a two-hour pupillage forum hosted by an ex-Manchester Law School graduate, who discusses how to prepare for the pupillage application and interview procedure. In term three there are a number of recruitment events, which can be especially useful for those who have been unable to secure a pupillage. Pro bono is also a big deal here, and there are opportunities with the Personal Support Unit at Manchester Civil Justice Centre and the Manchester Mediation Service on offer. There are also a range of mock trial, interview and negotiation competitions in place to help you hone your skills further.

Candidates who put Manchester Law school as their first or second-choice provider are eligible to receive a scholarship worth £4,000.

Northumbria University Law School

Number of places: 100 FT, 24 PT
Pro: the Student Law Office
Con: Gazza

Northumbria University boasts the largest law school in the North East and students are drawn to the £70m purpose-built campus complete with state-of-the-art teaching and learning facilities. Its location in Newcastle's city centre also means you should never be too far from a boozer if you need some time to let your hair down. The majority of BPTC students at Northumbria come from the region, but there's a decent international presence alongside them. However, with the teaching sessions involving a high degree of interaction, international students are expected to be fluent in both written and oral English, so will need to possess at least a 7.5 IELTS score.

Full-timers usually attend four days a week, with Friday left free for research, self-study or professional development opportunities. The part-time programme follows a flexible day release pattern and students can choose which day – either Monday, Tuesday or Thursday – they wish to attend. All subjects and skills are taught through practical sessions in which students work on case studies and carry out a range of tasks which replicate the demands of pupillage. Skills are taught in small group sessions, while evidence, criminal litigation and civil litigation are taught as discrete subjects, as well as being integrated with the main skill areas. Regular talks delivered by senior practitioners and judges are also worked into the timetable. The teaching staff are predominantly drawn from experienced barristers, many of whom are still practising in the region. A unique part of the course at Northumbria is the opportunity to get involved with the Student Law Office (SLO) at the option stage of the BPTC. Under the close supervision of a practitioner member of staff, students in the SLO provide pro bono legal services for members of the public. They can advise clients, take on cases, research and prepare for trials, and even represent clients at court and tribunals.

The school takes a keen interest in its students and looks to support them every step of the way in their quest for pupillages. Each student is assigned a personal guidance tutor whom they can regularly meet for information or advice. The careers service is on hand to organise networking events with local chambers and practitioners (each year the school hosts a number of dinners and social evenings) as well as group marshalling and a mentoring scheme with alumni. Mock pupillage interviews and a CV workshop upon induction are also in place to improve employability. The law school's 'Grey Society' organises mock trials and mooting competitions, as well as social activities such as pub crawls when a bit of liquid relief is required.

Northumbria provides the opportunity to study a four-year exempting law degree – something only a handful of providers nationwide offer – that incorporates the academic LLB and professional BPTC, great for those who know early on that the Bar is the career path for them. BPTC students can also study for a top-up LLM in Advanced Legal Practice once the course has concluded, or there's even the opportunity to undertake it simultaneously with the BPTC over a two-year stretch.

Nottingham Law School

Number of places: 120 FT
Pro: has the only FRU outside of London
Con: competitive entry

Nottingham is a consistently popular choice for aspiring barristers. A top-notch Bar course and city centre location make this a highly sought-after destination for students across the country and a steadily increasing number of internationals. As such, Nottingham can afford to be selective, and prospective candidates must show potential for a career at the Bar. This means most successful applicants will hold a 2:1 up their sleeve, while those with a 2:2 will need to show off additional evidence of achievement through awards or work experience. All applicants are expected to demonstrate commitment to the profession and an aptitude for advocacy, while it's also advisable to put Nottingham as your first-choice provider. Five scholarships worth £2,000 are on offer, as is a loyalty discount for former Notts undergrads.

The course consists of seven realistic briefs (three civil and four criminal) that students take on from start to finish to see how a case may progress in practice. These are supplemented by additional lectures and small group sessions, while knowledge and skills areas – which amount to roughly 60% of the BPTC – are taught and learned as the case studies progress. Teaching is conducted over four days each week, and there are no more 12 students in classes for written skills and no more than six students in advocacy classes. There are seven elective modules on offer: advanced crime, advanced civil, commercial, family, employment, immigration, and landlord and tenant.

To give students a better flavour for a career at the Bar, they are expected to wear suits and dress smartly when participating in advocacy or conferencing sessions to replicate real-life situations. All students have a one-to-one feedback session with a tutor prior to each skills assessment, which, wherever possible, are set in a practical

context. For example, actors are utilised to provide a realistic experience of examinations and the questioning and advising of clients. Students can also anticipate performing a chambers application before a district judge, who will interject with questions. Nottingham's BPTC is written by former practitioners in conjunction with judges, practising barristers and senior academics. Practitioners and judges assist with the delivery of the course as guest speakers and in practitioner workshops.

The law school was redeveloped in 2011, and students have access to mock courtrooms, moot rooms and top-of-the-range teaching facilities. Nottingham Trent University itself is currently undergoing a major expansion programme that will see brand-new student accommodation and a new student union built. All starters from September 2013 will be provided with an iPad as part of their teaching package. All course materials can be downloaded onto it, and students are allowed to keep it once the course is completed.

A dedicated careers and recruitment service is on hand to offer support and guidance during the search for a pupillage. A pupillage interview training day is organised before the course begins and subsequent trial interviews can also be sought throughout the year. Local chambers offer their support to the course by giving a number of presentations relevant to a life at the Bar, offering opportunities for mini-pupillages or by giving advice on CVs. Further to this, there are increasing opportunities for students to marshal a judge.

If you would like to dip your toe into the pro bono water then Nottingham houses the only Free Representation Unit (FRU) outside of London, and also runs an Innocence Project. To really show off some skills, there are two set-sponsored mooting competitions – one civil, one criminal – that students can participate in, and if after taking advantage of all these opportunities your CV is still looking a little sparse, then an LLM in Legal Practice can also be pursued.

The University of Law, London

Number of places: 240 FT, 48 PT
Pro: Future Lawyers Network
Con: built next to a plague burial ground

The University of Law runs the Bar course out of its London Bloomsbury and Birmingham centres. Successfully navigate the BPTC here and you'll earn 60 Masters credits and be a third of the way towards a top-up LLM.

The Bloomsbury branch is less aesthetically impressive than the other UoL outpost in London. The striking Moorgate centre in the heart of the financial district teaches the LPC to the future trainees of some leading law firms, but isn't validated to offer the BPTC. No need to feel disheartened, though; Bloomsbury is the largest UoL centre, and its central London location just off Tottenham Court Road gives students easy access to all the bustling hub-bub the capital can offer. On your doorstep you can find the West End, Oxford Street, Soho and Covent Garden, while major courts such as the Old Bailey are within easy striking distance too. If you're planning to stay on-site, the school offers a four-floor legal library, recently re-furbished IT suites and courtroom furniture in all BPTC workshop rooms.

Full-time and part-time weekend study options are avail-able. Teaching is delivered through small group sessions of no more than 12 students (although these groups can be much smaller for certain sessions, such as advocacy), each of which are three-and-a-half hours in duration. Classes closely follow the litigation process; in crimi-nal litigation you will begin by learning about offenders' rights in a police station and how to make a bail applica-tion. Court visits are no longer a BSB-required element of the BPTC, but UoL has retained this aspect of the course and expects its students to provide reports on their expe-riences. Students can also take part in mock trials held at the Inner London Crown Court and Blackfriars Crown Court. Practitioners play the role of judges, while local trainee police officers also participate to add to the sense of authenticity. *"Our ethos is learning by doing, so it's a very practice-based course. We want to apply knowledge by giving students the skills a barrister needs."* Therefore the school thinks that advocacy experience is of para-mount importance: in fact it thinks that *"no skill is more important."* UoL offers its students 32 advocacy sessions during their studies – three times as much as the BSB requires. You'll also study professional ethics and conduct as a discrete topic interwoven into the rest of the course. This helps students understand the core professional val-ues of practice at the Bar, and gives young practitioners experience of what they'll encounter as soon as they en-ter chambers. All teaching is supplemented by a range of multimedia resources, including podcasts, i-tutorials and video recordings that tend to cover niche areas of proce-dure.

The University of Law takes on students from a wide va-riety of universities, and successful students go on to pur-sue a range of pupillages. The school likes to be placed as first-choice provider by candidates and is looking for applicants with a minimum of a 2:2, although *"the whole academic profile, including A-level results, other qualifi-cations and relevant work experience"* is taken into con-sideration. An essay competition is in place to give one lucky student a full scholarship, while the runner-up will receive £4,000 off their fees. A Platinum Awards Scheme

is also in place to give academically gifted students a £3,000 discount.

The careers service is *"enormous and very active,"* and runs an 'employability programme' throughout the aca-demic year. For example, in the autumn term students can take advantage of employer talks, commercial awareness webinars, non-pupillage portal application workshops and BPTC-specific careers surgeries. In the spring and summer terms there's even more on offer, including a practitioner networking event, pupillage masterclasses, and leaving talks and events. Students also have access to a database *"that has thousands of job opportunities list-ed, including mini-pupillages and paralegal positions."* In addition, UoL run the Future Lawyers Network, an online community where students can network and seek special-ist careers advice.

The school offers a huge number of pro bono opportuni-ties, and students have been involved in initiatives such as Liberty Letters and the National Coalition Against Domestic Violence, among others. There's also a range of debating and mooting competitions to help you hone your skills.

The University of Law, Birmingham

Number of places: 132 FT, 36 PT
Pro: renowned pro bono programme
Con: New Street Station

UoL Birmingham opened in 2007 and is based in the city's historic Jewellery Quarter, near to the Second City's thriving legal hub and a great selection of cafés, bars, res-taurants and shops. The course is a mirror image of the one in London, meaning there is no deviation in the con-tent, timetable or teaching methods. Students here will also be able to access any of the school's national resourc-es, such as the employability and careers programme and the database full of job opportunities.

The centre is renowned for its pro bono initiatives, and its link-up with the Legal Advice Clinic was recently award-ed 'Best Partnership' by LawWorks. There are a number of other projects run in-house that students can partici-pate in, including the Birmingham Employment Rights Advice Line, The Refugee Council and The Birmingham TUC Centre for the Unemployed. UoL also has a long-standing partnership with the Streetlaw programme.

The facilities are on par with its London counterpart and a new wing was added to the school in 2010 along with an extension to the library.

How to fund law school

It's now completely plausible that you'll be saddled with upwards of £30,000 of debt by the time you complete your undergraduate degree. Given that a GDL, LPC or BPTC course is by no means cheap either, how can you ease the increasingly intimidating financial burden of law school?

Secure sponsorship before starting your training contract

If you're interested in commercial law or want to work at one of the larger firms in the UK, there's a chance you might be able to find a firm that will sponsor you through law school. These firms tend to recruit two years in advance of the start of the training contract, so you'll need to get your act together well ahead of time. Not only will such firms cover the cost of course fees (LPC and usually GDL too), they may well give you a few thousand pounds towards the cost of living. Details of what solicitors' firms are offering their future trainees are given in our **Salaries and Benefits** table.

The lucky minority of BPTC students will already have a pupillage lined up. At the more affluent sets, the size of the pupillage award is now comparable with City trainee/NQ salaries. Usually a decent chunk of the pupillage award can be drawn down to cover BPTC expenses. At the more modest sets there may be no money available for the BPTC at all. Further information about funding is given in the Bar section of this guide.

Local authority grants

Local Education Authority grants are hard to get and very limited. It's still worth finding the contact details for your LEA at www.studentfinance.direct.gov.uk and testing the water.

The Inns of Court

If you're training to be a barrister you can apply for a range of GDL and BPTC scholarships from the Inns of Court. Around a quarter of BPTC students get some funding, and there's just under £5m up for grabs. Check out page 634 for more details.

Law school scholarships

Individual law schools have scholarship programmes. Go to our website for details.

Where to study

Studying in London could set you back as much as double what it would elsewhere, say in Sheffield, Cardiff or Nottingham, and the quality of training isn't necessarily going to be any better. Go to our website for tables comparing the prices of all the law schools' courses.

Career Development Loans

First of all, if the loan isn't from Barclays or the Co-op then it isn't really a Career Development Loan (CDL), it's just a bank claiming there will be no repayments to make while you study. Though that may be the case, it doesn't mean there is no interest accruing – it could just be piling up, ready to swamp you once your studies finish. A true CDL allows you to borrow up to £10,000, with the interest paid by the Skills Funding Agency while you study. Because the CDL interest rate may be higher than another loan, some people recommend taking a CDL and, when the interest-free honeymoon is over, paying it off using another unsecured personal loan with a lower interest rate. Unfortunately, the GDL is no longer covered by the scheme, just the LPC and BPTC.

Bank loans

There's a good chance that you've already emptied the last pennies out of your student overdraft, but never fear – you may still be eligible for more debt. Despite the credit crunch, there's still money to be had, so check the interest rates of various banks.

Since 2010 most banks have withdrawn the special packages for customers entering the legal profession. However, check out graduate accounts, because they sometimes offer slightly better overdraft terms. Lloyds TSB provides loans of up to £10,000 with a repayment holiday of up to three months, and repayment is made over a maximum period of five years. RBS's FlexiLoan for Graduates goes up to £15,000 and comes with an interest rate based on your particular circumstances. Initial payments can be deferred for four or 12 months (if you have travel plans) provided you have a firm offer of employment. The repayment period is up to five or seven years depending on the amount of the loan. To be eligible, applicants must be or become RBS customers. Whatever you do, don't make any decisions lightly; loans involve a big commitment that only continues to grow once the debt starts to accrue.

Get a job!

Law firms are increasingly interested in applicants' commercial awareness and ability to cope in a professional office environment, so what used to be an undesirable option can now be deployed in an interview as proof of your suitability for a career in law. Course providers tell us that part-time enrolments are on the rise as students increasingly look to ease the financial burden of law school by working jobs alongside their studies. While this option does stall your legal career by another year or so, it does help you avoid the heavy debts accrued by the average law student. Even students on full-time courses will look boost their cash flow with evening shifts or weekend work. Be sure to set yourself a manageable schedule, though. You don't want to end up flunking your course for the sake of saving a few extra quid.

Benefits, benefactors, begging

So bunking up with ma and pa during your course isn't a dream come true, yet sometimes needs must. Forget ideas of declaring bankruptcy to evade student debt; consider other creative ways to ease the burden.

- A student card will get you low-cost travel, discount haircuts, cinema tickets and even drinks in some places. If nothing else, it'll make you feel young.
- Websites such as www.studentdiscountbook.co.uk and www.studentbeans.com have discounts and deals for meals, entertainment and more.
- Law books are pricey, so don't get overzealous before term starts. College libraries will have the core texts and you're sure to find former students hawking books. Check out notice boards and online for second-hand tomes.
- A number of law schools, chambers and solicitors firms run competitions. Do a Google search to find them. Winning may bring kudos as well as cash.
- Market research focus groups will pay decent money for an hour or two of your time.

Some scholarships

- Many law schools offer funding. For instance, national provider the University of Law offers various scholarships to those studying full-time LPC or BPTC courses. It also offers 35 Gold Awards worth £3,000 for students about to start a GDL who have a First or a distinction at Masters level.
- Universities also offer a miscellany of scholarships: Oxford, for example, has many for students wanting to take its BCL or MJur courses.
- The Law Society Diversity Access Scheme supports talented people who face obstacles to qualification.
- The Inderpal Rahal Memorial Trust supports women from an immigrant or refugee background. Contact irmt@gclaw.co.uk for more details.
- The Kalisher Scholarship works with each of the BPTC providers to ensure that every year at least two talented but financially disadvantaged students gain a free place on the course. In addition, it offers a variety of awards and bursaries, including a £5,000 essay prize. For more information: www.thekalisher-trust.org/contact.php
- The Leonard Sainer Foundation provides interest-free loans of £10,000 each to help fund either the LPC of BPTC. For further information go to www.charitiesdirect.com
- The Student Disability Assistance Fund can award up to £500 for people studying on a full-time or nearly full-time basis. See www.bahshe.co.uk/student-disability-fund/student-disability-fund.html
- Universities and publicly funded colleges have discretionary college access funds available to especially hard-up students. The major LPC/BPTC providers usually have a number of scholarships to assist select students with fees, etc.
- The HM Hubbard Law Scholarship is for trainees and solicitors who want to study the law and legal procedures in France, Spain or Canada.
- The Human Rights Lawyers Association will provide around ten awards from a maximum annual bursary fund of £10,000 to those who wish to undertake unpaid/poorly paid human rights work, either during their training or soon after.
- The Foreign and Commonwealth Office's Chevening Scholarships are available for overseas students wishing to study in the UK. In 2012 the scholarship fund totalled £22m.
- Postgrad Solutions offers a small number of £500 bursaries for LLM students.

"When I was at university I decided that I didn't want to join a corporate firm, but that I wanted to be involved in human rights law. When I graduated, I knew I had to gain some work experience first before I started applying for training contracts."

Trainee, top human rights firm

Solicitors' practice areas

Banking & Finance

In a nutshell

Banking and finance lawyers may work in any one of the specialist areas described below, but all deal with the borrowing of money or the management of financial liabilities. Their task is to negotiate and document the contractual relationship between lenders and borrowers and ensure that their clients' best legal and commercial interests are reflected in the terms of loan agreements. It is a hugely technical, ever-evolving and jargon-heavy area of law.

Straightforward bank lending: a bank lends money to a borrower on documented repayment terms. **Acquisition finance:** a loan made to a corporate borrower or private equity sponsor for the purpose of acquiring another company. This includes **leveraged finance**, where the borrower uses a very large amount of borrowed money to meet the cost of a significant acquisition without committing a lot of its own capital (this is called a leveraged buyout or LBO). **Real estate finance:** a loan made to enable a borrower to acquire a property or finance the development of land and commonly secured by way of a mortgage on the acquired property/land. **Project finance:** the financing of long-term infrastructure (eg roads) and public services projects (eg hospitals), where the amounts borrowed to complete the project are paid back with the cash flow generated by the project. **Asset finance:** this enables the purchase and operation of large assets such as ships, aircraft and machinery. The lender normally takes security over the assets in question. **Islamic finance:** Muslim borrowers, lenders and investors must abide by Shari'a law, which prohibits the collection and payment of interest on a loan. Islamic finance specialists ensure that finance deals are structured in a Shari'a-compliant manner. **Financial services regulation:** lawyers in this field ensure that their bank clients operate in compliance with the relevant financial legislation.

What lawyers do
- Meet with clients to establish their specific requirements and the commercial context of a deal.
- Carry out due diligence, an investigation exercise to verify the accuracy of information passed from the borrower to the lender or from the company raising finance to all parties investing in the deal. This can involve on-site meetings with the company's management, so lawyers can verify the company's credit profile.
- Negotiate with the opposite party to agree the terms of the deal and record them accurately in the facility documentation. Lenders' lawyers usually produce initial documents (often a standard form) and borrowers' lawyers try to negotiate more favourable terms for their clients. Lawyers on both sides must know when to compromise and when to hold out.
- Assist with the structuring of complicated or groundbreaking financing models and ensure innovative solutions comply with all relevant laws.
- Gather all parties to complete the transaction, ensuring all agreed terms are reflected in the loan and that all documents have been properly signed and witnessed. Just as in corporate deals, many decisions need to be made at properly convened board meetings and recorded in written resolutions.
- Finalise all post-completion registrations and procedures.

The realities of the job
- City firms act for investment banks on highly complex and often cross-border financings, whereas the work of regional firms generally involves acting for commercial banks on more mainstream domestic finance deals. If you want to be a hotshot in international finance, then it's the City for you.
- Lawyers need to appreciate the needs and growth ambitions of their clients in order to deliver pertinent advice and warn of the legal risks involved in the transactions. Deals may involve the movement of money across borders and through different currencies and financial products. International deals have an additional layer of difficulty: political changes in transitional economies can render a previously sound investment risky.
- Banking clients are ultra-demanding and the hours can be long. On the plus side, your clients will be smart and dynamic. It is possible to build up long-term relationships with investment bank clients, even as a junior.
- Working on deals can be exciting. The team and the other side are all working to a common goal, often under significant time and other pressures. Deal closings bring adrenaline highs and a sense of satisfaction.
- You need to become absorbed in the finance world. Start reading the *FT* or the City pages in your daily newspaper for a taster.

97

Current issues

- Suggestions that the UK slumped into a double-dip recession in 2012 have since been quashed, and the latest figures show that economic recovery is beginning to pick up momentum. However, experts say the country fell deeper into recession than previously thought in 2008 and 2009 (meaning an even longer road to recovery ahead), and the market is still feeling the effects of the credit crunch.
- With fewer deals being done, many law firms have downsized their banking and finance teams. The big City firms were no exception, but they have fared better than initially expected due to their ability to adapt quickly in tough market conditions. They've had to be flexible, advising clients on recapitalisations, restructurings and regulations.
- The Libor interest rate-fixing scandal has generated a considerable amount of work for major UK firms, many of which have been advising big-name institutions involved in high-profile cases.
- The ongoing European debt crisis, which has been paralysing deal markets in Europe, has also had an impact. Law firms are busy helping financial institutions to navigate current conditions, advising banks on how best to deal with their assets across the globe.
- In April 2013, off the back of the apparent regulatory failure of the banks during the financial crisis, the Financial Services Authority (FSA) was abolished and its powers were distributed to the Prudential Regulation Authority (PRA), the Financial Conduct Authority (FCA) and the Bank of England.
- Basel III, a package of measures intended to strengthen the regulation, supervision and risk of the banking sector, is to be implemented between 2013 and 2019. As a result of this, banks are seeking advice from risk and compliance experts on how to stick to the new rules.
- With minimal private sector growth and sovereign debt problems plaguing Europe and the USA, foreign investors are continuing to pile into emerging economies – the Middle East, Africa and BRIC countries in particular. Finance lawyers will increasingly need to get to grips with international matters.
- Commentators have observed a 'flight to quality' by clients, meaning magic circle firms are getting the lion's share of available work. Clients are also putting their faith (and money) into the hands of 'trusted advisers'.
- Secondments to banks are available, even for trainees, and subsequent moves in-house are common. In the past couple of years many banks have laid off large numbers of their own legal personnel, which has increased their demand for law firm secondees at all levels of seniority.

Read our True Pictures on...

Addleshaw Goddard	Linklaters
Allen & Overy	Macfarlanes
Ashfords	Maclay Murray & Spens
Ashurst	Mayer Brown
Baker & McKenzie	Memery Crystal
Berwin Leighton Paisner	Michelmores
Bird & Bird	Mills & Reeve
Bond Dickinson	Muckle
Brabners Chaffe Street	Nabarro
Browne Jacobson	Norton Rose Fulbright
Burges Salmon	Olswang
Charles Russell	Osborne Clarke
Cleary Gottlieb	Paul Hastings
Clifford Chance	Pinsent Masons
Clyde & Co	Reed Smith
CMS	SGH Martineau
Cripps Harries Hall	Shearman & Sterling
Dechert	Shoosmiths
Dentons	Sidley Austin
DLA Piper	Simmons & Simmons
DWF	SJ Berwin
Eversheds	Skadden
Farrer & Co	Slaughter and May
Foot Anstey	Squire Sanders
Freeth Cartwright	Stephenson Harwood
Freshfields	Stevens & Bolton
Gateley	Taylor Wessing
Gordons	TLT
Herbert Smith Freehills	Travers Smith
Hill Dickinson	Trethowans
Hogan Lovells	Trowers & Hamlins
Ince & Co	Veale Wasbrough Vizards
Irwin Mitchell	Walker Morris
Jones Day	Ward Hadaway
K&L Gates	Watson, Farley & Williams
Kirkland & Ellis	Wedlake Bell
Latham & Watkins	Weil, Gotshal & Manges
Lawrence Graham	White & Case
Lester Aldridge	Wragge & Co

Practice Areas

Capital Markets

In a nutshell

The world's capital markets are trading floors (either real or virtual) on which cash-hungry businesses obtain funding by selling a share of their business (equity) or receiving a loan (debt) from lenders. Capital markets lawyers advise companies ('issuers') and investment banks ('underwriters') on these complex transactions. Here are some of the terms you'll encounter.

Equity capital markets: where a private company raises capital by making its shares available to the public by listing itself on a stock exchange and executing an initial public offering (IPO), as a result of which it becomes a public company (or plc). The London Stock Exchange (LSE) and New York Stock Exchange (NYSE) are the most prestigious exchanges, but companies may list in many other exchanges worldwide. Once listed, a company's shares can be bought and sold by investors at a price determined by the market. **Debt capital markets:** where borrowers raise capital by selling tradable bonds to investors, who expect the full amount lent to be paid back to them with interest. **Structured finance:** this area can get gloriously complicated, but its aims are simple: to increase liquidity and limit or trade on risk, which in turn offers up extra funding for borrowers. **Derivatives:** financial instruments used by banks and businesses to hedge risks to which they are exposed due to factors outside of their control. The value of a derivative at any given time is derived from the value of an underlying asset, security, index or interest rate.

What lawyers do

- Carry out due diligence on issuers and draft prospectuses which provide information about the company and its finances, as well as past financial statements. A prospectus must comply with the requirements of the EU's prospectus and transparency directives.
- Negotiate approval of a listing on the stock exchange. This involves the submission of documentation, certifications and letters that prove the client satisfies the listing requirements. As soon as a company undergoes an IPO, it will be subject to all the rules and requirements of a public company, so the necessary organisational structure must be in place before then.
- Work with underwriters and issuers to draw up the structure of a security and help the parties negotiate the terms of the structure. The underwriter's lawyers draft most documents related to a bond issue. An issuer's lawyers will comment on them and negotiate changes.

- With derivatives, lawyers communicate back and forth with the client discussing legal issues and risks related to various possible structures for the product, as well as suggesting ways to resolve or mitigate those problems and issues.
- Issuer's and underwriter's counsel work together with a team of bankers, accountants, insurers and an issuer's management to get securities issued.

The realities of the job

- Capital markets lawyers are mostly based in the City. The biggest firms have specialist departments focused on capital markets or one of its subgroups, while mid-size firms may lump capital markets work in with corporate.
- Clients can be very demanding and lawyers work very long hours. On the plus side, large law firms usually have strong and close relationships with investment bank clients and financial institutions, meaning that trainees and NQs can get frequent client contact.
- Lawyers have to gauge the needs and personality of the company they're working with and require an aptitude for responding to and resolving issues as they arise.
- Capital markets lawyers feel all the highs and lows of market forces – if you're trying to get a deal done market conditions often matter more than the willingness of the parties involved. Even if a deal has been organised, unpredictable market conditions can mean it falls through.

Current Issues

- The effects of the 2008/09 recession and the ongoing European sovereign debt crisis continue to be felt by the markets.
- In the UK, at least, there has been some good news recently. According to research done by Ernst & Young, IPOs in London's premium market raised £2.4bn in the first half of 2013, against just £1.5bn in the whole of 2012. This puts the LSE behind only the NYSE and the NASDAQ in terms of capital raised.
- While the bond market has faired well in recent years, some of the biggest investment funds are wrestling with the prospect of the US Federal Reserve pushing up interest rates by 2015, and also bringing its $1tr a year bond buying programme to a halt before summer 2014. This could increase inflation and commodity prices and hinder the recovery of markets across the globe.

- In July 2013, the government unveiled plans to privatise the Royal Mail through a flotation on the LSE. It was announced that the public will be able to buy shares, alongside bigger institutional investors.
- An area of particular interest to the magic circle firms is high-yield financing and the European bond market, traditionally the stomping grounds of US law firms. High-yield products provide an increasingly popular alternative financing strategy for businesses struggling because of a lack of traditional bank lending. The growing popularity of high-yield financing has also contributed to the continuing success of US firms in the UK.

Read our True Pictures on...

Addleshaw Goddard	Linklaters
Allen & Overy	Mayer Brown
Ashurst	Memery Crystal
Baker & McKenzie	Nabarro
Berwin Leighton Paisner	Norton Rose Fulbright
Bird & Bird	Olswang
Burges Salmon	Osborne Clarke
Charles Russell	Pinsent Masons
Cleary Gottlieb	Shearman & Sterling
Clifford Chance	Sidley Austin
Covington & Burling	Simmons & Simmons
Dechert	SJ Berwin
Dentons	Skadden
DLA Piper	Slaughter and May
Eversheds	Squire Sanders
Freshfields	Stephenson Harwood
Herbert Smith Freehills	Taylor Wessing
Hogan Lovells	Travers Smith
Jones Day	Trowers & Hamlins
K&L Gates	Watson, Farley & Williams
Latham & Watkins	Weil, Gotshal & Manges
Lawrence Graham	White & Case

Practice Areas

Competition/Antitrust

In a nutshell
It is the job of the UK and EU regulatory authorities to ensure that markets function effectively on the basis of fair and open competition. The rules in the UK and EU are substantially similar, but the UK bodies concentrate on those rules that have their greatest effect domestically, while EU authorities deal with matters affecting multiple member states. The UK regulators are the Office of Fair Trading (OFT) and the Competition Commission (CC); on matters also affecting other EU countries, it is the European Commission. Additionally, there are industry-specific regulatory bodies, such as Ofcom for the media and telecoms industry. The CC and OFT are scheduled to be replaced by a single body, the Competition and Markets Authority, on 1 April 2014.

Competition authorities have extensive investigative powers – including the ability to carry out dawn raids – and can impose hefty fines. The OFT has become more proactive and litigation-minded in recent years, and the European Commission continues to dole out big fines.

What lawyers do
- Negotiate clearance for acquisitions, mergers and joint ventures.
- Advise on the structure of commercial or co-operation agreements to ensure they can withstand a competition challenge.
- Deal with investigations into the way a client conducts business.
- Bring or defend claims in the Competition Appeal Tribunal (CAT).
- Advise on cross-border trade or anti-dumping measures (preventing companies exporting products at a lower price than normally charged in the home market).
- Regulators investigate companies, bring prosecutions and advise on the application of new laws and regulations.

The realities of the job
- You won't get much independence; even junior lawyers work under the close supervision of experienced partners. In the early days the job involves a great deal of research into particular markets and how the authorities have approached different types of agreements in the past.
- You need to be interested in economics and politics
- The work demands serious academic brainpower twinned with commercial acumen.

- As a popular area of practice it's hard to break into. Work experience with a regulator or at the Commission in Brussels will enhance your prospects.
- Advocacy is a relatively small part of the job, though you could end up appearing in the High Court or the CAT.
- In international law firms you will travel abroad and may even work in an overseas office for a while, perhaps in Brussels. Fluency in another language can be useful. There is also a trend for lawyers to switch between private practice and working for the regulators.

Current issues
- Competition law continues to increase its profile as greater regulatory activity is undertaken by the UK, EU and USA. In 2012 the European Commission slapped a EUR1.5bn fine on a group of electronics companies, including Philips and LG, for agreeing to fix the price of cathode-ray tubes. The OFT recently ordered airlines and other travel companies to abolish hidden debit card fees.

Read our True Pictures on...

Addleshaw Goddard	Linklaters
Allen & Overy	Macfarlanes
Ashurst	Maclay Murray & Spens
Baker & McKenzie	Mayer Brown
Berwin Leighton Paisner	Nabarro
Bond Dickinson	Norton Rose Fulbright
Browne Jacobson	Osborne Clarke
Burges Salmon	Peters & Peters
Cleary Gottlieb	Pinsent Masons
Clifford Chance	Reed Smith
Clyde & Co	Shearman & Sterling
CMS	Shoosmiths
DLA Piper	Sidley Austin
DWF	Simmons & Simmons
Eversheds	SJ Berwin
Freshfields	Slater & Gordon
Herbert Smith Freehills	Slaughter and May
Hogan Lovells	Squire Sanders
K&L Gates	Stevens & Bolton
Kingsley Napley	TLT
Latham & Watkins	Travers Smith
Linklaters	Wragge & Co

Practice Areas

- The OFT has been criticised for offering immunity to competition whistle-blowers and has begun conducting more 'own initiative' investigations.
- Partly as a response to these criticisms, the Department for Business Innovation and Skills has announced reforms to competition law in the UK. The Enterprise and Regulatory Reform Act 2013 will bring together the CC and the OFT to create a new Competition and Markets Authority (CMA).
- BIS also plans to introduce a new regime for class actions to enhance access to justice for consumers who have suffered because of anti-competitive behaviour. The planned changes will see the introduction of 'opt-out' collective actions, which means a legal action can be brought on behalf of all affected individuals – for example by a consumer body.
- Competition lawyers are increasingly drawing on the experience of colleagues, such as financial regulation, tax, litigation and white-collar crime specialists.

- As the technology sector continues to grow it's coming under increasing scrutiny from regulators. Google is facing off against Microsoft and TripAdvisor over claims it had been giving itself an unfair competitive advantage by filtering search results.
- Online service providers are increasingly on the OFT's radar, especially for misleading pricing infringements, and the EU has passed a new Common European Sales Law to facilitate cross-border online transactions.

Confused by City finance? One trainee recommended Christopher Stoakes' All You Need to Know About the City – *"It's a great introduction to financial markets and can help you out on the commercial awareness front too."*

Construction

In a nutshell
Construction law can broadly be divided into non-contentious and contentious practice. The first involves lawyers helping clients at the procurement stage, pulling together all the contractual relationships prior to building work; the second sees them resolving disputes when things go wrong. In the past, the relatively high monetary stakes involved, and the industry trend for recovering building costs through the courts, made construction a litigation-happy practice. Since the 1990s most new contracts have contained mandatory procedures to be adopted in case of dispute. Adjudication of disputes has become the industry norm and these tend to follow a swift 28-day timetable. Others are resolved through mediation or arbitration; however, some disputes are so complex that the parties do still choose to slug it out in court.

What lawyers do
Procurement
- Negotiate and draft contracts for programmes of building works. Any such programme involves a multitude of parties including landowners, main contractors, subcontractors, engineers and architects.
- Work in conjunction with property lawyers if the client has invested in land as well as undertaking a building project. Together, the lawyers seek and obtain all the necessary planning consents as well as local authority certifications.
- Where the developer does not own the land, liaise with the landowner's solicitors over matters such as stage payments, architects' certificates and other measures of performance.
- Make site visits during development.

Construction disputes
- Assess the client's position and gather all related paperwork and evidence.
- Extract the important detail from huge volumes of technical documentation.
- Follow the resolution methods set out in the contracts between the parties.
- Where a settlement is impossible, issue, prepare for and attend proceedings with the client, usually instructing a barrister to advocate.

The realities of the job
- Drafting requires attention to detail and careful thought.
- It's essential to keep up to date with industry standards and know contract law and tort inside out.

- People skills are fundamental. Contractors and subcontractors are generally earthy and direct; structural engineers live in a world of complicated technical reports; corporate types and in-house lawyers require smoother handling. You'll deal with them all.
- The construction world is often perceived as a male-dominated environment, but while some clients might see a visit to a lap-dancing club as par for the business entertainment course, there are many successful female construction lawyers, architects and engineers who avoid such activities.
- Most lawyers prefer either contentious or non-contentious work, and some firms like their construction lawyers to handle both, so pick your firm carefully.
- A background in construction or engineering is a major bonus because you'll already have industry contacts and will be able to combine legal know-how with practical advice.

Current issues
- The construction industry continues to struggle with the effects of the recession. It lost £9bn in 2012 and is set to lose £2bn in 2013, thanks to cuts to government spending and difficulties in attracting private sector investment. Forecasts are cautiously optimistic for 2014, thanks to government stimuli and improving economic conditions.
- An up-tick in new housing construction has been prompted by incentive schemes including Help to Buy and the £450m Affordable Homes Guarantees Programme, which supports developers to build up to 30,000 homes.
- The huge demand for housing, combined with cuts to government spending on building affordable homes, has seen local authorities working with private developers more and more in a bid to increase cost efficiency. Social housing providers must now compete with the private sector for the government's £1bn Build to Rent fund, which will increase the supply of privately owned rental properties.
- Spending on private commercial property, the industry's largest sector, is continuing to fall – industry experts have expressed concern that construction is too reliant on residential building.
- Although government cuts have led to a falling off in health and education construction, big contractors are benefiting from investment in energy and rail infrastructure. Infrastructure activity is set to grow 7% in 2013, thanks to the ongoing work on Crossrail and on station refurbishments nationwide.

- Construction disputes are getting longer, lasting 12.9 months on average in 2012, compared to 8.7 months in 2011. This can be attributed to increasingly complex projects, and extra requirements placed upon litigants.
- One recent big High Court case saw a subcontractor forced to pay £800,000 in damages for delaying the construction of the Shard at London Bridge by 42 days.

Read our True Pictures on...

Addleshaw Goddard	Macfarlanes
Allen & Overy	Maclay Murray & Spens
Ashfords	Mayer Brown
Ashurst	Michelmores
Baker & McKenzie	Mills & Reeve
Berwin Leighton Paisner	Muckle
Bond Dickinson	Nabarro
Brabners Chaffe Street	Nabarro
Browne Jacobson	Norton Rose Fulbright
Burges Salmon	Olswang
Charles Russell	Osborne Clark
Clifford Chance	Pinsent Masons
Clyde & Co	Reed Smith
CMS	RPC
Cripps Harries Hall	SGH Martineau
Denton	Simmons & Simmons
DLA Piper	SJ Berwin
DWF	Slaughter and May
Eversheds	Speechly Bircham
Foot Anstey	Squire Sanders
Freeth Cartwright	Stephenson Harwood
Freshfields	Stevens & Bolton
Gateley	Taylor Wessing
Gordons	TLT
Herbert Smith Freehills	Trowers & Hamlins
Hill Dickinson	Veale Wasbrough Vizards
Hogan Lovells	Vinson & Elkins R
Jones Day	Walker Morris
K&L Gates	Ward Hadaway
Kennedys	Wedlake Bell
Lawrence Graham	White & Case
Lewis Silkin	Wragge & Co

Practice Areas

Corporate/M&A

In a nutshell

Corporate lawyers provide advice to companies on significant transactions affecting their activities, including internal operations, the buying and selling of businesses and business assets, and the arrangement of the finance to carry out these activities.

Mergers and acquisitions (M&A) involve one company acquiring another by way of a takeover (acquisition), or two companies fusing to form a single larger entity (merger). The main reasons for a company to execute an M&A transaction are to grow its business (by acquiring or merging with a competitor) or add a new line of business to its existing activities. During a recession, mergers are also a means of strengthening two or more existing companies facing financial trouble. M&A can either be public (when it involves companies listed on a stock exchange) or private (when it concerns companies privately owned by individuals). **Corporate restructuring** involves changes to the structure of a company and the disposal of certain assets, either because the company wants to concentrate on more profitable parts of its business, or because it is facing financial difficulties and needs to free up liquidity.

What lawyers do

- Negotiate and draft agreements – this will be done in conjunction with the client, the business that is being bought or sold, other advisers (eg accountants) and any financiers.
- Carry out due diligence – this is an investigation to verify the accuracy of information passed from the seller to the buyer. It establishes the financial strength of the company; the outright ownership of all assets; whether there are outstanding debts or other claims against the company; any environmental or other liabilities that could reduce the value of the business in the future.
- Arrange financing – this could come from banks or other types of investors; they will wish to have some kind of security for their investment, eg participation in the shareholding, taking out a mortgage over property or other collateral.
- Gather all parties for the completion of the transaction, ensuring all assets have been properly covered by written documents that are properly signed and witnessed. Company law requires that decisions are made at properly convened board meetings and recorded in written resolutions.
- Finalise all post-completion registrations and procedures.

The realities of the job

- The type of clients your firm acts for will determine your experiences. Publicly listed companies and the investment banks that underwrite deals can be extremely demanding and have a different attitude to risk than, say, rich entrepreneurs, owner-managed businesses (OMBs) and small to medium-sized enterprises (SMEs). To deal with such clients, a robust and confident manner is required and stamina is a must.
- Corporate transactions can be large and complicated, with many different aspects of the company affected in the process. Lawyers need to be conversant in a variety of legal disciplines and know when to refer matters to a specialist in, say, merger control (competition), employment, property or tax.
- Corporate deals involve mountains of paperwork, so you need to be well organised and have good drafting skills. Above all, corporate is a very practical area of law, so commercial acumen and a good understanding of your clients' objectives is a must.
- Corporate work is cyclical and therefore the hours lawyers work can vary depending on the general state of the market and the particular needs of the clients, whose expectations have risen even further since the widespread use of instant modes of communication. It's fair to say there can be some very late nights.
- The most junior members of a deal team normally get stuck with the most boring or unrewarding tasks. The banes of the corporate trainee's life are data room management (putting together and caretaking all the factual information on which a deal relies) and bibling (the creation of files containing copies of all the agreed documents and deal information). More challenging tasks quickly become available to driven junior lawyers.
- You need to become absorbed in the corporate world. If you can't develop an interest in the business media then choose another area of practice pronto.
- A sound grounding in corporate finance makes an excellent springboard for working in-house in major companies. Some lawyers move to banks to work as corporate finance execs or analysts. Company secretarial positions suit lawyers with a taste for internal management and compliance issues.

Current Issues

- The UK is traditionally Europe's biggest market for M&A deals, but since the start of the economic downturn it has been a story of gradual decline. In the first half of 2013 there were 485 UK targeted M&A deals valued at a total of £40.6bn, down 16.5% and 10.9% by volume and value from the first half of 2012.
- The value of total global deals dropped to $978.8bn in the first half of 2013, down from $1.07 trillion in the first half of 2012, marking the weakest performance since the first half of 2009. M&A deals in Europe accounted for just 22.6% of the global total, a 16 year low.
- Companies have been finding it more difficult and expensive to borrow money from banks, and there has been far less funding available from non-bank lenders such as hedge funds and pension funds. In such a volatile market, buyers and sellers are finding it hard to reach agreement on the value of assets. This, in part, explains the massive reduction in deal volume and value.
- Cash-rich investors have their pick of the best assets and often acquire businesses at a significant discount due to lower company valuations. There has been growing interest from emerging markets investors and sovereign wealth funds, particularly from the Middle East, in acquiring assets in the UK and elsewhere. Although the USA is still the largest overseas bidder for UK companies, emerging market bidders like China and India are catching up fast.
- Telecommunications was the most active sector by value in the first half of 2013 and recent large-scale transactions include Liberty Global's acquisition of Virgin Media for £16.34bn and Vodafone's planned purchase of Kabel Deutschland, Germany's biggest cable operator, for £6.5bn.
- Consumer and retail M&A has also been faring well and has been boosted by corporates taking advantage of improved credit conditions and ongoing consolidation among struggling companies.
- Big-ticket energy work – in both oil and gas, and renewables – is also on the up and up. Joint ventures between companies are increasingly popular on large projects, and government support for investments ensures greater regulatory stability.

Read our True Pictures on...

Addleshaw Goddard	Linklaters
Allen & Overy	Macfarlanes
Ashfords	Maclay Murray & Spens
Ashurst	Mayer Brown
B P Collins	Memery Crystal
Baker & McKenzie	Michelmores
Berwin Leighton Paisner	Mills & Reeve
Bird & Bird	Mishcon de Reya
Bond Dickinson	Muckle
BPE Solicitors	Nabarro
Brabners Chaffe Street	Norton Rose Fulbright
Browne Jacobson	Olswang
Burges Salmon	Osborne Clarke
Charles Russell	Paul Hastings
Cleary Gottlieb	Penningtons Solicitors
Clifford Chance	Pinsent Masons
Clyde & Co	Reed Smith
CMS	RPC
Covington & Burling	SGH Martineau
Cripps Harries Hall	Shearman & Sterling
Dechert	Shoosmiths
Dentons	Sidley Austin
DLA Piper	Simmons & Simmons
DWF	SJ Berwin
Eversheds	Skadden
Farrer & Co	Slaughter and May
Foot Anstey	Speechly Bircham
Freeth Cartwright	Squire Sanders
Freshfields	Stephenson Harwood
Gateley	Stevens & Bolton
Gordons	Taylor Wessing
Harbottle & Lewis	TLT
Herbert Smith Freehills	Travers Smith
Higgs & Sons	Trethowans
Hill Dickinson	Trowers & Hamlins
Hogan Lovells	Veale Wasbrough Vizards
Irwin Mitchell	Walker Morris
Jones Day	Ward Hadaway
K&L Gates	Watson, Farley & Williams
Latham & Watkins	Weil, Gotshal & Manges
Lawrence Graham	White & Case
Lester Aldridge	Wragge & Co
Lewis Silkin	

Practice Areas

Crime

In a nutshell

Criminal solicitors represent defendants in cases brought before the UK's criminal courts. Lesser offences are commonly dealt with exclusively by solicitors in the magistrates' courts; more serious charges go to the Crown Courts, which are essentially still the domain of barristers. Everyday crime is the staple for most solicitors – theft, assault, drugs and driving offences. Fraud is the preserve of a more limited number of firms, and the cases require a different approach from, say, crimes of violence. Criminal practice is busy, often frantic, with a hectic schedule of visits to police stations, prisons and magistrates' courts meaning plenty of face-to-face client contact and advocacy. The area is also known for having the lowest pay in the profession.

What lawyers do

- Attend police stations to interview and advise people in police custody.
- Visit prisons to see clients on remand.
- Prepare the client's defence using medical and social workers' reports, and liaising with witnesses, probation officers, the CPS and others.
- Attend conferences with counsel (ie barristers).
- Represent defendants at trial or brief barristers to do so.
- Represent clients at sentencing hearings, explaining any mitigating facts.
- Fraud solicitors need a head for business as they deal with a considerable volume of paperwork and financial analysis.

The realities of the job

- Hours are long and can disrupt your personal life. Lawyers who are accredited to work as duty solicitors will be on a rota and can be called to a police station at any time of the day or night.
- Confidence is essential. Without it you're doomed.
- In general crime you'll have a large caseload with a fast turnaround, meaning plenty of advocacy.
- The work is driven by the procedural rules and timetable of the court. Even so, in 2012 nearly 32,000 magistrates' and Crown Court trials did not proceed on the appointed day.
- Your efforts can mean the difference between a person's liberty or incarceration. You have to be detail-conscious and constantly vigilant.

- You'll encounter horrible situations and difficult or distressed people. Murderers, rapists, drug dealers, conmen, paedophiles – if you have the ability to look beyond the labels and see these people as clients deserving of your best efforts, then you've picked the right job.
- It can be disheartening to see clients repeat the same poor choices, returning to court again and again.
- Public funding of criminal defence means there's a good helping of bureaucracy. It also means you'll earn very little, certainly in your first few years of practice.
- Trainees in fraud find the early years provide minimal advocacy and masses of trawling through warehouses full of documents. Caseloads are smaller but cases can run for years.

Current issues

- Huge changes in legal aid funding are ongoing, and many firms that have previously excelled in crime are moving out of the area entirely or no longer accept publicly funded clients. Firms affected by the cuts (or those looking to pre-empt financial difficulties) are either abandoning legal aid altogether, merging, or shifting their focus from the high-street criminal cases to fraud and more serious financial crimes.
- The world of criminal legal aid is entering a long dark winter of despair. The Legal Aid, Sentencing and Punishment of Offenders Act 2012 came into force on 1 April 2013. It aims to cut £220m annually from the £1.1bn criminal legal aid budget by 2018/19 and remove entire areas – such as employment and immigration – from the scheme. In 2013 some groups of barristers went on strike in protest at the cuts, which will lead to 500,000 fewer instances of legal help to individuals and 45,000 fewer instances of legal representation.
- The number of legal aid firms has steadily declined in the past decade since the Legal Services Commission introduced a compulsory quality mark in 2000. In 2011, there were around 1,700 criminal legal aid firms, compared to 2,900 in 2000. The government's 'Transforming Legal Aid' proposals aim to cut that number to just 400, as well as require firms to bid on contracts to represent defendants, which will squeeze fee income. It's predicted that many smaller practices will be forced to merge as a consequence.

- The most controversial element of the Transforming Legal Aid proposals – depriving defendants of their right to choose their own solicitor – was quickly dropped after loud disapproval from the legal sector.
- Since the Jimmy Savile saga and the start of Operation Yewtree, there has been a huge rise in the number of historic sex abuse allegations being brought. The heat of the Savile case and the surrounding furore means that many cases are being brought on the strength of one allegation alone.
- When a company pays for private defence of any regulatory crime and is acquitted, it would normally get an award from the public purse as compensation for its costs. The capping up this pay-out (known as the defendant cost order) means that even if acquitted, defendants can end up severely out of pocket.
- The nationwide rollout of the Legal Services Commission's Criminal Defence Service Direct is affecting the amount of work available for solicitors. The CDS now provides telephone advice to those detained at police stations for less serious matters – for example drink driving, non-imprisonable offences, breach of bail and warrants.

Read our True Pictures on...

Foot Anstey	Kingsley Napley*
Forbes*	Peters & Peters*
Higgs & Sons	Slater & Gordon*
Irwin Mitchell	

* These firms have a particularly strong focus on crime

- More fraud cases are popping up, and with authorities pushing for criminal charges for competition regulation violations, corporations are facing greater criminal liability. This kind of work tends to go to the firms that have traditionally handled white-collar crime. The Bribery Act 2010 reformed criminal law to provide a comprehensive scheme of bribery offences in the UK or overseas. Companies are now liable for corruption among staff and – for the first time – associated third parties, so white-collar crime lawyers have been busy advising companies on anti-corruption policies and procedures.
- Check out www.clsa.co.uk for other news and discussion on major developments in criminal practice.

The criminal courts of England and Wales

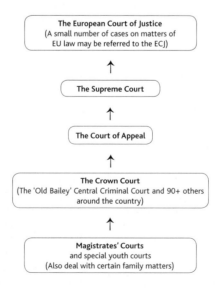

Employment

In a nutshell

Employment lawyers guide their clients through workplace-related legislation and are intimately involved in the relationship between employers and employees. The divide between employers' and employees' lawyers is often clear-cut so bear this in mind when you pick your firm. Most will work either largely for employers or largely for employees; a few will straddle both sides of the fence. Usually the job includes both advisory work and litigation.

Disputes are almost always resolved at an Employment Tribunal, or before reaching one, and appeals are heard at the Employment Appeal Tribunal (EAT). The grievances leading to litigation fall into the following broad categories: redundancy, unlawful dismissal, breach of contract, harassment and discrimination. This last type of claim can be brought on the grounds of race, religious or philosophical belief, gender, sexual orientation, disability and age.

What lawyers do

Employees' solicitors...

- Advise clients on whether they have suffered unlawful or unfair treatment and establish the amount to be claimed. This will either be capped or, in the case of discrimination, can include additional elements to cover loss of earnings, injury to feelings and aggravated damages.
- Gather evidence and witnesses to support the claim.
- Try to negotiate a payment from the employer or take the matter to tribunal. If there is a breach-of-contract element to the claim, it might be heard in a court rather than a tribunal.
- If the matter does reach tribunal, the solicitor may conduct the advocacy.

Employers' solicitors...

- Defend or settle the sorts of claims described above.
- Negotiate employment contracts or exit packages for senior staff.
- Negotiate with unions to avoid or resolve industrial disputes.
- Formulate HR policies and provide training on how to avoid workplace problems.

Realities of the job

- You quickly develop an understanding of human foibles. By their very nature employment cases are filled with drama.

- Clients may assume your role is to provide emotional support as well as legal advice, so you need to take care to define your role appropriately.
- Solicitors who want to do their own advocacy thrive here, although barristers are commonly used for high-stakes or complicated hearings and trials.
- The work is driven by the procedural rules and timetable of the tribunals and courts.
- The law is extensive and changes frequently. You'll read more than your fair share of EU directives.

Current issues

- The appetite for redundancy exercises has not tailed off completely, and although it's not as strong as it was in 2008, many clients are still looking to make cost savings by restructuring, outsourcing or simply cutting staff.
- There has been a rise in TUPE work as staff are transferred or outsourced by companies looking to cut costs. In cases where staff have been dismissed or made redundant, or have had changes made to their contracts, there has been more scope for proceedings.
- Employers are increasingly concerned about staff leaving to set up a competing business, leading to a rise in attempted enforcement of restrictive covenants and confidentiality agreements.
- Some law firms have a team of HR specialists or a dedicated hotline to deal with low cost, day-to-day employment queries.
- Many organisations have consolidated their employment legal spend by putting out to tender just one contract and are now looking for a sole legal provider to handle all their needs. This has naturally increased the level of competition between employment practices.
- Many companies are still leveraging the effects of the recession to make changes at board and senior management level. This has led to an increase in demand for advice on high-value contract termination work from both employees and respondents.
- The coalition government has introduced radical reforms to the tribunal process. More decisions can now be made by legal officers rather than employment judges or a full tribunal. Plus, from April 2012 the amount of time an employee needs to have worked at a company before being able to bring an unfair dismissal charge has been increased from one to two years. Employers naturally see these proposals as a good thing; trade unions are angry.

- As of April 2013, legal aid has been cut from all employment cases, except those related to discrimination. This is leading to more people representing themselves.
- The Enterprise and Regulatory Reform Act 2013 will bring about a number of changes to employment law and tribunal procedures. For instance, protection will be reduced for whistle-blowers, who now have to show that it's in the public interest to complain about an employer's unlawful act. Also, employers will be allowed to have a 'protected conversation' with an employee encouraging them to leave with a pay-off (settlement agreement).
- The government's new owner-employee contracts will offer employees shares in return for waiving employment rights including unfair dismissal, training rights and the right to ask for flexible working. It remains to be seen what the take-up rate for these new contracts will be, but observers say they will probably be unpopular with employers and employees alike.

Read our True Pictures on...

Addleshaw Goddard	Lester Aldridge
Allen & Overy	Lewis Silkin
Ashfords	Linklaters
Ashurst	Macfarlanes
B P Collins	Maclay Murray & Spens
Baker & McKenzie	Mayer Brown
Bates Wells Braithwaite London	McDermott Will & Emery UK
Berwin Leighton Paisner	Memery Crystal
Bird & Bird	Michelmores
Bond Dickinson	Mills & Reeve
BPE Solicitors	Mishcon de Reya
Brabners Chaffe Street	Muckle
Browne Jacobson	Nabarro
Burges Salmon	Norton Rose Fulbright
Capsticks Solicitors	Olswang
Charles Russell	Olswang Thames Valley
Clifford Chance	Osborne Clarke
Clyde & Co	Penningtons Solicitors
CMS	Pinsent Masons
Cripps Harries Hall	Reed Smith
Dechert	RPC
Dentons	SGH Martineau
DLA Piper	Shoosmiths
DWF	Simmons & Simmons
Eversheds	SJ Berwin
Farrer & Co	Slater & Gordon
Foot Anstey	Slaughter and May
Freeth Cartwright	Speechly Bircham
Freshfields	Squire Sanders
Gateley	Stephenson Harwood
Gordons	Stevens & Bolton
Harbottle & Lewis	Taylor Wessing
Herbert Smith Freehills	TLT
Higgs & Sons	Travers Smith
Hill Dickinson	Trethowans
Hogan Lovells	Trowers & Hamlins
Irwin Mitchell	Veale Wasbrough Vizards
Jones Day	Walker Morris
K&L Gates	Ward Hadaway
Kennedys	Watson, Farley & Williams
Kingsley Napley	Wedlake Bell
Latham & Watkins	Wilsons
Lawrence Graham	Withers
Leigh Day	Wragge & Co

Practice Areas

Environment

In a nutshell

Environment lawyers advise corporate clients on damage limitation and pre-emptive measures, and they defend them from prosecution. In other words, the majority of private practitioners work for, rather than stick it to, big business. Opportunities do exist at organisations like Greenpeace and Friends of the Earth, but these jobs are highly sought after. Another non-commercial option is to work for a local authority, a government department such as the Department for Environment, Food and Rural Affairs (Defra) or a regulatory body like the Environment Agency. However, be aware that hiring freezes and cutbacks having been hitting the public sector hard.

Environment law overlaps with other disciplines such as property, criminal law, corporate or EU law. Environmental issues can be deal breakers, especially in the modern era of corporate social responsibility. However, the small size of most law firms' environment teams means there are relatively few pure environmental specialists around.

What lawyers do

Lawyers in private practice
- Advise on the potential environmental consequences of corporate, property and projects transactions.
- Advise on compliance and regulatory issues to help clients operate within regulatory boundaries and avoid investigation or prosecution.
- Defend clients when they get into trouble over water or air pollution, waste disposal, emission levels or health and safety. Such cases can involve criminal or civil actions, judicial reviews and even statutory appeals. They may also be subject to damaging media coverage.

Lawyers with local authorities
- Handle a massive variety of work covering regulatory and planning issues plus waste management and air pollution prosecutions.
- Advise the authority on its own potential liability.

Lawyers working for Defra
- Are responsible for litigation, drafting of subordinate legislation, advisory work and contract drafting on any of Defra's varied mandates.
- Work in a team of 50 lawyers, including Government Legal Service trainees. Defra aims to promote sustainable development without compromising the quality of life of future generations.

Lawyers working for the Environment Agency
- Prosecute environmental crimes – this involves gathering evidence, preparing cases and briefing barristers.
- Co-operate with government lawyers on the drafting and implementation of legislation.
- Work in Bristol and eight regional bases and are responsible for protecting and enhancing the environment. They also regulate corporate activities that have the capacity to pollute.

The realities of the job
- In this competitive and demanding field, all-round skills are best complemented by experience in a specific area. The way in which environmental law spans disciplines requires commercial nous and a good understanding of corporate structures.
- Excellent academics are essential to help wade through, extrapolate from and present research and complex legislation; so too are sound judgement, pragmatism and the ability to come up with inventive solutions.
- A basic grasp of science helps.
- If you want to change environmental laws or crusade for a better planet, then stick to the public or non-profit sectors. The sometimes uncomfortable realities of private practice won't be for you.
- Client contact is key and relationships can endure over many years. Environmental risks are difficult to quantify and clients will rely on your gut instincts and powers of lateral thinking.
- With visits to waste dumps or drying reservoirs, and a workload that can span health and safety matters, corporate transactions and regulatory advice all in one day, this is neither a desk-bound nor a quiet discipline.
- Research constantly advances and legislation is always changing in this field, so you'll spend a lot of time keeping up to date.
- A taste for European law is essential as more and more EU directives prescribe the boundaries of environmental law in the UK.

Current issues
- The coalition government claims to be the 'greenest government ever' and the new Energy Bill 2012-23 commits it to investing in clean and low-carbon energy. However, the draft bill does not contain any mandatory targets to reduce carbon emissions. At the same time, the 2010 Carbon Reduction Commitment Energy Efficiency Scheme remains in place and requires large organisations to cap the amount of carbon they produce.

Practice Areas

- Regulatory work is on the up, and firms report an increase in supply chain and EU health and safety issues. For example, the EU's REACH (Registration, Evaluation, Authorisation & Restriction of Chemicals) regulations aim to control the use of chemicals and increase the amount of information available about them.
- The EU Environmental Liability Directive was updated in 2009, resulting in more companies taking up environmental insurance. Consequently, firms with an insurance focus have seen an increase in work on this front, and have witnessed more and more bespoke insurance products cropping up in this area.
- The Environment Agency has been taking a more stringent approach to clamping down on regulatory offences. Where businesses might previously have dealt with them in-house, lawyers are now being instructed to negotiate with the EA. The costs involved can run into the millions.
- An increasingly well-informed public also means an increasingly litigious public. The UN's Aarhus Convention, which has been ratified by the European Union, allows the public to participate in environmental decision-making and to access environmental information. When the public feels let down or barred from such knowledge, redress is sought from the courts. Monitoring the extent to which the UK is compliant with Aarhus is still generating activity for lawyers. A savvy public has also produced a surge in class actions, usually involving pollution, odour or other forms of nuisance.
- Some firms have been able to bring mass tort claims to UK courts. These have, for example, involved claims against parent companies on behalf of people who have allegedly suffered in the countries they have been working in. Lawyers have identified this as a potential trend which stems from a shift in the UK court's approach to accepting jurisdiction.
- The increased focus on renewable energy in the UK has resulted in more work involving alternative forms of power such as biomass, wind farm, nuclear and energy-from-waste projects. With the value of some recent deals reaching hundreds of millions, magic circle firms have been becoming more interested in the sector as well. The energy-from-waste projects are especially topical as they have brought up issues regarding whether waste should be labelled as waste or a fuel.
- Top-flight international firms are encountering climate change work more often, and international issues are coming to the fore. Corporate social responsibility is increasingly in vogue and as the bottom-up development of climate change regimes continues to evolve, firms have been advising on emissions reduction projects and also on a wider array of clean energy and energy efficiency projects.

Read our True Pictures on...

Addleshaw Goddard	K&L Gates
Allen & Overy	Leigh Day
Ashurst	Linklaters
B P Collins	Macfarlanes
Baker & McKenzie	Maclay Murray & Spens
Berwin Leighton Paisner	Mayer Brown
Bond Dickinson	Mills & Reeve
Brabners Chaffe Street	Nabarro
Browne Jacobson	Norton Rose Fulbright
Burges Salmon	Osborne Clarke
Clifford Chance	Pinsent Masons
Clyde & Co	Shoosmiths
CMS	Simmons & Simmons
Dentons	SJ Berwin
DLA Piper	Slaughter and May
DWF	Squire Sanders
Eversheds	Stephenson Harwood
Freshfields	Stevens & Bolton
Herbert Smith Freehills	TLT
Hogan Lovells	Travers Smith
Irwin Mitchell	Walker Morris
Jones Day	Wragge & Co

- The carbon trading sector, in Europe at least, seems to be near dead in the water thanks to the recession. Manufacturers have been producing less, which has consequently meant they have needed to buy fewer carbon credits. This is an endemic problem at the moment, and carbon trading specialists are witnessing an all-time low in this type of work. However, on the up is contentious work surrounding carbon trading, and firms report an uptick in disputes over carbon trading contracts, highlighting examples of carbon trading fraud.
- Keep on top of changes in environmental law courtesy of websites like www.endsreport.com. You should enhance your CV and prime yourself by joining organisations such as the Environmental Law Foundation (ELF) and the UK Environmental Law Association (www.ukela.org). Most environmental lawyers are members of UKELA and students are welcome to attend events across the country. The charity ELF (www.elflaw.org) provides a referral service for members of the public, organises lectures in London and produces regular newsletters for members.

Family

In a nutshell

Lawyers are involved with almost every aspect of family life, from the legal mechanics and complications of marriage and civil partnerships to divorce, disputes between cohabitants, inheritance disputes between family members, prenuptial and cohabitation agreements and all matters relating to children. Whether working in a general high street practice with a large caseload of legally aided work, or for a specialist practice dealing with big-money divorces and complex child or international matters, family solicitors are in court a good deal and fully occupied back in the office.

There is effectively a division between child law and matrimonial law, with many practitioners devoting themselves exclusively to one or the other; others plant a foot in each. Unfortunately, family law is one that has, and will be seriously affected by legal aid cuts.

What lawyers do

Matrimonial lawyers

- Interview and advise clients on prenuptial agreements, cohabitation arrangements, divorce and the financial implications of divorce. This can involve issues like inheritance and wills, conveyancing, welfare benefits, company law, tax and trusts, pensions and even judicial review.
- Prepare the client's case for divorce and settlement hearings, including organising witnesses and providing summaries of assets/finances, which will require dealing with accountants and financial and pensions advisers.
- Attend conferences with barristers.
- Represent clients in hearings or brief barristers to do so.
- Negotiate settlements and associated financial terms.

Child law lawyers

- In private cases – interview and advise clients on the implications of divorce with regard to child contact and residence. In some instances this will result in court action. Deal with disputes between parents or other family members over the residence of, and contact with, children.
- In public cases – represent local authorities, parents, children's guardians or children themselves on matters such as children's care proceedings or abuse in care claims. Social workers, probation officers, psychologists and medical professionals will also be involved in cases.

The realities of the job

- When it comes to relationships and families, no two sets of circumstances will ever be the same. Advocacy is plentiful.
- You will encounter a real mix of clients, some at a joyful moment in their lives, others facing deeply traumatic times. A good family law practitioner combines the empathetic, sensitive qualities of a counsellor with the clarity of thought and commercial acumen of a lawyer. You need to remain detached to achieve the result your clients need.
- Tough negotiating skills and a strong nerve are vital as your work has immediate and practical consequences. The prospect of telling a client that they've lost a custody battle does much to sharpen the mind.
- A pragmatic and real-world outlook is useful, however you'll also need to spend time keeping abreast of legal developments.
- On publicly funded matters you'll face your share of bureaucracy and it certainly won't make you rich.

Current issues

- London is arguably the divorce capital of Europe and the most generous jurisdiction in the world for (usually) women in a divorce situation. International instructions regarding divorce are on the rise as clients with a foot in two or more jurisdictions, not to mention a bundle of cash, seek to get the best outcome.
- There has been an increase in the popularity of prenuptial agreements following the Radmacher v Granatino divorce. Prenups aren't automatically recognised by the English courts, but this case saw the Supreme Court rule for the first time that they should have 'decisive weight'.
- The Supreme Court's landmark 2013 ruling in Prest v Petrodel Resources established that a divorced spouse can lay claim to an ex-partner's assets even if they are tied up in company assets.
- Legislation legalising same-sex marriages received royal assent on 17 July 2013 and is expected to come into force soon.
- The economic downturn has led to increased demand for advice on wealth protection.
- Taxation is a major theme as, more than ever, clients seek to reach settlements that are structured to mitigate unnecessary tax or other liabilities. As in many other practice areas, it's worth getting close to a tax specialist.

Practice Areas

- While family law isn't an area traditionally associated with City firms, some firms have been moving into or developing their family and private client practices during the recession to make up for losses from the corporate sector.
- These are challenging times for the publicly funded lawyer. Many firms are feeling the squeeze, and some are choosing to limit, or even cease, legally aided work. This is the case with both matrimonial finance cases and childcare proceedings, although some firms have stuck with the latter on idealistic grounds.
- Social workers are under increased scrutiny, and the family courts have been opened up to the press. Many lawyers say that this has made it much harder to do their jobs and has more to do with justice being seen to be done rather than anything else. The family courts have been heavily criticised for the length of time it takes to reach decisions in child law cases. In response, the government has implemented a six-month limit for the completion of child care cases. Critics say this will have an impact on the quality of decisions and on childrens' welfare.
- The government has also pledged to pour money into publicly-funded family mediation in the hope of diverting cases away from the courts. There's little optimism here either – 90% of cases are already resolved before they reach this stage, with only the most serious being heard by a judge.

Read our True Pictures on...

Ashfords	Kingsley Napley
B P Collins	Lester Aldridge
Bircham Dyson Bell	Michelmores
Boodle Hatfield	Mills & Reeve
Brabner Chaffe Street	Mishcon de Reya
Burges Salmon	Penningtons Solicitors
Charles Russell	SGH Martineau
Collyer Bristow	Slater & Gordon
Cripps Harries Hall	Speechly Bircham
DWF	Stevens & Bolton
Farrer & Co	TLT
Foot Anstey	Trethowans
Gateley	Ward Hadaway
Higgs & Sons	Withers
Irwin Mitchell	

Practice Areas

Human Rights & Immigration

In a nutshell

Human rights lawyers protest injustice and fight for principles at the point of intersection between the state's powers and individuals' rights. Cases usually relate in some way to the UK's ratification of the European Convention on Human Rights (ECHR) through the Human Rights Act and crop up in criminal and civil contexts, often through the medium of judicial review, a key tool in questioning the decisions of public bodies. Civil contexts include claims regarding the right to education or community care under the Mental Health Act, cases of discrimination at work and even family issues. Criminal contexts could relate to complaints against the police, prisoners' issues, public order convictions following demonstrations, or perhaps extradition on terror charges.

Immigration lawyers deal with both business and personal immigration matters – the former has been embraced by the government in its quest to manage economic migration. In this more lucrative area, lawyers assist highly skilled migrants to obtain residency or leave to remain in the UK and help non-nationals to secure visas for travel abroad. They also work with companies that need to bring in employees from overseas. Personal immigration lawyers represent individuals who have fled persecution in their country of origin. They also take on cases for people whose right to stay in the UK is under threat or indeed entirely absent.

What lawyers do

Business immigration lawyers
- Advise and assist businesses or their employees in relation to work permits and visas. They need to be up to speed on all current schemes, such as those for highly skilled migrants and investors.
- Prepare for, attend and advocate at tribunals or court hearings, where necessary instructing a barrister to do so.

Personal immigration lawyers
- Advise clients on their status and rights within the UK.
- Secure evidence of a client's identity, medical reports and witness statements, and prepare cases for court hearings or appeals. Represent clients or instruct a barrister to do so.
- Undertake an immense amount of unremunerated form filling and legal aid paperwork.

The realities of the job

- The competition for training contracts is huge. Voluntary work at a law centre or specialist voluntary organisation, or other relevant experience, is essential.
- A commitment to and belief in the values you're fighting for is essential in this relatively low-paid area. Work in the voluntary sector or taking on important cases pro bono can provide the greatest satisfaction.
- Because much of the work is publicly funded, firms do not usually offer attractive trainee salaries or sponsorship through law school.
- Sensitivity and empathy are absolutely essential because you'll often be dealing with highly emotional people, those with mental health issues or those who simply don't appreciate the full extent of their legal predicament.
- Strong analytical skills are required to pick out the legal issues you can change from the socio-economic ones beyond your control.
- In the battle against red tape and institutional indifference, organisational skills and a vast store of patience are valuable assets.
- Opportunities for advocacy are abundant, which means that knowledge of court and tribunal procedures is a fundamental requirement. Often cases must pass through every possible stage of appeal before referral to judicial review or the ECJ.
- If working within a commercial firm, the clients will be businesses and public sector organisations. As such there will be less of a campaigning element to the work and you will not necessarily feel you are 'on the side of the angels'.

Current issues

- Issues of asylum (including detention and deportation) and people seeking permission to stay in the UK on human rights grounds never cease to arouse strong opinions. The government is cracking down on all forms of immigration, but despite this – or perhaps because of it – the number of asylum appeals has been decreasing over the past few years.
- The advent of the Freedom of Information Act and increased transparency in the public sector in line with Article 6 of the ECHR mean law firms have seen a greater willingness from the public to challenge the decisions of authorities.

Practice Areas

- Many recent human rights and civil liberties cases have related to issues arising out of Guantanamo Bay, Iraq, terrorism, stop-and-search powers and national security. These cases have taken the form of judicial reviews and public inquiries. The much-publicised Binyam Mohamed judicial review, and the Baha Mousa and Al-Sweady inquiries are examples of such investigations.
- Other recent big social justice cases have related to equality rights, privacy rights and asylum seeker rights.
- The Points Based System (PBS) of immigration means every employer now needs to obtain an immigration licence under the PBS before being able to issue a Certificate of Sponsorship for each employee it wishes to employ. Some argue that the scheme is now so technical that employers are constantly at risk of unlawful employment. Critics believe that restricting highly skilled migrants from working in the UK is farcical.
- In early 2011 the government introduced an annual cap on non-EU immigration of 21,700 – all immigrants must be graduates with job offers or 'exceptional talent' like scientists and academics. All other non-EEA economic immigration has been halted.
- The past decade has seen an enormous growth in human rights litigation, in UK and European courts – like the General Court (formerly the Court of First Instance), European Court of Justice, European Court of Human Rights – as well as international tribunals. This case-driven development of human rights law is based on fundamental rights standards common to legal systems throughout Europe.
- The death of Jimmy Mubenga has shed light on deportation and the extent to which force can be used in immigration removals. A jury returned a verdict of unlawful killing regarding the incident in October 2010, when the husband and father of three suffered cardio-respiratory collapse on a flight to Angola after being restrained by three G4S guards.

Read our True Pictures on...

Baker & McKenzie	Leigh Day
Bates Wells Braithwaite	Lewis Silkin
Bird and Bird	Mishcon de Reya
Clyde & Co	Morgan Lewis
DWF	Penningtons Solicitors
Irwin Mitchell	Speechly Bircham
Kingsley Napley	Squire Sanders

- Trenton Oldfield, activist and disruptor of the 2012 Oxford and Cambridge boat race, faces deportation to his native Australia after serving two months of a six month sentence. With a British wife and young family, it remains to be seen whether the Home Office will make an example of him or relent due to public pressure.

Insurance

In a nutshell

Insurance is the practice of hedging against financial risk. This practice and its fall-out require a lot of legal work. Insurance and reinsurance (even insurers are vulnerable to financial risk and they transfer part of their risk on to reinsurers) are practised by a significant number of specialist law firms and general commercial outfits across the UK. Insurance can be split into many sub-specialisms (see below). Firms may offer all or some of these services. Personal injury and clinical negligence (including public liability, employers' liability, accident-at-work claims etc.) are also insurance-related practice areas – you can read more about them on **page 125**. Maritime insurance was the first type of insurance to exist. You can read more about shipping and trade law on **page 137**.

It's possible to insure pretty much anything against almost any eventuality. Put differently, insurance is taken out to cover risks: human error, accidents, natural disasters etc. The most common types of insurance which lawyers deal with are: insurance against the destruction of tangible assets (eg property); insurance against the loss of intangible assets (eg revenue streams); and insurance against mistakes made by professionals (professional indemnity – the insurance-related bit of professional negligence). So, insurance lawyers work on cases related to property damage, product liability, fraud, insolvency, director's liabilities (D&O), aviation, business interruption, mortgage losses, political events, technology, energy, environment, construction, finance... the list goes on. Disputes arise between the insured policyholder and the insurer; between the insured plus the insurer and another party; or between the insurer and the reinsurer.

Other lawyers specialise in the transactional aspects of the insurance industry, advising on tax, regulations, restructurings, drafting insurance policies, and M&A activity between insurance companies.

What lawyers do

Professional indemnity

- Represent professionals accused of malpractice and their insurers. Professions most often affected include engineers, architects, surveyors, accountants, brokers, financial advisers and solicitors as well as GPs, dentists, surgeons etc.
- Investigate a claim, assess its authenticity and look into the coverage of a given insurance policy to determine an insurer's degree of liability.
- Take advice from experts on professional conduct.
- Draft letters in response to claims.

- Prepare documents for court or out-of-court settlements.
- Attend pre-trial hearings, case management conferences and trials if a case goes to court.
- Attend joint-settlement meetings, arbitrations or mediations in out-of-court cases.

Commercial insurance disputes

- Work on claims related to things as varied as properties damaged by flood or fires, oil rigs destroyed by hurricanes, or gold mines nationalised by socialist governments.
- Work on disputes between insurers and the insured over insurance pay-outs and what insurance coverage consists of, or act for the insurer and the insured together in litigation with a third party.
- Assess coverage and the insurer's liability.
- Interview witnesses to find out how events occurred.
- Value the claim and build up the case for what the client feels is an adequate settlement.
- Attend court or mediations/arbitrations in order to come to a settlement.

Transactions

- Broadly similar to the work of a general transactional lawyer. There are extra rules and regulations governing insurance transactions which lawyers need to take into account.

The realities of the job

- While several legal practice areas fall under the insurance umbrella, the insurance industry itself is a distinct, single block within the City and the UK as a whole. There are a few big well-known insurance companies out there, but over 400 are registered with the famous insurance market Lloyd's of London.
- London is the global centre for insurance and reinsurance. It has been ever since Lloyd's of London was founded over 200 years ago. The industry is extremely well established and has its own rules, traditions and obscure terminology. Businesses based overseas will often be insured with a London firm, and the biggest disputes often have an international angle to them.
- The insurance industry has a reputation for being a bit dull; however, the legal side kicks in when calamities occur, making it quite eventful, as any 'wet' shipping lawyer will tell you. It is also home to plenty of colourful characters, and big companies organise many events, lectures and conferences for like-minded insurance-o-philes to rub shoulders.

- Insurance is a complex and technical area. Insurance policies are not the lightest reading material you'll ever come across. Stints in insurance seats are challenging for trainees, even those who have taken an insurance law elective on the LPC.
- Insurance lawyers are known for their precise and fastidious working style. Good organisational skills are crucial, because lawyers are often dealing with a host of claims at various different stages. There are often daily deadlines and clients need to be kept constantly informed.
- Lawyers have to pay special attention to potentially fraudulent claims or parts of claims.
- Insurance cases range from huge international disputes to small local squabbles. Trainees might run a small case themselves, but only work on a component of a large high-value dispute. Lower value work is usually done by small or mid-size regional and national firms, while the largest disputes are the preserve of City firms.
- Many firms regularly act for both insurance companies and insured policyholders. There is a trend towards firms specialising in either policyholder or insurer work.
- The insurance industry is regulated by the newly-established Financial Conduct Authority.

Current issues

- There is an increasing emphasis on using fixed-fee and capped-fee arrangements to save costs both for insurers and the insured.
- There have been many catastrophic events and natural disasters in the past few years. From the Arab Spring and the Fukushima earthquake to the aftermath of the Deepwater Horizon oil spill, the UK riots and 2013 European floods, all had massive insurance implications. In the long term such disasters will affect the reinsurance market too, causing reinsurance premiums to rise. The insurance market is called 'soft' when premiums are low and 'hard' when premiums are high because of a recent catastrophe or disaster. (For example, the market 'hardened' after 9/11.)
- The EU's Solvency II directive – aimed at harmonising EU insurance regulations to enhance consumer protection – is due to come into force in the next few years (1 January 2014 is the earliest possible date). It is already having a major impact on the insurance industry, as companies seek legal advice on compliance.

Read our True Pictures on...

Addleshaw Goddard	Holman Fenwick Willan
Allen & Overy	Ince & Co*
Ashurst	K&L Gates
Berwin Leighton Paisner	Kennedys*
Bond Dickinson	Lawrence Graham
Browne Jacobson	Linklaters
Clifford Chance	Maclay Murray & Spens
Clyde & Co*	Mayer Brown
CMS	Mills & Reeve
Covington & Burling	Norton Rose Fulbright
DLA Piper	Pinsent Masons
DWF	Reed Smith
Edwards Wildman Palmer*	RPC*
Eversheds	Sidley Austin
Freshfields	Simmons & Simmons
Herbert Smith Freehills	Slater & Gordon
Hill Dickinson	Slaughter and May
Hogan Lovells	

* These firms have a particularly strong focus on insurance.

- Much to the surprise of many observers, the insurance markets have held up well during the recession. Insurance firms are – for the most part – doing well. The recession has led to a slight increase in speculative and fraudulent claims by individuals and businesses looking to make a bob or two, but again not to the degree expected.
- The recession has caused an upsurge in the number of professional negligence claims against mortgage brokers and other financial advisers over their advice on investments and financial products.
- The Legal Aid, Sentencing and Punishment of Offenders Act 2012 has banned the use of referral fees for lucrative personal injury claims (often whiplash-related) from April 2013. There'll probably be a rise in insurance firms setting up alternative business structures to get around the ban.
- Telematics is a growing area in auto insurance. A device in the car can track the driver's behaviour and send that info to the insurance company, who will charge premiums accordingly based on that driver's risk of accident.
- The scandal of mis-sold payment protection insurance is ongoing, and claims continue to be dealt with. Add-on insurance is the next scandal-prone area. In 2013 a large insurer was fined for amassing £97m from policies that customers bought without being told that they were optional extras and separate from the core cover.

Intellectual Property

In a nutshell

Lawyers, patent attorneys and trade mark attorneys work to protect their clients' intellectual property assets. Technical solutions to technical problems are deemed to be inventions, usually protectable via **patents** that provide their proprietor with the exclusive right to stop others working in the claimed area for a period of usually up to 20 years. Preparing a patent specification is a highly specialised task requiring particular scientific/technical expertise and knowledge, combined with experience and knowledge of complex application procedures.

Trade marks used to sell goods or services are protectable by way of a registration procedure and provide a potentially perpetual monopoly right. The aesthetic shape and way a product is designed is also protectable via **registered design protection** for a limited period of time. **Unregistered** rights also exist for a time for various designs of products. Then there is **copyright** which lasts during the lifetime of the creator and for a period after their death, and which arises automatically on the creation of music, artwork, works of literature or reference, databases and web pages, for example.

A single product such as a mobile phone will be protected by several different forms of IP in countries all around the world. For would-be competitors wanting to make or sell something similar, a first costly hurdle is simply finding out what these rights are and who owns them. Worst-case scenario, getting it wrong or overlooking an IP right might result in being on the wrong end of a court injunction or costly damages (fearsomely so in the USA), and ignorance is no defence! The work of an IP lawyer is not only specialist in itself, but increasingly it requires close collaboration with other specialists in areas such as IT, media, competition, telecommunications, life sciences and employment.

What lawyers do

- Search domestic, European and international registers of patents, trade marks and registered designs to establish ownership of existing rights or the potential to register new rights.
- Take all steps to protect clients' interests by securing patents, trade marks and registered designs; appeal unfavourable decisions; attack decisions that benefit others but harm the lawyer's own client.
- Write letters to require that third parties desist from carrying out infringing activities or risk litigation for damages and an injunction.

- Issue court proceedings and prepare cases for trial by taking witness statements, examining scientific or technical reports and commissioning experiments and tests. Junior lawyers may find themselves conducting consumer surveys and going on covert shopping expeditions.
- Instruct and consult with barristers. Solicitor advocates can appear in the Patents County Court; the advantages of having a specialist IP barrister for higher court hearings are obvious.
- Draft commercial agreements between owners of IP rights and those who want to use the protected invention, design or artistic work. The most common documents will either transfer ownership or grant a licence for use.
- Work as part of a multidisciplinary team on corporate transactions, verifying ownership of IP rights and drafting documents enabling their transfer.

The realities of the job

- Lawyers must be able to handle everyone from company directors to mad inventors. Clients come from manufacturing, the hi-tech sector, engineering, pharmaceuticals, agrochemicals, universities and scientific institutions, media organisations and the arts.
- A degree in a relevant subject is common among patent lawyers. Brand and trade mark lawyers need a curiosity for all things creative and must keep up with consumer trends. Both need a good sense for commercial strategy.
- Attention to detail, precision and accuracy is important. You must be meticulous, particularly when drafting, as correct wording is imperative.
- In trade mark and design filings and prosecution, everything has a time limit. You will live by deadlines.
- In patent filing, procurement and strategy, you'll need to work seamlessly with a patent attorney. There are hardly any solicitors who are also patent attorneys (and vice versa).
- The volume of information and paperwork involved can be huge on patent matters, though on the plus side you could get the opportunity to visit research labs or factories to learn about production processes, etc.
- The stakes can be big. Commercial research and development in the pharmaceutical sector is motivated by profit not philanthropy. The investment involved will have been colossal, and even a day's loss of sales can be eye watering. Success or failure in litigation can dramatically affect a company's share price.

Practice Areas

- Manufacturing, pharmaceutical and research companies usually employ patent specialists and there tend to be in-house legal teams at all the larger companies. In the media, major publishers and television companies employ in-house IP lawyers.

Current issues

- UK copyright law has for some time failed to reflect the way that people use digital material and modern technology, and many questions have continued to occupy this ambiguous territory. Whether people infringe copyrights by linking to copyrighted material on websites, buying and selling second-hand digital content like MP3 files or imitating the layout of a photograph is still up for debate. The 2011 Hargreaves Report was commissioned to address problems like these, and the introduction of new statutory copyright exceptions is on the horizon. The changes will give individuals greater freedom to use copyrighted works such as computer games, paintings, films, books and music, while simultaneously protecting authors and right owners.
- The financial crisis led to a growing awareness of intellectual property as a valuable asset. Businesses have become more aggressive in protecting their rights and litigation is on the rise. The English courts' reputation for being patent-unfriendly has been challenged by recent judgments.
- International efforts are being made to harmonise aspects of patent procurement. The European, US and Japanese patent offices are testing out patent prosecution 'highways' to try and streamline the detailed processes of searching and examining patent applications. The European, US, Japanese, Korean and Chinese patent offices are looking at work sharing.
- After many years of discussion and planning, the EU has finally got closer to establishing a Unified Patent Court after a treaty was signed in February 2013. The court will hear cases involving European patents which are valid in the participating states, meaning that the need to organise separate litigation in each country will become obsolete. The court will be based mainly in Paris, but will also have sub-divisions in London and Munich. In the months before the treaty is ratified (by January 2014, potentially,) law firms are keeping busy advising businesses on the introduction of both the UPC and the attendant EU patent.
- Tech patents reached a record high in 2012. 14,205 applications were filed in this area – an increase of 19% from 2011. The high-profile US Apple v Samsung case – in which Samsung was found to have infringed patents which covered, for instance, the capacity to zoom into a picture by double-tapping the screen – has spurred on a ream of tech compa-

Read our True Pictures on...

Ashfords	Lewis Silkin
Addleshaw Goddard	Linklaters
Allen & Overy	Macfarlanes
Ashurst	Maclay Murray & Spens
Baker & McKenzie	Mayer Brown
Berwin Leighton Paisner	Michelmores
Bird & Bird*	Mills & Reeve
Bond Dickinson	Mishcon de Reya
Brabners Chaffe Street	Muckle
Bristows*	Nabarro
Browne Jacobson	Olswang
Burges Salmon	Pinsent Masons
Charles Russell	Reed Smith
Covington & Burling*	RPC
Cripps Harries Hall	SGH Martineau
Dechert	Shoosmiths
Dentons	Simmons & Simmons
DWF	SJ Berwin
Edwards Wildman Palmer	Slaughter and May
Eversheds	Speechly Bircham
Farrer & Co	Squire Sanders
Foot Anstey	Stevens & Bolton
Freshfields	Taylor Wessing*
Gateley	TLT
Harbottle & Lewis	Walker Morris
Herbert Smith Freehills	Ward Hadaway
Hill Dickinsons	Wedlake Bell
Hogan Lovells	Wragge & Co
K&L Gates	
Latham & Watkins	

* These firms have a particularly strong focus on IP.

nies to patent a whole range of screen gestures. This pick-up in patenting has, perhaps inevitably, led to an increase in litigation too, although a peak could soon be reached.

- In the trade mark arena many clients are seeking strategic advice on how to tackle the growing problem of counterfeit goods. L'Oréal's case concerning eBay's liability in relation to counterfeit goods sold on its auction site was referred to the ECJ by the French courts. Its decision was heralded as a triumph for luxury brand owners utilising selective distribution channels. The trend for digitalisation is bringing online IP issues to prominence; in its eagerly awaited ruling on Interflora v Marks & Spencer, the ECJ agreed with the High Court that M&S's use of the Google AdWords search term 'Interflora' infringes the flower business' trade mark.

Litigation & Dispute Resolution

In a nutshell

Litigation solicitors assist clients in resolving civil disputes. Disputes can concern anything from unpaid bills or unfulfilled contract terms to problems between landlords and tenants, infringement of IP rights, construction-related claims, the liabilities of insurers, shipping cases, defective products, media and entertainment industry wrangles… the list is endless. And that's just in the commercial sphere. The most common types of litigation involving private individuals are discussed at length in our personal injury overview.

If disputes are not settled by negotiation, they will be concluded either by court litigation or an alternative form of dispute resolution – thus litigation is a type of dispute resolution. The most common other methods are arbitration and mediation. The former is often stipulated as the preferred method in commercial contracts, while the latter is generally achieved through structured negotiations between the parties, overseen by an independent mediator. These methods can still be problematic: mediation is not necessarily adequate for complex matters, and some argue that opponents can use it as a means of 'bleeding' money from each other or as covert interrogation.

Confusingly, there are two divisions of the High Court dealing with major cases – the Chancery Division and the Queen's Bench Division (QBD) – and each hears different types of cases. For instance, the QBD hears various contract law and personal injury/general negligence cases, whereas the Chancery Division handles matters relating to trusts, probate, insolvency, business and land law.

What lawyers do

- Advise clients on whether they have a valid claim, or whether to settle or fight a claim made against them.
- Gather evidence and witnesses to support the client's position; develop case strategies.
- Issue court proceedings or embark on a process of alternative dispute resolution if correspondence with the defendant does not produce a satisfactory result.
- Represent clients at pre-trial hearings and case management conferences.
- Attend conferences with counsel (ie barristers) and brief them to conduct advocacy in hearings, trials and arbitrations.
- Attend trials, arbitrations and mediations with clients; provide assistance to barristers.

The realities of the job

- Work is driven by procedural rules and the timetable of the courts. Good litigators understand how best to manoeuvre within the system while also developing winning case strategies.
- The phenomenal amount of paperwork generated means that young litigators spend much of their time sifting through documents, scheduling and copying them in order to provide the court and all other parties with an agreed bundle of evidence.
- Litigators need to express themselves succinctly and precisely.
- Unless the claim value is small, the solicitor's job is more about case preparation than court performance. Solicitor-advocates are gaining ground, and once properly qualified they can appear in the higher courts. Nonetheless, barristers still dominate court advocacy and the performance of some solicitor-advocates has been criticised by the judiciary.
- Trainee workloads largely depend on the type of firm and the type of clients represented. Big City firms won't give trainees free rein on huge international banking disputes – they might not even go to court during their training contract – but they will be able to offer a small contribution to headline-making cases. Firms handling much smaller claims will often expect trainees to deal with all aspects of a case, from drafting correspondence and interim court applications to meetings with clients and settlement negotiations.
- There are a number of litigation-led law firms that handle cases of all sizes, and these present the best opportunities for a litigation-heavy training contract. The competition for litigation jobs at NQ level is fierce, so concentrate on litigation-led firms if you are certain of your leanings.
- The Solicitors Regulation Authority (SRA) requires all trainee solicitors to gain some contentious experience. People tend to learn early on whether they are suited to this kind of work. Increasingly in big City firms, SRA requirements can be fulfilled by a litigation crash course. It's also worth bearing in mind that more specialised areas, like real estate litigation and employment, can satisfy this contentious requirement.
- Despite a few firms starting up in-house advocacy units, the courts remain dominated by barristers, who are felt to have the edge when it comes to the skills and expertise needed to advocate. If you are determined to become both a solicitor and an advocate, certain areas of practice have more scope for advocacy – for example family, crime, employment and lower-value civil litigation.

Practice Areas

Current issues

- London has long been a popular forum for international litigation and arbitration, and the sheer volume of cases it receives (from places as disparate as Russia and South America) does not appear to be slowing. Research in 2012 showed that London was still the most preferred and widely used seat of arbitration.
- International arbitration is thriving at the moment, but not just in historically strong centres like London, Paris, Stockholm and Geneva; emerging arbitration hubs, such as Dubai and Singapore are also on the up. A survey by PwC released in April 2013 found that arbitration remains the most popular means of resolving disputes, with over 50% of respondents selecting arbitration as their preferred choice. Interestingly though, the popularity of arbitration varies depending on industry sector. In the same survey, arbitration was the outright winner in the energy and construction sectors, while litigation was the clear favourite in the financial services arena.
- London does face challenges as a venue for global dispute resolution, partly because of costs, but experts believe the popularity of English law across the globe means London will retain its position as one of the world's leading dispute centres. Additionally, it has become increasingly common for UK lawyers to spend time in places like Singapore to instruct on matters concerning English law.
- International arbitration hasn't been the only thing keeping lawyers busy in the past couple of years. White-collar fraud and internal investigations are two other areas which have experienced an upsurge in activity, especially off the back of the financial crisis, and cross-border disputes have similarly increased.
- Bigger UK firms and US firms in London are handling more arbitration advocacy in-house and not instructing the Bar. There is debate as to how successful and effective this is, but it's certainly something these firms are continuing to push, especially for more run-of-the-mill cases.
- Back in 2008, Lord Falconer of Thoroton QC famously predicted a 'tsunami of [post-credit crunch] litigation'. It may have taken longer than initially expected, but financial disputes are now dominating the English courts. It's not quite been the tsunami that Falconer suggested it would be but more of a steady flow, with cases spread out over a number of years as opposed to coming in thick and fast. What's more, the nature of these disputes has changed lately; many are now arising from the lack of liquidity in the financial markets, for example.
- The Libor scandal has been providing a lot of litigation activity for many firms, with several big-name financial institutions at the heart of allegations, including Barclays, Deutsche Bank and RBS.
- In April 2013, the majority of the Jackson reforms to costs in English civil litigation were introduced, representing the most significant changes to the English courts in more than a decade. Such changes include reducing the burden of costs on defendants as successful claimants will no longer be able to recover success fees from the losing party to pay their lawyers. Experts say the impact of these changes will largely depend on the extent to which they are acted upon over time.
- Third-party litigation funding has seen a rapid rise to prominence. Essentially, this means that an organisation that is not involved in a case – say a bank or private equity company – can choose to bankroll litigation for a share of the winnings.

Read our True Pictures on...

Addleshaw Goddard	Lawrence & Graham
Allen & Overy	Linklaters
Ashfords	Macfarlanes
Ashurst	Maclay Murray & Spens
Baker & McKenzie	Mayer Brown
Berwin Leighton Paisner	Michelmores
Bird & Bird	Mills & Reeve
Bond Dickinson	Mishcon de Reya
BPE Solicitors	Muckle
Brabners Chaffe Street	Nabarro
Bristows	Norton Rose Fulbright
Burges Salmon	Olswang
Charles Russell	Peters & Peters
Cleary Gottlieb	Pinsent Masons
Clifford Chance	Reed Smith
Clyde & Co	RPC
Covington & Burling	SGH Martineau
Cripps Harries Hall	Shoosmiths
Dechert	Sidley Austin
Dentons	Simmons & Simmons
DWF	Skadden
Edwards Wildman Palmer	Slaughter and May
Eversheds	Squire Sanders
Farrer & Co	Stephenson Harwood
Foot Anstey	Stevens & Bolton
Freshfields	Taylor Wessing
Gateley	TLT
Gordons	Travers Smith
Herbert Smith Freehills	Trethowans
Higgs & Sons	Veale Wasbrough Vizards
Hill Dickinson	Walker Morris
Hogan Lovells	Ward Hadaway
Holman Fenwick Willan	White & Case
Ince & Co	Wragge & Co
Irwin Mitchell	
Jones Day	
K&L Gates	
Latham & Watkins	

Pensions

In a nutshell

Pensions law revolves around long-term management of large sums of money. Pensions lawyers advise on the creation, structure and funding of pension schemes, their management and resolving any associated disputes. Often created under the form of a trust, pensions are highly regulated and governed by a vast amount of complex and ever-changing legislation. Solicitors typically advise employers, trustees of pension funds and pension providers.

There are several different types of pension scheme that individuals may buy into; broadly these can be divided into 'occupational pensions' and 'personal' or 'individual' pensions. All employers will soon be required to offer their employees membership of a pension scheme – roll-out of this system began in October 2012 with the biggest employers. An overwhelming majority of individuals who contribute to this form of retirement saving will be members of an employer-sponsored occupational pension scheme.

Most pensions are subject to specialist tax regimes, which makes them very attractive as long-term investments. Members are entitled to tax relief on contributions and a tax free allowance applies to pension income. Solicitors structure pension funds to take maximum advantage of the tax regime, and advise on compliance with the law and regulations in this area.

Pensions teams also work very closely with a firm's employment and corporate departments. Mergers and acquisitions of businesses may involve the movement of employees from one company to another, alongside the assets etc. of the target company. This change of ownership will have implications on who has responsibility for funding the pension schemes and raise questions over which employees (old or new) can become members of a scheme and whether the target company's pension scheme will even continue to exist or if it will be merged into or amended to mirror that of the bidding company.

Pension funds need to be well funded, managed and invested for the money to grow and support the fund's members in their retirement. The difficult economic climate recently has had an impact on pension schemes, with low return on investments contributing to funding deficits in pension funds. Pensioners are living longer than had been predicted or planned for, and some companies are struggling to find the resources to keep paying members' pensions for longer periods of retirement alongside funding the scheme for current employees. Such issues affect the public sector just as much as private enterprise – see Royal Mail, for example, which in 2009 had a £10.3bn deficit in its pension fund. Pensions lawyers help companies with restructuring and re-funding their pension schemes where there is such a shortfall and advise on the particular issues arising where companies collapse. Public sector occupational pensions are also subject to the will of the government, and lawyers have to be able to anticipate and negotiate amendments to schemes.

Most pension schemes are set up in the form of a trust and therefore strict rules apply to those in charge of administering the money. Trustees often seek legal advice on the discharge of their duties and litigation frequently occurs where they or other parties have failed to administer the funds diligently.

One of the best examples of financial mismanagement is the Equitable Life scandal, which lost its members millions of pounds.

What lawyers do

- Draft documentation relating to the creation, amendment, closure or freezing (closing funds to new members) of pension funds.
- Advise employers on their obligations towards members and pension funds.
- Advise on who can become a member of a pension fund and when to pay out of a fund.
- Advise on restructuring or securing pension funds which are underfunded or in financial difficulties, including on issues associated with the Pension Protection Fund.
- Advise on regulatory and legislative compliance with tax regimes.
- Handle disputes and litigation related to pension schemes.
- Advise trustees of pension funds on their duties.
- Advise companies, pensions providers and trustees on their interactions with the Pensions Regulator, which regulates UK work-based pension schemes.
- Assist the corporate teams on M&A deals by undertaking due diligence on potential liabilities.
- Negotiating amendments to pension plans with clients.

The realities of the job

- If you're working to corporate deal timetables then the hours can be long.

Practice Areas

- Pensions law is technical, highly regulated and often closely intertwined with tax law, which means a lot of time spent reading and interpreting complex statute books. A keen eye and ability to understand very technical information is essential.
- Pensions lawyers need to think long-term and anticipate what policy decisions and legislative proposals the government may make in the area.
- Contentious negotiations with employee/trade union representatives often arise over proposed amendments to employees' pension plans (especially in the public sector).
- Clients call every day for advice on small issues such as when to pay funds out of a pension scheme.
- Pensions lawyers need to be personable and able to explain complex law in layman's terms.

Current issues

- 2013 saw the announcement of proposals to radically reform the state pension system. The huge number of different state pensions are to be consolidated into a single rate (£144 in today's money), paid for by higher-income earners. Experts think this will encourage more people to save and boost the introduction of auto-enrolment for company pensions schemes.
- The new flat rate pension means entitlement is now solely down to each individual's contributions rather than things like the employment record of their spouse.
- The compulsory retirement age of 65 has been abolished, and the age at which an individual can access a state pension will be raised to 67 between 2026 and 2028.
- Automatic enrolment of employees on to company pension schemes began in 2012, making it compulsory for anyone between 22 and state pension age earning more than £8,105 a year to begin to put money away.
- As the UK population is living longer, defined benefit (or final salary) pensions are becoming unsustainable for employers to fund. Such schemes are either being closed to new members or wound up completely.
- In order to fund pension schemes, employers are having to find alternative funding methods such as using the company's assets as security for pension fund trustees.

Read our True Pictures on...

Addleshaw Goddard	Linklaters
Allen & Overy	Macfarlanes
Ashurst	Mayer Brown
Baker & McKenzie	Mills & Reeve
Berwin Leighton Paisner	Nabarro
Bond Dickinson	Norton Rose Fulbright
Burges Salmon	Osborne Clarke
Clifford Chance	Pinsent Masons
CMS	Reed Smith
Dentons	Shoosmiths
DLA Piper	Simmons & Simmons
DWF	Slaughter and May
Eversheds	Speechly Bircham
Freshfields	Squire Sanders
Gateley	Stephenson Harwood
Herbert Smith Freehills	Taylor Wessing
Hill Dickinson	TLT
Hogan Lovells	Travers Smith
Jones Day	Ward Hadaway
Lawrence Graham	Wragge & Co

Practice Areas

Personal Injury & Clinical Negligence

In a nutshell

Personal injury and clinical negligence lawyers resolve claims brought by people who have been injured, either as a result of an accident or through flawed medical treatment. The claimant lawyer usually acts for one individual, but sometimes a claim may be brought by a group of people – this is a class action or multiparty claim. The defendant lawyer represents the party alleged to be responsible for the illness or injury. In most PI cases the claim against the defendant will be taken over by the defendant's insurance company, which will then be the solicitor's client. Local authorities are common defendants in relation to slips and trips, while employers usually end up on the hook for accidents in the workplace. In a majority of clinical negligence cases, the defendant will be the NHS, although private medical practitioners and healthcare organisations are also sued.

What lawyers do

Claimant solicitors

- Determine the veracity of their client's claim and establish what they have suffered, including income lost and expenses incurred.
- Examine medical records and piece together all the facts. Commission further medical reports.
- Issue court proceedings if the defendant doesn't make an acceptable offer of compensation.

Defendant solicitors

- Try and avoid liability for their client or resolve a claim for as little as possible.
- Put all aspects of the case to the test. Perhaps the victim of a road traffic accident (RTA) wasn't wearing a seatbelt. Perhaps the claimant has been malingering.

Both

- Manage the progress of the case over a period of months, even years, following an established set of procedural rules.
- Attempt to settle the claim before trial or, if a case goes to trial, brief a barrister and shepherd the client through the proceedings.

The realities of the job

- The work is driven by the procedural rules and timetable of the court.
- There is a mountain of paperwork, including witness statements and bundles of evidence.
- Claimant lawyers have close contact with large numbers of clients and need good people skills.

- Defendant lawyers need to build long-term relationships with insurance companies. Clin neg defendant lawyers need to be able to communicate well with medical professionals and health sector managers.
- PI lawyers have large caseloads, especially when dealing with lower-value claims.
- There is some scope for advocacy, although barristers are used for high-stakes or complicated hearings and trials. Solicitors appear at preliminary hearings and case management conferences.

Current issues

- April 2013 saw the introduction of the majority of the reforms to civil litigation costs recommended by the Jackson Report. PI and clin neg are the two areas which are most affected. For example, successful claimants will no longer be allowed to recover success fees from the losing party. Instead, they will have to pay lawyers' fees from damages received, making controlling costs even more important. This will obviously have a profound effect on 'no win, no fee' arrangements. Successful parties can also no longer claim back after-the-event insurance premiums from the losing party, meaning that claimants have to either fund the premium out of their own pocket or risk having to pay out damages if their claim is unsuccessful.
- The reforms have also placed a ban on referral fees, impacting the relationship between lawyers and claims management companies. The fees were seen to be fuelling a growing compensation culture, and so far the ban appears to be having the desired effect: the Claims Management Regulation Unit (CMRU) posted figures which show that the number of companies handling personal injury claims fell from 2,435 in March 2012 to 1,700 in June 2013.
- At the same time, personal injury lawyers are being required to increase their use of the RTA Portal, which processes low-value personal injury claims. RTA claims are a significant source of work for PI lawyers, and the Motor Accident Solicitors Society estimates that 2,000 solicitors work in the sector, dealing with 500,000 cases each year. But the Portal is also facing a squeeze on costs.

- The expectation is that personal injury fee income will decrease significantly over the next couple of years. In this climate, larger PI firms may look to diversify their practice and branch out into different areas. Mergers may be the only option for some, continuing the trend for consolidation in the legal market. With the ban on referral fees, firms may decide to invest more time and money in marketing strategies in order to target clients directly.
- The opening up of the legal market to alternative business structures may have a significant impact upon this practice area, as individual clients on the claimant side could be an ideal target group for the kind of service which might be offered by high-street brands like The Co-op entering the legal market.
- Some concerns have been expressed about the quality of the defence available to clinicians. The NHS Litigation Authority has reduced the number of firms on its panel, and increasingly demands that those that remain adhere to very strict rules when responding to claims.

Read our True Pictures on...

Browne Jacobson*	Mayer Brown
Baker & McKenzie	Michelmores
Bates Wells Braithwaite	Mills & Reeve
London	Nabarro
Burges Salmon	Penningtons Solicitors
Capsticks Solicitors*	Pinsent Masons
Charles Russell	RPC
Clyde & Co	Shoosmiths*
DWF*	Slater & Gordon
Eversheds	Stevens & Bolton
Foot Anstey	Taylor Wessing
Freeth Cartwright*	TLT
Herbert Smith Freehills	Trethowans
Higgs & Sons	Veale Wasbrough Vizards
Hill Dickinson	Ward Hadaway
Irwin Mitchell*	Wragge & Co
Kennedys	
Kingsley Napley	
Leigh Day	

* These firms have a particularly strong focus on personal injury

Practice Areas

Private Client & Charities

In a nutshell
You have money. You need to know how best to control it, preserve it and pass it on: enter the private client lawyer. Solicitors advise individuals, families and trusts on wealth management. Some offer additional matrimonial and small-scale commercial assistance; others focus exclusively on highly specialised tax and trusts issues, or wills and probate.

Charities lawyers advise on all aspects of non-profit organisations' activities including the defence of legacies bequeathed to a charity in a will. These specialists need exactly the same skills and knowledge as private client lawyers but must also have the same kind of commercial knowledge as corporate lawyers.

What lawyers do
Private client lawyers
- Draft wills in consultation with clients and expedite their implementation after death. Probate involves the appointment of an executor and the settling of an estate. Organising a house clearance or even a funeral is not beyond the scope of a lawyer's duties.
- Advise clients on the most tax-efficient and appropriate structure for holding money and assets. Lawyers must ensure their clients understand the foreign law implications of trusts held in offshore jurisdictions.
- Advise overseas clients interested in investing in the UK and banks whose overseas clients have UK interests.
- Assist clients with the very specific licensing, sales arrangements and tax planning issues related to ownership of heritage chattels (individual items or collections of cultural value or significance).
- Bring or defend litigation in relation to disputed legacies.

Charities lawyers
- Advise charities on registration, reorganisation, regulatory compliance and the implications of new legislation.
- Offer specialist trusts and investment advice.
- Advise on quasi-corporate and mainstream commercial matters, negotiate and draft contracts for sponsorship and the development of trading subsidiaries, manage property issues and handle IP concerns.

- Charities law still conjures up images of sleepy local fund-raising efforts or, alternatively, working on a trendy project for wealthy benefactors. The wide middle ground can incorporate working with a local authority, a local library and schools to establish an after-school homework programme, or rewriting the constitution of a 300-year-old church school to admit female pupils. Widespread international trust in English charity law means that you could also establish a study programme in Britain for a US university or negotiate the formation of a zebra conservation charity in Tanzania.

The realities of the job
- An interest in other people's affairs is going to help. A capacity for empathy coupled with impartiality and absolute discretion are the hallmarks of a good private client lawyer. You'll need to be able to relate to and earn the trust of your many varied clients.
- Despite not being as chaotic as other fields, the technical demands of private client work can be exacting and an academic streak goes a long way.
- A great deal of private client work is tax-based, particularly involving income and estate tax. Specialists in this area also need their corporate tax knowledge to be up to scratch as it's not unusual for the families they work for to have multimillion-dollar businesses to their names.
- The stereotype of the typical 'country gent' client is far from accurate: lottery wins, personal injury payouts, property portfolios, massive City salaries and successful businesses all feed the demand for legal advice.
- If you are wavering between private clients and commercial clients, charities law might offer a good balance.

Current issues
- Private client and advisory work has become more popular in the City since the recession as a way of making up for losses from the decrease in the amount of corporate work available and taking advantage of the fact that private investors have been filling the void left by diminished corporate funds.
- The private client world is becoming increasingly international. Wealthy people are selecting a wider geographical spread of assets, and London has become a hub for the management of these assets. Many clients come from Russia, the Middle East, the USA, India and France.

- In an attempt to regulate businesses outside of the SRA's jurisdiction, The Law Society launched its first recognised quality standard for wills and estate administration in 2013.
- Recent controversies around tax avoidance (which, unlike tax evasion, is not illegal) have put the spotlight on private cash being ferreted away in offshore financial centres like Jersey and the British Virgin Islands. Still, financial arrangements related to these and other territories remain important, and a group of small specialist law firms deals with much of the related legal work. You can find them ranked in the 'Offshore' category in *Chambers UK*.
- The Charities Act 2011 consolidated most previous laws related to the sector but did not make any substantive changes to their content.
- Firms have dedicated teams handling legacy disputes. The RSPCA, for example, has been actively involved in these types of claim.
- Economic uncertainty has brought many challenges for charities, particularly the large ones that rely heavily on public donations and/or government funding. One in six charities surveyed in late 2012 feared they may have to close in 2013 because of falling donations and cuts to public spending. Some charities are restructuring or becoming more innovative with fund-raising, while others look towards collaborative working.
- There is a growing interest in mergers between charities. One of the most publicised combinations was that of Age Concern and Help the Aged to form Age UK.
- Other matters concerning charities are conflicts of interests, 'whistle blowing' and information management. A theme running through these areas is getting governance right – something that tends to come into focus in harder economic times.
- The introduction of Alternative Business Structures may harm the revenue streams of smaller firms working on will drafting and probate. Some may not survive the increased competition while others may merge, forming a united front against the challenge of 'Tesco Law' created by the Legal Services Act.
- Firms right across the country bemoan a dearth of young lawyers who can claim to be true private client specialists. It looks like a good time to put your hand up and be counted.

Read our True Pictures on...

Addleshaw Goddard	Irwin Mitchell
Ashfords	Lawrence Graham
B P Collins	Lester Aldridge
Baker & McKenzie	Macfarlanes*
Bates Wells Braithwaite London	Maclay Murray & Spens
	Michelmores
Berwin Leighton Paisner	Mills & Reeve
Bircham Dyson Bell*	Mischon de Reya*
Bond Dickinson	Muckle
Boodle Hatfield*	Penningtons Solicitors*
Brabners Chaffe Street	Pinsent Masons
Browne Jacobson	SGH Martineau
Burges Salmon	Shoosmiths
Charles Russell*	Speechly Bircham*
Collyer Bristow*	Stevens & Bolton
Cripps Harries Hall*	Taylor Wessing
DWF	TLT
Farrer & Co*	Trethowans
Freeth Cartwright	Trowers & Hamlins
Gateley	Veale Wasbrough Vizards*
Gordons	Ward Hadaway
Hewitsons	Wilsons*
Higgs & Sons	Winckworth Sherwood
Hill Dickinson	Withers*

* These firms have a particularly strong focus on private client and charities.

Private Equity & Investment Management

In a nutshell

Private equity and investment firms operate funds that pool the investments of anybody prepared to part with their money for a sustained period of time. Private equity firms use investors' cash (equity) in combination with money raised from banks (debt) to buy companies or other assets with the goal of selling them on at a profit. When the targeted company's assets are used as leverage and a significant amount of bank debt is employed, the transaction is known as a leveraged buyout (LBO).

Venture capital is a subset of private equity that sees investors put money into start-up companies or small businesses in the hope they will be sold to a private equity firm or taken public. Although this typically entails high risk for the investor, it has the potential for above-average returns. This high risk is typically offset by investing smaller amounts over a shorter timespan. **Investment management** is the professional management of various securities (shares, bonds, etc.) and assets in order to meet specified investment goals. Investment management lawyers advise on the structuring, formation, taxation and regulation of all types of investment funds. A **hedge fund** is a private, actively managed investment fund. It aims to provide returns to investors by investing in a diverse range of markets and financial products, regardless of whether markets are rising or falling. Using the derivatives market helps hedge funds achieve this. A **mutual fund** is a collective investment vehicle that pools money from many investors to purchase securities. The term is most commonly applied to collective investments that are regulated and sold to the general public. A **real estate investment fund/trust** is a publicly traded investment vehicle that uses investors' money to invest in properties and mortgages. Both hedge funds and mutual funds generally operate as **open funds**. This means that investors may periodically make additions to, or withdrawals from, their stakes in the fund. An investor will generally purchase shares in the fund directly from the fund itself rather than from the existing shareholders. This contrasts with a **closed fund**, which typically issues all the shares it will issue at the outset, with such shares usually being tradable between investors thereafter.

What lawyers do

- Advise private equity firms on how to structure new funds.
- Help private equity firms negotiate the terms on which investors contribute their money.
- Act for private funds when they buy and sell investments.

- Assist clients throughout the fund-raising process. This includes the preparation of offer materials and partnership agreements; advising on and documenting management and compensation arrangements; and closing fund formation transactions.
- Conduct diligence and negotiate contracts.
- Draft the numerous organisational documents necessary to form an investment fund. The private placement memorandum is key – it's a prospectus detailing the terms of the investment, minimum investor requirements, risk factors, who the investment manager is, and the strategy to be employed by the fund. If the fund is a limited partnership, it will need a limited partnership agreement, and if it's a limited liability company, it will need an operating agreement as well as an investor subscription agreement.
- Inform and advise clients on the constantly changing regulatory and compliance issues arising under UK and international securities and tax law.
- Provide day-to-day advice with respect to issues such as performance and advertising and brokerage and portfolio trading practices.

Realities of the job

- Small teams mean that trainees can get high levels of responsibility and client exposure rather than being stuck doing more mundane tasks. You can expect to be involved in drafting key documents and reviewing transfer agreements and to play a part in large-scale negotiations that could involve hundreds of parties at the same time.
- Structuring funds requires an intimate familiarity with the relevant securities and investment company rules. Understanding and being able to apply knowledge of key financial legislation is a vital skill.
- Setting up funds also requires a significant amount of tax and general finance industry knowledge. Funds lawyers often work in close collaboration with their tax and finance colleagues.
- Good people skills and a tough attitude are a must. Private equity lawyers work closely with clients to offer advice on a wide range of areas, and need to be able to explain the constantly evolving private fund markets to them, as well as understand the time-sensitive nature of fund organisation. Fortunately, clients are entrepreneurial and tend to have a good understanding of the world of business, meaning they can pick up on issues quickly.

Practice Areas

Current issues

- Recent years have been tough for UK private equity, as investors are reluctant to pay high fees – driven in part by very high management salaries – in an economic climate where returns are low.
- Private equity funds prefer to invest in real estate and companies with steady income streams but cheap stock prices. Any industry facing the need to increase efficiency, but with guaranteed demand for its products and services, is potentially a good investment.
- Economic conditions mean firms are finding it hard to find safe places to invest their money. Increasingly popular choices include consumer products and retail, technology companies – especially software providers – and the energy sector.
- The coalition government's spending cuts have led a move towards privatisation. Private equity firms and other commercial organisations are bidding against public sector providers for public service contracts. So far, the healthcare and social housing sectors have been the main targets for private equity buyouts, but firms are also moving in on educational institutions.
- Law firms are also finding that private equity firms are taking advantage of the new rules on alternative business structures to invest in public-facing areas of law like conveyancing, wills and personal injury.
- The EU and the Financial Conduct Authority (FCA) are looking to extend the same rules which already govern banks and investment firms to private equity firms. The EU's Alternative Investment Fund Managers Directive (AIFMD) puts hedge funds and private equity funds under the supervision of an EU regulatory body, with tougher rules on risk management and new limits on pay and bonuses.

Read our True Pictures on...

Addleshaw Godard	Macfarlanes
Allen & Overy	Mills & Reeve
Ashurst	Nabarro
Baker & McKenzie	Norton Rose Fulbright
Berwin Leighton Paisner	Olswang
Bird & Bird	Orrick
Burges Salmon	Osborne Clarke
Cleary Gottlieb	Pinsent Masons
Clifford Chance	Reed Smith
CMS	Sidley Austin
Covington & Burling	Simmons & Simmons
Dechert	SJ Berwin
DLA Piper	Skadden
Eversheds	Slaughter and May
Freshfields	Speechly Bircham
Herbert Smith Freehills	Squire Sanders
Hogan Lovells	Stephenson Harwood
Jones Day	Taylor Wessing
K&L Gates	Travers Smith
Kirkland & Ellis	Weil, Gotshal & Manges
Latham & Watkins	White & Case
Linklaters	

Projects & Energy

In a nutshell

Projects

Projects lawyers work hand in hand with finance and corporate lawyers to enable complex construction, redevelopment and infrastructure projects to come to fruition. A few City firms and the largest US practices dominate the biggest international projects, but there's work countrywide. Many projects relate to the energy sector (see below), while road, rail and telecoms infrastructure projects are also big business. UK lawyers also work on overseas natural resources and mining projects, while domestically waste and utilities projects provide work for many regional firms. The Private Finance Initiative (PFI) – an aspect of Public Private Partnerships (PPP) – has also been an important source of work. PFI introduced private funding and management into areas that were previously public sector domains.

Some law firms consistently represent project companies, usually through a 'special purpose vehicle' (SPV) established to build, own and operate the end result of the project. Often the project company is a joint venture between various 'sponsor' companies. An SPV could also be partially owned by a government body or banks. Other firms consistently represent organisations which commission projects. Then there are the firms that act purely on the finance side for banks, guarantors, export credit agencies, governments and international funding agencies.

Energy

If a firm has an energy practice, most of its work will be based around oil and gas. This breaks down into upstream and downstream work. Upstream refers to the locating and exploiting of oil and gas fields (think 'drill, baby, drill' and you get the picture). Downstream refers to everything related to transport, processing and distribution – pipelines, refineries, petrol stations etc. Many firms that do energy work trumpet their renewable energy and climate change expertise, but at any firm this will be a very small practice area. Power and utilities, and environment/regulatory are two other areas which are often considered to fall under the energy/projects umbrella.

What lawyers do

Projects

- The work of an energy or projects lawyer mirrors that of a corporate lawyer – drafting, due diligence, getting parties to sign agreements – with several added layers of complexity.
- There are several components to any project: financing, development and (often) subsequent litigation. Lawyers usually specialise in one of these areas, although they do overlap.
- The field also encompasses specialists in areas like construction, real estate, planning, telecoms, healthcare and the public sector.
- The financing of a project is riskier for lenders than other transactions are, as there is no collateral to act as security for the loan. For this reason risk is often spread across several stakeholders including the SPV, shareholders, the contractor, supplier etc. The agreements which govern the relationship between the parties are the primary domain of lawyers acting for the project company.
- Lawyers who act for lenders check over all project documentation, paying attention to the risks the lender is exposed to.
- Site visits and meetings on location are common.

Energy

- Internationally, energy lawyers work on the contracts and licenses agreed between international energy companies, governments and local companies. The upstream component of energy work often involves governments, as they have the exclusive rights to certain natural resources.
- Domestically, lawyers often interact with the Department for Energy and Climate Change (DECC). Energy is a highly regulated sector, and there are many government programmes and stimuli to encourage certain types of energy projects. EU regulations also frequently come into play.
- Some energy lawyers work on energy infrastructure projects, but usually an energy lawyer is someone who works on contracts and agreements over (oil and gas) resources already being tapped. For example, they might produce so-called Production Sharing Agreements, which detail which proportion of profits go to different parties.
- Because energy companies have very deep pockets, many energy financings happen without the need for a loan (this is called 'off-balance-sheet financing').
- Disputes in the energy sector are often resolved through arbitration, particularly when they have an international element to them (which is often).

The realities of the job

- Projects require lawyers who enjoy the challenge of creating a complex scheme and figuring out all its possibilities and pitfalls. Projects can run for years, involving multidisciplinary legal work spanning finance, regulatory permissions, construction, employment law and much more.
- The value of transactions can vary from a few million pounds for projects to build domestic waste plants to deals worth billions to exploit massive oil fields. You have to get your head around these big numbers and understand what they actually mean: often the sum of money involved is the (potential) value of a joint venture or natural resource deposit. One of the things projects lawyers like about their job is that the product of their dealmaking is tangible: they can usually watch a mine, bridge or oil refinery being built before their eyes.
- The world's energy resources have helpfully positioned themselves in some of the world's most politically unstable or dubious countries (Venezuela, Russia, Saudi Arabia, Iraq, Iran, Nigeria etc.). This adds an extra layer of interest and intrigue to many transactions. For example, the due diligence on building a diamond mine in West Africa might involve consideration of how many AK-47s and armoured personnel carriers the mine will need to operate.

Current issues

- The difficult market conditions caused by the recession have made it hard for companies to obtain financing for projects. After two years of decline, the volume of global project finance rose in 2010 and 2011 but reportedly slumped again in 2012.
- In July 2012 the coalition government announced it would underwrite up to £40bn of funding for infrastructure projects to kick-start the sector.
- In Europe, energy security is a key concern for governments as political actions in the recent past have highlighted the problematic nature of relying on a small number of countries (or just one) for domestic energy requirements. An obvious example of the interest in energy security is the development of LNG (liquid natural gas) storage and pipeline projects in Eastern Europe.
- The renewable energy sector is small but booming. Projects have mostly continued unabated despite the economic downturn due to their long-term nature. Renewable energy remains a key area of investment as it satisfies both government commitments to energy security and carbon emissions targets. The UK is already the world's number one offshore wind energy generator and several more massive wind farm projects are under construction or planned. Biomass also produces a significant proportion of

Read our True Pictures on...

Ashurst	Ince & Co
Addleshaw Goddard	Latham & Watkins
Allen & Overy	Linklaters
Baker & McKenzie	Maclay Murray & Spens
Berwin Leighton Paisner	Mayer Brown
Bond Dickinson	Memery Crystal
Burges Salmon	Mills & Reeve
Clifford Chance	Nabarro
Clyde & Co	Norton Rose Fulbright
CMS*	Pinsent Masons
Dentons*	Shearman & Sterling
DLA Piper	Simmons & Simmons
DWF	Skadden
Eversheds	Slaughter and May
Freeth Cartwright	TLT
Freshfields	Vinson & Elkins*
Gateley	Watson, Farley & Williams
Herbert Smith Freehills*	White & Case*
Hogan Lovells	Wragge & Co

* These firms have a particularly strong focus on projects & energy.

UK renewable energy, while solar remains of negligible importance.

- Nuclear technology is a key focus as being the most potent source of electricity for reducing carbon. Plans are currently underway to build four new nuclear power stations in the UK; construction of a £14bn plant at Hinkley Point in Somerset was given the go-ahead in early 2013. Investments are also being put in place to make old coal-fired power stations more carbon efficient.
- City lawyers are working on an increasing number of energy exploration and infrastructure projects overseas, especially in the BRIC countries, but also in Africa. The Middle East, with its oil reserves, continues to be a key area for investment.
- The USA is experiencing a shale gas boom – a technique called 'fracking' is used to blow the gas out of air pockets in layers of rock. The UK is now known to have the world's largest shale-gas field, the Bowland Shale, which lies beneath Lancashire and Yorkshire. According to some, tapping it could ensure massive cuts in carbon emissions as well as providing energy security and more jobs. Although natural gas is more environmentally friendly than coal, there are several environmental objections to fracking, but if these are overcome this will undoubtedly become a growth area.

Property/Real Estate

In a nutshell
Property lawyers, like their corporate law colleagues, are essentially transactional lawyers; the only real difference is that real estate deals require an extra layer of specialist legal and procedural knowledge and there aren't quite so many pesky regulatory authorities. The work centres on buildings and land of all types, and even the most oblique legal concepts have a bricks-and-mortar or human basis to them. It is common for lawyers to develop a specialism within this field, such as residential conveyancing, mortgage lending and property finance, social housing, or the leisure and hotels sector. Most firms have a property department, and the larger the department the more likely the lawyers are to specialise. Note: 'property' and 'real estate' are entirely interchangeable terms.

What lawyers do
- Negotiate sales, purchases and leases of land and buildings, and advise on the structure of deals.
- Record the terms of an agreement in legal documents.
- Gather and analyse factual information about properties from the owners, surveyors, local authorities and the Land Registry.
- Prepare reports for buyers and anyone lending money.
- Manage the transfer of money and the handover of properties to new owners or occupiers.
- Take the appropriate steps to register new owners and protect the interests of lenders or investors.
- Advise clients on their responsibilities in leasehold relationships, and on how to take action if problems arise.
- Help developers get all the necessary permissions to build, alter or change the permitted use of properties.
- Manage property portfolio investments and advise real estate funds.

The realities of the job
- Property lawyers have to multi-task. A single deal could involve many hundreds of properties and your caseload could contain scores of files, all at different stages in the process. You'll have to keep organised.
- Good drafting skills require attention to detail and careful thought. Plus you need to keep up to date with industry trends and standards.
- Some clients get antsy; you have to be able to explain legal problems in lay terms.

- Despite some site visits, this is mainly a desk job with a lot of time spent on the phone to other solicitors, estate agents, civil servants and consultants.
- Most instances of solicitor negligence occur in this area of practice. There is so much that can go wrong.
- Your days will be busy, but generally the hours are more sociable and predictable.

Current issues
- Arguably the most cyclical legal area around, property practice will always and has always followed the market. In a down economy there's less demand for properties and new developments, values plummet and conventional bank lending becomes increasingly hard to find. Still, the UK property market is getting a boost from alternative sources of investment and government stimuli – as the economy recovers, the real estate sector is bound to perk up too.
- Overall, global property markets are starting to grow again, but eurozone house prices continue to fare badly, with the blight spreading from Southern Europe to affect other countries too.
- Despite forecasts that UK house prices would stagnate in 2013, the average house price in the UK rose by 4% in the first half of the year. London prices are increasingly outpacing the rest of the UK – they are 5% higher than they were in 2007, pre-property crash, while across the country prices have fallen 9% since then.
- The residential property market has been boosted by recent government stimuli, including the Help to Buy scheme, which supports buyers of new-build homes.
- Apart from big government infrastructure projects like Crossrail and the Hinkley Point nuclear power station, the public sector real estate market has slowed. Social housing has been hit particularly hard.
- Commercial property – big office buildings, shopping centres – is seen as a good investment by overseas buyers, as it offers both high rentals and good liquidity, meaning that it can be sold quickly with minimal loss of value. The UK attracted £16bn worth of foreign investment in commercial property in 2012, up 61% from 2011. These foreign investors include cash-rich sovereign wealth funds, often from the Middle East, and private equity firms, which are often American.
- Generally, property litigation is a booming area at the moment, even though matters are not necessarily going all the way to court due to cost implications.

- The slow economy means more insolvency, with the knock-on result that some former tenants are being pursued when their assignees default. There are also more break clause disputes. The volume of general landlord and tenant dilapidations work is also up – with landlords looking for somebody to blame, they are picking over every last detail.
- There's been an upturn in professional negligence claims against valuers as home-owners are left in negative equity.
- There has been a shift towards the refinancing of existing deals in the wake of the general downturn in new transactions, with landlords having to be much more flexible than in previous years. Landlords are keen to avoid the dreaded 'empty rates' scenario, where they are forced to pay for buildings without occupiers.
- UK investors in real estate have been using pension funds, insurers and the bond market as alternative sources of finance – the value of non-bank debt grew by over a third in 2012. As the property market starts to recover, banks are also taking cautious steps to start lending again.

Read our True Pictures on...

Addleshaw Goddard	Macfarlanes
Allen & Overy	Maclay Murray & Spens
Ashfords	Mayer Brown
Ashurst	Memery Crystal
B P Collins	Michelmores
Berwin Leighton Paisner	Mills & Reeve
Bircham Dyson Bell	Mischon de Reya
Bird & Bird	Muckle
Bond Dickinson	Nabarro
Boodle Hatfield	Norton Rose Fulbright
BPE Solicitors	Olswang
Brabners Chaffe Street	Paul Hastings
Browne Jacobson	Penningtons Solicitors
Burges Salmon	Pinsent Masons
Charles Russell	Reed Smith
Clifford Chance	SGH Martineau
Clyde & Co	Shoosmiths
Cripps Harries Hall	Sidley Austin
Dentons	Simmons & Simmons
DWF	SJ Berwin
Eversheds	Speechly Bircham
Farrer & Co	Squire Sanders
Foot Anstey	Stephenson Harwood
Freeth Cartwright	Stevens & Bolton
Freshfields	Taylor Wessing
Gateley	TLT
Gordons	Travers Smith
Herbert Smith Freehills	Trethowans
Higgs & Sons	Veale Wasbrough Vizards
Hill Dickinson	Walker Morris
Hogan Lovells	Ward Hadaway
Irwin Mitchell	Wedlake Bell
Jones Day	Wilsons
K&L Gates	Winckworth Sherwood
Lawrence Graham	Wragge & Co
Lester Aldridge	
Linklaters	

Restructuring & Insolvency

In a nutshell

Insolvency law governs the position of businesses and individuals who are in financial difficulties and unable to repay their debts as they become due. Such a situation may lead to insolvency proceedings, in which legal action is taken against the insolvent entity and assets may be liquidated to pay off outstanding debts. Before a company or individual gets involved in insolvency proceedings, they will probably be involved in a restructuring or an out-of-court arrangement with creditors to work out alternative repayment schedules. The work of lawyers in the field can therefore be non-contentious (restructuring) or contentious (insolvency litigation), and their role will vary depending on whether they act for debtors or their creditors. What follows are some of the terms you'll come across.

Debtor: an individual or company that owes money. **Creditor:** a person or institution that extends credit to another entity on condition that it is paid back at a later date. **Bankruptcy:** term used in the USA to describe insolvency procedures that apply to companies, but not in the UK, where the term applies to individuals only. **Restructuring:** a significant modification made to the debt, operations or structure of a company with its creditors' consent. After a restructuring, debt repayments become more manageable, making insolvency proceedings less likely. **Insolvency proceedings:** generic term that covers a variety of statutory proceedings aimed at rescuing or winding up an insolvent company.

Insolvency proceedings include the following actions. **Company voluntary arrangement (CVA):** if it is clear that a business could survive if debt repayments were reduced, it can enter a CVA agreement with its creditors. Under this legally binding agreement, a struggling company is allowed to repay some, or all, of its historic debts out of future profits, over an agreed period of time. **Administration:** when in administration, a company is protected from creditors enforcing their debts while an administrator takes over the management of its affairs. If the company is fundamentally sound, the administrator will implement a recovery plan aimed at streamlining the business and maximising profits. If it is apparent that the company has no future then it can be sold or liquidation can commence.

Receivership: unlike administration, this is initiated by the company's creditors, not the company itself. A receiver is appointed by the court and must look to recover as much money as possible in order to settle the claims made by creditors. Under receivership, the interests of the creditors clearly take precedence over the survival of the company. **Liquidation:** procedure by which the assets of a company are placed under the control of a liquidator. In most cases, a company in liquidation ceases to trade, and the liquidator will sell the company's assets and distribute the proceeds to creditors. There are two forms: voluntary liquidation brought about by the company itself or compulsory liquidation brought about by court order. **Distressed M&A:** the sale of all or a portion of an insolvent business is an efficient way to preserve going-concern value and avoid the potential for substantial loss of value through a piecemeal liquidation. **Pre-pack sale:** refers to a deal made with an interested buyer to sell the insolvent company's business and assets, negotiated before an administrator is appointed and completed immediately on appointment. Such schemes are becoming increasingly popular and more frequently used in the current economic climate.

What lawyers do

Debtors' lawyers

- Meet with clients to assess the gravity of the situation, highlight the available options and advise on the best course of action to follow.
- In a restructuring, advise the insolvent company on the reorganisation of its balance sheet (such as closing down unprofitable businesses or refinancing its debt) and assist in negotiations with creditors.
- Assist in insolvency filings, and once proceedings have commenced, work closely with the insolvency officeholders (that is those appointed as administrators, receivers or liquidators) and accountants, to achieve the goals set for the insolvent company.
- Provide advice to directors of insolvent companies, explaining their duties to creditors.
- Advise on the sale of assets or mergers and acquisitions of troubled companies.
- Assist clients in insolvency litigation and appeals. Provide preventative advice to debtor clients on liability management and ways to avoid insolvency proceedings.

Creditors' lawyers

- Meet with creditor clients to assess the validity of their security over the insolvent company, the strength of their position in the creditors' pool and the best course of action to ensure full recovery.
- Assist in negotiations with debtors and insolvency officeholders.
- Represent clients in insolvency litigation and appeals.
- Assist in the tracing and valuation of debtors' assets.
- Provide training to their clients on how to deal with insolvent companies.

Practice Areas

The realities of the job

- Large City firms deal almost exclusively with large-scale corporate restructurings and insolvencies and the representation of creditor groups in these matters. Smaller regional firms mostly assist on smaller corporate and personal insolvency cases.
- Corporate insolvency as a practice area is extremely varied as proceedings affect every aspect of the insolvent company. Lawyers therefore need to be conversant in a variety of legal disciplines or know when to refer matters to specialists in employment, banking, property, litigation, corporate, etc.
- When financial difficulties arise in companies, the rapid deployment of a legal team is necessary to provide immediate assistance. This area of law is extremely fast-paced, and lawyers are often asked to deliver solutions overnight.
- Insolvency and restructuring involves mountains of paperwork, so lawyers need to be organised and able to prioritise their workload, particularly when dealing with multiple assignments. With so much at stake, attention to detail is paramount when drafting asset sale agreements or documents to be filed at court.
- Restructuring and insolvency situations are understandably tense for both debtors and creditors, and lawyers sometimes need to deal with difficult people, so they must be able to hold their ground and show they are not easily intimidated.
- You will need to immerse yourself in both the financial and corporate worlds. Get started by reading the *FT* or the City pages of a broadsheet.

Current issues

- Although the UK economy is showing signs of recovery, the restructuring market remains busy. Some major names to have entered administration over the past two years include Clinton Cards, JJB Sports, Comet, Jessops and HMV.
- Despite these high-profile cases, the number of corporate insolvencies has actually decreased considerably over the past year. There were just over 4,500 cases in the first quarter of 2013, nearly 19% lower than the same period in 2012.
- Sovereign debt defaults form an increasing threat to the world economy. More volatility in this market is having a marked effect on banks and investors.
- HMRC's Time to Pay (TTP) Scheme means debt-laden small and medium-sized entrepreneurs have been treated leniently in the last few years. As this scheme continues to wind down, it's likely to prove very harmful to small businesses.
- There's been a remarkable upsurge in the number of 'zombie' companies, a term used to describe those which are only able to repay the interest on their debt. Experts believe, however, that these businesses are surviving simply because of low interest rates

Read our True Pictures on...

Addleshaw Goddard	Mayer Brown
Allen & Overy	Michelmores
Ashfords	Mills & Reeve
Ashurst	Muckle
Baker & McKenzie	Nabarro
Berwin Leighton Paisner	Norton Rose Fulbright
Bingham McCutchen	Olswang
Bond Dickinson	Osborne Clarke
Brabners Chaffe Street	Paul Hastings
Browne Jacobson	Pinsent Masons
Burges Salmon	SGH Martineau
Charles Russell	Shearman & Sterling
Clifford Chance	Shoosmiths
Clyde & Co	Sidley Austin
CMS	Simmons & Simmons
Dentons	SJ Berwin
DLA Piper	Skadden
DWF	Slaughter and May
Eversheds	Speechly Bircham
Freeth Cartwright	Squire Sanders
Freshfields	Stevens & Bolton
Gateley	Taylor Wessing
Herbert Smith Freehills	TLT
Hill Dickinson	Travers Smith
Hogan Lovells	Veale Wasbrough Vizards
Irwin Mitchell	Walker Morris
Jones Day	Ward Hadaway
Kirkland & Ellis	Weil, Gotshal & Manges
Latham & Watkins	White & Case
Lester Aldridge	Wragge & Co
Linklaters	
Maclay Murray & Spens	

and will face serious difficulties when economic conditions change.

- The sectors hit hardest by the recession – and therefore the busiest in relation to restructuring – were construction and property. Nonetheless, insolvency cases have cropped up everywhere, so lawyers need to be up to speed with a wide range of industry issues.
- Figures show that individual insolvencies in the UK have fallen to their lowest levels since the start of the financial crisis, as roughly 25,000 borrowers resorted to personal insolvency in the first quarter of 2013 – almost a 13% drop compared to the same period in 2012.

Shipping

In a nutshell

Shipping lawyers deal with the carriage of goods or people by sea, plus any and every matter related to the financing, construction, use, insurance and decommissioning of the ships that carry them (or are arrested, sunk or salvaged while carrying them). Despite being the preserve of specialist firms, or relatively self-contained practice groups within larger firms, the discipline offers varied challenges. The major division is between 'wet' work relating to accidents or misadventure at sea, and 'dry' work involving the land-based, commercial and contractual side. In extension, disputes or litigation relating to contracts means there is also a contentious side to dry work. While some lawyers in the area may be generalists, it is more common to specialise.

What lawyers do

Wet lawyers
- Act swiftly and decisively at a moment's notice to protect a client's interests and minimise any loss.
- Travel the world to assess the condition of ships, interview crew or witnesses and prepare cases.
- Take witness statements and advise clients on the merits of and strategy for cases.
- Handle court and arbitration appearances, conferences with barristers and client meetings.

Dry lawyers
- Negotiate and draft contracts for ship finance and shipbuilding, crew employment, sale and purchase agreements, affreightment contracts, and the registration and re-flagging of ships.
- May specialise in niche areas such as yachts or fishing, an area in which regulatory issues feature prominently.
- Handle similar tasks to wet lawyers in relation to contractual disputes but are less likely to jet off around the world at the drop of a hat.

The realities of the job
- Wet work offers the excitement of international assignments and clients, so lawyers need to react coolly to sudden emergencies and travel to far-flung places to offer practical and pragmatic analysis and advice.
- Despite the perils and pleasures of dealing with clients and instructions on the other side of the world, the hours are likely to be steady beyond those international-rescue moments.

- Non-contentious work touches on the intricacies of international trade, so it's as important to keep up with sector knowledge as legal developments.
- Dealing with a mixed clientele from all points on the social compass, you'll need to be just as comfortable extracting a comprehensible statement from a Norwegian merchant seaman as conducting negotiations with major financiers.
- Contentious cases are driven by the procedural rules and timetable of the court or arbitration forum to which the matter has been referred. A solid grasp of procedure is as important as a strong foundation in tort and contract law.
- Some shipping lawyers do come from a naval background or are ex-mariners, but you won't be becalmed if the closest comparable experience you've had is steering Tommy Tugboat in the bath, as long as you can show a credible interest in the discipline.
- Though not an all-boys club, parts of the shipping world are still male dominated. Women lawyers and clients are more commonly found on the dry side.
- In the UK, shipping law is centred around London and a few other port cities. Major international centres include Piraeus in Greece, Hong Kong and Singapore. Some trainees even get to work in these locations.

Current issues
- The shipping market was quite severely blown off course in the recession. Some suggested that the top end of the market plummeted between 90% and 100% in a matter of weeks.
- The global shipping market remains volatile. Some areas areas are slowly recovering, but tanker and dry bulk rates are still dire.
- Decreased demand for raw materials has hit the industry hard. Because shipments and ships are big, slow and expensive, the shipping market is not very versatile. The recent fall in oil prices, however, has enabled shipping companies to operate more profitably.
- The tonnage on order at shipyards has increased over the past year, but shipping finance is still in the doldrums. New deals are being done though. For example, Singapore's Neptune Orient Lines recently secured $1.1bn worth of financing for the building of 12 new container ships. As this example indicates, the Asian market is doing better than most, with the Chinese government providing financial backing and Chinese commercial banks doing a lot of lending. 2012 figures

show freight turnover in China increased 12.4% year-on-year.

- The amount of contentious work arising directly from the economic crisis has tailed off as contracts have been renegotiated and remaining businesses have stabilised their positions in the market.
- Piracy remains a significant concern, although the number of incidents of Somali piracy off the coast of East Africa has fallen dramatically. In practice, shipping law tends to focus on the ships themselves rather than the pirates, and as yet, no pirates have been brought to trial in the UK (although this could happen in future).

Read our True Pictures on...

Ashfords	Lester Aldridge
Clyde & Co*	Norton Rose Fulbright
Eversheds	Pinsent Masons
Gateley	Reed Smith*
Hill Dickinson*	Stephenson Harwood*
Holman Fenwick Willan*	Thomas Cooper*
Ince & Co*	TLT

* These firms have a particularly strong focus on shipping.

Sports, Media & Entertainment

In a nutshell

Advertising and marketing lawyers offer advice to ensure a client's products or advertisements are compliant with industry standards, plus general advice on anything from contracts between clients, media and suppliers, to employment law, corporate transactions and litigation. Entertainment lawyers assist clients in the film, broadcasting, music, theatre and publishing industries with commercial legal advice or litigation. Strictly speaking, sports lawyers work in an industry sector rather than a specific legal discipline, and firms draw on the expertise of individuals from several practice groups. Reputation management lawyers advise clients on how best to protect their own 'brand', be this through a defamation suit or an objection to invasion of privacy.

What lawyers do

Advertising and marketing
- Ensure advertising campaigns comply with legislation or regulatory codes set out by the Advertising Standards Agency or Ofcom.
- Advise on comparative advertising, unauthorised references to living persons and potential trade mark infringements.
- Defend clients against allegations that their work has infringed regulations or the rights of third parties. Bring complaints against competitors' advertising.

TV and film
- Advise production companies on every stage of the creation of programmes and films.
- Assist on the banking and lending transactions which ensure financing for a film, as well as tax exemption rules for UK films.
- Help engage performers; negotiate a multitude of ancillary contracts; negotiate distribution and worldwide rights.

Music
- Advise major recording companies, independent labels and talent (record producers, songwriters and artists).
- Advise on contracts, such as those between labels and bands, or between labels and third parties.
- Offer contentious and non-contentious copyright and trade mark advice relating to music, image rights and merchandising.
- Offer criminal advice when things get old-school rock 'n' roll.
- Assist with immigration issues.

Theatre and publishing
- Advise theatre and opera companies, producers, agents and actors on contracts, funding and sponsorship/merchandising.
- Advise publishing companies and newspapers on contractual, licensing, copyright and libel matters.
- Assist with immigration issues.

Sports
- Assist with contract negotiations, be they between clubs and sportspeople, agents and players, sporting institutions and sponsors, broadcasters and sports governing bodies.
- Handle varied employment and immigration issues.
- Advise on corporate or commercial matters like takeovers, public offerings, debt restructuring and bankruptcy, or the securing and structuring of credit.
- Enforce IP rights in the lucrative merchandise market and negotiate on matters affecting a sportsperson's image rights.
- Work on regulatory compliance issues within a sport or matters relating to the friction between sports regulations and EU/national law.
- Offer reputation management and criminal advice.

Reputation management (incl. defamation and libel)
- Claimants' lawyers advise individuals – commonly celebrities, politicians or high-profile businessmen – on the nature of any potential libel action or breach of privacy claim, usually against broadcasters or publishers, before it either settles or goes to court.
- Defendants' lawyers advise broadcasters or other publishers on libel claims brought against them. With the burden of proof on the defendant, the lawyers must prove that what was published caused no loss to the claimant or was not libellous.
- Help clients stay out of hot water by giving pre-publication advice to authors, editors or production companies.

The realities of the job
- Advertising lawyers must have a good knowledge of advertising regulations, defamation and IP law.
- Clients are creative, lively and demanding.
- The issues thrown up can be fascinating and must be dealt with creatively.
- Many advertising disputes will be settled via regulatory bodies but some, particularly IP infringements, end in litigation.
- Entertainment lawyers need to be completely immersed in their chosen media and have a good grasp of copyright and contract law.

- Clients look to you for the rigour and discipline they may rarely exercise themselves.
- Sports lawyers need to be proactive, passionate and have bags of commercial nous. They must be able to deal with people involved at all levels of all sports.
- Reputation management lawyers need a comprehensive understanding of libel and privacy laws and an ability to think laterally. Individual claimants will be stressed and upset, so people skills, patience and resourcefulness are much needed.
- Solicitors prepare cases, but barristers almost always get the glory.

Current issues

- Web-based interactive, 'smart' advertising is throwing up all kinds of data protection and privacy issues. The attempt to regulate online content in the wake of the Digital Economy Act and the Audiovisual Media Services (AVMS) Directive is increasing demand for legal services.
- Although internet advertising is a big growth area, spending on magazine and newspaper adverts is falling sharply.
- There is an intensified public interest in sensitive areas such as gambling, alcohol and products targeting children. Various changes have been made to advertising codes by the Committee of Advertising Practice (CAP), which is the ASA's sister organisation.
- Overseas investment in UK film and television continues and has been boosted by government tax credits.
- Online television has grown a great deal and broadcasters are attempting to generate new revenue streams to offset a commensurate decline in advertising revenues.
- Efforts to tackle online piracy are gaining teeth. In the USA, pirate sites are being barred from hosting adverts by big companies like Google and Yahoo – the Internet Advertising Bureau (IAB) in the UK is working on a similar scheme.
- The rise of smart phones and tablets has created an explosion in demand for related services like apps, feeding a deluge of opportunities for new players in the market. It's also becoming clear which digital and audio-visual services consumers are and are not willing pay for. Media outlets are developing ways to negotiate the digital economy, deciding whether to offer free content online or put up pay-walls. This is directly affecting print media too, with online competition forcing *Time Out* to switch to free print distribution.
- The music industry continues to face challenges: illegal downloading and piracy are the biggest concerns. Sales of physical products are declining rapidly, so deals that combine physical sales with merchandising and live appearances are increasingly common.

Read our True Pictures on...

Addleshaw Goddard	Hogan Lovells
Baker & McKenzie	K&L Kates
Bates Wells Braithwaite	Lewis Silkin*
Berwin Leighton Paisner	Macfarlanes
Bird & Bird	Mishcon de Reya
Bond Dickinson	Olswang
Brabners Chaffe Street	Osborne Clarke
Bristows	Peters & Peters
Charles Russell	Pinsent Masons
CMS	Reed Smith
Collyer Bristow*	RPC
Dentons	Sheridans*
DLA Piper	Slaughter and May
Eversheds	Squire Sanders
Farrer & Co	Taylor Wessing
Gateley	Travers Smith
Harbottle & Lewis*	Withers
Herbert Smith Freehills	

* These firms have a particularly strong focus on media law.

- The 2010s have been hailed as a 'golden decade' of sporting events for the UK. Following on from the Olympics, there's the 2013 Ashes, the 2014 Commonwealth Games (in Glasgow), the 2015 Rugby World Cup, the 2017 Athletics World Championships and the 2019 Cricket World Cup.
- Football clubs' finances have continued to hit the headlines. Coventry City went into administration in 2013 following Rangers in 2012. Clubs have also been attracting interest from overseas investors.
- Enhanced TV deals are providing clubs with improved revenue streams and the Premiership's overseas broadcasting rights for 2010 to 2013 have doubled, from £625m to £1.4bn.
- The 2013 Defamation Act means that claimants can only sue for defamation if they have suffered serious harm to their reputation, and if they are companies they must demonstrate financial loss. It will also limit (but not halt) 'libel tourism' by making it much harder for individuals who live outside the country to be sued in the London courts.
- After Sally Bercow's notorious tweet 'Why is Lord McAlpine trending? *innocent face*' was ruled libellous, there's a new focus on what can and can't be said on social media. Defamation lawyers are involved in getting libellous statements taken off the internet fast.
- The aftershocks of the Leveson Inquiry are still being felt, with phone-hacking claims against News International continuing. Cross-party talks on implementing the Leveson Report broke down in March 2013 and it's unclear how any reforms will be carried forward.

Tax

In a nutshell

Tax lawyers ensure that clients structure their business deals or day-to-day operations such that they take advantage of legal breaks and loopholes in tax legislation. Although it's predominantly an advisory practice area, on occasion matters can veer into litigation territory. Tax law is most often used in private client and corporate matters.

What lawyers do

- Handle tax planning for clients, making sure they understand the tax ramifications of the purchase; handle ownership and disposal of assets, including advising on structuring corporate portfolios in the most tax-efficient way.
- Offer transactional advice when working with corporate lawyers on M&A deals, joint ventures and property portfolio acquisitions.
- Deal with investigations or litigation resulting from prosecution by Her Majesty's Revenue & Customs (HMRC). Litigation is always conducted against or brought by the government.
- Work alongside private client lawyers on matters of private wealth.

The realities of the job

- This is an intellectually rigorous, rather cloistered area of law and is ideally suited to the more academic.
- Corporate tax lawyers are very well paid, treated with reverence by their colleagues and find intellectual stimulation in their work.
- Lawyers must not only have the ability to translate and implement complex tax legislation, but must also be able to advise on how to structure deals in a legitimate and tax-efficient way to avoid conflict with HMRC.
- If you don't already wear specs, expect to after a couple of years of poring over all that black letter law. The UK has more pages of tax legislation than almost any other country, and there are changes every year.
- In time extra qualifications, such as the Chartered Tax Adviser exams, will be useful.
- Read our True Picture on the **Government Legal Service** to find out about working at HMRC.

Read our True Pictures on...

Addleshaw Goddard	Maclay Murray & Spens
Allen & Overy	Mayer Brown
Ashurst	Mills & Reeve
Baker & McKenzie	Nabarro
Berwin Leighton Paisner	Norton Rose Fulbright
Bond Dickinson	Olswang
Brabners Chaffe Street	Osborne Clarke
Burges Salmon	Penningtons Solicitors
Clifford Chance	Peters & Peters
CMS	Pinsent Masons
Dechert	RPC
Dentons	Shoosmiths
DLA Piper	Sidley Austin
DWF	Simmons & Simmons
Eversheds	SJ Berwin
Foot Anstey	Skadden
Freshfields	Slaughter and May
Gateley	Squire Sanders
Herbert Smith Freehills	Stephenson Harwood
Hogan Lovells	Stevens & Bolton
Irwin Mitchell	Travers Smith
Jones Day	Walker Morris
Kirkland & Ellis	Weil, Gotshal & Manges
Latham & Watkins	Withers
Linklaters	Wragge & Co
Macfarlanes	

Current issues

- Funds work remains active. The restructuring of existing funds, launches of new funds and increases in capital flow all have tax consequences.
- The fall in transactional work during the recession paved the way for other areas such as advisory and litigation to come to the fore. The significant savings achievable mean that tax lawyers' advice is valued more highly than ever.
- Law firms have come into their own in relation to tax advice. Pre-Enron it seemed accountancy firms were taking over. However, companies now prefer to take advice from sources independent from their auditors.
- Changes to corporate taxes and the introduction of anti-avoidance tax legislation have been keeping tax lawyers on their toes. Recent changes include the tightening of capital gains rules and an end to disguised remuneration – a method of paying employees by means of non-repayable tax-free loans.

Practice Areas

- Following controversy over the tax affairs of celebrities and major corporations like Starbucks, the government has hinted that members of tax avoidance schemes may be forcibly disclosed to tax inspectors.
- HMRC has introduced several 'amnesty' style initiatives, such as the Liechtenstein Disclosure Facility, the Offshore Disclosure Facility and New Disclosure Opportunity – these have resulted in over 50,000 voluntary disclosures of unpaid taxes.
- In recent years resources have been focused mostly on prosecution of indirect fraud – like carousel fraud – over and above direct tax fraud.

Technology, Telecoms & Outsourcing

In a nutshell

Technology lawyers distinguish themselves from general commercial advisers because of their specific industry know-how. They combine a keen understanding of the latest advances in various technologies with a thorough knowledge of the ever-changing law that regulates, protects and licenses them. As forms of media and new technologies converge, clients have come to rely on technology lawyers' innovation and imagination in offering rigorous legal solutions to maximise and protect income and ideas. The majority of the top 50 firms possess dedicated groups of lawyers. There are also specialists within smaller commercial firms and a number of niche firms.

What lawyers do

- Advise on commercial transactions and draft the requisite documents. There is a heavy emphasis on risk management.
- Assist in the resolution of disputes, commonly by arbitration or other settlement procedures as this is a court-averse sector. Many disputes relate to faulty or unsatisfactory software or hardware.
- Help clients police their IT and web-based reputation and assets. Cyber-squatting, ownership of database information and the Data Protection Act are common topics.
- Give clients mainstream commercial, corporate and finance advice.
- Specialised outsourcing lawyers represent customers and suppliers in the negotiation and drafting of agreements for the provision of IT or other services by a third party.

The realities of the job

- You need to be familiar with the latest regulations and their potential impact on your client's business. Does a website need a disclaimer? What measures should your client take to protect data about individuals gathered online?
- You need a good grasp of the jargon of your chosen industry, firstly to write contracts but also so you can understand your clients' instructions. Read trade journals like *Media Lawyer* and *Wired* or magazines such as *Computer Weekly* or *New Scientist*.
- In this frontier world, gut instinct matters. One in-house lawyer made what looked like a risky move from BT to little-known internet auction site, eBay. Six years later he moved to head up Skype's legal team.

- The ability to think laterally and creatively is a must, especially when the application of a client's technology or content throws up entirely new issues.
- High-end private sector outsourcing involves complex, high-value and increasingly multi-jurisdictional work. Mostly, it is the larger law firms that handle such deals. In the public sector, deals involve UK government departments, local authorities and the suppliers of services to those entities.

Current issues

- In the UK the technology sector has recovered well post-recession.
- As tech companies battle for the smartphone and tablet market, there has been an upsurge in patent disputes, most notably between Apple and Samsung.
- Digital convergence throws up many legal problems as the business opportunities created by new technologies move beyond the capacity of existing legal or regulatory structures: copyrighted content being transferred onto handheld devices, film or TV programme downloads from the internet… the list goes on.
- The public are becoming much more aware – or sceptical, rather – of how information is collected and dispersed in the digital sphere. In the wake of the controversy surrounding Edward Snowden's revelations about US spying capabilities, some of the world's most iconic technology companies (including Apple, Google, Facebook and Twitter) penned a letter to the US authorities asking for the ability to be more transparent about data requests and revealing how information is collated and used. It's a move which has won the support of Human Rights Watch and demonstrates the desire of tech companies to exhibit their independence.
- Many firms and their clients now believe that technology, media and telecoms are no longer three distinct markets and structure their departments accordingly.
- A trend for mergers and joint ventures in the telecoms sphere continues. Think of T-Mobile and Orange's UK operations merging to create 'EE' and Telefónica O2, Vodafone and EE entering a joint venture agreement to provide billing services to consumers.
- An EU law now requires websites to get consent from visitors to store cookie information on their device. The law was designed to make people aware of their right to privacy – whether it does is another matter.

- The most interesting telecoms work is taking place overseas, particularly in Africa and Asia. India's Bharti Airtel's $9bn takeover of Zain (South African telecoms) is the ultimate example of this. There is plenty of room for manoeuvre in the emerging markets, unlike Western Europe.
- Telecoms companies continue to try to chip away the infrastructure that gives BT a massive competitive advantage over its rivals, particularly in terms of how much it charges for its cabling.
- IT outsourcing began in the late 1980s, followed by business process outsourcings (BPOs) that involve handing responsibility to third-party service providers for functions like human resources, finance and accounting. Today the lines between technology outsourcing (TO) and BPOs are blurred. Smart outsourcing – the concept of outsourcing parts of a company, one part at a time, often using different suppliers – is in vogue at present, as is multisourcing (using many different suppliers on shorter term contracts).
- With the proliferation of cloud computing in business, data protection has become an area of huge expansion for many law firms. For example, if a New York-based official in a multinational company accesses HR data for staff based in London, they may well be in breach of the Data Protection Act because UK and EU laws are that much stricter than US ones.
- The government has announced plans to roll out a UK-wide super-fast broadband network by 2015. The government has earmarked £830m for the project but expects most of it to be paid for by private investors.

Read our True Pictures on...

Addleshaw Goddard	Macfarlanes
Allen & Overy	Maclay Murray & Spens
Ashfords	Mayer Brown
Ashurst	Michelmores
Baker & McKenzie	Mills & Reeve
Berwin Leighton Paisner	Muckle
Bird & Bird	Nabarro
Bond Dickinson	Norton Rose Fulbright
Brabners Chaffe Street	Olswang
Bristows	Osborne Clarke
Browne Jacobson	Pinsent Masons
Burges Salmon	Reed Smith
Charles Russell	RPC
Clifford Chance	Shoosmiths
Clyde & Co	Simmons & Simmons
CMS	SJ Berwin
Dentons	Slaughter and May
DLA Piper	Squire Sanders
DWF	Stephenson Harwood
Eversheds	Stevens & Bolton
Freshfields	Taylor Wessing
Gateley	TLT
Harbottle & Lewis	Travers Smith
Herbert Smith Freehills	Walker Morris
Hogan Lovells	Ward Hadaway
Irwin Mitchell	Wedlake Bell
Jones Day	White & Case
K&L Gates	Wragge & Co
Latham & Watkins	
Lawrence Graham	
Linklaters	

The True Picture

The True Picture reports on 115 firms in England and Wales, ranging from the international giants to small regional practices. Most handle commercial law, although many also offer private client experience.

The True Picture

Think all law firms are the same? They're not. Even superficially similar firms can be worlds apart in how they operate internally. Fortunately, one tool exists to sort the Christmas crackers from the old knackers, the breakthrough indie bands from the One Direction fans... the True Picture.

Between them, the 115 firms covered in the True Picture have thousands of training contract vacancies to fill. With luck, one of them could be yours. Even if none of these 115 firms wants you, reading the reports will teach you a great deal about the nature of legal training and the experience of working within a law firm.

How we do our research

Every year we spend many months compiling the True Picture reports on law firms in England and Wales, ranging from the international giants to small regional practices. Our purpose is to get to the heart of what you need to know about a prospective employer – what it can offer you in terms of work and working environment. You'll want to know how many hours a day you'll be chained to your desk, the tasks that will keep you occupied and who you'll be working with. Importantly, you'll want to know about a firm's culture and whether colleagues will turn into party animals or party poopers come Friday night.

Most of our chosen firms handle commercial law, although many also offer private client experience. There are a few general practice firms offering publicly funded advice to their local communities. To take part in the True Picture a firm must provide a complete list of its trainees. After checking the list is complete, we randomly select a sample of individuals for telephone interviews. Our sources are guaranteed anonymity to give them the confidence to speak frankly. The True Picture is not shown to the law firms prior to publication; they see it for the first time when this book is published.

If you'll allow us to blow our own trumpet for a minute, we're the only publication that conducts our research in this way. By chatting to trainees rather than sending them formulaic questionnaires, we can follow up on leads, delve deeper into what makes firms tick and what challenges they face. We think that leads to better, more detailed information for our readers.

Trainees tell us why they chose their firm and why others might want to. We put on our serious faces and talk about seat allocation, the character and work of different departments, the level of supervision and what happens to people on qualification. And we flirt shamelessly to get the gossip on firm politics, office oddities and after-hours fun. We look for the things trainees agree upon, and if they don't agree we present both sides of the argument.

We also speak to senior sources at every firm – managing partners, training partners, recruiters. You'll notice their comments scattered throughout the True Picture features and published in more detail online. We conduct these management interviews to get their insights on what their firm's strategy is for the coming years. We know that by the time you, our readers, hopefully begin your training contracts in 2016 and beyond, market conditions might be very different, so we've tried to make this a forward-looking guide. Additionally, True Picture feature isn't supposed to simply be a review of a training contract, but rather a broader picture of a firm as a whole. After all, it's not much use knowing that 'trainees are Firm X are happy/sad and work reasonable/terrible hours' but not having a clue about the commercial environment in which Firm X operates. Again, we're the only publication to go into this much detail.

What kind of firm do I choose?

Your choice of firm will be based on location, size and the practice areas available... then it's a matter of chemistry. Some firms are stuffier, some are more industrious and some are very brand-aware, involving trainees heavily in marketing activities. Some work in modern open-plan offices; others occupy buildings long past their sell-by date. Some focus on international business; others are at the heart of their local business communities. Some concentrate on contentious work, others transactional. The combinations of these variables are endless.

What we found out this year

The redundancies and falling profits of 2009 and 2010 are now fading into the mists of time, corporate activity has recovered somewhat and more firms are starting to talk about growth. This should not imply that the profession is out of the woods yet. The economy is still on shaky ground, government cuts are biting, the Eurozone crisis is lurching to goodness knows what conclusion – the effects on law firms have been and will continue to be profound. Read more about all this in our feature on Trends affecting the profession on page 19.

A word on law firm mergers or closures. Mergers are an increasingly regular occurrence in the profession. This is partly due to the recession – strength in numbers, and all that. However, it is also a result of globalisation. The firms with large international networks seem to feel that unless they have offices absolutely everywhere, they will be left out of an emerging global elite. When firms merge, trainees' contracts are honoured, though of course it does mean that new recruits find themselves in a different firm to the one they signed up to. Closures are rarer, but as we've seen with the cases of Halliwells in 2010, Dewey & LeBoeuf in 2012 and Cobbetts in 2013, they do happen and trainees can find themselves out on their ear.

Since the recession many firms are announcing their qualification job offers extremely late, making it difficult for those who needed to look elsewhere for employment. Pre-recession, usually just over 80% of qualifiers stayed with the law firms that trained them. After a dodgy couple of years, total retention at our True Picture firms recovered in 2011, and has remained fairly strong since then. It stood at 78.5% in 2013, slightly lower than the two previous years. At the same time, many firms have been cutting their trainee intakes it is to be hoped that firms have managed to 'right-size' themselves. If you intend to use retention rates as a determining factor in your choice of firm, do be wary of the statistics being bandied around. Law firms make their own rules on how to calculate retention rates – you may not be getting a full picture from them. We collect our own statistics and include them in each law firm feature. We have collated statistics since 2000 and publish them on our website.

What we hear every year

- Some seats are more popular than others and there are no guarantees of getting a specific seat. Employment and intellectual property are perennial favourites.
- Levels of responsibility vary between departments. In property you might have your own small files. In corporate you will generally work in a very junior capacity as part of a team.
- The experience in litigation depends entirely on the type of cases your firm handles; usually a trainee's responsibility is inversely proportionate to the value and complexity of a case.
- In times of plenty, corporate and finance seats mean long hours, commonly climaxing in all-nighters. The size and complexity of a deal will determine your role, but corporate and finance usually require the most teamwork.
- Most firms offer four six-month seats; some offer six four-month seats and others operate their own unique systems. Trainees switch departments and supervisors for each seat. Some share a room and work with a partner or senior assistant; others sit in an open-plan office, either with the rest of the team or with other trainees. Occasionally trainees have their own room.
- All firms conduct appraisals: a minimum of one at the conclusion of each seat, and usually halfway through as well.
- Client secondments help you learn to understand clients' needs. They can be the highlight of a training contract.
- The Solicitors Regulation Authority requires all trainees to gain experience of both contentious and non-contentious work. Additionally most firms have certain seats they require or prefer trainees to try. Some firms are very prescriptive, others flexible. Remember, a training contract is a time to explore legal practice to see what you're best at and most enjoy. You may surprise yourself.

And finally...

Use the True Picture to help you decide which firms to target. No matter how easy or hard securing a training contract is for you, you'll want to end up with the right one.

Jargonbuster

While we're not the biggest fans of legal jargon, the industry is flooded with it, and some of it actually means something. So if there are any terms you don't understand, or you just want to brush up on your legalese for an interview, then look no further.

- **ABS** – Alternative Business Structures: newly permitted arrangements for law firms, which allow non-lawyers to have a financial stake in the business.
- **ADR** – Alternative Dispute Resolution: a way of avoiding the cost or public exposure of litigation. The most common types are arbitration, mediation and negotiation.
- **Agency work** – making a court appearance for another firm that can't get to court.
- **AIM** – Alternative Investment Market: a 'junior' stock market run by the London Stock Exchange, which allows smaller companies and equities to float stock within a more flexible system.
- **Antitrust** – the US term for competition law.
- **Adjudication** – the legal process by which an arbiter or judge reviews evidence to come to a decision.
- **Arbitration** – a type of dispute resolution where the parties agree to abide by the decision of one or more arbitrators.
- **Associate** – a term used to denote solicitors not at partner level but more senior than an assistant solicitor.
- **Bench** – the judge or judges in a courtroom.
- **Best friends relationship** – a situation where two firms have no organisational or financial ties, but use each other as the first port of call when referring work. This is often found across international borders, eg between Slaughter and May (UK) and Hengeler Mueller (Germany).
- **Bibling** – putting together sets of all the relevant documents for a transaction.
- **Billing target/chargeable hours target** – the number of hours lawyers are required to record working for a client; time is usually recorded in six-minute chunks; trainees do not usually have billing targets.
- **Boutique** – a law firm which concentrates on one or a select few areas of law. They do not necessarily have to be small, but often are due to the scope of their work.
- **Brief** – the instructing documents given to a barrister when they are instructed by a solicitor.

- **Bundling** – compiling bundles of documents for a court case.
- **The City** – the commercial and financial centre of London; also known as the Square Mile, but can also include the Canary Wharf financial district.
- **CMC** – case management conference.
- **Coco** – corporate-commercial work.
- **Conditional fee arrangements** – also called 'no win no fee'; an arrangement whereby a solicitor acting in a claim agrees to be paid a fee only if they win the case; such payment is usually made by the losing party.
- **Contentious matters** – legal disputes between parties.
- **Conveyancing** – the transfer of the ownership of property from one person to another.
- **Counsel** – a barrister.
- **CSR** – Corporate Social Responsibility: the practice of companies taking responsibility for the impact of their activities on society; in reality 'CSR committees' at firms will run projects where lawyers paint schools, plant trees and clean playgrounds.
- **Damages** – a sum of money which one person or organisation has to pay to another for not performing a certain duty.
- **Data room duty** – used to involve supervising visitors to rooms full of important documents, helping them find things and making sure they don't steal them. With electronic data rooms the job becomes more of a desktop exercise.
- **Disclosure** – making relevant documentation available to the other parties in a dispute.
- **Dispute resolution** – litigation, mediation, arbitration, etc.
- **Document management** – dealing with the more administrative side of deal documentation.
- **Due diligence** – the thorough investigation of a target company in a deal.
- **Equity partner** – a partner who receives a contractually agreed share of the firm's annual profits. A part owner of the firm. The other type of partner is a salaried partner.

- **Fee earner** – a lawyer or a paralegal who bills time to a firm's clients. The term doesn't include lawyers who act in a more supportive role.
- **FTSE 100 (pronounced 'footsie')** – an index of the 100 most valuable companies listed on the London Stock Exchange; the value of these companies is used to give an indication of the health of the UK's business world.
- **Grunt work** – administrative (and boring) yet essential tasks including photocopying, bundling, bibling, paginating, scheduling documents, data room duties and proof-reading or checking that documents are intact.
- **High net worth individuals** – rich people.
- **Higher rights of audience** – the qualification necessary to become a solicitor advocate.
- **Highly leveraged** – the practice of having a ratio of few partners to lots of solicitors; leverage is also a term used in finance – the two are not connected.
- **Infant approval** – court authorisation for a settlement involving a minor.
- **In-house lawyer** – a solicitor or barrister who is employed by a company or public body rather than a law firm or barristers' chambers.
- **Injunction** – a court order requiring a party to do, or to refrain from doing, certain acts.
- **IPO** – the Initial Public Offering of shares in a company to the public on a stock market; also known as flotation.
- **Judicial review** – the legal process by which the actions of the government or public bodies can be challenged.
- **Junior Lawyers' Division** – a subgroup within the Law Society set up in 2008 to represent student members of the Law Society, trainees and lawyers up to five years' PQE (see PQE!).
- **Law Society** – the official representative body of solicitors in England and Wales.
- **Legal aid** – a government-funded system which pays for legal representation in criminal and some civil cases for individuals who would otherwise be unable to afford it.
- **Legal Disciplinary Partnership (LDP)** – a business structure whereby a law firm can take on non-lawyers as equity holders. Up to 25% of a partnership can be non-lawyers.
- **Legal Services Act** – the 2007 Act of Parliament encourages the development of one-stop shops that deliver packages of legal services at the convenience of consumers and provides an alternative path for consumer complaints.
- **Limited Liability Partnership (LLP)** – a way of structuring a professional partnership such that no partner is liable to any of the firm's creditors beyond a certain sum.
- **Litigation** – a method of settling disputes through legal proceedings in court.

- **Lockstep** – the practice of increasing solicitors' salaries based purely on seniority.
- **M&A** – mergers and acquisitions; the buying, selling and combining of companies; often the main focus of firms' corporate teams.
- **Magic circle** – the name given to five of the leading London-based law firms; it is generally held to consist of Allen & Overy, Clifford Chance, Freshfields Bruckhaus Deringer, Linklaters and Slaughter and May.
- **Managing partner** – the main boss of a law firm, who leads the partnership and/or management committee in running the business and devising its strategy.
- **Master (in the High Court)** – a judge in the High Court ranking lower than a High Court judge, chiefly responsible for case management. They are called 'Master' regardless of whether they are male or female.
- **Mediation** – a type of dispute resolution where a dispute is resolved with the help of a neutral third party.
- **Moot** – a mock trial used to train or test advocacy skills.
- **Nearshoring** – the outsourcing of work to another organisation, usually in a part of the UK where overheads and salary costs are lower.
- **Notary public** – a qualified lawyer appointed by the Archbishop of Canterbury, who is authorised to authenticate and certify estates, deeds, powers of attorney and other documents, especially for use abroad; the majority of notaries are also solicitors.
- **NQ** – a newly qualified solicitor.
- **Outsourcing** – hiring in an external organisation to perform a part of a company's activities. Frequently this is done overseas to take advantage of lower costs (offshore outsourcing).
- **Panel** – a group of law firms or lawyers chosen for regular consultation by a certain business.
- **Paralegal** – a non-lawyer, often with some legal training, who assists qualified lawyers on legal matters.
- **PFI** – Public Finance Initiative: a way of creating 'public-private partnerships' (PPPs) by funding public infrastructure projects with private capital.
- **Power of attorney** – the legal authority to act on someone else's behalf.
- **PQE** – post-qualification experience.
- **Pro bono** – from the Latin 'pro bono publico', meaning 'for the public good'; legal work done without payment as a public service.
- **Public procurement law** – regulates the purchasing by public sector bodies of products, works or services.
- **Profits per equity partner (PEP)** – the annual profits of a law firm divided by the total number of equity partners in the firm; this statistic is often used to indicate the financial health of a firm, but it can easily be

manipulated by altering the number of equity partners.

- **PSC** – Professional Skills Course: a compulsory course taken during the training contract.
- **Restructuring exercise (in the context of a law firm)** – the reorganisation of the firm to make it more efficient, to react to changes in income or to make the firm more attractive to clients; often a euphemistic way of talking about staff/lawyer redundancies.
- **Rights of audience** – the right of a lawyer (either a solicitor or barrister) to appear and conduct proceedings in court.
- **Salaried partner** – a partner who receives a salary but has no contractual claim on the firm's profits; the other type of partner is an equity partner.
- **Seat** – time spent by a trainee working in a department, usually four or six months.
- **Secondment** – the practice of 'lending' trainees and qualified solicitors to a firm's client to work in their in-house legal department for a certain period; is also used in the context of sending a lawyer to another office in the firm's network.
- **Silo-ing** – encouraging people to work in a specific field rather than being generalists; teams working very independently of others within a firm.
- **Silver circle** – a group of elite English law firms, generally considered as falling just outside the magic circle. This tends to include Herbert Smith Freehills, Ashurst, Berwin Leighton Paisner, SJ Berwin, Macfarlanes and Travers Smith.
- **Solicitor advocate** – a solicitor who is qualified to represent clients in the higher courts.

- **SRA** – Solicitors Regulation Authority.
- **Superinjunction** – the informal term for an injunction whose existence and details may not be publicly disclosed.
- **Swiss Verein** – a business consisting of a number of offices, each of which is independently liable for its own obligations.
- **Tesco law** – a nickname for the effect of the Legal Services Act.
- **Tort** – a breach of duty owed to someone else (a 'civil wrong') which leads to injury to a person or damage of their property.
- **Training contract** – a two-year period of working in legal practice in which someone who has completed their LPC is trained by an accredited organisation to become a qualified solicitor.
- **Training partner** – the partner who oversees the training scheme.
- **Trainee partner** – a trainee who acts like a partner. Not an entirely likeable peer.
- **Tribunal** – specialist judicial bodies that decide disputes in a particular area of law.
- **Vacation scheme** – a placement with a law firm designed to familiarise a prospective trainee with a firm and vice versa; sometimes called 'vac schemes' or 'summer placements', they are usually held during the summer or at Easter and can last between one and four weeks.
- **Verification** – the aspect of a deal in which lawyers ensure stated information is accurate.

Firms by size in the UK

		London	S & Thames Valley	South West	Midlands	East	Yorkshire & NE	North West	Wales	Overseas	Trainees	True picture	A-Z solicitors
1	DWF	●		●	●		●	●			98	245	537
2	GLS	●									c.45	278	548
3	Eversheds	●			●	●	●	●	●	●	52	251	539
4	Clyde & Co	●	●					●		●	73	220	526
5	Simmons & Simmons	●		●						●	85	409	596
6	Pinsent Masons	●			●		●	●		●	168	381	587
7	DLA Piper	●			●		●	●		●	173	242	536
8	Allen & Overy	●								●	190	159	506
9	Linklaters	●								●	229	329	567
10	Bond Dickinson	●	●	●			●				43	186	515
11	Clifford Chance	●								●	200	217	n/a
12	Freshfields Bruckhaus Deringer	●								●	187	270	545
13	Wragge & Co	●			●					●	51	484	622
14	Addleshaw Goddard	●					●	●		●	70	155	505
15	Herbert Smith Freehills	●								●	166	283	550
16	Mills & Reeve	●			●	●	●	●			34	347	574
17	Dentons	●	●							●	48	239	535
18	Hogan Lovells	●								●	129	391	554
19	Berwin Leighton Paisner	●								●	84	176	511
20	Norton Rose Fulbright	●								●	110	362	579
21	Irwin Mitchell	●		●	●		●	●			83	301	557
22	Hill Dickinson	●					●	●		●	41	288	553
23	Ashurst	●								●	95	167	508
24	Nabarro	●					●			●	50	359	578
25	Shoosmiths	●	●		●			●			42	403	594
26	Slaughter and May	●								●	167	419	599
27	Gateley	●			●		●	●			10	273	546
28	Kennedys	●	●	●		●	●	●		●	32	309	560
29	Taylor Wessing	●				●					47	435	605
30	Osborne Clarke	●	●	●							33	371	583
31	CMS	●		●						●	120	223	527
32	Squire Sanders	●			●		●	●		●	44	425	601
33	Baker & McKenzie	●								●	81	171	509
34	Burges Salmon	●		●							46	205	522
35	Charles Russell	●	●	●						●	37	211	524
36	Reed Smith	●								●	49	384	589
37	White & Case	●								●	53	473	618
38	SJ Berwin	●								●	77	412	597
39=	Browne Jacobson	●		●	●			●			16	201	521
39=	Reynolds Porter Chamberlain	●		●							33	389	590
41	Trowers & Hamlins	●		●	●			●		●	35	449	610

Firms by size in the UK

		London	S & Thames Valley	South West	Midlands	East	Yorkshire & NE	North West	Wales	Overseas	Trainees	True picture	A-Z solicitors
42	TLT	●		●			●				21	441	607
43	Macfarlanes	●									56	332	568
44	Mishcon de Reya	●								●	24	350	575
45	Freeth Cartwright	●	●		●		●	●			21	267	544
46	Travers Smith	●								●	41	444	608
47	Stephenson Harwood	●								●	32	429	602
48	Bird & Bird	●								●	18	183	514
49	Olswang	●	●							●	24	365	580
50	Farrer & Co	●									20	255	540
51	Mayer Brown	●								●	40	337	570
52	Latham & Watkins	●								●	40	317	563
53	Maclay Murray & Spens	●									8	335	569
54	Holman Fenwick Willan	●								●	35	295	555
55	Ward Hadaway						●	●			25	461	614
56	Brabners							●			13	195	519
57	Walker Morris						●				29	458	613
58	Capsticks	●	●		●		●				13	209	523
59	Speechly Bircham	●									25	422	600
60	Jones Day	●								●	30	304	558
61	Lewis Silkin	●	●						●		12	327	566
62	Ashfords	●		●							22	162	507
63	Withers	●								●	13	479	621
64=	Lawrence Graham	●								●	30	320	564
64=	Penningtons Solicitors	●	●			●					17	376	585
66	Ince & Co	●								●	31	298	556
67	Veale Wasbrough Vizards	●		●							16	453	611
68	SGH Martineau	●			●						17	393	591
69	Slater & Gordon	●	●	●	●	●	●	●	●	●	6	417	n/a
70	Michelmores	●		●							13	344	573
71	Shearman & Sterling	●								●	26	397	592
72	K&L Gates	●									16	307	559
73	Winckworth Sherwood	●	●					●			11	476	620
74	Watson, Farley & Williams	●								●	27	464	615
75	Dechert	●								●	23	234	534
76	Foot Anstey			●							13	261	542
77	Bristows	●									19	198	520
78	Bircham Dyson Bell	●									14	181	513
79	Weil, Gotshal & Manges	●								●	21	470	617
80	Stevens & Bolton		●								8	433	603
81	Sidley Austin	●								●	20	406	595
82	Kirkland & Ellis	●								●	14	315	562

The True Picture

Firms by size in the UK

		London	S & Thames Valley	South West	Midlands	East	Yorkshire & NE	North West	Wales	Overseas	Trainees	True picture	A-Z solicitors
83	Kingsley Napley	●									10	312	561
84	Wedlake Bell	●									12	468	616
85=	Forbes						●	●			8	264	543
85=	Gordons							●			8	276	547
87	Cripps Harries Hall	●	●								14	320	530
88	Leigh Day	●									14	323	n/a
89	Skadden Arps	●								●	15	415	598
90	Higgs & Sons				●						10	286	552
91	Lester Aldridge	●	●	●							13	325	565
92=	Bates Wells Braithwaite	●				●					8	174	510
92=	Cleary Gottlieb Steen & Hamilton	●								●	24	214	525
94	Muckle						●				8	355	577
95	Harbottle & Lewis	●									10	281	549
96	Edwards Wildman Palmer	●								●	13	248	538
97=	Boodle Hatfield	●	●								11	189	516
97=	Wilsons	●		●				●			8	475	619
99	Covington & Burling	●									14	228	529
100	Orrick	●									9	369	582
101	Trethowans		●	●							7	449	609
102	Memery Crystal	●									8	342	572
103	Collyer Bristow	●									9	226	528
104	Bingham McCutchen	●									4	179	512
105	Fisher Meredith	●	●								9	258	n/a
106	BP Collins		●								7	191	517
107	Sheridans	●									2	400	593
108	Morgan Lewis	●								●	6	353	576
109	BPE Solicitors			●							4	193	518
110	Paul Hastings	●									6	374	584
111	McDermott Will & Emery	●								●	7	340	571
112	Thomas Cooper	●								●	4	438	606
113	Vinson & Elkins	●								●	9	456	612
114	Peters & Peters	●									5	379	586
115	Curtis	●								●	4	232	531

Addleshaw Goddard LLP

The facts

Location: London, Leeds, Manchester

Number of UK partners/solicitors: 165/440

Total number of trainees: 70

Seats: 4x6 months

Alternative seats: overseas seats, secondments

Extras: pro bono – Springfield Legal Advice Centre Stockwell; language classes

On chambersstudent.co.uk...

How to get into Addleshaws

Berezovsky v Abramovich

Teambuilding in Romania

At Addleshaws the cases range from the ritz of Russian oligarchs to the rubble of Liverpudlian sewage works. This Northern giant has become a formidable force across the country with a prospering portfolio of offices abroad.

As 'shaw as the sun

Though it reported a slight drop in turnover in 2012/13, Addleshaw Goddard can't be accused of not keeping itself busy. Offices in Qatar and Oman became the latest additions to the firm's growing international interests, which also include recent openings in Dubai and Singapore, while back in Blighty Addleshaws was involved in two of the largest cases of the year. The firm launched Boris Berezovsky's £3.2bn damages claim against Chelsea FC owner Roman Abramovich and also defended Kazakh banker Mukhtar Ablyazov against claims that he embezzled £3.3bn of BTA Bank's money. The firm was also named in *The Times*' Top 50 Employers for Women list. Training principal Andrew Blower said: *"It's an exciting time for us and we're looking forward to developing the new offices,"* while one of our insiders said: *"There's a lot of international expansion, which is great for anyone about to join the firm."*

Spread between Leeds, London and Manchester, Addleshaws continues to maintain its TOOT ('Three Offices, One Team') policy and divides its work into commercial, corporate, finance/projects, international, litigation and real estate. Many of our sources cited the *"chance to work with FTSE 100 companies"* as part of what drew them to the firm in the first place, and Barclays, Sainsbury's and drinks giant Diageo are just some of the household names on its books. Our parent publication *Chambers UK* ranks the Leeds and Manchester divisions very highly, with the construction, corporate/M&A and private client departments making it into the top tier. Down south, London's real estate, employment and mid-market corporate/M&A divisions are also held in high regard by the guide.

The City of London HQ sits in the swish new glass-fronted Milton Gate building by the Barbican. *"It's really nice,"* one trainee told us. *"I'm proud to work here, proud to call it home."* It's open-plan, which *"stops people from being scary"* and at the subsidised canteen on the ground floor *"you can get a full plate of good grub for £4."* Up north the Manchester office is located close to the centre of town, just off Oxford Road, while in Leeds the office is built around a large atrium and situated close to the River Aire. At the time of our calls there were 31 trainees in the London office, 18 in Leeds and 18 in Manchester. The majority of those we spoke to had done the vacation scheme, offered by all three of the UK offices, prior to applying.

Mighty in Blighty...

The London HQ provides the widest spread of seats but each of the offices offers work in corporate, commercial, litigation, real estate, construction and banking/finance, although the subsets vary office to office. There are also occasional seats such as employment and pensions. Although there were a few grumbles about the allocation process it had mostly served our sources well and as a trainee *"you have the chance to map out your ideal training contract, which HR look at when placing people."* Our insiders had a lot of praise for the range of secondments, with one telling us: *"There are loads on offer and most of the clients are really big names."*

London's litigation department works on some very high-value cases and for that reason *"trainees work in a supporting role but they do try and get you involved wherever*

Chambers UK rankings

Banking & Finance	Healthcare
Banking Litigation	Information Technology
Capital Markets	Intellectual Property
Charities	Life Sciences
Competition/European Law	Local Government
Construction	Outsourcing
Corporate Crime &	Partnership
Investigations	Pensions
Corporate/M&A	Planning
Defamation/Reputation	Private Client
Management	Private Equity
Dispute Resolution	Product Liability
Education	Professional Negligence
Employee Share Schemes	Projects
& Incentives	Public Procurement
Employment	Real Estate
Energy & Natural	Restructuring/Insolvency
Resources	Retail
Financial Services	Social Housing
Fraud	Tax
Health & Safety	Transport

they can." The clients are *"a mix of large companies, including banks, and high net worth individuals."* As well as Boris Berezovsky and Mukhtar Ablyazov, the department recently worked for Diageo and British Airways. Much of the work is international and while trainees do get the chance to attend hearings there aren't opportunities for advocacy. *"I went to meetings where we interviewed witnesses,"* one trainee told us, while another shrugged off the suggestion of any boredom with the *"bundling, indexing and research"* they'd done, saying: *"The claims are of such high value, how could it be any other way?"*

The capital's real estate department does a lot of social housing work while its commercial clients include Primark, Sainsbury's and Travelodge. It was another regular stop for our insiders. *"I liked it because it felt like real preparation for becoming an associate. In social housing there's a mix of tenant and landlord work and I was drafting leases and licences. I was in charge of my own matters and the expectation is to react to cases as they develop and not be told what to do."* The department recently worked with the Co-operative Group in a deal worth £500m that will see the land around its iconic new Manchester HQ transformed into a 4 million sq ft mixed-use development site.

Banking was another top stop for the trainees we spoke to in London. Barclays, HSBC and Bank of Ireland are all on Addleshaws' books and many of the matters are multimillion-pound deals. One trainee told us: *"They start you off working on consent letters and minor charging*

documents but by the end I was handling my own transactions and I had the chance to draft the full suite of finance documents." Another said: *"There is some grunt work but a lot of the low-level work is outsourced to the support team based in Manchester."* Work varies from corporate to asset-based lending to real estate finance.

Manchester's stellar corporate department squares up to regional rivals like DLA Piper and Eversheds and does a lot of private equity and finance services work. The department has recently worked with Capita and Lloyds TSB, and also acted for plumbing supplier Wolseley on its acquisition of part of the utility group Burdens in a deal worth £30m. *"I had a really, really busy seat and there's loads of client contact,"* one trainee told us. Another said: *"At first I was co-ordinating due diligence, and drafting stock transfer forms and board minutes, but by the end of the seat I was managing some of the smaller transactions by myself. Some of the work is low-value but that means you get lots of responsibility and overall it was a great experience."*

...adored abroad

Over in Leeds the construction department acts for a lot of businesses in the energy and utilities markets and the work is split between the contentious and the non-contentious. One trainee praised the *"really interesting"* work on offer in the litigation arm of the department. *"Lots of the work is international and you get involved in work in Dubai and Singapore because there's so much growth in those parts of the world."* At a national level, the department advised United Utilities on its £200m refurbishment of waste water treatment facilities at Sandon, a sewage treatment station on the River Mersey. *"They're not shy about putting you in front of clients, and you're given as much responsibility as you want,"* one trainee told us.

Our interviewees were almost unanimous in their praise for the supervision on hand. *"They're always very keen to see how you're doing and make sure you're happy,"* one source said, while another told us: *"All the supervisors are good – you can see they've been chosen because they're genuinely interested in helping people out."* Working hours vary as much between departments as they do between offices but one London trainee summed it up well when they said: *"The bottom line is it's a City law firm so it's not 9am to 5pm, but if you end up staying late it's because everyone is staying late and they don't just leave you on your own."* In the Northern offices there can be some very late nights *"when a deal is running to a close"* and 2am finishes are certainly not unheard of in corporate and construction. This was the source of some dissatisfaction among those we spoke to but one insider said: *"They do try and give you days in lieu if you've worked extra hard."*

Our interviewees also felt like they had a good idea of where Addleshaws is going. *"Our clients aren't restricted by national boundaries, so why should we be?"* one source said. Another told us: *"I think we'll develop a greater presence in the Middle East – that's a big focus at the minute, but consolidating our base at home is still very important and we'll keep meeting the needs of our existing clients."* The firm has an 'Ideas Lab' which allows trainees to feed back via the intranet if *"you know how the firm could be run better or just have a suggestion for something you'd like to be done differently."*

Building teams and building houses

Before beginning their training contracts, trainees embark on a week-long trip to Cluj-Napoca in Romania where they help build homes for the international housing charity Habitat for Humanity. Our sources couldn't have spoken any more highly of the experience. One told us: *"It's brilliant. You get to know all the other trainees quickly and it's a great way of making connections. I came home when the week was over feeling like I had 35 friends."* Another agreed: *"It's really important because when you turn up on the first day you already know all the trainees – that counts."* Trainees are tasked with *"digging trenches, building walls and roofing,"* and when the day is done there's lots of fun to be had in the bars in the city centre.

Back home, socialising remains an important part of being a trainee at Addleshaws. In London, *"the firm puts on free drinks in the office on the last Thursday of every month which is a great chance to chat to people across* the office and catch up with anyone you've not seen for a while. Then we head out to the bars around CityPoint."* Last year's Christmas party was at the Oxo Tower and throughout the year there are regular netball, cricket and five-a-side football matches. In Leeds *"the social life is great,"* and they have their free drinks in the office on the final Friday of the month. When summer comes there are barbecues by the picnic area and after that it's a short stagger up to the drinking dens on Call Lane. Across the Pennines in Manchester trainees can be found in the pubs and bars around Deansgate and Spinningfields on a Friday night and last year's Christmas party was held at the grand Midland Hotel. At Christmas the firm's choir goes on tour and serenades each of the offices with carols while their colleagues eat minced pies and drink mulled wine. Friends and family are invited too.

There's also an emphasis on meeting and socialising with clients and juniors from outside the firm. *"Client events take place on a monthly basis and you're encouraged to meet with your contemporaries from other sectors. The idea is that it's a good chance to make contacts for the future of the firm. They also like you to attend events put on by the Junior Lawyers Division."* When asked what kind of person fits with the firm, Andrew Blower stressed the importance of *"interpersonal skills,"* while one London trainee told us: *"The work is client-focused so you need to be able to get on well with people at every level."* Several of our sources praised the inconspicuous hierarchy at Addleshaws and one told us: *"With the more senior figures, job title is proof of their experience, not how much you can expect them to talk down to you."*

And finally...

Since 2008 Addleshaws' retention rates have hovered at around the market average of 80%. In 2013 the firm kept on 25 of its 31 qualifiers.

Allen & Overy LLP

The facts

Location: London
Number of UK partners/solicitors: 181/668
Total number of trainees: 190
Seats: 3 or 6 months long
Alternative seats: overseas seats, secondments
Extras: pro bono – Toynbee Hall Free Legal Advice Centre, Battersea Legal Advice Centre, Fair Trials International, Amicus and many others; language classes

On chambersstudent.co.uk...

How to get into Allen & Overy
A history of the firm
An interview with Richard Hough, grad recruitment partner

If you're hankering after elite finance work and a vast international network, a stint at *"tough but rewarding"* A&O is the way to go .

Home-grown, away-bound

This magic circle mainstay is synonymous with top-shelf work. A fixture on the finance front, A&O is friendly with all the industry's top players – Barclays, Goldman Sachs, JPMorgan, you name it – and lends considerable credence to the term 'best of the best', scoring top-band *Chambers UK* rankings in everything from asset finance and derivatives to real estate finance and securitisation. The firm's know-how hardly ends there, though: A&O's scope is wide as it is tall, with practices as far flung as projects, pensions, employment, insurance and international arbitration all copping equally laudable ratings.

Like its elite peers, the born and bred Londoner's got serious game both home and away. The megafirm's wingspan covers all the inhabitable continents and includes some 42 offices, with Hanoi and Ho Chi Minh City rounding out the latest launches. *"It seems like we've got a new one opening every week!"* According to graduate recruitment partner Richard Hough, *"the strategy of opening more offices in a measured way in the right places using the right people is definitely bearing fruit."* That said, *"I imagine the next year or so will be a period of consolidation,"* he says, mentioning plans to hunker down on some of the new Asian offices *"in order to provide a full service to our clients."*

Considering this ever-expanding network, plus A&O's exhaustingly long list of 'best friend' firms, it comes as little surprise that the majority of undertakings are cross-border. In fact, more than two-thirds of A&O's work entails collaboration between multiple countries, with around a fifth involving five or more. *"I once worked on a deal that spanned 27 jurisdictions!"* one insider told us, adding: *"that's the kind of thing trainees and clients alike seek us out for."*

Gurus galore

Each of A&O's main departments hosts multiple subteams, so trainees have a sizeable pool of seat options to dip into. Seats are six months long (with the exception of litigation, which occasionally throws up three-month seats), and trainees are required to spend at least 12 months in the firm's core practice areas – corporate, banking and international capital markets (ICM). *"There's a lot of variety within and even beyond these groups, but you really shouldn't come here if you're not interested in corporate and finance work since those are our staples,"* one source warned. When it comes to seat allocation, most interviewees expressed confidence in the system, which sees first seats doled out according to general preferences and further ones determined following a seat planning event held before each rotation: *"It's like a little fair – representatives from each team show up to answer questions and fill you in on what will be expected of you in that seat."* Afterwards, trainees sit down with HR to highlight their preferences. Thanks to A&O's 'priority seat' policy, everybody gets to flag one choice *"that's virtually guaranteed. I don't know anyone who hasn't gotten theirs."*

At more than 800 lawyers-strong globally, A&O's banking team is one of the world's largest. The client cache includes over 800 institutions – with the likes of HSBC, Deutsche Bank, Heineken and CVC Capital splashed across the lenders, borrowers and sponsors fronts – and transactions regularly stray into the billions territory. Barclays is a regular client, with A&O recently leading the

Chambers UK rankings

Administrative & Public Law	Financial Services
Asset Finance	Fraud
Banking & Finance	Information Technology
Banking Litigation	Insurance
Capital Markets	Intellectual Property
Commodities	Life Sciences
Competition/European Law	Outsourcing
Construction	Partnership
Corporate Crime & Investigations	Pensions
Corporate/M&A	Private Client
Data Protection	Private Equity
Dispute Resolution	Projects
Employee Share Schemes & Incentives	Public International Law
Employment	Public Procurement
Energy & Natural Resources	Real Estate Finance
Environment	Restructuring/Insolvency
	Social Housing
	Tax
	Telecommunications
	Transport

The True Picture

charge on the megabank's £2.5bn refinancing of credit facilities for Motability Operations as well as its €4bn co-ordination of a revolving credit facility for Telecom Italia. Recent months have also seen banking lawyers oversee the financing for Global Infrastructure's £1.5bn bid on Gatwick Airport, and advise two Russian state-owned banks on a $3.45bn public-to-private financing. For all this high-flying wheeling and dealing, however, interviewees reported a *"surprisingly high"* amount of client contact and *"bona fide"* responsibilities, like taking a first stab at drafting and liaising with foreign counsel: *"Banking is our lifeblood, and everybody's at the top of their game – there's so much to be done that partners don't have time to pay attention to what you have or haven't done before; they just heap the work on and trust you to get on with it."* Of course, the ins and outs of a banking seat vary largely between sub-teams. Restructuring *"involves the most black letter law,"* so it's not uncommon for trainees to perform research tasks and draft memos, while funds and regulatory work is *"more technical – you'll probably spend most of your time working on one big deal because there's so much to get to grips with."* A stint with the structured finance team is similarly *"tricky,"* which means *"trainees are largely left to draft basic documents and manage files."* See our website to read more about our interviewees' experiences.

The ICM department handles derivatives and structured finance, debt capital markets, corporate trustee and securitisation work for financial behemoths like Bank of America Merrill Lynch, Credit Suisse and Morgan Stanley. As is the case with banking, the scale of transactions is huge – the third quarter of 2012 alone saw ICM lawyers

handle deals totalling a whopping $486bn. Recent highlights include advising RBS on capital issues related to insurance giant Direct Line's £2.9bn IPO on the London Stock Exchange and assisting private equity mogul Blackstone with a £1bn high-yield bond transaction in conjunction with holiday village whiz Center Parcs. *"The work is mostly transactional, so there's a big focus on getting a high volume of stuff done,"* said one source. This dynamic means a trainee's workflow can become *"pretty repetitive,"* though this was hardly a complaint among interviewees. *"That actually leaves you a lot of room for other responsibilities. I was trusted to liaise with listing authorities and participate in client meetings."* Our sources also reported reviewing documents, drafting board minutes and attending closings during their time with the group.

Field trip

M&A is the cornerstone of A&O's corporate practice, though lawyers also handle antitrust, private equity and non-financial regulatory matters for institutions as diverse as Shell, Thomson Reuters, News Corporation and Virgin. *"I engaged with more than 20 different jurisdictions during my seat,"* reported one trainee, emphasising the *"heavy cross-border slant"* of the department. *"The accompanying logistical and admin tasks add up pretty quickly."* Fortunately, these are balanced out by *"meatier"* undertakings like research, drafting and client contact in most seats. Sources on the projects team told of getting to grips with wind farm deals and construction contracts, while those in the M&A insurance group reported working closely with financial clients. *"The best part of my seat was working exhaustively on a big merger for several months and seeing the results printed in Bloomberg and all the other news sites after it closed – it really drove home how connected you are as an A&O trainee to that world."*

Though the firm's contentious work doesn't garner the same celebrity as its financial capabilities, A&O's growing litigation practice still manages to attract similarly upscale clientele – Sony, Honda, Amazon, eBay and News International are among the high-fliers that have sought out representation in recent years. The variety of seats within the department means there's an array of work for trainees to get their hands on, from IP cases and banking litigation to employment disputes and international arbitrations. We heard from sources who'd managed trade mark and copyright portfolios, participated in regulatory investigations, attended employment tribunals and worked on FCA matters. While the large-scale and long-running nature of most cases *"don't allow much opportunity for client interaction,"* our interviewees were chuffed with their experience attending hearings and meeting with counsel. There's also a lot of research, drafting memos, preparing court documents and bundling day-to-day.

The vast majority of trainees spend their last six months abroad or in-house with a client, *"something which really sets A&O apart."* A list of opportunities is circulated each seat rotation, and trainees submit a bid for their top choices – *"plus a short explanation of why you're a suitable candidate"* – in order to snag a spot. Overseas destinations shift from time to time and have recently included Hong Kong, Paris, Tokyo, Amsterdam, Moscow and New York, to name a few. *"You're swamped with choice!"* Client secondments also vary periodically, with trainees taking up stints at various banks and multinationals in recent years. Check out our website for more on overseas secondments.

The (best?) of the famous international playboys

"I can't think of anything I've worked on that's solely involved UK lawyers," said one trainee, touching on A&O's *"immense"* international ambit. *"I've worked with people in Paris, Hong Kong, Tunisia and Oman – and that was just in my last seat!"* Because *"it's given from the very beginning that you'll deal with colleagues or clients in other countries on a regular basis,"* it's imperative applicants make sure their people skills are up to scratch. *"A matter might involve liaising with four different counsels in four different jurisdictions, and that requires a positive attitude and professional approach."* Likewise, putting a good face forward is a must for those sent to represent the firm abroad: *"There's certainly scope for travel as a trainee – someone in my intake recently got sent to a Caribbean island to hand-deliver some documents!"*

Given its overseas presence, it's little surprise A&O's trainee intake represents a diverse range of nationalities. *"They don't care where you come from; they're only interested in the quality of your work,"* sources thought, telling us *"there seems to be less of a preoccupation with Oxbridge candidates than at other magic circle firms."* One detail that's non-negotiable, however, is a candidate's diligence: *"High standards of work are treated as the norm – if your work is below par, you'll be reminded right away."* A proactive personality doesn't hurt either, as *"a lot of responsibilities come down to what you put yourself forward for – the people who get interesting work here are the ones who seek it out."*

According to our sources, A&O is chock full of interesting characters: *"Everyone's got something exceptional about them aside from academic achievements. There's a trainee who used to study at the Royal Ballet School and* someone in litigation who just won a prize for her novel. You get the sense that people here actually have interests outside of work."* Interviewees agreed *"there aren't too many nasty individuals"* at the firm, and *"a collaborative, team-friendly environment"* prevails: *"No one tries to shine by climbing on others' shoulders; people seem to be more interested in getting the work done to a high standard and helping each other along the way."* For this reason, there's a substantial emphasis on training and supervision: *"All the trainers are great at explaining things rather than just telling them to you, and there's an open-door policy with respect to advice."*

Like its magic circle peers, the A&O headquarters are outfitted with all the trimmings, including a canteen, bar, dry cleaners, GP's office, in-house dentist, bike park, and gym with exercise classes and *"clean, fluffy towels in the changing rooms."* The trendy Spitalfields location garners much praise, as does the slick glass interior design, which is in keeping with the A&O's *"21st-century corporate machine image. The firm is keen on giving the impression it's forward-thinking and with the times, so they do everything they can to prevent it from feeling like you're entering the cigar room of a West End club. It's less stuffy than some other places in that respect."* Of course, no modern corporate machine would be complete without sleeping pods, and this one is no exception. Fortunately, nobody we spoke with had actually made use of the handful present, despite their admittedly *"gruelling"* schedule: *"I've worked 90-hour weeks before and know someone who's done four all-nighters in one week! You can't come to a big firm like this and not expect to work long hours. Still, the firm makes it as bearable as possible – people thank you for your hard work, and there's no expectation to stay past 6pm if you're not busy."*

In true work hard/play hard fashion, A&O lawyers raise a glass to closings whenever they can and always make time for Friday night drinks at Levanda, the firm's resident restaurant-cum-bar. Other opportunities for socialising crop up in the form of departmental dinners, team lunches, breakfast briefings, summer barbecues on the roof terrace, drinks trolleys and 'Cake Friday' (are you sensing a theme yet?). To balance out these epicurean events is a spate of sports teams – *"rugby, hockey, football, the works"* – and a few trainee dos from time to time, including the annual summer ball, a glam black tie shindy held this year aboard the ever-esteemed 'HMS Belfast.' *"There was a Champagne reception, a three-course dinner and disco! The partners bent over backwards to let us all out in time to enjoy that."*

And finally...
With a 190-strong trainee cohort, *"it's never difficult to find someone to sit with in the canteen."* Of the 107 qualifiers in 2013, 76 took up jobs with the firm.

Ashfords LLP

The facts

Location: Exeter, Bristol, London, Plymouth, Taunton, Tiverton

Number of UK partners/solicitors: 75/85

Partners who trained at firm: 21%

Total number of trainees: 22

Seats: 4x6 months

Alternative seats: secondments

On chambersstudent.co.uk:

How to get into Ashfords

Doing business in the South West

It's already got a widespread presence in the South West, but Exeter-based Ashfords is also gathering pace in the capital.

Sou'wester

Ashfords has a long history in the West Country which can be traced back to the 19th century. Alumni include one Denis Harward, noted for bringing his spaniel Bumble to work and skiing to the office during harsh winters. These days, trainees are unlikely to be accompanied to the office by any four-legged friends (or their skis), but interviewees did remark that the firm is *"quite rural, not metropolitan. Lots of people commute in from the countryside and have horses."* That's not to say that Ashfords is cut off from the capital besides five offices in the South West (Taunton, Tiverton, Exeter, Bristol and Plymouth) it has a London base too. The latter was strengthened by a 2012 merger with London private client outfit Rochman Landau – the combination created a firm with a total revenue of around £30m.

Corporate/commercial, litigation and property are the main areas of practice along with private client. The Plymouth and Exeter offices also have a significant shipping practice and other niche specialisms include leisure and tourism; agriculture and rural affairs; sport (which includes a top-notch equestrian team); and care homes. As you might expect, Ashfords attracts plenty of South West-based clients, including the Devon and Cornwall Police Authority, Exeter City Council, crowd-funding organisation Crowdcube, Viridor Waste and engineering company Centrax. Clients also include national outfits like Lloyds Banking Group and Age Concern, as well as several London boroughs and international companies like Vinci.

Trainees must complete seats in three out of the four core practice areas (corporate/commercial, litigation, property and private client). Within these groups, trainees

can do stints in insolvency, corporate/banking, projects, planning, commercial property, construction, trusts and estates, employment, personal injury, commercial litigation and property litigation. This *"diverse range of work"* attracted interviewees to the firm, as did the *"fantastic locations"* of the various offices – most of our sources were from or had actively sought a firm in the South West. Doing seats in more than one office is encouraged and *"from the start HR ask us how flexible we are about moving locations."* Nevertheless, new recruits can stay put if they want.

At the time of our calls there were 15 trainees in Exeter, six in Bristol, five in London, three in Taunton and one in Plymouth. Trainees are assigned their first seat, but from the first rotation onwards *"HR will give you a call and discuss your preferences. If there are any difficulties you're instantly told about it, but they do all they can to accommodate your first choice."* Our interviewees noted that *"in previous years there have been grumbles about seat allocation and how that's decided, but the firm has made great efforts to improve the system. I've seen an improvement in how it's dealt with since I've been here."*

Waste not, want not

The property and planning teams both receive top-spot rankings for the Exeter region in *Chambers UK*. The property team acts for clients such as Truro-based developer Poltair Homes, Persimmon Homes, Sovereign Housing Association, and the Homes and Communities Agency. The firm recently advised Exeter City Council on the redevelopment of the city's coach and bus station, valued at over £200m. Trainees also reported *"doing a lot of franchising work"* for clients like Subway. In Taunton,

Chambers UK rankings

Agriculture & Rural Affairs	Intellectual Property
Banking & Finance	Local Government
Construction	Planning
Corporate/M&A	Private Client
Dispute Resolution	Real Estate
Employment	Restructuring/Insolvency
Family/Matrimonial	Shipping
Information Technology	Sports Law

"some of the work is a lot more substantial and higher value than I expected," one trainee said. *"I was working for local clients and an international property company with an office in the South West. I also helped out on a property deal in London worth around £15m."* Sources also mentioned taking on chunks of research. *"I was looking into the risks associated with redevelopment of a derelict property by the Thames,"* said one trainee. *"The client was understandably cautious."* Trainees can also expect to get to grips with drafting leases and renewals.

In planning, trainees *"assist partners with both local government work and matters for private developers – there's a lot of negotiating section 106 agreements."* Meanwhile, the projects seat allows new recruits to work on *"large commercial deals with lots of interrelated contracts. You also get involved in research for pieces of advice on EU law."* Clients of the projects department include Balfour Beatty, the London Borough of Lambeth and North Yorkshire County Council. Ashfords also advised waste management company Urbaser on its bid for an £800m PFI project to construct a waste treatment plant in Essex capable of handling 350,000 tonnes of waste a year.

The corporate department also has a part-national, part-local clientele and acts for many businesses in the energy and waste sectors. The firm recently advised Viridor Waste on the £9m acquisition of recycling businesses Pulp Friction and SBS Paper. During their stint in corporate trainees get involved with all the large M&A deals as well as banking work. *"I dealt with everything from start to finish on one loan agreement,"* said one satisfied interviewee. The firm's banking activities include advising Lloyds on the £30m refinancing of Somerset Care, as well as counselling a subsidiary of Société Générale on providing a £1m loan to buy a luxury motor yacht.

Commercial litigation is *"a very popular seat."* Interviewees had taken on *"clinical negligence and contentious probate work as well as personal injury and commercial disputes."* One trainee told us: *"I did a lot of drafting and attended client meetings. And I was often travelling to London to submit documents to the High Court."*

Business park life

A regular trainee working day is 8.30am to 6pm. *"I'm very pleased that the firm's lived up to its reputation for having a civilised schedule,"* said one interviewee. *"I'm generally home at a decent time. The latest I have finished is 8pm or 9pm and that's only happened on a couple of occasions."* In fact, *"it's more likely that trainees will be told to go home rather than stay late!"* In litigation, *"you might stay to prepare for court the next day, but if that happens it's really exciting to be involved."*

In terms of training, several sources agreed that *"the firm's approach isn't that hands-on."* One trainee explained: *"I would say it's a bit sink-or-swim. As far as teaching or mentoring goes, this place isn't for people who want their hand held. You need to have good commercial awareness and are expected to get going instantly. Partners are generally receptive and willing to assist, but sometimes a bit more explanation would be good. Obviously if you desperately need to ask a question, it's your prerogative to seek help."*

On the whole trainees were happy with the support they received from supervisors but claimed that *"different partners expect different styles, so you have to be flexible."* The same source added that *"the firm could benefit from organising drafting lessons to help with consistency."* Sources also flagged up the fact that *"the small size of some teams means that you don't have the buffer levels of associates that you do at bigger firms. Instead you work directly with partners and have to adapt and get used to their particular style of signing off e-mails, for example."*

"I think the culture here varies from office to office," mused one interviewee, *"there's less of a monolithic corporate culture and more of a feeling that we are a collection of smaller businesses working together."* Overall, sources felt that in Exeter and Taunton *"everyone mucks in and there's a friendly buzz about the place."* These two offices are situated on out-of-town business parks, which means *"there's less of an after-work going-out culture and people are less likely to pop into town to run an errand at lunch."* However, the Exeter location does offer *"a gym, a car wash, dry cleaning and a very good café."* Inside, the open-plan office *"lends itself to being open and sociable. There's a lot of discussion and I can learn more just by listening to what's going on around me."* In Bristol the atmosphere is *"fairly informal because it's a small, intimate office. The kitchen is plastered with pictures of nights out!"* Meanwhile, in London Ashfords is steadily becoming established after the still-recent merger with Rochman Landau and trainees reported that *"everyone pitches in together."*

In the Exeter office there are *"departmental socials quite regularly"* as well as plenty of pub quiz outings and various sports teams including mixed netball and – unusually – darts. Since Ashfords is *"one of the biggest firms in the region, it takes a lead in the local law society"* and sources across offices mentioned that *"trainees are encouraged to get involved in networking events for young professionals."* In Bristol, there are *"drinks every Friday in the office, which is nice because partners join in and you can just have a chat."* Interviewees were also looking forward to another *"fantastic summer party"* – the event was introduced in 2012 when it took place in a field near Bridgwater in Somerset, where solicitors merrily partook of croquet games, lawn tennis and a hog roast, with musical accompaniment from a live band.

Finely matured

So is there an Ashfords trainee 'type'? Well, several of our interviewees were a bit older than average. *"There aren't too many fresh-faced people here who came straight from uni,"* observed one interviewee. *"A lot of us have a bit more life experience and are in their 30s or 40s. If you've already established yourself in another profession, that's valued by the firm."* However, there isn't a requisite age or background. *"Personality counts for a lot, rather* than just whether you are bookish and have the very best grades. In this economic climate the firm needs people who are more charismatic and willing to go out and network,"* asserted one trainee. *"The people here are really varied, but commercial awareness is important. You have to be fairly outgoing and able to hold your own in conversation,"* said another interviewee. *"When you work here you get to meet all sorts of people and put yourself about a bit."*

When it comes to the qualification crunch, trainees were pleased to report that, as with allocation, this process has been improved. *"A lot of people had complained that it wasn't very transparent. People would just get earmarked for a job and then get a tap on the shoulder."* Now, a jobs list is circulated and trainees apply with a CV and covering letter before going for interviews. Despite this improvement, our sources generally weren't very confident about their chances of being kept on. At the time we went to press the firm told us ten out of 17 qualifiers were taking up NQ jobs, although a few more could potentially be offered roles.

And finally...

Ashfords attracts a variety of trainees, and likes recruiting individuals with some career experience.

"As a trainee you have to do a lot more administrative work than you allow yourself to admit before you start. That's not highlighted much at careers fairs."

Trainee

"In my first week I was working on an IPO launch."

"Coming to an international office for my third seat has allowed me to work on some of the most exciting areas of corporate law, including M&As and IPOs. No two days here have been the same; I've attended client meetings and worked on drafting documents, including a Share Purchase Agreement.

The added responsibility that comes from working in a smaller team has allowed me more client interaction and greater exposure to a range of different deals. A definite highlight was working on an IPO launch, not to mention helping to close an oil and gas transaction during the first week of my placement. It's been a real learning curve but with the support of my supervisor, I've enjoyed every second."

Adrian Cheung
Seat: Corporate, Hong Kong
Studied: Law at Cambridge University

Ashurst is a leading international law firm and those joining us are encouraged to undertake an overseas placement. To find out more visit:
www.ashurst.com/trainees

make your presence felt

ashurst

careers in international law
f www.facebook.com/AshurstTrainees

Ashurst

The facts

Location: London

Number of UK partners/solicitors: 130/320

Partners who trained at firm: 33%

Total number of trainees: 95

Seats: 4x6 months

Altenative seats: overseas seats, secondments

Extras: pro bono – LawWorks, A4ID, TrustLaw, Toynbee Hall Legal Advice Centre, Reprieve; language bursary

On chambersstudent.co.uk...

How to get into Ashurst

Ashurst's beginnings

Overseas seats

This high-flying City firm handles top-end corporate and finance work and continues to build its cross-border clout.

Sterling silver

Imagine law firms are horses. If the magic circle were five powerful thoroughbred racehorses, Ashurst is in the stable right next door. He's also a pedigree horse and keeps up with the elite – but at the end of a long working day he'll readily let his mane down by the drinking trough.

So, while Ashurst is usually described as a member of the 'silver circle', trainees declared that *"the quality of work is pretty much the same as the magic circle. It's not the rung below."* Is this true? Ashurst is certainly capable of taking on absolutely massive, multi-jurisdictional matters – deals such as the $10.3bn merger of Indian firms Sesa Goa and Sterlite Industries, both subsidiaries of UK-based Vedanta Resources, confirm this. We would say that the largest, most global of deals do still tend to end up on the magic circle's desks more often than not, but certainly Ashurst trainees won't be starved of very big transactions involving well-known companies such as Tesco, Bank of America Merrill Lynch, RBS, Credit Suisse and BNP Paribas, to name but a few. What really seems to mark Ashurst out is a sense of approachability. It is a well-known name on campuses around the country, but has a less scary reputation than the magic circle. Trainees were attracted to a *"prestigious firm that's also positive and inclusive – it doesn't take itself as seriously as others."*

Since the 90s Ashurst has occasionally entertained the prospect of merging, but none of the prospective matches were quite suitable... until 2012 that is, when the firm's Asian practices were united with those of Blake Dawson, one of Australia's 'Big Six' – now known as Ashurst Australia. This tie-up adds significantly to the firm's interna-

tional capability, giving it a big boost in East Asia as well as Oz.

If you look at the *Chambers UK* rankings you'll get a good idea of what Ashurst's core strengths are: it's recommended for a host of areas related to corporate and finance: big-ticket M&A, capital markets, banking and funds work. The firm also has a good reputation for real estate, high-end litigation, projects and energy and all sorts of other areas, but any training contract here will probably be weighted towards those two core areas. *"Ashurst is big, so there's a whole host of seats available."* The finance department is the the only compulsory destination and is split into all sorts of subdivisions; additionally, there are seats in corporate; dispute resolution; energy, transport and infrastructure (ETI); employment, incentives and pensions (EIP); real estate; tax; and competition. There are also client secondments and overseas seats. The seat allocation process is a matter of *"e-mailing in preferences and hoping for the best"* or having a chat with HR. In most cases, trainees were satisfied with the outcome, although a few commented that *"it would be better to have more transparency, and perhaps a more personal approach regarding how you see your career developing and where you want to go."*

A profitable pickle

During the corporate seat, trainees can get involved with some hefty deals. Sources reported *"a lot of corporate work for Tesco"* regarding the supermarket's purchase of the Giraffe restaurant chain for £48.6m. Other toothsome projects include advising Japanese-based food manufacturer the Mizkan Group on its £92.5m acquisition of Premier Foods' sauce business (including the Branston

The True Picture

Chambers UK rankings

Banking & Finance	Information Technology
Banking Litigation	Insurance
Capital Markets	Intellectual Property
Competition/European Law	Investment Funds
Construction	Local Government
Corporate Crime &	Outsourcing
Investigations	Pensions
Corporate/M&A	Planning
Dispute Resolution	Private Equity
Employee Share Schemes	Product Liability
& Incentives	Projects
Employment	Real Estate Finance
Energy & Natural	Restructuring/Insolvency
Resources	Tax
Environment	Telecommunications
Financial Services	Transport
Fraud	

pickle brand and the factory in Bury St Edmunds which makes it). The corporate department also advised The College (now University) of Law on its £200m sale to Montagu Private Equity. Unsurprisingly, the department *"has a tendency to be busy"* and propels trainees up a *"steep learning curve."* One source remembered *"less than a month into the seat I was interacting with a pretty senior client on a call, which I thought was pretty cool."* Trainees found that *"the good thing about tasks such as due diligence, verification and research is that you end up knowing the most about what's going on."*

It's possible to get *"a lot of exposure to niche areas of banking and derivatives trading"* in finance seats. One source commented: *"Finance is quite jargon-heavy and conceptually difficult, so actually doing the proof-reading is the best way to get to grips with what's going on. People then work out how much you can handle. By the end of the seat I was probably doing associate-level drafting."* In the structured finance group, trainees described working *"mainly for very large banks like Credit Suisse, JPMorgan and Goldman Sachs on high-value, prestigious projects."* Likewise, those who'd sat in the securities and derivatives group noted that *"your clients are the largest banks in the world so the work is incredibly important, the backbone of the firm. But because the deals are so big, in the billions, you get less freedom to do stuff on your own. Instead you work on smaller, discrete tasks and document management, maybe drafting the occasional clause."* Ashurst's recent projects include advising a group of four banks on the £501m leveraged buyout of Mercury Pharma, and working on the refinancing of the acquisition of 1 Kingdom Street in London's West End.

All down the line

ETI is *"a headline practice which the firm is very proud of,"* thought trainees. *"There's a real buzz on the floor. People are working on big deals and when the firm pitches for a project they usually get it."* Sources reported *"taking on a real cross-section of matters"* here, including oil and gas corporate takeovers, assignments related to waste-to-energy as well as general project finance deals. Rail is a first-class team within the group. *"For most of my seat there I was working on one of the big Crossrail projects,"* one trainee revealed. Ashurst has been advising on London's Crossrail development since 2008, with a recent focus on the procurement of depots and rolling stock through public-private partnerships. A newer client is Virgin Trains – the firm is instructing the company on all rolling stock arrangements in relation to the new West Coast Passenger Rail franchise. As a part of this, one source had completed a *"small, self-contained project on which there was just me and a senior associate. All in all, it's a very interesting time to be in rail because of what's going on in government. The 'franchising fiasco' was very topical."* You may remember this story from 2012, when the government reversed its decision to award the West Coast Main Line franchise to First-Group, at a cost of £50m to the taxpayer. Involvement in the railway business *"made a good change from working with banks,"* according to trainees. *"You're working with people who're actually building things. The projects are so big and technical that as a trainee there are only so many things you're able to do. But by the end of the seat I felt able to do more interesting tasks, like drafting amendments to the main contract."*

A *"diverse range of work"* is also available in the real estate seat. *"There's a huge variety of clients and deal sizes. You could be looking at a small lease of a supermarket store and you could run with that yourself. On the other hand, you might be involved with a much larger transaction for an office in the City, worth about £300–400m. In those scenarios, you tend to be doing tasks like proofreading and document management, more standard trainee stuff."* The firm has some pretty whopping real estate matters on the go, including advising Sellar Property Group on the latest addition to the London skyline, The Shard, since 2006. Ashurst has also been working for Westfield in connection with the sale and development of the Broadway shopping centre project in Bradford. Trainees described attending meetings and handling clients as well as *"getting out and about a lot. I travelled to places like Huddersfield and Birmingham for judicial review hearings."* Sources had also worked on large planning applications for clients like Landprop, the real estate arm of IKEA, in relation to a mixed-use development near the Olympic Park.

High-profile work means tough hours. Trainees admitted that *"you don't go into a big City law firm not expecting to work late. Law isn't really a career where you can have flexible hours, and the clients are very demanding, especially in finance. You have to do what you have to do, I guess."* One source recalled *"one horrendous stretch for a day and a half where I didn't sleep. But I did get given days off in lieu."* However, *"although you'll sometimes be working crazy hours, until 4am for several consecutive days, this isn't the case all the time. The workload is cyclical."* Furthermore, toiling into the night creates *"such a sense of teamwork and camaraderie. It's very rare for there to be just one person staying late. Everyone is always pitching in."* Trainees might get tired, but they won't go hungry – the cafeteria is open until 10pm and free dinners are available after 7pm. Neither do trainees have to take the night bus home, as the firm pays for taxis after 10pm.

Not so Lashurst anymore?

With all this office exertion, Ashurst folk are often *"willing to go for a drink"* and there's lots to get involved in. Trainees are given responsibility for organising an annual themed ball, there are ski trips in various departments and summertime barbecues held at partners' country piles. *"A drama society has been mooted"* to complement the existing range of sports teams and language classes on offer.

"The old-boy atmosphere of the firm" that was a feature of Ashurst in the past *"has waned as Ashurst's tried to climb higher up the ladder of firms."* Sources commented that *"it does feel very international here, more so since the merger. It has a global approach now. Within the firm there's people from absolutely everywhere."* Crucially, *"people are interested in how hard you work rather than what Oxford college you went to."* The majority of our sources did attend bigger-name universities – but not all of them. *"What I found on the vac scheme and subsequently is that they like decent, sociable people. The people who didn't get in tended to be arrogant and very competitive, unnecessarily throwing their weight around,"* though one source. Other interviewees emphasised that *"everyone here is quite confident, bubbly and outspoken. It isn't a place for shy and retiring types who just want to shut the door and do their work."* All agreed: *"It's nice to be surrounded by smiley people. Even when the work – like bundling – is far from glamorous, you're doing it in a room with friends and chocolate. This might sound disgusting but I actually get up and want to go to work!"*

And finally...

Ashurst offers a top City experience and is able to combine it with a good atmosphere in the corridors. In 2013, it retained 43 of 57 second-years upon qualification.

Baker & McKenzie. Born global.

Join Baker & McKenzie and you'll have the best of all worlds.

Global is the first word people associate with Baker & McKenzie. We were established to offer a genuinely global perspective and operate without boundaries around the world.

Other law firms can open offices worldwide to try to match what we have. But they can't readily match how we think, work and behave.

Our global reach means we have well-known clients; we have fantastic relationships because we are business people who are great lawyers (not the other way around).

Our approach is friendly and inclusive; we are nice people and good citizens.

You'll find this a challenging and stimulating place to work, but one where you will also be inspired to always be your best.

Visit **www.bakermckenzie.com/londongraduates** to find out more.

BAKER & McKENZIE

Baker & McKenzie

The facts

Location: London

Number of UK partners/solicitors: 79/236 (+36 non-UK-qualified)

Partners who trained at firm: 37.5%

Total number of trainees: 81

Seats: 4x6 months

Alternative seats: overseas seats, secondments

Extras: pro bono – Bethnal Green Legal Advice Centre, Law-Works, A4ID and others

On chambersstudent.co.uk...

How to get into Baker Mac
Interview with training partner Simon Porter
From small firm beginnings to global giant
Understanding Swiss Vereins

Baker & McKenzie presents its gregarious trainees with a superlatively international outlook.

The American dream

Baker & McKenzie's co-founder Russell Baker sounds like a one-man embodiment of the American dream: in the 1920s he spent days stowed away in cold cattle cars to get to the University of Chicago, where he boxed at county fairs to pay his tuition. The same pioneering spirit was still evident after he founded the firm that bears his name. Along with partner John McKenzie, he made the decision to open its first office outside the States (in Venezuela) in 1956, and the Chicago firm soon expanded into Europe too – impressive in the days when flights were an expensive luxury and the English-speaking world traded among themselves in cheery self-sufficiency. These days, B&M's global approach is less of a rarity, more a necessity, and despite already being one of the two largest firms in the world, the firm is still growing – 2012 alone saw the launch of offices in South Africa, Morocco and Peru, and in 2013 B&M set up shop in UAE after absorbing a Dubai-based firm. In all, Baker has over 70 offices across 46 countries.

Although B&M London is built around corporate and finance, the office is an all-rounder and its employment, IT, administrative and public law, private client, outsourcing and telecoms departments all get top rankings from *Chambers UK.* The office has been around since 1961, and since B&M has never been the type of firm where everything is dictated from the USA, it makes sense the firm *"doesn't feel American,"* and *"there's no sense the Chicago office is a mothership."* In fact, London is now the firm's largest office.

Rich mix

Trainees are guaranteed their first-choice seat at least once, and our sources were happy with the *"transparent"* allocation system. Corporate is the only compulsory seat, and clients of this department *"range from the standard big names to weird and wonderful companies in industries you'd never have considered, like paper mills, cash changing and computer server maintenance."* Recent major deals include advising Carlsberg during its $1.2bn buy out of Russian and Eastern European brewing giant Baltika, and advising Siemens on acquiring part of Expro Holdings UK, which manufactures equipment necessary for a sea bed power grid that Siemens is planning.

The corporate department is a large one and, as well as standard M&A, depending on where they're sitting trainees might experience restructuring and insolvency work, private equity, capital markets, or even project finance and infrastructure matters, where they work for *"big mining and oil and gas companies, and governments as well,"* often in emerging markets. For example, the firm has recently advised clients on the $10bn development of an oil refinery in Angola, solar power projects in South Africa, a wind project in Namibia and the expansion of phospate mining operations in Saudi Arabia. The sale of a mine saw a trainee *"drafting ancillary documents, managing workstreams and keeping everyone up to date on the progress of the deal."* The capital markets seat, meanwhile, covers debt, securitisation and derivatives work. One trainee told of *"lots of big corporate reorganisation work"* on a bond issue for an overseas bank, working late nights *"unpicking transactions for things that had gone wrong, and offering advice."*

The True Picture

Chambers UK rankings

Administrative & Public	Immigration
Law	Information Technology
Banking & Finance	Intellectual Property
Banking Litigation	Investment Funds
Capital Markets	Media & Entertainment
Competition/European Law	Outsourcing
Construction	Pensions
Corporate/M&A	Pensions Litigation
Data Protection	Private Client
Dispute Resolution	Private Equity
Employee Share Schemes	Product Liability
& Incentives	Professional Discipline
Employment	Public International Law
Energy & Natural	Public Procurement
Resources	Real Estate
Environment	Restructuring/Insolvency
Financial Services	Sports Law
Franchising	Tax
Fraud	Telecommunications

B&M's banking department has been busy with a lot of international project finance and acquisition finance – 13 of the firm's offices were involved in wrapping up the €1.8bn financing of private equity group EQT for its acquisition of bandage supplier BSN Medical. It also handles major litigation for banks including JPMorgan Europe and Bank St Petersburg. There's plenty of smaller-scale work on offer, too – one trainee enjoyed a *"nice organic progression"* on a loan agreement, moving from a gentle start *"doing conditions precedent, getting all the documents together and drafting minutes"* to end up *"running quite a lot of aspects of the project."*

Trust auntie

The employment team is top-ranked in *Chambers UK*, and has recently made the news advising the BBC Trust on the high-profile departure of its Director General George Entwhistle, in the wake of the scandal surrounding the Newsnight child abuse investigations. Other work has included advising GM on its labour agreement with trade union Unite, and assisting BA's in-house employment team on security-related discrimination claims. It's *"hugely varied – not just corporate support,"* one source asserted. Trainees investigate interesting discrete points – *"someone might ask if they can put tracking devices in executive cars"* – and fourth-seaters *"get more opportunities to run the litigation themselves,"* especially for *"a fairly cost-conscious long-standing former pro bono client."*

The dispute resolution group has been *"kept busy with BBC work,"* which, thanks to the Leveson Inquiry and reviews into Savile-era practices on behalf of the BBC Trust, proved *"very interesting. We were working to 2 or 3am, but it didn't feel like that – it was a really great experience."* Other matters B&M has advised the Beeb on include challenges from the Lib Dems and independent candidate Siobhan Bonita regarding their allocation (or lack thereof) of party political broadcasts during the London mayoral election. Other clients include major banks such as JPMorgan, lottery operator Camelot, McDonald's and Sony. Trainees also experienced multi-jurisdictional arbitration work on behalf of big overseas clients: *"You really get to see the differences between the litigation system and how arbitration works."* A common feature of the seat is nipping out for court duty: *"At least once a week you have to go to the Royal Courts of Justice to check the pigeon holes or do filing."*

A seat in IT/commercial offers *"intellectual work; you learn a lot about the tech industry."* The team works for pioneering new businesses like Pinterest and Dropbox as well as more established players like Google and Netflix, and put *"a lot of trust"* in trainees, who are allowed to grapple with *"sophisticated questions, analysing quite detailed contracts for specific scenarios."* Over in IP lawyers provide clients with pre-contentious advice regarding trade mark and design infringement: *"That's very much the technical law side of the seat – the other side is working on anti-counterfeiting programmes, working with customs to identify counterfeits for clients."* Anti-counterfeit work often involves co-operation with foreign counsel: a trainee's experience might be *"a bit more administrative than legal, as it entails co-ordinating all the different parties."*

At B&M, *"you're expected to put in the hours,"* with most of our sources reporting regular post-11pm finishes or weekends visits to the office at busy times. That said, hard work doesn't go unnoticed. *"Everyone always expresses their appreciation."* Despite *"a really big feedback culture"* between supervisors and trainees, we did hear that mid and end-of-seat reviews are sometimes delayed; however, trainee principal Simon Porter says that's *"something we're working on."* Trainees often sit with partners, though *"you tend to get most work from senior associates, who act more as your line manager."* On the whole trainees are encouraged to be *"proactive"* and *"actively go out and get work from other people."* Because the firm *"runs a lean ship,"* responsibility levels are *"very good compared to magic circle firms with their armies of trainees,"* sources declared. In fact, some were *"shocked"* by how much they were given at times. *"I effectively ran the minor restructuring of a company."* B&M also offers trainees plenty of opportunities to *"build a rapport"* with clients. Reported one interviewee: *"In one seat clients dealt solely with me. I still keep in touch with a few."*

Rule the world

With a *"clear strategy"* of positioning itself *"on the cusp of emerging markets,"* B&M is constantly growing its overseas capabilities. *"Middle East expansion is really pushing ahead"* thanks to the recent merger in Dubai. The firm uses *"actual local lawyers"* wherever it goes, which means each office remains quite autonomous. Despite Baker's international ubiquity, there is this emphasis on using home-grown talent, so *"it isn't as common to go overseas"* for secondments as you might think. *"There's an open application process, but you really have to make the case to a department that it's worth their while to send you out somewhere."* Trainees have headed out for three-month stints in Sydney, San Francisco, Hong Kong and Moscow in recent months, and a handful recently got the chance to go to the new Johannesburg office for three weeks. In-house stints with various London-based clients are also an option.

Our interviewees reported the firm is *"pushing to improve its overall quality"* in order to compete with magic circle firms. One explained: *"Post-financial crash management has decided the firm will thrive best if it aims for the highest value work. In a recession you need to be a leaner, slightly harder place."* With all this status anxiety at play, it's little wonder that trainees seemed hyper-aware of how the B&M experience measures up to the magic circle. Interviewees noted that some departments *"tend to only take one qualifying trainee, so you really have to be the best. There's more of a margin at the magic circle."* To ease the pressure on smaller departments come qualification, trainee principal Simon Porter explains *"we've been trying to attract trainees with more of an interest in corporate work,"* so do bear that in mind. In 2013, B&M retained 28 out of 37 of its qualifiers.

Into the space age

Some of the *"relaxed and gregarious"* B&M trainees told us their friends working within the magic circle *"can't believe the level of informality there is between partners and trainees"* at this firm. Sources praised the *"very open culture, where you can voice your opinions even though you're a trainee."* Furthermore, the firm *"isn't full of old stuffy white men puffing away on pipes and making misogynist remarks; the firm takes diversity very seriously,"* backing its words up with *"every support group under the sun."* As a result, *"it really doesn't matter who you are and where you come from."*

A *"very sociable"* firm, B&M hosts monthly Friday drinks in the canteen and a much-loved firmwide Christmas party – the hijinks of last year's holiday do were such that firm higher ups would rather remain tight-lipped about them. Trainees told of recently discovering the City of London Distillery – *"the first working distillery to open in the City for over 200 years"* – and *"lots of little afternoon events. On one occasion people brought in their children for a party, which was lovely."* Sports on offer include hockey, netball and football, the last culminating in an inter-office European cup tournament held in a different city each year. *"They subsidise the kit and food and everything!"* We heard the Blackfriars-based office *"isn't particularly snazzy,"* though the *"nineties-looking"* digs have recently benefited from *"a huge IT update. We have screen monitors like massive spaceships now."*

The True Picture

And finally...
Insiders all agreed B&M *"feels like a firm on the up."*

Bates Wells Braithwaite

The facts

Location: London

Number of UK partners/solicitors: 31/49

Partners who trained at firm: 23%

Total number of trainees: 8

Seats: 2x6 + 3x4 months

Alternative seats: none

Extras: pro bono – South West London Law Centre

On chambersstudent.co.uk...

How to get into BWB

BWB's sector groups

More work highlights

With a lot of opportunities in corporate and commercial, there's more to this gem that just the charidee.

Goodfellas

If you're of a charitable disposition then chances are Bates Wells Braithwaite is already on your radar. This oasis in the City is well renowned for acting for charities of every kind – thousands in fact, ranging from tiny local enterprises and start-ups to the national and international big boys: the NSPCC, Christian Aid, Barnardo's and the RSPCA are all long-standing clients. Accordingly, the charity group is the only such department in London to be top-ranked by our parent publication *Chambers UK*. *"It's the firm's USP,"* confirm trainees, adding that Bates Wells professes to *"have a genuine conscience."* This conscience is all well and good, but it's important to mention that charity isn't the be-all and end-all of BWB – in fact, commercial work overtook charity as the firm's biggest earner in 2012, amounting to 31% to the latter's 23% of business.

Indeed, the corporate group, and M&A in particular, has seen a monumental surge over the last couple of years. M&A turnover has increased around 150%, and in 2012 BWB brought in former LG partner Richard Marke to bolster the corporate practice, bringing with him expertise in tech and outsourcing. One clued-up source summed up the changes: *"The firm is so dominant in the charities sector that it's hard to make much leeway in that market. So we have been pursuing commercial clients with a social aspect to their work – like crowdfunding – which is making the work more corporate. But we're never going to lose that founding ethos – if we lose that then we cease to be unique."*

Current trainees see BWB as *"a happy medium between a corporate firm and a human rights one."* Quite right. Despite all the talk of more corporate work, *Chambers UK* awards the firm high rankings for areas like immigration, public law, education and media (particularly theatre work).

Airplane!

Rather than individual seats, BWB newbies begin by picking a 'flight path'. These four set journeys are mapped out from the start and made up of five seats apiece – two six-month stints in the first year followed by three seats of four months each in the second. *"It gives you a good insight – especially if you're indecisive,"* said one trainee. Interviewees also appreciated being able to spend longer in the departments they visit in their first year. *"Initially you never know what you're doing when you join a department, but in your second year you can get off to a flying start,"* explained one. All of the paths include stints in dispute resolution and charity (which one trainee will visit twice), with a chance to include stops in immigration, employment, property and company/commercial. Trainees are also assigned a cross-departmental sector group such as arts, charities and education, allowing them to put a specific interest to practical use.

Charity – still *"the lifeblood"* of the firm – is *"always buzzing and always hectic."* Trainees sit with a partner whose speciality could be anything from education to sports to trusts to social enterprise. Rest assured there's a *"huge, huge variety of work"* going on – and not just the things you'd first expect. The team jumped in to help the Wikimedia Foundation – the charity set up to collect donations from visitors to Wikipedia – on a high-profile conflict of interests issue. It also advised Harry, Wills and Kate (okay, it was their Royal Foundation really) on the closure of the Diana, Princess of Wales Memorial Fund, and acted for Teach First on the organisation's tender for work in preparation for its recent major expansion. If a trainee is advis-

Chambers UK rankings

Administrative & Public Law	Employment
Charities	Healthcare
Data Protection	Immigration
Defamation/Reputation	Media & Entertainment
Management	Partnership
Education	Professional Discipline
	Real Estate Litigation

ing the board of an international charity – *"it's always so interesting when you're dealing with household names"* – there'll also be scope to simultaneously run their own small files. *"You get to deal with start-ups, and help them incorporate as a company or gain charitable status."* Interviewees told us that even when working with partner-supervisors *"at the top of their game,"* the group *"recognises it's their responsibility to educate trainees."*

All doggs go to heaven

"We mainly deal with tier two skilled migrant immigration cases," said one trainee of their time in this *Chambers* top-ranked department, *"although there is the chance to meet Snoop Dogg on his private plane."* Fo' shizzle! Head of department Philip Trott has, it turns out, a bit of a sideline in the rap game, advising Busta Rhymes, Kanye West, 50 Cent and convicted domestic abuser Chris Brown on entry to the UK. It's not all 99 problems though, and sources assert the main work of the department is corporate immigration. Corporate maybe, but when you're acting for the likes of Nike, Endemol, the Royal Shakespeare Company and News International things can't ever become dull. Trainees agree: *"It's all about the detail – when something in immigration goes wrong, it really goes wrong and the client may not be allowed into the country for ten years."* There's also the chance to work on human rights appeals *"and always some pro bono work – you'll research all the case law and draft the argument yourself."* While charity is known for its heavy hours, immigration was said to have *"a more comfortable pace, although by the time you're finished at the end of the day your mind is fried from thinking so hard."*

All the corporate expansion means there's plenty of M&A work on offer, which brings the *"inevitable late nights."* The firm's focus is still on small to mid-market private M&A, private equity and venture capital. *"On the bigger transactions you find yourself doing tasks like drafting

board minutes and ancillary documents."* There's plenty of commercial work to complement this – think commercial contracts and constitutional work.

Dispute resolution is a popular seat which is *"extremely varied – from commercial disputes in court to trade mark issues."* Employment, meanwhile, is *"almost completely contentious,"* and trainees here bear the brunt of trial work. *"There's always a lot of bundling and photocopying to be done,"* though interviewees assured us there are also frequent opportunities to attend trial and try your hand at drafting witness statements. Overall, sources emphasised the *"extraordinary levels of responsibility"* at BWB. *"It's always a surprise that I'm actually worth my charge-out rate, but I'm very grateful,"* one joked.

Another year

As you may imagine, lots of BWB lawyers *"are trustees of charities or involved with some form of social enterprise."* There's a strong pro bono culture too, with links to the South West London Law Centre. This work is *"more vital than ever with the cuts to legal aid."* Despite the strong altruistic angle to life at BWB, trainees thought that when it comes to recruitment *"previous charity work experience shouldn't be over-emphasised."* We spotted a real variety of backgrounds in our interviewee group – it's safe to say that people tend to be slightly older than your average City trainee and *"aren't the 'let's get wasted at 5.30' types."* There is, however, a flourishing social committee *"which organises a lot of events, from trips to museums to karaoke nights."*

Unfortunately, trainees told us unanimously that the NQ jobs process had been *"disastrous"* this year. The firm initially announced that only one of four qualifiers would be kept on, *"and there wasn't a proper internal process in place."* Eventually, *"another qualifier was offered a job, but by that time everyone had already secured places elsewhere."* To some, these events signal something of an identity crisis: *"We're moving towards being commercial but don't have the benefits, pay or full funding of the LPC to go with it,"* said a trainee, adding that *"while we're expanding, from an organisational point of view there's too little structure and not enough communication."* Despite these misgivings, trainees agreed that the poor retention figures shouldn't act as a deterrent: *"The most fundamental thing is securing good training, and that's what Bates Wells provides. Sitting with supervisors who've been partners for 15 years really ups the learning curve."*

And finally...

With corporate/commercial activities on the up and charities work less dominant (although still going strong), Bates Wells is going through a period of change.

Berwin Leighton Paisner LLP

The facts

Location: London

Number of UK partners/solicitors: 180/324 (+16 non-UK qualified)

Partners who trained at firm: 17%

Total number of trainees: 84

Seats: 4x6 months

Alternative seats: overseas seats, secondments

Extras: pro bono – Sonali Gardens Legal Advice Clinic

On chambersstudent.co.uk...

How to get into BLP

Interview with partners Tim Smith and Neville Eisenberg

This ambitious top-20 firm has enjoyed a successful decade in London and now has its sights set overseas.

Technicolour dreamfirm?

City firm Berwin Leighton Paisner has existed in its current form since the merger of Berwin Leighton and Paisner & Co in 2001. Since then, under the stewardship of managing partner Neville Eisenberg revenues have more than doubled – they stood at £233m in 2012/13, a slight drop from the year before. "*We are an ambitious firm and we are always trying to do better work and win more clients,*" a trainee said. "*And there is certainly an aggressive push from the senior levels if you look at what we are achieving. The biggest change I've noticed since I started is the increasing focus on all things international.*"

Indeed. Global expansion is now on the menu. BLP has opened five overseas offices in the past three years, most recently setting up in Dubai (2012) and Beijing (2013). It now has ten offices across Europe, the Middle East and Asia (Moscow is the largest). We've always said in the past that BLP's not a firm where the trainee experience is heavily influenced by the presence of large overseas offices, but it's clear this is changing. In 2011/12 revenues from the overseas offices grew by nearly 45% and there are also rumours that management is considering an international merger, possibly with a firm in the Asia-Pacific region. "*My own view is that that is unlikely to happen,*" graduate recruitment partner Tim Smith told us. "*Thus far, our international expansion has been successful without pursuing that strategy* [of merger], *but I would never rule it out.*"

BLP bases its work around five core 'pillars': corporate, real estate, finance, tax and litigation ("*a coat of many colours*" as one trainee observed). Historically, BLP has always been strongest in real estate and it arguably has

the most highly regarded property practice in the City. Qatari Diar, John Lewis, Tesco, Westfield and investment firm Blackstone are all clients. Given the firm's prowess in these areas, "*technically the line they push is that you should do a real estate and a corporate seat as well as a contentious seat. And you are now encouraged to do a finance seat too.*" In practice, many trainees we spoke to had deviated from this course. "*The HR team are showing themselves to be more and more flexible on what trainees can do.*"

There are presentations about each seat a few months into every rotation, and trainees also have meetings with HR to discuss their next move. "*There is a degree of advocacy involved – you have to make your case and give some background on why you want to do a seat.*" Corporate seats can be taken in M&A, public markets, funds and financial services, and private equity. The contentious requirement can be fulfilled in commercial dispute resolution, insurance/reinsurance, restructuring, IP, real estate disputes, employment, competition, contentious tax, planning or construction. The remaining seat options are commercial, tax, debt capital markets and asset finance.

Hot property

Real estate is "*what the firm does best*" according to trainees. BLP is ranked in the top two tiers of all four of *Chambers UK*'s London real estate categories: the only firm with that distinction. The department is split into three groups. "*Group two is retail-focused and does a lot of work for Tesco,*" a key client, while the others work on large corporate property deals – developments, acquisitions etc – for banks, investment funds, hotels and other institutional clients. "*A big driver recently has been the*

Chambers UK rankings

Asset Finance	Insurance
Banking & Finance	Licensing
Banking Litigation	Local Government
Capital Markets	Media & Entertainment
Charities	Outsourcing
Competition/European Law	Parliamentary & Public
Construction	Affairs
Corporate Crime &	Pensions
Investigations	Planning
Corporate/M&A	Private Client
Defamation/Reputation	Private Equity
Management	Projects
Dispute Resolution	Public Procurement
Employment	Real Estate Finance
Energy & Natural	Restructuring/Insolvency
Resources	Retail
Environment	Social Housing
Financial Services	Sports Law
Fraud	Tax
Healthcare	Telecommunications
Information Technology	Transport

cross-border work – a lot of overseas sovereign wealth funds [like Qatari Diar] are involved in big-ticket developments across London. I really enjoyed the number of 'skyline projects' we are involved in – you see things you've worked on popping up all over the city." The firm recently helped advise the landowners on arranging the £500m+ lease of a brand-new office building near King's Cross for Google's new UK headquarters. BLP also advised The FA on the £105m development of the National Football Centre in Burton-on-Trent and acted for the investor who has bought up Admiralty Arch in order to convert it into a hotel. "On the bigger deals I manage and review documents, complete conditions precedent check-lists, liaise with other lawyers, do the scheduling and deal with disclosure," one trainee told us. Another added: "Usually, you are also given your own files to manage. I dealt with leases and licences and helped sell two restaurants just working with a partner." It's "a challenge" to juggle both these types of work but "after the initial 'OMG! moment', it's amazing."

The various corporate teams each have around 30 to 40 lawyers and trainees usually join a single one (although they may end up taking work from several). The M&A team is top-ranked for mid-market work by *Chambers UK*. It recently acted for JPMorgan Cazenove and Canaccord Genuity on the £89m acquisition of famous jewellers Fabergé by gemstone firm Gemfields, as well as advising gaming company Playtech on the sale of its 29%, £424m stake in William Hill's online division to the bookie's main operation. "*I worked on some good mid-market deals,*"

one trainee said. "*It is the sort of work where you close a deal and then see it in the press the next day.*" Another added: "*I was the key trainee on a big deal for a major private equity client. There were a lot of less glamorous things to do like due diligence, transaction management and dealing with the ancillary documents. But when you see how that feeds into the purchase agreement and actually allows a merger to take place, it feels quite exciting.*"

AIM higher

The 'public markets' seat could equally be called 'equity capital markets'. The department is "*very strong in AIM work*" and recently advised asset managers Schroders on the £100m AIM flotation of its West End property trust WELPIC. There's main market work too. "*I had responsibility for the document management and other aspects of a deal in which we were helping a company raise funds and move from the AIM market to the London Stock Exchange,*" said one trainee. The firm also recently advised FTSE 250 property investment firm Raven Russia on raising $104m in the markets to help finance the takeover of a Moscow-based logistics company.

Commercial dispute resolution is by far the biggest contentious department. "*We do general breach of contract and misrepresentation work, but there is also a growing financial crime and fraud team,*" a trainee said. The firm recently defended HSBC Private Bank in a $300m High Court claim brought by a businessman who the bank had declined to perform various transactions for because of a pending SOCA case. A trainee told us: "*I got to go to court for one big six-week trial. It was great to see the final piece of the puzzle after putting in weeks of work. My task on that was predominantly bundling – there were 80 bundles in total – but on other cases I have drafted witness statements and application notices and I had the opportunity to appear before a Master to make a request for an application.*"

Another seat option we should give a mention are the stints overseas. "*The number of international opportunities is increasing fast, as we seem to be opening new offices every few months,*" one interviewee told us. Trainees can currently go to Brussels, Moscow, Abu Dhabi and Singapore to complete seats in competition, corporate, contentious construction and finance respectively. All but the Brussels placement are assigned a short while before the other seats, with interested trainees asked to give a brief written statement of why they want to go. No special qualities are needed to win an overseas posting, and once out there trainees can get involved in a "*broader range of activities*" than they would in an equivalent London seat.

In the first two to four weeks of each seat, trainees get the benefit of some "*excellent*" and "*well-organised*" training. "*In my first week in this seat I spent a third of my time in training and then today I did something that had been*" covered in that training," said one. There are mid-seat as well as six-monthly reviews, and with all the help available from supervisors, partner-mentors and other formalised networks trainees always "*feel like we know how well we are doing.*" Supervisors are either partners or associates, and trainees share an office with them.

Trainees are also kept well informed of the qualification process. "*The HR team and the partners don't like people trying to schmooze certain departments, but if you like a department you let them know you are interested in a job there and keep your face around.*" Second-year sources were relatively optimistic about qualification, even though retention rates were not as high in 2012 and 2013 as they had been in previous years. In 2013, 33 of 43 qualifiers were kept on. In other less good news, mid-2013 saw the firm announce a redundancy programme affecting 100 employees – over half of them lawyers – in a bid to cut salary costs. Keeping firm finances under strict control is clearly on management's mind. Perhaps this is in preparation for a merger or it could be a reaction to the continuing sluggishness of the real estate and corporate markets.

Trolley jolly

BLP is based in the Grade II-listed Adelaide House next to London Bridge. "*It is a lovely location – I'm looking at the Shard right now,*" cooed one trainee during our interview. But there's plenty more to do at BLP than stare at the view. A newly set-up choir performed a carol concert at Christmas. "*We started it because it previously always felt like you had to be a sportsperson to join a club,*" one trainee told us. The tag rugby, hockey, netball and football teams are indeed all very popular, and there's also an annual firm bike ride.

The corporate department has a weekly drinks trolley, while real estate's subdivisions into "*mini-teams*" makes informal socialising easier. And after a bit of pestering from trainees, there's now a trainee social budget for get-togethers every six months. "*When you first start as a trainee you do an awful lot with your intake – break-fasts, drinks, going travelling*" but as new recruits meet more people within the firm this tapers off – a testament to the "*inclusive*" character of BLP as a whole. Trainees can always head up to The Monument or The Fine Line as "*there will always be people from BLP in there on a Friday, even if it's just for one drink before heading off elsewhere.*"

BLP's extensive careers website says that what it is looking for in recruits is 'BerwinLeightonPaisnericity'. Once you get past this cringey bit of Newspeak, some nifty interactive tests will tell you that what this phrase (mostly) refers to is having excellent client interaction skills. So, take note of that and the fact that the snazzy new website is all part of an effort to "*increase awareness of BLP's brand – there is a lot of advertising and client pitching going on.*" You might also seek the firm out on Twitter, where it's been quite active running various competitions aimed at students.

Related to all this branding, pitching and advertising is another trend: over the past few years we've tracked something of a shift in BLP's firm's culture – or at least a shift in its reputation. "*We are becoming a more serious firm with a more corporate environment,*" said one trainee, "*and there is a sharp edge to our ambitions.*" An interviewee commented: "*There are times when you have to do long hours and maybe pull an all-nighter or work over the weekend, but that is not the norm. You work hard, have deadlines, but go home when you don't.*" Some trainees did demur at the suggestion there had been a 'culture shift', indicating that we mustn't over-egg any perceived changes. And anyway, sources believed "*the firm is still retaining its friendliness – people here are driven and hard-working but also very supportive. The senior people always want to integrate you into the team and when you talk to someone it doesn't have to be just about the task at hand.*" Another added: "*People here do like having a decent lunch break where they can not focus on work. And if there's a team social event the overwhelming majority of the partners get stuck in and some will start buying you Jägerbombs!*"

And finally...

BLP's efforts to big-up its brand, expand internationally and attract ever-better clients are attracting more and more applicants of an increasingly high academic calibre.

Bingham McCutchen (London) LLP

The facts

Location: London
Number of UK partners/solicitors: 19/29
Total number of trainees: 4
Seats: 4x6 months
Alternative seats: none
Extras: pro bono – LawWorks

On chambersstudent.co.uk...

How to get into Bingham
The firm's history
Bingham in America

Welcoming just a couple of new trainees each year, Bingham's 50-lawyer City branch provides an excellent training contract – and a mouth-watering NQ salary awaits those who stay on afterwards.

40 not out

As it puts away the party hats and sweeps up the confetti after its 40th anniversary, the City branch of this US-born firm can reflect on its position as a prosperous member of the Bingham family. Outperforming firm-wide results, the London office's revenue rose by 11.5% in 2012, and the verdict from trainees was that *"we're undoubtedly heading in the right direction. I think we're primarily looking to grow organically and in a gradual manner, but it's a strategy that has served us well so far."* The firm's London practice is relatively boutique-ey compared to some of its full-service offices elsewhere, and one source was right in saying: *"If you're looking to do something like employment law, then this isn't the place for you."* What the office does have is a financial restructuring group that's top-ranked in *Chambers UK*, alongside solid offerings in areas such as banking litigation, regulatory, debt capital markets and tax.

The four 'core' seats of financial restructuring (FRG), finance, litigation and corporate are accompanied by four recent additions: tax, regulatory, investment funds and competition. There's a bit more choice than in previous years when it comes to seats, though in actuality *"it's unlikely your first seat will be in either FRG or litigation because it's been fed back to the firm that these seats are a bit too fast-paced for the first six months – especially FRG."* While trainees don't have much of a say on where they start off, subsequent seat destinations are discussed before each rotation and *"there's always some talk among the trainees over who wants what."* There's also a lot of flexibility, as trainees are granted the possibility of splitting a seat, and *"if you express an interest to do a specific area of work then the firm will do its best to accommodate that."*

FRG is London's largest department and rakes in the most revenue – and trainees made its importance within the firm crystal clear. *"It's fair to say that a lot of our work as a whole is centred on restructuring,"* one told us, *"and we do take on some mega matters."* They weren't exaggerating when they said 'mega', by the way: Bingham has advised on some whopping cases lately, including the €1.6bn restructuring of Bulgarian operator BTC and the €1.3bn restructuring of the Quinn Group. Unsurprisingly, the *"tight deadlines and high-pressure nature of the cases"* make it a challenging seat to undertake. What's more, *"there's not really a lot that trainees can do because of how much is at stake."* This means *"you end up getting a good feel for documents,"* as trainees are tasked with collating information and often have a hand in due diligence, with drafting reserved for those *"who at the very least have a few years of experience behind them."* Still, we did hear from one interviewee: *"I had ample opportunity to speak to clients and was regularly in touch with bondholders, as well as being involved in a couple of negotiations."*

Bingham's gone to Iceland

The finance group *"has a lot of crossover with FRG,"* allowing trainees to sample a wide range of work – from distressed debt matters to credit arrangements and debt securities. Cross-border cases are part and parcel of the department, meaning *"it's rare for us to work solely on English law matters,"* and *"there's a lot of interaction with some of our other offices in Europe and Asia."* An insider revealed what they got up to during the seat: *"I drafted securities documents and helped out on low-level finance documents, but I also worked on things like securities filings and company searches. That kind of work is fairly basic but still forms an*

Chambers UK rankings

| Banking Litigation | Restructuring/Insolvency |
| Financial Services | |

essential part of the job." While it was agreed that *"you generally go to fewer client meetings compared to other departments,"* one source reported being in frequent contact with clients via e-mail – and *"when deals are nearing their completion you get a lot more client contact than usual."*

Bingham's litigation department is one of a small number in the UK that only handles financial disputes, particularly those arising from the likes of distressed debt, trading, investment banking, structured products, sovereign debt and regulatory issues. Many of the exciting cases taken on by the team are unfortunately kept under wraps, but we can tell you about one of them: Bingham has been acting for a group of around 70 leading financial institutions that hold more than $20bn of bonds issued by three insolvent Icelandic banks, with the long-running case expected to continue until 2015. A stint in the litigation seat entails *"a good mix of advisory and procedural work,"* like doing research into specific points of law and drafting memos, and *"you get a lot of exposure to the court process."* It's pretty unusual for trainees to be given the chance to do advocacy, but rest assured: *"You regularly sit in on client meetings and most of the work comes from the partners, so there's plenty of high-value work to go around."*

The corporate team *"tends to play a supporting role in tax and restructuring matters,"* which is demonstrated by the fact that much of its work concerns issues such as distressed M&A transactions. Sources were quick to point out, however, that *"the department draws in its own business too."* Its client base largely consists of hedge funds, investment funds and other financial institutions, and it occasionally collaborates with other offices like Hong Kong and Tokyo on cross-border M&A transactions. Those who spent time in the department were especially pleased with the amount of drafting they got to do, ranging from agreements and board minutes to *"complex cover letters that enclosed dozens of documents."*

Bingham down the house

With only 50 or so lawyers in Bingham's London office, it's hardly a shock that trainees *"get to know everyone here very, very quickly."* But this small environment doesn't just lend it-self to a tight-knit atmosphere – a high level of responsibility comes with the territory, and it's something our interviewees had at the forefront of their minds when they were mulling over which firms to apply for. *"I didn't want to go to a City firm where there are hundreds of trainees and most of them simply end up doing stapling and photocopying,"* remarked one, with another agreeing: *"There's a lot more responsibility on offer here than at many of the bigger firms."* So, does the challenging workload attract a particular type of person? *"I wouldn't say there's a Bingham 'type' as it were, but everyone here is definitely driven and focused on their careers."* In addition to these attributes, *"you need to be willing to give everything a try, as there'll inevitably be times when you don't really know what you're doing."*

Bingham pays an astronomical NQ salary of £100k (the highest in the City), and insiders explained to us: *"It's basically a reflection of the fact that our counterparts in New York are paid that amount."* Lawyers here do work hard for their money, but trainees consoled themselves with the fact that their hours were no longer than those of friends at the magic circle.

Bingham's London team occupies two floors of 41 Lothbury, which is just over a five-minute walk away from Moorgate station. An interviewee declared: *"I really hope we don't move from here any time soon, because we've got to be the most conveniently-located office in London."* The office itself is *"old yet impressive,"* and *"the first thing you see when you step into the building is a great marble hall."* It also houses a kitchen on both of its floors, and *"there's a lovely balcony area which people usually make the most of in the summer."* Sources speculated: *"Space might become a bit of an issue as we continue to grow, so we could start looking at the possibility of renting another floor within the building."*

Bingham doesn't exactly have the liveliest social scene in the world, but trainees quashed concerns that life at the firm is all work and no play. *"Maybe it's just me, but I didn't want to be somewhere that promoted forced fun,"* ventured one. *"Even so, we have brilliant summer and Christmas parties, and there are always events going on – whether it be a leaving do or happy hour drinks on the balcony."* We also heard tales of cocktail nights, departmental dinners and chocolatey treats when Easter comes around, all of which suggest that 'boring Bingham' is wide of the mark. Besides, *"how can we be dull when our logo is bright orange?"*

And finally...

Through the combination of high-quality work, a cosy environment, plenty of responsibility and a dazzling NQ salary, trainees deemed Bingham *"a fantastic firm to work for."* In 2013, it kept on one of its two qualifiers.

Bircham Dyson Bell

The facts

Location: London, Edinburgh

Number of UK partners/solicitors: 43/65

Partners who trained at firm: 30%

Total number of trainees: 14

Seats: 4x6 months

Alternative seats: secondments

Extras: pro bono – Migrants Resource Centre

On chambersstudent.co.uk...

How to get into BDB

Interview with training principal Nick Evans

Planning law

Based just a short walk away from the Houses of Parliament, Bircham Dyson Bell has a strong reputation when it comes to negotiating the trickier bits of government legislation.

Driving Miss Dyson

Bircham Dyson Bell's parliamentary law expertise has seen it profiting from the big, supposedly recession-busting infrastructure schemes that are being steered through the planning process. The West End firm is advising on the HS2 plans for a £33bn high-speed railway between London and Birmingham, which was recently granted the go-ahead even though it looks set to disturb the habitats of everyone from Camden Market punks to rare Chilterns water voles. Although losing its position on Network Rail's panel of law firms recently was *"a surprise – it could be a bit of a problem since they were a big client,"* BDB recently gained a spot on the government procurement service panel, which should see more work on major public projects rolling in.

One trainee saw Bircham Dyson Bell as a firm *"in transition – we're moving from being called Birchams to BDB, turning from a stuffy law firm to something a bit more modern and approachable."* Others didn't share the same confidence. Although the firm has explored mergers and boosting its corporate offerings in the past, they suggested that *"no one really feels the same drive any more."* Training principal Nick Evans explained: *"We're looking to continue to weather the worst of the recession steadily,"* and pointed to *"a return to growth in the most recent financial year."* The firm is aiming to move towards a fuller service offering, with new expertise in construction, IT and banking offering its existing clients a *"cradle to grave service."* The practice could also be shored up by the firm's increasing emphasis on links overseas: *"Partners are making constant trips to the Middle East and USA to bring in more work."*

Before trainees join, they choose their four preferred seats on the basis of presentations from each department. There

are no compulsory seats, but *"most people end up going to real estate, because they take three trainees at a time."* Other options include government and infrastructure, litigation, private wealth, charities, corporate/commercial and employment. Most trainees reported being happy with their allocated seats.

Riding the gravy train

The government and infrastructure (G&I) team works on big projects like the HS2 rail link and the planned Northern Line extension to Battersea, and the clients behind them are also the driver for *"a lot of work that falls into other departments."* The firm specialises in the fiddlier ins and outs of the 2008 Planning Act. A particular niche is in development consent orders (DCOs), which are government orders that straddle different areas of planning law, like compulsory purchase orders and planning permission, to grant permission for big infrastructure projects in one go. BDB recently secured a DCO for EDF Energy to build and operate the new Hinkley Point C nuclear power station. Trainees in the department find that there are *"always different things coming across your desk,"* and might find themselves researching *"plain packaging of cigarettes or harbour orders in Wales."* They also get to hone their skills in public law by working on the *"legislative drafting of statutory instruments"* for government ministers. Trainees are trusted to *"make presentations to clients,"* and one got to attend *"a very interesting public enquiry into the authorisation of a big transport project, taking detailed notes and offering general support to counsel."* The real estate team *"works closely"* with G&I, sharing the same big transport and industrial clients. It recently acted for the DLR on land and airspace acquisition for the new Thames-spanning ca-

Chambers UK rankings

Administrative & Public Law	Parliamentary & Public Affairs
Agriculture & Rural Affairs	Planning
Charities	Private Client
Family/Matrimonial	Public Procurement
Local Government	Real Estate Litigation
	Transport

ble car. There's also plenty of work with commercial and residential clients.

The litigation team handles a broad range of family, property, commercial, IP, contractual and other disputes. Trainees' experiences can be *"very much dependent on what your supervisor does,"* but one *"expressed an interest in family, so my supervisor went out and got that work for me."* There are lots of opportunities to run files, particularly in internal debt recovery, where trainees *"chase after clients who haven't paid us, and even send the bailiffs round, which can be quite depressing."* The firm particularly encourages advocacy, with trainees *"applying for a charging order in front of a master,"* or *"presenting at a magistrates court."*

Scouting for girls

BDB's business services practice has three arms: a small employment team, charities, and corporate/commercial. The charities team offers work with big household names like St John Ambulance, The British Film Institute and WAGGGS (the World Association of Girl Guides and Girl Scouts, not to be confused with the fashion-mad footballers' wives). There are also *"individual philanthropists running as a one-man band – they're very interesting to talk to."* Trainees get *"a wide variety of work; there's contract law, IP, drafting trust deeds, lots of tax, sales and mergers, and collaborative arrangements."* The matters have *"all the challenges of working with a normal company, but with an extra layer of regulation."* One trainee was involved with *"a charity converting to a newly introduced legal form – it was particularly interesting because no one knew how it would work."*

The corporate and commercial team handles *"a mix of public and private sector clients,"* including several charities and quite a few big healthcare providers, such as Nuffield Health. Corporate cases can involve anything from the acquisition of hospitals to *"struggling family*

businesses selling their assets off." There's also work on *"unusual human rights queries,"* and IP cases for individual clients – one trainee *"met a designer based overseas to consider how her designs could be transferred over here."* Trainees get *"less of the grind of due diligence and paperwork than at larger firms,"* taking on drafting, running small files and dealing directly with clients.

Ladies who lunch

Trainees explained that the day-to-day social scene at BDB is *"not particularly buzzing,"* since *"a lot of us are older, have families or live far away."* Recruits *"go for jolly lunches together"* most days, and get the odd drink in at firm local The Feathers. The firm's social committee go all-out for special events, though, exercising *"a lot of imagination and thought."* The ski lodge-themed Christmas party offered *"a vodka luge and a photo booth with lots of props – there was an alpine background, and antlers and woolly jumpers to wear."* The interdepartmental sailing regatta and carol service complete with a *"very keen"* firm choir are much-loved BDB institutions.

There's a trainee in-joke that the cohort's gender imbalance – with only one man to 13 women – is down to the fact that *"ladies are cleverer."* However, one recruit suggested that *"the nature of the firm might appeal more to women, as we don't have that brash City edge."* Perhaps. Anyway, a sizeable proportion of BDB's recruits have had previous careers, and there are *"quite a few quirky characters."* BDB is *"supportive of families, letting quite a few people work flexible hours."* Trainees tended to escape home at 6.30pm or so. One found that *"if you stay beyond a certain point someone will tell you to go home – there's no one cracking the whip,"* but trainees are still expected to work hard, as there's sometimes an assumption that *"if you stay late you've been inefficient, or not working correctly."*

BDB's qualification process is *"maybe too formal."* Trainees submit a CV and go for interview, and some departments have a written test too. Sources this year complained that the process was *"not particularly well managed – it was very rushed."* Training partner Nick Evans told us that the process was brought forward due to business needs, and that *"while trainees may have felt a bit more nervous than we would have hoped, the outcome was really good."* In 2013, six of seven second-years were retained.

And finally...

This is no place for shrinking violets: *"Trainees are expected to interact with clients and people higher up the firm almost like a qualified solicitor."*

Bird & Bird

The facts

Location: London
Number of UK partners/solicitors: 80/145
Partners who trained at firm: 9%
Total number of trainees: 18
Seats: 4x6 months
Alternative seats: overseas seats, secondments
Extras: pro bono – LawWorks, South Westminister Legal Advice Centre

On chambersstudent.co.uk...

How to get into Twobirds
Interview with training principal Christian Bartsch
Twobirds' sector focus

It's City law with a twist at Bird & Bird, where sector expertise makes for a flavourful workload.

The True Picture

Big bird

Our interviewees cut right to the chase when asked about Bird & Bird's professional identity. *"We're a bit like the Google of the legal world – we're more trendy than our competitors, and we're top dog on the media and technology side of things."* Indeed, the Londoner's with-it clientele – among them Microsoft, Amazon, EMI, Sega and Nokia – contributes to a *"cool, forward-thinking vibe"* and certainly lends some credence to interviewees' rather liberal use of the descriptor 'modern'. *"Basically, we do all the mainstream City work but with a more current edge; it's not just your standard M&A,"* one source summed up. A good example is the firm's recent win on behalf of the UKMMA, the representative body for UK media monitoring agencies, in a copyright case involving online news royalties.

Thanks to a sector-based approach, the firm (or Twobirds, as it's affectionately known) courts clients as diverse as media companies, sports bodies, food manufacturers and pharmaceutical brands. IP and commercial undertakings account for many of the acclaimed names on the roster, but impressive *Chambers UK* rankings in corporate, aviation, data protection, sports and telecoms demonstrate the range of the Londoner's strength. *"Within a single seat you can go from working on energy to media matters in a snap – that keeps your workload varied and helps you decide what you want to do in the long run,"* trainees said.

Though it's neither magic circle nor US-led, Twobirds maintains an expansive global reach, with 25 bases sprinkled across Europe, Asia and the Middle East. Strategic tie-ups with Australian, Danish and Swiss outfits in early 2013 served to further increase its wingspan. *"Each ven-* ture has been client-led and carefully thought through,"* training principal Christian Bartsch tells us, explaining the firm has *"historically tended to avoid major transformational mergers"* in favour of a strategy that *"combines organic growth with small bolt-on acquisitions. This allows us to retain a solid, consistent culture throughout our offices."* That said, management is certainly keen to *"internationalise"* the client base, he says, pegging Asia-Pacific and India as areas *"of massive interest to us"* at the moment.

Spread your wings

The HR team makes *"a real effort"* to take trainees' seat preferences into account, according to this year's flock. *"You're pretty much guaranteed to get three out of your four picks,"* and trainees' fourth seat choice is *"always honoured."* Several sources advised *"making your interests clear by talking with HR and forging relationships in the relevant departments."* Seats up for grabs each rota include commercial, dispute resolution, IP, corporate, banking, real estate, employment, aviation and the *"ever-popular"* sport. None are compulsory, although *"most people end up doing IP or commercial as they're the biggest groups."*

The IP department, once of Twobirds' stars, is big on the patent and life sciences front. The group is friendly with all of the top pharma companies, from Regeneron to Teva, and recently defended medical giant ConvaTec in a patent action over the production of wound dressings that contain silver. The team, known as *"one of the quirkier ones,"* also contends with 'soft' IP like trade marks and brand portfolio work. As its work advising on telecoms behemoth Everything Everywhere's rebrand to the sim-

Chambers UK rankings

Asset Finance	Intellectual Property
Aviation	Life Sciences
Banking & Finance	Media & Entertainment
Capital Markets	Outsourcing
Corporate/M&A	Private Equity
Data Protection	Product Liability
Employment	Public Procurement
Fraud	Real Estate Finance
Healthcare	Sports Law
Immigration	Telecommunications
Information Technology	Travel

Fly high

Bird & Bird's sports team is top-ranked in *Chambers UK* and handles corporate, commercial, regulatory and contentious matters on behalf of bodies as illustrious as the Premier League, Six Nations Rugby, the International Cricket Council and the World Anti-Doping Agency. "*Every day there are different issues to contend with, and a lot of the work is fast-paced,*" trainees said. "*A rugby citing that happened over the weekend will be waiting on our desk on Monday morning and settled by Wednesday.*" In addition to advising on sponsorship contracts and broadcasting rights, the team has recently kept busy with event organisation (such as helping the British & Irish Lions prepare for their 2013 Australasian tour) and anti-doping work in connection to last year's Heineken Cup and RBS Six Nations Championship. Unsurprisingly, our interviewees found the subject matter "*incredibly interesting,*" and they praised the "*good-quality work available. Sometimes you have to get on with dull things like bundling, but there's also some drafting, and the client exposure is really good.*" On the research side of things, one added, "*it can be good fun scouring the internet for information on certain clubs or governing bodies.*"

ple 'EE' and handling record label EMI's infringement action against rival BSkyB demonstrates, "*there's a wide breadth of contentious and non-contentious work to be had.*" Trainees described a "*busy workload*" and reported getting "*thrown straight into trial. Within a few weeks I was attending court, liaising with counsel and handling the document management.*"

Over on the commercial team, "*the work changes every day.*" The department operates as a standalone entity and covers telecoms, data protection, outsourcing and technology work for noted bodies like the Ministry of Justice and Department for Energy & Climate Change. "*We often work on big teams because of the size of the deals, so as a trainee you're often in charge of admin like preparing documents and proof-reading.*" That said, several interviewees reported "*sitting in on important meetings*" and "*taking a first crack at drafting contracts.*" Energy-related work is proving a boon of late, as are IT matters – lawyers recently advised European media platform Mecom on a cross-border IT outsourcing transaction concerning jurisdictions in Norway, Denmark and the Netherlands. "*The workload varies so much that you never know what to expect when a new matter comes through the door,*" one source said. Like IP, the department usually has around five or six trainees at any one time.

Dispute resolution lawyers have been "*insanely busy*" lately with a broad spectrum of cases, from contractual disputes to international arbitrations. Recent years have seen the firm score several significant successes for Nokia, including a claim against LCD cartel participants and a high-value arbitration against BlackBerry's parent company. "*Inevitably there's some bundling as a trainee, but everybody expects that,*" one interviewee shared. "*We're also drafting witness statements and defences, doing research into potential claims and corresponding with counsel.*"

A corporate seat also offers "*a good deal of client contact,*" this time with companies that span the financial, music, travel and food industries. Much of the work is mid-market M&A or joint ventures, plus "*some restructuring matters here and there.*" Recent successes on the advisory side include assisting Coca-Cola Hellenic Group (the iconic fizzy's bottling division) in an EU cross-border merger, and securing equity funding for online takeaway giant Just Eat. "*There are normally only two to three people working on a deal at once, so trainees are trusted with responsibilities like drafting and client calls,*" sources shared. "*I even got to run a small matter on my own, and the lawyers I was dealing with on the other side were ten years qualified.*" A small tax team operates within the corporate group and takes on a single trainee to assist with matters like stamp duty calculations and VAT leakage restructurings. "*About 90% of my work was purely tax, and the other 10% was corporate support work,*" a source clarified.

Three-month client secondments are available for trainees completing sports, commercial, IP or dispute resolution seat. "*I found the learning curve really steep,*" said one trainee of their in-house stint. "*The firm was great about keeping in touch and making sure I was getting on okay.*" A seat abroad in one of the many international offices is also an option, depending on language requirements and business need. "*There's no formal application process; you just speak up during your mid-seat HR talk to make your interest known, and the firm decides from there.*" Recent destinations include Madrid, Brussels and Hamburg.

Birds of a feather

Our interviewees were chuffed with Twobirds' *"hands-on"* approach to training. *"The partners do their best to get trainees as involved as possible, and HR provides really good mentoring,"* one summed up. Sources agreed: *"The firm does a great job on the supervision front,"* characterising the majority of partners as *"approachable, encouraging and forthcoming when it comes to feedback,"* and praised the scheme under which each trainee is assigned a 'buddy' two years above them – *"a handy resource throughout your LPC and training contract."*

When it comes to personalities at the firm, *"Bird & Bird doesn't do the boring lawyer stereotype,"* trainees told us. In fact, *"fun"* was how many sources described their colleagues, explaining: *"A key cultural aspect of the firm is friendliness"* and *"many people are a laugh to be around."* While interviewees acknowledged: *"A certain degree of hierarchy is present,"* they assured us: *"People of all levels get on and work well together – you can joke just as easily with a partner as you can with a fellow trainee."* In any case, *"there's a good group of young associates who bridge the gap between senior partners and young trainees,"* so issues with the pecking order *"rarely come up."* Thanks to partners' *"conscious efforts to make sure nobody's putting in too many long hours consistently,"* burnout isn't much of an issue either. *"It's clear that you work late because it has to be done, not just to be seen. Nobody's expected to be at their desk after 6pm if they don't have work to get on with."*

Insiders reported a *"diverse"* range of backgrounds represented among the current cadre, mentioning that *"the working environment allows for a lot of different characters. Our common bond is that everyone's a people person – the firm is really into people who are willing to engage with the firm on a broad scale by organising events, giving talks, that kind of thing."* Given Twobirds' strong techie platform, it's little surprise there are *"tons of people with science backgrounds,"* although *"there are also engineers, PhDs, art students – you name it,"* trainees added. *"The skill palette is impressively broad, which means we have a big database of knowledge to source*

from. They look for applicants with strong interests in subjects like technology or media – things that suggest they're passionate about the sectors we work in." Indeed, demonstrating your interest in such areas through extracurriculars *"is a must"* on the hiring front. Interviewees also suggested nabbing a slot on the summer vac scheme *"as it's a big means of recruiting."*

Bird & Bird lawyers flit between the firm's three offices: 15 Fetter Lane – *"the newest and nicest"* – houses the commercial, employment, banking and aviation teams, while number 90 covers dispute resolution, tax and corporate as well as being home to the famed Bird Table canteen; IP has a building to itself over on Furnival Street. *"We manage really well, but there are plans to get us all under one roof at some point,"* one insider revealed, and Two Birds has indeed struck a deal to move into numbers 12-14 New Fetter Lane in 2016.

Old Speckled Hen

The 31-trainee flock is a close bunch, thanks in part to the firm's bespoke LPC at Kaplan, *"which let us get to know each other early on and come in as friends."* Ad hoc events like pub quizzes are organised regularly, and Friday night drinks at the local pub are *"practically mandatory."* We even heard that some had been on holiday together. As for firm-wide get-togethers, there are plenty: drinks gigs for incoming trainees, charity events like raffles or marathons and summer and Christmas dos feature throughout the year, as do sports teams and occasional festivities planned by the social committee. *"We recently had a wine and cheese night with goodies someone brought back from France on the Eurostar."*

Historically, the firm's maintained a high retention rate, which trainees put down to a rigorous application process. *"It's clear they train to retain here, so there's not a lot of in-fighting among trainees when it comes to qualification."* Our second-year sources were pretty confident about their chances of staying on at the time of interviews, and it seems they had cause to be: in 2013 15 out of 16 were kept on.

And finally...

"I don't think we're the sort of place for people rolling off hundreds of applications," mused more than one source. *"You need to be interested in the sectors we focus on and not just in a legal sense."* So really do your research on this firm's chosen areas. There are some starting points on our website.

Bond Dickinson

The facts

Location: Newcastle, Stockton-on-Tees, Leeds, Plymouth, Bristol, Southampton, London, Aberdeen

Number of UK partners/solicitors: 146/562

Partners who trained with firm: c.30%

Total number of trainees: 43

Seats: 4x6 months

Alternative seats: secondments

On chambersstudent.co.uk...

How to get into Bond Dickinson
More on offices
More on seats

The result of a mid-2013 merger between two firms striving for national stardom, the brand-new Bond Dickinson covers much of the North and South.

Bonding with Dickie

Before Bond Pearce and Dickinson Dees joined together to form Bond Dickinson, they were perched side by side in the UK top 100. The two firms also had similar ambitions: Bond Pearce had a growth strategy known as 'Green Arrow', whereas Dickinson Dees' was called '2020 Vision'. If you looked at the two strategies next to each other you would have discovered a noticeable overlap. Bond Pearce's aim was to gain a place in the UK top 30 by 2015, while Dickie Dees targeted a spot in the top 20 by – you guessed it – the year 2020. With over 700 lawyers spread across eight UK locations and turnover in excess of £90m, the merged entity is currently around the 40th largest in the country. Ambitions, ambitions...

All this strategy talk makes the merger sound a wee bit like a marriage of convenience, but training partner Paul Stewart (formerly of Dickinson Dees) points to other similarities besides the legacy firms' plans for growth: *"There were a number of sectors where both firms had a good track record and other sectors where either Bond Pearce or Dickinson Dees had experience which complemented the other firm. For example, Bond Pearce had a lot of experience in the oil and gas sector, which complements Dickinson Dees' long-standing involvement in the chemicals industry."* This has translated into a focus on seven key sectors for Bond Dickinson: energy, waste and natural resources; retail and fast-moving consumer goods (FMCG); real estate; financial institutions; chemicals and manufacturing; transport and infrastructure; and private wealth.

They may have been neighbours in the UK law firm charts, but Bond Pearce and Dickie Dees weren't exactly hanging around the same parts of the country. The former was a South West native and had offices in Bristol, Plymouth and Southampton, as well as two small outposts in Aberdeen and London. Dickies had a tiny stronghold in the City too, but it was mainly viewed as the North East's go-to firm, with its headquarters in Newcastle and other bases in Stockton-on-Tees and Leeds. However, we shouldn't fail to mention that both firms acted for plenty of national and international clients too, and Bond Dickinson is no different. It's on the legal panels of widely recognised names like Network Rail, Colgate-Palmolive and the Crown Estate.

Love Actually

All in all, it's fair to say Bond Pearce and Dickinson Dees were pretty compatible work-wise. But how well did their personalities match up? It's a tough question to answer just by looking at the facts and figures. Thankfully, our interviewees were on hand to give us the inside scoop and, though some of them hadn't met their new comrades yet, those who had agreed *"it appears to be a very good fit. Generally speaking everyone's easy to get on with – if anyone had been standoffish then we wouldn't have gelled very quickly."*

We've already talked about office locations, but it's worth reiterating that one of Bond Dickinson's greatest challenges going forward will be trying to bridge the geographical gap between the legacy Dickie Dees offices in the North East and the legacy Bond Pearce ones in the South West. So far, integration efforts have mainly been carried out at department level, and this approach has generated solid results. *"Not every team has had its integration day yet, but the one organised by the commercial*

Chambers UK rankings

Administrative & Public Law	Intellectual Property
Agriculture & Rural Affairs	Media & Entertainment
Banking & Finance	Pensions Litigation
Banking Litigation	Planning
Charities	Product Liability
Competition/European Law	Professional Negligence
Construction	Public Procurement
Corporate/M&A	Real Estate
Dispute Resolution	Restructuring/Insolvency
Education	Retail
Employment	Social Housing
Environment	Tax
Information Technology	Transport

group worked out fabulously well," remarked a trainee. Similarly, another said: *"We had a firm-wide training day for dispute resolution, and all of us went to the Bristol office for that. It was really nice to see some of the new faces."* Just in case you wanted further proof that the two legacy firms seem to be a decent fit, it's interesting to note that whether they're partying it up in the North or boogieing on down in the South, trainees at the firm enjoy a lively social scene. Newcastle sources told us about pub quizzes, charity events, karaoke nights and a 'Stars in Their Eyes' evening – *"some of the partners dressed up as Britney Spears,"* apparently. And all the Southern offices have a social committee that organises fun-filled activities like barbecues, boat trips and Laser Quest. Even the merger was an excuse for some fun. Just before the nuptials Dickinson Dees hosted *"a massive firm-wide bash"* at the Hilton with *"free drinks and nibbles,"* while each office at Bond Pearce had its own 'goodbye to the firm' shindig. Then shortly after the merger was made official, everyone across the firm *"had balloons draped across their chairs with raffle prizes to be won, and there was a day on which everyone was asked to come in dressed in yellow, because that's Bond Dickinson's new corporate colour."*

Dickinson Dees and Bond Pearce both had small outposts in London. These teams have now been combined and are housed in Four More London on the south bank of the Thames. While the firm doesn't recruit trainees directly into its London office at the moment, that could well change in the future. Training partner Simon Hughes (formerly of Bond Pearce) confirms: *"It might happen within the next two years, and perhaps during the next recruitment round we'll be looking to address it."* With Bond Dickinson clearly intent on upping its status in the City, it does beg the question: how much importance will the London base have? *"The intention isn't to become a London-centric firm,"* says Hughes. *"We're using London as a hub from which to operate and will use it as a ful-crum to push work out from the centre."* As for the other offices, you can read more about them on our website.

Our interviewees hoped that trainees would soon be able to make the most of the merged firm's opportunities for North-South mobility, but Hughes told us: *"The probability of trainees in the North coming down to the South – or vice versa – is unlikely because of the practicalities and costs. Saying that, we're eager to ensure that if a trainee up North wants to do a seat in something like oil and gas, then there'll be a chance for them to travel to Bristol, Aberdeen or London to do so."* The firm currently recruits trainees into all its offices apart from Aberdeen and London, both of which serve as secondment locations.

There's something about property

Beyond its sector groups, Bond Dickinson is split into four 'business groups': real estate, corporate and commercial, dispute resolution, and private wealth. There are a multitude of seat options in each of these, but trainees in Newcastle and Bristol have the most to choose from, while *"the choices are a bit more limited"* in the smaller offices.

Real estate was Dickinson Dees' largest single department, while Bond Pearce had strong real estate teams in Southampton and Plymouth. The Southampton group serves as the Crown Estate's chief legal adviser on coastline and offshore property issues, while Newcastle lawyers recently acted for EDF Energy on the multimillion-pound purchase and development of a portfolio of wind farms in England. Trainees up North who had done a stint in real estate said that the team is *"always very, very manic – but in a good way!"* They also described it as *"fast-moving and fun,"* and some had experienced a mix of commercial property and social housing matters with *"loads of tiny transactions to handle ourselves."* Sources in the South worked exclusively on commercial property transactions, and were pleased to discover that *"the standard post-completion tasks tend to be done by paralegals."* Instead, they found themselves drafting leases, liaising with clients and conducting research.

Corporate was a particularly popular destination for the trainees we spoke to in the Northern offices. Prior to the merger, Dickinson Dees advised the departing shareholders of Energas and Engweld on the sale of both these companies' entire issue share capital to Air Liquide. The team also had a hand in Melrose's disposal of McKechnie Engineered Plastics to the Swedish-owned business Rosti for over £30m. Trainees in this seat draft ancillary documents, attend client meetings, and get involved in disclosure and due diligence. *"You're trusted to do a lot of the work without much supervision,"* mused one of the Newcastle lot, *"and that level of responsibility really brings you out of your shell."*

The True Picture

Bond Dickinson's commercial contracts, IP and IT team has done work for the likes of M&S, New Look and Sainsbury's. And do you remember those stamps released by the Royal Mail during the Olympics and Paralympics featuring Team GB gold medal winners? Well, Bond Dickinson's Bristol commercial team assisted with their creation. Trainees who do the commercial seat get to draft *"numerous different types of agreements"* and carry out bits of research, with many of our sources dabbling in a mix of IT and IP matters – from outsourcing deals to trade mark infringements.

Legally Bond

Contentious work was a real money-spinner for Bond Pearce. Its commercial litigation group represented clients like Virgin, British Gas and Carlsberg. Dickie Dees was no slouch in this department either, and the Newcastle team is top-ranked locally by *Chambers UK* for litigation. The commercial litigation seat is *"a relatively broad church,"* and some of the tasks trainees end up doing include preparing witness statements and going along to court.

Dickinson Dees had always had a strong private client practice in the North East. By contrast, Bond Pearce *"didn't really have a presence"* in this area, says Simon Hughes: *"One of the interesting aspects we discussed regarding the merger was the new opportunities it would present for both sides, and that was an area where we saw real potential for growth in the South."* It remains to be seen whether a seat in private wealth will trickle down to the firm's Southern bases any time soon, so for now we can only report on the experiences of trainees in the North. Many of them had handled wills, trusts and tax planning, and they could hardly be happier with the amount of drafting and client contact on offer. They also appreciated *"the personal side of it."* One recalled: *"I had a meeting that turned out to be incredibly emotional but the partner didn't even bat an eyelid, and I had to make sure I didn't rush over to the client to give them a hug!"*

You'll have to forgive us if this feature seems a little light on seat descriptions. Given that the merger's still relatively fresh, insiders had rather different experiences depending on where they were based and many seats were only up for grabs in certain offices. Simon Hughes told us: *"How the training contract will change is not yet set in stone and, at the moment, we're dealing with it on a North-South basis. But from March 2014 onwards we hope to have a homogeneous scheme."* For info on some of the other seats available, see the bonus features on our website.

This year's retention was sorted out before the merger took place. Although trainees on the Bond Pearce side had no complaints about the process, ex-DD sources described their experience as *"badly handled. We were told we'd find out a lot earlier because of the impending merger, but it just dragged on and on. In fairness, the merger plans meant that there was obviously a lot going on in the background and it certainly wasn't a case of people just sitting on their arses."* What's more, trainees were told before the merger went live on May 1st who was getting a job, and 25 out of 28 qualifiers were kept on.

And finally...
It's still very early days, but even just its yellow corporate colours make the future look bright for Bond Dickinson.

Boodle Hatfield LLP

The facts

Location: London, Oxford
Number of UK partners/solicitors: 32/37
Partners who trained at firm: 22%
Total number of trainees: 11
Seats: 4x6 months
Alternative seats: none

On chambersstudent.co.uk...

How to get into Boodle Hatfield
Digested Dukes of Westminster

This Mayfair institution specialising in private client and property is an appealing prospect for those seeking top-end work away from the bustle of the City.

What ho, Boodle!

Established in 1772 by the estate manager for the Grosvenor family, Boodle Hatfield has a long and illustrious history of serving the wealthy. The Grosvenors built many of the grand streets and squares across Mayfair and Belgravia and today the estate is worth almost £3bn. They sit side by side on Boodle's books with the Bedford Estate, owner of much of Bloomsbury. In fact, Boodle's Bond Street office works with four of the UK's top ten landed estates, while other major clients include Marriott International and the Telegraph Media Group. The litigation department is increasingly taking on high-value art disputes and was recently involved in a negligence claim to do with a painting by Renaissance master Titian.

While this may conjure up images of tweed-clad chaps quaffing claret in the Drones Club, the trainees we spoke to stressed Boodle's emerging modernity. "*There are lots of powerful women at the firm and just recently they made quite a few young associates into partners so we're shedding the image of the old boys' club.*" Another said: "*Everyone's really approachable and the office is pretty new. It doesn't feel old or stuffy at all and it's not like the hierarchy is alienating.*" The firm is by no means Oxbridge-only and Boodle's head of HR Katie Kirkhope told us: "*Our trainees come from a range of backgrounds – the most important thing is academic aptitude.*" As proof of Boodle's commitment to the cutting edge it's also worth noting that its maternity programme won the gong for Most Innovative Gender Diversity Initiative at the 2013 *Chambers UK* Women in Law awards.

Boodle offers seats in property, private client, litigation, construction, corporate and family. One trainee stressed that "*a strong interest in either private client or property and a good understanding of the kinds of clients Boodle works with is vital.*" The property department occupies a whole floor of the London office and the sheer volume of work pretty much guarantees one seat there while a second is also highly likely. Private client is also a regular stop for trainees. When asked about the allocation process for other departments, one trainee recommended "*making sure the partners are aware of who you are and your interests – that'll help when it comes to seat selection.*"

Angel of the South

The property department has three branches: Grosvenor/Bedford; other residential estate work; and commercial/development. The levels of responsibility vary but common tasks across each of the divisions are drafting leases and licences, conveyancing, and corresponding with surveyors and solicitors at other firms. One trainee told us they "*felt like a fee earner*" while working on Grosvenor cases and another expanded on this, saying: "*I had responsibility on my own files right the way through, from setting them up to sending out bills.*" The department has recently been involved with the development of a swish new Mayfair hotel in a listed art deco building reportedly worth more than £40m. When it opens, the hotel will host a unique habitable statue designed by sculptor Antony Gormley. The location of Boodle's office means "*you can walk down the streets you've been working on and see the properties you've been involved with – that's pretty cool.*"

Chambers UK rankings

Agriculture & Rural Affairs	Private Client
Charities	Real Estate Litigation
Family/Matrimonial	

The private client department regularly advises on matters exceeding £100m in value and for that reason "*you don't get the chance to handle your own files like you do in property.*" Trainees do get involved in "*drafting wills and documents for handovers but they're always checked by fee earners and rarely sent out in your own name.*" Much of the work in this seat is international and trainees are given the chance to work in supporting roles for clients with assets in France and Switzerland. Trainees also have the opportunity to go on secondment to the private client department in the firm's Oxford office. The overall level of responsibility is much higher than in London. "*You get to work with the big dogs,*" said one trainee. Accommodation costs are covered by the firm while trainees are over in the city of dreaming spires.

Fame and infamy

In the family seat there's a great deal of client exposure and trainees attend meetings and court hearings in the course of the high-value matrimonial, inheritance and succession cases they help with. One trainee commented: "*There's not quite the level of responsibility you get in property but it's a lot more than in private client.*" The department recently acted on behalf of West End star Don Gallagher in his headline-grabbing separation settlement from a City high-flier. As a relatively recent phenomenon, the law surrounding civil partnerships can be muddy and Gallagher's £1.7m settlement was both a landmark case and proof of how up-to-speed Boodle is when it comes to family law.

The litigation department is no stranger to high-profile cases either, and acted on behalf of the former deputy general director of Aeroflot, Russia's national airline, in response to the claim he stole money from the company. One trainee said of their time in the seat: "*I started here just as a big trial began. I've been going to court every day, doing some advocacy and I even got to make an appearance in front of a Master.*" Bundling and photocopying are inevitable but another trainee shrugged off the suggestion that the grunt work was dull: "*It was a good chance to muck in and get to know others across the firm.*"

It would be stretching things to say that Boodle is renowned for its corporate work, but we ought to mention that the firm does do work in this area as well and trainees can complete a seat here. The most well-known client is one that was cross-referred from the property department – Telegraph Media Holdings – while others include investment bank Canaccord Genuity and Luke Hughes & Co, which makes bespoke furniture for company boardrooms, churches and Oxbridge colleges (if you're reading this in the library at St Hugh's or Brasenose in Oxford, or Peterhouse or Pembroke in Cambridge you may be perched on a Luke Hughes chair).

Who's Bad?

In 2012 the firm held its inaugural Boodle's Got Talent competition, which the corporate team won, but the trainees came back with a vengeance in 2013, staving off stiff competition to take the crown. "*Two of the trainees taught the partners the dance moves for an Abba medley, but the trainees ended up stealing the show with their own Michael Jackson mash-up. It was incredible.*" For those not so keen on moonlighting as the King of Pop there are regular seven-a-side football matches, a netball team that includes Boodle and Grosvenor Estate employees, and yoga classes every Tuesday. The Christmas party was held at the Mayfair Hotel in 2012 and come July it's a short stroll over to a local bar for the summer bash. Those awaiting the start of their training contract are invited to both.

Office hours are favourable, with one source saying: "*9am to 6.30pm is the norm and I haven't done any overnighters or weekend work.*" There can be late nights in litigation but when the seat isn't so busy trainees can expect to finish promptly at 6pm. One trainee said: "*There's no face time and I would never stay on late if there was nothing for me to do.*"

In 2013 Boodle retained three out of its five second-years. Trainees told us that the family department has been hard to qualify into recently, but that the firm assured us in summer 2013 that it had addressed the issue.

And finally...

Head of HR Katie Kirkhope told us: "*We don't really have a type, but one characteristic among people at the firm is a strong academic record. The work here can be very complicated and it only gets harder the higher you go.*"

B P Collins LLP

The facts

Location: Gerrards Cross

Number of UK partners/solicitors: 16/35

Partners who trained at firm: 31%

Total number of trainees: 7

Seats: 4x5 + 1x4 months

Alternative seats: none

On chambersstudent.co.uk...

How to get into B P Collins

What goes on in Gerrards Cross

This full-service firm on the outskirts of London may prove the perfect fit for those looking to avoid the whirlwind intensity of the City.

Lifestyles of the rich and famous

Although Gerrards Cross may sound like the words of a Scouser eulogising about the oeuvre of Liverpool's Captain Marvel, it is in fact an upmarket little town in south Buckinghamshire. Located on the border of Greater London – and just a 25-minute train ride from Marylebone – it's often referred to as 'mini Hollywood' due to a number of celebrity residents – Gary Lineker, Des O'Connor, Fern Britton and Brangelina to name but a few. Among the glitterati – and more precisely in between the local library and a designer kids' clothes shop – you can also find B P Collins. Its six core practice areas – property, dispute resolution, corporate/commercial, private client, employment and family – are often charged with handling the affairs of the wealthy residents nearby. "*Gerrards Cross is an affluent area and that's reflected in our clientele,*" offered one trainee. "*We handle work for a lot of high net worth individuals, but also companies. We have a good reputation for that.*" Another source commented: "*I view B P Collins as operating like a London firm, with London clients, but without the London feel or London hours.*"

Pioneering pesto

Trainees usually complete four seats of five months each, with a final four months set aside for a "*return to where you want to qualify.*" No seats are compulsory but "*family and litigation are the main departments so you'll probably end up doing one of those.*" Trainees discuss their seat preferences with HR and indicate "*one or two seats you definitely don't want, and one seat you absolutely want. They try to take that into consideration, but obviously second-years get preference so things can be liable to change. The choices of one trainee can impact on eve-*ryone else. You may think you're going somewhere and then somebody wishes to change so it all moves around.*"

In dispute resolution the "*work is varied*" as the department handles anything from property or commercial litigation to environmental or IP dust-ups. The three-partner team looks after clients such as Biffa, HMV and Kawasaki Motors UK. Trainees agreed it's a "*good seat,*" although they did admit: "*You will get some banal tasks like bundling, checking documents and photocopying.*" However, on the whole "*you get work appropriate to your ability, and as much responsibility as you can take on. There's a lot of practical drafting – pleadings and letters to the other side. I also attended High Court hearings, issued claims at court by myself and helped instruct barristers.*" Partners also actively contribute to trainees' progression. "*I said I wanted to do more of a certain type of litigation and the fee earner tried to make sure I got more exposure to that,*" one source informed us.

The family team holds one partner, six associates and usually a single trainee, making it one of the the largest dedicated family teams in the Thames Valley. Due to the sensitive nature of the cases we can't name who the departments represents, but there's a fair few celebs and other "*high net worth clients*" on its books. Sources enjoyed the time they spent here: "*It's very hands-on, no day is ever the same and I didn't do mundane tasks,*" commented one. "*I was very fortunate to attend court a lot, either on my own with counsel or with my supervisor on the bigger cases,*" said another. One second-year concluded: "*The nature of family work generally means you deal with clients. I attended a lot of meetings, and would take calls from current and prospective clients to get to the bottom of what they need from us.*"

Chambers UK rankings

Charities	Family/Matrimonial
Corporate/M&A	Private Client
Dispute Resolution	Real Estate
Employment	

The property team also looks after Biffa – and advised it on gaining a lease for a new facility that allowed it to take on a £32m waste and maintenance contract with Winchester City Council and East Hants Council – as well as The Original Bowling Company and NYSE-listed Mini Mobile. The group handles commercial property primarily, although a smattering of residential property work also crops up. "*My responsibilities really increased here and I had the chance to run the day-to-day aspects of cases on my own,*" one trainee told us. "*I was ensuring things were ticking along nicely and the clients were always informed. I didn't attend meetings as such, but over the phone and via e-mail I was constantly communicating with them. I was also drafting lots of leases and other documents.*"

The employment department offers a variety of contentious and non-contentious work. The standout name on its list of clients – at least in our humble opinion – would have to be Saclá, the Italian sauce manufacturer and self-styled 'Pesto Pioneers'. "*It was a great seat,*" reflected a trainee. "*The employment team in particular is very keen to treat their trainees as junior lawyers. There's an emphasis on asking how you would run the case if you were in charge.*"

Corporate/commercial "*has more partners than any other practice group in the firm*" – a total of six. "*There's a few household-name clients,*" a trainee explained, "*then a lot of smaller local businesses and some charities. It was quite quiet when I was there, which hampered my experience a bit, but I got some reasonably interesting tasks such as drafting and providing advice on contracts and articles.*" Of the private client seat, one trainee said: "*The people in Gerrards Cross generally have a lot of money and most have estates in excess of £1m. This means we deal with a lot of complex situations involving money held abroad, tax and trusts. If you are keen and show yourself willing, then the team is really prepared to give you good work. If you don't put the effort in, then they're less forthcoming.*"

Bucking the trend

In B P Collins' quest for extremely talented, and also extremely dedicated, trainees, applicants are expected to submit a hand-written cover letter. Committing yourself wholeheartedly to this is a key factor in securing a training contract. "*Take some time with the covering letter,*" one source advised potential applicants. "*A great deal of importance is placed on it as it limits the number of applications the firm receives. Sitting down to hand-write a covering letter takes a bit longer and people aren't used to that, but it's a great chance to stand out and allows you to make more of an impression than on a computer application. The firm wants to see your personality and you've got the chance to show that in the letter.*" There's also a desire to see trainees progress through the ranks, rather than have them jump ship to the bright lights of the City. "*You need to show you're proactive, will take on responsibility and will make an effort to be part of the firm, as they want to see longevity in people,*" a source explained. "*A lot of people working here now, trained here, so the firm has shown it's willing to give trainees time.*" As such, retention rates are usually pretty healthy, and two out of four qualifiers were retained in 2013.

Most of the trainees live in Buckinghamshire or make the short commute from London and this does tend to have an effect on the social side of life at the firm. "*People go for lunch together but after work there's less interaction,*" elaborated one trainee. "*Most people drive to work or live in London and that makes it difficult to get everybody together to do things, as it's hard to decide on somewhere that will please everyone.*" However, we were assured that trainees "*do well given those handicaps,*" and the firm provides them a quarterly budget for socials, which usually means a group meal and drinks. In aid of Comic Relief the firm hosted a B P Collins Bake Off, with staff dishing up home-made cakes in the hope of becoming the next Mary Berry (and securing a natty new apron).

Trainees were chuffed to bits about their experience at B P Collins and the only grumbles we heard were limited to "*there's not loads to do in Gerrards Cross,*" and "*it would be nice if they paid the LPC fees.*" However, one source concluded: "*As long as you put in the work, prove yourself, show you're competent and understand the process of being supervised, then there's not much more you could ask for from a training contract.*"

And finally...

"*I was keen for my training contract to be a training process,*" said one source, "*and B P Collins is a mid-sized, full-service firm that offers that.*"

BPE Solicitors LLP

The facts

Location: Cheltenham
Number of UK partners/solicitors: 21/25
Total number of trainees: 4
Seats: 4x6 months
Alternative seats: none

On chambersstudent.co.uk...

How to get into BPE
All about Cheltenham

"If you want to find that elusive work/life balance along with hands-on experience and good clients," say trainees, *"BPE is a good choice."*

Bretherton Price Elgoods

The uninformed might not think that Cheltenham has much to offer in the way of law firms, but in fact this pleasant Gloucestershire spa town has its own legal market with a number of significant commercial outfits. Prominent among these is BPE Solicitors, formed in 1989 from the merger of Bretherton Price and Elgoods.

Historically strong in property work, it's only kept off the top of *Chambers UK*'s local corporate and litigation rankings by the presence of London interloper Charles Russell. *"Don't just look at BPE as a regional firm,"* trainees urged. *"We've got national clients."* The firm says 60% of its clients are national outfits while 40% are local. These include fashion brand Superdry and the Pure Gym chain. You can add to that list Lloyds TSB, the Yorkshire Building Society, BMW and a famous charitable organisation. There are local businesses on the books too, like AGD Systems and Worcester City Council.

This is the first time since 2008 that we've looked in on BPE and naturally we made comparisons between then and now. The firm's Birmingham office was perhaps too successful for its own good: opened in 2002, it grew rapidly and moved into larger premises but closed in 2009 after Irwin Mitchell came along and poached all its lawyers. There were nine trainees when we last called in 2008; that number is currently reduced to two.

Clearly life hasn't all been plain sailing for BPE in this recession – as one source said, *"we've not got shock absorbers like big City firms."* Still, *"our big clients haven't left"* and one gets the impression that BPE has turned a corner. *"On the first Friday of every month we have an informal gathering in the reception area,"* trainees say,

"where the firm lays on a drinks table and the results of the last month are read out – whether we are hitting or missing our targets. This year so far we are hitting them."

Big Property Expertise

One of the benefits of the smaller intake is that everything's very flexible. If a trainee asks to go to a particular seat, as long as the department's got the work it's more than likely they'll get their wish. Everyone has to visit property, though. A litigation seat fulfils the SRA's contentious requirement, while the other options include corporate, commercial, construction, employment and science/technology. The firm has a private client side and a new head of the matrimonial team arrived not long ago. Trainees can't do seats in these departments at present, but the firm told us that in future it will likely offer a combined matrimonial/private client option.

More often than not, property is a trainee's first seat and because of this *"you're not necessarily expected to be up and running and doing fee earning."* Nevertheless, by the end of the seat sources had taken on their own little caseload, after cutting their teeth on stamp duty returns and Land Registry applications. Property is the largest department in the firm, and a lot of the clients come from the retail and leisure sector, while others include Gloucestershire Airport and renewable energy company Ecovision.

Corporate is another relatively large department. It takes on *"a mix of limited company and plc work, not just provincial bits and bobs."* Many deals will be worth around £1–10m, although a few are much larger, such as Mears Group's recent £24m acquisition of the social housing business of Morrison Facilities Services. Trainees will handle the ancillary documents and post-completion

Chambers UK rankings

Corporate/M&A	Employment
Dispute Resolution	Real Estate

work on such matters, and they'll also have active involvement in client meetings and may well get a lot more responsibility on smaller transactions.

Bravo, Philip's Excellent!

The open-plan office is set up so that the litigation team is in the centre, as it feeds off all the other departments. One of the litigation partners is Philip Radford, who's also the firm's training principal, so naturally there's "*lots of interaction with and supervision from him.*" Radford handles "*big matters that go on for years, such as very interesting professional negligence cases that give you quite a good appreciation of how not to conduct yourself.*" The team's spotted some litigation opportunities within the high-value classic car market and it's looking to develop a niche there. Though trainees can't usually get huge responsibility on the long-running cases, they often go to court or mediations and sit in conference with counsel and are "*actively encouraged to do drafting and letter writing.*"

You're more likely to see matters from beginning to end in employment. Even though this doesn't count as a contentious seat, trainees here will prepare for tribunals – going through the documents, drawing the bundle together, writing particulars of a claim and then sit with counsel at the tribunal itself.

The commercial department is split between one partner who handles general commercial matters and another who handles IP. It works for "*a broad spectrum of clients, from local businesses* [nearby Stroud has a lot of small manufacturers] *right up to listed companies.*" If there's a certain type of work trainees are interested in, "*you are likely to be able to get it because they do such a variety.*" They won't be managing the files here because "*the partners do like to be the face of the matter,*" but trainees "*will be doing really good stuff behind the scenes.*"

Science and technology, meanwhile, is a newish department, created after the arrival of a partner with a tech following. It handles matters that are "*quite random*" for a non-City firm, like stem cell research-related issues and high-value medical devices.

Without actually complaining outright about their salaries, a number of interviewees expressed the opinion that "*everyone in the world would probably like to be paid a bit more money.*" When pressed, they half-heartedly accepted that their salaries were "*probably fair.*" If they're not raking in London dosh, then this is offset by the fact that office hours generally aren't much longer than nine to five, except at busy times in certain departments.

Brilliant: Previous Employment

Sometimes regional firms can come across as a bit old-school or stuffy, but we don't get the feeling that's the case here. "*During the recruitment process we had a tour of the office and what I remember when walking around is that people were laughing with each other,*" said one source. "*There's good humour on firm-wide e-mail chains that go around – you'll hear a general laugh go up as people read the joke.*"

We found the trainees themselves chatty and confident. "*In my daily work I deal with some very snobby City trainees who think I don't know what I'm talking about because my firm doesn't have an EC postcode,*" said one source. But none of the BPE people we spoke to were "*green*" – they'd seen a bit of life, often having travelled and/or worked as paralegals or in other law-related employment. Prior work experience is "*a big plus – I won't say it's essential but it certainly makes you stand out.*"

Common sense and "*an ability to use initiative*" are other prized assets – just as well, since we get the impression that BPE isn't the type of firm that imposes too much uniformity on its workers. We've mentioned that the seat allocation is pretty informal; so is the process of getting an NQ job. Both 2013 qualifiers stayed on with the firm.

The social life ticks over quietly – trainees go for dinner on a monthly basis and for drinks fairly regularly. The Number Seven wine bar near the office is "*usually full of BPE people,*" and Cheltenham offers all sorts of distractions that BPE can take clients to (see our website for details). Do also check out BPE's website for its CSR efforts – in 2012 a group including trainees went out to South Africa to help build an orphanage.

And finally...

BPE is a relaxed firm that nonetheless does some really good work, and as a trainee *"whatever you want to do can be done so long as you take the initiative."*

Brabners LLP

The facts

Location: Liverpool, Manchester, Preston
Number of UK partners/solicitors: 78/114
Partners who trained at firm: 30%
Total number of trainees: 13
Seats: 4x6 months
Alternative seats: secondments
Extras: pro bono – Liverpool University Pro Bono Clinic

On chambersstudent.co.uk...

How to get into Brabners
Recent cases and deals

Are you seeking a strong regional outfit with a superstar sports practice? If so, then North West firm Brabners could be just the ticket.

Two become one

When Brabners married Chaffe Street back in 2001, it kicked off a period of major expansion that is still going on today. But let's be clear: major doesn't mean rapid, as the word from trainees was that *"we've always been about steady growth and aren't like other firms that seem to keep on growing merely for the sake of it."* This emphasis on quality over quantity has seen Brabners (it dropped the 'Chaffe Street' from its name in a recent re-brand, by the way) emerge as one of the leading firms in the North West. It is particularly renowned for its work in areas like social housing, employment and private client, but it also has a solid corporate/commercial offering. And we mustn't forget to mention a sports law practice regarded as one of the best in the country by *Chambers UK.*

In keeping with Brabners' approach to growth, the firm doesn't take on dozens of trainees each year. In fact, at the time of our calls there were only six of them in Liverpool and another six in Manchester, with none in the firm's Preston office – though the latter does welcome trainees on occasion. A wide range of seat options includes corporate, commercial, commercial property, employment, family, litigation, private client, social housing and sport. Client secondments are also available, with a commercial seat at Manchester United FC offered every 18 months (which *"always gets rave reviews"*). First seats aren't discussed, but trainees have an input for the remaining ones and the system is very flexible: *"From day one we're encouraged to forge our own path,"* sources said, leading to the possibility of repeating or splitting a seat.

Putting the matter to bed

While it's not a compulsory seat, the firm still encourages its trainees to spend time in property at some point – and the majority of our interviewees did just that. Many of the team's clients come from the retail sector, such as Associated British Foods, Welsh fashion retailer Peacocks and Martin McCool Group, which owns the biggest chain of managed convenience stores in the UK. A recent highlight for Brabners' property group has been advising on matters concerning the development of brand-new student accommodation for Edinburgh Napier University, including the creation of 778 snazzy en-suite bedrooms. Given the largish size of the team, trainees tend to work for a lot of different partners and *"end up gaining a broad overview of the department."* A few declared that *"we're essentially seen as the masters of post-completion tasks,"* but *"every so often you'll work on something more thrilling, like drafting a lease."* Those who had completed the seat sensed a gradual progression when it came to responsibility: *"They want you to have the building blocks in place first, and then towards the end of the seat it's more likely you'll be running your own files."* In other words, *"once you prove that you're not a raging moron they're happy for you to take on a decent level of responsibility."*

One trainee described their stint in corporate as *"probably the busiest six months of my entire training contract, in terms of both hours and workload."* This may sound daunting, but that didn't stop another recommending it as a good first-year option: *"The long hours and huge piles of work provide you with a sizeable challenge, so it's better to experience that early on."* The department draws in business from the likes of small and medium

The True Picture

Chambers UK rankings

Agriculture & Rural Affairs	Intellectual Property
Banking & Finance	Media & Entertainment
Charities	Private Client
Construction	Real Estate
Corporate/M&A	Restructuring/Insolvency
Dispute Resolution	Retail
Employment	Social Housing
Family/Matrimonial	Sports Law
Information Technology	Tax

enterprises, entrepreneurs, and public and private companies, with deals typically ranging between £1m and £10m in value – although it does reel in deals exceeding that amount from time to time. The low-end transactions in particular allow trainees to get heavily involved, and *"you can sometimes find yourself juggling four or five of those types of transactions at once."* Some dabbled in company secretarial work, often carrying out tasks like filing accounts and returns, while others drafted shareholder agreements and board minutes, helped out with disclosures and due diligence, and went along to client meetings.

Employment was a very popular seat choice among our sources. The reason? *"It's a thriving department with a great reputation, but a lot of people choose it because of how supportive the team is. You can easily ask anyone for help and, while everyone at the firm has time for you, it's especially true in employment."* Mind you, it also doesn't hurt to have a client base that includes household names like Wetherspoon's, Typhoo Tea and Nando's. The group primarily acts for employers, but trainees reported working on behalf of both claimants and respondents. *"There was a lot of involvement in tribunal claims, whether it be an unfair dismissal or discrimination matter, but on top of that I drafted contracts, prepared witness statements, and instructed counsel. It felt like there was nothing I didn't do,"* mused one.

Robbing van Persie

With over three-quarters of the FA Premier League clubs on its books (plus the Professional Footballers' Association itself), we weren't really surprised to hear that seats in the Manchester-based sports team are always in demand. But be warned: *"If you have your heart set on doing a sports seat then you should apply to the Manchester office, because the chance is rare for trainees in Liverpool."* Brabners has advised on several headline-grabbing transfers, such as Chelsea's capture of Gary Cahill from Bolton Wanderers and Robin van Persie's £24m move from Arsenal to arch-rivals Manchester United, and it also helped to secure the loan deal that brought Arsenal legend Thierry Henry back to the club for a short spell.

The department isn't just suited to football fanatics, however; other clients include sports management agency ISM, which represents high-profile golfers and cricketers, and British Cycling. Sources explained that there are *"two distinct areas"* within the group. *"There's the side that handles things like sponsorship deals, image rights and stadium advertising. Then there's the regulatory work, which is mainly about the big-money transfers, but there are other types of matters too – like immigration issues surrounding overseas players who are coming into the country."* It all sounds quite glamorous on the surface, but one interviewee remarked that *"there's not a great deal trainees can actually do in the department. If a club's paying £30m or so for a marquee signing, then it's unlikely that they'll need to cut costs by getting the junior lawyers in on the action."* There are still plenty of tasks to get stuck into though, from drafting agreements and preparing witness statements to conducting research.

Not-so-mean machine

Insiders say: *"From the minute you walk through the door, everyone is incredibly warm and friendly towards you. People come across as actual people, rather than machines."* This was a view shared by those in both Liverpool and Manchester, where the working hours *"are by no means extreme compared to the likes of City firms – but that doesn't mean we don't work hard!"* Our sources told us that trainees normally get in at around 8.30am and leave just after 6pm, *"and if you do have to stay later for whatever reason, then the firm is highly appreciative of that."*

Trainees also had only good things to say about their respective offices. Brabners' Liverpool base is in *"a prestigious location right next to the town hall."* This *"lovely setting"* is complemented by the office's *"nice-looking"* interior, with dwellers commenting that *"everything is well kitted out. There isn't a canteen, but we have so many places on our doorstep that we genuinely don't need one."* Mancunians were every bit as complimentary about their home ground, as they said: *"The inside is very pleasant, and we're in the city centre too, so it's great for a spot of shopping."*

The two offices may be equally impressive in the eyes of trainees, but the social scenes in Liverpool and Manchester could hardly be more different from one another. While it's true that Liverpudlians aren't painting the town red every night, they did mention that *"there's a perfect amount of socialising. It doesn't take up all of our free time, but we have ample opportunity to mingle."* We heard tales of dress-down Fridays, weekly lunches, quiz nights, trips to the races and pay-day drinks at nearby Noble House. It would be unfair to label Manchester trainees as boring old farts in comparison, but it was agreed that the social life there is *"pretty dire. We don't have a Friday night drinks culture or anything like that, although there are departmental events every now and then. To be honest, it doesn't bother us that much because we all have lives outside of work.*" In 2013, four out of six qualifiers stayed with the firm.

The True Picture

And finally...

A trainee advised: *"We're perhaps best known for our sports law practice, but we also have some really strong departments elsewhere. If you can show that you're not just applying because you've seen the words 'Manchester United', then you're off to a good start."*

Bristows

The facts

Location: London
Number of UK partners/solicitors: 32/80
Partners who trained at firm: 25%
Total number of trainees: 19
Seats: 3 or 6 months
Alternative seats: secondments
Extras: pro bono – A4ID; language classes

On chambersstudent.co.uk...

How to get into Bristows
Unilever House
The Unified Patent Court

The True Picture

Working on fantastic matters from within a fancy office, Bristows is a fascinating firm with a particular strength in IP.

Bigger on the inside

Don't call Bristows an intellectual property firm. As numerous trainees pointed out to us, "*Bristows is full-service*" and possesses fully functioning corporate, commercial disputes and real estate departments, among others. But there's no denying that IP is this firm's forte. Just look at its *Chambers UK* rankings, which come for the most part in techy areas like patent litigation, life sciences, data protection and telecoms. This is the firm that drafted the patent agreement for the first electrical telegraph in 1837 and even gave Doctor Who (oh, all right, the BBC) a hand on the image rights for his TARDIS. Current clients include household names such as L'Oréal, Google, Sony, AstraZeneca, McDonald's and Guardian News & Media.

Boiling it down to the numbers, about 50% of Bristows' work is IP-related, and the firm divides its workload into eight areas: life sciences; consumer products; industrial markets; TMT; charities; financial services; public sector; and real estate. Trainees were quick to declare that not everyone comes to Bristows because of its IP reputation – many graduates are drawn here more because of its smaller size and affable atmosphere. More on that later.

The firm moved from Lincoln's Inn to 100 Victoria Embankment half a dozen years ago. This impressive neoclassical edifice overlooking the Thames is better known as Unilever House and is pretty swish inside. Bristows occupies two floors of the building, but sublets half of one of them to publisher Little, Brown. It sounds like it will need that space back before too long: "*I've noticed there are a few more three-people-to-a-room scenarios cropping up recently,*" said one trainee this year. Two to an office is standard procedure at most law firms but the

Student Guide knows that Travers Smith is very proud of its three-per-room set-up, thinking it makes law firm life more chummy, so maybe it will catch on at Bristows too.

Anyway, the fact that the firm's seams are starting to stretch a bit points to the fact that it has negotiated the recession quite well. Bristows seems to have found a business model that works so don't expect too much growth over the next few years.

Reliance on compliance

Seats last for either three or six months. Trainees' first seats are generally six-monthers, and the only compulsory seat, IP litigation, is usually that long as well. You might find that the most in-demand seats (commercial IP is perennially popular) are shorter to give everyone a chance to do them.

At the time of our calls, trainees told us how they had been presented with a big colour-coded spreadsheet showing not just their own seat plan for the next two years, but everyone else's as well. Though some sources were "*a little bit surprised not to be asked before I started what seats I was interested in,*" all declared themselves very happy with the efforts made by the HR team to accommodate their desires. It's a rare trainee who actually sticks to their preassigned seat plan: "*What inevitably happens is some people aren't completely happy. The HR team tends to be very receptive, especially if you approach them in a positive way with suggestions rather than bitching and moaning about the seats you don't want.*" In fact, when we spoke to HR sources in summer 2013 they told us they were trialing a new system under which seats are assigned at each rotation rather than in advance, so watch

Chambers UK rankings

Data Protection	Media & Entertainment
Dispute Resolution	Outsourcing
Information Technology	Partnership
Intellectual Property	Telecommunications
Life Sciences	

this space. No one had any complaints about the route that training contract had eventually taken, and sources noted a key way in which Bristows differs from larger firms: *"Our training contracts are not solely managed by graduate recruitment: the partners are so hands-on. You never feel like your fate is in the hands of one person."*

IP litigation always has several trainees working in it, and *"nobody's seat is identical"* here. There are two sides to the department. The patent part tends to be the most heavily contentious. Among many major cases the firm has taken on, Bristows represented SAMSUNG against Apple in the bust-up over the companies' smartphone and tablet technologies, and defended Cadbury against allegations of infringement from Nestlé, who claimed the former's Chocos range copied the shape of Rolos. The firm is also acting for pharma giant Novartis, which has a patent for a medicine that treats osteoporosis. Rivals want to copy the product and have applied to the High Court to have the patent revoked. Some of our sources had arrived at a point where they could work on a large part of a big trial, going to court towards the end of their seat. *"That was a mega-highlight of my training contract,"* said one, describing *"lots of drafting of witness statements and loads of time with counsel"* as well as the dubious *"joys of dealing with hundreds of bundles."* In one trade mark infringement case, meanwhile, a trainee's job was to search through a company's e-mails *"trying to find incriminating evidence."*

The other part of the IP lit department is softer stuff – often brands and advertising matters – and is more geared towards the prevention of litigation. *"We manage big companies' trade mark portfolios."* One interviewee had enjoyed working on advertising matters – *"we had a lot of clients who were official sponsors of the London Olympics, and others who weren't and were concerned about what they could and couldn't do."* Other sources had drafted terms and conditions for clients wanting to run big competitions, while yet another had examined the advertising law regarding electronic cigarettes, *"which aren't governed by the normal pharma regulatory rules."*

The commercial IP seat is more transactional in nature and handles data protection, IT and pure IP matters. One trainee spent time *"reviewing lots of documents in preparation for a deal. We had a client who was merging and they had thousands of contracts that needed to be looked at to see how they would work post-merger."*

An alliance with clients

Let's talk corporate. *"It's a solid department in its own right, not an ancillary practice,"* say sources, and several people have qualified here recently, proving not all Bristows trainees are IP-nuts. The deals aren't massive compared to what the biggest City firms are handling but they'll be valued in the tens of millions bracket. Typical mandates have included advising Accsys Technologies, an environmental science company, on a joint venture with petrochemical giant INEOS, and acting on Blue Diamond's acquisition of the Grosvenor Estate's Garden Centre Company. Trainees get *"good work"* both on *"lengthy ongoing projects"* and with discrete tasks – *"I remember spending quite a while analysing a charity's governance documents,"* recalled one.

The real estate group manages the property portfolios of the firm's major clients, like Capgemini and WPP. New arrivals in this seat are immediately handed numerous files to manage, *"so you have to get up to speed very quickly."* In fact, Bristows takes on a bit of residential property work to give trainees experience – *"sometimes the client will even be one of the partners, which makes things even more daunting!"*

Working hours at Bristows are generally about 9.15am to 6.30 or 7pm, or perhaps 8 or 9pm at busy times. Anything later is *"unusual,"* though a number of our sources had worked until the small hours of the morning and at weekends on occasion.

Virtually all trainees will head off on a three-month secondment to one of the firm's clients, such as WPP, McDonald's, Capgemini, Sony or Google. Interviewees described them as a *"really valuable"* experience. *"I think my drafting got better without me noticing it,"* said one. *"You do so much more and pick so much up."* Other available seats include commercial disputes, competition/EU, and regulatory.

The appliance of science

Bristows receives 2,000 applications a year for its ten training contracts. We reckon that makes it one of the most mathematically difficult firms in the country to get into – a 200/1 shot. Of course, the pure maths is slightly misleading, as many students will apply to multiple firms but can only accept an offer from one, but the point stands: you'll need to be a pretty impressive candidate to get a look-in.

Trainees declined to comment on what had made them stand out from the crowd, but highlighted *"modesty"* and a lack of pretension as key Bristows traits. *"I know it can get quite political at other firms, with trainees getting one over on each other and stabbing each other in the back to get the seat they want,"* opined one source. *"Here, there's a great camaraderie among the trainees – whenever any*

The True Picture

of us needs a hand they'll send round a general e-mail and usually four or five trainees will drop what they're doing to help out."

Bristows helpfully lists the backgrounds of its trainees on its website and we saw that of the 19 at the firm in summer 2013, only one studied law as an undergraduate. The rest were evenly split between those who'd been arts/humanities undergraduates (history, classics, journalism...) and those who had a science degree (physics, biochemistry, even veterinary medicine). Before all you law students throw in the towel in disgust, we must add that there are apparently several non-GDLers in upcoming intakes.

Though Bristows certainly does attract more science grads that most other firms, trainees were swift to counter the *"preconception that you need to be a scientist"* to get a look-in. *"I recently worked on a really complex piece of financial litigation, but lawyers aren't expected to have a degree in finance,"* one source pointed out. *"You do need to understand what the technology does, how it works, why it's patented and what features are important for that,"* but a science background isn't always an advantage. After all, what use is a MSc in Biology with Astrophysics on a patent case to do with boilers? In short, *"the ability to take in information quickly"* is what's most important.

Simmons is a winner

The qualification system, say trainees, is *"quite different to other places. You express a preference for where you would like to go and all the partners get together and discuss all of the trainees. I like that it's not just a department's decision – all the partners look at everyone."* Eight out of ten stayed on after qualification in 2013.

There's plenty going on socially – last Friday of the month drinks, the annual Bristows dinner dance, an autumn party, something whenever anyone leaves, or joins, or gets married, or has a baby. *"It's nice, because there's so much that you don't feel you that you have to make it to everything."* At the time of our calls the annual quiz had just taken place, clearly sparking strong feelings in some quarters. *"Who won? Ah, don't even ask... there were definitely people using iPhones,"* griped one competitive type. It sounded like fun, though, especially the 'creativity' round. *"Last year it was origami; it was face-painting this time. One team painted their person as Gene Simmons from Kiss. They got a good back-combing effect on her hair and she had quite a big tongue as well, so they got the ten points and won."*

Since Unilever itself is still resident in part of the building, Bristows employees get a discount on products in the company's shop. Thus, trainees enjoy unlikely perks such as *"cheap Marmite"* and 60p packets of face wipes. *"You might not appreciate this,"* our (male) researcher was told, *"but they cost £3.99 on the high street!"*

And finally...
For a firm doing work that's fascinating bordering on sexy, Bristows and its lawyers come across as pleasantly understated. IP fans will be in their element, but there's plenty more going on here too.

Browne Jacobson LLP

The facts

Location: Nottingham, Birmingham, London, Manchester, Exeter

Number of UK partners/solicitors: 90/183

Partners who trained at firm: 19%

Total number of trainees: 16

Seats: 4x6 months

Alternative seats: occasional secondments

Extras: pro bono – ProHelp, Planning Aid, Environmental Law Foundation

On chambersstudent.co.uk...

How to get into Browne Jacobson
Interview with training partner Brian Smith

Growing year on year but keen not to lose its welcoming atmos, Browne Jacobson's the place to be if you're aiming for health, public sector or insurance work.

Not in Nottingham

Arguably second only to Robin Hood as Nottingham's best export, Browne Jacobson is going places. Tracing its ancestry way back to 1832 (admittedly not as far back as Robin Hood, who has dibs on the twelfth century), BJ's only been growing in a major way over the past decade or so. Turnover's been steadily rising and in 2012/13, went from £41.3m to £45m. The firm opened its doors in Manchester in early 2012, and later that year took insurance and employment practices from South West firm Veitch Penny to start a fifth office in Exeter. London and Birmingham complete the picture which, according to trainees, shows a firm with very local roots *"moving towards becoming national."*

BJ, not unlike RH, has a strong history of working with services that give back. It's known for its healthcare and public sector work, as well as its very strong insurance, corporate, personal injury and commercial groups. With the seismic changes to the sector implemented by the coalition, Browne Jacobson is amassing a fast-growing education group. *"Resources are expanding all the time and there's a huge explosion in work,"* reported trainees.

"One of the things that attracted me most to Browne Jacobson was the wide range of seats – as a trainee, you can go pretty much anywhere," one source told us. There's more to choose from in Nottingham than over in Birmingham, but trainees in Brum can always go to Nottingham to sample seats not offered in their home office (Manchester and London don't offer any yet). Trainees have no say in the allocation of their first seat, though many were *"e-mailed before we start asking what we'd enjoyed the*

most on the LPC – they also take into account any prior experience like paralegalling."* For the remaining three seats, trainees list their top preferences.

The firm's business is divided into four: insurance and public risk (taking in healthcare, clinical negligence, personal injury, social care and environment); business services (corporate, commercial, private client, education); business and professional risk (commercial litigation, employment, IP, professional negligence and construction and property risk) and property (retail, development, public authority and health). *"There are always more seats than trainees and most departments want a trainee."* Current popular destinations include corporate, IP and employment – conversely, *"there's not much interest expressed in social care or private client – the latter hasn't been offered for a while."*

Medical matters

Insurance and public risk (IPR) first, and BJ's health group is renowned across the UK, in particular for clinical negligence and mental health. Much of what goes on in healthcare includes transactions and takeovers of health groups. Browne Jacobson is also a major panel firm, sitting on the NHS Litigation Authority and Medical Protection Authority panels – plus, there's a great deal of inquest, inquiry and public consultation work. A 24-hour helpline offers the availability of constant legal advice for medical clients. For trainees, there's a lot of good work on offer in the clinical negligence seat even though – due to the team's acclaim, it tends to be extremely high-value. Example cases: the team represented

Chambers UK rankings

Administrative & Public Law	Health & Safety
	Healthcare
Banking & Finance	Information Technology
Clinical Negligence	Intellectual Property
Competition/European Law	Local Government
Construction	Personal Injury
Corporate/M&A	Private Client
Court of Protection	Professional Negligence
Dispute Resolution	Projects
Education	Real Estate
Employment	Restructuring/Insolvency
Environment	Social Housing

a hospital trust in a multiparty inquest against a GP due to a teenage girl dying who had not being diagnosed with TB. It also represented a foundation trust after a female prisoner prescribed acne medication – alleged to have links with depression and suicide – took her own life. *"Claims like babies who've incurred cerebral palsy because of something going wrong during the birth are standard,"* explained one trainee. *"It's very sad, but the fact we're not on the side of the claimant means there's a barrier to prevent you being as emotionally involved."* You could see how cases like these may not prompt too much direct input from trainees, but our sources reported *"a lot of shadowing at the start, and then a lot of drafting work towards the end of the seat."* Said one: *"I attended witness interviews, reviews with the barrister and went to chambers with the solicitor and expert."*

Over in business services, the corporate seat is always popular. The Nottingham team is rivalled only by Eversheds in the locality, and acts for many family-run businesses with a smattering of international transactions. Sectors include *"retail, tech and education."* Predictably, there's a lot of crossover with healthcare – a major recent deal was the secondary buyout of CARE Fertility by BJ client General Healthcare for £60m. The work is *"predominantly M&A, with some corporate support work."* The team's partner-heavy, which means *"as a trainee you see lots of good work. One one deal I managed all the due diligence internationally and talked with lawyers across Europe and Asia."*

There's education sector work within corporate, but BJ is leading the field in developing a standalone practice in line with the changes to the sector made by the coalition. *"There's a huge amount of growth in this group, which permeates other teams as well."* The group works with institutions ranging from boarding schools and FE colleges to educational charities but is becoming best known for its work on Academy conversions. *"Because everything's so current, it's a more business-focused seat. You can watch the news every morning and there's something new from*

Michael Gove. It's about immersing yourself in the sector – even if it's not technically law-related it could be useful for the client. So, there's the chance to write articles, or opinions for the website, and help out on presentations to clients." There's also plenty of work on the pastoral side: *"Dealing with everything from admissions to exclusions."*

Risky business?

Business and professional risk (BPR) is home to commercial litigation and employment seats. The former can include a lot of insolvency work for trainees. *"We often get to manage a file, which can be daunting but is incredible experience. You could be working on a bankruptcy or winding-up petition – which when you've done one is applying the exact same principles to a different situation."* The commercial side of things *"could bring in anything – from partnership disputes to an employee who's failed to pay back a loan to an employer."* The team acts for councils, NHS trusts and companies from sectors such as electronics and pharmaceuticals. The size of disputes means *"you get an instant grasp of what being a solicitor actually is. Rather than just dipping in and out of something vast, you open the file, deal with the money and with billing the client – the full experience."*

The employment seat was praised by trainees for offering great responsibility on contentious and advisory work – *"like policy review and the drafting of handbooks, which is actually really enjoyable."* On the contentious side, trainees report working for *"mainly NHS clients, with some partners maintaining a private client base alongside them."* The team is *"respondent-heavy, and there are a wide variety of complaints – equal pay claims, tribunals involving discrimination and unfair dismissal."* Tribunals are made additionally problematic by the fact that many people are forced to represent themselves – *"which makes things more interesting but, equally, fairly frustrating."* Trainees naturally *"expect disclosure and prepping bundles,"* but *"attend a large number of tribunal hearings."* With crossover with education there's *"always Academy work. The trainee gets their own set of Academy files and you help them through the conversion process which is just transferring employment contracts over, though occasionally something unusual crops up, like someone could be mid-way through a disciplinary."*

Marrying litigation with property, the construction and risk team is interesting both legally and commercially, say our sources. *"You get a good exposure to the strategy of disputes, in the sense of delaying proceedings or putting pressure on the other side. You also get an insight into the fee quotation side of things, and estimating if you're going to meet them."* The team is instructed by huge retailers Wilkinson and Alliance Boots on issues ranging from unlawful occupation of premises and subtenants becoming insolvent. *"It's such a discrete area of law but it's unbelievable the amount of principles that can exist,"* said a source.

Property seats include retail (mainly tenancy leases for shopping centres), development (residential and social housing and some corporate support), public authority (predominantly Academy work) and healthcare. The health team is currently focusing on the transference of Primary Care Trusts into Clinical Commissioning Groups. See our online bonus feature for more on these changes to the healthcare system. Over in retail, there's a lot of work for high-end designer brands on their largest stores. The team acted for Le Coq Sportif on negotiations for its flagship European store in the Seven Dials district of Covent Garden. This kind of work is *"exciting by nature, and you also get proper legal work. I got to assist the fee earner throughout so I got to see variously the reviewing of title and preparation of first drafts for reports and leases, the documentation of store fittings, and at the end the closing, the finance and the payment of taxes."*

Harry Potter and the Inland Revenue offices of boom

Nottingham moved offices in mid-2012: its previous premises was *"three buildings put together – you'd constantly get lost and sometimes reception would give you a map just to find your way around!"* We're happy to report there's no such confusion at Castle Meadow, an office complex owned by the Inland Revenue, and given a £5m facelift before BJ set up shop there. Going from a creaky Hogwarts-like building to swish open-plan *"brings its own teething problems – some of the older partners still have to wear noise reduction headphones,"* but we're assured that they're transitional. *"It's created a change in the way people work, but in a good way. Everyone's out*

in the open, and working across departments is now more fluid – you cross work over and socialise more easily." The Birmingham hub in Victoria Square has *"a constant buzz of chatter and noise – everyone here is used to the open-plan vibe."*

It's worth noting that BJ has added 100 people to its ranks in the past year. With growth like this, comes inevitable change. *"They're trying to keep the culture the same,"* think trainees. *"They're keen on being viewed primarily as approachable – with things like trainees getting support from every single member of the team, rather than just their supervisor. There are no airs and graces here: you can speak to whoever you choose on a down-to-earth level and people appreciate your honesty. The best way to describe the firm is a national firm with the feel of a smaller, regional firm."*

This feeling of non-hierarchy seeps through to the firm's social life. *"Everyone here is willing to try new things with good humour. The trainees did a charity cycle ride between all of Browne Jacobson's offices. There was no sense that any one of us was going to rush off and try and beat the others – it was about working together."* There's a whole host of sporting activities (*"netball, football, a running club, pilates..."*) and networking opportunities for young hopefuls, along with a healthy Friday night pub scene, and a generous trainee budget. *"We go off once a year and have a weekend away in a cottage in the country."*

"There's clearly an emphasis here on putting out the same number of potential jobs as there are candidates – which meant that some of the jobs listed had pretty vague descriptions," said one interviewee, *"Despite this, they did make it clear that even though there may not be all the jobs we wanted, they've done their best to create roles for us."* In 2013, all eight qualifiers took up positions with BJ.

And finally...

"The firm really does what it says it's doing – it's growing quickly but trying to maintain its culture through conscious effort."

IT'S THE WAY WE WORK THAT MAKES US DIFFERENT

We work with **high profile clients** on well publicised deals

We give our trainees **early responsibility** to run their own smaller matters

We offer a **six seat training system** to allow trainees to make an informed decision

We have a **broad range of practice areas** so we can fit our expertise to our clients' needs

We think about the future – **we recruit future partners**, not just future trainees

We are based in the UK but that doesn't stop us having a **global reach**

We work together in a **collegiate environment**

For more information about trainee solicitor recruitment, please go to **www.burges-salmon.com/careers** or call the team on **0117 939 2229.**

f **www.facebook.com/burgessalmontrainee**

t **@burgessalmon**

Burges Salmon LLP is an equal opportunities employer

BURGES SALMON

Burges Salmon LLP

The facts

Location: Bristol

Number of UK partners/solicitors: 79/230

Partners who trained at firm: 32%

Total number of trainees: 46

Seats: 6x4 months

Alternative Seats: secondments

Extras: pro bono – Briston University Law Clinic

On chambersstudent.co.uk

How to get into Burges Salmon

Interview with trainee recruitment partner
 Keith Beattie

A rough guide to Bristol

Bristol's Burges Salmon remains fiercely independent – but watch out as it draws in more and more international work.

Bigger fish, smaller pond

You'd be very wrong to assume that Burges Salmon is just some quaint little regional firm. Despite only having one office, it has a broad reach and is increasingly tapping into the global marketplace too. Private individuals, government departments and many FTSE 100 companies appear on the firm's client list, including recognisable names like The Crown Estate, Eurostar, Lloyds Banking Group and BAE Systems. Burges Salmon can give established City firms a run for their money – as one trainee put it, *"in light of the current economic situation, we've still succeeded in bringing in the big-ticket work – and we can do it cheaper in Bristol."* Burges Salmon picks up top *Chambers UK* rankings in the South West for the banking, construction, corporate, dispute resolution, employment and real estate work that it conducts (a very condensed list; there are many more). It also concentrates its efforts on certain sectors, like education, energy, leisure, the public sector and transport.

Burges Salmon is a firm that has remained steadfastly independent throughout its existence, and has resisted the lure of potential hook-ups in a marketplace saturated by headlines announcing the latest mergers. It's a strategy that has served the firm well, and apart from a small client meeting space in London, Burges Salmon runs all operations out of its Bristol digs, located within One Glass Wharf. Bristol is in many ways the perfect location: it has bucked recession trends and is second to only London when it comes to economic growth (other firms, like Simmons & Simmons, have only recently cottoned on to this advantage). With 4% growth in revenue between 2012/13, trainees predicted that the firm's overall strategy wouldn't change much in years to come: *"I think there'll*

be a bigger push to target more international clients who are looking to invest their assets in the UK."

Trainees complete six seats throughout their training, with each one lasting four months. The first four seats will be in the firm's main departments. Real estate and a contentious seat are compulsory, and then trainees choose from options available in corporate and financial institutions; commercial; disputes, environment and planning; private client and wealth structuring. The fifth seat is an option seat, where trainees can try something new or revisit a department they enjoyed. Then the sixth seat is chosen on the understanding that it is the department a trainee wishes to qualify into. Sources felt that they were able to get a *"broad overview"* of the firm, and liked the idea of having a potential eight months in an area that they had eyed for qualification. The HR team's allocation efforts were also praised – *"they do work hard to place people where they want to be,"* and if someone's top preference can't be accommodated during one rotation, then the team try to ensure that they are next time round.

Salmon fishing in Bristol

The real estate group has an impressive client list which includes Aviva Investors, Lloyds, Nationwide and St Modwen (one of the UK's biggest developers). It is also the group which advises The Crown Estate most often, recently helping it to acquire Princes House in London, a mixed-use property which houses the BAFTA headquarters and the Princes Arcade. Trainees work mostly on these big commercial real estate transactions, and said that *"you play a smaller role on lots of different things – you have ten to 20 different matters and you'll be doing bits and bobs on all*

Chambers UK rankings

Agriculture & Rural Affairs	Intellectual Property
Banking & Finance	Investment Funds
Capital Markets	Outsourcing
Charities	Partnership
Competition/European Law	Pensions Litigation
Construction	Planning
Corporate/M&A	Private Client
Dispute Resolution	Professional Negligence
Employment	Projects
Energy & Natural Resources	Public Procurement
	Real Estate
Environment	Restructuring/Insolvency
Family/Matrimonial	Tax
Health & Safety	Transport
Information Technology	

of them." It can be "*quite hectic*," but the team are "*very nice and supportive.*" The subject matter is also interesting, and sources particularly enjoyed renewables work, helping to produce option agreements for developers who aim to construct wind farms or solar pods.

Burges Salmon's banking team has a reputation for high-value mid-market work, and also delves into more specialist areas such as project finance and Islamic finance. The team's sector expertise draws in clients from the hotels and leisure industry, and the group assisted YTL Hotels, which is owned by a Malaysian-based conglomerate, during the funding of its redevelopment plan to create a five-star hotel and spa in Bath. Trainees get "*quite a buzz from helping to make something happen, and to see a tangible end product: a building which has been funded because of our work.*" It also provides "*an interesting environment in which to look at contract law,*" and trainees will find themselves with "*a lot of document management*" to get to grips with, like managing conditions precedent lists, and in some cases they also visit "*people externally to get documents signed.*" Ultimately, trainees felt that they were "*really pushing the deal through – as if it couldn't happen without you.*"

The corporate perch

Those in corporate said that trainees become "*involved with two or three clients, and depending on who those clients are, you can have a completely different experience.*" Some had become involved with the transport work that comes into the department, while others had focused on the leisure and recreation sector. The department has a number of blue-chip corporate clients, including E.ON and FirstGroup, and it's not unusual for the team to be advising on transactions alongside magic circle firms. Corporate lawyers represented the Competition Commission (Slaughter and May acted for the purchaser) during the

sale of Edinburgh airport in 2012, for £807.2m. Trainees spend a lot of time "*researching companies and drafting the smaller documents in a transaction,*" while multinational deals enabled sources to "*manage relations*" between lawyers in all of the different jurisdictions.

Life in the commercial department is "*very varied,*" and there are "*lots of different elements that come under commercial, like IP, IT, projects and competition.*" Trainees said that "*they're very keen for you to keep your experiences quite broad, but you don't get to become an expert in one particular area.*" The commercial team is included on seven out of the eight panels appointed by the Government Procurement Service (more than any other firm), and the department has a mixture of private and public sector clients, including Ofgem, the Foreign & Commonwealth Office, Coca-Cola and Thomson Reuters. The latter appointed the firm to advise on an international contract in South-East Asia with Hewlett-Packard, which was worth over £100m. Trainees generally enjoyed the variety of the seat and had helped "*companies get their responses to the Competition Commission, following an investigation of their practices,*" and made amendments to "*large licence agreements for telecommunication companies.*"

Many trainees complete their contentious seat in commercial disputes. Once again, there are a number of specialist areas for trainees to dip into, including: arbitration; fraud and corruption; insurance; IP; professional negligence; real estate and agriculture; and sport. One source had been busy "*drafting cease and desist letters for an international food and beverage chain who had got wind of other businesses selling products with their name – it was the first letter of that type to be drafted for the client, so it will be used as the precedent going forward.*" Another had experienced an agricultural partnership dispute, in which they wrote "*all of the witness statements,*" and had become experts in "*20 years of quite complicated family history – in the end I knew more than the partner and the barrister!*" The department is "*always very busy,*" and has "*a London feel to it, with quite long hours and good cases.*"

Some of the smaller teams, like planning, employment and environment, can be "*oversubscribed, because they only take on one or two trainees.*" One of the seats that doesn't seem to suffer from that problem is pensions, which is perceived as "*dry and dull*" at first, but the feedback we received was unanimously positive: "*So many people have been sent there and they really enjoy it in the end.*" Chambers UK adorns the practice with a top ranking in Bristol, and sources had reaped the benefits of "*attending several trustee meetings, having direct client contact and drafting some challenging work – pensions is a technical area of the law.*" A tax seat is similarly technical, and is great for "*building up relationships with solicitors in other departments, because there are tax aspects to many of the matters we are involved in firm-wide.*"

Client secondments are often available, and trainees have recently completed them in banking real estate, environment and commercial clients. Trainees who had been seconded felt that firm support was there if they needed it, and enjoyed the chance to gain an insight into the kind of work that clients *"keep in-house, like consumer and regulatory work, which they have the internal know-how to deal with, so it doesn't make sense to get anyone external involved."*

And... this is Bert

Burges Salmon's new office is *"very bright,"* and trainees feel *"lucky to be in it."* The canteen is *"excellent,"* and serves some *"dangerously good americanos,"* while the ground floor is home to Bert, the *"resident gorilla"* – a statue which is decorated for St Patrick's Day and other special occasions (*"I always wonder: what is Bert going to be dressed as today?"*). Our sources concurred that having everybody based in one location was great for the firm, leading to a *"sense of cohesion and togetherness."*

However, with the move to the new office a couple of years ago, Burges Salmon left behind the city centre and set up shop in *"a more corporate area: we're right next to Temple Meads station, increasing our connectivity to London."* Some trainees felt that this physical move cemented atmospheric changes that have been occurring at the firm, as it pushes itself to become ever more established not just nationally, but on an international level as well: *"There's a more 'City' feel to the firm now. I remember that the advertising material used to highlight the combination of London-quality work with Bristol-quality life, but they've made a conscious effort to move away from that message. I suppose the point to pick up on is that you shouldn't expect to be leaving at 5pm."* Others agreed to a certain extent, but opined that *"City-firm atmospheres tend to go hand in hand with unhappy people, and that's not the case here – a sense of the regional remains, even if it isn't in the marketing materials any more."*

Trainees were certainly happy at Burges Salmon, and an active social life preserves their contented outlook. We heard of departmental *"kitchen parties,"* monthly charity 'dress down' days which culminate in firm-wide drinks in the canteen, vac scheme placement socials and many informal trainee get-togethers. The firm places an emphasis on charity fund-raising events, and hosts evenings which emulate some of the nation's most treasured TV formats, including 'Burges Salmon's Got Talent' and 'Strictly Le-

gal'. The former featured hula-hooping secretaries and a partner-shaped human pyramid, while the latter saw partners embark on a series of dance lessons to perfect their performance on the night. All of their efforts clearly paid off: the firm raised over £84,000 for charity in 2012.

"There's a real culture of grafting" at Burges Salmon, with people *"taking their work seriously"* but with *"humanity – people aren't robots here."* While trainees didn't specify a certain 'type', they did appreciate the mix of those with law and non-law backgrounds, as well as those with a previous career behind them: *"Other firms say that they have an equality and diversity policy in place, but in reality they only want people in their early 20s. Here, they actively welcome people who are older and have experience in other fields – they mean what they say."*

(Quali)flying high

The prevalence of training sessions which delve into the firm's sector specialities made trainees feel more enmeshed in what was going on as a whole. They run once a month, and are open for anyone to attend. *"They're really interesting, and there's a Q&A session at the end, which produces some good discussions, because everyone is coming at it from a different angle. I read the Farmer's Guardian for one! It just enables trainees to have a two-tiered perspective: first, of the work you're doing, and second, of the broader context in which it is occurring."*

Every trainee is allocated a partner principal who acts as a mentor. There's a budget set aside for mentors and mentees to meet up, but trainees said that *"in practice, the principals aren't particularly relied on, unless certain issues arise – mine wasn't a stranger by any means."* In the end, most trainees felt that they had enough support stemming from their supervisors and other colleagues at the firm.

With a 100% retention rate in 2012, trainees this year were quietly confident that a job would be waiting for them at the end of their contract. They liked the fact that the NQ recruitment round starts reassuringly early (some of our trainees knew where they would be qualifying by early April), and found the process very relaxed. *"You just go to HR and have a chat and express your feelings about where you would like to go. There are no interviews for positions, which takes some of the stress out, and they keep the decision focused on your performance throughout your training contract."*

And finally...

Trainees warn that this firm has an increasingly 'City' feel to it, so don't assume that life at Burges Salmon will be an easy ride. That said, trainees love this firm, the work and the location, and most wanted to stay on as NQs. 21 out of 23 did so in 2013.

The True Picture

"Pay attention to the culture of a firm and whether it suits you. A big M&A powerhouse will be very different to a firm with lots of smaller departments or one that focuses on an area like employment."

Trainee

Capsticks Solicitors LLP

The facts

Location: London, Birmingham, Leeds, Southampton
Number of UK partners/solicitors: 45/145
Partners who trained at firm: 22%
Total number of trainees: 13
Seats: 6x4 months
Alternative seats: none

On chambersstudent.co.uk...

How to get into Capsticks
Interview with training principal Majid Hassan
The Health and Social Care Act

Things are changing in the healthcare sector, and Wimbledon-based Capsticks is poised to surf the wave of reform.

Ch-ch-ch-changes

If you've got healthcare-related work on the brain, chances are Capsticks is already on your radar. More than three-quarters of this specialist firm's work is done on behalf of the NHS, advising various health authorities across the UK as well as national bodies like the NHS Confederation and Department of Health. Lawyers also act for hospitals, regulators and healthcare charities, and are damn good at what they do: *Chambers UK* recognises the firm as one of the best in the field.

Capsticks has called Wimbledon its home for almost three decades, though newly opened offshoots in Birmingham (2008), Leeds (2011) and Southampton (2013) now complement the London headquarters. The Southampton office was acquired from Coffin Mew and focuses on social housing. Trainees are now being recruited into all four offices, and insiders anticipate "*substantial*" growth across the firm in coming years, though not at the expense of the niche Capsticks has carved out for itself. "*It's clear management is calculating carefully to maintain our current shape.*" This expansion is set to coincide with some pretty major changes to the healthcare sector, not least of all the Health and Social Care Act 2012, a huge reorganisation of the NHS. "*People seem confident the changes will affect us positively, so spirits are high at the moment,*" said our sources, characterising the current mood at the firm as "*optimistic.*"

The training contract operates on a six-seat basis, with five options to choose from each rotation: clinical law (negligence and advisory), real estate, employment, dispute resolution and commercial. Most trainees experience five different practice areas before returning to the department into which they hope to qualify for their final four months. "*HR prioritises the second-years when making allocation decisions, but nobody's ever forced to go somewhere they don't want.*"

A healthy pulse

Clinical negligence is a cornerstone of Capsticks and has earned the firm top-band *Chambers UK* rankings on the defendant side. The team's prestige is such that it was called upon to advise the London Ambulance Services following the 7/7 bombings and recently began working with the Yorkshire Ambulance Trust in the infamous Hillsborough Inquest. Clin neg cases are wide-ranging and can include anything from routine knee injuries and hip replacements to perforated bowels following surgery and even "*the odd instance of tattooing gone wrong.*" Yikes. According to our sources, a good deal of matters err on the "*emotive*" side of the spectrum – for example, parents taking legal action because their baby has incurred brain damage during birth. Fortunately, such "*harrowing*" cases are balanced out by plenty of minor, less sobering (though no doubt traumatic for those involved) insurance claims "*like someone falling backwards off a massage chair or suing their guidance counsellor.*" With this wealth of work at their fingertips, trainees reckon "*you progress really quickly and get treated like a qualified lawyer from very early on.*" Interviewees reported liaising with medical experts, drafting instructions to counsel, witnessing negotiations and attending hearings throughout the "*fast-paced*" seat. "*I actually received instructions and prepared the direction of a case on my own towards the end of my time in the department. I was supervised of course, but they really let me run with it.*"

The True Picture

Chambers UK rankings

Administrative & Public Law	Employment
Clinical Negligence	Healthcare
Court of Protection	Professional Discipline

Work in dispute resolution consists of commercial, regulatory and property litigation for healthcare bodies like teaching hospitals, ambulance services and NHS trusts. "*You see different matters come in every day – it's a jack-of-all-trades department, which keeps things interesting.*" On the commercial side, lawyers contend with contractual disputes and "*procurement challenges, wherein we defend the client against private providers' claims that the process hasn't been carried out fairly.*" There's the chance to sample contentious IP work too. The property disputes team is currently keeping busy on the front lines following the abolition of Primary Care Trusts, a consequence of the coalition's new healthcare legislation. "*Old medical centres are being sold off, and we're seeing a lot of cases against squatters in disused properties.*" Dispute resolution lawyers also deal with primary care work, "*managing performance concerns and contract disputes for GPs and dentists.*"

Capsticks is home to the country's largest dedicated healthcare property team, which carries out commercial real estate work for both public and private sector clients. The firm recently advised on the redevelopment of St Bernard's, England's first purpose-built mental health hospital, assisting the hospital with the sale of several original buildings in order to make room for new facilities. Lawyers also acted for the Royal Institute of British Architects on its lease of a storage warehouse. While trainees admitted "*nobody comes here with the express intention of doing real estate,*" they agreed the seat is "*fantastic – the team is helpful and approachable, and you're put on the types of projects you can see all the way through to the end, which is a great confidence builder.*"

Commercial is an ideal seat for getting a handle on the big picture of NHS structure and its recent reforms: "*When you're the one working on actually advising on these reforms and implementing the results, you really come to understand the underlying principles of why and how certain bodies are changing.*" The team recently assisted the UK's largest mental health charity with its £52.5m refinancing and advised on the merger of Barts Health NHS Trust, the UK's largest, with several London hospitals to create Barts Health.

Just what the doctor ordered

Trainees are assigned an associate supervisor for each seat, the reason being "*seniors inevitably have more time to give you than partners,*" though the latter are "*still very approachable,*" we were assured. "*Supervisors are open about letting us know we can come to them if we get overwhelmed – it's clear they want us to grow as much as we can and see us as valued members of the team.*"

"*People do a good job of looking out for each other, so you always feel supported,*" one source told us. "*I've had supervisors who regularly left early to collect their kids, and it wasn't the big deal it might be at a firm less concerned with its employees' work/life balance.*" Despite the firm's expansion in recent years, our interviewees were confident this close-knit atmosphere will continue, pointing to "*people's tendency to spend their whole career here*" as a "*key factor in maintaining a positive culture that's lasting.*"

Staff of all levels gather outside of work for the odd game of rounders, pub quiz or wine and cheese do. With its "*lovely*" café, outside terrace and "*crazy*" art collection – indeed, work from the students of Wimbledon College of Art adorn each of the five floors – the flagship Wimbledon branch is conducive to regular get-togethers. "*They rotate the pieces every three months, at which point the firm hosts an evening for everyone to meet the artists.*" Come Christmas, however, it's all eyes on trainees as the cohort assumes the duty of "*dressing up as snowmen or giant presents and parading around the office to collect money for charity.*" Ritual humiliation aside, the firm makes a "*decent*" effort to create a welcoming atmosphere for its young 'uns, recently establishing a junior lawyers group to provide a forum for socialising and providing feedback on life at the firm.

Our sources recommended bagging a spot on the vac scheme or even trying your hand at paralegaling with the firm to get a true taste for life at Capsticks. When it comes to making applications, knowing your PCTs from your SHAs goes a long way (that's primary care trusts and strategic health authorities, by the way). "*My number-one piece of advice to people is to read up on the developments in the healthcare industry,*" offered one trainee. "*It'll help frame the questions you ask at interview and show you have a passion for this sector in particular.*"

And finally...

"If you work hard and show a keen interest in progressing, the firm will do its best to give you a job," trainees were convinced. In 2013, all six trainees were given a healthy prognosis and kept on.

Charles Russell LLP

The facts

Location: London, Cheltenham, Guildford
Number of UK partners/solicitors: 92/ 213
Partners who trained at firm: 15%
Total number of trainees: 37
Seats: 4x6 months
Alternative seats: overseas seats, secondments
Extras: pro bono – Bethnal Green law Centre, Surrey Law Centre, RCJ CAB, A4ID, LwwWorks; language classes

On chambersstudent.co.uk...

How to get into Charles Russell
Give it up for Guildford

If you're after a rich mixture of commercial and private client work, then Charles Russell might be the firm for you.

Family fortunes

Over two-and-a-bit centuries, Charles Russell has evolved a lot. Established in 1891 by the son of Lord Chief Justice, the firm traditionally served wealthy Roman Catholic families. Today the private client and family practices are still going strong but it's really corporate and litigation work that accounts for a hefty bulk of the firm's business. Since 2011, the firm has focused on nine key sectors: charities; energy; family; healthcare; private wealth; property; retail and leisure; sports; and technology, media and communications. This approach "*forms the key part of our strategy. We want to concentrate on areas where we have expertise,*" says training partner Eve Ellis.

As its practices have grown, the firm's expansion hasn't been totally seamless. In 2012, its Oxford office closed and its Cambridge branch was sold to another firm. "*From a UK perspective, we felt we were already well covered,*" explains Ellis. However, CR retains regional offices in Cheltenham and Guildford as well as overseas outposts in Geneva and Bahrain. Trainees have the opportunity to spend time in these international offices, as well as venturing out on secondment to big clients like Cable & Wireless, Actis, the FA and ITV.

At the time of our calls, 23 trainees were beavering away in the London office. There were eight more in Guildford and five in Cheltenham, while another two were out on secondment. In London, trainees can take seats in corporate commercial (coco), sports, IP, media/reputation management, healthcare, banking, dispute resolution, property litigation, family, private client, property, employment and pensions. In Cheltenham, new recruits can sit in private client, property, coco and dispute resolution, while in

Guildford coco, dispute resolution, insolvency, trusts and estates, family, employment, property, property litigation, private client and construction are on offer.

Many trainees were attracted to the variety of practice areas on offer at Charles Russell. "*I hadn't decided what area of law to go into and I liked the firm's diverse training contract,*" was the prevalent feeling among sources. Others pointed out that "*it's rare for a City firm to have a strong mix of private client and commercial work. Plus, it has a reputation for being one of the nicer places to work in the top 50.*" Those in Cheltenham and Guildford were drawn to the combination of a "*regional setting and high-quality work.*"

Russelling up business

The firm's corporate department works in the London mid-market, often advising on capital markets transactions for AIM clients from a whole range of sectors – mining and natural resources, telecoms, IT, manufacturing, real estate, biotech and transport. The firm recently advised Canadian gold mining company Yamana Gold on the acquisition of Extorre Gold Mines and acted for CIC Energy during its merger with Jindal Steel & Power. Other clients include Oxfordshire tech company Transense and another gold mining operation, Centamin. In corporate, "*you're encouraged to delegate where you can. Some trainees complain about photocopying and bundling, but you're encouraged to use secretaries: it's not looked down upon if you do delegate. It encourages you to step up.*" Of course, if there's a big transaction going on "*you can only take a back seat. But on smaller matters, you're expected to contribute.*" One source had amended articles and attended client meetings, and "*also did several com-*

Chambers UK rankings

Agriculture & Rural Affairs	Healthcare
Banking & Finance	Intellectual Property
Capital Markets	Media & Entertainment
Charities	Planning
Construction	Private Client
Corporate/M&A	Professional Discipline
Defamation/Reputation	Real Estate
Management	Restructuring/Insolvency
Dispute Resolution	Retail
Employment	Sports Law
Family/Matrimonial	Telecommunications
Fraud	

pletions, taking in the whole process of an M&A deal." Another described taking on "*some drafting of documents for deals, as well as letters and e-mails to clients. I also drafted the more simple sections of due diligence reports myself and worked on presentations for AIM companies.*"

Meanwhile, trainees in the commercial group "*did some work for online start-up businesses. We've got a good forward-thinking, energetic team, so there's lots of small new clients from digital and start-up businesses.*" The practice also includes significant sports and media-related work: the firm recently advised Paddy Power on an Olympic-related ad campaign. The online bookies cheekily sponsored a different athletics event in a French village called London and needed to ensure its billboards didn't contravene the strict rules prohibiting non-approved companies associating themselves with the 2012 Games.

Litigation at Charles Russell is "*a broad department that takes in pharma, IP and real estate matters.*" Clients are suitably varied and include the Central Bank of Bahrain, the government of the Republic of Trinidad and Tobago, the Welsh Rugby Union and Barclay Pharmaceuticals. "*I was the point of contact for some clients,*" remembered one trainee. "*I got involved in the day-to-day running of some files and went to court with counsel. I drafted letters of response and advice to clients, and drafted witness statements in the run up to a trial.*" Those who'd been in property litigation took on "*lots of small matters. You get given a lot of responsibility, which involves juggling a caseload. That's a good learning experience. It's heavy on actual law, so it helps to have an interest in the law rather than just soft skills like negotiating. I worked on a big trial, which was quite exciting. I drafted witness statements, prepared research and notes and dealt with the court printers and the transcription guys. I got to run areas of the case myself.*" It certainly sounds quite hectic. "*The workload was... impressive,*" laughed our source. "*There were a lot of late nights.*"

Though it's "*not unknown to be in until three in the morning or consistently be leaving at 11pm,*" the hours at Charles Russell are generally more "*reasonable*" than that. Trainees who'd toiled into the small hours felt that the firm makes up for it by offering time off in lieu. Overall, "*the focus is on willingness to get the job done, rather than showing face.*" One source confirmed this: "*I walked out at 5.30pm to play football and no one said anything.*"

Up close and personal

Private client is a "*dense area of law*" so trainees undertake "*a lot of really interesting research. You get a lot of supervision, but I did get to manage my own files and run with things if they were basic, like Lasting Powers of Attorney, which is really just form-filling.*" There's lots of drafting of wills, general estate and tax planning, too. "*Some big clients with landed estates might have businesses as well so there may be a corporate element to the seat. Or they might be selling family heirlooms or artworks.*" Trainees who head out to Charles Russell's Geneva office found themselves "*working largely on the Liechtenstein Disclosure Facility, whereby people declare UK tax that hasn't been paid,*" though they also see "*more typical private client work, like wills and probate.*" Upping and leaving to spend six months in the Swiss outpost "*isn't a stressful experience. The firm sorts out a flat and it's very easy to acclimatise to the office and get involved.*"

In the family department, "*the clients are generally high net worth individuals – people with Lamborghinis and international property – so it's quite glamorous, for want of a better word.*" Trainees work on divorces and financial settlements, as well as taking on "*some child-based work – protection and international kidnap. There's not really a late-hour culture, but it's quite intense. Because it's contentious and the clients aren't usually in the best point in their lives, it can get a bit stressy.*"

The seat allocation process involves trainees stating their top three preferences and giving reasons for their choice. "*They do their best to accommodate you. I only know of one person who hasn't got one of their three choices,*" said one interviewee. Appraisals take place in the middle of and at the end of each seat. "*They don't take an ambush approach,*" thought sources. "*If there's a problem, they'll tell you as soon as they notice.*" Most felt the appraisal is "*more of a constructive chat,*" though one or two others pointed out that "*appraisals are useful, but one-way. You get told what you can improve on but they're not too interested in what you have to say about the firm. Commercial imperatives triumph. But then we're paid a lot to be here, so you have to suck it up.*"

There's plenty of "*inter-office interaction. I wouldn't have a problem picking up the phone to London to ask for help. You don't feel like you're on your own,*" said one source outside the capital. Generally trainees appreciated the supportive atmosphere: "*It's an open-door environment. Partners are generally very receptive and approachable. I feel if I did have problems there are quite a few people I could go to. Charles Russell is not an intimidating place!*" CR's strong roots in family and private client influence the firm's culture today: "*It's more people-focused than other places,*" declared one source. "*It's very courteous. People are polite to each other and so it's retained a certain charm. Employees are treated well. There's a very friendly attitude. You don't really get hot-head partners that shout at you.*"

Million dollar questions

"*Low-key*" describes the Charles Russell social scene. Trainees tend to arrange "*informal drinks pretty regularly*" among themselves and the more junior solicitors, but "*it's not like we're down the pub every Friday.*" However, the small intake means that trainees form close relationships and sources at all offices reported going out en masse for lunch and dinner. We also heard about sports teams, a book club and film nights.

Firm-wide events are generally held in London, but Guildford and Cheltenham folk are encouraged to attend. While the firm's Christmas party is "*quite tame and comes in for criticism,*" the Charles Russell sports dinner is considered to be the "*event of the year.*" Apparently, "*it hasn't got anything really to do with sports – it's an excuse for a three-course dinner and a large bar tab.*" Consequently, "*a lot of shots are consumed*" and the ensuing jamboree "*provides gossip for the firm.*"

Despite historically good retention rates, trainees were nervy about qualification, pointing to the fact that several last year were initially given six-month contracts, or worrying that "*they've normally kept pretty much everyone on – perhaps it's our intake who will take the hit!*" The jobs list comes out in May and there was doubt at the time of our calls about where positions would be available. It was accepted that there's stiff competition to qualify into certain departments (family and employment in particular were mentioned), and once the list is released, rather than submitting preferences trainees must "*nail their colours to the mast,*" make a formal application and go through an interview. In the end, 14 out of 20 qualifiers stayed on as NQs in 2013.

The CR application form typically includes "*a quirky question*" that's designed to "*bring out your personality*" beyond the usual bland clichés and "*make the partner reading the form want to meet you.*" Examples of previous questions include: 'If you could shadow someone for a day who would it be?' 'What kind of animal would you be?' and 'What would your superpower be?' Representative and useless *Student Guide* team answers: Jack the Ripper; tapeworm; Lindy Hop dance ability. Regarding interviews, trainees advised that "*there isn't a set experience that you should have, like job experience or travelling. They want to know how your experiences have shaped you as a person.*"

And finally...

If you're applying for a regional office, interviewers are likely to want to know why. "*It helps to have links to the area rather than just not wanting to work long London hours,*" cautioned trainees.

Cleary Gottlieb Steen & Hamilton LLP

The facts

Location: London
Number of UK partners/solicitors: 14/52 (+14 non-UK-qualified)
Total number of trainees: 24
Seats: 4x6 months
Alternative seats: overseas seats; secondments
Extras: pro bono – LawWorks, A4ID, Lawyers in Schools

On chambersstudent.co.uk...

How to get into Cleary
Interview with grad recruitment partner Richard Sultman
Internationalists

An elite American outfit with serious international clout, Cleary is suited to *"self-starters"* who desire *"plenty of responsibility at the earliest opportunity."*

To Europe and beyond!

Born in the US in 1946, Cleary Gottlieb was only three years old when it set sail across the Atlantic to open a new office in Paris. It has established a further seven outposts in Europe since then, building on its early intentions of becoming an American firm with an extensive European network. Recently, however, Cleary has largely turned its attentions elsewhere: a new office in São Paulo in 2011, and another in Seoul the following year, have strengthened its presence in Latin America and Asia, while the Abu Dhabi office, also opened in 2012, represents the firm's first foray into the Middle East. The London base, founded in 1971, mainly focuses its efforts on M&A, finance and capital markets.

When we spoke to trainees, two things cropped up in conversation more than anything else. The first was the lockstep remuneration system that the firm has in place, whereby everyone in a class year earns the same regardless of the amount they bill – which is different from a lot of US firms. This *"takes away the competitive edge, because there's no pressure to hoard work: people are much more willing to help each other out and share the burden as a whole."*

The second was Cleary's *"eagerness for us to qualify as generalists,"* although those wishing to become specialists can qualify into litigation, competition, tax or employment. This generalist approach is emphasised by the fact that the firm has a non-departmental structure. For trainees this means that although they are assigned to specific seats, work will often derive from areas entirely unrelated to it during their six months there.

Our sources described this system as a *"double-edged sword."* On the one hand, trainees are able to carry work on through to their next seat, allowing them to *"actually see a deal through to the end"* and *"keep your finger in the pie if you've done a seat that you really enjoyed."* The downside is that, because work can come from anyone at any time, *"you sometimes feel like you're exposed and can't see the work coming before it hits you."* Thankfully, help is at hand: *"Your supervisor is there to ensure that you're not overburdened and usually has a good understanding of the demands being put on you."*

Workin' all over the world

"International' is definitely the word I would use to describe our M&A work," ventured one trainee. It's a fair statement when you look at Cleary's recent deal highlights. The firm is representing Bank of America Merrill Lynch in the sale of its non-US wealth management business to the Swiss private bank Julius Baer, involving the transfer of more than 2,000 employees and roughly $84bn of assets under management. With help from the Moscow and Brussels offices, the London team also represented Russian oil giant Rosneft in its $55bn purchase of Moscow-based oil company TNK-BP, making it the largest oil and gas producer in the world. If you still need convincing that 'international' is a fitting description, Cleary acts for global powerhouses Coca-Cola, American Express and Sony too.

Our interviewees initially carried out *"classic M&A tasks,"* such as reviewing documents, compiling checklists and monitoring due diligence, but this quickly made

Chambers UK rankings

Banking & Finance	Corporate/M&A
Banking Litigation	Dispute Resolution
Competition/European Law	Private Equity

way for greater levels of responsibility – from drafting documents to taking the lead on disclosures. One recalled: *"I spent the first couple of months working on a mixture of two or three deals that were fairly small in terms of my involvement, but then a deal came in that took up the remainder of my time in the seat and that was fantastic." "*

We were informed that the capital markets practice *"generates a lot of clients for the firm."* For instance, *"when we're managing an IPO, we'll hopefully establish a strong working relationship with the client. So, when that client becomes involved in something else, they may come back to us and will then be referred to the other relevant practices."* Be warned though: a seat in capital markets is an *"intense experience"* that involves *"a lot of hard, gruelling work."* Indeed, we asked one trainee to describe the tasks they took on and they mistily replied: *"That's difficult to answer because the tasks you're given are so huge from the beginning."* We did eventually hear about some, such as carrying out advisory work for public companies – as well as *"companies that are contemplating going public."* Trainees also draft prospectuses and liaise with clients.

Movin' on up

The litigation team has *"developed rapidly over the last couple of years,"* with the addition of two *Chambers*-ranked partners – banking litigation expert Jonathan Kelly and former Stephenson Harwood CEO Sunil Gadhia – fuelling this recent growth. *"They've brought so many years of experience to the table, which certainly helps with attracting high-profile clients and matters."* However, *"although it says a lot that we've made these key lateral hires, the firm tends to have an organic approach to growth and still encourages trainees to qualify into litigation if they're interested in doing so."*

"Invariably, the stakes are high in litigation," explained an interviewee. *"One wrong e-mail or badly worded phrase can cause untold consequences, so even as a trainee you're conscious of that."* While this means *"you'll be running a lot of things past your supervisor first,"* that doesn't stop trainees being handed a great deal of responsibility. *"They were always very happy for me to take on as much as I could handle,"* remarked one, *"so I never felt like I was limited in that sense."* In addition to drafting witness statements and helping with correspondence, trainees do *"a lot of legal research more so than in a transactional seat."* Cleary has recently acted for Iraq,

Argentina and Greece (concerning its historic €206bn debt restructuring), as well as corporations like Total and African Minerals.

Trainees in finance worked on derivative transactions, restructuring and project finance. They were also treated to the *"typical Cleary style"* of leanly staffed deals, meaning – you guessed it – plenty of responsibility from the get-go. *"You're given as much responsibility as you could imagine early on and are thrown in with very little background knowledge of the deal, but you learn to catch up quickly."*

This may sound daunting, but our sources revelled in the experience – an indication of the kind of person who truly thrives at the firm. *"It's so inspirational to be working on the front lines of a big deal, and I've really cherished that experience. It's very hard work, and I've pulled multiple all-nighters... I'm not sure the extent to which that's a good thing, but it's quite a common occurrence for trainees here."*

While Hong Kong, New York, Brussels, Moscow and Paris are usually the overseas secondments on offer, trainees sensed that *"anywhere is possible if you can provide a good rationale for it."* One shed light on their time abroad: *"It was an absolutely brilliant experience, and a perk of being part of a small team at a firm that has so many offices. If an issue comes up here now, I know that I can reach out to the people who I worked with overseas if they happen to be specialists in a relevant area."* Beijing, Washington DC, and Abu Dhabi are on the horizon, the firm tells us.

You don't need to go overseas to reap the benefits of Cleary's multiple offices. *"The firm prides itself on its international network, instead of just being a bunch of offices scattered around,"* commented one. *"You'll frequently have lawyers visiting from elsewhere, or be on the phone to them, and it has to be like that because almost every piece of work is cross-border. I've just realised how much I take that for granted, because I never have a meeting with only people from London!"* Trainees also attend seminars that take place in Brussels, Milan and Paris, where *"you discuss the latest developments in areas such as capital markets and M&A. It's a great opportunity to network while you're there."*

Here come the girls

In previous years we've found that male trainees have noticeably outnumbered female trainees – quite unusual these days. Although it was still the case at the time of our interviews that the majority were male, our sources tell us that the numbers are starting to balance better, and this trend continues. The signs are promising: in 2013, restructuring specialist Polina Lyadnova became the first female partner at the London office, with capital markets lawyer Sarah Lewis being made counsel in the same year. There's also a Women's Working Group, which organises *"all sorts of events – not only for the London office, but also for when female partners come over from the other offices."* While Cleary is making strides in this department, *"there's still work to be done and it needs to continue heading in the right direction."*

Trainees didn't beat around the bush when it comes to what the firm expects. *"Cleary knows what it is and doesn't make any bones about it; I wouldn't choose to go here if you want your hand held or to be in your comfort zone."* Despite this, one was quick to point out that *"it's not like they throw you in the deep end and watch you drown – you do get arm bands!"* Not literally, of course. They come in the form of *"an immediate support network,"* as *"the people here do make sure you're happy and coping with the work. There's a brilliant structure of support that goes all the way up to the partners."*

All future trainees complete the LPC at the University of Law in Moorgate (only a short distance from Cleary's office), creating a *"tight-knit group"* before arriving at the firm. *"It definitely brings you closer together,"* one remarked. *"You spend the year either being in the same classes, or classes that work closely with one another, so it makes it much easier to bond."* Others confirmed: *"We're a collection of pretty unique individuals, but doing the LPC together gives us a strong sense of group identity."*

The London office has a *"cosy"* feel to it, with interviewees praising its *"ideal location"* – situated between Mansion House and Moorgate. They were also fans of the *"heavily subsidised"* canteen, as one reported that *"you can feed yourself for under a fiver a day and the food itself is actually pretty good."* Trainees receive free access to Virgin Active gyms. Aside from that, the consensus was that the office is *"not spectacular by any means, but does the job... and at least it's not falling apart!"*

They may *"enjoy the challenge"* but, when Cleary trainees come up for air, *"we do spend the time wisely and socialise, as opposed to just sleeping."* There are occasional events organised by the firm, like pub quizzes, bowling trips and wine tasting sessions, but most agreed that socialising usually takes place on *"an informal basis depending on people's availability"* – which, due to a hectic work schedule, means *"the will is there but sometimes the way is not."*

Cleary *"has a very good track record of keeping people on,"* and in 2013 seven of eight qualifiers were retained.

And finally...
Simply put: *"If you want a slow-paced training contract and would prefer to be given responsibility gradually, this isn't the firm for you. But if you want to get stuck in from the start, you've come to the right place."*

Clifford Chance LLP

The facts

Location: London

Number of UK partners/solicitors: 159/531

Total number of trainees: 200

Seats: 4x6 months

Alternative seats: overseas seats, secondments

Extras: pro bono – various legal advice centres; language classes

On chambersstudent.co.uk

How to get into Clifford Chance
More about seats and secondments
A history of the firm

Big deals, international opportunities and *"a killer reputation"* – they all come as standard at global titan Clifford Chance.

Top of the Cliff

Magic circle heavyweight Clifford Chance is a leader among even the global legal elite and is one of the world's ten highest grossing law firms. Its 3,400 lawyers spread across 35 offices in 25 countries work together to make CC the world's best performer in the *Chambers Global* rankings. Its expertise ranges into areas as diverse as construction, employment and insurance, but it's best known for its transactional work, especially banking and finance. It frequently advises major financial institutions like Credit Suisse, JPMorgan and RBS on their biggest and most time-consuming ventures.

Unsurprisingly, the firm's international excellence was an enticing prospect for the majority of trainees we spoke to. The past couple of years alone have seen CC extend its reach to places like Sydney, Perth, Casablanca, Istanbul and Qatar, and in July 2012 it became the first UK firm to open an office in Seoul. In 2012/13 around 65% of revenue was generated outside the UK, with 37% coming from mainland Europe, 14% from the Asia-Pacific region, 11% from the Americas and 3% from the Middle East. Put simply, CC has its fingers in a lot of pies, and trainees are eager to reap the benefits: around three quarters do an overseas seat during their training.

Clifford Chance's raft of departments slot into six core groups: corporate; finance; capital markets; real estate; dispute resolution; and tax, pensions and employment. Trainees must spend at least two of their seats within the firm's core corporate, finance and capital markets groups, but our interviewees were quick to point out that *"these practices are very broad churches and there are dozens of subgroups within each one, so in reality you're not*

restricted that much." Seats like real estate, construction and employment are often oversubscribed and it can be difficult to win a spot there.

Project X

The finance group is split into general banking; asset and project finance; financial markets and structured products; derivatives; real estate finance; and insolvency, restructuring and liability management. As a trainee, you can expect to see *"huge piles of documents stacked up on your desk"* in all these seats, but each one entails more than just document management. In asset and project finance ('finance A') *"you get involved in really exciting stuff like big energy projects and aviation financing"* and, although the hours can be gruelling at times, *"you get to liaise with parties from all over the world via telephone."* What's more, *"deal closings often happen somewhere cool like an aircraft hangar."* The mysteriously named 'finance X' is a large general banking group. Trainees tend to play more of a support role here – *"proofing, preparing check-lists"* – but *"there's drafting on offer too"* and *"you can send e-mails to clients without someone looking over your shoulder all the time."* A prime example of CC's big-ticket finance work was when it acted for HSBC, Santander and a host of other well-known banks on the $7.2bn debt restructuring of global building materials supplier CEMEX.

The corporate group's main subdivisions are M&A; private equity; private fund formation; communications, media and technology; financial institutions; and European competition and regulation. As for corporate-related highlights: CC recently advised private equity firm Cinven on the £831m dual acquisition of two pharmaceuti-

The True Picture

Chambers UK rankings

Administrative & Public Law	Fraud
Asset Finance	Information Technology
Banking & Finance	Insurance
Capital Markets	Investment Funds
Commodities	Parliamentary & Public Affairs
Competition/European Law	Pensions
Construction	Planning
Corporate Crime & Investigations	Private Client
Corporate/M&A	Private Equity
Data Protection	Projects
Dispute Resolution	Public International Law
Employee Share Schemes & Incentives	Real Estate Finance
Energy & Natural Resources	Restructuring/Insolvency
Environment	Retail
Financial Services	Social Housing
	Tax
	Telecommunications
	Transport

cal companies, and International Power on its £6.4bn takeover by French energy giant GDF SUEZ. The work here is *"a mix of cross-border and domestic, although the international deals usually link back to the UK in one way or another."* For trainees, there's *"an awful lot of administrative and project management work to do,"* but *"you get to draft things like board minutes and purchase agreements"* too. In smaller teams like communications, media and technology, trainees are more in the thick of the action. One told us: *"I got to do a lot of foreign travel and face-to-face negotiations, with plenty of interesting drafting off the back of that."*

CC has been very busy on the capital markets front recently, advising Barclays and Deutsche Bank on Zambia's first Eurobond issue (valued at $750m), and counselling Bank of Tokyo-Mitsubishi UFJ on the $275m securitisation of a Russian car loan portfolio. The group also works on many IPOs. One trainee told us of their time in the department: *"At first I was picking up bits on the periphery – preparing amendments and checklists – but eventually I got to draft key documents and had direct contact with some major clients."* The structured debt seat earned praise for its varied workload. One interviewee said: *"I dealt with a tremendous range of matters. I did quite a lot of research on things like EU regulations, as this field of law is always changing."*

All hands on doc

"More and more people are beginning to view us as a firm with a top-notch litigation practice," trainees told us. Given CC's strong rankings for both litigation and arbitration in *Chambers UK* we can't argue with that. *"There's*

a lot of finance-related work doing the rounds at the moment," we were told. The team acts on behalf of numerous big-name institutions, such as BNP Paribas and Barclays. Still, there are many other types of disputes to get stuck into and because of this *"everyone who sits in the group has a unique experience."* One of our interviewee said: *"I was pretty lucky because I never had to do any doc review or bundling. Instead, I was primarily working on a regulatory investigation for a high-profile Libor case."* Another was slightly less fortunate, as they recalled doing *"lots and lots of doc review"* but did also *"get given more exciting stuff too, like carrying out advisory work on contracts."* Go to our website for more details on other seats, including overseas stints and secondments.

Responsibility levels vary from seat to seat, but trainees sensed that the onus was very much on them to nab the meatier work. *"Throughout my entire training contract, I've had the impression that if you establish a relationship of trust with your supervisor and show a willingness to handle a higher level of work, you will get the responsibilities you want."* Others agreed: *"As long as you're ready and up for the challenge, it's up to you how much you take on."*

Belly of the beast

Hard work, long hours – that's the nature of the CC beast. *"No one is under any illusions about just how much time and effort we have to put in here,"* a weary second-year remarked, *"and there has been an occasional horror story or two. The worst was probably staying until 5am on a Saturday and then coming back in again on the Sunday. That was unpleasant, to say the least."* It's safe to say our sources weren't exactly shocked to find themselves pulling multiple all-nighters, but we heard *"the biggest challenge is the unpredictability. You can't plan anything outside of work during the week because you can quite easily end up having to stay in the office past midnight at short notice."* It's worth noting that some seats have longer hours attached to them than others. Capital markets has *"the worst reputation."* Apparently *"its rep got so bad at one point that many trainees tried to avoid doing a seat there."*

While arduous hours come with the territory, it'd be wrong to suggest people don't take the time to appreciate the hard graft trainees put in. *"You'll always get a 'thank you' if you've worked really late or at the weekend, and if you've been constantly finishing late then you might get a couple of days off in lieu."* Besides, none could deny the benefits of training at a mega-firm like CC. *"When all is said and done, you're working on these awesome cases with some of the best in the business,"* mused one interviewee. *"That in itself spurs you on and makes you want to push yourself as much as you can."* Sources said that CC trainees are *"clever," "curious," "practical," "unflappable"* and *"ambitious."* Personalities asides, interviewees were keen to underscore the diversity on show at the firm. *"There are still plenty of Oxbridge people here, but when you look around you notice how diverse it is. We have trainees from all over the globe: India, Australia, Malaysia, the US – tons of places."*

Given the pressures of the job, it's refreshing to hear that *"there's a pretty relaxed atmosphere in the office. Most people can crack a joke and no one wears a tie all the time. And despite always being very busy, partners don't snap your head off when you ask a simple question."* It sounds like more of a necessity than a bonus, however: *"I don't think anyone could handle it for very long if we were overly stressed all the time; it'd cause everyone to have a breakdown!"*

Cut-and-dried

Clifford Chance is based in Canary Wharf, a place labelled as both *"somewhat soulless"* and *"very convenient"* by trainees. Location may not be a big selling point, but the office itself was praised for its *"fantastic"* facilities. Hairdresser? Check. Dentist? Check. Dry cleaner? Check. Other amenities on the list include a games room, sleeping pods, bar and canteen, as well as a gym that has squash courts, fitness classes and a swimming pool. *"I think there's a common misconception that we have no time to use any of these facilities,"* said one trainee, *"but that's definitely not the case and we're encouraged to* have a bit of downtime in between work." Trainees can also *"get a free meal in the canteen after 7pm, free food ordered to your desk if you are working past 10pm and – if you do stay really late – a free taxi-ride home."*

When not buried under heaps of work, CC trainees can enjoy a reasonably busy social calendar. Many shindigs – Christmas bashes, karaoke nights – take place at departmental level, and the office's handy basement Budgie Bar serves as the ideal setting for a post-work catch-up. *"It's a perfect starting point for nights out and, generally speaking, you'll find people from all different levels of seniority there, including partners."* Twice a year the trainee liaison committee organises an all-trainee social like ice skating or bowling, while athletic types are able to get involved in a variety of sports teams. Best of all, *"the fact that trainees do the LPC together means we've already got a massive group of friends at the firm before we even start."*

Trainees can state a preference for up to two seats which they'd like to qualify into. Our sources told us that there's been *"a notable shift towards greater transparency"* in the NQ jobs process. One advised that *"you can usually get a good feel for where the opportunities lie by speaking directly to the partners."* In 2013, 102 out of 126 qualifiers were kept on.

And finally...

If you're bold, proactive and in search of *"a firm that sits at the very top of the profession,"* then Clifford Chance is pretty much a perfect match.

Clyde & Co LLP

The facts

Location: London, Guildford, Oxford, Manchester
Number of UK partners/solicitors: 168/891
Total number of trainees: 73
Seats: 4x6 months
Alternative seats: overseas, secondments
Extras: pro bono; language classes

Clyde & Co is one of the UK's top litigation, shipping and insurance firms, and with more than 30 offices around the world, it continues to strengthen its global reputation.

Strong sails

The last five years have seen this firm grow significantly. A November 2011 tie-up with insurance rival Barlow Lyde & Gilbert (BLG) was the largest in a series of mergers that has bulked up Clydes to the extent that there are now few firms that can match it for sheer numbers of lawyers working in the UK. Since 2012, the firm has opened in Sydney, Perth, Madrid, Atlanta, Tripoli and Beijing, and trainees were nothing but thrilled. *"Clydes is a really respected firm and the expansion is very exciting. The potential of new opportunities, better work and possibly more secondments is great."* One source said: *"The growth also seems to be in a careful manner. We're aligning ourselves with firms of a similar character and ethos, so as not to lose that Clydes core. We're not aggressive, just ambitious."*

"Ultimately we do have a litigation focus, but Clydes is actually full-service," trainees said. *"Our transactional practices are constantly improving and the increased sector focus is aligning all practice areas."* This is reflected in the firm's *Chambers UK* rankings, which recognise Clydes for the likes of corporate and real estate as well as its contentious practices. Examine the Chambers website for a full list.

Clyde's cores

Before seat rotations, trainees are asked to prepare *"a summary of your experience in your current department. You put in who your supervisor was, the main clients and a general summary of the work."* Everyone's summaries are then circulated among the trainee group, *"which means you can make a really informed decision for your next rotation."* Trainees submit their three top choices and speak with graduate recruitment as to why they've made them. Thankfully, there's a lot of seat choice at Clydes and apart from the SRA contentious requirement, there are no departments trainees must sit in.

The transactional practice is split into 'cores'. For example, Core 3 is corporate insurance; Core 4 is general corporate; and Core 5 is energy, construction and projects, real estate, and banking/finance. For the transactional seats, trainees can either simply ask for a core or *"specify a team, such as 'Core 5, construction'."* On the contentious side trainees can choose from: professional commercial disputes (PCD) (which is a legacy BLG department and one of the largest at the firm); casualty and healthcare; aviation litigation; the dispute resolution group (DRG); shipping (another big department); employment and pensions.

Before we go any further, we need to talk about Guildford. Clyde has a small outpost there, and since certain departments are split between London and Guildford, trainees might have to undertake a seat outside the capital. Interviewees admitted facing Guildford with mixed emotions. One said: *"It's such an integral part of the firm and there are so many benefits, but realistically I've tried to avoid it like the plague."* Another said: *"There are actually several people that request a seat in Guildford – the hours are better and no one's ever been disappointed with the quality of work."* At the end of the day, *"the difficulty is we've all applied to be London trainees in a London firm,"* most sources agreed. *"Guildford remains a bit of an is-*

Chambers UK rankings

Asset Finance	Information Technology
Aviation	Insurance
Banking Litigation	Personal Injury
Clinical Negligence	Planning
Commodities	Police Law
Competition/European Law	Product Liability
Construction	Professional Discipline
Corporate/M&A	Professional Negligence
Dispute Resolution	Projects
Employment	Public International Law
Energy & Natural Resources	Real Estate
Environment	Restructuring/Insolvency
	Retail
Fraud	Shipping
Health & Safety	Transport
Healthcare	Travel
Immigration	

sue for trainees." Head of legal trainee recruitment and development Caroline Walsh said: *"The Guildford office is thriving and there is still the need for trainees to spend time there. The opportunities are second to none, especially in regards to working with much smaller teams."*

Budding litigators may be interested to know that *"there's a push at the firm to increase the amount of solicitor advocates."* Our sources in the employment and casualty and health teams had advocated on smaller cases: *"It's always a fantastic experience."* Although you can't take your Higher Rights as a trainee, if you're interested, Clydes has the ability to start you down that path.

Top-flight cases

"Insurance as a whole is a big department for the firm," trainees said, *"but the nice thing is you never feel lost in a massive sea because the department is split into smaller teams."* The department is split into several groups including political risk; general insurance; insurance/reinsurance; and marine, construction and energy. The latter two are the largest teams, *"but there is a lot of fluidity in the work. You're often liaising with other groups,"* interviewees observed. *"We're often working with mega-clients and on very large cases,"* trainees in insurance said. The group acted for AIG in an attempt to recover damages suffered in relation to a case regarding 'toxic sofas', where customers burned by seating made in China launched a group action against retailers Argos, Land of Leather and Walmsleys, who all admitted liability. It is advising on a $1bn claim concerning damage to the world's largest hydroelectric power construction project, based in the Amazon. *"Ultimately it's a contentious department, so there isn't going to be as much responsibili-*

ty," interviewees commented. That said, several had done *"plenty of drafting and a lot of research."*

PCD is *"probably the largest department at Clydes, and one the firm's very proud of,"* trainees said. One source claimed: *"It's so big that within six months of working there I don't think I actually met all the partners."* The subgroups are commercial litigation (which is predominantly made up of financial litigation work), professional negligence and regulatory. Currently the professional negligence work *"is really where the focus is, and a lot of our clients are banks and large insurers."* The PCD team has also acted for Eversheds against a claim brought by Newcastle International Airport, and advised entrepreneur Sir Keith Mills, the founder of Air Miles and Nectar loyalty cards, against Coutts. Trainees agreed: *"PCD is known for being a very friendly department. No matter the size, you never feel lost or submerged. They have regular drinks trolleys and people remember your name."*

The aviation litigation team has a *"strong reputation"* both inside and outside the firm. It predominantly acts for insurers and large airlines, and offers trainees a real variety of work. *"Of course there's the glamour of the large plane deals, but there's a range from small coffee-spill personal injury claims through to things like loss of cargo and major crashes. It's such interesting work."* Sources said the team *"makes a real effort to develop you and give you decent responsibility."* DRG, meanwhile, is divided into several subteams, including insolvency, fraud and business/banking litigation. By all accounts DRG is *"incredibly busy and really growing significantly, especially the insolvency work."* The team represents *"large banks and companies, but the fraud side means we also deal with some very interesting individuals."* Recent cases include acting for the former owners of Liverpool FC in the £300m proceedings from the sale of the club in October 2010.

Shipping work is still a big deal at Clyde. Among its recent shipping mandates, the firm acted for trading company Cargill on a charter hire dispute following the hijacking of a vessel by pirates off the coast of Somalia, and represented a group who bought a tanker and then discovered that it was in worse condition than was physically possible for a ship of its class. The buyers suspected that the ship's documentation had been falsified by the sellers, and Clyde won them millions in arbitration. There are a number of seats related to the shipping practice, including marine insurance and ship finance as well a general shipping team. General shipping is itself split into subgroups, including dry shipping, wet shipping and international trade/arbitration. *"The work is so interesting across the board,"* trainees said. *"The group deals with extremely high-value projects and the arbitration work is fascinating."* The ship finance group, meanwhile, is all about the sale and purchase of vessels and works with both private-client yacht owners and large commercial companies.

The overseas options at the time of our calls were Dubai, Abu Dhabi, Dar es Salaam, Rio, San Fran and Hong Kong. One source said: *"Realistically it's quite competitive, so there's no guarantee that you'll get to go abroad."* Caroline Walsh says: *"We are actually looking to increase the number of international secondments going forward; however, secondments aren't simply life experiences – they have to be tied in with business need. Currently we're busiest in the London and Guildford offices and need the majority of trainees here in the UK."* For those lucky enough to get out there, it's interesting to note that Clydes is actually *"the biggest international law firm in Dubai. We have about 170 fee earners out there and have built a great reputation. The experience and work out there is fantastic."*

Pastries, punch and putting

Although atmospheres vary between departments, on the whole *"everyone is extremely approachable and willing to help,"* trainees assured us. *"You never feel anonymous or ignored."* Following the BLG merger, interviewees did admit there were still *"teething problems. Certain departments haven't quite integrated with others and there is a bit of a divide between the two buildings, but ultimately we're all together under the amiable and social banner of Clyde & Co."*

Ah yes, the two buildings. Clydes is situated near Aldgate and split between *"new and swanky"* St Botolph Building, whose client rooms are so nice, *"even your mum would be impressed,"* and the older Beaufort House, which was home to BLG. Trainees affectionately reflected: *"Beaufort House is like an old friend that's a bit smelly, but nostalgia makes you still wanna hang out with them."* St Botolph's was actually in the James McAvoy film 'Welcome to the Punch'. It's the epitome of a modern City building. The canteen's also pretty amazing and we're treated to a professional pastry chef."*

Extracurricular offerings include a *"very popular and active"* football team. *"Clydes actually just won division three of the London Legal league. Before the merger, we were top of the legal Premiership, but changing teams mean we're starting afresh."* Clydes also partakes in rugby sevens, netball and cricket. The firm hires a tennis court for employees to use on a Wednesday and there's an annual golf tournament. The black-tie Christmas ball *"is always really excellent. Last year it was at Bishopsgate and was truly spectacular."* Every other Thursday, Clydes holds a drinks reception in the upstairs bar. *"Everyone's invited and it's always a relaxed affair."* Trainees themselves often head to the Bell or the Alchemist for a Friday night tipple.

And finally...
Clyde & Co *"does try and make the qualification process as stress-free as possible,"* trainees said. *"Retention rates have been good and the process is well organised."* In 2013 the firm kept on 35 out of its 37 qualifiers.

CMS Cameron McKenna

The facts

Location: London, Bristol, Scotland
Number of UK partners/solicitors: 130/232
Partners who trained at firm: 14%
Total number of trainees: 120
Seats: 4x6 months
Alternative seats: overseas seats, secondments
Extras: pro bono – LawWorks, A4ID, Islington Law Centre, TrustLaw Connect; language classes

On chambersstudent.co.uk...

How to get into CMS
CMS in Bristol and Scotland
More on overseas seats
Environmental expertise
Interview with grad recruitment
partner Simon Pilcher

'Everything that rises must converge', so says Flannery O'Connor's collection of short stories. But how will the CMS network come together in its bid for global recognition?

Keeping up appearances

With over 2,800 lawyers in 29 countries, 48 cities and 54 offices, CMS is an extensive network of ten independent member firms. The UK-headquartered arm – CMS Cameron McKenna – has a total of 14 offices in the UK, Central and Eastern Europe, China, UAE and South America. It concentrates on eight sectors (which you can find on its website) but is particularly known for energy work, as well as activities in the life sciences, technology and finance sectors. Reflecting its interest in these fields, 2012 saw CMS Cameron McKenna open an energy-focused Dubai office, and a Beijing branch initially looking to be active on life sciences matters.

Our interviewees had noticed that *"over the course of the past two years the CMS branding has strengthened. When I started it wasn't bedded in too well and there was confusion about the different firms and how they worked together, but they've made a good effort to sew things together and make it feel like one firm."* Part of that process involved collating and publishing a single revenue figure for the first time (total turnover reached £679.3m in 2012). Many interpreted this as a move to make the firm more attractive during its hunt for a US merger partner (which is by no means a secret), but it's also likely that the firm wants to be regarded as part of the global elite. *"At the moment we are seen as a European firm, but we are now looking at things more globally and starting to get the global footprint going – CMS is definitely going to get more international."* It will be interesting to see how the firm's structure and branding evolves in line with this.

The firm's desire to boost its London image is detectable in its upcoming move to Cannon Place, which should occur by 2015. The new office is a very swish new-build above Cannon Street station, and the move will physically embody the firm's ambitions – it has reportedly signed a 25-year lease.

The Good Life

Trainees are required to complete either a corporate or banking seat, but time in certain other departments (like energy) can also fulfil this demand. Our interviewees had completed a broad range of seats, including insurance, real estate, commercial litigation, energy, financial services, commercial/technology, EU and competition, employment and pensions, and tax.

All trainees (including new starters) list their top four preferences before each rotation. Previously, second-years were able to indicate a 'priority seat', but this has now been scrapped and some interviewees said the new system had been *"unlucky"* for second-years who had been banking on being able to do their priority seat. *"I understand the reasoning behind the change but it's unfortunate that one intake has ended up worse off than others."* Allocation was said to be *"a mixed bag, with some people coming out of it less well than others,"* but on the whole trainees do tend to get assigned one of their preferred seats.

Client secondments and overseas stints are usually done in the second seat. *"It's one of the best things about the firm,"* proclaimed one trainee. *"At other firms, trainees*

Chambers UK rankings

Banking & Finance	Insurance
Banking Litigation	Intellectual Property
Capital Markets	Life Sciences
Competition/European Law	Media & Entertainment
Construction	Outsourcing
Corporate/M&A	Pensions
Data Protection	PFI/PPP
Dispute Resolution	Planning
International Arbitration	Private Equity: Buyouts
Employment	Product Liability
Energy & Natural	Professional Negligence
Resources	Public Procurement
Environment	Real Estate
Financial Services	Restructuring/Insolvency
Information Technology	

worry about spending a seat away from the office, but everyone has to do one here, so you don't worry." Client secondments were *"flavour of the month"* among our interviewees: *"You have to be shrewd if you want to do one and make a good business case as to why you should go."* Positions are available at Amazon, IBM and Erste Bank. If you fancy an overseas stint then *"you're more likely than not to be able to do one."* Destinations include Prague, Sofia, Moscow, Munich and Rio de Janeiro. Those who had been abroad raved about the experience, enjoyed the enhanced responsibilities, and said that *"CMS is very good at providing everything you need to set you up your life abroad."*

At the time of our calls, eight trainees were based in the Bristol office (four places offered each year), where the seat options are real estate, insurance litigation, and banking litigation. In addition to overseas seats, English trainees can also spend time in the Edinburgh or Aberdeen offices. Read more about this on our website.

Bread

CMS's upper mid-market corporate practice has been busy thanks to the amount of M&A activity in sectors such as energy and technology. Lawyers advised TT Electronics on a number of transactions, one of which involved the disposal of the company's Ottomores business (including divisions in Mexico and Brazil) to a US buyer, Generac Holdings. The department is not divided into sub-teams, and partners have different areas of focus and interests. A trainee's experience and exposure depends on who they sit with, and could cover private equity, public M&A, private M&A and PFI transactions for clients across sectors. *"There are lots of trainees in the department, which provides a good sense of camaraderie,"* said one interviewee. *"Corporate is a good first seat because there is a lot of standard trainee work."* This can mean

"preparing ancillary documents like board minutes or powers of attorney," but also getting involved in business development and marketing. As a second-year, you get more responsibility in corporate, for example *"drafting amendments to an investment agreement."* The department is known for housing *"a lot of big personalities,"* but trainees insisted that *"it's completely wrong to presume that means the partners are arrogant – it just makes working there much more fun!"*

The banking department has traditionally been lender-oriented, but it also acts for borrowers, serving a spectrum of clients from large private equity houses to blue-chip companies. The client list contains names like HSBC, Santander, Lloyds and Barclays, as well as quite a number of healthcare and consumer products-oriented businesses. Lawyers recently advised the National Australia Bank on 'Project Morph' – the reassignment of £6bn worth of assets from its UK subsidiary Clydesdale to the main business. This involved analysing over 5,000 loans in Clydesdale's corporate real estate portfolio. The department is split into sub-teams (corporate recovery, leveraged finance, infrastructure and project finance, and banking litigation) and trainees sit with a specific one of these. Interviewees described the banking seats as *"a double whammy of lots of demands on the organisational front, and having to grapple with some very complex technical issues."* Those in infrastructure and project finance had responsibility levels which they found *"a bit scary,"* and endured their fair share of *"chasing people up and organising logistics."* In banking litigation there's a nice mix of smaller debt recovery cases, which involve *"working with the bank to get money back from debtors,"* and larger fraud cases, which see trainees do legal research and evidence analysis tasks. *"It's nice to have both on the go."*

Yes Minister

The energy, projects and construction department (EPC) is broken down into the following sub-teams: oil and gas; power and utilities; projects and construction; renewables and alternative energy; environment; and disputes. CMS acts for a large number of independent oil and gas companies, and works on some deals with an impressive geographical scope, encompassing Africa, the Middle East, Europe, India, Russia and Brazil. Closer to home, lawyers advised BP during a deal which saw the company dispose of its North Sea assets to TAQA for a whopping $1bn. It was one of the largest deals in the UK oil and gas sector in the last five years, and even David Cameron and George Osborne commented on it. Some trainees who had completed an oil and gas seat felt that they *"ended up taking on the role of an associate,"* and told us they had run *"weekly conference calls with the purchaser and their solicitor."* Energy disputes was described as *"one of the most international seats at CMS,"* and the work can involve *"disputes over everything from massive oil spills to joint venture agreements."*

Trainees also get involved in arbitrations and advisory work. *"Companies will approach us and ask: 'Here's what happened – what are our options?', and we'll give preliminary advice on the merits of their case, which involves looking at all the documents and contracts involved."* The environmental team is small and offers trainees a mix of contentious and non-contentious work, and while there may be a lot of bundling to be done, *"the subject matter of the cases is definitely enough to keep you interested."* The waste sector provides a steady stream of work, but other matters may touch upon environmental permits, contaminated land, cleantech and climate change.

The commercial/technology department has become an increasingly popular destination for trainees. Clients include Amazon, BT and MetLife, and the department is increasingly taking on work related to co-ordinating and managing outsourced services. *"I helped a major global energy company deal with its outsourcing requirements and introduce technology that would help it decide where to drill for oil in future."* More *"piecemeal"* work includes data protection matters and the drafting of terms of conditions for websites.

Insurance lawyers act for some of the biggest clients in the industry, including Chartis, Chubb and Swiss Re. A recent case involved representing Brussels Airport and its insurers in both civil and criminal proceedings following a fire in one of the airport's hangers. Trainees are able to do some *"great work"* here, and although a lot of cases settle, some do go to court and one trainee enjoyed *"being able to go to a barristers' chambers for conferences with a QC."* Other tasks include *"drafting letters and helping to track down documents for counsel."*

On the buses

CMS' culture *"varies hugely from one department to the next,"* from *"fun and dynamic"* corporate to *"relaxed"* financial services. A certain *"energy"* unites the departments, though: *"People are always striving to take an innovative approach; thinking of new ways to structure deals and new ways to explore emerging markets."* CMS'

"ethos," trainees say, is nurturing and supportive: *"It's very easy to find a mentor to push for you – my previous supervisors have continued to help me develop my career. You're not just treated as the nth trainee rotating through."* The firm also hosts a 'trainee of the year' award, and after nominations are put forward and a winner is chosen the successful candidate receives one-to-one coaching sessions with managing partner Duncan Weston.

Trainees are kept in the loop via regular (if ominous-sounding) *"sector group information seminars,"* as well as a string of internal publications. Interviewees underlined the primacy of CMS's sector approach: *"Anyone can get involved in a sector group – just because you're in corporate or competition doesn't mean that you can't do energy work, for example."*

The bars and restaurants around the Barbican and Smithfields provide plenty of entertainment for trainees. There are a fair few *"CMS pubs,"* including the Hand & Shears and the Butcher's Hook & Cleaver. *"Often an e-mail will go out asking who's finishing their work early – it's usually fairly easy to recruit people!"* There's plenty more going on too, including an annual firm-wide party and countless departmental events. We also heard of softball games, *"pub crawls around Fulham,"* *"day trips to Brighton on a Routemaster bus,"* *"barge trips around Camden lock,"* *"tapas Fridays"* and many *"jolly trolleys"* which do the rounds in the office. An annual trainee ball takes place each February, and was most recently held at the Waldorf Hotel. If trainees are on a secondment outside London, CMS will pay for travel and accommodation to attend up to three events a year.

For autumn qualifiers, an NQ jobs list is released in April/May after which applications are accepted. The process is over within about a month. It *"generally goes unspoken,"* but sources recommended speaking to departments you're interested in qualifying into before the jobs list is released. The commercial department was particularly popular in 2013. Eventually a total of 46 out of 61 qualifiers stayed with the firm.

And finally...

Trainees tend to join CMS because they have an interest in the firm's sectors, growing international coverage and secondment opportunities – if this combination appeals, then CMS comes highly recommended.

The True Picture

Collyer Bristow LLP

The facts

Location: London

Number of UK partners/solicitors: 25/29

Partners who trained at the firm: 11.5%

Total number of trainees: 9

Seats: 4x6 months

Alternative seats: none

Extras: pro bono – law centres, CAB, art gallery events, Zacchaeus Trust

On chambersstudent.co.uk...
How to get into Collyer Bristow

Can a tweet be libellous? How is the Leveson Report being implemented? Is it offensive to associate someone with Ken Livingstone? Collyer Bristow is the firm with the answers.

Telephone

We'll be honest. Some firms can be really vague about what they do and it can take loads of digging to get to the bottom of their practice. Not so at Collyer Bristow. Its website states: 'From property to popstars, from airlines to artists, the lawyers at Collyer Bristow work with a wide range of businesses and individuals, advising them on challenges of all shapes, sizes and complexity.' And that's a pretty decent summary of what makes this firm tick.

From its *"beautiful old building"* on London's historic Bedford Row, Collyer Bristow deals with both private client and commercial work. It wins *Chambers UK* rankings for private client, trusts and family work, but it's the defamation/reputation management practice which really stands out. Lawyers were heavily involved in the Leveson Inquiry, advising over 50 participants including Max Mosley, Charlotte Church, Kate and Gerry McCann, and Hugh Grant. In addition, partner Stephen Heffer and his team are acting for over 100 victims of phone-hacking using News International's fast-track compensation scheme to resolve claims outside the courts.

So what about those questions we asked in the stand-first? Well, yes, a tweet can be libellous. In the UK's first Twitter libel trial, CB won £90,000 damages for cricketing international Chris Cairns after the former chairman of the India's Twenty20 Premier League tweeted that Cairns had a 'past record of match-fixing'. Second, Leveson is having all kinds of consequences and the proposed Royal Charter could make blogging or tweeting legally equivalent to publishing an article in a national newspaper. And finally, no it's not offensive to link someone to Ken Liv-

ingstone (phew!), as Collyer Bristow established when it acted for Boris Johnson after he was sued by Bob Crow for putting the union boss's name on one of his London mayoral election posters.

Paparazzi

Seats are available in family, corporate/commercial, trusts and estate planning, real estate and the large dispute resolution group which covers employment, defamation/reputation management, IP, financial services and real estate litigation. *"You will most likely spend a year in dispute resolution"* – during that time trainees are a pooled resource for all teams. Although a year sounds like a long time, *"it's really worth it,"* interviewees agreed, because *"dispute resolution covers such a broad range of areas and encompasses some of the best teams."*

IP and reputation management teams are the largest within the dispute resolution group. *"They do everything from patent, copyright and trade mark work all the way through to the big injunction and libel cases."* All those juicy matters we mentioned earlier are the domain of this team and trainees boasted that *"you often get to meet famous people, which obviously makes everything more exciting."* The team also attracts businesses and other organisations as clients. *"Ultimately reputation and the media are important to everyone..."* commented one source. Unsurprisingly, *"the group is doing really well"* and the reasons for that are clear: *"Reputation management is becoming increasingly important because of the growth of Twitter and online media in general."* So what's in all this for trainees? *"Some of the work you get is relatively basic*

Chambers UK rankings

Defamation/Reputation Management	Private Client
Family/Matrimonial	Real Estate Litigation

– bundling, drafting – but on most cases you work directly with a partner, so you can be given some excellent responsibilities." For example, there's scope for advocacy. *"I've appeared before a Master, which was daunting, but I really like the fact that a partner had encouraged me to do it,"* said one interviewee. There's a court attendance rota and one trainee told us they had *"been out to court a couple of times to make applications."*

The financial services team is *"heavily involved in the Libor scandal, and those cases are primarily what trainees are working on at the moment."* This is the most *"heads-down"* disputes team, *"because a lot of the work is research-based."* The team recently acted for Northern Irish property developer Michael Taggart when he brought an £88m claim against two Irish banks because he blamed them for the collapse of his huge house-building company in 2008.

The employment team is known for being *"friendly and boisterous"* and the firm acts for both employees and employers. Trainees were *"surprised how much client contact you are given."* One said: *"I not only attended meetings, but was encouraged to contribute my thoughts and provide input."*

Trusts and estates deals with probate and wills, as well as charity work. Unfortunately the client list is entirely confidential, but we can tell you that there's both domestic and international work to get your teeth into. Trainees told us they were *"given more responsibility here than in any other department"* and got to run their own files, helping them *"feel like a key part of the team."*

The corporate/commercial group *"is mostly centred on M&A, but the group also deals with private equity, funds, restructuring and commercial contracts."* Deals are small in size – each worth a few million – and the firm mainly acts for clients in sectors like sports, media and health. For example, lawyers recently advised the administrators of Twickenham Film Studios on the £6.5m sale of the studios.

Born this way?

Collyer Bristow's Bedford Row townhouse is more likely to remind you of *Upstairs Downstairs* than NBC's lawyer romp *Suits* – say goodbye to shiny glass towers and hello to good solid Georgian brick. The street is lined with top-notch barristers' chambers – add to that CB's 250-year history and you may begin to wonder whether this firm's atmosphere leans towards the traditional. *"It's a balance,"* interviewees commented. *"Yes, we have some traditional elements – like our location and certain of our practice areas – but we are also at the forefront of legal developments in areas like media and finance, which means we are also modern and dynamic."* Indeed, step inside number four Bedford Row and *"you're immediately welcomed by an open-plan modern art gallery. We may be over 250 years old, but we have definitely moved with the times."* Another way the firm is moving with the times is the *"very encouraging growth"* in its international work. CB opened an office in Geneva ten years ago and it has Russian, Italian, and South and North American foreign desks. Several current trainees have international backgrounds and/or foreign language skills, both of which the firm values highly.

Trainees praised the open communications within the firm and said they'd *"never felt intimidated or segregated"* by superiors. *"Of course, you have respect for your seniors, but that's born out of regard for their professional expertise rather then fear."* Trainees said you'll often find a group from the firm at the Old Nick on the corner of Bedford Row on a Friday night, and other socials include *"wine-tastings, ping-pong nights at Bounce bar and pub quizzes."* One more unusual celebration sees to it that *"everyone is bought a lottery ticket for their birthday."* Happily, the qualification process is less of a lottery (see what we did there!) and after due process Collyer Bristow retained two of its three qualifiers in 2013.

And finally...

Good hours have always been one of the pluses of working at Collyer Bristow, although long days are not unheard of. *"There are times when you have to work late, and on one occasion I was here until 2am. But if I've finished my work leaving is not a problem."*

Covington & Burling LLP

The facts

Location: London
Number of UK partners/solicitors: 18/35 (+ 9 non-UK-qualified)
Total number of trainees: 14
Seats: 4x6 months
Alternative seats: secondments
Extras: pro bono – LawWorks, TrustLaw, A4ID, FRU, PILPG

On chambersstudent.co.uk...

How to get into Covington & Burling
Pro bono at Covington
Law firm retreats
Interview with training principal Grant Castle

Covington's *"highly intellectual"* and *"pretty inspirational"* London lawyers manage high-profile life sciences and corporate work on an international scale.

Global Cov-erage

Covington & Burling's bright and intimidatingly articulate trainees quote the firm's international presence as a big pull factor. It has newly opened offices in Seoul and Shanghai, and a significant number of London clients come from overseas. The firm's main areas of specialisation are life sciences and corporate law.

Compulsory six-month stays in corporate and dispute resolution are supplemented by seat options including life sciences, IT/IP, employment, tax, dispute resolution/international arbitration, and anti-corruption/white-collar crime. Trainees can also go on secondments to key clients GSK, Gilead and Vifor. The seat allocation process, sources said, *"hasn't been that transparent,"* with some reporting that they had been *"told on the Friday where we're going on the Monday."* But since trainees went and had a word with the HR team, *"the firm has been making a real effort"* and is now *"allocating two seats in advance."* Trainees also noted that the training is *"more flexible"* than at many firms: *"You can be sitting in one department but pick up work from others, and you're expected to be ready and willing in that regard."*

Jagged Little Pill

Life sciences is Covington's most high-profile London department, although work for pharma clients can be encountered across the firm. The firm handles work on that Wild West frontier, *"the boundary of law and policy,"* which makes it *"especially interesting because what you're doing is going to have a long-term impact on people for many years to come."* A seat focused on regulatory work proved perfect for one science graduate – *"regulatory law is quite black-letter and academic, but at the same time you might be reading a chemistry textbook."* There's plenty of advisory work in this department, meaning lots of research into new scientific developments is required, and trainees also get involved with *"judicial reviews involving public bodies – such as an NHS decision on suppliers of particular drugs, or a decision to refuse IVF to a patient."*

For many trainees the firm's life sciences work is a big draw, but they advised: *"Be aware that Covington is full-service. A lot of people see it as a life sciences firm and come to it with only that one interest, but our biggest department is corporate."* Corporate work often still has a life sciences flavour to it. For instance, Covington recently advised Merck and Schering-Plough on their post-merger integration across 70 international jurisdictions. Another high-profile deal for Armani was *"frantic,"* said one source, but partners *"took the time to brief me on everything."* Another trainee involved in a fund-raising transaction for a biotech company ended up *"doing the work of a five-year-qualified solicitor, drafting documents and advising directors."* Trainees also spend plenty of time *"reaching out to local counsel in about ten different countries."*

Litigation offers a mix of commercial dispute resolution and arbitration, along with bribery, anti-corruption and white-collar crime work. *"Partners come and find you and get you involved in whatever's going on!"* Turning the tables on crooked businessmen is *"quite interesting if you're nosy like me and enjoy digging round people's computers,"* said one source, and there's plenty of scope

Chambers UK rankings

Capital Markets	Investment Funds
Corporate Crime &	Life Sciences
Investigations	Parliamentary & Public
Data Protection	Affairs
Dispute Resolution	Private Equity
Insurance	Product Liability

Making a splash

"The firm is skewed more to liking you to behave like a barrister: they like you to advocate," claimed one source. Although we wouldn't overstate this aspect of the firm – these are still solicitors, after all – we've noted in the past that this firm attracts candidates who might otherwise have gone to the Bar and it's also true that *"they're very focused on your writing skills here. It's quite a big deal – they have stringent rules on how to write."* Trainees generally share a *"spacious"* office with a partner or senior associate, who make *"good teachers."*

Covington prides itself on being *"an intellectual firm,"* but under the *"self-assured,"* sharp-suited sophistication, trainees have found hearts of gold, appreciating that *"you'll end up having nice chats with partners"* in a firm that's keen to *"get to know and to appreciate"* its recruits' diverse range of international backgrounds and previous careers.

The *"brilliant, modern-feeling offices"* are *"spread over four floors"* with *"a breakfast bar on the first floor with a coffee machine, and a really nice terrace."* Seeing off stiff competition from *"fantastic nearby pubs,"* Daly's wine bar is probably the firm's favourite local. (*"We're right off the back of LSE so other places are swamped with students, so the partners prefer it there."*) On pay day there's an in-house *"lunch together instead of the usual Pret sandwiches,"* and even the busiest trainees emerge for the monthly drinks trolleys. A summer party on the roof of the National Theatre had *"a nautical theme so everyone was dressed up as sailors,"* while at Christmas *"we saw Superheroes 3D at the Planetarium, and a lot of people dressed up. The partners made a real effort – more than the trainees did!"* Captain America and Mighty Mouse were both present, we heard. A softball team shows *"it's not all drinking, wining and dining."*

Trainees had plenty of ideas about where the firm was going, and should go, perhaps thanks to close perusal of management notes, which give *"updates on the new Shanghai and Seoul offices,"* dissipating the feeling of the London office being a *"small piece of a larger puzzle."* They declared that *"it has the means to expand very rapidly without lateral hires,"* and their message for clients and future trainees was: *"We're more than just a life sciences firm – we're making a bigger noise and a bigger splash and hopefully the market will take notice."*

for independence. One intrepid soul even ventured to the High Court alone to *"apply for an extension to proceedings orally, though it's very rare that a trainee gets to do that."* Although some work can be *"research heavy"* and *"involve a lot of memorandum writing,"* contentious cases let you *"really see the interaction between barristers and lawyers."*

The international arbitration part of the department really benefits from the healthy number of multilingual trainees. Many deals are conducted partly or wholly in Spanish, like Occidental Petroleum's $2.3bn payout from Ecuador after a six-year arbitration – the largest award ever rendered against a sovereign State. One trainee got *"really stuck into"* a high-profile arbitration involving Russia, *"prepping a witness for cross-examination,"* getting *"the chance to work with the DC office"* and being *"taken to all the hearings that happened in London."*

Trainees agreed that Covington *"trusts you and let you run with things,"* and one had *"big clients calling"* in a partner's absence, safe in the knowledge that *"if ever things don't go right there's no hard come-down on you either."* They also said that the American influence sees trainees *"handle the same work as associates – they don't really differentiate between the two."* Alongside the responsibility, however, comes *"a lot of personal interaction"* with senior people. And after complaints that the formal appraisal process was *"confusing,"* the revamped *"timely and detailed reviews"* see partners and trainees discuss *"anonymous and summarised comments"* from people they've worked with.

Though one source *"couldn't think of a trainee who's worked a weekend,"* and *"there's no face time culture – if you're not busy you leave at six,"* it was acknowledged that the hours can be *"pretty unpredictable and that has a negative effect on your social life as you're not sure what you'll have to do on any given day."* We also heard the firm doesn't always give time off in lieu when nights get long, so perhaps this is a training contract for those who can show real dedication to the cause.

And finally...

This is a challenging training contract for brainy types who enjoy being pushed. The firm retained five of its six qualifiers in 2013.

Cripps Harries Hall LLP

The facts

Location: Tunbridge Wells, London
Number of UK partners/solicitors: 37/61
Partners who trained at firm: 22%
Total number of trainees: 14
Seats: 6x4 months
Alternative seats: none

On chambersstudent.co.uk...

How to get into Cripps
Interview with managing partner
Gavin Tyler
About Tunbridge Wells

The King of Kent indulges trainees with high levels of responsibility in a *"nurturing"* environment.

Delighted, of Tunbridge Wells

The mineral-rich waters of Royal Tunbridge Wells made it Queen Victoria's spa of choice. These days, it's the Cripps trainees who are basking in the *"relaxed"* milieu, rhapsodising about the freedom from *"busy, bustling City life."* As managing partner Gavin Tyler puts it, the firm offers *"all the benefits of working in an incredibly nice part of the country, while also having London-quality work coming in."* Although the firm has a London office to host client meetings, the Kent firm has no plans to base fee earners there; Tyler explains that the firm's strategy is to offer price-conscious companies *"a significantly lower cost, Tunbridge Wells-based service."*

Despite hard times for the property industry, the sector is thriving at Cripps, accounting for 40% of its revenue, and trainees get to try a wide variety of disciplines within real estate. The firm's other core strengths are in private client work and a whole host of corporate and commercial practices – in *Chambers UK*, Cripps rules Kent, leading the pack in anything from agriculture and construction to litigation and IP.

Cripps' unusual system sees trainees picking all their seats before starting, after *"presentations from current trainees and partners during the summer."* Trainees generally got at least four of their choices, and noted that the cohort *"are able to move and swap around."*

The plot thickens

Being the biggest department, property offers a portfolio of options, including residential conveyancing, commercial property, property dispute resolution, and plot sales. As well as working with private clients and developers, there's also a retail team that acts for companies including Wagamama, Mr Pretzels, and Jigsaw – one recent case involved bidding adieu to Kew, handling the disposal of the fashion brand's 18 stores.

The plot sales department offers residential work on *"new builds like housing developments and retirement homes, everything from social housing to million-pound plots in Surrey."* One trainee had *"five or six of my own clients – I had to do what a proper lawyer would be doing."*

The *"wide-ranging"* commercial property department *"deals with both run-of-the-mill sales and pretty complicated farm estate work."* The firm also works with developers on matters including the controversial £50m extension and refurbishment of listed modernist shopping centre thecentre:mk in Milton Keynes.

The property disputes seat unearths *"literally something new every day, including boundary disputes, house sales going wrong, and professional negligence."* Trainees escape the office for trips to court, and one broke up sessions trawling Google Earth *"to see the land involved in a rights of way dispute."*

The residential conveyancing seat works solely with high net worth individuals. One recruit did *"conveyancing specifically for Middle East clients buying in London, who come to us thanks to our relationships with the developers"* – *"you've got to deal with time differences and the language barrier in a lot of cases."* Trainees *"have a good amount of contact with clients,"* with one being *"given control of a couple of files under supervision,"* although they also warned that there was *"a lot of photocopying."*

There's also a general dispute resolution seat, offering cases including *"wills and estates disputes, personal injury and traffic offences."* Recruits are entrusted with

Chambers UK rankings

Agriculture & Rural Affairs	Intellectual Property
Banking & Finance	Partnership
Charities	Planning
Construction	Private Client
Corporate/M&A	Professional Negligence
Dispute Resolution	Real Estate
Employment	Restructuring/Insolvency
Family/Matrimonial	Social Housing

drafting *"letters before action, court documents, and preparing cases for trial up in London."* In a fatal injuries case, one got to *"find an expert witness to give an opinion in court – the case will go on for many months, if not years, so it was interesting to help set it all up."*

The wealth preservation group offers private client work, including *"a lot of will drafting, trust administration, estate administration, and tax advice – you get to experience all the different areas of the department."* The *"very, very busy"* trainees get *"a good balance between technical, complex drafting and client contact."* One *"went to London to visit clients at our offices, and got to play a part in explaining documents, rather than just sitting and listening."*

Sticking pretty

The advertising, technology and media department is one that the firm is looking to grow in coming years. Clients include global ad agencies Omnicom and ZenithOptimedia, football stickers manufacturer Panini UK, and the team has handled brand management for the producers of Pink Lady and Tenderstem apples.

The relatively small corporate finance group still manages to attract some sizeable international clients, including the world's oldest – and fourth largest – cosmetic company Shiseido, and French furniture brand Ligne Roset. Trainees enjoy the variety and responsibility: *"Advising clients on compliance issues and shareholders' agreements – there's nothing that I've not been allowed to touch!"*

Trainees generally reported leaving by 6.30pm, although at busier times they could end up staying till 8, but found that *"on the whole it is appreciated if you put the extra hours in."* The firm *"gives you a lot of feedback on how you can improve,"* with monthly reviews followed by an end of seat appraisal with the head of HR and the managing partner. Benefiting from *"having discussions*

throughout the two years" on where they'd like to qualify, recruits are *"told relatively early which departments are likely to have spaces."* In 2013, seven out of eight qualifiers were retained.

Goodbye Mr Cripps!

Fans of Jane Austen, Sharpe or both should enjoy Cripps' offices' historical charms – *"they're Regency period so they're very pretty, and they're all in different buildings in one road."* Tunbridge Wells might not offer the most bustling of night lives, but Cripps trainees enthused that *"the firm encourages people to be sociable and to see a lot of each other,"* laying on events including end of quarter drinks at the favoured local The Well Kitchen. There's also the firm Christmas party, hosted at bread-based French restaurant Dame Tartine – which roughly translates as Lady Stuff-on-Toast. The rather more glamorous summer ball has a James Bond theme complete with casino tables, although disappointingly for hardened gamblers, play is strictly for plastic chips.

For sporty types there's a triathlon, cricket, netball, lunchtime squash, Monday night football, and an impressive sounding *"dawn to dusk football marathon with other local firms."* Those with lower endurance levels can have their fun at periodic dress down Fridays, wine tasting, karaoke, and a Sussex Downs walk. Charity events are far from the corporate norm down here in Kent; trainees *"bake cakes for Valentine's day and Halloween to sell round the office,"* and host a firm-only Christmas fête. They've also been touting for small change as part of the schools' favourite Smarties challenge, *"where you fill a tube with 20ps"* – David Cameron recently attracted minor derision for guessing £3, but this'll actually raise a not too shabby £12 a packet.

Cripps' managing partner of 23 years has recently stepped down to be replaced by similarly long-standing partner Gavin Tyler, who explained that, escapees to London apart, "people tend to come here and stay here." The firm is planning business development initiatives to attract more City work, from both companies and private clients. Thanks to a dual-qualified partner, the firm has also built up a growing client base of French companies jumping the good ship socialism to set up shop in the UK, ahead of Hollande's feared 75% tax for the super rich. Although Tyler admitted that alternative business structures (ABS) pose a "significant challenge" in the future, he feels that "we started responding a long time ago" to changes in the landscape for firms, avoiding bank loans and turning a modest profit; the firm is in good financial health.

And finally...

The lure of bright lights has meant that *"in the past there's been an issue with people moving to the City after their training contracts – the firm is looking for people who are committed to developing their connections in Kent."*

Curtis, Mallet-Prevost, Colt & Mosle LLP

The facts

Location: London
Number of UK partners/solicitors: 1/3 (+ 8 US qualified)
Total number of trainees: 4
Seats: none
Alternative seats: New York

On chambersstudent.co.uk...

How to get into Curtis
Interview with deputy managing partner Winta Jarvis
Curtis in America

The pint-sized London branch of this American firm is looking to embark on a course of *"steady, organic growth"* in the capital.

All around the world

One of the first American firms to branch out overseas, Curtis has a long-running history of international expertise. Today the firm's got 15 outposts around the globe, some in lands as far-flung as Turkmenistan, Argentina and Turkey. The petite London office, founded in the 70s, trades largely in complex, multi-jurisdictional matters, representing an array of multinationals, financial institutions and foreign governments – the government of Uganda and Ghana National Petroleum Corporation are two of the capital's biggest clients. Curtis London's strengths lie in international arbitration and corporate work, and the hub acts as a gateway to the firm's practice in Africa. You won't find any personal injury or media cases here, but if heaps of cross-border work and a firm with a *"tight-knit family feel"* sound up your alley, do keep reading.

At the time of our calls London housed just 13 qualified lawyers, and three trainees (none of whom were due to qualify in 2013). As such, trainees reported working very closely with resident partners and associates. The small team is hardly isolated from Curtis's vast global network, however; our sources insisted the bevy of offices is well integrated and the distance between them means nothing in the the digital age. *"You hear loads of different languages in the office, and American and other European partners are always passing through."* To keep up with this global setting, *"trainees need to be internationally minded,"* says deputy managing partner Winta Jarvis. Indeed, exposure to cross-border matters from day one is very much the norm at Curtis. *"Getting so much high-quality international work at such an early stage in your career is incredible."*

A quirk of the Curtis training contract is the absence of a regimented seat system. *"At the beginning you're allocated a department to sit in, usually international arbitration or corporate, and you stay there for most of your training contract."* That said, sources were quick to assure us *"you do still get a taste of at least four different areas; otherwise we'd be in trouble with the SRA!"* As Jarvis explained, trainees could be working *"on an arbitration case, a finance matter or a corporate transaction at any one time."* Said one insider of the system: *"It's not for everyone, but I love it. You really get stuck in, and they accommodate your preferences if you're vocal about what you'd like to work on."*

Arbitration, arbitration, arbitration

The international arbitration practice *"does a lot of work with foreign governments as well as international oil and construction companies."* Lawyers have worked extensively in Algeria, Ghana and Uganda in recent years as well as the Middle East and recently represented the Ugandan government in an epic $404m capital gains tax dispute launched by oil and gas magnate Tullow. Our sources told of attending client meetings, conducting research, drafting witness statements, handling doc review and liaising with specialists and agencies. *"I had to get my head around 300-odd files for one matter! Luckily you're doing more than just the legwork."* According to one trainee, *"there isn't a lot of English or black letter law; this stuff requires working out a strong narrative in order to argue a better case than the opposition, so you have to be able to think creatively. It's never dull."*

Over in corporate, lawyers work with private and public companies, hedge funds, governments and state-owned companies on *"really wide-ranging matters – on any given day you might be working on a finance deal or an employment issue or a joint venture."* Our interviewees' experience largely centred around funds, though the department also deals in M&A. *"A lot of our clients are US-based and have offshore funds in places like the Cayman Islands,"* one trainee told us. *"I've also been helping colleagues in New York and Asia. The global spread lends itself to some long hours and late nights – you have to be quite versatile to work in this department."* On the plus side, *"nobody expects you to be an expert right away. You get to work alongside partners who have tons of experience, and there's plenty of support."* As far as day-to-day tasks go, *"there's a lot of due diligence and checking over financial documents and prospectuses for banks. You can also get involved in writing memos."* To give you an idea of just how leanly staffed the London operation is, consider the following anecdote: we heard of one associate working with just two of the firm's Omani lawyers on the acquisition of 40% of shares in a large Omani holding company by a wealth fund owned by the Sultan's government.

A bite of the Big Apple

Another twist to the Curtis experience sees final year trainees dispatched to the firm's New York HQ, where they join the US summer associate programme for up to ten weeks. *"They're treated very well out there,"* Jarvis says, informing us trainees *"stay in the firm's apartment and get to attend a lot of events."* According to one experienced source, *"you get tons of contact with the partners."* Said another: *"I'm really looking forward to going – I've worked a lot with the New York office already, so it'll be good to meet them face to face."* Back in Blighty our insiders were pretty happy with the hours they'd been keeping. *"You don't go into the corporate department of a practice like this expecting to finish at 5.30pm everyday, of course! Still, while I finish at 10pm some days, I'm mostly done by about 7pm."* Likewise international arbitration can entail some finishes in the a.m., *"but that's only when something absolutely needs to get done,"* insiders insisted. *"You're not expected to check your BlackBerry constantly unless you're working on something really urgent."*

Situated on Gresham Street with views of The Bank of England, the London office is *"nice and modern though pretty spartan in terms of facilities,"* bar *"a sociable kitchen area where you can catch up with colleagues before work and at lunch."* Trainees are given their own *"spacious"* rooms from the off, a policy that substantiates Jarvis's view that *"trainees are effectively treated as associates."* Being the small firm it is, we should point out Curtis doesn't command a raging social scene; however, trainees *"get on really well"* and *"organise a fair amount of get-togethers,"* from karaoke to bowling to quizzes. On the glitzier side of things are cocktails and steak dinners at the nearby Hawksmoor Guildhall – a staple to trainee life at the firm. *"I was a bit worried before I started that there might not be much of a social life because the intake is so small, but that definitely hasn't turned out to be the case."* On the contrary, sources said the firm encourages them to form *"lasting relationships"* with colleagues as *"the firm wants people who are 'Curtis for life'. Ideally you'll be working with these people for the rest of your career."*

The True Picture

And finally...
"It's interesting that none of us in the current intake have an undergraduate law degree," mused one insider. *"I think the firm is looking for people with a broad base of knowledge and international interests."*

Dechert LLP

The facts

Location: London

Number of UK partners/solicitors: 33/74 (+11 non-UK-qualified)

Partners who trained at firm: 10%

Total number of trainees: 26

Seats: 6x4 months

Alternative seats: overseas seats, secondments

Extras: pro bono – A4ID, Islington Legal Advice Centre, Prince's Trust

On chambersstudent.co.uk...

How to get into Dechert

Interview with grad recruitment partner Andrew Hearn

US firm Dechert's rapid international expansion means trainees combine the benefits of a small office with access to high-quality work with a global flavour.

Double Dechert

After adorning the map of the US with 13 American offices, Dechert has been venturing out into markets both emerging and established – recently, it has opened offices in Frankfurt, Almaty, Dubai, Tbilisi and Chicago. The firm's London trainees have benefited from the expansion – part of an intake that isn't *"overwhelmingly huge,"* they still have access to *"a lot of good work coming in from the US,"* and are able to work on high-value cases with an *"international scope."*

Financially, trainees felt: *"We're very well placed – we don't have a lot of debt, and haven't carried out expensive large-scale mergers."* Instead, Dechert has expanded through an aggressive campaign of lateral hires – the London office's revenue grew by 44% in 2012, following some big hires, including Miriam Gonzalez (Nick Clegg's wife) from DLA Piper and a heavy-hitting capital markets team from collapsed firm Dewey & LeBoeuf. Andrew Hearn, co-head of graduate recruitment, explained that *"we've added a large white-collar crime team, a completely new government affairs and EU trade team, a finance team, and an emerging markets team – its all very international in flavour."* Dechert's biggest departments are corporate and finance, but the firm has plenty of smaller practice areas for trainees to sample. The new white-collar team gets top rankings in *Chambers UK*, which also recognises the firm for investment, dispute resolution, real estate, IP, employment and tax.

Trainees find Dechert's six-seat system *"really appealing as it offers a bit more variety."* It gives them the chance to sample practice areas including corporate; financial services; finance and real estate; employment; IP; international litigation and arbitration; tax; and white-collar crime. *"You're expected to do at least one of financial services or corporate,"* while there's hot competition for seats in smaller departments where *"trainee numbers will fluctuate"* and going abroad is *"tricky because everyone wants to do a secondment: it would be easier in a larger firm."* On the plus side, the system was seen as *"transparent"* and *"quite flexible: you can stay on in a seat if you enjoy it."*

A song for a sovereign

Trainees keep things general in the corporate securities department – *"you're just 'corporate' and volunteer for what you're interested in."* In terms of work, *"you're looking at mid-sized M&A rather than big magic circle transactions."* The firm specialises in life sciences, especially the biotech sector – recent deals have included acting for drug development company Cellzome as it was acquired by GlaxoSmithKline for £61m. Trainees get involved in *"drafting first-level board minutes and writing notes to the client – one matter took place over about a month, and involved quite a lot of work in keeping the client up to date, and liaising with lawyers internationally."* The multi-jurisdictional nature of the cases saw one trainee involved in *"setting up a global legal panel: they needed lawyers in 17 other jurisdictions."*

The finance department is divided into capital markets, financial services, and the finance and real estate group. Clients include Standard & Poor's, France Telecom and Investec. The new capital markets team from Dewey &

Chambers UK rankings

Banking & Finance	Employment
Capital Markets	Financial Services
Corporate Crime &	Intellectual Property
Investigations	Investment Funds
Corporate/M&A	Tax

LeBoeuf have brought in a new focus on emerging markets – they *"issue bonds for a lot of sovereign nations in the Middle East and North Africa – no one else in the area can hold a candle to them."* One trainee found it *"much more interesting to research for a country than for a company – you get to look at national statistics, and even find out how many goats, sheep and cows they have!"* The high values involved are an added excitement: *"I'm not used to seeing that many zeroes on a sheet of paper!"* Financial services offers *"quite a lot of variety"* in a *"quite interesting, very intense"* department. Dealing with big investment fund managers in multiple jurisdictions, *"the skill is mainly in keeping the whole thing together – making sure the papers go out correctly, and that the documentation is all organised."* The finance and real estate group might seem like a slightly odd combination, but one trainee explained that *"over here the departments aren't terribly linked, but it's led by the US, where there's more crossover."*

As seen in court

The IP team works with household names including Vauxhall Motors, Thomas Cook and Brake Brothers (Britain's largest supplier of frozen food to restaurants and schools). Recently, Dechert represented the online fashion giant ASOS against claims of trade mark infringement by cycling gear retailer Assos of Switzerland, and represented broadcasting company Starbucks – no relation to the frothy coffee merchants – in its dispute with BSkyB over the use of the name Now TV. The seat offers trainees a variety of contentious and non-contentious work. One source *"mainly worked on compliance regarding new EU regulations relating to how you store cloud data – it's quite a big task,"* while on the contentious side, another *"sifted through"* a document mountain during a High Court claim for breach of EU trade marks.

Dechert's sizeable litigation department offers seats in international arbitration, white-collar crime, employment and commercial litigation. The international arbitration seat involves some high-profile work for government clients; London is working closely with the new Tbilisi office in a dispute between the Georgian administration and the opposition regarding $150m of foreign investment. Trainees get involved in *"reviewing documents, and drafting affidavits and witness statements,"* and *"quite a lot of correspondence with local counsel"* across the world, even if a focus on pre-action work meant that some were

"not actually in court much." Recently poached from DLA Piper, the white-collar crime team is top-ranked in *Chambers UK,* handling *"some of the largest corporate scandals."* Trainees wouldn't kiss and tell, but loved *"being on the Tube seeing people reading about something you'll be working on that day."* Trainees were involved in *"attending interviews, writing notes and compiling bundles"* – document review is *"driven and managed by trainees, working with about 12 paralegals."*

Partner Duncan Wiggetts' cinematic prowess lends the department a bit of industry sparkle, although we're not exactly talking Legally Blonde – he recently wrote and produced his fourth film, exploring how companies should deal with allegations of fraud from whistle-blowers. Trainees especially interested in litigation have the option to complete a secondment at the Royal Courts of Justice, which saw one trainee *"sitting with two judges, going to court with them to take notes and help them draft their judgments."* There are also international seat options including Brussels, Dublin and a new seat in Moscow – although trainees did raise the point that the likelihood of getting them was *"kind of oversold"* by the firm, as some options are heavily oversubscribed.

Trainees found themselves doing *"a lot of routine work"* at first – *"people are quite tentative initially but they'll give you more responsibility once you've gained their trust."* Pro bono is a good way to get a bit more independence. It's *"really encouraged"* – work for The Prince's Trust has seen trainees providing advice to antique furniture dealers and music video makers. Dechert's review system was praised as offering *"extensive and thorough feedback"* – an independent panel partner *"acts as a mediator in a very informal way"* for trainees throughout their training contract, and further support is offered by a trainee buddy system.

The fewer men, the greater share of honour

One trainee saw Dechert as *"a US firm with a UK ethos – the guys from the States will be around the office quite a lot, but I don't think the London office feels like a satellite."* Thanks to Dechert's rapid global expansion, *"the US distinction is now becoming a lot less potent: it's much more of an international firm."* With 26 *"well-connected"* offices around the world, one trainee found that *"pretty much everything I've done has had an international element."* Now that *"corporate and litigation have expanded massively"* through lateral hires, trainees had a sense that *"the game plan is to get ourselves out there a bit more"* and *"raise our brand relative to other firms at the same level – the work we do is top-notch."* Trainee numbers are also increasing, but co-head of graduate recruitment Andrew Hearn told us: *"We aim to be parsimonious in the number of trainees we take on, in order to maintain the quality of the training."*

Although one first-year trainee counselled: *"Don't get put off by the myth that American firms work you a lot harder – that's definitely not the case here,"* most of the more seasoned recruits had battle stories of working through the night on big cases, especially in the frenetic corporate department. A *"horrendous week"* of working until the small hours then returning in time for breakfast left one trainee temporarily *"questioning my career choice,"* but it helps that the trainee salary outstrips the magic circle. The high workloads are due to *"smaller teams – there aren't enough trainees for anyone to laze around."* The new teams arriving from other firms have also caused *"a bit of a divide in culture"* – trainees see them as *"more intense,"* with longer hours.

Trainees find *"any excuse for a drink"* – the misleadingly named local pub Shaws Booksellers gets business *"from the newest trainees right up to partner level: a lot of the hierarchy you might expect to see isn't here."* The firm *"pulls out all the stops"* for its Christmas party – last year's was held at Terence Conran's upmarket French bistro Lutyens, and was enlivened by *"nail painting, magicians, karaoke and a band."* There are also departmental events, including a summer party held in Stationers' Hall.

Several corporate trainees enjoyed heading to the countryside for a Europe-wide departmental retreat – they *"aren't allowed to shrink into a corner"* during negotiation exercises, but were rewarded by a *"fun night out in Windsor."* Out of doors, there's various sports teams, though one trainee said: *"Sport isn't as much of a big deal as I thought, as the hours mean that it's difficult to get a whole team out by 6pm."*

Lawyers here are *"very sociable"* and *"normal – everyone's quite human: they're not super-super-high-achieving."* Maybe so, but these guys are no slouches and most attended Russell Group universities. Trainees do tend to be *"fresh out of uni and law school,"* rather than having had previous careers.

Trainees felt that *"retention rates are really good,"* which just shows how much things have improved recently, because until a couple of years ago Dechert's retention figures were notoriously poor. It kept on a measly 56% of the 96 trainees that qualified between 2003 and 2010, but clearly took a conscious decision to up its game because it managed to retain 81% of the 16 qualifiers of 2011 and 2012. In 2013, the firm fell back again with just five out of nine second-years retained upon qualification. However, trainees did praise the *"fair"* and *"transparent"* qualification system.

And finally...
You do need to be interested in corporate or financial services to work here. If you are, then this is a hard-working but not unpleasant environment in which to train. Emerging markets are clearly a big focus for Dechert at the moment, so have a think about that too.

It's good to take an interest in particular practice areas. But don't join a firm only wanting to do very specific seats. You are unlikely to get all your preferences. Be flexible and open to new experiences. You may discover a passion for something you never knew you cared for!

Dentons

The facts

Location: London, Milton Keynes
Number of UK partners/solicitors: 117/422
UK partners who trained at firm: 22%
Total number of trainees: 48
Seats: 4x6 months
Alternative seats: overseas seats, secondments
Extras: pro bono – PopLaw Clinic, RCJ CAB, UNICEF

On chambersstudent.co.uk...

How to get into Dentons
More about seats
The Milton Keynes office

From cuddly mid-sizer to global mega-firm within a couple of years – welcome to Dentons, the world's newest legal giant with a huge international footprint.

Ménage à trois?

You don't need to be Miss Marple to figure out this firm has had two things on its mind of late – getting bigger, and getting bigger fast. In 2010, Denton Wilde Sapte (DWS) was a 610-lawyer City outfit. Three years on, it's morphed into Dentons – a 2,600 attorney strong mega-firm with a CEO in Washington, DC. So, what happened?

Well, in 2010 DWS hooked up with US lothario Sonnenschein Nath & Rosenthal (SNR). This brought the firm's head count up to 1,400 lawyers with 16 offices across the globe. In late 2012, however, the firm felt the urge to merge again. Having batted its eyelashes at the now-defunct Dewey & LeBoeuf, in November 2012 it announced its rather saucy three-way engagement to French-founded international firm Salans, and Canada's Fraser Milner Casgrain (FMC).

The new entity is called Dentons (handily, that was DWS's nickname anyway) and was launched in March 2013. By head count it's the seventh largest firm on the planet, boasting 79 offices in 52 countries. In addition to the usual suspects (New York, Hong Kong, Moscow), the adventurous operation also has offices tucked away in the likes of Manama, Tashkent and Ashgabat. Oh, and Milton Keynes (does it get any more exotic?). Like a number of large international firms that came about through merger: Dentons is structured as a 'Swiss Verein', meaning that its regions won't combine profit pools. At least, not for the foreseeable future.

Trainees in the 250-lawyer London office reckon the transformation *"can only be a good thing."* The consensus is that *"it's part of strengthening the firm for the future. As DWS, it was easy to get lost in the global marketplace when everyone else was growing. This will solidify our position and bring in new clients."* They feel it will bolster the firm's brand, attract high-profile clients and enable them to reach new corners of the legal market.

"I remember the previous merger and there's a much more positive atmosphere now," mused one trainee. *"People are definitely excited and I think it's great."* Other than a small number of former Salans trainees joining their ranks, it seems unlikely there'll be too many changes to the firm's training experience. *"In theory, it should mean more work for everybody,"* they predict.

Pre-merger, Dentons focused on eight core sectors; post-merger that has tripled. We're not going to run through them all but you'll find the sectors listed, along with Dentons' offices and practice areas, in a pleasing Venn diagram on the firm's new and extremely purple website. We'd also advise you to get on over to *Chambers UK*'s website to explore Dentons' various strengths in greater detail. But in short, banking, real estate and energy have long been the pillars here in the UK, and trainees will usually pass through the banking and real estate departments at some stage.

Milton Keynes is the firm's second (and only other) UK office. Ringing in at about 50 lawyers, it's relatively small but packs quite a punch. It's currently undergoing an enormous project: *"There's a buzz in the office because all the administrative functions that are needed as a result of the combination fall to the Milton Keynes corporate*

Chambers UK rankings

Administrative & Public	Local Government
Law	Outsourcing
Asset Finance	Pensions
Banking & Finance	Planning
Capital Markets	Professional Negligence
Commodities	Projects
Construction	Public Procurement
Corporate/M&A	Real Estate
Data Protection	Restructuring/Insolvency
Dispute Resolution	Retail
Employment	Sports Law
Energy & Natural	Tax
Resources	Telecommunications
Environment	Transport
Information Technology	

team. It's nice to be involved." The small bunch of trainees here can choose between seats in corporate, dispute resolution, real estate, property litigation, construction and employment, and give the firm glowing reviews. Check out our website for more info on this training gem in the East Midlands.

Aeroplanes and rollercoasters

In recent years we've heard grumbles about the seat assignment system. Recently, it's undergone some tweaks but our sources remain unconvinced about its effectiveness: *"It's a bit hit and miss."* Second-years express their top three preferences, but said that *"like all training contracts, there's an element of mystery as to who gets put where and why."* That said, pretty much all of our interviewees admitted: *"It's worked out okay for me,"* so hopefully the HR team have managed to iron out most of the system's lumps and bumps.

Every trainee at Dentons should expect to pass through the banking department. It's probably the firm's best-known group, for good reason. Firstly, its sheer size – over 100 Dentons lawyers in the UK are dedicated to financial institutions. Secondly, its clients – Commerzbank, JPMorgan, Deutsche Bank and a host of other big names have passed through its doors at some stage. And finally, the enormous range of expertise available. In London, the department is split into subgroups. Very broadly speaking, Group 'A' consists of general banking, including real estate finance. Group 'B' is asset finance, known to be *"aeroplane geek"* heaven. Group 'C' works on the regulatory and capital markets side, while Group 'F' is trade finance, *"a niche module dealing specifically with structured loans for companies dealing in commodities."*

Each subgroup contains a number of trainees at any one time. Whichever one they're in, trainees are gener-

ally happy with the work on offer. *"Making bibles can get a bit wearing, but I've never been told to just do a ton of photocopying,"* said one source, plus *"there have been a few deals I've basically just got on with myself – drafting documents and effectively running the closing."* The group is renowned for its rollercoaster hours – one trainee said they'd left the office by 7pm most days, while another found them *"just dire."* Fortunately, banking is also known for its vibrant social life, and *"while there are times you're required to work very late, you're never on your own."* Partners and trainees often grab lunch together, and *"you really feel part of the team."* In fact, across the entire firm, we're informed: *"When big deals come in people have to work hard, but there's no US-style culture. There's no shame in leaving early if you can."*

The real estate group is another of the firm's big guns, and one of its largest departments. It has been involved in some enormous deals in recent years – advising the likes of Sainsbury's, the London Borough of Hammersmith & Fulham, and the owners of Argos and Homebase. It's also working for Bombardier Transportation as it bids to win a contract to build a depot for Crossrail. *"You get more responsibility than you do in banking, for lower-key matters,"* explained one source. Another said: *"It's actually quite scary how much you're trusted to get on with things. There are some smaller matters you can completely run with on your own."*

The corporate group is *"a competitive one to get into,"* and hence mostly populated by second-years, who get preference over their juniors in the seat-picking stakes. Split into two parts – public and private company work – clients consist of *"big supermarkets, and quite a few gym brands, down to smaller clients too. It's really good to work for them as you can get to know the individuals involved."* The firm recently advised Virgin Group on a strategic partnership agreement to merge its South African mobile telecoms business with a Middle East telecoms operator to become Virgin Mobile Middle East & Africa. This deal highlights two Dentons hallmarks: expertise in telecoms work and a significant and long-standing presence in Africa and the Middle East. The firm also worked for Nokia on the worldwide sale of its luxury mobile phone division, Vertu, to a Swedish investment company. On the bigger cases there can be *"some administrative stuff that needs doing,"* but trainees find that responsibility tends to ramp up with time and *"there's a lot of meaty work"* up for grabs, both domestically and on the international front.

Secondments are worth a mention. The firm sends trainees to a changing handful of overseas offices – in Muscat, Abu Dhabi and Dubai in 2013 – and has a few cracking client secondments on offer. At the moment there are opportunities to spend a seat with a French engineering firm, a well-known travel company or one of Dentons' many London-based bank clients. *"Our overseas second-*

ments are always over-subscribed," said one source, *"but if you play your cards right and state your case well, it's definitely possible."*

There are plenty of other big departments at Dentons – read about the likes of energy, TMT and litigation on our website.

Currying favour

The old Denton Wilde Sapte was known for having a relaxed, close-knit character. *"This is a firm for those who expressly don't want to work in the magic circle and wouldn't want to be just a number,"* we wrote back in 2010. So, how is this culture holding up now that the firm's head count has ballooned by a couple of thousand?

According to one source, *"they've been trying to become more business-focused since the SNR merger – building up profits and ensuring that everyone's taking responsibility for the success of the firm."* Even as outsiders, this shift is obvious. Take the firm's graduate recruitment ads, for example. Back in 2010, DWS beckoned interested students to its website www.friendly-firm.com. Since the SNR merger, however, it features a young chap looking at a plate of chillies with steely-eyed determination below the tag-line: 'Can you take the heat?' *"I've noticed a marked difference between the people taken on now, and those when I started,"* mused one second-year. *"The most recent intakes are perhaps stronger on paper, but less in keeping with the 'friendly firm', as it used to be."*

In general though, the firm's traditional quirks and sense of humour have served as a bulwark against too many incoming changes. *"There's always a bit of banter about the Americans and the way they do things,"* said one trainee. *"We understand we have to make money as a business, which is very much the American way, but we can also make a bit of fun out of it."* Others agreed: *"It's still a very friendly place to work. Everyone's really easy to talk to, which is great when you're learning. And you never feel you can't ask a partner a question just because they're a partner."* As for the future? Well, hopes are high that a healthy shot of Canadian and European influence from Salans and FMC will help to temper SNR's US-law tendencies. *"Maybe over time there'll be changes, but I can't envisage anything happening in the immediate future."*

Groups of trainees can be found grazing together in the canteen at lunch, and a substantial cohort will be spotted at the Corney & Barrow under the office on any given Friday. *"When we go to the bar there are nearly always staff from all different departments and levels of qualification having a drink with each other."* The firm has recently been focusing on its social side with renewed vigour, arranging no end of events. We heard about an upcoming merger party, a Halloween event, weekly drinks trolleys for the banking department, charity quizzes, loads of sports teams, a choir (*"that's a big thing"*) and fortnightly yoga sessions on the seventh floor. *"The banking department even went white-water rafting. That was the first event of this new drive."* You'd be hard pressed to squeeze all this frolicking into your schedule. Luckily, *"it's up to you how much you go to – you make of it what you want."*

Hang tough

Last year we reported that SNR Denton had slimmed down its rather convoluted qualification process. Thankfully, the current batch of Dentons trainees are reaping the rewards. *"The process is much better than it was,"* one source judged. *"When I started, qualifiers were finding out whether they were staying a week or two before the end of the training contract, and there were lots of fake obstacles to trip up on."* An NQ jobs list is published in May and sources said the process *"seems fair and organised."*

Retention rates used to be a perennial bugbear at SNR Denton. *"There's a slight fear among trainees, and we don't have that sense of security that we're more likely than not to get a job,"* commented one interview. It didn't help our sources' confidence that in 2013 a few incoming trainees from Salans would also be competing for NQ spots. Then again, trainees pointed out that *"last year the firm had a great retention rate, so it's a matter of keeping that trend up."* 'Great' might be pushing it – in 2012 the firm kept on 29 of its 39 qualifiers, which might be good by Dentons' standards over the past few years, but is decidedly average compared to the City as a whole. In 2013, the firm managed to retain a similar number: 26 out of 35 qualifiers.

And finally...

The future of this firm will become clearer once the post-merger dust settles. For now, however, it seems Dentons could offer that elusive combination – top-class training in a global firm, with a slightly more personal feel.

DLA Piper UK LLP

The facts

Location: Birmingham, Leeds, Liverpool, London, Manchester, Sheffield, Edinburgh
Number of UK partners/solicitors: 274/589
Seats: 4x6 months
Total number of trainees: 173
Alternative seats: overseas seats, secondments
Extras: pro bono – LawWorks, CAB, A4ID, Bar Pro Bono Unit, FRU, BPP Legal Advice Clinic, i-Probono, several legal advice centres and much more

On chambersstudent.co.uk...

How to get into DLA Piper
Interview with training principal Siân Croxon

This global heavyweight has a vast array of offices and offers a broad spectrum of work, a fantastic roster of clients and *"a dynamic environment. You can never quite predict what will happen year on year, but you can guarantee it will be entertaining."*

Indoctrination of the DLA nation

It's fair to say that at some of the firms we cover, trainees can often be riddled with unease when we ask about what their employer is trying to achieve. It came as a breath of fresh air, then, to find the current intake at DLA Piper so fully signed up to the visions of the global juggernaut. As if reading straight from a DLA pamphlet, one Leeds trainee told us: *"I think the firm is very ambitious on an international and national level. It doesn't want to be magic circle. It wants to the leading global business law firm and that is where it's going."* One of their London counterparts offered: *"I am impressed with its drive, its growth and its vision. It wants to be the world's leading global business law firm."*

Given the standing of DLA it's easy to see why such attitudes filter through the ranks. With nearly 8,000 people – including roughly 4,200 lawyers – across nearly 80 offices in over 30 countries, this is a truly global law firm. These figures actually earmark DLA as one of the two biggest firms in the world by head count, and considering the firm only came into being as recently as 2005, that's a pretty impressive feat. A tie-up with Indonesian firm Ivan Almaida Baely & Firmansyah in May 2013 saw DLA extend its network yet further, although trainees felt this formidable rate of growth would not be maintained. *"I think there is a general push to increase our coverage in emerging markets,"* considered one second-year. *"However, after such rapid expansion the real goal now is to maintain the quality across offices. 'Trusted advisers'*

is the term that's bandied about. We're generally trying to become a one-stop shop for high-quality clients."*

It hasn't all been plain sailing, though. The firm's Glasgow office closed in April 2013 – at the cost of 45 jobs – while significant cuts to staff numbers were made across the UK in the document production and defendant insurance teams. This created a sense of unease among some trainees. One said: *"It's quite a nervous environment to be in at the moment. The firm's hoping to become bigger and better and I think it will bring in relationship firms in emerging markets. However, I think some further UK offices may be closed. [Senior partner] Tony Angel joined [in 2011] and he has a reputation for closing offices and shutting down departments."* Training principal Siân Croxon responded: *"I can understand their concern. The Scottish position was always difficult and you never like consolidation that results in offices closing. A huge amount of thought and planning went into it though and it wasn't a decision taken lightly."*

No Brum deal

DLA has offices in London, Birmingham, Manchester, Liverpool, Leeds, Sheffield and Edinburgh. Don't be fooled into thinking that it's only the capital that sees any action though, as all the regional offices offer fantastic opportunities. *"I considered applying to the London office but you get the same quality of work in the regions,"* said a trainee in Brum. *"Even in Birmingham, you get high-calibre, high-value deals. From that point of view*

Chambers UK rankings

Asset Finance	Investment Funds
Aviation	Media & Entertainment
Banking & Finance	Outsourcing
Banking Litigation	Parliamentary & Public
Capital Markets	Affairs
Commodities	Pensions
Competition/European Law	Planning
Construction	Private Equity
Corporate/M&A	Projects
Data Protection	Public International Law
Dispute Resolution	Real Estate Finance
Employment	Restructuring/Insolvency
Financial Services	Retail
Fraud	Tax
Healthcare	Telecommunications
Insurance	Transport
Intellectual Property	

it doesn't matter if you're in London or the regions so I chose to stay closer to home." All the offices handle a mix of local/regional, national and international work – the latter being a main draw for the current crop of trainees.

Seat options are broad and only differ slightly between offices, with London generally offering *"more specialisms"* within certain departments. An interviewee explained: *"In IPT (intellectual property and technology), for example, you might get to do sport and media in London, whereas the regions just offer straight IPT."* From another source: *"In Leeds you can sit in finance, but in London you have to pick which stream of finance you want to be in."* Some sources were drawn to the capital because of this, but others preferred the broader regional seats: *"It means I can do the whole scope rather than being limited."* Before each rotation, trainees submit three or four seat preferences – sources emphasised with vigour the correct terminology is *"preferences"* rather than *"choices"* – and *"graduate recruitment tries to maximise the people who get at least one of those."* One trainee added: *"There's no compulsory seats or firm-led preferences so we get quite a free rein. As long as you do your mix of contentious and non-contentious there is great variety in the seats you can do."*

Location also has no bearing on who can take advantage of the *"very popular"* client and international secondments. *"Because most client secondments are centred in the South East it can give the impression that London trainees are preferred for those roles,"* a trainee told us. *"But there is a focus on getting people from regional offices to go on them and anyone is eligible to apply."* Overseas seats in places such as Singapore, Hong Kong, Sydney, Dubai, Abu Dhabi and Bangkok are also available to any trainee, although *"you have to put forward a busi-*

ness case saying why you'd be suited to working abroad." What trainees won't generally do, however, is move round DLA's UK offices during their training contract.

Exactly what it says on the tin

DLA Piper has maintained – for the sixth time in seven years – its position as the UK's busiest legal adviser for M&A. There are currently over 150 corporate lawyers dedicated to this practice across the country. Deals are often international, although London and Leeds tend to shoulder a greater share of these ones than the other offices. The London branch recently advised Discovery Communications on its acquisition of ProSieben's SBS broadcasting business in Scandinavia for £1.35bn, and its €850m investment in Eurosport. Even though less of their M&A work is international, the regions still advise some big-name clients: Birmingham represents Barclays Ventures, Manchester looks after Warburtons and Matalan, and Sheffield handles Lynx and Ronseal. Due to the nature of the deals, *"the usual trainee tasks"* can be expected. *"I did all the standard things like board minutes, resolutions, powers of attorney, due diligence, organising data rooms and going to a couple of completion meetings,"* said a second-year. However, *"if you show enthusiasm, the more they'll trust you and the more responsibility you'll get."* Some of our interviewees had some great exposure. *"I was dealing with an international company and there were 25 countries involved,"* said a Manchester source. *"We had clients from France, clients from Germany – all these different countries communicating with translators to me and my supervisor about disclosures. It's not just your bog-standard tasks!"* It's not just London that's at the mercy of chaotic corporate closings. *"You're on a Leeds salary, but working London hours,"* one of Yorkshire's finest disclosed. *"People often think we don't put a shift in, which would be my one real bone of contention."*

DLA's litigation department has a range of specialist subgroups, such as commercial, real estate, sport and aviation. London looks after RBS, Lloyds and Barclays, as well as the government of Georgia and the Republic of Turkey among others. Other interesting clients include the City of St Petersburg (Leeds), Liverpool Football Club (Liverpool), Honda (Manchester) and ITV (Sheffield). Trainee experiences generally depend on the size of the matters at hand. *"On some of the bigger cases it's a smaller role, assisting on various tasks,"* said a source in Leeds. *"Mainly I was researching points of law we could turn our case on, but I was actively encouraged to attend calls and mediations, too."* A London trainee added: *"There was a lot of smaller files I was given responsibility for. They were keen for me to get good experience and make sure I got the most out of my six months."*

Although *"the most popular seats tend to vary year on year,"* the IPT department is a current favourite. The team

The True Picture

handles matters for a variety of industry sectors including: life sciences; hospitality/leisure; media/sport; fashion; and food and drink. The firm recently advised the Premier League on the use of satellite decoder cards by other EU member states to watch top-flight football and on its sponsorship arrangements with Barclays, together with all other aspects of its commercial IP licensing programme. Other clients on the books include Channel 5, Polo Ralph Lauren, Kraft Foods and The Savoy Hotel. On the technology side, the work involves things like *"big public sector procurement contracts. I was mostly reviewing schedules, provisions and working on certain areas of ongoing contracts."* In the sphere of IP, there is a lot of *"support work for corporate mergers,"* said one source. *"I did plenty of research, proof-reading and document checking. My associate was very good at talking me through things though and I got to see how a deal progressed from start to finish."*

Real estate takes on a good number of trainees. *"As the deals are smaller than the corporate or finance transactions, there's lots of different matters to juggle which can be quite challenging,"* one source informed us. *"On bigger files I was doing due diligence and helping the clients with queries, whereas on smaller matters like the sales of garages I got a lot more freedom. If you show you are a capable they are happy to give you responsibility and let you get on with it. My supervisor left me to prepare the pre-completion for a multimillion-pound building sale."*

Orange squash

With recruitment adverts featuring an orange and talk of how much DLA squeezes into a training contract, it is also up to trainees to try and squeeze the most out of their experience. *"My supervisor came to me before I started and said I would either sink or swim here,"* a trainee recalled. *"If you make the most of it, you will swim, but if you're scared to make decisions or worry about your actions it's probably not the place for you."* The schedule can be tough here, and the hours long. *"There's no point people coming in and expecting a nine-to-five,"* warned a source. *"No one's ever said I needed to stay, and I haven't had to cancel plans, but if there's the opportunity to get involved in good work you generally just keep working."* From another interviewee: *"You can't avoid the all-nighters. During completions it went crazy and no one remem-*

bered they had a watch or clock. In all fairness though, if I finish at 6pm and there isn't anything else to do they do let you go. There's no culture of sitting around twiddling your thumbs."

Despite the array of offices and vast number of individuals, trainees actually said DLA *"is quite like a family. You see each other in the corridor and can have a chat. Most senior people are very approachable – there's no power hierarchy in how people speak to each other."* A source elaborated: *"You can have a joke and laugh with people as long as you're doing your work. You can be a person, a human being. Trainees are allowed to experience the most that they able to and are helped to develop. We're well looked after."* On this subject, one interviewee said: *"My supervisor went as far as pretending she was a client so my work would be perfect. She took the role really seriously!"*

Creating a family atmosphere is not something that's restricted to individual offices: it seems that DLA is pushing for greater integration across its whole UK network. *"One ambition that's been voiced recently is for it not to be about the regions and London, but about being lawyers at DLA,"* a source explained. Another concurred: *"DLA sees itself as one UK firm and to a client it shouldn't be obvious what office they're dealing with. We're all essentially delivering one product."* As such, a second-year told us that *"you're encouraged to get to know the other trainees; not just those in your office, but nationwide."*

Although there is currently little cross-office trainee socialising – *"it doesn't occur that much as you have to get over 90 people in one place"* – the whole intake does congregate at the start of the training contract for a week-long professional skills training course and induction. Last year this took place in the lavish Crewe Hall, a Jacobean mansion in the heart of Cheshire. No need to fret though – all the individual offices have hearty social scenes. All run Friday-after-payday drinks and the regional offices are closely affiliated with their local Trainee Solicitors Groups, which put on Christmas and summer balls. In the Manchester office we also heard of Halloween parties and plenty of karaoke, while down in London charity ping-pong tournaments, ice skating at Somerset House and a variety of sports teams are just some of things that keep trainees active.

And finally...

DLA has posted decent retention rates over the past few years, but this dropped off somewhat in 2013 with 56 out of 77 qualifiers staying on.

DWF LLP

The facts

Location: Birmingham, Bristol, Coventry, Leeds, Liverpool, London, Manchester, Newcastle, Preston, Teesside, Scotland

Number of UK partners/solicitors: 296/1520

Total number of trainees: 98

Seats: 6x4 months

Alternative seats: occasional secondments

On chambersstudent.co.uk...

How to get into DWF
Training principal Carl Graham on
DWF's stratospheric growth

It's mergers galore at DWF, where a taste for tie-ups has propelled the national unit ever closer to the coveted circle of UK top 20 firms.

Growth spurt

Native Mancunian DWF is no stranger to steep growth. A spate of strategic tie-ups and savvy lateral hires over the last six years has transformed the enterprising firm – once a four-office regional shop up north – into a national behemoth with coverage across England, Scotland and the Republic of Ireland. At last count, a whopping 11 outposts made up the DWF family, thanks in large part to combinations with no fewer than five firms between January 2012 and February 2013. DWF's most recent undertakings – the acquisitions of professional indemnity experts Fishburns and a large part of fellow Northerners Cobbetts in early 2013 – have more than doubled its turnover, prompting management to scrap previous dreams of being UK top-30 material for a crack at the top 20. Revenue now stands at £200m and head count in excess of 2,500 people.

At the time of our interviews, DWF was in the midst of welcoming more than 500 ex-Cobbetts and Fishburns folk to its clan. *"We're used to taking on new groups, but this has been an especially big undertaking,"* a few sources admitted. Luckily, *"we're fairly good at synching people now that we've done it several times,"* training partner Carl Graham chimes in. *"It's a big effort to make sure everyone is taken care of, but despite the scale we haven't had any major issues."* Having taken the decision to honour existing and future training contracts for each firm, DWF's trainee cohort in autumn 2013 numbered 98 all in. Little's changed in Liverpool and Newcastle, but Manchester, Leeds, London and Birmingham have all incorporated new trainees into their ranks. *"The firm's done well to make sure there's no 'them and us',"* interviewees agreed. *"All the changes have been*

for the better – there's a real buzz about the place, and it's an exciting time to be here."

Insurance work has always been DWF's backbone, historically accounting for around half of its revenue. The firm's personal injury defence practice is especially well regarded, as evidenced by nationwide *Chambers UK* rankings, while its non-contentious insurance arm is making strides following the 2012 hire of ex-Barlow Lyde & Gilbert partner Douglas Howie in London. As a trainee, *"it's likely you'll end up with an insurance seat as there are so many available,"* though *"it's not compulsory."* There's also the chance to spend time in the real estate, banking and finance, corporate, commercial/IT, private client, employment, family, construction and litigation departments.

DWF's six-seat system means trainees receive a *"panoramic"* view of the business. Seat options vary by location, though *"you're not restricted to your home office; before each rotation they release a national list, so you can apply for seats in any office if they're not offered at yours."* Manchester and Liverpool offer the biggest spread – *"we generally have around 15 or 16 seats to choose from"* – though Leeds and London provide a *"fairly diverse"* pool as well. When it comes to allocation, legacy DWF, Cobbetts and Fishburns trainees alike praised the *"fantastic HR support. They make it clear they're keen to help us get our top choices, and have made the transition following the mergers as smooth as possible."* Indeed, *"we're all being treated just like any other trainees at DWF,"* one ex-Fishburns source confirmed. NQ decisions are typically made in the spring, so *"it's policy to return to the seat you're qualifying into for your last rotation."*

The True Picture

Chambers UK rankings

Administrative & Public Law	Insurance
	Intellectual Property
Banking & Finance	Licensing
Banking Litigation	Local Government
Charities	Parliamentary & Public Affairs
Civil Liberties & Human Rights	
	Partnership
Competition/European Law	Pensions
Construction	Personal Injury
Consumer Finance	Planning
Corporate/M&A	Police Law
Dispute Resolution	Product Liability
Education	Professional Negligence
Employment	Projects
Energy & Natural Resources	Real Estate
	Restructuring/Insolvency
Environment	Retail
Family/Matrimonial	Social Housing
Health & Safety	Tax
Information Technology	Transport

Horses for main courses

DWF's insurance work is far-reaching and includes relationships with many of the industry's top dogs, from Aviva and Ageas to Zurich and QBE. The work is mainly defendant-side (usually on behalf of insurers, brokers or claims organisations) and spans the full spread of the firm's specialist sectors including food, retail, engineering, pharmaceutical and automotive – last year's merger with Birmingham insurance specialists Buller Jeffries helped DWF beef up its presence in that last field, adding prestigious clients like Aston Martin and Jaguar Land Rover to its base. Common seats within the department include commercial insurance, occupational health, fraud and catastrophic personal injury.

The commercial insurance team handles both contentious and non-contentious issues, including professional negligence claims, professional indemnity disputes and corporate transactions. Within DWF's food sector, lawyers deal with product recall and operational risk matters for a number of noted retail and food brands – the infamous horsemeat scandal of early 2013 proved a boon for business thanks to myriad claims arising on the product liability side. Trainees completing a commercial insurance seat *"tend to work across multiple discrete matters rather than one big one – you end up with a good perspective on what the team does as a whole,"* they said. In addition to *"organisational tasks such as arranging client meetings and ascertaining partners' availability for mediation,"* there's *"a fair bit of drafting,"* sources reported. *"I got to draft instructions to counsel and a few reports updating insurers on the progress of certain matters. Likewise, if*

there are letters to go out off the back of research, people come to you for the first draft."

A stint in occupational health is a *"purely litigation-focused seat. We always act for the insurer, often in workplace accident or public liability cases – for example, if someone's hurt themselves at a sports ground or some other business premises."* According to trainees, *"the work is really interactive. On low-value cases, trainees get to take witness statements, watch video surveillance, talk to medical experts and attend sessions with counsel."* An insured property seat means *"working for one arm of the illegal expenses insurance team."* Work is high-volume and *"can be emotionally draining,"* insiders warned. *"The clients are really demanding and expect constant correspondence. I was running nearly 30 files by the end of my seat."* A standalone professional indemnity seat is now available in London thanks to the Fishburns tie-up. *"We essentially work as an outsourced function for the insurer by defending them against claims that come their way,"* sources explained. The spectrum of claims is broad – *"cases involve architects, accountants, engineers, financial advisers"* – and client contact is plentiful. *"Trainees communicate directly with the insured parties."*

Commercial crusades

DWF's commercial real estate team is one of its biggest, so *"most people sit in the department at some point."* The firm is especially big in the retail, technology, energy, education and public sectors, with clients as wide-ranging as Santander, Liverpool John Moores University and Manchester City Council. Property finance, *"a big focus"* of late, means there's *"quite a bit"* of overlap with the banking team. Recent projects include advising The Co-operative Bank on the development of a new Hilton hotel as part of the £40m revamp of Southampton's Ageas Bowl and acting for the trustees of the Irish Diaspora Foundation throughout the development of Manchester's Irish World Heritage Centre. *"There's also a lot of commercial leasing work for companies who own town shopping centres,"* one trainee revealed. *"It's a good seat for gaining transactional experience – I was working with clients constantly and got to hone my drafting skills."*

A stint in corporate entails *"a real variety of work,"* from *"straightforward"* M&A transactions to capital markets and AIM-related matters. Recently, the firm advised Acenta Steel Holdings on an acquisition of equity held by a mid-market private equity house and acted for German manufacturer Burg-Wächter KG on its acquisition of British-owned peer Sterling Locks. *"My seat was all over the place – I assisted with a completion, did some research into initiatives targeting AIM companies and amended some documents pertaining to public markets work,"* one source shared. Likewise, a commercial seat is *"really broad,"* incorporating data protection, IT contracts and regulatory work. *"I got to help draft some distribution documents and also completed a number of dis-*

crete research tasks," said another. Both seats are *"great for developing time management skills,"* interviewees agreed, *"as you're often being yanked back and forth between projects."*

On the commercial litigation front, there's *"anything from negligence and breach of contract cases to IP, probate and pensions litigation. Every day you're doing something different."* As such, *"it's a fast-paced seat – one minute you're preparing bundles and making applications to the court, and the next you're drafting instructions to counsel or put in a car to deliver the court bundle. There's the odd photocopying task you can't get out of, but most of the trainee work is good-quality,"* sources said. While interviewees who'd sat in commercial litigation invariably enjoyed it, the seat is not in particularly high demand. *"Most people prefer to fulfil the contentious requirement through one of the insurance seats,"* we were told.

May the odds be ever in your favour

Occasionally, some in the profession seem to view rapidly growing firms like DWF as pushy upstarts and make vague warnings about expanding too far, too fast. Still, we don't think DWF is in the same mould as Halliwells, another Manchester-founded firm that rocked up the rankings in the 2000s only to come to a sticky end. Our interviewees made it clear that DWF's ambitious recent moves have been well received across the firm. *"All of a sudden, everyone knows who we are, which is an amazing development to witness and be a part of – we're current, fresh, constantly changing and getting better every day."* Sources described an *"energetic buzz"* and *"buoyant atmosphere visible day to day,"* and felt long-term prospects appear promising. *"From a trainee perspective it seems like there will be increased opportunities for us now that we're part of this bigger and better brand."*

Thanks to *"a similar approach to culture"* between DWF and its acquired firms, lawyers have had little trouble assimilating. Explained one legacy DWF source: *"DWF sustains an atmosphere that's both relaxed and professional, and as much as we've grown, we've never lost that balance. Cobbetts and Fishburns were also known for having pleasant environments, so throwing us all together under one roof has worked out just fine."* Sources firm-wide praised *"the incredible effort put into making*

sure trainees are happy and kept up to date with firm on-goings,"* mentioning the biannual trainee dinners hosted by managing partner Andrew Leaitherland in Manchester. *"It's a great forum to raise comments and concerns in – we get the chance to be open and honest, and they really listen to our input. I don't think that access to senior people is available everywhere."*

Digs in Manchester, Liverpool and Leeds are largely similar, *"especially in the client areas – they're light and airy, with lots of glass panels and a very contemporary feel."* Each is kitted out with communal kitchens, a bistro and *"plenty"* of break-out areas. Amenities vary among the smaller offices, but interviewees agreed DWF's open-plan set-up helps consolidate an *"approachable"* vibe. *"It doesn't matter whether you're a senior partner or a trainee – you're sitting at the same desk. That lessens the hierarchy and means support and feedback are easily accessible."* In order to help the newly ballooned trainee cohort integrate, the firm's ramped things up on the social side, organising various after-work drinks and lunch dos to complement the already *"full-on"* scene. *"I'm playing football tonight with some ex-Cobbetts guys,"* one Leeds source told us, adding: *"It might be a showdown!"* In addition to 'Friday fridge' – a monthly free drinks event held in each office – we heard about sundry after-hours activities across the firm: sports teams, charity events, wine tastings, craft sessions, trips to the Lake District, yoga classes. There's also an annual trainee quiz in Manchester for the whole intake, *"future trainees included."*

According to Carl Graham, further growth is on the cards, *"though I can't see another five mergers in the next year! Still, we'll continue pursuing more sectors and diverse clients as we focus on making the most of the recent mergers."* Despite the *"inevitable uncertainties"* accompanying DWF's rapidly changing structure, this year's bunch was nothing but optimistic. *"The firm is pretty different from the one I applied to back in 2009, but at the end of the day it's nice people working with other nice people – that sold me in the beginning, and that'll keep me here in the future,"* one concluded. Luckily, historically high retention rates mean *"the odds seem to be in our favour"* with respect to qualification, and *"the HR team is doing their best to keep us as informed as possible – you can't ask much more than that."* In fact, 30 out of 40 qualifiers were kept on in 2013.

And finally...

When it comes to getting hired, *"there's no set mould for the firm,"* trainees thought. That said, they urged applicants to keep in mind *"this is a people-oriented business – a positive personality goes a long way."*

Edwards Wildman Palmer UK LLP

The facts

Location: London

Number of UK partners/solicitors: 28/42

UK partners who trained at firm: 21%

Total number of trainees: 13

Seats: 4x6 months

Alternative seats: secondments

Extras: pro bono – LawWorks, Fair Trials International, RCJ CAB; language classes

On chambersstudent.co.uk...

How to get into Edwards Wildman

Pro bono at the firm

A series of ambitious tie-ups has spurred various changes to Edwards Wildman's structure, but trainees insist this London office's friendly ethos is here to stay...

Pencils at the ready?

The lineage behind this transatlantic outfit is somewhat convoluted, so you might want to take notes. Back in 2008, Edwards Wildman Palmer's American precursor Edwards Angell Palmer & Dodge – itself the progeny of a 2005 merger between respective Rhode Island and Boston firms – linked up with London insurance buffs Kendall Freeman in order to gain access to the European market. The firm plodded along swimmingly as EAPD until 2011, when native Chicagoan Wildman, Harrold, Allen & Dixon entered the mix, thus spawning Edwards Wildman Palmer as we know it today. Under this latest stewardship, Tokyo, Hong Kong and London bases top off the dozen stateside offices.

Big strides have been made to bring the London practice into line with the US side of the firm, including the addition of IP, competition and private equity/venture capital teams to complement the office's historical metier in the insurance sector. Edwards Wildman's City branch has also bulked up its litigation capabilities thanks to Wildman Harrold's formidable strength on that front, and now commercial litigation accounts for one of the firm's four cornerstones (along with IP, corporate and insurance work). Since 2008, revenue has more than doubled – ringing in at a healthy £26m in 2012 – and the firm has made huge leaps on the client front, welcoming institutions as varied and illustrious as Amazon, Citibank and the government of Nigeria to its customer base.

A few interviewees expressed concern at the potential side effects of Edwards Wildman's shifting landscape – *"with all of our name changes, I worry that clients won't immediately recognise our brand,"* said one – but our sources all agreed that the pluses of the firm's evolution to this point *"far outweigh"* any drawbacks. *"We have all the benefits of an international network, like increased resources and a robust US client base, and everyone feels confident about our future,"* one pointed out. *"We just need to make sure we work to solidify our brand so people instantly associate us with the quality work we do."* Trainee recruitment manager Sarah Warnes agrees: *"Communicating that whilst we have a new name our legacy is over a century of experience working with clients in all industries and of all sizes is a priority at the moment. More than anything, we want to be seen as a business-minded, approachable, entrepreneurial firm that is easy to work with and understands the challenges our clients face."*

Seats are available in the insurance, commercial litigation, business law, employment, IP and competition departments. Before each rotation, trainees meet with the HR team to discuss their options, and from there it's a *"shuffling exercise"* that takes both business needs and personal preferences into account. *"Things don't always work out perfectly,"* sources revealed, *"but it's clear they take what we say into consideration and do their best to place us where we want to go."* No seats are compulsory, but *"it's generally expected"* that most trainees will spend time in both commercial litigation and insurance as well as going on one of the many client secondments on offer.

Chambers UK rankings

Dispute Resolution	Intellectual Property
Insurance	Public International Law

Can you keep up?

Edwards Wildman's insurance practice errs towards contentious work, covering a range of insurance and reinsurance disputes. Cases often span multiple jurisdictions and tend to be *"massive and long-running,"* and many are *"highly specialised,"* like the £500m asbestos liabilities dispute the firm recently handled on behalf of European companies Centre Re, Swiss Re and Munich Re. Still, teams usually comprise just one partner, associate and trainee, a set-up that offers a *"front-row view"* for those in training. *"We go to all the court sessions and meetings with counsel,"* sources said. In addition to performing research, drafting correspondence and undertaking the odd analytical task, there's *"a good deal"* of doc review, we were told. *"It's up to us to make sure everything's perfect with the bundles. Luckily they reward us by letting us attend the hearings."* The insurance team also contends with a fair whack of non-contentious matters of the corporate, M&A, regulatory and restructuring persuasion. A recent deal saw solicitors advise AmWINS, an American-led wholesale broker, on its £32m takeover of risk management group THB.

Over in commercial litigation, lawyers tackle a wide spectrum of issues, from contractual disputes to international arbitrations to anti-corruption matters. A recent success on that last front saw the litigators land the coveted spot of lead counsel for the Turks and Caicos Islands government in one of the largest asset recovery programmes currently pending. Other high-flying clients include Shell, Tata Steel and Bambino Holdings, the family trust of Formula One baron Bernie Ecclestone. As a trainee, *"you do a million and one different things,"* including drafting research memos, visiting client sites, attending hearings, and managing doc review and bundling duties. Luckily, *"a fair amount of the work is proper,"* we were assured. One interviewee told of writing a response to a counter-claim – *"a real meaty piece of work!"* – while others mentioned interacting with counsel and even travelling abroad for cross-border trials.

London's business law department covers corporate, M&A, banking and private equity matters across multiple sectors, including telecommunications, life sciences, insurance and financial institutions. In 2012 alone, the team handled over 100 transactions worth a collective £2bn-plus, acting for the likes of JPMorgan, Bank of America and Citibank. Our interviewees characterised their time in the department as *"completely different"* from contentious stints in that *"you work a lot more closely with clients, often on discrete matters like share agreements or small investments."* Like business law, the growing IP team contends with an array of issues, from patent and trade mark cases to IT and copyright disputes. Big-name clients include Amazon, MasterCard and Warner Bros. – which the firm advises on all trade mark and design-related matters – and much of the work *"falls into the litigation or regulatory category."*

A client secondment is *"more or less guaranteed"* as part of the training contract, *"though the firm doesn't force you to go; most people just apply with the intention of doing one because they're very prevalent here."* Recent destinations includeCitibank and Amazon, and those who'd spent time in-house characterised the opportunity as an *"overwhelmingly positive"* experience with *"lots of scope to manage your own matters."* Likewise, pro bono work is *"an excellent way to develop your skills."* According to insiders, it's *"a big priority for Edwards Wildman – if you have the time, it's basically expected."* Fair Trial clinics – *"where much of the work is done on behalf of people arrested abroad"* – and CAB sessions at the Royal Courts of Justice feature regularly on the docket, as do ad hoc LawWorks cases circulated by the firm's pro bono co-ordinator.

Cakes with gherkins

Despite Edwards Wildman's robust stateside presence, *"we're not your typical American firm"* was an insistence we heard time and again. As one trainee elaborated: *"Kendall Freeman was a legacy UK firm, so the partners and culture from the old days are still present. That dynamic would be different if we had originated as the London office of a big US firm."* Indeed, our interviewees placed Edwards Wildman's City branch *"more in the bracket of a small UK firm"* when it comes to working environment, explaining: *"We don't have the high salaries or unbearable hours associated with places like Bingham or White & Case."* Of course, the boost in transatlantic matters hasn't gone unnoticed – *"it's certainly great to have those contacts,"* trainees agreed – but it's said the UK crowd tends to operate *"pretty independently"* from its comrades across the pond.

Insiders told of an open, *"welcoming"* atmosphere present day-to-day, one in which *"the hierarchy isn't stiff at all – there's an understanding you can knock on anyone's door and they'll make time for you."* Most interviewees attributed this *"excellent"* dynamic to the firm's small scale, which ensures *"everybody knows everybody else's names; you're never walking past strangers who ignore you in the corridor."* What's more, there an extensive support network that includes trainee buddies, partner mentors, department mentors and supervisors, so *"you've always got someone to turn to if a problem crops up."* At Edwards Wildman's Liverpool Street digs, brand-new catering and a Thursday cake trolley are big hits, as are *"the insane views of the Gherkin"* and the fact that *"we don't have sleeping pods, thank goodness."*

The current cohort comprises quite a variety of backgrounds, degrees and ages, with 11 different universities represented among the 15-strong bunch. *"The trend you'll notice among us is that we're all very personable,"* one said. *"People who get in tend to be chatty, warm and down-to-earth."* Getting along isn't a problem for this year's class, although several sources warned applicants to *"consider the impact of pursuing a firm where there are only seven or eight others in your year. You're more likely to get good client contact and access to partners, which is great, but on the flipside there's no escaping the people!"* Indeed, judging by Edwards Wildman's crowded social calendar, lawyers see rather a lot of each other. In addition to a *"fairly active"* sports scene that culminates in an internal football tournament held each summer in Regent's Park, there's a spate of committee-planned dos like quiz nights and payday drinks, *"the usual rush of things at Christmas,"* plus a blast of a summer party by the sound of things. *"This year the theme is 'I'm a Wildman, Get Me Out of Here!' I heard there will be challenges and everything!"* A big effort is made to include future trainees, who are invited to most events and are even thrown a dedicated social in their honour. Last year's was Wild West-themed, complete with a bucking bronco that we heard one partner (we won't name names) was *"surprisingly good at riding – like, questionably good..."*

And finally...

With only one female partner in London, *"the firm's highlighted gender diversity as an issue and is working hard to address it. We're now doing in-house dinners for women across the firm, which have been really useful and inspiring."* In 2013 Edwards Wildman kept on three of its eight qualifiers and two of them were female.

Eversheds LLP

The facts

Location: Birmingham, Cambridge, Cardiff, Leeds, London, Manchester, Newcastle, Nottingham, Ipswich, Scotland

Number of UK partners/solicitors: 280/1084

Total number of trainees: 52

Seats: 4x6 months

Alternative seats: overseas seats, secondments

Extras: pro bono – LawWorks, TrustLaw, Battersea Legal Advice Centre and others; language classes

On chambersstudent.co.uk...

How to get into Eversheds
Interview with head of lawyer development Ian Gascoigne
CSR at the firm

Ambitious, auspicious and growing by the day, Eversheds is a good shout for those crazy for cross-border work.

Eversheds state of mind

At just 23 years old Eversheds is a relative youngster in the legal market, but the UK unit is hardly a novice. The mega firm has over 40 offices worldwide and posted a whopping £376m in revenue alongside a record increase in net profit in 2012/13. That year also saw the firm open a brand spanking new Beijing base, nabbing energy specialist Ingrid Zhu-Clarke and top corporate partner Jay Ze (no relation) along the way. Things haven't been entirely rosy for Eversheds, however; in 2013 the firm closed its 29-strong Copenhagen base and announced impending redundancies for 116 lawyers and support staff – the firm's sixth round of lay-offs since September 2008. Unfortunate, though hardly unheard of in the current climate. As head of lawyer development Ian Gascoigne points out, *"it's always regrettable, but by taking action at an early stage we've made the impact as cushioned as possible."*

When it comes to the current atmosphere at the firm, one trainee noticed *"a strong sense of momentum at present. Our managing partner keeps us in the loop in terms of firm strategy, and all the changes feel well co-ordinated and communicated."* Many sources expressed confidence in the firm's growth over the years and *"focused"* approach going forward. *"There's a big international drive, with a special focus on the legal market in the Far East, and management is also trying to make sure our service is tip-top across the board in the UK."* According to Gascoigne, *"the underlying goal is to make Eversheds a global law firm that sets the standard for other firms. By 2015, when readers of the Chambers Student Guide will be ready to join, I hope we'll have more offices in a few more countries."*

Eversheds' main divisions are company commercial, litigation/dispute resolution, human resources and real estate. Commercial work is the firm's backbone, and it's none too shabby on that front – its corporate/M&A, capital markets and investment funds practices have all nabbed top-tier scores from *Chambers UK*. That said, Eversheds remains well regarded for its work across areas as varied as employment, education, parliamentary and pensions litigation. Check out our global directories to see the firm's rankings galore. London undoubtedly attracts the biggest matters, but trainees were keen to point out that the firm's regional offices are far from stagnant backwaters. For years now Eversheds has operated a canny policy of outsourcing London work to its smaller offices in order to offer attractive rates to clients, so it's not uncommon for regional lawyers to get to grips with weighty domestic matters and even some substantial international ones. Case in point: a partner in Cardiff recently led the way on Network Rail's high-value joint venture with Ballymore to establish a 200-home development in north London.

Training contracts are available in London, Birmingham, Manchester, Cardiff, Cambridge, Leeds, Newcastle and Nottingham. Trainees in the capital – the largest branch of the Eversheds family tree – get the lion's share of seats. Still, a variety of departments are up for grabs across the UK, with some of the regional offices offering stints in unique practices like education (Birmingham) and environment (Manchester).

A shed load of deals

Seat allocation goes as follows: a vacancy list is circulated each rotation, and trainees are asked to list their top three preferences. *"If you don't get what you wanted*

The True Picture

Chambers UK rankings

Administrative & Public Law	Investment Funds
Banking & Finance	Licensing
Banking Litigation	Local Government
Capital Markets	Media & Entertainment
Competition/European Law	Outsourcing
Construction	Parliamentary & Public
Consumer Finance	Affairs
Corporate Crime &	Pensions
Investigations	Planning
Corporate/M&A	Product Liability
Data Protection	Professional Discipline
Dispute Resolution	Professional Negligence
Education	Projects
Employment	Public International Law
Energy & Natural	Public Procurement
Resources	Real Estate
Environment	Restructuring/Insolvency
Financial Services	Retail
Health & Safety	Shipping
Healthcare	Social Housing
Information Technology	Tax
Insurance	Telecommunications
Intellectual Property	Transport

for your first two seats they try and make up for it in the third and fourth. Everyone's pretty sympathetic to HR as they have a pretty difficult job trying to place us all!" We heard some murmurs of discontent surrounding the process, but no sources were truly unhappy. Said one: *"At times placements can seem arbitrary, but it's worked out well for most."* It's also worth mentioning that trainees whose desired seats aren't available in their home office can apply to sit in that department elsewhere – we heard of London trainees taking seats in Manchester and Birmingham juniors sitting in London.

In 2013 a handful of overseas seats were available in Paris, Hong Kong, Shanghai and Abu Dhabi, with plans to offer places in Madrid and Singapore come autumn of that year. According to insiders, *"the Paris-based international arbitration seat is the hardest to get,"* though one reckoned *"that's a testament to the quality of work on offer out there."* Beyond that we heard *"there's a lot of scope for putting together your own ideas and suggesting a new secondment – the firm is very open to that."*

The firm handles commercial work across a spread of sectors, including retail, media, telecoms, health, education and sport. As such, a diverse array of clientele abounds, from Papa John's Pizza and Rolls-Royce to Lego, Heinz and John Lewis. The firm recently assisted GAME with its first international franchise and advised HSBC on a global outsourcing agreement that involved a whopping 55 jurisdictions. In London, the practice is split into sub-

teams like general commercial, outsourcing, and IT/tele-communications. *"We work on a lot of huge international contracts, but within those are smaller agreements that trainees get to manage on their own occasionally,"* said one trainee in the latter group. There's a big focus on renewable energy in Cardiff, where trainees are responsible for *"lots of research into industry rules and regulations. The legislation is so new that there's lots to find out."*

Eversheds' corporate department at large specialises in private equity and capital markets work, with trainees nationwide telling of project management tasks and *"regularly"* drafting ancillary documents, board minutes and verifications. A Manchester source who'd sat in corporate estimated that *"around 75% of juniors' work is high-volume, unsophisticated M&A matters, while the other 25% is top-shelf stuff like preparing companies for IPOs."* Mancunian lawyers recently advised on the £850m sale of Four Seasons Health Care to Terra Firma and assisted Matalyn Investments on its £14m disposal of Neales Waste Management. *"We do a lot of work with the big PLCs of the North West and some international names too."* Over in Birmingham, sources sang the praises of their *"highly regarded"* team, which acts for local private equity houses as well as some London-based names like Carlyle. *"The firm sent me on site visits during a sale I was working on, and I got to field loads of different queries by myself."* Cardiff lawyers handle a good deal of solar power deals and wind farm purchases, recently overseeing the £170m purchase of a straw-fired renewable energy plant in Lincolnshire. *"There are great opportunities for networking at renewable energy conferences and meeting clients."*

London's competition practice *"deals with a lot of large EU investigations into sanctions and exports control and also works with the Office of Fair Trading on price-fixing cases."* Over in the contentious arm of the department it's all about damage claims and *'dawn raid' investigations against cartels. There's quite a bit of corporate support work too."* Insiders agreed the seat offers *"excellent"* client contact and reported getting to grips with research, attendance notes and non-disclosure agreements on a day-to-day basis. The department regularly deals with *"very far-reaching"* and *"incredibly interesting"* matters.

The capital's financial services dispute resolution team wields an *"incredible client list"* that includes the likes of Barclays, UBS and Deutsche. Like all the big players, Eversheds has cashed in on the Lehman Brothers saga, recently assisting the German administrator of Lehman on claims totalling $1bn. *"The department seems terrifyingly technical at first, but you really do get into it,"* we heard. Trainees are typically tasked with drafting board minutes and ancillary documents, *"though you occasionally get the chance to advise big foreign banks on UK regulatory requirements. It's great to be trusted with something so important."*

Grabbing the Bullring by the horns

Along with corporate, real estate is a *"main pillar"* of the Birmingham office. The team recently advised Land Securities, the largest property company in the country, on its £144m acquisition of two massive multiplexes: the Printworks in Manchester and the Cornerhouse in Nottingham. Lawyers also played an important role in the £600m redevelopment of New Street Station – welcome news to anyone who's had the misfortune of catching a train there. Clients include both occupiers and developers, and Brum trainees are likely to get involved with Bullring-related work at some point as the firm regularly advises the mega shopping complex on leasing matters. *"We also work on applications to the Land Registry,"* a source reported. Juniors across the firm told of a bit of grunt work here and there but agreed a stint in real estate *"really stretches you and helps you grow as a trainee."*

Manchester's employment team – the biggest of the bunch – largely handles contentious work like discrimination cases. *"They throw you in at the deep end and expect you to keep on top of the work,"* according to our sources. *"The lawyers in the department do all their own advocacy, and trainees help with some of the initial instructions. I got to attend hearings, draft witness statements and deal with clients."* The office is also the only one to have an environment team, which has a particular focus on shale oil and gas in Europe. *"It's an extraordinarily complex area of law, real cutting-edge stuff, and involves a lot of EU legislation. Most of the work trainees do is research and answer ad hoc queries on specific issues."*

In Nottingham there's a big focus on IP and IT work. *"I got involved in writing cease and desist letters, doing the due diligence on patent and trade mark applications and looking out for infringements of our clients' brands,"* said one trainee. *"They're very good at dishing out responsibility on an individual basis if you show you're up to it."* While Eversheds has scaled down its Nottingham operation in recent years – already one of the smallest offices, the branch recently lost its real estate department to Birmingham – insiders nonetheless insisted *"we're not just a regional support outpost; lots of our clients are big international blue-chip names and have long-standing relationships with partners here."*

Eversheds, I will go with thee

Trainees firmwide agreed *"there certainly isn't a set mould for people here;"* still, most sources used the terms *"ambitious"* and *"driven"* to describe their colleagues. Considering Eversheds' huge international network and growing focus on cross-border work, we suspect language skills don't go amiss either.

Understandably hours vary between offices and departments, but it's fair to say a corporate seat demands the longest days and latest nights. One Cardiff source recalled *"a whole week of 3am finishes"* during their time in the department, while another in Manchester told us *"you can easily find yourself working until 10pm most days."* That said, there are plenty of other seats with a less taxing schedule. Final word goes to the numerous trainees who told us *"everyone still manages to have a life outside of the firm. If you've finished your work by 6pm, partners are good at telling you to take your foot off the gas."* On the training front we heard *"supervision varies among partners in terms of style but not quality. You tend to get really constructive feedback."*

Despite the upheaval accompanying the firm's rapid growth in recent years, inter-office ties are still strong at Eversheds. *"They've done a great job of bringing us all together and making the offices feel connected,"* said a Nottingham source. *"Last week I visited Birmingham and Manchester, and it was clear we're all part of the same Midlands team."* The firm-wide open-plan set-up also helps on the cohesion front. *"You can overhear all the office gossip."* Thanks to lawyers' constant proximity, the prevailing atmosphere at most offices is *"not too formal. Partners right down to deli staff all get along, and you don't get the feeling anyone's standing on ceremony."* The facilities in Cardiff score highly on the food front, owing to the *"really nice"* top-floor canteen, while the Manchester massive praised the *"huge corporate atrium"* in their building just off Oxford Road and Brum sources extolled their proximity to Victoria Square and canteen, *"which turns into a bar on Fridays."* The award for swankiest office definitely goes to London, which has a rooftop terrace, cafe, canteen and shower facilities.

"Your social life is as good as you want it to be," we were told. Most offices put on a fair smattering of departmental meals and drinks events, and there are football, netball and softball teams across the firm as well as the usual celebrations in the summer and at Christmas. London trainees told of trips to comedy clubs, bowling alleys and the zoo while the Brum cohort regularly attends drinks arranged by the Birmingham Solicitors Society. Meanwhile in Manchester it's all about Friday night drinks at the nearby Rain Bar and forays to Chester races. There's also quite a bit in the way of charity events – see our bonus feature online for more information.

And finally...

"We're not a one-size-fits-all kind of place; the trainees here come from a variety of unis and all have interesting stories to share." In 2013 the firm kept on 45 of its 55 qualifiers.

"Think about the broader picture of where a firm's work comes from. Be ready to get involved in marketing and business development – those things are increasingly important to law firms."

Trainee

Farrer & Co LLP

The facts

Location: London

Number of UK partners/solicitors: 77/143

Partners who trained at firm: 60%

Total number of trainees: 20

Seats: 6x4 months

Alternative seats: secondments

Extras: pro bono – Battersea Legal Advice Centre, LawWorks; language classes

On chambersstudent.co.uk...

How to get into Farrer & Co

Charles Dickens' lawyer

From its elegant townhouse in Lincoln's Inn Fields, this royally endorsed firm handles work for both corporate entities and private clients.

Pedant's corner

The substantial page on Farrer's website devoted to its past claims that 'Our history could fill a space a thousand times larger'. Since, at two million words, that would be longer than the Bible and the whole Harry Potter series combined, there may be a bit of exaggeration going on. Still, the Queen's solicitors have plenty to boast about, thanks to royal connections going back hundreds of years, famous clients including Charles Dickens and an only recently broken 230-year run of Farrers in the firm.

Top-ranked by *Chambers UK* for private client, agriculture, employment and education work, Farrer is also recognised in many other areas including family, corporate, IP and charities. Trainees were attracted by the firm's *"really unique work for higher education bodies, charities and museums,"* with *"slightly different and quirky"* cases making for *"really interesting questions of law."* Rather than being *"dependent on a hard corporate centre,"* business is driven by lots of cross-referrals between departments – especially from large charities with complex structures, and from relationships with private clients that have been developed over many years. Among the organisations that turn to Farrer for advice are the Bill & Melinda Gates Foundation, Save the Children, the British Library, the National Gallery, the Duchy of Cornwall and the Kennel Club.

Farrer's six-seat system requires trainees to choose an option from each of the private client, litigation, property and commercial practice areas, a *"wildcard"* seat, and then a final repeated seat which they will (hopefully) qualify into. Trainees praised the system as giving them *"that extra bit of wriggle room,"* and felt that Farrer makes seat

selection *"higher priority than anywhere else,"* giving due credit to trainee recruitment manager Donna Davies as someone *"willing to bash heads together so you get the seats you want."*

Go wild in the country

Private client work is *"at the heart of the firm,"* and thanks to a thriving practice stretching back hundreds of years, the department is seen as *"so established it's reassuring"* by its trainees, and presumably its clients too, who include old-money aristos as well as wealthy entrepreneurs. Cases range from the prosaic – acting for a *"family who had a lovely dog, when the man who lived next door decided it was dangerous"* – to an international fraud case which saw one trainee *"sent to Spain to search our client's house for documents"* following a court order. Working closely with high-profile individuals means that trainees need to be highly personable and in possession of a *"good bedside manner"* – maybe even literally, when visiting aged clients to *"draft wills and receive instructions."* Trainee tasks can be *"academically challenging,"* potentially involving *"trust structuring, tax planning and complex cross-jurisdictional issues."*

The property department is divided into commercial property, and estates and private property, which includes Farrer's leading agricultural estates and rural affairs team. The firm keeps up its royal connections through its work for the Duchy of Cornwall, the Prince of Wales's landowning giant and pre-eminent organic biscuit provider. Other clients include the Joseph Rowntree Housing Trust, Great Portland Estates and London Underground. Thanks to the team's work with major landowners, more standard work on tenancies, sales and leases is complemented by

The True Picture

Chambers UK rankings

Agriculture & Rural Affairs	Fraud
Charities	Intellectual Property
Corporate/M&A	Media & Entertainment
Defamation/Reputation	Partnership
Management	Private Client
Dispute Resolution	Real Estate
Education	Real Estate Finance
Employment	Sports Law
Family/Matrimonial	

more arcane and research-heavy cases, such as identifying the lawful owners of *"unregistered land – people skim over it at law school but actually there's quite a lot of it left!"* – or advising on the complex legislation governing mineral rights registration. One trainee had a *"day trip to the country,"* visiting the site of a disputed village green and interviewing local witnesses, while back in the office *"disposing of the property of people who've died without any heirs"* proved *"quite poignant."*

The soul of discretion

Farrer's media team parted ways with a major client, Rupert Murdoch's News Group, in the wake of the phone-hacking scandal – since then, trainees feel that *"the team is repositioning itself to do a lot more claimant work with high-profile individuals."* The growing media defamation practice offers fast-paced work *"representing individuals trying to get something defamatory taken off Twitter,"* or *"writing to Microsoft or Google or other blog providers"* to get libellous blogs removed, often within 24 hours. There's also *"pre-publication work checking through stories before they go to press"* for long-term clients including Bauer – the publisher of *Heat* and *Closer* and broadcaster of Magic FM. One source was *"dying to tell my friends about what I've been working on"* but in vain, as they have to remain tight-lipped. Trainees were particularly discreet about the firm's work in the field of super-injunctions: *"We have been at the forefront of the development of privacy law, but I can't talk about it any more,"* said one. The media team also works with Farrer's wide range of museum and gallery clients – including the Museum of London and the V&A, as they seek to put their content onto new media platforms and digital technologies. Recent cases have involved looking into legal deposit law for the British Library as part of its major database project of archived newspaper materials, and advising the Royal Collection on an app that provides a smart look at Leonardo da Vinci's anatomical drawings.

Chambers UK puts Farrer in the top five in the country for charities, singling out its work with those with *"more complex trading structures."* The group advises on the merger, rationalisation and restructuring of major charity clients, and also works with individuals just starting to set up their own charities and trusts. Farrer was recently involved in the unusual case of the acquisition of Wycombe Wanderers FC by its supporters' trust, while work for major educational institutions including Oxford University and Eton can throw up any number of unusual matters – maybe sorting out filming agreements with media companies wanting to do location filming, or maybe putting an end to a *"crazy person stalking a professor."*

As well as working for charities, the corporate department also handles mid-market M&A work for private companies and banks. A multi-jurisdictional deal saw one trainee unravelling a tangled web of *"who owned what"* in a £90m takeover of a Russian plc, while another ended up *"verifying all the documents for five hours with the trainee on the other side."* Trainees noted that although corporate is *"not as busy as it was five years ago, we've refocused – young entrepreneurs are the new target market"* – as demonstrated by the teams' recent £1.5m fundraising for the new online pocket money site PKTMNY.

Other seats include employment, banking and finance, family and general litigation. Insolvency is *"high-octane, a really enjoyable mix of transactional work, black-letter law and client contact."* IP handles *"really intellectual"* matters to do with patents as well as softer trade mark work, *"like what happens if a museum sees images of its prize painting being sold on a postcard outside."* Partners here *"use trainees really well: they'll involve you even if it's not time-effective to do so."* Although *"traditionally it hasn't trusted clients to give trainees supervision up to Farrer's standards,"* the firm has made a small range of *"really carefully picked"* secondments available, including ones at Oxford University and the Lawn Tennis Association.

Sources welcomed the absence of a *"breakneck working atmosphere,"* citing 9am to 6.30pm as the *"really reasonable for the City"* average, although hours will stretch longer at busy times. Trainees sit in open-plan offices, sharing a pod with a supervisor who *"acts as a shield to make sure you don't get too bogged down"* when receiving work from *"most people in the department."* Trainees do end up doing a lot of more mundane work such as bibling, but *"supervisors are careful to mix things up,"* and *"generally you get to work on very interesting things. There are lots of discrete bits of research, where you'll write a two or three-page memo on what you've found. There's a lot of all kinds of drafting."*

English heritage

Farrer's history made a real impression on the trainees – *"as a family name, going through generations, it really feels more personal than a bigger place that just has three random partners' names stuck together."* The firm sticks to *"some old-fashioned values – I know that could sound like a bad thing, but here it isn't,"* a trainee argued. *"There's a bit of integrity,"* seen in policies such as not overly aggressive billing for long-standing clients. Although *"we are traditional and that gives us a lot of character,"* trainees stressed that *"we're up to date: the reputation of being stuffy is quite untrue."* They highlighted the firm's work with entrepreneurs and its growing new media expertise.

Farrer has also had a reputation for being a bit posh – *"RollOnFriday says we've all got double-barrelled surnames."* Although trainees admitted that the firm is home to some *"rugby lads,"* and those with public school backgrounds, this aspect of the firm mustn't be overstated. The trainee group is not overloaded with Oxbridge candidates and we also chuckled at the anecdote of the trainee who *"once whipped by the office in red chinos"* only to be papped by a partner for the Sloane-baiting blog lookatmyfuckingredtrousers.blogspot.com (and presumably to the disappointment of the firm's client Boden, pre-eminent russet leg-wear supplier).

Forget soft skills, it's *"softly-softly skills"* that are *"extra-valued here,"* and a *"good friendly handshake"* is essential when it comes to dealing with high-profile private clients. *"I think they look for people who are quite personable and can be quite front-facing and deal with being with clients,"* one source declared. Interviewees had experienced Farrer's personable nature first-hand when applying to the firm. One source described the training contract interview: *"It was a genuine conversation with me as an individual – they'd read my application really closely. It felt really personal."* As a result, the firm brings in a select group of *"well-rounded"* people. *"Maybe because there's only ten of us in a year, there's no sense of oneupmanship. We're hard-working but not in an aggressive way,*

and everyone seems to rub along well. We've all become really good friends."*

The 17th century office at 66 Lincoln's Inn Fields is *"really old-school"* – there's no bold corporate logo emblazoned on the front of the building here, just the firm's name, rather worn, on the letter box. Trainees waxed lyrical about the Peacock Room, with its ornate moulded plaster ceiling, and suggested that clients even *"have some sort of reverence about the building, which makes them easier to advise."* The ancestral home has now been joined by a new office, *"a nice little three-minute walk across the Fields."* Sunny lunch breaks are enlivened by *"throwing a frisbee about"* in Lincoln's Inn Fields. On Friday, *"without fail, everyone gathers in the pub"* – generally the Olde White Horse – *"partners, trainees and associates all together: there's not the hierarchy you might expect, there's lots of joking."* The trainee revue at the firm's Christmas party pushes first-years into the limelight as they write and perform sketches satirising the partners – last year's offering, for example, sent up two finance partners in a rendition of Abba's 'Money Money Money'. Cricket and rugby are the most common sports, but there's also football on Thursdays, charity bike rides and easy access to the tennis courts in Lincoln's Inn Fields. At Farrer, *"people have a sense of community spirit"* – all employees are given a paid day off a year to spend doing something charitable.

Despite some *"rattling"* redundancies recently, particularly in the property department, trainees were confident about qualification. One loyal recruit felt that *"they'll go to hell and back to keep you: it's amazing, really, that they take that kind of chance on a piddly little 21-year-old."* Farrer's excellent retention record continued in 2013, when it held on to all nine of its qualifiers.

The True Picture

And finally...
It might be over 300 years old, but Farrer's efforts in the new media sphere show that when it comes to work, it keeps bang up to date.

Fisher Meredith LLP

The facts

Location: London, Richmond-upon-Thames
Number of UK partners/solicitors: 13/39
Total number of trainees: 9
Seats: 4x6 months
Alternative seats: occasional secondments
Extras: pro bono – Gaia Centre, UKLGIG

On chambersstudent.co.uk...

How to get into Fisher Meredith
Interview with managing partner Stephen
 Hewitt
More on seats

In light of ongoing government cuts, this firm is bringing its legal aid expertise to a broadened spectrum of clients.

Widening the net

Fisher Meredith has made a name for itself in the legal aid field and at any one point has a colourful array of cases in its docket, from human rights matters and family disputes to public law issues and criminal cases. The firm recently scored a payout for an East Londoner held unfairly at Heathrow by a customs official insisting – despite seeing his UK passport, birth certificate, bank statements and driving licence – that he was an illegal immigrant. Actions against the police also fall under FM's radar, be they false imprisonment charges or cases concerning injuries sustained during political demonstrations. Thanks to the South London firm's long history of providing assistance to those with limited resources, FM has developed *"particular expertise in dealing with difficult cases. Clients come to us because of our reputation, and many have problems that have proved challenging to other firms."*

Unfortunately, the government's ongoing £220m cost-cutting exercise – which entails significant chops to government-assisted legal representation – means *"legal aid will form an [increasingly] smaller part of what we do,"* according to managing partner Stephen Hewitt, who estimates such cases will go from comprising half of FM's workload to accounting for *"around a third of what we do in 18 months' time."* While civil actions against the police and community care, landlord/tenant and court of protection cases are largely safe from the cuts, legal aid-funded family and education matters have *"effectively gone out of scope"* for the firm, insiders noted sadly. That said, FM lawyers are not taking the changes lying down. *"We're quite a politically aware and socially active bunch, and have been turning out for legal aid protests lately."* Still, Hewitt's hint that future applicants will need to *"find it*

just as easy speaking to a company director as to a vulnerable person" suggests the tides are indeed turning.

At the time of our calls the firm was entering a *"transitional phase,"* implementing a series of marketing initiatives in the hopes of luring in more private and commercial clients. First up: a rebranding exercise, complete with a new website designed *"to differentiate ourselves from the rest of the mid-sized market,"* says Hewitt. *"Our website is our online shop front. We want to show we're a City-quality firm that offers the level of fees you'd associate with a mid-sized provincial firm."*

In safe hands

Trainees have quarterly meetings with HR to find out which seat options will be available in coming rotations, after which they note down three preferences along with the reasons why they're interested in particular departments. Stints are typically up for grabs in police and prison law, housing, children, dispute resolution, immigration and public services law (PSL). *"We usually work it out among ourselves to decide who's going to apply where,"* sources said, mentioning it's the norm for second-years to get priority.

Children cases are largely confidential, but some are considered grave enough miscarriages of justice to be in the public interest, like that of Ben Butler, a young father the firm recently helped exonerate following false accusations of child abuse. Much of the department's work involves representing parents during care proceedings, working out contacts and residence for children of divorced parents and handling domestic violence cases, all of which *"can be a bit scary. You have to learn how to*

Chambers UK rankings

Civil Liberties & Human	Immigration
Rights	Police Law
Court of Protection	Social Housing
Family/Matrimonial	

deal with awkward questions and manage clients' expectations without promising them the world." Trainees' supervisors determine their specific workload, though "you get to manage your own cases whether you're a first or fourth-seater." Because there's no administrative support in the department, trainees often "end up doing a lot of admin" on top of tasks like meeting with clients and reading through reports. Luckily, there are plenty of opportunities for advocacy experience – one of our sources told of going before a district judge to get a case transferred and, on another occasion, to apply for non-molestation orders. The majority of matters are handled in the magistrates' courts, but a few – such as non-accidental injury cases – make it to the High Court.

The firm recently rechristened its housing team in an effort to reflect an anticipated shift in workload: "We now refer to the department as landlord and tenant as we're trying to attract more work from private landlords." Indeed, the firm has seen an uptick in the number of foreign clients investing in residential property, though the team still spends most of its time acting for tenants in housing disputes against social landlords. "It's a good seat for learning the tactics of defending a weak position," said one trainee, explaining that "you have to find imaginative ways to explain why someone hasn't paid their rent, often by delving into their personal history and medical reports. Some clients are very vulnerable, so it's important to build up a really good rapport with them and make sure they understand what's going on." Others told of attending possession hearings, meeting clients and making applications for funding. "You're down at Lambeth County Court all the time, supporting counsel or the client." For most, saving tenants from evictions or helping those who are homeless proves "very rewarding," but insiders took care to point out the job is "a bit like being a doctor – you kind of have to have a calling to do it in the long run."

Won't somebody please think of the children?

The PSL department team is split into two branches. The first revolves around community care work, with lawyers handling "challenging, wide-ranging issues" related to the Children Act – for example, supporting children of parents with no recourse to public funds, working with child asylum seekers and "getting care plans put in place for disabled children." Like much of the work FM does, "it can get quite tough emotionally as you're helping re-

ally vulnerable and sometimes neglected individuals, but it's gratifying as well – you can see the direct results." For instance, one interviewee triumphantly told of getting a mother and disabled child off the streets within the day. Most cases are settled with local authorities, but occasionally litigation arises, particularly when it comes to age assessment cases for young immigrants. "Science can only give you a window of five years, so in that case an independent social worker comes in to make an assessment and a judge decides." The team also handles education matters like plagiarism claims, though insiders anticipate a drop-off in such cases in the face of recent legal aid cuts. "It's a shame, and stupid really because we have all this expertise which will go to waste."

The other PSL branch works primarily on Court of Protection matters – again, an area that's had its funding ring-fenced. "We handle work on behalf of people who lack the capacity to make their own decisions – they often have very little understanding of what the case is and who we are." As such, the matters at hand are often emotionally taxing, like that of a married couple in their eighties who were separated after one partner's dementia progressed. There's also quite a bit of work for parents and siblings of disabled people who are concerned about their relatives' treatment in local authority homes. "We have to go through medical, educational and social records, and often visit clients in residential homes. It's a very collaborative kind of law – there's generally a lot of back and forth."

Soul food

Unlike City firms, Fisher Meredith's South London office "doesn't blow you away with how shiny it is. The space is fine, but sometimes you think 'I wish I had a better computer'." One trainee described Kennington as "not the most cosmopolitan" of neighbourhoods, but we think they must just have meant it's not the best place to slurp pink cocktails – after all, the area is very multicultural. It's also "great transport-wise" and handily positioned for court attendances. What's more, FM lawyers are spared the soulless parade of Pret a Mangers and Eats that plague the Square Mile. "At lunch everybody heads to the park nearby or to the nice little shops and cafes." A lot of trainees take advantage by renting nearby and walking or cycling to work. "We're a big firm of cyclists – there's a lot of bike talk going on." The firm's Richmond office is a small, private client operation and doesn't host trainees, although a seat there may be available on an ad hoc basis.

Trainees summed up FM's atmosphere as follows: "This is the kind of place where you can speak up and put your view across. It's relaxed in terms of hierarchy, and people get on across all levels." Rather unusually the firm has more women than men – according to Hewitt two-thirds of solicitors are women, plus three of FM's five equity partners and its senior partner. Social offerings usually take on a down-to-earth feel, with lawyers occasionally descending on a meeting room for studenty-sounding *"beer and pizza nights"* and regularly heading out to the pub, where *"there's quite often a contingent present until closing time."* The Christmas party – a dinner and disco do held last year in a function room at local cricket ground The Oval – also makes for *"a good bash,"* we heard.

Many in the current cohort have previous careers or experience as paralegals; it's *"rare to come here straight from uni."* Dealing with vulnerable clients can be gruel-ling business, but it's a challenge that future FM trainees need to be committed to. *"People here are very dedicated and able, which is something they look for. Most could get jobs elsewhere with fewer headaches and better pay, but they've chosen to work here."* When it comes to qualification, we heard the firm *"tries to give you a good idea of your chances quite far in advance"* and *"offers support throughout the process."* In 2013 the firm retained just one if its four qualifiers – legal aid cuts are likely affecting the firm's ability to offer NQ positions.

And finally...

The general attitude towards salaries, which start at £21,000?
"We've all spent too long at uni and built up too much debt to be paid what we're paid, but the amount isn't unreasonable given the difficulties the firm faces from government cuts."

Foot Anstey LLP

The facts

Location: Bristol, Exeter, Plymouth, Taunton, Truro
Number of UK partners/solicitors: 51/63
Total number of trainees: 13
Seats: 4x6 months
Alternative seats: secondments

On chambersstudent.co.uk...

How to get into Foot Anstey
One foot in the West Country

Don't go mistaking Foot Anstey for a quiet backwater firm in the picturesque South West; this is a firm with ambition and the drive to compete for large national and international clients...

Footprint stamping

Foot Anstey's roots can be traced back to the wonderfully named Isaac Foot, who together with his pal Edgar Bowden set up the Plymouth-based Foot and Bowden in 1903. Today, the firm has grown to house nearly 200 lawyers, in offices which span all the hotspots in the South West: Bristol, Exeter, Plymouth, Taunton and Truro. Most of Foot Anstey's growth has occurred in the last decade, and the firm virtually doubled in size during the latter half of it, thanks to a string of mergers and lateral hires, making it the biggest firm in the region. Core practice areas include corporate, commercial, real estate, employment and dispute resolution, and *Chambers UK* ranks each of these highly in the region. The firm's excellent clinical negligence and personal injury practices shouldn't be forgotten either, as Foot Anstey is among the largest claimant-focused practices in the South West. Sectors specialisms are broad, and cover areas such as healthcare; media; financial services; agriculture; energy and infrastructure; and retail and leisure. Clients are equally diverse, and range from big names like Lloyds TSB, Odeon Cinemas and the Royal Shakespeare Company, to more local entities like the Eden Project and Cornish Sea Salt.

Trainees had recently attended a strategy meeting and had been privy to *"the new three-year plan."* According to our sources, the aim is still very much the same as it has been in previous years – to be *"the premier law firm in the South West"* – but in the coming years the firm wants to *"increase contact with big clients and take on a lot of additional work: we are affordable and offer the same quality as the bigger firms who charge much more."* The intention is *"not to move away from our South West cli-* ents," but instead to push the firm further as a commercial contender, in an attempt to pick up more national and international clients: *"We are definitely a commercial firm – if you want to do family this is not necessarily the firm for you. Corporate, commercial and commercial property are all growing and that is very much the direction the firm is headed in."* This direction can be gleaned quite clearly in the firm's decision to transfer its non-core childcare teams to three smaller firms in the South West.

Bristol was cited as an ever important office for Foot Anstey, and was viewed as a crucial link to those bigger clients that the firm is seeking: *"They tend to like firms that can service them from a Bristol base."* With one of the biggest economies outside of London, Bristol is certainly a good location to be in right now, and Foot Anstey's move there in 2011 looks like it is paying off: the office is growing rapidly, and the firm has managed to pinch lawyers from Bristol heavyweight Burges Salmon (including Islamic finance partner Imam Qazi). The commercial team there, in particular, *"is very exciting – it's getting more and more established, and the various subteams are really finding their feet."*

Touring the West Country

Second-years get preference when it comes to seat allocation, and, of course, it all depends on good ol' business need as well, but trainees do get to list their top three choices. *"Generally if you don't get your preference in your first seat that's quite normal,"* said one source, who recommended before subsequent rotations *"speaking to a fee earner in a specific department that you are interested*

Chambers UK rankings

Agriculture & Rural Affairs	Dispute Resolution
Banking & Finance	Education
Banking Litigation	Employment
Charities	Family/Matrimonial
Clinical Negligence	Information Technology
Construction	Intellectual Property
Corporate/M&A	Licensing
Court of Protection	Personal Injury
Crime	Real Estate
Defamation/Reputation	Real Estate Litigation
Management	Tax

in. Discuss it with them and they will often be supportive and speak to HR: it's in their interest to get a trainee who is interested in their area." Trainees also usually move around at least two of the Foot Anstey offices throughout their training contract: "It's encouraged but not essential. It's good to get a broader experience and meet people across the different offices. Sometimes there can be a bit of a commute, but the firm never made me do it!" Ultimately, sources felt that the future benefit of getting their face known across the network of offices outweighed the potential fatigue of a longer commute. Common seats this year included commercial property and clinical negligence, but our sources had also completed seats in the corporate, commercial, dispute resolution and employment teams. Secondment opportunities also crop up from time to time, and around a quarter of the current intake had been able to sit in-house with a client.

Corporate lawyers have been busy seeking out those more national and international clients – like the International Finance Corporation and UBM – but still cater for more local outfits like Axminster Power Tools. Offices have varying client bases, so, for example, Exeter draws in a number of healthcare clients, while Bristol and Plymouth have more media-related clients. Trainees here worked on deals both big and small, and, as you might expect, were able to "get more exposure assisting on the smaller sale of a company – on the larger deal you do feel lower in the pecking order." Some enjoyed their corporate seat because of "the combination of media elements and acquisitions," and were able to get involved in the sale and purchase of some famous brands. UBM, a multinational media company, is now a top ten client for Foot Anstey and recently corporate lawyers helped the company sell some of its magazine titles and associated websites (including that publication we all like to keep up to date with, the Farmers Guardian) to a new business, Briefing Media.

The media influence continues in the firm's commercial department, which is particularly thriving: "It's growing all the time, and over the last year it has tripled in size – it's a big focus for the firm and great to be a part of."

Clients include Silvergate Media, Which?, Johnston Press and Mama Group. One interviewee had spent "most of the time working with a large cinema chain," but commented on the mix of IP and IT work as well, which can have more of an international dimension. Others had really got their teeth stuck into the licensing and gaming side of things, especially in relation to mobile phone apps: "We work with clients who are developing certain products and we help to bring them to market and make sure that they comply with the various regulations – it's interesting stuff." Lawyers here advised Betfuse/Social Formats on regulatory issues surrounding the Gambling Act, in the run up to the launch of a new social media-based product. Overall, there's "good, detailed work" on offer, and trainees had helped to draft terms and conditions for cookie policies, as well as "amendments to a contract worth around £80m, between a public body and a private sector company."

Foot in the door

When it comes to commercial real estate, it's mostly "commercial, but there is the odd residential piece every now and again, which can be enjoyable because as a trainee you get to run it with supervision and make the key decisions." On the more commercial side, trainees were "not left to sink or swim, but had supervision when needed." Sources had been able to work with different fee earners, and had encountered matters which touched upon the agricultural, leisure and retail spheres. Santander is a big client, and one team acted on behalf of the bank during the £5.1m refinancing of a mixed retail and leisure scheme, geared toward rejuvenating the Eversham County Shopping Centre.

Those who had spent this seat in Bristol had been able to work for the "new Islamic finance department" there, and said that it was "great to be involved in an area of work that is not commonly found outside of London." Trainees "assisted on some key documents in relation to a property development which was subject to Shari'a law – it was a big deal and took up most of the six months, but it was good to work on something with an international focus." One such deal involved representing 90 North Real Estate Partners during the £42m acquisition of the Parham Road student village in Canterbury: the investors were from Kuwait, and lawyers had to set up a Shari'a-compliant investment structure and profit rate swap.

What trainees get up to in clinical negligence depends on the office. For example, "Taunton specialises in still births" while in Exeter there's "wide variety, including brain injury claims, misdiagnosis of cancer, and child abuse claims." Sometimes the "cases go on for so long that you only tend to touch one aspect of it," but still sources felt that the responsibility levels were good. Typical tasks might include applying to a patient's GP or hospital in order to obtain medical records, "to put together a picture of what a client's treatment should have been, and whether that path was followed or not." Trainees also take witness statements, contact medical experts, help to assess costs and draft instructions to counsel. It can be a tough seat emotionally, but sources did say that *"you can distance yourself from it – it's funny that you can do that but at the end of the day you know and are driven by the fact that you are helping someone with a severe disability get money, so that they can have a better quality of life."*

Trainees said that the formal training had *"come as a surprise"* to them, precisely because of the lack of it: *"I was expecting to turn up into each new department and have this very structured training at the beginning, but actually you just muck in with the existing team members and pick up a lot of knowledge on the job."* It's a system that works well, and trainees liked it because of the responsiveness of those around them – *"you sit in open plan offices, so when you have a question you just ask it: that's the kind of training that happens here."* This more informal mentoring is complemented by monthly departmental training sessions, which are designed for lawyers at all levels, and are usually delivered via video-conferences across offices. There's a similarly relaxed stance when it comes to feedback, and each supervisor has their own style (some do mid-seat reviews, some don't; some have fortnightly 'catch up' sessions) – but all trainees do get an end of seat review, and interviewees felt that their supervisors had made the effort *"to build up a good relationship"* throughout the seats.

Devon is a place on Earth

Given that you're quite likely to spend time in various offices if you join this firm, here's a quick run down of what they're like: Plymouth was seen as *"the best office,"* because it *"looks impressive"* and has *"excellent views over Sutton Harbour – you can sit there and look at the sea and yachts."* Taunton, on the other hand, isn't quite as idyllic, as it overlooks that beautiful pathway to the South West, the M5... Nonetheless there's a *"lovely atmosphere"* and it is *"convenient in terms of commuting, but if you want to go anywhere the only option really is the petrol station."* The Exeter office is *"bigger, quieter, not as modern and has more of a corporate feel to it,"* but it's based in Southernhay, close to the cathedral green, which makes a great place to eat lunch and is very close to the city centre. Truro is a small but *"really modern office, which overlooks the river,"* while Bristol has grown significantly, *"from seven to 50 people in 12 months,"* and is based close to Temple Meads station, along with a host of other firms.

The offices feel *"fairly integrated,"* and sources elaborated by saying that *"there will always be a geographical sense of separation, especially between places like Bristol and Truro, but also the kinds of clients we act for in different departments and offices does change, so that the real*

estate team in one office may pick different kinds of work from another." However, some departments, like clinical negligence, hold training days which bring everyone together in one office, and trainees also pointed out that *"it's not just the trainees that move around the offices: there are a lot of hot desks and people jumping around all the time."* In the end, *"every office has a different feel to it, but they don't form cliques or feel too separated."*

Lifestyle (for a while)

Culturally, it's *"a very pleasant place to be,"* and trainees especially enjoy the clear *"first name policy"* that is in place. *"It helps to get rid of those first nerves, and there's no confusion over what you call people – you just go straight in there with the first name."* The small intake of trainees means that *"people do know who you are, and you're treated by the fee earners as someone who can actually help, rather than just someone to do all the dogsbody work."*

Sources also loved the fact that they get a 'lifestyle hour' to take off each week, and said that *"it's really useful if you want to go and meet friends, come in a bit later, or do some Christmas shopping,"* but qualified this by adding that they wouldn't use it if they were too busy. Lifestyle hours aside, trainees were keen to correct what they saw was a misconception about Foot Anstey: that the firm is just a lackadaisical, rolling-around-the-idyllic-sunlit-moors-instead-of-working-hard kind of place. Yes there's a lifestyle hour, but trainees did not feel that this firm was necessarily a 'lifestyle' one: *"There's an emphasis on progression here, and a focus on being commercial and client-driven – it's hard work, and you get rewarded for that."*

Others rolled out the *"work hard, play hard"* description (that old chestnut), but it certainly sounds as if there's a good social scene at Foot Anstey. Each office has an annual 'flagship event' – Bristol's was held in the Zoo, for example – and there's a Christmas party which brings all of the offices together, although this may be shifting to a summer party to *"make the most of a great South West outdoor event"* (weather permitting). Departments were described as friendly and meet up for team drinks and lunches as and when the time crops up. The trainees do have a social budget, and they seem to have overcome *"the problematic side of having trainees spread out in different offices"* quite well. Most trainees base themselves in Exeter, which tends to form a *"central point to meet up more informally, and go to a barbecue at someone's house."* Trainees are often heavily involved in the firm's charity work and organise events. This year's charities are AGE UK and the Dame Hannah Rogers Trust, and we were impressed by the array of events that have been held (or are in the pipeline), all in the name of charity fund-raising: space hop races, 10k runs, abseiling competitions, quiz nights, auctions, treks across Dartmoor, camping out on roofs...

While quite a few interviewees had roots in the South West, there were also those that didn't, and they said that *"there isn't a need for you to already be based in the region – we get applications from people all over the country – but what they want to see is a commitment to the region. If you're a 'London person' that just wants to come here, get a training contract and leave again, well that won't go down so well. They want people to get involved, take responsibility and help to push the firm forward."*

Qualification preferences shift with each intake, and *"last year a number of trainees wanted to qualify into clinical negligence – this year there has been more of a focus on commercial."* The process itself was described as *"transparent and structured,"* and after a jobs list is released, trainees have about a month to decide what positions they would like to apply for, before being interviewed. Sources felt confident that the firm was trying its best to keep them: *"There are five trainees. And they've made five jobs in different practice areas. They are keen."* In 2013, all five of the firm's qualifiers were kept on.

And finally...

Trainees were confident that good things were on the horizon for this firm, so if the chance to do some quality work while moving around a few locations in the South West appeals, then definitely give Foot Anstey a try.

Forbes

The facts

Location: Blackburn, Preston, Chorley, Accrington, Manchester, Leeds
Number of UK partners/solicitors: 36/63
Partners who trained at firm: 33%
Total number of trainees: 8
Seats: 4x6 months
Alternative seats: secondments
Extras: pro bono – legal advice clinics in Blackburn, Preston, Chorley and Accrington

On chambersstudent.co.uk...
How to get into Forbes
Lancashire life

Blackburn born and bred, this buzzing firm offers top-quality work and training with a regional feel.

North by Northwest

Proud of its North-Western roots, Forbes has grown its original Blackburn office into three branches in the town, as well as six further offshoots in the North. The firm's excellent local reputation has been confirmed by *Chambers UK* rankings, which lists its sizeable crime department among the top five in the North West, alongside a respectable showing in dispute resolution and a growing prominence in social housing.

Regional links were generally key to both encountering and selecting the firm: as one trainee said, *"I'm from the North West so Forbes was the obvious choice for me."* The firm's wide range of practice areas relative to its size offers further incentive. *"A real strength of Forbes,"* declared one source, *"is that you get experience of private client and commercial."* The spectrum of work available ranges from traditional high-street fare such as conveyancing and personal injury right up to commercial work with major clients such as Blackburn Rovers, Liverpool and Manchester United football clubs, supermarket chains The Co-operative and Asda, and a range of local and national authorities.

The four trainees taken on each year complete four seats of six months each, the first of which is assigned by the firm. The options at Forbes are: crime, family, personal injury, insurance, commercial property, employment, business law, commercial litigation, housing litigation, domestic conveyancing, and wills and probate. Since the different offices each have their own specialisations, *"expect to move around."* Blackburn is the heart of the firm and does the widest range of work, and Preston comes next in terms of number of lawyers. Chorley (crime and

family), Accrington (crime and PI/clin neg) Leeds and Manchester (both insurance only) are all relatively small operations, though trainees do spend seats there. Although Forbes' offices are spread over a wide base, the firm makes an effort to get everyone together – *"even though we're far away, we still feel like we're part of Forbes."* The seat allocation process is straightforward. *"They ask you what you'd like to try next,"* but business needs and *"what they think might be good for you"* are taken into account as well.

Although business law is a popular choice among this year's batch of recruits, *"all the people who wanted to do it have had the opportunity – it's expanding so there'll be even more opportunities in the future."* Work undertaken involves both litigation, and advising on *"day-to-day running"* of matters for long-term clients from *"Premiership football clubs and partnerships, all the way down to sole traders who are just starting up."* In the Leeds and Manchester offices, there's the opportunity to do secondments for a few days a week at major clients.

Crime and fun-ishment

In the last couple of years, Forbes trainees seem to have been more interested in business law than the firm's excellent criminal practice. It's fair enough: you have to be a certain type of person to handle this area of law. Forbes takes on the real gritty stuff down in the dark corners of the local community. One source described going to prison *"on my own"* during the seat, and meeting some *"tough clients,"* although there was *"always someone as back-up."* Trainees get to grips with a wide range of duties, including initial instructions after arrest and liaising with the Crown Prosecution Service. The option to do a

Chambers UK rankings

Crime	Real Estate Litigation
Dispute Resolution	Social Housing
Local Government	

Crown Court seat gives those with a special interest in qualifying into criminal law the option to work on more serious cases, such as murder, rape and robbery. For those whose love of crime doesn't stop at five o'clock, Forbes also offers the chance to complete the Police Station Accreditation Course, which enables trainees to qualify as a police station representative, advising and assisting detainees in their spare time at evenings and weekends.

Trainees often sit with partners, meaning that *"rather than sitting at your desk thinking, 'Can I go and ask about this?' you just chirp up and ask for help."* The nine different offices make for real diversity of experience during the course of the training contract, but a common theme was that trainees were particularly impressed with *"how much free rein they give you – they'll build you up slowly, but they do trust you very quickly."* Sources described a *"nurturing"* atmosphere where there's *"no sense that the trainees are competing with each other,"* which they perceived as a contrast to the more cut-throat nature of London firms.

Although there are higher salaries around, trainees seem to view the pay as a fair trade-off for a *"better work/life balance."* With hours not stretching far past 9am to 5pm, *"you can still have a life outside work, and keep up with family commitments,"* and it might be hard to overburden yourself, even if you want to: *"If bosses see you with a file in your hand on Friday they'll say, 'No, put that back, don't do that over the weekend!'"*

Alley pally

Forbes has deep roots in the North West and as such it is very involved in the local community. Among other worthy projects, it offers twelve-month apprenticeships and training in office skills to local young people. Trainees saw charitable activity as a good way of meeting people from across the firm – we heard about mock trials in schools, a ten-strong firewalk to raise funds for a local youth club and sponsorship of local darts champion Fred Carter – nicknamed the Jolly Green Giant – to compete in the Isle of Man Championships. The investment in the areas reaps dividends too: *"It attracts a lot of clients."*

Reflecting Forbes's sporty outlook, one trainee boasted that *"we're infamous for our bowling."* Alley socials include supervisors, mentors and two intakes worth of future trainees, so they'll know *"few friendly faces"* by the time they arrive. The whole-firm Christmas party at Ewood Park, Blackburn Rovers' stadium, was fondly remembered: *"We finished at noon that day, the firm put on a minibus over for us, then a free bar, buffet and disco."* Should you need further convincing of Forbes' frivolous side, head to its website and check out the personal profiles of its lawyers to discover their fantasy dinner party guests, revealing dream careers (we learn that joint managing partner Winston Hood aspires to be masseur to the Dallas Cowboys Cheerleaders) and most embarrassing moments – take as awful warnings the stories of the lawyer whose skirt fell apart in court and the one who crashed the firm's car into a lamp post. And props to the partner who answered: *"Being mistaken for my wife's father."*

Trainees all emphasised the importance of being *"down to earth,"* and local connections are an advantage – as one source pointed out, *"the shared background really helps you relate to your clients. Maybe it's the Northern grit that means people here have the same outlook."* Despite a challenging climate for high-street law, there's a real sense of optimism among trainees for the firm's future – *"it has really diversified a lot,"* said one. *"In family we're moving to more fixed-fee work to combat legal aid cuts, and the commercial side is definitely coming through now."*

And finally...

If you're keen to find a friendly North West firm with a good work/life balance, there's a sporting chance Forbes is right for you. In 2013, all four qualifiers were welcomed into the Forbes family.

Gateley

The facts

Location: Birmingham, Nottingham, Leicester, London, Manchester, Leeds, Scotland

Number of UK partners/solicitors: 150/244

Total number of trainees: 30

Seats: 4x6 months

Alternative seats: none

On chambersstudent.co.uk

How to get into Gateley

A history of mergers

Despite a push into the top 50, Gateley is sticking closely to its Midlands roots.

Father and son

Geographically speaking, Gateley is a somewhat unusual firm. Formed by the merger of Scotland's Henderson Boyd Jackson and Birmingham's Stephen Gateley & Sons, it has masses of lawyers both north and south of the Scots-English border, as well as a small outpost in Dubai. Birmingham, Edinburgh and Manchester are the three largest offices. The last of these grew substantially with the arrival of a host of commercial lawyers from defunct firm Halliwells in 2010. Glasgow, Leicester, Nottingham, London and Leeds complete the picture – the final one of those is the latest addition to the Gateley family, having been opened in 2012.

The firm picks up sturdy *Chambers UK* rankings across the board, with recognition mostly in the mid-market. Gateley plays to different strengths in each of its localities: its tax practice comes top of the market in Birmingham, for example, and Manchester has a strong IP/IT group.

There's a reasonably structured frame to Gateley's training contract. Trainees must stop off in corporate, real estate and a contentious seat, leaving them one *"open choice"* from the remaining departments offered. *"We list three preferences and HR do the rest,"* reported one trainee. Employment and commercial are always popular choices, and there are ad hoc opportunities for client secondments. Birmingham and Manchester both have around the same number of trainees (nine apiece at the time of our calls), while London has five, Leicester three and Nottingham two. Unsurprisingly, there are fewer seat options in smaller offices like Leicester and Nottingham. Trainees can request to do seats in other offices, but *"we're advised to*

be realistic. If we're assigned to a specific office, the feeling is that we're an asset which belongs to that location."

Mid-market Marmite

Corporate accounts for the largest proportion of Gateley's practice at just under a quarter. Its staple is in mid-market deals – think multimillions rather than billions – such as Gazprom's £13.5m disposal of its subsidiary Gazprom Global Energy. The team is well regarded in Manchester and Birmingham and comes top of the *Chambers UK* charts in Leicester. Gateley trainees find corporate *"a bit of a Marmite experience."* One said: *"Day to day, you're not really dealing with the law – you're helping businesses. The work is practical because it's commercial – and you're often under pressure."* Another interviewee had a somewhat different experience. *"I spent my time trying to get my head around what it was that we were doing! I was working on paying off a director's loan, but there was no actual loan... That's when it got complicated."*

Trainees who work in corporate during busier periods get the *"badge of honour"* of doing heavy hours, while those who spend time there when it's quieter *"get more supervision on the meatier assignments – the busier partners get, the less time they have to spend with you."* Despite this, trainees assured us that *"supervisors make sure you get a variety of work: shareholder agreements, due diligence and post-completion tasks are all standard fare."* The corporate group is known for its camaraderie, propelled by frequent client events. *"You're often out and about twice a week – that was probably my favourite part of spending time in corporate!"*

273

Chambers UK rankings

Banking & Finance	Private Client
Construction	Real Estate
Corporate/M&A	Real Estate Litigation
Dispute Resolution	Restructuring/Insolvency
Employment	Shipping
Family/Matrimonial	Social Housing
Intellectual Property	Tax
Pensions	Transport
Planning	

Trainees can also fulfil the requirement to do a corporate seat by spending time in banking – the team is well regarded in the Birmingham and Nottingham areas. It acts for all the major players: Lloyds, HSBC, RBS and Santander. For trainees, there's the opportunity for crossover with real estate finance: *"You work closely with the property team, which is great for honing your skills in that area too."* The team recently represented Birmingham-native property manager Hortons when it secured a £30m finance package from Sweden's Handelsbanken. Tasks range from *"registering securities at Companies House and drafting board minutes"* right through to *"drafting facility agreements and security documents for real estate transactions."*

Commercial dispute resolution and corporate recovery are the main contentious seats; other options include employment, property litigation or construction litigation. CDR offers work on *"shareholder, contentious probate, claimant professional negligence and fraud disputes."* The latter is an area that's grown a lot recently. For example, the firm has been acting in a fraud dispute for a charity founded to regenerate Nechells Baths in Birmingham. Suspicions were raised when £1.2m worth of funds appeared to have gone missing – during a period when the charity was chaired by a member of clergy no less! *"It's a really lively, busy team,"* trainees told us of their time in CDR. *"Each office acts for a number of household names and international clients, but trainees are also given responsibilities on smaller claims – things like boundary disputes, smaller professional negligence claims and contract litigation."*

The employment department acts for businesses from many sectors, most notably manufacturing (Tyrrells Crisps), retail (discount bookstore The Works) and telecoms. Trainees enjoy the contentious/non-contentious mix – there's a lot of corporate support work like *"compromise agreements, social media policies, drafting employment handbooks and extra stuff like running client seminars."* Over on the litigious side, tribunal work *"will always be the juicy part."* Trainees frequently get to take notes while taking in any drama that ensues. *"I saw one case recently where the claimant was obviously lying and*

the judge saw right through it – it's great that a judge can do that as it really reaffirms my faith in the system."* The Leicester and Nottingham offices run a joint employment seat, and the trainee travels between offices. Solicitors in the East Midlands team *"do their own advocacy, which is great to watch."* Ringside seats aside, trainees reckon they get to do *"nearly everything"* when it comes to employment disputes. *"You can be as involved with the nitty-gritty of claims as you want,"* proffered one. *"I've drafted claims forms and responses, instructions to counsel and witness statements, and been to client meetings."*

High flyers

In Birmingham the real estate team is split into residential development, commercial real estate and retail. In some locations, a trainee will devote time to planning and property finance too. The residential team acts for many of the major national housebuilders – Taylor Wimpey, Barratt Homes, Bellway – and deals with the acquisition of vast areas of land. *"It can be hard to pass parts of these huge matters down to trainees,"* sources admitted, *"but if there's interesting stuff going on – like advising farmers on grazing or cropping licences – they make sure we get to see it."* Over in the commercial group, the team recently acted for Bloc Hotels on its acquisition of a swanky property at Gatwick's South Terminal. There are always smaller matters being dealt with too, so trainees *"run their own files for smaller clients and get to deal with issues directly like a proper solicitor."*

Gateley trainees *"aren't easily phased by anything. We're a bunch of people who can approach strangers and have a perfectly decent conversation. If we are phased by something, we don't show it readily."* To this end, sources agree that *"everyone here has something else going on – either a previous career or a big outside interest."* Birmingham trainees told us that *"most of the group here aren't from the local area, which is unusual for a regional law firm. Recruiters evidently look at what each individual can bring to the table and approach recruitment nationally – we're all seen as part of the same firm."*

Trainee sources felt this idea carried fully through into the working ethos of the whole of Gateley. *"When you're applying for training contracts you quickly realise there are two types of firm: firms that look for blank canvasses to paint their image onto, and firms that are interested in you for how your particular personality can be utilised for their business. Gateley is the latter – you could tell on the assessment days that they really wanted to hear what you had to say."* Day to day this ethos equates to *"being able to speak to anyone and always feeling part of the team."* One trainee believed: *"It's almost like being part of a family – which is a bit embarrassing to say. But we're down to earth and socially very interesting. There's always a lot happening."*

The True Picture

We asked a hundred people to name something associated with Gateley...

Here's one interviewee's view on the support they received from colleagues: *"The firm assumes that if you're intelligent enough to get here, then you're intelligent enough to do the job. If you come out the other end and you're a hot-shot lawyer then obviously that's great, but they don't put pressure on you in terms of time or billable hours. There are targets, but it's no problem if you miss them. They want you to develop – this starts internally by building up how you ask for work, and learning how to deal with people. Anything technical is picked up in appraisals, but it's never any cause for concern. What would be worrying is if you have poor interpersonal skills or can't be trusted to be left alone with a client."*

Appraisals were described as being very helpful. *"You always get criticisms but they're constructive and never horrible."* When it comes to day-to-day supervision *"some supervisors are very proactive in making sure you're always getting good work. In other groups it can be a nightmare to get your work checked, but supervisors do explain things in a way that gives you confidence going forward."* At the start of the training contract, newbies complete two weeks of training covering all the compulsory PSC modules; after that, formal training varies between departments.

The vibe across the Midlands offices is that *"it's a fun place to work. The teams are close knit and – although it's a cliché – there is a work-hard, play-hard mentality."* Over in Manchester – where we heard stories of continuing loyalties to the dearly departed Halliwells last year – it seems most have agreed it's time to make peace with

history. *"There is some occasional nostalgia, but it's all pretty much forgotten now. I mean, none of us trainees ever actually worked there!"* Quite. It seems that some of Halliwells' sociable, rambunctious side remains, however. *"No one here takes themselves too seriously,"* said one Mancunian. *"You work very hard, but people are always happy to have a giggle about something. That's important because it means you always feel like you can be yourself."*

Birmingham and Manchester trainees are heavily involved in their respective cities' trainee solicitor groups. *"There are a lot of drinks receptions to go to... and we often do!"* proclaimed one. In-firm, there's a cross-office social club run by the trainees. With barbecues, pool tournaments, karaoke, bingo, pub quizzes and other fun and games, there's a lot going on besides the traditional 'drinks at the local'. There's plenty of sport too – cricket, netball, football and rounders – as well as Christmas, summer and trainee induction parties. This year's welcome party had a Family Fortunes theme, with the part of Les Dennis being played by two current trainees (although not at the same time, we point out). Trainees in smaller offices told us that the social scenes there are vibrant too. *"There's more responsibility to push things forward socially, so more ends up happening."*

After some pretty poor retention figures last year, trainees were slightly taken aback by the 2013 jobs list. *"There were pretty much the same number of jobs as qualifying trainees, but not in the locations we expected."* However, there was *"scope to talk to people and fix the issue,"* meaning more jobs were created. Ultimately, nine of the 12 qualifiers stayed with the firm.

The True Picture

And finally...

Charity and CSR are a big deal at Gateley. A dedicated CSR committee is headed up by trainees in each office. *"We go for lunch with reps from charities all the time!"*

Gordons LLP

The facts
Location: Leeds, Bradford
Number of UK partners/solicitors: 35/64
Partners who trained at firm: 17%
Total number of trainees: 8
Seats: 4x6 months
Alternative seats: none

On chambersstudent.co.uk...
How to get into Gordons
The Yorkshire legal market
Where to bury Richard III?

A formidable force in Leeds, Gordons' new strategy aims to raise the firm's profile and win work nationwide.

Now are our brows bound with victorious wreaths

After a turbulent decade of expansion and rapid growth Gordons has emerged hot on the heels of the so-called 'Big Six' in Leeds. Yet while the majority of these firms are big national beasts, Gordons has stayed true to its no-nonsense Yorkshire ethos: honest, plain-speaking and personable. *"It's about being people first and lawyers second,"* explained one trainee, while another declared it *"very Yorkshire – we've got that spirit."* But let's make no mistake: while Gordons values its community connections, the firm's desire for recognition on a national level is palpable. With big clients such as Morrisons, Santander and Lloyds TSB on its books and a number of new departments popping up, it looks like Gordons is on the rise. The firm even made national headlines in 2013 when it acted for the Plantagenet Alliance, challenging the Ministry of Justice's decision to allow recently unearthed monarch Richard III to be buried in Leicester Cathedral rather than York Minster.

There's no winter of discontent chilling Gordons. After bagging a selection of regional and national gongs in the past two years, the firm's trophy cabinet is growing as rapidly as the Leeds office. *"It's been nice to have the recognition,"* said partner Barbara Rollin. When asked if there was swagger in Gordons' step, one source replied: *"We're facing forward and it definitely feels like there are plans for the future."* What are these plans? *"To get bigger and better and be the best in Yorkshire,"* replied another confidently. And if they're confident at Gordons, it's for a reason: there's been a steady rise in both revenue and staff numbers.

Property and personal law remain the two largest departments at Gordons, but recent acquisitions, including a charities team led by *Chambers UK* star lawyer Ros Harwood, have further enhanced a firm that already has a range of expertise. First-year trainees don't get a say in the allocation process and are usually sent to personal injury and either commercial property or commercial litigation. There were no complaints about this, and our interviewees said every effort had been made to place second-years in their desired departments. The other seats on offer include employment, family, personal, construction and corporate/banking.

Alas, why would you heap this care on me?

With offices in Bradford and Leeds, trainees can expect to spend time in both, and although the steel and glass exterior of the Leeds office is pretty much the polar opposite of Bradford's brown sandstone building, the same welcoming open-plan atmosphere prevails at both. Trainees will spend the majority of their two years in the Leeds office, though, which is located by the river, close to the station. Leeds is home to most of the commercial property department, the largest team at Gordons, and insiders said lots of the work they did was for Morrisons (the supermarket's recent £2.4m purchase of three petrol filling station sites was a typical deal), but they had also acted on behalf of local landlords and tenants. Other clients include brewer Molson Coors and H2O Urban, a company which develops sites next to rivers and canals. Gordons advised on its development of a mixed-use scheme at Northwich Marina. Typical trainee tasks include drafting lease and tenancy forms and assisting with post-completion documents, and our sources agreed that while they had mostly been confined to supporting roles there were plenty of chances to interact with clients.

Chambers UK rankings

Banking & Finance	Employment
Construction	Private Client
Corporate/M&A	Real Estate
Dispute Resolution	

Commercial litigation, spread across both offices, is another likely stop and insiders spoke glowingly of the support to hand, particularly in the pint-sized Bradford division. The contentious work on offer here deals mostly with debt recovery and right-of-way disputes, and candidates can expect to work for a variety of clients ranging from Yorkshire construction giants GMI to small and medium local enterprises. Responsibility is pitched high: *"I ran a couple of disputed debt claims and was doing my own hearings,"* revealed one source.

Trainees typically spend six months in Bradford as part of the personal injury team. The department is split down the middle into claimant and defendant cases, although trainees will only do defendant work. Our sources were unanimous in acknowledging the degree of autonomy they'd been trusted with as well as the chances they'd had to manage cases independently from start to finish, though the work can be quite basic and *"monotonous – I felt more like a claims handler than a trainee solicitor,"* one said. The final word should perhaps go to the interviewee who found the chance for independent advocacy *"invaluable"* and commented: *"If you show you're capable and the firm has faith in you they'll put you on the bigger higher-earning cases."*

With Morrisons never far from anything Gordons does, it was no surprise to hear that the supermarket brings a lot of work to the employment seat. Trainee tasks in the contentious branch of this department include bundling and attending hearings, and non-contentious tasks involve drafting contracts of employment. The banking seat was held in high regard for similar reasons and another trainee fondly recalled the *"hands-on"* role they'd had in one of Gordons' highest-earning matters that year. Among the banking team's recent deals, it advised Santander on investment facilities in connection with the acquisition of a hotel at Legoland.

The idle pleasures of these days

Common among our interviewees was a sense that they'd been trusted with more responsibility than their friends and contemporaries in national and multinational firms. *"I didn't want to feel like a cog in a corporate machine – that's why I chose Gordons,"* thought one. Others were impressed by the extent of the firm's personable approach, with one commenting: *"They're all about people here: they don't want robots."* The firm's supervision and mentoring system was praised, with one source saying that aside from the routine appraisal at the end of every seat, each supervisor has a different approach and they organise sessions.

For most of our sources a normal day started at 9am (unless they were on post duty), and it's rare to still be in the office after 7pm. While the 8am post duty has been a sore spot for Gordons intakes of previous years, our interviewees this time round were more enthusiastic and one praised it as *"a good chance to meet trainees and catch up with people in other departments."* Sources also spoke favourably of the opportunity charity events gave them to socialise. In the past these have included quizzes, long-distance cycling and a talent show. More informally, local bars Roast, Toast and Lazy Lounge are staples on a Friday evening, with lawyers in the Bradford office often coming over to Leeds.

Sons of York

It was no surprise to find out that all of the trainees we spoke to were either born or educated in Yorkshire. Similarly, almost all of them had paralegal experience. While there's no policy in place barring inexperienced candidates from outside God's Own County, applicants without a palpable passion for the locale will need to be exceptional in other areas to win the training contract. Anything else? *"Gordons wants brand ambassadors and people who can go out and represent the firm in the wider community,"* one source stated. Partner Barbara Rollin clarified Gordons' criteria: *"It's about having a can-do attitude – we want people with a hunger to forge a career here and make connections with local businesses."* Though not of direct relevance to people searching for a training contract, we think it's also worth noting Gordons' admirable apprenticeship programme, which offers school leavers a chance to train as chartered legal executives.

In 2012 the retention rate at Gordons dropped dramatically, and while concerns over this still linger, our sources agreed that the hiring process has become more transparent in response to their anxieties. The intake in previous years has been as high as seven trainees but this figure has now been cut to four, which should hopefully mean there will be enough NQ positions for future qualifiers. Five out of the seven qualifiers stayed with the firm in 2013.

And finally...

While a can-do attitude is the most desirable trait in trainees, some experience of paralegal work will certainly make your application stand out.

Government Legal Service (GLS)

The facts

Location: London
Number of solicitors: c.1,550
Total number of trainees: c.50
Seats: 4x6 months
Alternative seats: none

On chambersstudent.co.uk...

How to get into the GLS
Much more about the work of the GLS

The GLS famously has only one client. But it's one helluva customer that keeps its 2,000 lawyers busy with some awesome work – Her Maj's Government.

'And Now for Something Completely Different'

You might see the words 'government' or 'civil service' and think immediately of the Ministry of Silly Walks, bowler hats, bureaucratic red tape stretching to the moon and back, acronyms aplenty and cutbacks... but also a job for life, cushy hours and generous holidays. Is any of this true at the GLS?

"Not enough students know about the GLS," one trainee lamented (actually, 3,000 applications for just 20 to 25 training contracts suggest that quite a few of you will get to know about it). *"The public sector hadn't really occurred to me,"* another confessed. *"But as soon as you start looking into the GLS you see it's very broad. I have friends at law firms who aren't enjoying their training contracts as much as me, and don't feel the same passion. It is so different."*

How's it different? Imagine watching ministers you've just advised debate a Bill (that you've part-drafted) in Parliament live on TV. Or working on judicial reviews (JRs) into whether high-profile alleged terrorists should be deported from the UK. Or investigating the dodgy offshore tax arrangements of famous companies and individuals, then prosecuting them. Or perhaps even attending the House of Commons, the Lords or the Supreme Court yourself. On your own... Hardly your typical trainee fare, and moving seats here *"is like starting a new training contract at a firm that does something completely different. It's like doing a training contract with four different firms."* The

GLS also hires pupil barristers – for more, read our Bar feature on page **659**.

Add to the mix a decent work/life balance, genuine teamwork (*"there's no backstabbing or one-upmanship. There's not the same kind of competitiveness you get at firms"*) and job security. It's true the GLS has experienced cutbacks in recent years, but the training programme has been relatively ring-fenced, and this year's NQ retention rate was once again 100%. Suddenly working for the government seems very appealing indeed.

OK, so not all the work is always as glam, but much of it is. Admittedly the pay is lower than many private sector firms, *"but we do have more responsibilities,"* trainees said. They praised the *"straightforward"* application process, and if you bodged your A-levels don't worry because recruiters don't ask about these. However, a 2:1 is essential (though the GLS is in the process of reviewing its eligibility criteria). Trainees also liked the competency-based approach to testing candidates (for which work experience of some kind is a big plus). It's a process that *"reviews ability and intellect rather than allowing you to blag it at interview."* Read our bonus feature on applying here online.

Merger mania

The largest department and the one with most trainees is the Treasury Solicitor's Department (TSol for short), and it just got bigger: thanks to the Coalition's cost-saving initiatives, TSol is currently undergoing a transformation and is in the process of merging the legal teams from various government departments – such as the Home Office, the Department for Energy and Climate Change, the Department for Transport, the Department for Work and Pensions, the Department of Health and the Ministry of Defence – into a new, enlarged organisation. This is in addition to the TSol advisory teams already supplying legal services to HM Treasury, the Cabinet Office, the Department for Culture, Media and Sport, the Department for Education, the Department for Communities and Local Government, the Department for Food, Environment and Rural Affairs (Defra) and the Ministry of Justice – some of which previously offered their own trainee posts. By the time the process is completed in October 2014, the new organisation will comprise around 1,700 lawyers.

Future trainees interested in departments that used to take their own trainees should still be able to gain experience here (if they are needed); it's just that from now on they will be part of TSol rather than individual departmental teams. As one interviewee put it, in TSol *"you can stick your fingers in a lot of different pies"* – and this has never been truer. *"The mergers have opened more doors for me,"* another source reckoned. Apart from *"the initial awkwardness while working out who people are,"* teams have integrated well, sources felt.

TSol provides legal advice to an absolute plethora of government departments and agencies, both on litigation (for example, *"when someone sues a government department, we will defend it"*) and advisory matters. *"That means advising the government on the legal implications of policies – the potential risks of a certain policy decision, overarching concerns regarding the EU, issues related to the Freedom of Information Act... all the things you read about,"* a trainee explained. *"Clients are policy officials and, ultimately, the Secretary of State."* Trainees do two litigation and two advisory seats. Work includes immigration, prisons, employment and education. Fairly often trainees will spend their seat at the offices of their client team, especially in advisory seats. TSol itself is located inside a 1960s concrete *"doughnut"* at One Kemble Street, just off Kingsway near Holborn tube.

In litigation seats, clients could (among many) be Home Office caseworkers (in immigration cases) or the Ministry of Justice in prison cases (for example, *"defending Her Majesty's Prison Service against personal injury claims brought by prisoners"*). Naturally, trainees find that *"often the clients are other lawyers."* On the advisory side, lawyers recently advised the Health and Safety Executive on simplifying and streamlining workplace regulations following publication of the Löfstedt review. Another high-profile new piece of legislation being passed when we did our interviews was the same-sex marriage act. In other words, GLS work can be *"really important politically"* and actually change lives.

Responsibility-wise, *"it's different to private practice. I'm either the joint lawyer on a big project or, mostly, have my own work. Most of the time you act like a qualified lawyer. They keep an eye on you, but there's not the same partner-supervisor-trainee hierarchy as in law firms, where you can't send an e-mail without having to run it past someone senior first."* Another revealed: *"Today I had a meeting in Whitehall with heads of HR, senior lawyers and other senior people. You're not just an assistant taken along to take notes – you get asked your opinion."*

Call of duties

After TSol, HM Revenue & Customs Solicitors' Office (HMRC) takes the next most trainees. The department's top lawyer, Anthony Inglese, is also its training principal and takes an active interest in his trainees' development: *"The word 'patriarch' is used! We have a lot of contact with him and meet one-to-one in the middle and end of every seat."* Reviews aside, Inglese *"really likes to be involved."* As about half of HMRC's work is litigation, trainees here usually do two contentious seats. The department is big enough not to have to farm anyone out to gain other necessary experience: *"We stay within the department for two years. Some other departments do secondments."*

Here's a whirlwind tour of some HMRC seats. VAT and duties litigation (based at Bush House on the Strand, not far from the Royal Courts of Justice) is *"fast-paced"* and involves *"lot of tribunal cases."* Responsibility's good, with trainees getting their own caseloads and appearing at hearings themselves. VAT work involves *"people who didn't agree with their VAT assessments,"* while duties litigation includes *"customs and excise type stuff"* – seizures of fags and booze – *"so you meet a lot of customs officers"* (we're imagining scenes from daytime TV staple *UK Border Force*). In VAT advisory (based at 100 Parliament Street, *"one of the huge Whitehall buildings"*), a policy wonk *"might come to you and ask about a point of law."* You need to have your wits about you and have done your homework, mind, because funnily enough these clients already *"know the law pretty well"* themselves. They might, for example, seek your counsel on how a court might interpret a particular EU directive.

The criminal and information law advisory work (also based on Parliament Street) is *"wide and varied"* and includes *"search warrants, investigations, legal professional privilege and human rights ... they come up quite a lot."* Personal tax litigation (based at Bush House) works on bigger tax avoidance cases – for example *"people who've moved assets to tax havens abroad"* but, naughtily, haven't actually moved themselves. Some cases are *"worth millions,"* some involve well-known names and *"some go all the way to the Supreme Court."*

The True Picture

As well as TSol and HMRC, the Department for Business, Innovation and Skills (BIS) is the third and final department which still recruits its own set of trainees. The department provides legal advice on policies and projects, and investigates and prosecutes business cases where the law has been broken (such as fraud arising from insolvency). During the application phase you'll express your departmental preferences and be placed where you're needed.

Interviewees repeatedly stressed that the GLS *"is really different to anything else out there. You work on cases that appear in Parliament and the Supreme Court. It's made me politically aware. There's a work/life balance – it's nine-to-five, more or less. Everyone's really nice. Photocopying is rare; I did it once. In litigation I ran my own cases; in advisory I'm advising on my own areas. They let you run with things, though I can go to someone if needed. You're not expected to specialise, unlike some of my peers at firms who have done conveyancing as a trainee and know they'll end up doing that when they qualify."* Qualified lawyers join teams they haven't worked in before, and thereafter move teams every few years, *"so you keep learning as your career progresses."*

"There was one department which definitely stretched me the most," said one interviewee. *"I got to do incredibly complicated things with very smart people, very quickly. It wouldn't suit everyone. I got exposure to work like nowhere else: I can't imagine private sector trainees giving feedback on senior partners' work! Having so much responsibility certainly grew my confidence."*

Question Time

If you want to work for the GLS an interest in politics and government is obviously beneficial, although as a civil servant you have to be politically impartial once you're on the job. So we asked trainees: do you have to have a passion for the public sector? *"For me, I liked the feeling of doing something useful and worthwhile and that*

I'm contributing," was one answer. Another thought GLS *"attracts a certain type of person compared to City law firms."* What does that mean? *"It's far less competitive – once you're in. People look to help each other. At the end of two years you know they'll offer you a job."* Well, at least *"they certainly told us they hire for the long term."*

We've covered the GLS in this guide for several years now and must say that it has always looked after its trainees and pupils when cost-cutting changes were afoot elsewhere. During the worst of the recession, for example, when the GLS faced job cuts of 20 to 40%, the training scheme was protected, the view being that it was necessary to recruit fresh talent now to fill important government jobs in the future. Diversity is pretty good, especially regarding gender (just under 60% of GLS employees are women), and the Treasury Solicitor, Sir Paul Jenkins KCB QC, is the most senior openly gay civil servant.

And what of the social life? Do civil servants have fun? Yes they do, actually, but don't expect Champagne binges expensed on the company credit card or team-building days at the races. A training committee across the GLS organises things like trips to galleries, museums, the zoo, picnics in Lincoln's Inn Fields and pub jaunts. People chip in themselves for things that cost money. Some take part in a civil service sports day. More informally, trainees like to link up from time to time for so-called UGLY drinks (which stands for 'the Union of Government Lawyers who are Youngish'). Sometimes trainees from the Crown Prosecution Service come along too. There's also a social committee for all GLS lawyers; a recent event was a chocolate tasting. *"Some teams are extremely sociable, and some less so – although I don't want to give the impression there are party teams!"* a trainee was quick to point out. As for Crimbo, *"I ended up going to about three different festive meals for different teams and one for trainees."*

And finally...

Some trainees told us they would like *"bit more consistency between supervisors,"* but there were virtually no gripes. If money is your fetish, don't apply. Otherwise: *"Do it! It's been an absolutely brilliant training contract."*

Harbottle & Lewis LLP

The facts

Location: London
Number of UK partners/solicitors: 35/41
Partners who trained at firm: 10%
Total number of trainees: 10
Seats: 4x6 months
Alternative seats: secondments

On chambersstudent.co.uk...

How to get into Harbottle
More on media, show business and entertainment

Media mavens are drawn to this West End firm, which has bountiful big-name clients from the world of entertainment.

Stars in their eyes

In 1951 in Guildford, a couple of showbiz enthusiasts met at law school. They were Harbottle and Lewis (Laurence and Brian respectively), and four years later they set up shop in Mayfair, specialising in the legal aspects of film and theatre production and representing dashing thespians like Laurence Olivier and Dirk Bogarde. As we've morphed from the era of the matinee idol into the digital age, the firm has kept pace with the ever-evolving media and entertainment sector. Today its reputation management team deals with dodgy tweets and texts as well as what's published the traditional print way. A digital media team handles data protection, IP and privacy issues, while the interactive entertainment group specialises in video gaming.

Along with all the newfangled digital platform business, the firm has maintained its position in the theatre and film industries, as well as taken in clients from the music, TV, publishing, broadcasting, sport, fashion and advertising sectors. Harbottle may have the media and entertainment arena mastered (as evidenced by top-notch *Chambers UK* rankings) but it isn't some one-trick legal pony. This is a full-service place that can sort out corporate, litigation, tax, employment, property, family and private client issues for its creative industry clients, and even has some more niche areas in its armoury, such as 'charity and philanthropy', 'entrepreneurs' and 'LGBT community'.

As you might expect, Harbottle has a whole host of household names on the books. To mention a few, there's Kate Moss, David and Victoria Beckham, the National Theatre, Sir Alex Ferguson, Microsoft and the publishing house Penguin. The firm recently represented cricketer Kevin Pietersen over a libel issue in which he was accused by national papers of

match-fixing via text message. It was also involved in two massive 2012 privacy cases involving the Royal Family in various states of undress – acting for the Duchess of Cambridge regarding those photos of her sunbathing published in French magazine *Closer* and dealing with those other photos of Prince Harry cavorting in Las Vegas.

There's no business like legal business

There are six seat options – litigation; corporate; employment; property; media; and family, private client and tax (all three in one seat) – as well as a client secondment at Virgin Atlantic. No seat is strictly compulsory, although *"you pretty much have to do litigation to get the contentious box ticked, and everyone does corporate because they need trainees."* Before starting at the firm, future trainees put in a request for a top choice of seat. On arrival, their four seats are already mapped out: *"You don't have so much choice about the other three seats, but they try their best to take your preference into account. If you have an issue with a particular seat, they're good about rearranging things."*

Litigation is split between commercial work and the media and information group (MIG). The latter deals with privacy or defamation issues and is currently working on behalf of phone hacking victims. Commercial litigation might involve trainees *"going on the weekly court run – I went before a master a couple of times, which was pretty nerve-racking."* As well as this there'll be the usual trainee fare of bundling and photocopying, but the chance to extract unpaid legal fees offers up a greater level of responsibility: *"You get decent exposure to the nuts and*

Chambers UK rankings

Charities	Information Technology
Corporate/M&A	Intellectual Property
Defamation/Reputation	Media & Entertainment
Management	Real Estate
Employment	Sports Law

bolts of litigation when you run debt management files by yourself." The department recently acted for one of the founders of Skype and his wife when their luxury coastal home was found to be defective. Litigators also represented Virgin Atlantic Airways in a dispute with its UK catering suppliers, Sky Chefs.

Trainees praised the *"very friendly, quite young"* corporate team, whose clients tend to come from the media sectors. For instance, the department advised Penguin Books on the acquisition of shares in Snowman Enterprises, the company which owns the rights to Raymond Briggs' famous character and brand. New recruits face up to *"research, drafting ancillary documents and board minutes"* as well as *"company secretarial work – doing annual returns and looking at shares."* One more lugubrious interviewee stated: *"It's largely about document management and keeping the machine well-oiled. I did an awful lot of photocopying, a few verification tasks, due diligence and data rooms. That's the trainee's lot really – it's pretty standard stuff."*

And now on to media, undoubtedly *"the reason people apply to the firm and the seat that most have their eyes on."* The seat is divided into two – there's theatre, film and television or music, sport and IP. One interviewee told us: *"I sat at the film and theatre end of it. It's very much a commercial seat and I worked on all sorts of production deals, both big and small."* Trainees can expect to take on *"first drafts of opinions or getting bibles together for film financing transactions. I also did a lot of ad hoc commercial research into relevant points of law that emerged, like the licensing regime theatres go through when hiring child actors."* Along the way, trainees appreciated the partners' input: *"They were keen to show me all the different stages of a financing."* Among others, Harbottle represents Universal, Working Title and DreamWorks, and recently advised Neal Street Productions on BBC fave *Call The Midwife* and Shakespeare series *The Hollow Crown* (featuring the *Student Guide*'s actor of choice Ben Whishaw). Theatre-wise, the firm worked on the Broadway production of *Breakfast at Tiffany's* and new play *The Audience*, starring Helen Mirren as the Queen.

A contented source declared: *"The high points were working on films like Steven Spielberg's Lincoln and helping with the War Horse film and play."* Interviewees also mentioned *"mingling with celebrities"* at the British Comedy Awards. The hours seem to be another bonus – *"it's a lot more civilised than the City. The latest I've worked is 9pm and that was completely voluntary!"*

The man with the golden bundle

It's best to keep the jazz hands at bay. Despite the glitzy client list, all our sources warned potential trainees not to get any flashy delusions of life at Harbottle. *"Don't apply to a media firm because you think it'll be glamorous or sexy. They're not interested in gossipy people who want to meet celebrities. They want intellectually capable people who have a clear interest in the business and legal side of media and entertainment."* Many trainees had prior work experience or careers in creative industries, although this isn't strictly necessary. *"The key thing is a proven interest."* What else characterises a Harbottle trainee? Aside from having attended *"a really good uni"* and being *"proactive, outgoing and easygoing,"* the new recruits here are *"nice – I know that sounds wishy-washy but it's true. They don't want backstabbing people who try to get one over on each other."*

Harbottle folk work in a *"lovely building"* in Hanover Square. *"It's great to be so central with Soho just next door."* The different departments are separated over five floors. However, everyone gets to mix together in the James Bond-themed kitchen, the notorious room 007, decorated with *"Bond posters from the 60s and 70s, back when Harbottle worked on the films."* The kitchen comestibles are *"another massive perk – we get a free home-cooked lunch every day and you can have as much as you like."* The firm's quiz nights are held in the kitchen, and there's a summer treasure hunt that involves the unusual sight of solicitors *"running around the Oxford Circus area solving riddles"* in a bid to win a day's holiday. *"It's pretty entertaining and gets quite competitive."* As well as this, there's a Christmas party and fairly regular Friday drinks.

When it comes to the serious business of qualification, sources felt *"it's not as clear-cut and open as at other places. There isn't a jobs list. During the review at the end of the third seat, your supervisor will ask you where you want to end up."* As such, *"if you enjoy an area and want to work there, don't be too quiet about it."* The firm retained three of its five qualifiers in 2013.

And finally...

Unsurprisingly, media is a highly popular area. A trainee warned: *"You need to keep an open mind. All the clients are media-based but it's not wise to be focused solely on a media department job because it's so competitive."*

Herbert Smith Freehills

The facts

Location: London

Number of UK partners/solicitors: 159/439

Partners who trained at the firm: 61%

Total number of trainees: 166

Seats: 4x6 months

Alternative seats: overseas seats, secondments

Extras: pro bono – Whitechapel Legal Advice Centre, RCJ CAB, FRU, death row appeals; language classes

On chambersstudent.co.uk...

How to get into HSF

The rush to Seoul

Herbies' in-house advocacy unit

Overseas seats and client secondments

Herbert Smith Freehills' expansion plan is well under way, but will it be hitting the brakes any time soon?

Seoul searching

The result of 2012's merger between Herbert Smith and Australia's 'Big Six' member Freehills, this is now an £800m firm with 2,800 lawyers operating out of Asia, Australia, Europe, the Middle East and the USA. The merger supports the view by some that, in years to come, the market will be dominated by a few global power-houses. The tie-up fell under the remit of the old Herbert Smith's 'Project Blue Sky' – its ambitious plan to take the firm global by targeting countries like Australia, the USA, South Korea and Germany.

Project Blue Sky's hit-rate is quite something, ticking off country names with stunning rapidity. The Freehills merger has made HSF the biggest firm in the Asia-Pacific region, taking the crown from Baker & McKenzie. A disputes-focused office in New York opened for business in 2012, broadening access to US clients. April 2013 saw the firm open the Seoul office, hot on the heels of the country's relaxation of its restrictions to foreign firms. HSF has also set the foundations for its own offices in Berlin and Frankfurt. Herbies also has its eyes on Latin America, says training partner Matthew White: *"Brazil is probably where we will focus our attentions on developing an energy-led office."*

Corporate and dispute resolution are the big beasts at the firm, and both practices are ranked up there with the best by *Chambers UK*. A host of industry expertise – in areas such as energy, financial services, technology, pharmaceuticals and leisure – runs alongside HSF's full-service offering. Energy and mining had for some time been a focus for legacy Herbies, and the merger with Freehills

has boosted that side over in the mineral-rich land that is Australia.

"They're still looking at ways to pool together client bases and forces," added one source, but by May 2013 the two legacy firms had already worked on around 250 joint advisory and cross-referral matters since the merger in October. This includes advising China National Offshore Oil Corporation on its $1.9bn acquisition of interests in a liquefied natural gas project in Australia. We'll have to wait and see until the revenue figures are published, but so far Herbies' Aussie tie-up looks like it has got off to a good start.

Litigation nation

HSF is organised around five divisions: corporate; dispute resolution; finance, real estate and projects; employment, pensions and incentives; and competition, regulation and trade. Trainees will complete a corporate and litigation seat throughout their training contract, and stints in real estate and finance are also likely. On top of that, there are more specialist seats on offer in employment, pensions and incentives; competition, regulation and trade; tax; and IP. Trainees get to list *"between three and six preferences"* at each seat rotation, and *"it's quite unusual not to get one of your top three."* HR *"do take into account your general development,"* and *"they'll ask if you have a qualification preference, and if so what."* There's also the opportunity to go on an international or client secondment – check out the *Student Guide* website to find out more.

There's plenty of choice when it comes to litigation at HSF. Trainees can be placed in three or four large litiga-

The True Picture

Chambers UK rankings

Administrative & Public Law	Life Sciences
Banking & Finance	Local Government
Banking Litigation	Media & Entertainment
Capital Markets	Outsourcing
Competition/European Law	Partnership
Construction	Pensions
Corporate Crime & Investigations	Pensions Litigation
Corporate/M&A	Planning
Data Protection	Private Client
Dispute Resolution	Private Equity
Employee Share Schemes & Incentives	Product Liability
Employment	Professional Discipline
Energy & Natural Resources	Professional Negligence
Environment	Projects
Financial Services	Public International Law
Fraud	Public Procurement
Health & Safety	Real Estate
Information Technology	Real Estate Finance
Insurance	Real Estate Litigation
Investment Funds	Restructuring/Insolvency
	Retail
	Tax
	Telecommunications
	Transport

tion groups, *"but within those there are some more niche things, so in group one there's a lot of Russian disputes, in group two there's more oil and gas work, while group three does some media and a lot of insolvency, and group four encompasses public law, but also financial services regulation and banking litigation."* Sources said that *"there's a good mix of work, which is a positive thing as you get to be very busy,"* but the potential downside is that the *"groups are not particularly cohesive – there's not a common thread that unites them."* There's a mixture of international and domestic clients, like London Underground, Chevron and Abbott Laboratories, as well as the chance to work in more specific groups focusing on insurance, construction, international arbitration and advocacy.

Rogue traders and financial misbehaviours

In the larger groups, *"who you work for depends on your supervisor and how territorial they are – but it is encouraged that you work on with other people as well."* Increased work on the banking/financial services regulatory side (regulatory scrutiny is where it's at these days) means that litigators have been helping retail and investment banks with mis-selling claims, derivatives litigation and disputes arising from the Libor scandals. One such case involved advising Credit Suisse in a mis-selling claim brought against it by a high net worth individual, whose investments suffered in the midst of the 2008 fi-

nancial crisis. *"It's a fascinating group,"* said one source who had worked on a mis-selling claim and *"got a hands-on look at the documents on the case; you get to immerse yourself in the evidence, draft witness statements and put together the materials – it's very interesting."*

Regulatory and corporate crime lawyers united over the 'rogue trader' Kweku Adoboli case (Adoboli's 'unauthorised trading incident' resulted in the loss of £1.5 bn to UBS and the arrest of Adoboli). Trainees here told us how work fell mostly into three categories: *"General advice on things like money laundering rules; investigations work, which is sometimes anticipatory and sometimes occurs when a client is being investigated by the Serious Fraud Office; and finally corporate support, when an M&A transaction is going through and we need to design questionnaires for both buyers and sellers on corporate crime, practices and related topics."* Sources felt there was *"good exposure and the chance to work with foreign lawyers – we were dealing with projects going on in North Africa and the Middle East."*

International arbitration clients include BP, Alstom and the Kingdom of Spain. This is a popular choice because *"the team is very small, so you get to have more responsibility"* It's also a *"very academic team which focuses on a lot of publishing, networking events, lectures and webinars to give to clients."* It's also *"very research-based – it's basically what you think law is like when you're in law school. You're choosing the things that support your view and preparing counter-arguments."* Trainees had prepared witness statements, attended hearings and, inevitably, done their fair share of disclosure as well.

Stake 'n' markets

The corporate group serves a roster of FTSE 100 and 250 companies, including names like G4S, Virgin Group and Moneysupermarket.com. There has been a bit of a reshuffle in the corporate division of late: *"The idea is to give people a greater breadth of experience so that you don't become super-specialised."* Most of our sources had spent time in a group that dealt with general public and private M&A, as well as equity capital markets. *"The work is so varied; I've helped to sell chicken farms – anything can come up!"* Trainees don't get *"to draft the big headline points, but you do get bits of discrete drafting and get a good experience of the more ancillary documents."* Some had found themselves in groups which encompass more of the firm's sector specialisms, like energy and TMT. This can involve *"working on technology outsourcing agreements for major clients, as well as doing profit work on a mobile licensing deal."*

The real estate and finance groups combined to form one division in 2012 in the aftermath of the Freehills' merger. Finance is *"not our strongest department, but it's definitely a growing division and a lot busier recently – plus it's quite nice to be in a place where people are striving to get better and you're considered to be a player much more."* Again, there are a smaller number of groups which work on a broader range of financial transactions and activities. One group encompasses securitisation, debt capital markets and derivatives work, which went down well with trainees as *"at other big finance firms they put all of those things into separate groups, but here you get to do a bit of everything."* Clients include well-known banks and financial institutions like BNP Parabas, Citibank, Credit Suisse and Standard Chartered Bank. Trainees had worked on securitisation deals and had been able to *"do the first reviews of a suite of documents, like an agency agreement and a trust deed, and put my comments on them."* Sources generally agreed that because the finance teams are smaller, *"there are more opportunities as a trainee."*

Real estate comprises general, construction, property litigation and planning groups. Long-standing clients include FTSE 100 property company Hammerson, Standard Life and EDF, but the teams have also won new international clients like Sime Darby from Malaysia and the Renaissance Group from Russia. Lawyers advised Hammerson on the sale of its London office portfolio to Brookfield Office Properties, a large North American developer, for £518m. Construction lawyers then stepped on board to assist Brookfield on its joint venture with Oxford Properties to redevelop London Wall Place for office and retail space in the City. The construction group has a wide range of clients in the energy, transport and infrastructure, and commercial spheres. Trainees had got involved in *"a number of nuclear power plant deals,"* and loved them because *"there are few projects in the construction industry that are as complex as a nuclear power station as the consequences of something not being correct are huge."* Tasks included making amendments to construction contracts, which addressed the appointment of architects and engineers, as well as assisting on the drafting of collateral warranties.

Fun direction

"The morale is really good at the moment," said one trainee: *"The merger has given us a shot in the arm, and people are feeling energetic."* Others felt that *"the firm has more direction now, more focus – not that there wasn't a plan before, but now it's more visible."* The merger has also cranked communication levels up a notch as well, with regular group sessions and *"monthly CEO updates"* to keep everybody updated. Sources cited the recent *"firm-wide consultation"* on the firm's values as an example of this improved quality

of communication, and now a refreshed set of post-merger values have been shaped to steer *"the way the firm will go in the future."* Ultimately, *"people have been pleased about how, culturally, there's a lot of similarities between the legacy firms."*

There's quite an academic culture, with an *"emphasis on intellectual engagement with law and society – you'll walk past people having conversations in the corridors and hear someone say '... and ninthly...'."* There's also a nice balance between individual striving and broader considerations: *"It's not a stereotypically aggressive environment, but it's still an entrepreneurial place. There's an energy and intensity here, but it's often directed in a collective movement to get things done – there's not an unhealthy competitive atmosphere."* Traditionally, the firm has been painted as a more formal one, but the formality appears to be more associated with the litigation groups, where *"it's more hierarchical – corporate teams tend to be friendlier, but that's a broad-stroke generalisation."*

While there may not be too much socialising going on at an office-wide level, there's still lots going on at HSF. Each group has its own entertainment budget, meaning that departmental socialising is common. We heard of well-attended Christmas and summer parties; pizza and proscecco nights in conference rooms; group traditions like *"going out for a new-joiner curry on Brick Lane"* ; and karaoke nights: *"After you've left the karaoke bar with the partners you've been singing with all evening, there's not much hierarchy left."* Trainee-specific events tend to dip, but the group still comes together to organise things like its own Christmas party each year: *"We assign co-ordinators from each intake and everyone chips in 25 quid."* Being *"fortunately located in Exchange Square"* makes it easy to find somewhere to grab a few drinks after work as well.

Trainees heaped praise on the firm for the way it handled the qualification process: *"They've done really well and kept us regularly updated."* That's quite some feat, considering the number of trainees hoping to progress through the ranks. A clear timetable alerts trainees to when things will happen, and a jobs list indicates how many positions will be available in each division. *"Everyone hears the outcome of the decisions on the same day, and they even give everyone an allocated appointment to deliver the news – mine's at 11.05.am*

And finally...

At the time of our calls in mid-June, our sources were just a couple of days away from finding out their future employment status. 54 out of 66 eventually found out that they had jobs in September.

Higgs & Sons

The facts

Location: Brierley Hill, Kingswinford

Number of UK partners/solicitors: 28/54

Partners who trained at firm: 57%

Total number of trainees: 10

Seats: 4x4 + 1x8 months

Alternative seats: none

Extras: pro bono – Birmingham Employment Advice Centre, Birmingham CAB

On chambersstudent.co.uk...

How to get into Higgs

Interview with David, the firm's last Higgs

Higgs' new home

Higgs & Sons is a Black Country native that can provide training which mixes private and commercial work.

The firm in Black

Higgs & Sons was established in 1875 in the heart of the Black Country, an area characterised by steel mills and iron foundries. Much has changed since then, not least the firm's stature: it has grown to become one of the most prominent outfits in the region, with fancy headquarters in Brierley Hill alongside a smaller office in Kingswinford.

Some things remain the same, however; there's still a Higgs at the firm – David, great-grandson of the founder. Now employed as a consultant, he spent some time reflecting with us on how far the firm has come: *"The total number of staff now working for the firm is in the region of 200, and it continues to grow and evolve."*

Despite the expansion, Higgs appreciates there's no place like home. Trainees said: *"Despite the growth and success we've had, we're not moving towards becoming a big corporate firm or looking to extend ourselves geographically. In terms of the future, it's about striking a balance between trying to keep our community roots and continuing to expand."* David Higgs again: *"It is certainly my hope that we retain our Black Country roots."* So don't apply here expecting a Birmingham office to crop up any time soon.

This is how we do it

When it comes to seats, Higgs does things a little differently. Trainees undergo four seats consisting of four months each, followed by the finale of an eight-month seat, which gives trainees the opportunity to experience their preferred practice area once more, with the hope of qualifying into it.

The seats themselves are largely determined by the six preferences that trainees rank prior to starting. Of course *"you can't expect to get every single one of your top choices,"* but there was an overall feeling among our interviewees that *"the system is fair and the firm tries to give everyone what they want."*

While Higgs has *"a huge range of practice areas,"* it is traditionally strongest on the non-commercial side. The firm has an excellent reputation for its private client work and *Chambers UK* ranks this practice as one of the best in the region. However, one source was quick to point out that *"it isn't only a popular choice with trainees due to its reputation – everyone has such a brilliant time there as well."* The work is *"generally very interesting, but you also get exposed to a wide range of tasks – something that's really important to a trainee."* Such tasks include drafting wills and Lasting Powers of Attorney. There's also Court of Protection work and a considerable amount of tax and estate planning to carry out, with the latter often involving estates worth *"an incredible sum of money."* The larger office tends to handle matters for these high net worth individuals, but the smaller Kingswinford branch still gets ordinary people who just walk in off the street.

The private client department rakes in roughly one-quarter of Higgs' total revenue, and the same is true of the firm's personal injury and clinical negligence work. Trainees will undoubtedly get to tackle both PI and clin neg. Personal injury work can involve things like meeting prospective clients and evaluating their claims, which one said was a *"very different"* experience, adding: *"The onus is basically on you to make the decision as to whether it's a reasonable claim or not."* Trainees also visit accident sites and prepare locale reports, take wit-

Chambers UK rankings

Corporate/M&A	Family/Matrimonial
Crime	Personal Injury
Dispute Resolution	Private Client
Employment	Real Estate

ness statements and attend trial with counsel. The clinical negligence team enjoyed a particularly busy year during 2012, completing a record number of claims for the department – one of which resulted in its highest ever settlement figure of over £4m. Cases often relate to the likes of brain and spinal injuries, respiratory arrest, fatal accidents and delayed cancer diagnosis. Besides attending inquests and settlement meetings, trainees also perform tasks such as drafting letters of claims to hospitals.

Have no fear, corporate is here!

Those hoping to do corporate and commercial work needn't fret. The firm has a team of about a dozen lawyers working on transactions mainly in the £1–10m range. Recent deals include advising jewellers T.H. Baker on the sale of its online business The Watch Hut. Many clients come from the manufacturing and engineering sectors – names like Floors 2 Go, Metalrax and Mackwell Electronics should give you an indication of the sort of companies we're talking about. A number of well-known banks also instruct the firm, NatWest being one such example. Trainees are able to *"help run deals from start to finish."*

Dispute resolution provides a mixed bag of work, including IP disputes (like a bust-up between the similarly named washroom accessory manufacturers Frost Products and FC Frost), professional negligence (defending a partner of another law firm), franchising disputes, product liability and more. Trainees are granted regular client interaction *"from the outset"* and *"get to experience all sorts, from drafting witness statements and court forms to attending mediations. There's a little bit of photocopying as well, but I definitely don't mind doing a few hours of photocopying if I get to go to court."* Trainees do also get to do a bit of advocacy, and while *"you're obviously not in court every day,"* they are able to take the lead on smaller hearings. *"If you show that you're capable of handling the responsibility, there's not much the firm won't let you have a go at."* Other seat options include commercial property, family, employment, conveyancing and motoring and private criminal/regulatory.

Trainees receive formal feedback through *"highly detailed"* monthly appraisals with a departmental supervisor, as well as a review at the end of each seat with the head of department and HR. There's an open-door policy that exists as much through necessity as anything else: *"If you close the door the air conditioning can make the rooms a little bit cold."*

Higgs and giggles

Higgs moved to posh new offices on the Waterfront Business Park in Brierley Hill back in 2010. *"I think it better reflects the calibre of work we do and how far we've come,"* one trainee opined. Interviewees described its *"lovely and spacious"* interior – a *"huge"* atrium serves as a social hub where trainees gather for drinks and lunches in addition to being the ideal space for games like Giant Connect Four and Scalextric. Trainees share an office with a supervisor (most likely a partner), which one referred to as *"an immediate support network. It means you have someone constantly looking over your shoulder – in a good way!"*

"You walk around the office, and the overall atmosphere is great," mentioned one source. *"You're able to chat with everyone in the building, and that's something which I think is invaluable. It brings out the best in you, as you're working in a place where you feel like you can have a good time."* While David Higgs bemoaned the fact that the male lawyers don't always wear ties, there were no such complaints from our trainee sources.

The Birmingham Trainee Solicitors Society and the Wolverhampton Junior Lawyers Division provide trainees with the opportunity to attend dinners and sporting tournaments. The firm does its bit too, with Christmas and summer parties (those who have not yet begun their training contracts are also invited). One interviewee recalled that *"at first you don't know who anyone is, but then people get up and have a good dance – even the equity partners end up having a little bit too much to drink!"*

Unfortunately, only two out of six qualifiers stayed with the firm in 2013. *"You do have discussions and know what to expect, both in terms of what the firm is looking for and whether there is likely to be a position for you at the end."* One source mentioned an important statistic: *"There's a large emphasis on organic growth from trainee to partner – over half of the partners actually trained with the firm."*

And finally...

Aside from bringing in *"a magic photocopier that can do all the copying, sorting and hole punching for you,"* our sources struggled to think of anything Higgs could do better.

Hill Dickinson LLP

The facts

Location: London, Liverpool, Manchester, Sheffield

Number of UK partners/solicitors: 159/293

Total number of trainees: 41

Seats: 4x6 months

Alternative seats: overseas seats, secondments

Extras: pro bono – Liverpool and Manchester University Legal Advice Clinics, LawWorks St Hilda's Legal Advice Clinic

On chambersstudent.co.uk...

How to get into Hill Dickinson

The firm's history

The story of Halliwellls

North West firm Hill Dickinson combines its long-standing reputation in the likes of insurance, professional negligence and marine law with an increasingly impressive corporate practice.

HD ready

Hill Dickinson trainees were quick to point out that *"there's been a lot of change around here over the last few years."* The driving force behind this change came about in 2010 with the acquisition of collapsed firm Halliwells' offices in Sheffield and Liverpool, a move that considerably beefed up its corporate and commercial offerings. But let's not forget where HD's traditional strengths lie: areas like insurance, professional negligence and marine remain as crucial as ever to the firm's success. In fact, the firm recently opened a Monaco office in March 2013 – its third one overseas – which *"mainly serves as an extension of our marine practice."*

A major reshuffle in 2011 saw seven practice groups condensed into four 'business units'. Insurance was coupled with professional risks to form one unit, while property, construction, employment, commercial litigation, banking, pensions and company commercial now all fall under the 'business services' banner. The marine and health groups were both unaffected by the changes and complete the set.

It was founded in Liverpool, but HD has greatly expanded since then and now includes other domestic offices in Manchester, London and Sheffield. The firm's two foreign outposts we haven't named yet are in Singapore and Piraeus, both of which offer shipping secondments. Sources speculated that the newly opened Monaco office might soon follow suit. The firm told us this is a medium to long-term possibility. While London trainees usually have first dibs on these overseas opportunities, it's worth noting that they are open to trainees in all offices. Domestic client secondments are also available.

Candidates apply to individual offices, and there are significant differences between each base when it comes to seat options. Liverpool and Manchester have a wider selection to choose from, plus the possibility of switching between those two offices to complete certain seats. Trainees who end up in the London office should be prepared to stay there for the duration of their training contracts as, with the exception of secondments, moving between offices is a rarity for them. London trainees always end up completing at least one seat in marine law.

Risks and rewards

The insurance department rakes in around one-third of the firm's total revenue. HD recently strengthened its teams in Manchester and Sheffield by acquiring the majority of DLA Piper's defendant insurance practice in the two cities, which added 30 or so staff to its ranks (with the Sheffield office taking on most of the new employees). The group is split into numerous sub-teams that concentrate their efforts on specific areas such as fraud, casualty claims, catastrophic injury, motor claims, regulatory, and professional and financial risks.

Fraud is a popular seat choice and one of the largest groups within insurance. This area of law is *"naturally really interesting,"* said some, but that isn't always reflected in the work trainees are given. *"If you're able to get involved in the investigations side then that is exciting, although the administrative tasks – like inputting data*

Chambers UK rankings

Agriculture & Rural Affairs	Intellectual Property
Banking & Finance	Pensions
Clinical Negligence	Police Law
Commodities	Private Client
Construction	Professional Discipline
Corporate/M&A	Real Estate
Court of Protection	Real Estate Litigation
Dispute Resolution	Restructuring/Insolvency
Education	Shipping
Employment	Social Housing
Health & Safety	Transport
Healthcare	Travel
Insurance	

into spreadsheets – aren't quite as fun." However, it was agreed that *"you are handed a great deal of responsibility early on and end up gaining a vast amount of experience as things can get phenomenally busy."*

Professional risks involves *"defending professionals over any cock-ups that they may or may not have made."* The professional in question could be a solicitor, surveyor, financial adviser or even a vet, with the team representing clients such as Aviva and the Veterinary Defence Society. Trainee tasks range from assisting with disclosures to attending hearings and client meetings, and a few of our interviewees were fortunate enough to have managed their own small matters. There's also plenty of research, often revolving around *"trying to get the dirt on someone."*

Marine law is where HD made a name for itself, after founder Edward Morrall opened his small practice in Liverpool in 1810 – the city was considered to be the second port of the British Empire at the time. The firm swiftly became known as a leader in maritime law, and has taken on some historic cases over the years: it represented White Star Line, owners of the 'Titanic', following the ship's famous sinking in 1912 and acted for the owners of the 'Lusitania' after it was torpedoed and sunk by a German U-boat during the First World War. Marine law remains an important area for HD and brings in a quarter of revenue. The marine, trade and energy department includes several sub-groups like shipping, personal injury and regulatory, commodities, cargo and logistics, and a specialist yacht team. Contentious shipping covers a range of 'dry' and 'wet' matters, from bill of lading and charter-party disputes to collisions and salvage awards, with those who had completed the seat reporting a lot of research but not a lot of client contact. *"I reckon it's due to the cases being typically high in value and importance,"* remarked one. *"Saying that, you're still able to go along to meetings and take attendance notes."* We also heard that *"most of our shipping clients are international, so there's a fair*

amount of collaboration with the Singapore and Piraeus offices in particular."

That's why clients go to Hill Dickinson

The property and construction department contains three property teams: corporate and investment; public sector and energy; and retail. Corporate and investment *"tends to deal with commercial and residential conveyancing, property investment portfolios and corporate transactions that have a property component."* Meanwhile, the retail team draws in business from a number of household names, including the Co-operative and Poundland. It also does a lot of work for Iceland, and assisted the supermarket chain with the purchase of seven UK stores that previously belonged to Welsh fashion retailer Peacocks after the latter chain entered administration in January 2012. On the public sector and energy front, the firm acts for local authorities, NHS trusts, educational establishments, charities, church bodies and social housing providers, as well as major utilities and energy companies. Regardless of which team they were in, sources noted that *"you're handed a decent level of responsibility without ever feeling out of your depth. Of course, there's always going to be the occasional SDLT return or Land Registry application that needs to be completed, but you get to do plenty of meatier work too."*

HD's corporate group is *"exceptionally robust now"* as a result of the Halliwells takeover. *"A large proportion of our team is made up of people who came from there, and it seems to have become a popular seat choice – especially when you take into account the clients you get to work with."* Such clients include the alcoholic beverages manufacturer Halewood International, Chester Zoo, and Everton and Sheffield Wednesday FCs. In addition to these, the firm recently advised the Stobart Group on its £12.4m acquisition of the vehicle logistics company Autologic. Given the size of the deals taken on by the team, which often exceed £10m in value, trainees are *"more of a cog in the machine as opposed to being in the thick of the action."* Despite this minor niggle, interviewees had few complaints about the variety of work on offer. *"One minute you might be helping out on a mega-M&A deal, while the next you could be assisting with a smaller matter on behalf of a start-up company or partnership. There are all sorts of things to prepare too, both before and after a transaction, and I was pretty lucky in that I saw a couple of deals through from beginning to end."* Aside from the standard tasks like drafting board minutes, compiling documents and going along to client meetings, trainees may find themselves receiving work from elsewhere. *"You quickly realise that a key part of your role is acting as an intermediary as there's a good chance you'll be advising other departments on corporate-related issues."*

Hill Dickinson has a prestigious healthcare practice in the North, representing more than 100 NHS and private sector clients across the nation. The department itself is made up of various subsets with expertise in certain areas, such as mental health and 'offender healthcare' (ie healthcare in prisons), and is retained by the NHS Litigation Authority to defend healthcare professionals and NHS bodies against malpractice claims and other contentious issues. *"These types of cases always have a lot at stake in terms of both money and reputation,"* a source explained. The group also acted for the West Midlands Strategic Health Authority on the public inquiry that arose following the discovery of unusually high mortality rates among patients at Stafford Hospital, regarded by many as one of the biggest scandals in the history of the NHS. Those who had spent time in the department got to work on clinical negligence matters, attend GMC hearings, draft court applications and review medical records. *"There was so much to get stuck into, not to mention the fact that I had my own collection of small cases to manage on top of helping out with the larger matters,"* recalled one interviewee.

Beyond the wall

Rather ironically, our interviewees were very much divided over whether a North-South divide exists within the firm – a topic that has reared its head in past years. *"It's simply not true,"* declared one of the Mancunians. *"The phrase we use here is 'one HD' and it's something that's strongly applied."* Another source in the North labelled it *"bit of a myth"* too, but conceded that *"getting everyone in the same place isn't exactly a common occurrence." "* Meanwhile, Londoners had no doubts about just how different life is down South – especially after making the trip to one of the Northern bases. *"It was like visiting an alien planet when we went to Liverpool for the first time, because our working cultures are worlds apart. The trainees up North usually finish work earlier than we do and it's okay for them to leave at, say, 5pm on a Friday, whereas we can't really do that here,"* one opined. *"It seems as if all the activities are centred around there as well, so it's easy for us to feel left out."*

The firm's Liverpool base is located at No 1 St Paul's Square. Trainees described it as *"a lovely place to work. It's really contemporary and has lots of huge glass windows, and to one side you've got spectacular views of the Mersey. You do feel like a bit of a big-shot when you walk through the door."* There was also plenty of praise for the *"absolutely brilliant"* subsidised café situated on the first floor of the building, which serves up *"fantastic food and a delicious selection of cakes."* In London the firm moved into three floors of Broadgate Tower on Bishopsgate in summer 2013. This skyscraper was only completed in 2009 so should be everything a 21st-century trainee could wish for.

Although inter-office events are fairly rare (apart from the occasional departmental shindig or charity fund-raiser), each base does have its own busy social calendar. This includes payday drinks towards the end of every month which, depending on the office, either take place internally or at a local venue. Speaking of pay, the NQ salary is up to £36,000 in the Northern offices and £58,000 in London.

Alongside events organised by the firm, trainees are actively encouraged to get involved in the local Junior Lawyers Division, and HD even covers their membership fees. Sources mentioned weekly activities like wine-tasting sessions and pub quizzes, and the JLD also hosts formal events such as Christmas parties and summer balls. Trainees in Liverpool have further opportunities to socialise through their close ties with the Merseyside Young Professionals organisation, while those in Manchester mingle with the Manchester Trainee Solicitors Group. *"It gets drilled into us before we start about the importance of going out and networking,"* one source informed us. *"Obviously you're trying to promote the firm, but at the same time it provides a great chance to meet new people."*

And finally...

Hill Dickinson has had *"excellent retention rates in the past,"* although 2013 was a bit of a blip with only 14 of 20 qualifiers kept on.

Hogan Lovells

The facts

Location: London

Number of UK partners/solicitors: 153/368

UK partners who trained at firm: c.33%

Total number of trainees: 129

Seats: 4x6 months

Alternative seats: overseas seats, secondments

Extras: pro bono – British Paralympic Association, various charities; language classes

On chambersstudent.co.uk...

How to get into Hogan Lovells

More on the old Hogan & Hartson

Interview with training partner Ailbhe Edgar

This international beast continues to grow its brand and is now hot on the heels of the magic circle.

A magic touch

Hogan Lovells is the bumper baby of a 2010 merger between American colossus Hogan & Hartson and City heavyweight Lovells. As well as gaining the firm a good deal of attention within the legal world, the transatlantic tie-up endowed it with massive manpower and an expansive global platform: at last count, Hogan Lovells boasted more than 2,400 lawyers across 40-plus offices around the world. *"Having a truly significant US presence has really borne fruit,"* training partner Ailbhe Edgar tells us, explaining the firm *"can now more effectively cross-sell between the States and other jurisdictions,"* a capacity that's proved particularly lucrative on the regulatory front considering the rise of cross-border libel investigations in recent years. While the firm's currently more interested in bedding in what it's got than *"running around doing further mergers,"* that's not to say further growth isn't on the agenda. *"We're not in the business of planting flags around the world. However, we have a clear interest in the emerging markets of South East Asia and Latin America, as can be seen through our recent expansion into markets such as Indonesia and Brazil,"* Edgar says.

With a solid reputation across Europe, Lovells historically occupied a spot on the fringes of the magic circle. Now that it's tapped into the US market and become a top ten firm by revenue, insiders believe the bulked-up Londoner has enough critical mass to offer a training contract that approaches the magic circle's sheer clout. *"There's a lot of potential that comes along with us building up our name and getting it out there,"* trainees from the current cohort said, pointing to the *"growing influx of big-ticket international matters."* Indeed, the ability to roll with the big boys remains a perceptible plus of the merger – global

hard-hitters like Johnson & Johnson, Nintendo, News International and Amazon all appear in the firm's recent client cache. Likewise, enviable roles such as legal adviser to the 2012 Paralympics and counsel to BTA Bank in a set of multibillion-pound fraud proceedings – just a few of the big instructions that have made headlines recently – indicate a vote of confidence from the well-to-do.

Corporate is Lovells' biggest department, though its litigation and finance arms make sizeable contributions to turnover, with both achieving multiple top-tier rankings in *Chambers UK*. IP and government regulatory groups round out the firm's five main practices. A wide variety of seats across that quintet proved a main draw for our interviewees, who felt *"this is a good firm to come to if you want a well-rounded City experience."* Multiple strengths – as evidenced by more than 50 *Chambers UK* rankings across the firm – are also a plus. *"It's one of our main selling points, actually; we're not just a corporate machine or a finance house."* Trainees are required to sit in one of the many corporate or finance seats as well as a contentious one. There are also a number of niche seats to explore, from public law to share schemes to employment, though competition for each is tough. As such, sources cautioned against *"coming here with the intent of specialising in a small department. There are lots of different areas you can have a go at, but if you have a burning desire to be an IP lawyer, you'd be better off at a specialist firm."*

Seat allocation works as follows: new starters express a preference for their first seat, and the rest of their training contract is mapped out within a few months of joining. *"We receive lunchtime presentations from all the groups and then rank six preferences, including secondments,"* one interviewee explained. *"There's a lot of anxiety*

The True Picture

Chambers UK rankings

Administrative & Public Law	Intellectual Property
Asset Finance	Investment Funds
Banking & Finance	Life Sciences
Banking Litigation	Media & Entertainment
Capital Markets	Outsourcing
Commodities	Parliamentary & Public Affairs
Competition/European Law	Pensions
Construction	Pensions Litigation
Consumer Finance	Planning
Corporate/M&A	Private Equity
Data Protection	Product Liability
Dispute Resolution	Professional Negligence
Employee Share Schemes & Incentives	Projects
Employment	Public International Law
Energy & Natural Resources	Public Procurement
Environment	Real Estate
Financial Services	Real Estate Finance
Fraud	Real Estate Litigation
Information Technology	Restructuring/Insolvency
Insurance	Retail
	Tax
	Transport

The True Picture

as to what goes on that form because once you get the schedule for your remaining three seats, it's fixed." While some agreed "the bird's eye view" this system offers is a positive, the majority complained about "the difficulty of planning out your entire training contract so early on. It's a shame we can't let our experience shape our opinions as we go along." On the plus side, trainees can request specific supervisors to study under. "We usually get together with those leaving the seat to find out who specialises in what and who's known for being difficult so we can make informed requests."

Hogging all the deals

Lovells' corporate department excels in M&A work, with particular strengths in the energy, financial services and life sciences sectors. The firm's recent representation of SABMiller during its £7.8bn acquisition of Aussie brewer Foster's garnered much attention from the press, as did its advisory role during Northumbrian Water's £4.7bn takeover by Cheung Kong Infrastructure. Barclays, ExxonMobil and Santander are among other high-flying clients. Seats in the department correspond with various subgroups like private equity, regulatory and M&A, and most offer "an incredibly varied experience" by the sounds of it. "I was doing everything from helping set up charities to assisting companies going insolvent," said one. On the private equity side, there's the chance to get involved in energy transactions and IPOs, which translates into "a lot of detective work for trainees – we're the

ones doing the research into shareholder structures and due diligence on companies." Luckily, "nobody's chained to the photocopier," sources assured us. In addition to drafting board minutes, memos and articles, interviewees spoke of a "surprising" amount of client contact. "I got to liaise with a few Americans and other foreign lawyers during a cross-border acquisition," one said.

Finance seats also cover a range of practice areas including banking, project finance, capital markets and asset finance. Thanks to the firm's global coverage, lawyers are friendly with many of the industry's bigwigs, from Barclays and HSBC to RBS, Deutsche Bank and Lloyds. Trainees on the project finance front spoke of drafting shareholder agreements and attending negotiations for deals across a range of industries. "The research is so in-depth for each matter that you leave the seat super enthusiastic about topics like gas or waste or electricity," we were told. Over in asset finance it's a "document-heavy workload" that revolves mainly around aviation and shipping-related matters. "A lot of time is spent putting amendments into documents, checking them over and bibling." That said, "things kick off when it gets busy – I got to draft documents, make some changes to loan agreements and even deal with a few clients directly," said one source.

Almost all trainees go on secondment at some point, usually in corporate, finance or commercial roles. Each rotation sees around eight people head to international seats in Hong Kong, Paris, Dubai, Brussels, Singapore and New York, while another 20 or so take up in-house positions with companies like John Lewis, Prudential and ExxonMobil. "When you get your seat plan at the beginning, it'll say whether you have a secondment or not. Later down the line they invite applications for international seats, and once those are sorted out everyone else is assigned to client secondments." While there have been new opportunities in New York from 2012, some grumbled about "being forced to do a client secondment when you wanted an international one." Fortunately, the experience is "really valuable, even if you're not mad keen on the role – we're relied on a lot."

Baby, you're a star

Litigation has always been one of Lovells' star departments. The firm's fraud team is among the City's best – recent successes include issuing multiple claims on behalf of BTA Bank in one of the biggest set of fraud proceedings in the UK and advising several major companies on the impact of the UK's Bribery Act 2010. On the pensions front, litigators are acting for the trustee of the BT Pension Scheme, the UK's largest private sector scheme, in a £23bn liabilities case. "The pace is generally slower than corporate or finance," trainees said of a stint in the department, "although things can get hectic in the run up to trial, particularly when it's a big case." Trainees' day-to-day roles vary depending on which subgroup they work for – those in employment contend with *"research and quite a lot of black-letter law,"* while their peers over in the construction disputes team mentioned *"preparing bundles and dealing with clients pretty frequently."* All contentious seats are accompanied by a three-day advocacy training course that *"covers the basics like building a case and how to argue."*

Our sources appreciated that *"the role of the firm's niche departments is more than corporate support work."* Indeed, the real estate practice has a rich client list of its own, advising the likes of Waitrose, KPMG and News International. Among the bigger highlights of recent times was overseeing the £200m sale of BBC Television Centre in White City to development giant Stanhope. Likewise, Lovells' IP arm is strong in its own right, particularly on the patent side. Lawyers have enforced patents for the majority of the world's top pharmaceutical companies and recently became embroiled in the smartphone wars by advising Qualcomm, supplier of iPhone chips, on how to protect its trade secrets during the ongoing litigation between SAMSUNG and Apple. *"I was able to gain a good grasp of court procedures during my seat,"* one trainee said, mentioning the seat *"also covers trade mark work."*

The majority of our interviewees had become involved with pro bono work at some point, calling it *"a fundamental part of the firm – there are lots of full-time employees working on matters at any given time."* Projects tend to fall into one of two categories: *"general"* ones open to anyone, such as form-filling assistance for non-native English speakers or obtaining injunctions for domestic violence victims; and seat-specific undertakings *"where the matter is more relevant to the billable work you're doing."* We heard from trainees who'd assisted charities on constitutional issues, helped laid-off employees pursue wrongful dismissal claims, advocated for victims of disability discrimination and more. *"It's amazing to have your own client as a trainee – if their case goes to trial, you're the one representing them in court."* While pro bono work is *"certainly heralded"* across the firm, *"ultimately your fee-earning work has to come first,"* trainees conceded. *"People mostly take it on when their department is slow."*

Lovely Lovells

Despite its *"palpable emphasis on top-quality work,"* Lovells assumes a *"sensible"* attitude when it comes to work/life balance, we were told. *"Partners are reasonable in their expectations. When things are busy, you have to stay until the work is done, but if it's quiet you're free to go home instead of sitting around until everyone else is gone."* When frenzied periods of long hours do occur, they're usually tempered by *"little rewards in recognition of your hard work – a day off in lieu, for example."* Trainees share an office with their supervisor, which means direct feedback is readily available and *"help is only ever*

a desk away if you need it." While some supervisors are more hands-on than others, *"the firm as a whole does a good job of keeping an eye on trainees. Almost everybody is open to chatting and answering questions, and we're each assigned a partner mentor we can talk to about things like our qualification options."*

The moniker 'Lovely Lovells' has been bandied about in years past, but insiders told us the firm is keen to shake off its 'friendly' reputation. Explained one: *"It's really a matter of making sure we present an honest view of our culture. We're not a firm with easy working hours and hugs all around; people take their work seriously and aim to push forward all the time."* That's not to say the atmosphere's not a positive one, however. *"People are very nice and treat each other well,"* interviewees insisted. *"It's just that there's a lot more to us than the generic description 'friendly' suggests."* Considering the sheer size of the London branch, which houses nearly 700 solicitors (including trainees), it's little surprise certain aspects of the working environment vary depending on who you're sitting with. *"Each department has its own ethos. Some are more open then others, but overall it's a pretty relaxed place,"* one interviewee clarified. *"My tie lives on my desk!"* Said another: *"It's rare to come across someone who's unreasonable or difficult to work with. In fact, I get partners who say hello to me whose names I don't even know!"*

With 129 trainees all told, our interviewees found it hard to put their finger on a certain Hogan Lovells type. *"I'd say we're reasonably diverse in terms of people's backgrounds,"* sources said, mentioning *"a lot of nationalities and personalities represented"* as well as a 50/50 split between law and non-law degrees. With respect to universities, *"there's a heavy Oxbridge tilt,"* though *"the firm has expanded the number of institutions they target as well as their outreach at the school stage."* Trainees counted commercial awareness and a client-oriented demeanour among the top priorities for recruiters, a point Edgar agrees with. *"Understanding how to deliver the service that our clients expect is really key. As a former colleague used to say, this job is comparable to being a waiter at a top five restaurant: you have to be able to anticipate what the client wants, make recommendations as to other options they might try that they might not have thought of, and deliver a first class service that hopefully leaves them wanting to come back again."* Fortunately, such skills lend themselves to a wide range of characters. *"We've got non-lawyers, people who are a bit older and even a Trekkie or two among us!"* insiders reported. *"There's a refreshing lack of typecasting here."*

Trainees raved about Lovells' City digs, which contain *"lots of little perks"* including an in-house Starbucks, a gym with showers and free classes, cookie-filled client rooms and, *"best of all,"* a wine bar in the basement, complete with a secret entrance in the canteen. *"I've spent so much time there they've given me a loyalty card! Don't go in if you don't want to bump into another Lovells lawyer,"* one source suggested. Basement boozing aside, social activities tend to be organised by department and are often charity-related – we heard about cake-baking contests, exercise bike spin-a-thons and even a dance competition called 'Legally Ballroom,' all held in the name of fund-

raising. By far the year's biggest event is the summer party, which is *"renowned for being awesome."* The 2012 do coincided with retirement of co-chair John Young, who cemented a legendary status for himself by zipwiring in wearing a Braveheart outfit. *"Fingers crossed someone steps up to fill his shoes this year, though that'll be a hard act to follow!"*

And finally...

NQ jobs lists are posted in April and October, and trainees are welcome to apply for a seat they haven't sat in. We heard departments take differing attitudes to the hiring process, but *"quite a few favour a strict approach"* that includes panel interviews. In 2013, 51 out of 74 trainees were kept on.

Holman Fenwick Willan LLP

The facts
Location: London
Number of UK partners/solicitors: 74/122
Total number of trainees: 35
Seats: 4x6 months
Alternative seats: overseas seats, secondments
Extras: pro bono – Morden Legal Advice Centre, LawWorks

On chambersstudent.co.uk...
How to get into HFW
Interview with training principal Toby Stephens
Piracy: an international problem

Shipping specialist Holman Fenwick Willan offers trainees a wealth of international opportunities, and all the responsibility they can handle.

Preparing for takeoff

Holman Fenwick Willan was founded by two mariners during the panic of 1873, which was largely triggered by the discovery that the newly completed Suez Canal couldn't be used by commercial sailing vessels, because the winds blew in the wrong direction. Rough winds are buffeting the shipping industry again these days, but as one trainee explained, shipping's *"countercyclical nature means we're always going to have work – in good times parties will be making contracts; in bad times they'll be breaking them."*

Along with fellow specialist Ince & Co, HFW is top-ranked for shipping by *Chambers UK* – trainees saw this practice as *"the beating heart of Holmans, even though they're marketing themselves as able to do lots of other things."* Recently, HFW has been promoting its growing corporate offering, alongside strengths in transport, trade and energy, which have been bolstered by new aerospace and construction departments. The firm's heavy-duty client list includes RSA and Barclays, alongside a huge range of industrial giants like British Airways, Rolls-Royce, Glencore and Eni. With recent new offices opened in Perth and São Paulo, the firm is *"really ambitious abroad."* Thanks to the firm's strong international ethos, training principal Toby Stephens advised that recruits *"need to be open to working or travelling abroad at some point in their career – if you don't like getting on aeroplanes this is probably not the place for you."*

The first seat is allocated by the firm, then trainees put down three choices for each subsequent seat, choosing from a heavily contentious set of options including trade and energy; shipping and transport; insurance and rein-surance; aerospace; and commercial banking disputes. There's also a compulsory corporate projects and finance seat. Stephens explained that thanks to HFW's new offices abroad, *"we guarantee each trainee an overseas placement"* – the flip side of which is that going abroad, if not technically compulsory, is *"more than encouraged"* by the firm. There's *"hot competition for the shipping seat,"* meaning that *"persistence is key"* – although being willing to go overseas to do shipping raises the odds.

Setting sail

Shipping offers trainees *"a very dynamic, very active"* environment in a department with impeccable pedigree. The practice is divided into 'wet' work and 'dry' work. The former involves perils at sea like collisions, groundings, piracy and salvage and lets trainees *"get stuck into some interesting problems – you have to pick up the background quite quickly so it helps having a mariner in the office who you can ask technical questions of."* Piracy is naturally *"the first thing that grabs your attention"* said one trainee, who explained that, unfortunately, due to strict confidentiality *"everybody knows we do it but we can't really talk about it."* Somali piracy might be subsiding, but there are still *"problems"* in the Horn of Africa – HFW's work involves *"not actually getting the crew off"* a stricken ship so much as *"dealing with the vessel stuck there, the contract, the charter party."* HFW lawyers also advise on anti-piracy efforts, including drafting the international maritime council's standard form for the use of armed guards onboard vessels. In salvage cases stakes are similarly high, thanks to a trend towards cargo ships getting bigger – HFW recently acted for the salvors of a $1.2bn BP drilling vessel which almost capsized in the Gulf of Mexico. In another case, after *"a fire on board*

The True Picture

Chambers UK rankings

Asset Finance	Insurance
Aviation	Shipping
Commodities	Transport
Dispute Resolution	Travel

The True Picture

a vessel, we had to deal with the ship owners and cargo owners to get the salvors a decent reward in the salvage arbitration – it was quite a reactive, tactical case to work on." HFW benefits from having a flotilla of international offices close to major shipping routes – one trainee was *"working on a pollution claim – the lawyers nearby in Singapore have taken witness statements, while we're making the defence back in London."*

Responsibility levels for trainees in the London office weren't that high, perhaps because of the specialist nature of the work – the 19 master mariners on staff *"tend to get sent off to go and look at things, because they'll know what they're talking about"* – but trainees on secondment in the smaller overseas teams get a wider range of work and responsibilities. One was *"left in control of a case"* deciding which jurisdiction to hear a dispute in, and another went to *"get things signed by surveyors, and had conferences with counsel."* Dry work generally deals with contractual disputes, particularly about charter parties, which are the contracts by which boats are let by their owners to cargo carriers. In one such dispute, *"our clients hired a vessel for a four-year period – on giving it back the owners claimed it hadn't been maintained properly."*

In the pipeline

Trade and energy trainees also end up handling some dry shipping: one *"high adrenaline"* case involved *"using all angles of attack after our client's ship had been arrested,"* while another trainee *"got to initiate the arrest of a vessel which had our client's goods on it – the threat meant we ended up getting paid and got the goods back, but it was still fun!"* The bulk of trade and energy work, though, is in shareholder or trade disputes subject to international arbitration, with work for industrial clients in mining, oil and gas joined by commodities work *"including grain, wheat, cotton and oil – not the kind of thing you do at university; it was all new to me."* Sources' experiences had been *"pretty intense"* and offered high levels of responsibility – one trainee handling petroleum sales *"that had gone a little bit wrong"* was entrusted with *"preparing the questions and interviewing the witnesses directly."* Trainees were also set to taking notes at hearings, *"then translating them into a more understandable form to send to the client," "phoning counsel to discuss our case,"* and one had even *"gone before a master asking him to give permission for a worldwide freezing order."* Overall, trainees in trade and energy benefited from being *"involved in*

fewer cases to a much greater extent – your input is a lot more valuable, and you really learn case management."

Corporate projects and finance is the firm's only transactional department and is *"divided into two halves – one side does shipping and aviation, the other does general corporate."* HFW's client base still has a strongly international and industrial flavour – in a recent deal it advised the Cameroon Oil Transportation Company on the €75.3m refinancing of a pipeline. Recent lateral hires have almost doubled the size of the department and diversified HFW's corporate offering. Capital markets work now brings a *"new capability to the firm: we're working on IPOs, debt issuing and Islamic finance, a real variety of projects."*

The competition team involves technical work regarding *"complaints to the EU Commission"* on issues including abuse of dominance. One trainee had the opportunity to *"attend four hearings in my first week."* Clients of the team include UEFA and Air China.

Stormy weather

Trainees felt that *"high levels of responsibility are common throughout HFW – they get you involved with proper work rather than just chucking bits of research at you."* While some trainees really thrived on the opportunities offered, others saw *"a need to be a bit more nurturing and maybe a bit less hands-off."* The firm doesn't really have an official mentoring system, which training principal Toby Stephens puts down to not being a large firm where that formality is necessary: *"It's more the sort of culture where it's about picking someone you're comfortable talking to."* Sources also warned of certain partners with *"very big personalities who have a reputation for working trainees very hard,"* and several felt *"there isn't an attitude of sharing work around the department"* as some partners are very possessive of 'their' trainees. Stephens admitted that *"some seats generally get the tougher tag"* but felt that those experiencing them *"come out better trainees"* as a result. We've said in the past that the secret of success as an HFW trainee is to be thick-skinned enough not to be bothered by the occasional rough-and-tumble of life here, confident enough to shine and so pick up more interesting work, yet humble enough to accept that the partners rule the roost.

One trainee *"had a misconception that because we aren't corporate-heavy we wouldn't do long hours, but that's not the case."* Although on average trainees work from 9am to 7.30pm, which they saw as *"pretty reasonable,"* a couple of seats involve much later hours and some weekend work, with a culture where *"you feel obliged to stay until the partners go home."* The firm provides mid and end-of-seat reviews – some trainees were pleased with the *"really good"* level of detail these entail, though others found the ten-page review forms *"quite frustrating"* – you can't please everyone, we suppose.

HFW inhabits a majestic 1980s Gothic pile in concrete and pink granite, with life-size sculptures of crutched friars paying homage to Tower Hill's monastic history. *"Every Friday,"* trainees habituate *"the Habit, just below the offices,"* which offers wine, traditional pub grub, and sawdust and barrel medieval theming a little at odds with all the tinted glass and marble outside. Trainees raved about the subsidised canteen – *"we all congregate down there for lunch"* – with its *"daily theme, like curry day or Mediterranean food"* and *"barbecues outside in the summer."* In addition to various departmental drinks trolleys, every two months there's a big firm-wide buffet lunch with wine and a chocolate fountain. Big events like Christmas and summer parties are held every other year, alternating with smaller departmental dos. As well as a trainee-led running club and a football team with a dashing new blue and gold kit, there are more unusual opportunities like *"dinghy racing in the Docklands organised by one of our mariners."* The international offices each have a flavour of their own – the Brussels one *"is in an old architects' office, so it's quite snazzy, with cool art-*

work and strange lights hanging down and a lovely view over the city," while Geneva offers the lure of *"looking out of your office window to see the Alps."*

Plenty of trainees have had previous careers in *"industry, insurance, shipping, or the navy,"* although most come straight from uni, making for *"a few more down-to-earth characters, rather than everybody being pure lawyer."* HFW is diversifying rapidly due to the tough economic conditions – one trainee noticed that where *"the firm had felt a lot more London-centric and like a family"* during their vac scheme, *"that's giving way to a more corporate atmosphere – it's more business-oriented now."*

Trainees had mixed feelings about qualification – one suggested that *"they will make an attempt to take everyone on, but whether that will be in London is debatable."* In the past some trainees have gone to competitor firms rather than qualify abroad, but Toby Stephens offered reassurance that although *"we want people to go to a jurisdiction where there's the potential to grow the business there are still more jobs in London than through the international network."* In 2013, HFW kept on 13 out of its 14 qualifiers.

And finally...

Trainees opined that successful applicants are now *"not only bright but very commercially aware, and abreast of issues in the industries of their clients."* The big publication for the shipping industry is TradeWinds – maybe take a look at that.

Ince & Co

The facts

Location: London

Number of UK partners/solicitors: 53/90

Partners who trained at firm: c.70%

Total number of trainees: 31

Seats: 4x6 months

Alternative seats: occasional overseas seats

On chambersstudent.co.uk...

How to get into Ince & Co

An insider's view of the insurance industry

Consider getting on board with Ince & Co if you want to make a splash in the shipping, insurance and energy sectors.

Salty sea dogs

The international market relies on shipping, but it can be a perilous business. Any number of disasters are waiting to strike when sailing the deep blue sea with a few thousand tonnes of precious cargo – collisions, pirate hijackings, exploding freights, a man overboard. But never fear! In the wake of calamity, it's the wise mariner who's got the folks at Ince & Co on speed dial to sort through the ensuing flotsam and jetsam with their expert maritime lawyering.

Ince has been at the helm of shipping law for 143 years, racking up a steady streak of top *Chambers UK* rankings in the practice area since 2004. Accordingly, the firm reels in the big fish when it comes to high-profile matters. It was Ince to the rescue in the legal aftermath of the sinking of the 'Costa Concordia' cruise ship in 2012, and lawyers have dealt with some significant piracy cases in Somalia, the Niger Delta and the Malacca Straits with the help of the firm's 24-hour emergency hotline and accompanying app, both of which are poised to respond to watery dramas with haste.

Such misadventures at sea comprise Ince's 'wet' shipping undertakings, while 'dry' work refers to contractual and commercial matters as well as disputes within the industry. In total, shipping accounts for half of the firm's work. Beyond this, the firm told us its work is approximately 20% energy, 20% insurance and 10% international trade and aviation. Generally, litigation is the name of the game at Ince, so aspiring transactional lawyers have traditionally been encouraged to set their sights elsewhere. That's not to say non-contentious work is off-limits, however. In fact, *"it's a growing part of the practice,"* our inter-

viewees said, claiming: *"The firm's actually starting to encourage people to take up transactional work."*

"I don't think I've ever been involved in a case here that was purely British," noted one source enthusiastically; *"there's always an international angle."* Indeed, Ince's global clout is substantial and consistently proves a draw for trainees keen to get their hands on multi-jurisdictional matters. In addition to the London base, suitably located in St Katherine Docks, the firm has shops in Paris, Hamburg, Le Havre, Monaco, Piraeus, Beijing, Shanghai, Singapore, Hong Kong and Dubai. Our sources spoke fondly of their experience *"constantly dealing with the other offices"* and working for a range of geographically disparate companies, from those in Holland and Korea to Greece and even good old Aberdeen.

Different ports of call

Ince has a *"fairly unique way of doing things"* when it comes to set-up: instead of designating strict departments, the firm is arranged into groups, but no lawyer is strictly confined to any one of them. So, trainees sit with a single partner each rotation, but they're actually free to take work from any group. This fluid structure offers the *"flexibility to move around and focus on areas that interest you most"* and makes it possible to carry over cases into the next rotation. After all, *"it doesn't make sense to abandon a big bit of litigation three days before a hearing begins or hand it off to another trainee who hasn't been involved with any of the legwork,"* pointed out one insider. *"Plus, you get to build up your relationship further with the client."* That said, *"having work follow you around can prove a drawback as you might get stuck with the same ongoing case for a long time; you're not guaran-*

Chambers UK rankings

Asset Finance	Fraud
Aviation	Insurance
Commodities	Professional Negligence
Dispute Resolution	Shipping
Energy & Natural Resources	

teed the broad exposure those plonked in brand-new departments every six months get." In any case, the training contract emphasises a generalist experience, so it's only after a year or so of being an NQ that Incies choose *"an interlinked primary and secondary"* specialism.

Trainees use a 'traffic light' system to update their availability each week, but they're also required to take an proactive role in finding work. *"You have to go out there, make contacts and market yourself by chatting to partners in the lift and approaching people at drinks gatherings; you can't expect good-quality work to just land on your desk."* Sources admitted that the process of doorknocking and networking *"isn't everyone's cup of tea,"* but most took the pragmatic view that it's positive training for the future: *"Sitting quietly and only doing what's given to you will just make it harder to market yourself to clients as a qualified lawyer."* Fortunately, *"partners are approachable and keen to get you involved. From that perspective, there's a lot of support."*

Batten down the hatches

Thanks to the fluid boundaries between departments, trainees often find themselves *"keeping multiple plates spinning."* Said one: *"I started off my training contract with an energy dispute between two large companies, at the same time handling aviation matters like insurance claims, registration issues for private airfields and settlements for mid-air collisions."* Fortunately, weekly lectures are put on to guide trainees through the technical intricacies of Ince's sector coverage. *"The partners appreciate you might not have much pre-existing knowledge on certain subjects,"* sources said, with one admitting: *"My first time on a ship was only last year!"*

"There's quite often a pure contractual dispute at the heart of a shipping case, as opposed to an incredibly complex energy dispute or large M&A deal, so it's possible to run most matters with just a few people," a source informed us. As such, shipping teams tend to err on the lean side, with high levels of responsibility for new recruits. *"I've corresponded with clients and counsel, drafted bits and bobs and done the bundling, doc review and admin work,"* one said. Another source mentioned *"having input into the advice giving. I got to attend several client meetings, including a seven-hour one, which was invigorating to witness."* Indeed, drama often runs high during shipping cases. *"When there's hostility between sides, both*

thrash it out to settle on a figure that's commercially suitable. I'd say observing negotiations has been the highest point of my training contract so far,"* one interviewee noted. Recent years have seen the firm represent leading marine insurer Gard in a $143m unsafe port claim following the loss of a cargo ship during inclement weather, and act for Novoship in a $170m litigation to recover losses arising from fraudulent chartering arrangements. The latter matter is *"a landmark case"* that's spawned a good deal of follow-on work, according to trainees. *"The judgment came out in December, but we're still dealing with various issues connected to it."*

Wet work is *"seen as the sexy side of shipping,"* insiders agreed, telling us: *"Cases are glamorous and fast-paced."* When emergency calls comes in, *"you see partners running from their offices into the meeting room in order to deal with the barrage of information and piece together what's going on. The initial moments are hectic, especially if it's a collision or grounding, which involves a lot of parties."* Trainees told of liaising with some *"colourful, interesting characters"* from the shipping world, many of whom require *"a sensitive touch"* in order to sustain their relationship with Ince. *"Clients aren't always faceless corporate entities; quite often they own their own businesses and tend to take the advice we offer very personally."*

Ince's energy practice is well rounded, covering everything from charter party disputes, real estate and employment issues to corporate M&A matters, operational insurance claims and gas and renewables financing. The firm recently represented energy company BlueWater in an €11m contractual dispute against Mercon Steel over the faulty assembly of a mooring platform. There's a special emphasis on offshore exploration and production issues within the practice – a sizeable chunk of clientele is comprised of drilling contractors, whom lawyers advise on day-to-day operational issues like crewing as well as contract negotiations. Trainees *"don't get loads of client contact"* on the energy front, *"but we're relied on pretty heavily during the disclosure stages to make sure all the documents are ready to go."*

Around half of all Ince's work is underpinned by insurance in some way or another, with lawyers working across myriad sectors including the aviation, space, energy, engineering, professional indemnity, fine art and, unsurprisingly, marine industries. On the contentious side, Ince acts for big-ticket names like RSA and Faraday – the firm recently represented the latter in a $40m case involving asbestos claims. One interview described *"a document management-focused role involving doc review and bundling"* during their time on a professional negligence case, while another reported *"drafting letters to both sides"* during a reinsurance dispute.

The firm periodically sends trainees on six-month stints to overseas offices. Recent destinations include Paris, Hamburg, Shanghai, Piraeus and Dubai.

Three sheets to the wind?

Our interviewees described a schedule averaging from 9am until 7pm *"most days."* That said, many were quick to note that *"occasional troughs and crests"* are inevitable, telling us: *"There are times when things kick off and you find yourself here at midnight."* Luckily, *"nobody's beasted all the time,"* and forays into the early hours are largely improved by the provision of some hearty fare. *"There's a chef who prepares home-cooked and quite healthy meals for people working late, which is a much better motivator than greasy takeaway pizza."* Other perks in the *"amazing"* Docklands office include a *"huge"* balcony, a dockside café and a stellar view from the top of the building. *"You can see yachts being parked in the wharf from some windows and the City, the Tower and the Shard from others."*

The old-school industries Ince has traditionally rubbed elbows with *"have definitely left their mark on the firm's culture,"* thought trainees. *"It's no secret we've got a conservative exterior."* That said, many noticed *"some very marked changes"* in recent years that suggest the tides are shifting. *"Since becoming an LLP, management has started modernising to fit in with the the general legal* market – for example, there's a push to become more inclusive in terms of gender,"* one source felt. Indeed, while the older generation remains *"a boys' club,"* women outnumber men two to one in the current class of trainees. Likewise, *"the firm isn't just comprised of white people from Oxbridge;"* in fact, the current trainee cohort represents a range of universities, international backgrounds and languages. According to insiders, unifying factors among Incies include *"a fairly strong personality"* and a high degree of confidence (not to be confused with arrogance, a sure way to *"get people's backs up"*). When it comes to interview, sources agreed a *"tenacious attitude"* comes in handy as *"some partners come off as quite fearsome. You have to show you're not easily flustered and can stick to your guns."*

Thanks to a prevailing 'work hard/play hard' attitude, a *"rowdy"* social life awaits successful applicants. *"People here attack drinking with the same verve that accompanies their work, which means things can get pretty raucous!"* Client events and department dos complement regular trainee get-togethers and monthly 'Ince Drinks', which see *"the walls just fall down between partners and trainees – suddenly you find yourself swigging from somebody's gin and tonic like you've known them for years!"* The firm also pushes the boat out with its *"amazing"* London Marathon party and *"spectacular"* May Ball – the latter is a glitzy hotel affair reliably followed by an unofficial after-party in a club.

And finally...

A historically pragmatic approach to retention had many interviewees in high spirits when it came to discussing qualification, though some expressed concern the market might not keep everyone afloat. In the end, ten of 15 qualifiers took up jobs with the firm in 2013.

Irwin Mitchell

The facts

Location: Birmingham, Bristol, Leeds, London, Manchester, Newcastle, Sheffield, Scotland

Number of UK partners/solicitors: 148/357

Total number of trainees: 83

Seats: 3x4 + 1 x 12 months or 4x6 months

Alternative seats: none

Extras: pro bono – CAB, LawWorks, ProHelp and others

On chambersstudent.co.uk...

How to get into Irwin Mitchell

The firm's conversion to an ABS

Pro bono opportunities at Irwin Mitchell

Newly transformed into an ABS, Irwin Mitchell is on an ardent mission to reinvent its image by *"beefing up"* its business-related capacities.

Redressing the balance

"Unusual," "unique" and *"innovative"* were words trainees frequently bandied around when sharing their thoughts on Irwin Mitchell. We tend to agree: for starters, it's not terribly common for a bulky national firm – one of the UK's top 25, in fact – to maintain headquarters in Sheffield (point one for 'unusual'). Likewise, IM's extremely broad scale of both personal and business legal services makes it hard to put your finger on a comparable peer ('unique' – tick), and its long-awaited conversion to an Alternative Business Structure, or ABS, is nothing if not progressive (here's looking at you, 'innovative').

While the firm dates back to 1912, it's IM's recent history that's shaped the 500-lawyer institution as we know it today. IM's national scope has broadened in recent years to encompass offices in Birmingham, Bristol, Glasgow, Leeds, London, Manchester, Newcastle and Sheffield. And while this firm had its beginnings acting for claimants in PI and clin neg cases, its work for business clients has also increased, particularly on the corporate, real estate and commercial litigation fronts. Growth has been fuelled by a desire to give both City and other national firms a run for their money. Still, the firm's commercial side – around a quarter of its business – has yet to invoke the levels of esteem its personal services enjoy (though to be fair, IM has been honing those for a much longer period). In addition to leading medical negligence and personal injury practices – which *Chambers UK* adorns with many a ranking – IM garners much respect in the areas of public law and court of protection work.

IM celebrated its centenary in 2012, which was marked by a 7% rise in turnover and the firm's receipt of five ABS licences (if you don't know about ABSs yet, see page 19). Among other things, they allow non-lawyers to have a stake in solicitors' firms, and since August 2012 IM's management has brought on board three such people to help steer the firm forward – senior practitioners from PricewaterhouseCoopers, KPMG and Dart Group. Lisa Jordan, training partner, explains that *"we have the legal expertise, but we want to be able to balance that with experience and knowledge from other sectors."* It's no secret the firm's hoping to secure cash from external investors, but insiders recently dispelled rumours that an imminent stock market flotation is on the cards, with managing partner John Pickering emphasising a focus on lateral hiring going forward. A lot of new faces have certainly come in over the course of 2012 and early 2013, especially within the commercial groups. Lawyers from Nabarro, Squire Sanders and DLA Piper have all recently joined to help balance up this traditionally litigation-heavy firm.

Business or personal?

Trainees settle on a specific 'stream' before joining the firm: either 'personal legal services' (PLS) for an experience rooted in clin neg, PI and private client, or the more corporate/commercial 'business legal services' (BLS). *"It's impossible to request seats in the other stream,"* said one trainee, emphasising the need for applicants to be *"100% sure"* of the direction they wish their careers to take. For PLS trainees, three seats of four months each are followed by a year-long 'qualification seat'. Many of our interviewees appreciated this set-up for its emphasis on providing experience prior to qualification, but some found the idea of a year-long seat rather *"restrictive"* as *"it forces you to make qualification decisions very early in your training contract."* That said, we heard those par-

Chambers UK rankings

Administrative & Public Law	Family/Matrimonial
	Fraud
Banking & Finance	Health & Safety
Charities	Information Technology
Civil Liberties & Human Rights	Personal Injury
	Police Law
Clinical Negligence	Private Client
Corporate Crime & Investigations	Product Liability
	Professional Discipline
Corporate/M&A	Professional Negligence
Court of Protection	Real Estate
Crime	Real Estate Litigation
Dispute Resolution	Restructuring/Insolvency
Employment	Tax
Environment	Travel

ticularly unhappy with their final seat assignment have the option of splitting it into two, though this is very rare. *"It's understood if you stomped your feet hard enough then you'll have got what you wanted in the first place."* Following some rejigging over the past year, those in the BLS stream now complete a more traditional four seats of six months each.

Before joining, trainees discuss their seat choices with the grad recruitment team team, who *"ask questions about your preferences but also stress the importance of business need."* While the majority of our sources failed to get exactly what they'd requested, they were largely content with their lot, having *"known the score from the beginning."* Certain seats are only available in some locations, so trainees urged hopefuls to *"tailor your application to the right office."* See our website for a full list of seat options.

Claimant compassion

Most of our PLS sources had completed a seat in IM's clinical negligence department, alternatively known as 'medical law and patient rights'. The practice – which *Chambers UK* top-ranks across Birmingham, London and Sheffield – is *"incredibly busy"* and offers *"huge variety of cases,"* including injuries sustained during operations or birth, misdiagnoses and instances where hospital staff have failed to spot preliminary signs of severe illnesses. *"We've got some experts among us, so you really feel like you're working with the best people in this area."* Work is always claimant-side, typically in costly cases against GPs, NHS foundation trusts or other medical professionals. *"There's also a small team that specialises in low-value claims,"* one source added, mentioning trainees tend to get *"lot of responsibility"* on such matters. *"We do everything from setting up funding to approaching experts for evaluation to drafting letters to the defendant*

laying out the allegations." For the high-stakes matters, trainees have *"a more supportive role,"* helping review medical records, filing claim forms and other supportive documents, preparing letters of instruction to experts and attending conferences with counsel.

In addition to *"great deal of tact,"* a clin neg stint requires the ability to adapt to various situations, trainees took care to point out. *"Approaching the failure to diagnose someone's cancer is inevitably different from the way you approach a death that's been caused as a result of a procedure. Each situation is different, as is the terminology involved, and it's up to you to put it in simple terms for clients who are understandably upset and angry. Some of these people have been left with injuries that will affect them for the rest of their lives."* A similar skill set is required of those spending time in IM's serious injury or industrial/asbestos disease practices. The former *"pretty much does what it says on the tin"* – lawyers contend with cases involving *"catastrophic"* injuries sustained from road or workplace accidents. According to insiders, both seats offer *"a lot of court time,"* and trainees assume *"an active role – they encourage us to take on a lot."* Asbestos-related cases in particular are accompanied by *"real sense of urgency,"* as *"sometimes the client hasn't got long left – you've got to do your utmost to help them and do it quickly."*

The court of protection team deals with *"people who don't have the ability to handle their own affairs"* – clients can range from elderly people with dementia to cerebral palsy patients. It's up to trainees to make court applications, attend meetings with financial advisers and *"keep on top of things like clients' outgoing expenses and doctor visits. There's so much client contact."* Over in a public law seat, lawyers are faced with *"some novel challenges"* relating to health, welfare, prison, education and professional regulation issues. *"It's a really exciting seat – I was going to court almost every day,"* said one source. *"Unfortunately, cuts to legal aid make such cases increasingly difficult to fund."* Read our online bonus feature to find out more.

Other seats in the PLS stream include travel litigation, armed forces claims, fast-track claims, public liability, employers' liability and workplace injury, as well as private client options like family, and contentious probate.

What's your business?

Recent lateral hires from DLA Piper and Nabarro have boosted IM's corporate department, which handles *"mainly private M&A work"* across the manufacturing, precision engineering, financial and digital and IT sectors. The London team recently oversaw the €200m sale of a Turkish shopping centre business, while lawyers over in Sheffield advised a subsidiary of AES Engineering on the acquisition of share capital of Ultimate Vacuum – Denmark's leading hoover pump distributor, apparently. Some BLS

The True Picture

trainees reported a *"quiet and not overly exciting"* corporate experience, but others relished the *"extra drama"* they encountered on the transactional side. *"You're not just doing the strict ancillary documents,"* said one interviewee, who mentioned drafting the *"bespoke clauses in an SPA. As the seat progresses you get more involved, especially with clients."*

The real estate team handles a fair whack of development and property finance work and also advises businesses on their operational property portfolios. Clients include banks like HSBC, Santander and the Co-operative, plus large property development companies such as Henry Boot Developments. Sources reported *"some big deals in the works,"* especially in light of IM Manchester's January 2013 hire of four commercial property partners from DLA Piper. Trainees told of *"brilliant"* supervision in the department and plenty of formal training: *"I must have attended 12 different sessions!"* Initially, *"there's a bit of grunt work, like putting together title packs and deeds,"* one explained, *"but the more you prove yourself, the more you're given – by the end of my seat I got stuck into some big real estate finance matters."*

IM's commercial litigation team is known for its expertise in the insurance field, working for big industry names such as Aviva, AXA and Allianz. However, litigators deal with disputes in areas as varied as competition, construction, defamation, product liability and professional negligence. A lucky few sources who'd seen a case through as far as trial told of *"drafting court documents like the pleadings and the particulars of claim."* Other seats in the BLS stream include employment, pensions, banking & finance IP, insolvency and regulatory.

So far, IM's conversion to an ABS *"hasn't had much impact on our day-to-day job,"* trainees agreed, though *"things could change going forward on that front,"* some thought. *"IM has traditionally been known as a PI firm, but management is really trying to improve the external perception and credibility of our business side by recruiting lawyers from firms above us in the corporate league table,"* said one. *"They know PI work alone wouldn't keep us afloat much longer."* According to some, this push on the BLS side is starting to add more of a *"corporate edge"* to IM – a few insiders described a shift in atmosphere from the *"friendly and relaxed"* vibe cultivated by a history of people-oriented services towards one more in line with *"a big corporate firm."* However, others

dismissed this notion entirely, emphasising *"there's not much interaction"* between the two streams as *"each sustains a separate working environment"* in most offices. That said, this may not be the case forever, as they admitted: *"There's a big push to further integrate the BLS and PLS streams so the firm can cross-sell its practices."*

Salt of the earth

Our interviewees proudly characterised IM as *"not posh, potentially because management focuses on recruiting a diverse range of people."* Thanks to an open-plan layout – present in all offices – *"a healthy degree"* of communication is sustained across the firm: *"It's easy to pop over to someone's desk to ask a quick question or go speak with a partner."* When it comes to working hours, sources were largely satisfied. *"We're not worked to the bone when it's not necessary. No one will tell you to cancel your theatre plans or watch you like a hawk."* However, there's a trade-off: *"Our salary's not the greatest,"* a few pointed out. *"We don't do magic circle hours, but it's not like we're working nine to five, either."* For the record, salaries have increased in 2013; first-seaters in the regions pick up £25,000 while their counterparts in London start on £33,000.

Firm-wide social activities aren't terribly common, but we did hear about a *"smashing"* annual charity quiz, which sees all the offices compete via videolink. Occasional departmental away-days also bring people together across the firm, but most socialising occurs within the individual offices. Office-wide Christmas, summer and end-of-financial-year parties are thrown each year and supplemented by ad hoc departmental dos and diversity-related events like drinks and film nights. Luckily, *"there's no pressure to be part of the crowd. How much you get involved is up to you."*

IM's qualification process divided opinions among interviewees, some of whom wished to be *"informed more regularly about what's going on."* Indeed, without an official jobs list, *"you kind of have to do your own digging and fight for what you want."* Still, many highlighted the lack of a formal interview as a plus and took comfort in the firm's historically high retention rates. In 2013, 38 out of 46 qualifying trainees stayed on.

And finally...

PLS trainees love IM for its *"rewarding"* spread of work, while BLS trainees envisage a future where the breadth of the firm's business capabilities matches that of the personal teams.

Jones Day

The facts

Location: London

Number of UK partners/solicitors: 60/110 (+12 non-UK-qualified)

UK partners who trained at firm: over 50%

Total number of trainees: 30

Seats: none

Alternative seats: Dubai, occasional secondments

Extras: pro bono – LawWorks, Waterloo Legal Advice Clinic, Reprieve, Amicus

On chambersstudent.co.uk...

How to get into Jones Day

More on the non-rotational training

Headline cases and deals

Jones Day's non-rotational training contract sets it apart from other firms in the City. *"People who lack confidence and like to work with their doors closed will struggle here."*

The Goulden Rule

Now over 120 years old, Jones Day has grown to become one of the largest law firms in the world. February 2012 saw it open a base in Düsseldorf, and in 2013 it followed this up by establishing two more outposts: one in Miami and another in Amsterdam. That takes the firm's office tally to 40. So, how crucial is the London office to this legal giant's success? *"I wouldn't say we're necessarily the flagship outside of the USA,"* says graduate recruitment partner David Smith, *"but we're certainly considered critical and are seen as a hub for a lot of our other European offices."* JD has had a presence in London for more than 25 years, but things really started to pick up steam when it took over a firm called Gouldens in 2003. Today, the London team has numerous *Chambers UK* rankings to its name, with a formidable reputation in areas like corporate/M&A, litigation, civil fraud and private equity.

It's hard not to be impressed by Jones Day's size and stature, but perhaps you still need convincing that it truly stands out from the City crowd. Well, when it comes to training JD offers something that most other City firms don't: a non-rotational training contract where trainees don't complete seats. Instead, they are expected to seek out their own work from the off. This might sound scary, but the trainees we spoke to knew exactly what they were getting into. In fact, most of them had chosen the firm with the non-rotational system in mind. *"That sold it to me straight away,"* a first-year recalled. *"I loved the idea of having the freedom to work on whatever I wanted to."*

Knock, knock...

From day one *"you literally just walk into people's offices to introduce yourself and let them know that you'd be interested in working for them. There's a chance you won't get work from them straight away, but in the beginning it's all about establishing relationships."* The system does suit those who enter with a spread of interests but, ordinarily, trainees try out a variety of practice areas in their first year and then concentrate on the department they hope to qualify into in their second. *"I think the main point to make is that you really feel like you're progressing because you take on more responsibility as you go along,"* stated one source, *"whereas in the seat system, you spend six months in one group and then essentially start again from scratch."*

It's worth bearing in mind that the system does have its drawbacks: *"There are definitely inherent risks in that you're solely in charge of your own workflow, so it's easy to take on either too much or too little. What's strange is that the quieter days can be the most stressful, as you're eager to impress and are left wondering why you don't have any work coming in."* When trainees become overburdened they can sometimes be reluctant to offload some of their work, and David Smith tells us: *"One of the biggest challenges we face is persuading trainees that it isn't a sign of weakness to let others help you out, and it's more of a weakness if you don't speak to someone about having too much work."* The 'free market' system requires trainees to be *"proactive"* and *"confident,"* but *"that doesn't mean you have to be pushy or loud. Someone who is very brash and arrogant won't fare any better here than someone who shies away from talking to people."*

Chambers UK rankings

Banking & Finance	Fraud
Banking Litigation	Pensions
Capital Markets	Private Equity
Commodities	Real Estate
Construction	Real Estate Finance
Corporate/M&A	Restructuring/Insolvency
Dispute Resolution	Tax
Employment	Telecommunications
Environment	

We would normally reel off the seat options available to trainees, but seeing as there are no formal seats to list we'll tell you that the London office's work is roughly 20% disputes; 30% corporate; 20% finance and restructuring; 15% real estate; and 15% 'other' (including energy, construction, competition and IP). The non-rotational system also means there are no overseas 'seats' on offer, although the firm occasionally sends trainees to Dubai for four to six months.

Read all about it!

JD's corporate practice is top-ranked by *Chambers UK* for its work in the London mid-market, advising the likes of national and multinational corporations on both domestic and cross-border transactions. Recent deals the team's worked on include property developer British Land's £1.525bn joint venture with Norwegian sovereign wealth fund NBIM and private equity firm JF Lehman's multimillion-pound acquisition of emergency locator devices manufacturer ACR Electronics. *"One of the best things about corporate is being able to work on huge cases that could eventually appear on a page in the* Financial Times," declared an interviewee. We were informed that the department contains three sub-groups: M&A, private equity and capital markets. Every trainee we spoke to had received work from at least one of these groups, though some went the extra mile and took on matters from all three.

One of our sources *"started off by managing the due diligence process and multi-jurisdictional elements revolving around a massive acquisition,"* while another described carrying out *"the fairly basic stuff"* like drafting company forms and board minutes. *"Your role tends to vary depending on the size of the transaction. You take more of a back seat on the bigger deals, but the smaller matters are leanly staffed, which means you can get heavily involved in drafting documents and liaising with the other side."*

The banking and finance team is especially strong in areas such as structured finance and derivatives, property finance and cross-border emerging markets transactions. We heard from one trainee: *"I initially got given a lot*

of classic trainee tasks like shuffling papers and co-ordinating with banks,"* but *"on subsequent deals they were more than happy for me to draft the documents."* Another reported working with *"some pretty big hitters in terms of partners,"* many of whom *"have long-standing relationships with quite a few of our major clients,"* which include Bank of America, Goldman Sachs and RBS.

Our sources labelled real estate as *"the most outgoing department at the firm, and it's why so many of us are keen to get work from them."* The group acted on behalf of Metric Property Investments over the purchase and development of Bishop Auckland Retail Park in County Durham, which included advising on pre-lets with Next, Boots, M&S and Costa, and it also worked for Hansteen Holdings on the investment trust's £60m acquisition of 33 UK industrial estates and trade parks. Some trainees mentioned drafting leases and licences, while others worked on portfolio sales and purchases and tackled property elements surrounding corporate transactions. *"In general you get a little bit more client contact compared to other teams because, in addition to these very large deals, there are small files that you can run yourself,"* explained one interviewee. *"In those cases, you're likely to be the client's first port of call."*

"A lot of trainees who prefer transactional work are surprised by how much they enjoy litigation," a second-year said. *"That's because, rather than simply doing bundling for hours on end, there's an opportunity for you to do plenty of meatier work."* This was backed up by another source, who did admit to *"going through bundles of documents during my first couple of weeks"* but then got involved in *"a thrilling fraud case that saw me go to court and witness some of our lawyers in action."* Trainees told us that specialist areas like fraud provide *"the more exciting work"* and *"enable you to draft things like witness statements and claim forms under very little supervision."* The litigation team recently defended oil and gas company Texas Keystone in a dispute concerning exploration rights to oilfields in Iraqi Kurdistan, with the case itself worth over $1.5bn. Other noteworthy clients include Procter & Gamble, Standard Bank and Total.

Fifty shades of grey

Although the non-rotational system means it's important for trainees to get in people's good books, interviewees were quick to point out that *"it's very much a two-way thing. If a partner's picked up a reputation for being horrible then no trainee will go to them for work, so everyone has to be respectful and easy to approach."* This has paved the way for a *"flat hierarchy"* whereby *"the partners are used to having us bustling around the building and badgering them. You get to know most of your other colleagues too, as you're always up and about."*

The True Picture

Trainees typically arrive for work at around 8am and depart from the office just after 7pm. At other times they can be found beavering away in the office until the early hours of the morning, which happens more often when they have corporate-related matters to attend to. *"Even during the high-pressure situations people manage to crack a joke, which shows you how calm the atmosphere is here,"* remarked one, and *"the firm appreciates that you don't want to be stuck in the office purely for the sake of it when you're having a quieter period."*

The workload may be cumbersome at times, but JD trainees are still a sociable bunch. Really sociable, actually. *"We have so many departmental Christmas parties each year that they've now moved our annual firm-wide party to the summer,"* an insider revealed, *"and there are lots of impromptu nights out – even if it's just to the pub."* The pub of choice is usually The Harrow, described by some as *"legendary"* and by others as *"bit small and smelly."* However, those who were less complimentary about it did concede: *"It's a good place to round everyone up before we see where the night takes us."* Trainees are also treated to several events organised by the firm. This includes a week-long stay in Washington DC for the 'New Lawyer Academy', which takes place shortly after the beginning of their training contracts. Aside from being taken out on a party bus and having drinks on the office's *"amazing rooftop balcony that overlooks Capitol Hill,"* the trip allows new starters to *"gain a real understanding of the 'one firm worldwide' motto. It makes you realise how big*

we are on a global scale as you don't just meet people from the US; I also mingled with lawyers from places like Beijing, Sydney and Frankfurt."

There were a couple of trainees who grumbled about the London office being quite noisy, but this wasn't due to any wild shenanigans or boisterous partners: the place was actually undergoing refurbishment at the time of our calls. *"Everything is slowly but surely looking better as a result,"* according to one dweller. *"We have brand-new coffee machines and seating areas, plus the walls are now decorated in cool shades of grey – which gives the office a bit of a sci-fi look."* The new look hasn't gone down well with everyone, however, as some claimed that *"the office used to have a warm and personal feel but, since the renovation, it's adopted more of a clinical appearance."*

The biggest change has arguably been the fact that trainees no longer get their own office but now share with a fellow trainee or other junior lawyer. Smith explains the decision: *"We wanted to increase the capacity of the building and keep us all in the same place, but trainee feedback from our pilot has shown that sharing an office, with a peer or near peer, has some genuine benefits. If you have a quick question, for example, then it's a lot easier to lift your head up and ask the person opposite you rather than walk all the way down the corridor."* Our interviewees agreed and said that *"sitting with someone who's close to your age means they can act as your informal mentor."*

And finally...
Jones Day's unique training contract is not to everyone's taste, but bold and independent types will flourish. In 2013 the firm kept on 14 out of 17 qualifiers.

K&L Gates

The facts

Location: London

Number of UK partners/solicitors: 52/69 (+3 UK non-qualified)

UK partners who trained at firm: 7%

Total number of trainees: 16

Seats: 4x6 months

Alternative seats: occasional secondments

Extras: pro bono – Battersea Legal Advice Centre, LawWorks, Amicus

On chambersstudent.co.uk...

How to get into K&L Gates

One New Change for K&L

Words from top K&L partner

Tony Griffiths

K&L Gates is an American firm with an *"international outlook,"* but the London office *"still maintains its English ways."*

Merging machine

K&L Gates' latest merger with Aussie firm Middletons, plus the opening of a new office in Texas, now takes its total office count to 48, making it the 16th largest law firm worldwide by number of lawyers. Expect that tally to rise soon enough: *"One thing you can say about this place is we're always looking to expand,"* reported one trainee. *"If you look at the trends of the past, it's safe to say the firm is going to get bigger and better."* The history of K&L is one of mergers: the most significant ones from a UK perspective came in 2005, when Pittsburgh-based Kirkpatrick & Lockhart established itself in London by merging with Nicholson Graham & Jones, and two years later when it combined with US West Coast heavyweight Preston Gates & Ellis (and in case you were wondering, the 'Gates' in K&L is Bill Gates' dad).

Given the firm's global scale, the lawyers in London could be forgiven for feeling like little fish in a big pond but, as our interviewees pointed out, it still manages to make a splash. *"We're perhaps torn between being steadily good at what we're doing and trying to find our place within this global giant, but if you speak to our American colleagues about the firm they'll always stress how important London is. It's kind of the European linchpin as well as being an important financial centre."* While there's still work to be done, the London office's continuing growth is evident: revenue rose to £35.6m during 2012, an 8% increase on the previous year, with recent lateral hires strengthening the projects, finance and corporate practice groups in particular. A move to the fancy new One New Change complex in 2010 has also boosted morale.

The London office retains its historic focus on corporate and property transactions, and one trainee noted that *"when I joined I thought that real estate and corporate were compulsory, but they're actually just encouraged."* Similarly, *"although there are certain requirements with regards to doing a contentious seat, that doesn't mean you have to do straight litigation."* Areas such as insurance coverage, employment and the construction secondment satisfy the contentious requirement.

Many revealed their initial concern over not getting to choose their first seat. As one commented: *"I was a bit wary of being put somewhere I didn't want to be,"* but *"looking back, the firm did a remarkably good job of putting us in places where we were likely to get on well."* Trainees get greater input when it comes to their remaining seats. The two appraisals that take place with a supervisor – one halfway through each seat, the other at the end – cover the expected topics.

Workin' 9 to... 10?

Some mentioned the corporate group's reputation for working arduous hours, but the reality's actually a little different: *"You do work some late nights and can occasionally find yourself in the office until 10pm on a Friday evening, but I can't say I ever had it that bad,"* recalled one. *"The flip side of that is it's a great, fun department to be in."* Sources were particularly pleased with the variety of work they had been able to take on, which is mainly split between M&A and capital markets. *"It can range from normal trainee tasks, such as working on verification and drafting ancillary documents, to assisting with the completion process on M&A deals."* Cross-border work occurs often and reflects K&L's international dimen-

Chambers UK rankings

Banking & Finance	Intellectual Property
Capital Markets	Investment Funds
Competition/European Law	Licensing
Construction	Parliamentary & Public
Corporate/M&A	Affairs
Dispute Resolution	Projects
Employment	Real Estate
Environment	Real Estate Finance
Information Technology	Sports Law
Insurance	Travel

sion – Halliburton, Brightstar and Hitachi Consulting are just three of the global companies it acts for. The firm also advised Arena Leisure, which runs several racecourses across the UK, on its purchase by Aldersgate Investments.

One trainee stated that real estate provides *"the most direct client contact out of any seat at the firm."* Others concurred: *"Although you're supervised, there's a lot of day-to-day responsibility in terms of managing your own files."* The department works for clients ranging from FTSE 100 corporations to middle-market companies and entrepreneurs including *"some big institutional clients that own a portfolio of properties, so you'll often deal with management matters on those."*

Trainees in the litigation department take on a mix of work including white-collar crime, financial litigation and ADR as well as general commercial litigation. You may remember the Farepak collapse of 2006, in which many people who had purchased Christmas hampers were left out of pocket. This long-running dispute reached a dramatic conclusion in 2012: the disqualification case brought against K&L's client, the directors of Farepak's parent company European Home Retail, ended up collapsing at trial. Responsibility levels vary, as trainees generally have *"less input on the bigger cases"* but are able to run smaller matters on their own.

Competition is *"quite a small department"* where trainees *"get a lot of exposure to international work."* Cases often relate to *"trade regulation, UN sanctions and merger assessments"* – such as advising chemical multinational Orica on merger control laws over a proposed joint venture in Australia. The insurance coverage group, highly ranked by *Chambers UK*, acts exclusively for policyholders and is *"fundamentally a contentious seat,"* although there are additional aspects like policy review and corporate support work. Other seats include employment, tax, IP and finance.

The United Gates of America

K&L's international network plays a key role. *"We have all the US and international offices to rely upon, and so much of the work is derived from them – and, equally, a lot of what comes through to us we refer to other offices. We also get people visiting from other offices, and that's actually quite rewarding because you can properly service a client by using other peoples' expertise."* It seems a shame, then, that there are currently no overseas opportunities for trainees. *"There could potentially be future opportunities in the Far East, but something definitely needs to be done as a lot of us want the chance to do an overseas seat,"* one source opined. So far nothing concrete on this from management.

"It's an easy line to say that we're an American firm, but we're definitely not typical in that sense," remarked a trainee. *"We don't have a hawkish, aggressive or intimidating culture at all."* Trainees thought the firm's friendly character stems from the legacy of Nicholson Graham & Jones, which had a reputation as a fairly sedate City midsizer: *"It's still got some of the NGJ feel about it and has retained that collegial atmosphere."* One source did feel that *"it's becoming more and more Americanised – I've certainly seen the difference in the time I've been here. In terms of personalities, there are a lot of characters left over from NGJ, but they are going to gradually disappear and the people coming through are increasingly going to be shaped in the K&L mould."* Cultural change has been slow here since the 2005 merger, but in the past couple of years we have definitely noticed a certain something in the air at this firm: if not quite the winds of change then certainly the light breezes.

While there are some *"pretty lively"* office-wide events laid on for occasions like Christmas and Bonfire Night, interviewees agreed *"there's less of an organised social life compared to other firms."* Thankfully, recent efforts have been made to remedy this: a committee has been set up to arrange more trainee-specific social events, with a budget put aside for *"drinks and nibbles"* every couple of months at a nearby pub. Trainees don't just leave it up to the firm as *"e-mails are always going around on Fridays about meeting up for drinks. You're not at all pressured to attend though; it's encouraging that people have their own lives outside of work."* Our sources almost shamefully confessed that Ping Pong remains the office's regular local: *"There's been a small attempt at an uprising to go somewhere else, but it's still where we usually end up. I blame the two-for-one cocktails!"*

In 2013, the firm retained seven of its eight second-years upon qualification, up a whole one on last year.

And finally...

If you're looking for a large international firm without too much of a cut-throat atmosphere, you'll find K&L a good fit.

Kennedys

The facts

Location: London, Manchester, Birmingham, Cambridge, Chelmsford, Maidstone, Sheffield, Taunton, Belfast

Number of UK partners/solicitors: 145/247

Partners who trained at firm: 23%

Total number of trainees: 32

Seats: 4x6 months

Alternative seats: Hong Kong, secondments

On chambersstudent.co.uk...

How to get into Kennedys
Interview with partner
Andrew Coates
The firm's regional offices

Kennedys is a rapidly growing national firm that offers a contentious-heavy training contract.

Grow Kenny, grow!

Kennedys may have started slowly – the firm opened its second office, in Belfast, almost a hundred years after it was founded in London in 1899 – but it has expanded rapidly since the millennium, opening 16 new offices worldwide in locations including Hong Kong, Dubai, Sydney and, most recently, Dublin. And there's no sign of Kennedys stopping there. "*We have ambitious growth targets for the next five years – we want to improve turnover and continue our expansion by opening more offices in North America, South America and Asia. We're also looking to expand further into the aviation and marine industries,*" professional practice partner Andrew Coates told us. In June 2013 specialist aviation and aerospace firm Gates & Partners stepped under the Kennedys umbrella, bringing 20 new partners to the firm.

The vast majority of the work Kennedys does is insurance and litigation-based, and *Chambers UK* ranks the firm's domestic clinical negligence, professional negligence and health and safety departments as some of the best in the country. Kennedys has been one of the fastest-growing law firms by revenue over the past five years, and our interviewees said the sense of momentum is palpable. "*It definitely feels like we're in growth. There are new people starting all the time, which gives it that sense of energy. I think we're only going to get bigger and bigger.*"

Kennedys' London office is tucked away on Fenchurch Avenue, in the "*heartland of the insurance world.*" This comes as no surprise – we once heard a partner say that insurance lawyers' heads explode if they get further than 100 yards from the famous Lloyd's building. The firm acts on behalf of more than 50 of the world's leading insurers,

including AIG, AXA and Zurich. Owing to the size of the department, Kennedys takes on cases of the highest value, both at home and abroad. The insurance department worked for a number of clients whose property was damaged by the 2011 earthquake and tsunami in Japan. More recently, the department acted on behalf of several reinsurers after a munitions explosion in Cyprus caused catastrophic damage to the island's main power station. The matter exceeded €100m in value.

The London office is the largest and for that reason accommodates the majority of trainees. There were 23 in the capital at the time of our calls in May 2013, while the remaining nine were spread between regional outposts in Birmingham, Cambridge, Chelmsford, Manchester and Sheffield. "*London is clearly and obviously the main office. The others are essentially satellites and sometimes it does feel like a number of different firms with a loose connection,*" said one trainee. In London, the main departments are insurance, clinical negligence, personal injury, company/commercial and the mysteriously named 'workplace' (a mix of employment and health and safety matters). Half of the clinical negligence department is based in Cambridge, while the Chelmsford office focuses solely on liability claims, working closely with local authorities. The Birmingham, Manchester and Sheffield offices are largely contentious in nature and offer a slightly wider spread, concentrating on personal injury, litigation and commercial. Two trainees each year have the chance to spend six months in the Hong Kong office.

London calling

The seat allocation process varies across the firm, with one London trainee explaining: "*Second-years will al-*

Chambers UK rankings

Aviation	Partnership
Clinical Negligence	Personal Injury
Construction	Product Liability
Dispute Resolution	Professional Negligence
Employment	Real Estate
Health & Safety	Transport
Insurance	

ways get preference, but first-years are usually happy. It's done pretty fairly and HR always knows who has and hasn't had their first choice." In the regional offices there is much less choice, but the competition for seats is considerably lower and we found that most trainees had been placed in their first choice from their second seat onwards.

The insurance department in London is best described as gargantuan and houses 39 partners and more than 150 associates. There are subseats in clinical negligence, professional indemnity reinsurance, construction and insurance litigation (among others), and it's likely that trainees will spend time in at least one of these. One trainee said of the construction department: "*This is where the massive claims come in. Most of it involves negligence and property damage claims against companies in the industry. I was working on a case worth a few hundred million pounds and, although it can be quite document-heavy for trainees, if you get involved you can become the go-to person for facts and data on a given file.*" The department acted for insurers in the fallout of the Buncefield oil depot fire in 2005. It was the biggest explosion to have happened in peacetime Europe and, at more than £1bn, the most costly industrial accident in British history.

Professional indemnity is another important division within insurance and was a popular stop for our interviewees. The department works across finance, construction, education and the media, representing professionals accused of errors or omissions. "*You're not running your own files, even in your second year, because most of what trainees do is assisting. I was attending meetings, taking attendance notes, researching for fee earners and doing bits of bundling. That's a standard task for trainees at Kennedys. I did attend hearings, though, and the workload is quite varied: you get to learn about all the various niche aspects of the job,*" said one trainee. "*It can be quite document-heavy, but I know people who've got lucky and started the seat just when a big case went to court,*" another told us.

Special K

The clinical negligence department's main client is the NHS Litigation Authority. "*The work is very high-value and a lot of the cases involved babies with brain damage*

and wrongful births. It can be harrowing but also really rewarding. I went to trial with a case, which was a great experience, and I got to run my own file on medical insurance,*" one trainee told us. Another said: "*You have a hands-on role from the beginning. A lot of the work involves drafting instructions and witness statements, and the team gives you lots of encouragement. I worked on a million-pound brain damage charge.*"

Non-contentious work can be hard to come by, but the employment seat offers some scope for it. The majority of clients in this seat are from the rail industry, and household names include Virgin, East Midlands Trains, London Overground and First Great Western. Sheffield United FC is also on the books. "*It was really interesting. A lot of the work has to do with redundancy and discrimination claims, but there is advisory work too. The team is lovely,*" one trainee told us. The corporate/commercial seat also offers non-contentious work. "*I was drafting board minutes, helping with purchase agreements and doing due diligence. Most of it was background work, and you'd never be the one dishing out advice.*"

While the value of the cases in London means trainees often play supporting roles, in the regional offices the cases are smaller and trainees have more responsibility. One trainee in Sheffield's cost litigation department told us: "*I was running about 30 of my own files, from the moment they came in right up to settlement. I was also attending hearings.*" Another was "*sent to London to do advocacy in the Senior Courts Costs Office in the Royal Courts of Justice. I got to negotiate on behalf of a defendant, which was a real rush.*" Some of the trainees we spoke to in Manchester had also been given the chance to do advocacy, with one telling us: "*I've been running files on my own.*"

Trainees were mostly happy with the level of supervision they had received, but the sheer size of the firm meant some felt they had been forgotten. "*It depends on what seat you're in, but my supervisors have been hands-on and really good. I know some people who feel there hasn't been enough support on offer though,*" said one London trainee. Another trainee outside of London told us: "*There are times when people are just too busy to help.*" At the very least, trainees have a formal sit-down meeting with their supervisor at the middle and end of every seat, and this is a chance to check progress and raise any issues.

A fruitful office

While all the offices have the same furnishings and decor, the London headquarters is undoubtedly the slickest. "*We have a café on the fifth floor called The Ritz where you can get hot food, and we get smoothies and baskets of fresh fruit delivered every day. There's an awesome balcony on the ninth floor that goes round the whole building – you can see every London landmark from up there and* it's a great place to wind down and have a drink." Sheffield, on the other hand, only gets fruit delivered "*twice a week.*" And that's not the only difference. Trainees in London earn up to £9,000 more than their regional counterparts each year, with one of our interviewees describing this as "*frustrating.*" Overall though, trainees didn't seem to mind too much, with one regional source saying: "*Although it's a big difference, we're still paid more than trainees in a lot of other regional firms.*"

Salary gripes aside, the trainees we spoke to were fond of their colleagues across the firm, and a yearly inter-firm charity event keeps ties strong. In 2012, employees organised their own torch relay (in honour of the Olympics), starting from the Belfast office and passing the baton on to those in Dublin, Manchester, Sheffield and Cambridge before ending in London. The event raised more than £10,000 for charity and the next target is to raise £15,000 for War Child by doing the Three Peaks challenge. The trainees we spoke to raved about the relay, with one saying: "*Kennedys is a great firm to be part of if you want to get involved in fund-raising.*"

Working hours are similar across the offices, with a normal day being 9am to 6pm. In London, certain seats demand longer hours, and one trainee recalled "*a week of 11pm finishes when I was at trial in clinical negligence. But I was happy to stay – I was the partner's number two!*" Most of our sources hadn't worked into the night and in the regional offices weekend work is unheard of. Naturally, this means there's plenty of time to fit in a good social life. "*It's a really sociable place to work, and we go out all the time,*" said one trainee. The Londoners regularly slope off to The Lamb in Leadenhall Market on a Friday night. There are also football, netball, softball and rugby teams playing on a weekly basis. Up north, staff

from the Manchester office can usually be found in the bars around Deansgate and Spinningfields on a Friday night, while a trainee in the Sheffield office told us: "*The partners organise monthly drinks in the boardroom as a way of saying thanks. There's always stuff going on.*"

Can a firm as large and spread out as Kennedys possibly retain any kind of common identity? "*We have family values,*" one trainee told us. "*You can see that in everyone who works here – they're all good people.*" Another remarked: "*I don't know how they do it! Everyone is so nice,*" while several others told us there are "*no egos*" at the firm. When asked what kind of person thrives at Kennedys, Andrew Coates said: "*You'll find that the same kind of person does well at the firm irrespective of which office or department they're in. Our lawyers are commercially oriented and non-esoteric.*" Trainees also praised CEO Guy Stobart for his involvement and interest in their development, with one describing him as "*brilliant*" and another saying: "*He's always going around the offices keeping people up to speed with what's happening across the firm.*"

In the course of our interviews it became apparent that many of the trainees had previous experience of paid insurance or paralegal litigation work. One trainee told us: "*Past experience definitely helps – it shows you're committed and interested in the practice areas.*" Andrew Coates stressed that trainees should be "*articulate both in writing and verbally. The insurance sector is all about communication.*" He also said the firm is looking for trainees who are "*sociable*" and "*able to go out and represent the business.*" This was backed up by trainees, with one telling us: "*You're encouraged to meet clients and build lasting working relationships.*"

And finally...

Retention rates at Kennedys are reassuringly high. In 2013, 20 out of 21 qualifiers stayed on with the firm as NQs.

Kingsley Napley LLP

The facts

Location: London

Number of UK partners/solicitors: 40/63

Partners who trained at firm: 8%

Total number of trainees: 10

Seats: 4x6 months

Alternative seats: none

Extras: pro bono – CAB, Family Division

On chambersstudent.co.uk...

How to get into Kingsley Napley

Interview with training partner Nicola Hill

Senior partner Jane Keir on women in law

Kingsley Napley's criminal practice might deal with some horrible crooks, but the firm's sunny atmosphere sees trainees nicknaming it *"kind and nice."*

Luck be a lady

Kingsley Napley's co-founder Sir David Napley earned his knighthood with a royal flush of causes célèbres, working for General Pinochet, for Princess Michael of Kent and on the famous one-armed bandit case that inspired the film *Get Carter*. The firm's sizeable criminal practice, top-ranked in *Chambers UK*, still hits the news as the go-to choice for the great and not-so-good. Among KN's latest scoops is representing Rebekah Brooks in the criminal case springing from the News International phone hacking scandal. Other clients range from international war criminals right down to misbehaving footballers like Arsenal's André Santos, recently arrested on a dangerous driving charge, and Constance Briscoe – the barrister and confidante of Vicky Pryce charged with perverting the course of justice in the Chris Huhne speeding points affair.

Less well-known areas at KN are equally thriving, driving the firm's turnover up by 10% in 2011/12. One trainee felt that *"we're rightly associated with our criminal past, but we're becoming more focused on other areas."* In particular, KN's immigration team has been swelled by new hires recently. Clinical negligence and crime are both popular with trainees, hosting two at a time. Other seat options include regulatory, public law, private client, dispute resolution, immigration, corporate and commercial, family, real estate and employment.

Trainees complete four seats of six months each, which are chosen before the start of their training contracts. Trainees explained that *"you conduct your own research"* into departments and, although some struggled to choose,

they noted that *"a couple of trainees have been able to swap their seats."*

Eye of the tiger

KN's criminal litigation practice handles general criminal work ranging from harrowing rape and assault cases to the frankly bizarre: the firm recently advised a taxidermist accused of supplying a stuffed tiger to an Alexander McQueen photoshoot without the proper papers. There's also high-value white-collar crime, like advising Russian bank group Otkritie after it was defrauded to the tune of $180m by London-based traders. Trainees are closely supervised by partners, who are *"very good at getting you involved – you're in it together."* They reported interviewing witnesses and drafting statements, liaising with counsel, tracking down experts to give evidence in court and meeting clients, whether slumming it down at the police station or up at the firm's rather more fancy offices. There are also opportunities for trainees to take on the odd small file of their own. One trainee handling a drink-driving case – *"I met the client on my own, attended the Magistrates' hearing with the barrister, and got the toxicology report: it was nice to get a small case I could manage myself."*

KN's clinical negligence team is top-ranked in *Chambers UK* and works for claimants in complex, high-value compensation cases that *"often take years to resolve, so you never really see anything from beginning to end."* Recently, it joined up with the public law team to represent Action against Medical Accidents (AvMA) and The Patients Association in the public inquiry into shocking

Chambers UK rankings

Administrative & Public	Employment
Law	Family/Matrimonial
Clinical Negligence	Financial Services
Competition/European Law	Fraud
Corporate Crime &	Immigration
Investigations	Professional Discipline
Crime	

patient abuse and mortality rates at Stafford General Hospital. Trainees often start out involved in administrative tasks – *"there's quite a large element of sorting records."* As the seat progresses, they are entrusted with research, drafting statements for claimants and high levels of client contact. One trainee *"went to the hospital to talk the claimant through the process."*

The whole tooth and nothing but the tooth

KN's regulatory department acts for organisations including The Law Society, the Architects Registration Board, and the General Dental Council, which *"refers work to us when they have doubts about an individual."* Trainees run their own caseloads – *"from the first day you interview witnesses and liaise with the client; it's very hands-on."* One recruit found: *"You certainly do get a bit cynical when you see what all these naughty professionals get up to: some have been inappropriately looking at things on the internet, convicted by the police for offences or harming patients."*

A seat in the growing private client team offers a mix of contentious and non-contentious work for high net worth clients that include *"a couple of celebrities. It's nice to be sent out to those – you get to be nosy!"* Dealing with deceased peoples' estates means trainees *"get the occasional soap opera – it's horribly traumatic for the families, but it does give it that edge for us."* Trainees enthused about the *"fantastic levels of responsibility"* on offer.

The small corporate and commercial team makes for varied work, and lots of collaboration with other departments. A trainee involved in the sale of a heliport found themselves *"going to client meetings and dealing with insurers and banks: I learnt a lot,"* while work on a international construction contract *"was very good for my technical knowledge of law in different jurisdictions."* Smaller cases on offer include working on litigation for small tech

start-ups and overlapping with the private client department to negotiate production agreements. There's also an immigration seat, which sees trainees running their own files, working for *"big commercial law firms and City institutions"* and on the odd bit of *"interesting appeal work with a human rights element."*

The great British bake off

Trainees raved that the firm's Farringdon location is *"brilliant – you can just roll out to all the bars, so a lot of people go out on Fridays."* The firm's Christmas party is *"normally a very boozy occasion,"* and judging by the fact that none of the trainees could remember where it was held, the most recent jolly was no exception. The firm's recent 75th anniversary saw it regressing to seven, five or younger with *"a massive Scalextric set and a photo booth with fancy dress,"* while a *"big Jubilee tea party with loads of decorations"* featured a baking competition aced by a super-keen trainee who entered two flag-themed sponges. There are also charity cake sales, and a recent tasting has introduced *"special posh biscuits"* and *"retro snacks"* to the office. KN's choir has been busily building up a growing YouTube discography (*"they get wheeled out at every possible opportunity,"* one source grumbled).

Jane Keir's recent appointment as senior partner makes the firm unique in the top 100 for having both a female senior and managing partner as well as a female-dominated executive management committee. Sources attributed the similarly high proportion of women in the trainee cohort to the firm having less of a focus on *"the big City rough and tumble stuff"* – although working in criminal law isn't exactly flowers and kittens. Trainees identified a *"more helpful, less political and maybe less hard-nosed"* environment, feeling that *"you can have a family and still get on at the firm."* The *"very sociable"* hours tend to run from 9am to 6.30pm, and no one reported staying more than a couple of hours after that.

A lot of KN trainees have had previous careers or have a few years of paid legal experience under their belts – *"you have to be quite confident and willing to get stuck in because you're the only trainee in a department."* Trainees generally share a room with their supervisor and were full of praise for the effort the firm invests in their training. Mid and end of seat reviews are *"constructive, but there's general feedback as you go along so there are no surprises."* Trainees praised the *"fairly formal"* interview-based qualification process, saying that *"we've been kept informed at every step of the way."* In 2013 KN retained all five of its qualifiers, as it did in 2012.

And finally...

One trainee advised: *"We're a leading criminal firm, but applicants shouldn't limit themselves by just wanting to do crime – we have so many other departments that are real players."*

Kirkland & Ellis International LLP

The facts
Location: London

Number of UK partners/solicitors: 28/58 (+18 US-qualified)

Total number of trainees: 14

Seats: 4x6 months

Alternative Seats: overseas seats

Extras: pro bono – LawWorks, A4ID

On chambersstudent.co.uk...
How to get into K&E

"Quiet ambition and drive" fuels this firm, which we'd say is a good match for hard-working, entrepreneurial trainees in search of a small firm feel.

Exceptional candidates

London is home to the largest European office of American powerhouse Kirkland & Ellis. Known for its formidable private equity prowess, the UK unit is one of an elite handful of firms that consistently receives top *Chambers UK* rankings for investment funds. Recent years have seen the firm's banking and finance team fetch equally high rankings.

Despite Kirkland's Chicago roots, *"we're not dominated by our colleagues in the States,"* trainees said, insisting the relationship's *"a collaborative one"* and *"it's great to have a network of people across the pond."* That said, certain Americanisms remain inherent to the firm's approach – the famed Yankee paycheck, for instance. *"Uncle Kirkland takes very good care of his employees,"* one insider confirmed, *"because he expects a lot out of you. With all the responsibility and great opportunities comes some very hard work."* Indeed, that leads us to another trope the firm doesn't eschew – tough hours: *"It does fulfil that American stereotype of working late and having your BlackBerry on you at all times, but people here don't mind that. Most are type A personalities who clearly want to be the best they can be."* To be clear, *"that ambition doesn't manifest itself through aggression or competition,"* sources took care to point out. *"We're meticulous but not cut-throat."*

As of 2013 K&E London is 130 attorneys strong and growing, both in size and reputation. According to graduate recruitment partner Rajinder Bassi: *"Typically we have taken on six to seven trainees a year, and this year we are taking on nine trainees in September. This is not necessarily setting a trend for the future. It's simply that* for 2013, there were some exceptional candidates, and we felt it made sense to make some additional offers."

K&E's seat system is *"really quite flexible,"* sources observed. Standard seats are in corporate (a mandatory seat), banking (aka debt finance), tax, funds, restructuring, IP and litigation, while the competition team takes on the occasional trainee. *"There's a lot of freedom in terms of making requests – smaller departments that don't always take trainees are open to taking on people who show a real interest if the work is there."* Tax and IP are only available in your second year. Interviewees agreed people are *"generally happy"* with the set-up, pointing out *"there's not a massive selection of seats, so you know what you're getting into."* Thanks to the small intake – *"you're either the sole trainee in your seat or one of two"* – levels of responsibility tend to be high, a prospect that *"doesn't really suit people who are slightly reticent,"* Bassi points out. *"There's nowhere to hide, so you have to be someone who's dynamic and wants to achieve from the outset."*

A private heart

"Split over two floors" of the firm's über-swanky office inside the Gherkin, the corporate department is K&E's largest. *"There aren't any specific sub-groups as the bulk of the work is either private equity or general corporate stuff like SPAs and shareholder agreements,"* insiders informed us. *"We're encouraged to work with a variety of people and ask for work we're interested in."* Clients are predominantly large private equity houses and investment portfolio companies – *"some of the biggest names in the City,"* in fact, including Terra Firma and Lion Capital. *"It's*

Chambers UK rankings

Banking & Finance	Restructuring/Insolvency
Investment Funds	Tax
Private Equity	

mostly high-end stuff. The only thing we don't do a lot of is AIM listings." High-end indeed: recent successes include acting for Vista Equity Partners on its £1.27bn takeover of software giant Misys and representing Bain Capital in its €1bn acquisition of a global call centre from Telefonica. Trainees aren't quite exempt from due diligence duties, *"but even the big deals are staffed very leanly, so you're trusted with a lot from the get-go,"* they reported. Luckily, *"partners are really good at sitting with you and explaining exactly what's going on so nobody's lost."*

As evidenced by its *Chambers UK* rankings, Kirkland remains top of the game when it comes to funds work. *"It's really the core of the London office,"* interviewees commented. *"The work you're exposed to is nothing short of superb, and the team is great at getting you involved."* As is the case in a corporate seat, *"you're encouraged to put yourself out there and really get into the work."*

Despite having just five partners, debt finance is considered *"a pretty large department in the context of the firm,"* and our interviewees dubbed the team *"a pretty mighty set. Many of the partners have come from magic circle firms."* Matters are *"primarily"* acquisitions finance-focused and, unsurprisingly, often private equity-related. *"A significant amount is portfolio work, including refinancing, recapitalisation and so forth,"* sources added, claiming *"the exposure is great as a trainee. You get to draft portions of agreements and liaise with counsel, often across several jurisdictions."*

Though it's not the key focus of the office, we ought to add a word on litigation/arbitration. *"Without taking anything away from any of the others, it is probably the nicest team,"* said once source enthusiastically, *"and the nature of the work is that you have the full array of clients – banks, private equity houses, Russian individuals and their businesses."* Work on huge arbitrations allows for less responsibility than in other departments, but trainees can get involved in discrete research tasks.

Thanks to K&E's extensive global network, trainees typically have the option of heading to Hong Kong or New York City. *"Typically, people who go abroad head off in their third seat,"* trainees said, mentioning that *"those really interested have a good chance of landing a spot."* Hong Kong tends to be the most popular destination, though we heard *"you can make your case for going to a totally different office as long as it makes business sense – the firm is open to that kind of thing."*

Burgers with gherkins

While our interviewees praised the firm's American backing – with many citing it as a reason for joining – they did suggest applicants consider the implications of K&E's *"long"* hours culture. *"You will genuinely earn your paycheck here,"* one remarked, highlighting the fact that *"because of all the international work, you're often expected to function through multiple time zones."* Fortunately, there's an upside in that there's *"a real appreciation for everyone's efforts"* and *"absolutely no facetime. The firm treats everyone like an adult, so it's up to you to manage your schedule."*

Insiders described Kirkland's day-to-day atmosphere as *"open and amiable,"* agreeing *"this really isn't a hierarchical place."* Down at the trainee level, people get along *"swimmingly,"* a dynamic most put down to the cohort's small size and the *"motivated and outgoing"* nature of those attracted to the firm. Due to its small size things are *"slightly limited"* on the social front, but the social committee *"does a grand job, all things considered."* Alongside a yearly quiz – which we heard is taken *"surprisingly seriously"* – there's a *"great"* Halloween party, *"complete with pumpkin-carving competitions and everything. We've obviously been influenced by the States on that front!"* Another American import is the annual 'Burger Day', a gastronomic tradition enjoyed by all. An autumn retreat to the countryside is a real crowd-pleaser, as are *"random little treats"* like Easter breakfasts and Pancake Day jubilations. Those who prefer more spontaneous hangouts will be pleased to know *"e-mails are always going around inviting everyone to ad hoc drinks."* Indeed, Searcys, the Gherkin's exclusive top-floor bar, proves *"very handy"* on a Friday afternoon.

And finally...

Trainees were heartened by the notion that *"the firm never seems to take on more trainees than it can handle. If there's no room in your department of choice, HR will try to find another suitable one."* In 2013 four out of five stayed qualifiers on at K&E. Big thumbs up all round.

Latham & Watkins

The facts

Location: London

Number of UK partners/solicitors: 44/102 (+56 non-UK-qualified)

Total number of trainees: 40

Seats: 4x6 months

Alternative seats: overseas seats

Extras: language classes; pro bono

On chambersstudent.co.uk...

How to get into Latham

Interview with training principal Catherine Drinnan

Latham's pro bono

The flat hierarchy at US firms

Latham is a place where *"very, very ambitious"* trainees with an interest in international corporate and finance work will thrive.

Giant strides

With 31 offices across the US, Europe, Asia and the Middle East, and annual turnover exceeding £2bn, Latham is one of the world's most successful firms. The London office *"has grown to be quite independent"* and is the firm's second largest after New York. It has carved out a space in the City working on high-end transactional and contentious matters, usually with an international element.

Standout deals of recent times on which the office has worked include Qatar Holdings' acquisition of a significant shareholding in mining company Xstrata (worth $45bn), Watson Pharmaceuticals' purchase of Actavis (€4.25bn, the largest leveraged buyout of 2012), retail conglomerate Landmark's acquisition of Iceland Foods (£1.55bn) and private equity firm KKR's acquisition of Capital Safety Group ($1.1bn). All those billions of pounds, dollars and euros should tell you that this is a firm that's operating with the big boys, and if you brought the topic up with a Latham lawyer, they'd consider the firm as of equivalent stature to the magic circle – though with lots of differences. More on those later. For trainees, three out of the four six-month seats are compulsory, but interviewees reflected that since the firm is *"led by corporate and finance"* and is *"trying to bulk up litigation,"* if you didn't do them, *"you wouldn't get a true experience of the firm."* The full list of seat options is: corporate M&A, finance, litigation/arbitration, property, tax, banking, restructuring, project finance, technology transactions, private equity, capital markets, competition and employment. *"With only one free choice you do have to be careful what you pick,"* thought sources: apparently, some trainees had their chances of experiencing one of the firm's popular overseas seats scuppered by picking incompatible niche seats early on. To avoid this scenario, sources advised: *"Get the compulsories out of the way early."*

Baby steps

Most of Latham's corporate clients are large financial institutions – banks, private equity houses and the like. Barclays, Merrill Lynch and Credit Suisse are some examples, though the likes of Virgin Media and Yahoo! offer some variety. As we've already mentioned, Latham works on some *"really big deals."* We'll only mention one more – Bob the Builder, Fireman Sam and Angelina Ballerina can now all play happy families in Barbie's dreamhouse thanks to Latham's work on toy manufacturer Mattel's $680m acquisition of HIT Entertainment. *"The highlight of my seat was a deal where it was just me and a mid-level associate working on it for a month and a half,"* said one source. *"That was a very interesting experience. The associate dealt with main documents, and I was responsible for all the ancillary ones. I negotiated with the other side about what was going in them and what wasn't."* Working on the case from start to end meant our interviewee *"also had to do the post-closing and bibling as well."*

The work in finance is *"more project management, less about the law,"* so as well as plenty of *"proof-reading, verification and memorandums,"* trainees might research the logistics of *"which firms we should use in other jurisdictions"* on international deals then *"ring them up, send across documents and brief them."* The project finance team has been working on Project Ichthys, a multibillion-dollar financing deal for an Australian oil and gas plant, while in an acquisition finance deal the firm acted for a private equity firm taking a stake in Topshop and Topman.

Chambers UK rankings

Banking & Finance	Information Technology
Banking Litigation	Investment Funds
Capital Markets	Outsourcing
Competition/European Law	Private Equity
Corporate/M&A	Projects
Dispute Resolution	Public International Law
Employment	Restructuring/Insolvency
Energy & Natural Resources	Tax

The high-stakes nature of the litigation Latham takes on means a lot of cases are confidential, but we can tell you it acted for the Republic of Macedonia in an ICSID arbitration brought by a Swiss investor who alleged that the country's government expropriated and unlawfully interfered with the his investment in an agricultural business. There's also white-collar criminal work resulting from the Bernard Madoff affair. Research-heavy, it offers "*a good transition from studying,*" and alongside "*quite routine*" work like due diligence there is the opportunity to "*go to hearings and see barristers in action.*" Tax, meanwhile, offers its trainees something more "*academically challenging – it's quite black-letter.*" Latham has advised on the tax aspects of big matters such the $233m IPO of Manchester United onto the New York Stock Exchange.

Busy bees

Every law firm inevitably has to have people on the bottom rung of the ladder, but Latham & Watkins was founded in laid-back California on a principle of non-hierarchical management, and trainees still see this influence today when they talk of a firm that's "*definitely a meritocracy,*" with rewards for "*entrepreneurial flair.*" This is the chief distinction between Latham and the magic circle, sources thought. Despite working on mega-deals opposite the Freshfields and Linklaters of this work, "*our office is still small enough for you to be a named face – I didn't like the idea of being an anonymous worker bee.*" And all qualified lawyers, from the most prolific rainmaker to the most measly NQ, have the same billing targets and holiday allowance.

Don't be fooled into thinking this is some kind of hippy commune where anything goes, though. Perhaps as a consequence of that non-hierarchical structure, Latham's "*obsessed with committees.*" And trainees are held to "*very high standards.*" One trainee explained: "*When talking about pieces of work with friends at other law firms, I get the sense that things that would be acceptable at other firms are not acceptable here. People here would ask you to do it again – it's not acceptable to not push yourself.*"

And those egalitarian billing targets? They're "*incredibly harsh,*" said one source: after qualification lawyers must aim to record 1,900 hours annually, "*the highest requirement in the City.*" Trainees themselves must aim for 1,200. One source recalled their first day in the corporate department: "*I was there until 2am going through correspondence documents.*" The spectre of "*long hours*" looms over many departments, with home time during busy periods sometimes reaching "*10 or 11pm, and some late nights of 2 or 3am,*" and occasionally people "*work for 40 hours flat.*" Fortunately, Latham attracts the sort of lawyer who views extended hours with equanimity: "*People here don't want to go home; the long nights don't really affect them.*"

In short, "*anyone doing the job just for money will be in trouble,*" but there's no denying that the pay packet is ample reward for all the hard work Latham lawyers put in. The NQ salary is among the very highest in the UK (a wallet-bursting £98,000), and "*anyone who says they don't care about the pay is lying.*"

If you're at work until the wee small hours, you need to both "*feel you can joke around*" with partners and be someone they'd want to joke around with, so it's easy to see why Latham has a "*no dickheads policy.*" Fraternising between partners and trainees tends to vary between departments, but in general the atmosphere was praised as "*unstuffy,*" with "*people bouncing in and out of people's rooms – I've never seen anyone flying off the handle.*" And, "*I'm treated as more of an adult and more of an asset than I would be at other places,*" one source thought. "*People always say thank you, and partners actually want to know what I think.*" The offices themselves are kitted out to give hard workers every luxury – including an all-day, fry-up dispensing canteen, where a "*whizzy, iPad-controlled new coffee machine*" sits in state.

Though the firm naturally looks for high academic achievers, it's not over-reliant on Oxbridge as a source of candidates, and we spoke to many trainees who'd graduated elsewhere. Sources believed that Latham is looking for "*all-rounders*" who possess the "*independence*" that often comes from prior work experience – along with the "*willingness to work really hard,*" of course.

Wohhhh sexy Lathies

One thing US firms are historically strong on is pro bono, and those with a passion for this type of work will find plenty of opportunities to get involved. Hard workers win the title "*Guardians of Justice*" and get "*a sticker on their door.*" We suspect the slightly cheesy title is an American innovation, but we shouldn't sneer – the ethos is admirable, and Latham's commitment to pro bono is evidenced by the fact that "*it all counts towards your billable hours.*" Pro bono mainly comes in the form of legal advice to charities – a regional mental health charity, an inner-city youth group, the BFI – and allows trainees *"more free rein"* on higher-level work.

Mentoring is a big deal at Latham, with one second-year source we talked to acting as mother hen to three mentorees – an undergraduate, a future joiner and a current vac schemer, with *"a budget to take them out for lunch."* Trainees get an associate mentor of their own as well as a partner supervisor. Trainees were positive about the review system – supervisors sit them down for *"an informal chat"* mid-seat about *"how you can develop"* followed by summarised feedback from three other people a trainee has worked with at the seat's end. But it isn't all softly-softly – afterwards, there's a *"follow-up review with an independent person who you haven't worked for: they'll give you a more honest critique than your supervisor who you have to see all the time."*

Though *"there's not an en-masse exodus to a certain local on Fridays,"* Heron Tower across the road has a couple of fancy bars where Latham hosts client events, which *"we're definitely encouraged to go to."* As a change from desk-bound research, trainees went on *"a taxi treasure hunt with a Christmas theme"* in December – *"we had to drive around across London answering clues"* and complete tasks like *"recording videos of us performing"* and *"busking"* for rather unneeded pennies. A masquerade-themed party offered more opportunity for Christmassy fun, courtesy of partners' faces photoshopped onto Gangnam Style music videos – and if you prefer your fun a bit muddier, there's also football, and *"cricket in the spring."* Retention is usually good here and second-year trainees were confident about their prospects when we spoke to them. 13 out of 14 were eventually kept on as NQs in 2013.

And finally...

Trainees readily admit that *"the firm's culture probably isn't for everybody"* but described the Latham training contract as a *"challenging and rewarding"* experience for those with the drive to take it on.

Lawrence Graham LLP

The facts

Location: London

Number of UK partners/solicitors: 65/90

Partners who trained at firm: 12%

Total number of trainees: 30

Seats: 4x6 months

Alternative Seats: Dubai

Extras: pro bono – Big Issue, End Child Poverty, Environmental Investigation Agency

On chambersstudent.co.uk...

How to get into LG

The AIM market

More London

LG's private capital/client work

These are testing times for one of London's oldest firms, but with international growth on the rise and a rebranding exercise in 2013, will Lawrence Graham quell those persistent merger rumours?

Mid-market middler?

Dealing with Napoleon's will, facilitating the divorce between King George IV and Queen Caroline and advising Princess Diana's estate in the aftermath of her death are just a few examples of the matters Lawrence Graham has handled since its registration in 1730. Since then the firm has developed a solid reputation for its real estate and private client work and has also honed its services in key sectors, including (but not limited to): energy, renewables and cleantech; financial institutions; healthcare; insurance and reinsurance; public sector; retail; and technology.

In 2007 Lawrence Graham ditched its old premises along the Strand, moved into the swanky new development of More London and rebranded itself under the moniker 'LG'. However, the recession hit, and the firm experienced sliding revenue figures, expensive overheads (the cost of residing in More London drains £5.1m a year) and many accusations of simply 'middling' around in a legal market which requires firms to adapt quickly. 'Middling' is not a great thing to be doing in the middle market: in recent years bigger firms, starved of mega-deals, have sought to snap up transactions lower down the pecking order, encroaching on Lawrence Graham's turf. In other words, the middle market is a difficult place to be.

How has LG responded? Well, it's recently opened a new office in Singapore and in early 2013 decided to revert to the original 'Lawrence Graham' branding in order to increase international recognition of the firm. That's probably a good idea given that revenue derived from overseas clients is just over 42%. The Dubai office has posted the highest revenue increase, growing by 40% in 2011/12, and an association with Brazilian firm Motta, Fernandes Rocha Advogados has recently been formalised. Domestically, the firm engaged in merger talks with Field Fisher Waterhouse in 2012. A deal wasn't struck, but not many in the market would be surprised if another one was further down the line.

Getting what you want

Trainees complete four seats, three of which must be within property, contentious and transactional teams. Trainees said that these prerequisite areas are *"broad schools with a lot of variation within them."* There are smaller departments within the firm like employment, projects, pensions and private client, which are more competitive to get into. A stint in Dubai, which mainly focuses on construction work, is available; *"if you want to do it then it's a good idea to express an interest early on."*

Most sources were happy with the way in which the HR team allocates seats and had been able to list three preferences before each rotation. *"I've always got something that I've put down, but second-year preferences are accommodated more,"* revealed one interviewee. Trainees also have the option to add the supervisor they would like to work with within a department, and our sources recommended doing precisely that: *"I always specify as it seems that there's more guarantee of getting what you want if you are more specific and have spoken to people beforehand."*

Chambers UK rankings

Banking Litigation	Insurance
Capital Markets	Investment Funds
Construction	Pensions
Corporate Crime &	Planning
Investigations	Private Client
Corporate/M&A	Public Procurement
Dispute Resolution	Real Estate
Employment	Real Estate Finance
Fraud	Real Estate Litigation
Information Technology	

Getting real

Partners from Linklaters and Herbert Smith Freehills joined the real estate team in 2012, and the firm describes its strengths in this area as being in retail, real estate finance, offices and hospitality/leisure. Clients include Sainsbury's and The Crown Estate, and the team recently advised Development Securities on its £800m regeneration project with Cathedral Group, which aims to transform the Greenwich peninsula into a top-notch entertainment zone.

Trainees can complete a general real estate seat, which all trainees found kept them *"very busy."* Sources said that *"you get the best of worlds,"* working on *"small matters involving leases and licences and the alterations you have to make to them,"* as well as on *"big developments and the disposal of major properties – it's a rounded seat."* Many found that they received the most responsibility in this department and were given ample opportunity to run files and enjoy a nice amount of client contact: *"You deal with agents and run matters all the way through from start to finish."* On the larger transactions, trainees get *"good exposure and go to all the client meetings,"* but play more of a role in the data room. However, working with the *"big institutional clients"* enables them to gain insight into key transactions: *"We sit on Sainsbury's legal panel and help them with their purchasing of large stores and get involved on the planning side as well."*

Those who had completed a seat in construction said that there's *"a nice mix of contentious and non-contentious work."* Trainees described taking witness statements as *"exciting"* but also slaved away on the disclosure process, *"the bane of a trainee's life."* Some cases have involved suing building contractors who laid the foundations of a development in the wrong place, meaning that developers *"had to redesign the entire building."* Non-contentious work allows trainees to get to grips with warranty documents and construction reports, and sources felt that they were *"supervised well and could always ask questions."* The team has an appointment to The Crown Estate's urban portfolio's legal panel and also advises high net worth individuals on the construction and refurbishment of private residences.

Tell me lies, tell me sweet little lies

Trainees who spent a seat in dispute resolution found themselves *"running around, helping the team attend the trials and with the general day-to-day progression of the case."* Some described the department as more hierarchical than others, with *"a lot more admin and bundling to be done."* While the tasks themselves might not be fascinating, the details of the cases are: many trainees have been involved in the culmination of a case concerning claims of corruption against the former mayor of São Paulo, Paulo Maluf. The trial ended in 2012, and the Royal Court of Jersey gave judgment in favour of LG's clients, the Federal Republic of Brazil and the Municipality of São Paulo – Maluf was found guilty of stealing millions from Brazilian taxpayers, and hiding it in a secret bank account in Jersey. Other notable cases have included the collapse of Bernard L. Madoff Investment Securities following the arrest of its principal (the eponymous Bernie Madoff) for fraud, which resulted in investors losing around $65bn. LG is representing professional trustees in the case.

Trainees had also been involved in matters surrounding the Libor investigations, and given the magnitude/significance of all the cases described above, sources *"felt much more closely supervised"* than in other departments. Work revolves around doc management, legal research and drafting memos, but sources did say that they felt *"really included and very much part of the team – they would take us all out for drinks."*

Some trainees had sat within Lawrence Graham's insurance and reinsurance dispute resolution team. One source had been involved in *"an arbitration with a major US company: I was dealing with US lawyers all the time, sitting in on conference calls, attending case management sessions and drafting part of an offer letter to the other side."* Other seats which fulfil the contentious requirement are construction, employment, real estate litigation, and restructuring and insolvency.

AIM high

Lawrence Graham's long list of AIM clients has helped to keep its stream of M&A work flowing, and the firm acted on two of the largest public M&A deals of 2012: one for Cove Energy during its £1.22bn takeover by PTTEP Africa Investment and the other during AIM-listed uranium miner Kalahari Minerals' £650m sale to Taurus Mineral. Trainees flagged insurance, hotels, healthcare and energy as key sectors in which the group has expertise. There's a *"good range of public and private"* M&A deals as well as *"a lot of AIM investment funds work"* to get stuck into. Trainees are *"involved in the case management process,"* draft ancillary documents and complete board minutes, but are also able to write more substantial sections of reports: *"It's a really supportive team, and I've never been worried about asking a single question."*

Corporate tax is *"interesting and challenging"* and throws up some *"fantastic pieces of research involving places like Singapore and Monaco."* Trainees here found themselves *"in the library reading up on statutes"* and brushing up on *"lots of black-letter law."* The team feels *"very much a part of corporate"* but also deals a lot with *"specific queries from real estate and the finance team there,"* meaning that a trainees can get a feel for how tax connects with different departments in the firm.

On the banking and finance side, Lawrence Graham works with familiar names from the sector, including HSBC, RBS Group and Santander. The firm is also popular with German banks and represented DG Hyp and Deutsche Postbank during the refinancing of the Lloyds of London building. Trainees said that they *"were thrown in at the deep end"* during their banking seat and that *"you have to put in the hours."* Tasks included running conditions precedent lists, which can lead to *"being stuck in a room for 13 hours straight"* as the completion date nears. *"Bundling comes with the territory,"* but sources felt that *"it's a good department to work in,"* with opportunities to have *"a first stab"* at more complex drafting and some client contact. It also introduces trainees to the potentially confusing world of mezzanine financings. Seats can also be taken in private capital/client, projects and employment/pensions.

LG? L-NO!

In early 2013, the firm decided to drop its 'LG' branding (which had been introduced back in 2007 to coincide with the move to More London) and revert to its original name of Lawrence Graham. *"The name change was bizarre,"* said one trainee, who added: *"When I told people where I was working, they just said, 'What, the electronics manufacturer?'"* Sources concurred that *"it's a good move to go back to the original name,"* and were pleased that *"we now sound like a law firm again!"* Trainees thought that the rebrand was a good way for the firm to showcase its long history and *"traditional roots,"* and everyone we spoke to viewed it as a step in the right direction.

Rumours of imminent mergers for this firm have abounded recently. Training principal Caroline Walker says: *"You can't just sit there waiting for a merger – that is madness. We are concentrating on our own strategy., but on the other hand we are alive to opportunities and don't sit navel gazing."* The firm will continue to invest in its *"key service areas"* while also keeping a look-out for international opportunities in South America and India. Walker also emphasised that London is still of major im-

portance to the firm. *"International investors continue to pour money into UK real estate, and this remains an important focus for us."*

Trainees thought that a merger was *"likely"* and that *"with all the talks around mergers, morale has been up and down at the firm – but that's a common situation for mid-tier firms at the moment."* With expensive property costs, the firm has sublet some of its office space in the More London development in order to ease the burden on its finances. Trainees do love the South Bank location: *"It's much nicer being this side of the river: you get amazing views, and you can sit outside in The Scoop during the summer."*

While Lawrence Graham's uncertain future may have *"dulled the atmosphere"* of late, trainees felt a genuine attachment to the firm and described it as *"a friendly place – everybody is approachable and there are no absolute nightmares here."* They were impressed with the *"high-quality"* formal training which greets them at the beginning of each seat; they *"couldn't complain"* about their salary; liked that there wasn't a *"face-time culture"*; and praised the *"amazing feedback"* they'd received from their supervisors.

There's a good social life too, and although trainees' Christmas party budget was axed a couple of years ago, they still get together to organise their own gathering: *"It's turned into a firm-wide party now, and everyone's invited. Last year it took place in a hotel near London Bridge."* The social committee also organises lots of events, including *"quiz nights and games evenings,"* while individual departments host welcome drinks and invite trainees to client parties as well. The last real estate one was held at The Savoy, and quite a few trainees attended: *"They really encouraged us to go and chat and build connections – you are trusted and, in comparison to my friends at bigger firms, I've had a lot more client contact."*

Ultimately, given the choice, most interviewees expressed a strong desire to stay with the firm, but one trainee spoke for all when they said: *"I don't think anyone in my year is overly confident. There is a nervousness which stems from the trainees, and a lot of us are aware that it will be hard, but if they want me I'll definitely stay!"* In the end, there was no need to be too nervous as ten out of 13 eventually remained with the firm on qualification in 2013, which is in line with the national average.

And finally...

Who knows what Lawrence Graham will look like in a year or two's time, but there's no doubting the affection trainees have for it.

Leigh Day

The facts

Location: London
Number of UK partners/solicitors: 29/67
Partners who trained at the firm: 28%
Total number of trainees: 14
Seats: 2x12 months
Alternative seats: secondments

On chambersstudent.co.uk...
How to get into Leigh Day
Cycling and the law

Ethical lawyering is the name of the game at claimant firm Leigh Day, which handles complicated and often ground-breaking PI and clinical negligence cases along with international and human rights work.

Defeating the giant

What if the oyster bars of the City don't call out to you? What if tinkering with the tax arrangements for oligarchs' offshore funds makes you feel a bit queasy? What if you believe that justice isn't some lofty ideal to be left at the door of academe and trampled upon by the financial and political power-brokers of our age? What if you want to Stick It To The Man? Well, you can. At Leigh Day.

The firm was created in 1987, when Martyn Day joined his former Bindmans colleague Sarah Leigh at her specialist PI practice. While Leigh concentrated on clinical negligence cases, Day initially led a case against British Nuclear Fuel for a family in Sellafield who claimed to have discovered traces of plutonium in their home. Over time the firm's clinical negligence department has grown to become one of the largest in London – alongside lawyers (some of who are former doctors), the firm employs nurses and forensic accountants. As well as taking on complex claims relating to illness and injury, the firm has a human rights department and an international group that works on behalf of people worldwide, often against UK-based multinationals and government bodies. Across all its practices, the Leigh Day ethos is clear – to strive for justice on behalf of those who might otherwise be denied a voice. Indeed, the firm sees itself as embarking on 'David and Goliath' struggles against the commercial and public powers-that-be. *"I wanted to do claimant work, especially for vulnerable clients against bigger defendants. I really wasn't interested in the corporate world or transactional work,"* emphasised one of our interviewees. *"People at the firm are very passionate about the work they do. You feel that everyone is pursuing the same goal – seeking justice."*

Litigate to compensate

Cases undertaken here are certainly diverse, and some attract significant media coverage. For instance, the international and group claims department recently acted for Kenyans who were tortured during the 1950s and 1960s by British colonial officials during the Mau Mau uprising. The British government failed in its attempts to strike out the case in 2011 and 2012. Leigh Day lawyers are also managing a case relating to the Rwandan genocide. And a number of claims have arisen from the recent war on terror – the firm is acting for Iraqis civilians who suffered human rights abuses when detained by the UK military. Similar cases involving Afghan citizens are also being pursued. As well as this, solicitors are working for an individual detained indefinitely in Guantanamo Bay.

Unlawful environmental damage is another concern of the international group. Lawyers, led by Martyn Day, are bringing a case against Shell Oil on behalf of 15,000 members of the Nigerian Bodo community after two major oil spills – yet to be cleaned up – damaged their fishing industry and land. The firm is also representing Colombian farmers who are suing BP – the farmers allege that a pipeline built by the company through their land in the 1990s has resulted in erosion and contamination of the soil and water. Leigh Day also handles age and race discrimination issues. For example, it represented TV presenter Miriam O'Reilly over her dismissal from BBC programme *Countryfile*. Other clients in this field include

Chambers UK rankings

Administrative & Public Law	Education
	Employment
Civil Liberties & Human Rights	Environment
	Personal Injury
Clinical Negligence	Product Liability
Court of Protection	Travel

the RNIB, the Citizens' Advice Bureau and the British Humanist Association.

Personal injury and clinical negligence cases at Leigh Day are usually complex and high-value. They could involve brain or spinal injury sustained during medical treatment or cerebral palsy arising from mismanaged births. The firm's other healthcare matters include challenges to the privatisation of the NHS and cases relating to access to healthcare in prison or for people with learning disabilities. Cases have arisen in the wake of the recent Mid-Staffs hospital scandal and from the widespread abuse of patients at a Bristol care home, exposed by *Panorama*. Leigh Day advises organisations such as Dignity in Dying on right to die or right to life cases – solicitors have represented a client suffering from 'locked-in syndrome' in this regard. Plus there's a group dedicated to working for cyclists, another *"massive draw"* for some trainees. In 2012 the head of the PI and accident claims team recovered more than £22.5m in damages for injured clients.

The court of conscience

Trainees complete just two year-long seats. There are spots available in personal injury; clinical negligence; international and group claims; and human rights (which comprises traditional human rights cases and employment work). Within employment, there's a chance to do six months with a trade union, and a six-month secondment with the Shadow Attorney General, Emily Thornberry, is open to all trainees. The first seat is allocated to new recruits, but HR will ask for preferences when it comes to the second seat. Sources concurred that the seat structure means *"there's a real emphasis on depth,"* although *"on the flipside, it does leave you wanting to see other departments because all the work is so exciting."*

Nearly all of our interviewees had undertaken a seat in clinical negligence. *"I was helping a partner who does a wide variety of claims, including birth injury, surgical malpractice, lack of consent and misdiagnosis cases. I*

also worked on an inquest," said a source. Tasks include *"drafting letters, e-mails, pleadings and witness statements, and liaising with clients and experts."* A key element is *"sorting and reviewing medical records."* While training is provided on *"what to look out for"* in these documents, new recruits will inevitably spend time decoding unfamiliar medical terms and learning on the fly: *"I spent half of my days on Google working out what things meant, and by the end of the seat I felt like I had a medical degree! It's very intellectually challenging but also rewarding because you get to see the tangible results, like a family getting funds for their child's wheelchair."*

In the human rights seat, trainees *"work on most parts of a case, whether that's drafting instructions to counsel, applying for funding or being the general point of contact for the client."* As in clinical negligence, *"you build a working relationship with people who've had very distressing things happen to them. It's hard. The cases are always shocking – you never get used to it. But that motivates me to work hard and obtain justice."*

Trainees described the firm as a *"progressive, energetic place full of like-minded, passionate people. It's exciting when big cases are won – when the Mau Mau judgment was handed down; there was a real buzz in the office."* One source commented: *"I worked briefly at a City firm and, oh god, it's the polar opposite! It's not about money, it's about the clients and fighting for justice."* Speaking of money: Leigh Day is one of the firms which has publicly voiced its concern over the recent legal aid reforms. While the cuts are affecting areas like judicial review, the firm told us that only 10% of its work is publicly funded, so the impact on its business will be minimal.

Most trainees at Leigh Day aren't fresh out of university. *"Lots of people here have prior career experience, maybe with NGOs, volunteering, working abroad or paralegalling. You need to show you're genuinely committed to working with vulnerable people."* One interviewee remembered that on the assessment day *"a lot of people were quite loud, and I was worried that I wasn't loud enough! However the people who shouted loudest didn't actually get a job."* Nevertheless, the firm *"attracts people who are feisty and daring. It's not a place for shrinking violets."* When it comes to qualification, the firm releases a list of positions, and trainees can apply for any of the jobs, even if they haven't sat in that department. In 2013 five out of eight qualifiers were retained.

And finally...

"To work here you need the sensitivity and empathy to be able to deal with people going through difficult times while still maintaining a professional distance."

Lester Aldridge LLP

The facts

Location: Bournemouth, Southampton, London
Number of UK partners/solicitors: 40/41
Partners who trained at firm: c.20%
Total number of trainees: 13
Seats: 4x6 months
Alternative seats: none

On chambersstudent.co.uk...

How to get into Lester Aldridge
Life in Bournemouth

South coast supremo Lester Aldridge offers trainees *"wide exposure to different areas of law"* and multi-office postings.

Welcome to LA

Despite its small size, Lester Aldridge isn't some parochial small-fry outfit – its *Chambers UK* scores are significant, with rankings in the South for areas such as family, real estate and charities, and UK-wide recognition for its consumer finance, healthcare and shipping practices. Indeed, our sources were attracted to the firm's reputation as a full-service *"regional heavyweight."* Location was an important factor – most interviewees were Bournemouth or Southampton-bred and wanted a career in the South.

However, trainees aren't confined to a single base but often switch offices during their training contract. As such, new recruits can expect a fair bit of commuting (a driving licence is a requirement here) or some reshuffling of accommodation. Seats are usually six months long and the range on offer reflects LA's broad spread of practices – there's real estate, corporate, care, employment, family, dispute resolution, personal injury, marine, and trusts, tax and wills (TTW). At any one time, most trainees can be found in the Bournemouth office, which is just a bundle's throw from the beach.

Coasting on the coast? Shorely not!

Real estate is a hefty king prawn in the seafood medley that is LA's mixture of practices – it's a dominant force in Dorset and one of the largest property departments in Southampton. The latter office deals with insolvency matters, while Bournemouth folk take on commercial transactions and residential work. *"On the insolvency side of real estate, we were acting for liquidators,"* said a source. *"I got to do an exchange of contract and completion on my own."* Meanwhile, those in Bournemouth reported

working on the special sub-team devoted to McCarthy & Stone, a locally based developer of retirement homes and one of the firm's key clients. Work involved *"sales and purchases, standard form contracts and the odd bit of research – they might call up with a question about rights of way or a neighbourhood dispute."* The firm has also acted for Care South, a provider of nursing and residential homes, on the £10m acquisition of another business. Other notable clients include FTSE 100 engineering group Meggitt (another Bournemouth native), Marina Developments and Big Yellow, the storage company with the unsurprisingly big and yellow warehouses.

The care seat covers *"both contentious and non-contentious work. I did a lot of research into different care home regulations and supported living. The litigation element meant I got to go to court and draft witness statements. Plus I did a due diligence report for the acquisition of a home."* The care seat can be combined with employment work: *"The areas intertwine when owners and managers of care homes have issues with employees. It can be quite hard if there's a case of abuse."* Among others, the firm works for National Care Association, NHS Nottinghamshire County and Kent Autistic Trust. It might not sound like a particularly glamorous seat, but the UK's aging population means that this will become an ever-more significant area of law.

"I've done a lot of professional negligence work and even managed to do some advocacy," one source said when asked about their time in the dispute resolution team. Bundling is to be expected here, but trainees can also find themselves handling their own files and meeting clients without supervision. Meanwhile, the corporate seat might involve a few *"reasonably big transactions,"* which means getting

Chambers UK rankings

Charities	Partnership
Consumer Finance	Planning
Corporate/M&A	Private Client
Dispute Resolution	Real Estate
Employment	Real Estate Litigation
Family/Matrimonial	Restructuring/Insolvency
Healthcare	Shipping

stuck into some due diligence. Trainees became immersed in *"setting up companies from scratch – the Companies House side of the law – as well as commercial aspects like drafting licence agreements."* Corporate clients include Mobil oil supplier Wessex Petroleum, Bournemouth University and hair product manufacturer Herb UK.

On to marine matters. LA recently advised Portuguese holiday company Douro Azul on the purchase of 'The Spirit of Chartwell', which was used as the royal barge by the Queen during that drizzly jubilee pageant in 2012. LA's shipping practice also counts prominent insurers RSA and Allianz Global Corporate as clients. *"On my first day in the seat I was given a folder to read through, and by that afternoon I'd already drafted advice to the client, which was scary but exciting!"* exclaimed one happy source. *"I got to draft boat build contracts, mooring contracts, charter and skipper agreements. There's a lot of work for private clients relating to their yachts."* As well as all this, sources reported *"a bit of contentious work, such as getting involved with an instruction from a client whose vessel had been stolen from the marina."*

Allocation, allocation, allocation

In previous years we've reported some grumbles that trainees were bypassing the official list and approaching partners directly to secure their seat of choice. When asked about the procedure, this year's sources raised similar issues: *"It's meant to be quite a fair system, but it doesn't seem very transparent. I don't really understand it."* Each department only takes one trainee at a time, and halfway through each seat, the list of upcoming options is circulated. Trainees state their preferences to the training principal, who then allocates the spots. However, it was felt that *"some people who've done vac schemes or worked as paralegals here seem to have a head-start on those who've come here fresh, which isn't fair."* One source said: *"It doesn't surprise me that people would go to partners as some always get the seats they want. I've never got my pref-*

erence. *I wanted to do a seat, but when the list came round it said 'already allocated'. It's tough because the seats you do have such a big effect on your career."* While several trainees felt the system is *"secretive,"* others took a more laissez faire attitude: *"People can see it as unfair, but inevitably someone will lose out."* Luckily, some co-operation between trainees can smooth the way: *"All six of us get on really well, so we all met up to figure out where everyone could go. This time round we've all asked for different seats."* Repeating a seat is not uncommon.

The salary was another troublesome issue. *"I could be earning more working in Topshop,"* grumbled one source. *"It's really bad having to live like a student after paying rent and bills. But then you put it in perspective – so many people don't have a training contract, and I'm not working crazy hours."* And on the topic of qualification, sources said: *"The processes aren't that clear. You're left in the dark. There's no jobs list and there aren't interviews. You have to make it known to a partner if you're interested in qualifying into that team."* In 2013 five out of six trainees stayed on upon qualification.

Despite their gripes, interviewees were largely happy and relished the favourable work/life balance on offer at LA. Working hours tend to range between 9am and 6 to 6.30pm. *"Just after 7pm is the latest I stay until,"* declared one source, while another said: *"The Southampton office is very relaxed and most days I get out about 5.45pm."*

The three offices have their own social traditions. Friday lunchtimes in Southampton typically involve *"going to The Cricketers with partners. They're fascinated by this pub and always get the chilli chips. It's like a cult, but it's keeping the place in business!"* The London office is *"very lively and sociable,"* with frequent lunchtime outings around Chancery Lane. The two smaller offices were viewed as *"close-knit and less formal because we're all on one floor and everyone mixes."* According to one source, the Southampton office is *"like a family."* Meanwhile, in Bournemouth *"it's more segregated because there are seven floors, so you sometimes feel like you only see people in your department."* However, trainees make an effort to arrange lunches and trips to the beach. 'Happy hour' drinks take place on the first Friday of each month in the boardroom, arranged by trainees. Teams hold their own Christmas parties, and there's a firm-wide summer event too.

And finally...

If you're fond of sand dunes and salty air and fancy a good mixed training on the South Coast, you would do well to give Lester Aldridge a closer look.

Lewis Silkin LLP

The facts

Location: London, Oxford, Cardiff

Number of UK partners/solicitors: 62/100

Partners who trained at firm: 23%

Total number of trainees: 12

Seats: 6x4 months

Alternative seats: occasional secondments

Extras: pro bono – National Pro Bono Centre, Own-it; language classes

On chambersstudent.co.uk...

How to get into Lewis Silkin

Interview with training principal Lisa Patmore

Social housing at Lewis Silkin

Best known for its social housing, employment and media work, Lewis Silkin sits between the West End and the City and offers an eclectic training contract.

Left right, left right

Latterly an MP in Clement Attlee's Labour government, Mr Lewis Silkin founded the firm that bears his name in 1920 and in doing so initiated its long-standing commitment to social housing projects. Then, in the 1980s the firm was the first to advertise its services on a billboard, and today the burgeoning media department works with leading figures across the ad industry, including Labour and Tory favourites Saatchi & Saatchi. The firm recently opened a new office in Cardiff, and training principal Lisa Patmore told us: *"We want to keep growing our core areas in employment, creative industries, and real estate development and regeneration."*

The employment, media and mid-market corporate/M&A departments are all top ranked by *Chambers UK*, and the firm offers trainees seats in employment, reward and immigration; media, brands and technology; real estate/development; corporate; and litigation. If there was any dissatisfaction among the trainees we spoke to it was to do with the seat allocation system. One trainee described the process as *"a game of luck,"* while another said: *"The decision-making process doesn't seem all that clear. They're not very open about it."* Most of our insiders, however, were fairly happy with where they had been placed, and Lisa Patmore told us: *"We give each trainee two priority seats between their second and fifth seats, but we do also try to accommodate them in their desired departments for the rest of their training contract."*

House of Fazer

Employment is a regular stop for trainees, and the department accounts for 40% of the firm's revenue. It hosts 86 employment law specialists, making it the largest department of its kind in the South of England, and attracts names like Nokia, MTV and Marks & Spencer. *"It's a great seat because of the range of work on offer to trainees,"* one source said. *"You get to run some smaller claims by yourself, but then you also get the experience of working as part of the team on the high-value litigation disputes. I was drafting witness statements and correspondence and getting involved in giving advice to clients."* Another trainee mentioned *"really interesting work for major football clubs,"* while a senior associate in the department was recently quoted by the BBC on points relating to the law surrounding unpaid internships after it transpired that David Gauke, HMRC minister and MP for South West Hertfordshire, was advertising for an unpaid graduate position in his constituency office.

The media department was another popular stop for our interviewees. It deals with film/TV, music, theatre, advertising/marketing, publishing and interactive content matters. One trainee told us: *"The work is contentious and non-contentious, and there's a huge amount of scope and variety in terms of the cases you might be working on. You get a lot of responsibility, and it feels like there's loads going on."* Another said: *"The media side of the firm is booming – it's a really exciting seat to be in."* The department recently represented both Fazer and Tulisa from N-Dubz, winning an undisclosed six-figure sum for Tulisa after her sex tape was leaked online. It also won a settle-

Chambers UK rankings

Construction	Intellectual Property
Corporate/M&A	Media & Entertainment
Defamation/Reputation	Partnership
Management	Real Estate
Dispute Resolution	Real Estate Litigation
Education	Retail
Employment	Social Housing
Immigration	Sports Law

ment for Holly Willoughby when the Sunday Sport faked an up-skirt shot of the TV presenter.

Over in real estate/development, the work is split between social housing and commercial projects. *"I found that you had a lot of responsibility,"* one trainee told us. *"You're given your own small files to manage, which might be something like a property sale, and you keep control of them right up to completion."* Another said: *"I managed four different cases from start to finish in the course of four months. Each was the sale of a residential property. The supervision is really good, and I was left to do as much as I possibly could so as to get the experience, but I knew help was always on hand if I needed it. You have to be quick, efficient and responsive."* The commercial branch has advised Fulham FC on plans to expand its Craven Cottage stadium, and helped EDF Energy with a National Grid tunnel-building project worth £6bn. The social housing branch works on regeneration and development projects in areas including Elephant and Castle and Notting Hill.

Fulham FC works closely with the firm on immigration matters, and trainees seeking plenty of client exposure need look no further: *"I was regularly spending two days a week with clients independently. Most of the work involves preparing visa applications for employees at large companies, and I was drawing up contracts for foreign professional footballers and rugby players who were coming to play in the UK. I also got to go to the Border Agency's Public Enquiry Office, and there's lots of scope for advocacy. Sometimes the work gets repetitive, but it's really satisfying when one of your applications is granted."* Speaking of advocacy, another trainee said of their time in the litigation department: *"I went up in front of a Master at a bankruptcy hearing. It was terrifying. I was on my own, and I had only just started the seat! That said, it was such a great experience."*

A quick word on the corporate department: it has carved out a spot of its own in London's lower mid-market. It has *"a lot of advertising agencies"* on the books and also acted for United Agents on its acquisition of the share capital of AP Watt, one of the oldest literary agents in the business. It's a *"really nice department,"* said sources, and *"good to be in as a trainee because you can get involved in the smaller cases, drafting share-holders agreements and board minutes."*

Benevolent bee-haviour

One of our sources said *"it's a really positive place, and you feel that at all levels."* Although this may sound like we've merely mic'd-up the marketing channels, the fact that Lewis Silkin regularly appears on The Sunday Times' '100 Best Companies to Work For' list lends some weight to the suggestion that it's an enjoyable place to work. Charity work is *"really important"* to the firm, and one recent money-spinner saw the firm keeping bees on the roof of the Chancery Lane office and selling the honey they made to raise funds for a London children's hospice. Staff across the firm also completed the Three Peaks challenge for charity, and there has been talk of a sponsored cycle ride to Amsterdam.

Trainees spoke very highly of the social life, which includes dinner in a swanky West End hotel around Christmas, regular departmental curries and Friday night drinks across the road at Baranis wine bar, where *"there are always people from across the firm, and the bar staff know us by name now, for better or worse."* While late nights in the office are not unheard of, particularly in litigation, *"a normal day is 9am to 7pm,"* so there's plenty of time for getting acquainted with staff (and local bar staff, apparently) after hours.

The current trainee intake includes a former literary agent, a one-time antiques dealer and a couple of round-the-world explorers. So what do Lewis Silkin's trainees have in common? *"If there's anything, it's that the people here are all really interesting and most have a particular talent of some kind, whether it's playing sport or a certain instrument."* Another source said: *"We're all good with people."* Perhaps the final word should go to the trainee who told us: *"Everyone is here to be part of the firm and part of the team; there's never any kind of competitiveness or one-upmanship."*

And finally...

Lewis Silkin offers a training contract that's a bit different from the standard. In 2013 the firm was happy to report it retained all of its seven qualifiers.

Linklaters

The facts

Location: London

Number of UK partners/solicitors: 179/535

UK partners who trained at the firm: 35%

Total number of trainees: 229

Seats: 4x6 months

Alternative seats: overseas seats, secondments

Extras: pro bono – Mary Ward Legal Advice Centre and others; language classes

On chambersstudent.co.uk...

How to get into Linklaters

The Linklaters LPC

Linklaters in America

"The all-nighters go so fast that you look at your watch at 3am and think: 'How did this happen?'"

Big is best

Law doesn't get much more globally connected than Linklaters. *"It's got the widest base of the premium clients, is top in terms of kudos and the opportunities for travel are second to none,"* say trainees. *"You know you won't be the biggest fish in the pond, but you know it will give you the best foundation possible."*

It has many excellent practices, and we really recommend you take a look at the firm's full *Chambers UK* rankings online, but any discussion of this firm really has to start with the corporate and finance departments, which take on the biggest deals around. It's a cliché to bandy about words like 'powerhouse', but really, what else are we supposed to say? The latest list of advisers to the FTSE companies was published as we were writing this article, and Links acts for 28 of the top 100 – more than any other firm except magic circle peer Slaughter and May. Also at the time of writing, it was lining up alongside Slaughters and Freshfields on the IPO of Royal Mail and advising the largest utilities company in the world, China's State Grid Corporation, on its $4bn acquisition of Australian power assets.

At any one time, nearly half of Linklaters' 230 trainees will be sitting in banking, corporate or capital markets. The remainder are split between litigation, real estate, projects, pensions, restructuring and insolvency, tax, competition, investment management, IP, TMT, financial regulation, trusts, environment and employment/incentives. There are options aplenty, but it's important to remember that *"Links is heavy on corporate and finance."* That said, *"if you've got a really good reason to sit in a smaller department, the firm takes it into account."*

Links trainees list four preferences before they start at the firm, one of which they'll ideally get as a first seat. A few months later they put down another eight options, from which their remaining three seats will be allocated. *"It gives you the opportunity to plan out the two years you have. If there's one you don't want, you can try and use that to go abroad, or swap into a department you do want to go to."* If a seat's very oversubscribed, networking never hurts. *"I met with a partner in the group before I went there,"* said one trainee in a smaller department; *"I got to grips with the kind of work that was going on and made it known that I really wanted to do it."*

Living in the future

Linklaters' corporate group is split into a handful of sector-focused teams, including *"energy, private equity and a niche group which covers things like insurance work."* The energy deals that Linklaters works on are predictably Herculean. Ongoing are the $70bn merger of Glencore and Xstrata and the sale of BP's share in Russian oil company TNK-BP. Trainees only see the briefest snapshot of deals in this league, and the tasks they're given, understandably, can be basic. *"Often the context of the deal is so international that doing the bundling really helps you grasp what's going on."* On shorter-term deals of less high value, trainees do manage to *"build respect and get trusted with phoning clients or turning around documents."* Private equity work *"won't be as huge as the energy deals, but there are enough zeros to still make it all pretty mindblowing."* Tasks here are marked by their variety, and when it comes to grunt work, *"it's always explained to you."* If responsibility is limited, Links trainees all say the same: *"My role was minor, but what was being created overall by the little tasks was fascinating."*

The True Picture

Chambers UK rankings

Asset Finance	Insurance
Banking & Finance	Intellectual Property
Banking Litigation	Investment Funds
Capital Markets	Life Sciences
Commodities	Outsourcing
Competition/European Law	Partnership
Corporate Crime &	Pensions
Investigations	Pensions Litigation
Corporate/M&A	Planning
Data Protection	Private Equity
Dispute Resolution	Projects
Employee Share Schemes	Public Procurement
& Incentives	Real Estate
Employment	Real Estate Finance
Energy & Natural	Real Estate Litigation
Resources	Restructuring/Insolvency
Environment	Retail
Financial Services	Tax
Fraud	Telecommunications
Information Technology	Transport

It would be wrong to detail the corporate life without including a 411 on late nights. *"You have to be willing to be there,"* explained one corporate trainee, *"and have flexible plans."* So, for every period *"of leaving at 6pm on the dot,"* there are *"weeks where you're consistently in until 3am."* But that's the thrill of working on deals this big and deadlines this tough: *"You don't have a typical day – which is one of the main draws. It's always exciting, and there's always something going on to be swept up in."* Another explained: *"People are quite good at telling you to have a day off after a deal wraps up. The other kind of late hours are less fun – perhaps you've taken on too much work, or someone lands something on your desk at 6pm. Still though, you have the sense that you're taking control of things and pushing them forward."*

Transactional work may appeal to the kind of person who thrives under seven hours of heat, but it wouldn't be right and just to conclude that Links trainees *"are obsessed with punishing hours."* Sources do agree, though, that *"everyone here is out to impress. All-nighters are incredibly tough, but if there's work to be done, there's nobody here who wouldn't bend over backwards to do it."* Unusually, there is a trainee bonus scheme to reward those who put serious time in. *"It's nice to know that if you do work crazy hours, you will get something for it."*

Late nights are alleviated not just by 24-hour admin support but by *"free dinners and a guaranteed taxi home."* When late nights become all-night-longs, there are always the office sleep pods, *"which my flatmates think are crazy but are actually really useful!"* But this isn't even the start of Links' utopian dwelling. There's an on-site cash point,

gym, doctor, dentist and beautician *"you can book for eyebrow threading or waxing,"* and a 24-hour shop. *"We view the Barbican over the road as some sort of futuristic commune, but in reality we probably have more facilities than they do,"* one trainee joked.

EDM, DSP, SFG... WTF?

Finance is the other strand of Linklaters' transactional double helix. It's split between banking (= private loans) and capital markets (= raising money publicly). A banking seat can involve insolvency and restructuring, though the mainstay will always be advising lenders and borrowers on taking out loans. It's very international by nature, and even if the basic trainee job *"is matter management, it makes for a fascinating legal experience. Trainees look after the CP process, but because a lot of it is cross-border you get to understand the requirements for registering securities in other countries and see what kind of board structures they have."*

Linklaters being one of the very few firms with multiple capital markets seats means that true public finance bods can opt to sample more than one. On the cards are equity and debt markets (EDM) – *"mainstream bond issuances, primarily capital markets"* – derivatives and structured products (DSP), and the structured finance group (SFG), *"which essentially involves transactions that end with a bond issue."* The team recently assisted Barclays, HSBC and JPMorgan in various structured equity transactions (such as total return swaps, prepaid collars and call spreads) that relate to the public stake holding of Iberia airlines in Amadeus IT in order for the former to protect the value of its shares while simultaneously participating in any appreciation the shares could incur in the future.

If that sounds more WTF than SFG, get used to it – it's a seat renowned for its stretching, slightly intangible intellectual requirements. *"It takes a lot of brain power, but everyone there is very good at getting you up to speed,"* say its enthusiasts. Equally though, the relatively small department size and iterative nature of deals means trainees get buckets of responsibility *"and amazing work"* from the off. *"You're able to see things through to their end, and although it's repetitive, fresh things arise each time."* The amount of client contact *"is a massive shock – you're not just copied into e-mails; you're the person the client calls."* Different by nature to the adrenaline rush of corporate, there's *"real pleasure in not wondering what the hell is going on as soon as you get to your desk every morning."* Additionally, *"it's always topical now the financial crisis put the industry in the spotlight, yet it's far less orthodox than M&A work."*

Lehman or Leveson

When the bread and butter of a department involves either the Lehman Brothers bankruptcy or the Leveson Inquiry, it's understandable that the trainee role will be limited. In litigation (*"the silver island in a sea of transactional departments"*) trainees do get pretty friendly with the concepts of doc review and disclosure. The latter, we hear, becomes more tricksy every year that technology allows daily communication to exponentially rise. *"When everything was hard copy, people thought twice before writing something down. Now people send hundreds of e-mails every day and accessing them all from the past two years is like pulling teeth."* Doc review *"admittedly has its highs and lows,"* but *"the issues are always in a legal grey area or Linklaters wouldn't be on the case – the clients are high-profile, the issues are complex and you are the first pair of eyes deciding what's favourable or unfavourable about it."* Sources were also keen to point out the role of training principal here: *"They check in with you once or twice a week, because if you spent six months bored, there's no way you'd want to qualify there."*

The firm's got a great rep for its training. There are e-learning modules and interactive sessions most weeks. There's also *"fantastic"* PSL support and *"a real drive towards people sharing knowledge when they've done something."* The training integral within the trainee-supervisor relationship is often of an equally high standard. *"Some are more focused on teaching than others, but they're great at stopping what they're doing and drawing out a diagram on their whiteboard."* We heard good things about the use of formal appraisals, although some sources felt *"partners can wait until appraisal time to give constructive feedback when it could have been given sooner."* That said, there are different experiences when it comes to getting day-to-day feedback. *"It can be hard to get it out of some people at first, but the onus is always on the trainee to request it."*

Overseas opportunities at Linklaters are such that *"if you want to go, you'll be able to."* Around two-thirds of the trainee cohort will spend a full seat abroad, with numerous ad-hoc positions cropping up during seats in London. Hong Kong, Dubai, Paris and New York are all very popular. In addition to laid-on accommodation and an overseas stipend, trainees see multiple benefits to spending time in another office. *"It's useful to understand how the overseas outposts co-ordinate with London. It's also exciting because there are so many Asian opportunities; being able to go there and find out what all the hype is about is exciting."*

Silky smooth

"You notice types of trainee in other firms, but on the face of it here, there's just a bunch of very interesting people." Linklaters' new starters are marked by their internationality, with dedicated intakes from Australia and India. Oxbridge grads make up around a third of incoming trainees. *"There are lots of Redbricks represented, which is made apparent in the non-stuffy atmosphere."* Opinion varied as to whether the firm was doing enough to bring in socio-economic diversity, though. Some were surprised that *"many people here are the first in their family to go to university."*

The accelerated LPC at the University of Law means *"loads of people are in London for the first time and want to make friends. If you're not in touch with everyone after the LPC, you know someone who is, which is how the gossip gets around."* A trainee social committee *"has a healthy budget to play with,"* though there aren't too many regular events for everyone as *"when you've got 200 people, it enters into 'hiring out a nightclub' territory."* There is, however, a trainee summer ball and drinks every seat swap. Departmentally, there are *"the famed drinks trolleys"* and plenty of overseas away days and team-building retreats. On Thursday nights staff canteen Silks becomes 'Sunset Silks', somewhere to get a drink and antipasti. Regular Silks sounds pretty exciting to us – *"it has everything you could ever possibly want to eat: DIY salad or noodles, a pizza oven, a milkshake bar...."*

Maybe it's the eloquent nature of Links trainees, but we always seem to be able to end our feature on this firm with some pithy quotes as to what makes it tick. This year we heard some interesting thoughts about the nature of the people who thrive here. The level of ambition *"is obviously higher than in an average sample of the population. Everyone here wants to absolutely smash it – though there's no sense that people would step over one another in order to get there."* The other side of that ambition is a level of self-critique *"which comes from everyone naturally being a bit of a perfectionist and becomes clear on the first day – no matter how amazing you thought you were, you'll be humbled."*

And finally...
With no job lists or interview system, *"the feeling is if you're good enough and want to stay the firm will find space for you."* In 2013 97 out of 111 qualifiers stayed at Linklaters.

331

Macfarlanes LLP

The facts

Location: London
Number of UK partners/solicitors: 76/180
Partners who trained at firm: 55%
Total number of trainees: 56
Seats: 4x6 months
Alternative seats: none
Extras: pro bono – Cambridge House, LawWorks, Impetus Trust, Carbon Leapfrog and others; language classes

On chambersstudent.co.uk...

How to get into Macfarlanes
Interview with grad recruitment partners John Hornby and Seán Lavin

> **Classy and restrained Macfarlanes continues to whirr along with the charm, reliability and pedigree of a Victorian pocket watch.**

Silver service

Founded in 1875, this firm first welcomed a member of the Macfarlane family in 1894. Several generations of the clan have since worked here but this is no family business. Macfarlanes is a City big-shot and a member of the elite group of firms sometimes call the silver circle. Corporate is king here, bringing in 37.5% of revenue in 2012/13. Unusually for such a high-end City firm, Macfarlanes still has a large and highly-regarded private client practice, which brought in a further 14.7% of turnover in 2012/13. The other main earners are finance (20.8%), litigation (17.2%) and real estate (11.6%). This *"variety of practices and clients"* coupled with the firm's medium size is the draw for many graduates.

Macfarlanes impressed observers with double-digit revenue growth in 2012/13, and we weren't surprised to hear trainees say the firm is *"not changing direction"* any time soon. But sources did notice *"a lot more focus on regulatory advice and litigation."* The firm has recently been working on some interesting matters in these areas. It was appointed to advise the independent commission looking into the use of doping in cycling set up by the Union Cycliste Internationale. It was also brought in by mining giant Bumi to produce a report into dodgy financial dealings worth £1.25bn in its Indonesian operations. Why the focus on these areas? *"It is a response to market conditions,"* says grad recruitment partner John Hornby. *"There are not as many M&A deals happening in the market as there used to be, and we have found we have been able to leverage our reputation to attract regulatory and litigation work, of which there is a lot around."*

Still, transactional work remains at the heart of Macfarlanes and its training contract, and that is not going to change any time soon. Six months in 'mainstream' corporate M&A is obligatory, as is a stint in a 'specialist' corporate seat: investment funds; banking and finance; employment, pensions and benefits; commercial; competition; derivatives and trading; or financial services. For their remaining two seats, trainees can spend time in real estate, private client, tax and dispute resolution/litigation. Seats are allocated before each rotation, and *"at the start of your training you nominate one main preference,"* a trainee reported. *"None my peers have had any problems with seat allocation or being allowed to do their first choice."* At the start of every seat there is an *"excellent, tailored"* training programme running to *"15 seminars over the course of three or four months."*

Hermes, Heinie and high-end deals

Macfarlanes' corporate practice actually has two rankings in *Chambers UK*: one placing it at the very top of the mid-market – *"the sweet spot which is doing well economically"* – and the other recognising its strength in high-end deal making. The department has a private equity and a public M&A side and *"nominally trainees sit within one of these, but generally you get access to both parts of the department."* On the private equity side the firm recently advised fund manager Hermes on the transfer of its $800m Focus Asset Management fund team to investment manager RWC, while the M&A team acted for new client Heineken during its acquisition of a 50% stake in an African joint venture. *"Despite the fact we only have the one office in London, pretty much everything I have worked on has had an international element to it,"* one

Chambers UK rankings

Agriculture & Rural Affairs	Fraud
Banking & Finance	Information Technology
Banking Litigation	Intellectual Property
Charities	Investment Funds
Competition/European Law	Media & Entertainment
Construction	Pensions
Corporate/M&A	Private Client
Dispute Resolution	Private Equity
Employee Share Schemes	Real Estate
& Incentives	Real Estate Finance
Employment	Real Estate Litigation
Environment	Tax
Financial Services	

trainee pointed out. Other clients include Virgin, Trafigura and brokerage firm ICAP.

"On most deals it's the trainee's task to co-ordinate all the different components, organise the document list and keep track of what has and hasn't been agreed. You also draft the ancillary documents like board minutes and powers of attorney, and I am often the first port of call for clients calling to check on the progress of a deal." Another interviewee added: *"If there is time, the partner will give you the chance to do a first draft of the purchase agreement, even if they don't end up using it."*

With so much to do, trainees who'd worked in corporate cautioned that *"the hours are long and unpredictable but that just comes with the territory."* One added: *"You do get a bit of a buzz when you are working on something late into the night,"* while another said: *"I had a gentle start and rarely worked past 9pm or 10pm, but my second three months involved staying until the early hours and getting in early the next day for a few days in a row."* In other departments, trainees *"usually leave between 6 and 8pm."*

Together with the M&A team, the investment funds department recently represented Four Seasons Health Care during its £825m acquisition by private equity firm Terra Firma. *"Trainee tasks include amending the partnership agreement and prospectuses and sometimes providing discrete pieces of advice on things like FSA regulation."* Generally, the work involves *"more repetition"* than regular deal work, which can mean *"more admin-based tasks"* for trainees, but at the same time one interviewee said: *"My supervisor did their best to vary the tasks I was given."*

Outlandish gentry

"It is an outdated perception to think of our private client practice as thriving off the landed gentry in England!"

said one trainee. True, but we don't want to undersell the firm's pedigree: *"We do have some old-money clients who have been with us an awfully long time,"* though the clients are now *"almost exclusively international entrepreneurs."* Impressively, Macfarlanes wins a top-tier global-wide ranking for this area in *Chambers Global* and *"people jet in from around the world for our services – from Arab sheikhs to Russian oligarchs."* Of course, *"the partner is the face of the firm when it comes to the private clients,"* and as a trainee *"90% of what you draft goes out under someone else's name."* But trainees are taken to client meetings whenever possible and enjoyed the day-to-day tasks of drafting wills and trusts. They also help advise on individuals' tax arrangements, where *"the line between efficiency and avoidance is a fine one..."*

Trainees interested in real estate can complete seats in private client property and commercial real estate. A property seat used to be obligatory, but the market slowdown – things continue to be *"quieter than normal"* – has seen this policy scrapped. In commercial real estate the work *"ranges from simple licence and lease renewals all the way through to purchases of huge industrial plots and mansions in Mayfair."* The firm recently advised a consortium of two property firms (one English, one Japanese) and a Canadian investment management corporation on the £200m purchase and redevelopment of BBC Television Centre in White City. *"I have been very involved with some high-spec deals,"* a trainee said. *"On those I do things like the Land Registry application and submitting the Stamp Duty Land Tax forms."* There are more opportunities on offer on smaller matters. *"I ran 18 of my own files on a day-to-day basis – they were things like licences to sublet and to redevelop."*

When it comes to disputes, one trainee said the firm is *"winning more and more large-scale commercial litigation mandates."* There are private equity and financial services-related cases as well as general commercial matters. The firm recently acted for Salford Capital Partners as one of three defendants in a case brought by the late Russian oligarch Boris Berezovsky over the ownership of the multibillion-dollar Patarkatsishvili estate. Trainees have a variety of responsibilities including, of course, *"preparing bundles for court on the bigger cases."*

If the shoe fits

"There is a real sense of the importance of training here," interviewees agreed. Supervisors – who trainees share an office with – can be partners or senior/mid-level associates. *"My supervisors have all been very hands-on,"* a trainee said. *"They have been keen to give me as much responsibility as possible and they make a concerted effort to give feedback."* Sitting with an associate, trainees tend to work mostly with that individual, while with a partner they'll probably receive tasks from a broader range of colleagues. Each trainee has their own

The True Picture

training principal – a partner-mentor available for career support and advice. *"They are in place to stop anything going wrong"* but also *"provide a very good network of support"* for career development and *"informal discussions"* about qualification.

The qualification process itself is a fairly speedy one. September qualifiers apply for jobs in early May, are interviewed two weeks later and hear whether they have a place two weeks after that. Prior to this *"the importance of internal networking is noticeable,"* and chats with partners about where there will be (and won't be) NQ jobs are common. There is also the opportunity to talk about qualification prospects during the *"long and detailed"* reviews trainees receive halfway through and at the end of each seat. But *"just acting buddy-buddy and having coffee with a partner will not make a difference."* In 2013, 20 of 28 qualifiers were kept on.

At the start of this feature we compared Macfarlanes to a pocket watch. One trainee didn't really agree with our comparison: *"I would describe the firm more as a brogue: dependable and serious."* It's a good comparison, and the guarded sobriety implied by this piece of footwear is apt. *"We are a traditional firm in the sense that we are committed to certain long-standing values: there is a huge focus on quality, attention to detail and getting things right. I wasn't attracted to the type of firm that's all flashy and throws glossy publications at you left, right and centre,"* one source averred. Trainees recognised the firm's reputation for having a more traditional culture, but said that in practice *"it's not a stuffy place – the old-school reputation lingers in the background, but in reality it is very similar to other City firms."* Another trainee added: *"The majority of partners are actually incredibly approachable and will address you directly."* Our interviewees reported having a lot of free-flowing partner contact and admitted that there are some *"eccentric characters"* among the partnership. We laughed at the story of a partner who *"sometimes walks into the centre of the secretarial pool and randomly starts singing."*

His home is his Castle

You mustn't be afraid of a song or two at Macfarlanes: we heard a rumour that at one department's Christmas party trainees are asked to sing Christmas carols to the partners. Not that this was a form of hazing; it's just that Macfarlanes is an engaging and sociable place. QUACC (the QUasi-Articled Clerk Committee) organises a trainee Christmas party, summer ball and drinks every six months to welcome new joiners. There are plenty of other activities to join in with, including departmental socials at partners' houses, skiing trips, art history lectures, five-a-side football and a firm-wide Christmas party (held at Kensington Roof Gardens in 2012).

We were saddened to hear that the annual cabaret – previously held at KOKO in Camden and including dragged-up partners – was off the menu for 2013. *"Everyone always loved getting stuck in, but we felt that it would be more fun to do something different for a change."* Glum at the fact they won't get to see the partners showing off their legs in sheer stockings, trainees can drown their sorrows at Macfarlanes' watering hole, The Castle. *"If you go there on a Friday night, there will always be a lot of people there from different departments. You can share a drink with a random partner you have never met before, and you might realise afterwards they are actually the head of their department!"*

Interviewees stressed that it's not frowned upon if trainees want to opt out of office social life for whatever reason, but it's clear that 'joining in' is appreciated at Macfarlanes. Is there anything else we can say about a typical trainee here? Well: *"Macfarlanes used to have a reputation for its intakes being very Oxbridge,"* interviewees said, *"but that's not the case any more."* Some 80% of trainees with the firm in 2012/13 were non-Oxbridge graduates, and trainees said the firm has *"made an effort"* to attract trainees from a greater variety of universities and ethnic backgrounds.

And finally...

Macfarlanes has operated as a single close-knit stable of thoroughbreds for donkey's years, but *"it is willing to embrace change and knows that it may even have to tweak how it approaches its international operations in the future."*

Maclay Murray & Spens LLP

The facts

Location: London, Scotland

Number of UK partners/solicitors: 59/141

Total number of trainees: 8 (in England)

Seats: 3x8 months

Alternative seats: none

Extras: pro bono – RCJ CAB

On chambersstudent.co.uk...

How to get into MMS

Interview with training principal Roger Tyrnan

This large Scottish firm has one foot in the City, with a London office that's clearly getting into its stride.

Your MMS

Scottish law students are no stranger to Maclay Murray & Spens, one of Scotland's 'big four'. The firm is headquartered in Glasgow and has further bases in Edinburgh, Aberdeen and London, the last of which sources likened to *"a teenager growing under the parental guidance of the more established Scottish offices. The general feeling is that it's young and eager."* Indeed, there are plenty of 'parents' hovering around the London digs – *"we've got a lot of Scottish lawyers about, and I wouldn't be surprised if at least half of the partners are dual-qualified."* According to London training principal Roger Tyrnan, the London office is currently *"the focus of the whole firm's effort, which is why you see a lot of faces on the ground."* That's not to say the City branch is milling with a swarm of stereotypically dour Scots, however; sources told us their neighbours from the North are *"really friendly"* and *"not frosty at all. They're all happy to have a drink and a laugh, and they understand the importance of letting your hair down."*

Trainees welcomed MMS's first appearance in the *Student Guide* as many *"found it hard to get enough info"* about the London training contract during application season. *"We need to make sure we shout a bit about how great MMS is."*

Unusually, MMS juniors complete three eight-month seats during their time as trainees. Insiders had this to say of the set-up: *"It's swings and roundabouts. The system is fantastic if you like your seats, and you're pretty much treated like an NQ during your last two months. That said, eight months is a very long time to spend in a department you find you don't like."* The tiny intake fluctuates between three and five trainees each year, with seat allocation methods altered to reflect the number. Smaller intakes don't get a say in which seats they're placed, but the latest five-person class benefited from *"a presentation before the start of the training contract regarding seat options for trainees."* Insiders told us *"pretty much everyone does either dispute resolution or employment at some point,"* and *"at any one time there are first and second-years sitting in our core areas of corporate, litigation, and banking and finance."* The other seat options are property and employment.

Crunch corner

There's plenty of mid-market M&A work for corporate trainees to sink their teeth into. The team recently advised Scottish milk mogul Robert Wiseman Dairies during its £280m takeover by German yoghurt-monger Müller, and represented LM Funerals' during Duke Street Capital's acquisition of the Wolverhampton-based funeral company. Our sources relished the high responsibility levels they encountered, with one recounting the *"fantastic experience"* they had *"working all hours of the day on a multimillion-pound deal. I got to draft the disclosure letter and all the ancillary documents – I was essentially running the deal on my own."* Of course, lower level work is not inescapable. *"Admin tasks are very common for trainees. We update the books and file documents at Companies House."*

Interviewees were similarly keen on the banking and finance seat, *"which entails a lot of responsibility and encourages you to think for yourself. You get to deal with clients every day,"* many of which are big international banks – think Santander, Barclays and RBS – and finan-

Chambers UK rankings

Public Procurement	Social Housing

cial institutions. Lawyers recently assisted insurance giant Aviva with long-term debt finance provisions following the £282.5m purchase of the iconic Tower 42 estate. *"I got to run the organisational elements of a big matter that involved lots of property across the country, drafting countless securities documents and authorisations."* We also heard from sources who'd drafted board minutes, prepared notices and *"liaised with lawyers on the other side."*

All wool and no shoddy

MMS is top-ranked in *Chambers UK* for its real estate practice in Glasgow. The London RE team is less established but accesses some fairly high-quality cases through its collaboration with colleagues over the border. One trainee told of their time on a UK-wide multiple property, explaining: *"I dealt with the English side of things while a Scottish trainee worked out stuff from his end. On big deals it's impossible for the senior staff to monitor everything, so we were largely left to get on with it ourselves."* When it comes to asset disposals, real estate lawyers link up with their counterparts in restructuring and insolvency. The combined forces were recently instructed by your gran's favourite jumper providers Edinburgh Woollen Mill during the company's purchase of 388 Peacocks stores following the fashion chain's bankruptcy. There are also links to the firm's housing and care practice, which acts for social landlords like Family Mosaic and Peabody, a residential charity with a history stretching back to Dickensian London.

A stint in dispute resolution offers *"a complete mix of commercial work,"* from technical disputes to commercial arbitrations to bribery claims. *"I don't think I've done anything twice – there's been property, tax and fraud work. Yesterday I spent the whole day researching the legality of private parking tickets."* One exciting dispute regarding commission fees for a national airline resulted in *"a Chinese wall in our department – half of the team acted for one party while the others acted for the other side. Things got pretty interesting."* According to trainees, such *"exciting"* large-scale cases are complemented by less complex matters that afford juniors *"lots of independence."* Indeed, there's even the chance to run small files – for example, debt collection cases.

Ode to a haggis

The axe of 30 jobs in June 2013 caused some to question the overall health of MMS. According to Roger Tyrnan, the recent redundancies were *"part of a very clearly defined strategy. You never want to lose people, but as a business we need to focus on areas we can really be profitable in."* Trainees chimed in to lament the way *"sometimes you'll find out something online that you should have got an e-mail about"* but agreed the latest layoffs were handled well. *"They didn't really affect morale, and it was just business as usual soon afterwards."*

Despite these trying times, an atmosphere of optimism prevails at MMS, in London anyway. The office has recently relocated to the snazzy new Norman Foster-designed One London Wall development, with one lucky recruit reporting a glorious view of St Paul's from their desk. MMS lawyers might be high up on the twelfth floor these days, but the climb hasn't gone to anyone's heads; on the contrary, our sources insisted people remain *"down to earth"* as ever, explaining the firm *"doesn't want people who are snotty about their intelligence. They prefer a confident and good-humoured approach to clients."*

It seems there's been a *"bit of a lull"* in terms of organised events lately, but sources expected more going forward thanks to a new committee chock full of *"fresh ideas."* Luckily, the *"partners are pretty spontaneous about things like going out for drinks,"* and the small size of each department means plenty of chances to socialise across hierarchies. Among the formal dos we did hear about were a summer ball at a local bar and a spring fair, which was relocated indoors this year due to a bout of *"rubbish weather. We still had car racing, a coconut shy and that game with all the plastic ducks you have to fish out."* Trainees also had fond, if somewhat hazy, memories of the firm's *"big annual Scottish dinner,"* which involves a three-course meal followed by a club night, *"about two hours sleep and an early morning flight back to London. Certain partners who do like a drink always go up."*

Qualifying positions in London are open to applications from Scottish trainees and vice versa. As a result, there's a bit of pressure on London jobs, and trainees explained that *"the vast majority of us have no intention of moving to Scotland as it involves a 50% pay cut, but many Scottish trainees are keen to come down here."* The firm didn't tell us how many of its three London qualifiers it kept on, but UK-wide the figures were 15 out of 19.

And finally...

"Keep in mind there's not a lot of say in seats here, so don't fixate on one area in particular. You've got to show a willingness to get involved in all areas of the firm."

Mayer Brown International LLP

The facts
Location: London
Number of UK partners/solicitors: 85/130
Total number of trainees: 40
Seats: 4x6 months
Alternative seats: overseas seats, secondments
Extras: pro bono – LawWorks, A4ID

On chambersstudent.co.uk...
How to get into Mayer Brown
Mayer Brown in Asia

Lots of firms are ambitious, but you can really sense the drive at Mayer Brown as it attempts to compete with the magic circle in London.

International relations

More than a decade on from Chicago native Mayer Brown's tie-up with old-school Brit Rowe & Mawe, the global expansion goes on. A combination with Asian outfit Johnson Stokes & Masters in 2008 gave the firm a strong Asian presence, and that was followed by the take-over of a French litigation shop in 2009. Frankfurt, Düsseldorf and Brussels complete the European contingent, and seven US offices bring Mayer Brown's total global network to 20, and that's not counting alliances with firms in Brazil and in Spain. Trainees report constant exposure to international work but also to the business development side of law. *"If there's a huge case on the go, we learn how they're using that to bring in further work – they teach you very early on what it means to run a law firm."*

The London office has taken a few blows in the recession. Revenue fell dramatically in 2009 and again in 2011 and 2012, prompting partner moves, a round of redundancies in mid-2012 and trainee deferrals. However, our sources felt optimistic about London's future, and there's evidence of things being back on track with the arrival of new talent, including the *Chambers*-ranked Alistair Graham, who joined the litigation team from White & Case.

Mayer Brown operates a pretty structured training, trainees being obliged to pick a contentious, non-contentious and 'wildcard' option in addition to their mandatory secondment. Contentious seats include commercial dispute resolution, employment, insurance and construction, while transactional ones include real estate and the huge departments of corporate and finance. Other more niche areas include IP, tax, pensions and EU/competition. Most of our sources had got what they wanted most of the time.

"If you have one particular top choice, it would be surprising if you didn't get to sit there at some point. Plus, if HR can't place you in one of your choice seats, they contact you directly and apologise."

You may have heard about Mayer Brown's glamorous overseas seats, but trainees think the primary factor that sets the firm apart from the crowd is the obligatory secondment. *"They don't trumpet them enough. The international posts are obviously glamorous, but if you're starting to look at developing your own professional network, the client secondments are where it's at."* For the record, trainees have the chance to apply to spend six months in Hong Kong or New York. These are predominantly finance-based seats, so they're only open to trainees who've completed a London seat in finance already. Client-wise, there's just under a dozen spots open each rotation at banks, corporate clients and even a record company. There are two reasons MB places such an onus on spending time with clients. First, *"it's good marketing for the firm – these clients need to remember who we are, so the firm is trusting us with making a great impression."* Others added that *"the firm values the client above everything else, so sitting with them is the best way to work out the quirks in the service you're giving them – to try and understand what would be more helpful and how to acquire a sound base of knowledge."* Most importantly for the training contract, sources who had returned from secondment thought: *"As a junior you often don't have the whole picture in view, but when you're with a client, you see it all. You also get all the responsibility – to which you must step up or fail. People return from secondment and say it was the making of them."*

Chambers UK rankings

Banking & Finance	Intellectual Property
Banking Litigation	Outsourcing
Capital Markets	Pensions
Competition/European Law	Pensions Litigation
Construction	Product Liability
Corporate/M&A	Professional Discipline
Dispute Resolution	Professional Negligence
Employment	Real Estate
Energy & Natural	Real Estate Finance
Resources	Real Estate Litigation
Environment	Restructuring/Insolvency
Information Technology	Tax
Insurance	Telecommunications

The staples

The corporate department's got a strong securities flavour, and there's "*lots of public and private M&A and capital markets work.*" The group's part of Mayer Brown's global practice, so there's frequently a cross-border aspect to deals. Take the £144 million acquisition of Alliance Films by Entertainment One, for example – the former a Canadian, UK and Spanish distribution company; the latter, an entertainment group with bases in Europe, Australia, the US and Canada. Other clients like credit rating outlet Moody's and mining company African Eagle are evidence of the group's global reach. Sources report getting the majority of their work through the speciality of their partner supervisor, although "*if there's an area you particularly desire exposure to, you can ask.*" There's always the standard trainee-level tasks to deal with, but a bit more responsibility will be offered should newbies step up to the challenge. Naturally, this is a department renowned for its heavy hours – partly due to the amount of interaction with the US.

The same goes for finance – a seat where 'late' constitutes "*36 hours straight*" or "*frequent days that run past midnight and then involve you coming back at 9.30am the next day.*" For those who can take the heat, the large team offers exposure work ranging from project finance to restructuring to derivatives – and as trainees aren't allocated to any of these sub-groups, they'll have a bespoke experience. "*There's no attempt to make you focus straight away. The kind of work you do is based on who you sit with as certain partners are keen to give you what they're doing and others are keen for their trainee to get a broad exposure.*" Typically, "*every single deal will have at least one international element to it.*" Mayer Brown advised UBS in relation to a dispute that came from a credit default swap and involved several parties in Germany, culminating in proceedings in both London and the Leipzig Regional Court. There's also work advising banks in respect of bonds guaranteed by the Greek government after haircuts had been imposed. Rather than being a spe-

cial kind of Athenian mullet, this is actually a term that describes the markdown of debt that debtor banks agree to in order to pull through the financial crisis. Sources emphasise that though "*there's an element of luck in the deals you end up working on determining the tasks you'll get,*" ultimately "*the team judges you on how well you can do certain tasks, and if you step up, you'll be trusted with more.*" There's always the "*awful trainee work to do, which here is probably going to be bibling,*" but sources also waxed lyrical about their direct client contact and sojourns abroad.

Mayer Brown's dispute resolution group has particular expertise in finance, construction and insurance litigation, and is top-ranked by *Chambers UK* in London's mid-market. Clients include HSBC, KPMG and Ernst & Young. The team acted for the independent valuer of Northern Rock in assessing the value and amount of compensation owed to shareholders when the bank was nationalised. Trainees are assigned to specific cases, "*which is a really good way of doing it as you know exactly what you're working on, get to find your way around all the documents and build up good relationships with those teams.*" Responsibility-wise, sources admitted "*there's always the bundling and running around, but there's also good research available.*"

Multimedia Mayer

Trainees who get to sit in IP relish their experience in a small department with a strong focus on high-end technology and life sciences. "*It's often just you and the partner, so there's opportunity to get very involved with everything and to do all the small things. There's the opportunity to draft, and when arbitrations are held at the office, the trainee attends with the client and counsel.*" Clients include EMI, Studiocanal/Canal+ and Google, and the group recently acted for Hachette in a litigation against a website which was creating pirated versions of almost 1,000 ebooks – this was possibly the first ebook litigation in England.

Trainees think that Mayer Brown has a reputation for providing very strong training. "*The firm spends time on the soft skills stuff. We learn how people all work in different ways and how to deal with that. There are also presentations in many groups, and in others there's a thing called 'question time', which allows you to fill in the gaps of your knowledge.*" Supervision-wise, sources see the standard as high. "*Even if you're designated something pretty menial to do, people will still take half an hour out of their day to explain the whole case to you.*"

Before arriving at Mayer Brown, most trainees wondered "*if it'd feel like a punishing American working culture.*" After integrating, however, sources seemed to concur "*that it feels more City than US,*" though many said: "*In-*

ternational is the way to describe it. The fact is, we don't have a head office in Chicago any more, and we also have a Hong Kong office that is huge. We work so regularly with Germany or the Paris office that things seem connected."

There may be a broad overarching vibe to MB London, but this is also an office where each department has a very different feel. There's a hard-nosed edge to finance and corporate, but also a clear sense of camaraderie. *"They're the home of louder, bigger personalities and things get informal pretty quickly, which is nice. When you're in those seats, you have to accept that you're going to work hard whatever you do, so you might as well play hard too and enjoy yourself."* Dispute resolution may have *"an image of not being very fun"* due to its slightly more introverted personalities. *"They're more reserved initially, but once they've warmed to you, you're in the club."* Groups like pensions and IP, which are *"naturally more advisory, mean that you're very closely supervised and you build up relationships that way."* Overall, though, trainees thought: *"Across the board, the values are the same – as a place, it's practical and pragmatic. It may not be the right place for very shy and retiring types. We do big-ticket work and we're not a huge office, so often if you want someone's time, you have to go and get in front of them. You need to have the ability to do that in your nature, and partners appreciate it when you do take initiative."*

Mine's a cosmopolitan

On that note, trainees think the fact that *"there's no clear Mayer Brown type reflects the idea behind the firm. There are such different departments here; it would be foolish to*

recruit a certain type of person only." Saying that, there's a natural bias towards *"people with an international aspect, be it languages or the experience of living abroad."* Though sources state that the firm's *"great at picking people who've done something else beforehand or studied to an advanced level,"* we also noticed a high Oxbridge contingent with a strong showing of Durham alumni. But, as one trainee put it, you'll find both *"bookish and jockish"* people here.

For a few years we've reported on the firm's opaqueness in communicating vital info to our trainee sources. This is something we're happy to note has improved hugely. *"They are really trying to open up communication channels. We got invited to a talk given by the head of the London office about the nuances of the firm's strategy for the next two years. The idea is to let us know exactly where they want to be going. Even in terms of work, the trainee is never left off the e-mail chain."*

Sources do admit that *"post-credit crunch, there's not much of a budget for us to socialise,"* though trainees do a lot of informal drinking come Thursday and Friday night, and drinks trolleys do still roll round each department. There's a lot of sport available for those that way inclined, but a plethora of other activities too – for instance, *"an annual challenge which this year involved biking from London to Paris, a talent show, and there's a book club too. Basically, if there's something you want to do, the firm will finance it."* Some people even did the Tough Mudder, an endurance challenge designed by British Special Forces and billed as 'probably the toughest event on the planet'.

And finally...
Mayer Brown is an ambitious firm that is not giving up its fight to push on in the City despite some recessionary setbacks. In 2013 it kept on 17 out of 28 qualifiers.

McDermott Will & Emery UK LLP

The facts

Location: London

Number of UK partners/solicitors: 20/24

UK partners who trained at firm: 0%

Total number of trainees: 7

Seats: 4x6 months

Alternative seats: overseas seats, occasional secondments

Extras: pro bono – LawWorks, Lawyers Without Borders, Citizenship Foundation, TrustLaw

On chambersstudent.co.uk...

How to get into McDermott

Headline cases and deals

About Heron Tower

The City arm of this American heavyweight grants its trainees *"a starring role – but that doesn't mean the quality of work is rubbish."*

Shuffling the pack

Chicago-born McDermott Will & Emery has been around for almost 80 years, but it didn't set foot in London until 1998. That was actually the firm's first voyage into Europe, and since then it has established a further seven outposts across the continent – the latest of these was a shiny new Frankfurt office in May 2012. In other news, MWE made a total of 54 lateral partner hires over the course of 2012, a handful of which joined the ranks of the London base. Private equity duo Mark Davis and Russell Van Praagh arrived from collapsed firm Dewey & LeBoeuf, while Tom Scott was brought in from KPMG to head up the office's tax practice group.

Insiders also revealed that *"we've had a bit of a reshuffle over the past couple of years or so and are heading in a slightly different direction now,"* with private clients cited as one of the main areas of focus going forward. They added: *"The plan is to establish the London group as a leader in a small number of areas rather than going mainstream and expanding merely for the sake of it."* MWE's IP and employment practices in the City come highly recommended by *Chambers UK*, with its commodities and data protection teams renowned for their work on a national level.

That private client practice we just mentioned is one of the seat options available to trainees, as are corporate, employment, IP, energy and tax. The seat allocation system is quite informal – there's basically a quick chat with HR and the training principal before each rotation – though *"trainees will typically start off in corporate."* So, corporate is where we shall head to first.

Jumping through (Hula) Hoops

MWE's corporate practice revolves around the middle and upper-middle M&A markets, with the team in London representing a multitude of publicly and privately held businesses. As for sector expertise, it has an increasingly impressive presence in the food and drink sector to go alongside its collection of energy, healthcare, sports and technology clients. For instance, some of the firm's City lawyers had a hand in Intersnack's acquisition of KP Snacks (the maker of Hula Hoops), which was one of 2012's largest M&A deals in the UK food sphere. Intersnack is a German snacks group and therefore serves as a pretty good indicator of the department's international dimension; the majority of its clients are in fact international companies with UK offshoots, and as such a sizeable portion of the deals worked on are cross-border in nature. Much of that cross-border activity derives from Asia, and a recent example of this was when the team advised Singapore-headquartered company Olam International on its $170m purchase of the Nigeria-based OK Foods Group.

Our sources revelled in the chance to work on deals with an international flavour, and while *"the time differences can get frustrating,"* they deemed it a small price to pay for the *"interesting and high-quality work"* on offer. What's more, they were pleased to discover that *"you aren't just stuck by the photocopier"* and were able to handle some of the meatier tasks once they'd proven themselves. One trainee elaborated: *"There are the more basic tasks like drafting board minutes and corporate governance, but I also attended plenty of meetings and drafted memos from scratch, and in many cases I was essentially the client's first point of contact."*

Chambers UK rankings

Commodities	Employment
Data Protection	Intellectual Property

The firm is a major player in the energy sector, as demonstrated by some of the big-name clients it acts for – from institutional investors like Goldman Sachs and JPMorgan to giant utility companies such as Thames Water and EDF Energy. In 2012, the London team advised the latter on its joint venture agreement with Eneco Wind UK for the development of an offshore wind farm near the Isle of Wight. An interviewee was right to point out that *"energy is a very broad term,"* meaning the seat itself entails *"a sizeable mix of work"* including project finance, regulatory, trading and renewable energy matters. Trainees also reported a lot of research in particular; as one of them told us: *"Energy laws change so much, especially in Europe, so you prepare a lot of memos containing the latest updates."*

Despite being *"a smallish department,"* MWE's IP offering in London is *"right up there with some pretty mega firms."* It advises on a raft of contentious and non-contentious issues, encompassing the likes of copyrights, trade marks, patents, designs and trade secrets, and is complemented by the firm's growing reputation in the data privacy arena. In one noteworthy matter, the group represented Swiss pharmaceutical company Novartis in a dispute against GlaxoSmithKline over several patents and vaccines. Insiders mentioned *"a lot of drafting on a variety of subjects"* as well as attending court sessions and *"writing articles which get sent either to the client or somewhere else."*

The *Chambers*-ranked employment team, which acts exclusively on behalf of employers, is perhaps best known for handling high-end litigation, but it also advises on other types of matters such as complex restructurings, senior executive departures and the UK employment implications of domestic and cross-border transactions. Its client base includes famous names like Expedia.com, Formula One Management and Callaway Golf. On top of attending tribunal hearings and conducting research, there's *"a fair amount of corporate support work"* to carry out in this seat.

MWE trainees have the extra option of an overseas seat, and there are two of them available: one in Paris (which *"is usually a corporate seat"*) and another in Düsseldorf. If either of these sounds appealing, then pay attention to the following words of advice: *"You are expected to speak the local language,"* one source warned. *"Put it this way: it's definitely not a holiday."*

Howdy partner!

One trainee thought: *"Based on what I've heard about other US firms, we have quite a chilled atmosphere here. It's natural to have a hierarchy because human nature dictates it, but there are no weird lines of communication. It's not like I have to get permission from a partner's secretary in order to speak to them, or talk to an associate who then passes the message on to the partner in question."* Indeed, our sources seemed especially pleased with the amount of direct contact they had with partners, leading to more responsibility than they could shake a stick at. *"They're also not that interested in getting you to do the administrative tasks. Instead, they'd much rather you do more meaningful work like drafting and liaising with clients."*

However, it'd be wrong to jump to the conclusion that greater responsibility equates to gruelling working hours. On the contrary, *"the hours aren't bad at all compared to City firm standards,"* and *"if you play your cards right then you can be gone by 7pm most nights."* The only real exception to this rule is the corporate department. *"When a deal's closing you might end up working until midnight, but you won't find yourself pulling constant all-nighters."*

Putting trainees in the thick of the action understandably attracts a specific 'type', and it was agreed *"you need to have confidence. If you're prone to shying away then you will struggle."* We've noted over the past few years that – perhaps because of this – MWE does attract quite a few trainees who already have a bit of life experience.

Heron Tower has been the London team's home ground for over two years now, and it's fair to say the novelty hasn't worn off just yet. The *"bright and airy"* office features *"full-length windows looking out onto the City,"* with break-out areas and changing facilities. We mustn't forget to mention the 70,000 litre aquarium either, which contains more than 1,200 fish (and no, we didn't count them ourselves). The aquarium's kept in tip-top condition by divers, who apparently got in the festive spirit around Christmas time by *"dressing up as Santa Claus."*

The social life at MWE appears to be in equally good spirits. There used to be a drinks event every other Friday, but this now takes place on the last Thursday of every month instead. *"A survey was sent around asking if we'd like to have them less often but with a summer party introduced as a result. Most people voted in favour of it."* Speaking of the summer party, it was held in a *"really posh restaurant"* in Devonshire Square, and trainees labelled it a *"fantastic success."*

The True Picture

And finally...

MWE's London branch will suit those who want to be part of a small trainee intake and have an interest in employment, IP or corporate. In 2013 the firm kept on three of its five qualifiers.

Memery Crystal LLP

The facts

Location: London
Number of UK partners/solicitors: 21/33
Partners who trained at firm: 5%
Total number of trainees: 8
Seats: 4x6 months
Alternative seats: none
Extras: pro bono – A4ID

On chambersstudent.co.uk...

How to get into Memery Crystal
More on seats
AIM explained
Memery Crystal's website

This *"young and vibrant"* Chancery Lane firm stands out for its excellent AIM-focused corporate department.

A trip down Memery lane

Memery Crystal's journey began in 1978 when it was founded by John Memery and Peter Crystal. And as it blows out its 35th-anniversary candles, this small but successful City firm can be proud of how far it has come. *Chambers UK* regards it as one of the best in the country for its capital markets/AIM work, with the real estate department also held in high esteem. MC has a strong standing in other areas too like commercial contracts, M&A, employment and litigation. Over the past couple of years, the firm has made a deliberate effort to build up a private client practice, starting with the 2011 hire of a top-notch family team from Howard Kennedy. The seat options are private property (also part of MC's private client offering), corporate, real estate, dispute resolution, real estate litigation, tax and employment/commercial contracts.

Everyone does at least one seat in corporate, while dispute resolution, real estate litigation and employment are among those that satisfy the SRA's contentious requirement. The seat allocation system is *"quite informal,"* and *"there's a lot of discussion among ourselves over who wants what,"* with second-years' preferences getting priority. It's possible for trainees to repeat a seat in the department they wish to qualify into, and *"you can sometimes get called back to a department if there's a lack of bodies there."* There's also the possibility of splitting a seat.

Claim to AIM

Given MC's considerable strength in the capital markets/AIM arena, it's hardly surprising that the corporate department's work is largely centred on this sort of work. Just in case you're not familiar with AIM, a brief explana-

tion: the Alternative Investment Market operates below the main market of the London Stock Exchange and was launched in 1995 to enable smaller companies to raise cash by going public. We asked trainees whether prior knowledge was a necessity for this type of work, and one told us: *"You don't have to know the ins and outs but it definitely helps to understand the general background of it."* You can read more about AIM on our website. One of the firm's AIM-related highlights in 2012 was assisting long-standing client Gulf Keystone Petroleum with its $300m offering of senior unsecured convertible bonds, the largest bond offering ever carried out by an AIM-listed company.

The team works for a number of clients belonging to the natural resources sector (mainly in oil and gas and mining) and has an equally impressive reputation in the technology sector. It's also worth mentioning that much of the work has an international dimension, with the department drawing in business from many overseas clients looking to tap into the UK markets – recent examples of this include the Tanzanian gold producer Shanta Gold and Canada-based oil and gas company Edge Resources. We mustn't forget to add that Memery Crystal does a fair bit of M&A work as well and often has a hand in deals close to the £10m mark, such as Grant Thornton UK's £7m acquisition of a professional insolvency division that belonged to the professional services firm RSM Tenon.

We heard that trainees in corporate tend to start off with a lot of administrative tasks like *"company searches, Companies House filings and verification."* A source explained that verification is basically *"fact-checking a company's prospectus before it lists on the* [London AIM] *market. It's something that every trainee in the seat will do – and*

Chambers UK rankings

Capital Markets	Energy & Natural Resources
Corporate/M&A	sources
Dispute Resolution	Real Estate
Employment	Real Estate Litigation

yes, it is as dull as it sounds!" While these sorts of tasks feature heavily in the beginning, they become less prominent towards the end of the seat and are by no means the only things trainees find themselves doing. There's plenty of drafting on offer, for example, ranging from ancillary documents to shareholder agreements, as well as *"lots of running around for partners to help out with stuff like research and gathering documents."*

The dispute resolution department has grown by leaps and bounds over the past few years and now accounts for nearly one-third of the firm's total revenue. *"It's become a really popular seat choice,"* according to our interviewees, *"especially after one case in particular."* The case they were talking about was the mammoth $1.65bn Gulf Keystone litigation, which revolved around exploration rights to oilfields in Kurdistan, and received widespread coverage in the press (and was included in *The Lawyer*'s 'top 20 cases in 2012'). *"Pretty much every trainee worked on that at some point and it was incredibly interesting to get involved in."* In another monumental matter, the team defended two former owners of Kazakhstan-based Alliance Bank in a $1.1bn claim brought against them for alleged conspiracy and fraud.

It's little wonder that our sources jumped at the chance to work on such colossal cases, though *"the only slight negative with these is you only really get to see a tiny proportion of them."* Even so, trainees are able to prepare court applications and attend the all-important hearings – plus there are a lot of smaller cases that allow for more responsibility in comparison. Other typical tasks include liaising with clients and conducting research, with the latter proving to be a particularly enjoyable experience. *"It's so fun just to delve into a completely new subject matter and try to get to grips with it."*

Tax *"feeds into most elements of the firm's overall work."* More specifically, there's a lot of crossover with the real estate and corporate departments – and trainees informed us that *"the bulk of the work we do in tax is on employment incentives like employee share schemes."* On top of *"managing many documents"* and doing bits of drafting, there are *"various form and letters to send to HMRC."* Some also mentioned conducting research, which can be a sizeable challenge because *"tax law seems to move so quickly."* And, like in private property, *"you're a key member of the group from day one."*

We've limited space here, but on our website there's an extended version of this feature with details about the private property and employment/commercial contracts seats.

Tie or no tie?

Our sources agreed: *"We have a very casual atmosphere here. It's not like you need to wear a tie all the time, and you can always hear people chatting away in the corridors."* There was also a feeling that *"everyone genuinely cares about how the trainees are getting on. It's a bit mundane to call the place 'friendly', but on the whole people are certainly willing to share their words of wisdom with us."* While insiders had only nice words to say about their colleagues, they did make a minor complaint about the *"fragmented"* layout of the office – *"there isn't much communication between some of the departments that are situated on different floors."* However, *"as a trainee you move around a lot and mingle with more or less everyone, so it's something we don't notice as much."*

Interviewees also admitted: *"There isn't exactly a culture of everyone going out after work all the time,"* an issue that has been brought up in previous years too. But sources were quick to play down concerns about the social scene and said: *"We often go out with the more junior members of the firm for lunch or coffee, and there are plenty of events to get everyone socialising."* The annual summer shindig is usually well attended, and the Christmas bash in 2012 was deemed a great success, mainly due to its Olympic-style awards ceremony. MC's chief executive Lesley Gregory *"gave a lovely speech and then handed out medals to people for their extracurricular activities, which was brilliant fun but pretty embarrassing for the winners!"*

And finally...

If you're after a smaller-scale corporate experience at a firm that *"gives you the attention you need,"* then Memery Crystal very much fits the bill. In 2013, two out of four second-years were kept on as NQs.

Michelmores LLP

The facts

Location: Exeter, London, Bristol, Sidmouth
Number of UK partners/solicitors: 56/73
Total number of trainees: 13
Seats: 4x6 months
Alternative seats: secondments

On chambersstudent.co.uk...

How to get into Michelmores
Interview with training principal Emma Honey
Working in the South West

This Devon native is heading upstream with an ambitious programme of expansion.

Riding the wave

According to one excited Michelmores trainee, *"our aim is to grow, grow, grow!"* A look through the firm's recent press coverage certainly reflects this intention. November 2012 saw the Exeter-headquartered mid-sizer take over the Bristol branch of rival South-West firm Wilson Solicitors, a move that boosted revenue a healthy 15% in 2012/13 and nudged Michelmores into the UK top 100 by turnover. The new office is headed up by a highly regarded agricultural team – top-ranked in *Chambers UK*, in fact – and also includes a small but growing private client practice. Training principal Emma Honey divulged that plans to add corporate, TMC and insolvency teams are in the works.

Michelmores may well be considered a regional unit, but trainees insisted its full-service operation and respectable band of clients mean *"you're not missing out on anything."* The firm is a veritable force in the South West, scoring top-band *Chambers UK* recognition for its local banking and finance, corporate/M&A, IT, IP and restructuring work, among other areas. Its lawyers in London represent capital institutions like NHS London and the Met Office, while its presence in Exeter and beyond gives the firm access to reputable regional shops such as Dorset County Council, Cornwall Hospice Care and Plymouth College of Art and Design.

Michelmores had six trainees at the time of our calls, one of whom was an ex-Wilsons recruit. Trainees largely operate out of Exeter, though there's a litigation seat offered in London, and the firm hopes to offer an additional one in Bristol in the future. This set-up offers *"the best of both worlds,"* insiders felt, telling us *"people travel up and down to London a lot but still get to enjoy the beautiful countryside."* Indeed, there's a lot to love about life in Devon: the weather's mild, the nearby coast is a surfer's paradise, and on a good day you might just get out of the office in time for a clotted cream tea (cream before jam of course).

The seat allocation system sees trainees list three preferences a month before each seat rotation. Options include clinical negligence, dispute resolution/contentious probate, employment, corporate, government property, insolvency, IP/IT, planning and private client.

Fit as a fiddle

Most trainees pass through Michelmores' sizeable real estate team, which handles both public sector work for local councils and some big commercial matters. As one wide-eyed new arrival pointed out, the team has solicited work from some *"huge"* clients of late, including Santander, University of Exeter, and Exeter and Devon Airport. Lawyers recently advised New Fitness Exchange on the acquisition of five London and Surrey health clubs from Fitness First, and assisted Barratt Homes on a £45m regeneration project in Plymouth. Trainees praised the team's approach to supervision – *"you can make your own mistakes, but they take the time to go right through everything with you"* – as well as the tasks at hand, which include *"a lot of drafting of licences and deeds of variation."*

Interviewees who'd sat in planning were likewise impressed by the work on offer: *"I worried it would mostly involve people complaining about their neighbours' conservatories, but actually I encountered a lot of big com-*

Chambers UK rankings

Agriculture & Rural Affairs	Information Technology
Banking & Finance	Intellectual Property
Clinical Negligence	Planning
Construction	Private Client
Corporate/M&A	Projects
Dispute Resolution	Real Estate
Employment	Real Estate Litigation
Family/Matrimonial	Restructuring/Insolvency

mercial clients." Indeed, in addition to representing local authorities like Portsmouth City Council – which the firm recently assisted on a £250m home-building deal – the team has acted for the likes of Blackpool Airport, Leander Developments and Cavanna Homes in recent years. According to our sources, *"there's a lot of marketing stuff that you're expected to get involved with – for example, we hosted a huge planning conference last year, and it was my job to liaise with the speakers beforehand and write the introduction to the event."* Others told of running *"smallish jobs like changing payment allocations,"* sitting in on client meetings and even attending court: *"It's great to get to interact with clients and other solicitors in that setting."*

The commercial litigation seat is available in both Exeter and London. The latter team handles disputes for a mix of corporate names like global nursery brand Gro Group and satellite provider Intelsat as well as the odd private client. Lawyers recently represented Lord Coleridge in a professional negligence claim against Sothebys following allegations the auction house undervalued one of the peer's family heirlooms. In addition to *"frequent court runs,"* future joiners in either office can look forward to preparing bundles, attending hearings, and drafting documents like witness statements and applications for summary judgments. We heard there's *"a lot of client contact, especially when you're working on smaller claims,"* and even the chance to get some advocacy experience: *"I had to make an application on short notice for a certificate that would allow a judgment here to be enforced abroad. It's a bit daunting to get up there but really good experience."*

Ticket tussles

According to our sources, a stint with the insolvency department involves *"reviewing lots of documents and drafting letters to the other side."* The Exeter team is top-ranked in *Chambers UK* and specialises in dealing with high net worth individuals. Lawyers recently advised Deloitte on the high-profile bankruptcy of Gary Lineker's brother and, continuing the football theme, scored a victory on behalf of Ticketus ticket agency against the scandal-hit former owner of the Glasgow Rangers, who tipped the club into administration with some dodgy financial dealings.

Michelmores' corporate team is one of the best in the Exeter area, with a fittingly impressive client list that counts big names like NatWest, Santander and the Met Office among its ranks. The firm recently assisted with the UK's first ever publicly listed solar finance bond and represented Devon County Council in a £125m procurement deal to manage its inclusion support services in schools. That said, most work is done in the private sector – recent undertakings include advising Mole Valley Farmers on the company's acquisition of pet products retailer Farmway and assisting with Media Corporation's acquisition of online gaming platform Intabet. The team's also spent a good chunk of time working for various international development funds investing in projects in Africa. *"They really make an effort to get you involved,"* said trainees of the team, telling us *"you work with a lot of different fee earners and get to progress really quickly."* Tasks range in responsibility from routine due diligence to *"drafting all kinds of agreements"* and *"getting involved in client meetings."*

The firm runs occasional secondments, including a part-time in-house stint at the Met Office doing *"IP and public sector matters. You get to work with really well-recognised bodies and end up with some high-level contacts."* One trainee reported *"going down to London to meet clients for prospective collaborations and conducting some meetings internally. I got a lot of experience doing stuff myself."*

Knights who say Mi...chelmores

Michelmores' headquarters are hidden away on a business park outside of Exeter proper, but luckily the firm compensates for its remoteness with an impressive range of perks. We heard tale of a subsidised cafe with a *"huge conservatory and nice patio area to eat in,"* a gym with a personal trainer, dry cleaning services and even rumours of a masseuse doing the rounds. A few sources lamented their inability *"to nip down the pub like you could in London,"* but most were satisfied with the custom of *"sticking together for lots of partying at the weekends"* in the town centre. For those who prefer a classier approach, there's always the annual summer ball, an undeniable highlight of the social calendar – last year's was held at Exeter Castle and bore an unseasonal ice theme, with trainees slipping from blue Champagne cocktails to quality local nightspot Timepiece for afters. The firm also makes a real effort for quarterly drinks – we heard one jungle-themed jolly incorporated *"real reptiles and snakes. I was terrified!"*

Trainees agreed the firm maintains a family-friendly ethos, as evidenced by functions like camp-outs and treasure hunts organised for lawyers and their kids. *"We're really sporty as well,"* insiders revealed, mentioning the many sailing races and cycling events held each year, *"and get really involved in the community."* Indeed,

The True Picture

lawyers participate in numerous pro bono initiatives and fund-raising schemes involving local schools and charities: *"Everyone mucks in to organise our annual charity run through Exeter,"* which culminated last year in two chivalrous fee-earners winning a special prize for their Monty Python-themed knight costumes.

According to insiders, the firm makes *"a real effort to build a healthy, happy environment,"* which generally results in *"a cheery bunch; no one stays grumpy for long*

here." Trainee hours don't stray wildly from the surfer-friendly schedule of 8am to 6.30pm, though the corporate and London seats tend to be more demanding, with some trainees bringing their work home in the evenings. Fortunately the training contract is *"monitored very well as a whole – there's lots of support,"* including mid and end-of-seat appraisals and regular sit-downs with HR. In 2013 Michelmores kept on three out of four trainees upon qualification.

And finally...

Ties to the Exeter area are certainly an advantage at this firm, though natives from elsewhere are still encouraged to apply: *"I think the firm is increasingly willing to look further afield to find good people."*

Mills & Reeve LLP

The facts

Location: Norwich, Cambridge, Birmingham, Leeds, London, Manchester

Number of UK partners/solicitors: 112/455

Partners who trained at firm: 12.5%

Total number of trainees: 34

Seats: 6x4 months

Alternative seats: occasional secondments

Extras: pro bono – Birmingham FLAG, LawWorks, ProHelp

On chambersstudent.co.uk...

How to get into Mills & Reeve
Birmingham FLAG pro bono

Mills & Reeve takes on high-quality work, often with an educational or healthcare slant. *"Whereas in the past there has been more of a focus on the Cambridge and Norwich offices, you really get the sense it's a national firm now."*

Grist to the mills

Originally from Norwich, Mills & Reeve has gradually transitioned from a local to a national firm, opening five other UK offices, first in Cambridge, then Birmingham, Leeds, London and Manchester. Currently, only the larger, full-service offices in Norwich, Cambridge and Birmingham host trainees, but the others are on the up – the Manchester branch, for example, has the wind in its sails thanks to a recently announced merger with local firm George Davies, which will bring it full-service capabilities and a new specialist sports team.

The firm stands out for its work with the NHS and major educational clients, including lots of top-20 universities and schools converting into academies. London and European connections help funnel international work the firm's way, making for plenty of interesting corporate cases. Mills & Reeve also helps out when Mills & Boon romances go wrong, thanks to its top-notch divorce practice, which offers both contentious and collaborative services. *Chambers UK* gives regional top rankings to the majority of the firm's departments, especially in Cambridge – other strengths include private client, real estate, banking/finance, employment, litigation and tax.

The firm is structured along what the firm calls 'National Service Lines', which are overarching department divisions that stretch across offices: *"We're all the same team wherever we are"* – *"everyone has found themselves spending at least a few days in another office,"* and there's a spirit of *"inter-office collaboration."*

Trainees are only permanently based in Norwich, Cambridge and Birmingham, but the firm's six-seat system gives them plenty of chances to explore the other offices – *"Manchester, London and Leeds are always looking for trainees."* The firm picks trainees' first seat for them, and generally speaking they get more and more choice the further through the training contract they get. There were a few gripes about seats being assigned at less than a week's notice, and some trainees felt the system *"could be a bit more transparent"* – occasionally complaining about being *"given seats I didn't request."* However, trainees who aren't happy are sometimes given the option to do the seat in another office – *"the firm is willing to provide accommodation and travel expenses."*

Stone the crows!

The private tax seat lets trainees encounter clients *"ranging from the Sunday Times Rich List to people walking in off the street wanting a will drafting."* The firm, especially the Norwich office, also deals with landed estates: *"We had to register succession settlements with the House of Lords – it's quite unusual, not something that many firms would deal with,"* one trainee recalled. A recent matter involved the Right Honourable Patrick Fourth Baron Fisher of Kilverstone – he's instigating a multimillion-pound land pooling arrangement among local landowners to build 50,000 new homes. One trainee *"ran several small files and got to know several clients very well,"* and others had trips out to nursing homes to draft wills.

Chambers UK rankings

Administrative & Public Law	Healthcare
	Information Technology
Agriculture & Rural Affairs	Insurance
Banking & Finance	Intellectual Property
Charities	Licensing
Clinical Negligence	Pensions
Construction	Planning
Corporate/M&A	Private Client
Court of Protection	Private Equity
Data Protection	Professional Discipline
Dispute Resolution	Professional Negligence
Education	Projects
Employment	Public Procurement
Energy & Natural	Real Estate
Resources	Real Estate Litigation
Environment	Restructuring/Insolvency
Family/Matrimonial	Tax

The family team is the *"biggest in the country"* and is led by star matrimonial lawyer Roger Bamber – one trainee gushed that *"I'd read all about him, it was amazing getting to work with him!"* Bamber took the far-sighted decision to buy the domain www.divorce.co.uk back in 1997 – the cornerstone of a Mills & Reeve e-empire that includes 30 videos of the man himself, a YouTube channel, a smartphone app and a 'divorce calculator' which, after going viral in bastardised form, has been credited with pushing down divorce rates among cash-strapped Chinese couples.

Trainees felt that *"you can be very involved with minimal supervision"* in this seat – one source was typical in being *"given my own files to manage, taken along to court hearings, and attending conferences with counsel."* For another, the work was *"not as draining as I thought it might be – it's sad but clients want you to give advice, not to listen to them cry."* Still, trainees were entrusted with some heavy-duty responsibilities. One was sent to attend a hearing alone with the mother of a small child: *"It was my job to provide her with emotional support and guide her through the process, especially as English wasn't her first language."*

The agriculture team has recently switched from being part of the private client team to being part of real estate. Clients include *"a lot of big landowning institutions"* like the Wellcome Trust, Northumbrian Water and the Universities of Oxford and Cambridge.

Back to school

Mills & Reeve's corporate and commercial departments have *"good relationships in Holland and France which bring us a lot of European referrals"* and an agreement which sees them taking on overspill work from Freshfields. These high-level cases *"definitely exercised the little grey cells"* of one trainee – one cross-jurisdictional matter involved *"restructuring a multinational company's businesses and cleaning up its accounts."* The firm also counts plenty of universities, including King's College London, Nottingham, Oxford and Cambridge, among its clients – recent work has included advising the University of Cambridge on its first ever venture into capital markets fund-raising as it launched a £350m public bond issue. Mills & Reeve has also benefited from the trend for converting schools into academies, with a dedicated team advising on over 100 cases in the past few years.

Employment is split into three strands: *"Corporate clients, NHS and education."* Cases are often high-profile – Mills & Reeve's client Henning Berg hit the news after winning £2.25m in compensation from Blackburn Rovers FC after being sacked from the club he was brought in to manage. Other contentious cases have seen trainees *"helping fee earners with tribunal claims, managing documentation and tribunal bundles"* in discrimination and unfair dismissal claims, as well as getting a bit more responsibility by *"going to several tribunal hearings. That was brilliant, being at the live end of the law."* Sources had *"drafted lots of witness statements too."* The non-contentious side of the seat involves the *"more day-to-day work"* of advising on *"restructuring and redundancies"* at companies.

The professional indemnity insurance disputes team is *"really big"* and works for insurance companies like Chartis and Aviva to handle claims against clients including solicitors, brokers, architects, engineers and doctors. Trainees found it *"interesting to look at the mistakes other solicitors had made,"* and one revelled in the drama of a case where a litigant in person sent a deputy to *"play Judge Judy – there was lots of abuse flying around!"* In the *"very, very busy"* department, responsibility levels are high – one trainee got to *"go to court on my own and liaise with the client and the judge. It was a really good way of introducing me to the litigation side of things."*

Across all Mills & Reeve's branches, the offices are open-plan and employees sit in pods of four, making for *"a really good learning environment – you can pick up on things that are going back and forth as well as get one-on-one supervision."* Responsibility levels are high, with plenty of small files around to handle – one trainee felt that *"people went out of their way to give me interesting work."* Supervisors are also *"keen for you to get a rapport going with clients – it's good for them to put names to faces."* Recruits have their training contracts supervised by *"completely independent"* partner training principals, who are *"full of great advice, particularly during the qualification process."* Mid and end-of-seat reviews with supervisors are *"very different"* from seat to seat, but generally provided *"a nice record of your four months' hard work."* Trainees also largely approved of the qualification system – they find out if they'll be kept on in September by the end of April, giving those who miss out *"ample opportunity to brush up their CVs."* In 2013 17 out of 20 qualifiers stayed on at the firm.

Garden parties

The Cambridge office is newly ensconced in a *"massive six-floor glass building"* with *"floor to ceiling windows"* and *"lovely views of Cambridge University Botanic Garden."* In Cambridge, *"there are more trainees mixing with partners after work than at Norwich"* and *"everyone goes to the local, The Flying Pig – you'll often get drinks bought for you."* As well as the odd barbecue, there are sports including cricket, rounders, football, netball and hockey. The sociable Norwich trainees reported that *"the group has gelled really well,"* ganging together at the weekends for events like the Norfolk and Norwich junior lawyers' ball – *"we all showed up where other firms might not make the effort."* The *"quite grand"* art deco Birmingham office was *"fancy enough"* for one trainee, even if the inside isn't as *"swish and shiny"* as the firm's other branches. The office is *"not the wildest place – it's quite family-oriented,"* so the social committee has put

its budget to good use subsidising a trip to *The Phantom of the Opera* and a guided museum tour as well as on the usual pay-day drinks.

Several trainees pointed to a *"collaborative culture"* at the firm – *"it's not too hierarchical"* – and felt: *"We're not corporate aggressive lawyery people."* It was agreed that *"people here have made a choice not to be in London; they're after a quieter life,"* as demonstrated by the *"pretty regular hours"* of about 9am to 6.30pm that trainees tended to work. A few noted that *"people in the Cambridge office might work a bit longer,"* though, thanks to the branch being *"busier – maybe we need to share the work around other offices better."* The trainee salary isn't mindblowing – in Norwich it's seen as *"very fair for the area,"* but it's on the *"slightly lower end of the scale in Birmingham."* However, said one source, *"at qualification we're completely competitive with the other firms, so I haven't felt too hard done by."* Professional skills courses are hosted by each office in turn, so trainees get regular road trips – *"we get put up in a hotel and given a subsistence allowance."* Otherwise, they felt that *"we really could do more firm-wide get-togethers."*

And finally...

One Cambridge trainee counselled: *"Even though you're outside London, the quality of work here is still really good. There may be less pay, but the responsibility you're given and the life you can have outside work are excellent."*

Mishcon de Reya

The facts

Location: London

Number of UK partners/solicitors: 83/172

Total number of trainees: 24

Seats: 4x6 months

Alternative seats: occasional secondments

Extras: pro bono – Queen Mary and Mary Ward Ward Legal Advice Centres, Reprieve

On chambersstudent.co.uk...

How to get into Mishcon de Reya

Mishcon's history

Interview with training principal Daniel Levy

The past few years have borne witness to healthy expansion and a robust hike in financials for Mishcon de Reya.

Pop princess

Under an ambitious three-year plan launched in 2010, Mishcon de Reya – no longer content being pegged as a quirky West End player – has steadily made moves to relabel itself as a solid, *"serious"* mid-size practice. Management's put in an application to convert to an Alternative Business Structure and begun offering various non-legal services under Mishcon Private, a brand designed to cater to high net worth individuals. The firm also launched a boutique litigation practice in New York and has been working to build up work in new areas like private equity and competition law. The results of these efforts are quickly becoming visible, and we have to say things are looking pretty promising for Mishcon: turnover was up 14% in 2012/13, clocking at an impressive £83.4m – overshooting the firm's £80m target.

While Mishcon's transformative endeavours have certainly upped its stock across the City, the firm's reputation for big-name, *"sexy"* media and entertainment work prevails. Among its star-studded clientele of years past are Cat Deeley, Matt Lucas, Thierry Henry and even Princess Di (it famously was the firm she used for her divorce). Pop princesses like Lady Gaga, Britney Spears, Rihanna and Pink have all come to the firm for IP and trade mark advice in recent years, and Mishcon was the first port of call for profanity-prone celeb chef Gordon Ramsay during a noxious family dispute with his father-in-law. For all its street cred, however, Mischon actually sources the vast majority of its undertakings from the business realm. Litigation is the firm's biggest driver, generating close to a third of turnover by way of big clients like Microsoft, American Express and Dell. Real estate and corporate

follow closely behind, with each notching up enviable rankings in *Chambers UK*.

Banking on the veritable success of the last revitalisation programme, management unveiled a new three-year plan in 2013 *"to consolidate our growth,"* training principal Daniel Levy tells us: *"We'll focus on making sure our success is sustainable and investing in the parts of the firm that could help facilitate that,"* particularly litigation – *"one of our greatest selling points."*

Mish mash

Mishcon's home to a host of seats, but those with eyes only for the popular ones *"might run into some problems."* Prior to each rotation, trainees choose three seat preferences from a *"huge range"* of options across Mishcon's core practice areas (corporate, litigation, employment, real estate, family and private client). *"A lot of people come here solely for one or two niche practices like IP, family or art law,"* but because of the breadth of practices on offer trainees advised *"not to come to Mishcon for one very specific area unless you're interested in the wider work the firm does as well."* They also mentioned *"a lot of politics goes into the allocation process – much of the decision-making actually rests with partners."*

Fraud is the largest division of Mishcon's litigation group. The highly lauded practice – recognised in the top tier of *Chambers UK* – courts a wealth of high-profile clients, from Microsoft and American Express to Pfizer and RBS. Trainees can pick up work on both the defence and claimant side. The first is the smaller of the two and has a reputation for sustaining a *"more manageable"* pace. Lawyers recently defended a former property agent against claims

Chambers UK rankings

Corporate/M&A	Immigration
Defamation/Reputation	Intellectual Property
Management	Licensing
Dispute Resolution	Private Client
Employment	Real Estate
Family/Matrimonial	Real Estate Litigation
Fraud	Sports Law

of bribery and dishonesty brought by budget pub chain extraordinaire Wetherspoon's. There's also a good deal of criminal cases involving civil freezing orders. Claimant cases *"tend to be larger and more drawn out."* One source told of working on a data theft case in which *"an employee of a public limited company was sacked and went to a rival company with valuable information on a memory stick. We managed to prohibit the rival company from using the data unlawfully."*

A seat in corporate is *"more fluid"* and occasionally entails interaction with the real estate group: *"We regularly work with small private companies, many of which are owned by the very people that run them, so they often come to us for all their legal needs."* This means the team could be running a company's takeover one day and helping the same client purchase a small property the next. Trainees agreed the crossover *"is great for getting to know people and very useful in the long run."* Responsibility-wise, sources admitted *"a corporate seat can become pretty admin-heavy,"* though fortunately *"that entails a lot of client contact, which is always great to have."*

Over in employment, the group deals with huge corporations like Aviva, Universal Music and the Bank of Ireland, though there are also *"distinct, smaller matters – for example, someone leaving one job for another might hire us for a few hours to look over their proposed employment contract. Doing both employer and employee work helps you become sympathetic to both sides and understand the best approach for each."*

Headlines and bylines

Mishcon's real estate group is split into commercial, residential and litigation teams. Major clients on the commercial front include Delancey, UBS Global and CAPCO – the latter owns *"the vast majority of Covent Garden"* and has flooded the team with property lets and deed variations in the area in recent years. One of the bigger projects of late saw lawyers advise real estate investment mogul Delancey on the £557m development of what was formerly the Olympic Village in Stratford. There's no dedicated residential seat at the moment, though the team handles *"plenty"* of residential purchases for corporate clients. The contentious real estate seat has a great reputation for *"responsibility coupled with support."* Many put

this down to the varied nature of the practice, with clients ranging *"from small businesses and individuals with their own properties all the way up to large companies that own vast amounts of land across London. There's a great balance between huge litigations and tiny matters you can take ownership on."*

In the coveted family seat trainees encounter *"quite a lot of responsibility"* due to the prevalence of small matters that *"allow you to interact directly with clients and the problems they have."* Many felt this dynamic means *"it's easy to get invested in the matters at hand and actually envision yourself as part of the team a few years' time."* While most low-level tasks *"start to look the same after a while,"* they're still tempered by the individual needs and quirks of each client: *"Filling in a divorce petition is just that, but knowing the people you're dealing with care so much about it means the work starts to take on a different image."*

Seats are available on both the contentious and non-contentious sides of the private client team. The litigious crew deal with art law, trusts and media disputes, while reputation management lawyers *"advise people on the untrue or defamatory things the press have said about them. We also take a proactive role in teaching publications how to err on the right side of the line. It's not so much about showing them how to get away with stuff as it is demonstrating what constitutes responsible journalism."* A well-publicised case of late saw litigators bring harassment claims against the Daily Mail on behalf of Carina Trimingham, partner of the until recently incarcerated MP Chris Huhne: *"We had to review particular terms that were being used in the media, so much of the work was going through headlines and bylines searching for those."* The art law team advises on matters as diverse as art funds investment structures, sales of pieces of work and auctions law, as well as the criminal side of things – that is, the dastardly world of fakes, forgeries and theft.

There's also a private client seat that deals with tax, wealth planning and immigration matters for high net worth individuals. *"It's a fascinating mix of the very famous and people who spend their time trying not to be,"* said one trainee of the clientele. *"The planning and management aspects can get pretty juicy – when you're writing someone's will, you're privy to all their deepest, darkest secrets."*

Growing pains

Several interviewees told us that *"everybody looks out for you, and your specific supervisor mainly acts as the conduit for feedback when appraisals come round."* Another source had had a different experience: *"One of my supervisors really did their best to teach me things like how to manage my expectations and never to cut corners.*

It's those peripheral bits of advice that help you become better at the job."

With care like this, it's no surprise a jovial, personal vibe abounds in most practice groups: *"It can almost feel like a small firm in some senses – it's easy to forge relationships, and the bonds between people seem quite strong."* That said, it's worth remembering how quickly the firm is growing. *"It's getting to the point where you occasionally find you have no idea who the person next to you in the lift is."* Still, while Mishcon's expansion in recent years has certainly contributed to the rise of slight cultural difference between groups – for example, we heard transactional teams tend to be *"mellower"* than those on the *"more established"* private client side – interviewees assured us the firm nevertheless manages to provide a comfortable home for all. As one source put it, *"the firm's kind of like an adolescent in a much bigger body right now – we're still working through the growing pains of having shot up so quickly."* High up on the list of priorities is sorting out a new, unified office space, a move our interviewees welcomed: *"We're currently split between three buildings and running out of space pretty quickly."*

The firm favours a lively social scene, with occasional trainee get-togethers, weekly drink trolleys and a stand- ing tradition of Friday night drinks at the Bountiful Cow near Mishcon's Red Lion Square digs. Christmas is when much of the year's festivities take place. Trainees are in charge of organising a party for all the employees' children and traditionally take on the role of entertainers during the firm-wide Crimbo party. This year's bunch opted for a dance medley, which one characterised as *"a highly choreographed journey through the evolution of music, taking in Beyoncé, Tom Jones and 'N Sync, and culminating with a rousing dose of 'Gangnam Style'. It was a great bonding experience and actually so well put together that people didn't know whether to laugh or applaud."* As such traditions illustrate, *"there are a lot of big personalities at Mishcon – they naturally favour the brave, though it's never a good idea to be too pushy."*

Last year's qualification round only saw a mere half of trainees land NQ positions, but things are looking up for the 2013 cohort, which fortunately isn't padded by recession-driven deferrals. Still, we heard the firm has begun running skills sessions in order to *"get us to start thinking about all of our options in the event things don't work out here."* In the end, Mishcon kept six out of seven of its 2013 qualifiers.

And finally...

The *"great variety of personalities"* at Mischon ranges from *"the very old-school to the super-progressive."* Still, it's clear confidence and enthusiasm are non-negotiable qualities trainees must possess.

Morgan, Lewis & Bockius LLP

The facts

Location: London

Number of UK partners/solicitors: 18/24 (+6 non-UK-qualified)

Total number of trainees: 6

Seats: 4x6

Alternative seats: Moscow

On chambersstudent.co.uk...

How to get into Morgan Lewis

ML's international ambitions

"Morgan Lewis has traditionally been focused on its home ground in the US, but it's now reaching out in order to become more international and London is poised to play a big role in that."

Philly spread

Philadelphia-headquartered Morgan Lewis took in its first crop of London trainees in 2012. Meanwhile, qualified lawyer headcount in London grew from 21 to 48 between mid-2011 and mid-2013. Chief cause was the arrival of eight partners, ten associates and seven trainees from Dewey & LeBoeuf at the time of its demise in May 2012. The firm also hired partners from Pinsent Masons, Speechly Bircham and Proskauer Rose during 2012. At the same time, Morgan Lewis announced it would be recruiting its own first cohort of five trainees in summer 2013.

This expansion is no accident. *"Morgan Lewis is a big and highly regarded firm in the US, and it has a strong US network,"* says London office co-managing partner Peter Sharp, *"but compared to some of its US peers it had not achieved massive international growth. So while the firm will continue to grow in the US, the real growth opportunities are international. The changes and lateral hires at Morgan Lewis London in the past two years are a reflection of that."* Sharp is also training partner (as well as the former head of Dewey & LeBoeuf's London office) and won plaudits from our interviewees for his support and supervision.

Trainees can do seats in litigation, employment and business and finance. There's also an overseas seat in Moscow. *"Getting the department you want is not difficult because the trainee group is small – we tend to discuss what we want to do among ourselves."* Some seats are in departments which moved over from Dewey & LeBoeuf, while others – like employment – are in legacy ML areas which hadn't worked with trainees prior to 2012. *"I can tell that things are changing fast and that the office has expanded*

very quickly," observed one trainee. *"At first, HR had to get used to having trainees around, but they picked up on things quite quickly and have put in place important provisions like training seminars."*

"It's a very exciting time to be with the firm," said one trainee. *"Management have realised that to flourish they need to take chances – like recruiting trainees. The more the firm grows internationally, the more opportunities that will bring, and the more I will benefit."* In summer 2013, ML announced it was opening an office in Dubai, and firm sources told us that an overseas seat there may soon be in the offing. In addition, Peter Sharp told us that he expected the London lawyer headcount to be pushing 100 within two to four years. Trainees are part of this expansion too: the firm retained four out of five qualifiers in 2013.

The Sharp end

The 30-lawyer business and finance department has sub-teams specialising in investment funds, M&A, banking and finance, energy, and capital markets. While trainees sit with one of these teams *"there is no bar to taking work from elsewhere in the department."* Peter Sharp told us that one of the firm's main aims is to *"further develop this office's transactional practices."* Lots of work relates to the energy industry, Russia and the CIS countries. The firm recently advised Kazakhstan's state oil company KazMunaiGas on a $1.1bn loan from the China Export Import Bank to finance the upgrade of two of its oil refineries. *"It's really interesting that the work is so international and that you get to visit clients in Russia and the CIS,"* said one trainee. In part, this is a Dewey & LeBoeuf legacy, but there's more to it than that. In summer 2013

The True Picture

Chambers UK rankings

Immigration

the firm added an eight-lawyer banking team to its Moscow office from French firm Gide Loyrette Nouel.

Litigation is currently home to two trainees, one of whom sits with Peter Sharp. *"It is considered slightly daunting,"* said one trainee. *"You get to hear and see a lot and you are expected to have an overview of all Peter's cases."* At the same time *"the team is very good at allocating challenging work to trainees."* Its small size means that trainee activities vary from note-taking and bundling to *"drafting a hardcore 20-page memo for a client."* The team often acts on banking and insurance disputes and – as in the transactional teams – some work relates to the former Soviet countries.

In the US, Morgan Lewis can boast of having one of the country's biggest and best employment practices. In London, the seven-lawyer team sees to businesses' litigation and advisory needs. The team recently acted for Willis in a sex discrimination case, advised the Commonwealth Bank of Australia on a bankers' bonuses dispute and counselled Amnesty International when its mooted redundancy round saw Unite threaten a strike. The team also provides general legal advice to HR departments. A trainee reported: *"I have drafted policy agreements and helped prepare presentations to educate people on employment law – lots of international businesses in London need basic training on what something like TUPE actually is."*

Not bowling alone

Given the make-up of the office's DNA, we wondered to what degree it had the same atmosphere as Dewey & LeBoeuf's London office did. (The *Student Guide* once wittily nicknamed the firm 'Dewey & LeTough', because of its hard-nosed culture, long hours and hands-off supervision model.) *"It is definitely a very different firm to Dewey,"* said one trainee, *"and I think Morgan Lewis suits me better: it is smaller and there is more of a team atmosphere."* Another interviewee added: *"There is an effort to make the firm feel cohesive and a strong atmosphere of respect which includes the support staff and cleaners."* Perhaps this atmosphere can be traced back to the fact that ML did not start out as a corporate Wall Street firm, instead having its roots in Pennsylvania and a strong employment practice.

But ML's training contract is not a cushy nine-to-five affair. *"There is less structure than I thought there would be,"* said one trainee. *"I expected all my work to come from my supervisor, but I actually work with the whole team."* Another added: *"I've noticed that trainees here are often treated more like associates. Once you are given something you are expected to run with it – but the support is there if you need it."* The hours can be demanding too. *"8pm is a pretty standard time to leave,"* said one trainee, *"and it isn't that unusual to stay until 10pm."* One interviewee was happy to point out the benefits of this: *"I want to be learning as much as possible, and staying late gives me that chance."* It's clear that the opportunities are there for the taking at this firm, and we highly recommend Morgan Lewis to entrepreneurial graduates who want big rewards for hard work.

Given the long hours, *"people are usually working so hard during the week that there isn't a huge opportunity for socialising in the evening."* Nevertheless, there are occasional *"impromptu socials,"* and *"the Shaws Booksellers pub just down the road is a favourite."* What's more, trainees and others *"like to get together for lunch in the cafeteria"* and *"every fortnight all the trainees try to meet up for lunch at GBK or Pizza Express."* The firm organises *"getting-to-know-you"* drinks when new hires join, as well as a Christmas and summer party. In 2013, the latter saw ML employees show off their sweet skills at bowling alley All Star Lanes.

And finally...

Trainees can play an active role in shaping the culture of the growing London office of this ambitious US firm.

Muckle LLP

The facts

Location: Newcastle

Number of UK partners/solicitors: 27/52

Total number of trainees: 8

Seats: 4x6 months

Alternative seats: none

Extras: pro bono – LawWorks

On chambersstudent.co.uk...

How to get into Muckle

The Newcastle legal market

The boosters are on and Newcastle's Muckle is boldly going out to find business.

Ahead, warp speed

This full-service Geordie outfit was formerly known as Robert Muckle, but in 2007 the first name was dropped as it was felt it made the firm sound too small. While this still isn't one of Newcastle's largest players, it packs a punch that's hard to ignore. *Chambers UK* regards Muckle as one of the best firms in the city for banking work, and for corporate transactions it competes with larger firms like Ward Hadaway and Eversheds. It also scores well in many other areas, including real estate, dispute resolution and IT/IP. Major national organisations sit alongside regional companies in the firm's client list.

What's the goal for Muckle, we asked trainees. "*It's not to be the number-one law firm in Newcastle.*" What's that? Pricking up our ears, we started drafting sensationalist tabloid-style headlines along the lines of 'Geordie firm lacks ambition!' But our source continued: "*That's because we don't want to compare ourselves to our competitors – we're nothing like Bond Dickinson or Eversheds.*" Ah, right. Instead, the aim is a more tangible one: to hit specific revenue targets year on year.

It may not want to compare itself with them, but Muckle will undoubtedly be keeping a close eye on its rivals at the moment. The merger of Bond Pearce with Dickinson Dees – long seen as the grand-daddy of the Newcastle legal scene – shakes things up. The new Bond Dickinson will be a truly national firm, and trainees suggested that Muckle has an opportunity to expand into the resulting gap in the regional market. "*We've grown so much even since I've started,*" said one, "*and that will probably continue.*" It's likely Muckle will remain firmly anchored in its open-plan Tyneside office, though. "*We are very much a regional firm – I don't see a desire to move into York or Leeds.*"

We khan do it

The large corporate and real estate departments are highly likely to be trainee stop-offs – all our sources did one or both of them. Other seat options are banking, commercial, construction, dispute resolution and employment. Trainees talk to graduate recruitment head Kevin Maloney mid-seat and then again towards the end to talk about where they could go next. Business needs play a big part, and second-years tend to get priority, but we heard no complaints about the system.

It's recognised that "*some seats are more challenging than others*" and banking is regarded as a good one to start off with because it's "*quite niche, you learn a lot of the basis skills, manage a file, and sit next to Kevin Maloney, who's a banking lawyer himself.*" Clients include HSBC, Santander, Lloyds TSB and the Port of Tyne. "*It's a really good seat,*" one source enthused. "*I got the technical drafting, and there's a lot of business development work too. We'd have regular catch-ups with clients in the region – getting to meet some high-level people within banks was really good.*" The department also has an insolvency element, so trainees could potentially even go to court in this seat as well.

Property has recently been re-dubbed real estate and does development and corporate real estate work. Trainees help clients develop plots of land, such as a big matter for Project Genesis. Wait, wasn't that in *Star Trek II*? Alas, Project Genesis isn't the advanced technology capable of transforming barren worlds and resurrecting Mr Spock, but rather a business seeking to develop a new Tesco superstore in Consett. Corporate real estate work involves transactions such as the £9.1m acquisition by Northumberland Estates of the Denbigh Hall Industrial Estate in Milton Keynes, but there are smaller files too, such as act-

Chambers UK rankings

Banking & Finance	Information Technology
Charities	Intellectual Property
Construction	Real Estate
Corporate/M&A	Real Estate Litigation
Dispute Resolution	Restructuring/Insolvency
Employment	

ing for "*a couple who wanted to start up their first business and came to us to sort out a lease.*" In either property seat trainees will run their own files. They'll also draft ancillary documents in corporate transactions, and "*one of the main tasks is registrations at Companies House. It might sound a trivial task, but you have to register within a specified time and if you don't it's effectively negligence, so it teaches you to be really organised.*"

All aboard the Enterprise

Construction is a rapidly growing department with contentious and non-contentious aspects to it. One source enjoyed the "*technical side*" of the work reading expert reports – "*obviously the emphasis is on the legal side but you're encouraged to build technical expertise and if the case depends on technical points then it's an obligation.*" Fortunately, "*the senior lawyers are very knowledgeable.*" Trainees get exposure to "*all three types of dispute resolution: normal litigation, mediation and adjudication,*" and work on e-disclosure and bundling in the run up to trial. Away from litigation, the team recently represented London Southbank University on the construction of its new £7m Enterprise Centre.

Corporate is the department that "*links with all the others in the firm.*" In the course of 2012, the team worked on well over 100 matters with a combined value of more than £550m. Among them were Kitwave's acquisition of Huddersfield-based confectioner Teatime Tasties, the admission of Utilitywise to the AIM market, and Quantum Pharmaceutical's acquisition of UL Medicines. The "*broad*" commercial team, meanwhile, has expertise in areas like charities, IP, data protection and sport. In this last area, Muckle acts for some world-famous individuals from the world of football, and clubs including Arsenal, Man City and Liverpool, and The FA has appointed it to run a legal helpline for the 5,246 FA Charter Standard clubs (ie all those outside the Football League). In the rest of the department, trainees might spend time "*drafting terms and conditions for local businesses*" or helping protect the intellectual property of pharmaceutical companies.

BEAM me up

After becoming managing partner in 2004, Steve McNicol visited the States and investigated how various different companies deliver good customer service. His finding, in a nutshell, was that the secret is to have employees who are committed to the firm and its business. This might not sound particularly ground-breaking, but we know other law firms where the motto is 'The client, then the firm, then you.' Muckle's ethos fundamentally rejects the view that employees' needs should somehow be a tertiary consideration.

The result is that this is a firm that's strong on joined-up thinking and does an awful lot to keep its employees motivated. There's a dedicated 'Being Engaged At Muckle' (BEAM) team made up of staff from across the firm. This arranges social events, raises issues with management on behalf of employees and carries out an annual engagement survey once a year. Furthermore, "*we have a regular Monday morning firm-wide e-mail*" with details of what's going on, while "*a business development list of who's catching up with what clients*" is also circulated to all staff to keep everyone in the loop.

Furthermore, inspired by a talk from Olympic swimmer Chris Cook, all Muckle lawyers are ascribed "*two lengths and five keys*" to keep in mind. From what we can work out, the 'lengths' are the chief goals that employees and teams should be aiming for (for trainees it's "*to become an outstanding newly qualified Muckle lawyer, technically able and commercially aware*") and the keys are how they can achieve these goals (in brief, the five trainee keys are: have pride in providing an excellent service; display dedication in every seat; be part of the team and listen and learn from feedback; continually improve technical knowledge; and be positive).

You might be thinking this talk of US fact-finding missions and 'keys' all sounds a bit hokey but it's clear that trainees genuinely buy into the Muckle manifesto and really feel invested in the firm's success. The lengths and keys are "*really about stripping things down to basics*" rather than getting "*bogged down*" by overly elaborate mission statements.

It's a social life Jim...

Among the social events organised by the BEAM team are country hikes, curry nights, "*lads' and lasses' Toon nights,*" and a family day at Gosforth Rugby Club, with magicians and bouncy castles. A grow-your-own veg competition resulted in some impressive marrows but a follow-up contest with leeks was a casualty of the Newcastle weather. Trainees kick back in 'Time Out', the social area of Muckle's city centre offices, which has TVs, radios and pool tables.

Odds and ends: the trainee salary is good (*"the best in Newcastle,"* sources thought). Meanwhile, the hours aren't terrible – 8.30am to 6pm sounds about standard and although *"30-hour stints in the office"* aren't unheard of we didn't speak to anyone who'd actually done one. The qualification process is an informal affair with no jobs list circulated but it all seems to work out okay and two of three qualifiers were retained in 2013.

And finally...

Muckle's our 'dark horse' selection for this year: with the changes in the Newcastle legal market we reckon it's one to watch.

Average trainee salary: £26,739
In central London: £34,787
In outer London: £27,0027
In South West: £22,133
In South East: £20,975
In Yorkshire: £20,637
In the Midlands: £20,046
In the North West: £19,512
In Eastern England: £19.149
In the North East: £18,648
In Wales: £17,943

Figures provided by the SRA, summer 2013

Nabarro LLP

The facts

Location: London, Sheffield
Number of UK partners/solicitors: 106/319
Partners who trained at the firm: 13%
Total number of trainees: 50
Seats: 4x6 months
Alternative seats: Brussels, secondments
Extras: pro bono – LawWorks; language classes

On chambersstudent.co.uk...

How to get into Nabarro
Interview with training principal James Snape
The Sheffield office

Both the London and Sheffield offices of this mid-market firm continue to sing its praises.

Nabarro moves house

Still flying the flag for strong and successful mid-size firms, Nabarro is a happy place to be. Training principal James Snape says: *"In the past 12 months, we have seen continued success is all our practices, and seen our Singapore office double in size. Our real estate practices – particularly funds and indirect real estate – continue to do well, and the construction litigation team has acted on one of the largest arbitrations of the past year."* In 2012, turnover rose for the first time in years, and 2013 is no different, with revenue increasing by 2.6%. Newly appointed senior partner Graham Stedman intends to *"maintain Nabarro's open and inclusive culture."* 2013 saw the announcement of a move to new premises in October 2014, from the firm's Holborn spot to the *"totally redeveloped"* 125 London Wall, right in the heart of the City.

Nabarro continues to stand tall in property, maintaining top real estate rankings in *Chambers UK*. There are, however, several other practices on offer, aptly reflected in rankings. Nabarro scores highly across a broad cross-section of practices, from public procurement and local government to capital markets and venture capital.

What does a move to the City mean for the culture? *"It's clear Nabarro has a strategy in place to push forwards, but it's step-by-step,"* interviewees reflected. *"The general mood about the firm is very positive and everyone wants Nabarro to grow, but we're thankfully never going to be some aggressive American giant."* There are whispers of potential mergers – *"which are welcome and interesting"* – (and reports of a broken one with Addleshaws), but interviewees assured us *"a merger would never be a snap, rapid decision. Nabarro continues to be a solid and good*

environment to work in." Training principal James Snape commented: *"Our intention is for the move not to change what we're like to work for. Yes, we're moving to the City and people will draw their own conclusions from that, but we're proud of our culture and intend to maintain it. We have put a great deal of effort into our rebranding, and hope that it will mean that Nabarro is recognised as an international firm – and the new premises will reinforce that"*

Nabarro still holds true to its six-seat system, much to the trainees' delight. *"It's such an asset for the firm,"* they agreed. *"It's brilliant to be able to get a broad experience of the law, and there is the option of doing multiple seats in a similar field."* Naturally, *"chopping and changing so frequently can be difficult at times, but the positives outweigh any real struggles,"* interviewees said.

Realty check

Seats in London are organised as follows. There are four real estate teams, each taking two trainees; separately, there are teams in real estate disputes, construction (contentious and non-contentious), and funds and indirect real estate. There are also teams in pensions, commercial litigation, corporate, financial regulation, banking, restructuring/insolvency, tax, employment, IP and EU/competition, planning, environment and projects. The Sheffield office has seats in real estate, corporate/banking, employment, projects, property litigation, construction, commercial litigation (which includes Medical Defence Unit MDU work, clinical negligence and healthcare) and environment. Trainees in both offices undertake a contentious seat and a seat in real estate. *"The property seat is non-negotiable,"* interviewees confirmed, and *"Nabarro*

The True Picture

359

also requires you to gain some sort of corporate/transactional experience." Trainees submit four seat choices per rotation and agreed that *"from your third seat onwards, people often get their first or second choices."*

The construction team, *"although not large,"* works with some of the firm's most prominent clients. This includes advising client Mitsubishi on the £100m redevelopment of its prime City office site to create a new 250,000 sq ft office and retail building, and working with the corporate team for Google in the (reported) £650m purchase and development of the new one million sq ft Google UK HQ site in King's Cross. *"The contentious construction team is the bigger of the two,"* interviewees said. *"They've had some massive cases on this year, so their need for man-power has grown."* Both teams sit together but work *"completely separately, as it's often conflicting cases. The non-contentious people almost exclusively do employer development work, while the contentious work for contractors."* The department *"is seen as a whole and attorneys between teams get on well, and they throw a great Christmas party"* interviews assured us. All agreed: *"The department is particularly good at involving trainees."* One said: *"I drafted appointments and warranties, and liaised with counsel."* Another added: *"You're always taken to meetings and, if necessary, to court. You're never just left in the dark."*

The real estate teams combined make up Nabarro's largest department. Occupying an entire floor of the London building, there are about 75 fee earners and *"all are top of their game,"* interviewees said. The teams are split by client and partner speciality, and all *"deal with commercial real estate ventures. Most teams have two or three main clients, alongside a host of smaller clients."* Although each team takes on a variety, *"one does predominantly development work, while another sees a lot of lease/landlord management work."* Nabarro's *"bread and butter is asset management work, and that's mostly what trainees see,"* interviewees said. *"The department often works closely with the construction department, and has some very interesting clients."* This includes advising BNP Paribas on the £300m forward sale of its King's Cross development scheme to a joint venture. Meanwhile up North, the team is unofficially split between asset management and development work, with trainees concentrating on one or the other. *"You can always ask for work on the other side if you're interested. It's not a hard and fast divide."* interviewees assured us. The team acted for London & Stamford in the £1.6bn sale of its 50% stake in Sheffield's Meadowhall shopping centre to Norway's sovereign wealth fund. Both offices concurred: *"Even from day one, you're thrown into the deep end and expected to take on responsibility. On the bigger transactions you're managing documents, but you're often given your own licence work – which includes all drafting and dealing with clients."* One said: *"It's not always easy, but nevertheless a terrific learning curve."*

Chambers UK rankings

Capital markets	Local Government
Competition/European Law	Pensions
Construction	PFI/PPP
Corporate/M&A	Planning
Dispute Resolution	Private Equity
Education	Professional Discipline
Employment	Public Procurement
Environment	Real Estate
Healthcare	Retail
Information Technology	Tax
Investment Funds	

Real estate disputes trainees busy themselves with *"major asset management work,"* interviewees explained. *"They advise on the validity of break notices, schedules of dilapidations and large planning cases."* One said: *"We also have a growing rights to light practice."* The two offices have *"weekly video meetings,"* and both *"often work closely together. Sheffield trainees are sometimes supervised by London partners and vice versa."* Although neither team is particularly large, the client list is still pretty impressive, including acting for Saatchi & Saatchi against its landlord regarding its headquarter premises off Tottenham Court Road. *"Although it's contentious work, so always more difficult to get good responsibility, you're never spending hours bundling,"* trainees said. *"You do learn a lot and there's also the potential of advocacy if you qualify into the team."*

A 'barro load of business

Nabarro's corporate offering continues to be a *"growing"* field for the firm. Trainees reflected that both teams have *"a lot of work on at the moment, especially on the restructuring side, unsurprisingly."* The highly regarded restructuring/insolvency team does a mixture of both private and public work and covers the full range of corporate work, including equity capital markets, M&A and securities. The Sheffield trainees said: *"They've taken on several NQs over the last year and seem to be particularly interested in growing our insolvency speciality."* Speaking of insolvency, the team in the North led on the restructuring of UK Coal Group. Meanwhile in London, Nabarro acted for Care UK on its £48m purchase of Harmoni, a large GP out-of-hours provider.

Commercial lit encompasses everything from banking litigation and pensions to general commercial. *"The variety is great and I can get stuck into a range of work,"* trainees said. The Sheffield office prides itself on the niche MD Unit, which takes its own trainee every round. *"MDU is a small but mighty team,"* essentially acting for doctors in disciplinary actions. *"As a trainee, you're exposed to really great drafting, conferences with clients and taking on your own short applications. It tends to be more responsibility than on the com lit side."* There are some big-name clients in both cities, including Molson Coors Brewing Company and IBM UK Pensions Trust, *"but also individuals and smaller companies."* For instance, Nabarro represented Nicholas Gilodi-Johnson, the managing director of Farepak Food and Gifts, in defence of directors' disqualification proceedings. *"The range of clients means you often see the full litigation process and really learn from it."* All agreed: *"The levels of client contact are great, and you're often drafting and doing research."* One said: *"Com lit is known for being one of the nicest teams in the firm. They're very sociable and approachable, and people frequently stop to ask how you're doing."*

Although a secondment to Brussels is currently the only overseas opportunity on offer, the firm is mulling over sending a trainee to Singapore. At present, there are also several client secondments, including stints at Mercedes Benz and Serco.

The social network

"Honestly, it's even friendlier then you can hope for," trainees agreed. *"Nabarro really isn't some cut-throat place where you're shouted at. Of course people are serious and they work hard, but you feel like you're included right from the start."* One said: *"A lot of that attitude is embodied in our involvement in business development."* Even vac scheme students at Nabarro are required to host their own networking evening, while trainees continue to run their 'Contact Nabarro' event. *"It's an evening where we invite friends and contacts, with the potential of engaging the clients of the future."* One interviewee added: *"You feel like Nabarro wants to involve you in its progression, and they always want to hear your business development thoughts. You really get the sense that everyone is welcome to have their voice."* Partners are *"never a different breed. They're always open and approachable."*

"Although you can't go so far as to say it's truly 'one firm', Nabarro does really make the effort between offices and we feel very connected," trainees agreed. *"There are several video-linked meetings, and Sheffield lawyers of-ten travel to London for departmental training."* All commended the *"really fun"* 'Trainees in the North' weekend the firm continues to run. London trainees head up to Sheffield for *"corporate bonding exercises"* as well as *"general drinks and fun."* One said: *"You do feel trainees are friends, and it's great to socialise with everyone."* Sheffield trainees also invite their London counterparts to a summer ball. Ultimately, *"Nabarro is committed to improving relationships and taking very positive steps. The geographical differences always make things difficult, but it's much better than you'd expect."*

Both offices have an array of sports teams, including football, hockey and cricket. *"They've also recently revived the language classes,"* trainees said. Otherwise, Nabarro's lawyers have *"hidden musical talents,"* and re-entered the Battle of the Bands/Law Rocks competition this year. Musical capabilities also extend to a *"lovely"* Christmas choir. The summer ball, held in Sheffield, is the big event of the year. *"It's a black-tie, sit-down-dinner do for charity,"* interviewees said. *"The twist this year is several groups took part in a dance competition to raise even more money. There were some silky moves happening."* Informally, there's less going on in Sheffield *"as people are often driving or commuting,"* but London trainees are *"normally"* out on a Friday night. The Dolphin and The Enterprise are still firm favourites, and you'll regularly see *"a partner or senior associate out as well."*

Although retention stats are pretty good, London trainees agreed that *"more transparency is necessary."* There *"isn't a formal application process, and everything seems to happen slightly behind the scenes. It's stressful."* One said: *"Although we appreciate the firm is still trying to confirm where jobs are, a little more structure would really help."* The firm commented that it is reviewing the NQ process with a view to boosting transparency. Sheffield trainees painted a slightly sunnier picture: *"Ultimately there are only four or five of us, so there is more scope for space. We also talk to each other, so it's all pretty open."* The firm says it's aware of these issues and is looking into how the process functions. This year Nabarro retained 22 out of 27 qualifiers.

And finally...

"Get on the vac scheme," was the overwhelming advice. *"Nearly 100% of trainees did the vac scheme, and it's a great programme."*

361

Norton Rose Fulbright

The facts

Location: London
Number of UK partners/solicitors: 149/360
Total number of trainees: 110
Seats: 4x6 months
Alternative seats: overseas seats, secondments
Extras: pro bono – Tower Hamlets Law Centre, South West Law Centre, Liberty Advice Line, FRU; language classes

On chambersstudent.co.uk...

How to get into Norton Rose Fulbright
Going global: Norton's internal network
Duncan Batchelor's thoughts on the merger

Peer through this firm's glass-fronted exterior on London's South Bank and you'll see two gigantic flags hanging in the atrium. The Union Jack and Stars & Stripes pay tribute to the most significant transatlantic combination of 2013.

The future is Fulbright

"As a result of our growth and development, we are now a top-ten global legal practice by revenue and number of lawyers." So training principal Duncan Batchelor told us this year, revealing the transformation this famous old City firm has gone through. Fresh from a merger with Texan giant Fulbright & Jaworski in June 2013, the newly minted Norton Rose Fulbright counts 3,800 lawyers in more than 50 cities across the world. The UK part of the firm was known primarily for its financial prowess, but the merger will undoubtedly open a lot of new doors.

Why Fulbright? Duncan Batchelor again: *"Cultural fit is incredibly important in any large organisation or combination. Ours is a people business and it was one of the key criteria from the outset that we would join with a firm with a similar culture, ethos and outlook."* He adds: *"Looking at the international axes of trade (such as the axis between Africa and China, which few firms are able to service in the way we can), the inclusion of the Fulbright practice is perfect to complement our existing network."*

As you can tell, Batchelor gave us some detailed responses: visit our website for management's further thoughts on the merger. *"Ultimately, we can't yet tell how the merger will affect our culture and vibe, but our American expansion feels very exciting,"* trainees said, alluding to a 2010 merger with Aussie firm Deacons and not mentioning in all the excitement the recent tie-ups with Canadian and South African firms that have been equally important in NR's recent expansion. *"The deal with Fulbright is seen* as a relationship rather than a takeover. Fulbright is such a big fish in the States: we know we're joining a good thing."* One source said: *"Wealth and clients are global, and we were lacking a US presence. The merger make a lot of sense."*

Six becomes four

Norton Rose was unusual among the largest City firms in that it ran a six-seat training contract. This was always a big draw for students who liked the idea of sampling lots of different areas of law. However, the firm recently switched to the more common system of four seats lasting six months each. *"I think the idea is to create uniformity across offices, particularly in light of 2010's Australian merger,"* one trainee said. Training principal Duncan Batchelor explains: *"First, the sixth seat often lost its value as qualification decisions were usually made during the course of the fifth seat. Second, we noticed that people often repeated a seat which they had previously done in their last four months. Third, and from a client perspective, clients were often keen to take trainees for a six-month secondment rather than a four-month period."* We were expecting a lot of griping about the change from the current trainees, but in fact they appear to have taken it on the chin and appreciated the logic behind the decision. They did say: *"The transition to the four seats could have been handled better. It was all done very quickly and many of us applied here specifically for the six seats. That will be different with new intakes, of course."* All agreed: *"The*

Chambers UK rankings

Asset Finance	Insurance
Aviation	Investment Funds
Banking & Finance	Outsourcing
Capital Markets	Pensions
Commodities	Planning
Competition/European Law	Professional Negligence
Construction	Projects
Corporate Crime &	Public Procurement
Investigations	Real Estate Finance
Corporate/M&A	Real Estate Litigation
Employee Share Schemes	Restructuring/Insolvency
& Incentives	Tax
Employment	Telecommunications
Environment	Transport
Financial Services	Travel
Information Technology	

HR team do really try and get you the seats you want, but it's important to make your wishes known early on."

Seats now fall broadly into the following categories: banking; dispute resolution; corporate; real estate; competition and regulatory; employee incentives and pensions; and tax. In future *"all trainees will have to undertake one of the banking seats, one corporate and one disputes,"* interviewees said. *"Within each team there are subspecialisms and partners that have their own niches. It means there's a lot of choice."* For example, banking covers a wealth of options including asset finance, general banking, project finance, derivatives/capital markets and Islamic financing, while real estate includes the likes of planning, construction and property litigation. One source explained: *"There's an internal publication detailing what each partner does, so you have the ability to make an informed decision when it comes to seat changes."*

We've mentioned in passing NRF's prowess when it comes to matters financial, but perhaps we understated it. *Chambers UK* awards the firm rankings – often top rankings – in every type of finance category going. The corporate and litigation practices are also genuinely high-end and don't look out of place on magic circle-sized deals. Check our the *Chambers UK* website for a full list of the firm's many rankings. The only other area we'll single out for special mention is projects and energy work. Norton Rose has long had a decent reputation in this area, but this will be significantly boosted by the US merger. Fulbright & Jaworski was a Texas native and energy law is the stock-in-trade of all the biggest Texan firms.

Coming up Roses

"There are two large asset finance teams, and in both areas Norton Rose Fulbright are leaders," trainees said. *"The teams have some incredibly long-standing clients, and asset finance is at the core of the firm."* The split is between an *"exclusively"* marine-focused group and an aviation/rail team. Shipping was one of Norton Rose's first departments, and has been a part of the firm for over 200 years. The UK practice is very connected to the firm's Athens and Paris office and works with *"all the big names"* in the shipping world, including advising Talbot, Hiscox and other Lloyd's syndicates in defence of $77m worth of claims following an alleged piracy attack on a crude oil tanker. The aviation and rail practices act for the likes of easyJet, KLM and Transavia, and recently advised China Aircraft Leasing on its Airbus order. Interviewees agreed the teams *"instil real discipline and attention to detail."* One said: *"Although there is a lot of document management, the teams are relatively small, so there's good scope to get involved and get very early responsibility."*

Almost every trainee we spoke to had taken a seat in the project finance department. *"It's one of the largest groups at the firm,"* and *"the department is incredibly dynamic and consistently fluid. There are partners from all over the world that fly in and out."* One subteam focuses on energy and projects; the other is more geared towards mining, infrastructure and construction. Basically, *"the energy stuff is financing the building of power stations or acquisitions of energy companies,"* interviewees explained. *"It's predominantly international work."* The other team is involved in matters like *"the building of airports and roads, and the financing of mining companies."* The department is *"notoriously hard-working and you can get some crazy hours,"* interviewees admitted. *"It's punishing at times, but the work you're doing is interesting."* One said: *"Realistically, you will be proof-reading, but there's actually quite a bit of drafting."* Another added: *"These are mega-transactions, so it's hard to get that full amount of responsibility, but you are involved, and the training is comprehensive."*

Corporate is still a *"big driver"* for the firm. *"NRF isn't as well known for its corporate work because of our finance and projects expertise, but the teams are very strong."* Interviewees thought the departments were doing well: *"The telecoms practice is expanding internationally and the insurance practice is working on several big deals."* The private equity team recently worked on the $315m sale of the Oxford Aviation Academy, while the insurance group advised on the $300 sale of Brit Insurance to Riverstone to Fairfax. M&A deals continue to be big-ticket work: the firm advised The Royal Bank of Canada on the $2bn acquisition of Latin American, Caribbean and African private banking businesses; and the general corporate team acted for Muller Dairy UK on the £279.5m public

The True Picture

takeover of London Stock Exchange-listed Robert Wiseman Dairies.

NRF's disputes practice is split into four teams, covering broadly but not exclusively: financial and general commercial litigation; construction, transport, energy and trade; insurance (including marine litigation); regulation and investigations; and white-collar crime. The teams do however, cover the firm's full spectrum of practices. *"The insurance and regulatory teams have had a heavy influx from Fulbright,"* trainees said. *"Following the merger, disputes on the whole is growing. It's not always been a focus for NRF, but there is a lot of new potential."* Recently, NRF has represented law firm Collyer Bristow in an £100m claim against insurance brokers, and is acting for the US trustee of Lehman Brothers in the protection of interests in the UK and other jurisdictions outside the US.

Flying potential

The opportunities to go on overseas secondments are second to none. Options currently span three continents and no doubt more will open up in the future. See **page 500** for a full list. *"The options really are incredible,"* interviewees said. *"Going overseas is very much encouraged by the firm – it's almost compulsory. To be perfectly honest, it'd be strange to come to NRF and not want to go abroad. We're such an international entity."* Training principal Duncan Batchelor said: *"We're a global firm and are looking to hire people with a global outlook. That is reflected in our selection for candidates. Those coming to Norton Rose should expect to work with international clients and colleagues and to travel overseas from time to time – not only as a trainee, but throughout their careers. The chance to work in another office and with our clients in another region gives people a wider exposure to the business. Applicants need to think beyond the two years of the training contract and think about the benefits working overseas can bring to their careers."*

The East Asian placements continue to be very popular, as is Paris. The option of heading to Australia is new on the table, much to the delight of trainees. NRF also runs a variety of client secondments, mostly at *"a mix of banks and energy companies."*

Do the hula

"Although we're a massive City firm, people are very down to earth and inclusive," trainees said. *"You're never treated as a low-life trainee. Common sense prevails and people respect each other. People are reasonable and helpful."* Our sources had all made *"good friends"* at the firm. *"People meet up for lunch as often as they can, and some are even holidaying together this summer."*

Norton Rose loves sport, and mixed hockey, rugby, cricket, sailing, football, netball, tennis and softball clubs are all knocking about. Music and language lessons are held in the office, while the firm won 'Business Choir of the Year' in 2013 and interviewees reflected how *"lovely it is to hear them practising in the atrium."* Although there's no official Christmas party, teams put on their own events. *"One held an American line-dancing do and the corporate department threw a Hawaiian-themed party. Grass skirts and flip-flops were heavily encouraged."* NR also held a 'welcome Fulbright' drinks function, *"to help with early integration."* Informally, the Brigade bar and the Bridge pub, both on Tooley Street, are firm favourites.

Retention rates at NR are pretty good, interviewees admitted. *"They don't release job lists, because it's about showing that initiative and nurturing good relationships with the team you want to work with."* One said: *"It's probably the correct way to run things, but can make the process stressful. Some departments decide earlier than others and it all gets a bit mad."* All agreed: *"If you're a good candidate and you don't get your first choice – they will make every effort to place you elsewhere, which is great. You never feel abandoned."* Some 24 out of 26 qualifiers were kept on in 2013.

And finally...

Long respected as a top City firm that treats its employees with respect, Norton Rose is now entering a new phase. Hopefully the Fulbright merger will bring all the benefits of globalisation without compromising the firm's pleasant nature.

Olswang

The facts

Location: London, Reading

Number of UK partners/solicitors: 83/139

Partners who trained at firm: 6%

Total number of trainees: 24

Seats: 4x6 months

Alternative seats: overseas seats, secondments

Extras: pro bono – RCJ CAB, various charities; language classes

On chambersstudent.co.uk...

How to get into Olswang

Why Malaysia?

CSR at the firm

Founded in the midst of the yuppie-minded '80s, this firm is no *"media boutique"* and has its expansionist eye set firmly on the Asian markets in the years ahead...

Go East, where there's work to do

Olswang's origins can be traced back to property law firm Brecher & Co, which Simon Olswang and senior partner Mark Devereux broke away from in order to form an outfit with a distinct media focus. That was 1981. Since then, this firm has transitioned through phases which have seen it become well known for its TV, film, technology and telecoms expertise, as well as for cultivating a 'quirkier' atmosphere.

Today, Olswang consists of nearly 700 people, 110 of which are partners (quite a jump, given that in 1991 there were just ten). This is a firm that has, over the years, become full-service, and its practice now encompasses a broader range of sector areas such as banking, real estate, retail, life sciences and leisure. Sectors come first at Olswang, and the firm makes it clear that it advises primarily from *"a sector point of view"* – the various departments are all tailored to cater to the specific clientele of the firm. The corporate and litigation departments are the standout areas, and there are the usual teams that you'd expect from a full-service firm, like employment, finance, tax and competition.

2013 has seen the re-election of CEO David Stewart for a second three-year term. During Stewart's first term, the firm expanded internationally and offices were opened in Paris, Munich, Madrid and, most recently, Singapore. So what we can expect from Mr Stewart in round two? His next three-year plan is ambitious, and he has already stated his aim to be in the UK's top 20 firms by 2016. He's also slimmed down the executive committee (for clarity's sake) and turned his sights onto expansion in Asia.

The former 'head of China' at CMS Cameron McKenna, Andrew Halper, has been brought on board to focus on the firm's potential future in – you guessed it – China, as has Fasken Martineau corporate partner Azlinda Ariffin-Boromand, who's a Malaysian specialist and former barrister in the region for 12 years. Olswang recently lost out on a qualifying foreign law practice licence in Singapore (meaning that they can't practise permitted areas of Singapore law) which may have put a bit of a dampener on things, but Olswang still earns a band-one ranking for its Singapore TMT practice in *Chambers Asia*. Financial results in 2012/13 have not been quite as impressive as the year before – up by 3% instead of a 17% climb in 2011/12 – but to be fair that's a pretty tough act to follow.

It's easy to see why ambitious would-be solicitors are easily drawn to Olswang – over the past few months fashion lawyers have hosted 'dinner discussions' in Belgium on the globalisation of fashion; film lawyers have been busy discussing the impending Cinema Communication Review at the International Berlin Film Festival; and the media partner who advised on the phone hacking scandal will now be representing a group of Apple users who claim that Google has secretly tracked their browsing habits. Is there ever a dull moment, one wonders?

So Olswang

There's a *"standard four six-month seat system"* at Olswang, and trainees will complete a seat in the corporate department, often in their first year. Preferences are listed before each rotation, and *"generally speaking most people get close to what they want."* Trainees also have a

Chambers UK rankings

Administrative & Public Law	Intellectual Property
Banking & Finance	Licensing
Capital Markets	Life Sciences
Construction	Media & Entertainment
Corporate/M&A	Outsourcing
Data Protection	Planning
Defamation/Reputation Management	Private Equity
	Real Estate Finance
Dispute Resolution	Real Estate Litigation
Employee Share Schemes & Incentives	Restructuring/Insolvency
	Retail
Employment	Sports Law
Information Technology	Tax
	Telecommunications

chance to list a 'priority seat' in a department that they are especially keen on, but *"you can't manipulate when you get it – although most people want it in their third seat – and it can mean that a there has to be a trade-off somewhere else. They never guarantee it."* Seats available include commercial litigation, finance, tax, construction, employment, IP, real estate, real estate litigation and MCT (media, communications and technology).

Olswang also takes on two trainees each year in the Thames Valley office, where seats in real estate, real estate litigation, commercial and employment are available. Reading trainees can also apply to complete seats in London.

The *"busy"* mid-market corporate department takes on the most trainees at each rotation, and is subsequently *"quite used to providing us with work."* The department is *"structured around sectors,"* and most clients are drawn from the media, technology, leisure, retail and real estate industries. Clients include BBC Worldwide, Vodafone and Alpha Flight Group, and lawyers here recently advised ITV on its acquisition of So Television – the independent production company behind *The Graham Norton Show* – as part of its five-year, 'transformation plan'. Some trainees complained that there was *"a lot of doc management, which can become repetitive,"* while others were more positive, and described being able *"to have a first crack at drafting the articles of association for a shareholder's agreement, which involved a small start-up company."* Generally, *"the partners and seniors will run the main sales docs, while you'll work with juniors and mid-levels to handle the disclosure process and ancillary docs – but they are keen to make sure that you stay involved and know how your work fits in."*

The hours in corporate – as you might expect – can be *"very up and down, and when a completion happens it's not unheard of to leave at 4.30am, but it's a rarity to stay beyond midnight."* Phew.

Life in commercial litigation means that trainees encounter a broader array of sectors than in corporate, and disputes here may touch upon areas such as manufacturing, energy, pharmaceuticals and financial services. The team has been kept busy acting for Ildar Khazhaev, a Russian national who has had proceedings brought against him by JSC BTA Bank (Khazhaev's former employer), which has accused him of being involved in allegedly sham loans. It's a complicated case, with several other claims involved, which together form one of the largest set of proceedings brought before the commercial court.

Trainees said that *"there's a fair amount of bundling"* to be done, but there's also the chance to hone drafting skills as well, and they had been able to draft claim forms, letters to the other side, and also *"an entire facts section of the defence during an arbitration."* Sources had been to court *"two or three times,"* and advised that *"if you want to get decent exposure then seek out the responsibility."* These were sage words, as another (perhaps more reticent) trainee bemoaned that they had *"only got disclosure exercises to do."*

There are some *"cool clients"* like Microsoft and Kudos Film and Television (who produced *Life on Mars* and *Spooks*), and there can be the chance to sit within the media litigation team, where there's *"a lot of defamation and libel work, which is fascinating and topical."* The firm's defamation work, incidentally, is ranked in band-one by *Chambers UK*.

MCT 4 ME

MCT is the hot seat of all hot seats and *"the one that people go for."* It's easy to see why, of course; Olswang originally made its name in this area of work, and *Chambers UK* ranks several strands of its expertise in film and television, music, publishing, digital media, and advertising and marketing. Sources said that: *"You get involved within a wide range of those areas, so you might be helping out on the terms and conditions of a video game one minute, and then working for a large telecoms company the next."* Some had got more involved in the *"telecoms and technology stuff that is hitting the headlines lately,"* and found that this strand in particular came with some *"fast-moving deadlines; with telecoms there's a lot of outsourcing required, so clients want certain services outsourced for the sake of efficiency and cost cutting."*

There are pros and cons to a seat in MCT. The structure of the team means that *"a high percentage of partners are specialists in their area, and it's great to get exposure to them"* (one trainee raved about the training they had received in each sub-team during the seat). However, because of the nature of the tasks, *"it can be tricky to give trainees bits of work,"* as often *"ad hoc niche agreements crop up, which are easier to keep just between the associate and the partner, but they do try to keep you involved."*

Most of our interviewees had been more involved in the telecoms/tech/sports side of the department, and one pointed out that *"sometimes people come here and think that they'll spend all their time working on Hollywood blockbusters and wind up disappointed – you've got to be realistic."*

We'll give you a taste of that kind of work regardless, just to be cruel: media lawyers have advised the producers of the new Stephen Frears film, *Philomena* (which stars Dame Judi Dench and Steve Coogan), by reading the script to check for any potentially contentious subject matter (as the film is based on a true story). They also advised the producers of *Skyfall* to ensure that the film was classified as British, so that it could qualify for UK tax credit. Sounds great, doesn't it? But don't forget that there's far more to MCT than just film and TV, and trainees here loved the seat especially because such a variety was on offer.

It might be easy to forget that Olswang has a real estate department in the midst of such perceived glamour, but it actually generates 25% of the firm's turnover. It's also a common destination for trainees, and most of our sources had completed a stint there. At the moment, there's a push to develop a pan-European practice in certain key cities, but London real estate lawyers (of which there are 40) have been busy over the past year working on shopping centres, London offices, hotels and student residencies. Clients include UBS, BP and Legal & General, which the firm represented during the sale of St Martin's Court, which provides a mixture of office and retail space right next to St Paul's cathedral.

Trainees *"loved"* their time here, and found the responsibility levels to be much higher than they were elsewhere: *çYou get your own files to run, which can be intimidating at first, but you learn fast, and you're involved in everything from start to finish – conducting conflict checks, agreeing fees, contacting the other side if there's a lease involved, agreeing the terms of the lease, drafting the contracts etc."* At the end of the day, a seat in real estate *"provides excellent training, as the team is friendly and approachable, and the work is more manageable – you're in control of your time."*

Both client and international secondments are available – *"there are usually around four or five opportunities at every rotation."* For now, trainees can go to Paris and Brussels, or choose to sit in-house at key media clients.

Surviving and social-skiving

Trainees described the Olswang culture as *"forward-thinking and progressive,"* and repeatedly pointed out the firm's more meritocratic stance on development: *"We're modern in our approach, and we've cut out those olde-worlde legal stereotypes."* Being in a *"legacy media firm"*

means that there are some *"very eccentric characters"* to work alongside, and sources added that *"we're quite geeky as well – the fee earners understand so much about the sectors and the technology used within them. It goes above and beyond what they need to know, and you really get to see how passionate people here are."*

People may well be *"very open, friendly and welcoming,"* but trainees couldn't deny that the social life at the firm had dampened down a bit over the past year: *"The social scene has not been fantastic, and people just don't seem to be going out as much – my intake went for a Christmas meal and that was it."* Others agreed, and said that *"it has been difficult to keep the momentum going – we're probably not the most social bunch, but we are trying to make more of an effort now. There's a trainee social committee and we do things three or four times a year, like hiring a bar and having drinks, or organising a soft ball event in the summer."*

While Olswang *"may not be the sort of place where you can rely on fellow trainees to go out on a Thursday night,"* interviewees did concede that *"the firm is really great at organising firm-wide events."* End of month drinks in the office are *"well attended,"* and last year's Christmas party was held in *"an underground venue which was decked out like a ski lodge. That was classy and cool, and everyone had a fun night."*

Trainees were also invited to a 'Fee Earners Retreat', which brought together people from all over the international offices, as well as some of the firm's clients. Add to this a bi-annual 'State of the Nation' address by the CEO David Stewart and a weekly newsletter, and trainees felt that they were *"generally kept fairly up to date, and not just in relation to London, but internationally as well."* So what's on the agenda then? The general game plan revolves around not just focusing on existing clients, but also developing some new relationships, and *"each department has a target list of clients they want."* It doesn't look like Olswang will be branching out into other sectors any time soon, and instead *"the emphasis is on cross-selling – we want to use our existing clients and offer them a full service."* Internationally, the firm will be *"consolidating a period of quite rapid expansion,"* but sources reiterated that there's a *"big push for branching out in Asia, which will tie in nicely with our new-ish Singapore office."*

Ultimately, sources felt that the firm *"is moving in a more corporate direction (you can tell from our lateral hires of late) and people expect it do so."* Some felt that the downside to this was that Olswang had lost something: *"People used to think of the firm as quirky, but it's losing that personality now – which is maybe just a survival thing."*

It's also true that Olswang was traditionally seen as a *"media-focused boutique"* before *"painting itself as full-*

The True Picture

service and more grown-up." Trainees emphasised that *"it's really the case now,"* and some who had been to law fairs said that students still suffer from displays of *"mistaken identity"* over Olswang: *"We had students coming up to us and assuming that we were purely a media firm – we were told to firmly market ourselves as full-service."*

When it comes to qualification, trainees are told *"relatively early in the final seat what the process will be,"* and *"each department has its own interview process."* Sources this year felt *"fairly optimistic,"* and we noticed quite a divergent set of interests throughout our interviews, so perhaps MCT wasn't saturated with applications after all. In the end, 12 out of 20 stayed with the firm.

And finally...
Remember this vital point if you are about to apply to Olswang: yes, the firm advises clients in the media sector, but it offers them a full service nonetheless. Full service. Full service. Full service. Got it?

Chambers UK rankings

Capital Markets	Restructuring/Insolvency
Real Estate Finance	

a variety of tasks – some things are administrative, like making bibles, but there's a lot of drafting as well."

London calling

Corporate clients mainly come from the technology, finance and real estate sectors, and include Samsung, Capita, Apollo and Visa to name a few. Cross-border work is rife: London lawyers recently represented California-headquartered engineering giant Jacobs in its $913m acquisition of a Norway-based construction business and advised international investment unit Blackstar on its reverse takeover of a South Africa-listed company. Our sources told of completing *"due diligence exercises for high-value international cases"* and *"drafting sale and purchase agreements,"* among other tasks. Although trainees occasionally run into *"a lot of bibling,"* insiders assured us there's plenty *"that requires quite a lot of thought put into it."* What's more, trainees *"get to deal with clients every day – they'll call you the moment you put your name on an e-mail."*

The majority of trainees head to client secondments at financial institutions like Credit Suisse or Hatfield Philips, often continuing relationships they've already formed during a previous seat. Most welcomed the opportunity for *"a front row view of how legal advice is interpreted,"* calling the experience *"underrated – people don't always realise how helpful it is to see things from a client's point of view."* Another plus? The *"much shorter"* schedule, which provides a welcome respite from the frantic pace back at the firm.

It became clear to us during our interviews that the trainee experience can differ dramatically depending on how much responsibility you're saddled with. According to our insiders, *"the biggest compliment you can get is to be busy all the time – it means they trust you."* When it comes to hours, our interviewees insisted *"everyone has a crazy schedule at some point,"* with more than one reporting regular 10pm finishes. These time-strapped recruits explained *"PH is top-heavy in terms of partner-to-associate ratios"* and warned future joiners to keep in mind that *"trainees are shared resources – anyone can give you work, and everyone thinks theirs is the most important."* On the plus side, helping out other departments means

"the work is always really varied; you're never stuck for six months doing the same stuff over and over." PH recently added some extra office space to its London digs, prompting speculation that the firm is planning to ease the pressure by taking on more associates soon. Still, *"don't apply here if you're looking for an easy ride; you've got to be prepared to work very hard."*

Special kind of magic

One trainee expressed surprise at the discovery that *"it's not massively hierarchical here. You are expected to work hard and be respectful of the people above you, of course, but overall it's quite chill."* Several of our interviewees chose Paul Hastings over magic circle options, telling us despite the firm's small size *"there are actually loads of partners from different backgrounds, which is encouraging when you're applying."* We suspect the generous £88,000 qualifying salary is no small incentive, either. That said, PH is first and foremost an American firm, and its high wages are not the only marked Stateside influence. *"You definitely feel like things are being run out of the US here,"* said insiders, mentioning senior management's twice yearly visits to London to *"keep everyone up to date."* Yankee influence also trickles down in the form of *"long hours, certain ethics and even our pictures on the website – they've made us look a bit more American by whitening our teeth a bit!"*

Appropriately, *"Thanksgiving is a big thing here. We have a big lunch followed by a guest speaker who talks for a good while about the history of the holiday."* Fortunately, such ramblings are largely forgiven in the face of vast quantities of turkey and other such treats. *"Any excuse to eat pecan pie is fine by me!"* A Fourth of July picnic in Regent's Park rounds out the American shindigs, while quarterly trainee socials and a *"spectacular"* Christmas party prove good fun on the home front. Day to day there's *"not a huge culture of going out because people are usually too busy,"* but trainees did share some stories of attending quirky client events like fashion exhibitions and virtual golf.

Sources were largely satisfied with PH's *"buzzy"* Spitalfields location as well as the firm's approach to trainee appraisals, which include *"a quite relaxed mid-seat sit-down with your supervisor"* followed by a more formal review at the end of each rotation that sees trainees scored on various competencies. In 2013, both of PH's two qualifiers were kept on.

And finally...

Owing to small trainee numbers, *"we haven't got the robust training framework that other firms do. Supervisors don't hold your hand very much, and they expect you to educate yourself when you begin a seat."*

Penningtons Solicitors LLP

The facts

Location: Basingstoke, Cambridge, Godalming, Guildford, London

Number of UK partners/solicitors: 67/88

Partners who trained at firm: 15%

Total number of trainees: 17

Seats: 4x6 months

Alternative seats: occasional secondments

Extras: pro bono – LawWorks

On chambersstudent.co.uk...

How to get into Penningtons
The magic circle firm that never was

Still flying high after two recent mergers, this South East firm serves up a tasty mix of commercial and private client work.

One for all, all for one

Penningtons has been busy of late. Mergers with Wedlake Saint and Dawsons bolstered its London presence in 2011. These were followed by two new offices in March 2012: one in Guildford to complement the firm's existing Godalming base, and another in Cambridge to boost its growing reputation in the education and technology sectors. These recent developments have clearly paid dividends, with Penningtons posting a turnover in excess of £30m.

If our sources are to be believed, Penningtons isn't about to rest on its laurels. *"I reckon we're probably on the lookout for further mergers,"* one speculated, *"but only if they happen to fit the Penningtons mould."* There was also a feeling that the firm *"will target more international work over the next few years,"* which could pave the way for its first overseas office. Others were a bit more cautious: *"I don't think there's anything else pending. It's still about cementing the mergers, gaining a greater market share and expanding organically, while keeping our personality at the same time."*

Interviewees did agree that *"one of the best things about Penningtons is its mix of corporate/commercial and people-based work."* The firm is split into three parts – business services, real estate and private individual divisions.

At the time of our calls, there were eight trainees plying their trade in London, five in Guildford/Godalming – the two Surrey offices are *"treated as one,"* we were told – and four in Basingstoke. While the London office is the largest, trainees were adamant that *"all the offices are on an equal footing"* and *"the quality of work, profile of cli-*ents and level of responsibility remain the same regardless of where you are. There's a 'one firm' mentality at Penningtons, with lots of interaction between the offices on a daily basis."*

However, there are slight differences between the offices when it comes to seats. In London, trainees can pick from commercial dispute resolution, corporate, employment (a seat shared with Cambridge), immigration, professional regulation, commercial real estate, private client and clinical negligence. Basingstoke's seat choices are corporate/commercial, clinical negligence, private client and commercial real estate, while Guildford/Godalming offers a similar selection but with the added option of a seat in personal injury, with a lot of overseas cases, we were told.

The firm encourages its trainees to take seats across the three business divisions, with both private client and commercial real estate being likely destinations at some point. *"You don't have to do them, but you would be in the minority if you didn't. Besides, if you've chosen Penningtons then the likelihood is you'll be interested in those two areas anyway."* Trainees may also be able to split a seat or, if business needs allow, swap with someone in another office. They list their preferences before each seat, then the HR team *"will try and accommodate us all as best they can,"* but *"we also discuss it among ourselves and everyone is usually clued-up on who wants what."*

Roots Manuva

Penningtons' business services division rakes in a sizeable portion of the firm's revenue, and the majority of our sources had completed an entire seat in corporate or done a corporate/commercial split. The corporate team's work

Chambers UK rankings

Clinical Negligence	Private Client
Corporate/M&A	Professional Discipline
Employment	Real Estate
Family/Matrimonial	Social Housing
Immigration	Tax
Partnership	Travel
Personal Injury	

spans a number of sectors, including education, technology, transport, travel, healthcare, and hotels/leisure. Interviewees found the department to be *"either frantically busy or fairly quiet,"* with not much middle ground. *"It's not exactly rocket science in terms of the level of work; there's just a lot of it to do,"* one source had found. Trainees draft board minutes and articles of association, prepare documents, assist with disclosures and due diligence, and occasionally attend client meetings. You may even be fortunate enough to *"see a couple of transactions through from beginning to end."* Some claimed that *"there's more interaction with the other offices in corporate than any other department. Every Monday morning, we have a live video meeting involving everyone in corporate from across the firm. It's a great way to start the week, and you really get the sense that you're part of the team."* The commercial group handles IP matters for the likes of sauce magnate Levi Roots and the American Institute for Foreign Study, focusing on trade mark, design and copyright issues.

In commercial dispute resolution, *"there are huge cases that you can get really involved in, which take up a lot of your time, or you can be working on discrete tasks for several different matters. The variety of work is really impressive."* You may remember that in September 2012 the UK Border Agency revoked London Metropolitan University's right to sponsor international students for UK visas. Penningtons acted for the university and secured a reprieve for its existing overseas students. Trainees can undertake work from other teams such as property litigation and professional regulation, which adds *"a real element of flexibility"* to the seat. In terms of responsibility, trainee tasks include preparing witness statements, reviewing documents, attending court and drafting court applications.

The mergers with Dawsons and Wedlake *"practically doubled the size"* of Penningtons' private client department, with *"every aspect of our private client work strengthened as a result. The partners from both firms also brought plenty of international work with them, which is a lot more interesting than drafting wills... although some of us do love a good will-drafting session!"* It's worth noting that nuggets of specific work can be found in each office: Basingstoke *"deals more with the contentious side"* and, along with Godalming, takes on most of the Court of Pro-

tection cases, while much of London's private client work has an international component. The firm says many of its overseas clients come from India, the US, South America, continental Europe and, increasingly, South Africa.

Aside from drafting wills, trainees prepare Lasting Powers of Attorney, deal with probate matters, carry out trusts work, handle estate and tax planning, and conduct research. Our interviewees raved about the level of client contact available in this team, with one declaring it *"among the best at the firm."* Others gave further details: *"You get to sit in regularly on client meetings, and even have the chance to take control of some as the seat progresses. By the end of it you'll be dealing with clients head-on – they'll be calling you before the partners."* This largely depends on the client: with high net worth individuals, for instance, *"you're still able to get involved but have to accept that you're not going to be the first port of call."*

Life of PI

The well-reputed PI and clin neg team is spread between Basingstoke, Godalming and London. Its clin neg work covers a number of specialist areas, including cerebral palsy and cosmetic surgery cases. On the personal injury side, there's a considerable focus on serious injury cases (mainly brain and spinal injuries and fatal accident claims), with settlement figures ranging from five-figure sums to millions of pounds.

Sources informed us that the department is *"incredibly busy,"* meaning trainees are left to handle the smaller matters – *"albeit under close supervision"* – and are in regular contact with clients. *"You're constantly on the phone to them, either to organise a meeting, ask them to provide more information, or update them on the case,"* stated one interviewee. Trainees get to experience *"all aspects of the work,"* such as preparing witness statements, drafting schedules of loss, retrieving medical records and instructing medical experts.

Penningtons' real estate division includes construction, banking and finance, property litigation, property tax and social housing (among others), with trainees often finding themselves *"doing little bits of work for lots of people."* A seat here is *"primarily commercial"* in nature but many sources had also experienced the residential side. Responsibility levels tend to vary depending on the type of work trainees are doing: *"The residential transactions are normally less complicated and shorter in duration, so you're likely to run the files yourself and see them through from beginning to end,"* an interviewee remarked. *"The commercial transactions are usually pretty large though, so you take more of a back seat on those."* Trainees carry out *"post-completion formalities,"* such as completing Land Registry applications and filing SDLT returns, but are also treated to *"all the fun stuff"* like drafting leases and negotiating lease terms.

Pens down

When we asked sources to describe the firm's culture, they unanimously declared: *"I'd say it's friendly and approachable, if that doesn't sound too out there."* We did groan a bit when they all trotted out this ultimate cliché, but our job is to report what trainees think, and Penningtons' do all agree that there's *"a brilliant buzz"* around the place. *"It's not doom and gloom at all,"* added one. *"No one dreads coming to work."*

The firm's approach to working hours plays an important part. *"None of us feel like we need to leave our jackets on the back of our chairs, or stay late just for the sake of it,"* commented a source. Indeed, most of the trainees we spoke to revealed that it's fairly rare to be in the office after 6.30pm – including those in London. *"At 7.30pm the lights go out anyway,"* one reported, *"and at that point you'll probably only have the cleaners for company."*

Penningtons' open plan set-up makes it *"incredibly easy to work well with each other and, if you'll pardon the pun, speak openly. You don't have to face the scary prospect of knocking on a partner's door, as you're sitting a few desks away from them."* It also means *"there's no sense of hierarchy here; you can joke in equal measure with partners and secretaries."*

Each office has its own sports and social committee, which is responsible for putting on several events throughout the year. London trainees spoke of quiz nights, karaoke outings, walking tours of London and a particularly memorable trip to a cooking school *"just around the corner from the office, where we learnt how to make a couple of dishes before sitting down to eat them with a few glasses of wine."* Those in Godalming mentioned evening drinks and a monthly cinema club, while trainees in Basingstoke have been showing off their sporty side lately by organising cricket and football matches.

The offices don't just keep to themselves, as departmental Christmas parties are accompanied by two firm-wide events each year: the first is an annual sports day –held in Guildford this year – involving a barbecue and *"silly sports like three-legged races,"* with the second being a spring party that usually occurs in June. There's also 'Trainee Thursday' to look forward to once a month, usually in London, in which trainees gather for a training session followed by drinks – providing *"a great excuse to catch up with everyone."*

And finally...
If you're already tempted by Penningtons' combo of commercial and private client work, then the possibility of further expansion in the near future might just seal the deal. In 2013, eight out of nine qualifiers were kept on.

Peters & Peters Solicitors LLP

The facts

Location: London

Number of UK partners/solicitors: 8/23

Partners who trained at firm: 80%

Total number of trainees: 5

Seats: notionally 4x6 months, but flexible

Alternative seats: transactional secondment

Extras: pro bono – CAB

On chambersstudent.co.uk...

How to get into Peters & Peters

The firm's different areas of work

Litigation boutique Peters & Peters is a star in the world of white-collar crime.

Handbags and gladrags

Fighting extradition? Fraud investigators at the door? Major international contract dispute looming? Unfairly cut out of a business deal? Peters & Peters is the firm you need. Its *Chambers UK* rankings indicate exactly which areas this firm practises in – fraud, corporate crime, commercial litigation and regulatory disputes – and it excels at all of them. It is also strong on corruption, competition, tax and extradition cases, as well as acting for corporations and individuals embroiled in global investigations. A typical matter might involve *"working for a massively high net worth individual in a breach of contract case."* Or *"handbags at dawn between the oligarchs,"* as one interviewee put it.

Peters & Peters is split into business crime and commercial litigation/civil fraud departments. The *"official line"* is that trainees spend two six-months seats in business crime, one in civil litigation and one on secondment to another firm or in-house in order to complete the non-contentious part of their training. In practice the system is flexible, so a trainee might spend nine or ten months in both departments, and then do a secondment that only lasts four or five months. As far as the secondments are concerned, *"some people have an idea about where they'd like to go and the firm helps them find something,"* while for others their stint away was *"something the firm suggested."* In all cases the firm organises and arranges everything.

Dirty money

In business crime, *"the vast majority of the work is white-collar crime – there is a small percentage of general crime work, but that is on the periphery of what we do."* Lawyers work on cases related to competition, corruption, insider trading, tax fraud, cartel and money laundering offences, including FCA, SFO and HMRC investigations. Extradition cases are also common: Peters & Peters has successfully helped at least 13 individuals resist extradition to Russia in recent years. Trainees get exposure to all these areas, and often work on cases from start to finish. *"I was involved with the hearing, judgment and now post-judgment proceedings of one case,"* a trainee said. *"I have also attended a police interview, where I took notes but was chiefly present because my supervisor wanted me to see how things work."* Another said: *"I started out doing document management, but as the matter progressed I found myself drafting witness statements, doing complicated bits of research and liaising with counsel in a foreign jurisdiction."*

The international nature of the work is a hallmark of Peters & Peters' practice. *"It is rare to find a case which does not have an international link,"* a trainee said. Training partner David McCluskey estimated that 65% of his clients were non-British and 90% of his cases were international. This leads to some challenging and unusual work and international travel. *"I once went with a partner to interview some witnesses, who we couldn't talk to in the country where they lived because they feared for their lives, so we had to meet in a third-party jurisdiction."*

The civil fraud and commercial litigation team acts for individuals and businesses, both as claimant and defend-

Chambers UK rankings

Competition/European Law	Dispute Resolution
Corporate Crime	Financial Services
& Investigations	Fraud
Crime	Tax

ant, often in cases involving the alleged misappropriation of large sums of money. One of the firm's biggest recent commercial cases saw it defending steel magnate Lakshmi Mittal in a suit brought by rival Manmohan Varma over the latter's alleged exclusion from a multimillion-dollar oil deal in Nigeria. The case eventually settled out of court. Lawyers also work on banking claims, insurance fraud cases, international asset tracing and things like "*a case in which the defendant was accused of artificially inflating the value of a company.*" Recently, the firm also acted for property agent Charles Lissack, who was seeking to reclaim a share of the profits made by the Manhattan Loft Corporation in refurbishing the St Pancras Renaissance Hotel, as he claimed he had introduced the opportunity to them back in the 1990s.

Trainees enjoyed their commercial seat just as much as their criminal one. "*You do stuff that associates at others firms don't do until they are three years PQE,*" one said. "*This morning I have drafted two letters, the terms of a settlement agreement and a consent order. I have a lot of client contact as well.*"

Perhaps as a result of how much Peters & Peters expects from its trainees off the bat, past work experience is common among trainees. "*The work we do is so unusual and challenging, that it's difficult to comprehend it without prior knowledge,*" a recruitment source told us. All four trainees at the time of our research had worked either as paralegals or legal researchers – three of the four at Peters & Peters itself. "*It is unusual for us to take on someone who doesn't have some sort of previous work experience,*" a recruitment source commented. Having said all this, neither of the two trainees starting in September 2013 had had paralegal experience with Peters & Peters, so it's clear there are no hard and fast rules. The application process is a challenging one, but we've got some useful hints about how to negotiate it on our website.

West End duckling to White Swan

Nearly all supervisors are partners, and trainees share an office with them for the duration of each seat. "*Sitting with a partner is great as you get to see how they talk on the telephone and so on. And if you have any questions they can always answer them.*" Workwise, trainees interact with everyone in their department, and most of the time may not be working with their supervisor. "*I think I worked with everyone within the department,*" one trainee recalled. Interviewees found their colleagues approachable and easy to ask for help and training. There is also a "*constant stream*" of internal and external training opportunities.

Interviewees put the firm's supportive training atmosphere down to the fact that "*the firm is small enough that everyone knows you by name.*" Another added: "*It is not one of those places where you just know a couple of people who you get on with. Everyone knows everyone and gets on well.*" It's no surprise that in this environment people enjoy coffee and lunches together or "*have friends from the office who you go out with on a Saturday.*" Recent socials include an outing to play table tennis and a skiing trip. More regularly, you'll find employees of the firm having a drink together at the White Swan pub just up the road.

To round off, a word on business matters. Firm revenue has been on the up recently, rising to £11.1m in 2012/13, an increase of 8.8% on the previous year. "*In the past ten or 15 years, Peters & Peters has changed its image and the move to Fetter Lane* [in 2007] *was a huge boost to that,*" one trainee believed. Previously, the firm was based in "*fashionable but shabby*" West End digs. Its new offices are pretty slick and are home to an sharp-suited partnership which takes decisions collectively. "*There is a divide in the legal profession between successful monster firms which try to be all things to all men, and successful specialists who do one thing very well. There is no doubt which we are,*" says training partner David McCluskey. According to interviewees, the firm's specialisation is serving it well post-credit crunch, and allows it to "*seek out new areas.*" A trainee explained why: "*If we haven't worked in an area related to our core expertise before, chances are that's because it's something completely new, like challenges to EU sanctions. When a case like that comes up, businesses and investigations fall back on an expert in a related field: us.*"

And finally...

In 2013 the firm kept on its single qualifier, as it did in 2012.

Pinsent Masons

The facts

Location: London, Birmingham, Manchester, Leeds, Scotland
Number of UK partners/solicitors: 317/712
Total number of trainees: 168
Seats: 4x6 months
Alternative seats: overseas seats, secondments
Extras: pro bono – Amicus, Pathways to Law, PRIME, UNIQ

On chambersstudent.co.uk...

How to get into Pinsent Masons
All about McGrigors
Interview with HR director, Jonathan Bond

Off the back of a 2012 merger and with a growing international network, Pinsent Masons now has *"the bling factor"* as well as a *"down-to-earth environment"* to give its training contract that extra sheen.

Ain't no mountain high enough!

PM combined forces with Scottish firm McGrigors in May 2012, and the resultant firm now has over 1,500 lawyers in 18 offices across the UK, mainland Europe, Asia and the Gulf. In the UK the firm has been splashing its brand around – even going so far as to advertise on the Tube – and combined firm revenue rose by 5% in 2012/13. *"The merger has worked out incredibly well in that it did what we hoped it would do,"* claims director of HR and learning Jonathan Bond. *"It was about building a greater platform for international expansion, and what McGrigors has given us is not only a stronger presence in the UK, but also in places like Qatar and the Falkland Islands – locations that complement the overseas offices we already had."* Indeed, since the merger, PM has opened shiny new offices in Munich, Paris and Istanbul (meaning that over half of its bases are now outside the UK), and trainees sensed more are likely to follow as the firm continues its upwardly mobile ascent. *"Our goal is to have a truly global reach by 2020 and we're certainly heading in the right direction. I don't know when the next overseas office is going to arrive, but it's fair to say it won't be too far off."*

Even though PM's talking big internationally, it'd be silly of us not to highlight its top-notch work at home. Our parent publication *Chambers UK* illustrates the breadth of expertise the firm has at its disposal. It chalks up dozens of rankings in areas as varied as capital markets, healthcare and pensions – not to mention its exceptional construction team, which is one of the biggest and best in the country. As if it didn't already have enough to shout about, the merger with McGrigors also beefed up PM's offering in other areas. Tax, for example, *"was the absolute jewel in the McGrigors crown,"* says Jonathan Bond. *"It's now a jewel in the crown of the new Pinsent Masons and we're delighted to be making the most of it."*

You may have read the unfortunate news that the firm has made a number of job cuts across its UK offices after three post-merger redundancy rounds, though it's worth noting these were mainly to remove duplicated roles. The latest round was the only exception to this and affected the employment practice, which Bond tells us *"needed to be restructured to meet client demands."*

Ain't no valley low enough!

At the time of our interviews, there were 60 trainees plying their trade in London, 25 in Birmingham, 24 in Leeds and 15 in Manchester. We asked insiders whether there was much chance for trainees to switch between offices to complete seats, and the overwhelming response we got was that *"it's technically possible but doesn't really happen a lot. It used to be something they went for at McGrigors, but it's not the norm now."* Still, it'd be wrong to suggest trainees never see anyone from other parts of the PM network. In fact, *"there's a lot more cross-office interaction than I thought there would be. It does vary depending on the department you're in, but you'll often see certain characters popping down to London when a massive deal is on, and some teams hold cross-office meetings and events."*

There's an extensive selection of seats on offer, and each of them belongs to one of the firm's seven core practice

Chambers UK rankings

Administrative & Public Law	Licensing
	Life Sciences
Banking & Finance	Local Government
Capital Markets	Media & Entertainment
Charities	Outsourcing
Competition/European Law	Parliamentary & Public
Construction	Affairs
Corporate Crime &	Partnership
Investigations	Pensions
Corporate/M&A	Pensions Litigation
Data Protection	Planning
Dispute Resolution	Private Client
Education	Private Equity
Employee Share Schemes	Professional Negligence
& Incentives	Projects
Employment	Public Procurement
Energy & Natural	Real Estate
Resources	Restructuring/Insolvency
Environment	Retail
Fraud	Shipping
Health & Safety	Social Housing
Information Technology	Tax
Insurance	Transport
Intellectual Property	

groups: construction advisory and disputes; corporate; financial institutions and human capital; property; litigation and compliance; projects; and strategic business services. Trainees list three preferences before each rotation and, on the whole, interviewees felt the process *"is as transparent as it can be. It's easy to whine if you don't get your first choice, but sometimes you have to take that on the chin. As you go along, you're more likely to get your top preference."* What's more, *"there is a slight element of networking involved"* and one trainee advised: *"It never hurts to let a department know you really want to work for them."*

Ain't no river wide enough!

Pinsent Masons has a stellar reputation in the construction arena. The practice employs nearly 200 specialist lawyers, making it the biggest construction team in the country, and handles both advisory and contentious matters – clients include Thames Water, the London School of Economics and Westfield. The firm acts for 18 of the UK's top 20 contractors and over half of the world's top 50, and has had a hand in some truly mega infrastructure projects, from Wembley Stadium to the London Array wind farm in the Thames Estuary. A stint in construction litigation entails *"a lot of research"* and, although there are the usual trainee tasks to carry out (bundling, proof-reading), this is balanced out by more exciting undertak-

ings like *"drafting pieces for adjudications and arbitrations."*

Projects is *"kind of a hybrid seat,"* according to one insider. *"You have some work related to LLP and joint venture agreements, but there's also an energy and regeneration side of things."* Another chipped in: *"It's all about facilitating the contracts and sub-contracts, and making sure that if something goes wrong the parties involved are able to seek redress."* Our sources reported *"doing plenty of research into technical points of law,"* *"putting together advice papers"* and *"going along to negotiations."* There's a *"decent amount of client contact"* too, *"whether it be a conference call or face-to-face meeting."*

Those who spent time in corporate described the work there as *"short, sharp and sexy."* (Try saying that without sounding like Sean Connery.) In London, the team advises on the likes of IPOs, corporate governance and M&A deals in both a domestic and cross-border context, and has a growing presence in the natural resources and energy sectors (as demonstrated by instructions from clients like Regal Petroleum and Sirius Minerals). The Brum team recently acted for UK Coal on its £20.3m sale of Harworth Power, while Leeds lawyers have been advising Lupus Capital on the £75m sale of the group's oil services division to Phoenix Equity Partners. Trainees mentioned drafting board minutes and ancillary documents, managing due diligence, attending completion meetings and *"keeping on top of hundreds of documents and checklists."* Project management was deemed *"the worst part of the seat,"* but it was agreed corporate is *"a good seat to start off in because you're kept really busy throughout and get to learn about how big companies operate."*

PM's banking practice, part of the financial institutions division, has a strong reputation in areas like leveraged finance, corporate lending, syndicated finance and property finance. The team represents several major institutions including HSBC, Santander and BNP Paribas, and in 2012 it acted for Lloyds TSB and Sweden's Handelsbanken on the £49m refinancing of international engineering group Renold. *"Things move incredibly quickly"* in this seat and trainees' sleeping habits can take a turn for the worse, as one declared: *"They're probably the longest hours I'm ever going to work, and you end up staying especially late when the deals are drawing to a close."* However, our interviewees were keen to stress the fact that *"you're seen as a crucial member of the team straight away."*

The employment team deals with a multitude of issues, including high-profile senior departures, restrictive covenants and redundancies. Trainees who had completed this seat *"absolutely loved it,"* which is understandable given the department's fabulous list of clients – John Lewis, Manchester United, Bupa and Monsoon Accessorize are just a few of the big names the team works for. The group advised Jack Wills on the employment implications surrounding the axing of its Aubin & Wills brand, as well as counselling the Ministry of Justice on various projects involving the transfer of prisons to the private sector. There's contentious work too. One trainee reported: *"I got to go out to tribunals with counsel and drafted pretty much every document arising from the tribunal process."* Another said that they had spent their time preparing witness statements, conducting research and *"constantly updating clients on what was happening with their respective cases."*

To keep me from you!

Trainees usually aren't able to go on secondment until their second year but, once they are able to, many take up the opportunity. The firm says roughly 25% of its trainees undertake a secondment during their training contract. Secondments are open to individuals in all locations and stints at BP, John Lewis and RBS are among the available options. On top of these, there's a chance to do an overseas seat in either Dubai or the Falkland Islands – the second of these is McGrigors legacy – and trainees speculated that more locations could be on the cards soon. Jonathan Bond added: *"We're looking at not only having trainees from the UK spending time overseas, but also welcoming trainees from other offices to the UK – like Hong Kong, for example. There'll definitely be an increasing number of overseas opportunities for trainees in future, but it's something we want to think about carefully."*

Over a year on from the merger, legacy PM and McGrigors trainees agreed *"personality-wise both sides fit perfectly together. A lot of people waffled on about how we were aligned in terms of values and all that, but it actually turned out to be true. Everyone's fun and down-to-earth, and there's always a bit of banter being thrown about."* While most said that *"you can't really tell the legacy Pinsent Masons and McGrigors people apart,"* a few of sources could still differentiate between the two. *"Most departments have been integrated quite nicely, but of course there are some that are either Pinsent-heavy or McGrigors-heavy,"* revealed one, *"and some old-school partners still treat the firm as if it's two separate entities."* Nonetheless, the vast majority said there had been

"a pretty smooth transition overall" and praised PM for *"retaining a regional feel despite the great heights we're striving towards."*

In London, trainees purred approvingly about their *"plush"* Crown Place office which, in addition to having *"uninterrupted and fantastic"* views of the City, houses *"lovely and convenient"* shower rooms, a Costa coffee *"where you can head for a drink and a quick chat,"* and a subsidised restaurant on the seventh floor. The latter has *"excellent food cooked up by a superb chef"* – the *"Thursday roast"* and *"Wednesday home-made burgers"* were both recommended by our interviewees. Mancunians are based on the top floor of a 16-storey high-rise in the *"really lively"* Spinningfields areas. *"Our office has a similar feel to the Crown Place one,"* trainees noted. *"We've got our own little deli and Costa coffee on site, and there's a gym underneath the building so you can nip down there in your lunch break."* The Leeds base has recently been quasi-revamped. *"We have an amazing terrace overlooking the city, with a stylish and arty coffee shop attached to it. On a summer's evening it's a great place to entertain."* By contrast, PM's Birmingham office is in a *"bog-standard"* building with *"decor that looks like it's from the 1980s... it's fair to say it do could do with some work."* It's also the only office not to have a 'fully' open-plan layout.

PM trainees enjoy a healthy social life at the firm and *"you'll always find someone who's up for a drink after work on a Friday."* As for the ex-McGrigors lot, they're *"a bunch of party animals"* apparently, and plenty of legacy PM trainees had joined them on *"some brilliant nights out"* since the merger. Londoners shared stories with us of an *"awesome"* Christmas bash, a range of sports activities (including a softball team *"which never wins any matches"*) and *"a wonderful party held in our auditorium to celebrate the merger's one-year anniversary."* Things are just as merry outside the City, with Brum trainees partaking in regular football, netball and cricket matches, the Manchester crew putting on charity bake sales and fancy dress shindigs, and those in Leeds hosting summer barbecues and drinks on their office's rooftop terrace.

And finally...

Pinsent Masons is *"growing and has a lot of ambition,"* and trainees mused *"it's an exciting time to hop on board."* In 2013, the firm kept on 68 of its 84 qualifying trainees.

Reed Smith LLP

The facts

Location: London

Number of UK partners/solicitors: 113/183 (+2 non-UK qualified)

UK partners who trained at firm: 45%

Total number of trainees: 49

Seats: 4x6 months

Alternative Seats: overseas seats, secondments

Extras: pro bono – 50 hours per year expectation, Queen Mary Legal Advice Centre, Dellow Centre, A4ID; language classes

On chambersstudent.co.uk...

How to get into Reed Smith

Interview with training principal Peter Hardy

As the largest office of this US heavyweight, Reed Smith London plays a significant part in a wider global network.

A special relationship

Reed Smith is a big firm. Originally a Pittsburgh operation, it now has 25 offices spanning three continents. Its London arm was born out of a 2007 merger with an old-established City firm named Richards Butler and currently houses more than 290 attorneys.

"The best way to define Reed Smith in London is as an Anglo-American firm," trainees argued. *"Yes, we're under the banner of an American name, but considering our heritage and the fact that we're the largest office worldwide, there's a balance between cultures. The established Richards Butler culture is still prominent. We don't adhere to that 'American firm' stereotype at all. The hours aren't horrible and people aren't aggressive. We're far more akin to the silver circle."* One source even joked that London was the firm's *"rogue"* office, before quickly adding: *"That doesn't mean we're not connected or integrated with the US. We don't have that 'beast you and then spit you out' mentality, but we do get a lot of excellent benefits that come with being part of a large international operation. The work coming through is of a very high level and we're consistently being exposed to international law."* For his part, training principal Peter Hardy says: *"We see ourselves as an international firm, rather than an American firm."*

Despite a post-merger push to build up the corporate department, Reed Smith's *Chambers UK* rankings still reflect Richards Butler's historic reputation as a jack of all trades but with a particularly strong grounding in litigation. A top-notch shipping group is perhaps the jewel, but other rankings come in many other areas, from banking to

media; life sciences to pensions. This really is your classic all-rounder.

Of course, some areas are more central to the business than others, and Reed Smith London stated key client sectors are shipping, energy & natural resources, financial services and media/technology. Peter Hardy says: *"The firm continues to make significant investments in our core sectors. In the last year we've opened offices in Singapore and Houston. Houston is, of course, one of the geographical centres for energy work, while Singapore will allow us to build on our shipping and trade capabilities."*

Departments at Reed Smith fall under larger *"umbrella"* groups – the financial industries group (FIG); commercial disputes; corporate (which includes media, private equity and M&A); shipping; and energy & natural resources.

Trainees entering their final seat get priority when it comes to choosing where they want to go, followed by those entering their third seat and so on down the line. Predictably therefore, *"you're probably not very likely to get even your second or third choice as a first-year,"* trainees said, *"but that's how it should be."* Second-seaters onwards can select preferences from *"not only specific subgroups, but supervisors as well, so you can really request a speciality."* The SRA's contentious requirement can be satisfied by taking seats in general litigation, certain shipping teams, employment and certain energy practices. *"There are also a litigation-based client secondment."* Beyond this, *"seat choice is relatively free. Of course you're not guaranteed anything, but on the whole the HR team is very good at listening to your choices and reasons."*

Chambers UK rankings

Banking & Finance	Information Technology
Banking Litigation	Insurance
Commodities	Intellectual Property
Competition/European Law	Life Sciences
Construction	Media & Entertainment
Corporate/M&A	Pensions
Data Protection	Product Liability
Defamation/Reputation	Professional Negligence
Management	Public International Law
Dispute Resolution	Real Estate Finance
Employment	Shipping
Fraud	

Casting off

Shipping *"is a big department for the firm."* The 'wet' shipping team deals with accidents at sea and is informally known as 'the Admiralty', as it's filled with ex-mariners who've re-trained as lawyers. Among the recent accidents they've helped to mop up have been the groundings of the containership 'Bareli' off the coast of China in March 2012, and the freighters 'Sunrise' and 'Celia', beached near Valencia later the same year. The 'dry' work is almost entirely litigious and revolves around contract claims and disputes, but *"there's also the occasional drafting of charter parties and contracts carriage type work."* Interviewees agreed: *"You're always slightly worried going into the department for the first time, and the initial lingo is completely confusing, but you'll have your 'shipping law moment', when it all clicks."* The majority of trainees are placed in the various dry groups and all were extremely happy with the levels of responsibility afforded to them. *"It's one of the best departments in the firm for substantive trainee work,"* one said. *"We have several paralegals in the group, so you're never stuck with endless photocopying. The cases and value of the claims tend to be smaller, so there's more scope for trainees to be trusted."* Another added: *"You really either sink or swim, for want of a better phrase. It is a really steep learning curve and the department expects you to perform."*

The large FIG group covers insolvency/restructuring, funds, regulation, banking finance, structured finance and real estate finance, and is *"a growth sector"* for the firm. *"Although we're currently on one floor, the practice is definitely growing out of the space. The different groups are distinct entities, but there are constant overlaps of work, so a trainee can get exposure to a variety of practices."* Responsibility levels tend to vary and *"definitely"* grow in the third and fourth seats. *"Most people tend to leave about 8.30 to 9pm in this department,"* trainees divulged. *"We're a busy department and it's the price you pay for interesting work."*

Enter the dragon

The mid-market corporate group has worked on some interesting deals. It helped *Dragons' Den* investor Theo Paphitis, through a newly incorporated entity named Gladys Emmanuel, acquire the home appliance retailer Robert Dyas, and advised AIM-listed emerald producer Gemfields on its acquisition by way of merger of Fabergé, of egg fame. Officially a subgroup of the corporate department, the always-popular media and technology department is *"fairly small, but a big pull for applicants"* and as such is competitive to get into. It is predominantly a transactional practice, working on film financing, production and artist agreements and advertising. The group advises McDonald's on advertising and marketing law and is representing Virgin Media in anti-piracy blocking cases. Trainees receive good responsibility. *"It's an extremely busy department and if you show you can handle the substantive work, you'll be given it. It's probably a better department in your third or fourth seat, as it's incredibly fast-moving."*

The energy and natural resources department *"has grown massively over the last couple of years,"* trainees observed. It was originally an offshoot of shipping, but now has 17 partners of its own. Trainees have sat more on the litigation side in the past, though there are several transactional groups too. *"The transactional work is taking off, such as derivatives trading and renewables work."* The department also includes environment, construction and projects lawyers. The firm recently advised Kellogg Brown & Root in multimillion-dollar court proceedings against Fina Antwerp Olefins relating to an ethane production plant in Antwerp.

There are several secondments available, both in overseas offices and with the firm's clients. *"They are popular, but never impossible to get on. If you're interested, there's a good chance you'll get to go on one at some point during your two years."* All secondments require trainees to make a formal application and do an interview, *"but it's never a very stressful process."* Overseas placements can include Paris, Abu Dhabi, Dubai and Piraeus. Dubai is the only litigation seat. *"For a shipping seat, obviously you need to head to Greece."* Trainees raved about the options, saying: *"It's absolutely fantastic how much is on offer, and they're always looked on very favourably by the firm. You can also potentially qualify abroad."* Training principal Peter Hardy says: *"We intend to keep all those secondments we currently have, but are also looking to Singapore and the US. All could be wonderful opportunities for the trainees, but we have to adhere to SRA requirements and decide whether such secondments will add value to the business."*

Actions for justice

"Every department has its own atmosphere at Reed Smith," trainees said. *"Shipping's more traditional, real estate's slightly quieter, whereas FIG, energy and media tend to be a bit chattier and sociable."* On the whole, however, *"people are extremely down to earth. We're a good size, so you'll always see faces you know and everyone is very respectful of each other."* Trainees also confirmed that they'd made *"real friends"* at the firm. *"We were all in the same class at law school, so you come in having made good relationships with people. We even see each other at weekends."*

Socially, *"there's a lot on offer,"* with football, cricket and netball teams, language classes including a popular French business course, a choir, and not one but two *"excellent"* bands. *"They're called Class Actions and Rough Justice – brilliant legal names,"* sources laughed. *"They include a couple of partners and are actually really good."* Interviewees also praised the *"great"* summer barbecue on the roof terrace. Informally, trainees *"regularly meet up and you'll always find someone in the bars of Broadgate Circle."*

Pro bono is *"really encouraged"* and our sources had taken part in several projects. *"The pro bono co-ordinator sends out e-mails every day and you're pushed to take part. Your contribution is also taken into account in your bonus review."* There's also the option of a three-month secondment to human rights charity Liberty through the litigation department.

Rigorous selection

Although not a prerequisite to getting a training contract, Reed Smith does hire *"quite heavily"* from its vac scheme. The firm has two vac scheme places for candidates with disabilities. *"They invest a lot in the two weeks and choose people very carefully for it."* Peter Hardy says: *"We have seen some hugely talented people coming in at entry level. The standard of academic results has gone up and hugely impressive backgrounds and credentials are now a given."* Trainees agreed that you'll need top marks, but stressed that Reed Smith *"looks outside the box. It's not all Oxbridge people, and you don't have to be getting a double First to get a look-in."* One source said: *"Reed Smith wants people who are gregarious and interesting. A lot of people here are well travelled, and good at connecting with others."*

The qualification process is an equally thorough experience. All applicants submit a CV and cover letter for each department, which is followed by interviews. Certain departments also require case studies and presentations. *"It's a really long process here, and can get frustratingly difficult, but it's as fair as it can be,"* trainees reflected. *"There aren't any backhand offers and you know what's going on at every step."* There were grumblings about the length of the process, which the firm is aware of – Hardy says: *"We are very sensitive to the tension qualification creates. We believe we have a system that as far as humanly possible provides for equal opportunity."* 26 out of 32 qualifiers were retained in 2013, and sources added that *"Reed Smith is really good at also helping those they didn't take on. The HR team looks out for you and people have successfully found other jobs through client and departmental connections."*

And finally...

Reed Smith is one of the first firms requiring students to take up the new combined LPC/MA course at BPP. Peter Hardy says: *"We believe this will ensure an absolute commitment to clients and increased business awareness. It will give future trainees an advantage from day one."*

"Always keep thinking about networking. Just because you start a training contract doesn't mean you should rest on your laurels. Keep being that person who was so impressive in the first place that they got a training contract."

City training partner

Chambers UK rankings

Banking Litigation	Insurance
Clinical Negligence	Intellectual Property
Construction	Life Sciences
Corporate Crime &	Media & Entertainment
Investigations	Partnership
Defamation/Reputation	Product Liability
Management	Professional Discipline
Dispute Resolution	Professional Negligence
Education	Real Estate
Employment	Retail
Health & Safety	Tax
Information Technology	

presentation on what they're currently working on and what trainees can expect. It gives you an idea of everything the firm is doing."

The general liability and medical insurance team primarily works for defendants on *"medical negligence and high-value personal injury claims. We represent the insurers of doctors, nurses, chiropractors, spiritual healers – literally all sorts!"* Due to their confidential nature we can't give you the scoop on any juicy cases, but trainees were highly impressed by the seat. *"I was thrown into interesting tasks straight away and by the third week I was phoning up clients and taking statements myself,"* said one. Another said: *"The associates I sat with were very keen to get me involved. I was drafting instructions to counsel and experts, looking at policy reviews and assessing claims. I even went along to trial and lots of hearings. There wasn't much bundling at all, thank goodness!"* The professional negligence team works for professionals in the financial, insurance, construction, legal and technology sectors. *"Partners were really keen to get me involved, take me along to meetings and allow me to draft documents for clients,"* a trainee said of the seat. *"There's a lot of interesting and weird cases which aren't run-of-the-mill. Recently I've seen a wasted costs case against a solicitor and I've done lots of negligence claims against tax advisers. There's also a real push at the moment for the more complicated, higher-value cases."*

Both the real estate and construction departments have contentious and non-contentious offerings. Each facet has been helping to advise Hadley Mace on the Heart of East Greenwich development, an urban renewal project set to create 650 new homes as well as health and leisure facilities. On the construction insurance side, trainees said: *"Our main clients are big contractors, but we also work for private clients – usually wealthy individuals who built holiday homes or annexes and things have gone wrong with damp or their planning permission."* The real estate litigation team counts Sports Direct as a long-term client and recently acted for the retailer in relation to its acqui-

sition of 19 stores from failed rival JJB in a case worth £25m. On the financial side, RPC advised Student Cribs on the formation of a property investment fund for the acquisition of student accommodation throughout the UK. *"I was dealing with the Land Registry Office on a regular basis and filling in stamp duty,"* a second-year informed us of the seat. *"However, I also ran my own file involving a significant transaction. I was doing all the paperwork for the completion of a property sale."* Another said: *"If you do a good piece of work they let you send it out in your name so the client will come back to you. It meant a partner at another firm rang me directly, which was great!"* Real estate also has a bit of rep for being *"the most social seat."*

Tissue issues

Training principal Simon Goldring told us that RPC's commercial group – which takes on a broad spread of work, from corporate/M&A and real estate, to commercial litigation and IP –*"had its best ever year, and for the first time contributed more than 50% of the firm's turnover."* The team mainly handles mid-market deals for clients such as Fox News, HMV and the Daily Mail Group, but it sees some mammoth transactions as well. Recently, it advised Sweden's SCA Hygiene Products on its $1.32bn acquisition of Georgia-Pacific's European tissue operations in 22 jurisdictions. Trainees offered mixed opinions of their time in the seat. *"It was classic corporate,"* reflected one. *"You get some quiet weeks, but then also some really long hours. I generally got good responsibility and was very clearly told what I needed to do, which is crucial on big deals otherwise you can get lost."* Unfortunately another source felt much more out of the loop: *"I wasn't included in any internal meetings. I was just given discrete tasks and didn't know the context or what value I was adding, which was a bit demoralising. I understand the pace of the work means there isn't always time to sit down with the trainee, but I still would have appreciated feeling more involved in the bigger picture."* In all fairness, that source did add: *"I worked on a couple of banking deals which were completely different. They were much more interesting purely because the associates involved gave me a lot more responsibility."*

A seat with the media group is *"always popular"* as the team *"works for a lot of the national newspapers and high-profile tech clients, primarily on defamation, privacy and contempt of court claims brought by people in the public eye."* The roster of clients RPC hold in this area is mightily impressive – News International, *The Financial Times*, Amazon, Google (including YouTube), Twitter and Betfair are just some that roll off the tongue. The defamation/reputation management branch is the real star – it picks up top recognition from *Chambers UK* – and it recently played a key role in advising Associated Newspapers (in particular its *Daily Mail, Mail Online* and *Mail on Sunday* titles) throughout the Leveson Inquiry. *"It's a very busy seat,"* a source informed us. *"The claims aren't always worth a huge amount so they can be very short. There are some menial tasks, like bundling, photocopying and logistics, but they give you the chance to take the lead on some smaller claims too. On bigger cases I also got to draft quite a lot of court documents like applications for the defence."* IP is another seat that is *"incredibly popular"* across intakes. The team mainly focuses on trade mark, copyright and design litigation but handles transactional work as well. Clients hail from the sports, media, technology, retail, insurance and pharmaceutical sectors, and names such as Newcastle United FC, Dunlop, Waterstones and the National Trust all seek out RPC's expertise. *"You get involved in good work from day one,"* chirped a happy trainee. *"It's not sitting down doing the photocopying. I was drafting witness statements and pleadings, but the best thing was that I could do research, give feedback and offer opinions on the matter at hand. They really got me involved with team meetings and there's no separation in roles. Everyone works together."*

If you're desperate to get experience outside of RPC HQ, then there's the opportunity to go on secondment to the in-house teams of certain construction, IP and media clients. *"It's a case of speaking to the relevant partner and then they'll take it up with HR and discuss who is best for the role,"* explained a second-year. *"The only prerequisite is that you've done the relevant seat beforehand."*

Rules are made to be broken

Our sources were adamant that the open-plan offices *"make a massive difference"* to the trainee experience. *"It's the best thing about RPC,"* eulogised one. *"It's been incredibly valuable sitting with partners and senior associates and it's a great learning experience just to sit and listen to them."* Another appreciated the integrated atmosphere it creates. *"You get to know each other very quickly. It's not like you're having to wander up and down the corridors knocking on doors to introduce yourself to everyone. People just do the meerkat and pop their head up over the pod, which makes it more social."*

This also plays a central role in what trainees described as a *"collaborative"* culture. *"There's a sense everyone is working together and there's definitely an effort to encourage team-playerism,"* offered one noun-inventing source. *"Everyone helps each other out and the degree you see different partners from different departments interacting is great."* With the current intake seeing their training contracts play out during a time of transition for RPC, some worried its favourable aspects may be diluted. *"As we're growing so rapidly and there have been a number of lateral hires, there is concern over the culture,"* explained a second-year. *"It hasn't changed yet, but you do sense there will be a discernible shift."* Another source added: *"As RPC moves towards being full-service and tries to*

get in the bigger, higher-value work, you do anticipate the hours might become longer and the atmosphere won't be quite as relaxed." Simon Goldring was quick to allay such fears: *"Growth generated through laterals always carries the risk of people coming in who don't share our culture, but that's so far not been a problem at RPC,"* he says. *"Senior management are rigorous in making sure that any new hire is a cultural fit with RPC, and their judgement has proven to be spot on over the years."* Other trainees did echo Goldring's sentiments. *"To be an integrated firm with one culture is very important to senior management and it shows in the people they hire,"* commented one.

Reynolds Porter and the Chamberlain of Secrets

One way in which the culture is safeguarded is through RPC's Hogwarts-style house system, which sees each lawyer placed into either 'Reynolds', 'Porter' or 'Chamberlain'. The houses compete in a variety of competitions and quizzes throughout the year in aid of charity and – more importantly – for the glory of winning the house cup. *"It's a great way to get to know people who you might not work with every day,"* concluded a source. *"The firm-wide competitions also allow everyone to have an evening together and there's always a great atmosphere."* The much-vaunted 'RPC's Got Talent' night is the *"highlight of the social calendar"* and sees a range of credible and novelty acts unleash their own brand of on-stage wizardry. One embarrassed source mumbled about a *"terrible"* dance they'd performed to a well-known pop hit. *"It was highly humiliating."* It's not entirely fun and games though: apparently each house is *"very competitive."*

The buzzword *"innovative"* is currently flitting around RPC so much that it's to the chagrin of some. *"You actually get a bit fed up of hearing how innovative and incredible we are,"* joked one source. We asked Simon Goldring what this – along with recruitment phrases such as 'Ripping up the rule book' and 'Breaking the mould' – actually says about life at the firm. *"What we really mean is that we think that the traditional approach to delivering legal services has had its day, and at RPC we're looking to create something new and refreshing, fit for the future needs of our clients,"* he told us. *"We genuinely want to facilitate trainees to bring in their own ideas to the firm, to be dynamic and improve what we offer. Aside from work we see trainees putting on fantastic shows at the Christmas party, rolling up their sleeves for our charity work and setting up new clubs. We're trying to foster an environment where they have the confidence to be individuals and do innovative things, as it gives them all the kinds of skill like communication and project management which are necessary to be a good lawyer."* As such, sources agreed that *"as long as you are enthusiastic and keen to jump in with both feet – whether that means with bundling or just trying your hand at something new – then RPC will like you. We're not looking for shrinking violets, but neither are we looking for Sir Alan Sugar's apprentices. RPC wants people who can work in a team without being abrasive."*

And finally...

RPC has historically excellent retention rates. *"We're very rigorous in our recruitment, ensuring we bring in the best possible people with the expectation they will stay on and develop their careers at RPC,"* says Simon Goldring. *"We're pleased that this has been borne out in our retention figures over the last few years."* In 2013, 13 of 16 qualifiers were retained.

SGH Martineau LLP

The facts

Location: Birmingham, London
Number of UK partners/solicitors: 56/79
Partners who trained at firm: 20%
Total number of trainees: 17
Seats: 6x4 months
Alternative seats: occasional client secondments

On chambersstudent.co.uk...

How to get into SGHM
A beginner's guide to Birmingham

A Birmingham native that's gradually making strides in London, Martineau offers *"high-quality work without the horrible hours."*

Weighing up the facts

'So, what can you tell us about SGH Martineau?' we asked its trainees. *"Well, we're a heavyweight Brummie firm with international ambitions,"* replied one, *"and recently merged with a firm in London "giving us a stronger presence in the capital."* It's a decent answer – let's examine it more closely. December 2011 saw Martineau combine forces with City-based firm Sprecher Grier Halberstam to form SGH Martineau, which did considerably strengthen its existing London presence. The move also bulked up several of Martineau's key practices such as corporate and real estate, and the merged entity today employs over 300 staff and has turnover in excess of £30m.

In October of the same year, the firm demonstrated the international ambitions our source was talking about by opening a Brussels office in collaboration with Germany's Becker Buttner Held, housing a team of energy and competition law specialists.

The only word we might take slight issue with in our source's quote is 'heavyweight'. While certainly no minnow, Martineau is a medium-sized outfit in a competitive Birmingham market and, while it has plenty of *Chambers UK* rankings to its name, the majority of them are in the second or third tiers of the tables dedicated to the Midlands – the top tiers are dominated by big nationals like DLA Piper, Eversheds and Pinsent Masons. So 'middleweight' might be a better description. The firm does stand out for its education practice though, and is considered to be one of the best in the country at acting for colleges and universities (the latter accounts for around 15% of the firm's overall work). For the record, Martineau concentrates on seven industry sectors in particular. These are:

banking and restructuring; energy; private wealth; investment funds; education; industry and manufacturing; and leisure.

Trainees complete six four-month seats, which *"gives you the opportunity to get a flavour of many different areas of law. The only downside is that, when you feel like you're just getting to grips with the work, you get whisked away into another seat – although if you end up doing a seat that you don't enjoy, it means you can get out of there fairly quickly!"* While the system allows for trainees to pursue a spread of interests, it's worth bearing in mind that *"you can potentially repeat a seat in the department you're hoping to qualify into."* Trainees have to complete a corporate, a property and a contentious seat, but some seats satisfy two of these requirements at once.

First seats *"aren't really discussed,"* but *"the decision is usually based on your background and previous working experience."* For the remaining seats, trainees sit down with the HR team before each rotation and discuss where they would like to go next. Managing partner Bill Barker has also *"become highly involved in the process and helps to determine a sensible route for trainees."* A second-year explained: *"It's all well and good tailoring your training contract towards something you're interested in, but if the chances of qualifying into that area are slim then what's the point?"*

99p acquisition

The property team *"occupies more floor space than any other department,"* meaning it can accommodate a lot of trainees at once, and is *"a really common place to end up for your first seat."* Our sources felt that *"there's plenty*

Chambers UK rankings

Agriculture & Rural Affairs	Employment
Banking & Finance	Family/Matrimonial
Charities	Intellectual Property
Construction	Private Client
Corporate/M&A	Professional Negligence
Dispute Resolution	Real Estate
Education	Restructuring/Insolvency

of work to go around and you're not simply a small cog in the machine. One minute you might be helping out on a mega-deal, while the next you could be drafting a lease or liaising with the Land Registry. You also get to manage your own files from beginning to end, so you're certainly given a fair amount of responsibility." Interviewees informed us that work "comes through various avenues," with the department focusing mainly on the education, finance, leisure and energy sectors. Martineau acted for the University of West London on the multimillion-pound sale of its Crescent Road campus in Reading, and is assisting 99p Stores with its acquisition of seven shops from the Co-operative. Other noteworthy clients include Heineken and Lloyds TSB. If a 'traditional' property seat doesn't sound up your street, then it can be avoided by spending time in property disputes – a department that primarily handles work in the retail sector, advising household names such as Claire's Accessories and Wetherspoon's.

The commercial disputes group "has grown to become one of the biggest departments at the firm" and "acts for a multitude of clients, from gigantic energy corporations to rich individuals involved in settlement disagreements." It recently defended London South Bank University in a £1.8m damages claim, based on numerous allegations including racism, harassment and assault – all of which were dismissed with costs awarded in the university's favour. The team also represents French chemical corporation Air Liquide and Accrington Stanley FC, among others. One trainee remarked that "there's never a dull day during this seat" but, according to another, that isn't strictly true: "You do spend quite a bit of time doing bundles, which is the most boring aspect of the work... but hey, it's got to be done." Trainees also get to carry out more exciting tasks, like drafting consent orders and attending settlement meetings, and may even be given the chance to run their own matters.

Trainees that complete a seat in construction get to experience a mix of contentious and non-contentious work. The department has lots of energy and education clients, and has recently focused its efforts on a number of universities, venture capital trusts and developers in the renewable energy market, advising on the likes of wind and solar projects. "You're heavily involved in drafting things

like construction contracts and warranties," sources said, "but at the same time you're just trying to wrap your head around the work in general... it's not exactly a straightforward area of law." On the contentious side, trainee tasks range from drafting court letters to conducting background research for impending court cases.

With great power comes great responsibility

The energy, projects and commerce seat falls under the firm's commercial banner alongside education, employment and pensions, and IP and technology. The team acts for two of the 'big six' energy suppliers – npower and EDF Energy – as well as the British electricity and gas giant National Grid. It assisted the latter with contract issues concerning the newly opened East-West Interconnector, which links the power grids of Ireland and Britain (allowing electricity to be bought and sold between the two countries). The 'projects and commerce' part of the seat "covers general commercial matters," such as drafting website terms and conditions, reviewing commercial contracts and addressing client queries. On the energy side, trainees take on plenty of research and draft agreements that "often have a commercial outlook – hence the firm combining it with projects and commerce." Regardless of the type of work they were doing, our interviewees had no complaints about the amount of responsibility that was given to them: "You're kept really busy throughout and, although the work does get checked by your supervisor, it's not like they rewrite the whole thing before sending it off to the client."

Trainees enjoy IP and technology for the "brilliant spread of work" on offer which, like construction, includes both contentious and non-contentious matters. The Chambers-ranked IP team deals with licensing and infringement cases on behalf of universities, and handles trade mark, design and patent matters for trendy clothing brands like Californian fashion retailer Wet Seal and Scottish knitwear outfit Lyle & Scott. The technology side "mostly relates to data protection and other similar issues," with the group advising education clients on IT, web and social media matters.

We mustn't forget that "Martineau is one of the major players in Birmingham when it comes to private client work," a claim supported by the fact that Chambers UK regards its private client practice as one of the best in the Midlands. The department acts for wealthy individuals and families with landed estates, and also specialises in personal injury trusts – where clients have received large sums of compensation after serious accidents. Although our interviewees didn't have their own cases to manage, they did agree that "the team is very accommodating and more than happy to let trainees get stuck into the work. Whereas some departments are either too busy or too *quiet, private client sits perfectly in the middle."* Trainees draft wills and deeds of appointment, prepare Lasting Powers of Attorney, and *"work on the nitty-gritty tax issues that inevitably come up when dealing with estates."* There's also plenty of client contact available, with trainees regularly attending meetings. *"It seems to me that you get to know the clients a lot better in this seat,"* commented one. *"A lot of the time you're only working for an individual, so you really feel like you're directly affecting their lives."*

The corporate choices in Birmingham are M&A, banking and corporate finance, while trainees can travel to London to spend time in banking, corporate or a banking/commercial litigation mixed seat.

New look

Reflecting on the 2011 merger, sources told us that *"it sometimes feels like it never actually happened, as we're all primarily based in Birmingham and most of us don't travel to London very often. Culturally there hasn't exactly been a massive transformation, so it's difficult to pin down what has changed – apart from the branding."* However, with the promise that graduates will be recruited directly into the London office from 2014 onwards, the firm might begin to attract a different breed of trainee. In London trainees can spend time in restructuring and insolvency, real estate or commercial disputes. One source mused: *"There's a possibility we'll adopt the more aggressive nature that City firms are known for having – but fingers crossed it remains a nice place to work."* Two trainees have already qualified into the London office.

We're willing to bet, however, that Martineau will retain its pleasant working environment, where there's *"no sense of anybody trying to step on other people's toes. You can quite easily have a conversation with partners about the football that was on at the weekend, and there's certainly room for a bit of downtime in between work."* Indeed, the vast majority of those we spoke to had chosen the firm because of its reputation for providing a good work/life balance: *"I applied to the main firms in Birmingham, but was especially on the lookout for the ones that appreciate a life outside of work,"* said one. *"Martineau was top of my list in that regard and it hasn't disappointed. I haven't found myself constantly in the office until late and, most importantly, I've never had to work weekends."*

The Birmingham HQ occupies two floors of No 1 Colmore Square, at one end of Brum's main lawyer drag. It's *"an ideal location for commuters,"* as it's situated opposite Snow Hill station. *"Clients are definitely impressed when they walk through the door, particularly when they enter our state-of-the-art reception area which is draped in orange and grey,"* interviewees agreed, veering slightly into estate-agent-speak. Orange and grey are the the firm's corporate colours, by the way. Employees sit in pods of four, though partners *"usually sit around them by the windows,"* including MP Bill Barker. There are also quiet rooms and break-out areas on each floor which have *"snack machines, sofas and free fruit."* Trainees visiting Martineau's London base at One America Square, near Tower Hill, are provided with nearby accommodation.

A couple of social secretaries are elected every year to organise events. *"They're usually pretty inventive, and mix it up quite a bit in terms of where we go on a Friday,"* revealed one source. *"My personal favourite is probably Primitivo, a snazzy wine bar that's only a few minutes away from the Birmingham office – although it tends to get pretty busy in there."* There's also the Birmingham Trainee Solicitors Society, which *"the firm is heavily involved in"* and *"has something going on every week or so."* Following the merger, Martineau arranged a 'firm away day' in Oxfordshire in an attempt to get the two offices to mingle. *"We got to do a bunch of outdoor activities like clay pigeon shooting, archery, go-kart racing and falconry, and they also put on a massive barbecue with a free bar. It was very well organised and didn't involve any horrible team-building exercises."* While this hasn't yet turned into a annual event, some trainees speculated that more firm-wide events could be on the horizon – *"there's been talk of a summer ball, for instance."*

The True Picture

And finally...

It may not be a heavyweight, but with a broad range of seat options, a strong standing in several sectors and a healthy work/life balance, SGH Martineau has a lot to offer. In 2013, eight out of 11 qualifiers were kept on.

SHEARMAN & STERLING LLP

Perform on the big stage

Abu Dhabi

Beijing

Brussels

Frankfurt

Hong Kong

London

Milan

New York

Palo Alto

Paris

Graduates are afforded early responsibility and work at the highest level within the firm. You will play a part in headline-making deals for some of the world's leading organisations, and enjoy many opportunities for international travel.

But don't just take our word for it – go online:
ukgraduates.shearman.com

Rome

San Francisco

Sao Paulo

Shanghai

Singapore

Tokyo

Shearman & Sterling LLP

The facts

Location: London

Number of UK partners/solicitors: 25/71 (+5/24 non-UK-qualified)

Seats: 4x6 months

Total number of trainees: 26

Alternative seats: overseas seats

Extras: pro bono – LawWork, legal clinics; language classes

On chambersstudent.co.uk...

How to get into Shearman

A history of Shearman

Shearman & Sterling has been operating in the City for over 40 years, allowing this US firm to establish a *"stronghold"* in the London finance market.

Shear class

When Thomas G. Shearman and John W. Sterling opened a firm back in 1870s New York, it's probably safe to assume they wouldn't have anticipated what Shearman & Sterling would look like 140 years down the line. With offices spanning five continents, this is a firm with a truly global footprint. Its first international office opened in Paris in 1963, while the London branch arrived in 1972. The international opportunities Shearman can provide were a major draw for the current crop of trainees. *"I wanted to do a lot of cross-jurisdictional work, and be at the cutting edge of the market,"* said one recalling their application. Another commented: *"It obviously has a good reputation, but I liked that there was a big focus on international deals and the chance to do overseas seats as well."*

This may be a US firm, but don't expect the London office to be blaring out the Star-Spangled Banner on loop. *"We certainly see ourselves as an international firm,"* commented HR manager Mariyam Hassan. *"However, I think a lot of students have this perception of US firms being dominated by US lawyers – but 80% of our lawyers in London are UK-qualified, and 60% of the London partners were associates in the office. There really is the chance to develop your career here."*

The corporate, finance and projects departments are the main drivers at the firm and all pick up recognition from *Chambers UK* – the latter achieving a top ranking nationwide. The magnitude of deals Shearman gets involved in showcases its expertise in these areas. Not only is it advising the Dow Chemical Company in connection with a $20bn joint venture with Saudi Aramco to build a chemical complex in Saudi Arabia, it's acting for Liberty Global on its acquisition of Virgin Media in a deal valued at $23.3bn. *"I think US-headquartered firms often have the same reputation as the magic circle, we just operate in a much smaller environment,"* concluded one source.

Predilections for jurisdictions

"Because we're mainly known for finance and projects, you have to sit in two of either corporate, finance, or project finance," a trainee explained. Jetsetters can join up with the transactional teams in Shanghai, Singapore, Abu Dhabi, Brussels, New York or Hong Kong to fulfil one of these compulsory elements. For the remaining two seats, trainees can choose from the firm's 'advisory' teams: litigation/arbitration; employment; competition/antitrust; tax; real estate; and financial services regulation/asset management. A contentious seat is not essential, as *"you can complete a two-week course at the University of Law to fulfil the SRA requirements."*

The finance group has roughly five trainees working in it at any given time. Clients include well-known names from the banking industry – Barclays, Standard Chartered and Citi are just some of those represented. *"In finance it can either be really busy or dead,"* one source recalled. *"I came in right as something was closing so that was quite exciting and I got to cut my teeth quite early. That means I was sorting documents for signings, corresponding with foreign counsel, handling corporate authorisations and drafting."* The department handles both leveraged and structured finance matters, although trainees usually experience either one or the other.

The True Picture

Chambers UK rankings

Banking & Finance	Energy & Natural
Banking Litigation	Resources
Capital Markets	Financial Services
Competition/European Law	Projects
Corporate/M&A	Restructuring/Insolvency

As a large proportion of the cases are *"really high-value,"* trainees can expect to do *"a lot of research, get documents together and collect bibles."* However, sources enjoyed the international nature of the deals. One reported liaising with 16 jurisdictions on a case, while another bested them by working with 20: *"New York, Paris, Milan and Germany were all involved. One of the main training tasks was liaising with client counsel and it's a massive organisational responsibility."* They continued: *"When deals cover different jurisdictions you will tend to be working with our offices in those areas. You build up a rapport with people all over the place, and can replicate those relationships on different matters. It makes the firm feel much more integrated."*

The projects team is smaller than finance but is a *"major area for the firm and the London office in general."* This is shown by Shearman getting its teeth stuck into some seriously meaty transactions. It advised the Egyptian private equity firm Citadel Capital and the Egyptian Refining Company on financing the redevelopment of its hydrocracking refinery in Mostorod, in a deal worth $3.7bn. It also advised a consortium of lenders led by HSBC and Barclays Capital on the permanent financing of the $1.1bn Tamar gas development project in Israel. As these examples show, a lot of projects work has an energy slant to it. *"There's a lot of very big transactions – prestigious work with lots of international aspects – so you have to muck in with anything given to you,"* one trainee told us. *"You get given a lot of good work as well. You can have a first go at drafting, you can do diligence reports – it's so busy that they're willing to let you take the lead on things."*

The corporate team recently advised on the successful bid by General Electric to acquire the Avio Group for $4.3bn. *"It's very busy,"* one trainee informed us. *"It's pretty demanding both in terms of the amount you have to focus on and work you do. There's a heavy research element involved, which means you can advise on the structuring of deals and how things unfold. The size of the team is much smaller than you'd find at magic circle firms so you get all hands on deck and work together to get stuff done."*

Yu-kos to be kidding me

The advisory teams at Shearman are often tasked with providing *"corporate support work,"* but also have their own standalone projects. For example, the tax team played an integral role in assisting its M&A counterparts during Vivendi's £487m sale of Parlophone Label Group to Warner Music. Trainees in the financial regulatory services practice said their time was evenly split between *"real regulatory work and corporate support. I was doing applications for FSA approval and standard applications to authorities across Europe, but the firm was also advising on an acquisition with regulated entities. On that side there wasn't much due diligence but I was working out what the regulatory implications were. As a trainee it was left to me to look at that and report back."* The real estate group was another popular pick for our sources. One said: *"While you can't avoid the basic trainee work, the fact there's a small number of trainees means you're often needed to do things you haven't done before, so they will push you to see how far you can get."*

Shearman & Sterling *"is pretty famous for its litigation and arbitration work worldwide."* The firm continues to represent the majority shareholders in the now-defunct Yukos Oil Company in a series of three arbitrations against the Russian Federation – the largest arbitration case ever in terms of amount at stake – an eye-watering $114bn! *"I was worried that trainees wouldn't get to do that much, but it's the total opposite,"* one litigator beamed. *"I've been able to run my own work stream, write reports, and draft both witness reports and statements. There's not much difference between a trainee's and a junior associate's work load."*

Each of the overseas seats has a particular transactional focus. *"Singapore is a projects seat, New York is capital markets, Brussels is antitrust, Abu Dhabi is projects, corporate and anything else going, and Shanghai is a mix as well,"* explained one interviewee. A second-year added: *"You're encouraged to go away at some point and the people who want to generally do. You specify an office you'd like to go to and put it down as one of your preferences during the seat allocation process. It was the complete and utter highlight of my training contract. I've enjoyed all my seats, but going away really forces you to stand alone. It was definitely a step up in responsibility, which then helped me progress here in London and grow in confidence."*

Time is invested in trainees to aid their progression. *"You sit with your supervisor and that's normally a partner or senior associate,"* commented one source. *"You tend to work quite closely with that person, though you are encouraged to work for other people in the department too. When you're working on transactions closely with your supervisor you can listen in on calls and attend meetings. They are 100% willing to give you feedback and comments and mark up your work. They're a complete source of support."* Due to the consistency of day-to-day performance updates, the reviews are considered *"very helpful, but you wouldn't expect to be told anything you weren't already aware of."* The mid-seat appraisal *"is pretty informal and useful for a touch up on how you've been doing,"* while the end-of-seat review is a more structured affair with *"a partner, your supervisor and a member of HR. They assess the work you've done and then let you know if you've met, exceeded, or fallen below expectations in different categories of performance."*

When it comes to qualification the firm refrains from communicating which departments have vacancies, leaving second-years to apply where they would actually like to work, rather than implementing any sort of Mourinho-esque tactics. *"They want people to put down where they want to work rather than trying to play the game and hedge their bets,"* explained one source approaching the end of their training contract. *"There are so few people here that if someone is good enough they might try to find a space even if there might not originally be one. It also eliminates that element of competition."*

Biscuit big boys

"US law firms are not just eat-what-you-kill, solitary environments, where people stay in their office all the time," one trainee stressed. *"There's just as much teamwork here as you'll find at any English firm, and perhaps even more so – there's no fear of knocking on a partner's door with a question."* Despite the big deals, late nights and big city setting, *"people tend to be very laid-back,"* a source concluded. *"I haven't worked with anybody whose stress has been that apparent. They might be working on stressful deals and haven't had enough sleep, but the general ambience is to get on and deal with things rather than snapping and creating a difficult working environment."*

There's no immediately apparent commonality in the backgrounds of Shearman's trainees. There's a wide variety of universities represented, and among our sources there was roughly a 50/50 split between those who came through a vac scheme and those who applied cold. Aside from an interest in the international aspect of life at the firm, what else unites this disparate bunch? *"There's an entrepreneurial feel here,"* suggested one source. *"Everyone is willing to just get up and give it their best shot."*

Shearman's offices are located on Appold Street, just a short walk from Liverpool Street station and Exchange Square. *"It does everything that it needs to,"* reflected a first-year. *"This isn't the HQ of the firm so I suppose in comparison with the magic circle it's not absolutely magnificent or spectacular, but we don't have the need for the London office to be like that. It's very practical and they recently refurbished all the kitchen and break-out areas."* When it comes to biscuits though, not even the magic circle can hold a candle to Shearman. Gossip website Roll on Friday's firm of the year 2013 survey ranked the firm second in this most illustrious of categories.

This is a firm that isn't shy of socialising either. *"There's definitely usually a pub visit every Friday,"* we were told – often to The Fox, The Light Bar or any other of Shoreditch's trendy haunts. *"All levels will happily socialise together. It would be weird if it was only trainees out and about as there isn't that division within the office."* However, there are *"official trainee socials"* for which the firm provides a budget. One trainee elaborated: *"There's normally four a year and often there's money put behind the bar, but there's also a social committee where people can say what they'd like to do."* An array of sports teams are also available to help you take your mind off the job.

The True Picture

And finally...

Shearman has a solid track record when it comes to retention, and in 2013 it kept on 11 of its 13 qualifiers.

Sheridans

The facts

Location: London
Number of UK partners/solicitors: 29/21
Partners who trained at the firm: 20%
Total number of trainees: 2
Seats: 4x6 months
Alternative seats: occasional secondments

On chambersstudent.co.uk...

How to get into Sheridans
Recent work highlights
The amazing life of Bernard Sheridan

A true media boutique, *"Sheridans certainly doesn't fit the mould of what you perceive law firms to be like."*

The Bloomsbury set

Bernard Sheridan set up shop in 1956 in a small office on London's Red Lion Square. Though known for his human rights acumen, he soon branched out to tap the potential of swinging London's pop scene. The move was a success and over the decades Sheridan negotiated the record deals of acts as diverse as The Hollies, Kate Bush and Pink Floyd. Back in the old days, Sheridan's USP was to act only for the artists – a crucial point meaning he could never be cowed by the clout of record labels. Equally, he was held in renown for his intricate knowledge of the copyright law that underpinned these negotiations. Trainees in the star-studded Sheridans of today concur that the spirit of '56 remains alive and well. *"It's great to get involved with exciting clients and sectors but what runs through all the work here is basic contractual and commercial knowledge – the underlying law is key to everything."*

From skiffle to Spotify, Sheridans has moved with the times. Now based in Bloomsbury, it's no longer solely a one-stop shop for recording contracts: the firm has full-fledged film, TV and theatre groups, in addition to catering to sectors including fashion, telecoms, advertising and sport. Departments like real estate, employment and company/commercial source a lot of work directly from these creatives, although they're increasingly generating their own work. A fast-growing 'interactive' team focuses on gaming and digital media (most prominently, the development of apps) and this year took on its first trainee. The other seats available are a litigation and employment joint seat; film, TV and sport; music, theatre and media; and company/commercial. There's a great deal of cross-department work, helped by the petite size of the office and its open-plan layout.

"Interactive is the current growth spot, as is the sports group," sources said. *"The firm is poised to move in the direction that these industries are moving, so things are always adapting. Rather than suddenly acquire, say, a new advertising department, the firm will probably just work with what it has in order to cover all the areas in media it needs to continue working with these high-end clients."*

Surfing the digital wave

The TV, film and sport group offers its trainee a balance of work from each of the three very separate areas: *"Although they are all concerned with copyright each brings a very different focus,"* sources explained. Film work involves working with production companies (and big-ticket producers Channel 4 and the BFI) on making movies happen. For trainees, this can mean experiencing *"the drafting of production agreements and writers' agreements to script reads, insurance and getting clearances for the film."* Though there's *"more hands-on experience on lower-budget films,"* sources assured us that *"you always get your hands dirty"* with plenty of client contact along the way. Over in TV, there's *"quite a lot of format-related work, like looking into rights ownership, as well as discrete research tasks such as looking into the Ofcom code."* The team works with HBO and Channel 4 and helped get Ricky Gervais' latest project *Derek* onto the small screen. *"As the lone trainee, there's always the bibling when transactions are going through, but equally the chance to take a stab at drafting key documents,"* said sources.

Chambers UK rankings

Media & Entertainment	Sports Law

The interactive team is expanding, recently bringing on board a specialist in digital media, IP and e-commerce. It's a practice that by its nature changes by the day. How to sum it up? *"It's anything online, basically,"* explained a source. *"That could be digital music, advertising or marketing. Mainly though, it's gaming and apps."* Tasks can range from working on contracts for app developers to handling disputes on behalf of games manufacturers, with plenty of infringement work in between. *"IP is becoming a huge part of interactive – in the broadest sense it's drafting licences or drafting letters in relation to contentious matters before they reach litigation."* Infringement work is just *"helping really big clients protect their brand online – for them the virtual world is an opportunity, but also a big threat. We go through the major platforms like Apple and Google and look for infringing material."* Overall, it's a great seat *"to put key legal skills like contracts and knowledge of IP law into practice in a new and exciting area that's developing all the time."*

There are some internal shifts going on at the moment, with some fee earners who built their practice in 'traditional' music moving over into the interactive department. The music practice proper continues apace, with clients like Robbie Williams and Paul McCartney proving that the department still has much clout. There's a lot of work for McCartney's company MPL Communications – *"doing their outsourced business affairs, so sorting clearances for the tour, clip licensing, approaching rights holders and negotiating with people who approach us for rights."* There's also plenty of media and theatre work going on in this seat. Sheridans acts for theatre production powerhouses Judy Craymer (*Mamma Mia!* and *Viva Forever!*) and Andrew Lloyd Webber's Really Useful Group.

The coco seat at Sheridans *"is more the corporate side of things, as interactive now encompasses a lot of commercial work."* There's much work from the film and TV side *"when clients want to buy or sell a company,"* and standalone clients like Glamoo, Java Investments and Outer Capital.

Eighties throwback

Even if they do get constant feedback as they go, trainees appreciate the formal system Sheridans has. *"They collate all of the team's comments and you then get to reflect on the work that you've done, and whether you've enjoyed it or not."* Generally, though, the small size of teams means *"you're never just handing in a piece of work – and if you don't get feedback on something, it means you're doing it right."* Trainees say being a boutique firm creates an environment where there's simultaneously *"lots of different personalities,"* yet *"people also tend to be quite similar in outlook – a key trait is that people are incredibly into their particular niche."*

Christmas and summer parties bookend the Sheridans social calendar: the most recent seasonal bash was held at a private members club on Shaftesbury Avenue *"where a partner's band provided the entertainment – I think they're called the 'After Eighties'."* Organised drinks at a local bar are also a staple of firm life, but more so are *"the impromptu drinks, where it's not just juniors but a proper cross-section of everyone here – you're able to get to know everyone you work with socially, be they another trainee or a partner."*

Getting a job at Sheridans is an informal affair. *"You speak to the training partners about where the positions are likely to be. It's not like picking options, so it can get sorted pretty early on in the year."* In 2013, the lucky qualifier bagged a job in the TV, film and sport department.

We'll finish with our standard warning about media firms. Apply for the right reasons, not because you want to meet Dappy (or another celebrity of your choice). At the end of the day, Sheridans is a law firm not a media agency and you'll need a strong interest in commercial law to land one of the few training contracts on offer.

And finally...

Stay up to date with developments in the media world if you want a shot at Sheridans – current trainees pointed to the tax credits introduced by the coalition government to encourage more TV drama to be shot in Britain as one major talking point.

Shoosmiths

The facts

Location: Basingstoke, Birmingham, Fareham, London, Manchester, Milton Keynes, Northampton, Nottingham, Reading, Scotland

Number of UK partners/solicitors: 132/282

Partners who trained at firm: 5%

Total number of trainees: 42

Seats: 4x6 months

Alternative seats: secondments

Extras: pro bono – Legal Launch Pad, LawWorks

On chambersstudent.co.uk...

How to get into Shoosmiths
Interview with chairman Andrew Tubbs
Reading: why it won't do your head in

This national outfit has come a long way since its modest Northampton beginnings, but it still retains *"the chummy and supportive atmosphere of a smaller firm."*

Big Shoos

It's been around for the better part of two centuries, but Shoosmiths has picked up most of its steam over the past decade or so. The Northampton native doubled its turnover between 2002 and 2008 and these days sits squarely in the UK top 40, posting a revenue of £87m for 2012/13. Since our last edition, the firm's reach has extended north of the border, bringing the total office count to ten following a merger with Edinburgh-based firm Archibald Campbell & Harley in autumn 2012.

Previously known mainly for its debt recovery and personal injury work, Shoosmiths now runs a full-service operation, with core practices like corporate, employment, litigation and property all present in the majority of its bases. *Chambers UK* offers nods to the firm's strength across the board, awarding it top-tier rankings in IP/IT (Milton Keynes), banking litigation (Manchester), employment (Reading) and real estate (Nottingham) amongst scores of others.

The 2012/13 financial year kicked off with an unfortunate round of redundancies in the Basingstoke branch, but insiders insist the firm is ploughing forward with a plan for *"UK domination"* (as one trainee put it). *"We have a 30% growth strategy over the next three years and that applies to all the offices. Our aim is to be the go-to firm in the UK and continue punching our weight with the big boys on a national level."* A major rebrand, unveiled in August 2012, gave the world a new website, a new logo incorporating an arresting lime green infinity symbol, and a new emphasis on cross-office collaboration, all confirm-

ing Shoosmiths means business. *"There's definitely been a push to get into everyone's minds that we're a national firm and should rely on the expertise of our colleagues,"* explained one source. *"The Fareham and Reading teams work quite closely together now, for example, and we're sharing more work between the offices than we ever have before."*

Trainee places are available in Nottingham, Birmingham, Reading, Fareham, Manchester, Northampton and Milton Keynes (seeing as they're essentially neighbours, the last two are *"more or less treated as one"* for the purposes of the training contract). Elsewhere, London operates primarily as a client meeting point, while Basingstoke is a base for Shoosmiths' private client arm Access Legal. When it comes to seats, only those already paralegalling at the firm – a good 20 to 30% of each intake – get a say in the first one, though everybody's allowed to list preferences for the remaining three. An initial meeting in Birmingham provides a chance for juniors to get to know their counterparts across the firm, though they tend to keep to their own offices in their early years.

The Shoo's on the other foot

Our sources had noticed a considerable shift of power from the Northampton digs – dubbed The Lakes – to Milton Keynes. The entire regulatory department has moved out of Northampton, *"so the only key teams left there are private client and debt recovery,"* we were told. A Lakes source who'd completed a stint in asset finance – part of the recovery services umbrella – reported *"getting into*

Chambers UK rankings

Banking & Finance	Pensions
Clinical Negligence	Personal Injury
Competition/European Law	Planning
Corporate/M&A	Private Client
Dispute Resolution	Product Liability
Employment	Real Estate
Environment	Restructuring/Insolvency
Health & Safety	Retail
Information Technology	Tax
Licensing	

the nitty-gritty of proper litigation" and enjoying "close client relations. Once a week I work on a bespoke project with one of our big names." The only seat available in Northampton now is recovery services.

The Milton Keynes practice, on the other hand, largely falls within "the commercial side of Shoosmiths" and is "renowned for its IP work in particular." Indeed, the team has a terrific reputation in the retail, automotive, education and technology sectors and acts for an all-star cast of clients, among them H&M, McDonald's, Ann Summers, Thorntons and Samsung. In one of the many highlights of 2012, MK lawyers secured a victory for Red Bull in a trade mark infringement case against supermarket distributor Sun Mark involving the Austrian giant's 'Bullit' brand. The MK office is also home to the "very technical" pensions team, as well as a top-notch property litigation group which represents the likes of Thomas Cook and Almacantar (the owner of London's Centre Point). "You get exposed to cases of the highest order in that seat," mused one trainee, "whether it's an enforcement proceeding or lease review. You're able to work for a really wide range of clients too." This city centre office has a bit of a "commuter culture," (more at partner level) but trainees sensed "a real drive lately to retain younger people in here in the evenings," mentioning a handful of fun-filled activities like poker nights, networking events, cocktail evenings and Friday drinks at nearby plaza The Hub.

Shires and shires of Shoos

Reading offers "the full spectrum of commercial work," with seats available in corporate, commercial, litigation, IP, banking, employment, regulatory, tax and real estate. Things are thriving on the corporate front and the group doesn't just work on behalf of regional clients; lawyers advise big-hitters like Krispy Kreme and GAME. According to trainees, some token administrative tasks are required, "but later on you have the chance to do more drafting and legal research." Those who'd sat with the employment team – which stands tall in the higher education, retail, logistics and IT sectors and wields an impressive client list that includes Hewlett-Packard and the National Trust – described it as "a really lively department"

and reported "a brilliant experience" attending tribunals, researching technical points and drafting witness statements and compromise agreements. The Reading hub is split across two floors, and its trainees – of whom there were eight at the time of our calls – enjoy a social scene that largely revolves around monthly Thursday lunches and Friday night drinks. A number of sports teams cater to athletic types, and there's also New Friday, a quarterly informal networking event set up by juniors, a version of which takes place at all the offices.

In Nottingham real estate, real estate litigation, corporate, commercial and employment seats are all up for grabs. "Each of these teams pulls its weight; I wouldn't say one is necessarily any better than the others," one insider remarked. As far as Chambers UK rankings are concerned, however, the real estate practice is the office's highest achiever, with trainees revealing "it's been constantly busy." The team regularly acts for household names like HMV and Waterstones. One source recalled: "I helped out with the due diligence on a few massive deals, and reviewed and drafted various leases. There were some post-completion tasks like Land Registry applications and SDLT returns, but they don't all simply get dumped on the trainees." The office usually houses around five trainees and, like Milton Keynes, has "a youthful feel to it. We have a lot of laughs, and I can't even count how many dinners, lunches and nights out we go on. The summer and Christmas parties are always memorable occasions too."

Birmingham's eight-strong trainee cohort has a wide range of seats at its disposal, with recovery services, commercial, litigation, corporate/insolvency, personal injury, employment, construction and real estate all on the menu. The corporate practice serves up "a nice mix of one-off acquisitions and longer-term investment work" and "offers the chance to add some gloss to your CV" through its work with well-known regional institutions like Midlands Co-operative and Birmingham City FC. "I worked alongside some venture capitalists and got to do a disclosure exercise on my own." Meanwhile, the specialist construction team is a small but mighty force in the area, handling a raft of local development issues, including a few major regeneration schemes. Lawyers recently advised UK investment company Seven Capital on the £60m conversion of a vacant building into a 290-bedroom hotel and conference facility. In spring 2013 the Brum team picked up sticks and relocated to shiny new digs at Two Colmore Square, which holds the distinct honour of housing the largest single floor of office space in the city – a whopping 40,000 square feet. "There are so many meeting rooms here, and they all have snazzy flat-screen TVs. And extra-special client toilets – they really are something else." We'll take their word for it.

Shoosmiths' Manchester base turned four years old in 2013 and recently hit the 100 employee mark. "Every week there's a new face in the kitchen." "Our roots are *in debt recovery work, but we've more or less become full service, and all our teams are looking to grow further."* Manchester currently welcomes two trainees a year, who are *"immediately absorbed into the practice"* and benefit from *"a good deal of responsibility."* At the moment juniors can spend time in the real estate, commercial, corporate/banking, finance litigation and employment/pensions departments, though insiders speculated that *"future trainees will likely have a lot more choice as we continue to grow."*

Fareham, otherwise known as Solent, houses six or seven trainees and offers seats in commercial, commercial litigation, corporate, employment and property/planning. The corporate team has *"a very strong presence in the local market,"* with specialities in private equity, M&A, public company and acquisition finance work, while the top-ranked planning practice draws in business from builders, developers, local authorities and retailers along the lines of IKEA and English Heritage. The office's business park location *"can make it difficult to go for drinks after work or pop out to networking events,"* but sources reckon this could soon change as *"a new shopping centre with lots of bars and restaurants has just opened up nearby."*

One of the key features of a Shoosmiths training contract is the *"virtually guaranteed"* opportunity to do a client secondment. *"There are so many of them available, both locally and nationally,"* with Home Retail (operators of Argos and Homebase) among the national options. *"It gave me a really good insight into how clients work on a day-to-day basis,"* said one trainee. Others agreed: *"It's incredibly beneficial to understand how these huge companies operate, and that's something you can't really comprehend unless you've had direct exposure to it."*

The Shoo people

Regardless of the local quirks, our sources agreed *"it's very clear we're all part of the Shoosmiths family. The firm has really pushed for uniformity, especially since the rebrand."* So does Shoosmiths attract a certain 'type' of would-be lawyer? The vast majority of interviewees answered 'yes': *"You'll find that nobody here takes themselves too seriously. Everyone's the kind of person who can have a bit of a laugh but is also willing to knuckle down when they need to."* What's more, *"there's no place for arrogance here. Those who come in with a cocky attitude simply won't succeed."*

On the whole, interviewees across the offices gave their Shoosmiths experience the thumbs up. That said, we did hear quite a few grumbles pertaining to salaries, which start at £24,000 for all trainees and rise to £25,000 in the second year. Some deemed this pay *"reasonable,"* but others felt *"it should more accurately reflect each location. It's not like living expenses are the same in every place."* Still, the firm's *"ethos of providing a great work/life balance"* was much appreciated among our sources. We're pleased to report insiders had no real horror stories to share regarding their working hours, with an average day seeing most out the door by 7pm.

Barring a minor blip in 2009, retention rates at Shoosmiths have been pretty good in recent years, as demonstrated by the 100% retention posted in 2012. However, the outlook for 2013 was hardly optimistic at the time of our calls, with one second-year describing their chances as *"bleak"* and another admitting *"it's looking a bit doom and gloom. The number of jobs being advertised are relatively low."* Still, trainees praised the firm for showing *"a genuine desire to keep as many of us on as it can"* and emphasised the *"wonderful level of support in place for those who aren't successful."* In the end, nine out of 20 qualifiers were retained. Trainees sense that this is down to the previously pristine figures catching up with the firm.

The True Picture

And finally...

Considering Shoosmiths' plans for national growth, trainees foresee *"an increasing importance on future joiners' ability to network and liaise with clients."*

Sidley Austin LLP

The facts

Location: London

Number of UK partners/solicitors: 34/59 (+12 non-UK-qualified)

Partners who trained at firm: 8%

Total number of trainees: 20

Seats: 4x6 months (occasional three-month seats)

Alternative seats: Brussels, occasional secondments

Extras: pro bono – LawWorks

On chambersstudent.co.uk...

How to get into Sidley

Capital markets explained

Structured finance aficionado Sidley Austin has developed more strings to its bow than securitisation.

Variety is the spice of life

The year was 1974. There was feathered hair, flares and Bagpuss on TV, and two very weighty, but very different, American imports arrived in London. One was McDonald's, which ensconced itself down in Woolwich. The other was Sidley & Austin, a fast-expanding legal contender with roots back in Chicago. Now, both are global giants – if you want top-notch corporate legal advice, with a side of fries, you don't have to go far, whatever the jurisdiction.

Today's Sidley Austin comes from the 2001 merger with New York's Brown & Wood, a combination that created a colossus. Now it's one of the ten biggest law firms in the world, with offices in eight US cities plus Beijing, Brussels, Frankfurt, Geneva, Hong Kong, Shanghai, Singapore, Sydney and Tokyo. Until the credit crunch, the London office concentrated on quite a specialist area of structured finance work – securitisation and derivatives. Since then, it has developed and broadened its practices to cover more economically buoyant areas, such as insurance, dispute resolution, regulatory, insolvency and capital markets.

For new recruits, this means an increasingly *"diversified"* training contract. Besides finance, which is no longer a compulsory seat, there are seats in corporate, capital markets, disputes, funds, competition, employment, regulatory, tax and insolvency. However, sources stressed that *"there's no point applying if you don't have a keen interest in finance and what's going on in the market."* There's a *"good range of transactional and regulatory seats but most matters are still tailored towards corporate and finance. For example, in employment the work is often part* of a bigger transaction or restructuring."* Trainees assured us that *"despite the post-recession feeling, people are desperate to sit in finance, which is what the firm's renowned for."*

Indeed, Sidley's reputation for finance work was a major draw for all our sources, who were looking for *"an international firm with big deals and big clients but, in comparison to other City firms, a relatively small trainee intake and high levels of responsibility."* While Sidley does draw in big-ticket clients, it's not working on those mammoth matters that are the preserve of Linklaters et al. As one trainee put it, *"the workload here is so different to other firms. It's amazing to deal with a really niche area of finance."* One specialised project the firm took on recently was advising Santander on a bond offering worth 4.5bn Swedish kronor by a Swedish auto financing firm and an Irish SPV (special purpose vehicle) to buy a portfolio of loans taken out to buy cars.

True finance

Six-month and three-month seats are available. HR sits down with trainees to have *"lengthy discussions"* about their options and preferences. *"They do it fairly and they try really hard to give you what you want."* There was some mixed opinion over the value of three-month seats, but most had a positive take on them. *"Doing three months gives you more exposure to different areas. The split seats tend to be in the most popular departments, so it's no disadvantage, because when you qualify you'll want to have good relationships across the firm. You're inevitably helping yourself – you learn a lot more."*

Chambers UK rankings

Capital Markets	Investment Funds
Competition/European Law	Real Estate Finance
Corporate/M&A	Restructuring/Insolvency
Dispute Resolution	Tax
Insurance	

"The firm doesn't break down the finance department, which is something it prides itself on. They try not to pigeon-hole anyone, so there's associates working on lots of different matters. In my seat I saw about 60% banking work, along with some restructuring and securitisation – a bit of everything really," explained a source. On the banking side of things, one trainee was *"managing a due diligence process for 180 loans, which was a pretty huge task, so obviously I've become very familiar with securitisation documents."* According to interviewees, banking work offers plenty of responsibility *"because the transactions aren't the most complex. I did a lot of work like suggesting amendments for important documents. The highlight was when I got to negotiate over certain documents on my own with the other side."*

Within the global finance department, securitisation sits *"at the heart of the firm."* Most sources reported rolling up their sleeves and getting a grip on the copious documents. *"I haven't had much client exposure so far, mostly just working on spreadsheets, compiling data and assisting with discrete research tasks,"* explained one, while another talked of *"doing commercial-backed mortgage securities and getting involved in a big headline deal."* One excitable source exclaimed: *"The guys in the team are awesome. As individuals they're really dynamic and they work you really hard. I've been doing some doc management, drafting a lot of ancillary documents, taking board minutes and working with the property group."* Exposure to the firm's fairly niche financing projects should be on the cards: *"The deal I've been most involved in is the securitisation of revenues for a solar park. It's been very compelling to see how the renewable sector works and how companies go about raising finance."*

Down on the pharm

In capital markets, trainees reported taking on *"a real mixture"* of matters. *"I did some equity work for a Peruvian renewable energy company and got to do the closing by myself, so I felt like I had a lot of responsibility. I worked for some pretty large, well-known clients as well, so that was rewarding."* Familiar names on the books include Bank of America Merrill Lynch, Credit Suisse, Morgan Stanley and pharmaceutical giant GlaxoSmithKline. Another interviewee mentioned getting to grips with *"a restructuring of a major bank in Central and Eastern Europe, which has been going on for the last four*

years. I was involved in arranging a series of meetings at our office and making sure they ran smoothly, plus I was drafting, reviewing and amending memos." Sources also noted that *"the firm does a lot of debt capital markets work for clients in the life sciences sector."*

Several sources enjoyed the corporate department *"because the work isn't so niche."* For example, the firm worked on the fairly comprehensible sale of various assets and marketing rights by Teva Pharmaceuticals to Acino Pharmaceuticals for ,€94m. One grateful trainee declared: *"I was very lucky because I was involved in a £650m merger. I created execution documents and liaised with clients. It was very international – spread across a number of jurisdictions."* Others got off to a quieter start in corporate, but said that when things do kick off, *"it's pretty intense, but a very rewarding learning curve. The client contact experience is phenomenal. I went to a couple of board meetings, which was my first introduction to face-to-face client contact, plus there were clients from the States coming over for lunch. I would be calling clients and guiding them through what I knew as a trainee, and so I'd be researching beforehand what on earth I'd say during the call!"*

The investment funds seat allows trainees to take on varied tasks, often with an international aspect. *"I was looking at tax vehicles that would be viable for US and non-US investors as well as working on issues around fund establishment or restructuring and helping with regulatory advice to managers of onshore and offshore funds."* One source remembered squaring up to *"a really big due diligence task. It was like a perfect storm really, because there was only me and a junior associate who was away, so I had a lot on my plate."* And if that wasn't enough, *"I was researching the responsibilities of fund directors, especially with regard to Cayman law."* The small size of Sidley's employment team means that trainees *"can get involved with everything. I helped with unfair dismissals, immigration matters and transactional work like the employment aspect of an M&A deal. It's extremely varied – the team does corporate support but also has standalone clients that bring in contracts."* Similarly, the competition seat gave one trainee insight into *"the work the firm does as a whole"* when they dug up *"competition advice needed for corporate deals."* Trainees can also sample life in the contentious arena. Recently, Sidley's litigation department has represented industrial corporation Federal-Mogul over asbestos insurance claims. Other clients include Bermudian reinsurance company Pulsar Re and Illinois-based hedge fund Magnetar Capital.

The Great Gatsby: solicitor-style

Trainees tended to agree that *"the hard thing is not staying late but the uncertainty, so you can't plan anything and you have to get used to that. I've stayed late at short no-*

The True Picture

tice lots of times," said one. This being a City firm, *"you'll inevitably work long hours, and at the end of a deal you get a rush of adrenalin and the time passes quickly. But when you randomly have to work long hours, that's more frustrating."* Trainees typically worked between 9am and 7pm, with periods of staying into the early hours of the morning and occasionally coming in at weekends.

"A few partners are American, there's an intensity and American style about the office," enthused one source, while another declared: *"I don't think it's very American in terms of being brash. It feels like they've taken the benefits of having a large firm and big clients and stamped a British identity on it."* Generally, our sources agreed that it's a *"friendly, collegial, open-door"* sort of place where *"you see smiling faces every day and you're made to feel welcome."* Others pointed out that the firm's international presence impacts on day-to-day London office life: *"One of the advantages of having a global firm is that there are so many fantastic colleagues around the world who are willing and able to help you out. I was working on a pro bono matter and corresponding with the Palo Alto offices. My US colleagues really made me feel that the firm is bigger than the London office and the ease with which you can communicate is very comforting."* A source noted: *"One thing that does feel American is the women's committee. There's a huge drive for women and America are about ten years ahead of us in that respect."* The commit-

tee organises talks and events including a recent trip to a Man Ray exhibition and a tour of the Royal Opera House.

On the subject of committees, Sidley's social one seems to have upped its game recently. *"In the past I'd read negative things about the social life but lots of new things have been put on,"* one interviewee told us. A wine and cheese evening expected to muster a desultory turnout was overhauled by proactive trainees and turned into a *"spectacular 1920s speakeasy-style cocktail soirée"* with 130 in attendance. There's also a big family-friendly Halloween party, a Christmas bash at a fancy venue, plus bake sales, karaoke and *"a lot of sporty things"* going on. There doesn't seem to be a 'Sidley type', however. Trainees come from a range of ages and backgrounds, though a large proportion do have *"some kind of international background."*

Although *"retention was a concern for people because it has fallen in recent years,"* in the most recent jobs round there were more positions available than actual qualifiers. Although spots in certain departments are *"hotly contested,"* our sources felt generally positive about the whole process. A list of openings is sent around and trainees are interviewed in the departments they'd like to apply for. Sidley retained all nine of its 2013 qualifiers.

And finally...
Real responsibility isn't a myth at Sidley, according to trainees: *"We're are an integral part of the firm and you actually do get responsibility. You're relied upon and that makes the job better."*

Simmons & Simmons LLP

The facts

Location: London

Number of UK partners/solicitors: 230/800

Partners who trained at firm: undisclosed

Total number of trainees: 85

Seats: 4x6 months

Alternative seats: overseas seats, secondments

Extras: pro bono – Battersea Legal Advice Centre; language classes

On chambersstudent.co.uk...

How to get into Simmons

Simmons' art collection

Interview with Alex Brown, graduate recruitment and development partner

"When you think of your quintessential City law firm, we most probably fit the model," interviewees said. Simmons & Simmons is a top name in the City, especially when it comes to all things financial.

Financially yours

Simmons & Simmons has been knocking around London since 1896, and has long been a large and well-respected all-rounder. The firm experienced some turbulence during the downturn, and 2012-13 revenues dipped slightly to £250.3m following several years of solid growth. Known primarily for its stellar financial practice, the firm also enjoys *Chambers UK* top rankings for its employment, life sciences and IP work.

The firm's current strategic plans revolves around five core sectors. These are: financial services; life sciences; TMT; asset management / investment funds; and energy and infrastructure. Graduate recruitment and development partner Alex Brown says: *"Everything we do is driven by our sectors and the focus is part of our three-year growth strategy. During the last twelve months, we have made significant moves. We've opened in Munich, which makes three bases in Germany, and we announced that we're opening in Singapore. Aside from this, there's been growth in regards lateral hiring."* Closer to home, the firm also opened an office in Bristol in 2012. *"We wanted to have another UK location that could replicate our specialities, while offering lower costs,"* Brown says. *"It is a fully functioning office; however we're not currently running a training programme there."*

In the last few years, Simmons trainees have had the option of doing an MBA before joining the firm. This is no longer the case, but over the course of their LPC and training contract they'll take extra business courses which will give them the option to complete an MBA post-qualification. For more about this unique Simmons selling point, take a look at the bonus feature on our website.

14 and counting

"There are 14 seat choices and every rotation you rank your preferences from one to 14," trainees explained. Seats are organised into four groups: contentious, corporate/commercial (CoCom), financial markets and *"other."* The contentious group includes IP, pensions, employment and dispute resolution. CoCom covers corporate, projects and ICT. Financial markets has financial services, banking, asset finance and capital markets, while the 'other' category includes real estate, EU/competition and tax. Trainees are expected to complete one finance and one CoCom seat. A two-week litigation course can circumvent the SRA's contentious requirement, *"but it isn't that encouraged and not many people do it."* Realistically, *"finance is what we're known for, so people want experience in that field anyway. The restrictions makes sense."* Trainees thought *"the HR team do actually listen to your choices although the element of business need always plays a part."* Several had approached the departments directly, saying it helps *"to really express an interest and show how serious you are about the work."*

The financial services (FS) department is *"the strongest department we have, and one of the largest in the City,"* trainees asserted. It's split into three groups including funds, regulatory and derivatives, and trainees are allocated to one of these. *"Funds is probably the biggest and most revered team of the three,"* interviewees reflected, *"but the regulatory group is really growing."* The funds

Chambers UK rankings

Asset Finance	Fraud
Banking & Finance	Health & Safety
Banking Litigation	Information Technology
Capital Markets	Intellectual Property
Commodities	Investment Funds
Competition/European Law	Life Sciences
Construction	Outsourcing
Consumer Finance	Pensions
Corporate Crime	Product Liability
& Investigations	Professional Negligence
Corporate/M&A	Projects
Dispute Resolution	Real Estate Finance
Employment	Restructuring/Insolvency
Energy & Natural	Retail
Resources	Tax
Environment	Telecommunications
Financial Services	Transport

team busies itself with events in the life of a hedge fund – setting them up and restructuring them. Clients are top hedge funds and large financial institutions: *"We continuously work for the top funds in the world."* The *"really research-heavy"* regulatory part of the department involves true black-letter law. *"We often work on market abuse issues and frequently liaise with the litigation teams."* Trainees said: *"You'll probably be working some of the longest hours in the funds group, but it thankfully isn't just adminny-type work."* Though one source opined that *"these teams are perhaps slightly less friendly than others,"* it was agreed that there's *"a lot of client contact and you can get really involved."*

Capital markets is another strong team at Simmons and *"serves some of our biggest clients."* It's no secret that the capital markets... er... market... isn't quite what it used to be in the City, *"but the team still seems to be doing good work and has great secondment connections,"* trainees reflected. It's expanding, too, with two partners joining the group from Linklaters in 2012. *"Obviously there's the grunt work to be done at the lower level,"* trainees said, *"but you progressively get better and better opportunities."* One thought: *"There's a lot of training, because it's a complex area, and the team are so good at explaining everything along the way."*

Apple grapple

Dispute resolution at Simmons is is split between commercial and financial litigation. *"Although the split is quite pronounced, as a trainee you do work for both. You might be more focused on one camp, but you're officially a pooled resource."* One source added: *"Trainees can also put themselves forward for work they're interested in."* Work in the commercial group covers a variety of

different specialities including insurance, professional negligence and white-collar crime, and there's *"a well-regarded arbitration practice."* The financial litigation side predominantly involves asset management and banking disputes: clients range from Russian individuals to large corporations and major banks. The team acted for Sharp on the defence of two claims brought by Nokia in the High Court for antitrust damages and is representing Samsung Electronics on its much-publicised EU design right and patent disputes with Apple. Trainees agreed: *"In this team, if you have the ability and maturity, you can get a lot of responsibility."* One said: *"Everyone is incredibly busy, but people try and include you. Due to the nature of the work, you're not going to get quite the same levels of responsibility, but you will get access to drafting and research."* Another added: *"You even spend time in court and attend several client meetings."*

The employment and intellectual property departments are always popular with trainees. Employment *"has a very strong reputation"* and acts for the likes of AXA, Visa and ratings agency Moody's. *"The work is a fairly balanced split between contentious and non-contentious, although at the moment disputes seem to be more dominant,"* interviewees said. Trainees *"draft witness statements and frequently liaise with counsel."*

Pills, pop and rock

The IP team covers copyright, trade marks and patents, and it's fair to say is heavily flavoured with life sciences clients, such as Eli Lilly, GlaxoSmithKline and Bayer Pharma, which Simmons represented in patent litigation relating to a range of oral contraceptive pills. There are still plenty of names from other sectors – like Samsung and British American Tobacco, for example. One source said: *"The seat is popular partly because the clients are household names, so the work is immediately more interesting."* For example, Simmons advised Coca-Cola in litigation against Media Village Entertainment (MVE). The latter company sued Coke for trade mark infringement, because Coke had sponsored music festivals to promote its RELENTLESS energy drink, while MVE has a stake in Relentless Records, the label behind Joss Stone, KT Tunstall and So Solid Crew. *"There's a lot of drafting and research to be done,"* trainees said of this seat, *"and thankfully very little adminny stuff."* For the first few years, lawyers in this team work on a mix of everything, and so trainees are encouraged to take on as much variety as possible.

The hours trainees are expected to work are *"essentially what you'd expect from City law. Yes, there are all-nighters and some weekends, but it's not commonplace. In several departments you'll be out by 7 or 8pm."*

Secondments are *"encouraged at Simmons, and realistically about 80% of people head out on one."* Overseas seats include Tokyo, Hong Kong, Dubai, Abu Dhabi, Qatar and Paris. Client secondments are *"generally London-based,"* and destinations include Barclays, Credit Suisse, Shell, GSK and a number of hedge funds. *"Realistically, if you want to go there's a great chance you'll get to,"* interviewees said. *"The client secondments are probably actually more competitive to get on."* Those that had gone abroad had nothing but good things to say: *"The learning curve is challenging, but it's always an interesting experience,"* and Simmons *"always put you up in these great flats."*

Going on the piste

There has been some suggestion in the legal press that Simmons has sat still while some of its peer firms have pushed on, but interviewees reflected: *"There does seem to be more emphasis on ambition and energy recently. There are constant initiatives to encourage practice area expansion. From the inside, it doesn't feel like Simmons is resting on its laurels."* One said: *"We have an entrepreneurial side to us and the firm feels modern and progressive,"* while another added: *"People want to get the job done and push ahead, but without the aggression of the magic circle or American firms. There's no lack of ambition, but people aren't overly competitive and you're never beasted."* But where next for Simmons? This is a firm that has looked at mergers in the past (most notably, there were talks with Mayer Brown in 2010). It has never gone all the way and we don't get the sense that anything is imminent for Simmons, but long-term we wouldn't bet against it ending up hitched to a nice American or Australian.

When it comes to qualification, trainees thought: *"The HR team are as open as they can be throughout the process. Of course it's a stressful process, but the firm is organised, and is clear about where the jobs are. You put down your first, second and third choice and take it from there."* In the end, 27 out of 34 were kept on as NQs.

"You're never exposed to that 'old boy' banter," one source said, and we get the impression that this is a very civilised working environment. All sources agreed: *"Ultimately, this is a lovely place to train. You're not allowed to treat people badly: it's a respectful, friendly and open place."* Simmons is clearly quite committed to diversity and has won awards for its LGBT-friendliness in particular.

Trainees themselves are *"a really tight-knit group. You have to remember that as a result of the LPC and MBA, there are some very strong friendships at the firm."* One said: *"We often go for drinks and several people actually live with each other."* Sports teams include hockey, rugby, netball, cricket and even rounders. *"There's also a choir which performs at Christmas."* Departments have regular drinks and run their own ski trips, and the firm puts on a biannual summer ball and hosts *"rather poncily named 'soirées' once a month or so, which are basically just a whole load of booze in the canteen."* There's also a women's society and a human rights group. *"Both regularly have speakers that come in, and they are often followed with a social."* Informally, *"you'll always find someone in the Corney & Barrow on a Friday night."*

And finally...

The firm is looking for *"gregarious, high-energy"* personalities, thought trainees. *"You need to have a willingness to get the job done, but also understand that there are things in life beyond the law."*

SJ Berwin LLP

The facts

Location: London
Number of UK partners/solicitors: 93/184
Partners who trained at firm: 22%
Total number of trainees: 77
Seats: 4x6 months
Alternative Seats: overseas seats, secondments
Extras: pro bono – Toynbee Hall Debt Clinic, International Lawyers for Africa; language classes

On chambersstudent.co.uk...
How to get into SJB
Private equity explained

"No one rests on their laurels" at SJB: now the firm is joining forces with Asia-Pacific superfirm King & Wood Mallesons.

What's in a name?

This younger sister of Berwin Leighton Paisner was formed by the ambitious lawyer Stanley Berwin in 1982. At only 31 years old, that means it's still a relative baby among the ranks of the top City firms. *"We are a young firm that's grown very quickly. Our attitude towards hard work and perseverance is why we've been so successful,"* trainees believe, repeatedly describing their workplace as *"dynamic"* and *"go-getting."* One said: *"Everyone's very driven and high-energy. We're about moving the firm forwards together."* Though sources admitted the firm has taken a bit of a beating in the recent recession, they argued that *"SJB's desire to push forward is a powerful force. People are very motivated and no one rests on their laurels. We're not a relaxed place. There is a lot of ambition in the air."*

Let's talk mergers. KWM is an interesting firm. Chinese in origin, it never had any partners called King or Wood – they were made-up names designed to sound appealing to Western ears. Mallesons was a leading Australian firm taken over in 2012. As such, this is a major force in the Asia-Pacific region, and a tie-up with SJB would be its first major foray into Europe, and equally sets SJB on a far more solid international footing, with an expected 2,000-odd lawyers.

Although known predominantly for its private equity prowess – *"which is still an incredibly important driver for the firm"* – there are several growth areas at SJB. Graduate recruitment partner Nicola Bridge says: *"We continue to develop our countercyclical practice groups. Our EU and competition team is very highly regarded and we're looking to strengthen the contentious side of* our business. Our energy and infrastructure team is doing very interesting work, and we have seen several notable hires in our financial markets and financial services practice."* Away from SJB's corporate/finance core, areas such as real estate, IP and tax also pick up rankings in *Chambers UK*.

In common with a lot of firms, SJB is also increasingly talking about 'sector focus'. It is now concentrating on seven industry sectors: real estate; private equity; technology, media and telecoms; consumer; financial institutions; energy and infrastructure; and life sciences and healthcare, and its lawyers are informally being realigned within them. *"It's good for business and a way to create a cohesive firm that makes sense for clients."* interviewees agreed.

The power of three will set us free

Seats fall under three headings: corporate, contentious and 'other.' The contentious requirement can be fulfilled by spending time in straight litigation, IP litigation, restructuring, employment, EU/competition, planning or environment. The 'other' category includes real estate, commerce/tech, financial markets, construction and tax. *"HR says that you'll most likely get three out of your four top choices,"* trainees said. *"Although that might not be entirely accurate, they really do try to accommodate you and it's very rare that people are upset."*

The large and *"very important"* corporate department is separated into three teams. They are all *"massive, each rivalling whole other departments in size."* Although the teams are distinct, *"they are ultimately cohesive and often work together on matters."* The first team used to be

Chambers UK rankings

Banking & Finance	Investment Funds
Banking Litigation	Life Sciences
Capital Markets	Parliamentary & Public
Competition/European Law	Affairs
Construction	Partnership
Corporate/M&A	Planning
Dispute Resolution	Private Equity
Employment	Real Estate Finance
Financial Services	Real Estate Litigation
Fraud	Restructuring/Insolvency
Information Technology	Retail
Intellectual Property	Tax

dominated by capital markets and public work, but *"as there is less of that in the market, it's now more focused on M&A, real estate finance and investment work – general corporate stuff."* Clients include Universal and Associated British Foods, and the team recently advised Westfield on the £159m sale of three shopping centres in the UK. A very *"work-heavy"* department, the team runs on slightly *"unsociable"* hours, however they're also *"really great and make sure to try and develop you as an attorney."*

"The second team is the largest of the three and possibly the highest-performing for the firm," trainees said. SJB advised Apollo Global Management on its acquisition of luxury jewellery group Arum Holdings, and acted for Lion Capital on the acquisition of hair-straightening brand GHD from Montagu Private Equity. *"There were probably times when I had too much responsibility,"* one trainee laughed. *"The team's so busy that you'll definitely get involved in high-level matters. There's a lot of client-facing stuff, and by the end of the seat you're drafting SPAs and liaising directly with opposing teams."* One said: *"Of course, you need to build up people's trust, but the team are very willing to give you experience."*

The final team (aka 'funds team') is the private equity and fund formation group for which SJB is famous. Consistently highly ranked by *Chambers UK*, *"this team is almost at the core of SJ Berwin and is incredibly important to the firm."* It is often the first point for private equity clients, who then progress to the second team for their private M&A and investment work. Clients are funds houses, private equity firms and large investors – including those in the financial and healthcare sectors. *"As soon as you enter 'funds team' you're aware of the high calibre of the work. It's sort of ridiculous how much some of the partners know,"* trainees said. Known to attract *"bookish and technical types,"* this team *"pride themselves on the intellectual nuances in their work."* The work itself *"is quite complex,"* but trainees are supported through *"excellent associates"* and weekly training sessions. Interviewees confirmed getting a good amount of substantive

work: *"Obviously there's admin stuff to do, but the client contact is great and they encourage you to be proactive and get stuck into the work."*

The EU/competition department is a *"real growth sector"* for the firm. *"There are now about a dozen partners,"* with two having joined in 2012. Clients include banks, pharmaceutical companies and other blue-chip corporations, and the work has a strong regulatory focus. Sources here all said they did a lot of research and project management of documents: *"It's a relatively contentious seat, so there are the standard low-level trainee tasks, but you always feel very much part of the team and work with a variety of partners."*

Michelin-starred squabble

Litigation is another *"growing"* department for the firm: *"It's becoming more and more established and, although it's one large team, specialisms such as arbitration and fraud are doing very well."* As a trainee *"you're doing a real variety. Although there are different practices, the lines between them are very informal, so you get a real breadth of matters."* Commercial litigation makes up the largest proportion of work, however. Clients include everything from large companies to individuals, and *"the work is also very multi-jurisdictional."* The team is representing tyre manufacturers such as Michelin, Continental and Bridgestone against synthetic rubber manufacturers in a £350m cartel case. *"Due to the nature of the work perhaps, the department is slightly more hierarchical and there's less for junior lawyers to do,"* interviewees admitted. *"The team does really try and keep you up-to-date and they will genuinely listen to your suggestions. You also get a bit of drafting to do."* The real estate department, meanwhile, has *"an excellent client list"* which includes Marks & Spencer and British Land. It advised the latter on the £340m development and letting of the 'Cheesegrater' skyscraper currently going up in London. The department is known for its *"warm atmosphere."*

There are several overseas seats on offer. Trainees have a choice between Paris, Dubai, Luxembourg, Madrid, Frankfurt, Munich, Brussels and Hong Kong. Several require trainees to speak the local language, but all *"are very popular."*

SJ Berwin is known for the drive that has seen it become a major corporate player in its relatively short lifetime. This drive does occasionally translate into *"what can be perceived as aggression,"* trainees admitted. One said: *"I remember hearing the stories when I first applied and being terrified they were going to eat me alive, but it actually isn't like that at all."* Another source added: *"Yes, there are a few characters who fulfil that hard-nosed stereotype, but on the whole people are extremely approachable and friendly."* We particularly liked the musings of this next source, and reckon the following quote is a summary of

The True Picture

the firm that's as relevant as any comments about aggression: *"Culture is a powerful force, and even though none of us were here 30 years ago it's passed down through behaviour patterns. The firm does still have that dynamic culture. I mean, we suffered a lot through the recession, but people are always looking up and looking forward."* All agreed: *"In terms of general rapport, things have definitely improved since the new management came in."* Managing partner Rob Day took on the role in 2011 and is well-liked about the firm: *"He engages and communicates with people on a daily basis. There is a definite push to ensure a cohesive, happy firm."* Interviewees also insisted: *"People always stop to say hello or to chat. SJB is full of energetic, strong, outgoing people, so it's never going to be deathly quiet."*

The Banker, the Anchor and the Oyster Shed

The rumours of tough hours are pretty accurate, however. *"Look, the hours aren't great,"* sources said, *"but not any worse than you'd expect."* Although several interviewees had worked the *"occasional"* weekend and all-nighter, they *"aren't the norm."* Finance and corporate are notoriously the worst departments for stockpiling midnight oil, *"but that's the nature of the work. Partners and senior associates do also look after you and appreciate your effort."*

The qualification process didn't get rave reviews from trainees this year, even though retention at the firm is usually alright. *"SJB doesn't release job listings because they say they don't want to turn away talent, but all that means is that you have no idea where the jobs are or if there are any at all in certain departments,"* one source grumbled. *"It creates paranoia and competition among trainees, and that isn't handled well."* Another added: *"Applying to more than one department – as you naturally would in order to hedge your bets – also seemed to be a disadvantage last year, as people weren't seen as 'committed' enough to one team."* All agreed: *"We appreciate it's a difficult system to work out and there can never be full transparency, but the way it's run it needs to change."* The firm commented: *"The process is assessed continually, and any changes are based on trainee feedback, which we seek throughout and after each qualification round."* It kept on 25 out of 36 qualifiers in 2013.

SJB offers a good social scene: *"We have football, netball, cricket and rugby teams,"* trainees said. *"They're always well-subscribed, and people do actually get involved."* There's also a choir. *"It's called 'Sounds Just Brilliant'. Do you see what they did with the initials there? Genius."* Sarcasm aside, *"they're really good, and have an external choirmaster that comes in."* So good in fact, that they won 'Singingworks' Choir of the Year. The most recent big event was 'SJB's Got Talent', which was *"a lot of fun. There was singing and classical violin playing. People even choreographed a dance with LED lights."* Otherwise, trainees are treated to regular 'trainee networking' drinks on the terrace. *"It gives us the opportunity to really get to talk to people in both years and normally turns into a great night. We were all on the LPC together anyway, so it's a fun evening with friends more than anything."* After-work pints will be at the Banker, the Anchor or the Oyster Shed.

And finally...
Interviewees say the people who succeed here *"understand SJB's drive and are ready to work hard. It's not all about being the most bookish, or technically gifted; it's showing energy and enthusiasm for the work and a will to achieve what's best for the firm."*

Skadden, Arps, Slate, Meagher & Flom (UK) LLP

The facts

Location: London

Number of UK partners/solicitors: 25/61

Seats: 4x6 months

Total number of trainees: 15

Alternative seats: overseas seats

Extras: pro bono – LawWorks, TrustLaw Connect, Child Rights Information Network

On chambersstudent.co.uk...

How to get into Skadden

Interview with grad recruitment partner Danny Tricot

Disney and Lucasfilm

Abramovich v Berezovsky

This American idol's Canary Wharf office does tip top corporate and international arbitration work and acts as the hub of the firm's European operations.

Another day, another 30 billion dollars

It goes without saying that at the *Student Guide* reasoned, considered thought is our modus operandi, but if we were to drop all that and apply an impulsive playground logic to law firm rankings Skadden would surely come top of the charts: not only did the firm advise on the most expensive private court case in the world – Roman Abramovich's recent rebuttal of the $6bn claim brought against him by Boris Berezovsky – but it won as well. Both a victory and a validation, though certainly not the first of either, for a firm founded by immigrant Jewish lawyers who'd been snubbed by the legal elite of 1940s New York. Today Skadden is one of the most profitable and powerful firms in the world. With 23 offices around the world and an international network of 1,800 lawyers, it's no surprise that the *Chambers UK* and *Chambers Global* guides put many of Skadden's departments in the top tier.

Considering Skadden's reputation for working exclusively on the biggest, costliest, toughest cases and deals, the firm's UK graduate recruitment website makes some pretty bold promises to prospective trainees: *"You can expect early responsibility, significant client exposure and the opportunity to work on cutting-edge cross-border transactions sooner than you could expect elsewhere."* How much of this is just hot air? Let's take it apart, bit by bit. Early responsibility? Check: *"I found out that on one case I worked on the client on the other side was represented by a magic circle firm. They had their NQs managing the photocopying and due diligence, while I was making calls to our client in Africa and working through negotiations."* Significant client exposure? Check: *"One trainee was working on an arbitration matter nominally worth £20bn.*

It was just them, a partner and a senior associate, and they sat through at least ten hours of client meetings, face to face." Cutting-edge, cross-border transactions? Check: *"This one major M&A case I've been working on is based across 16 jurisdictions. It's a top-level deal between two household names. I've had to go to Europe a couple of times to help oversee completion."*

The firm recruits almost exclusively from the vac scheme – we say almost because one of the 12 trainees at the time of our research in summer 2013 hadn't done it. Potential vac schemers should know about the *"3am test,"* which sees paid-up staff judging vac schemers on *"whether or not they'd be good to share an office with at that time of night."* Sources cited the *"tiny trainee class sizes"* as part of what drew them to Skadden in the first place, as well as the firm's *"global prestige."* But it's best to be clear: Skadden isn't for everyone. Our insiders showed a streak of masochism when asked what life is like at the firm, glowingly telling us that *"there's nowhere to hide"* and *"you can never afford to take a back seat."* While these could sound like criticisms, our sources were sharing them as badges of honour. In their first year trainees do a seat in corporate and a seat in litigation, while second-years have the chance to revisit corporate or branch out into funds, restructuring, tax and banking. Overseas seats in the capital markets and litigation departments in Hong Kong are also offered to two second-years.

The force is strong with this one

Corporate mainly deals in M&A and capital markets work. Our interviewees had largely sat in M&A, where

Chambers UK rankings

Banking & Finance	Energy & Natural Resources
Capital Markets	Investment Funds
Corporate Crime	Private Equity
& Investigations	Restructuring/Insolvency
Dispute Resolution	Tax

the work *"is about 60% private equity and 40% public M&A, and the teams that trainees work with usually consist of a partner, a senior associate, a junior associate and a trainee. All the work is international – I didn't work on anything that was just based in England."* There can be some low-level work to begin with, such as due diligence and drafting board minutes, but this progresses quickly to attending client meetings, arranging signings, liaising with specialists, drafting non-disclosure agreements and assisting negotiations. In London, the department managed Nike's sale of Umbro to Iconix for $225m, while the American arm made headlines when it was instructed by Disney on its $4.05bn acquisition of Lucasfilm, the production company that gave the world 'Star Wars' and 'Indiana Jones'.

The dispute resolution department handles both litigation and international arbitration, with work coming in from all sorts of sectors including energy, real estate, telecoms and finance. One source sagely commented: *"A lot of these cases last two or three years, so the level of involvement you have depends on when you land in the seat."* But everyone we spoke with had high praise for their time with the team: *"I was lucky enough to join just as we started work for a huge real estate developer on an arbitration case. I had the chance to draft witness statements, and I oversaw that whole process from start to finish. I was calling the client directly, so they knew me by name."* Another recalled the *"high-adrenaline"* work they'd done on a freezing injunction. As well as representing Roman Abramovich, the department acted for the government of South Sudan (the world's newest country) on its recovery of oil cargoes worth hundreds of millions of dollars after they were reportedly snatched by the neighbouring Republic of Sudan. Skadden also won the 2013 *Chambers Global* award for Dispute Resolution Law Firm of the Year.

One trainee spoke of *"the almost vertical learning-curve"* in the banking department, which *"primarily works for borrowers rather than banks. There's a great variety of work and a lot of it comes from new businesses, although we do other acquisitions, restructurings and refinancings too. There's also a good portion of private M&A deals coming over from corporate, and we work closely with the US offices."* The department advised international metal magnates Outokumpu in the financing of its €2.8bn acquisition of steel supremes Inoxum, resulting in the creation of one of the world's largest metal businesses. Over in tax, there's also *"a lot of crossover work with the corporate team,"* and the department deals with big banks and financing companies such as Barclays and BlackRock.

Wharf side story

When asked if trainees get any time away from work, one source told us: *"I remember saying to my friends I'd got a training contract at Skadden and them telling me I should wave goodbye to my social life, but it hasn't been that way at all. I still finish earlier than a lot of my friends at other top firms."* That said, *"it's not abnormal to be leaving the office at 8pm,"* and *"there are some sleepless nights and weekend work in litigation and corporate,"* but one insider stressed: *"Colleagues are generally very understanding of the fact that trainees have a life outside the office."*

Most Fridays, trainees go for an after work drink *"somewhere around the Wharf,"* while there are firmwide drinks on the last Wednesday of every month in the canteen and occasional departmental forays to The Narrow, Gordon Ramsay's restaurant on the banks of the Thames. Back in the office, almost all of our insiders touched on Skadden's *"collegial"* feel, with one telling us: *"I know I can speak with anyone in every department – even those I haven't worked with. You get to spend time directly with people at all levels, so it feels very integrated."* Another added: *"While it's not the case that we're all best friends, people do genuinely get on very well."* It's also worth noting that Skadden recruits trainees from a global market: more than half of our interviewees were born abroad.

And finally...

Skadden's *"famously high"* retention rates mean that if you've got yourself a training contract you've pretty much got yourself a job. In 2013, the firm kept on all five of its qualifying trainees.

Slater & Gordon Lawyers

The facts

Location: Birmingham, Bristol, Cardiff, Edinburgh, London, Manchester, Milton Keynes, Newcastle, Sheffield, Wakefield, Cambridge

Number of UK partners/solicitors: 48/82

Partners who trained at firm: 15%

Total number of trainees: 6

Seats: 4x6 seats

Alternative seats: none

On chambersstudent.co.uk...

How to get into Slater & Gordon

S&G's acquisition of Russell Jones & Walker

In 2012 UK firm Russell Jones & Walker was acquired by Australia's Slater & Gordon, the world's first publicly traded law firm.

Public interest

A lot gets written ever year about changes to the legal profession. But few firms are really making major alterations to the traditional law firm model. Australia's Slater & Gordon is one big exception. In early 2012 it acquired Russell Jones & Walker for £53.8m, making the UK firm part of its publicly listed business and effectively giving RJW – where revenue had flatlined since 2007 – a big cash injection. *"I am chuffed that I got a training contract at a firm that is leading the way and is at the forefront of consolidation in the legal market,"* one trainee told us. *"I hope and believe that the firm will maintain its historic integrity and ethos in the future."*

Personal injury, clinical negligence, employment, crime, family and commercial disputes are the main areas of practice. Nearly all work revolves around *"claimant litigation for individuals, rather than acting for big corporates."* Several major trade unions are big clients and the firm is very proud of its focus on 'personal legal services'. One trainee said: *"As cheesy as it sounds I really do want to help the little man. That is a passion that everyone at this firm shares. To know that a client who had their leg amputated will get a prosthesis thanks to my work gives me a lot of satisfaction."*

The firm has 11 offices in the UK. London is the largest and the firm recruits trainees here every year, as it does in Manchester. Birmingham, Cardiff and Sheffield have also all recruited newbies in recent years – check the firm's website for the latest on where it's hiring. As we went to press, S&G had just agreed to acquire three more PI-focused entities – Goodmans Law, Fentons and part of Taylor Vinters. This expands the firm's presence in London and Manchester and adds a new office in Cambridge.

Line of duty

At the time of research there was one trainee each in family, crime and clin neg and two in both employment and personal injury. There are also seats in group litigation (aka class actions), trusts and estates, and property. The latter too (along with employment) can be used to fulfil the SRA's non-contentious requirement.

Personal injury handles a lot of work for unions, but it saw a 31% increase in referrals from individuals in 2012. The Police Federation is a major client, and the firm also acts for the Union of Shop, Distributive & Allied Workers (Usdaw) and the Royal College of Nursing. Some work is pretty high-profile: PI practice leader Liz Dux is acting for 50 Jimmy Savile sex abuse victims in negligence claims against the BBC and Stoke Mandeville hospital. Another major – but more typical – case saw the firm win £1.35m in compensation for a bus driver who lost a leg after he was hit by a car while standing at a bus stop. Most cases *"have the same trajectory,"* one trainee explained. *"You interview the client, take a statement, send out the letter of claim, obtain medical records, research the quantum of damages, negotiate with the other side over the offer of settlement, and then follow up with court proceedings if it comes to litigation."*

The clin neg team works on a large number of cases related to negligent operations and birth defects. *"When you meet the parents of a baby who suffered brain damage because they weren't delivered correctly, you realise what is at stake,"* reflected one trainee. S&G is one of several firms advising claimants in a case against a surgeon who allegedly performed over 1,000 faulty mastectomies on women with breast cancer. One more unusual case saw the widower of a psychiatric patient who hanged

The True Picture

417

Speechly Bircham LLP

The facts

Location: London

Number of UK partners/solicitors: 75/113

Partners who trained at the firm: 8%

Total number of trainees: 25

Seats: 4x6 months

Alternative seats: occasional secondments

Extras: pro-bono – Blackfriars Settlement, Kings Legal Clinic

On chambersstudent.co.uk...

How to get into Speechlys

This London mid-sizer prides itself on its commercial approach to the private wealth sector.

Multi-trick pony

Speechly Bircham has been a favourite among the super wealthy for many years. Known for its private wealth prowess, the 138-year-old firm maintains one of the biggest private client practices in the City, with its contentious trusts work consistently scoring highly in the *Chambers UK* stakes. That said, management is keen to emphasise the firm's flourishing commercial practices in an effort to posit Speechlys as a balanced entity rather than a one-trick pony. *"Although we're very proud of our private client capabilities, traditional private client work only accounts for 25% of our practice,"* training principal Chris Putt tells us, mentioning that *"corporate and finance are growing. We also expect to see an increase of work from family offices."* After speaking with this year's cohort, it appears incoming generations of applicants are beginning to reflect this shift: *"I actually applied to Speechlys because of its corporate and IP work,"* admitted one, while another estimated *"only around half of trainees come to the firm intent on a private client seat; the rest are more interested in the breadth of practices available."* In addition to top-band rankings in lower mid-market corporate/M&A, *Chambers UK* also offers nods for the firm's investment funds, real estate litigation and data protection work, among others.

The 2012/13 financial year saw a small growth in net profit somewhat dampened by a similarly slight drop in both turnover and PEP. A number of partner departures – 23 since January 2012 in fact – and the May 2013 announcement that the firm was abandoning its merger talks with London private client whiz Withers further disrupted things. *"Ultimately the merger with Withers just wasn't right for either side,"* comments Putt. Not to be downtrodden, however, Speechlys has held its head high and proclaimed an intention to channel resources into international expansion instead. *"You can feel the push,"* insiders said, revealing *"our Zürich branch is doing well, and our Luxembourg base has just moved to larger premises to cater to growth."* What's more, *"we've got plans in place to open other offices. The ambition to grow is clearly there."* Back at home *"things definitely feel like they're moving forward. Lots of departments seem keen to take NQs, and we've had some lateral hires too. The general feeling is pretty optimistic."*

Family matters

Around 14 seat options are available across Speechlys' private client, real estate and business services divisions. The only compulsory seats are one in business services and one in a contentious area like real estate litigation to satisfy SRA requirements. Our interviewees agreed *"HR does a really great job"* when it comes to seat allocation. Before starting and before each rotation trainees list their top four preferences, and *"most people get their first or second choice. They usually call you in for a little chat to discuss what you're thinking and try to accommodate you the best they can."* We heard the family and employment teams can be *"slightly harder to get into"* than others owing to their small size – sources suggested those keen on such seats *"make your interest known to HR from the beginning."*

The tax, trusts and succession practice is *"pretty large,"* occupying a whole floor of Speechlys' New Street Square digs and playing host to several sub-teams: onshore, offshore, probate, trust administration and property. *"As a trainee, you get exposure to all of these. Onshore work*

Chambers UK rankings

Agriculture & Rural Affairs	Intellectual Property
Charities	Investment Funds
Construction	Pensions
Corporate/M&A	Private Client
Data Protection	Projects
Employment	Real Estate
Family/Matrimonial	Real Estate Litigation
Financial Services	Restructuring/Insolvency
Immigration	

tends to be a little more accessible for first and second seaters, while offshore work is more suited to people further along as it can get very complex." Still, we heard there's scope for juniors at any level to express an interest in certain types of work. *"This is a good seat for client contact,"* said our sources. *"We get to to run certain files and act as the first point of contact in some instances. I can't remember the last time I touched the photocopier!"* So-called 'landed gentry' comprise a good chunk of the clientele, though the bulk is made up of self-made entrepreneurs and wealthy international individuals. *"We also service several family offices that make use of our capabilities."*

The firm *"bundles together"* its small family and contentious trusts teams to give trainees *"a good view of the contentious side of private client work."* The practice covers a *"complete mix"* of matters, from pre-nups and cohabitation agreements to childcare disputes and divorce petitions, often for clients who frequent the firm's other services. *"We tend to focus on divorces and the ensuing financial issues more than anything,"* an insider clarified. Our interviewees were happy with the responsibilities at hand, telling us *"the team is always keen to get trainees involved. There's a lot of drafting of wills and lasting power of attorneys and plenty of research to get stuck into."* Some told of attending court sessions when applicable, *"which involves some bundling, though never an overwhelming amount."*

Elle 'The Body of Law' Macpherson

The well-regarded corporate finance team is *"fairly big and definitely growing,"* interviewees said, mentioning that *"we've taken on several NQs and laterals recently."* According to insiders, *"there's a lot of client crossover between corporate and our other departments, so sitting with the department gives you a good appreciation of the firm at large."* Work predominantly consists of mid-market M&A, quoted company and private equity-related matters for clients as varied as family offices, healthcare companies and natural resources corporations. The firm recently advised primary care provider Harmoni on its £48m sale to Care UK. *"Often trainee work involves*

drafting ancillary documents and board minutes, but occasionally you're able to take the lead on small fundraisings."* Additionally *"there's lots of client contact and exposure to big-scale deals."*

Speechlys' banking and finance work is *"complementary to both the corporate and property teams,"* trainees said, *"and we act for both borrowers and lenders."* The team recently advised administrators on the preservation of live music venue London Pleasure Gardens and assisted with the sale of a Yorkshire renewable energy power plant following its liquidation. Matters may range *"from small business expansions all the way up to huge financings,"* but trainees are *"always made to feel integral to the team. Even as a first seater you're encouraged to go along to client meetings and lead the way on document management."*

The IPTD (IP, technology and data) department operates as a single unit, though *"there are clear divisions"* between contentious IP and data protection work, we were told. The former largely involves copyright infringement and other commercial disputes. A long-standing client is the illustrious Elle Macpherson, whom the firm advises on sponsorship and endorsement arrangements as well as any issues connected to the exploitation of her Elle Macpherson Intimates brand. Lawyers also recently acted for greetings card giant American Greetings on a variety of copyright and trade mark-related licensing matters. *"I got to draft letters of claim and attend conferences with counsel,"* reported one source. Over on the data protection side, trainees get to grips *"cutting-edge"* privacy and information security matters, *"often for clients who own their own websites. The team is brilliant and really inclusive – I felt like part of the group from day one."*

Speechlys' real estate practice was significantly bolstered following the firm's 2009 merger with Campbell Hooper and remains *"incredibly busy,"* according to insiders. Work is primarily commercial, though the firm occasionally makes room for a few of its more prominent private clients' residential matters. The team acts for investors, developers and tenants, many of whom reside overseas, and recently advised Henderson Global and P&O Estates on their pre-let agreements to Macmillan Publishing for space in an urban regeneration project in Kings Cross. There's a good deal of crossover with the nearby construction team, which handles both contentious and non-contentious across the development, regeneration, infrastructure and projects sectors. *"The majority of the work is UK-centric, and we can count some of London's finest property developers among our clients."* Trainees agreed both departments offer *"brilliant amounts of responsibility"* in the way of direct client contact and *"opportunities to run small files by yourself."*

The firm offers a handful of client secondments, which are reviewed each rotation and cater to specific departments like IP, employment and construction. *"They're very popular and seen as a positive experience. You have to go through a formal application and interview process to get onto one."* Those who'd spent time away from the office reassured us *"you never feel disconnected from the firm. They're managed very well, and you're in touch with people here throughout."* Although trainees don't go abroad, there is potential for NQs.

Speech easy

Nabbing a training contract at Speechlys isn't just about stellar academics (though grades are important, of course); our sources emphasised that personality plays a crucial role in the decision. *"The amazing egghead with the limited personality is not who we're looking to recruit,"* training principal Chris Putt says, telling us the *"overriding qualities"* in successful applicants include an ability to collaborate with colleagues and *"a high degree of emotional intelligence. We're looking for drive, but not for ruthless, aggressive types."* Also up there in importance is commercial awareness. *"The contrast between Speechlys and other firms of the like is that our clients tend towards new-moneyed, international entrepreneurs,"* continues Putt. *"On the whole we take a commercial approach to private wealth. Candidates need to be aware of potential growth and market development and demonstrate how their skills are applicable. We're looking for candidates who want to learn business skills alongside black-letter law."*

Interviewees praised the office's open plan set-up, which *"lends itself to an approachable atmosphere. Trainees sit among people of all levels, so it's easy to keep an open dialogue with partners and forge relationships."* As another pointed out, *"it really encourages comradery. You see some teams bringing in baked goods for each other, while others get together for Friday night drinks on the regular."* We also heard the firm has *"a good attitude towards hours and efficiency. There are some late nights of course, but people tend to head off between 7pm and 8pm. Luckily when you're here beyond that it's appreciated."*

Speechlys hosts an array of social forums that trainees can get on board with. In addition to football, netball, hockey and cricket teams, there's a *"popular"* reading club and a no doubt melodious Christmas choir. Speaking of Crimbo, the holiday party that accompanies it is the year's biggest event, complete with a champagne reception, sit-down meal and *"dancing bonanza. The dinner jackets come out, and people get really involved."* There's also an annual summer do – last year's was held at Canon Street Roof Gardens – as well some *"great"* vac scheme events like speedboating on the Thames and quarterly drinks events. On the informal front, a merry band of Speechlys folk can almost always be found kicking off the weekend at one of the office's many nearby pubs.

Our interviewees were pretty relaxed about the qualification process. *"Of course it's always nerve-racking, but HR will fight your corner if you're good enough. The system seems as fair and open as possible."* In 2013 Speechlys retained 9 of its 13 new qualifiers.

And finally...

Speechlys' vac scheme functions as *"an extended interview"* and *"is probably the safest route to getting a training contract,"* according to insiders. *"They rely heavily on the feedback from partners and trainees."*

Squire Sanders

The facts

Location: London, Leeds, Birmingham, Manchester

Number of UK partners/solicitors: 132/226

Partners who trained at firm: 28%

Total number of trainees: 44

Seats: 6x4 months

Alternative seats: overseas seats, secondments

Extras: pro bono – Paddington Law Centre, Birmingham and Hillside Legal Advice Clinics; language classes

On chambersstudent.co.uk

How to get into Squire Sanders

The SSD/Hammonds merger

> **Having taken a gargantuan merger in its stride, Squire Sanders is** *"growing and busy... which can only be good!"*

Transatlanticism

English rose Hammonds exchanged vows with Yankee Squire Sanders & Dempsey in early 2011, and things are yet to lose their honeymoon sheen. There was a bit of fiddling around with names – 'Squammonds' was always going to be easier than 'Squire Sanders Hammonds' – but a stern rebrand got rid of the fun and left us with just plain 'Squire Sanders'. For trainees, it's safe to report, there are real positives, not least more international work. *"The US heads of department come over regularly to meet us – it's quite exciting to be part of the grand scheme of things,"* said one trainee.

Overall trainees don't see a loss of Hammonds' congenial ethos. *"The hours haven't changed, morale hasn't changed and the social scene is still the same. But everyone here is thrilled to be part of a bigger firm. The work is going to be far more juicy and we now get cross-referrals from other offices. So the calibre of people we're going to be employing will naturally also be higher."* If there are any bones to pick, it's with the issues that come with size. *"It can be harder to make yourself known when bonuses and promotions are determined by a committee."* And the Squire Sanders behemoth keeps getting bigger, adding Singapore, Seoul, Sydney and Riyadh in 2012. *"You do feel this big global push,"* trainees agreed. *"Before, the partners were the big bosses, now there's this higher, almost unspoken force which has the final word. Before, we focused on the hours we recorded, but in the US that doesn't mean anything – they want to know how much money you've actually brought in. So now the focus is on billing rather than recording hours, but that's nothing negative."*

With six seats to sample the wares of Squire Sanders, trainees are still spoilt for choice. *"Plus, with the job market as it is, sampling that many departments really opens up your options."* There are seats on offer in more than 15 groups, which are all present in the majority of the four UK offices. We heard good things about the *"accommodating"* HR department – for example, in some seats trainees have recently been able to divide their time between London and the regional offices. *"Within the trainee group, we all have slightly different interests – it's clear that HR plans each intake,"* sources said. Squire's trainees are split fairly evenly between its four offices; at the time of our calls there were 18 in London, 12 in Leeds, 11 in Birmingham and ten in Manchester.

Sandwiches and the City

New recruits to Squire Sanders now complete a fast-track LPC at a branch of BPP law school. *"It's a lot of hard work, but it does get it out of the way."* This is followed by a three-month client secondment before trainees start at the firm proper. During the training contract, there's also the opportunity to do a six-month client secondment or spend a seat in Paris or Brussels. *"It's great for business development if the firm can place someone with a valued client, but it also gives the trainee a commercial advantage over others who have not spent time in-house."*

Corporate does *"a lot of M&A, a little bit of public company work as well as private equity."* Trainees like the seat as *"it's easy to get up to speed straight away – you can hit the ground running from the off. There's a buzz and it's so busy it makes you happy to work the hours it demands – days fly by."* Clients include national companies and banks, though there's a slightly different slant to the

Chambers UK rankings

Capital Markets	Intellectual Property
Corporate/M&A	Media & Entertainment
Data Protection	Pensions
Dispute Resolution	Pensions Litigation
Employment	Private Equity
Immigration	Real Estate
Information Technology	Sports Law

work in each office, increasingly with an international flavour. *"We often give discrete advice to US-based clients, and there's lots of work for European companies too."* The team worked on the £274m takeover of UK-based Umeco by US chemical technology company Cytec, and on the takeover of Schneider Foreign Exchange by Mexico's Monex. Trainees told us they often get client contact on these large international buyouts. *"It's good, as you often only have a partner above you, so you get to correspond directly with the other side. And my work is checked minimally – I'm supervised but not stifled."*

Commercial dispute resolution works on international arbitrations as well as courtroom disputes. The firm is currently acting for trustees of the Siemens Benefit Scheme in negligence claims worth £7m against an investment management company. Again, trainees emphasised how involved they get, even if the trial is huge. *"Because of the stage the case was in when I joined the team, all I'm doing is bundling,"* said one. *"But I'm included in absolutely everything, so if there's an opportunity to take me to a mediation, they will."*

Sherlock homes

Each office offers a property seat, and in some locations trainees have access to planning and construction work too. The department acts for investors, councils and developers across the country. *"The bread and butter work is post-completion and all the registration formalities and form filling that entails. If you show willing, you get to do more: draft leases and contracts of sale, or look at title investigations for big old plots of land."* Trainees tend to like this seat if they enjoy document-heavy investigations. *"Someone will give you a task to run with and then it becomes your puzzle to sort out and piece together – eventually you will go back to them with four lever arch files..."*

A seat in restructuring and insolvency can be a lot more dynamic than it may sound, sources told us. There's both contentious and non-contentious work, the former being the sexier stuff – *"like when someone's run off with a Saudi princess and he's a devil worshipping alcoholic... for example."* There's a great deal of international work, but *"the firm still prides itself on keeping hold of its local Yorkshire clients."* Instructions come from Deloitte

and KPMG as well as smaller companies. *"We're spread across the spectrum in terms of where our income comes from and that means the dynamics of every matter you work on are different."* Insolvency is still a very active area in the post-recession world, which means *"interesting issues crop up all the time – banks are cautious to take action and you learn the politics of the insolvency game."*

IP offers the chance to work for clients like Google, Panasonic and the Telegraph Media Group on a range of trade mark and copyright infringement cases. The team also does a lot of work for the National Grid, advising on soft IP – branding, design – as well as trade mark and patent issues, like those surrounding the company's new 'smart meter' – a revolutionary way of measuring electricity use that communicates back usage without the need for a manual reading. One of the group's other strengths is advising luxury brands like Cath Kidston, Hobbs and DAKS on branding protection and domain name issues. *"As those brands are global, you get to liaise with external and internal counsel around the world, which means you get a good feel for Squire Sanders' international operations."* Our sources reported that the team offers trainees *"a huge number of drafting opportunities"* on various projects. *"I've produced terms and conditions, supply-of-goods contracts and service agreements – all for clients with very different demands,"* reported one trainee.

The pensions department does both contentious and non-contentious advice work. *"It's enjoyable to explain the provisions of a pension scheme to trustees,"* said one trainee. *"Usually, a fee earner will send me away to produce a research note and then I will see it being passed to the client with hardly any amendments."* The group acts as counsel to the trustees of funds from ICI Chemicals, Thames Water, Fiat and infrastructure conglomerate Mouchel. *"Being in pensions is like going back to university, it's so technical,"* said one trainee. *"You get to delve down into one tiny little clause in a 200-page document, which is actually really interesting because so much turns on it."* Luckily, people who practise pensions *"tend to be really lovely, which certainly helps as there are so many hair-pulling moments when you are doing such detailed research."*

Earth Wind and Squires

All the trainees we quizzed conveyed a genuine excitement to be part of something *"with such a big global reach. It's in everyone's thinking and consequently the level of business development is really high."* There was an assertion, though, that alongside this *"Squires offers something different."* Take the in-house rock band 'Earth Wind and Squires', currently competing in Law Rocks – *"that isn't the kind of thing you'd see at the big boys in the magic circle."* There are also *"plenty of sports activities and things for crazy fitness people like a charity bike ride to Paris."* There's plenty to keep trainees busy out of hours, with summer and winter parties, charity quiz nights, team breakfasts and regular Friday drinks. There's a head trainee in each UK office, who *"makes the effort to get everyone involved by getting us to go for dinner once a month."* Manchester trainees harnessed the power of transatlanticism by organising an Independence Day fête at a hotel *"with sweet stalls, sponge-the-partner and a barbecue."* Best of both worlds, we say.

Supervision style and support differ a bit between departments. *"On the whole, supervision is really good,"* said one trainee. *"Personalities and interest in teaching vary, but there's a base level of help which is always offered."* In departments with more time pressures, *"it's daunting but you rise to the challenge. You can always come back to ask questions, and after you do something well you get praised for it."* We didn't hear any complaints about the qualification process either. A jobs list is announced nationally, and trainees can apply to any of the UK offices. In 2013, 19 out of 27 trainees were kept on.

The True Picture

And finally...

"Since the merger, there's now a blend of international and more local work. But the atmosphere hasn't changed – the support and friendliness which was historically our selling point is still present."

shine

STEPHENSON HARWOOD

Invest your talents in a firm that's growing and regularly delivering groundbreaking deals. For our size, our international reach and client base are exceptional. Get right to the heart of the action alongside associates and partners in tight, focused teams. Add the chance to complete a six-month seat in Hong Kong or Singapore, and it's clear we're a firm that can help you perform brilliantly. Find out how at www.shlegal.com/graduate

Stephenson Harwood

The facts

Location: London

Number of UK partners/solicitors: 92/150

Partners who trained at the firm: 15%

Total number of trainees: 32

Seats: 4x6 months

Alternative Seats: overseas seats, secondments

Extras: pro bono - PRIME, Lawyers in Schools; language classes

On chambersstudent.co.uk...

How to get into SH

SH overseas

The 1979 Iranian hostage crisis

Stephenson Harwood continues to expand after kicking off 2013 with moves that will boost its presence in Asia, signalling no desire to rest on its laurels...

O Pioneers!

It's unfortunate that many people still view Stephenson Harwood primarily through the lens of its shipping work. It's easy to see why, though, and in the last three years the firm has handled the biggest maritime navigation claim to ever hit London's insurance markets, and helped to finance the largest vessel built in China. But there's a lot more to SH. It's international (with offices and associations spanning Asia, Europe and the Middle East) and, despite being full-service, it has been especially recognised for its work in five key areas: asset finance, commercial litigation and arbitration, corporate finance, marine and international trade (of course) and real estate. It was also one of the first UK firms to take the plunge and enter the Asian market, by opening shop in Hong Kong back in 1979. That, incidentally, was the same year that SH lawyers played a pivotal role in freeing hostages during the Iranian hostage crisis (by helping to unfreeze Iranian assets), a case which earned the firm praise from US Secretary of State Cyrus Vance.

Today, over 25% of SH people are based in the Greater China and South-East Asia offices, a figure which reflects relationships cemented ever since SH's inception: co-founder William Harwood established the firm back in 1875 upon his return to London after practising law in China. 2013 has seen SH inject further investment into the region, and in May the firm announced its launch in Beijing (to further draw in clients from China's financial and administrative centre), as well as two new associations with firms in Singapore and Myanmar. SH is playing the pioneer again, by becoming the first UK firm to establish connections in the latter location – although it is also playing it safe by forming an association instead

of merging and opening up a fully fledged office (which Myanmar currently permits). In Singapore it's a different story, and the new association was formed in light of the firm's unsuccessful application for a qualifying foreign law practice licence: it lost out to American big boys Sidley Austin, Jones Day and Gibson Dunn. For now, the association complements an office which specialises in offshore maritime arbitration work (for which it doesn't need a licence).

Elsewhere, SH has also been busy of late, establishing a new office in Dubai and beefing up its Paris offering by adding a disputes team to the transactional-heavy office, after dissolving a former alliance with French firm BCTG & Associes. These moves occurred as part of an ongoing plan to boost the firm's international arbitration capability across several locations in the network, which makes sense, given that litigation was the biggest fee generator in 2011/2012.

Speaking of turnover, the figures have been good, all things considered. SH reported a flat turnover for the second quarter of the 2012/13 financial year – a quarter which Deloitte described as one of the slowest for law firms in seven years, with many firms posting disappointing results.

Hold your horses!

Before each rotation trainees list three seat preferences. *"The firm certainly does try to match people,"* said one source, *"but it doesn't always work out, and sometimes things are out of our control."* Some people had been *"left unhappy,"* but the majority of our contacts felt that their preferences had often been met.

Chambers UK rankings

Asset Finance	Fraud
Aviation	Information Technology
Banking & Finance	Investment Funds
Banking Litigation	Outsourcing
Capital Markets	Pensions
Commodities	Pensions Litigation
Construction	Private Equity
Corporate Crime	Professional Negligence
& Investigations	Projects
Corporate/M&A	Real Estate Finance
Dispute Resolution	Real Estate Litigation
Education	Shipping
Employment	Social Housing
Environment	Tax
Financial Services	Transport

Commercial litigation *"has been the most popular department in terms of receiving NQ applications, and it is by far our largest department, too."* It covers insolvency, IP, regulatory, arbitration, property litigation and general litigation. *"This department has all these teams developing within it, which are big enough and busy enough to keep each trainee exclusively for the duration of the seat."* The focus of the group's high-end litigation has revolved around the energy, investment and banking sectors, and headlines were grabbed when SH acted for Rabobank in relation to acase involving a horse named London, who was due to compete in the 2012 Olympic Games as part of the Dutch equestrian team. As it turns out, London was in fact an asset embroiled in the collapse of Eurocommerce – a major Dutch real estate group – and owners of the group were attempting to place London out of reach of Rabobank, to whom pledges were owed. Plans to sell London to a Qatari sheikh were foiled and SH managed to get an injunctive relief to prohibit removal of the horse, but not before London triumphed at the Olympics, winning two silver medals.

The IP team does a mix of litigation and advisory work, and works with some very well-known UK and global brands. In regulatory, *"the vast majority of our work is financial services-related, and can involve insider-trading market abuse – many of these cases are high-profile. I've been going to client offices to take witness statements, as well as going to FSA meetings with clients and drafting advice."* In comparison, insolvency comes with *"an awful lot of research – one of the biggest tasks I've had is reviewing documents for potential disclosure."* Arbitrations *"happen every now and again,"* and when they do *"it's a very good experience."*

A seat in MIT (marine and international trade) is *"excellent,"* and it's a *"very successful team – the one that the firm is well known for."* The team recently advised

Groupama, a lead insurer on a claim received relating to engine damage sustained by a Greek vessel called the 'Navios Apollon': the original claim was for $44m, but SH managed to wrangle it so that the final amount paid was $5.8m. Trainees said that *"it's not just shipping litigation – there's a significant amount of international trade and a lot of shipbuilding contract work. I was working on the contracting of raw materials and there was only a short window to conduct negotiations. My supervisor and I were writing supply contracts and altering them to the specific needs of each transaction – it was quite technical stuff."* Others had been involved in a *"large shipbuilding arbitration"* and had spent the majority of their time coordinating the disclosure process. Some had also mentioned the opportunity to *"travel and write articles for certain publications."*

Boeing somewhere?

Trainees can also get their shipping fix in SH's shipping finance team, which is a part of the broader finance department: *"There's a lot of responsibility here if you want it – you can be sent to closing meetings abroad, and often trainees are sent somewhere in Europe. We're basically helping to structure and draft supporting documentation for high-value loans which are backed by vessel securities. You might also be responsible for registering a vessel and making sure everything is compliant."* Other teams in the finance department include aviation, rail, banking and real estate. SH worked on one of the largest deals in aviation history in 2011, advising Lion Air on the purchase of 230 Boeing aircraft in a deal worth $21.7bn. The deal was so big that Obama himself oversaw the signing of it. Sources said that *"we tend to work for airlines rather than banks, and we've been working with many of the emerging low-cost airlines in the Asian region, buying planes from Boeing and Airbus. You have quite a regular delivery schedule, and the pace picks up quite a bit in the run up to a delivery. The only drawback is that Airbuses are delivered in Toulouse and Boeings in Seattle, so things can get a little stressful!"*

SH's mid-market corporate department is split into the following potential seats: corporate finance (which is a general seat covering M&A and securities work); tax; funds; competition; projects; and commercial, outsourcing and technology. On the M&A side, SH attracts many companies in the energy sector, and advised Eland Oil & Gas on its $154m acquisition of a 45% stake (from Shell, Total and Agip) in a Nigerian oil mining lease. Those in corporate finance said that *"the first half of my seat was taken up by due diligence, for a massive transaction which involved the listing of a London company on the Hong Kong stock exchange, but the second half of my seat was more enjoyable, and I was engaged in more drafting and attended shareholder meetings."* The projects team is a *"fairly new addition to the firm,"* and have most recently overseen projects in the UK, Singapore, Greece and Ireland. They'll help out on bidding strategies, risk management and procurement, and trainees told us: *"I did join at a quieter time of year, but it still feels quite different to corporate, even though you're considered a corporate trainee."* Funds trainees, however, *"really enjoyed"* their seat and said that *"it's extremely varied and you'll never do the same thing twice. It's a nice mix of research and transactional stuff, and I've worked on setting up new funds, going to the market to get money for existing ones and restructuring funds as well."*

When it comes to real estate, SH is taking the lead, along with Berwin Leighton Paisner, on the purchase and development of Amersand, an 80,000 sq ft site on the corner of Oxford and Wardour Street in London. SH are advising Hong Kong real estate and private equity specialists Peterson Group on the £121m acquisition, its very first property investment in Europe. Sources said it was a *"terrific and extremely busy department. As a trainee you get given your own transactions to work on, and the level of client contact is superb."*

Singa-snore? Don't think so...

The overseas secondments to Singapore and Hong Kong are *"extremely popular"* and there's *"a lot of competition for spaces."* At each rotation, two spots are open to trainees in each location: *"Hong Kong is always very popular, while Singapore is less so, as it has a reputation for being crazy busy all the time, which puts people off a bit."*

Sources who had completed a stint in Singapore said that the hours were *"comparable to London, but possibly longer because they don't always have the manpower, so they really need the two trainees."* The office covers a range of shipping finance, aviation finance, MIT and corporate work, and trainees added that SH was *"very popular with clients"* in this region, meaning that *"they pile on the work and you just have to muck in and get on with it – you get thrown in at the deep end but the partners are fantastic."*

Those who had been to Hong Kong said that *"it's really interesting to look at a different legal system which is based on English law, but at the same time it does mean that there are limitations in what you can do."* Nonetheless, the office's small size means that *"there's less division between teams, so you can take on a variety of work that in London you wouldn't be able to do unless you were sitting in that specific department."* Corporate/finance will form the bulk of the work, but litigation and real estate work is sometimes available. All sources that had been seconded commended the support they received and were especially grateful for *"the very nice apartments"* they temporarily resided in.

Harwood's way

Going forwards, the aim is to *"get above being a mid-tier, mid-sized City firm: we don't want to be a magic or silver circle firm, but we do want to be one of the top firms in the City."* It looks like SH will be focused on *"continuing to build a good name and shouting louder. We're so much more than a 'shipping' firm – just look at our litigation and finance practices."* Among trainee predictions were the anticipated expansion of the real estate practice, as well as *"targeted growth in Africa."* the firm does have long term intentions to grow internationally, but can't confirm anything concrete at this stage.

Sources praised CEO Sharon White for giving speeches and sending emails which highlight *"how we're doing, who the new hires are and why we're moving in a certain direction – she even holds a trainee-only session which goes into what our role as a trainee is in that wider strategy."* White was also commended for *"acknowledging the firm's weaknesses and where we need to improve."* One such perceived weakness was that *"the firm is not very good at marketing itself, despite the good work that we do – many clients are surprised when they come to the building and they see how great it is. It's a sign of where the firm is and where it is going."* Others added that *"there's scope to grow within this building. There's a clear strategy and there's room to accommodate it – I can't think of any area that will contract."*

"The building may well influence the atmosphere as well," suggested another trainee: *"The offices are big, and it's all very light and airy, which contributes to an environment which is very friendly and collaborative – there's none of that competitive nonsense!"* There's little sense of hierarchy at social events, in which *"you'll find trainees chatting to partners,"* and there are plenty of chances to mingle as well.

The Christmas party – most recently held at The Marriott hotel – is *"always nice,"* while many departments hold monthly lunches. *"We're really into the team stuff,"* said sources, who enthusiastically described a *"thriving"* netball league, cricket matches in the summer and football games every Monday night. For those with a more peaceful disposition, yoga classes are held every Friday. The trainee intake is close because *"it's small compared to a magic circle firm; everyone knows each other and people go out every week for drinks, not just on a Friday, but mid-week as well..."* Trainees also receive a budget for *"young professionals events,"* in which they invite *"potential contacts"* for food and cocktails at the firm. They're designed to stimulate networking and business development, which sources said was promoted throughout their seats as well: *"There's no pressure, but they do encourage us to get to know the clients and attend events."*

Trainees get *"very useful"* induction sessions each time they join a new department. Most cram these sessions into the first few days, but commercial litigation *"is different – the training is stretched throughout the course of the seat."* There are also *"regular know-how sessions"* in each department, as well as external seminars which help to *"make you alert and aware of things that you're not directly working on."*

The qualification process is *"generally handled quite well,"* but things can get quite tricky because *"many trainees want a place in commercial litigation and they can only take on so many people!"* There are, of course, *"exceptions to that trend"* who prefer more transactional work, and sources said that *"if they like you and you're not successful in your first interview for an NQ position, then they'll try to offer you something else."* In 2013 the firm kept on 13 out of 16 qualifiers.

And finally...

"Anyone who applies here will get a damn good training contract," said trainees, who bemoaned a reality where this firm too often gets overlooked. If you're looking for international opportunities and a broad mix of expertise then don't be too quick to dismiss Stephenson Harwood.

Stevens & Bolton LLP

The facts

Location: Guildford
Number of UK partners/solicitors: 37/69
Partners who trained at the firm: 11%
Total number of trainees: 8
Seats: 6x4 months
Alternative seats: none

On chambersstudent.co.uk...

How to get into Stevens & Bolton
All about Guildford

S&B trainees can sample high-calibre private client and commercial fare in a serene Surrey setting.

Well on the Wey

City-standard lawyering in genteel Guildford might seem like an impossible dream, but the folks at Stevens & Bolton think otherwise. *"A lot of people see us as a regional firm and before I started I was a bit concerned that I'd just be working on really small matters. But that's not been the case at all,"* revealed one trainee. *"The work is high-quality and we compete with City firms – the other side on our deals will often be a magic circle firm."* Among S&B's ranks are many partners who've escaped the Thames-side rat race for greener pastures on the banks of the Wey, bringing along notable clients which they can serve at more affordable regional rates. Familiar names on the books include Kia Motors, Cineworld and pizza chain Papa John's.

S&B's commercial credentials are matched by a strong private client practice. *"I like that we represent individuals as well as companies. When I applied I hadn't decided what area I wanted to specialise in, so I wanted a broad range of experience at a well-rounded firm,"* was the feeling of one interviewee.

Trainees complete six seats of four months, allowing them to sample all available options, *"which is really good if you're feeling circumspect."* However, it is possible to complete two seats in one department. Time in coco is compulsory; the other seats available are dispute resolution/IP, real estate, tax and trusts and employment. *"The allocation system is the best I could think of,"* enthused a source. *"My friends at other firms are jealous of how lucky we are over seats. The HR team will bend over backwards to accommodate you."*

Brewers, Babycham and bribery

In coco, trainees *"inevitably end up doing admin tasks. There isn't a way of getting round that."* Fortunately, our sources concurred that *"partners make a big effort to keep you involved and give you experience if you show interest. You're not brought into a deal and then left in the dark. You feel like part of the team rather than someone just doing boring tasks."* Transactions can be hefty – the firm recently advised Veolia Water on the £1.236bn sale of its regulated water companies. During the commercial component of the seat new recruits might take on *"drafting franchise agreements, research into the Data Protection Act or anti-bribery work on a compliance procedure questionnaire."* Although the ideal coco seat would include *"an even mix of corporate and commercial,"* in reality *"it doesn't usually work like that and depends on how busy the departments are."* Sources weren't too fussed, however: *"I was more interested in the corporate side anyway, but my supervisor made it clear that they'd try and get me more commercial exposure if I wanted it,"* said one.

In the real estate department, a trainee reported *"handling a lot of my own transactions on smaller property files. There were a couple of instances where I was handling all the correspondence with solicitors from the other side and the clients. I was always supervised, but I was doing all the leg work. Being able to handle all the aspects of a matter makes you feel like a real solicitor."* When they're not *"drafting leases or letters of advice to clients or doing complicated bits of research,"* trainees can also *"get involved with construction litigation."* Lately, the firm has acted for property developers Vfund on a £60m joint venture with Epping Forest District Council to create a fashion retail park.

The True Picture

Chambers UK rankings

Banking & Finance	Immigration
Competition/European Law	Information Technology
Construction	Intellectual Property
Corporate/M&A	Partnership
Dispute Resolution	Private Client
Employment	Real Estate
Environment	Restructuring/Insolvency
Family/Matrimonial	Tax

Recent contentious matters at S&B include representing Canadian freight company Chaulk Air in a £6.2m dispute with a UK shipyard. Other clients include Dairy Crest, Hiscox Insurance and brewing company SABMiller. For trainees, the dispute resolution seat is likely to involve a portion of *"the more mundane tasks like filing and organising documents."* But aside from bundling and *"massive disclosure exercises,"* our sources had drafted witness statements and spent plenty of time at arbitrations and in court. One emphasised that *"if you look for opportunities and make a play for them, they're there. I was part of conference calls with clients and counsel and asked to give my opinion, which was taken into consideration. It's not like you've just got a lowly status and robot function."* The IP disputes department *"has got quite a few high-profile clients, so it's a bit more glamorous,"* asserted one trainee. *"I got to draft complex particulars of claims and letters before action, plus complex pieces of research for the client, although there was still a lot of document management."* The firm recently acted for global drinks company Accolade Wines in a trade mark and passing off dispute with retailer Cath Kidston over the Babycham logo. The IP department *"has a bit more of a City mentality in the way it's run,"* claimed a source, alluding to a more pronounced internal hierarchy. However, *"when something good happened with a case we went for an expensive lunch, which isn't the usual style of a regional firm like this. We don't tend to have that high-rolling lifestyle!"*

Grounded in Guildford

So lavish City-style wining and dining might not be on the menu all that often, but does the regional setting mean a pay off in terms of hours? After all, sources mentioned that they were attracted to the notion of a *"work/life balance that you don't get in the London firms."* Well, don't expect a solid nine to five routine at S&B. The coco department *"gets very busy towards year-end, and then you're looking at working City hours. I know some trainees did all-nighters."* Others endured heavy patches in litigation bundling into the night *"with a big deadline coming up for the exchange of witness statements."* But this interviewee looked on the bright side: *"It wasn't that awful because I was in a team and we helped each other out. It was a nice example of S&B doing high-quality work which requires you to put in the hours, but going about it in a supportive way."* Really late stints are *"unusual,"* however, and most sources reported leaving the office at around 6.30 or 7pm on average days.

"Not being in the City means that people are a lot more willing to have a chat. They're not wrapped up in work all the time," mused one trainee. *"It's welcoming and relaxed – there's nobody here that's particularly intimidating. It's a place where no one's lost perspective and people still know how to have a good time."* Sources thought: *"There's a good informal culture of getting out of the office and popping to the pub."* More officially, there are firm-wide monthly drinks, departmental summer socials and a Christmas party on the top floor of the office. This space also hosts lunchtime pilates and *"not too rigorous boot camp sessions"* with a personal trainer. Recently, the coco department went on an excursion to Cambridge and real estate folk did a spot of wine tasting. *"There's always something or other going on."*

Trainees here come from a range of universities but sources thought a Russell Group background *"is becoming more and more important"* during selection. They also say S&B looks for *"confident, calm and diligent"* types with *"a bit of personality."* The qualification process is *"quite informal"* and interviews occur *"only if there's more than one person who wants a job in a certain department."* The main concern for trainees was not the number of positions but *"whether the firm can match up people with the departments they actually want a job in."* This fear proved true in 2013, as the firm offered four NQ jobs (three in coco and one in real estate), but none of the three qualifiers took them up.

And finally...

Happy interviewees agreed that S&B has *"all the bonus points of being smaller. People know your name. You're more than just a trainee with a two-year contract. A massive effort is made to get you involved with the highest quality work possible."*

Taylor Wessing LLP

The facts

Location: London, Cambridge

Number of UK partners/solicitors: 104/281

Partners who trained at firm: 23%

Total number of trainees: 47

Seats: 4x6 months

Alternative seats: secondments

Extras: language classes

On chambersstudent.co.uk....

How to get into Taylor Wessing

Silicon Roundabout and tech start-ups

More on seats

Taylor Wessing *"may not be the best-advertised name on campus,"* but this IP-focused firm still manages to attract *"energetic and creative"* trainees to join it in its bid for international expansion.

Let's get digital!

Art lovers might recognise the name Taylor Wessing from the National Portrait Gallery Photographic Prize it sponsors. A recent winner might have struck gold capturing a reclusive woman shying away from the camera, but the firm is making a serious effort to seize the limelight, and make a name for itself for innovation and creativity. The former Taylor Johnson Garrett may have broadened its scope beyond its IP, life sciences and technology specialism since its merger with German firm Wessing back in 2002, but the firm's London office is pushing to attract new internet start-up clients. A recently opened Shoreditch office joins the HQ on Fetter Lane and a tech-focused offshoot in Cambridge as the firm bids to snare the next Google as a client. It already represents the actual Google.

Taylor Wessing combines *"aspects of a small firm, like taking on private client work, with having big clients and an international scope."* The firm's *"international presence is one of the reasons we get repeat instructions from clients,"* and having lawyers in other offices on hand makes for an *"extra level of support"* when dealing with multi-jurisdictional cases. The firm has built on a strong Western European base, including six offices in Germany, to make a recent foray into Singapore, and a partnership with Europe's ENWC has brought offices in Austria, the Czech Republic, Hungary, Poland, Slovakia and Ukraine on board.

Taylor Wessing's trainees pick four six-month seats, one of which must be corporate or financial in nature. Although trainees were reasonably happy with the seats they ended up with, they noted that *"there just aren't enough seats around in some departments"* – particularly in the popular trade marks, copyright and media department, and in employment. Some found that *"some rotations you won't get any of your choices,"* but when that happened, the HR team were praised for *"making proposals – rather than just sticking you somewhere, they try and get you exposure to the type of work you want, even if it's outside your seat."*

Diamonds in the rough

Taylor Wessing's trade marks, copyright and media (TCM) department works with big manufacturing clients including Ferrero – makers of the ambassador's chocs of choice – and *"creative individuals, like sculptors or interior designers."* Trade mark opposition litigation saw trainees doing *"a lot of research, drafting cease and desist letters, and attending two hearings"* – one got the chance to witness *"a settlement meeting where the opposition agreed to change certain things about their trade mark to make it less similar to our client's, which is a fascinating interaction to see."* Trainees recognised that *"we're unusual in having a huge TCM department, then a separate patent litigation group."* Nearly all partners and associates in the patent department have at least one degree in science or engineering, since *"the work's very technical,"* working on *"huge multinational patent cases."* The firm also offers its life sciences clients – which include gene therapy experts Oxford BioMedica and global pharmaceutical manufacturer Abbott Laboratories – regulatory, licensing and venture capital services.

Chambers UK rankings

Agriculture & Rural Affairs	Intellectual Property
Banking & Finance	Life Sciences
Banking Litigation	Media & Entertainment
Capital Markets	Outsourcing
Construction	Pensions
Corporate/M&A	Pensions Litigation
Defamation/Reputation	Private Client
Management	Private Equity
Dispute Resolution	Product Liability
Employee Share Schemes	Professional Discipline
& Incentives	Professional Negligence
Employment	Real Estate Finance
Financial Services	Restructuring/Insolvency
Fraud	Telecommunications
Information Technology	

Taylor Wessing's sizeable corporate department is split into subgroups, including the corporate, commercial and projects team, which works for *"incredibly varied clients"* including healthcare, hotel, renewable energy and private equity companies. One trainee working on a billion-dollar IPO got sent out to the offices of a client based in the Middle East, to do *"due diligence work and verification working with the client's in-house legal counsel – not many firms would trust a trainee to be in all-day meetings with clients in foreign jurisdictions."* The firm's recent M&A work has included advising private equity firm Rutland Partners on the acquisition of Pizza Hut's UK Dine-In Restaurant business – anyone who's been a victim of the chain's sticky seating and crusty carpets will welcome Rutland's planned investment in a £60m refurbishment and restructuring programme. Taylor Wessing also worked on the $130m restructuring of African mining giant Namakwa Diamonds, and on Nokia's sale of Vertu, which puts the world's most valuable stones to good use encrusting the phones of the super-rich.

The corporate technology team is partly based at the firm's recently opened office in Shoreditch's Tech City development. Set up with the idea that it will promote links with new businesses in the area, the office offers venture capital advice to *"start-ups that might be literally one app developer with an idea."* More established IT clients include techy takeaway favourites Just Eat, Spotify and Google. There's also international work on *"inward investment, which involves companies from overseas who want to set up in the UK."* Responsibility levels are high across the seat – *"in my first week I was down at the offices of the client helping out with a disclosure exercise, and I also got to do a first draft on an M&A deal."*

Random house

The private client department is *"really well renowned."* Clients are split between *"high net worth individuals who are old, with trusts that have been going for a long time,"* and *"new clients coming in from abroad – there are a lot of Saudi clients whose estates are enormous, so they're quite impressive to deal with!"* The work is varied, and allows for lots of responsibility: *"You can talk to half a dozen different clients in one day."* One trainee found themselves dealing with the fallout from *"a couple of clients whose deaths have been in the press, administering their estate and their assets, but also liaising with the coroners and the family, which has been really interesting."* It's a seat where *"you'll find yourself doing really random things, like going to a rural town to get a man who's a bit of a recluse to find some documents. I'd go on regular trips to clients' houses; it's more interesting than sitting at your desk all day."* There's also a private client litigation seat, which saw one trainee *"attending court quite regularly, meeting barristers, and helping them prepare for court,"* along with conducting some *"quite technical research into one client's agricultural property, and helping restructuring another's small companies."*

London readers will no doubt be familiar with the Foyles bookstore on the Charing Cross Road. Family-owned, it was known for its bizarre arrangement where books were sorted by publisher, not author, and a payment system where customers were required to queue three times. Anyway, the Foyle family sold the premises in 2012, and Taylor Wessing's real estate team acted for Soho Estates on the £70m purchase of the site. Trainees are allowed *"a lot of responsibility"* in this seat: *"You can sort of run your own matters, as there are quite a lot of low-value transactions."* In the related real estate litigation seat, *"I was sent to court on my own for small cases, like rent disputes and rights of light,"* said one source. *"My supervisor had negotiated beforehand, but I was there to support the client."*

Other seats include tax and incentives, hotels, private equity and financial institution. Head to our website for more details on the finance seats, which are a big part of Taylor Wessing.

Recruited, suited, booted

Taylor Wessing *"invests a lot of time in developing trainees – it's recognised you have to have the right level of training in place to build a firm of talented lawyers."* After feedback from trainees that *"it's nicer to have intensive training at the start,"* the firm is rolling out *"a boot-camp whenever you move seats – it's an intensive training session that gives you all the information you need."* There are also weekly departmental meetings where trainees *"have to present to the whole group on recent updates and case law. I was nervous but it's really good to practice your presentation skills."* At this firm, *"you have to* schedule your own appraisals, and pester your supervisor – some people haven't got round to organising their reviews, but I think it's right that the impetus should be on us."

High responsibility levels and frequent client contact means trainees *"feel responsible for the work you're doing: you're not a nameless part of a massive machine."* Although the work can be *"challenging"* (*"Gosh, I'm trying to keep a lot of plates spinning here!"* exclaimed one source), trainees were glad to avoid *"doing paperwork and bundles all the time."* Despite the heavy workloads, one interviewee felt that *"firms of a similar standard have a lot worse hours."* Trainees tended to head home at 7 or 8pm, with periodic late nights, but one found that after a heavy few days, *"my supervisor told me to take the next day off – you get recognition for putting the hours in."* Another reported: *"If I have tickets booked for something, partners are very flexible: they understand you have other things to do in the evenings."*

A room with a view

As part of *"a genuinely nice firm – it's not just marketing,"* trainees felt *"involved within your department – you're not the bottom of the pile, and everyone's very easy to talk to."* One trainee suggested that because they've sought out Taylor Wessing rather than going to the magic circle, people are *"a little bit more adventurous or creative"* – *"no one's a stuffy lawyer"* and *"you are allowed to be creative and to think outside the box."* The trainee cohort includes *"quite a lot of interesting people that maybe haven't done the traditional law route – they've acted, worked in the arts, played international sport or run companies."* In the course of our interviews we certainly spoke to several trainees who'd worked for a few years in other jobs.

Trainees felt that *"it's a difficult economy, so we've got to be creative and entrepreneurial"* to keep up with the competition – *"it's probably what's helped us to succeed with smaller start-ups."* Sources viewed Taylor Wessing as *"ambitious, with more get-up-and-go than bigger firms"* and thought that *"moving forward, expansion is*

probably the strategy." There's also *"more focus on getting the offices to work together and to integrate – there'll often be at least three or four offices involved in any one deal."* Still, although partners will *"pop back and forth,"* the lack of international secondments has meant that trainees have had fewer opportunities to make contacts overseas. However, the latest news coming out of the firm is that international secondments, especially to Asia, are likely to be on the menu in the near future.

Business development is a big deal and trainees are encouraged to get involved in hooking new clients. Quarterly firm-wide awards include a prize for *"having a good BD idea – they're very inclusive, and trainees have won them."*

Sources said that the *"fair"* qualification process comes *"very much down to merit."* One felt confident that *"even if there were no jobs here, I'd still feel I'd been given good enough training to go and work in any City firm."* Fortunately, there was space at Taylor Wessing for 19 out of 23 qualifiers in 2013.

Taylor Wessing inhabits *"a lovely glass-fronted building"* and trainees raved about the firm restaurant, Cloud Nine, which has *"a terrace overlooking the river and Big Ben."* There are plenty of nice bars on nearby Fleet Street, and at the end of the week *"there's always a handful of trainees in the pub."* They head to City favourite Corney & Barrow, or for something a bit less slick there's Ye Olde Cheshire Cheese, *"a wonky old pub where the ale doesn't cost about £6."* Trainees fondly remembered the firm's annual party at high-rise restaurant Skylon, *"looking out over the South Bank and seeing all the Christmas lights."* And a touch of the traditional is maintained in the private client department, where they have a monthly tea party – *"one of the trainees has to ring a gong to announce the party, then everyone sits around and chats over cucumber sandwiches."* Sports include rugby, rounders and there was recently a football tour to Paris. The fun on offer isn't enforced, though: *"There's not so much happening that you can't have your own life outside work – you get a life/life balance as well as a work/life balance."*

And finally...

A trainee summarised: *"Taylor Wessing is a great option for students that want the big City experience, with exposure to big corporate deals and clients, but don't want to work all hours without much recognition."*

Thomas Cooper

The facts

Location: London
Number of UK partners/solicitors: 17/21
Total number of trainees: 4
Seats: 4x6 months
Alternative seats: overseas seats

On chambersstudent.co.uk...

How to get into Thomas Cooper
P&I clubs

If the idea of being a maritime maven appeals, then this compact international shipping firm might just fit the bill.

International waters

Thomas Cooper has been dealing with seafaring matters since 1825. The eponymous Mr Cooper was expert in an area of admiralty law called prize, which refers to the capture of an enemy ship and its cargo during conflict. Obviously, this isn't high on the agenda any more. Nowadays, the maritime lawyer will be immersed in some quite different problems encountered on the waves, such as piracy, collisions and oil spillages, as well as tricky contractual issues surrounding the shipment of cargo. The firm today is a familiar name in maritime law, and recognised by *Chambers UK* – and indeed our *Asia, Europe* and *Global* guides – for its shipping and commodities work.

As well as these two main specialisms, the firm's practice areas include finance, corporate finance, international arbitration, insurance and reinsurance, oil and gas, private client and aviation. However, new recruits won't be exposed to all these elements. Thomas Cooper offers a truly salty maritime-based experience for its trainees, so if you think shipping really won't float your boat it's probably best to apply elsewhere.

Are all trainees here maritime boffins prior to joining, then? In short, no. *"I didn't know much about shipping when I started, but I was interested in it because everything in shipping is so heavily tied to commerce in general,"* confirmed one source. *"They don't expect knowledge of shipping, but looking at headlines on Lloyd's List is useful to get a feel for the industry."* Those looking to train at a *"small firm with international offices"* found that shipping outfits tended to fit this bill, and were attracted to the prospect of getting to grips with *"a specialist area."*

Trainees complete one seat in finance, one in marine and commercial litigation, and two stints in shipping, with one of those often spent overseas. TC's international presence is considerable for such a small firm. Alongside the London office, you'll find TC outposts in Madrid, Paris, Singapore, São Paulo and Piraeus (a common trainee destination).

Charter party time...

Over the course of their shipping seats, trainees receive exposure to both wet and dry work. The former is *"all about salvages; if something goes wrong during a voyage, if the vessel is sunk or the cargo is lost,"* while the latter relates to land-based contract disputes or commercial issues. Turn to page **137** for more information on this. Recently, the firm's dealt with some significant matters such as pollution claims arising from the explosion of the 'Stolt Valor' off Bahrain, and liability issues connected to the collision of the AHTS 'Intersand' with a rig in the gulf of Saudi Arabia. Due to the firm's petite size, *"you don't have multiple hierarchical layers of lawyers, so you get direct access to the partners dealing with big cases."* In the shipping seat, the work of a trainee really *"depends on the partner you're sitting with – they all have their own way of organising and delegating."* While trainees staffed on bigger matters will inevitably be *"helping out with organising documentation,"* all our interviewees noted that *"on the smaller cases you participate very actively and you're given a lot of freedom to try and organise the matter as you think it should progress."* One source *"was encouraged to take on drafting – settlement agreements, legal advice or correspondence with the other side – and then my supervisor would check it."* Another described

Chambers UK rankings

Commodities	Shipping

journeying to court to *"square up to a barrister"* and present an argument relating to a salvage case.

A seat abroad is *"not compulsory in the strictest sense, but it's sort of expected that you'll go and lend an extra pair of hands."* Out in Madrid, trainees appreciated a discernibly high level of responsibility *"on matters for big clients."* As well as shipping work, interviewees sampled *"a bit of everything else, because there's only one trainee there at a time. I did some insurance and some oil and gas work, mainly for large South American companies. The Madrid office is our gateway to South America."* In Piraeus, one trainee took on *"some dry, but mainly wet, shipping work. It's a smaller office than London, so it was more client-facing for me. I acted as an associate in terms of tasks like drafting, but at the same time it's well supervised."*

The marine and commercial litigation seat *"encompasses a range of work depending on who you're sitting with. It could be general commercial litigation, contract disputes or issues arising from personal injury on a ship."* Meanwhile, the finance seat might throw up projects that *"aren't necessarily anything to do with shipping."* In this area, the firm does lots of work for the London branches of foreign banks. Sources got involved with *"a lot of trade finance transactions, standard loans and receivables finance – I did a lot of drafting and got to go to client meetings, which surprised me,"* said one source.

A voyage of discovery

Training and teaching are top priorities at Thomas Cooper. *"The partners understand that the firm's mainstays are niche topics. Sometimes it's the basics that you want to get your head around,"* explained a trainee. *"I wanted to understand commodities finance because I hadn't had much exposure to it, and a partner offered to meet me in the mornings to go over it."* There are weekly internal lectures in which *"one of the partners will give a series of five or six talks on a particular topic,"* plus a monthly external lecture *"often done by barristers or experts, who*

come in and talk on some aspect of shipping or insurance, like what cargoes blow up when you transport them."* Our sources confirmed that partners are *"always approachable and open to questions. If a partner tells you to read into the actual law, they don't mind if you take lots of time over it. It's important to have knowledge; you're not just here to bill."*

On the subject of billable hours, trainees described the amount of time they spend in the offices as *"really civilised – although it does depend on what's going on at any given moment."* In general, trainees will be in the office between roughly 9am and 7pm, with longer stints on occasion: *"In shipping you can expect longer hours because of the time difference between London and overseas."*

While shipping might have a reputation as a traditional sort of industry, the firm today isn't the preserve of gents in braces. One trainee mused: *"There are lots of young female assistants. Certainly at the lower levels there are more girls than boys. But you can't get away from the fact that there aren't many female partners, so in that sense it's very male-heavy. I guess that's a reflection of what it was like 25 years ago, and they're probably trying to get away from that."* Another pointed out that *"lots of partners trained at Thomas Cooper. They're very loyal to it and they've created their own culture."* Interviewees praised the atmosphere as *"very relaxed and sociable. You get to know absolutely everyone."* Although *"it's not a formal environment,"* the dress code is strictly business. Ties are a must for the menfolk, and looking artfully dishevelled simply won't cut it. *"I was asked if I owned a comb,"* admitted one formerly rumpled trainee.

While the firm doesn't organise heaps of get-togethers, there's a Christmas party, occasional departmental drinks and lots of client events including a summer boat trip. The close-knit trainee groups tend to go out for lunch or drinks – *"we're all quite like-minded in the respect,"* thought one source. *"With such a small crowd, it's more about what you make of it yourself. It's all quite laid-back."* As such, *"it's not über-competitive"* either. There tends to be space for everyone on qualification. *"They seem to want to keep hold of the trainees they've got,"* declared a source. *"There's so few of us and they see us as investments. They want to keep you happy and in turn that makes you want to stay."* All five qualifiers did so in 2013.

And finally...

Some trainees thought that *"outgoing, positive people"* thrive at the firm, while others took a more nuanced view: *"We're a disparate group, but everyone has got something of value. There are quiet, scholarly types and louder, more sociable people. I think because it's a small firm, they're looking for someone who's easy to get along with. An all-right chap or chapette, really."*

The True Picture

TLT LLP

A NEW KIND OF LAW FIRM

Real clients.
Real cases.
Real experience.

www.TLTcareers.com/trainee

Training Contracts & Vacation Schemes

A growing top-100 law firm with a fresh, open outlook. The chance to work on live cases and learn rapidly working alongside senior staff. No, really…

TLT is a truly great place to start your legal career. Trainees tell us they're surprised at how different we are to other law firms – open plan, open minded and open to new ways of doing business. We believe in breaking down barriers and encouraging creativity. And we've had accolades from the best in business who agree that our way is the way forward.

Whether you join us for your training contract or a one-week vacation scheme placement, you'll work on live cases for real clients. You'll have real Partner contact too, not just a quick hello in the corridor. It's designed to help you develop a broad range of skills across the full legal and business spectrum.

It's a great springboard for a future career in law. We've got a good record for retaining as many trainees as we can and we have big plans to develop. With new offices opening in Belfast, Scotland and Manchester, there's plenty of opportunity here for the right people.

Our vacation scheme is open to second-year law students, final-year law or non-law students as well as graduates and mature candidates. It's held every Easter and summer in Bristol, and every summer in London. We're also recruiting for trainees to join us in September 2016 and March 2017.

Find out more and apply at www.TLTcareers.com/trainee

TLT LLP

The facts

Location: Bristol, London, Manchester, Scotland, Northern Ireland

Number of UK partners/solicitors: 82/177

Partners who trained at firm: c.18%

Total number of trainees: 21

Seats: 4x6 months

Alternative seats: secondments

On chambersstudent.co.uk...

How to get into TLT

Recent growth and mergers

This up-and-comer is, in its own trainees' words, *"driven," "energetic"* and *"unhindered by stuffy traditions."*

Wunderkind

With steep ambitions and a pocketful of moxie, TLT isn't a place content with standing still for long. Since its conception in 2000 off the back of two merging Bristol firms, the Y2K baby's built itself into a sturdy operation with six domestic offices, plus a hub in Piraeus. Along the way it's steadily scaled the revenue ranks, posting a healthy £49m in turnover in 2012/13 – a 10% rise from the year prior and more than triple that of a decade ago.

The firm shows no signs of slowing down, either; TLT kicked off its teen years by opening three offices across Scotland and Northern Ireland in 2012, supplementing the Bristol headquarters and London branch, and upgrading the firm's status from South-West powerhouse to bona fide national entity. Most recently, a new Manchester base debuted in summer 2013. According to training principal Maria Connolly, the Mancunian digs will initially focus on commercial contracts and disputes, and will *"hopefully"* recruit trainees in due course. *"They're really focusing on strengthening our brand identity as a UK-wide firm,"* insiders said of all this recent expansion. *"We're growing and regularly winning new clients, which suggests trainees have a lot to look forward to in the future."* A spurt of new lateral hires and promotions across the board has also turned heads, both internally and in the legal press.

TLT has upped its game in the financial services sector in recent years, widening its client cache to include household names like Barclays, Lloyds Banking, The Co-operative Bank and RBS. Such clients now account for more than 40% of the firm's overall undertakings. TLT's sector-focused strategy also lends itself to specialities in the retail and leisure, housing, renewables, public and technology, and media industries, encompassing a diverse swath of name-brand clients, from EDF Energy and WHSmith to Ladbrokes and TUI Travel.

Trainees get no choice in their first seat, but from there on they submit five preferences each time rotations roll around: *"We're prioritised as we go along, so by your third or fourth seat you can expect to get one of your top choices."* In Bristol, *"there are plenty of seat options,"* but things are *"a little more limited"* in London, home to just five trainees at the time of our calls. On the upside, Londoners *"have it a bit easier in that we can sit down with each other and chat about where we want to go. The whole process is pretty transparent."* No seats are compulsory, but *"the vast majority"* of trainees spend time in a property or banking seat at some point during their training contract.

Key assets

The banking and finance team advises numerous financial institutions in the UK, plus a good deal of international banks. A recent cross-border matter saw lawyers strike a deal for a syndicate of lenders including Bank of India and Punjab National Bank (Hong Kong) in a $110m loan to an oil and gas exploration company. Retail and leisure is an area of expertise, as is the renewables sector – TLT regularly advises Dutch ethical bank Triodos on projects such as its £2.2m financing of a Dagenham wind farm extension and £1.8m funding of a hydroelectric project in Wales. *"Both clients and transactions are usually pretty big, so your role as a trainee often revolves around file management,"* insiders reported. *"Partners deal with the*

Chambers UK rankings

Banking & Finance	Intellectual Property
Banking Litigation	Licensing
Competition/European Law	Partnership
Construction	Pensions
Corporate/M&A	Planning
Dispute Resolution	Private Client
Employment	Professional Negligence
Energy & Natural	Real Estate
Resources	Restructuring/Insolvency
Environment	Retail
Family/Matrimonial	Shipping
Franchising	Social Housing
Information Technology	

main loan agreements, and ancillary tasks like drafting minutes and overseeing share charges are left to us."

According to trainees, *"you can't do much better than a BFSL seat when it comes to responsibility."* The BFSL team – that's banking and financial services litigation, by the way – is one of the country's largest and acts for insurers, banks and mortgage lenders across the commercial, corporate and retail sectors. The details of most cases are kept under wraps, but the majority tend to revolve around recovering fraudulent losses and deterring similar mishaps in the future. *"Sometimes you're chasing up the bank because somebody can't afford their mortgage, and other times you're dealing with complicated lending that needs securing."* In keeping with its *Chambers UK* top-tier recognition, sample clients include big names like Bank of Ireland, Nationwide Building Society and Lloyds. Despite this high-profile rep, however, *"trainees really get the opportunity to think for themselves in this department,"* one said. *"We're constantly running our own files and corresponding with clients. I even got to conduct my own advocacy at a hearing and attend a trial."*

Financial services regulation is a *"small but growing"* team in London. *"The work is pretty technical – we respond to ad hoc regulatory queries by reading through documents like the FSA Handbook or the Consumer Credit Act and drafting the advice. You end up performing a lot of intensive research on very specific subjects."* TLT occasionally seconds trainees to financial services clients such as Barclays, though placements only occur *"as and when the client needs."* Said one trainee who'd completed a secondment: *"I got to deal with a huge variety of matters every day and see how the client operates from the inside out. That exposure proved beneficial when I returned to the firm and resumed dealing with them from the other side."*

Rewarding renewables

TLT's regional property capabilities – including its planning, real estate litigation, construction and social housing work – are deemed among the best in *Chambers UK*. Department successes of late include scoring the role of sole property legal adviser to the BBC – whose portfolio includes more than 300 properties – and acting for the Canal and River Trust in an arrangement to allow a luxury boating service ferry sport fans to and from the 2012 Olympic site. On the client front, commercial giants like WHSmith, EDF Energy and Everything Everywhere complement public sector pillars like the Environment Agency, Energy Saving Trust and the Mayor's Office for Policing and Crime (the new name for the Metropolitan Police Authority).

In Bristol, trainees are assigned to sub-teams such as residential or social housing, while the London team operates as a one-stop shop. *"I did everything from lease renewals and high-value residential conveyancing work to property sales and commercial licensing matters,"* a source in the capital said. *"You're pretty much left to your own devices – I ran numerous files myself and conducted my own client meetings."* Over in Bristol, we heard from trainees who'd negotiated leases, handled property registrations, worked on insolvency issues and performed corporate support roles: *"The responsibility's yours for the taking. Very early on, I worked alongside a partner to devise a social housing project implementing solar panels. I got to meet with the client regularly and even had a sub-team at my disposal."*

Those on the construction side of things get involved in a mix of contentious and transactional matters, *"quite often"* renewables-related ones: *"I've drafted framework agreements and negotiated building contracts, as well as taken witness statements for a contract dispute."* Meanwhile, over in professional negligence it's mainly claimant work for financial services clients. *"Seeing how claims get put together is really interesting,"* said one source. *"I was involved in a mediation and got to attend settlement discussions for a residential mortgage claim on behalf of a bank."* The team works closely with its colleagues over in BFSL, particularly in the fraud arena, and handled more than 2,000 different matters in 2012.

Much of TLT's corporate work falls into the renewables sphere – in fact, there's a specialist team devoted to handling fundraising and M&A work for clean energy projects involving wind, wave, hydro and solar technologies. Lawyers recently advised on a finance vehicle's £4.2m acquisition of a solar farm in Buckinghamshire, as well as kitchen and washroom system provider The Frank Artemis Group's acquisition of a water-saving technology specialist company. The firm's also big in the private equity and retail industries – sample matters include advising on the sale of professional indemnity firm Prime Professions and that of Rileys, Britain's biggest pool and snooker club chain. Trainees praised their role as *"not too prescriptive,"* reporting a variety of *"standalone tasks"* such as drafting collaboration agreements and powers of attorney, and running data rooms during the disclosure process.

Eyes on the prize

Our sources were quick to praise the firm for its emphasis on trainee development: *"We're encouraged to take our own initiative, but there's quality control – partners are receptive to trainees' needs and make it clear they're interested in our progression."* As one pointed out, *"they regularly ask us what we'd like to work on next, which suggests they value our interests and input. Some firms look to bend trainees to a certain mould, but TLT is more interested in encouraging people to shape their own path."* When it comes to supervision, efforts are *"more structured than they used to be – we now have a supervision meeting once a month to review our progress and set objectives."* What's more, the open-plan office set-up means *"you end up with multiple supervisors because there are always senior people around to ask questions to and observe."* Insiders agreed all these factors contribute to *"an environment where trainees can settle quickly and contribute a lot."*

Likewise, interviewees had nothing but positive comments on the firm's recent growth, insisting *"it's an exciting time to be here. Everybody's first thoughts of the Bristol legal market involve Burges Salmon or Osborne Clarke, but TLT is really making a name for itself lately."* Indeed, many pointed to *"innovative pricing structures"* and the recent *"abundance"* of lateral hires from the likes of DLA Piper and Eversheds as evidence of TLT's determination to land a bigger market share. *"The general level of optimism and excitement surrounding our development contributes to a great atmosphere – people all over the firm are striving to better themselves and take us forward."* On another promising note, NQ vacancies in 2013 outnumbered the amount of qualifying trainees, with ten of 12 kept on in the end.

Relaxin' all cool

Trainees acknowledged a *"technical hierarchy"* but insisted *"there's little need to take a different approach with people more senior than you."* Indeed, we heard about *"plenty"* of banter and sport and entertainment-related chatter, largely facilitated by the open seating plan: *"Lots of people approach each other face-to-face rather than by e-mail."* There *"isn't loads"* of crossover between London and Bristol, but we detected a similarly comfortable vibe present in each. *"It's clear they look for applicants with good people skills,"* sources from both locations agreed.

The Bristol office – or *"TLT Towers,"* as one interviewee put it – is housed in a 1970s tower block adjacent to the Avon: *"I think we can agree it's not very attractive from the outside, but the inside is fine – we have great panoramic views of the city."* We paid a little visit not so long ago and can attest to the fact that there are few buildings with such good prospects of Bristol. That said, *"it would be nice to have a place to sit down for lunch – we have a little room upstairs, but it's not big enough to congregate."* London trainees had similar opinions of their Cheapside digs, praising the *"modern, clean"* interior and *"excellent views"* while lamenting the lack of canteen. On the upside, hours are *"reasonable"* at each branch, so lawyers have plenty of time to take advantage of the myriad social activities on offer.

"A lot of people get involved in wider firm life," we heard, with third-seaters taking on the task of organising occasional trainee events like Laser Quest and bowling outings. In Bristol, extracurricular highlights include the football league and networking events, while Londoners have monthly drinks dos and impromptu nights at their local. An annual trainee gathering in Bristol each June sees new and future joiners welcomed to the firm, and there's also a *"cracking"* firmwide summer party held every other year. Last year's shindig was held at Ashton Court Mansion, complete with *"doughnuts, drinks, funfair rides and great weather."*

And finally...

We reckon this is a firm that's going places. Current trainees recommend getting on board *"if you're someone who wants to contribute to and be part of a growing entity."*

The True Picture

Travers Smith LLP

The facts

Location: London
Number of UK partners/solictors: 63/185
Partners who trained at firm: 48%
Total number of trainees: 41
Seats: 4x6 months
Alternative seats: Paris, secondments
Extras: pro bono – Paddington Law Centre, Private Equity Foundation, death row cases, A4ID; language classes

On chambersstudent.co.uk...

How to get into Travers
Interview with graduate partners Anthony Foster and Caroline Edwards

Suave, sophisticated, charming – and that's just the trainees.

Travers-ing the market

There's something reassuring about how comfortable Travers Smith is in its own skin. *"It will always be Travers,"* reflected one source when contemplating the firm's future (unintentionally quoting a line from *Student Guides* past). *"It won't branch out into America or anything like that. It has an identity that won't change and I like that."* With a small, subsidiary office in Paris its only nod to an international presence, Travers is more than happy to remain steadfastly London-based.

It may only be a mid-sized operation of roughly 250 fee earners but Travers packs an almighty punch, primarily through its corporate offering, which for over 200 years has defined the firm. Back in 1801 one of the firm's partners drafted the constitution for the first Stock Exchange, and the department today is consistently ranked as one of the best around by *Chambers UK*. Advising on deals such as NDS Group's $5bn sale to Cisco Systems and Metric Property's £811m all-share merger with London & Stamford Property serves to indicate its capabilities in the mid-market arena. *"It might be a 'smaller firm',"* commented one trainee, *"but it has a cracking reputation."* Travers has a further 16 specialist practice areas besides, and *Chambers UK* hasn't been shy in handing out rankings to the large majority of them.

You wouldn't want it any other way

Perhaps unsurprisingly, a bout in corporate is compulsory during the four-seat training contract, as is a visit to a contentious team, which is a choice between either litigation or employment. For their third and fourth seats trainees give four preferences, choosing from banking, real estate or any of the wildcard options: competition; commercial, IP & technology; pensions; funds; tax; and

financial services. One of the choices must be banking or real estate. From these preferences trainees are assigned two seats. This system was introduced after we spoke to trainees and graduate recruitment sources told us *"it allows greater flexibility in seat allocation from both our trainees' and the firm's point of view."* Trainees did tell us that some wildcard options are *"more difficult to get as they are heavily oversubscribed."* Commercial, we heard, is one option that is particularly sought after. Although preferences are submitted at the start of a trainee's time at Travers, *"you can change them as you go along. Nothing is set in stone."*

Corporate is the largest department within Travers Smith and houses roughly ten trainees at any given time. The department is split into two primary subteams: corporate finance and private equity. The latter is one of the largest private equity teams in London. Sources who'd spent time in corporate agreed their workloads were prone to fluctuation. *"I felt like I was either in fifth gear or stationary,"* explained one. *"When it was fifth gear I was terrified, but looking back I wouldn't have had it any other way. My supervisor was keen to get me stuck in and give me as much responsibility as I could handle."* Typical tasks include *"drafting ancillary documents rather than getting involved with the drafting of share agreements."* However, this is offset with a good amount of client contact and the scope to *"run processes on your own."* Trainees also play a part in some pretty large transactions, with one source reporting their involvement in a £300m deal.

Travers' litigation team represents clients such as the Argentine Republic and Rosneft Oil, while *"big banking insolvency cases"* were dominating the department's schedule at the time of our calls. Trainees can expect to find a mix of *"rubbish tasks"* as well as *"interesting,*

Chambers UK rankings

Banking & Finance	Fraud
Banking Litigation	Information Technology
Capital Markets	Investment Funds
Competition/European Law	Media & Entertainment
Corporate/M&A	Outsourcing
Dispute Resolution	Pensions
Employee Share Schemes	Pensions Litigation
& Incentives	Private Equity
Employment	Real Estate Finance
Environment	Retail
Financial Services	Tax
Franchising	

substantive work." One reported: *"I was in till 11.30pm one night checking bundles that were due at the Court of Appeal. It wasn't the greatest Friday evening but things like that are par for the course here."* Another reflected: *"I know that some people have done grunt work but they do try to balance it out. You're never stuck doing that for more than a few weeks at a time. In my six months here I didn't spend many hours photocopying and I had some very good responsibilities such as drafting witness statements, attending court regularly for updates and speaking on the phone to clients, including one 'celebrity'."*

Touche Rugby

The employment team works for the likes of Deloitte and the RFU. Lawyers here work across three practice areas: transactional support, contentious work and general advisory. Trainees agreed it's a *"great department."* One gleefully reminisced: *"My favourite bit about it was the amount of drafting you're able to do and the ability to write angry letters to people."* Another commented: *"I didn't necessarily think it would be my thing, but I found I was given a lot of responsibility from day one. That's partly because there's a lot of small matters to deal with rather than just one larger transaction. You'll be juggling a lot of balls, but the excellent supervision means you can just run with it."*

Time in banking is like a *"mini corporate seat"* in terms of workload. The group counts RBS, Lloyds and Macquarie Bank among its roster of clients, meaning that *"deals can be quite full on – including 4am finishes – but you feel really part of something so it's very enjoyable."* Sources are impressed by how quickly responsibility is handed over. *"You get thrown right in there,"* reported one. *"Trainees are used as a resource, not just work experience students. They expect you to do proper work and help advise clients. There's a lot of trust placed in you."*

The real estate team also picks up rankings from *Chambers UK* and is home to roughly 20 fee earners. Banking

generally proved a more popular pick based on the sources we spoke with, but those who spent time delving into property law agreed there is *"a lot of responsibility early on. They throw you in at the deep end and you eventually get your own matters to handle."*

Wild thing... you make my rotation sing

Of the wildcard seats on offer *"commercial is hugely popular and if you want to do it you should make sure it's your number-one choice."* The department has an extensive list of well-known clients on its books, such as TSL Education, Channel 4, Pret A Manger and Pinewood Studios. A recent deal saw Travers Smith advise Taylor Street Baristas on its joint venture with Tesco for the creation of new coffee shop chain Harris+Hoole. The tax team advises on private equity, funds and employee incentive matters. It is *"more research-driven than other departments,"* and *"a technical area in which you can feel a little daunted."* Another source commented: *"It's one of the loveliest teams in the firm – you really feel at home."* Pensions might not have many chomping at the bit, but those who'd sat here found it *"absolutely fascinating."* A second-year elaborated: *"Most people would go, 'OMG, pensions, really?' but it's actually great as it relates to real people."* It's at the opposite end of the spectrum to corporate, *"where everything is super-urgent. Pensions is more academic and generally operates at a slower pace."*

There are two alternative seat options for people who want to spread their wings beyond Travers' base. A jaunt to join up with the corporate team in Paris is on offer at every rotation – *"it's an amazing gig if you do get it"* – while a secondment to private equity client 3i is frequently available too.

One element of life at Travers that's widely praised is the three-person-per-office sharing system. *"I actually found that having three to an office has lived up to what I thought it would be,"* beamed one. *"You have a partner who is over ten years' qualified who will help you with certain things, but they can also be extremely busy so if you don't want to ask a silly question and be embarrassed it's nice to have an associate in the room who can handle those more basic requests."* The real key to learning and progressing, trainees agreed, comes from the ability to watch their seniors first-hand. *"It's not just about direct feedback,"* reflected one. *"It's about being able to observe senior solicitors and how they deal with certain situations."* Another commented: *"Just sitting with an associate and a partner shows you how they interact with clients and manage their workloads, and allows you to understand the context of what they are working on. By osmosis you pick stuff up without even realising."*

The True Picture

Formal reviews are conducted both mid-seat and end-of-seat. *"They strike a good balance between being serious but not scary,"* pondered a second-year. *"Both reviews are with the immediate supervisor in your room, then a week or two later you'll have secondary review with the training principals."* Trainees agreed these were more detailed than they initially anticipated: *"You get a written review form which lists strengths, areas for improvement, and things to work upon during your next seat. Every supervisor I've had has really taken their time at writing those and they are a lot more observant than you think. They really pick up on the little things."*

The in-crowd

Although there's no denying that a stint at Travers demands a lot of you – *"don't expect to get through your training contract without at least a few late nights"* – this is also somewhere that *"recognises a work/life balance. I never feel the firm wants me to work myself into the ground. I think they realise they don't get the best out of people doing that."* One trainee added: *"When I was absolutely swamped the partners took work off my to-do list and told me to take a day off. It was a really nice touch."*

"There's a bit of a perception about the people who work here," one trainee told us. What perception is that? *"That we all went to Bristol, Durham or Oxbridge."* In fairness, half of the current trainee group hail from these institutions, but this doesn't define Travers' recruiting. *"I think most of the partners just want people who will do a good job and they don't really care about your background, race or gender,"* commented one. Another offered: *"It's really not a 'you have to go to this uni' type of place, but you do need the grades. It's inevitable that you end up with people who are slightly geekier or more intelligent than your average workforce."* The firm has made efforts to diversify its intake and a good smattering of universities are represented in the 2013 cohort – 14 in all.

One way and another, we've encountered more than our fair share of Travers trainees over the years, and have identified one very noticeable trait. These are seriously charming people, and not in an oily, City-slicker way but in a bright-eyed and unremittingly cheerful way. Invariably eloquent and unfailingly polite, they tend to have the gift of putting people at their ease: there'd never be an awkward silence if you found yourself seated next to them at a dinner party, and by the end of the night you'd find yourself wishing you were part of their friendship group. In short, Travers values the old-fashioned quality of social grace – the ability to get on with clients is vital, after all. Our guess is that it's that more than anything which will get you through the interview stage.

I wanna drink with somebody

If Travers has a motto, it's that *"this is a place where people take their work but not themselves seriously."* This is something that transcends the demarcations of seniority at the firm. *"The atmosphere is very open and the hierarchy is pretty flat,"* a second-year said. *"If I got stuck in the lift with anyone, I would feel comfortable speaking with them even if they were head of a certain department. There's no ivory tower where all the partners sit."*

There may be no ivory tower, but Travers does occupy two premises in London. The corporate department is based in a modern building on Smithfield Street, while the rest of the firm is right next door on Snow Hill. The latter *"could do with sprucing up,"* trainees declared. *"It's not a flashy type of firm with the latest chic or technology. The client spaces aren't spectacular either but I guess that keeps in line with the down-to-earth culture of the firm. Some partners would prefer a bit more impact but others think that it's a massive expense for not much purpose. It's our work that ultimately defines us."* Situated in between Farringdon and City Thameslink, trainees felt that the location more than makes up for any shortcomings in the decor.

It's common to see *"most of the firm"* at local watering hole the Bishop's Finger on a Friday night, while for those who fancy themselves as the next Whitney, there's the ever favourite Karaoke Box as well. There is a good spread of sports teams to sign up for, while individual departments usually organise events as well. Travers' last Christmas party saw them attend The Dorchester. *"The food was good; the alcohol was even better."*

And finally...
Travers brings a touch of class to the London corporate market. It kept on an impressive 22 of 23 qualifiers in 2013.

Trethowans LLP

The facts

Location: Southampton, Salisbury
Number of UK partners/solicitors: 24/32
Partners who trained at firm: 17%
Total number of trainees: 7
Seats: 4x6 months
Alternative seats: occasional secondments

On chambersstudent.co.uk...

How to get into Trethowans
Interview with managing partner Simon Rhodes

With one foot in Hampshire and the other in Wiltshire, Trethowans is a strong performer in the South's legal market.

Rhodes to glory

The road goes ever on for Trethowans. Its 'Destination 2012' strategy having recently come to fruition, managing partner Simon Rhodes has now launched a new three-year plan called 'Becoming Premier'. The aim? To make this *"a premier firm ranked in the top three across the board in the Solent area. To do this we'll be investing more money into our systems, our profile and further targeted recruitment."*

How far is Trethowans from gaining that 'top three' status in its many different practice areas? We turned to the only rankings that count – *Chambers UK*'s, obviously. The firm's employment and personal injury departments are both ranked in the top tier for the Southampton region – a good start. The clin neg and family teams are also there or thereabouts when it comes to being in the top three locally; however, the corporate and real estate teams feature lower down the rankings and have some work to do yet. Given that Trethowans is duking it out with big boys like Bond Dickinson, Shoosmiths and Blake Lapthorn, one might theorise that the firm needs to do some growing if it wants to be consistently challenging for 'top three' status in the region by 2015. Still, national clients including sugar daddy Tate & Lyle and Stannah, of stairlift fame, show that Trethowans has some genuine clout. One trainee said of the firm: *"It's big enough that you get to work with national names but not so big you get lost in the system."*

Personal injury and corporate/commercial together account for a good deal of Trethowans' workload. Most of our interviewees had spent time in both. The other seats on offer are commercial litigation, insurance litigation, commercial property, employment, family, private client, residential property and agriculture and rural property. Before they start each seat, trainees are asked to complete a wish list of their desired departments and those they want to avoid. Second-years get priority if there's competition, but each of our interviewees had been allocated either their first or second choice in every seat. *"You have to do a contentious seat, and they like it if you spend time in both offices, but they're the only real requirements."*

Welcome to the Solent quarter

Personal injury is split between both offices, with each handling clinical negligence work on behalf of claimants with head and spinal injuries. Lawyers also get to grips with defendant claims and encounter a lot of road traffic accident work. The seat proved to be a favourite among our interviewees. One happily reported the team *"wasn't shy about giving me meaty tasks right from the start."* Trainees have the chance to draft pleadings, give instructions to counsel, attend settlement meetings and take witness statements, and the work can be very rewarding, if emotionally draining at times.

"I was working for both large nationals and regional start-ups," one insider said of the Southampton-based corporate/commercial department. Big names on the books include Bacardi and Ladbrokes, which it advised on around 60 commercial contract instructions over the course of 2012. Trainees mostly act in supporting roles drafting memorandums, helping with due diligence and taking minutes, but they are also invited to attend client meetings. Our sources heaped praise on the team's *"work hard, play hard"* attitude. The hours in this seat are the longest, particularly in the weeks leading up to com-

Chambers UK rankings

Agriculture & Rural Affairs	Family/Matrimonial
Banking & Finance	Licensing
Clinical Negligence	Personal Injury
Corporate/M&A	Private Client
Dispute Resolution	Real Estate
Employment	

pletion, although none of the trainees we spoke to had worked late into the night or at weekends.

Managing partner Simon Rhodes is a key figure in Southampton's employment department and plays an active role in trainees' development. One source lauded both the quality of work on offer here, which includes drafting letters, tracking witness statements and independently running meetings, and Rhodes' efforts to develop soft skills like *"commercial awareness."* Those seeking advocacy experience will be interested in the commercial litigation seat, which gives trainees the opportunity to attend hearings in both Southampton and London. According to one trainee, the quality of the cases in this seat *"more than made up for the bundling and research."* In one recent case, Trethowans represented a couple who sued their surveyor for professional negligence after buying a house that was later discovered to have a construction fault that rendered it essentially valueless.

The commercial property department does a lot of work for banking giants Santander and has a particularly good following in the world of pensions, acting for the likes of Legal & General. One trainee praised the *"variety"* of work on offer and said they'd been *"supported at all times, but given the freedom and ownership to talk to clients and take control."* As well as meeting with clients, trainees draft leases and licences, and help with purchase and sale agreements.

Trethowans' appraisal process is a thorough one and trainees sit down and map their progress four times in the course of each seat. They meet with their designated supervisor twice during each seat and with *"Nicky"* – HR partner Nicola Richards – midway through the seat and then again at the end.

Let them eat cake

When asked to describe the character of the firm, two trainees said *"forward-thinking."* At the *Student Guide* we hear this a lot, but it was surprising to find out how involved trainees are in planning the firm's future. *"We*

were consulted on the design of the new website," and *"if you know how a job can be done better they're keen to hear your ideas."* The new website, by the way, is a tasteful white and grey number – nothing too snazzy, but a big improvement on the rather basic prior incarnation.

"There's loads going on in Southampton," and bustling Bedford Place with its pubs and bars is close to the office and popular with trainees and solicitors alike on a Friday night. The most recent Christmas party was a black-tie event at the Marwell Hotel, while at the summer barbecue recently the two offices competed in a tug-of-war as part of a mini-Olympics (Southampton won). The charities committee organises events all year round, with trainees participating in a sleep-out on the steps of Salisbury Cathedral one year in order to raise money for a homelessness charity. Cake Bake Friday, a Trethowans tradition, takes place on the final Friday of every month and restores blood sugar and blood pressure to a golden mean. Staff at every level bring in their home-baked goods and sell them to their hungry colleagues, with the proceeds going to local charities.

Trainees praised the *"lovely"* old-fashioned aesthetic of the listed Southampton building, where fee earners have their own offices, but there were a few grumbles about the Salisbury office. *"It's so quiet you can't help feeling people can overhear your phone calls – that can be daunting as a trainee."* Another of our sources mentioned the lack of local amenities in Salisbury, owing to the office's location on a business park two miles from the city centre. Working hours allow for plenty of time away from the office, though, and one trainee told us they'd jokingly been told off when a partner had found them still at work at 6.30pm. The hours in employment and corporate/commercial can be long in the weeks leading up to completion, but this is the exception rather than the rule.

We couldn't help but notice that of the 13 trainees who started at the firm between 2010 and 2012, just one was male. That said, the firm confirmed that the autumn 2013 intake contains two men. When asked how to impress at the assessment day, one trainee said candidates need to show they fit with *"team Trethowans."* Make sure your handwriting is up to scratch – applicants are asked to complete a gruelling seven-page application form by hand before they are invited to interview. Anyone with big ideas should not be afraid to apply – Rhodes wants people with *"entrepreneurial spirit and business acumen,"* and stressed the strength of an application that shows off these skills: *"If you've done a paper round, tell us; or if you've set up a business selling stuff on the internet, that's a big tick in the box too."*

And finally...

Trainees at Trethowans have historically enjoyed high retention rates.

Trowers & Hamlins LLP

The facts

Location: London, Manchester, Exteter, Birmingham

Number of UK partners/solicitors: 108/154

Partners who trained at firm: c.33%

Total number of trainees: 35

Seats: 4x6 months

Alternative seats: overseas seats

Extras: pro brono – Kaplan Legal Advice Centre; language classes

On chambersstudent.co.uk...

How to get into Trowers

The Middle East

Interview with training principal Tonia Secker

Trowers & Hamlins has over 700 staff, and offices spanning the UK, the Middle East and South-East Asia. It offers quite a unique mix of public sector, private sector and international work.

Lawyers of Arabia

While many firms felt the brunt of the recession during 2008/09, the impact hit Trowers a little later. After a rough patch in 2010/11, revenue increased by 3% in 2011/12 to £80.5m. This dip was largely down to the Arab Spring, public sector cuts and sluggishness in the social housing market, all of which are still ongoing. Out in the Middle East, the firm closed its Jeddah office in 2011 after just one year, and also withdrew from its Riyadh alliance outfit. Add news of seven announced redundancies in early 2013, and we can't say that it has all been plain sailing for the firm recently.

But it's not all doom and gloom either. Retention figures are high, and the London office moved from Tower Bridge to Bunhill Row in 2012. It's a location with more corporate associations: trainees can now sit in the cafeteria and *"wave across to Slaughter and May."* The move has *"really shaken things up. The new office has given us all a focus, and now people can visualise where we are going."* Perhaps they can in some respects, but in others maybe not so well, as the new computer screens are *"eye-wateringly big."* All in all, it's a *"big, swanky office,"* with plenty of *"Haribo in the meeting rooms and all mod-cons."* Meanwhile, the elevation of a corporate finance lawyer, Jennie Gubbins, to senior partner excited trainees, who said she *"is robust and has a vision. She wants us to be a front runner as a City firm and there is going to be a corporate push – that was obvious when we moved offices."*

High up on the agenda is promoting the real estate practice and seeking out further international opportunities,

in the Middle East, sub-Saharan Africa and South-East Asia. Progress has already been made on that front, and Trowers became the first Western law firm to open up a representative office in Malaysia in 2012. Malaysia's domestic market is quite small, meaning that the country's wealthy businessmen have been spurred by the slump in Euro and Sterling exchange rates to seek investment abroad: Trowers has already advised Malaysian asset management company Permodalan Nasional Berhad on its £500m property acquisition of One Exchange Square and Olswang's London offices from German fund manager KanAm.

With the new corporate address, further international expansion and a push to develop private sector work, what will happen to the practices that Trowers has traditionally been known for? *"We're already a big player in the public sector,"* stated trainees, *"so if anything we will be investing more time in maintaining that as well."* Judging by the recent work Trowers has done in this area – advising Newham Council on a deal which aims to rejuvenate the Olympic Stadium for the benefit of the surrounding residents, for example – the firm certainly hasn't forgotten its roots.

What is clear is that Trowers is a firm – like many others – that is adapting to survive, but perhaps marrying its very diverse strands of work complicates things somewhat. It will be interesting to see what kind of balance is struck in the years ahead.

The True Picture

Chambers UK rankings

Administrative &	Employment
Public Law	Healthcare
Banking & Finance	Local Government
Capital Markets	Projects
Charities	Public Procurement
Construction	Real Estate Litigation
Corporate/M&A	Social Housing
Education	

Strangers on a trainee

As well as London, the firm also has offices in Manchester, which recruits four trainees a year, and Exeter, which takes on one, but a second will join from September 2014. International and London seats are available for trainees in these locations. The Manchester office is a *"little tired,"* but based in a *"brilliant location, just opposite the town hall,"* while the Exeter base is situated just off the picturesque green surrounding the cathedral. Trainees in these locations said that the firm *"makes an effort to make us feel like part of the overall firm, via the three-week induction in London, regular video conferences and mid-seat meals."* Trowers also contributes to expenses if the trainee group in London is hosting a social event.

Trainees liked the fact that they could combine both private and public sector work in their training contracts, and said: *"You have to keep an open mind. Some people come here thinking about the public sector, and then find that private sector work interests them more."* Seats available include: housing and regeneration; public sector commercial; banking and finance; corporate (including tax and pensions); employment; litigation; international London; commercial property; and projects and construction. Overseas seats are also available, in Oman, Dubai, Abu Dhabi and Bahrain.

There's no choice when it comes to the first seat, but subsequently trainees are able to state three preferences before each rotation. Mid-seat chats with the graduate manager help trainees to plot their course: *"He will sit down with everyone and get a good picture of what a person is about and what they want."* Sources also raised the point that *"because there are three legs to the firm – public, private and international – then you're pretty much guaranteed to do seats in at least two of those legs. Many trainees will do a public seat, often in housing and regeneration."*

Fizzy Heights

Sure enough, the majority of our interviewees has completed a seat in housing and regeneration. Trainees said: *"You get a lot of responsibility early on – it's a remarkable place to be."* The work touches on the mechanics of funding and delivering housing, as well as policy issues affecting the sector. Clients include a variety of registered providers (RPs), local authorities, institutional investors, private entities and government agencies. Sources encountered *"a mix of transactional property work, and you get involved in everything: drafting development agreements, putting together reports on title for clients, liaising with the Land Registry... you get to learn about the whole process, from entering into a housing association development agreement to procuring and granting a lease."* Given the current climate, lawyers here have helped to formulate new projects by introducing clients to private equity houses and institutional investors: the team recently helped Thames Valley Housing Association to establish its 'Fizzy Living' commercial subsidiary (which aims to rent affordable homes to young professionals), by orchestrating a structure which could allow private investors to get involved.

A seat in public sector commercial is closely related, and *"a lot of it involves simply advising public bodies on commercial transactions, some of which are pretty sizeable and can be worth hundreds of millions – you have to give these public bodies a clear idea of their position in commercial contexts."* Sources added: *"You're still doing commercial transactions, like you would do in corporate, but you're approaching them from another angle."* The documents in these transactions are *"really quite complicated,"* so instead of *"drafting the entire document, you'll be drafting discrete provisions within it."* When it comes to advising public bodies, there's *"a lot of research involved,"* as transactions are complex and sometimes without any precedent (the Fizzy Living example above required a 'first-of-its-kind' structure to be devised).

Many trainees had completed a seat in commercial property or projects and construction. Those in commercial property said that *"actually there's a mix of commercial and residential work – you can work across both fields and keep it broad."* The residential element involves advising *"high net worth individuals on their larger residential ventures,"* while commercial work mixes *"institutions and individuals and their various commercial interests."* The work is international in scope, and sources had helped to assist *"Malaysian clients on large property purchases in London, both beforehand by helping out on preliminary investigations, and afterwards on the post-completion side."* Trainees can get a *"good level"* of responsibility, negotiating leases and working on their own files.

Some like it hot

"The litigation department is split into three teams, which work on construction, commercial and property disputes." Some trainees focused on the construction side, while others split their seat between commercial and property work. Construction disputes are *"really interesting"* and trainees get to *"liaise with clients, draft witness statements, take forms down to the RCJ and do a lot of research: it's a research-heavy seat and you'll advise cli-*

ents on what risks they may face – fascinating stuff." One recent dispute involved representing One Vision Housing, which was pursuing a claim against three parties after cladding collapsed at several tower blocks in Sefton.

Corporate trainees expected their workload to be "quite stressful: the standard hours here are 9am to 8:30pm – it has been a very technical seat, hectic, and full-on." Trowers' mid-market corporate practice has expertise in the hotel/leisure, social care, real estate and logistics sectors, and in 2012 completed M&A deals with an aggregate value of over £800m. There are many international clients: the firm advised three Bahrain-based banks (Capivest, Elaf Bank and Capital Management House) on a three-way merger that created an entity with assets in excess of $400m. It's the first deal of its kind in Bahrain, and should go some way to strengthening the country's banking sector. As you might expect, Trowers' banking and finance lawyers were in on this deal too, and trainees come across their fair share of Islamic finance work while sitting in that department. It's not just Islamic finance though, and sources broke it down into "four big areas: advising the public sector on their loans and borrowings; advising the private sector on similar issues; Islamic finance; and asset finance." Overall, it's a "great six months, as you get a lot of exposure to each of these areas, and have a lot of responsibility: you draft complex security documents and deeds of release, and there's a high degree of client interaction too."

Half our interviewees had been on secondment in the Middle East, and said that they "weren't affected" by the turmoil created during the Arab Spring: "The offices are definitely open for business." Read more about Trowers' offices in the Middle East on our website.

A briefing encounter

Some found it difficult to sum up Trowers in a pithy phrase, "because of the two contrasting areas at the firm: there are the people who are interested in the public sector work, and those who are interested in more of the international, private work." Some sources suggested that the two contrasting areas of the firm attracted two different types of personality. Many others dismissed this theory out of hand. One trainee with a sustained interest in public sector work insisted that "it's not as black and white as that. The quote [from a trainee published in last year's Student Guide] about us being Guardian readers in sandals is a bit far-fetched. I read the Times." In the end, trainees summed up Trowers as "a firm of personalities – that's the great thing about the place, and it keeps it dynamic and interesting."

While some said that "relative to an average law office, Trowers is quite relaxed," others stated that, "as banking and corporate up their game, there has been more stress here." Some offered words of warning: "You often read that our firm has a great work/life balance and it often gets misinterpreted. People think that we all leave the office at 5pm, but that's not the case at all. We are a City law firm and we have to work long hours, but what makes it okay is that it's easy to get on with people and people are appreciative when you do stay. What work/life balance means is that there is no 'stay at your desk' culture."

During interviews it became clear that "trainee involvement in social events has gone down a bit lately," but fortunately "it has been flagged as an issue and people are making an effort to bring it back." Traditional 'mid-seat meals' for trainees are still going strong, and the group recently had a slap-up meal at Tiger Tiger, followed by a trip to a nearby comedy club. The cafeteria is a social hub, and "you'll always bump into people there," while a Christmas party in February (yeah, that happens at Chambers, too) and a firm-wide quiz help to inject a dose of integration. 'Business Briefings' drinks take place at the firm once every quarter: "After a round of billing we get a speech from the senior partner, and then there's a drinks party afterwards."

The True Picture

And finally...
Second-years praised the HR team for its efforts during the qualification process, and Trowers kept on a promising 19 out of 20 qualifiers in 2013.

You've read the book, now visit the website. Chambersstudent.co.uk has bonus features for every firm covered in the True Picture, including details of their recruitment process.

Veale Wasbrough Vizards

The facts

Location: Bristol, London

Number of UK partners/solicitors: 45/93

Partners who trained at firm: 27%

Total number of trainees: 16

Seats: 4x6 months

Alternative seats: none

Extras: pro bono – Bristol CAB, Avon & Bristol Law Centre, BRAVE

On chambersstudent.co.uk...

How to get into VWV

Trends in the education sector

Dickens and the law

The product of a 2009 merger, Veale Wasbrough Vizards conjures up an enchanting offering of sector-based work – especially in education and charities.

A tale of two firms

November 2009 saw Bristol's Veale Wasbrough and London's Vizards Tweedie combine forces to form the magical-sounding Veale Wasbrough Vizards. The former was renowned for its education and charities work; the latter had a history in the capital that stretched back over 200 years, with solid private client, property and family practices and a fascinating literary connection: the firm gave Charles Dickens his first job as a legal clerk in 1828. The merged entity today employs around 300 staff and has turnover in excess of £20m.

VWV targets five sectors in particular, which are: education and charities; healthcare; public sector; private wealth; and family businesses. The vast majority of our sources had chosen the firm with at least one of these in mind, often education or charities – areas which account for a hefty chunk of VWV's revenue and are top-ranked in *Chambers UK*. The work from the five sectors is spread across the firm's four departments: litigation and employment; charities, corporate and commercial (CCC); private client; and real estate.

It's worth noting that the London office now has commercial seats on offer – which wasn't the case in previous years – in addition to its corporate, private client, litigation/employment, real estate and charities groups. Meanwhile, Bristol trainees said that *"couple of seats seem to have vanished here."* More specifically: *"The pastoral seat* [a niche area dealing with issues between teachers, pupils, parents and schools] *doesn't exist at the moment, simply because other areas have more work going on, and personal injury has practically fizzled out as well."* The

firm told us both of these seats may be on offer again in future. There's also the possibility of moving between offices, although trainees are not actively encouraged to do this.

The adventures of Oliver Twist, LLB, LPC

The charities team advises over 1,000 charitable organisations, largely concentrating on those in the education and healthcare sectors. It also works with national charities like the Royal British Legion, as well as organisations associated with the arts – including the Bristol Music Trust and the London Symphony Orchestra. In one notable matter, VWV acted for Wallace and Gromit's Grand Appeal, a charity that raises funds for the Bristol Children's Hospital, on its public art trail known as 'Gromit Unleashed', in which giant sculptures of the famous animated dog were let loose in Bristol during July 2013. The department is *"roughly split into two,"* we were told. *"One half involves a lot of work for educational institutions, like advising independent schools on various charitable issues and dealing with academy conversions. The other half pretty much concerns all other charitable organisations, such as assisting charity trustees with management matters."* Our interviewees agreed that the team is especially charitable when it comes to handing out responsibility to trainees. *"They've always been very relaxed about us getting in touch with clients under no supervision whatsoever,"* remarked one. *"You're certainly given the chance to attend a fair few client meetings too."*

The True Picture

Chambers UK rankings

Banking & Finance	Employment
Charities	Partnership
Construction	Personal Injury
Corporate/M&A	Private Client
Dispute Resolution	Real Estate
Education	Restructuring/Insolvency

There are two seat options in corporate. One of them is more general but has a considerable focus on mid-tier M&A work and matters concerning family-run businesses, while the other revolves around company secretarial work – it's also possible to split a seat between the two. A stint in the general seat *"entails more than just administrative duties,"* with tasks ranging from drafting shareholder agreements to providing advice to start-up companies. *"Things can get pretty exciting, particularly if you're lucky enough to help out with the completion of a major deal. That's something which definitely gets your adrenaline going!"* On the company secretarial side, trainees manage company accounts, file annual returns and draft corporate forms.

The old voracity shop

The group devoured its way through over 110 deals in 2012, with a combined value of around £450m (typically, though, it advises on deals which are between £1m and £10m in value). VWV does a lot of work for early-stage tech companies in the South West region, such as children's luggage retailer Trunki and mobile app developer Mubaloo, and acts for a number of family businesses, including Weston's Cider and Cornish fish merchant W Stevenson & Sons.

Insiders reported that the firm's commercial department *"has seen a lot of investment lately, and is constantly growing in size and stature."* Trainees in this seat get to review and draft contracts, and examine terms and conditions *"which occasionally have some absolutely bonkers clauses in them."* The team takes on plenty of IP work too, specialising in licensing and trade mark matters, and regularly assisting with corporate transactions that have a strong IP element. It advises many schools across the country on licensing issues, and handles trade mark portfolios for the likes of coffee business consultants Beyond the Bean and the Royal Mint.

Employment deals with both contentious and non-contentious matters, from workplace disputes and discrimination cases to general advisory work. The group acts on behalf of charities, higher and further education institutions, schools and nurseries, and has a strong standing in the public sector – such as advising the Crown Prosecution Service on various tribunal claims. Other noteworthy clients include Italian shoe designer Fratelli Rossetti and

Bristol Zoo. Aside from carrying out tasks like reviewing policies and drafting compromise agreements, trainees are sometimes given the opportunity to attend tribunal hearings, which one source described as *"the sharp end of the process."* Some also took on a sizeable portion of immigration work, as *"we're usually the first port of call for those types of enquiries."* An interviewee explained: *"The team is highly conscious of ensuring that you cover all aspects of employment law and other areas relating to it. There's a real effort to give trainees in the seat a well-rounded experience."*

Commercial litigation is broken down into several sub-teams that cover areas like debt recovery (chasing unpaid school fees is a VWV specialism), professional negligence and insolvency. *"Trainees tend to work on the low-end matters but there's a lot of them to get through, and the level of responsibility is great because you're given free rein in terms of running your own cases."* Those who had spent time in the department also got to attend court on more than one occasion. *"It's a fantastic experience that stands you in good stead for the future, as you get to see how the whole thing plays out."*

Hard times

Property litigation *"can be a drastic change of pace if the seat you were in before happened to be fairly quiet."* Indeed, one trainee rather poetically declared: *"It's such a busy seat and you're really rushed off your feet, but the quality of work is truly a treat!"* Sources handled dilapidation claims, drafted lease notices and regularly attended meetings, with a few mentioning that *"it's pretty common for you to be put in front of some big-name clients."* The team has acted for the Ministry of Defence, Bath Spa University and Esso, and represented the global accountancy giant PricewaterhouseCoopers in a number of estate management disputes.

VWV's private client practice encompasses estate and tax planning, trusts and Court of Protection work, as well as contentious trusts and probate matters. *"The clients that we reel in vary enormously,"* trainees informed us. *"It could be an elderly couple who aren't very wealthy but want help preparing a will, or a middle-aged man who's got heaps of cash and doesn't want his first wife getting access to his riches. You honestly don't know who is going to walk through the door next."* The department even advises celebrities and politicians every now and then – though the names of such clients are unsurprisingly kept under wraps.

Real estate remains an important area for the firm. Much of the work is centred on academy conversions, and VWV was recently appointed by the Education Funding Agency to assist with matters concerning the creation of numerous free schools across the country. In addition, the group helps government departments with property-related

The True Picture

issues, carries out work for healthcare practices on surgery development plans, and advises on town centre regeneration schemes and partnering arrangements. Trainees who spend time in the department *"are kept very busy throughout. Even if a project you've been working on is coming to a close, or has been sent off to the Land Registry, there are still hundreds of other tasks to get stuck into – whether it be drafting deeds of assignment or leases, or helping out with the property elements of a corporate transaction."* Client contact is also plentiful, though *"it tends to take the form of telephone calls and e-mail exchanges rather than actual meetings."*

Great exaltations

VWV has three 'core values' listed on its website. These are: working as a team and thinking collaboratively; putting clients at the centre of everything it does; and taking a commercial approach. Our sources had clearly had the first of these core values impressed upon them, because they repeatedly referred to it, occasionally veering into marketing-speak: *"We embody the brand message of teamwork and collaboration – and that's the main reason why there's such a relaxed and supportive atmosphere."* The firm's managing partner Simon Heald appears to lead by example in this respect, with trainees in Bristol commenting that *"he's particularly visible and doesn't simply hide away. He always makes sure he takes the time to engage everyone and there's no doubting that he's a great guy."* London trainees had similarly kind words to say about the office's managing partner David Emanuel: *"I remember him coming over and introducing himself to all of us during our first week here, which I didn't really expect. There are absolutely no qualms about the most senior person at the firm saying hello to the most junior person."* This is aided by the open-plan set-up that both offices have. *"You get to know people far better and, while it may seem like a minor point, when you're en route to your desk there are so many people you speak to who you otherwise wouldn't normally see."*

Situated just behind the Hippodrome Theatre, VWV's Bristol base is *"tucked away slightly in a small cobbled courtyard – but we're still right in the city centre so location-wise it's brilliant,"* one source said. *"It's out on its own a bit compared to many of the other big Bristol firms, who have migrated to Temple Quay."* However, while the office *"actually looks pretty nice from the outside and has a lot of character,"* interviewees were less complimentary about its interior. *"It's a bit dated, the facilities are poor, and the kitchen is badly designed... it could definitely do with some improvements."* Thankfully, it sounds like employees won't have to put up with the building for too much longer: the word from trainees is that the firm plans to move in 2015, although this is not yet official.

In contrast, the London office *"undoubtedly looks smarter and cleaner, with snazzy computers and comfy chairs. It's the epitome of a modern-day law firm."* Trainees were also fans of its location: *"We're on Fetter Lane, which is only a few minutes away from Chancery Lane tube station, plus there are loads of other law firms nearby – we're right in the heart of things from a lawyer's point of view."*

The social life in Bristol *"comes and goes in waves. One month we might go out every Friday night, while other times we'll find that we haven't been out for a good few weeks."* Trainees do regularly attend events organised by the Junior Lawyers Division though – VWV even pays for their JLD summer ball tickets – and *"there are several sports teams that we're encouraged to get involved in."* London trainees go out for Friday night drinks as well but, as in Bristol, *"it happens more from time to time as opposed to every single week."*

Individuals from both offices work together to try and arrange firm-wide gatherings. The majority of those we spoke to felt that *"the effort is there but in practice it's a difficult thing to pull off, seeing as we're pretty far apart in terms of location."* Although trainees would like to see more of these events take place, there have been some recent successes: *"We had a quiz across London and Bristol that was done via a video link, so everyone was able to participate. Surprisingly, it actually worked as planned – the IT crew did themselves proud!"*

And finally...

VWV *"strongly encourages its trainees to experience as many different areas of law as they can,"* so if you're looking for a broad training contract then this could be the perfect place for you. In 2013, seven of nine qualifiers were kept on.

Vinson & Elkins LLP

The facts

Location: London

Number of UK partners/solicitors: 11/18 (+ 3 non-UK-qualified)

UK partners who trained at firm: 10%

Total number of trainees: 9

Seats: 4x6 months

Alternative seats: overseas seats

Extras: pro bono – Toynbee Hall Legal Advice Centre, Trust-Law

On chambersstudent.co.uk...

How to get into V&E

A brief history of the firm

Energy law

This friendly Texan in London offers trainees hard work and hoedowns.

Positive energy

Founded in Houston in 1917 by the aloof Mr Vinson and practical joker Mr Elkins (see our website), V&E is a leading light in the world of energy law. The firm was built on the product that Texas is famous for – oil – and it is still heavily invested in the energy sector, though it has branched out into gas, electricity, alternative energy, and of course all those staple practices of international firms, like corporate, litigation, banking and so on. Check out the firm's rankings in *Chambers USA*, *Chambers UK* and *Chambers Global* to get a better picture or what the firm excels at, in what jurisdictions.

An international outfit with some 15 offices worldwide, V&E was one of the first American firms to venture into London, taking up residence in the City in 1971. The office is situated on the 32nd and 33rd floors of the CityPoint tower, and contains just 41 lawyers. But this isn't some small, isolated offshoot. The trainees we spoke to were drawn to the *"high-quality work and calibre of deals"* as well as by the London office's petite size, noting that *"you'd attribute the range of work we do to a much bigger outfit."* Recent projects include advising Uz-Kor Gas Chemical on the development of a $3.9bn energy complex in Uzbekistan, and representing Norwegian energy company Statoil in its acquisition of land in Ghana. It's not all about energy though. Despite its diminutive size, the London office has several other practices, including international dispute resolution, tax and intellectual property.

In the saddle

Trainees are officially assigned to four seats – corporate; litigation; energy, transactions and projects (ETP); and finance. There's a tax option too. However, sources concurred that in reality V&E runs a *"fluid"* and *"incredibly* *flexible"* system that *"allows you to seek out and pursue work that really interests you."* As such, *"you're not stuck in one area. You can dive between them, dipping in and out as you like – everyone's very welcoming of that."* So, a trainee can be formally in the M&A seat but *"if you express an interest in litigation, you can pick up that work and carry on with it. Even if you then get offered corporate work, you can turn it down."*

Departments usually have around three partners, a few associates and one or two trainees, who will sit with a supervisor for each six-month period. Fortunately, *"trainees aren't there to be put away in the cupboard. We're not photocopying or scanning."* Instead, they're exposed to *"heavy amounts of drafting"* and receive *"a lot more client contact than expected. Even on the vac scheme I sat in client meetings, and this is a consistent feature of working here, not some façade they rolled out for the internship. I've worked with partners from the Abu Dhabi, Dubai and Washington offices."*

Of course, corporate work does involve *"a lot of due diligence,"* which trainees argued *"sounds boring but is actually pretty interesting."* One remarked: *"You always think you can do more, but then when you're tasked with something you've never done before you have a minor heart attack. You're thrilled to be asked but also dying. Trainees are always going to feel a bit held back but it's for your own good. You have to be realistic when you're fresh out of law school – the responsibility levels are fair, not massive."* Sources also cited work on deal closing, drafting and legal research while on corporate assignments.

In litigation, *"most of the work is international arbitration."* We can't reveal much due to the sensitive nature of such matters, but will say that if you arrived at Vinson

Chambers UK rankings

Construction	Projects
Energy & Natural Resources	

hoping to work on contract disputes in the energy sector, you wouldn't be disappointed. Key clients include Essar, Cairn India, Centrica and Kinder Morgan. Sources noted the number of overseas companies that V&E's arbitrators represent, and the firm itself says: *"In particular the last year has seen the majority of work arising from India, across the MENA region and Latin America."* Trainees take on *"a fair share of bundling and lots of research,"* as well as taking part in witness preparation, helping to draft witness statements and *"having bits of communication here and there with the other side."*

V&E's *"international focus"* was something trainees highlighted as an important factor in attracting them to the firm. As well as working on global deals from London, most also go on secondment to Hong Kong or Dubai for six months. This year a secondment in Houston is also being trialled for one trainee *"pioneer"* who'll do energy and finance work and hopefully spot some cowboy boots along the way. We heard on the grapevine that this trainee has been watching episodes of *Dallas* in preparation and were pleased to learn that V&E boasts a partner who *"looks just like Bobby Ewing"* from said TV series.

The firm's Texan heritage *"feeds into the attitude and atmosphere"* of the London office. Certain partners hop between US and UK offices regularly, so trainees are cheered to *"always hear a Texas drawl from down the corridor"* even in drizzly Moorgate. Sources agreed that *"there's a sense of Southern hospitality"* at the firm. *"It's so friendly and laid-back, not like a New York firm. Cheesy as it sounds, the environment here is genuinely supportive."* The small numbers mean that everyone gets to know each other and it's normal for trainees to chat to associates or partners in the kitchen, which can often be a trainee's chance to make an engaging *"30-second pitch for work."*

Burning the midnight oil

Do trainees need gallons of coffee to fuel frequent all-nighters? Sources were sanguine about their time spent in the office. *"Of course there's going to be long hours. But it's a cliché that you'll be forced to work crazy hours at an American firm. You always have support here: you're nev-*er alone at 4am thinking 'what does this mean?'"* Even in the early hours, *"partners have the patience to sit down with you and explain things."*

Interviewees noted that *"every department is different depending on what's going on, how busy they are with a deal or how demanding a client is. So you'll work as long as you have to."* In quieter periods, there's *"no obligation to stay beyond 6.30pm if you've done all your work."* One source put it this way: *"If you take on a corporate training contract you have to expect to sometimes stay late and just suck it up. You have to commit to it. But it's not like you'll be staying until midnight every night. Also, in a weird way, you start to want those late nights because it means you're working really hard and learning."*

They might work hard, but V&E lawyers still have time for fun. *"We celebrate anything we can,"* said trainees, recalling firm-wide parties for Thanksgiving, Australia Day, Chinese New Year and Burns Night, and summer and Christmas gatherings. There's even a special Texas Independence Day celebration for lawyers and clients, with cowboy-style games like horseshoe flinging and a fast-draw shooting contest (bullets not included). Aside from this, V&E employees can often be found after hours in the Corney & Barrow or involved in some kind of energetic activity. Trainees mentioned an annual ski trip, badminton, bowling and an *"upcoming ping-pong night,"* plus there's a five-a-side football team, which regularly competes against the shambling soccer lads of Chambers and Partners.

Trainees come from a range of backgrounds and we couldn't identify any particular traits, except for one. You might think that energy and projects work is a laddish area of law but actually at the time of our calls in early 2013 female trainees outnumbered males six to one. Gents, you have been warned.

"I think they like people who have really found the firm for themselves, rather than just taking a punt on it," declared one source. V&E doesn't have a lot of slots to fill, so it can afford to be picky about who it takes on. Potential trainees don't need to be John D. Rockefeller (or Sheikh Mansour for want of a less 19th-century oil baron), but being able to demonstrate a genuine interest in energy work will definitely stand you in good stead.

The True Picture

And finally...
Generally, V&E lawyers *"all really care about their work and know how to enjoy a good Texan party."* Two out of three qualifiers were retained in 2013.

Walker Morris LLP

The facts

Location: Leeds
Number of UK partners/solicitors: 51/140
Partners who trained at the firm: 40%
Total number of trainees: 29
Seats: 6x4 months
Alternative seats: secondments

On chambersstudent.co.uk...

How to get into Walker Morris
Interview with grad recruitment partner Nick Cannon
The Yorkshire legal market

This profitable firm knows what it's good at – offering *"City service outside the City,"* with a dash of Yorkshire charm.

Roll with the punches

"It stood out as a different proposition to the other main firms in Leeds," mused one trainee. It's easy to see why. The Leeds market is largely dominated by national players such as DLA Piper, Eversheds, Pinsent Masons and Addleshaw Goddard. While they have embarked to a greater or lesser extent on the road to global expansion, little Walker Morris is the only one to keep it local in its Leeds-based single-site office. *"While the others are all exceptionally good firms, they're tending to become more homogenised."* says grad recruitment partner Nick Cannon. *"They're part of larger and ever-expanding organisations. That has advantages, but it makes the experience more impersonal."*

It almost seems inappropriate to call Walker Morris 'little' – ringing in at roughly 200 lawyers – but then, all things are relative. That's still about 400 fewer than Addleshaws in the UK, and any comparison with the omnipresent DLA Piper would just be silly. Given its size, the firm performs well. It's ranked among the best firms in Leeds for dispute resolution, planning, real estate and restructuring by *Chambers UK*, and is nipping at its rivals' heels in banking and finance, corporate and M&A, employment, environment, IT and tax, among others.

A cursory glance at the firm would suggest expansion is on the cards. A 27-strong banking litigation team from now-defunct Cobbetts jumped on board in February 2013, the firm's profit margin remains healthy and, well, all its peers are at it. Nick Cannon, however, is adamant: *"We'll get bigger, but only if it's the right thing at the right time. If we find a perfect fit, it'd be considered, but we're not actively courting merger partners."*

In the meantime, the firm continues to excel at what it does best. *"Property is still doing extremely well,"* Cannon says. In 2013 it picked up new client ASDA and now handles pretty much all of the retail giant's real estate work. The influx of ex-Cobbetts lawyers also gave the firm's banking litigation team *"a big shot in the arm."*

Corporate kraftwerk

Rather than the conventional four, trainees at Walker Morris rotate through six different seats on their training contract. Sources were pleased: *"The most important thing for a trainee is to get exposure and see where your skill set is most suited."* This system means they're able to get a feel for a large chunk of the firm, get to know a wide range of people and learn how different groups interact. Current seat choices include corporate, commercial contracts, IP, regulatory, banking litigation, property litigation, construction litigation, commercial dispute resolution, banking, restructuring and property, plus a couple of client secondments. While none are mandatory, trainees are almost certain to pass through a transactional, litigation and real estate seat at some point.

In their first year trainees don't get much choice over seats, while second-years submit a few preferences stating their department and supervisor of choice. *"We sit down every four months to work out seat assignments,"* says Cannon. *"It's like doing brainteasers at the back of the Sunday supplement. One of our strengths is that we'll try and get to know people and hopefully do what's best for them. We'll consider if they're likely to gel with that supervisor and take into account their interests and aspirations."* Trainees appreciate the effort. *"I've tried nearly everything I wanted to, and they volunteer you for ones*

Chambers UK rankings

Administrative & Public	Intellectual Property
Law	Local Government
Banking & Finance	Pensions
Banking Litigation	Planning
Construction	Projects
Corporate/M&A	Real Estate
Dispute Resolution	Real Estate Litigation
Employment	Restructuring/Insolvency
Environment	Retail
Information Technology	Tax

you might not necessarily pick," explained one source. *"It's good as you get to try things you might not have thought you'd enjoy."*

"Post-recession, the corporate group was a bit quiet, but it's picked up a lot now," trainees said. In fact, the group is seriously active, working for a whole range of clients inside and outside its local area. *"I loved it,"* said one source. *"You get diverse work from public companies, start-ups and anything in between."* The firm has recently advised Leeds-based private equity house Endless on its acquisition of retail chain Bathstore as well as on the purchase of a German music catalogue from Universal Music Group for new client BMG. *"The hours can get pretty lengthy,"* we're told, *"but the adrenaline pumps, hours whiz by and suddenly it's 3am."* Plus, it helps that *"partners are always there until the same time, if not later."*

The finance commercial group offers two seats – banking and insolvency. It's one of the firm's medium-sized groups, with some partners working distinctly in one area and others multi-tasking between the two. On the banking side, WM works mostly with big-name financial institutions – Yorkshire Bank, Santander, HSBC and RBS among others. The insolvency team advised Lloyds as rival firm Cobbetts went into administration. The firm has also made quite a name for itself helping football clubs going into insolvency, acting for Portsmouth, Crystal Palace, Plymouth and Darlington in the last few years. *"I had long hours, but it was great,"* said one trainee. *"I was able to see a deal through from start to finish, and had a large amount of responsibility."*

REBL with a cause

Corporate dispute resolution is one of WM's bigger groups. *"It does a really broad range of work,"* trainees said. That's everything from contractual disputes through to professional negligence claims for a bunch of different sectors including food, energy and retail. Of course, there's the odd bit of doc review, but trainees also get to take witness statements and go to court, where *"the firm ensures we have quite close contact with the barristers."*

Another big contentious seat is real estate and banking litigation (or REBL as it's fondly known internally). *"You think they'd be two quite different things, but it works,"* trainees explained. That's largely thanks to the group's clients – the majority are banks and financial institutions. *"We deal with all their lending problems, but also with problems over mortgages and real estate issues."* The 27 new recruits from Cobbetts have bolted onto this group, bringing it up to about 50 lawyers. *"I had very little menial work,"* said one trainee. *"I was drafting witness statements and managing expert witnesses."* In fact, throughout the group, *"when it's fast-paced you get to see how far you can push yourself and really step up to the plate."*

The transactional side of real estate is big news at Walker Morris. The department hosts five trainees every four months – *"pure maths says everyone will spend some time there, but there's no written rule,"* says Nick Cannon. That said, as one of the firm's most prominent groups *"it's an excellent training ground,"* where newbies get to work for the likes of ASDA, Bupa, Debenhams and Starbucks. Student accommodation company UNITE is also a major client. Trainees get to run their own smaller matters – *"I felt I was being useful, but I didn't feel swamped,"* said one source.

The firm's menu of secondment opportunities is also worth a mention. *"There tend to be about three secondments available for every seat, and about half of all trainees do one at some point,"* we're informed. London-based positions at companies in the energy and banking sectors come up regularly, as do occasional stints in Edinburgh. *"I was initially a little nervous,"* said one trainee, *"but I was pleased they showed trust in me. Going in-house brings the law to life, and you find out what commercial awareness really is."* While other secondment opportunities crop up on a needs basis, bear in mind that *"Walker Morris is a single-site, medium-size firm, so it's not like you'll get a secondment to Singapore any time soon."*

One office wonder

It's all swings and roundabouts, however. The lack of any exotic outposts in the Asia-Pacific region means there's an intensive focus on trainees at home, and the attention paid to professional development really is top-notch. Trainees share office space with their supervisors, who *"are really good at picking up when you're catching on to work and you've understood something. They make an effort to give you something different so you don't get stuck doing the same thing over and over again."* There's rigorous training: *"In the first couple of weeks they're quite intensive,"* and after that the schedule varies between departments. In general, however, expect a substantial dollop of training every week or two. *"There's a lot available, and it's left to you to decide what to go to. There are occasionally workshops and various training events aimed specifically at trainees, but no one's breathing down your neck."*

Walker Morris acts for *"the full spectrum"* of clients, from regional companies to huge multinationals, and trainees' working hours mirror this. *"I've had some pretty horrendous hours in the transactional departments but you expect that,"* said one source. *"It's how the job works. But, no one expects you to be here if you have nothing to do. People will respect you more if you go home."* The only real grumble from trainees concerns their pay cheque. At a grand or two less than their rivals, our sources worried: *"If they don't keep up with Eversheds in Leeds they'll lose the best trainees."* That said, the consensus is: *"You feel a bit hard done by at first, but we do work much better hours than other firms on a day-to-day basis."*

It may have *"a unique, old-school law firm feel,"* but it's hard to emphasise quite how much pride this cosy firm takes in being in one location. It really is the beacon that sets it apart from its rivals in the Yorkshire market. *"Although it's very much a marketing ploy, there's truth in it too,"* revealed one trainee. *"It feels like we are one team. If you're working on a multidisciplinary transactions you can always pop over for a chat. It brings a level of cohesion that's slightly different to firms with lots of offices."*

Most trainees do have some sort of local connection, or can at least demonstrate a commitment to the area, and several insiders took care to point out that Walker Morris is *"very Yorkshire and proud – straight-talking, with a lack of pretension."* This may sound like the firm's simply playing up to flat-cap and whippet stereotypes, but we do get the impression that in the past one or two trainees haven't quite fitted the firm's no-nonsense ethos. Anyway, *"partners expect you to be competent, but above and be-* *yond that they want someone who is personable and able to build relationships inside and outside of the firm. This is a place where personality shines."*

Walker on the wild side

Unsurprisingly then, this is a fairly outgoing, chatty bunch. That's probably for the best as Walker Morris is definitely a social sort of firm. *"They take the social side just as seriously as they take the work side, but in the completely opposite direction,"* trainees told us. As well as regular drinks at local bar Toast, the firm hosts summer sports days, quiz nights and a collection of Christmas parties and encourages everyone to get involved in its sports teams. It appears that partners are just as up for partaking in frivolities as the trainees. *"One construction partner was particularly zealous in a tug-of-war contest at the summer party and gave a rousing speech when his team won,"* a source recounted. *"It's nice to get a glimpse of their personalities. It's like seeing your teachers outside of school."*

It's hardly surprising that every trainee we spoke to was eager to stay on at the firm, and the qualification process is relatively stress-free. *"The jobs list comes out in April, and we have a couple of weeks to put applications in."* Interviews are held, and jobs are confirmed by the end of April. Partners are happy to chat with trainees about their chances. *"If you build a good relationship, there's no problem knocking on their door and giving your thoughts on the job list. People appreciate that and it shows that you're keen."* In 2013, 11 out of 16 qualifiers nabbed an NQ job at the firm.

And finally...
If working with top-class clients in a close-knit environment sounds up your street, make sure you apply for the firm's vac scheme as the firm recruited about 80% of its trainees from the summer programme in 2012.

Ward Hadaway

The facts

Location: Newcastle, Leeds, Manchester
Number of UK partners/solicitors: 82/111
Total number of trainees: 25
Seats: 4x6 months
Alternative seats: secondments

On chambersstudent.co.uk

How to get into Ward Hadaway
The Newcastle legal market

"People underestimate Ward Hadaway – I expected to work for major North East companies, but there are even international clients..."

Beyond the toon

Things look bright for Ward Hadaway as it turns 25. Accelerated growth over the past five years has seen a firm that's long played second fiddle to Dickinson Dees in Newcastle open hubs in Leeds and Manchester. The latter office has a focus on finance, litigation, property, employment, insolvency and corporate recovery. A Leeds office opened in 2008 and now houses over 70 staff. Graduate recruitment partner Paula Myers explains how the Yorkshire contingent fits in: *"Leeds will quickly grow. We're now full-service there, which means we can give trainees a very varied training and also the responsibility and care that they need."*

Employment, property and litigation form this firm's backbone. Also notable is a long-standing relationship with the NHS, from which WH picks up plenty of clinical negligence, employment and commercial work. Trainees say: *"We've got a public sector streak, but that's not everything we do. We're full-service, and our growth means you've got to be prepared to be fluid and dynamic and go along with changes."*

The last point is indicative of where the firm is currently at. *"We know the firm wants to do in Manchester what it's done in Leeds,"* thought one Newcastle trainee. *"We now get a lot of work from Leeds and likewise refer work there ourselves. We started out with a creative industries unit in Manchester and now have a full office. We also have space on Oxford Street, which isn't an office but is a useful meeting place. But the firm's also conscious of the fact that we don't want to be distracted from Newcastle."* To that end, some trainees think that *"the firm is expanding so quickly that people need to be prepared that they won't get to know everyone."* There wasn't much negativity among those we spoke to, however. *"It's exciting how fast we're growing,"* said one source. *"The market's changing all the time, and things like Tesco Law mean we have to adapt with it. There's a feeling here that we all have a say, and if you wanted to take a department in a certain direction there's the flexibility to do so, as there's no precedent."*

In Newcastle, the seat options remain commercial litigation, property, banking, corporate, healthcare, property litigation, employment, private client, IP/IT, insolvency, matrimonial and coco. There used to be a policy of staying put from third to final seat, and it's still sometimes a possibility but is dependent on business needs. Choice-wise, *"nobody's been consistently disappointed – one person was put in a seat they knew nothing about, but they now want to qualify there!"* First-years get some say in where they want to go, but the caveat is that more senior trainees get priority.

Leeds trainees have a slimmer selection of seats to choose from, checking off employment and property – *"the office's two big areas"* – along with corporate, and commercial. There's also room for a trainee in insolvency and with a private client team *"expanding on a weekly basis,"* trainees hope there'll be a seat there in the not-too-distant future. There's only one trainee in Manchester at the moment, who started in September 2012 and is *"taking on a bit of everything"* from property, commercial litigation, corporate finance and employment.

The True Picture

Chambers UK rankings

Agriculture & Rural Affairs	Healthcare
Banking & Finance	Information Technology
Charities	Intellectual Property
Clinical Negligence	Licensing
Construction	Pensions
Corporate/M&A	Planning
Dispute Resolution	Private Client
Employment	Real Estate
Family/Matrimonial	Restructuring/Insolvency

The True Picture

Pets at home and away

The litigation department is *"the biggest in the North East, if not the North."* The group works across WH's three offices and has a particular focus on shareholder disputes, professional negligence, IT, insurance and reputation management. Clients include *"loads of national organisations like breweries and telephone companies, but also a lot of local wealthy individuals,"* such as Sir John Howard Lawson, whom WH defended when the baronet's son claimed he had been *"swindled out of his rightful inheritance"* (the son was eventually awarded a whopping £5.60). Newcastle trainees sit in a room with their supervisor *"and get most work from them, along with ad hoc tasks from other fee earners."* Many will be trusted with their own smaller matters, *"like breach of contract claims or Twitter defamation."* On huge disputes, such as Newcastle Airport's professional negligence claim against Eversheds, trainees naturally *"do what's given to you. But everyone's very keen to give you work that will interest you and that you haven't done before."*

Corporate's divided into M&A and banking/finance teams. Trainees may sit with a partner who does one of these specifically or gather work across both. Banking trainees could see venture capital and private equity work in addition to tax and capital markets. Over in M&A, Ward Hadaway recently represented equestrian supplier Ride-Away during its takeover by Pets At Home and fishing tackle specialist Hardy and Greys in its sale. These business are York and Alnwick-based, respectively, but trainees added that there are also national and international businesses represented: ASDA, UK-founded pharma group Aesica and German sugar maker Südzucker are some of them. One source mentioned the substantive work they received in the department: *"Often it was just a partner, a junior associate and me – it's not just due diligence; I had very good experience working on ancillary documents, and had day-to-day exposure to the client."*

Ward Hadaway's healthcare group is nationally ranked alongside the likes of BLP, Clyde & Co and Eversheds. The group is a staple of the firm's practice, and it acts for more than 70 NHS organisations. It is also one of very few firms appointed to both the NHS's litigation liabilities

and clinical negligence panels. The firm acts for numerous foundation trusts in the region and recently for many primary care trusts on transferring their properties following the shake-up of the NHS structure. *"As a trainee you're involved with many of the different areas, but also with day-to-day advice for the NHS. Especially in your first year, partners are very good at taking you out with them and meeting people."*

Fog on the Tyne

The property group at Ward Hadaway is subdivided into public sector, residential, business and development teams – trainees in Newcastle focus on one area, while those in Leeds and Manchester take on a mix of work from both the transactional and contentious sides. Development work is both *"tangible and complex,"* say trainees. *"There are regular site visits, so you might go and stand in a field, but know that you can go back in a couple of years and it'll be a massive development."* Regular clients include major developer Barratt as well as Aldi and software manufacturer Sage UK. Public sector work involves selling properties for dentists, opticians, pharmacists, GPs and PCTs. *"There's a lot of land transfer, and we also brought quite a few properties to auction. It's fascinating to see old schools turned into surgeries."*

Property litigation runs from boundary quibbles to professional negligence and leaseholder disputes. *"Most interesting,"* said trainees, *"are the personal ones – neighbour disputes or nuisance claims. When you've got people saying they can't access their home properly things get heated very quickly."* Prop lit's also great for those keen on black-letter law. *"The trainee's job is to dig through everything and apply the law to it – you could be looking at a map, or the specific wording of a right of way – it's pure law."* This kind of work *"teaches you how to be really thorough. A mere word out of place on a form can make everything void."*

Employment clients include housing association Home Group, the Department for Work & Pensions, numerous NHS organisations, many local schools and academies, and Newcastle United FC itself. Trainees think that no matter what size the client, *"disciplinary proceedings or employee grievances are always personal and real to the individual who's dealing with it."* Equally, *"there's a set procedure come what may, but within that the full range of matters and clients means that no two sets of pleadings are the same – which makes it fascinating."* A seat in coco, meanwhile, can mean either support work such as *"joint ventures and initial drafts of T&Cs"* on behalf of corporate clients, or public sector work. The latter deals with education providers (there's a team specifically for academies in the Leeds office) and hospitals.

Far from *"just dealing with rich people making wills,"* a seat in private client gives trainees access to court of protection and mental capacity cases in addition to the standard estate planning and wills and probate work. Happily, *"there's a big variety in the value of cases,"* meaning some juniors get their own clients and files to run autonomously. *"It's not just partners who have long-standing relationships with old landowners. The whole team has its own clients, and trainees are encouraged to build relationships too."*

Ward Had-howay

The atmosphere varies across Ward Hadaway's departments, partly because in Newcastle operations are split between two offices. Sandgate House has individual offices which trainees share with their supervisor. Keel Row House is open plan and houses staff in pods *"with two partners and a secretary."* Funnily enough, it's the latter that has a subdued, library vibe, while the individual offices of the former foster *"an open-door policy, with people popping in and out and constant hustle and bustle."* Despite these differences, trainees concur that supervision is of a very high standard. *"There are scheduled appraisals for the middle and end of seats, but it's really an ongoing thing. There are ample opportunities for people to flag up where you're going wrong, which helps build confidence as you always know when you're going in the right direction!"*

Aside from departmental quirks, our sources thought the common theme at WH was *"client care, in a friendly, straight-talking way."* *"There's a priority here that you're*

a reasonable human being – it's by far the friendliest place I've ever interviewed at," was something we heard repeatedly. *"If you worked here and didn't come across as outgoing, it could be your downfall."* Despite there being senior partners *"who've been here 35 years,"* sources also concurred on two points. Firstly, *"if you walked in off the street and tried to work out who was who, it'd be difficult to see a hierarchy."* In the words of one trainee, *"you could equally be out on a Friday with a partner or a secretary. There are no real divisions."*

There's a major emphasis on networking in the non-public sector departments. *"The partners warm up to you quickly if you're out and being sociable, and the marketing guys are really keen to support ideas that we have."* Two entrepreneurial current trainees started a 'Beer and Burger' night to network with peers every month. *"I can't believe how full my calendar is now I've started,"* laughed one interviewee. *"The North East isn't a massive area, so we can get to know key clients pretty quickly and they start giving us work instead of the partner."* Meet and greets aside, there's plenty of socialising to keep trainees occupied on other nights of the week. Along with sports such as football, squash and tennis, there's a charity challenge – for the Percy Hedley Foundation in 2013 – invoking trainees to creatively turn £500 into as much cash as possible. Regular drinks at the Pitcher and Piano *"are an almost religious activity come Friday, as we all wait for the senior partner to walk around and say, 'right, off to the pub'."*

And finally...

NQ jobs are the one bugbear among this otherwise cheerful bunch. WH publishes its jobs list in May, *"which causes a certain degree of unrest as other firms publish way before this."* The firm is open about its timings, however, and in 2013 eight out of 11 qualifiers stayed on.

Watson, Farley & Williams

Challenging.

Nick Payne, Newly Qualified

Distinctive.

Opportunities.

Integrated.

Real.

"From my first seat I enjoyed the challenge of working closely with senior associates, partners and clients on every project."

Vacation Placements
31st January 2014
Training Contracts
31st July 2014 (to start 2016)

www.wfw.com/trainee

Watson, Farley & Williams

The facts

Location: London

Number of UK partners/solicitors: 51/70

Partners who trained at firm: 10%

Total number of trainees: 27

Seats: 6x4 months

Alternative seats: overseas seats, secondments

Extras: language classes

On chambersstudent.co.uk...

How to get into WFW

P&I clubs explained

Overseas travel is an option at smaller firms too! Watson, Farley & Williams is a compact City firm with a significant international network and a focus on asset finance.

Ship shape

In late 1981 Alistair Farley and Martin Watson, two shipping finance partners at Norton Rose, decided to strike out on their own. This was a boom time for shipping, and these lawyers were keen to build up foreign contacts and take on international deals but were frustrated by NR's cautious approach to overseas expansion (how times change, eh?). Another colleague, aviation specialist Geoffrey Williams, came on board, and by May 1982 their new firm was launched in the City.

Today the firm maintains its traditional maritime strength, with the largest shipping finance practice in the world and a top-tier ranking in *Chambers UK*. However, the firm has expanded beyond its traditional forte. In 2010 an aviation team joined the ranks, and the shipping finance department was renamed 'asset finance'. But it's not all about boats and planes. Other assets include power plants, mines, rail equipment, satellites, telecommunications and property, and the firm works on matters involving all of these. And WFW has other departments too, including employment, real estate, corporate and tax.

In 2012/13 the firm saw revenue top the £100m mark for the first time. In less good news, it announced it was deferring the start-date of a small number of individuals in its September 2013 intake. However, the firm denied rumours that it would be downsizing the training scheme as a consequence and said it had no intention of decreasing the size of future intakes.

In addition to its compact London HQ, WFW has a network of overseas offices, mainly based in key shipping hubs (New York, Hamburg, Hong Kong, etc.). This robust international presence shored up the firm during the recession and helped it to flourish financially. The international outlook is an integral part of WFW's identity. A seat abroad is guaranteed (indeed, compulsory) for trainees, who will head off to the Paris, Piraeus, Singapore or Bangkok office.

WFW runs a six-seat training contract. As well as the spell overseas, there are seats available in asset finance; projects, commodities and export finance (PCEF); corporate; litigation; tax; employment; property; and competition. *"The compulsory seats are litigation, asset finance and overseas... the others aren't absolutely compulsory, but they like everyone to do corporate or PCEF,"* one trainee declared. Seat allocation is a *"collaborative process."* Three-quarters of the way through each seat, trainees meet with the HR department to discuss where they want to go next.

All hands on deck

Asset finance is *"the bread and butter of the firm."* Unsurprisingly for a department with such a good reputation, it takes on some *"big-ticket"* projects. Recent highlights include advising Citibank and Bank of America Merrill Lynch on a loan agreement with the wonderfully named Sovcomflot to finance the construction of two very large crude carriers (VLCCs). Meanwhile, the aviation team acted on behalf of Lloyds Banking Group on a pre-delivery payment (PDP) financing of three AgustaWestland helicopters for LCI Aviation.

Chambers UK rankings

Asset Finance	Dispute Resolution
Capital Markets	Employment
Commodities	Energy & Natural Resources

"This is a very strong department, and the work you get is very involved, no matter where you sit," thought trainees. *"You get a lot of responsibility. I went to closing meetings and worked on ship deliveries, plus I did a lot of drafting, so I really honed those skills."* Trainees might also find themselves *"managing files and dealing with international clients in different time zones."* Other sources reported that *"there's a lot of admin"* as well – *"a lot of bibling at the end of transactions."* However, trainees are given the chance to *"run with and lead small parts of transactions, always with appropriate supervision."* Trainees tend to sit with a partner and split their time between shipping and aviation.

In PCEF, trainees might handle *"a lot of work in trading commodities."* One source was pleased to note that *"the partner I sat with was very pedagogical and took time to explain things and make sure I did high-level work. I was drafting trust agreements, corresponding with counsel and questioning points of their legal opinion."* Sources also pointed out that projects work also involves *"handling data rooms and due diligence, which no one smiles about."* Another interviewee mentioned that they had *"spent a lot of time assisting on big corporate reorganisations, drafting amendments to contracts. It was pretty full-on because they were large-scale deals."*

Corporate matters involve *"lots of crossover between departments."* In this seat one trainee *"assisted with a couple of joint venture agreements and worked on a shipping transaction involving a private equity group and a company that buys distressed ships. I also got involved in some energy work."* Among the deals the team has worked on of late was Albwardy Investments' $26m purchase of Westcliff Hotel (in South Africa, not the seaside town in Essex).

In the litigation department, *"a lot of matters are based around finance or industries like shipping, aviation and energy."* For instance, WFW litigators recently acted on behalf of global oil trading company Vitol on a claim concerning a long-term supply agreement for crude oil. During the seat, trainees found that *"cases go on for a lot longer* [than deals] *and the advice you give needs to be very specific. There's less you can run with yourself. It's more academic, more research-based."* One interviewee had attended an arbitration, and had been to court to get orders, *"as well as grappled with bundling tasks."*

Bon voyage

Overall, trainees waxed lyrical about their spells abroad. One content source stated: *"It was incredible; one of the best things I've ever done. Definitely the highlight of my training contract."* Trainees can jet off to Paris, Piraeus or Singapore to do an asset finance seat, while the Bangkok stint is in litigation. There's also the option of a corporate or contentious seat in Singapore. Before venturing abroad, they'll ideally have completed a London seat in the corresponding department. Trainees enthusiastically emphasised that *"the quality of exposure that you get in these front-line offices is markedly different to the training experience in London."* While there's *"client contact and a high level of responsibility"* on home soil, things get a lot more intense overseas. *"It was completely different. Whereas in London a junior associate watches your every move, overseas you pretty much run transactions yourself."*

One source elaborated further: *"It was extremely busy, but I loved every minute of it. The hours are longer, but the client contact is amazing. You go out to client dinners, cocktails, networking events. I'd be allowed to negotiate a point on transactions. The partners were great because every time I had a problem, I could query them in a very casual, relaxed way. It's very open. It was definitely the most developmental seat."* Interviewees agreed that *"you definitely feel like a junior associate rather than a trainee."* Of course, this can be a double-edged sword: *"The hours can be tough overseas because as well as doing almost NQ-level work, you're still expected to do all the trainee tasks as well."*

Away from the office, trainees shouldn't get lonely. *"There's quite a big trainee social network in Singapore,"* said one who'd been out to East Asia. *"I got put on an e-mail list of about 60 or 70 people. We'd arrange things for the weekend, like going to the beach and having drinks. I also did a bit of travelling around the region."* Trainees in Greece, meanwhile, appreciated that *"the office is really busy, and you get loads and loads of client contact. I went to all the signings, plus I worked with the London office – it's good to still be linked with them."*

A whale of a time?

Back in Britain, what's firm life like generally? The office *"doesn't have the bells and whistles of other offices. There's no water feature or extra pizazz. It's not like the Norton Rose office!"* However, it's *"functional"* and in a *"very practical"* location near Liverpool Street.

Trainees felt that working hours are *"on the whole, pretty good."* A 6 or 7pm finish might be standard at quieter times, stretching to 9 or 10pm when there's a big deal on and later at very busy times. Asset finance *"probably has the toughest hours,"* but sources were pleased to note that when they stayed late into the evening *"there's an acknowledgement that we've worked hard. It's not just expected."* During quieter patches *"the partner I sat with actively shooed me out of the door."*

WFW isn't massive, so incomers don't get lost in a crowd of clamouring trainees. Instead, sources *"know most people by name, and that makes you feel welcome. I felt a part of it within a couple of months."* Despite being just 31 years old, WFW is *"a little bit traditional, but not in the sense that it's conservative or doesn't want to change."* The atmosphere may arise from the fact that the firm's got shipping finance at its heart. *"The shipping industry is quite a fraternal, handshake-based industry. Finance is what the firm's all about, and in this area with our kind of clients you need that traditional approach."* As such, *"it isn't a law firm that's trying to be really cool."* So while partners and associates are described as approachable, you won't find them zipping down the corridor on a Segway. *"I've heard the expression 'It is what it is' a lot,"* said one trainee. *"So when a client says they want something done before the end of the tax year and we have loads to do, this phrase pops out. It kind of sums up the firm's understated, get-on-with-it approach."*

This attitude seems to influence the type of person WFW is looking to hire: *"At the assessment day, you have to be* able to hold your ground, explain an idea and listen to someone else. They want people who can just get down to work, but then are also jovial and relaxed."* Within the current trainee group there's a whole spectrum of personalities ranging from *"wallflower to extrovert with everything in between."* It's important to remember that *"the firm sends trainees abroad, so they want people who are enthusiastic about going overseas and engaging in new things. They're looking for someone who's pretty outgoing, but not necessarily in the sociable sense. You need to be confident, but that doesn't mean loud. There are a lot of people here who are more reserved but have the courage of their convictions."* One source summarised: *"Trainees need to be willing to get stuck in. They don't want people who'll start acting like mini-partners."*

The firm puts on a Christmas and summer party plus a fee earners' dinner, but it's really up to trainees to organise their own social events week to week. One trainee reeled off an impressive list of boozers: *"the Whistling Stop, the Light Bar, the Queen of Hoxton, McQueen, Golden Bee – we're trying to push away from All Bar One."* As well as venturing out to Spitalfields or Shoreditch for drinks, they'll often have lunch together in the popular canteen, sampling the wares of French chef Philippe. *"He's a great asset to the firm,"* declared sources, speaking highly of his canapés, cookery classes and wine-tasting sessions.

And finally...

A guaranteed overseas seat might float your boat, but bear in mind that there's a *"heavy bias towards asset finance"* at WFW. In 2013, 12 out of 14 second-year qualifiers were kept on.

Wedlake Bell LLP

The facts

Location: London
Number of UK partners/solicitors: 52/48
Partners who trained at the firm: 17%
Total number of trainees: 12
Seats: 4x6 months
Alternative seats: secondments

On chambersstudent.co.uk...

How to get into Wedlake Bell

Financially sound and among the friendliest of firms, Wedlake Bell's more than worth a look for its healthy spread of seat options and petite size.

A marriage made in Gray's Inn

Gaze up at its listed building on London's Bedford Row and you'd be forgiven for surmising that Wedlake Bell is a bit of a traditional place. But first impressions can be wrong: step inside and it's all glass sliding-doors and modern art. This sums up Wedlake Bell – excellent at private client and family, but also sporting ever-expanding corporate and commercial practices. Property (which makes up 32% of the business and is the firm's biggest group) plays to the two halves of the firm's strengths by advising both commercial contractors and established landowners.

A 2012 merger with Cumberland Ellis pulled both firms out of the credit-crunch blues. In 2012/13 Wedlake Bell not only posted net profits of £6.74m (up from £2.2m the previous year) but also a mega-rise in profits per equity partner (to £324,000 from £135,000 last year) – no mean feat given there are now a third more partners than there were previously. *"It's like we've always been the same firm,"* say trainees, and by way of evidence, new senior partner Simon de Galleani is legacy Cumberland Ellis. With bolstered property, family, private client, litigation, corporate and commercial groups, the rejuvenated firm does not look remarkably different from the WB of yore. Trainees still have the pick of these groups, plus, as before, pensions, employment, tax and construction.

Through sheer size, a stint in property remains *"unavoidable."* There's plenty of variety though, and trainees can spend this six months in commercial, residential or property litigation. There's also a dedicated construction team *"which is heavily contract-based, so it tests very different skills to regular property."* For that reason, *"if you do con-* *struction, chances are you'll end up doing another seat in property too."*

Commercial and residential property offer different experiences – the former's *"one of the busiest seats,"* and accordingly there are always two trainees supporting the group, *"which is nice because if one of you is drowning, you can share the load out – plus, there's always someone you can bounce ideas off."* The seat involves liaising with all the people involved in the buying process of anything from large soon-to-be malls to *"the sale of a small shop or the purchase of a garage."* These things will be given to the trainee pretty much straight away. *"You walk in and get a filing cabinet full of small matters: licences to alter and assign and some bigger leases that aren't too complex."* It's fast-paced, the hours can be heavy, but the support from the team *"is constant. Your knowledge is assumed to be pretty much zero, and you're made to feel from the start that you can approach anyone. They're careful to ensure you're not just running with something because you fancy yourself as a hot-shot property lawyer."*

The residential seat offers the chance to work with *"individuals who the firm already has a relationship with through private client work"* on *"vast residential portfolios."* Property lit *"offers pretty straightforward disputes,"* some more exciting than others. Rent arrears, service charges and the ins and outs of land law, yes, but also think squatters and arguments involving wills and property assets.

McEmployment

The all-female construction department offers a slightly different experience, as part of the trainee role is being the

Chambers UK rankings

Construction	Intellectual Property
Employment	Real Estate Finance
Information Technology	Real Estate Litigation

main point of contact on a helpline for contractors. *"The firm provides an hour's free legal advice for the members of a trade union. It's a bit daunting when you start, but it's the best way to learn how to offer legal advice that's actually helpful. You man the helpline, go off and do the research and respond."*

The corporate team is growing, and trainees reckon *"there are ambitions to become the biggest group in the firm."* Still *"predominantly M&A,"* the team's developing other areas *"through a couple of partners who have expertise in public company and private equity work."* The deals aren't huge, but one of the successes of the group is the way it capitalises on internal cross-referrals. *"Work comes in from private client, and conversely every corporate client brings in employment, pensions, property and IP work."*

As if to evidence the importance of cross-referrals, trainees in employment estimated doing *"about 70% non-contentious corporate support and advisory work."* The team assists glamorous names like the Royal Academy, Jaeger and *cough* postage stamp supply business Stanley Gibbons on a range of contract matters. The team seems to have a particular niche in the individuals it acts for: it recently represented the former head of Selfridges food and restaurants Ewan Venters in his appointment as CEO of Fortnum & Mason, and former McDonald's PR Steve Easterbrook on his departure for pastures healthier to become CEO of Wagamama. We'd better leave it at that, as Steve was head honcho during the infamous McLibel case in the 1990s and we don't want Wedlake Bell to pick up any litigation on his behalf....

"I thought I'd enjoy my private client seat for all the contact with people but I didn't actually have that many meetings," mused one trainee. *"What I've actually enjoyed the most has been the detailed research I've done for every step of each process."* In a department that was already large, and is now *"far larger post-merger,"* the private client seat involves much more than drafting wills. *"I've never been asked to do the same thing twice!"* laughed a source. Expect plenty of wills, sure, but the department

also deals with *"anything that comes up in people's personal affairs: probate, trusts, Court of Protection work and lasting powers of attorney."*

Tissues, no issues

We heard nothing but great things about the family seat and its head, the *"amazing"* Charmaine Hast. Expect non-stop client contact here. *"Often the things you're saying on the phone aren't anything legal – you're just providing a listening ear... you do a lot of counselling, but do have to know when to cut the conversation short."* The team deals with some rich clients, though be assured *"no matter how much money someone earns, having divorce proceedings served is very dramatic."* There's plenty of opportunity for drafting here, plus much time spent out of the office at court and meeting clients. *"You learn on your feet how the litigation process works."*

Trainees intimated that the hours lawyers work have become slightly longer in recent years, but there's still *"no sense that you ever have to work really late – all I'd say is that you may now be leaving at 7pm when it's busy as opposed to 6pm a few years back."* WB has always been one of the loveliest firms on our radar, and we're pleased to report that nothing's changed there. *"There's a focus across the firm on employees being well-rounded individuals who have a lot of personality. Part of the reason we attract the clients we do is that we offer expertise but we're also approachable."* Training is, as you'd expect, pretty personal. *"HR are great,"* say trainees, *"and training principal Hilary Platt is the top dog – it's amazing how many minute details she knows about each trainee...."*

With such a variety in practice groups, it's no surprise that *"every floor feels different – almost like microfirms within a whole,"* but rest assured – this is *"never a problem."* We were told that *"private client is studious, family is noisier, but the number of cross-referrals makes it clear that our variety is a strength."* Come Friday, *"there are often impromptu drinks,"* and *"if you're out with someone senior they will always pay."* Good show!

Wedlake Bell goes for trainees *"who are doers, who can talk to anyone about anything. They don't go for the Oxbridge hockey-playing captain of the rugby team type. We're a mixed bunch age-wise, and we're better for it."* Consequently, sources report the firm interviewing *"as many people as it can, as recruiters can't tell what you're like until they've met you."*

And finally...

With no jobs list released, this year's set of qualifiers felt there wasn't a *"particularly clear message"* about NQ prospects. However, five out of seven qualifiers managed to secure jobs with Wedlake Bell. Lucky them, we say.

Weil, Gotshal & Manges

The facts

Location: London
Number of UK partners/solicitors: 25/82
Total number of trainees: 21
Seats: 4x6 months
Alternative seats: New York, secondments
Extras: pro bono – CAB, Battersea Legal Advice Centre

On chambersstudent.co.uk...

How to get into Weil
More on private equity

If intense hours and a demanding workload don't put you off, elite Weil may well be up your street...

Tough talkers

Weil makes no apologies for its image as a tough City establishment. In fact, 'Working at [Weil] is not for everyone' is splashed unabashedly across the front of its recruiting brochure. While our interviewees preferred to phrase this sentiment a little more delicately – *"The thing about this firm,"* said one carefully, *"is nothing's handed to you on a plate"* – the fundamental message rings loud and clear: this is a no-nonsense place of business. Indeed, there's a veritable streak of diligence and entrepreneurial moxie to the American-led unit. At just 17 years old, the teen's already jostled its way into the City's premier corporate and finance ranks and scored some magic circle-worthy accolades along the way – *Chambers UK* singles out Weil as one of the country's top contenders for private equity buyouts and banking/finance work on the sponsors side. Need further proof Weil belongs in the ring with the big boys? Consider the origins of its recent lateral hires: the last two years have seen the firm onboard several high-flying partners from Freshfields and Linklaters, not to mention an entire funds team poached from Clifford Chance. *"This is a place with opportunities for the future,"* trainees confirmed. *"There's definitely a plan to expand and get bigger and better."*

Weil's London operation may be linked to the firm's New York roots, but it's by no means secondary to its progenitor across the pond. The British unit is Weil's second largest office and is stocked almost exclusively with UK-qualified lawyers who undertake a majority spread of home-generated work. In fact, the chief indicator of the firm's American heritage is its hefty NQ salary, which is among the highest in the City.

Weil's plate of work is undeniably upper-crust, but comparisons to the magic circle largely end here. For starters, there are only around ten trainees in each intake – a reason many cited for joining up. *"It's easy to make a name for yourself when you don't have to fight 100 other trainees for visibility,"* sources agreed. Seat choices are varied, but *"with some restrictions"* – a corporate seat is required, as is a stint in finance (which can take the shape of a banking, structured finance or funds seat). Other options include property, IP, tax, employment and pensions, litigation and business finance/restructuring (BFR). Seat allocation *"isn't the clearest process,"* though *"it's fairly relaxed – you're assigned your first seat, and then at some point midway through your seat you have a conversation with HR about where you'd like to go next."* More than one source hinted that speaking directly with the relevant partners beforehand *"can increase the likelihood of getting your top choice – they like to see you take some initiative."*

Corporate cornerstones

Corporate work, as multiple trainees took care to point out, *"is what Weil's famous for."* As such, it's little surprise London's managing partner, Mike Francies, is one of the City's most prominent corporate forces. The *"main cornerstone"* of the practice is private equity work, though lawyers also handle private and public M&A, equity capital markets, joint ventures and corporate governance matters across a multitude of sectors, including healthcare, retail and energy. The final has proved particularly lucrative of late: 2012 saw the team lead on one of the year's biggest transactions – the $28bn sale of Access Industries' and Renova's stake in Russian TNK-BP to oil giant Rosneft, which is now the world's largest public

Chambers UK rankings

Banking & Finance	Investment Funds
Capital Markets	Private Equity
Corporate/M&A	Restructuring/Insolvency
Dispute Resolution	Tax

oil producer. Other recent roles of note include playing co-counsel to GDF SUEZ in its £6.84bn acquisition of a stake in International Power and advising General Motors on the company's famed $4.2bn buy-back of its finance and leasing operations.

According to our interviewees, *"big part of your job as a corporate trainee is admin stuff – keeping on top of completion agendas, chasing up documents, that sort of thing."* Still, *"you're not kept on the sidelines,"* they insisted, mentioning a host of drafting and research-based tasks. *"There isn't a ton of client contact, but the chance to produce a first draft of an ancillary document is exciting,"* one source recalled. *"I worked on a multi-jurisdictional deal that entailed liaising with lawyers in several different countries and co-ordinating the document flow,"* offered another. *"Attending the completion meeting was a real high."* All in all, trainees agreed a corporate stint is *"pretty engaging,"* not least because *"it allows you to see a primary department in action."* The downside? *"Very long hours! An early night for me was getting out of the office before ten."*

There's a regular secondment to New York, which is understandably popular. Luckily, the smallish intake means *"you've got a good chance of going if you're interested."* According to our sources, the Big Apple seat *"was traditionally just corporate-focused, but now people are starting to go for other practice areas."* Applicable language skills and a *"solid"* business case make a secondment to the firm's European offices *"a possibility."* In true Weil fashion, posts are *"not just handed out; you have to go speak to the relevant people and convince them you're suitable."* Client secondments are *"slightly more ad hoc"* and *"not really advertised: you have to raise the interest yourself."*

Refinanced tastes

What used to be a general finance seat has now been split into two separate ones: structured finance and banking finance. The former is *"a relatively small team"* with *"somewhat niche and more technical work"* than the latter. *"You have to get to grips with concepts like derivatives, which can be tricky."* Our interviewees reported a good deal of asset finance and securitisation work as well as *"lots of Lehman-related matters. Our peers on the other side are normally magic circle firms."* Trainees with a taste of banking reported an *"immensely varied workload"* accompanied by high levels of responsibility. *"I was running check-lists, drafting board minutes,*

analysing documents and interacting with clients regularly," one said. The *"lean structure"* of the team is such that *"trainees are often working opposite associates and sometimes even partners on the other side. You feel like you're contributing valuable work."* Banking clients can be found on both the lender and borrower side and include international finance superstars like Bain Capital, Morgan Stanley and Goldman Sachs.

If there's any con to a finance stint, it's the intense schedule required. *"Let's just say you'll quickly get to know and love the sleep pods!"* one source joked of the department's *"workaholic"* atmosphere. *"There are periods where people don't go home for a few days at a time."* Fortunately, sustained periods of 3am finishes are balanced out with a reasonable approach to face time – *"you don't have to stick around if there's nothing on."* What's more, our interviewees all accepted their crazy schedules as part and parcel of the Weil experience. In fact, their only complaint revolved around the quality of the firm's canteen grub. *"It would be nice if it was better, seeing as we eat dinner there rather frequently!"*

While trainees distinguished Weil from its peer firms by pointing out *"the broad practice beyond corporate,"* they urged applicants to bear in mind most of the firm's teams provide some kind of corporate support work and so are *"considered somewhat ancillary to corporate. If you're keen on pure IP work, for example, this might not be the best place."* To satisfy the SRA's contentious requirement, a seat in litigation, employment and pensions or BFR will do; alternatively, trainees can opt for a two-week litigation course, such is the focus on transactional work. We heard much praise for the litigation team, though, which trainees described as *"friendly and great fun."* Recent years have proven lucrative for the department, with Weil leading the way on several notable matters including Littlewoods' £1bn High Court case regarding interest repayments on overpaid tax. The range of work – which includes *"some advisory stuff for corporate clients"* as well as *"true"* contentious work – lends itself to *"tons of different tasks,"* sources reported, mentioning doc review, bundle prep, drafting and *"some black-letter law"* research. There's also a good chance of attending court. *"I got to go to a hearing for an arbitration one month in, and later went to the Royal Courts of Justice on multiple occasions."*

Looking for a challenge?

The workload may be *"rather demanding,"* as one trainee put it politely, but a training contract at Weil is not without its rewards. Our interviewees spoke of *"valuable"* learning experiences and top-notch supervision, much of which they chalked up to the firm's size. *"They let you run as far as you can with something because otherwise there might not be somebody else to do it,"* one testified. Said another: *"I applied because it was clear this is* the kind of place where you get high responsibilities and exposure to a challenging environment from the beginning. People come here ready to be pushed." Fortunately, there's a "huge" level of support to make sure nobody's in over their head. "We have personal mentors plus a 'responsible' partner, who acts as a resource for discussing career progression." What's more, "there's a real team environment which subverts the hierarchy a bit – people are constantly going in and out of each other's offices, and day to day you're working alongside partners, so the notion that trainees are lemmings doesn't really hold true here." While people are "generally good-natured," there's "an expectation you'll only come to them with questions if you truly can't work out the answer yourself. Being self-sufficient is valued highly, so you have to be circumspect when it comes to bothering someone who's busy."

There "aren't tons" of firm-sponsored social events, but our sources liked Weil's scene just fine. In addition to "standard" dos like welcome drinks and charity events, there's a Christmas party at Lincoln's Inn and a summer bash (complete with petting zoo) held at managing partner Mike Francies' house for lawyers and their families. The women's committee Women@Weil organises occasional outings such as bowling and ice skating, and trainees have a budget that allows for a couple of get-togethers each year. Much anticipated is the annual quiz, which includes a "hilarious" karaoke component. "Each team assigns itself a crazy name and dresses up according to the song they've bid on," a source explained. "Last year the trainee team ended up dressing in rags to perform a song from Oliver Twist!"

This year's intake is "pretty diverse," with a "decent mix" of universities, nationalities and men and women united in large part by a diligent work ethic – "everybody's a hard worker, and nobody minds that a job at the firm will be difficult in lots of ways." On a broader scale, "the key qualities they're looking for in trainees are confidence and a willingness to be seen," trainees thought. "This is one of the major differences between us and a firm with 100 trainees – you have to be proactive and comfortable stepping into the spotlight because there's nowhere to hide." Indeed, "timid people would not fare well," one interviewee suggested. "Self-promotion is an important part of your job here, which requires a certain level of determination. It's up to you to talk to the right people when you need something, and nobody's going to do that for you." Considering the firm's "love of self-starters," eagerness and a good attitude "get you quite far," as does "a genuine interest in corporate work – you've got to be serious about that as your career here will revolve around it."

Self-promotion aside, trainee dynamics remain "fairly relaxed and uncompetitive," particularly when it comes to qualification. In keeping with Weil's go-getter culture, it's an "unspoken rule" that trainees will take it upon themselves to seek out the relevant partners in their department of choice and speak with them off the record before formally announcing their preferences to HR. "That way, your interests are out in the open and you can find out whether you have a good chance of getting your top choice in advance," we were told. This year's class anticipated little competition for NQ spots "as we're smaller than the usual intake and have our interests staked across a range of departments." In fact, six out of eight trainees were kept on in 2013.

And finally...
Applicants should know *"a lot is expected of you in terms of work ethic,"* current trainees warned. That said, *"as long as you try your best and show yourself as willing to learn, it's a great place to be."*

White & Case LLP

The facts

Location: London

Number of UK partners/solicitors: 56/200 (+25 non-UK-qualified)

UK partners who trained at firm: 5%

Total number of trainees: 53

Seats: 4x6 months

Alternative seats: overseas seats

Extras: pro bono – A4ID, Innocence Network, Lawyers Volunteering for the Arts and others; language classes

On chambersstudent.co.uk...

How to get into White & Case

Overseas seats

A potted history of the firm

White & Case provides exposure to top-quality work and the opportunity to learn your trade abroad.

Fright & Case?

White & Case appears to have built up quite a fearsome reputation among the law school masses. The current crop of trainees certainly didn't sign up expecting a two-year stint of feet-on-desk, thumb-twiddling. *"If I'm honest, I was partially fearing coming here because at law school the reaction was always that I was going to be worked into the ground,"* commented one second-year. From another trainee: *"I had this idea it would be a cold, corporate environment. They say you won't see the light of day, but that's just scaremongering. When you say you work at a US firm people pull a face and say it must be terrible, but it's nowhere near as bad as people think."* With all these horror stories bandied about you may wonder how White & Case manages to attract so many applicants. Simple really: *"The international work, the focus on emerging markets and obviously the guaranteed overseas seat."*

White & Case was founded in New York back in 1901 but now has a global footprint comprising 40 offices across five continents. The international trailblazing started back in 1926 when it opened in Paris, while the London office has been in operation since 1971. The most recent addition came in March 2013 when the firm opened in Madrid – the first international firm launch in Spain for several years. *"The international offices aren't just outposts, and that's especially true of the London branch,"* one trainee explained. Having expanded very rapidly in the noughties, the London office has nearly as many lawyers as the New York one, and *"because it's so large it's almost like a stand-alone law firm in some respects. It's not like we bang the American drum or anything like that."* Having achieved

near-global coverage, the firm is now focused on filling in what gaps still remain. Until this year, Spain was one of those, and there are still some emerging markets that W&C has yet to tap. Likewise, the firm hasn't seen the right opportunity in Australia yet, but the situation is constantly being monitored. W&C is also keen to ensure a degree of uniformity across its offices rather than having them operate independently from one another (as is the case at some other global firms). This has been a stated aim for several years now, but talking to higher-ups at the firm, it's clear this is seen as vital to the firm's continued success.

While the firm is perhaps best known for its expertise in banking and finance, recent years have seen the energy and projects teams pick up more recognition, with both awarded top rankings by *Chambers UK* and *Chambers Global*. Advising on deals such as Saudi Aramco's $20bn Sadara Petrochemical Project joint venture with the Dow Chemical Company serves to illustrate the firm's capabilities in these areas. *Chambers UK* isn't shy in handing out rankings to a wealth of White & Case's practices, and everything from capital markets to construction gets a mention.

Brief Case

Trainees generally don't get the choice of their first seat; thereafter, they submit three preferences, and most are allocated their top choice. *"When we give our seat choices we often put down our preferred supervisor as well,"* a source revealed. *"The best way to decide is just to talk to previous trainees. If someone has sat with someone they've really liked, then it's probably a good sign."* At

Chambers UK rankings

Asset Finance

Banking & Finance

Banking Litigation

Capital Markets

Commodities

Construction

Corporate Crime
& Investigations

Corporate/M&A

Data Protection

Dispute Resolution

Employee Share Schemes
& Incentives

Energy & Natural
Resources

Financial Services

Information Technology

Private Equity

Projects

Restructuring/Insolvency

Transport

least one finance seat must be completed during the training contract, but *"there's so many to choose from."* Seats such as construction, employment or real estate accommodate far fewer trainees, but are also less in demand. *"If you want to go into corporate, finance, or banking then White & Case is great, but for the more niche departments – especially if you want to qualify there – it might not be the best place."*

The finance practice has three strands: banking; capital markets; and energy, infrastructure, project and asset finance (EIPAF). Within those, seats in project finance, asset finance, capital markets, bank finance and restructuring are available. These house the majority of trainees at any one time, while most of the rest will be in corporate or litigation/arbitration. Day-to-day work in EIPAF allows you to *"get a sense of White & Case as an international firm."* One source explained: *"I've worked on projects involving jurisdictions like Mozambique, Kazakhstan and Malawi – the work consistently has that global element."* White & Case advised Enerjisa in connection with the €1.1bn development, construction and financing of the 450 MW Tufanbeyli Thermal Power Plant in Turkey, as well as Qatar Petroleum and Exxon Mobil on the $10.3bn Barzan Gas Project in Qatar. *"On bigger deals the majority of work is creating tables and proof reading, but on smaller deals where there is one associate and a partner you get a bit more exposure."* In asset finance, *"deals come and close very quickly – they only have a lifespan of about three weeks."* One interviewee said: *"During my time there there were about 15 closings. By the end of the seat I had been given four cases to run by myself with partner and associate guidance. On the flip side, as there are only two trainees, and because deals close so quickly, you get a lot of post-closing work such as bibling."* Various trainees noted W&C employs relatively few legal support staff, so it does often fall to trainees to take on lower-level tasks. The firm told us it is aiming to recruit more paralegals in future.

On the Case

The deal flow in bank finance increased by roughly 50% this year, with both the size and number of high-end deals jumping sharply. For example, the team represented Deutsche Bank and HSBC Securities in connection with the $2.1bn senior secured credit facility provided to Colfax Corporation. *"I was on the team for a really complex deal, but I wasn't merely there assisting my supervisor. You are part of the team and expected to contribute. It's a bit daunting, but a very good learning experience."*

Sources agreed it's common for first seaters to be packed off to capital markets. *"Nine out of 16 people from my intake went there first,"* said one, *"probably because it has a reputation for slamming its trainees."* Is that fair? *"They work you hard but they are very nice and most supervisors go about it the right way."* The team recently represented the Republic of Zambia in its ten-year, US-denominated bond which raised $750m from a global investor base. A seat here involves *"a lot of transaction management mainly. I was keeping things in check, doing lots of bibles and proofreading.* However, despite the fair share of *"mundane"* tasks, there is also scope to expand your repertoire of skills. *"I got recognition for doing well, and then I was given some junior associate-type work, with a lot of client contact – maybe sometimes too much, but I prefer to be pushed and challenged,"* one source said. Another *"liaised with foreign counsel in 13 different jurisdictions, giving advice on key securities law memos. I actually had to call a founding partner at one of South America's leading law firms and tell him his memo was wrong."*

Time in the corporate department is a bit of a mixed bag. *"If you prove you're good then they're prepared to give you decent work, but there is a ceiling to what you can do as a trainee,"* a source commented. With the team largely handling *"very high-value cases with big corporations"* – such as representing Morgan Stanley as financial adviser to advertising agency Dentsu on its £3.2bn offer for Aegis Group – trainees are often clearly at the bottom rung of the ladder. *"There's a lot of doc pushing,"* an interviewee moaned. *"Honestly, I've been in very late just printing, scanning and stapling. It's very boring stuff but someone has to do it."* One source took a more positive stance on their time in the seat: *"We've got a very good position in M&A in emerging markets, and I don't think I've done a single UK-only deal. It's all under UK law, so I feel I get the English training I need, but then I also get the international elements and see a different way of approaching these matters."*

Outside of White & Case's most well-known practice areas, there's still good work to be found. The dispute resolution group picks up a top ranking from *Chambers Global* and is acting for Russian mobile telecoms provider Mobile TeleSystems in a dispute against various Turkmen State entities and the State of Turkmenistan in a case worth in excess of $900m. *"I've done a lot of interesting*

The True Picture

tasks like drafting a memo that formed a key component of our strategy," said one trainee. *"It's not all glamorous, though. One time I had to stay around till 2am putting folders together and checking that 114 documents for a structured finance transaction were all the same. People do depend on you though, and you get to see the exciting, funky stuff."* Even niche areas such as construction get involved in some incredibly meaty deals. The team is currently providing advice for The Qatar Integrated Railway Project, a $37bn infrastructure development for when the World Cup comes to Qatar in 2022.

The guaranteed overseas seat *"is a massive plus point about White & Case. It makes us stand out above other firms and really does appeal to people."* Trainees give their destination preferences a few months after starting, before venturing abroad – usually in their fourth seat – to places such as Paris, Hong Kong, Singapore, Abu Dhabi, New York, Moscow, Tokyo and Johannesburg. Singapore generally takes the most trainees while New York, the most popular choice, hosts just one and is often oversubscribed. *"Trainees receive a spreadsheet outlining everyone's preferences,"* a source explained. *"When there are clashes it's a case of drawing names out of a hat. Everyone realises that's the fairest method as noone has more validity than anyone else."* It almost goes without saying that trainees have a fantastic time once overseas. Read more on our website.

A Case of identity

There's no denying that White & Case is a demanding place. *"It's hard-working, and a lot is expected of you at any level,"* said one trainee of the firm's culture. With the partnership operating an 'eat-what-you-kill' remuneration system, some felt that a *"clear hierarchy"* and *"dog-eat-dog mentality"* is evident. *"Some partners would shoot themselves in the foot to complete a deal,"* commented a second-year. In all fairness, other sources spoke of *"no hierarchy"* and an *"incredibly friendly and down-to-earth"* atmosphere: we think those who pointed out that *"every department is like its own organisation"* probably hit the nail on the head. *"It's hard to generalise about the firm as every team has a very different vibe or way of working."*

Schedules can often be gruelling: *"In my first seat I was doing no less than a 60-hour week for four months,"* and *"in my last two months in asset finance it went crazy, and I was doing 16 or 17 hours days, every day,"* we heard. *"The nature of the work means you can go home at 8pm every day in some departments, but finishes generally range from*

6.30pm to very late at night. 8.30pm is about average," one source concluded. Trainees don't have a problem with working hard; however, they did flag up *"some work distribution issues."* One informed us: *"I feel that work just isn't allocated efficiently,"* while another cited *"big problems when I was drawn into a corporate deal. I was doing stupid hours quite regularly but nobody said I shouldn't be doing it. I wasn't even in that department and some other corporate trainees were leaving at 6pm!"* Other sources expressed similar concerns: *"There are people who take a two-hour lunch and leave at 6pm, and others who stay until midnight every night."* Frustration came from the perception that *"the departments make no attempt to make it fairer."* When we talked to partners Philip Stopford and Justin Benson about this, we found they were aware of this issue. They said that steps are already been taken to address trainees' concerns: efforts have been made to improve supervision, while Stopford and Benson are personally meeting with trainees more frequently. They also have detailed hours reports showing how hard people are working, so hopefully this is something that can be smoothed out.

Our considered conclusion is that this is a training contract of extremes. Hours, responsibility and departments can all vary wildly. *"You just have to take the rough with the smooth,"* advised sources, and trainees who can do so will reap rewards as they progress. One tangible reward we haven't mentioned is the salary. White & Case outpays the magic circle by some margin.

Open and shut Case

White & Case is pretty diverse, with *"a wide range of nationalities and cultural backgrounds"* represented. *"In my intake there are only two fully 'British' people,"* one source asserted (though many trainees from overseas studied in the UK). Many people here have the travel bug, and sources said that applicants should demonstrate an international outlook.

There is a chance for White & Case trainees to get away from their desks after hours. *"We work extremely hard all the time, but we have some absolutely cracking parties where we drink very large bottles of booze in big nightclubs. One partner went in and ordered all of one club's Sambuca – there weren't even that many of us."* All new starters head to Brussels for a three-day training programme, and every year a White & Case World Cup is held – 2013's was in Berlin – with lawyers from all corners of the firm's global network competing in events such as volleyball and football.

The True Picture

And finally...

The international nature of this firm is something that can't be understated. *"Another big selling point of White & Case is the high retention rate."* The firm kept on 23 of 28 qualifiers in 2013.

Wilsons

The facts

Location: Salisbury, London

Number of UK partners/solicitors: 33/36

Partners who trained at firm: 20%

Total number of trainees: 8

Seats: 4x6 months

Alternative seats: occasional secondments

On chambersstudent.co.uk...

How to get into Wilsons

Wilsons' commercial and eduction work

The London office

What's Salisbury like?

Salisbury's finest revs itself up in the wake of changes which will steer it in *"the direction of expansion."*

You win some, you lose some

Almost 300 years have moulded the Wilsons we know today, but it wasn't until the mid-1970s that the firm launched its private client business, the area – along with charities work – with which Wilsons has become most synonymous. *Chambers UK* top-ranks the firm regionally for these practices, along with its expertise in agriculture and rural affairs. Other practices not to be sidelined include commercial, property and litigation.

2012 was in many ways a good year for Wilsons. Turnover rose to £13.3m, returning it almost to pre-recession levels; a new managing partner, Andrew Roberts was appointed; the firm moved into Alexandra House (formerly home to the Courts of Justice) near the cathedral; and a rebrand saw Wilsons adopt green and black as corporate colours. A sour point arrived when Wilsons decided to offload its Bristol office – which was only acquired in 2011 – to Michelmores following a dispute with two partners.

This is a firm that intends to grow nonetheless, and 2013 has seen lateral hires bolstering Wilsons' expertise in commercial litigation and education. The move to Alexandra House has given Wilsons 31,000 sqft to play around with, and trainees said that *"this office has been designed for more people – we still have empty desks."* A London office was opened in 2009, and is set to be an increasing point of focus in years to come. *"If all goes to plan we will expand in London and develop our client base there, but we will have to do so in a manner that suits the current financial climate."* The emphasis will remain on the key strengths of private client, charities and agricultural work, but will also encompass growth of the commercial practices.

Get a handle on it

Trainees have to complete a property seat, either in the residential, commercial or farms/estates teams. Other seat options include private client, contentious trusts/probate (charities), non-contentious trusts/probate, family, employment, company/commercial and litigation.

Private client is divided into two teams: offshore/new wealth and landed estates/old money. The department deals exclusively with super-wealthy 'top-drawer' clients, with estates that in some cases exceed £100m, offering advice which caters to the complex tax, trusts and probate needs of clients in this income bracket. Many are owners of farms and estates, and due to Wilsons' move into the Big Smoke, the firm has seen an increase in the number of clients with US-related issues, meaning that lawyers have been working alongside US tax consultants. A seat here is *"heavily drafting-based,"* and trainees had been able to cut their teeth on a range of wills, codicils, deeds of appointment, oaths for executors and inheritance tax forms. Advice on corporate structuring may be thrown into the mix depending on the client in question, and sources said that they were *"expected to consider the commercial implications when drafting documents."* There's *"not so much client contact"* because wealthy clients prefer to deal with partners or other senior lawyers. And when it comes to issues like complex tax advice, *"trainees may be less involved, but colleagues are always keen to give us bits of research to do to, and to prompt us to think about the types of questions clients may ask."*

The non-contentious probate/trusts team deals with private clients who are more humble financially, and there's more client contact here. Trainees are kept busy research

Chambers UK rankings

Agriculture & Rural Affairs	Private Client
Charities	Real Estate
Employment	

ing inheritance tax issues and embarking on *"fact-finding missions"* when someone dies without a will. There's also mental capacity work with elderly clients and, of course, *"lot of will drafting."* Dealing with clients is a *"hand-holding process – you have to be able to deal with people crying."* Contentious trusts/probate, on the other hand, shows trainees *"what happens when it all goes wrong."* It's *"complex work, and there are a lot of grey areas and situations where there may not be a clear right or wrong."* A lot of the work revolves around representing charities in legacy disputes, when claimants contest the amount of money left by the deceased to a certain organisation. Lawyers successfully represented Cancer Research UK and Arthritis UK during a claim for rectification of someone's will, which the court denied. Other charities represented include Oxfam, Macmillan Cancer Support and the British Heart Foundation.

Wilson's real estate department acts for some of the oldest landed estates in the country, as well as for charities and specialist companies. Wilsons represented RSM Tenon – one of the largest accountancy firms in the UK – on the £3.5m reorganisation of its Reading operations so as to bring everyone under one roof. In residential property, trainees draft transfer deeds, licences for alterations and final reports to clients. *"The phone is ringing all day, and the client contact is brilliant. It's not just about the churning out of forms and procedures; people get really stressed out when they move – I once had a client phone me up to ask if it was okay that they had removed all the handles from the doors in their old house."* Those in farms/estates had *"assisted fee earners on the sale and purchases of agricultural land,"* and came away from the seat *"understanding the rules and restrictions which affect such land, including registration rules."*

Cosy hub

Sources praised the firm for its efforts to move into and renovate Alexandra House: *"It's good that they were able to find somewhere in the centre of Salisbury – we haven't had to move into a business park like other firms."* The move has *"improved the relationships between the different departments* [which used to be housed in separate buildings] *– they had to a certain extent formed cliques, but being in one office has forced them out of it."* Some

suggested that each department had nonetheless retained elements of its distinct character or personality. Wilson's website proudly flags up the firm's traditional values as well as a Darwinian knack for adaptation. Interviewees said they *"wouldn't exactly describe the firm as informal"* and instead classified it as a *"smart place"* that had been given a boost of slickness by the recent move and rebrand. There's a sense of rootedness too, with a loyalty not only to the cathedral city but also to the firm: *"a lot of the people have been here for a long time, and they command respect – they are very proud of the firm, which in turn makes everyone proud."*

Don't go making assumptions about the Salisbury social scene: *"It's actually very vibrant and good fun – there's no shortage of places to go."* The trainees *"are very sociable, and will go out for drinks after work – we're in the centre of Salisbury, so you have to walk past at least five pubs before you make it home."* One favourite is The Cosy Club, which has *"hunting motifs all over the wall – it's very Salisbury."* A Christmas party came complete with *"a choir singing carols and mulled wine in the reception area,"* while themed summer parties are also a staple. *"The new senior partner invited the entire firm to his house for one summer party,"* said one trainee. *"The weather was amazing and you could feel the 'cliquey department' thing evaporate away."*

"The expectation is not that you have to work really late," and the official working hours are nine-to-five. One trainee, who decided to stay a bit later during a busy couple of weeks, said that *"the partners were telling me that I shouldn't still be here; they were keen for me to hurry off!"* As in previous years, interviewees believed that communication is still something that *"the firm could improve on, and not just in relation to trainees, but in the firm generally – there have been a couple of things which we've heard on the grapevine, when they should have come from the top."* Others felt that *"it's important that trainees make sure that they take responsibility for their own interests – I've always been able to speak to a supervisor or head of a department."*

"The chances of getting a job on qualification aren't as high as we would like them to be," trainees admitted, and all sources were realistic about their options, given what they saw as Wilson's recent not-so-strong retention record. In 2013, two out of four qualifiers were kept on, but we heard that the firm is good at letting trainees know about retention on time. *"The fact that there was disappointment shows how much people wanted to stay."*

And finally...

Come to Wilsons for *"high-quality work, a healthy work/life balance and a range of practice areas."*

The True Picture

Winckworth Sherwood

The facts

Location: London, Oxford, Manchester
Number of UK partners/solicitors: 43/79
Total number of trainees: 11
Seats: 4x6 months
Alternative seats: none
Extras: pro bono – CAB

On chambersstudent.co.uk...

How to get into Winckworth Sherwood
The firm's history

If you're looking to avoid the corporate chaos but still fancy a taste of life in the City, Winckworth Sherwood offers *"a range of different and interesting practice areas."*

Saints and sinners

"Don't look at the niche areas and think that's what Winckworth is primarily about," one trainee succinctly advised. *"We do have niche specialisms, which are great and provide interesting work, but we're also grounded in solid practice areas such as commercial, property and private client."* So this is a full-service firm – Winckworth's website lists 15 core areas – but there's no denying that it's the quirky range of not-oft-seen, do-they-really-exist practices that make the firm stand out. Never has the word *"niche"* cropped up in our interviews with such painstaking regularity. Among others, Winckworth Sherwood delves into the esoteric areas of ecclesiastical and parliamentary agency law. Other *Chambers UK*-ranked teams include charity, social housing and planning.

Among the firm's *"eclectic"* client base you'll find the Department for Transport, St Paul's Cathedral, Sainsbury's and The London Diocesan Fund. As one source chuckled: *"We have clients ranging from the Church of England all the way down to night clubs."* In fact, new senior partner John Rees serves as provincial registrar to the Archbishop of Canterbury and is legal adviser to the Anglican Consultative Council.

Winckworth runs small operations in Oxford and Manchester, but its heart is the London office – located just a stone's throw from London Bridge on the South Bank since moving from Westminster in 2009. It was around this time that the firm pursued cautious growth and new practice areas began to take on greater significance. As one trainee explained, *"we have a very up-and-coming employment department, and the same can be said for*

corporate/commercial. It used to just be known as commercial, so it seems like they've been expanding." One source said of these changes: *"This firm, like any other in the City, is about making money after all."*

Niche and easy?

Trainees have a wealth of seats to choose from. Options include: parliamentary agency; planning; housing and regeneration; private client; ecclesiastical; education; employment; corporate/commercial; property and licensing; institutional property; construction; and dispute resolution. For the first seat *"you're basically stuck where they put you,"* but for the remainder *"you say where you'd like to go and the firm makes every effort to accommodate those wishes."* One source concluded: *"It's rare a trainee would go through the contract and not experience their first-choice seat."*

"Even though we have a lot of niche (there's that word again) *work and departments, the golden thread is that they're all property-based,"* one source informed us. *"This firm would be a dream for someone who wants to be a property lawyer. You can do ecclesiastical, institutional – there's literally all sorts in the realm of property."* As such, sources agreed it's *"incredibly unlikely you won't do something in property. As the firm does so much work in that area it prefers us to have that experience."* In a similar vein, *"most trainees do the housing seat as it's the firm's largest department."*

The social housing team works for 12 of the 15 largest housing associations in London and the South East,

Chambers UK rankings

Charities	Planning
Education	Real Estate Litigation
Local Government	Social Housing
Parliamentary & Public Affairs	Transport

including Catalyst Housing, A2Dominion and Genesis. It recently advised Grahame Park and Network Housing on their separate negotiations with the Homes and Communities Agency for Get Britain Building funding, a £400m+ deal intended to kick-start stalled residential developments. Time here can include *"a lot of stamp duty. There are plenty of tax returns and property registrations, and you'll spend a lot of time on the phone to the Land Registry Office."* However, *"towards the end of your seat they lengthen your leash a lot and you get your own files to deal with. It's one of those places where you can get loads of responsibilities once you get to grips with the nuts and bolts. You get tasked with a lot of low-level senior work where you have full control, with supervision."*

Since the Academies Act was introduced in 2010 Winckworth's education team has led 248 schools (as of April 2013) through the Academy conversion process – that's roughly 10% of all schools that have reorganised. Therefore, we weren't hugely stunned when a trainee told us: *"I was primarily dealing with the Academy conversions of schools."* However, individual workloads offer great variety. *"I did a mix of work,"* recalled an interviewee. *"The team delves into many matters that all fall under the umbrella of education, and I was helping with land transactions and negotiating agreements. There was a huge range of diverse research tasks."*

The parliamentary department's principal work is in drafting and promoting legislation of all kinds, including Acts of Parliament. For example, it worked alongside Eversheds to advise the Department for Transport and HS2 on the Bill to construct and operate the proposed high-speed railway between London and Birmingham. Law firm Shepherd & Wedderburn also sought Winckworth's assistance when it needed a Development Consent Order drafted for a wind farm off the Yorkshire coast. *"We mainly handle big infrastructure projects,"* one source said of parliamentary agency. *"Unfortunately, that affords less responsibility as the work is much more intellectual. I was properly getting into the nitty-gritty of law and Acts of Parliament. It's a very academic seat, but you do get small matters that you can manage yourself."*

Sex and the City

"Employment is a relatively new department, but it's already proven very popular with trainees," a second-year informed us. Why's that? *"The head of department is enormously respected, the quality of training is excellent, and if you love insider stories and lascivious goings on in the City then it's a great way to go. We're dealing with libel and dodgy sex scandals resulting in people getting fired."* Another source concurred: *"I think it is probably one of the best-managed teams in the firm, and the department functions as a coherent whole. My supervisor is very good at giving me stuff to do but also making sure I don't cock it up."* The 2012/13 financial year is expected to be another record breaker for the team, following on from an 8% rise in income in 2011/12.

The corporate/commercial team is another of the firm's rising stars. It's currently *"not one of the biggest departments"* but *"it is a brilliant seat that offers the right amount of supervision and the right amount of responsibility."* One source elaborated: *"When you're confident they let you have a bit of free rein. It's a very trusting department. I was talking to clients directly and drafting documents and negotiations for big, high-value transactions. The other lawyers were very interested in getting me to do substantive work. I felt like a useful team component."*

Laborem habemus!

With roughly 120 lawyers, Winckworth Sherwood is far from the biggest law firm in the capital. However, the smaller headcount is a primary reason we heard the standard quotes about the firm having a *"friendly,"* *"collegiate"* and *"collaborative"* culture. Delving deeper, what really makes Winckworth stand out? *"We're a very diverse firm,"* offered a trainee. *"The partnership is half women and half men. There are older partners, younger partners, gay and straight partners."* One source elaborated: *"That means each seat and department is quite different. There's obviously an overriding sense of professionalism, but I feel I can talk to partners easily. You have a lot of access to them and they take an interest in you. It's generally pretty relaxed – you don't feel like you're walking on eggshells."*

An important facet of the *"inclusive team culture"* is that *"people stay here a long time,"* sources agreed. *"We constantly get updates on the intranet congratulating people for being here for ten, 20 or 30 years,"* one said. *"The firm likes people to progress from within rather than hiring from outside. We also see lots of people leave and then return. A combination of the work and the culture lures them back."* Thus, retention rates are usually pretty healthy and in 2013 five of six qualifiers were kept on. There was a bit of a moan over the *"lack of transparency"* in qualification decisions, although sources did say the firm *"does its best to keep people on, even if it's in places they didn't want to go."* One interviewee provided this analogy: *"It's sort of like how they select the Pope. No one really knows how it's done, but white smoke will soon start billowing from the training partner's office."*

Interviewees said the firm isn't for those *"just looking to get rich"* but is perfect if you want *"a job you can enjoy, where you can leave at a decent time"* – sources

said 9.30am to 6 or 7pm is about standard – *"and have a family."* Sources were keen to stress that the firm employs *"no criteria checklist"* when it comes to recruiting. This is exemplified by a large portion of the current intake *"not doing law at university"* and by Winckworth *"frequently offering its paralegals training contracts as well. That's nice to know if you haven't done that well at uni."*

And finally...
"Quite honestly I felt that a number of other firms blended into one," said a source of their search for a training contract. *"They all did the same work, in the same areas. Winckworth has something a bit different about it."*

Withers LLP

The facts

Location: London

Number of UK partners/solicitors: 59/97

Partners who trained at firm: c.33%

Total number of trainees: 13

Seats: 4x6 months

Alternative seats: overseas seats

Extras: language classes

On chambersstudent.co.uk...

How to get into Withers

Landmark divorce cases

Unconventional literary heroines

Withers continues to attract the richest of the rich with its top-quality private client service.

Something old, something new

One of London's older firms, Withers set up shop back in 1896 and today promotes itself as *"the first international firm dedicated to serving successful individuals, families, and their personal, business and philanthropic interests."* Well, Withers certainly does that, and has represented over a third of the *Sunday Times* Rich List and for 20% of the top 100 in the Forbes Rich List to boot. A 2002 merger with American outfit Bergman Horowitz & Reynolds instigated a decade of steady international expansion, and WithersWorldwide (as it's now referred to) has nine overseas offices in some of the key financial hotspots dotted around the globe. Most recently, Withers opened in Zürich (this was 2011, adding a second base in a country which contains a third of the world's privately-held wealth) and then Singapore, following a trend which has seen a flurry of firms scramble to establish a base after the city-state relaxed its rules to allow international firms in.

Withers' most recent figures show a global revenue of £113m in 2011/12, and just over half of that amount is derived from the international offices. The family and private client groups (both top-ranked in London by *Chambers UK*) together continue to be the most profitable areas for the firm, but the contentious practice in London is performing particularly well of late (drawing in almost half of the revenue generated in that office), and Withers' other expertise shouldn't be sidelined either: on the corporate side, the firm acts for listed and private companies and is popular with fashion and luxury brands, whereas its property know-how covers commercial, residential and agricultural interests.

At the time of our research in May 2013, Withers had set up a pan-European funds practice after hiring a partner from offshore firm Appleby (in anticipation of the EU's alternative investment fund managers directive, which was implemented later in 2013) and had also launched an international family consultancy group. That's not it though. Merger talks between Withers and Speechly Bircham were being conducted: a tie-up would have created one of the world's largest private client firms. Nothing came of these talks in the end, but they do give a clue as to how Withers sees itself developing in the future.

Quite apart from merger considerations, *"Withers has strong ideas that it wants to implement. It did well to get ahead of other private client firms by going international some years ago. We're chasing the new money, the new international entrepreneurs. We're not sitting about in men's clubs drinking port – no one's in the Garrick Club!"* Sources suggested that the firm would be developing a *"stronger focus"* on the *"luxury brand front,"* while at the same time *"looking for new markets and jurisdictions in which our expertise would be needed – we're a very forward-looking firm."*

Public apologies and high-class teas

The family team at Withers is the largest in London, and most of its clients are City professionals. Matters could involve negotiating hefty nuptial agreements, appealing a children order with tricky international dimensions or advising billionaires on divorces which involve corporate structures in multiple jurisdictions. The department is a *"slick, professional operation – it's very precise and ordered, and by the time you finish the seat you have that diligence and awareness of detail honed into you."* The

Chambers UK rankings

Administrative & Public Law	Employment
Agriculture & Rural Affairs	Family/Matrimonial
Charities	Private Client
Defamation/Reputation Management	Professional Negligence
	Tax

"human" element of cases makes them *"easy to understand or relate to, even if there are complex financial matters"* to contend with. The seat does come with an *"inevitable"* amount of *"court work and doc management,"* and sources found that they didn't have as much responsibility here as elsewhere. Most found that they were able to draft the more *"complex documents only toward the end of the seat,"* but did nonetheless enjoy *"lots of client contact."*

The reputation management team regularly acts on high-profile matters, including cases relating to the phone-hacking scandal and subsequent litigation against News International. Lawyers here recently acted for Baroness Shriti Vadera, securing apologies from the *Financial Times*, the *Daily Mail* and BBC *Question Time* (among others) after allegations were made against the Baroness, citing her involvement in the fixing of LIBOR rates. Trainees here said that it's *"quite a small team. You get to write opinion pieces and there's lots of networking events to attend."*

Most trainees end up completing a stint in the large wealth planning department, which is divided into three potential seats: the family and business planning team (FAB); the international team (INT); and the funds, investment, trusts and tax team (FITTs). FITTs lawyers recently advised the management of Premium Credit – a UK financing company – on its private equity-backed buyout, which involved constructing management incentive plans and remuneration structures. FITTs trainees said it feels like *"a hybrid seat of wealth planning and corporate work,"* and is potentially the most complex seat at Withers. FAB has a reputation for being a *"sleepier"* team, but trainees found it just as challenging and said that they were *"treated as an associate."* Some had worked on the *"tax structuring of a property development deal,"* and were *"in touch with the client directly. There's always a wealthy individual behind these things, and I've been out to see a landed estate client on my own – having tea with them can be very interesting...."* The INT team works on *"lots of trust structures with an international element,"* and there's the possibility of getting involved in the US tax team as well. Sources said that *"responsibility was quite high,"* and they were able to have a crack at first drafts of wills and trusts, balancing out the seat with some *"technical research"* as well.

The contentious trusts on successions group (CTSG) is a popular destination, with one enthusiastic source going as far to say that it's *"easily the world's best department."* Interviewees mentioned that *"trusts is different to probate: trusts is like corporate law, and you deal with these enormous structures which are complicated and technical and interesting, in comparison to probate cases, which are smaller and easier to get a handle on."* Trainees had been involved in cases that went all the way to the Supreme Court and said that *"large disputes can be worth $100m."* There's also a charities team – *"we act for charities when someone has left lots to them in their will, and subsequently a disgruntled relative gets involved and disputes it"* – and a growing Court of Protection practice.

Full-blown leases and hedgerow diseases

A seat in commercial litigation is another popular option for trainees, and the department has built up a reputation for financial services disputes, fraud and professional negligence cases, and arbitration expertise. Trainees remain generalists throughout the seat and take on work from the various sub-groups. *"It's exciting stuff,"* and some sources had encountered a case where *"we had to get an interim prohibiting injunction because protesters had infiltrated a GM crop farm – we had just two or three days to turn it around and deliver it to the High Court."* The trainee role *"is essential,"* and sources had drafted witness statements, application notices and *"lots of covering letters."*

Corporate at Withers *"covers a bit of everything – we've got some corporate, some commercial and some banking as well."* A trainee documented some *"high-adrenaline, high-octane days"* where *"I got a call late on a Thursday, and the client wanted an answer as to whether they should pay out 'X' amount of millions based on a certain guarantee – the team let me do the legwork, and it was seriously good fun."* Others said that the nice thing about the deals in corporate is that *"they're not always so massive, so you haven't got a three-month due diligence process, meaning you can see the whole thing from start to finish."* The department has a sector-focused approach, and is popular with fashion and sports clients: recent deals include the sale of Nottingham Forest FC to the Al-Hasawi family and advising British designer Christopher Kane on securing investment from PPR.

The employment team's work on behalf of senior executives is top-ranked in London by *Chambers UK*, and the group recently advised Andrew Moss, the CEO of Aviva, on his resignation from the company, in light of the 'Shareholder Spring'. Sources here said: *"You feel like you're doing the real job – I got to negotiate a whole deal on my own and had lots of client contact."* Those in real estate, meanwhile, come across quite a *"mixed batch"* of work including residential and agricultural/rural matters. The latter can involve some *"bizarre pieces of research on hedgerow diseases, which is always handy knowledge to keep at the back of your mind...."* Commercial property work is *"good fun"* and can involve working on *"under-lettings of real estate in Central London – I had eight full-blown leases and licences to assign."* Other seats on offer include charities, intellectual property and property litigation.

Wandering around with no shoes on

"I suppose the outside view of us is that we are a traditional firm," ruminated one source, adding: *"That view of us is true in some ways, but in positive ways. They like a bit of personality and eccentricity here; they appreciate people who are a breath of fresh air."* The wealth-planning lawyers, for example, are *"old-school in some respects but are also relaxed and wander around with no shoes on,"* while in CTSG *"there are some people who could've had a career in stand-up comedy – it's true that there are a lot of characters."*

Characters there may be, but sources claimed that *"we're over-represented by Oxbridge"* and that there *"are a lot of public school types knocking around."* We can't speak for school backgrounds, and we didn't examine the details of Withers' qualified solicitors, but in the interests of accuracy we should say that the firm publishes details of where its trainees went to uni on its website and as of May 2013, we counted that while 12 of the 26 trainees in London did attend Oxbridge, though 11 other universities were also represented.

Sources insisted that Withers *"doesn't feel stuffy – the firm has an idea of how it is viewed and has a wry sense of humour about it."* Others felt that *"the firm doesn't have an openly 'City' culture, but I guess in some ways it has sneaked in, without us realising it."* Although the hours are by no means terrible, with trainees describing an average working day as lasting between 9am and 7pm, it was made clear that *"Withers does not want to be seen as a lifestyle firm,"* and there are periods when trainees work later into the night.

Parlez-vous Withers?

Another thing it was hard to miss when we were examining Withers trainees' web-bios was the number of foreign languages they speak. We've said for many years that the firm likes to recruit a couple of Italian speakers in each intake, and there are indeed three Italian-educated trainees out in the Milan office. But there are plenty of Spanish and French speakers too. Linguists take note.

Socially, there is *"enough"* going on, with firm-wide quarterly drinks and Christmas parties (2012's was held at the Gherkin), departmental drinks and away days (*"wealth planning have an annual ski trip which they invite all the trainees to, even though you're not a permanent fixture of the department"*) and a trainee budget which allows the intake to go out for a curry on Brick Lane every now again. The trainees are close and regularly go for drinks in Jamies Wine Bar and Corney & Barrow. They've also recently set up a new trainee networking event, which involves *"inviting two or three of your City contacts to the firm for cocktails – it has been successful and the firm is supportive of that kind of thing."* The more athletically inclined can join the cricket, softball and hockey teams, while those of a more delicate disposition can find fulfilment in the *"special workshops"* that the firm puts on, during which some trainees fondly remember flower arranging.

Withers was described as a *"female friendly"* firm, with *"lots of women in positions of power"* (Margaret Robertson is managing director, and 40% of the firm's global offices are headed by females) and an active women's group – one source quipped that *"soon we'll need a men's group!"* Generally, trainees felt that they were looked after well, with a trainee buddy to *"really help you settle in"* and a mentor who *"will make sure that your preferences are known"* at each seat rotation. Training sessions were also praised, with sources stating that *"if you're in a tier-one-ranked department like family or wealth planning, then you're going to get two hours training a day at the beginning of the seat, and you'll be taught by partners, some of whom are editors of practitioner texts."*

Since *"our financial year ends in July"* – later than other firms – departments *"don't have the figures"* to know if they have capacity for NQ jobs until quite late in the day. This, and the fact that there's no official jobs list circulated, provoked a few grumbles. Still, sources said that *"there's no sense of panic among the trainees, and when you look at the figures the business is doing pretty well."* In 2013, ten out of 15 second-years stayed with the firm upon qualification and qualified into all departments.

And finally...
The typical Withers applicant *"isn't straight out of uni – it's not unusual to have trainees in their forties."*

483

Wragge & Co LLP

The facts

Location: Birmingham, London
Number of UK partners/solicitors: 121/288
Partners who trained at firm: 29%
Total number of trainees: 51
Seats: 4x6 months
Alternative seats: secondments; China
Extras: pro bono – Birmingham Legal Advice Centre, charities, Account3 Community Business Law Clinic

On chambersstudent.co.uk...

How to get into Wragge...
Interview with Baljit Chohan

Top Birmingham firm Wragge & Co is becoming an established national player.

Movement forward

"The true highlight of this year is the consolidation of our international presence," training principal Baljit Chohan tells us. *"We've expanded in Germany, and our China office is now an established fixture."*

However, around 75% of Wragges' 500-plus lawyers are still based in its Midlands HQ. *"The Birmingham office is embedded in the scenery here,"* trainees remarked. *"We're very well established in the Midlands and have reached a good size."* Chambers UK gives the firm top rankings in Birmingham for several of its teams, including real estate, tax, employment, environment, IP, IT and corporate, while it also has a number of national rankings – notably for construction, healthcare and life sciences.

All agreed: *"Any [UK] growth is probably centred in the London office, although we are moving premises in Birmingham in 2014."* One said: *"It's kind of sad as we're leaving this beautiful Victorian building, but heading to Two Snowhill is the right move."* Wragges will occupy the top eight floors of this new building, which has been slowly going up in the city centre.

The London office *"has been growing quite steadily for several years,"* and hires its own intake of trainees. *"We feel comparable to other City firms, and the office here isn't just an outpost,"* they said. This is no idle boast: the London office scores a number of *Chambers* rankings in its own right – not necessarily at the top of the market, but certainly enough to show that Wragges is about more than just Birmingham.

Brum and the Big Smoke

In Birmingham trainees must undertake one contentious and one real estate seat: *"There's really no wiggle room there."* The practices themselves are divided into four large groups. First, there's REG – the real estate group, which includes: residential development; commercial development and investment (CDI); property litigation; planning; retail/energy/leisure/management; and a specialist sector property team. Then there's HRG (human resources group), which includes employment and pensions. CCFP (corporate/commercial/finance/projects) covers corporate, commercial, IT, outsourcing, banking/finance, energy/projects and insolvency. Finally, the dispute resolution group (DRG) handles commercial litigation, contentious IP, antitrust, construction and finance litigation. London seats *"are quite similar to those in Birmingham; there are just fewer of them,"* trainees said. We won't go into details of the various acronyms that London departments are known by because it just gets confusing, but simply put, options include IP; employment; corporate/banking; project finance; *"a large and well-established pensions group;"* a *"small"* commercial litigation team; commercial, IT and outsourcing; commercial development and investment; and property litigation.

Getting a particular seat is *"luck of the draw really,"* trainees admitted. *"The HR team does try, but there are a lot of people to satisfy. If you really push for a certain department from the very beginning you'll probably sit there eventually."* Pleasingly, *"all departments are open for NQ applications, even those you haven't sat in."*

Chambers UK rankings

Banking & Finance	Local Government
Banking Litigation	Outsourcing
Competition/European Law	Pensions
Construction	Pensions Litigation
Corporate/M&A	Planning
Dispute Resolution	Projects
Employment	Public Procurement
Energy & Natural Resources	Real Estate
Environment	Real Estate Litigation
Health & Safety	Restructuring/Insolvency
Healthcare	Retail
Information Technology	Social Housing
Intellectual Property	Tax
Life Sciences	

Property storeys

Real estate has long been a core area for the firm, and there are several prominent property teams. Contrary to what you'd expect in this difficult economy, all are performing well. Among the local projects the firm is working on are the redevelopment of Paradise Circus site, the £30m redevelopment of Warwickshire County Cricket Ground, the development of a new engine plant at Jaguar Land Rover and the development of Birmingham City University's Eastside City centre campus. We mustn't forget the London team, which recently took on a quirky little instruction: advising the NSPCC on its ArtBox project – a public art exhibition where leading artists and designers re-styled the classic red telephone box. You might not immediately imagine that a project like that would have property aspects to it, but the boxes were displayed out on the streets, so of course it did, and Wragges was on hand to help. A more conventional matter was the £204.5m acquisition of 19 industrial estates by a US private equity house.

Trainees join one team within real estate, but *"the real estate group as a whole is quite close, so while you're in, say, residential development, you might work in conjunction with the planning team or seek advice from property litigation."* Residential development itself is one of *"the busiest teams at Wragge,"* one source averred. *"It acts for the UK's top ten house builders and essentially acquires plots of land – often fields from farms – that the developer then uses."* On some of the smaller deals trainees run their own files: *"It's like running a small corporate deal, and as such it's a good base for your learning. I was the primary contact with the client and did pretty much all the contract drafting myself."*

CDI is *"basically the general transactional and commercial part of our real estate practice, with a bias towards development work."* As one of the larger property teams, across both offices, it boasts large clients, including

Marks & Spencer and The Olympic Park Legacy Company. *"The projects you work for are exciting and often have a lot of history behind them,"* one trainee said. Take, for instance, Derbyshire County Council and High Peak Borough Council's £35m development of Britain's first new spa hotel in 100 years.

Although *"the hours are actually relatively difficult, because of how busy the team is,"* trainees loved the department. *"There are very late nights and constant calls and e-mails, but you learn so much,"* one said. Closely related to property, construction is *"very strong focus at Wragges and an area the firm is developing."* Clients are all big guns, including Amec Group, E.ON and the Royal London Mutual Insurance Society. Interviewees agreed: *"There is more responsibility in the non-contentious work,"* but in both, trainees are given *"great access to clients and real learning experience."*

"Litigation has some really great cases coming in across the board, with some very interesting clients," trainees said. These include the Department of Business, Innovation and Skills; Philips; Vodafone; and Dyson. *"Commercial litigation is important to the firm and takes the most trainees of any seat in Birmingham."* Trainees get involved with work across the board and reported a great amount of responsibility for a contentious seat. *"I reviewed documents, yes, but also briefed the team, liaised with the other side and drafted witness statements,"* one said. Another added: *"I took telephone hearings and got to dabble in advocacy."*

From Germany to Guangzhou

"Although it's essentially focused on mid-market M&A," the corporate team covers just about everything, from public companies work and restructuring to private equity. Clients include Mercedes-Benz and GlaxoSmithKline, *"and we undertake their mid-market work,"* trainees explained. Wragges advised Lloyds TSB Development Capital on the £56.4m management buyout of Forest Holidays, for example. *"Because the teams are still relatively small, there's actually a good amount of responsibility,"* interviewees agreed. *"You're much more active in the deal."*

The pensions and employment teams are *"always popular seats."* In Birmingham, trainees swap between departments at the three-month mark. The employment team does *"mixture of contentious tribunal work and corporate support, so there's a lot of interaction with the corporate team."* Clients are *"from all over the country, although we tend to work for large employers and pension funds,"* trainees said. *"The pensions partners are very distinguished in their fields, but the work is quite complex. That means you're not going to be doing the best work, but the team involves you as much as they can."* The employment team, on the other hand, has several smaller files

Applications and Selection

Firm Name	Degree Class	Number of Contracts	Number of Applications
Addleshaw Goddard	2:1	30	2,000
Allen & Overy	2:1	90	2,500
Ashfords	2:1	10	400
Ashurst	2:1	40	2,500
Baker & McKenzie	2:1	34	Not known
Bates Wells Braithwaite	2:1	4	750+
Berwin Leighton Paisner	2:1	40-45	Not known
Bingham McCutchen	High 2:1	Up to 4	Not known
Bircham Dyson Bell	2:1 preferred	5	700
Bird & Bird	2:1	16-18	2,000
Bond Dickinson	Not known	Not known	Not known
Boodle Hatfield	2:1	5	Not known
B P Collins	2:1	Not known	Not known
BPE Solicitors	2:1	4	100
Brabners	2:1 or postgraduate degree	7	Not known
Bristows	2:1 preferred	Up to 10	2,000
Browne Jacobson	Not known	8	800
Burges Salmon	2:1	25	1,700
Capsticks	2:1	8	300
Charles Russell	2:1 preferred	18	1,500
Cleary Gottlieb Steen & Hamilton	High 2:1	13-15	Not known
Clifford Chance	2:1	100	Not known
Clyde & Co	2:1	35-40	1,500
CMS	2:1	60	1,000
Collyer Bristow	2:1	Not known	Not known
Covington & Burling	2:1	6	Not known
Cripps Harries Hall	2:1	8	200
Curtis Mallet Prevost	2:1	2	300
Davenport Lyons	2:1	8	400
Davis Polk & Wardell	2:1	4-6	Not known
Dechert	2:1	10-12	1,000+
Dentons	2:1	15	1,500
DLA Piper	2:1	90	3,800
Dundas & Wilson	2:1 preferred	12 (London)	600
DWF	2:1	48	3,000
Edwards Wildman Palmer	2:1	Up to 8	c. 700
Eversheds	2:1	50-60	4,500
Farrer & Co	2:1	10	1,000
Fladgate	2:1	4	Not known
Foot Anstey	2:1	4-6	300
Forbes	2:1	4	350+
Freeth Cartwright	2:1	10	750
Freshfields Bruckhaus Deringer	Not known	90	2,000

Applications and Selection

Firm Na me	Degree Class	Number of Contracts	Number of Applications
Gateley	2:1	11	Not known
Gordons	2:1	4	400
Government Legal Service	2:1	20-25	2,000+
Harbottle & Lewis	2:1	5	500
Herbert Smith Freehills	2:1	Not known	Not known
Hewitsons	2:1	10	850
Higgs & Sons	2:1 preferred	4-6	350+
Hill Dickinson	Not known	Up to 14	Not known
Hogan Lovells	2:1	Up to 60	1,500
Holman Fenwick Willan	2:1	15	Not known
Ince & Co	2:1	15	1,000
Irwin Mitchell	None	40	2,000-2,500
Jones Day	2:1	15	1,600
K&L Gates	2:1	Not known	1,000
Kennedys	2:1	c.18	900
Kingsley Napley	2:1	5	250
Kirkland & Ellis	2:1	Not known	Not known
Latham & Watkins	2:1	20	Not known
Lawrence Graham	2:1	c.10	600
Lester Aldridge	2:1	6	Not known
Lewis Silkin	2:1	6	600
Linklaters	2:1	110	4,500
Macfarlanes	2:1	25	1,000
Maclay Murray & Spens	2:1	20-25	450
Mayer Brown	2:1	c. 20	2,000+
McDermott Will & Emery	Not known	Not known	Not known
Memery Crystal	2:1	4	300
Michelmores	2:1 preferred	6	200
Mills & Reeve	2:1	15	c. 850
Mishcon de Reya	2:1	8-12	1,000+
Morgan Lewis & Bockius	High 2:1	5	Not known
Muckle	2:1 preferred	4	230-240
Nabarro	2:1	25	1,000
Norton Rose Fulbright	2:1	Up to 55	2,000+
Olswang	2:1	12	2,000
Orrick, Herrington & Sutcliffe	2:1	5	Not known
Osborne Clarke	2:1	20	1,200
Paul Hastings	2:1	3-4	Not known
Penningtons Solicitors	2:1	8-10	1,300
Peters & Peters Solicitors	2:1	2	200
Pinsent Masons	High 2:1	80	2,000+
PwC Legal	2:1	9	Not known
Reed Smith	2:1	c. 24	1,000

Applications and Selection

Firm Na me	Degree Class	Number of Contracts	Number of Applications
RPC	2:1	24	Not known
SGH Martineau	2:1	10	800
Shearman & Sterling	2:1	15	900
Sheridans	2:1	1	Not known
Shoosmiths	2:1	20	1,600+
Sidley Austin	2:1	10	600
Simmons & Simmons	2:1	c. 40	2,000
SJ Berwin	2:1	30	2,000
Skadden	2:1	10-12	1,000
Slaughter and May	High 2:1	c. 75-80	c. 2,000
Speechly Bircham	2:1	12	800
Squire Sanders	2:1	20	1,500
Stephenson Harwood	2:1	16	1,300
Stevens & Bolton	2:1	4	300
Sullivan & Cromwell	2:1	4-6	750
Taylor Wessing	2:1	c. 22	Not known
Thomas Cooper	2:1	Up to 4	Not known
TLT	2:1	Up to 15	c. 700
Travers Smith	2:1	25	2,000
Trethowans	2:1	3-4	100+
Trowers & Hamlins	2:1	20	c. 1,500
Veale Wasbrough Vizards	2:1 preferred	8-10	Not known
Vinson & Elkins	2:1	3-4	450
Walker Morris	2:1	15	c. 800
Ward Hadaway	2:1	10	600+
Watson, Farley & Williams	2:1	12-14	700
Wedlake Bell	2:1	6	Not known
Weil, Gotshal & Manges	2:1	Up to 14	Not known
White & Case	2:1	30	1,500
Wilsons	Not known	4	Not known
Winckworth Sherwood	2:1	6	300
Withers	2:1	11	900
Wragge & Co	None	20	1,000

Refine Your Search

Salaries and Benefits

Firm Name	1st Year Salary	2nd Year Salary	Sponsorship/Awards	Other Benefits	Qualification Salary
Addleshaw Goddard	Not known	Not known	GDL & LPC: fees + £7,000 (London) or £4,500 (else-where)	Corporate gym m'ship, STL, subsd restaurant, pension, pte healthcare	Not known
Allen & Overy	£39,000	£44,000	GDL: fees + £8,000 (London), £7,000 (elsewhere) LPC: fees + £7,000, financial incentives for first-class degree and/or distinctions in LPC	Pte healthcare, PMI, in-house medical facilities, STL, gym, music rooms, prayer rooms, subsd restaurant	£61,500
Ashfords	£20,000 (re-gions, London uplift will apply)	Not known	LPC: £9,000 grant towards LPC	Pension, life ass, holiday pur-chase scheme, childcare vouch-ers, CTW, free legal services	£31,000 (regions)
Ashurst	£38,000	£43,000	GDL & LPC: fees + £6,500, £500 for first-class degree, language bursaries	Pension, life ass, STL, subsd gym m'ship, PMI, income protection, in-house medical facilities, restaurant, CTW	£61,000
Baker & McKenzie	£39,500 + £3,000 bonus	£44,000	GDL: fees + £6,000 LPC: fees + £8,000	Health ins, life ins, pte medical ins, group pension, subsd gym m'ship, STL, subsd restaurant	£63,000
Bates Wells & Braith-waite	£32,000	£34,000	GDL & LPC: £6,000, interest paid on student loans	STL, subsd gym, subsd restau-rant, one month's unpaid leave on qualification, pension	£46,575
Berwin Leighton Paisner	£37,000	£41,000	GDL & LPC: fees + £7,200	Not known	£61,000
Bingham McCutchen	£40,000	£45,000	GDL & LPC: fees + £8,000	Travel ins, disability ins, STL, life ass, critical illness scheme, subsd gym m'ship, discretion-ary bonus, PMI	£100,000
Bircham Dyson Bell	£32,000	£33,500	Not known	Bonus scheme, group health-care, life ass, pension, STL	£52,000
Bird & Bird	£36,000	£38,000	Not known	Not known	£59,000
Bond Dickinson	Not known	Not known	Not known	Not known	Not known
Boodle Hatfield	£33,500	£35,500	GDL & LPC: fees + main-tenance	Pte healthcare, life ass, STL, pension, enhanced maternity pay, childcare vouchers, convey-ancing grant, PHI, CTW, EAP	£52,000
B P Collins	£24,500	£25,500	Not known	Not known	Not known
BPE Solicitors	£20,000	£20,000	Not known	Pension, income protection, death in service benefits, sab-batical scheme	Not known
Brabners Chaffe Street	No less than £21,000	No less than £21,000	Assistance with LPC funding	Not known	Not known
Bristows	£34,000	£37,000	GDL & LPC: fees + £7,000	Life ass, pension, PMI, PHI, childcare vouchers, EAP, CTW, STL, health assessment	£58,000
Browne Jacobson	£24,500	£25,500	GDL & LPC: fees + £5,000	Life ass, income protection ins, pension, PMI, corporate discounts	Not known
Burges Salmon	£31,000	£32,000	GDL & LPC: fees + £7,000	Bonus scheme, pension, pte healthcare, life ass, mobile phone, Xmas gift, gym m'ship, sports and social club	£41,000
Capsticks	£29,000	£30,000	GDL & LPC: financial support	Pension, income protection, PMI, life ass, CTW, gym m'ship, childcare vouchers, STL, bonus scheme	£46,000

Salaries and Benefits

Firm Name	1st Year Salary	2nd Year Salary	Sponsorship/Awards	Other Benefits	Qualification Salary
Charles Russell	£32,500	£33,500	GDL & LPC: fees + £6,000 (London)	Bupa, PHI, life ass, pension, STL, subsd canteen	£56,000
Cleary Gottlieb Steen & Hamilton	£40,000	£45,000	GDL & LPC: fees + £8,000	Health club m'ship, pte healthcare (personal & family), life ins, disability ins, EAP, subsd restaurant	£92,150
Clifford Chance	£38,000	£43,000	GDL: fees LPC: fees + maintenance (£4,900 for accelerated LPC)	Subsd restaurant, fitness centre, pension, up to 6 weeks' leave on qual	£61,500
Clyde & Co	£36,000	£38,000	GDL & LPC: fees + maintenance	Pension, life ass, dental ins, PMI, subsd gym m'ship, STL, optional interest free loan, subsd restaurant	£59,000
CMS	£37,000 (London) £32,000 (Bristol)	£42,000 (London) £34,000 (Bristol)	LPC & GDL: fees + £7,500	Pte healthcare, life ass, pension, STL, subsd gym m'ship, subsd restaurant, confidential careline	£61,500 (London) £45,500 (Bristol)
Collyer Bristow	£28,500	£31,500	LPC: fees + £4,000	Not known	Not known
Covington & Burling	£40,000	£44,000	GDL & LPC: fees + £8,000	Pension, PMI, life ass, STL, EAP, PHI	£80,000
Cripps Harries Hall	£23,000	£25,000	(Discretionary) LPC fees: 50% interest-free loan, 50% bursary	Not known	£37,500
Curtis Mallet Prevost	£38,000	£42,000	Not known	Pte healthcare, STL, pension, income protection	Not known
Davenport Lyons	£33,000 - £33,666	£34,332 - £35,000	No	STL, client intro bonus, subsd gym m'ship, discretionary bonus, life ass, EAP, pension, PHI	Not known
Davis Polk & Wardwell	£50,000	£55,000	GDL & LPC: fees + maintenance	PMI, life ins, pension, STL, subsd gym m'ship, EAP	£100,000
Dechert	£41,000	£46,000	LPC: fees + £10,000	Not known	£68,000
Dentons	£37,000 (London) £25,500 (Milton Keynes)	£40,000 (London) £27,500 (Milton Keynes)	GDL & LPC: fees + £6,000 (London) or £5,000 (elsewhere)	Flexible: pension, pte health ins, income protection, life ass and others	£59,000
DLA Piper	£37,000 (London) £25,000 (Regions)	£40,000 (London) £27,000 (Regions)	GDL & LPC: fees + up to £7,000	Not known	£60,000 (London) £37,000 (Regions)
DWF	£35,000 (London) up to £25,000 (Regional)	Not known	LPC: fees	Flexible: life ass, pension and others	Not known
Edwards Wildman Palmer	£38,000	£42,000	GDL & LPC: fees + £7,000 (London) or £6,500 (elsewhere)	Bupa, STL, subsd gym, bonus, pension, life ass, subsd cafe, CTW, EAP	£61,000
Eversheds	£36,000 (London) £25,000 (Regions)	£37,000 (London) £26,500 (Regions)	GDL: Fees + £7,000 (London) or £5,000 (Regions) LPC: Fees + £7,000 (London) or £5,000 (Regions)	Not known	NQ Salary £59,000 (London) £37,000 (Regions)
Farrer & Co	£34,000	£37,000	GDL & LPC: fees + £6,000	STL, income protection, life ass, company doctor, subsd gym	£57,000
Fladgate	£32,000	Not known	Not known	Pension, PHI, life ass, STL, PMI, sports club loan	£55,000

Salaries and Benefits

Firm Name	1st Year Salary	2nd Year Salary	Sponsorship/Awards	Other Benefits	Qualification Salary
Foot Anstey	Not known	Not known	LPC: fees + maintenance	Holiday purchase scheme, pension, life ass, CTW, childcare vouchers	£33,750
Forbes	£16,500	£19,500	Not known	Not known	Not known
Freeth Cartwright	£21,500	Not known	GDL & LPC: interest-free loan	PMI, pension	£35,000
Freshfields Bruckhaus Deringer	£39,000	£44,000	GDL & LPC: fees + maintenance	Flexible scheme	£65,000
Gateley	£20,000 - £22,000 (Midlands)	£22,000 - £24,000 (Midlands)	LPC: £5,000	Life ass, STL, library, pte healthcare	£33,000 (Midlands)
Gordons	£20,000	£22,000	LPC: £5,000	Pension, life ass, STL, childcare vouchers, sports club, interest-free travel loan	£31,000
Government Legal Service	£23,900 - £25,500	£25,300 - £27,000	LPC and BPTC: fees + £5,400 - £7,600	Pension	£32,000 - £40,000
Harbottle & Lewis	£30,000	£31,000	LPC: fees + interest-free loan	STL, lunch, life ass, pension, CTW, EAP, childcare vouchers	£50,000
Herbert Smith Freehills	£39,000	£44,000	GDL + LPC: fees + maintenance	Not known	£63,000
Hewitsons	£23,500	£23,500	No	Not known	£35,000
Higgs & Sons	£21,500	£24,000	No	PMI, pension, life ass, BTSS m'ship	£32,000
Hill Dickinson	£32,000 (London) £24,000 (North)	£34,000 (London) £26,000 (North)	LPC: fees + maintenance	Pension, holiday purchase scheme, PHI, life ass, STL, Bupa	Not known
Hogan Lovells	£38,000	£43,000	GDL & LPC: fees + maintenance	PMI, life ass, STL, gym, dentist, GP & physio, subsd restaurant, local retail discounts	£61,500
Holman Fenwick Willan	£36,000	£38,000	Not known	Pension, subsd gym m'ship, STL, life ass, medical ins	£58,000
Ince & Co	£36,000	£39,000	GDL: fees + £6,500 (London & Guildford) or £6,000 (elsewhere) LPC: fees + £7,000 (London & Guildford) or £6,500 (elsewhere)	STL, corporate health cover, pension, subsd gym m'ship, PMI	£58,000
Irwin Mitchell	£33,000 (London) £25,000 (outside London)	£35,000 (London) £27,000 (outside London)	GDL & LPC: fees + £4,500	Healthcare, pension, death in service + critical illness cover	Not known
Jones Day	£41,000 increasing to £46,000 after 10 months	£46,000 increasing to £50,000 after 22 months	GDL & LPC: fees + £8,000	Pte healthcare, STL, subsd sports club m'ship, life cover, salary sacrifice scheme, pension	£72,500
K&L Gates	£35,000	£38,000	GDL: fees + £5,000 LPC: fees + £7,000	Subsd sports club m'ship, STL, life ass, pension, PHI, GP service	£60,000
Kennedys	£34,000	£37,000	Not known	PHI, pension, PMI, life ins, STL, gym m'ship, CTW, child care assistance, EAP, corporate GP	Not known
Kingsley Napley	£28,000	£30,000	Not known	Pte health ins, income protection ins, life ass, pension, corporate cash plan	£49,000
Kirkland & Ellis	£41,000	£44,000	GDL & LPC: fees + £7,500	PMI, travel ins, life ins, EAP, gym m'ship	£97,560

Salaries and Benefits

Firm Name	1st Year Salary	2nd Year Salary	Sponsorship/Awards	Other Benefits	Qualification Salary
Latham & Watkins	£42,000	£45,000	GDL & LPC: fees + £8,000 + £500 for LPC distinction	Healthcare & dental, pension, life ass	£96,970
Lawrence Graham	£35,000	Not known	GDL: fees + £6,500 (London) £6,000 (elsewhere) LPC: fees + £6,500 (London)	STL, life ass	£54,000
Lester Aldridge	Not known	Not known	Not known	Not known	Not known
Lewis Silkin	£32,500	£34,500	GDL & LPC: fees + £5,000	Life ass, health ins, STL, pension, subsd gym m'ship, bonus, income protection	Up to £52,000
Linklaters	£39,500	Not known	GDL & LPC: fees + maintenance	Bonus, pensions, PMI, life ass, income protection, STL, subsd gym m'ship and others	£64,000 + discretionary bonus
Macfarlanes	£38,000	£43,000	GDL & LPC: fees + £7,000	Life ass, pension, pte healthcare, STL, bonus, childcare vouchers, subsd restaurant and others	£61,000
Maclay Murray & Spens	£32,000 (London)	Not known	Not known	Pension, death-in-service benefit, income protection, discounted medical/dental plans and others	Not known
Mayer Brown	£37,500	£42,300	GDL & LPC: fees + £7,000	STL, sports club m'ship, pte healthcare, PMI, life ass, pension, STL, EAP, subsd gym m'ship	Not known
McDermott Will & Emery	£39,000	£43,000	GDL & LPC: fees +maintenance	Pte medical and dental ins, life ass, PHI, STL, pension, EAP, subsd gym m'ship	Not known
Memery Crystal	£30,000	£32,000	GDL & LPC: fees	Not known	Not known
Michelmores	£20,000	£21,000	LPC: fees up to £8,000	Pension, subsd restaurant, subsd gym with personal trainer, free parking	£33,000
Mills & Reeve	£25,000	£26,500	GDL & LPC: fees + maintenance	Life ass, pension, bonus, sports and social club, STL, subsd restaurant	Not known
Mishcon de Reya	£32,000	Not known	GDL & LPC: fees + £5,000	Life ass, dental ins, PMI, travel ins, critical illness cover, gym m'ship, STL, pension, childcare, in-house doctor, bonus and others	Not known
Morgan, Lewis & Bockius	£40,000	£43,000	GDL & LPC: fees + £7,500	Life ins, health ins, dental ins, disability ins, STL, travel ins	£75,000
Muckle	£22,000	Not known	LPC: fees subject to eligibility	Pension, PHI, life ass, corporate discounts, salary sacrifice scheme, car parking discount	£34,000
Nabarro	£37,000 (London) £25,000 (Sheffield)	£40,000 (London) £28,000 (Sheffield)	GDL & LPC: fees + (or 50% retrospectively)£6,000 (London GDL) £5,000 (Regions GDL) £7,000 (London LPC) £6,000 (Regions LPC)	PMI, pensions, STL, subsd restaurant, subsd gym m'ship	£59,000 (London) £38,000 (Sheffield)
Norton Rose	£38,000	£43,000	Not known	Not known	Not known
Olswang	£37,000	£41,500	GDL & LPC: fees + £7,000 (London) £6,500 (outside)	Life cover, medical/dental schemes, subsd gym m'ship, subsd restaurant, STL, pension, PHI	£60,000

Salaries and Benefits

Firm Name	1st Year Salary	2nd Year Salary	Sponsorship/Awards	Other Benefits	Qualification Salary
Orrick, Herrington & Sutcliffe	£38,000	£42,500	GDL & LPC: fees + £7,000 (if applicant is no more than half-way through)	Pension, health ins, subsd gym m'ship, STL, PMI, dental care, childcare voucher scheme	Not known
Osborne Clark	Not known	Not known	GDL & LPC: fees + £6,500 (if applicant is no more than half-way through)	Pension, PMI, PHI, life ass, STL	Not known
Paul Hastings	£40,000	£45,000	GDL & LPC: fee sponsorship + maintenance	Pte healthcare, life ass, pension, STL, gym subsd	£88,000
Penningtons Solicitors	£32,000 (London)	£34,000 (London)	LPC: fees + £5,000	Life ass, critical illness cover, pension, PMI, STL	£47,000 (London)
Peters & Peters	£37,000	£40,000	Not known	Pension, Bupa, STL, subsd gym m'ship, life ass, childcare vouchers, CTW	£52,000
Pinsent Masons	Not known	Not known	Not known	Not known	Not known
PricewaterhouseCoopers Legal	£37,000	£42,000	GDL & LPC: scholarship for fees + maintenance	Not known	Not known
Reed Smith	£37,000	Not known	GDL: fees + £6,000 LPC: fees + £7,000	Pension, life ins, STL, bonus, subsd restaurant, conveyancing allowance, pvt health ins, CTW	£59,000 + bonus
RPC	£37,000 (London) £32,000 (Bristol)	£40,000 (London) £35,000 (Bristol)	GDL & LPC: fees + up to £7,000	Not known	£58,000 (London) £44,000 (Bristol)
SGH Martineau	c. £23,000	c. £25,000	LPC: fees + maintenance	PHI, life ass, PMI, pension, STL, CTW	£36,000
Shearman & Sterling	£39,000	£44,000	GDL & LPC: fees + £7,000	Life ass, long term disability ins, pension, subsd gym m'ship, PMI, travel ins, dental ins	£78,000
Sheridans	Not known	Not known	Not known	Not known	Not known
Shoosmiths	£24,000	£25,000	GDL & LPC: assistance + maintenance	Pension, life ass, corporate discounts	£38,000
Sidley Austin	£41,000	£43,000	GDL & LPC: fees + £7,000	Life ass, contribution to gym m'ship, STL, income protection scheme, pension, subsd restaurant, pte health ins	Not known
Simmons & Simmons	£37,500	£41,750	GDL & LPC: fees + £7,500	Not known	£59,000
SJ Berwin	£37,500	£41,500	Not known	Pte healthcare, subsd gym m'ship, life ass, pension, STL, lunch	£60,000
Skadden	£42,000	£45,000	GDL & LPC: fees + £8,000	Life ins, pte health ins, travel ins, subsd gym m'ship, technology budget, EAP, PMI, subsd restaurant	Not known
Slaughter and May	£39,000	£44,000	GDL & LPC: fees + maintenance	PMI, STL, pension, interest-free loan, subsd gym m'ship, accident cover, CTW and others	£63,000
Speechly Bircham	£33,000	£35,000	GDL & LPC: fees + maintenance	PMI, life ass, pension, STL, subsd restaurant, corporate discounts, gym m'ship	£56,000
Squire Sanders	£35,000 (London) £23,500 (Regions)	£37,000 (London) £26,000 (Regions)	GDL & LPC: fees + £6,000 (GDL London) £4,500 (GDL Regions) £7,000 (LPC London) £5,000 (LPC Regions)	Flexible: pension, life ass, subsd gym m'ship, STL	£58,000 (London) £37,000 (Regions)

Salaries and Benefits

Firm Name	1st Year Salary	2nd Year Salary	Sponsorship/Awards	Other Benefits	Qualification Salary
Stephenson Harwood	£37,000	£40,000	GDL & LPC: fees + maintenance up to £6,000	Subsd gym m'ship, pte health ins, pension, life ass, private GP, critical illness cover, subsd cafe, STL and others	£60,000
Stevens & Bolton	£30,000	Not known	GDL & LPC: fees (College of Law, Guildford) + £4,000	Pension, pte healthcare, life ass, loan for travel or car parking	Not known
Sullivan & Cromwell	£50,000	£55,000	GDL & LPC: fees + maintenance	Pte health ins, dental ins, life ins, travel ins, pension, subsd gym m'ship and others	£97,500
Taylor Wessing	£37,000	£41,000	GDL & LPC: fees (BPP London) + maintenance	Not known	£60,000
Thomas Cooper	£33,000	£36,500	LPC: fees	PMI, life ass, PHI, pension, loan for dental ins, STL, loan for gym m'ship	Not known
TLT	Not known	Not known	GDL & LPC: fees + maintenance	Flexible scheme	Not known
Travers Smith	£39,000	£44,000	GDL & LPC: fees + £7,000 (London) £6,500 (Regions)	PHI, life ass, subsd restaurant, STL, pte health ins, CTW	£63,000
Trethowans	Not known	Not known	No	Pension, death in service benefit, PHI, bonus, car parking, new recruit bonus, childcare vouchers, EAP	Not known
Trowers & Hamlins	£36,000	£39,000	GDL & LPC: fees + maintenance	Not known	£58,000
Veale Wasbrough Vizards	£23,000	£25,000	LPC: fees + interest-free loan	Not known	£35,000
Vinson & Elkins	£40,000	£42,000	GDL & LPC: fees + up to £7,500 (LPC)	Pte medical and dental, pension, STL, life ass	£80,000
Walker Morris	£24,000	£26,000	GDL & LPC: fees + £5,000	Not known	£36,000
Ward Hadaway	£20,000 (Newcastle) £23,000 (Leeds)	£20,500 (Newcastle) £23,500 (Leeds)	GDL & LPC: fees + maintenance	Flexible: death in service ins, pension, travel scheme	£32,000
Watson, Farley & Williams	£35,000	£40,000	GDL & LPC: fees + £6,500/£5,500 (dependent on location)	Income protection scheme, life ass, EAP, pension, STL, subsd gym and healthcare m'ship	£60,000
Wedlake Bell	Not known	Not known	LPC: funding available	Pension, travel loans, gym m'ship, life ass, PMI, PHI, CTW, EAP	Not known
Weil Gotshal & Manges	£41,000	Not known	Not known	Not known	Not known
White & Case	£42,000 + £2,000 welcome bonus	£45,000	GDL & LPC: fees + maintenance + awards for commendation and distinction on LPC	Flexible: PMI, dental ins, life ass, pension, critical illness ins, travel ins, STL and others	£72,500
Wilsons	Not known	Not known	Not known	Pension, life ass, PMI, optional benefits	Not known
Winckworth Sherwood	£32,000	Not known	LPC: financial support in certain circumstances	Not known	Not known
Withers	£34,000	£36,000	GDL & LPC: fees + £5,000	Not known	£56,000
Wragge & Co	£35,750 (London) £26,250 (Birmingham)	£38,750 (London) £29,250 (Birmingham)	GDL & LPC: fees + maintenance + prizes for first class degree, and distinction GDL/LPC	Pension, life ass, PHI, PMI and others	£61,000 (London) £38,000 (Birmingham)

Refine Your Search

"My experience definitely exceeded expectations. I was nervous about what City office culture would be like. But it's completely different to what I expected. Everyone is really approachable and I never hesitate to ask partners a question." Trainee, US firm in London

Picking a firm for its overseas opportunities

The idea of the international law firm is far from new; UK firms have ventured overseas since the 19th century. What has changed is the number of firms with offices overseas and the increasing desire to plant flags around

Big firms are canny operators. They understand that thriving in a competitive international legal market requires a network of overseas offices (or relationships with overseas firms) in regions with strong economic growth. China and the Far East are of real interest at present, as are Central and Eastern Europe, the Middle East, Africa and resource-rich parts of Central Asia. Despite its economic draws, India has so far avoided invasions due to its strict Bar Association rules. The downturn in the world economy has, largely, not dampened this thirst for expansion, with firms becoming ever more determined to invest in developing countries where growth has been affected less. The global recession did, however, see some of the magic circle firms retreating in regions such as CEE.

There are so many firms with overseas networks that keeping track of the fluctuation of office openings and closings is almost a full-time occupation. Wherever possible, we've mentioned the main changes from the past year in our True Picture reports. Predicting which firms will open new overseas offices and who will merge with whom is always a gamble, but palpable trends crop up here and there. Anglo-American mergers are particularly in vogue – Squire Sanders, Norton Rose Fulbright and Dentons are all the product of transatlantic tie-ups in recent years. Several firms – Ashurst, Norton Rose, Clifford Chance, DLA Piper and most recently Herbert Smith Freehills – have made similar gestures towards the Australian market, while SJ Berwin's tie up with King & Wood Mallesons makes the first global firm headquartered in Asia.

There is no question that practising abroad does make your CV shine. Of course, competition for seats can get tough, and not all firms can guarantee opportunities abroad ahead of time, but the True Picture reports should give you a better idea of where your luck lies. An important thing to bear in mind is language capability – some firms earmark their fluent Russian speakers for Moscow, regardless of whether they'd prefer to head to New York. Language skills in general are undeniably attractive to recruiters, particularly those who actively recruit with certain needs in mind. International private client firm Withers, for example, likes to enlist a few fluent Italian

speakers in each intake to fill its coveted corporate seat in Milan.

Although time abroad gives you experience of working in another jurisdiction, chances are you won't actually practise foreign law. Still, an overseas seat is without a doubt a very rewarding and challenging experience. For UK firms at least, your overseas outpost will be smaller than your home office, so you're likely to receive a greater amount of responsibility. Securing the most popular overseas seats often involves waging a campaign of self-promotion back at home. Sometimes you'll also need to gain experience in a certain department in the UK office before you go.

Overseas trainees need not worry about feeling isolated in their host country as the local lawyers and staff invariably give a warm welcome to newcomers. In cities with a large influx of UK trainees there's usually a ready-made social scene, so it's likely the first thing to pop up in your inbox will be an invitation to meet other new arrivals. In Singapore, it's not unheard of for trainees to jet off for group weekends on Indonesian islands. Another big plus is free accommodation on the firm. Trainees are usually housed in centrally located private apartments. In fact, it may be some time before they can afford such plush digs and domestic perks back home. For more on life as a trainee in an overseas seat, check out our website.

The following table outlines where the overseas seat opportunities are this year. Back in the UK, a firm's international footprint will determine what trainees do day to day. At White & Case there's project finance work conducted in conjunction with Eastern European offices, while Dentons' energy and natural resources work across Africa and the Middle East rakes in heaps of work for London lawyers. Likewise, Trowers & Hamlins' predominance in Islamic finance keeps its City side busy, as do Curtis Mallet's and Lawrence Graham's respective relationships with Middle Eastern governments and major film studios in Los Angeles. See our True Picture reports for more details on each.

Overseas seats: Who goes where?

Location	Firms
Abu Dhabi	Berwin Leighton Paisner, Cleary Gottlieb Steen & Hamilton, Clifford Chance, Clyde & Co, Dentons, DLA Piper, Eversheds, Herbert Smith Freehills, Latham & Watkins, Linklaters, Norton Rose Fulbright, Reed Smith, Sherman & Sterling, Simmons & Simmons, Trowers & Hamlins, White & Case
Amsterdam	Clifford Chance, Freshfields Bruckhaus Deringer, Linklaters, Slaughter & May
Athens	Norton Rose Fulbright
Auckland	Slaughter & May
Bahrain	Charles Russell, Trowers & Hamlins
Bangkok	DLA Piper, Watson Farley & Williams
Barcelona	Slaughter & May
Beijing	Cleary Gottlieb Steen & Hamilton, Clifford Chance, Norton Rose Fulbright, White & Case
Berlin	Freshfields Bruckhaus Deringer
Brussels	Baker & McKenzie, Berwin Leighton Paisner, Bird & Bird, Cleary Gottlieb Steen & Hamilton, Clifford Chance, Dechert, Freshfields Bruckhaus Deringer, Herbert Smith Freehills, Hogan Lovells, Holman Fenwick Willan, Latham & Watkins, Linklaters, Nabarro, Olswang, Sherman & Sterling, Sidley Austin, SJ Berwin, Slaughter & May, Squire Sanders, White & Case
Bucharest	CMS (Cameron McKenna)
Dar es Salaam	Clyde & Co
Doha	Lathams & Watkins
Dubai	Ashurst, Clifford Chance, Clyde & Co, Dentons, DLA Piper, Freshfields Bruckhaus Deringer, Herbert Smith Freehills, Hogan Lovells, Holman Fenwick Willan, Jones Day, Latham & Watkins, Lawrence Graham, Linklaters, Norton Rose Fulbright, Pinsent Masons, Simmons & Simmons, SJ Berwin, Trowers & Hamlins, Vinson & Elkins
Dublin	Dechert
Düsseldorf	McDermott Will & Emery
Falkland Is.	Pinsent Masons
Frankfurt	Ashurst, Clifford Chance, Freshfields Bruckhaus Deringer, Linklaters, SJ Berwin
Geneva	Charles Russell, Holman Fenwick Willan, Withers
Guangzhou	Wragge & Co
Hamburg	Bird & Bird
Helsinki	Slaughter & May
Hong Kong	Ashurst, Baker & McKenzie, Bird & Bird, Cleary Gottlieb Steen & Hamilton, Clifford Chance, Clyde & Co, DLA Piper, Eversheds, Freshfields Bruckhaus Deringer, Herbert Smith Freehills, Hogan Lovells, Holman Fenwick Willan, Kennedys, Kirkland & Ellis, Latham & Watkins, Linklaters, Mayer Brown, Norton Rose Fulbright, Shearman & Sterling, Simmons & Simmons, SJ Berwin, Skaddan Arps, Slaughter & May, Stephenson Harwood, Vinson & Elkins, White & Case, Withers
Houston	Vinson & Elkins
Kyiv	CMS (Cameron McKenna)
Luxembourg	SJ Berwin
Madrid	Ashurst, Bird & Bird, Clifford Chance, Eversheds, Linklaters, SJ Berwin, Slaughter & May
Melbourne	Holman Fenwick Willan, Norton Rose Fulbright
Milan	Clifford Chance, Linklaters, Norton Rose Fulbright, Slaughter & May, Withers
Moscow	Baker & McKenzie, Berwin Leighton Paisner, Cleary Gottlieb Steen & Hamilton, Clifford Chance, CMS (Cameron McKenna), Dechert, DLA Piper, Freshfields Bruckhaus Deringer, Herbert Smith Freehills, Latham & Watkins, Linklaters, Morgan Lewis, White & Case
Munich	Bird & Bird, Clifford Chance, CMS (Cameron McKenna), Norton Rose Fulbright, Slaughter & May
Muscat	Dentons , Addleshaw Goddard, Trowers & Hamlin
New York	Cleary Gottlieb Steen & Hamilton, Clifford Chance, Freshfields Bruckhaus Deringer, Hogan Lovells, Kirkland & Ellis, Latham & Watkins, Mayer Brown, Shearman & Sterling, Slaughter & May, Weil, Gotshal & Manges, White & Case

Overseas seats: Who goes where?

Location	Firms
Oslo	Slaughter & May
Paris	Ashurst, Bird & Bird, Cleary Gottlieb Steen & Hamilton, Clifford Chance, Eversheds, Freshfields Bruckhaus Deringer, Herbert Smith Freehills, Hogan Lovells, Holman Fenwick Willan, Ince & Co, Latham & Watkins, Linklaters, McDermott Will & Emery, Norton Rose Fulbright, Olswang, Simmons & Simmons, SJ Berwin, Slaughter & May, Squire Saunders, Travers Smith, Watson, Farley & Williams, White & Case
Perth	Holman Fenwick Willan
Piraeus	Hill Dickinson, Holman Fenwick Willan, Reed Smith, Thomas Cooper, Watson Farley & Williams
Prague	Clifford Chance, CMS (Cameron McKenna), White & Case
Riyadh	Latham & Watkins, White & Case
Rio de Janeiro	Clyde & Co, CMS (Cameron McKenna)
San Francisco	Baker & McKenzie, Clyde & Co
São Paulo	Clifford Chance
Shanghai	Clifford Chance, Eversheds, Holman Fenwick Willan, Ince & Co, Linklaters
Singapore	Ashurst, Baker & McKenzie, Berwin Leighton Paisner, Clifford Chance, DLA Piper, Eversheds, Freshfields Bruckhaus Deringer, Herbert Smith Freehills, Hill Dickinson, Hogan Lovells, Holman Fenwick Willan, Latham & Watkins, Linklaters, Norton Rose Fulbright, Shearman & Sterling, Stephenson Harwood, Watson Farley & Williams, White & Case
Stockholm	Slaughter & May
Sydney	Baker & McKenzie, DLA Piper, Norton Rose Fulbright, Slaughter & May
Tokyo	Ashurst, Clifford Chance, Freshfields Bruckhaus Deringer, Herbert Smith Freehills, Linklaters, Norton Rose Fulbright, Simmons & Simmons, Slaughter & May, White & Case
Vienna	CMS (Cameron McKenna)
Warsaw	Clifford Chance, Linklaters
Washington DC	Baker & McKenzie, Cleary Gottlieb Steen & Hamilton, Freshfields Bruckhaus Deringer

"My experience definitely exceeded expectations. I was nervous about what City office culture would be like. But it's completely different to what I expected. Everyone is really approachable and I never hesitate to ask partners a question."

Trainee, US firm in London

A-Z of Solicitors

Addleshaw Goddard

Milton Gate, 60 Chiswell St, London EC1Y 4AG
Sovereign House, PO Box 8, Sovereign Street, Leeds LS1 1HQ
100 Barbirolli Square, Manchester M2 3AB
Website: www.addleshawgoddard.com/graduates

Firm profile

Addleshaw Goddard is a dynamic, international law firm committed to doing all it can to help its clients and its people succeed in their ambitions.

Lots of law firms say they are different and talk about the reasons why. Those reasons sound the same.

Addleshaw Goddard tries to be different. By listening. By innovating. Through a combination of technical excellence, market insight and commercial decision-making and importantly, by being fun to work with and for.

The firm is an FT Innovation Award winner and is pioneering new ways of delivering services which bring outstanding value to its clients and exciting career opportunities for its lawyers. Wherever you are based, you'll also be part of the team from day one, getting first-hand experience of working with blue-chip clients within a supportive yet challenging environment, and benefit from a structured training programme designed with your future success in mind.

Main areas of work

The firm's client portfolio is testament to its strength and range of expertise, and includes financial institutions, public sector bodies, successful businesses and private individuals. It is a leading advisor to FTSE100 companies, and a market leader across its business divisions – commercial services, corporate, finance and projects, litigation and real estate – as well as in specialist fields such as private capital, and across its chosen sectors: financial services, government, energy and infrastructure, retail and consumer and real estate.

Trainee profile

Graduates who are capable of achieving a 2:1 and can demonstrate commercial awareness, teamwork, motivation and drive. Applications from law and non-law graduates are welcomed, as are applications from students who may be considering a change of direction. We also have a Legal Access scheme for applicants on GDL or LPC with less conventional academic backgrounds. Further details can be found on our website.

Training environment

During each six-month seat, there will be regular two-way performance reviews with the supervising partner or solicitor. Trainees may have the opportunity to spend a seat in one of the firm's other offices and there are a number of secondments to clients available. Seated with a qualified solicitor or partner and working as part of a team enables trainees to develop the professional skills necessary to deal with the demanding and challenging work the firm carries out for its clients. Practical training is complemented by high-quality training courses provided by both the in-house team and external training providers. A trainee buddy programme is in place with the trainee predecessor for the first seat. All trainees have a mentor for the duration of training contract and beyond.

Placement Schemes

Places for 2014: 70; Duration: 1 or 2 weeks; Location; all UK offices; Apply by 31 January 2014. Interviews for our placement schemes start early January.

Sponsorship & benefits

GDL and LPC fees are paid, plus a maintenance grant of £7,000 (London) or £4,500 (elsewhere in the UK). Benefits include corporate gym membership, season ticket loan, subsidised restaurant, pension and private healthcare.

Partners 160
Associates 500+
Trainees 70

Contact
grad@addleshawgoddard.com

Closing date for 2016
31 July 2014
Interviews for our training contracts start in early June.

Application
Training contracts p.a. 30
Applications p.a. 2,000
% interviewed 8%
Required degree grade 2:1

Overseas Offices
Dubai, Hong Kong, Oman, Qatar and Singapore. The firm also has a formal alliance with Tokyo-based Hashidate Law Office, and a world-wide network of strong relationships with chosen firms in North America, Europe and other emerging jurisdictions.

ADDLESHAW GODDARD

Allen & Overy LLP

One Bishops Square, London E1 6AD
Tel: (020) 3088 3399
Email: graduate.recruitment@allenovery.com
Website: www.aograduate.com
Facebook: www.facebook.com/AllenOveryGrads Twitter: @allenoverygrads

Firm profile
Allen & Overy LLP is an international legal practice with approximately 5,500 people working across 42 major centres worldwide. The firm's client list includes many of the world's top businesses, financial institutions and governments.

Main areas of work
Banking, corporate, international capital markets, litigation and dispute resolution, tax, employment and benefits and real estate. Allen & Overy partners frequently lead the field in their particular areas of law and the firm can claim both an enviable reputation amongst clients and unrivalled success in major deals.

Training contracts
We recruit 90 trainee solicitors each year across two intakes (March and September).
Final year non-law undergraduates and graduates can apply from 1st November 2013 to 14th January 2014. From 1st June 2014 to 31st July 2014, penultimate year law undergraduates and graduates can apply. We are currently recruiting for our March/September 2016 intakes.

Trainee profile
You will need to demonstrate a genuine enthusiasm for a legal career and Allen & Overy. The firm looks for a strong, consistent academic performance and you should have achieved or be predicted at least a 2:1 degree and 340 UCAS points (AAB), or equivalent. At Allen & Overy you will be working in a team where you will use your initiative and manage your own time and workload, so evidence of teamwork, leadership and problem solving skills are also looked for.

Training environment
Allen & Overy offers a training contract characterised by flexibility and choice. The seat structure ensures that you get to see as many parts of the firm as possible and that your learning is hands-on, guided by an experienced associate or partner. Your choice of a priority seat is guaranteed unless exceptional business needs or other extenuating circumstances arise. Given the strength of the firm's international finance practice, trainees are required to spend a minimum of 12 months in at least two of the three core departments of banking, corporate and international capital markets. The firm offers its trainees the option of completing a litigation course. This means that trainees do not need to spend time in the firm's litigation and dispute resolution department to gain their contentious experience if they are sure their interests lie elsewhere. There are also opportunities for trainees to undertake an international or client secondment during their final year of training.

Vacation placements
Allen & Overy offers 60 vacation placements across the year. The winter placement is for finalists and graduates who should apply from 1st October to 31st October 2013. Summer placements are for penultimate year undergraduates who should apply from 1st November 2013 to 14th January 2014.

Benefits
Private healthcare, private medical insurance, in-house medical facilities, interest-free season ticket loan, free in-house gym, subsidised staff restaurants, multi-faith prayer rooms and music rooms.

Sponsorship & awards
GDL and LPC course fees are paid in full along with contributions towards your maintenance costs. For the Allen & Overy LPC, a £7,000 maintenance grant is provided. For the GDL, £8,000 is provided in London and £7,000 elsewhere. Financial incentives are also offered to future trainees achieving a first class undergraduate degree and/or a distinction in every module of the LPC.

Partners 525 worldwide
Associates 2304 worldwide
London Trainees 190

Contact
Graduate Recruitment
Method of application
Online application form
Selection procedure
Interviews
Closing date for 2016
Non law candidates
14 January 2014
Law candidates 31 July 2014
Application
Training contracts p.a. 90
Applications p.a. 2,500
% interviewed p.a. 10%
Required degree grade 2:1
(or equivalent)
Training
Salary
£39,000 – Year 1
£44,000 – Year 2
£61,500 – NQ
Holiday entitlement 25 days
% of trainees with a
non-law degree p.a. 50%
No. of seats available
in international offices
36 seats twice a year;
9 client secondments
Post-qualification
Salary £61,500 (2013)
% of trainees offered job
on qualification 83%
International offices
Abu Dhabi, Amsterdam, Antwerp, Athens, Bangkok, Beijing, Belfast, Bratislava, Brussels, Budapest, Bucharest*, Casablanca, Doha, Dubai, Dusseldorf, Frankfurt, Hamburg, Hanoi, Ho Chi Minh City, Hong Kong, Istanbul, Jakarta*, London, Luxembourg, Madrid, Mannheim, Milan, Moscow, Munich, New York, Paris, Perth, Prague, Riyadh*, Rome, Sao Paulo, Shanghai, Singapore, Sydney, Tokyo, Warsaw, Washington DC.
* associated office

Ashfords LLP

Grenadier Road, Exeter EX1 3LH
Tel: (01392) 333634
Email: GraduateRecruitment@ashfords.co.uk
Website: www.ashfords.co.uk

Firm profile

We are a leading law firm, providing a full range of legal and business services to clients worldwide, and our ambition is to be nationally recognised as a leading provider of legal services and interrelated professional services.

Our aim is straightforward – to provide high calibre, cost effective and practical solutions to assist our clients and deal with the issues they face. We are plain speaking and innovative. Committed to building and developing a lasting relationship with our clients, our goal is to understand their needs and to deliver a solution which achieves their objectives.

Our three core work groups - Commercial Services, Real Estate and Infrastructure, and Private Client - cover a wide range of practice areas, including corporate, commercial property, dispute resolution, projects, local government, employment, intellectual property, information technology, trusts and estates, family and equity release.

Recognising our responsibility for our business behaviours, our corporate social responsibility strategy is based on the principles of positive engagement, inclusion and corporate/internal investment, to promote and develop an Ashfords culture providing a positive and inclusive working environment for staff and partners at all levels; developing, recognising and rewarding talent, commitment and contribution amongst our staff and partners; and takes our corporate responsibilities as an employer and member of our local business communities seriously.

Trainee profile

We don't care where you come from, what degree you did or what you look like as long as you are passionate about a career at Ashfords, are confident, a creative thinker with excellent communication skills and a strong academic background.

Training environment

Your training contract will comprise of four six-month seats. Seats are allocated following a face to face trainee meeting with our Trainee Recruitment Manager to ensure that your training contract is structured to suit you. We expect trainees to complete seats in three of our four core areas of commercial, property, litigation and private client.

Seats are available in our Bristol, Exeter, London and Taunton offices and as our training contract is not location based your seats may be in any or all of these locations.

We'll give you as much hands-on experience as possible from the start of your training contract as we believe it is a critical part of your training contract. You will have the full support of your supervisor and other lawyers in your team.

We're proud to have been voted a Guardian UK 300 employer by students and graduates in the UK for the second year running.

Benefits

Pension scheme (5% employer contribution), life assurance, holiday purchase scheme, childcare voucher scheme, access to corporate rates and discounts, cycle scheme, free legal services.

Sponsorship

£9,000 grant available towards your LPC.

Partners 73
Total Fee Earners 261

Contact
Katherine Wytcherley
01392 33 36 34

Method of application
Online application form

Selection procedure
Assessment centre, including
group exercises and interviews

Closing date for 2016
Vacation Scheme & Training
Contract 31 March 2014
Training Contract only 1 July
2014

Application
No. of training contracts pa 10
Applications per annum 400
% interviewed 10%
Required degree grade 2:1

Training
Basic Starting Salary (2013)
£20,000 (London uplift will
apply)
Holiday Entitlement 30 days

Post Qualification
Market Rate

Offices
Bristol, Exeter, London,
Plymouth, Taunton and
Tiverton

Ashfords
Incorporating   Solicitors
ROCHMAN LANDAU

Ashurst LLP

Broadwalk House, 5 Appold St, London EC2A 2HA
Tel: (020) 7638 1111 Fax: (020) 7638 1112
Email: gradrec@ashurst.com
Website: www.ashurst.com/trainees
Facebook: www.facebook.com/AshurstTrainees

Firm profile

Ashurst offers clients and trainees alike a clear alternative to the other elite international law firms. With 25 offices spanning the world's leading financial and resource centres in Europe, Asia-Pacific, the Middle East and the USA, we offer the scale to attract global mandates. We operate at the cutting edge of financial, corporate, infrastructure, disputes and resources markets. What marks us out from our competitors, however, is our team work and care for the individual. For our trainees it means a chance to make your presence felt right from the outset. Our strong culture of collegiality means you will be encouraged to take greater responsibility during your training contract and beyond.

Trainee profile

As with other law firms at the top of the market there will be challenges, late nights and pressure to perform. However, we also prize our culture of teamwork, client service, innovation and fun. We are looking for exceptional people who can contribute fully in all these areas. You will need to be totally committed to delivering for our clients and at home expressing yourself on paper and out loud, with your team and within a client's board room. If you share our vision, have a track record of achievement and are determined to be the best, multi-faceted lawyer you can be, we would like to hear from you.

Training environment

In addition to the obvious legal skills taught by all leading law firms, we will help you to develop the broad based acumen that will one day make you a trusted advisor to governments and the world's leading businesses. Your role at Ashurst will require you to become not only a highly technical lawyer, but also a shrewd negotiator, an incisive reader of any balance sheet and a business strategist with deep understanding of specific industries. In setting out to learn these skills you will complete four seats of six months, each of which will be planned in collaboration with you. You will also be encouraged to join an overseas office or go on secondment to one of our most valued clients.

Benefits

Private medical cover, pension, life assurance, income protection, interest-free season ticket loan, cycle to work scheme, in-house medical facilities, subsidised gym membership and staff restaurant and 25 days holiday per year during training.

Vacation placements

The best way to learn what it's really like to work at Ashurst is to join one of our placement schemes. Have a look at our website to find out which one would be best for you to join us on.

Sponsorship & awards

Full fees paid for the GDL and LPC fees plus maintenance allowances of £6,500 per annum. First class degree awards of £500 and language tuition bursaries.

Partners 400+
Assistant Solicitors 1700
Total Trainees 100+ (London)

Contact
Emma Young, Graduate Recruitment and Development Manager. For general enquiries contact us on
gradrec@ashurst.com

Method of application
Online

Selection procedure
An assessment day - see our website for full details

Closing date for 2016
31 July 2014

Application
Training contracts p.a. 40
Applications p.a. 2,500
% interviewed p.a. 10%
Required degree grade 2:1 (or equivalent)

Training
Salary (2013)
First year £38,000
Second year £43,000
Holiday entitlement 25 days
% of trainees with a non-law degree 50%
Number of seats abroad available p.a. 10

Post-qualification
Salary (2013) £61,000
% of trainees offered job on qualification 77%

Overseas offices
25 offices in 14 countries:
Australia, Belgium, China, France, Germany, Italy, Japan, Papua New Guinea, Singapore, Spain, Sweden, UAE, UK and USA.

A-Z of Solicitors

Baker & McKenzie LLP

100 New Bridge Street, London EC4V 6JA
Tel: (020) 7919 1000 Fax: (020) 7919 1999
Email: londongraduates@bakermckenzie.com
Website: www.bakermckenzie.com/londongraduates

Firm profile

Baker & McKenzie is a leading global law firm based in over 70 locations across 46 countries. With a presence in nearly all of the world's leading financial and commercial centres, our strategy is to provide the best combination of local legal and commercial knowledge, international expertise and resources. Our trainee solicitors are a vital part of that strategy, exposed to the international scope of the firm from the moment they start. There is also the possibility of an overseas secondment, recent secondees have spent time in Tokyo, Brussels, Moscow, Chicago and Hong Kong.

Main areas of work

London is home to the firm's largest office where Baker & McKenzie has been well established since opening in 1961. With more than 400 legal professionals, we have a substantial presence in the legal and business community.

We deliver high-quality local solutions across a broad range of practices and global advice in conjunction with our international offices. Our client base consists primarily of multinational corporates, based in the UK and elsewhere, and financial institutions. As may be expected of a firm with a very strong international client base, we have considerable expertise in acting on, and co-ordinating, cross-border transactions and disputes.

Our Corporate and Finance teams regularly advise on, and co-ordinate, complex, cross-border transactions for our clients. As a full service office, we cover all the practices expected of a major law firm in the UK, many of which are acclaimed and market-leading.

Trainee profile

The firm strives to enable trainees to be the best they can be. We are looking for trainees who are stimulated by intellectual challenge and respect and enjoy the diversity of cultural, social and academic backgrounds found in the firm. Effective communication skills, together with the ability to be creative and practical problem solvers, team players and to have a sense of humour, are qualities which will help them stand out from the crowd.

Training environment

The two-year training contract comprises of four six-month seats which include a corporate and a contentious seat, usually within our highly regarded dispute resolution department, together with the possibility of a secondment abroad or with a client. During each seat you will have formal and informal reviews to discuss your progress and regular meetings to explore subsequent seat preferences. Your training contract commences with a highly interactive and practical induction programme which focuses on key skills including practical problem solving, presenting and the application of information technology. The firm's training programmes include important components on management and other business skills, as well as seminars and workshops on key legal topics for each practice area. There is a Trainee Solicitor Liaison Committee which acts as a forum for any new ideas or concerns which may occur during the training contract.

Benefits

Permanent health insurance, life insurance, private medical insurance, group personal pension, subsidised gym membership, season ticket loan, subsidised staff restaurant.

Sponsorship & awards

CPE/GDL funding: fees paid plus £6,000 maintenance.

LPC funding: fees paid plus £8,000 maintenance.

Partners 83
Assistant Solicitors 210
Trainees 81

Contact
The Graduate Recruitment
Team 020 7919 1000

Method of application
Online via our website
www.bakermckenzie.com/londongraduates

Selection procedure
Online application, online tests, telephone interview and assessment centre

Application
No. of training contracts p.a 34
Required degree grade 2:1 or equivalent
AAB at A Level or equivalent.

Training
Salary for each year of training
1st year £39,500 + £3,000 'joining bonus'
2nd year £44,000

Post-qualification
Salary £63,000

Overseas Offices
Over 70 offices across 46 countries

BAKER & McKENZIE

Bates Wells Braithwaite

2-6 Cannon Street, London EC4M 6YH
Tel: (020) 7551 7777 Fax: (020) 7551 7800
Email: training@bwbllp.com
Website: www.bwbllp.com

Firm profile
Bates Wells Braithwaite is a commercial law firm servicing a wide range of commercial statutory, charity and social enterprises. The firm is expanding, progressive and is doing high quality work for clients and providing high quality training for those who work with the firm.

Whilst the firm is ranked first in three areas of law by the Legal 500 and ranked by them or Chambers in 15 other areas of law, the firm also believes in its staff enjoying a good work/life balance and living a life outside as well as inside the office.

Main areas of work
The firm is well known for its work for a wide range and variety of clients. This includes working with the charities and social enterprise sector, commercial organisations, regulators and individuals. The firm also has particular expertise in the arts and media, sports and immigration arenas together with strong departments dealing with employment, property and dispute resolution.

Trainee profile
The firm is looking for trainees with not only a sound academic background and the ability to communicate clearly and effectively, but most importantly it is looking for trainees who positively want to join a firm such as Bates Wells Braithwaite. We want the applicant with the character and ability to prosper anywhere, who is positively looking to be in a firm with our work mix and approach.

Training environment
In the first year there are two six month seats, whilst in the second year there are three four month seats which, between them, cover a wide range of the work with which the firm is involved. From time to time the firm arranges secondments to clients on an ad hoc basis.

The firm runs a programme of internal seminars specifically addressed to trainees and operates a mentoring system, all designed to ensure that the trainees enjoy their time with the firm and to maximise the opportunities that are available for them during their training contract and beyond.

Benefits
Firm pension scheme with match funding provided, interest-free loan for season ticket travel, Permanent Health Insurance (PHI), Death in Service Scheme, subsidised use of gym/corporate gym membership, wellbeing classes and squash court access, cycle to work scheme, subsidised restaurant, Buying Annual leave and one month's unpaid leave on qualification.

Vacation placements
Places for 2014: 12 people for a duration of two weeks each (£300 paid expenses). Closing date: March 2014. See website for details and to apply.

Sponsorship & awards
We will provide financial support to the value of £6,000 for LPC course fees which commence after the offer has been accepted. Similar support is given for the GDL on a discretionary basis. We also pay interest on student loans on either of these courses from the signing of the training contract to the contract end.

Partners 31
Assistant Solicitors 49
Trainees 8

Graduate recruitment contact
Peter Bennett (020) 7551 7777

Method of application
Online via website

Selection procedure
Interviews

Closing date for 2016
June 2014 - see website

Application
Training contracts per annum 4
Applications p.a. 750+
% interviewed p.a. 5%
Required degree 2:1

Training
Salary
1st year £32,000
2nd year £34,000
Holiday entitlement
5 weeks
Post-qualification
Salary £46,575
% of trainees offered job
on qualification (last 3 years)
92%

Bates Wells Braithwaite

Berwin Leighton Paisner

Adelaide House, London Bridge, London EC4R 9HA
Tel: (020) 3400 1000 Fax: (020) 3400 1111
Website: www.blplaw.com/trainee

Firm profile
BLP is an exciting, ambitious, and dynamic full service international law firm with over 850 fee-earners, including more than 215 partners. BLP currently has offices in eleven international locations, and has acted for or completed work in 130 countries in the last two years. BLP has a reputation as one of the most respected and innovative law firms, recording an eight percent increase in revenue growth in 2011-12 to £246 million and an increase in net profit to £93 million.

Main areas of work
Our client base includes more than 30 FTSE 100 companies and seven of the world's top 10 banks. We support each of the country's largest retail, water and construction companies. There are over 70 legal disciplines in which we are ranked. These include: commercial contracts; corporate finance; dispute resolution; energy and natural resources; EU and competition; finance; hotels, leisure and gaming; human resources; insurance; intellectual property; outsourcing; public sector; real estate; retail; regulatory and compliance; restructuring and insolvency; tax; and transport and infrastructure.

Trainee profile
In addition to talented individuals with brilliant minds and bright attitudes, we are looking for people who can take complex, often pressurised, commercial situations in their stride. The sort of people our clients want on their side and will ask for by name. People they can trust to help them succeed. In other words, people with BerwinLeightonPaisnericity.

Training environment
Trainees spend six months in four seats and progress is reviewed every three months. Client secondments are a popular choice, and there is the opportunity to undertake an international seat in either our Brussels, Moscow, Singapore or Abu Dhabi offices.

LPC+/ GDL+
The firm developed and runs the UK's first tailor-made LPC Course, called the LPC+. All trainees study at the College of Law, where tutors are joined by BLP lawyers and trainers who help to deliver some of the sessions, using BLP precedents and documents, and discussing how theory is applied to real cases and transactions. In 2011 we also introduced the GDL+; a programme of BLP led workshops which supplement the content that you study on the GDL course.

Sponsorship
CPE/GDL and LPC+ fees paid and £7,200 maintenance p.a

Partners 215
Assistant Solicitors 435
Associate Directors 30
Total Trainees 85

Contact
Claire England, Graduate Recruitment & Trainee Manager

Method of application
Online application form

Selection procedure
Telephone interview, assessment centre, partner interview

Closing date for 2016/2017
31 July 2014

Application
Training contracts p.a. 40-45
Required degree grade 2:1
Required UCAs points 340

Training
Salary
1st year (2012)
£37,000
2nd year (2012)
£41,000
Holiday entitlement 25 days
% of trainees with a
non-law degree p.a. 50%
No. of seats available
abroad p.a. 4

Post-qualification
Salary (2013) £61,000
% of trainees offered job
on qualification (Sept 2012)
85%

Offices
Abu Dhabi, Beijing, Berlin, Brussels, Dubai, Frankfurt, Hong Kong, London, Moscow, Paris and Singapore

A-Z of Solicitors

BERWIN LEIGHTON PAISNER

Bingham McCutchen (London) LLP

41 Lothbury, London EC2R 7HF
Tel: (020) 7661 5300 Fax: (020) 7661 5400
Email: graduaterecruitment@bingham.com
Website: www.bingham.com

Firm profile

Bingham London offers you the opportunity to work alongside outstanding individuals in a personal and collegial environment. Our team of over 50 finance, litigation and corporate lawyers is dedicated to providing a seamless and responsive service to the firm's international financial institution clients. Our London office capabilities have been carefully shaped to meet the complex needs of a demanding client base. Through practical experience and in-depth study of the legal and business issues facing these clients, the firm's London lawyers provide counsel in an intelligent and focused way. Widely recognised as one of the world's top-tier financial restructuring firms, Bingham has played a leading role representing creditors in numerous high-profile, precedent-setting workouts and restructurings throughout Europe. Clients include many of the world's largest insurance companies, pension funds, investment banks, hedge funds, distressed debt investors, international agencies, governments and multinational corporate groups. The firm has recently represented the senior noteholders on the restructurings of Uralita, Technicolor S.A. (formerly Thomson S.A.), the Quinn Group, Connaught Plc and Phoenix Pharmahandel; the public noteholders of Wind Hellas, Preem, Petroplus, Sevan Marine, the Icelandic Banks (Kaupthing, Landsbanki and Glitnir), Anglo Irish Bank and Irish Nationwide Building Society; the mezzanine lenders to Gala Goral, Bulgarian Telecommunications/Vivacom, Alinta Energy, Crest Nicholson, European Directories, Alliance Medical, Findus Foods and Dometic; and the bondholders on the majority of restructurings of high yield bonds in Norway including Petrojack and Remedial Offshore. Our Financial Restructuring Practice, which includes recognised leaders in the profession, is ranked in Band 1 by both UK Chambers and Legal 500 and was awarded a top-tier ranking in the UK by PLC in its Restructuring and Insolvency Handbook 2012-13 for the sixth straight year. We have approximately 1,000 lawyers in 14 locations in the US, Europe and Asia.

Main areas of work

Bingham's London office capabilities include financial restructuring, finance, securities and financial institutions litigation, financial regulatory, UK funds, corporate, EU/UK competition and tax.

Trainee profile

We are looking for high-quality candidates who have an exceptional academic record combined with evidence of extracurricular achievement. Prospective trainees will show initiative, be solution-driven and seek to be part of a challenging, yet friendly, environment.

Training environment

We recruit up to four trainee solicitors each year. The training contract currently consists of four six-month seats, rotating between the following practice areas: financial restructuring, finance, corporate, financial regulatory, competition, tax and litigation. The intimate nature of our London office means that you will benefit from a bespoke training programme with a high level of partner involvement. You will assume responsibilities from day one.

Benefits

The firm offers an extensive compensation programme for trainees. As well as a highly competitive salary, the firm offers private health insurance, travel insurance, long-term disability insurance, season ticket loan, life assurance, a critical illness scheme and subsidised gym membership. A discretionary bonus is also payable.

Sponsorship & awards

On acceptance of our offer for a training contract, we will provide LPC and PgDL fees and a maintenance grant of £8,000 per year.

Assistant solicitors 31
Total Trainees 4

Contact
Vicky Widdows, Legal Recruiting/Learning and Development Manager
(020) 7661 5300

Method of application
Online application via firm website at www.bingham.com or via CV Mail

Selection procedure
Currently face to face interviews

Closing date for 2016
31 July 2014

Application
Training contracts p.a. up to 4
Required degree grade High 2:1 from a leading university and excellent A-levels

Training
Salary
1st year £40,000
2nd year £45,000
Holiday entitlement 25 days

Post-qualification
Salary (2013) £100,000

Overseas offices
Beijing, Boston, Frankfurt, Hartford, Hong Kong, Los Angeles, New York, Orange County, San Francisco, Santa Monica, Silicon Valley, Tokyo, Washington

BINGHAM

Bircham Dyson Bell LLP

50 Broadway, London SW1H 0BL
Tel: (020) 7227 7000 Fax: (020) 7222 3480

Partners 43
Fee Earners 109
Total Trainees 14

Contact
Graduate Recruitment Team
(020) 7227 7000

Method of application
Please visit the firm's website,
www.bdb-law.co.uk/graduates

Selection procedure
Two interviews with members
of the Graduate Recruitment
Panel, comprising of a number
of partners, associates and HR.
In addition you will be required
to complete an online test and
assessment centre exercise.

Closing date for 2016
31 July 2014

Application
Training contracts p.a. 5
Applications p.a. 700
% interviewed p.a. 5%
Required degree grade
2:1 or above degree preferred

Training
Salary
1st year £32,000
2nd year £33,500
Holiday entitlement
25 days

Post-qualification
Salary £52,000
% of trainees offered job
on qualification (2012) 86%

Firm profile

Bircham Dyson Bell is a leading London law firm. The firm's approach and track record has enabled it to attract and retain some of the most talented people in the profession. This is achieved through the breadth and variety of work that the firm does. As part of the firm's commitment to providing a high level of service, it has been accredited with the Law Society's Lexcel quality mark and is one of the first law firms to be awarded ISO 14001, the internationally recognised standard for Environmental Management Systems. The firm is a leading member of Lexwork International, a network of 34 mid-sized independent law firms with over 1,700 lawyers in major cities across North America and Europe.

Main areas of work

Bircham Dyson Bell is recognised as having leading practices in the charity, private wealth, parliamentary, planning and public law fields. The firm also has strong corporate, commercial, employment, litigation and real estate teams.

Trainee profile

Applications are welcome from both law and non-law students who can demonstrate a consistently high academic record. The firm is looking for forward thinkers with a practical outlook and lots of initiative to join the firm's friendly, hard-working environment. If you're focused, positive and a confident leader, get in touch. Many of the firm's current trainees have diverse interests outside law.

Training environment

The firm's training is designed to produce its future partners. To achieve this they aim to provide a balance of both formal and practical training and will give early responsibility to those who show promise. The two-year training contract consists of four six-month seats during which you will work alongside partners and other senior lawyers, some of whom are leaders in their field. As the firm practises in a wide variety of legal disciplines, trainees benefit from a diverse experience. Trainees undergo specific technical training in each seat in addition to the mandatory Professional Skills Course (PSC). Great emphasis is also placed on interpersonal skills training and development so when you qualify you have the breadth of skills required to be an excellent solicitor.

Benefits

Bonus scheme, group health care, life assurance, pension scheme, season ticket loan.

A-Z of Solicitors

Bird & Bird

15 Fetter Lane, London EC4A 1JP
Tel: (020) 7415 6003 Fax: (020) 7415 6111
Website: www.twobirds.com/londongraduates

Firm profile

Over the course of nearly 190 years, Bird & Bird has evolved into a respected global business, serving clients in 118 countries from 25 offices across Europe, the Middle East and Asia. Today, our clients include the owners of seven of the ten most valuable brands on the planet and more than half of those listed by Forbes as the world's 100 most innovative companies. They need legal advisors who can work in partnership with them, develop a deep understanding of their sector and add real value to their business. It's the reason they turn to Bird & Bird.

The firm is ambitious and it manages to combine a resilient business approach with a hugely supportive attitude to its employees. With offices in Abu Dhabi, Beijing, Bratislava, Brussels, Budapest, Copenhagen, Düsseldorf, Frankfurt, The Hague, Hamburg, Helsinki, Hong Kong, London, Lyon, Madrid, Milan, Munich, Paris, Prague, Rome, Shanghai, Skanderborg, Singapore, Stockholm and Warsaw and close ties with firms in other key centres in Europe, Asia and the United States, the firm is well placed to offer its clients local expertise within a global context.

The firm is proud of its friendly, stimulating environment where individuals are able to develop first class legal, business and interpersonal skills. It has an open and collegiate culture reflected in its strong retention rate and assistant involvement. The firm is structured with a very strong international perspective to its culture - integrated teams working for cross-border clients as well as a range of international sport and social activities enables this.

At Bird & Bird, there is a genuine commitment to acting as a responsible employer and also as a proactive member of its local and wider international communities. The firm has a full programme of corporate social responsibility initiatives and policies in place, which fall under three broad areas: people, community and environment.

Main areas of work

We operate at the forefront of a range of sectors including: aviation and defence, automotive, communications, electronics, energy and utilities, financial services, food, healthcare, information technology, life sciences, media and sports.

Across these sectors, we cover the following practice areas: arbitration, banking and finance, commercial, corporate, corporate restructuring and insolvency, dispute resolution, EU and competition, intellectual property, international HR services, outsourcing, privacy and data protection, public sector, real estate, regulatory and administrative, tax, trade and customs and pro bono.

Trainee profile

We look to recruit trainees who have the potential and ambition to meet our clients' exacting standards. Not only will you need to develop technical legal skills to deliver high-quality legal advice, but you must also have an inquisitive, down-to-earth and pragmatic approach. If you think you have what it takes, we can offer you a challenging career in a fast-paced international environment. It's your chance to help shape the future of the clients we work for and the industries they serve.

If you are interested in a training contract at Bird & Bird, the summer placement scheme is a fantastic way to get started. We take on 34 students for two three-week schemes throughout June and July. Apply online at www.twobirds.com/londongraduates by 31 December 2013 for summer placement applications or by 31 July 2014 for training contract applications.

Partners Over 230*
Assistant Solicitors Over 580*
Total Trainees 33 in London
*denotes worldwide figures

Contact
Graduate Recruitment and
Trainee Development Team
london.graduates@twobirds.com

Method of application
Online application form via the
firm website

Selection procedure
Insight and Selection days in
February and March 2014 for
summer placements and
August 2014 for training
contracts

Closing date for 2016
31 July 2014 for law and non-
law students

Application
Training contracts p.a. 16-18
Applications p.a. 2,000
% interviewed at first stage
p.a. 20%
Required degree grade 2:1

Training
Salary
1st year (2013) £36,000
2nd year (2013) £38,000
Holiday entitlement
25 days
% of trainees with a non-law
degree p.a. Varies

Post-qualification
Salary (2013) £59,000
% of trainees offered job
on qualification (2012) 92%

Overseas offices
Abu Dhabi, Beijing, Bratislava,
Brussels, Budapest, Copenhagen,
Düsseldorf, Frankfurt, The Hague,
Hamburg, Helsinki, Hong Kong,
Lyon, Madrid, Milan, Munich,
Paris, Prague, Rome, Shanghai,
Singapore, Skanderborg,
Stockholm and Warsaw

A-Z of Solicitors

Bond Dickinson

St. Ann's Wharf, 112 Quayside, Newcastle upon Tyne NE1 3DX
Tel: (0844) 984 1500 Fax: (0844) 984 1501
Email: graduates@bonddickinson.com
Website: www.bonddickinson.com

Firm profile
Although we have only been in existence since 1 May 2013, you will probably be very familiar with the two firms who created this exciting new proposition. Bond Pearce and Dickinson Dees have both had a strong profile in the legal market and agreeing the merger was a major step in delivering the growth strategies for both firms. It is this new scale that will give us the strength, depth and sector insight to support our clients' commercial objectives. Both firms identified early in the discussions a shared culture and core values and with this at the heart of Bond Dickinson, together with ambitions for further growth, there's no doubt that it is an exciting time to be starting your career with us.

We have more than 1200 people nationwide, including 146 partners and over 580 other legal professionals.

Main areas of work
We are a full service law firm with a focus on 7 major sectors: energy, waste and natural resources; retail and fast moving consumer goods (FMCG); real estate; financial institutions; chemicals and manufacturing; transport and infrastructure; private wealth. We also have 3 other areas which are growing: technology; hospitality and leisure; education.

Trainee profile
The firm is looking for intellectually able, motivated and enthusiastic graduates from any discipline. Successful applicants will understand the need to provide practical, commercial advice to clients. You will share the firm's commitment to self-development and teamwork and its desire to provide clients with services which match their highest expectations.

Training environment
Our approach to trainee recruitment is one of long-term investment.

Trainees at Bond Dickinson will have an opportunity to spend six months in four Business Groups, gaining a real breadth of experience along the way. Your personal preferences are taken into consideration during the seat rotation process.

Our supervisors are trained and fully supported on an on-going basis. You will have access to high quality work and senior client contacts. We regularly second trainees to our most high profile clients.

We keep our trainee intake relatively small which is great for you. You are generally one trainee in a team which provides you with some great opportunities. We're looking for trainees across six of our locations, namely, Bristol, Leeds, Newcastle, Plymouth, Southampton and Tees Valley, with opportunities to spend time in our Aberdeen or London offices.

Work placements
The firm's work placement weeks are part of the recruitment process and all applicants should apply online at www.bonddickinson.com.

The first stage is an on-line application form which assesses the core competencies we look for: analytical thinking, communication and influencing skills, an ability to build strong and lasting relationships, commercial awareness, an ability to adapt and innovate and drive and motivation. If you are successful in getting through this stage, you will be invited to complete an online SHL verbal reasoning assessment. The next step will be to attend an assessment day in the location of your choice.

The day consists of a number of exercises as well as time to meet with trainees, partners and other people from around the business. By the end of the day we hope that you can make an informed decision about whether we are right for you.

Partners 146
Total Staff 1,200
Total Trainees 45

Contact
Graduate Recruitment Team

Method of application
Apply online at
www.bonddickinson.com

Selection procedure
Online application, aptitude and ability tests, assessment day, presentation, interview

Closing date for 2016
31 July 2014 for 2016
31 January 2014 for Easter and Summer placements

Application
Training contracts are based in Newcastle, Tees Valley, Leeds, Bristol, Plymouth and Southampton

Training
Salary
1st year Please see the firm's website
2nd year Please see the firm's website
Holiday entitlement 25 days
% of trainees with
a non-law degree p.a. 50-60%
No. of seats available abroad 0

Post-qualification
% of trainees offered job
on qualification (2013) 89%

Other offices
London, Aberdeen

Boodle Hatfield LLP

89 New Bond Street, London W1S 1DA
Tel: (020) 7629 7411 Fax: (020) 7629 2621
Email: traineesolicitors@boodlehatfield.com
Website: www.boodlehatfield.com

Firm profile
Boodle Hatfield is a highly successful law firm which has been providing bespoke legal services for nearly 300 years. They still act for some of their very first clients and are proud to do so. The firm has grown into a substantial practice, serving the full spectrum of commercial and private clients, both domestically and internationally.

Main areas of work
The ethos of facilitating private capital activity and private businesses underpins the work of the whole firm. The interplay of skills between five major areas – private client and tax, property, family, corporate and litigation – makes Boodle Hatfield particularly well placed to serve these individuals and businesses.

Trainee profile
The qualities the firm looks for in its trainees are commitment, flexibility and the ability to work as part of a team. Applicants who have obtained, or who are predicted to obtain a 2:1 degree in any discipline and a minimum of ABB at A-level should apply.

Training environment
Trainees spend six months in up to four of the firm's main areas: property, corporate, family, private client and tax and litigation. Boodle Hatfield is well known for the high quality of its training. All trainees are involved in client work from the start and are encouraged to handle their own files personally as soon as they are able to do so, (with the appropriate supervision). The firm's trainees therefore have a greater degree of client contact than in many firms with the result that they should be able to take on more responsibility at an early stage. Trainees are given formal appraisals every three months which are designed as a two-way process and give trainees the chance to discuss their progress and to indicate where more can be done to help in their ongoing training and development.

Benefits
Private healthcare, life assurance, season ticket loan, pension scheme, enhanced maternity pay, conveyancing grant, permanent health insurance, employee assistance line, childcare vouchers, cycle to work scheme, give as you earn scheme.

Vacation placements
Two week placement in July, for which six students are accepted each year. Applicants should apply via the application form on the website at www.boodlehatfield.com. The form will be available from 1 November 2013.

Sponsorship & awards
LPC and GDL fees paid in full plus maintenance grant.

Partners 32
Other Fee-earners 50
Total Trainees 11

Contact
Nicky Goodwin
(020) 7079 8240

Method of application
Online application

Selection procedure
Interviews with the Training Principal, a Partner and the HR Director plus an ability test in verbal reasoning

Closing date for 2016
Graduates and non-law students 30 June 2014
Law students 31 July 2014

Application
Training contracts p.a. 5
Required degree grade 2:1

Training
Salary
1st year £33,500
2nd year £35,500
Holiday entitlement
25 days

Post-qualification
Salary £52,000

Regional offices
Oxford

Boodle Hatfield.

B P Collins LLP

Collins House, 32-38 Station Road, Gerrards Cross SL9 8EL
Tel: (01753) 889995 Fax: (01753) 889851
Email: jacqui.symons@bpcollins.co.uk
Website: www.bpcollins.co.uk

Firm profile

B P Collins LLP was established in 1966 and has expanded significantly to become one of Buckinghamshire's largest and best-known practices with an enviable reputation within the Thames Valley Region. Based to the west of London, our easily accessible offices in Gerrards Cross are close to the M25/M40 interchange and city rail links as well as Heathrow airport. This location enables us to deliver city quality legal services at highly competitive rates.

The firm's emphasis is on offering the full range of commercial and private client legal services to all our clients from business start-ups to multi-nationals, successful entrepreneurs to retired professionals.

Most of our partners and associates have worked in London but have now opted to work in more congenial surroundings and enjoy a higher quality lifestyle. Gerrards Cross is a very pleasant town surrounded by beautiful countryside but within 30 minutes commuting distance of central London. It is an affluent area and we are conveniently located to serve the extremely active business community which includes West London, Heathrow, Uxbridge, Slough and High Wycombe.

Types of Work
- Corporate and commercial
- Commercial and residential property
- Employment law
- Family law
- Litigation and dispute resolution
- Private client

Training programme

The firm aims to have six to eight trainee solicitors at different stages of their training contracts at all times. Trainees complete five months in four different practice groups of their choice. The final four months is spent in the practice group in which the trainee intends to specialise. The firm has a partner with overall responsibility for all trainees and each practice group has its own supervisor who is responsible for day to day supervision. Trainees are given early responsibility which includes plenty of client contact and professional work. There are regular meetings between the supervisors and trainees to monitor progress as well as a review meeting with the training partner both midway through and at the end of each practice group seat. Trainees are encouraged to participate in social and marketing events. The firm has a very high trainee retention rate.

Trainee profile

Bright, hard working, lateral thinkers who are good communicators with plenty of initiative will thrive in the B P Collins environment. You should be adaptable and self starting in approach and possess a degree of robustness to cope with the changing demands which you will face during the contract.

Partners 16	
Assistant Solicitors 30	
Total Trainees 7	
Contact	
HR Manager Mrs Jacqui Symons	
Method of application	
Handwritten covering letter & CV	
Selection procedure	
Screening interview & assessment day	
Applications for the firm's 2015 intake will be accepted from 1st March to 31 May 2014	
Application	
Required degree grade 2:1, Grades A & B at A level	
Training	
Salary	
1st year £24,500	
2nd year £25,500	

bpcollins
SOLICITORS

BPE Solicitors

St James' House, St James' Square, Cheltenham GL50 3PR
Tel: (01242) 224433   Fax: (01242) 574285
Email: bpe@bpe.co.uk
Website: www.bpe.co.uk

Firm profile

BPE thrives on being different to many other law firms.

It is prepared to pioneer new approaches to provide a better service for its clients, and invests time and resources in new teams where it sees potential for growth. The firm's partners do not hide behind closed doors but instead work alongside their assistants and trainees so you have an opportunity to learn from their experience every step of the way. Our only office is in Cheltenham but we have access points in Cirencester, Oxford, Bristol and London.

Main areas of work

BPE offers a full range of services including: corporate, commercial property, commercial, employment, commercial litigation, construction and engineering, private client, science and technology, and family. Clients range from blue-chip multi-nationals, property developers and entrepreneurs to charities and local authorities.

Trainee profile

BPE looks for high-calibre, commercially astute individuals with character. The firm's 'work hard, play hard' ethos makes it an ideal workplace for dedicated and driven lawyers-to-be who are keen to socialise with colleagues outside of the office. Applications from law and non-law graduates are welcome provided you have a 2:1 degree.

Training environment

BPE adopt a flexible approach to your training. If you suspect commercial property may be your eventual specialisation or you have a passion for corporate work the firm will try to accommodate you.

Trainees at the firm are required to spend a six month seat in each of the following disciplines and are encouraged to spend their last six-month seat in the team of their choice: corporate; commercial property; commercial litigation; commercial. Although your training will be hands-on, the firm offers a comprehensive trainee induction programme to help you understand the firm's style of working, its culture, policies and procedures.

Benefits

A contributory pension scheme, 25 days holiday, income protection to cover long-term illness, death in service benefits and a sabbatical scheme.

Sponsorship & awards

BPE supports trainees in attending the Professional Skills Course (PSC).

Equity Partners 6
Partners 15
Associates 7
Total Trainees 4

Contact
Amanda Coleman
(01242) 248231

Method of application
Application form, available on website

Selection procedure
Shortlisted applicants are invited to attend an open day in August/September each year. A final shortlist of applicants is invited to attend an assessment day which includes formal interview, case studies and a numerical and verbal reasoning test.

Closing date for 2016
31st July 2014

Application
Training contracts p.a. 4
Applications p.a. 100
% interviewed p.a. 25%
Required degree grade 2:1

Training
Salary
£20,000
Holiday entitlement 25 days

Post-qualification
Salary Market rate
% of trainees offered job on qualification 80%

Brabners LLP

Horton House, Exchange Flags, Liverpool L2 3YL
Tel: (0151) 600 3000 Fax: (0151) 227 3185
55 King Street, Manchester M2 4LQ Tel: (0161) 236 5800 Fax: (0161) 228 6862
7-8 Chapel Street, Preston PR1 8AN Tel: (01772) 823921 Fax: (01772) 201918
Email: trainees@brabners.com
Website: www.brabners.com

Firm profile
One of the top North West commercial firms, Brabners LLP, in Liverpool, Manchester and Preston, has the experience, talent and prestige of a firm that has a 200-plus-year history. Brabners LLP is a dynamic, client-led specialist in the provision of excellent legal services to clients ranging from large plcs to private individuals.

Main areas of work
The LLP carries out a wide range of specialist legal services and Brabner's client base includes plcs, public sector bodies, banks and other commercial, corporate and professional businesses. The LLP's client focused departments include banking, corporate, commercial (including sports law), employment, litigation (including media and sports law), property (including housing association and construction) and private client.

Trainee profile
Graduates and those undertaking CPE or LPC, who can demonstrate intelligence, intuition, humour, approachability and commitment.

Training environment
The LLP is one of the few law firms that holds Investor in People status and has a comprehensive training and development programme. It is listed in the Sunday Times Best 100 Employers to work for in 2006, 2007, 2008, 2009, 2010 and 2011. Trainees are given a high degree of responsibility and are an integral part of the culture of the firm. Each trainee will have partner-level supervision. Personal development appraisals are conducted at three and six-monthly intervals to ensure that trainee progress is valuable and informed. The training programme is overseen by the firm's Director of Training, Dr Tony Harvey, and each centre has a designated Trainee Partner. It is not all hard work and the firm has an excellent social programme.

Sponsorship & awards
Assistance with LPC funding is available.

Partners 77
Associates 51
Assistant Solicitors 46
Fee Earners 50
Total Trainees 14

Contact
Liverpool office
Dr Tony Harvey
Director of Training, Risk and Compliance

Method of application
Online

Selection procedure
Interview & assessment day

Closing date for 2016
Apply by 30 June 2014 for training contracts commencing in September 2016

Application
Training contracts p.a. 7
Required degree grade
2:1 or post-graduate degree

Training
Salary
Not less than £21,000
Holiday entitlement 25 days

Offices
Liverpool, Manchester, Preston

Brabners

Bristows LLP

100 Victoria Embankment, London EC4Y 0DH
Tel: (020) 7400 8000 Fax: (020) 7400 8050
Email: trainee.recruitment@bristows.com
Website: www.training.bristows.com

Firm profile

Bristows is a medium-sized firm that handles the kind of work that might normally be associated with only the very largest firms. Established over 175 years ago, the firm has built up a client list that includes leading businesses from a variety of sectors, whether global corporations, growing start-ups, charities or financial institutions. Working with so many ambitious organisations, the firm is often advising on issues that shape entire industries and on which a company's future might depend. For example, advising on whether the business is entitled to launch a new product or assisting a client to buy a rival business.

Main areas of work

Bristows might be known as one of the foremost intellectual property firms in the UK, but this only tells part of the story. The firm's lawyers are also recognised as leading authorities in a wide variety of other legal disciplines and as a firm offer a true breadth of expertise. These are our core practice areas: intellectual property; information technology; corporate; commercial disputes; real estate; regulatory; EU and competition; media and marketing; employment and tax.

Trainee profile

The size of the firm makes this an ideal environment for trainees. As part of a small intake, the trainees work alongside the partners dealing directly with clients right from the start. There's plenty of responsibility but this is matched by an extremely supportive and friendly culture so you're never far from encouragement and advice when you need it. The firm recognises that its reputation as a leading city law firm is entirely down to the individuals who work here, so it places great stock in attracting talented people and doing all it can to make sure they enjoy life at Bristows.

Training environment

Each year the firm asks up to 10 graduates to join its team. The firm is extremely selective because it's looking for the people who will be its future partners. As part of such a select and high calibre intake the firm will give you real responsibility earlier than you might expect. During the two years' training, you'll spend time in each of the firm's main departments, developing your skills and knowledge. You'll also work closely with its partners and senior associates. Part of this training may also involve a secondment to one of a number of leading clients. With the international spread of the firm's clients, the probability of overseas travel is high, especially following qualification.

Benefits

Life assurance; pension scheme; private medical insurance; permanent health insurance; eye care; health assessment; employee assistance programme; cycle to work scheme; childcare voucher scheme; and season ticket loan.

Work experience

For opportunities to spend time with the firm during Winter, Spring and Summer, please see the firm's website for full details.

Sponsorship & awards

GDL and LPC fees paid in full, plus a maintenance grant of £7,000 for each.

Partners 33	
Assistant Solicitors 81	
Total Trainees 19	
Contact	
Graduate Recruitment Officer	
Method of application	
Online	
Selection procedure	
2 individual interviews and a written exercise	
Closing date for 2016	
31 January 2014 for February interviews,	
31 July 2014 for August interviews	
Application	
Training contracts p.a. Up to 10	
Applications p.a. 2,000	
% interviewed p.a. 4%	
Required degree grade 2:1 (preferred)	
Training	
Salary	
1st year (2013) £34,000	
2nd year (2013) £37,000	
Holiday entitlement 23 days	
% of trainees with a non-law degree p.a. 90%	
Post-qualification	
Salary (2013) £58,000	
% of trainees offered job on qualification (2013) 88%	

BRISTOWS

Browne Jacobson LLP

Nottingham, Birmingham, London, Manchester, Exeter
Tel: (0115) 976 6000 Fax: (0115) 947 5246
Email: traineeapplications@brownejacobson.com
Website: www.brownejacobsoncareers.com

Firm profile

Browne Jacobson a full service national law firm with offices in Nottingham, Birmingham, London, Manchester and Exeter.

With over 700 people, Browne Jacobson is large enough to attract some of the best talent in the country, but small enough to foster a supportive and flexible working environment. The firm's people are the key to its success and it has a track record of attracting and retaining outstanding people.

Browne Jacobson focuses on long-term relationships that are friendly, flexible and straightforward, with its people, clients and suppliers. The firm's forward thinking environment and its friendly and open culture mean that its people really enjoy working here. This allows good working relationships to develop and provides consistency for clients. It's a simple tactic yet one that works; a large proportion of the firm's client base has been with the firm for a number of years.

Main areas of work

Browne Jacobson offer a comprehensive range of specialist legal services with real strength across the commercial, public, health and insurance sectors.

Trainee profile

Browne Jacobson is looking for talented law and non-law graduates who can bring with them enthusiasm, tenacity, commitment and client focus combined with a flexible and friendly attitude. For more information about life as a trainee visit their blog at www.traineetalk.co.uk or follow them on twitter at www.twitter.com/brownejtrainees.

Training environment

Trainees start with a comprehensive induction programme, a fast track professional skills course and then go on to undertake an extensive internal trainee development programme. They spend four periods of six months in some of the principle areas of the firm, gaining an overview of the practice. Trainees get great training, a friendly and supportive working environment and real career opportunities. They are also given quality work and exposure to clients from early on, but are supported in achieving results and recognised for their contribution.

Sponsorship & awards

LPC/GDL tuition fees paid, plus £5,000 maintenance grant.

Open days

Browne Jacobson runs an open day in the spring - application deadline for the 2014 open day is 17 March 2014. Apply online at www.brownejacobsoncareers.com

Benefits

Browne Jacobson offer life assurance, income protection insurance, pension, private medical insurance, dental insurance, travel insurance and corporate discounts.

Partners 90
Associates 77
Assistant Solicitors 79
Total Trainees 16
Total Staff 705

Contact
Sophie Potter, HR Manager

Method of application
Apply online at
www.brownejacobsoncareers.com

Selection procedure
Telephone interview,
assessment centre and partner
interview

Closing date
31 July 2014 for 2016 training
contracts

Application
Training contracts p.a. 8
Applications p.a. 800
% interviewed p.a. 8%

Training
Salary
1st year (2012) £24,500
2nd year (2012) £25,500
Holiday entitlement 25 days
% of trainees with a
non-law degree p.a. 40%

Post-qualification
Salary Market Rate
Holiday entitlement 25 days
% of trainees offered a job on
qualification (2013) 100%

brownejacobson
law less ordinary

Burges Salmon

1 Glass Wharf, Bristol BS2 0ZX
Tel: (0117) 939 2229 Fax: (0117) 902 4400
Email: frances.lambton@burges-salmon.com
Website: www.burges-salmon.com

Firm profile
Burges Salmon is consistently ranked among the UK's most successful commercial law firms. We pride ourselves on delivering an excellent standard of legal and business advice to our clients, which has led to many of our practice areas winning awards and recognition as best in class.

Main areas of work
We provide a full commercial service through five main departments: corporate and financial institutions (CFI); commercial; real estate; private client and wealth structuring; and disputes, environment and planning. Our sector specialisms include energy, infrastructure, financial services, real estate, food, farming and land and transport.

Trainee profile
We recruit future partners, not future trainees and recognise that developing talent is critical to our success. Burges Salmon lawyers are hardworking and motivated with a strong academic background and a genuine enthusiasm for a career in commercial law.

Training environment
Our training contract incorporates six seats as opposed to the usual four which we believe ensures our trainees gain maximum exposure to our varied practice areas. This dedication to trainee development is demonstrated in our consistently high retention rates.

Vacation schemes
We run two assessment days in February and offer 36 places over 4 two-week vacation schemes during the summer. Individuals visit two departments of their choice supervised by a partner or senior solicitor. Current trainees run skills training sessions, sports and social events. Remuneration: £250 per week.

Sponsorship and awards
The firm pays GDL and LPC fees. Maintenance grants of £7,000 are paid to LPC students and £14,000 to students studying for both the GDL and LPC (£7,000 p.a.).

Benefits
Annually reviewed competitive salary, 24 days paid annual leave, bonus scheme, pension scheme, private health care membership, life assurance, mobile phone, Christmas gift, corporate gym membership, sports and social club.

Partners 79
Assistant Solicitors 350
Trainees 46

Contact
Frances Lambton, Trainee
Solicitor Recruitment Advisor

Method of application
Application form available via
our website

Selection procedure
Assessment centres held in
August include a psychometric
test, a group exercise and a
written exercise. Successful
candidates will be invited back
for an interview conducted by
a partner and member of the
HR team.

Closing date for 2016
31 July 2014

Application
Training contracts p.a. 25
Applications p.a. 1,500 approx.
% interviewed p.a. 10%
Required degree grade 2:1 in
any discipline

Training
Salary
1st year (2013) £33,000
2nd year (2013) £34,000
Holiday entitlement 24 days

Post-qualification
Salary (2013) £42,500
% of trainees offered job
on qualification (2013) 91%

BURGES SALMON

Capsticks

1 St George's Road, Wimbledon SW19 4DR
Tel: (020) 8780 2211 Fax: (020) 8780 4811
Email: career@capsticks.com
Website: www.capsticks.com

Firm profile
Capsticks is the leading provider of legal services to the health and social care sector and in the field of professional discipline. In June 2013 the firm also acquired a highly rated social housing practice, creating a firm with over 230 fee earners across 4 offices in London, Birmingham, Leeds and Southampton.

Main areas of work
The firm acts for over 200 clients, including all forms of NHS provider and commissioner organisations, the Department of Health, the NHSLA, regulatory bodies, charities, independent healthcare providers, housing associations, medical malpractice insurers and defence organisations.

Trainee profile
The firm is committed to recruiting the best people to maintain its market leading position. The firm plans to recruit eight (five in London, one in Birmingham, Leeds and Southampton) trainee solicitors in 2016 and welcomes applications from candidates who are either on course for or have achieved at least a 2:1 (or equivalent) in their undergraduate degree. The firm expects candidates to be committed to a career in healthcare law and to be able to demonstrate they are highly driven, but well rounded, team players, with good problem solving and communication skills.

Training environment
The firm's broad range of practice areas and health and social care clients enables it to give its trainees an opportunity to experience a wide variety of legal work. Trainees are therefore able to acquire an in-depth knowledge of both health and social care law and industry, in addition to developing the skills that any good lawyer needs.

The training contract is designed to give trainees maximum exposure to the work of the firm and trainees undertake seats in all of the firm's practice areas, including clinical law, corporate/commercial, dispute resolution, employment and real estate.

Benefits
Bonus scheme, 25 days holiday, pension contribution, income protection, private medical insurance, life assurance benefit, cycle to work scheme, corporate gym 'membership', childcare voucher scheme and season ticket loan.

Vacation placements
The firm's vacation scheme in each office runs from the end of June through to the middle of August and placements last for two weeks each. In order to be eligible for the 2014 vacation scheme you should be looking to secure a training contract with the firm in September 2016. The firm welcomes applications for a place on its 2014 vacation scheme between 11 November 2013 and 14 February 2014. Further details are available from the website.

The firm encourages all prospective trainee solicitors to participate in the vacation scheme as this is their primary means for selecting future trainee solicitors.

Sponsorship & awards
The firm offers its future trainees financial support for both the Graduate Diploma in Law and the Legal Practice Course.

Partners 45
Assistant Solicitors 145
Total Trainees 12
Other Fee-earners 38

Contact
HR department,
career@capsticks.com

Method of application
Application form, CV and covering letter

Selection procedure
Interview with Partner and Director of HR

Closing date for 2016
11 August 2014

Application
Training contracts p.a. 8
Applications p.a. 300
% interviewed p.a. 7%
Required degree grade
2:1 or above

Training
Salary
1st year £29,000 p.a. (London)
2nd year £30,000 p.a.(London)
Holiday entitlement
25 days p.a.
% of trainees with a
non-law degree p.a. 50%

Post-qualification
Salary (2013)
£46,000 p.a.
% of trainees offered job
on qualification (2013) 100%

Capsticks

Charles Russell LLP

5 Fleet Place, London EC4M 7RD
Tel: (020) 7203 5000 Fax: (020) 7203 5307
Website: www.charlesrussell.co.uk

Firm profile

Charles Russell is an ambitious, independent law firm with wide expertise and a long heritage. We offer a range of legal services, including advising on routine day-to-day issues to managing more complex, strategic matters for both businesses and private individuals in the UK and internationally.

The practice is well known as a friendly place to work and is committed to fostering a strong team spirit and encouraging personal development, which, combined with good quality work and good quality people, makes it a winning combination.

Charles Russell people are actively involved in CSR; helping to promote and organise pro bono, volunteering and fundraising initiatives.

Main areas of work

There are experts in a number of legal service areas, including: corporate and commercial; employment and pensions; litigation and dispute resolution; family; private client; property.

These services are focussed on the following sector areas: charities and not-for-profit; energy and natural resources; family; healthcare; private wealth; property; retail and leisure; sport; technology, media and telecommunications; financial services.

Trainee profile

Trainees are expected to get involved with all aspects of the role, so aside from the drafting and research tasks which are a given, trainees can also expect to get more involved directly with clients, run their own files with close support, develop their commercial awareness and participate in business development.

The firm wants to recruit trainees of the highest standard. Trainees will usually have a consistent and strong academic background and will have demonstrated other key attributes outside of academia, such as teamwork, leadership, communication skills and initiative. These attributes can be demonstrated in lots of different ways. The firm is looking for a diverse make up of trainees and welcomes individuals who will bring something different to the role.

Training environment

A small number of trainees are recruited and this allows trainees to undergo the best possible training.

The opportunities to get involved and the experience offered are second to none. Trainees can expect to be challenged and encouraged to go beyond their comfort zone, all with the full guidance, support and encouragement of the team. Trainees are seated with a partner/senior solicitor; there will always be close support at hand. Formal training is in place from day one and the first two weeks are spent completing induction and Professional Skills Course modules. This training provides trainees with the key skills required for their first day in the service area.

Regular feedback is important and mid and end seat appraisals take place to discuss performance and to give guidance on how to develop further. This does not, of course, replace the regular on the job feedback trainees can expect.

Benefits

BUPA; PHI; life assurance; pension; season ticket loan; 25 days' holiday; subsidised canteen (London).

Sponsorship & awards

GDL/LPC funding plus £6,000 maintenance grant (London) whilst you are at law school.

Partners 95
Other fee earners 252
Total trainees 39
Total staff 613

Contact
trainee.recruitment@
charlesrussell.co.uk

Method of application
Online application via
www.charlesrussell.co.uk

Selection procedure
Assessment day includes an interview and other exercises designed to assess identified performance criteria

Closing date for 2016
31 July 2014

Application
Training contracts for 2016 18
Applications p.a. Approx 1,500
% interviewed p.a. 7%
Preferred degree grade 2:1

Training
Salary (London)
1st year £32,500
2nd year £33,500
Holiday entitlement 25 days + additional day for house moves

Post-qualification
Salary £56,000

Regional / Overseas offices
Guildford, Cheltenham, Geneva and Bahrain

CHARLES RUSSELL

Cleary Gottlieb Steen & Hamilton LLP

City Place House, 55 Basinghall Street, London EC2V 5EH
Tel: (020) 7614 2200 Fax: (020) 7600 1698
Email: longraduaterecruit@cgsh.com
Website: www.cgsh.com/careers/london

Firm profile
Cleary Gottlieb is one of the leading international law firms, with 16 closely integrated offices located in major financial and political centres around the world. For more than 60 years, the firm has been pre-eminent in shaping the internationalisation of the legal profession. Its worldwide practice has a proven track record for innovation and providing advice of the highest quality to meet the domestic and international needs of its clients.

Main areas of work
Core practice groups in London are mergers and acquisitions, financing, capital markets, international litigation and arbitration and competition, plus additional self-standing practices in tax, financial regulation, intellectual property and information technology.

Trainee profile
Cleary looks for candidates who are enthusiastic about the practice of law in a challenging and dynamic international setting. Whilst academic excellence is a pre-requisite, the firm places particular emphasis on recruiting candidates that they and their clients will enjoy working with. A sense of humour is as important as the ability to think critically and creatively about cutting-edge legal issues.

Training environment
By limiting its graduate intake to just 13-15 trainees a year, Cleary is able to offer bespoke training that is individually tailored to the interests, experience and aptitudes of the exceptional individuals that join them. The firm does not believe that the transition from trainee solicitor to associate occurs overnight on qualification, but rather that the transition should be a smooth and gradual one. It therefore encourages its trainee solicitors to accept increased responsibility as soon as they are ready to do so. With appropriate levels of supervision, trainees operate as lawyers of the firm from the day that they join.

Benefits
Health club membership, private healthcare cover (personal and family), life insurance of twice annual salary, long-term disability insurance, employee assistance programme and subsidised staff restaurant.

Vacation schemes
The firm's London office offers 35 vacation places each year (five in winter, ten in spring and ten in each of two summer schemes). The firm actively encourages all candidates that are seriously considering applying for a trainee solicitor position to undertake a vacation placement with the firm. Applications for winter vacation placements should be received by 15 November. The deadline for spring and summer vacation scheme applications is 28 January.

Sponsorship & awards
Cleary funds the LPC for all future trainee solicitors. For non-law graduates, the firm also funds the GDL. A maintenance grant of £8,000 is paid for each year of professional study.

Trainees 27	
Partners 197	
(21 in London)	
Total Staff 2500	
(200 in London)	
Contact	
Graduate Recruitment	
Method of application	
Cover letter and CV	
Selection procedure	
Future trainees are primarily selected from among those having completed a vacation scheme with the firm	
Closing date for 2016	
July 31 2014	
Application	
Training contracts p.a. 13-15	
Required degree grade	
High 2:1	
Training	
Salary	
1st year £40,000	
2nd year £45,000	
Post-qualification	
Compensation £92,150	
Overseas offices	
New York, Washington DC, Paris, Brussels, Moscow, Frankfurt, Cologne, Rome, Milan, Hong Kong, Beijing, Buenos Aires, Sao Paulo, Abu Dhabi and Seoul	

A-Z of Solicitors

CLEARY GOTTLIEB

525

Clyde & Co

The St Botolph Building, 138 Houndsditch, London EC3A 7AR
Tel: (020) 7876 5000 Fax: (020) 7876 5111
Email: theanswers@clydeco.com
Website: www.careers.clydeco.com/trainees

Firm profile

Clyde & Co is an international law firm with a pioneering heritage and a resolute focus on its core sectors of aviation, energy, healthcare, infrastructure, industrials, insurance, professional practices, shipping and trade. With over 1,400 lawyers operating from 33 offices and associated offices across six continents, the firm advises corporations, financial institutions, private individuals and governments on a wide range of contentious and transactional matters.

Main areas of work

Core sectors: aviation, energy, healthcare, industrials, infrastructure, insurance, professional practices, shipping, trade and commodities.

Core practice areas: commercial, competition, corporate, dispute resolution, employment, finance, global governance, insolvency and reorganisation, international arbitration, projects and construction, real estate.

Trainee profile

An excellent academic record (including a 2:1 degree) are expected but equally important are your commercial and transferable skills. We look for trainees who take an interest in our clients' business, can apply their knowledge and intellect to practical legal problems, have the confidence to build relationships with clients and colleagues and are committed to a career in commercial law.

Training environment

You will gain early responsibility and be supported through close personal supervision and day-to-day coaching complemented by a wide range of training courses. You will undertake four six-month seats, which will cover both transactional and contentious work. You may also choose to be seconded to one of our overseas offices or have the opportunity for a client secondment.

Benefits

An optional £1,000 interest free loan on joining, pension, life assurance, dental insurance, private medical insurance, subsidised gym membership, interest-free season ticket loan, 25 days holiday per year, we also have a subsidised restaurant.

Vacation placements

The firm runs two-week summer and Easter schemes. Applications are made online at www.apply4law.com/clydeco. The closing date for applications is 31 January 2014. The vacation students have the opportunity to get involved in a range of training sessions along with a tour of Lloyd's of London and the Royal Courts of Justice. In addition to working in their chosen practice group, students have the opportunity to network with employees at a variety of social events.

Sponsorship & awards

GDL and LPC fees paid plus a maintenance grant.

Partners 289*
Assistant Solicitors 1,426*
Trainees 100*
*denotes worldwide figures

Contact
Caroline Walsh, Head of Legal Trainee Recruitment and Development

Method of application
Online

Selection procedure
Assessment day

Closing date for 2016
31 July 2014

Application
Training contracts p.a. 35-40
Applications p.a. 1500
% interviewed p.a. 10%
Required degree grade 2:1

Training
Salary
1st year £36,000
2nd year £38,000
Holiday entitlement 25 days

Post-qualification
Salary (2013) £59,000
% of trainees offered job on qualification (2013) 92%

Overseas offices
Abu Dhabi, Atlanta, Beijing, Caracas, Dar es Salaam, Doha, Dubai, Hong Kong, Madrid, Montreal, Moscow, Mumbai*, Nantes, New Delhi*, New Jersey, New York, Paris, Perth, Piraeus, Rio de Janeiro*, Riyadh*, São Paulo, San Francisco, Shanghai, Singapore, St Petersburg*, Sydney, Toronto, Tripoli
*associate offices
Alliances: Mongolia - Khan Lex Advocates, Zimbabwe - Scanlen and Holderness

---

CLYDE&CO

CMS Cameron McKenna

Mitre House, 160 Aldersgate Street, London EC1A 4DD
Tel: (020) 7367 3000   Fax: (020) 7367 2000
Email: gradrec@cms-cmck.com   Website: www.cms-cmck.com/chambers

Firm profile
What's in a name? A lot, when it's CMS. Firstly, CMS Cameron McKenna forms part of a leading network of firms known as CMS. We have 54 offices across 29 countries, with the most extensive footprint in Europe of any other firm. Secondly, we take a genuine, client-focused approach that attracts some of the world's biggest organisations. Last but not least, we know how to take talented people much, much further – geographically, intellectually and professionally.

Main areas of work
Our lawyers advise international clients across all types of commercial law, including corporate, banking and finance, energy, intellectual property and real estate.

Trainee profile
We welcome both non-law and law graduates who can contribute fresh thinking, an international outlook and formidable communication and analytical skills. The work we do is intellectually demanding and professionally stretching – something you'll find provides you with an excellent grounding for your career in law.

Training environment
We offer two-year training contracts in London, Bristol, Edinburgh and Aberdeen. During this time you'll undertake four seats across our broad range of practice areas, such as energy, intellectual property, corporate or EU competition. Alongside this, you're guaranteed to spend a seat outside of your 'home' office – an exciting prospect. You might be seconded to one of our top clients based in London or Europe, or spend time in one of our international offices including Rio de Janeiro, Edinburgh or Moscow.

Vacation placements
Places for 2014: 60 over spring and summer. Duration: 2 weeks. Remuneration: £250pw. Closing date for applications: 31 January 2014.

Benefits
Gym membership/subsidy, life assurance, pension scheme with firm contributions, private healthcare, season ticket loan, confidential care line, subsidised restaurant and 25 days' holiday with options to buy a further five days. You are also guaranteed to spend a seat outside your home office on a client, regional or international secondment.

Sponsorship & awards
The firm will cover fees for the GDL and LPC (or PEAT for Scotland) and provide you with a maintenance grant of up to £7,500. Please see our website for further details.

Partners 750 (global)
Assistant Solicitors 2,800
Total Trainees 120

Contact
Jess Heading (020) 7367 3000

Method of application
Online

Selection procedure
Stage one: online application and psychometric testing.
Stage two: assessment day (commercial analysis, group exercises and partner interview)

Closing dates
Training contracts
London & Bristol
31 July 2014
Aberdeen & Edinburgh
12 October 2014
All vacation schemes
31 January 2014

Application
Training contracts p.a. 60
Applications p.a. 1,000
% interviewed p.a. 10-15%
Required degree grade 2:1

Training
Salary
1st year
London £37,500
Bristol £32,000
Scotland £22,500
2nd year
London £42,000
Bristol £34,000
Scotland £26,000

Post-qualification
Salary
London £61,500
Bristol £45,500
Scotland £38,000
% of trainees offered job on qualification 82%

Overseas/regional offices
Aberdeen, London, Bristol, Edinburgh, Prague, Rio de Janeiro, Bucharest, Moscow

Collyer Bristow LLP

4 Bedford Row, London, WC1R 4TF
Tel: (020) 7242 7363 Fax: (020) 7405 0555
Email: recruitment@collyerbristow.com
Website: www.collyerbristow.com

Partners 26	
Trainees 9	
Total Staff 130	
Contact	
recruitment@collyerbristow.com	
Method of application	
Application form	
Selection procedure	
Testing & interview	
Training	
Salary	
1st year (2013) £28,500	
2nd year (2013) £31,500	
(Both reviewed annually)	

Firm profile
This long-established London firm provides a complete legal service to businesses and private individuals. Collyer Bristow is committed to providing a commercial and innovative approach to clients' legal issues, combined with a discrete and personal service, often not available from a large city practice. The firm's client base includes: multinationals, public and private companies, partnerships, entrepreneurs, public sector organisations and high net worth individuals, both in the UK and throughout the world.

The firm's Geneva office provides a base from which to serve clients in Switzerland, Europe and worldwide and, increasingly, to service its expanded private client offering.

The firm is well known for its ground-breaking in-house art gallery and is passionate in its support for the contemporary arts.

Main areas of work
Collyer Bristow has an impressive client base in such diverse sectors as real estate, media and sports, hotels and leisure, financial services and fashion, as well as a substantial private client practice. The firm's main areas of practice include corporate and commercial, real estate, dispute resolution, tax and estate planning, family, defamation and reputation management.

Trainee profile
The firm is looking for individuals who are able to demonstrate a strong academic performance, having gained a 2:1 or at least on track to achieve this. Successful candidates will be motivated individuals who possess strong commercial awareness, common sense and an ability to understand a client's needs.

Training environment
The firm's trainees spend six months in four of the firm's five key practice areas, working with a range of people from senior partners to more recently qualified solicitors. The firm has mentoring, training and appraisal programmes which nurture the development of technical expertise and client advisory skills. Trainees are encouraged at an early stage to take responsibility for their own files and to participate in managing the client's work with appropriate supervision.

Benefits
25 days holiday and usual benefits.

Sponsorship & awards
Full LPC funding and maintenance grant of £4,000.

Covington & Burling LLP

265 Strand, London WC2R 1BH
Tel: (020) 7067 2000 Fax: (020) 7067 2222
Email: graduate@cov.com
Website: www.cov.com

| Partners 261* |
| Associate Lawyers & Others 632* |
| Total Trainees London |

2010	14
2011	13
2012	13
2013	14

*denotes worldwide figures

Contact
Graduate Recruitment Team
(020) 7067 2000
graduate@cov.com

Method of application
Online application form
See website www.cov.com

Selection procedure
1st & 2nd interview

Closing date for 2016
31 July 2014

Application
Training contracts p.a. 6
Required degree grade 2:1

Training
Salary
1st year £40,000
2nd year £44,000
Holiday entitlement 25 days

Post-qualification
Salary
currently £80,000 p.a

Overseas offices
Beijing, Brussels, New York, San Diego, San Francisco, Seoul, Shanghai, Silicon Valley, Washington

Firm profile
Covington & Burling's LLP London office, situated next to the Royal Courts of Justice, encompasses a broad range of expertise and practice areas. The office, established in 1988, combines deep industry knowledge with lawyers experienced in advising on a wide variety of pioneering legal issues. The firm has over 800 lawyers globally, in offices in Beijing, Brussels, London, New York, San Diego, San Francisco, Seoul, Shanghai, Silicon Valley and Washington.

Covington has been rated a Top Ranked Leading Law Firm in Chambers UK 2012 and appears in The Lawyer Top 30 International Law Firm survey. The firm is also rated as one of the leading firms by the American Lawyer. Ranked in 'The A-List', Covington & Burling is part of a listing of twenty elite US law firms which are assessed on financial performance, pro bono activity, associate satisfaction and diversity.

At Covington & Burling, you will have an opportunity to work on cutting-edge deals for international and UK corporates such as Microsoft, Merck and Samsung, Fortune 100 businesses and leading technology, life sciences and media companies.

Main areas of work
Corporate advisory (including capital markets, M&A, finance, private equity, venture capital and funds), commercial litigation, data privacy, employment, financial services, insurance coverage disputes, intellectual property, internal investigations and compliance, international arbitration, life sciences, tax, technology and media. In addition, all our lawyers, including trainees, are encouraged to undertake pro bono work.

Trainee profile
We are looking for consistently high academic results (on target for a 2:1 degree or above and with strong A level results), commercial awareness, strong interpersonal skills and ability to work well in a team.

Training environment
You will do four six-month seats, rotating between departments. All trainees will undertake a seat in corporate and a seat in dispute resolution. We can offer optional seats in the following areas: employment, intellectual property, life sciences regulatory, life sciences transactional, tax, technology and media. Client secondments may also be available.

We aim to distinguish our trainee programme by offering a genuine support network which includes assigning associate buddies and undertaking regular performance reviews. We have an excellent record of retaining trainees on qualification and we aim to recruit trainees who are interested in making a long term commitment to the firm.

Benefits
Private medical insurance, life assurance, permanent health insurance, pension, 25 days holiday, season ticket loan and access to an employee assistance programme. We also have an active social calendar which includes regular firm drinks and sports activities.

Vacation placements
Summer Placements for 2014: We offer 24 summer placements, split into three, week-long programmes. You will be paid £300 per week. Apply by 31 January 2014, online at www.cov.com.

Sponsorship
GDL and LPC course fees and a maintenance grant of £8,000 are paid.

COVINGTON
COVINGTON & BURLING LLP

A-Z of Solicitors

Cripps Harries Hall LLP

Wallside House, 12 Mount Ephraim Road, Tunbridge Wells TN1 1EG
Tel: (01892) 515121 Fax: (01892) 598206
Email: graduates@crippslaw.com
Website: www.crippslaw.com

Firm profile
A leading regional law firm and one of the largest in the South East, the firm is recognised as being amongst the most progressive and innovative regional practices.

The firm's organisation into client-focused, industry sector groups promotes a strong ethos of client service and ensures the firm's solicitors are not only excellent legal practitioners but also experts in specialist business sectors. The firm is regarded by many businesses, institutions and wealthy individuals as the natural first choice among regional law firms. Although long-established, the firm's profile is young, professional, forward-thinking, friendly and informal.

Main areas of work
Commercial 20%, dispute resolution 20%, private client 25%, property 35%.

Trainee profile
Individuals who are confident and capable, with lively but well organised minds and a genuine interest in delivering client solutions through effective and pragmatic use of the law; keen to make a meaningful contribution both during their contract and long term career with the firm.

Training environment
The firm offers a comprehensive induction course, a well structured training programme, frequent one to one reviews, regular in-house courses and seminars, good levels of support and real responsibility.

The training programme is broader than most other firms and typically includes six seats in both commercial and private client areas. Trainees usually share a room with a partner or an associate and gain varied and challenging first hand experience.

Sponsorship awards
Discretionary LPC funding: Fees – 50% interest free loan, 50% bursary.

Partners 37
Assistant Solicitors 60
Total Trainees 16

Contact
Alan Geaney
Director of HR & Development

Method of application
Application form available on website

Selection procedure
First stage interview with a partner and an associate, followed by a closing session with the Director of HR. Successful candidates are invited back to a second stage interview with the Managing Partner and another Senior Partner.

Closing date for 2016
31 July 2014

Application
Training contracts p.a. 8
Applications p.a. up to 200
% interviewed p.a. 20%
Required degree grade 2:1

Training
Salary
1st year (2012) £23,000
2nd year (2012) £25,000
Holiday entitlement 25 days
% of trainees with a non-law degree p.a. 25%

Post-qualification
Salary (2012) £37,500
% of trainees offered job on qualification (2013) 100%
% of assistants/associates (as at 2012) who joined as trainees 60%
% of partners (as at 1/5/2012) who joined as trainees 22%

**Cripps
Harries
Hall.**

Curtis, Mallet-Prevost, Colt & Mosle LLP

99 Gresham Street, London EC2V 7NG
Tel: (020) 7710 9800 Fax (020) 7710 9801
Website: www.curtis.com

Firm profile
Curtis is one of the longest established international firms in either London or New York. Operating out of 15 offices across Europe, the Middle East, Asia and the Americas, Curtis was one of the first US firms to open in Mexico City in 1985. It remains the only US-headquartered law firm licensed to practice in Oman and was the first international law firm to open an office in Turkmenistan.

Main areas of work
Curtis' core practices in London are: international arbitration, investment management and corporate/commercial law, which includes mergers and acquisitions, private placements, public offerings, venture capital and private equity, fund formation, joint ventures, infrastructure projects and debt finance. The firm is well known for representing state-owned energy companies and governments around the world.

Trainee profile
Curtis provides an international and dynamic environment, so applicants will need energy, enthusiasm and an ability to get on well with people of all kinds as well as excellent academics. A pro-active approach is a plus, as are languages and a willingness to travel.

Training environment
Curtis' London office is small and friendly as well as diverse and internationally minded. As a key hub for Curtis' European and African activities, many of our overseas partners and colleagues visit regularly. Instead of a traditional four seat method, we offer a flexible but non-rotational training. It allows a higher degree of flexibility for individuals and their particular interests or talents. Our second year trainees participate in the summer associate programme in New York for up to 10 weeks.

Benefits
The range of benefits includes: private health care, travel season ticket loan, pension and income protection.

Partners 6
Counsel 1
Associates 6
Total Trainees 3

Contact
Tuula Davis, Office Manager
(020) 7710 9800

Method of application
Candidates should e-mail a CV and cover letter to
recruitmentlondon@curtis.com

Selection procedure
Three rounds of interviews with partners and the chance to meet current associates and trainees.

Closing date for 2014/5
Applicants for September 2014 should apply by end March 2014. We are also currently accepting applicants for September 2015.

Application
Training contracts p.a. 2
Applications p.a. c. 300
% interviewed p.a. 8%
Required degree grade 2:1

Training
Salary
1st year £38,000
2nd year salary £42,000
Holiday entitlement 25 days

Post-qualification
100% of trainees offered job on qualification

Overseas and regional offices
We have offices in Astana, Almaty, Ashgabat, Buenos Aires, Dubai, Frankfurt, Houston, Istanbul, Kuwait City (Associated Firm), London, Mexico City, Milan, Muscat, New York, Paris and Washington DC

A-Z of Solicitors

CURTIS
Curtis, Mallet-Prevost, Colt & Mosle LLP

Davenport Lyons

30 Old Burlington Street, London W1S 3NL
Tel: (020) 7468 2600 Fax: (020) 7437 8216
Website: www.davenportlyons.com

Firm profile
A leading business law firm offering a partner-led service. The firm provides commercial advice to its clients across a broad range of market sectors. The firm offers a unique combination of very strong corporate, tax, litigation and property capabilities coupled with specialist media and intellectual property expertise. If you want to train in a firm that has a warm and friendly environment, then Davenport Lyons is the ideal place to start your career as a successful solicitor.

Main areas of work
The firm provides comprehensive advice from its 18 legal services covering: corporate; intellectual property/rights; dispute resolution; property; commercial; tax; film and TV; employment and immigration; competition; defamation and privacy; information technology; insolvency and corporate reconstruction; licensing; aviation and travel; music; private client and wealth management; family and children and banking and finance.

Trainee profile
Davenport Lyons is looking for candidates with excellent academic qualifications (2:1 and above, good A level results) and interesting backgrounds, who are practical and can demonstrate good business acumen. Candidates should have a breadth of interests and foreign language skills are an advantage. In short, the firm is looking for well-rounded individuals.

Training environment
The training programme consists of four six-month seats. During each seat trainees receive mid and end of seat reviews, and each seat has a dedicated trainee supervisor. Davenport Lyons has an on-going in-house training and lecture programme. The firm prides itself on offering interesting, hands-on training with trainees being encouraged to develop their own client relationships and to handle their own files under appropriate supervision, therefore being treated as junior fee earners. The firm aims to make its training contract informative, educational, practical, supportive and as enjoyable as possible.

Benefits
Season ticket loan; client introduction bonus; contribution to gym membership; discretionary bonus; 23 days holiday; life assurance; Employee Support Programme; pension and private health scheme.

Vacation placements
A limited number of places are available on the summer vacation scheme, which runs during July and August. Remuneration is £250 per week.

Sponsorship & awards
The firm does not offer financial assistance.

Partners 41
Fee Earners 57
Total Staff 191
Trainees 17

Contact
Dawn McEwen
Operations Director
Michael Hatchwell
Training Partner

Method of application
Apply online at
www.davenportlyons.com

Selection procedure
Interviews

Closing date for 2016
30 June 2014

Application
Training contracts p.a. 8
Applications p.a. c. 400
% interviewed p.a. 10%
Required degree grade 2:1, AAB
at A Level (340+ UCAS Points)

Training
Salary
1st Year trainee
£33,000 - £33,666
2nd Year trainee
£34,332 - £35,000
Holiday entitlement 23 days
% of trainees with a
non-law degree p.a. 70%

Post-qualification
% of trainees offered job
on qualification
(2012) 60%

Office
London

Davenport Lyons

Davis Polk & Wardwell London LLP

99 Gresham Street London EC2V 7NG
Tel: (020) 7418 1300 Fax: (020) 7418 1400
Website: www.davispolk.com/careers/uk

Partners 9	
Counsel 3	
Associates 33	

Contact
martha.jeacle@davispolk.com

Method of application
If interested in applying for a training contract or a place on our vacation scheme, please visit our website at www.davispolk.com/careers/uk for information on how to apply.

Selection procedure
Interview

Closing date for 2016
31 July 2014

Application
Training contracts p.a.
4-6
Required degree grade 2:1

Training
Salary
1st year £50,000
2nd year £55,000

Post-qualification
Compensation £100,000

Overseas offices
New York, Menlo Park, Washington DC, Paris, Madrid, Hong Kong, Beijing, Tokyo and Sao Paulo

Firm profile
Davis Polk is a global law firm. For more than 160 years, its lawyers have advised industry-leading companies and major financial institutions on their most challenging legal and business matters. Davis Polk ranks among the world's preeminent law firms across the entire range of its practice. With more than 750 lawyers in New York, Menlo Park, Washington DC, London, Paris, Madrid, Hong Kong, Beijing, Tokyo and Sao Paulo, the firm operates from key business centres around the world to provide clients with seamlessly integrated legal services of the highest calibre.

Main areas of work
We advise European companies, private equity firms, financial institutions and governments on all areas of business and finance, and we are regularly involved in the largest and most important securities offerings and M&A transactions in Europe.

Trainee profile
We seek to hire applicants from a variety of backgrounds with outstanding academic and non-academic achievements, personal skills and creativity, and with a demonstrated willingness to take initiative. We strive to find exceptional lawyers who share our commitment to excellence and who will be collaborative and supportive colleagues.

Training environment
Davis Polk trainees will work closely with and learn from our senior lawyers in London and in our offices around the world as we advise leading British, European and global corporations across the spectrum of their most complex legal matters. Given the quality of instruction, the meaningful legal experience gained on major global transactions and the opportunity to be a part of a dynamic and rapidly expanding practice at one of the world's truly preeminent law firms, there is no better place than Davis Polk for an aspiring solicitor to begin a career. Davis Polk trainees will also have the opportunity to work for a period in our New York office.

Benefits
Private medical insurance, life insurance, pension scheme, season ticket loan, subsidised gym membership, Employee Assistance Programme.

Vacation schemes
Davis Polk offers two-week vacation schemes in the summer for students interested in training contracts. During each vacation scheme, students will have the opportunity to work on international transactions for a variety of the firm's clients and attend training programs designed to teach skills required to become an effective solicitor as well as information sessions focused on the work of our UK practice. Students will also have the opportunity to experience Davis Polk's culture through interactions with lawyer mentors and attendance at social events.

We will be accepting applications for 2014 summer vacation schemes (please visit our website at www.davispolk.com/careers/uk for information on how to apply) from 1 November 2013 through 31 January 2014. We expect to offer 16-20 places on our vacation schemes in 2014.

Sponsorship & awards
GDL and LPC fees and maintenance grants are paid.

Davis Polk

Dechert LLP

160 Queen Victoria Street, London EC4V 4QQ
Tel: (020) 7184 7000 Fax: (020) 7184 7001
Email: application@dechert.com
Website: www.dechert.com www.careers.dechert.com

Firm profile
Dechert LLP is a dynamic international law firm, with 2,000 professionals across the USA, Europe, Middle East and Asia. London is the third largest office, after Philadelphia and New York.

Main areas of work
The London office has particular strengths in investment funds, corporate and securities (including private equity), litigation (including international dispute resolution, white collar and securities, EU trade and government affairs and arbitration), and finance and real estate; and smaller teams in employment, IP and tax.

Trainee profile
Dechert looks for enthusiasm, intelligence, an ability to find practical solutions and for powers of expression and persuasion. Undergraduates and graduates from any discipline are welcome to apply.

Training environment
The highly personalised six seat rotation system allows trainees to structure their training contract to their interests and aspirations and allows opportunity for secondments to overseas offices as well as to clients. Your seat plan and professional development are guided by the graduate recruitment manager, the graduate recruitment partners and your dedicated trainee partner. Your trainee partner is allocated to you when you start your training contract and acts as a sounding board and a source of support until you qualify.

Vacation placements
Dechert runs a two week vacation placement in the summer and Insight Days in the spring. The firm's vacation placement programmes are aimed at penultimate year law students. During our placements visitors are supervised by a partner or senior associate and they undertake a variety of tasks such as research projects and attending client meetings. Training sessions are also hosted throughout the scheme, on a range of topics, such as presentation and client pitch skills. The closing date for applications is 31 January 2014. The Insight Days are designed to give participants an overview of the firm, its practice areas and its work. Participants also have the opportunity to meet trainees and associates and take part in a legal case study.

Sponsorship & awards
The firm pays LPC fees plus £10,000 sponsorship.

Partners 41*
Assistant Solicitors 87*
Total Trainees 26*
*denotes London figure

Contact
application@dechert.com or
Graduate Recruitment Team
020 7184 7576

Method of application
Online

Selection procedure
An assessment morning or afternoon which includes interviews with partners, associates and recruiters and written tests

Closing date for 2016
31 July 2014

Application
Training contracts p.a. 10-12
Applications p.a. 1,000+
% interviewed p.a. Approx 5%
Required degree grade 2:1 (or capability of attaining a 2:1)

Training
Salary Current trainee salaries as of September 2013 £41,000 and £46,000. Trainee salaries are reviewed annually.
Holiday entitlement 25 days
% of trainees with a non-law degree p.a. Varies
No. of seats available abroad p.a. varies (Brussels, Dublin, Moscow, and client secondment and judicial secondment opportunities)

Post-qualification
Salary £68,000
% of trainees offered job on qualification 89% (2013)

Overseas offices
Almaty, Austin, Beijing, Boston, Brussels, Charlotte, Chicago, Dubai, Frankfurt, Hartford, Hong Kong, LA, Luxembourg, Moscow, Munich, New York, Orange County, Paris, Philadelphia, Princeton, San Francisco, Silicon Valley, Tblisi, Washington

Dentons

One Fleet Place, London EC4M 7WS
Tel: (020) 7242 1212 Fax: (020) 7320 6555
Email: graduaterecruitment@dentons.com
Website: graduates.dentons.com

Firm profile
Dentons is a client-focused global legal practice delivering quality and value, with lawyers and professionals in 79 locations worldwide. We have disciplined focus on meeting the evolving needs of our clients, in 24 sectors.

Main areas of work
Dentons offers an international legal practice focused on quality in the following industry sectors: energy, transport and infrastructure, financial institutions and funds, government, health and life sciences, insurance, manufacturing, real estate, retail and hotels, technology, media and telecommunications.

Trainee profile
We're looking for people with talent, personality and ambition to join our London, Milton Keynes and Middle East offices. We accept candidates from any degree discipline, but you must have a strong academic and extracurricular record of achievement. Dentons lawyers are good team players with excellent interpersonal skills and the flexibility to grow with the firm.

Training environment
As a trainee you will undertake four six-month seats, including a contentious seat or attending an external litigation course. Your transactional experience will include banking (if in London) and corporate, construction or real estate (if in Milton Keynes). Middle East trainees will spend two seats in the UK and two in the Middle East.

Benefits
You'll earn a competitive salary. In London £37,000 in your first year, rising to £40,000 in your second year. In Milton Keynes you'll earn £25,500 in your first year, rising to £27,500 in your second. On top of that you'll enjoy numerous benefits – and you'll get to choose the ones that best fit your lifestyle, from 24 days' holiday, private health cover, income protection insurance, life assurance, pension and many others.

Vacation placements
We offer a one-week summer scheme in Milton Keynes for both law and non-law (July) and in London for law students (July).

In London we also offer open days for non-law students (December).

These placements consist of business games, department visits and social events, giving potential trainees an insight into commercial law and our way of life at SNR Denton.

Sponsorship & awards
We'll also pay your GDL/LPC law school fees during actual years of study, as well as study maintenance grants of £5,000 per year of study (£6,000 in London).

Partners 151
Fee-earners 615
Total Trainees 60

Contact
Alexandra Mundy

Method of application
Online application form

Selection procedure
Selection test; occupational personality questionnaire; first interview; second interview and case study

Closing date for 2016
Non-law – 31 March 2014
Law – 31 July 2014

Application
Training contracts p.a. 15
Applications p.a. 1,500
% interviewed p.a. 10%
Required degree grade 2:1

Training
Salary in London
1st year £37,000
2nd year £40,000
Salary in Milton Keynes
1st year £25,500
2nd year £27,500
Holiday entitlement 24 days
% of trainees with a
non-law degree p.a. 30%
No. of seats available
abroad p.a. Currently 2

Post-qualification
Salary (2012) £59,000
% of trainees offered job
on qualification (2013) 90%

SNR Denton Offices
London and Milton Keynes in the UK and across Europe, Middle East, CIS, America, Canada, Africa, South East Asia and Central Asia. For more location details please see our website.

DENTONS ▸

DLA Piper UK LLP

3 Noble Street, London EC2V 7EE
Tel: (0870) 0111 111
Email: recruitment.graduate@dlapiper.com
Website: www.dlapipergraduates.co.uk

Firm profile
DLA Piper is a global law firm positioned to help companies with their legal needs anywhere in the world. They want to take care of the world's business and believe in building long-term client relationships by being accessible; responsive; straightforward; smart; decisive and focused. They want their people to develop commercial and business skills, but this has to make a positive impact on local communities. This is why they have an extensive corporate responsibility programme that includes pro bono work as well as charitable projects.

Main areas of work
Corporate; employment; finance and projects; intellectual property and technology; litigation and regulatory; real estate, restructuring; and tax

Trainee profile
Every year DLA Piper recruits a diverse group of talented individuals who have a consistently strong academic performance, formidable commercial acumen, who are articulate, ambitious, driven and dynamic with sharp minds, enthusiasm and intellectual curiosity.

Training environment
As a trainee you will complete four six-month seats and are given an opportunity to express which areas of law you would like to experience. There are also opportunities to do a seat abroad, or a client secondment.

If you want responsibility, and display the right level of aptitude, you will be given as much as you can handle. This approach, combined with an open door policy, provides DLA Piper trainees with an excellent foundation on which to build their careers.

Sponsorship & awards
Where training contracts are secured prior to course completion, DLA Piper offers full funding for the LPC and the GDL, as well as a maintenance grant of up to £7,000.

Work placement scheme
DLA Piper offers placements to 130 people across our UK offices and use these to recruit their trainees. Attendees sit with two different departments and are fully immersed into life at DLA Piper. They are given real work to develop legal, and wider workplace skills and take part in work shadowing, court visits, bespoke presentations, group activities and social events with the firm's trainees.

Partners 280*
Fee-earners 620*
Total Trainees 182
*denotes UK figures

Contact
Sally Carthy, Head of Graduate Recruitment

Method of application
Online

Selection procedure
Interviews, group exercise, assessment days

Closing date for 2016
31 July 2014

Application
Training contracts p.a. 90
Applications p.a. 3,800
% interviewed p.a. 13%
Required degree grade 2:1

Training
Salary 2012
1st year
£37,000 (London)
£25,000 (English Regions)
£22,000 (Scotland)
2nd year
£40,000 (London)
£27,000 (English Regions)
£24,000 (Scotland)
Holiday entitlement 25 days

Post-qualification
Salary 2012
£60,000 (London)
£37,000 (English Regions)
£34,000 (Scotland)
% of trainees offered a job on qualification 83% (2012)

Regional / Overseas offices
Australia, Austria, Bahrain, Belgium, Birmingham, Brazil, China, Czech Republic, Edinburgh, France, Georgia, Germany, Hong Kong, Hungary, Italy, Japan, Kuwait, Leeds, Liverpool, London, Manchester, Mexico, Netherlands, Norway, Oman, Poland, Qatar, Romania, Russia, Saudi Arabia, Sheffield, Singapore, Slovak Republic, Spain, Thailand, Turkey, UAE, Ukraine, USA

DWF LLP

1 Scott Place, 2 Hardman Street, Manchester M3 3AA
Tel: (0161) 603 5000 Fax: (0161) 603 5050
Email: trainees@dwf.co.uk
Website: www.dwf.co.uk

Firm profile
DWF is a UK business law firm with international reach. Our legal experts combine real commercial understanding and deep sector knowledge to help clients anticipate issues, create opportunities and achieve the outcomes they need.

DWF was ranked 2nd for the quality of its legal advice in the 2012 Client Satisfaction Report by Legal Week.

The firm employs over 2,450 people, including 296 partners and 1,520 fee earners.

Main areas of work
Our legal teams are arranged under four core practice groups, providing a broad range of expertise which enables us to meet the varied needs of our clients. These practice groups are Corporate and Banking, Insurance, Litigation and Real Estate.

We align ourselves with our clients through our sector groups which reflect the specific service needs of our clients in those sectors. These sector groups include energy and industrials; financial services; food, retail and leisure; local and central government; technology, media and telecoms; and transport.

Trainee profile
We're looking for people who are committed to a career in law, who enjoy working as part of a busy team and respond positively to a challenge.

Our trainees share ambition and the ability to bring something new and valuable to our team. Commercial acumen, good organisational skills and a fresh way of thinking about client needs are all hallmarks of a DWF team member. We also like to see candidates who have spent some time pursuing interests outside of academia.

Training environment
Our unique training contract is divided into six four-month 'seats'. This allows trainees to get a real taste of the variety of work we offer and make informed decisions about their future career. Trainees have the opportunity to sit in specialist departments within all of our practice groups and return to a preferred department for their final seat; enabling up to eight months pre-qualification experience in their chosen field.

Halfway through each seat, a senior member of our dedicated HR team will meet with each trainee to discuss progress. Trainees are also able to discuss which practice area they would like to target for their next seat rotation. We always do our best to accommodate seat preferences. Having completed four seats our trainees have a detailed discussion with the training principal about their future aspirations.

Vacation placements
The summer vacation scheme is an excellent way to learn more about the firm and experience first-hand life as a DWF trainee. During the week you will become fully immersed in one of our many practice groups, complete legal skills training and attend numerous social events.

Partners 296
Other fee-earners 1,520
Total Trainees c. 96

Contact
Katherine Elam
Graduate & Apprentice Talent
Specialist

Method of application
Apply online via www.dwf.co.uk

Selection procedure
First interview, assessment
centre and final selection day

Closing date for 2015/2016
Undergraduates 31 July 2014

Application
Training contracts p.a. 48
Applications p.a. c. 3,000
% interviewed p.a. 10%
Required degree grade 2:1

Training
Salary
1st year (2013)
up to £25,000 (Regional)
£35,000 (London)
Holiday entitlement
25 days p.a.

Post-qualification
% of trainees offered job
on qualification
2011 100% 2012 79%

Benefits
Flexible benefits scheme
including insurance, life
assurance, contributory pension
and others

Sponsorship & awards
LPC / Scottish Diploma

Offices
Birmingham, Bristol, Edinburgh,
Dublin, Glasgow, Leeds,
Liverpool, London, Manchester,
Newcastle, Preston

A-Z of Solicitors

Edwards Wildman Palmer UK LLP

Dashwood, 69 Old Broad Street, London EC2M 1QS
Tel: (020) 7583 4055 Fax: (020) 7353 7377
Email: swarnes@edwardswildman.com
Web: www.trainee.edwardswildman.com

Firm profile

Edwards Wildman is a growing international firm working with Fortune 500, FTSE 250 clients and start-up companies alike, in a full spectrum of industries. Our clients know us as trusted legal and business advisers. The firm has been fortunate to receive a number of recent accolades including 2012 London Office of the Year by Legal Week in addition to 2012 Most Innovative Law Firm by the Financial Times in recognition of the firm's litigation practice.

Main areas of work

Our lawyers are known internationally for their work in private equity, venture capital, corporate and finance, complex litigation, insurance and reinsurance and intellectual property. We also have a number of other specialisms in our London office. The firm is involved in the highest quality work with an international context. We advise multi-national corporates, financial institutions and governments worldwide on a range of multi-jurisdictional and cross-border disputes, transactions and regulatory matters.

Trainee profile

Our trainees need to be stimulated by solving business and legal challenges, therefore academic excellence, great analytical skills and a rigorous approach are essential. We seek engaging individuals with a sense of humour in addition to the initiative and drive to make their mark. We value good commercial judgement, adaptability and those capable of thinking on their feet. Understanding teamwork, evidence of leadership and taking on responsibilities, interesting achievements and making the most of non-academic opportunities will help applicants stand-out.

Training environment

We believe you learn best by doing, with trainees valued for the substantive contributions they make to the matters they work on. Trainees meet clients, develop responsibility for their own work and get involved in marketing and client development activities. Trainees spend six months in four of the firm's practice areas being supervised by a partner or senior associate. There are also secondment opportunities to clients. Our tailored training programme develops the technical skills and knowledge needed in those areas. Supervisors, buddies, partner mentors and the trainee recruitment team, ensures you have a variety of guidance and support enabling you to build on and maximise the knowledge and skills gained.

Benefits

Bupa, STL, subsidised gym membership, pension scheme, life assurance, subsidised café, cycle to work scheme, EAP, eye tests, social events and sports.

Vacation placements

Two-week placement for 8 students in June/July of each year. We also host open days at Easter, Summer and Christmas – check website for dates and details. Closing date for summer placements - 31 January 2014. Closing date for open days - check website.

Sponsorship

GDL and LPC funding, plus maintenance allowance of £7,000 (London) / £6,500 (outside London).

Partners 29
Assistant Solicitors 39
Total Trainees 15

Contact
Sarah Warnes 020 7556 4414

Method of application
Online applications only
www.trainee.edwardswildman.com

Selection procedure
Assessment centre involving business case study, verbal and numerical critical reasoning tests. Successful candidates are interviewed by partners/senior associates.

Closing date for 2016
31 July 2014

Application
Training contracts p.a. up to 8
Applications p.a. 700 approx
% interviewed p.a. 5-8%
Required degree grade 2:1

Training
Salary
1st year £38,000
2nd year £42,000
Holiday entitlement 25 days

Post-qualification
Salary £61,000
Trainees offered job on qualification 75% (2012)

Summer placements
No. of places p.a. 8
Open days 4 accomodating up to 100 students in total.
Closing date for open days check website

Overseas & Regional Offices
UK: London, US: New York, Boston, Chicago, Hartford, Los Angeles, Orange County, Providence, Stamford, Washington, West Palm Beach, Madison, Ft Lauderdale, Asia: Hong Kong, Tokyo.

A-Z of Solicitors

Eversheds

1 Wood Street, London EC2V 7WS
Tel: (0845) 497 9797 Fax: (0845) 497 4919
Email: gradrec@eversheds.com
Website: www.eversheds.com

Firm profile

Eversheds is one of the world's largest corporate law firms. Committed locally, but connected globally, with over 40 offices based in the world's major economic centres, with a proven track record of delivering consistently high quality legal services across jurisdictions.

Eversheds operates as one team, from 44 offices in 26 countries. Our people share a distinctive culture which has deep client relationships at its core. Whether providing advice which is complex or straightforward, multi-national or local, an attitude of delivering only the very best underscores everything we do.

Main areas of work

Core work: company commercial, litigation and dispute management, real estate, human resources (employment and pensions).

Trainee profile

Our firm attracts great people and we've created an environment where they can achieve great things.

True, you will need a strong academic background and proven ability to apply your intellect to complex problems. But that's just the start. Eversheds trainees need to be multi-faceted people who combine extreme professionalism with outstanding expertise, genuine approachability and real personality.

Training environment

Our training contracts consist of four seats of six months each over two years. At least one seat must be in a contentious area. As part of your training contract, you can also apply to do a secondment at a client office or at another Eversheds office in the UK or internationally. You will also take part in a full programme of personal and commercial development skills training, including finance and business, communication, presenting, business writing, client care, professional standards and advocacy.

Vacation placements

Two week summer placements are available across Eversheds' UK offices. Applications can be made at www.eversheds.com. The application deadline for the 2014 Schemes is 31 January 2014. Please visit the website for the dates of when these will take place.

Sponsorship & awards

GDL fees paid, plus maintenance grant of £7,000 (London) or £5,000 (other regions).

LPC fees paid, plus maintenance grant of £7,000 (London) or £5,000 (other regions).

Offices

Amman, Abu Dhabi, Amsterdam, Baghdad, Berne, Birmingham, Bratislava, Brussels, Bucharest, Budapest, Cambridge, Cardiff, Doha, Dubai, Dublin, Edinburgh, Geneva, Hamburg, Hong Kong, Ipswich, Johannesburg, Leeds, London, Madrid, Manchester, Milan, Munich, Newcastle, Nottingham, Ostrava, Paris, Prague, Riga, Riyadh, Rome, Rotterdam, Shanghai, Singapore, Stockholm, Tallinn, Vienna, Vilnius, Warsaw, Zurich. In addition the firm has close relationships with preferred law firms across Europe, Middle East and America. Further details are available on the firm's website.

Partners 347
Lawyers 1,800
Total Trainees 120

Contact
gradrec@eversheds.com

Method of application
Apply online at
www.eversheds.com

Selection procedure
Application form and online tests, telephone interview, face to face interview, assessment day

Closing date
31st January 2014 for 2014 Summer Vacation Placement
31st July 2014 for 2016 Training Contracts
Applications open for both on 1st October 2013

Application
Training contracts p.a. 50-60
Applications p.a. 4,500
% interviewed p.a. 40%
Required degree grade 2:1 and 320 UCAS points

Training
Salary
1st year (2013)
London £36,000
Other regions £25,000
2nd year (2013)
London £37,000
Other regions £26,500
Holiday entitlement 25 days
% of trainees with a non-law degree p.a. 45%
No. of seats available abroad p.a. 6+

Post-qualification
Salary (2013)
London £59,000
Other regions £37,000
% of trainees offered job on qualification (2013) 85%

EVERSHEDS

A-Z of Solicitors

Farrer & Co LLP

66 Lincoln's Inn Fields, London WC2A 3LH
Tel: (020) 3375 7000 Fax: (020) 3375 7001
Email: graduaterecruitment@farrer.co.uk
Website: www.farrer.co.uk

Firm profile
Farrer & Co is a mid-sized London law firm. The firm provides specialist advice to a large number of prominent private, institutional and commercial clients. Farrer & Co has built a successful law firm based on the goodwill of close client relationships, outstanding expertise in niche sectors and a careful attention to personal service and quality.

Main areas of work
The firm's breadth of expertise is reflected by the fact that it has an outstanding reputation in fields as diverse as matrimonial law, offshore tax planning, employment, heritage work, charity law, defamation and sports law.

Trainee profile
Trainees are expected to be highly motivated individuals with keen intellects and interesting and engaging personalities. Those applicants who appear to break the mould – as shown by their initiative for organisation, leadership, exploration, or enterprise – are far more likely to get an interview than the erudite, but otherwise unimpressive, student.

Training environment
The training programme involves each trainee in the widest range of cases, clients and issues possible in a single law firm, taking full advantage of the wide range of practice areas at Farrer & Co by offering six seats, rather than the more usual four. This provides a broad foundation of knowledge and experience and the opportunity to make an informed choice about the area of law in which to specialise. A high degree of involvement is encouraged under the direct supervision of solicitors and partners. Trainees attend an induction programme and regular internal lectures. The training partner reviews trainees' progress at the end of each seat and extensive feedback is given. The firm has a very friendly atmosphere and regular sporting and social events.

Benefits
Flexible benefits scheme, sporting teams/clubs, season ticket loan, 25 days' holiday, group income protection, group life assurance, company doctor, subsidised gym membership, subsidised yoga/pilates, pension scheme, private medical insurance after one year, wellwoman/wellman checks.

Vacation placements
Places for 2014: 30; Duration: 2 weeks at Easter, two schemes for 2 weeks in summer; Remuneration: £275 p.w.; Closing date: 31 January 2014.

Sponsorship & awards
CPE Funding: Fees paid plus £6,000 maintenance. LPC Funding: Fees paid plus £6,000 maintenance.

Partners 73
Assistant Solicitors 147
Total Trainees 20

Contact
Trainee Recruitment Manager

Method of application
Online via the firm's website

Selection procedure
Interviews with Trainee Recruitment Partner and partners

Closing date for 2016
31 July 2014

Application
Training contracts p.a. 10
Applications p.a. 1000
% interviewed p.a. 5%
Required degree grade 2:1

Training
Salary
1st year (Sept 2013) £34,000
2nd year (Sept 2013) £37,000
Holiday entitlement 25 days
% of trainees with non-law degrees p.a. 40-60%

Post-qualification
Salary (2013) £57,000
% of trainees offered job on qualification (2013) 100%
% of partners (as at 2013) who joined as trainees over 60%

FARRER&Co

Fladgate LLP

16 Great Queen Street, London WC2B 5DG
Tel: (020) 3036 7000 Fax: (020) 3036 7600
Email: trainees@fladgate.com Website: www.fladgate.com

Firm profile
Fladgate LLP is an innovative, progressive and thriving law firm which prides itself on its friendly and professional working environment. We are based in modern, attractive offices in London's Covent Garden.

Main areas of work
The firm provides a wide range of legal services to a portfolio of prestigious clients in the UK and overseas, including multinationals, major institutions and listed companies, clearing banks, lenders and entrepreneurs. Fladgate LLP's lawyers have experience in most major areas of practice and the firm combines an accessible and responsive style of service with first-class technical skills and in-depth expertise.

The firm has a strong international dimension based on multi-lingual and multi-qualified lawyers working in London and complemented by access to an extensive network of overseas lawyers. The firm operates specialist teams which serve continental Europe, India, Israel, South Africa, the US and the Middle East.

The firm's principal departments comprise corporate (which includes tax, private capital, restructuring, employment, IP and technology), litigation and real estate (which includes planning, construction and real estate litigation). These are supported by specialist cross-departmental teams that provide co-ordinated advice on a range of issues.

Trainee profile
Fladgate LLP seeks trainees with enthusiasm, confidence and excellent interpersonal skills. You must be able to work both independently and in a team, and will be expected to show common sense and initiative. Awareness of the commercial interests of clients is essential. You will have a minimum of a 2:1 degree, although not necessarily in law, together with three excellent A levels or equivalent.

Training environment
Typically, you will complete four six-month seats. Each seat will bring you into contact with new clients and colleagues, and you can expect to gain real hands-on experience of a variety of deals and projects, both large and small. In each seat you will work alongside senior lawyers who will supervise your development and ensure that you are involved in challenging and interesting work. In addition to on-the-job training, each department has a comprehensive training schedule of seminars and workshops covering a range of legal and skills training.

The firm has a modern culture and an open-door policy where trainees are given early responsibility and encouraged to achieve their full potential.

Benefits
Pension, permanent health insurance, life assurance, season ticket loan, sports club loan, private medical.

Partners 57
Assistant Solicitors 38
Total Trainees 8

Contact
Mrs Annabelle Lawrence, Senior Human Resources Manager

Method of application
Information and an application form are available at the firm's website www.fladgate.com

Selection procedure
Assessment day plus interview

Application
For more details please visit www.fladgate.com
Training contracts p.a. 4
Required degree grade 2:1

Training
Starting salary £32,000
Holiday entitlement
25 days

Post-qualification
Salary £55,000

Foot Anstey LLP

Salt Quay House, 4 North East Quay, Sutton Harbour, Plymouth, PL4 0BN
Tel: (01752) 675000 Fax: (01752) 675500
Email: trainingcontracts@footanstey.com Website: www.footanstey.com

Firm profile
Delivering exceptional client service has enabled Foot Anstey to expand rapidly in recent times, notably establishing a strong Bristol office which has doubled in size in less than two years. Under the leadership of managing partner John Westwell, the firm continues to invest in people and technology to ensure value and quality, focussed on helping clients to achieve their strategic objectives and manage risk. Targeted talent acquisition has seen Foot Anstey recruit 15 new partners from national, City and international firms in the past 18 months. Our growing client base comprises of national and regional businesses and public sector organisations. The firm is truly committed to strengthening relationships with local communities and actively engages in corporate social projects from conventional fund raising, to support for the long-term unemployed.

Main areas of work
Corporate: the firm's respected corporate team supports a wide range of clients, from global businesses to entrepreneurs and business owners. Our corporate team is comprised of leading experts in private equity, banking, restructuring and insolvency, international transactions, tax, and company secretarial.

Commercial: the team are trusted experts to private, public and third sector organisations, advising on all aspects of business, including research and development through to the post sales environment.

Dispute resolution: the rapidly growing dispute resolution team looks after a wide range of commercial disputes, with highly specialist teams offering advice in a number of niche areas.

Employment: the firm's employment law team is the largest in the South West, working with major national and regional employers.

Real estate: the property team supports a large portfolio of public sector and private clients handling prestigious city work alongside large regional and local projects.

Clinical negligence: the highly rated clinical negligence team has over 25 specialists with vast experience in handling high-value and complex cases.

Wealth and succession: the firm also has a strong wealth and succession team advising on a range of work from tax planning to wealth and succession management and family law.

Trainee profile
The firm welcomes applications from all law and non-law graduates who have a good academic background, exceptional communication skills and the ability to work as part of a dynamic team.

Training environment
Trainees undertake four seats of six months. Regular communication between the trainees and supervisors ensures an open and friendly environment. The Professional Skills Course is sponsored by Foot Anstey and provided by a highly regarded external training provider.

Benefits
Our flexible benefits package includes: 25 days' holiday (plus BH) and the option to buy/sell holiday, contributory pension scheme, life assurance, cycle scheme and childcare vouchers. In addition, non-contractual benefits are offered (such as the 'lifestyle hour' where employees benefit from enjoying one hour off work each week to promote a healthy work/life balance).

Vacation placements
Please see the website for the deadline and application form for the 2014 summer placement scheme.

Sponsorship & awards
Grant available towards LPC and living expenses.

Partners 51
Assistant Solicitors 63
Trainees 13

Contact
Emma.Watts@footanstey.com

Method of application
Online at www.footanstey.com

Selection procedure
Online Training Contract Application Form and Assessment Day

Closing date for 2016
Applications for a 2016 training contract should be made by 1 June 2014. The deadline for the 2014 summer placement scheme is 28 April 2014.

Application
Training Contracts p.a. 4-6
Applications p.a. 300
% interviewed 10%
Required degree grade Usually 2:1 degree

Training
Starting salaries TBC

Post-qualification
Salary (2013) £33,750
% of trainees offered job on qualification (2013) 100%
% of assistant solicitors who joined as trainees 42%
% of partners who joined as trainees 9%

Offices
Bristol, Taunton, Exeter, Plymouth, Truro

Forbes

73 Northgate, Blackburn BB2 1AA
Tel: (01254) 580000 Fax: (01254) 222216
Email: graduate.recruitment@forbessolicitors.co.uk

Firm profile

Forbes is one of the largest practices in the north with 36 partners and over 360 members of staff based in nine offices across the north of England. The firm has a broad based practice dealing with both commercial and private client work and can therefore provide a varied and exciting training contract. The firm is however especially noted for excellence in its business law, social housing, insurance crime, family and employment departments. It has a number of Higher Court Advocates and the firm holds many Legal Aid Agency Contracts. Underlying the practice is a strong commitment to quality, training and career development – a commitment underlined by the fact that Forbes was one of the first firms to be recognised as an Investor in People and its ISO 9001 accreditation. For applicants looking for a 'city' practice without the associated hassles of working in a city then Forbes could be it. The firm can offer the best of both worlds – a large firm with extensive resources and support combined with a commitment to quality, people and the personal touch.

Main areas of work

Business law, civil litigation, social housing, insurance, crime, family and employment services.

Trainee profile

Forbes looks for high-calibre recruits with strong North West connections and good academic records, who are also keen team players. Candidates should have a total commitment to client service and identify with the firm's philosophy of providing practical straightforward legal advice.

Training environment

A tailored training programme involves six months in four of the following: crime, insurance in Leeds, Manchester or Blackburn, social housing, family, employment, business law, wills, trusts and probate, conveyancing (domestic and commercial). Trainees may also be given the opportunity to experience secondments at major clients.

Partners 36	
Assistant Solicitors 62	
Total Trainees 8	
Contact	
Graduate Recruitment Manager	
Method of application	
Online application	
Selection procedure	
Interview with partners	
Closing date for 2016	
31 July 2014	
If no invite to interview is received by 31/08/14 applicants to assume they have been unsuccesful.	
Application	
Training contracts p.a. 4	
Applications p.a. 350 plus	
% interviewed p.a. Varies	
Required degree grade 2:1	
Training	
Salary	
1st year £16,500	
2nd year £19,500	
Holiday entitlement	
20 days p.a.	
Post-qualification	
Salary	
Highly competitive	
% of trainees offered job on qualification (2012) 100%	

forbessolicitors.

Freeth Cartwright LLP

Cumberland Court, 80 Mount Street, Nottingham NG1 6HH
Tel: (0845) 634 2600 Fax: (0115) 859 9600
Email: carole.wigley@freethcartwright.co.uk
Website: www.freethcartwright.co.uk

Firm profile

Freeth Cartwright is a national law firm offering services to a wide range of commercial and private clients. The firm has clients throughout the UK and many of those clients have strong international connections. The firm is the 68th largest in the UK, with a team of over 600 operating from offices in Birmingham, Derby, Leicester, London, Manchester, Milton Keynes, Nottingham, Oxford, Sheffield and Stoke on Trent.

In recognition of organisations that demonstrate high levels of employee engagement, the firm has been awarded star status by Best Companies for 2013. The Legal 500's UK rankings also put the firm as a regional leader in no less than 12 categories and 42 partners are recognised by Chambers UK as leaders in their field. The firm has also won awards for training and recruitment and its IT infrastructure.

Main areas of work

Real estate and construction; commercial services; private client and personal litigation.

Trainee profile

Individuality. There's no such thing as a typical Freeth Cartwright candidate! We are open-minded and interested in people who share this quality. We are looking for individuals who can demonstrate strong academic performance — and would expect candidates to be able to demonstrate the ability to achieve a 2.1 degree or higher at university, in any degree discipline, and have 320 UCAS points (ABB) at A Level (or equivalent). Beyond this we want to see evidence of teamwork, motivation and drive, communication skills, planning and organisation, critical thinking, commercial awareness and commitment - both to a career in law and to a career with Freeth Cartwright.

Training environment

Your training contract will be based on six month rotations through a number of departmental or practice seats. You will sit with a partner or an associate and actively contribute to the day-to-day work of that department - working on transactions and cases, taking real responsibility and gaining plenty of client exposure. Your supervisor will give you regular feedback and conduct an appraisal with you at the end of the seat so you are fully aware of your progress.

Benefits

Trainees with the firm are entitled to 25 days annual holiday, private healthcare and a non-contributory pension.

Sponsorship & awards

An interest free loan is available to cover the cost of the GDL and LPC.

Partners 119
Assistant Solicitors 129
Total Trainees 20

Contact
Carole Wigley, Principal HR Manager
0845 274 6815

Method of application
Online application form
selection procedure
Interview and selection day

Closing date for August 2016
13/07/2014

Application
No. of training contracts p.a 10
Applications p.a. 750
% interviewed 10%
Required degree grade 2:1

Training
Salary for each year of training
Starting salary £21,500
(September 2012)
Holiday entitlement 25 days

Post-qualification
% trainees offered job on 90%
Salary £35,000

Overseas / regional offices
Birmingham, Derby, Leicester, London, Manchester, Milton Keynes, Nottingham, Oxford, Sheffield and Stoke on Trent.

Freeth
Cartwright
LLP

Freshfields Bruckhaus Deringer

65 Fleet Street, London EC4Y 1HS
Tel: (020) 7785 5554 Fax: (020) 7832 7001
Email: uktrainees@freshfields.com
Website: www.freshfields.com/uktrainees

Firm profile

As an international law firm, Freshfields Bruckhaus Deringer advises some of the world's most well known businesses. For graduates keen to pursue a career in commercial law, we offer challenging work that demands a strong intellect and a desire to help ambitious businesses achieve long-term success.

Our lawyers provide clients with a global service from our network of offices across Europe, the Americas and Asia. It is essential that our service is consistent and of the highest quality.

Main areas of work

Our lawyers work in teams, often of no more than three: a partner, an associate and a trainee. Whatever our clients want to achieve, the team's job is to work out how. Is it possible? What will be the most effective way of structuring the deal or tackling the problem? What are the risks? How should it be documented? The team has to provide real commercial solutions, not just what is right or wrong in law.

Organisationally, our lawyers work in one of seven practice areas: antitrust, competition and trade; corporate; dispute resolution; employment, pensions and benefits; finance; real estate; and tax.

Trainee profile

Background, university and the degree studied are immaterial. But every successful candidate has three qualities that are non-negotiable: intellectual talent, excellent English (written and verbal), and a generous spirit.

We pursue premium, cross-border work that is nearly always complicated. This means that the learning curve is steep, so the graduates who do best are those who like to be challenged.

Training environment

Graduates who accept a training contract with us have the opportunity to experience up to eight areas of law – twice the number offered by most law firms. The training is largely provided from our London office but many trainees will also spend time on secondment to a client or to one of our US, European or Asian offices.

Benefits

The firm offers a flexible and competitive benefits package.

Vacation placements

We normally take students on our vacation schemes who are in their penultimate year of an undergraduate degree. Again, you will need to submit an online application. The application window for our 2014 schemes is from 1 October 2013 to 6 January 2014. Since we offer places as we go along, the sooner you apply the better.

Sponsorship & awards

Before a training contract starts all graduates complete the Legal Practice Course; and non-law graduates also need to take the Graduate Diploma in Law before the LPC. The firm meets the cost and provides a maintenance grant for both.

Partners 439
Associates 2,187
Total Trainees 188*
(* London based)

Contact
uktrainees@freshfields.com

Method of application
Online application form

Selection procedure
Online verbal reasoning test,
2 interviews and written test

Closing date for 2016
Please see website

Application
Training contracts p.a. 90
Applications p.a. c.2,000
% interviewed p.a. c.12%

Training
Salary
1st year £39,000
2nd year £44,000
Holiday entitlement 25 days
% of trainees with a
non-law degree p.a. c. 40%
No. of seats available
abroad p.a. c. 42

Post-qualification
Salary £65,000
% of trainees offered job
on qualification 83% (across
February and August 2013)

Overseas offices
Abu Dhabi, Amsterdam,
Bahrain, Barcelona, Beijing,
Berlin, Brussels, Cologne, Dubai,
Düsseldorf, Frankfurt, Hamburg,
Hanoi, Ho Chi Minh City, Hong
Kong, Madrid, Milan, Moscow,
Munich, New York, Paris, Rome,
Shanghai, Singapore, Tokyo,
Vienna, Washington DC

A-Z of Solicitors

 **FRESHFIELDS**

Gateley LLP

One Eleven, Edmund Street, Birmingham B3 2HJ
Tel: (0121) 234 0000 Fax: (0121) 234 0079
Website: www.gateleyuk.com

Partners 150 (firmwide)	
Vacancies 11 (England)	
Total Trainees 30 (England)	
Total Staff 716 (firmwide)	

Contact
HR Department

Closing date for 2016
Training contracts
31 July 2014
Vacation placements
31 January 2014

Training
Salary
1st year £20,000-22,000
(Midlands)
2nd year £22,000-24,000
(Midlands)

Post-qualification
Salary £33,000 (Midlands)

Offices
Birmingham, Dubai, Edinburgh, Glasgow, Leeds, Leicester, London, Nottingham and Manchester.

Firm profile
A 150 partner, UK commercial based practice with an excellent reputation for general commercial work and particular expertise in corporate, plc, commercial, employment, property, construction, insolvency, commercial dispute resolution, banking, tax and shipping.

The firm also offers individual clients a complete private client service including FSA-approved financial advice. The firm is expanding (716 employees) and offers a highly practical, commercial and fast-paced environment. Gately LLP has built an outstanding reputation across the UK for its practical approach, sound advice and professional commitment to its clients. The firm is a full range, multi-disciplinary legal business with expertise in many areas.

Gateley LLP has an enviable reputation as a friendly and sociable place to work. The firm is committed to equality and diversity across the firm.

Trainee profile
To apply for a placement in England: applications are invited from second year law students and final year non-law students and graduates. Applicants should have (or be heading for) a minimum 2.1 degree, and should have at least three Bs (or equivalent) at A-level. Individuals should be hardworking team players capable of using initiative and demonstrating commercial awareness.

Training environment
Four six-month seats with ongoing supervision and appraisals every three months. PSC taken internally. In-house courses on skills such as time management, negotiation, IT, drafting, business skills, marketing, presenting and writing in plain English.

Benefits
Current trainee offered as a 'buddy' – a point of contact within the firm, library available, private health, life assurance (death in service) and season ticket loan.

Vacation placements
Two-week placement over the summer. Deadline for next year's vacation placement scheme is 31 January 2014 and the closing date for 2016 training contracts is 31 July 2014. Apply online at www.gateleyuk.com. Paper/email applications not accepted.

Sponsorship & awards
LPC maintenance grant of £5,000.

Gordons LLP

Riverside West, Whitehall Road, Leeds, LS1 4AW
Tel: (0113) 227 0100 Fax: (0113) 227 0113
Forward House, 8 Duke Street, Bradford, BD1 3QX
Tel: (01274) 202202 Fax: (01274) 202100
Email: recruitment@gordonsllp.com
Website: www.gordonsllp.com

Firm profile
Gordons is a UK Top 100 law firm and one of the largest law firms based entirely in Yorkshire, with offices in Leeds and Bradford. The firm provides commercial and personal legal services to a wide range of businesses and individuals across the region and beyond, from the individual entrepreneur and small family business to the large PLC, and the firm's private client service is equally as comprehensive. The firm's approach is that of a straight-talking, hard-working, ambitious law firm that puts its clients' success before its own. They aim to be the law firm of choice in their region, providing a genuine alternative to the national firms.

Main areas of work
Commercial property; planning and environmental; construction; corporate; pensions; banking; insolvency; commercial litigation; intellectual property; employment; personal injury; private client; family law and residential property.

Trainee profile
The firm is looking for trainees who are eager to learn, have good interpersonal skills, can relate well to clients and who welcome responsibility at an early stage. Initiative, commercial awareness, IT skills and a friendly and professional manner are all essential qualities along with ambition to succeed. The firm sees its trainees as its partners of tomorrow!

Training environment
The firm's trainees spend a minimum of six months in at least three different departments. During the second year of the training contract trainees may state their preference for a particular department and the firm will try to accommodate the request where possible. The firm's trainees work closely with a partner or senior solicitor in each seat and get 'hands on' training with plenty of client contact. They are actively encouraged to get involved with marketing, networking, training, and other events hosted by the firm and/or clients, and the firm itself has regular social activities on offer, both formal and informal. The environment is supportive and friendly with an open door policy across the firm, and the trainees have regular meetings with their supervisors to ensure their progress. The firm aims to offer its trainees positions within the firm on qualification wherever possible.

Benefits
Group personal pension; life assurance; interest-free travel loan; childcare vouchers scheme; 24 days holiday per year plus statutory holidays; free fruit; sports and social club.

Sponsorship & awards
The firm contributes £5,000 towards LPC course fees.

Partners 34
Assistant Solicitors 70
Total Trainees 8

Contact
Karen Mills, HR Manager
Philip Paget, Training Partner

Method of application
Online application via website
www.gordonsllp.com

Selection procedure
One stage interview process, including practical exercise and opportunity to meet current trainees

Closing date for 2016
31 July 2014

Application
Training contracts p.a. 4
Applications p.a. 400
% interviewed p.a. 8%
Required degree grade 2:1

Training
Salary
1st year £20,000
2nd year £22,000
(Reviewed annually)
Holiday entitlement 24 days and statutory
% of trainees with a non-law degree p.a. 50%

Post-qualification
NQ Salary £31,000 p.a.
(Reviewed annually)

GORDONS

Government Legal Service

Tel: 0845 3000 793
Email: glstrainees@tmpw.co.uk
Website: www.gls.gov.uk

Firm profile

The Government Legal Service (GLS) is the collective term for the 2000 lawyers who deliver legal services to an extensive range of Government departments and agencies. These include departments such as the Department for Business, Innovation and Skills, Department of Energy and Climate Change, HM Revenue and Customs, the Home Office, the Ministry of Justice and agencies such as the Treasury Solicitor's Department but there are many more.

Although the legal teams are organisationally separate, together they form the GLS.

Main areas of work

Enabling investment in low carbon energy supplies. Transforming the way in which offenders are managed in the community. Removing the barriers preventing same sex couples from marrying in civil ceremonies. These are just some examples of the legislation our lawyers have been involved in recently. Providing a wide range of legal services to the Government of the day means that GLS lawyers and trainees operate at the cutting edge of law and politics. Regardless of whether they are advising Government ministers on the legality of proposed policy, creating new legislation or representing the Government in high profile litigation cases, it's fair to say that our work is unique, fascinating and challenging in equal measure.

Trainee profile

To join the GLS as a trainee solicitor or pupil barrister, you'll need at least a 2:1 degree (which need not be in law). You must also provide evidence of strong analytical ability, excellent communication and interpersonal skills and motivation for working in public service.

Training environment

The GLS provides a unique and varied training environment for trainees and pupils. Generally, trainee solicitors work in four different areas of practice over a two-year period in the government department to which they are assigned. Pupil barristers divide their year's pupillage between their department and chambers. The GLS prides itself on involving trainees and pupils in the full range of casework conducted by their department. This frequently includes high profile matters and will be under the supervision of senior colleagues.

Benefits

These include professional development opportunities, pension scheme, civilised working hours, generous holiday entitlement and flexible working opportunities.

Vacation placements

10-15 placements are usually available each year. Please check www.gls.gov.uk for further information.

Sponsorship & awards

LPC and BPTC fees as well as other compulsory Professional Skills Course fees. If you intend to study for your LPC or BPTC on a full time basis, you may also be eligible for a grant of about £5,400-£7,600 for the vocational year. The GLS is unable to provide funding for the GDL.

Total Trainees around 50 currently working for the Government Legal Service

Contact
glstrainees@tmpw.co.uk or visit www.gls.gov.uk

Method of application
Online application form, situational judgement test, verbal reasoning test and critical reasoning test

Selection procedure
Half day assessment centre involving a written exercise and competency based interview

Closing date for 2016
31 July 2014

Application
Training contracts p.a. 20-25
Applications p.a. 2000+
% interviewed p.a. 6%
Required degree grade (need not be in law) 2:1

Training
Salary
1st year salary £23,900-£25,500
2nd year salary £25,300-£27,000
Holiday entitlement 25 days on entry

Post-qualification
Salary
£32,000-£40,000
% of trainees accepting job on qualification (2012) 100%

Harbottle & Lewis LLP

Hanover House, 14 Hanover Square, London W1S 1HP
Tel: (020) 7667 5000 Fax: (020) 7667 5100
Email: kathy.beilby@harbottle.com
Website: www.harbottle.com

Firm profile

Harbottle & Lewis provides pro-active legal advice to dynamic and creative clients operating primarily in the following sectors: media and entertainment; technology; advertising, marketing and sponsorship; sport; charities; retail; property; travel and leisure.

Recent highlights include acting for Emirates on the terms of its 10 year sponsorship of the Transport for London cable car, "Emirates Air Line"; acting for Zattikka on its initial incorporation and the acquisition of other gaming companies; advising Comic Relief on matters relating to Comic Relief television programmes, fundraising and challenges overseas; undertaking all financing and production work on "Call the Midwife", advising Conor Maynard in relation to his recording and publishing agreements; and advising Tom Daley on the establishment of his image rights company and on endorsements deals.

In 2012 the firm won the FT's award for the Most Innovative Law Firm in Private Client work and became the British Legal Awards' Private Client / Family Team of the Year.

Main areas of work

Harbottle & Lewis advises businesses and other organisations on corporate, commercial, charity, data protection, employment, family, finance, intellectual property, litigation, property, reputation management and regulatory matters. It advises individuals on issues including asset freezing, family law, high-value residential property, mediation, personal injury, philanthropy, privacy, probate, tax and trusts.

Having been at the centre of many of the entertainment industries' largest and most high profile transactions and cases it has a strong reputation for providing specialist advice to clients in industries such as broadcasting, digital media, fashion, film, interactive entertainment, live events, media finance, music, publishing, television and theatre.

Trainee profile

Trainees will have demonstrated the high academic abilities, commercial awareness, and initiative necessary to become part of a team advising clients in dynamic and demanding industries.

Training environment

The two year training contract is divided into four six-month seats where trainees will be given experience in a variety of legal skills. Seats include, corporate, employment, family/tax/private client, litigation, property, a secondment to a long-standing client as well as a seat in the firm's core industries, including film, interactive entertainment, music, publishing, sport, television and theatre. The firm has a policy of accepting a small number of trainees to ensure they are given relevant and challenging work and are exposed to and have responsibility for a full range of legal tasks. The firm has its own seminar programme in both legal topics and industry know-how. An open door policy and a pragmatic entrepreneurial approach to legal practice provides a stimulating working environment.

Benefits

Lunch provided; season ticket loans; group personal pension scheme; life assurance; 23 days holiday; childcare vouchers; cycle to work scheme; employee assistance scheme.

Sponsorship & awards

LPC fees paid and interest-free loans towards maintenance.

Partners 35
Assistant Solicitors 37
Total Trainees 10

Contact
Kathy Beilby

Method of application
Application form to download from website

Selection procedure
Interview

Closing date for 2016
31 July 2014

Application
Training contracts p.a. 5
Applications p.a. 500
% interviewed p.a. 15%
Required degree grade 2:1

Training
Salary
1st year £30,000 (2013)
2nd year £31,000 (2013)
Holiday entitlement
in the first year 23 days
in the second year 26 days
% of trainees with
a non-law degree p.a. 40%

Post-qualification
Salary (2013) £50k

Harbottle & Lewis

Herbert Smith Freehills LLP

Exchange House, Primrose Street, London EC2A 2EG
Tel: (020) 7374 8000
Email: graduatesuk@hsf.com

Partners 469
Total Trainees 168

Contact
graduatesuk@hsf.com
020 7374 8000

Method of application
Online at
www.herbertsmithfreehills.com
/careers/london/graduates

Selection procedure
Online tests: Verbal reasoning,
critical reasoning and
situational judgement
Assessment Centre: Group
exercise, case study
presentation and a competency
interview.
Required degree grade 2:1

Closing date for August 2016
London training contract
applications should be
submitted between 1 October
2013 and 15 January 2014 for
finalists and graduates and
between 1 June and 31 July
2014 for penultimate-year
students.
Training
Salary
1st year £39,000
2nd year £44,000
25 days holiday (rising to 27
on qualification)

Post Qualification
Salary £63,000
Post-qualification
75% trainees offered job on
qualification - March 2013

Overseas Offices
Asia, Australia, Europe, the
Middle East and the US

Firm profile
As one of the world's leading law firms, Herbert Smith Freehills advises many of the biggest and most ambitious organisations across all major regions of the globe. The firm's clients trust it with their most important transactions, disputes and projects.

The firm is committed to excellence, providing tailored legal advice of the highest quality to major corporations, governments, financial institutions and all types of commercial organisations.

Main areas of work
Herbert Smith Freehills' disputes practice is acknowledged as the number one in the UK and Asia and includes the firm's leading international arbitration practice and award winning in-house advocacy unit, offering a complete litigation service and a realistic alternative to the bar. The firm is a market leader in corporate with a particular strength in the energy sector. Allied to this is a deep vein of quality that runs through its other practice areas, including finance, competition, regulation and trade, real estate and employment, pensions and incentives. The firm also has specialist areas such as intellectual property and tax.

Trainee profile
The firm seeks to recruit people with the desire to be exceptional at what they do. As well as a solid academic record, applicants should have a strong level of commercial awareness and understand the importance of building relationships with clients and colleagues. Herbert Smith Freehills chooses people who are assured, perceptive, ambitious and empathetic. Combine these qualities with a creative and questioning mind and Herbert Smith Freehills will offer you great challenges and rewards.

Training environment
The strength and breadth of the firm's practice areas guarantees excellent training and development opportunities for trainees. Trainees rotate through four six month seats and are encouraged to go on international or client secondments.

Sponsorship & awards
The firm provides funding and a maintenance allowance for GDL and LPC courses.

Vacation placements
Herbert Smith Freehills run winter, spring and summer vacation schemes. The firm also runs two day workshops exclusively for first year students around Easter time, designed to give students an early insight into a career at an international law firm.

Hewitsons LLP

42 Newmarket Road, Cambridge CB5 8EP
Tel: (01604) 233233 Fax: (01223) 316511
Email: mail@hewitsons.com (for all offices)
Website: www.hewitsons.com (for all offices)

Firm profile
Established in 1865, the firm handles mostly company and commercial work, but has a growing body of public sector clients. The firm has three offices: Cambridge, Northampton and Milton Keynes.

Main areas of work
Three sections: corporate, property and private client.

Trainee profile
The firm is interested in applications from candidates who have achieved a high degree of success in academic studies and who are bright, personable and able to take the initiative.

Training environment
The firm offers four six-month seats.

Benefits
The PSC is provided during the first year of the training contract. This is coupled with an extensive programme of Trainee Solicitor Seminars provided by specialist in-house lawyers.

Vacation placements
Places for 2014: A few placements are available, application is by way of letter and CV to Caroline Lewis.

Sponsorship & awards
Funding for the CPE and/or LPC is not provided.

Partners 40	
Assistant Solicitors 33	
Total Trainees 12	
Contact	
Caroline Lewis	
7 Spencer Parade Northampton	
NN1 5AB	
Method of application	
Firm's application form	
Selection procedure	
Interview	
Closing date for 2016	
31 August 2014	
Application	
Training contracts p.a. 10	
Applications p.a. 850	
% interviewed p.a. 10%	
Required degree grade	
2:1 min	
Training	
Salary	
1st year £23,500	
2nd year £23,500	
Holiday entitlement 22 days	
% of trainees with a	
non-law degree p.a. 50%	
Post-qualification	
Salary £35,000	
% of trainees offered job	
on qualification (2013) 50%	

Hogan Lovells

Hogan Lovells, Atlantic House, Holborn Viaduct, London EC1A 2FG
Tel (020) 7296 2000 Fax (020) 7296 2001
Email: recruit@hoganlovells.com
Website: www.hoganlovells.com/graduates

Firm profile

Hogan Lovells is a top global law firm, with over 2,200 lawyers working in over 40 offices in Asia, Europe, Latin America, the Middle East and the United States. Our unique balance of ambition and approachability attracts prestigious clients and creates a working culture where the ambition of our trainee solicitors is supported to ensure their success.

Main areas of work

Our global diversity and wide range of practice areas gives us a strong reputation for corporate finance, dispute resolution, government regulatory and intellectual property. Exposure to a variety of legal disciplines provides good training and development opportunities for those joining us.

Trainee profile

We are looking for graduates whose combination of academic excellence and desire for specialist knowledge will contribute to developing business and taking it forward. Although we are one of the largest global legal practices, we work in small, hard-working teams where everybody is committed to our collective success.

The personal qualities our people possess are as important as their qualifications. You need to be happy collaborating with a team yet capable of, and used to, independent action. You will need to demonstrate an ability and desire for lateral thinking, be capable of close attention to detail, and have the energy, resilience and ambition to succeed in a top global law firm.

Training environment

As a trainee solicitor at Hogan Lovells, you will be offered work that sharpens your mind. You will take on as much responsibility as you can handle relating to client work, as well as a comprehensive legal skills training programme, regular reviews and appraisals. After qualification, continuous training and development remain a priority – you will deepen your professional and business expertise throughout your career. Making the best of your expertise enhances the quality of advice we provide to clients, maintains our reputation and helps you build your career.

We require every prospective trainee solicitor to undertake the accelerated LPC at BPP London. The course will prepare you for practice in the City.

Our two-year training contract is split into four six-month periods of work experience known as 'seats'. As a trainee solicitor, you will move around four different practice areas during this time to gain as much experience as possible – one of your seats will be in either our corporate or finance group, and another in one of our litigation teams. You will also have the option of spending time in the second year of training on secondment to one of our international offices or to the in-house legal team of a major client.

Benefits

PPP medical insurance, life assurance, season ticket loan, in-house gym, access to dentist, doctor and physiotherapist, subsidised staff restaurant, discounts at local retailers.

Sponsorship

GDL and LPC course fees are paid and maintenance grants are provided for both the GDL and LPC.

Partners 800+
Assistant Solicitors 2,200+
Total Trainees 143

Method of application
Online application form

Selection procedure
Assessment day

Closing date for February & August 2016
Law applications 31 July 2014
Non-Law applications 30 April 2014

Application
Training contracts p.a. up to 60
Applications p.a. 1,500
% interviewed p.a. 25%
Required degree grade 2:1

Training
Salary
1st year (2011) £38,000
2nd year (2011) £43,000
Holiday entitlement 25 days
% of trainees with a non-law degree p.a. 50%
No. of seats available abroad p.a. 25

Post-qualification
Salary £61,500

International offices
Alicante, Amsterdam, Baltimore, Beijing, Berlin, Brussels, Budapest, Caracas, Colorado, Denver, Dubai, Dusseldorf, Frankfurt, Hamburg, Hanoi, Ho Chi Minh City, Hong Kong, Houston, Jakarta, Jeddah, London, Los Angeles, Madrid, Miami, Milan, Moscow, Munich, New York, Northern Virginia, Paris, Philadelphia, Prague, Rio de Janeiro, Riyadh, Rome, San Francisco, Shanghai, Silicon Valley, Singapore, Tokyo, Ulaanbaatar, Warsaw, Washington DC, Zagreb

Holman Fenwick Willan LLP

Friary Court, 65 Crutched Friars, London EC3N 2AE
Tel: (020) 7264 8000
Email: grad.recruitment@hfw.com
Website: www.hfw.com

Firm profile
We are an international law firm with over 450 lawyers worldwide and a market leading reputation for advising businesses in all aspects of international commerce. We have developed our transactional, regulatory and dispute resolution services across a number of core sectors, including aviation, commodities, energy, mining, insurance and shipping and transport. We offer our trainees an environment where you will be working alongside some of the most respected and talented lawyers in their field, embracing opportunities that may include international seats and client secondments. If you enjoy challenges, are driven, and have an outgoing personality, then we would like to hear from you.

Main areas of work
Admiralty and crisis management; arbitration; asset finance; aviation; commercial litigation; competition law - EC and UK; commodities – soft and hard; construction; corporate; corporate finance; dispute resolution and mediation; employment; energy; environmental; fraud; information technology; insurance and reinsurance; intellectual property; logistics; marine litigation and claims; personal injury; professional negligence; port development; real estate; restructuring and insolvency; space; ship finance; world trade.

Trainee profile
We look for trainees with sharp minds, common sense, enthusiasm, ingenuity and a good sense of humour. We look for team players and good communicators who work hard and are client focused. As our training contract is truly international, we look for individuals who have a global perspective and an interest in completing international work. We accept applications from all disciplines and backgrounds; from students and experienced graduates alike.

Training environment
Trainees are involved in a combination of trainee workshops, departmental know-how discussions, mentoring by experienced lawyers and on-the-job training. All our trainees are also encouraged to spend time on our numerous worldwide pro bono and CSR initiatives.

Each year we recruit only a small number of trainees – 15 per year split across a September and a March intake. This enables us to give every trainee our full attention, and means that your individual contribution makes a big difference. You will do interesting, stretching work, very often with an international element. During your training you will have four six-month seats, sitting with a partner or a senior associate. Most trainees have the opportunity to work in one of our overseas offices (recently trainees have completed seats in Brussels, Dubai, Geneva, Hong Kong, Melbourne, Paris, Perth, Piraeus, Singapore and Sydney), or to be seconded to a client.

Benefits
Our salaries are highly competitive. Trainees receive an annual salary of £36,000, increasing to £38,000 after the first year of the training contract. On top of that we offer additional benefits, which include: study assistance and grants; generous contributory pension; subsidised gym membership; season ticket loan; life assurance; medical insurance.

Vacation placements
We run a 1 week spring vacation scheme and 2 x 2 week summer vacation schemes. We have up to 10 places on each scheme (30 in total). Vacation scheme participants gain practical experience and exposure, as well as attending a final round interview for a training contract as part of the scheme.

The closing date for 2014 vacation schemes will be 14 February 2014.

Partners 151
Associates 236
Total Trainees 36

Contact
Sarah Burson

Method of application
Online application form

Selection procedure
Online application form, assessment centre, vacation scheme (if applied for), final round interview with 2 partners

Closing date for September 2016 / March 2017
31 July 2014

Application
Training contracts p.a. 15
Required degree grade 2:1

Training
Salary (2013)
1st year £36,000
2nd year £38,000
Holiday entitlement 25 days
Number of seats available abroad Variable - 10 (2013)

Post-qualification
Salary £58,000 (2013)

Overseas offices
Rouen, Paris, Brussels, Geneva, Piraeus, Dubai, Shanghai, Hong Kong, Singapore, Perth, Melbourne, Sydney, Sao Paulo

A-Z of Solicitors

Ince & Co LLP

International House, 1 St Katharine's Way, London E1W 1AY
Email: recruitment@incelaw.com

Firm profile

With over 140 years of experience, Ince & Co is one of the oldest law firms in the City. We've built our success by always taking an innovative approach, looking for new ways to apply legal strategies and create new law. Ince & Co is frequently at the forefront of developments in contract and tort law.

Main areas of work

With a world leading reputation initially built on shipping and insurance, over the decades we have successfully explored new territory and established our expertise across a number of specific industries. We have five core business groups: aviation, energy and offshore, insurance and reinsurance, international trade and shipping.

Trainee profile

Hardworking, competitive individuals with initiative who relish challenge and responsibility within a team environment. Academic achievements, positions of responsibility, sport and travel are all taken into account. Not only do we regard our trainees as future solicitors and potential partners, but our training programme is different too. Ince trainees get involved in real legal work from day one, and the cases they assist on stay with them throughout their training period and sometimes beyond.

Training environment

Our training contract is unique as we do not have a rigid seat structure which confines trainees to a specific department. Instead, trainees are encouraged to be proactive and take on tasks from any of our business groups.

Our open and friendly culture allows our trainees to make a real contribution and get involved in all aspects of our practice. Trainees will sit with four different partners for six months at a time throughout their training. Under close supervision, trainees are encouraged from an early stage to meet and visit clients, interview witnesses, liaise with counsel, deal with technical experts and handle opposing lawyers. As a result they quickly build up a portfolio of cases from a number of partners involved in a cross-section of the firm's practice.

Benefits

Season ticket loan; corporate health cover; private health insurance; contributory pension scheme; Well Man/Well Woman health checks; subsidised gym membership.

Vacation placements

Places for 2013 > 10; Duration > 2 weeks; Remuneration > £250 p/w.; Closing Date > 31 January 2014.

Sponsorship & awards

LPC fees; £7,000 grant for study in London and Guildford, £6,500 grant for study elsewhere.

GDL fees; £6,500 grant for study in London and Guildford, £6,000 grant for study elsewhere.

Partners 98*
Senior Associates 40*
Solicitors 145*
Total Trainees 30*
* denotes worldwide figures

Contact
Rebecca Withers, Recruitment and Resourcing Manager

Method of application
Online at
http://graduates.incelaw.com

Selection procedure
Interview with HR and a Partner from the Recruitment Committee & 4 tests

Closing date for 2016
31 July 2014

Application
Training contracts p.a. 10
Applications p.a. 823
% interviewed p.a. 10%
Required degree grade 2:1

Training
Salary
1st year £36,000
2nd year £39,000
Holiday entitlement 25 days
% of trainees with a
non-law degree p.a. 50%

Post-qualification
Salary £58,000
% of trainees offered job
on qualification (2012)
83%
% of partners (as at 2012)
who joined as trainees approx
70%

Overseas offices
Beijing, Dubai, Hamburg, Hong Kong, Le Havre, Monaco, Paris, Piraeus, Shanghai, Singapore.

INCE & CO | INTERNATIONAL LAW FIRM

Irwin Mitchell

Riverside East, 2 Millsands, Sheffield S3 8DT
Tel: (0870) 1500 100 Fax: (0870) 197 3549
Email: graduaterecruitment@irwinmitchell.com
Website: www.irwinmitchell.com/graduates

Firm profile
Irwin Mitchell is unique, both in its culture and its approach to law. Nationally acclaimed, it is one of a few law firms to provide a diverse range of legal services to businesses and private individuals. It has a strong customer service culture and a high level of client retention. It has an established office network and employs more than 2100 staff. In August 2012, it was one of the first firms to become an Alternative Business Structure (ABS), and the first to be granted multiple ABS licences by the SRA. The firm was awarded the best graduate trainee recruitment campaign and most effective diversity programme (gender) at The Lawyer Workplace & Diversity Awards (2012). Other accolades include being ranked in the Stonewall Workplace Equality Index for 2013, as well as being one of the leading companies to sign up to the Business Compact scheme to create fairer job opportunities for all.

Main areas of work
Personal Legal Services: The firm remains one of the leading personal injury and medical negligence litigation practices in the UK, covering all the key injury types from road traffic accidents, to product liability claims and serious head/spinal injury cases. A comprehensive range of private client services are also provided, including a national family team. In addition, it provides a national probate, contentious probate, public law and conveyancing service and is the UK's leading court of protection practice.

Business Legal Services: The firm offers a wide range of commercial services and in recent years has expanded its corporate, commercial litigation and real estate services. The aim is to develop a cutting edge commercial service that will challenge the traditional City and national firms. Areas of expertise include business investigations, commercial litigation and dispute resolution, construction, corporate, employment, environmental, finance, insolvency, international, pensions, planning, real estate, recoveries, restructuring and tax.

Trainee profile
The firm is looking for ambitious and well-motivated individuals who have a real commitment to the law and who can demonstrate a positive approach to work-life balance. Irwin Mitchell recruits law and non-law graduates and views social ability as important as academic achievement.

Training environment
The firm's training contracts are streamed so that as a trainee you would either undertake a training contract based within the Personal Legal Services or Business Legal Services divisions. Trainees will have three training seats and a qualification seat. This allows trainees to gain practical experience in diverse areas of law, whilst maximising retention opportunities.

Benefits
Pension, professional subscriptions, health plan, death in service and critical illness cover.

Sponsorship & awards
GDL and LPC funding, if you have not started or completed your studies when offered a training contract, plus a maintenance grant of £4,500.

Work placements
Each summer the firm runs a formal work placement programme which is a great way to get a real insight into what life is like as a trainee at Irwin Mitchell. An increasing number of training contracts go to people who have undertaken a work placement, so the firm encourages all those interested in joining to apply. Closing date for applications is the 31 January 2014.

Partners 176
Other fee-earners 900+
Total Trainees 83

Contact
Helen Cannon
Graduate Manager
graduaterecruitment@
irwinmitchell.com

Method of application
Please visit the firm's website
www.irwinmitchell.com/gradua
tes and complete the online
application

Selection procedure
Telephone interview and
assessment centre

Closing date for 2016
31 July 2014

Application
Training contracts p.a. 40
Applications p.a. 2,000-2,500
% interviewed p.a. 20%
Required degree grade: The firm
does not require a specific
degree grade

Training
Salary
Outside London
1st year £25,000
2nd year £27,000
London
1st year £33,000
2nd year £35,000
reviewed annually in July
Holiday entitlement
24.5 days

Post-qualification
% of trainees offered job on
qualification 80%+

Overseas / Regional offices
Birmingham, Bristol, Leeds,
Leicester (consulting office),
London, Manchester,
Newcastle, Sheffield, Glasgow,
Madrid and Malaga.

A-Z of Solicitors

Jones Day

21 Tudor Street, London EC4Y 0DJ
Tel: (020) 7039 5959 Fax: (020) 7039 5999
Email: recruit.london@jonesday.com
Website: www.jonesdaylondon.com

Firm profile
Jones Day is a truly global law firm - probably the most integrated in the world. Our 2,400 lawyers across 39 locations worldwide have vast transactional and contentious experience and are at the forefront of globalisation and the advancement of the rule of law. Our strengths in London reflect those of the firm: our 200 London lawyers (including around 60 partners and 30 trainees) have a sophisticated understanding of risk and draw on specialist insights and skills from across the globe to guide clients through their toughest challenges and most significant, corporate life events.

Main areas of work
In London's critical financial centre, our lawyers are perfectly placed to address the most demanding and complex global matters; including cross-border M&A; real estate and finance transactions (including banking, capital markets, investment funds, private equity and structured finance); English law disputes; and regulatory matters involving the UK, US and other authorities. Additional specialist areas include business restructuring; competition/antitrust; corporate tax planning; employment and pensions; energy; intellectual property; and projects and infrastructure.

Trainee profile
We look to recruit people who want to work on global deals, be challenged on an international level, and can become partners of the future, not just candidates who will qualify with us. Successful candidates have either a law or non-law degree; strong intellectual ability; good communication skills; and demonstrate resourcefulness, drive and dedication.

Training environment
The firm operates a unique, non-rotational system of training (whereby trainees receive work simultaneously from all departments) to provide flexibility, responsibility, faster development of potential and the opportunity to compare and contrast different disciplines alongside one another. Work will vary from small cases which trainees may handle alone (under the supervision of a senior lawyer) to larger matters where they will assist a partner or an associate solicitor. The firm runs a structured seminar programme to support the practical teaching trainees receive from associates and partners they work with.

Placement schemes
64 places for two week placements. Allowance of £400 per week. Apply for a placement if you want to train at Jones Day. We expect to recruit all trainees from our placement candidates, who see how the firm's non-rotational training system works in practice by taking on real work from a variety of practice areas. They also meet a range of lawyers at various social events. All our placement schemes are open to final year law and non-law students, graduates and postgraduates; our summer placement schemes are also open to penultimate year students undertaking a qualifying law degree. We recruit on a rolling basis, so cannot guarantee availability. Final deadlines (unless places fill earlier) are 31 October 2013 (winter scheme); 31 December 2013 (spring scheme); 31 January 2014 (summer scheme).

Trainee benefits
Private healthcare, season ticket loan, subsidised sports club membership, group life cover, salary sacrifice schemes and access to stakeholder pension.

Sponsorship & awards
GDL and LPC fees paid and £8,000 maintenance p.a. Fast track LPC for sponsored students from August to February each year, allowing for a 6 month gap before training starts.

Partners approx 60
Assistant Solicitors approx 110
Total Trainees approx 30

Contact
Diana Spoudeas
Manager - Trainee Recruitment / Development

Method of application
Online via our website:
www.jonesdaylondon.com

Selection procedure
We recruit all trainees from our placement schemes:
1 interview with 2 partners for placement scheme; further Interview with 2 partners for training contract whilst on placement scheme.
Applications open early on 1 September 2013.

Closing date for 2016
For placement schemes and 2016 training contracts: 31 January 2014 (unless places fill earlier). We close when we are full so apply early.

Application
Placements p.a. 64
Training contracts p.a. 15
Applications p.a. 1,600
% interviewed p.a. 20%
Required degree grade 2:1
Required A-Levels/IB AAA/36

Training
Salary (2013)
Start £41,000
After 10 months £46,000
After 22 months £50,000
Holiday entitlement
5 weeks

Post-qualification
Salary (2013) £72,500
% of trainees offered job on qualification (2013) 100%

Overseas offices
Continental Europe, Asia, USA, Latin America, Middle East, Asia Pacific

JONES DAY | One Firm Worldwide™

A-Z of Solicitors

K&L Gates LLP

One New Change, London, EC4M 9AF
Tel: (020) 7648 9000 Fax: (020) 7648 9001
Email: traineerecruitment@klgates.com
Website: www.klgates.com

Partners 60	
Trainees 16	
Total Staff 275	

Contact
Hayley Atherton

Method of application
Online at www.klgates.com

Selection procedure
Online testing, full assessment centre and interview

Closing date for 2016
31 July 2014

Application
Training contracts p.a. TBD
Applications p.a. 1,000
% interviewed p.a. 10%
Required degree grade 2:1

Training
Salary
1st year £35,000
2nd year £38,000
% of trainees with a non-law degree p.a. Varies

Post-qualification
Salary £60,000
% of trainees offered job on qualification 80%

Firm profile
K&L Gates LLP comprises more than 2,000 lawyers who practice in over 48 offices located on five continents. K&L Gates represents leading global corporations, growth and middle-market companies, capital markets participants and entrepreneurs in every major industry group as well as public sector entities, educational institutions, philanthropic organisations and individuals. The firm's practice is a robust full market practice – cutting edge, complex and dynamic, at once regional, national and international in scope. Over each of the last 4 years our revenues have exceeded $1 billion and, as stated in the July 2010 issue of the UK publication Legal Business, the firm 'has further cemented its position as the Global 100's fastest growing firm.'

Main areas of work
K&L Gates is active in the areas of corporate/M&A, capital markets, private equity, restructuring and insolvency, finance, derivatives, funds, antitrust, competition and trade regulation, real estate, planning and environment, intellectual property, media and sport, construction, insurance coverage, regulatory, tax, employment, pensions and incentives, litigation, international arbitration, white collar crime and other forms of dispute resolution.

Trainee profile
The firm welcomes applications from both law and non-law students. Law students should generally be in their penultimate year of study and non-law students should be in their final year of study. The firm also welcomes applications from relevant postgraduates or others who have satisfied the 'academic stage of training' as required by the Solicitors Regulation Authority (SRA). You should be highly motivated, intellectually curious, with an interest in commercial law and be looking for comprehensive training.

Training environment
The firm ensures each trainee is given exceptional opportunities to learn, experience and develop so that they can achieve their maximum potential. Trainees spend six month seats in four of the areas mentioned above. Each trainee sits with a supervisor and is allocated an individual mentor to ensure all round supervision and training. The firm has a thorough induction scheme, and has won awards for its career development programme. High importance is placed on the acquisition of business and professional skills, with considerable emphasis on client contact and early responsibility. The training programme consists of weekly legal education seminars, workshops and a full programme of skills electives. Pro bono and corporate social responsibility activities are also encouraged.

Benefits
25 days holiday per annum, subsidised sports club membership, season ticket loan, permanent health insurance, life assurance, GP service and pension.

Legal work placements
The firm's formal legal work placement scheme is open to penultimate year law students, final year non-law students, other relevant post graduates or others who have satisfied the 'academic stage of training' as required by the SRA.

Sponsorship
GDL funding: fees paid plus £5,000 maintenance grant. LPC funding: fees paid plus £7,000 maintenance grant.

Overseas offices
Anchorage, Austin, Beijing, Berlin, Boston, Brisbane, Brussels, Charleston, Charlotte, Chicago, Dallas, Doha, Dubai, Fort Worth, Frankfurt, Harrisburg, Hong Kong, Houston, Los Angeles, Melbourne, Miami, Milan, Moscow, Newark, New York, Orange County, Palo Alto, Paris, Perth, Pittsburgh, Portland, Raleigh, Research Triangle Park, San Diego, San Francisco, Sao Paulo, Seattle, Seoul, Shanghai, Singapore, Spokane/Coeur d'Alene, Sydney, Taipei, Tokyo, Warsaw, Washington and Wilmington.

K&L GATES

Kennedys

25 Fenchurch Avenue, London, EC3M 5AD
Tel: (020) 7667 9667 Fax: (020) 7667 9777
Email: r.bubb@kennedys-law.com
Website: www.kennedys-law.com

Firm profile
Kennedys is a specialist national and international legal firm with unrivalled expertise in litigation and dispute resolution. The firm has over 1000 people globally, across nine UK and 10 international locations. Kennedys is a top 30 law firm. Kennedys is regarded as a leader, not just because it has some of the most respected legal minds in their field - but because they know the importance of being practical, commercial and approachable. Kennedys prides itself on offering its clients clear legal advice.

Main areas of work
Kennedys lawyers provide a range of specialist legal services for many industries including: insurance/reinsurance, healthcare, construction, rail, local government, maritime and international trade – with a particular focus on dispute resolution and litigation.

Trainee profile
The firm is looking for graduates who are articulate, self aware and resourceful. Kennedys' trainees experience early responsibility and client contact, therefore it essential to have a mature and confident approach. Trainees with the firm must have commercial awareness and a strong appreciation of the interests of the client. As Kennedys has a vibrant and supportive working environment it is also looking for sociable, energetic team players.

Training environment
The purpose of the training contract is to give the trainees a mix of experience and skills that will set them up in their legal career as a solicitor with Kennedys. The firm's ability to consistently offer the majority of its trainees positions on qualification is attributable to producing newly qualified lawyers who are competent, confident and commercially driven. A balance of responsibility, supervision and formal training achieves this. Kennedys ensures that their trainee solicitors are given sound training in the core disciplines. All partners and supervisors are readily accessible and always ready to offer support when needed.

Placement schemes
Kennedys runs summer vacation schemes during June and July. Applications should be made online for the 2014 schemes by 31 January 2014.

Benefits
Permanent health insurance, pension, private medial insurance, life insurance, 25 days holiday increasing to 27 days after five years, interest-free season ticket loan, gym membership, cycle to work scheme, child care assistance scheme, employee assistance scheme, corporate GP, contribution towards conveyancing fees and eye care vouchers.

Partners 173
Fee Earners 565
Total Trainees 32
Total Staff 1205

Contact
Rowena Bubb
Graduate Recruitment Advisor
r.bubb@kennedys-law.com

Method of application
Online Application Form

Selection procedure
Assessment Day

Closing date for 2015/2016
31 July 2014
Applications will reopen for 2016 training contacts on 1 October 2014

Application
Training contracts approx 18
Applications 900 (London)
Required degree grade 2:1 and 300 UCAS points or equivalent at A-level

Training
Salary
1st Year £34,000 (London)
2nd Year £37,000 (London)

Post-qualification
% of trainees offered job on qualification 95%

Offices
Auckland, Belfast, Birmingham, Brussels, Cambridge, Chelmsford, Dubai, Dublin, Hong Kong, Lisbon, London, Madrid, Maidstone, Manchester, Miami, Sheffield, Singapore, Sydney, Taunton

Kennedys
Legal advice in black and white

Kingsley Napley LLP

Knights Quarter, 14 St John's Lane, London EC1M 4AJ
Tel: (020) 7814 1200 Fax: (020) 7490 2288 DX 22 Chancery Lane
Website: www.kingsleynapley.co.uk

Firm profile
Kingsley Napley is an internationally recognised law firm based in central London. Our wide range of expertise means that we can provide support for our clients in all areas of their business and private life. Many of our lawyers are leaders in their field and our practice areas are highly ranked by the legal directories.

We are known for combining creative solutions with pragmatism and a friendly, sensitive approach. The relationship between lawyer and client is key. We work hard to match clients with lawyers who have the right mix of skills, experience and approach in order to achieve the best possible outcome.

Main areas of work
Clinical negligence and personal injury, corporate and commercial, criminal litigation, dispute resolution, employment, family, immigration, private client, public law, real estate and regulatory and professional discipline.

Trainee profile
The firm looks for candidates with a strong academic background. A trainee will also need to demonstrate commercial awareness, motivation and enthusiasm. To be successful you will need excellent communication skills with the ability to be a creative practical problem solver, and to be a team player with a sense of humour.

Training environment
Your training contract will consist of four seats which aim to provide a wide range of practical experience and skills in contentious and non-contentious work. Our training programme is broader than most other firms due to the wide range of law practiced here.

Individual preference for seats is sought and will be balanced with the firm's needs.

Trainees work closely with partners and solicitors in a supportive team structure, and have regular reviews to assist development. The firm maintains a friendly and open environment and it is the firm's policy that each trainee sits with a partner or senior solicitor whilst working for a department as a whole.

The firm gives trainees the chance to meet clients, be responsible for their own work and join in marketing and client development activities.

Benefits
Private health insurance, income protection insurance, life assurance, pension, corporate cash plan and 25 days holiday per year during training. Trainees are also eligible to participate in the firm's flexible benefits scheme.

Partners 40
Assistant Solicitors 63
Total Trainees 10

Contact
Jemimah Cook, HR Director or Kim Austin, Recruitment Manager
Tel 020 7814 1200

Method of application
Online application form

Selection Procedure
Assessment centre. Candidates who are successful at this stage will then be invited to an interview.

Closing date for September 2015
31st May 2014

Application
Training contracts p.a. 5
Applications p.a. 250
% interviewed p.a 10%
Required degree grade 2:1

Training
Salary (2013)
First year £28,000
Second year £30,000
Holiday entitlement 25 days
% of trainees with a non-law degree 60%

Post qualification
Salary (2013) £49,000
% of trainees offered job on qualification 100%

Kingsley Napley

Kirkland & Ellis International LLP

30 St Mary Axe, London EC3A 8AF
Tel: (020) 7469 2000 Fax: (020) 7469 2001
Website: www.kirkland.com/ukgraduate

Firm profile
Kirkland & Ellis International LLP is a 1,600-attorney law firm representing global clients in offices around the world.

For over 100 years, major national and international clients have called upon Kirkland & Ellis to provide superior legal advice and client services. The firm's London office has been the hub of European operations since 1994. Here, approximately 130 lawyers offer detailed expertise to a wide range of UK and international clients.

Main areas of work
The firm handles complex corporate, debt finance, restructuring, funds, capital markets, tax, intellectual property, antitrust and competition, litigation and counselling matters. Kirkland & Ellis operates as a strategic network, committing the full resources of an international firm to any matter in any territory as appropriate.

Trainee profile
Your academic record will be excellent, probably culminating in an expected or achieved 2:1. You will have the initiative, the drive and the work ethic to thrive in the firm's meritocratic culture and arrive with an understanding of the work undertaken in the firm's London office.

Training environment
As one of a select number of trainees, you will be given early responsibility to work on complex multi jurisdictional matters.

The principal focus of your training will be on corporate law with a specialism in private equity. You will complete four, six month seats and obtain training in areas such as debt finance, funds, arbitration, IP, antitrust and competition, restructuring and tax. In addition there will be opportunities to undertake an overseas secondment to enable you to experience the international resources and capabilities of Kirkland & Ellis.

Your on the job training will be actively supported by an extensive education programme, carefully tailored to meet your needs.

Benefits
Private medical insurance, travel insurance, life insurance, employee assistance plan, corporate gym membership.

Vacation placements
Places for 2014: up to 20. Duration: 2 weeks. Remuneration: £350 per week. Closing date for applications: 15 January 2014.

Sponsorship & awards
GDL and LPC course fees and a maintenance grant of £7,500 p.a.

Partners 738
Assistant solicitors 833

Contact
Kate Osborne

Method of application
Online application form

Selection procedure
Interview

Closing date for 2016
31 July 2014

Training
Salary
1st year (2013) £41,000
2nd year (2013) £44,000
Holiday entitlement
25 days

Post-qualification
Salary
1st year: £97,560
% of trainees offered job on qualification 100%

Overseas/ regional offices
Chicago, Hong Kong, Los Angeles, Munich, New York, Palo Alto, San Francisco, Shanghai, Washington DC

KIRKLAND & ELLIS

Latham & Watkins

99 Bishopsgate, London EC2M 3XF
Tel: (020) 7710 1000 Fax: (020) 7374 4460
Email: london.trainees@lw.com
Website: www.lw.com

Firm profile
Latham & Watkins has more than 2,100 lawyers in 31 offices across Europe, the US, the Middle East and Asia and the London office advises on some of the most significant and groundbreaking cross-border transactions in Europe. The firm believes that its non-hierarchical management style and 'one firm' culture makes Latham & Watkins unique.

Main areas of work
Latham & Watkins provides clients with a strong, full-service offering, including banking and finance, corporate, capital markets, litigation, real estate, employment and tax practices. Many of the firm's practice groups are award-winning industry leaders, as are many of the firm's partners. The firm offers clients unrivalled legal resources and strategic commercial thinking to provide innovative solutions to even the most complex issues, and serves multinational companies, start-ups, investment banks, private equity funds, venture capital firms, sovereign wealth funds, governments and other organisations around the world.

Trainee profile
Candidates should be entrepreneurial and thrive on early responsibility. Those with a strong academic background, excellent communication skills and a consistent record of personal and/or professional achievement will be rewarded with first-class training in a stimulating environment. The firm is dedicated to diversity and equal opportunity and values originality and creative thinking.

Training environment
Latham & Watkins can provide a very different training experience to that offered by other elite law firms. Each trainee receives bespoke supervision and outstanding support while being encouraged to recognise that they have their own part to play in the growth and success of the firm. Each trainee also has meaningful responsibility from the outset and significant legal experience on qualification. It is also common for trainees to be given the opportunity to spend one of their four six-month seats in one of the firm's overseas offices.

Benefits
Healthcare and dental scheme, pension scheme and life assurance.

Sponsorship & awards
All GDL and LPC costs are paid and trainees receive a maintenance grant of £8,000 per year whilst studying. A bonus of £500 is provided by the firm if a distinction is achieved in the LPC.

Vacation placements
The firm runs vacation schemes during Easter and summer. Students are paid £350 per week. Please visit our website www.lw.com for application deadlines and eligibility requirements as well as for further information regarding other recruitment opportunities and events.

Partners 58
Associates 142
Trainees 40

Contact
Graduate Recruitment Team

Method of application
Online application form at www.lw.com

Selection procedure
3 x 30 minute interviews with a partner and an associate

Closing date for 2016
31 July 2014

Application
Training contracts p.a. 20
Required degree grade 2:1

Training
Salary
1st year (2013) £42,000
2nd year (2013) £45,000

Post-qualification
Salary £96,970

Overseas/regional offices
Abu Dhabi, Barcelona, Beijing, Boston, Brussels, Chicago, Doha, Dubai, Frankfurt, Hamburg, Hong Kong, Houston, London, Los Angeles, Madrid, Milan, Moscow, Munich, New Jersey, New York, Orange County, Paris, Riyadh, Rome, San Diego, San Francisco, Shanghai, Silicon Valley, Singapore, Tokyo, Washington DC

LATHAM&WATKINS

Lawrence Graham LLP

4 More London Riverside, London SE1 2AU
Tel: (020) 7379 0000 Fax: (020) 7173 8694
Email: graduate@lg-legal.com
Website: http://graduates.lg-legal.com

Firm profile

Lawrence Graham is a distinctive legal practice with a leading reputation in its chosen services and sectors. The firm's approach is relationship-driven and internationally minded, with great people dedicated to their clients.

The firm services its clients from international offices in London, Dubai, Monaco, Russia and Singapore, and also through its close relationships with other advisers in its key jurisdictions. Together, Lawrence Graham advises seamlessly on the most complex cases, cross-border deals and disputes.

Main areas of work

Lawrence Graham offers a full range of legal services with particular focus on commerce and technology, corporate, dispute resolution, employment and pensions, finance, real estate and tax, private capital and projects. It has a specific understanding of the issues facing businesses and individuals operating in its key sectors: energy and natural resources, financial institutions, healthcare, hospitality and leisure, private capital, publishing and media, real estate, support services and technology.

Over 42% of the firm's transactions are now handled for companies outside the UK. The emerging markets of India, South East Asia, the Middle East and South America remain of critical importance to the firm and its clients, while exciting new business opportunities in the more mature markets of Europe and North America keep it firmly centred on those regions.

Lawrence Graham is proud to have a culture that is open and refreshingly straightforward. It employs highly talented individuals, while valuing a strong team ethic - and that is fundamental to the way it works as a business.

Trainee profile

The firm is looking for individuals from a variety of backgrounds with refined communication skills who can demonstrate a commitment to a career in the commercial application of law. A strong academic track record with a minimum of 320 UCAS tariff points and a 2:1 degree is a basic requirement. Also required is a good record of achievement in other areas – indicative of the ability to succeed in a demanding career – and evidence of team working skills and the ability to handle responsibility.

Training environment

Under partner supervision, trainees will be given early responsibility. Training is structured to facilitate the ability to manage one's own files and interact with clients. In addition to the Professional Skills Course, there are departmental training and induction sessions as well as a two year rolling training programme, designed to develop well-rounded lawyers. Training consists of four six-month seats: real estate, transactional and contentious seats are compulsory.

Benefits

Season ticket loan, life assurance.

Vacation placements

Places for 2013: 10; Duration: 1 x 2 weeks between June and July; Remuneration: £350 p.w; Closing date: 31 January 2014.

Sponsorship & awards

GDL Funding: Course fees and maintenance grant. £6k outside London, £6.5k in London.

LPC Funding: Course fees and maintenance grant. £6.5k in London.

Partners 69	
Assistant Solicitors 98	
Total Trainees 30	

Contact
Vicki Thompson
Graduate Recruitment Manager

Method of application
Firm's online application form

Selection procedure
Verbal reasoning test, Partner interview and assessed case study

Closing date for 2016
31 July 2014

Application
Training contracts approx 10
Applications p.a. 600
Required degree grade 2:1

Training
Salary
£35,000
% of trainees with a
non-law degree p.a. 50%

Post-qualification
Salary £54,000
% of trainees offered job
on qualification (2013) 77%

Overseas offices
Dubai, Monaco, Moscow and Singapore

LawrenceGraham

A-Z of Solicitors

Lester Aldridge LLP

Russell House, Oxford Road, Bournemouth BH8 8EX
Tel: (01202) 786161 Fax: (01202) 786110
Email: humanresources@LA-law.com
Website: www.lesteraldridge.com

Firm profile

Lester Aldridge LLP is an energetic business providing both commercial and private client services on a local, regional, national and international scale. The firm's reputation rests on the expertise of its people who are first-class in every respect, and on the firm's astute approach to its clients. Client satisfaction is always the firm's aim.

History is important in any business – it shows a commitment to its industry and its clients and the firm is proud of its own history. Lester Aldridge's positioning on the south coast offers a positive working environment and a great work life balance; while providing opportunities to work with first class lawyers, impressive clients and opportunity for City experience via LA's London office.

Excellent legal advice is standard. Each client can expect a commitment to excellent service from its staff, a partner led approach, leading legal expertise, comprehensive and cohesive advice, innovative and technological support and value for money.

Main areas of work

LA's work is divided up into 5 groups – Dispute Resolution, Corporate and Commercial, Banking and Finance, Real Estate and Private Client. Within these groups the firm has a number of sectors which offer a cross section of these work types – these include marine, charities, fertility and same sex couples, development, care and medical practices. As a trainee, you will get involved in the broad range giving you choice and experience for your future career in law.

Trainee profile

Candidates should have a consistently strong academic record, be commercially aware and possess a broad range of interpersonal skills. Applicants should be highly motivated and have a desire to succeed working with teams to advise clients in dynamic and demanding industries.

Training environment

When you start at LA you'll be given responsibilities and real jobs to get your teeth into. Direct client involvement is encouraged and you will become an integral part of each team you join.

During the course of your two year contract you will complete four seats of six months duration. This gives you exposure to different areas of the firm and hopefully will help you decide what you would like to specialise in.

Giving constructive feedback is always encouraged at LA, so you can expect to hear the good things about your work from your team (and a few things you need to improve). LA also has an appraisal system where you work with your team leader to set objectives and create an action plan that will measure your progress. In addition each trainee is assigned a mentor to provide guidance and encouragement and regular review meetings are arranged with the Managing Partner where you'll be encouraged to voice your views and opinions.

Vacation placements

The firm offers 2 week work placements in the summer of each year. The application deadline is usually 31 March but please check the firm's website for further details on how to apply.

Sponsorship

LPC loan currently under review.

Vacancies 6
Trainees 13
Total Staff 290

Contact
HR Team

Method of application
Apply to human resources application form

Selection procedure
Interview by a panel of partners as part of assessment and development day

Closing date for 2016
30 June 2014

Application
Training contracts p.a. 6
Minimum required degree grade 2:1

Training Salary
Starting salary Competitive market rate for a south coast firm plus additional London allowance where appropriate
Holiday entitlement 22 days

Offices
Bournemouth (2), Southampton & London

LesterAldridge LLP

Lewis Silkin

5 Chancery Lane, Clifford's Inn, London EC4A 1BL
Tel: (020) 7074 8000 Fax: (020) 7864 1200
Email: train@lewissilkin.com
Website: www.lewissilkin.com

Firm profile
Lewis Silkin is a commercial firm with 60 partners. Due to its expertise and the number of leaders in their respective fields, it has an impressive list of household name clients, ranging from large multinational corporations to brands to government agencies and entrepreneurs, across a wide range of sectors. What distinguishes them is a matter of personality. For lawyers, they are notably informal, unstuffy…well, human really. They are 'people people'; as committed and professional as any good law firm, but perhaps more adept at the inter-personal skills that make relationships work and go on working. They place a high priority on the excellent technical ability and commercial thinking of their lawyers and also on their relationships with clients. Clients find them refreshingly easy to deal with. The firm has a friendly, lively style with a commitment to continuous improvement.

Main areas of work
Lewis Silkin provides services through five departments: Corporate; Employment, Reward and Immigration; Litigation and Dispute Resolution; Real Estate and Development; and Media, Brands and Technology. The major work areas include: commercial litigation and dispute resolution; corporate services, which includes company commercial and corporate finance; intellectual property; media and entertainment; reputation management; employment; marketing services, embracing advertising and marketing law; real estate (including social housing); and technology and communications. They are recognised by commentators as a leading firm in employment and all aspects of brand management.

Trainee profile
They are looking for up to six trainees with keen minds and personalities, who will fit into a professional but informal team.

Training environment
The firm provides a comprehensive induction and training programme, with practical hands-on experience from day one. You will sit with either a partner or senior associate giving you access to day-to-day supervision and guidance. The training contract consists of six four-month seats, working in the firm's five departments and/or client secondments.

Benefits
These include individual and firm bonus schemes, life assurance, group income protection, health insurance, season ticket loan, group pension plan and subsidised gym membership.

Work placements
Please refer to the firm's website for further information.

Sponsorship & awards
Funding for GDL and LPC fees is provided plus a £5,000 maintenance grant for each.

Partners 60	
Assistant Solicitors 90	
Total Trainees 12	
Contact	
Human Resources	
Method of application	
Online application form	
Selection procedure	
Assessment day, including an interview with 2 partners, a group exercise, analytical and aptitude test	
Closing date for 2016 intake	
Please refer to website	
Application	
Training contracts p.a. 6	
Applications p.a. 600	
Required degree grade 2:1	
Training	
Salary	
1st year £32,500	
2nd year £34,500	
Holiday entitlement 25 days	
Post-qualification	
Salary (2013) up to £52,000	

lewissilkin

Linklaters LLP

One Silk Street, London EC2Y 8HQ
Tel: (020) 7456 2000 Fax: (020) 7456 2222
Email: graduate.recruitment@linklaters.com
Website: www.linklaters.com/ukgrads

Firm profile
Join Linklaters and you become part of one of the world's most prestigious law firms – a global network of exceptionally talented, highly motivated lawyers working as a team and learning from one another to fulfil its ambition of becoming the leading global law firm.

Main areas of work
While many law firms are strong in particular areas, Linklaters is the only firm to have market-leading global teams across the full range of corporate, finance and commercial practice areas.

This, partnered with its culture of innovation, teamwork and entrepreneurship, means that it has built strong relationships with the world's leading companies, financial institutions and governments and is asked to advise them on their most important and challenging transactions and assignments.

Trainee profile
A truly global firm, Linklaters has 19 practices across 29 cities worldwide, giving you the opportunity to connect with a diverse range of international colleagues and clients on a daily basis.

As part of your training contract you will have the opportunity to be seconded to one of the firm's international offices or to the offices of one of its clients, giving you first hand experience of this global dimension.

Linklaters has high expectations of its trainees and recruits talented and motivated graduates who expect a lot from themselves. In return, the firm offers its trainees global opportunities, entrepreneurial freedom, world-class training and incredible rewards.

Training environment
Linklaters recruits a diverse mix of the most talented graduates from a wide range of universities and backgrounds. Non-law graduates spend a conversion year at law school taking the Graduate Diploma in Law (GDL) and all graduates complete the Legal Practice Course (LPC) before starting their training contracts. The firm meets the cost of the GDL and the LPC and provides a maintenance grant for each. The training contract is structured around four six-month seats, designed to build your knowledge, experience and contacts in a broad range of practice areas and to equip you for your long-term career.

Sponsorship & benefits
GDL and LPC fees are paid in full, plus a maintenance grant. Benefits include eligibility for a personal performance-related bonus, pension, private medical insurance, life assurance, income protection, in-house healthcare services, family friendly benefits, in-house gym, subsidised staff restaurant, interest-free season ticket loan, holiday travel insurance, time bank scheme, cycle2work and give as you earn.

Vacation placements
Linklaters offers vacation schemes for penultimate year students at UK and Irish universities (law and non-law), which take place over the summer. The firm also offers first year law undergraduates structured work experience through a two-day insight programme called Pathfinder. All applications begin with an online application form.

Partners 460
Associates 2,200
Trainees 230+*
*(London)

Contact
Graduate Recruitment

Method of application
Online application form

Selection procedure
Critical thinking test, work simulation exercise and two interviews

Application
Training contracts p.a. 110
Applications p.a. 4,500
Required degree grade 2:1

Training
Salary
1st year trainee £39,500
Holiday entitlement 25 days
% of trainees with a non-law degree p.a. 40%

Post-qualification
Salary £64,000 + discretionary performance-related bonus

Offices
Abu Dhabi, Amsterdam, Antwerp, Bangkok, Beijing, Berlin, Brussels, Dubai, Düsseldorf, Frankfurt, Hong Kong, Lisbon, London, Luxembourg, Madrid, Milan, Moscow, Munich, New York, Paris, Rome, São Paulo, Seoul, Shanghai, Singapore, Stockholm, Tokyo, Warsaw, Washington DC

Linklaters

Macfarlanes LLP

20 Cursitor Street, London, EC4A 1LT
Tel: (020) 7831 9222 Fax: (020) 7831 9607
Email: gradrec@macfarlanes.com
Website: www.macfarlanes.com

Firm profile

Macfarlanes is a leading City law firm. The firm is recognised for the quality of its work, not just in dealing with a full range of corporate and commercial matters, but in advising clients on their private affairs. Clients trust Macfarlanes' judgement and the firm is in a unique position to advise on their most complex matters, whilst at the same time remaining smaller than its competitors.

As advisers to many of the world's leading businesses and business leaders, the firm manages international matters in an effective and seamless manner. It gives clients a single point of contact and co-ordinates advice across all relevant jurisdictions.

Main areas of work

The firm's main areas of practice are in banking and finance; commercial; competition; corporate and M&A; corporate and regulatory investigations; data privacy; employment; financial services regulation; hedge funds; investment funds; IP and IT; litigation and dispute resolution; pensions; private client; private equity; real estate; restructuring and insolvency; and tax.

Trainee profile

Macfarlanes believes the strongest firm is achieved by choosing a mix of people – reflecting different styles so as to meet the needs that it – and its varied range of clients – will have in the future. The firm looks for a rare combination of intellectual curiosity, character and drive. It is looking for ambitious trainees who will thrive on responsibility and challenge and who are ready to begin their careers on day one.

Training environment

Woven into every aspect of life at the firm is an enduring commitment to the development of trainees. Training begins with tailored electives on the LPC and a week-long induction course at the start of your training contract.

During the two-year training contract you'll be working on real cases, doing real work for real clients from day one. As a trainee you will complete four six-month seats in different areas of practice; typically it is one seat in corporate and M&A, two seats in either private client, litigation, commercial real estate or tax, and then a seat in one of the firm's specialised practice areas within corporate. The precise allocation of seats is flexible so that it can offer you as broad a legal training as possible. Support and guidance are, of course, vital and you will find your supervisor a valuable source of information and inspiration.

Benefits

Life assurance, pension scheme with company contributions, private healthcare, discretionary performance related bonus scheme, season ticket loan, subsidised restaurant, gym membership subsidy, eyecare vouchers and childcare vouchers.

Vacation placements

Places for 2014: 55; Duration 2 weeks; Remuneration: £300 p.w.; Closing date: 31 January 2014.

Sponsorship & awards

CPE/GDL and LPC fees paid in full and a £7,000 maintenance allowance.

Partners 76
Assistant Solicitors 180
Total Trainees 61

Contact
Lisa De Simone

Method of application
Online via website

Selection procedure
Assessment day

Closing date for 2016
31 July 2014

Application
Training contracts p.a. 25
Applications p.a. 1,000
% interviewed p.a. 15%
Required degree grade 2:1

Training
Salary
1st year £38,000
2nd year £43,000
Holiday entitlement 25 days, rising to 26 on qualification
% of trainees with a non-law degree p.a. 55%

Post-qualification
Salary (2012) £61,000
% of trainees offered job on qualification (Sept 2013) 79%
% of partners (as at 1/7/13) who joined as trainees 55%

MACFARLANES

Maclay Murray & Spens LLP

1 George Square, Glasgow, G2 1AL
Website: www.mms.co.uk

Partners 60	
Assistant Solicitors 145	
Total Trainees 43	

Contact
Karen Falconer, HR Assistant
karen.falconer@mms.co.uk

Method of application
Application forms only,
accessed at
www.mms.co.uk/careers/
traineeship

Selection procedure
Two stage interview process.
During the second stage
candidates will be asked to
complete a role-play and
research exercise.

**Closing date for 2015 and
2016**
London traineeship August
2014
Scottish traineeship October
2014

Application
Training contracts p.a. 20-25
Applications p.a. 450
Required degree grade 2:1

Training
Salary (2012)
(Scotland) 1st year £18,000
(London) 1st year £32,000
Holiday entitlement 34 days
per year, including public
holidays

Firm profile
Maclay Murray & Spens LLP is a full service, independent, commercial law firm offering legal solutions and advice to clients throughout the UK and beyond. With offices in Aberdeen, Glasgow, Edinburgh and London the firm's objective is to provide a consistently excellent quality of service across the firm's entire service range and from every UK office.

Main areas of work
Banking and finance, capital projects, commercial dispute resolution, construction and engineering, corporate, employment, pensions, EU, competition and regulatory, IP and technology, oil and gas, planning and environmental, private client, property, public sector and tax.

Trainee profile
Applicants should have a strong academic background (minimum 2:1 degree) as well as demonstrate a number of key skills including an inquiring mind and a keenness to learn, commitment, professionalism, determination to see a job through, first class communication skills, the ability to get on with colleagues and clients at all levels, an ability to operate under pressure in a team environment, as well as a sense of humour. The firm welcomes bright non-law graduates.

Training environment
Trainees will have three seats of eight months where you will be provided with a very broad range of practical experience, including legal writing, drafting, research work and an element of client contact. This is one of the firm's strengths as a business and a long standing attraction for candidates.

In addition to on-the-job training, the firm also offers trainees the opportunity of attending in-house seminars and workshops in order to develop their legal and general business skills. By working as a team member on more complex transactions, you are given the opportunity to gain experience over a broad range of work. You will also be encouraged to meet and work alongside clients from different backgrounds and diverse areas of industry and commerce. The firm has an open plan office environment which allows trainees the benefit of working closely alongside solicitors at all levels. This promotes greater communication and team working. Trainees are also able to participate in CSR activities which take place across our offices.

Benefits
At MMS trainees are paid competitive salaries as well as provided with an attractive benefits package. All of the firm's employees receive a combination of fixed and variable holidays totalling 34 days each year. The firm also offers a contributory pension scheme, death in service benefit worth four times your annual salary, support with conveyancing fees, enhanced maternity and paternity pay, income protection insurance, cycle to work scheme, Give As You Earn, season ticket loan for travel, childcare voucher scheme and discounted access to medical and dental plans.

Vacation scheme
MMS offers students the opportunity of a three week summer placement. To apply please visit our website for more details on our application process. The closing date is 31 January 2014.

Sponsorship
Assistance with LPC is available.

mms | maclay murray & spens LLP

Mayer Brown[1]

201 Bishopsgate, London EC2M 3AF
Email: graduaterecruitment@mayerbrown.com
Website: www.mayerbrown.com/london

Firm profile

Mayer Brown was one of the first law firms to develop a global platform in recognition of the fact that many of its clients increasingly needed an integrated, cross border legal advice. The firm is now one of the world's leading global law firms with offices in key business centres across Asia, Europe and the Americas. In Brazil, the firm has an association with Tauil & Chequer Avogados. Through the association, the extensive international expertise of its lawyers and its presence in the leading financial centres around the world, Mayer Brown provides high quality legal advice and client-focussed solutions to support many of the world's leading businesses, governments and individuals. This includes a significant proportion of the Fortune 100, FTSE 100 and DAX and Hang Seng Index and organisations in the banking, insurance, communications, industrials, energy, construction, professional services, pharmaceuticals, chemicals and mining sectors.

Main areas of work

Our lawyers have expertise across a wide range of areas including corporate, finance, litigation and dispute resolution, real estate, insurance and reinsurance, pensions and employment, competition and trade, tax, intellectual property and information technology.

Trainee profile

We are looking for candidates who not only have a consistently strong academic record, but also who have a wide range of interests and achievements outside their academic career. Additionally, the firm would like to see innovative candidates who can demonstrate a drive for results, good verbal and written communication skills and an ability to analyse, with good judgement and excellent interpersonal skills.

Training environment

One of the advantages of joining Mayer Brown are the choices available to you. As a trainee at the firm, you will be able to tailor your training contract across a broad range of seats, including our main practice areas in London (as listed above), and international secondments in either Hong Kong or New York. If you don't want to stray too far, you have the option to gain valuable in house experience by going on secondment to one of the firm's major clients. Whilst Mayer Brown is a global law firm, our London office remains a tightly knit team with an open and inclusive culture. You will be given significant opportunities to assist on matters which may be multi-disciplinary, cross-border, complex and high-profile in nature.

Benefits

Benefits include 25 days holiday per annum, an interest free season ticket loan, subsidised sports club membership and membership of private health scheme.

Work experience programmes

The firm runs three work experience programmes each year; two three-week schemes in the summer and one two-week programme in the spring. You will gain experience in two key practice areas and be involved in seminars and social events, including a trip to one of our European offices.

Sponsorship & awards

The firm will cover the cost of the GDL and LPC fees and provide a maintenance grant of £7,000.

[1] Mayer Brown International LLP operates in combination with its associated Illinois limited liability partnerships, a SELAS established in France, a Hong Kong partnership, and its associated entities in Asia, and is associated with Tauil & Chequer Advogados, a Brazilian law partnership.

Partners 100
Assistant Solicitors 130
Total Trainees 40

Contact
Caroline Sarson,
Graduate Recruitment Manager

Method of application
Online application form

Selection procedure
One stage assessment process including an interview, a written exercise, a group exercise and an online verbal reasoning test

Closing date for September 2016/March 2017
31 July 2014

Application
Training contracts p.a.
approx 20
Applications p.a. 2,000+
% interviewed p.a. 8%
Required degree grade 2:1

Training
1st year £37,500
2nd year £42,300
Holiday entitlement 25 days
% of trainees with a non-law degree p.a. 50%

Post-qualification
% of trainees offered job on qualification 65% (March 2013)

Overseas offices
Bangkok, Beijing, Brussels, Charlotte, Chicago, Dusseldorf, Frankfurt, Guangzhou, Hanoi, Ho Chi Minh City, Hong Kong, Houston, London, Los Angeles, New York, Palo Alto, Paris, Shanghai, Singapore and Washington DC

MAYER · BROWN

McDermott Will & Emery UK LLP

Heron Tower, 110 Bishopsgate, London EC2N 4AY
Tel: (020) 7577 6900 Fax: (020) 7577 6950
Website: www.mwe.com
Email: graduate.recruitment@mwe.com

Partners 570 (worldwide) Associate Lawyers & Other Fee-earners 711 (worldwide) Total Trainees 7 (London)	
Contact Graduate Recruitment	
Method of application Apply online at www.mwe.com	
Selection procedure Assessment day, written test and Partner Interview	
Closing date for September 2015 31 July 2014	
Training Salary 1st year £39,000 (2013) 2nd year £43,000 (2013)	

Firm profile
McDermott Will & Emery UK LLP is a leading international law firm with offices in Boston, Brussels, Chicago, Düsseldorf, Frankfurt, Houston, London, Los Angeles, Miami, Milan, Munich, New York, Orange County, Paris, Rome, Seoul, Silicon Valley and Washington DC, and a strategic alliance with MWE China Law Offices (Shanghai). The firm's client base includes some of the world's leading financial institutions, largest corporations, mid-cap businesses, and individuals. The firm represents more than 60% of the companies in the Fortune 100 in addition to clients in the FTSE 100 and FTSE 250. Rated as one of the leading firms in The American Lawyer's Top 100, by a number of indicators, including gross revenues and profits per Partner.

London Office: The London office was founded in 1998. It is already recognised as being in the top 10 of the 100 US law firms operating in London by the legal media. The firm has around 50 lawyers at present in London, almost all of whom are English-qualified. The firm provides business oriented legal advice to multinational and national corporates, financial institutions, investment banks and private clients. Many of the firm's partners were head of practice at their former firms and are recognised as leaders in their respective fields by the most respected professional directories and market commentators.

Main areas of work
Energy and commodities advisory; corporate advisory; financial institutions advisory; employee benefits, compensation, labour and employment; US and international tax; private client; international dispute avoidance and resolution; and IP litigation. London is the hub for the firm's European expansions and the firm coordinates legal advice from here for all multinational clients across Europe and elsewhere.

Trainee profile
The firm is looking for the brightest, best and most entrepreneurial trainees. You will need to convince the firm that you have made a deliberate choice to apply to McDermott Will & Emery.

Training environment
The primary focus is to provide a practical foundation for your career with the firm. You will experience four seats over the two-year period and a deliberately small number of trainees means that the firm is able to provide a degree of flexibility in tailoring seats to the individual. Trainees get regular support and feedback.

Benefits
Private medical and dental insurance, life assurance, permanent health insurance, pension, season ticket loan, subsidised gym membership, employee assistance programme, 25 days holiday.

Sponsorship & awards
GDL and LPC funding and maintenance grant.

McDermott Will&Emery

Memery Crystal LLP

44 Southampton Buildings, London WC2A 1AP
Tel: (020) 7242 5905 Fax: (020) 7242 2058
Email: hseaward@memerycrystal.com Web: www.memerycrystal.com

Partners 21	
Assistant Solicitors 36	
Total Trainees 8	
Contact	
Helen Seaward	
Method of application	
Online application form	
Selection procedure	
First interview followed by assessment centre	
Closing date for 2016	
31 July 2014 for training contracts	
Application	
Training contracts p.a. 4	
Applications p.a. 300	
Required degree grade 2:1	
Training	
Salary	
1st year (2012) £30,000	
2nd year (2012) £32,000	
Holiday entitlement	
25 days p.a.	
% of trainees with a non-law degree 50%	
Post-qualification	
Competitive Salary	

Firm profile
Memery Crystal LLP has an enviable reputation as a commercial legal practice. We have a strong internal culture, based upon a set of core values, which underpins our individuality, our emphasis on long-term client relationships and our collegiate and entrepreneurial approach. We act for a broad range of clients, from individual entrepreneurs and owner-managed businesses, to City institutions, educational organisations and multi-national corporations.

We offer a partner-led service and pride ourselves on the strength of our client relationships. We set ourselves apart from our competitors through our pragmatism and pro-activity and we have a reputation for punching well above our weight. Unusually for a single-office firm, we have a strong international focus, which we see as vital to our vision of remaining independent in a globalising economy. We have considerable cross-border transactional experience and have built strong relationships with other independent law firms around the world.

Our key strength lies in the quality of our award winning people. We seek to recruit and retain leading individuals, who provide the highest level of service to our clients.

Main areas of work
Our main practice areas are corporate, dispute resolution, employment, family law, real estate and tax. We have particular expertise in a number of industry sectors, including natural resources, education, financial services, retail and technology.

Trainee profile
We welcome applications from candidates who have achieved a high standard of education in any discipline and who demonstrate a willingness to take on responsibility. We are looking for enthusiastic and ambitious individuals, who are commercially aware and want to build a career at the firm.

Training environment
During your training contact you will rotate departments every 6 months with the aim to give second year trainees their choice in seats. You will sit with a partner or associate who will monitor your progress on a regular basis, with appraisals being carried out every three months. You will also have support from a mentor (normally a junior lawyer) for guidance throughout your training contact. We run a high number of internal legal, client focused and soft skill training courses throughout the year which all trainees are invited to.

We believe that trainees should be integrated into the firm from their first day; you are encouraged to get involved in various firm initiatives and committee groups. Ultimately, we believe that if you accept a training contract here then you are worth investing in. We are looking for individuals to become and remain Memery Crystal career lawyers.

Work Placements
We offer an Open Evening in July, which aims to provide an insight to the firm and the trainee recruitment process. Please see our website for more details and for information on how to apply.

Sponsorship
The firm funds the GDL and the LPC.

Memery Crystal

Michelmores LLP

Woodwater House, Pynes Hill, Exeter EX2 5WR
Tel: (01392) 688 688 Fax: (01392) 360 563
Email: careers@michelmores.com Website: www.michelmores.com
48 Chancery Lane, London, WC2A 1JF
Tel (020) 7659 7660 Fax: (020) 7659 7661

Firm profile
As a top 100 law firm, Michelmores is a dynamic, full-service practice with a total complement of
nearly 400 staff. From its Exeter, Bristol and London offices, the firm provides a first-class service to
a wide range of local, national and international clients (including several central government
departments). Our teams include corporate and commercial, real estate and private client and cross
practice sector focused teams including energy and renewables, manufacturing, and international trade.
The firm has an established track record of attracting quality lawyers at every level, enabling its trainees
to learn from solicitors who are leaders in their fields. Michelmores has created a great place to work
and attracts and retains some of the very best lawyers. The partnership has retained a collegiate style,
which has helped to foster a happy law firm renowned for the enthusiasm of its lawyers, from the
managing partner to the first-year trainees. We have won a number of awards and accolades, including
Corporate Law Firm of the Year at the Insider Awards 2012 and winner of the Regional Law Firm of
the Year 2013 at the City Wealth Magic Circle awards. Furthermore we have just achieved our 'One
Star' accreditation in the prestigious Best Companies Awards 2013, improving the law firm's status
from last year's 'Ones to Watch'.

Main areas of work
The firm has an excellent reputation for its work in company commercial law, dispute resolution and
commercial property while the firm's Private Client Group (including the firm's Family Team)
continues to thrive. The firm also has specialist teams in areas such as projects/PFI, technology, media
and communications, construction and medical negligence.

Trainee profile
The firm welcomes applications from both law and non-law graduates. The firm is looking for trainees
with a strong academic background who are team players and who genuinely want to share in the firm's
success and help it to continue to grow. We are looking to recruit future associates and partners of the
firm. Retaining our trainees on qualification is very important to us and we have an excellent retention
track record.

Training environment
As a Michelmores trainee you will usually spend six months in each of the firm's main departments
(business, real estate and private client). You will work closely with your supervisor in each department
and will be pleasantly surprised at the level of client exposure, responsibility and client involvement. The
firm's trainees are given both the opportunity to handle work themselves (while under supervision) and
to work as part of a team. The quality of the firm's training is high. You will be expected to attend relevant
training sessions on areas such as marketing, IT skills and time management, and will also be
encouraged to attend conferences, seminars and marketing events. As well as the Exeter office we also
have thriving Bristol and London offices where trainees have the opportunity to spend six months of
their training contract. We run a structured trainee training development programme, which aims to
equip our trainees with the key skills needed to be a successful solicitor, on a technical and personal level.

Sponsorship & benefits
Optional private medical insurance, pension scheme, payment of LPC fees (up to £8k), subsidised staff
restaurant, subsidised gym with personal trainer (Exeter), free parking.

Vacation placements
The firm runs an annual vacation placement scheme in July in the firm's Exeter office for one week.
The application form is available on the website. Completed forms should arrive by 28 February 2014.

Partners 57	
Total Staff (inc. Partners) 375	
Assistant solicitors 70	
Contact careers@michelmores.com	
Method of application Online application form	
Selection procedure Assessment days	
Closing date for 2016 1 July 2014	
Application Training contracts p.a. 6 Applications p.a. 200 % interviewed 15% Required degree grade 2:1 (occasional exceptions)	
Training Salary 1st year (2013) £20,000 2nd year (2013) £21,000 Holiday entitlement 25 days p.a. % of trainees with a non-law degree 10% Number of seats available abroad 0 (although occasional foreign secondments available)	
Post-qualification Salary (2013) £33,000 % offered job 75%	

A-Z of Solicitors

Michelmores

Mills & Reeve

100 Hills Road, Cambridge CB2 1PH
Tel: (01223) 222336 Fax: (01223) 355848
Email: graduate.recruitment@mills-reeve.com
Web: www.mills-reeve.com/graduates

Firm profile

Mills & Reeve is a major UK law firm operating from offices in Birmingham, Cambridge, Leeds, London, Manchester and Norwich.

Our business model is straightforward - the highest quality advice, outstanding client service and value for money. We advise more than 70 universities and colleges, over 100 healthcare trusts and NHS bodies, 65 local authorities as well as leading international insurers. Our commercial clients include global and UK-based businesses, FTSE and AIM listed organisations, private companies and startups. We have the largest private tax team outside of London and one of the largest family teams in Europe.

For 10 consecutive years Mills & Reeve has been listed in The Sunday Times Top 100 Best Companies to Work For, which recognises that we put people at the centre of our business.

Main areas of work

Mills & Reeve's services are delivered through firm-wide core groups: corporate and commercial, disputes, employment, family, health, insurance, private wealth sectors, projects and construction and real estate. Further specialist sector teams focus on agriculture, charities, education, food and farming and real estate investment.

Trainee profile

We welcome applications from penultimate year law students, final year non-law students or graduates. Candidates should already have or expect a 2:1 degree or equivalent.

You'll have a good balance between academic ability, interpersonal skills, drafting skills, common sense, commercial awareness, confidence and a professional attitude.

We look for candidates who have the potential to develop into our solicitors of the future.

Training environment

Trainees complete six four-month seats and are recruited to the Birmingham, Cambridge and Norwich offices. Trainees work alongside a partner or senior solicitor. Regular feedback is given to aid development. Performance is assessed by a formal review at the end of each seat.

Training is supported by a full induction, in-house training programme developed by our team of professional support lawyers and the professional skills course (PSC).

Benefits

Life assurance, a contributory pension scheme, 25 days holiday, bonus scheme, sports and social club, subsidised staff restaurants, season ticket loan. The firm runs a flexible benefits scheme.

Vacation placements

Applications for two week placements during the summer must be received by 31 January 2014.

Sponsorship & awards

The firm pays the full costs of the CPE/GDL and LPC fees and a maintenance grant during the GDL and LPC.

MILLS & REEVE

Partners 112
Assistant Solicitors 455
Total Trainees 37

Contact
Fiona Medlock
01223 222336

Method of application
Online

Selection procedure
Normally one day assessment centre

Closing date for 2016
31 July 2014 for training contracts
31st January 2014 for work placements

Application
Training contracts p.a. 15
Applications p.a. Approx 850
% interviewed p.a. 10%
Required degree grade 2:1

Training
Salary
1st year £25,000
2nd year £26,500
Holiday entitlement
25 days p.a.
% of trainees with a non-law degree 40%

Post-qualification
% of trainees offered job on qualification 85%

Offices
Birmingham, Cambridge, Leeds, London, Manchester, Norwich

A-Z of Solicitors

Mishcon de Reya

Summit House, 12 Red Lion Square, London WC1R 4QD
Tel: (020) 7440 7000 Fax: (020) 7430 0691
Email: trainee.recruitment@mishcon.com
Website: www.mishcongraduates.com

Partners 81	
Assistant Solicitors 146	
Total Trainees 24	
Contact	
Ann-Marie Comer, HR Manager	
Method of application	
Online application form	
Closing date for August 2016	
15 July 2014	
Application	
Training contracts p.a. 8-12	
Applications p.a. 1,000+	
% interviewed p.a. 5%	
Required degree grade 2:1	
Training	
Salary	
1st year £32,000	
Holiday entitlement	
25 days p.a.	
Occasional secondments	
available	
Overseas / Regional Offices	
London, New York	

Firm profile
Founded in 1937, Mishcon de Reya is a law firm with offices in London and New York offering a wide range of legal services to companies and individuals.

Our clients are dynamic and sophisticated and we reflect that in our belief in challenging the conventional or accepted ways of working. We like to solve problems quickly. To achieve this consistently, we employ a diverse collection of talented people, from varied backgrounds with differing perspectives, who are capable of addressing issues in a collaborative, non-hierarchical environment.

In every area of the law that we operate, Mishcon de Reya prides itself in providing a best in class service to its clients. Our expertise covers five areas: analysing risk, protection of assets, managing wealth, resolving disputes and building business.

Main areas of work
We are organised internally into six different departments: corporate, employment, dispute resolution, family, Mishcon private and real estate. The firm also has a growing number of specialist groups which include: art; betting and gaming; finance and banking; fraud; immigration; insolvency and IP.

Trainee profile
Our trainees are typically high-achieving and intelligent individuals with good interpersonal skills and outgoing personalities. Strength of character and ability to think laterally are also important.

Training environment
Trainees have the opportunity to gain experience, skills and knowledge from across the firm in four six-month seats involving contentious and non-contentious work. Because of the relatively few training contracts offered, trainees can be exposed to high-quality work with lots of responsibility early on. Trainees are supported with a wide ranging training and development programme in addition to the Professional Skills Course. Trainee performance is monitored closely and trainees can expect to receive regular feedback in addition to mid-seat and end-of-seat appraisals.

Sponsorship & benefits
The firm provides full LPC and GDL funding, and a maintenance grant of £5,000 payable in the GDL and LPC year. Benefits include 25 days holiday, health screening, life assurance, dental insurance, income replacement insurance, private medical insurance, travel insurance, critical illness cover, gym membership, season ticket loan, stakeholder pension scheme, yoga classes, childcare vouchers, cycle scheme, in-house doctor, bonus scheme and give-as-you-earn schemes.

Vacation placements
Places for Easter 2014: 10

Places for summer 2014: 20

Duration: 2 weeks; closing date: 15 January 2014

Our Easter and Summer Vacation Schemes have been designed to provide students with an opportunity to gain an insight into the role of a trainee, our culture and our people. We run a fun and informative workshop programme covering all practice areas of the firm, combined with individual and group work sessions.

Mishcon de Reya

A-Z of Solicitors

Morgan Lewis & Bockius

Condor House, 5-10 St. Paul's Churchyard, London EC4M 8AL
Tel: (020)3 201 5000 Fax: (020)3 201 5001
Email: Londontrainingprogramme@morganlewis.com
Website: www.morganlewis.co.uk

Firm profile
With 25 offices in the United States, Europe, Asia and the Middle East, Morgan Lewis provides comprehensive corporate, transactional, regulatory and litigation services to clients of all sizes and across all major industries. Founded in 1873, Morgan Lewis comprises more than 1,600 legal professionals—including lawyers, patent agents, benefits advisers, regulatory scientists and other specialists. The firm has expanded significantly in London in the past year through the addition of several new teams.

Main areas of work
Debt and equity capital markets; finance and restructuring; labour and employment including employment litigation and immigration advice; private investment fund formation and operation; UK and US tax planning and structuring; international commercial dispute, arbitration, insurance recovery, and white collar matters: life sciences, financial services, energy and technology sector work.

Trainee profile
Morgan Lewis is seeking candidates with a consistently strong academic record, who would respond with confidence to opportunities to work on challenging assignments across a wide variety of areas. Candidates should be able to demonstrate strong interpersonal, communication and client service skills and analytical ability, as well as a proven ability to work effectively both independently and within a team.

Training environment
Our new training programme is led by an experienced training principal. Following a full induction into the firm, including legal research training, the programme will provide trainees with consistently high quality, challenging assignments, working with senior lawyers on complex and frequently cross-border matters. Through this hands-on experience, trainees can expect to gather a thorough understanding of the firm's business and of working with international, high profile clients.

In addition to formal appraisals, the office environment allows regular contact with the training principal, supervisors and other lawyers. Trainees will attend Professional Skills Courses throughout their contract and will have the opportunity to participate in all associate training sessions, pro bono work and business development activities.

Vacation scheme
There will be 20 spaces available on the 2014 Spring Vacation Scheme. The deadline for applications is 31st January 2014.

Benefits
Life insurance, health and travel insurance, dental insurance, long-term disability insurance and season ticket loan.

Sponsorship & awards
Sponsorship of LPC and GDL. A maintenance grant of £7,500 will be provided.

Partners 20
Assistant Solicitors 28
Total Trainees 6

Contact
Georgia Shearman
0203 201 5620

Method of application
Via our website

Closing date for 2016
31 July 2014

Selection procedure
Interviews

Application
No. of training contracts 5 p.a
Required degree grade
high 2:1

Training
Salary
1st year £40,000
2nd year £43,000
Holiday entitlement
25 days p.a

Post-qualification
Salary £75,000

Overseas offices
Almaty, Beijing, Boston, Brussels, Chicago, Dallas, Dubai, Frankfurt, Harrisburg, Houston, Irvine, London, Los Angeles, Miami, Moscow, New York, Palo Alto, Paris, Philadelphia, Pittsburgh, Princeton, San Francisco, Tokyo, Washington, Wilmington

Morgan Lewis

A-Z of Solicitors

Muckle LLP

Time Central, 32 Gallowgate, Newcastle upon Tyne NE1 4BF
Tel: (0191) 211 7777 Fax: (0191) 211 7788
Email: tracy.murray@muckle-llp.com Website: www.muckle-llp.com

Firm profile
Muckle LLP is a leading commercial law firm in the North East of England. The firm has an excellent client base of successful private and public companies, property investors and developers, financial institutions and public sector and educational organisations, which recognise that its innovative commercial skills are a major benefit in enhancing its service delivery to them.

Main areas of work
The firm provides the following services – corporate, banking and restructuring, commercial, construction and engineering, real estate, employment, dispute resolution and private client.

Trainee profile
The firm recruits four trainees a year. The firm is looking to recruit talented individuals who can demonstrate their enthusiasm and desire to become business advisers and a commitment to building their career in the North East. Trainees must have good academic qualifications, interpersonal skills, be team players and embrace our culture and values.

Training environment
The firm runs an excellent training programme that focuses on the trainees' legal, IT, management and business development skills. During your training contract you may experience training within the following areas: corporate finance, commercial, property, employment, dispute resolution, construction and banking. Training is a combination of on-the-job experience, partner and other lawyer mentoring as well as in-house and external courses. Trainees are encouraged to participate in all aspects of the firm which include engagement, community and 'green' teams.

Benefits
25 days holiday a year and flexible holiday option; pension after six months service; permanent health insurance; life assurance; corporate discounts; salary sacrifice schemes; car parking discounts.

Sponsorship & awards
LPC fees are paid subject to eligibility.

Partners 27
Fee earners 83
Total Trainees 9

Contact
Tracy Murray HR Assistant
0191 211 7843

Method of application
Apply online via our website
www.muckle-llp.com

Selection procedure
Interviews and an assessment day

Closing date for 2014 summer vacation scheme
Friday 31st January 2014

Closing date for 2016 training contracts
Thursday 31st July 2014

Application
Training contracts p.a. 4
Applications p.a. 230-240
% interviewed p.a. 25%
Required degree grade preferably 2:1

Training
Salary
Starting salary £22,000 (2012) with regular reviews throughout training contract
Holiday entitlement
25 days holiday a year and flexible holiday option

Post-qualification
Salary
Starting salary £34,000 (2013) with regular reviews
Aim to retain 100% of trainees on qualification

Office
Only Newcastle upon Tyne

muckle LLP

PricewaterhouseCoopers Legal LLP

6 Hay's Lane, London SE1 2HB
Tel: (0808) 100 1500
Website: www.pwclegal.co.uk

Firm profile

PricewaterhouseCoopers Legal LLP (PwC Legal) is an independent member of the PwC international network of firms. We combine the best of both worlds. A firm that's not so large it's impersonal, yet as part of the wider PwC network, we can call upon the support of professionals in PwC when our clients are looking for rounded solutions incorporating multidisciplinary advice. Combined with our ambitious growth plans, this makes us an exciting place to launch your career.

Main areas of work

We offer a wide range of domestic and international clients both project-based, specialist legal advice and on-going general day-to-day counsel. Our areas of expertise include advising on mergers and acquisitions, corporate restructuring, intellectual property, information technology, commercial and tax litigation, immigration, pensions, employment, banking, commercial contracts, real estate, wills and trusts, environment and sustainability.

Our solicitors often work directly alongside PwC tax advisers, human capital consultants, corporate finance experts, actuaries, management consultants and of course, accountants. In terms of global reach, the PwC network is unsurpassed, having access to legal expertise in over 75 countries and immigration expertise in 116 countries. Thanks to resources like this, we can deliver a superior service to our clients. One that really addresses their business needs, while offering our lawyers a unique working environment.

Trainee profile

Penultimate-year law students and final-year non-law students with at least a 2:1 honours degree (or equivalent), a 320+ UCAS tariff (or equivalent) and a keen interest in business law.

Training environment

Trainee solicitors have the opportunity to develop their skills in any of our practice groups. At the same time, exposure to the diverse skill sets of professionals in PwC will help you hone strong business advisory skills. You're definitely training to be a lawyer, but you'll do it in an exciting multi-disciplinary environment. You'll develop lateral thinking skills, gain practical, hands-on experience at a very early stage in your traineeship and be part of teams delivering creative solutions. During your training contract, you'll take the core and elective modules of the Professional Skills Course between your second and fourth seats and receive extensive training internally on business development and networking, management and interpersonal skills.

Vacation schemes

Our paid, three-week summer vacation scheme is a great way to find out how we work and why we're unlike any other legal firm. You'll spend time in several of our practice groups, gain invaluable work experience and develop a real flavour for life as a solicitor in PwC Legal. The summer vacation scheme is also the biggest source of candidates for our trainee solicitor intake.

Sponsorship & awards

Trainees can apply for a scholarship award to help with the costs of the Graduate Diploma and the Legal Practice Course. If successful, you'll receive the total cost of the tuition and examination fees plus a significant contribution towards living expenses. You can find out more on our website.

Vacancies 9
Trainees 19
Partners 23
Total staff 210
Work placement Yes

Method of application
Visit www.pwclegal.co.uk to submit your online application form.

Closing dates
For training contracts starting in 2016 apply by July 31 2014
For our summer vacation scheme apply by January 31 2014

Application
Penultimate-year law students and final-year non-law students with at least a 2.1 honours degree (or equivalent), a 320+ UCAS tariff (or equivalent) and a keen interest in business law

Training
Salary London
1st year (2012) £37,000
2nd year (2012) £42,000

Reed Smith

The Broadgate Tower, 20 Primrose Street, London EC2A 2RS
Tel: (020) 3116 3000 Fax: (020) 3116 3999
Email: graduate.recruitment@reedsmith.com
Website: www.reedsmith.com

Firm profile

Key to Reed Smith's success is its ability to build lasting relationships: with clients and with each other. United through a culture defined by commitment to professional development, team-work, diversity, pro bono and community support, the firm has grown to become one of the largest law firms in the world. Its 25 offices span three continents and London is currently the largest with over 500 people. While the offices benefit from an international framework, each one retains key elements of the local business culture.

Main areas of work

The firm is particularly well known for its work advising leading companies in the areas of financial services, life sciences, shipping, energy and natural resources, advertising, technology and media. It provides a wide range of commercial legal services for all these clients, including a full spectrum of corporate, commercial and financial services, dispute resolution, real estate and employment advice. Much of the work is multi-jurisdictional.

Trainee profile

The firm is looking for individuals with the drive and potential to become world-class business lawyers. They want 'players' rather than 'onlookers' with strong intellect, initiative, the ability to thrive in a challenging profession and the personal qualities to build strong relationships with colleagues and clients.

Training environment

Given the range of different work undertaken in the London office, trainees get the chance to have a varied training contract and develop a wide range of skills. The firm runs a 4 seat rotation system and trainees will be supervised by either a senior associate or partner. In addition to seats in the London office, trainees have the opportunity to spend six months on secondment, either abroad or with a client.

The firm has developed a new version of the Legal Practice Course (LPC) that fully integrates legal and business learning and leads to a unique Master's qualification, the MA (LPC with Business). This bespoke programme was the first of its kind and allows students to study commercial and legal aspects in parallel, and not separately, so that they complete the course before entering a training contract with the firm.

There are vacancies for training contracts commencing in August 2016 and February 2017.

Benefits

Permanent health insurance, subsidised cafeteria, life insurance, lifestyle discounts and concierge service, contributory pension scheme, season ticket loan and a flexible benefits package.

Vacation placements

Every summer, the firm offers the opportunity for up to 20 students to experience working life at Reed Smith as part of our vacation scheme. It is also an excellent opportunity for the firm to meet with prospective trainees in a relaxed environment and to provide them with a realistic representation of what trainee life may be like. The schemes are two weeks in duration and students will have the opportunity to work in two different practice areas. On arrival, students will have completed at least two years of undergraduate study.

Sponsorship & awards

GDL Funding: Fees paid plus £6,000 maintenance. LPC Funding: Fees paid plus £7,000 maintenance.

Partners 113*
Fee-earners 297*
Total Trainees 51
* denotes UK figures

Contact
Lucy Crittenden

Method of application
Online application form

Selection procedure
Selection exercise, interview, verbal reasoning assessment

Closing date for 2016/2017
31 July 2014

Application
Training contracts p.a. approximately 24
Applications p.a. 1000
% interviewed p.a. 7%
Required degree grade 2:1

Training
Salary
1st year (2013) £37,000
Holiday entitlement 25 days
% of trainees with a non-law degree p.a. 40%
No. of seats available abroad p.a. 4

Post-qualification
Salary (2013)
£59,000 plus bonus
% of assistants who joined as trainees 43%
% of partners who joined as trainees 45%

Overseas offices
New York, London, Hong Kong, Chicago, Washington DC, Beijing, Paris, Los Angeles, San Francisco, Philadelphia, Pittsburg, Munich, Abu Dhabi, Princeton, N Virginia, Dubai, Century City, Piraeus, Richmond, Silicon Valley, Shanghai, Houston, Singapore, Kazakhstan, Wilmington

ReedSmith

RPC

Tower Bridge House, St Katharine's Way, London E1W 1AA
Tel: (020) 3060 6000
Website: www.rpc.co.uk/manifesto

Firm profile

Leading lawyers. Great clients. And an unrivalled commercial approach to business. At RPC we offer a depth of knowledge and creativity that few firms can rival and combine this with high quality training programmes that are consistently lauded in the leading directories.

Headquartered in a state of the art site in the City of London, we also have stunning offices in Bristol, Hong Kong and Singapore. Our open plan, collaborative working environment – where knowledge is easily shared and access to partners an everyday reality – is designed to bring out the best in our people and to ensure that the service we offer our clients is second to none. And it is.

We provide top quality legal services to global businesses across a wide range of industry sectors and practices, including insurance, commercial litigation, construction, engineering and projects, corporate/M&A, IP and technology, media, real estate, employment and pensions, outsourcing, regulatory, tax and competition.

Twice nominated as Law Firm of the Year in 2013, in 2012 we won Insurance Team of the Year at the Legal Business Awards, Corporate Team of the Year (midcap) at The Lawyer Awards, and Service Provider of the Year at the British Insurance Awards, as well as being voted by the Financial Times as one of the most innovative firms in Europe.

Main Areas of Work

Banking and finance, commercial litigation, corporate, commercial insurance, competition, construction, corporate finance, corporate insurance, dispute resolution, employment, energy/transport/infrastructure, insolvency, insurance and reinsurance, intellectual property, IT, media, personal injury, pensions and benefits, real estate, regulatory, tax, technology and outsourcing.

Trainee Profile

Although proven academic ability is important (we require a 2:1 degree or above, not necessarily in Law) we value energy, enthusiasm, business sense, commitment and the ability to relate well to others just as highly.

Benefits

We feel it is important to offer our employees a creative and competitive benefits package with choice and flexibility. Our full range of benefits can be viewed via our website.

Funding

Bursaries are available for the GDL, if applicable, and the LPC. Bursaries comprise course and examination fees and maintenance grants of up to £7,000. We request that all our trainees complete their LPC and GDL at BPP law school.

Partners 80
Associates 266
Total trainees 33

Contact
Trainee Recruitment Team
020 3060 6000
RPC, Tower Bridge House,
St Katharine's Way,
London, E1W 1AA
www.rpc.co.uk/manifesto

Method of application
Online or by post

Selection procedure
First interview face to face, presentations, aptitude tests, case studies

Closing date August 2016
Training contract
31 July 2014
Vacation scheme
31 January 2014

Application
Training contracts p.a.
London 20
Bristol 4
Required degree grade London & Bristol 2:1

Training
Salary
London 1st year £37,000
Bristol 1st year £32,000
London 2nd year £40,000
Bristol 2nd year £35,000

Post-qualification
Salary
London (2012) £58,000
Bristol (2012) £44,000
% of trainees offered job on qualification (2012) 87%

Overseas/Regional offices
Hong Kong and Singapore

SGH Martineau

No 1 Colmore Square, Birmingham B4 6AA
One America Square, Crosswall, London EC3N 2SG
Tel: 0800 763 1000 Fax: 0800 763 1001
Email: training.contracts@sghmartineau.com
Website: www.sghmartineau.com

Firm profile
We are a top 70, commercially orientated law firm that services a diverse range of clients across a number of key sectors, offering the full spectrum of legal services.

Main areas of work
Corporate, corporate finance, capital projects, private capital, commercial disputes, commercial property, employment, mergers and acquisitions, charities and trusts, construction and engineering, professional negligence, intellectual property, technology, property disputes, and retail. Our key sectors are energy, education, banking, leisure, private wealth, industry and manufacturing and investment funds.

Trainee profile
We work in partnership with our trainees and provide mentoring, supervision, support and exposure to the key areas of the firm's practice. Trainees are encouraged to deliver legal solutions to clients while benefiting from quality work.

Trainees benefit from a structured career training programme tailored to their personal development needs. It covers not only legal technical matters but also a business and commercial approach which has never been more central to successful professional careers.

Trainees rotate every four months which results in gaining a broad experience and also the possibility of repeating a seat.

Benefits
Permanent health insurance, life insurance, private medical insurance, pension, season ticket loan, cycle to work.

Sponsorship
LPC fees are paid and a maintenance grant available.

Vacation placements
Our 2 day mini vacation schemes give an excellent opportunity to meet a range of people from the firm and see what life is like as a trainee. They involve presentations, interactive workshops and legal activities from various teams, networking opportunities and much more.

Partners 60	
Fee earners 130	
Total Trainees 20	

Contact
Jennifer Nicholson

Method of application
Online application form
www.sghmartineau.com/
trainingcontracts

Selection procedure
Mini vacation scheme and assessment centre

Closing date for 2016 training contracts
31 July 2014

Closing date for 2014 mini vacation schemes
24 February 2014

Application
Training contracts p.a. 10
Applications p.a. 800
& interviewed p.a. 10%
Required degree grade 2:1

Training
Salary
1st year (2013)
c. £23,000 (regional)
2nd year (2013)
c. £25,000 (regional)
Holiday entitlement 25 days
% of trainees with a non-law degree 32%

Post-qualification
Salary (2012) £36,000 (regional)
% of trainees offered job on qualification (2012) 100%

Overseas offices
Belgium

Shearman & Sterling LLP

Broadgate West, 9 Appold Street, London EC2A 2AP
Tel: (020) 7655 5000 Fax: (020) 7655 5500
Email: graduates@shearman.com
Website: www.shearman.com

Firm profile

Shearman & Sterling is one of the world's leading premier global law firms and was established over a century ago. The London office opened over 40 years ago and quickly became one of the leading practices, covering all aspects of English, European and US corporate and finance law. Globally there are approximately 900 lawyers, including around 200 partners.

Main areas of work

Our main areas of work include: European corporate (including mergers and acquisitions, equity capital markets and US capital markets), project development and finance, global finance (including capital markets, structured, acquisition and leveraged finance), international arbitration and litigation, antitrust, tax, financial institutions advisory and asset management, real estate and executive compensation and employee benefits.

Trainee profile

We look for trainees from a broad range of backgrounds who can bring their unique experiences to the firm. Working closely with partners and associates, trainees have the opportunity to become an integral team member, taking on real responsibility from day one. Our trainees are enthusiastic and ambitious, and show a real willingness to learn and develop their skills across both technical and soft skill areas.

Training environment

The two year training contract consists of four seats, each lasting six months. Two of these seats will be in our core practice areas (European corporate, global finance or project development and finance), while the remaining two are selected from the other practice areas. Trainees typically share an office with a partner or senior lawyer allowing informal learning on the job, while the structured training programme at the firm ensures trainees get exposure to all the information they need to be a success now and in the future. In addition to the cross-jurisdictional work trainees do in London, they are also encouraged to spend a seat in one of our overseas offices, allowing them to further build their global networks.

Benefits

Life assurance; long term disability insurance; annual eye test; matched pension contributions; subsidised gym membership; private medical insurance; travel insurance; private dental insurance.

Sponsorship & awards

Full sponsorship for the GDL and LPC, and a maintenance grant of £7,000 during each year of these courses.

Partners 30
Assistant Solicitors 120
Total Trainees 26

Contact
Charlotte Hannan
Tel (020) 7655 5000

Method of application
Online at www.shearman.com

Selection procedure
Psychometric test
Interview with HR and a senior lawyer/partner
Assessment centre

Closing date for 2016
31 July 2014

Application
Training contracts p.a. 15
Applications p.a. approx 900
% interviewed p.a. 7%
Required degree grade 2:1 or international equivalent

Training
Salary
1st year (2013) £39,000
2nd year (2013) £44,000
Holiday entitlement
24 days p.a.

Post-qualification
Salary (2013) £78,000
% of trainees offered job on qualification (2011) 84%

Overseas offices
Abu Dhabi, Beijing, Brussels, Dusseldorf, Frankfurt, Hong Kong, Milan, Munich, New York, Palo Alto, Paris, Rome, San Francisco, Sao Paulo, Shanghai, Singapore, Tokyo, Toronto and Washington, DC.

SHEARMAN & STERLING LLP

Sheridans

Whittington House, Alfred Place, London WC1E 7EA
Tel: (020) 7079 0100 Fax: (020) 7079 0200
Email: enquiries@sheridans.co.uk
Website: www.sheridans.co.uk

Firm profile
Sheridans is a leading leisure, media and entertainment law firm with an established reputation across the creative industries. The firm represents a number of leading organisations, brands and talent across sectors including computer games, entertainment, fashion, film, interactive media, music, sport, television and theatre. Sheridans complements this expertise with a thriving commercial practice offering corporate, dispute resolution, real estate and employment services.

Main areas of work
Media & Entertainment: The music department advises recording artists and recording and management companies, on contract negotiation, popular and classical music publishing, merchandising and sponsorship. The film and television departments advise broadcasters, television and feature film production companies, distribution and sales agents, financiers and talent. Other specialist areas include theatre, sport, advertising and branding, fashion and design, trade marks and domain names, technology, computer games and interactive and digital media.

Dispute Resolution: The firm provides advice and representation in relation to disputes arising in the media and entertainment industries. The disputes typically range from privacy and defamation claims against the national press to rights disputes.

Corporate/Commercial: The firm advises on commercial contracts, mergers, acquisitions and disposals, management buy-outs and buy-ins, corporate finance, joint ventures, corporate reorganisations, company formations and insolvency.

Real Estate: Services include the sale and purchase of commercial property, involving investment, leasehold and planning matters, secured lending, building and development schemes and property financing, as well as domestic conveyancing for high net worth individuals.

Employment: The employment practice handles contentious and non-contentious matters, representing both employers and senior executives on a wide range of matters from recruitment to severence and change management to TUPE.

Trainee profile
Excellent academic background (2:1 and above, good A levels), commercial awareness, great interpersonal skills and an ability to think strategically. Trainees should have an enthusiasm for, and a demonstrable commitment to, the firm's areas of practice.

Training
The training contract is divided into four six-month seats, although trainees are expected to be flexible and assist any department as required. Trainees are given a challenging range of work and exposure to a significant level of responsibility.

Partners 28
Consultants 1
Assistant solicitors 20
Total trainees 2

Contact
Claire Lewis (Training Principal)

Method of application
CV and covering letter, by email to
trainees@sheridans.co.uk

Selection procedure
2 stage interview process

Closing date for 2016
31 July 2014

Application
Training contracts p.a. 1
Required degree grade 2:1

Training
Salary
1st year competitive with similar firms
2nd year competitive with similar firms
Holiday entitlement
20 days

Post-qualification
Salary Competitive with similar firms
% of trainees offered job on qualification (in last two years) 100%

SHERIDANS

A-Z of Solicitors

Shoosmiths

The Lakes, Northampton NN4 7SH
Tel: (0370) 086 3075 Fax: (0370) 086 3001
Email: join.us@shoosmiths.co.uk
Website: www.shoosmiths.co.uk
Twitter: www.twitter.com/shoosmithsgrads

Firm profile

Shoosmiths is a full service law firm offering you experience in a variety of areas, including commercial, corporate, employment, real estate, intellectual property, banking, planning and dispute resolution. Through our Access Legal consumer brand, we also offer private client, personal injury, medical negligence and conveyancing.

Trainee Profile

You'll be open-minded, forward-thinking, creative and innovative, and be trained in a non-hierarchal, open plan environment.

As a trainee, you will value a social life outside the office. Work-wise, you will care about the quality of service you give to clients, and will want to make a real and direct contribution to the firm's success.

Your experience will be built around a practical workload, complemented by technical and business skills training. We allocate no more than one trainee to each team, which means trainees enjoy high levels of involvement with the team, and are given good quality work and contact with clients.

Over two years, you will complete four, six-month placements, one of which could be an external secondment to a client's in-house legal team, providing an invaluable insight from the client's perspective.

Training environment

There's nothing like diving straight in and having a go and, while we would not ask you to do something you are not comfortable in tackling, we expect you to relish the opportunity to get experience of real cases and deals from the start. In our opinion, it's the best way to learn.

Shoosmiths Trainees take an active part in the CR (Corporate Responsibility) around the firm, and they also create and drive initiatives of their own including "New Friday" a networking event for young professionals.

Your experience will be built around a practical workload, complemented by technical and business skills training. Over the two years, you will complete four six-month placements, one of which possibly being an external secondment to a clients in-house legal team, which provides an invaluable insight into the clients perspective.

Benefits

Regular involvement in sporting and social events, flexible holiday, pension, life assurance, corporate discounts. Please see our website for more benefits.

Vacation placements

Placements provide invaluable experience, allowing you to choose the right firm for you, and can even fast track you to a place on the assessment day for a training contract.

During your time with us, you'll be buddied with a trainee and spend time working with clients, partners and qualified lawyers, making a valuable contribution to the business.

Sponsorship & awards

We are happy to offer you financial assistance in relation to your GDL and/or LPC. We will also provide a living allowance whilst you are studying.

Partners 130
Total Staff 1,300
Total Trainees 42

Contact
Samantha Hope

Method of application
Online application form

Selection procedure
Application & assessment day

Closing date for 2016
31st July 2014

Application
No. of Training Contracts 20
Applications pa 1600+
% Interviewed 10%
Required degree grade 2:1

Training
Salary
£24,000 / £25,000
Holiday entitlement p.a
23 days + flex

Post-qualification
Salary £38,000
% of trainees offered job on qualification (2012) 100%

Offices
Birmingham, Edinburgh, Manchester, Milton Keynes, Nottingham, Northampton, Reading, Solent (please see our website for locations we are currently recruiting to)

SHOOSMITHS

Sidley Austin LLP

Woolgate Exchange, 25 Basinghall Street, London EC2V 5HA
Tel: (020) 7360 3600
Email: ukrecruitment@sidley.com
Website: www.sidley.com

Firm profile
Sidley Austin LLP is one of the world's largest full-service law firms. With approximately 1,700 lawyers practising on four continents (North America, Europe, Australasia and Asia), the firm provides a broad range of integrated services to meet the needs of its clients across a multitude of industries.

Main areas of work
Corporate, competition, corporate reorganisation and bankruptcy, debt restructuring, debt finance and structured finance, equity capital markets, employment, financial services regulatory, hedge funds, insurance, IP/IT, litigation, real estate and real estate finance, tax.

Trainee profile
Sidley Austin LLP looks for focused, intelligent and enthusiastic individuals with personality and humour who have a real interest in practising law in the commercial world. Trainees should have a consistently strong academic record and a 2:1 degree (not necessarily in law).

Training environment
The firm is not a typical City firm and it is not a 'legal factory' so there is no risk of being just a number. Everyone is encouraged to be proactive and to create their own niche when they are ready to do so. Trainees spend time in the firm's main groups. In each group trainees will sit with a partner or senior associate to ensure individual training based on 'hands on' experience. You will be encouraged to take responsibility where appropriate. Regular meetings with your supervisor ensure both the quality and quantity of your experience. In addition, there is a structured timetable of training on a cross-section of subjects.

Benefits
Private health insurance, life assurance, contribution to gym membership, interest-free season ticket loan, income protection scheme, pension and subsidised restaurant.

Sponsorship & awards
Tuition fees for the GDL/CPE and the LPC. Maintenance grant of £7,000 p.a.

Partners 43
Assistant Solicitors 75
Total Trainees 20

Contact
Lucy Slater
Graduate Recruitment Officer

Method of application
Apply online at
www.sidley.com

Selection procedure
Interview and verbal reasoning test

Closing date for 2016
31 July 2014

Application
Training contracts p.a. 10
Applications p.a. 600
% interviewed p.a. 15
Required degree grade 2:1

Training
Salary
1st year (2013) £41,000
2nd year (2013) £43,000
Holiday entitlement 25 days
% of trainees with a
non-law degree p.a. 50%

Overseas offices
Beijing, Boston, Brussels, Chicago, Dallas, Frankfurt, Geneva, Hong Kong, Houston, Los Angeles, New York, Palo Alto, San Francisco, Shanghai, Singapore, Sydney, Tokyo, Washington DC

A-Z of Solicitors

Simmons & Simmons LLP

CityPoint, One Ropemaker Street, London EC2Y 9SS
Tel: (020) 7628 2020 Fax: (020) 7628 2070
Email: recruitment@simmons-simmons.com
Website: www.simmons-simmons.com/graduates

Firm profile

Simmons & Simmons is a leading international law firm with fully integrated teams working through 22 offices across Europe, the Middle East and Asia. The firm's strategy is designed to ensure it provides its clients with high-quality advice and delivers value through new ways of working.

Main areas of work

Simmons & Simmons applies considerable expertise to all business sectors, but focuses on: asset management and investment funds, energy and infrastructure, financial institutions, life sciences, and technology, media and telecommunications. These five sector teams are drawn from the core practice areas of: corporate, dispute resolution, EU, competition and regulatory, employment, pensions and employee benefits, financial markets, IP, projects, real estate, information, communications and technology, and tax.

Trainee profile

Simmons & Simmons is interested in finding out about your academic successes but will also explore your ability to form excellent interpersonal relations and work within a team environment, as well as your levels of motivation, drive and ambition. Show us evidence of a rich 'life experience' as well as examples of your intellectual capabilities and we will provide you with everything you need to become a successful member of our firm.

Training environment

The training programme is constantly evolving to build the skills you will need to be successful in the fast moving world of international business. Our groundbreaking MBA programme is designed to provide our trainees and junior lawyers with a unique opportunity to gain valuable business and commercial skills early in their career. During the training contract we will also ensure trainees have a broad legal experience, and a balanced, integrated approach to gaining the knowledge, expertise and abilities you will need to qualify in the practice area of your choice.

Vacation placements

The firm's internship schemes are one of the primary means of selecting candidates for a career at Simmons & Simmons. Your placement will enable you to gain a first-hand experience of a busy and dynamic international law firm, with exposure to the deals and transactions the firm works on.

The firm's three week summer vacation scheme is open to penultimate year law students, final year non-law students and graduates. Applications open 01 November 2013.

The spring vacation scheme is a great opportunity for first year law students and penultimate year non-law students to get an in-depth view of the firm. Applications open 01 November 2013.

Simmons & Simmons also runs a winter vacation scheme aimed specifically at final year non-law students, graduates of non-law subjects and career changers. Applications open 01 October 2013.

Finally, a series of open days, available to all students and graduates run throughout the year.

Sponsorship

The firm will cover your full tuition fees at law school and offer a maintenance grant of £7,500.

Partners 230+
Fee earners 800+
Total Trainees 80+

Contact
Andy Renouf, Graduate Recruitment Advisor

Method of application
Online application form, at www.simmons-simmons.com/graduates

Selection procedure
Online application, remote online critical reasoning test, assessment day

Application dates for Training Contracts in 2016/17
Non law finalists and all graduates
1 Nov 2013 - 31 March 2014
Law undergraduates
1 June - 31 July 2014

Application
Training contracts p.a. circa 40
Applications p.a. 2,000
Required degree grade 2:1

Training
Salary
£37,500 1st and 2nd seat
£41,750 3rd and 4th seat
Holiday entitlement 25 days
% of trainees with a non-law degree p.a. 50%
No. of seats available abroad p.a. varies

Post-qualification
Salary (2013) £59,000

Overseas offices
Abu Dhabi, Amsterdam, Beijing, Bristol, Brussels, Doha, Dubai, Düsseldorf, Frankfurt, Funchal*, Hong Kong, Jeddah*, Lisbon*, London, Madrid, Milan, Munich, Paris, Rome, Shanghai, Singapore, Tokyo
*Associated office

Simmons & Simmons

SJ Berwin

10 Queen Street Place, London EC4R 1BE
Tel: (020) 7111 2268 Fax: (020) 7111 2000
Email: graduate.recruitment@sjberwin.com
Website: www.sjberwin.com

Firm profile
SJ Berwin is the youngest of the large international law firms and we've always prided ourselves on our modern, creative and service-driven approach. Our lawyers are recognised as leaders in their field. We have 164 partners and more than 1,100 staff with a total of 12 offices across the world in Europe, Asia and the Middle East.

Main areas of work
We work for some of the world's leading brands from multi-national companies and financial institutions to funds and private equity houses, advising on the full range of legal services including: commerce and technology, corporate, employment and pensions, EU, competition and regulatory, finance, financial markets, intellectual property, investment funds, litigation, real estate, restructuring and insolvency and tax. We also have deep industry expertise in the following sectors: consumer, energy and infrastructure, financial institutions, life sciences and healthcare, private equity, real estate and technology, media and telecoms.

Trainee profile
The firm wants ambitious, commercially minded individuals who seek a high level of involvement from day one. Candidates must have a strong academic record, be on track for, or have achieved, a 2:1 or equivalent in their undergraduate degree, and have demonstrated strong team and leadership potential.

Training environment
The two-year training contract is divided into four six-month seats. Trainees will spend two seats (which may include a seat abroad or client secondment) within the following areas: finance, mergers and aquisitions, equity capital markets, private equity, venture capital and investment funds. Trainees are given early responsibility and are supported throughout the training contract.

How to apply
The firm welcomes applications from all disciplines and all universities. Applications must be made using the firm's online form available at www.sjberwin.com. The same form can be used to indicate your interest in an open day, a vacation scheme and/or a training contract.

Benefits
25 days holiday, private healthcare, gym membership/subsidy, life assurance, pension scheme, season ticket loan, free lunch.

Partners 164
Assistant Solicitors 348
Total Trainees 77

Contact
Graduate Recruitment Team

Method of application
Online application form

Selection procedure
2 interviews / case study /
critical reasoning test

Closing date for 2016
31 July 2014
2014 Easter & summer
vacation schemes 31 January
2014

Application
Training contracts p.a. 30
Applications p.a. 2,000
10% interviewed p.a.
Required degree grade 2:1

Training
Salary
£37,500, 1st year
£41,500, 2nd year
Holiday entitlement 25 days
% of trainees with a
non-law degree p.a. 50%

Post-qualification
Salary (2013) £60,000
% of trainees offered job
on qualification (as March
2013) 79%

Overseas offices
Berlin, Brussels, Dubai, Frankfurt,
Hong Kong, Luxembourg,
Madrid, Milan, Munich, Paris,
Shanghai

A-Z of Solicitors

Skadden, Arps, Slate, Meagher & Flom (UK) LLP

40 Bank Street, Canary Wharf, London E14 5DS
Tel: (020) 7519 7000 Fax: (020) 7519 7070
Email: graduate.hiring@skadden.com
Website: www.skadden.com/uktraineesolicitors

Firm profile

Skadden is one of the leading law firms in the world with approximately 2,000 lawyers in 24 offices across the globe. Clients include corporate, industrial, financial institutions and government entities. The London office is the gateway to the firm's European practice and has some 250 lawyers dedicated to top-end, cross-border corporate transactions and international arbitration and litigation. The firm has handled matters in nearly every country in the greater European region, and in Africa and the Middle East. The firm is consistently ranked as a leader in all disciplines and amongst a whole host of accolades, the firm has been voted 'Global Corporate Law Firm of the Year' (*Chambers and Partners*), 'Best US Law Firm in London' (Legal Business) 'Best Trainer' and 'Best Recruiter' in the US law firm in London category (Law Careers.Net Training and Recruitment Awards).

Main areas of work

Lawyers across the European network focus primarily on corporate transactions, including domestic and cross-border mergers and acquisitions, private equity, capital markets, leveraged finance and banking, tax, corporate restructuring and energy and projects. The firm also advise in international arbitration, litigation and regulatory matters.

Trainee profile

The firm seeks to recruit a small number of high-calibre graduates from any discipline to join their highly successful London office as trainee solicitors. The firm is looking for candidates who combine intellectual ability with enthusiasm, creativity and a demonstrable ability to rise to a challenge and to work with others towards a common goal.

Training environment

The firm can offer you the chance to develop your career in a uniquely rewarding and professional environment. You will join a close-knit but diverse team in which you will be given ample opportunity to work on complex matters, almost all with an international aspect, whilst benefiting from highly personalised training and supervision in an informal and friendly environment. The first year of your training contract will be divided into two six month seats where you will gain experience in corporate transactions and international litigation and arbitration. In the second year of your training contract, you will have the opportunity to discuss your preferences for your remaining two seats. The firm also offers the opportunity for second year trainees to be seconded to our Hong Kong office for a six month seat.

Benefits

Life insurance, private health insurance, private medical insurance, travel insurance, joining fee paid at Canary Wharf gym, subsidised restaurant, employee assistance programme and technology allowance.

Work placements

Skadden offers the opportunity for penultimate year law and non-law students to experience the culture and working environment of the firm through two week work placements. Placements are paid and take place during Easter and over the course of the summer. The deadline for applications is 12 January 2014 for placements in 2014.

Sponsorship & awards

The firm pays for GDL and LPC course fees and provides a £8,000 grant for each year of these courses.

Partners 31*
Assistant Solicitors 115
Trainees 15*
*London office

Contact
Aidan Connor
Graduate Recruitment
Specialist

Method of application
Online application

Selection procedure
A selection event comprising of an interview and a short exercise

Closing date for 2016
31 July 2014

Application
Training contracts p.a. 10-12
Applications p.a. 1000
% interviewed p.a. 8%
Required degree grade 2:1

Training
Salary
1st year £42,000
2nd year £45,000
Holiday entitlement 25 days
% of trainees with a
non-law degree p.a. 50%

Overseas offices
Beijing, Boston, Brussels, Chicago, Frankfurt, Hong Kong, Houston, Los Angeles, Moscow, Munich, New York, Palo Alto, Paris, San Francisco, São Paulo, Shanghai, Singapore, Sydney, Tokyo, Toronto, Vienna, Washington DC, Wilmington

Skadden

Skadden, Arps, Slate, Meagher & Flom (UK) LLP

Slaughter and May

One Bunhill Row, London EC1Y 8YY
Tel: (020) 7600 1200 Fax: (020) 7090 5000
Email: trainee.recruit@slaughterandmay.com (enquiries only)
Website: www.slaughterandmay.com

Firm profile

One of the most prestigious law firms in the world, Slaughter and May enjoys a reputation for quality and expertise. The corporate, commercial and financing practice is particularly strong and lawyers are known for their business acumen and technical excellence. As well as its London, Brussels, Beijing and Hong Kong offices, the firm nurtures long-standing relationships with the leading independent law firms in other jurisdictions in order to provide the best advice and service across the world.

Main areas of work

Corporate, commercial and financing; tax; competition; financial regulation; dispute resolution; technology, media and telecommunications; intellectual property; real estate; pensions and employment.

Trainee profile

The work is demanding and the firm looks for intellectual agility and the ability to work with people from different countries and walks of life. Common sense, the ability to communicate clearly and the willingness to accept responsibility are all essential. The firm expects to provide training in everything except the fundamental principles of law, so does not expect applicants to know much of commercial life.

Training environment

Each trainee completes four or five seats of three or six months duration. Two or three seats will be spent in one of the firm's corporate, commercial and financing law groups. The remaining time can be divided between some of the specialist groups and can also include an overseas secondment to one of the firm's offices or to one of its best friend firms. In each seat a partner is responsible for monitoring your progress and reviewing your work. There is an extensive training programme which includes the PSC. There are also discussion groups covering general and specialised legal topics.

Benefits

Private medical insurance, season ticket loan, pension scheme, interest free loan, subsidised membership of health club, 24 hour accident cover, Cycle to Work scheme, childcare vouchers, subsidised restaurant and coffee bar, concierge service and health screenings.

Vacation placements

Work experience schemes are available at Easter and during the summer period for penultimate year students. We also offer a first year open day for law students at Easter and workshops for finalists and graduates at Christmas. Please visit the website for full details.

Sponsorship & awards

GDL and LPC fees and maintenance grants are paid.

Partners 113
Associates Over 400
Total Trainees 178

Contact
The Trainee Recruitment Team

Method of application
Online (via website)

Selection procedure
Interview

Application
Training contracts p.a. approx 75-80
Applications p.a. 2,000 approx
Required degree grade Strong 2:1

Training
Salary (May 2013)
1st year £39,000
2nd year £44,000
Holiday entitlement
25 days p.a.
% of trainees with a non-law degree Approx 50%
No. of seats available abroad p.a. Approx 30

Post-qualification
Salary (May 2013) £63,000
% of trainees offered job on qualification (March 2013) 90%

Overseas offices
Brussels, Beijing and Hong Kong, plus 'Best Friend' firms in all the major jurisdictions.

SLAUGHTER AND MAY

Speechly Bircham LLP

6 New Street Square, London EC4A 3LX
Tel: (020) 7427 6400 Fax: (020) 7427 4456
Website: www.speechlys.com

Partners 75
Assistant Solicitors 125
Total Trainees 25
Contact
Rosalyn Bowler
HR Officer
Method of application
Online application via
www.dolawthinkbusiness.co.uk
Selection procedure
Interview and psychometric
testing
Closing date for 2016
31 July 2014
Application
Training contracts p.a. 12
Applications p.a. 800
% interviewed p.a. 15%
Required degree grade 2:1
Training
Salary
1st year 33,000
2nd year £35,000
Holiday entitlement 25 days
Post-qualification
Salary (2013) £56,000

Firm profile

Speechly Bircham is an ambitious, full-service City firm, with over 250 lawyers working with a fascinating mix of clients. We do not see ourselves purely as legal advisers to our clients. Instead, we aim to offer a more rounded, tailored service, where our insight and expertise helps clients achieve their wider aims. We combine expertise, professionalism and hands-on involvement to help our clients both in the UK and internationally with a complete offering across four sectors – financial services, private wealth, technology and real estate and construction.

The firm's international capabilities span three key European centres, with offices in London, Luxembourg and Zurich, making it one of the few UK law firms to offer intergrated corporate, tax, regulatory, funds and private client work to companies, banks, fund managers, wealthy individuals and private offices in Europe.

Main areas of work

Banking and finance, corporate recovery and restructuring, construction, engineering, projects, contentious trusts, corporate finance, corporate tax, employment, family, financial services, IP, technology and data, pensions, private client, real estate and real estate litigation.

Trainee profile

We require candidates to achieve a minimum of a 2:1 in their degree and look for smart, ambitious and intellectually curious individuals. People come to us from all backgrounds and degree disciplines, with a range of views that combine to give us our distinctive perspective on the law.

Training environment

Speechly Bircham divides the training contract into four six-month seats. We only take on 12 trainees per year and emphasis is given to early responsibility and supervised client contact to provide you with a practical learning environment. Trainees are supported by a partner or solicitor and are given in-house legal training complemented by regular performance reviews to promote development. Most of our trainees are selected from our summer schemes however we also accept direct training contract applications and interviews for these take place during August each year.

Vacation scheme

Our scheme is a three-week scheme offering a detailed introduction to the legal world. Each week is spent in a different practice area where you will carry out fee-earning work that could include attending client meetings and going to court. Support is always close at hand, with a current trainee as mentor and an assistant solicitor sponsor for each placement. Our summer scheme also has a programme of sports and social events which help both parties see if we are right for each other personally as well as professionally.

Benefits

Benefits include private medical insurance, life assurance, pension scheme, 25 days holiday, interest-free season ticket loan, subsidised restaurant, 4 weeks unpaid leave on qualification, corporate discount for gym membership.

Sponsorship

GDL and LPC fees paid together with a maintenance grant.

SpeechlyBircham

Squire Sanders

Rutland House, 148 Edmund Street, Birmingham B3 2JR
7 Devonshire Square, Cutlers Gardens, London EC2M 4YH
2 Park Lane, Leeds LS3 1ES
Trinity Court, 16 John Dalton Street, Manchester M60 8HS
Tel: (0800) 163 498
Email: traineerecruitment@squiresanders.com
Website: http://trainees.squiresanders.com

Firm profile
We combine sound legal advice with a deep knowledge of our clients' businesses to resolve their legal challenges. We care about the quality of our services, the success of our clients and the relationships that are forged through those successes.

With over 1,400 lawyers in 39 offices located in 19 countries on five continents, our global legal practice is in the markets where our clients do business. We also have strong working relationships with independent firms in Europe and the Middle East, as well as the Squire Sanders Legal Counsel Worldwide Network, which includes independent firms across Latin America.

The client base of our global legal practice spans every type of business, both private and public, worldwide. We advise a diverse mix of clients, from Fortune 100 and FTSE 100 corporations to emerging companies and from individuals to local and national governments.

Main areas of work
Banking and financial services, corporate/corporate finance, environment, safety and health, intellectual property, commercial and IT, international dispute resolution, labour and employment, litigation/disputes, pensions, real estate, regulatory, restructuring and insolvency and tax.

Trainee profile
Squire Sanders seeks applications from law and non-law graduates, and we also welcome applications from individuals seeking a career change. A strong academic background will be key and you will have, or would expect, a 2:1 degree. It is an advantage for applicants to have language skills, but this is not essential. You should also be motivated and ambitious and have a wish to succeed in a client-focused business. Evidence of work experience in the legal sector, excellent communication skills and significant achievement in non-academic pursuits is advisable.

Training environment
20 trainee solicitors recruited each year. Trainees undertake six four-month seats during their training contract. Trainees have input in choice of seats and are encouraged to undertake a broad selection of seats to benefit their knowledge on qualification. Trainees benefit from two-tier supervision and challenging work. The firm provides a comprehensive induction programme including on-going departmental training, seminars and workshops throughout the training contract. Trainees undertake formal appraisal meetings with their supervisors during each seat. Trainees also benefit from exposure to clients, cross-border work and opportunity for seats on secondment. Trainees are involved in all aspects of professional life.

Benefits
Pension, life assurance, subsidised gym membership, interest free season ticket loan and a flexible benefits package.

Vacation placements
Places for 2014: 40 summer scheme; Duration: 2 weeks; Remuneration: £230 p.w. (London) £215 p.w. (Birmingham, Leeds, Manchester); Closing date: 31 January 2014.

Sponsorship & awards
PgDL and LPC fees paid and maintenance grant provided. Maintenance grant presently:

GDL: London, £6,000; Regional, £4,500

LPC: London, £7,000; Regional, £5,000

Partners 450
Assistant Solicitors 1050
Total Trainees 55

Contact
Graduate Recruitment Team

Method of application
Online application form

Selection procedure
Assessment and interview

Closing date for 2016
31 July 2014

Application
Training contracts p.a. 20
Applications p.a. 1,500
% interviewed p.a. 10%
Required degree grade 2:1

Training
Salary
1st year (2013)
£23,500 regional
£35,000 London
2nd year (2013)
£26,000 regional
£37,000 London
Holiday entitlement 25 days
% of trainees with a non-law
degree p.a. 30%
No. of seats available abroad
p.a. 6

Post-qualification
Salary (2013)
London £58,000
Other £37,000
% of trainees accepting job on
qualification (2012) 80%

Overseas offices
Squire Sanders Legal Counsel
World Wide has offices in the
USA, South America, Asia,
Europe and the Middle East. For
a complete list of our offices,
please visit our website.

SQUIRE
SANDERS

Stephenson Harwood LLP

1 Finsbury Circus, London EC2M 7SH
Tel: (020) 7809 2812 Fax: (020) 7003 8346
Email: graduate.recruitment@shlegal.com
Website: www.shlegal.com/graduate

Firm profile

Stephenson Harwood is a thriving, international law firm with over 100 partners and more than 600 staff worldwide. We act for a wide range of listed and private companies, institutions and successful entrepreneurs. We also offer a full range of services in a wide variety of sectors. What's more, when it comes to delivering sound commercial solutions to complex business challenges, we punch well above our weight.

Main areas of work

Commercial litigation; corporate (including corporate finance, funds, corporate tax, business technology); employment and pensions; finance; marine and international trade; and real estate.

Trainee profile

Firstly we look for a quick intellect. As well as at least a 2:1 in any discipline plus 320 UCAS points or equivalent, you'll need strong analytical skills, sound judgement, imagination and meticulous attention to detail.

Also vital are the communication skills to be persuasive and build rapport, plenty of drive and determination, plus a keen interest in business. Mandarin Chinese language skills are useful.

Training environment

We take just 16 trainees on each year. So you can look forward to a huge amount of individual attention, coaching and mentoring. Your structured programme involves four six-month seats in our contentious and non-contentious practice groups. You can expect on-the-job training complemented by in-house seminars; to share an office with a partner or senior associate; and to benefit from a continuous review of your career development. You could also have the chance to spend one of your six-month seats in Hong Kong or Singapore and to take advantage of client secondment opportunities. We'll give you your own caseload and as much responsibility as you can shoulder – not forgetting free language tuition where appropriate.

Benefits

These include subsidised health club membership, private health insurance and screening, pension, life assurance, private GP services, critical illness cover, dental insurance, retail vouchers, concierge service, subsidised cafe, season ticket loan and 25 days' paid holiday a year.

Vacation placements

Places for 2013/2014: 40

Duration: 1 week winter; 2 weeks spring and summer

Remuneration: £260 p.w.

Closing date: 3 November 2013 for winter; 31 January 2014 for spring and summer.

Open days

15 January 2014, 12 February 2014, 19 March 2014, 23 April 2014

Closing date: 31 January 2014

Sponsorship & awards

Fees paid for GDL and LPC at BPP Law School London and maintenance awards of up to £6,000 (if still studying).

Partners 100+
Associates 200+
Total Trainees 32

Contact
Sarah Jackson
(graduate.recruitment@shlegal.com)

Method of application
Online application form via
www.shlegal.com/graduate

Selection procedure
Application screening, online verbal and numerical testing, face to face interview and assessment centre

Closing date for TC
commencing March/Sept 2016
31 July 2014

Application
Applications p.a. circa 1,300
Training contracts p.a. 16
Required degree grade 2:1

Training
Salary
1st year £37,000
2nd year £40,000
Holiday entitlement 25 days
% of trainees with a
non-law degree p.a. 50%
Overseas secondment opportunities

Post-qualification
Salary £60,000
86% of trainees offered job

Overseas offices
Paris, Piraeus, Hong Kong, Singapore, Shanghai, Guangzhou, Dubai, Beijing

Associated offices
Athens, Bucharest, Kuwait, Jakarta, Yangon

Stevens & Bolton LLP

Wey House, Farnham Road, Guildford GUI 4YD
Tel: (01483) 302264 Fax: (01483) 302254
Email: julie.bounden@stevens-bolton.com
Website: www.stevens-bolton.com

Partners 37
Associates 69
Total Trainees 8

Contact
Julie Bounden
(01483) 302264

Method of application
Online application form
available from website

Selection procedure
Two interviews and other
processes

Closing date for 2016
31st July 2014

Application
Training contracts p.a. 4
Applications p.a. 300
% interviewed 10%
Required degree grade 2:1

Training
Salary
£30,000
Holiday entitlement 25 days

Overseas/regional offices
Guildford only

Firm profile

Stevens & Bolton LLP is recognised as a leading national law firm, offering a full range of commercial legal services. We are recommended in 24 specialist practice areas by leading legal directories and have received widespread awards recognition. Over the years we have been named and shortlisted Best Recruiter and Best Trainer in the LawCareers.Net Training & Recruitment Awards.

Based in Guildford, our single office approach ensures excellent communications and efficient co-ordination of our resources. We provide legal services both nationally and internationally, with unswerving focus on quality. From the outset, our trainees get first class experience of the business world. We advise a number of the top 100 and other UK FTSE companies, as well as many other substantial international groups, owner managed businesses and SMEs. As such, the work we carry out is both interesting and challenging and equal to work handled by City firms.

Main areas of work

Corporate and commercial; finance; real estate; dispute resolution; IP; employment, pensions and immigration; tax, trusts and charities; and family.

Trainee profile

We welcome applications from candidates with either a law or non-law background, with at least 320 UCAS points and one grade A at A level, who have achieved (or expect to achieve) a 2:1 degree or higher. Essential qualities include: very good communication skills, drive and ambition, intelligence, attention to detail, business interest and genuine enthusiasm for wanting to be a lawyer.

Training environment

Our trainees have genuine responsibility and experience of dealing with clients – and are made to feel part of the team from day one. Trainee seats will be available in most of the key business areas we specialise in, namely M&A and other corporate work, finance, commercial contracts, tax, real estate, IP, commercial disputes and employment. We do our best to maximise your ability to experience as many of those areas as possible as part of our six, four month seat rotation.

We are dedicated to encouraging continuous professional development, delivered in a variety of ways to give our trainees the best chance to become rounded, assured and respected professionals. Training in technical and business skills and early exposure to stimulating work with a variety of clients is instrumental in providing a solid foundation. Our unique combination of factors – supervision when you need it, support from colleagues and the opportunity to embrace early responsibility as soon as you are ready - creates a compelling proposition at the outset of your career.

Benefits

25 days holiday, pension, private healthcare, life assurance and an interest free loan for rail travel or car parking.

Sponsorship & awards

We pay the fees for the CPE/GDL and LPC and a £4,000 maintenance grant for each course of study. Any future trainees who are yet to take their LPC or the GDL are required to attend the College of Law Guildford.

Vacation placements

We run two programmes each summer of one week duration. Applications are accepted between 1 December 2013 and 31 January 2014.

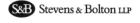
S&B Stevens & Bolton LLP

A-Z of Solicitors

Sullivan & Cromwell LLP

1 New Fetter Lane, London EC4A 1AN
Tel: (020) 7959 8900 Fax: (020) 7959 8950
Email: traineesolicitors@sullcrom.com
Website: www.sullcrom.com/careers/opps/trainee/

Firm profile

Sullivan & Cromwell provides the highest quality legal advice and representation to clients around the world. The results we achieve have set us apart for over 130 years and become a model for the modern practice of law. At S&C, there is no such thing as second best – our culture of meritocracy, responsibility and opportunity ensures the success of each and every new employee. S&C has more than 700 lawyers across an international network of 12 offices on four continents. We maintain a unified firm culture worldwide and provide clients with highly integrated advice on a global basis. The office locations represent our strategy to be present in key financial and business centres where our clients are active. The London office, established in 1972, is S&C's largest office after New York. There are approximately 75 English, US and dual-qualified lawyers working in the office across a number of practice areas.

Main areas of work

S&C London is perhaps unique in the scale, complexity and significance of the work carried out in an office of its size. Our practice areas include: M&A and private equity; capital markets; project finance; leveraged finance and restructuring; real estate; competition law; criminal defence and investigations; and tax.

Trainee profile

We seek trainees who have strong academic credentials (including a projected or achieved First or Upper Second Class honours degree (or equivalent)) as well as an excellent prior academic record. Most important, however, you should also have genuine intellectual curiosity, integrity, common sense, commercial awareness and an ambition to succeed as a lawyer at one of the world's leading law firms. Strong interpersonal skills will also be important: we are looking for genuine team players. If you are interested in working with the worlds leading companies on their most challenging matters, and you feel that you have the qualities we are looking for, we encourage you to apply.

Training environment

We will offer our trainees the opportunity to do superior work, meet exceptional people and grow in a supportive culture. We aim to distinguish our trainee programme by offering genuine mentoring from partners and senior lawyers who will take a keen interest in your career development.

Benefits

Include private health insurance; dental insurance; life insurance; travel insurance; group personal pension scheme with option to contribute via salary sacrifice; subsidised gym membership; concierge service; and 24 days vacation each year.

Vacation placements

Places for 2014: a two-week summer placement scheme primarily aimed at penultimate-year law undergraduates and final-year non-law undergraduates. Remuneration £500 p.w. Apply by CV (including a full classification and percentage breakdown of all academic results) and a covering letter. We will be accepting applications for our 2014 summer vacation scheme from 1 November 2013 through 31 January 2014.

Sponsorship & awards

GDL and LPC funding plus a maintenance grant.

Partners 16
Assistant Solicitors 65
Total Trainees 4

Contact
Kirsten Davies, Trainee Solicitor
Recruitment Manager

Method of application
CV and covering letter

Selection procedure
Interview with Graduate
Recruitment and two Partners,
meeting with 1-2 associates

Closing date for 2016
31 July 2014

Application
Training contracts p.a. 4-6
Applications p.a. 750
Required degree grade 2:1

Training
Salary (2013)
First year - £50,000
Second year - £55,000
Holiday entitlement – 24 days
Post-qualification
Salary (2013) £97,500

Overseas/regional offices
Beijing, Frankfurt, Hong Kong,
London, Los Angeles,
Melbourne, New York, Palo Alto,
Paris, Sydney, Tokyo,
Washington DC

SULLIVAN & CROMWELL LLP

A-Z of Solicitors

Taylor Wessing LLP

5 New Street Square, London EC4A 3TW
Tel: (020) 7300 7000 Fax: (020) 7300 7100
Website: www.taylorwessing.com/graduate
Email: graduate@taylorwessing.com

Partners 365
Trainees 47
Vacancies Circa 22
Application All candidates are required to complete our online application form, which can be found on our website, www.taylorwessing.com/graduate
Training Salary 1st year £37,000 2nd year £41,000
Post qualification Salary £60,000
Offices Berlin, Bratislava, Brussels, Budapest, Cambridge, Dubai, Dusseldorf, Frankfurt, Hamburg, Kiev, London, Munich, Paris, Prague, Singapore, Vienna and Warsaw Representative Offices Beijing, Brno, Klagenfurt and Shanghai

Firm profile

Taylor Wessing is a leading international law firm where you can move your career forward, faster. We are looking for the trusted advisors of tomorrow who can think creatively, be proactive and stay close to our clients and identify and deliver innovative solutions that help their businesses grow.

Our clients include large and medium size, private and public companies, financial institutions, professional service firms, public sector bodies and wealthy individuals. Our focus is on the sectors that we believe are the industries of tomorrow: energy; life sciences; private wealth; technology; media and telecoms.

We are experts in providing a seamless, high-quality service to global clients across many jurisdictions. Combining a pan-European network with a strong presence in the Middle East, India, China and North America, we are the leading firm for inward investment from North America and experts in IP protection and enforcement rights across the globe. That's why we work for 60% of the world's Top 50 brands.

Main areas of work

We offer industry-focused advice and in-depth sector experience by grouping together lawyers from different legal disciplines including: banking and finance; capital markets; copyright and media law; corporate; commercial agreements; construction and engineering; employment and pensions; EU competition, IT and telecoms; litigation and dispute resolution; patents; planning and environment; private client; projects; real estate; restructuring and corporate recovery; tax; trade marks and designs.

Trainee profile

We look for people with a minimum of ABB grades at A-level and a 2:1 degree in any discipline. You'll need to be a team player with the communication skills to build vibrant relationships with our clients. You'll have the energy, ambition and creativity to take early responsibility and have a real impact on our business and our clients' business. You'll also be committed to a career in law, with a genuine drive to learn and explore new boundaries.

Training environment

Our training programme combines the in-house Professional Skills Course with six-month seats in four different practice groups, including one contentious seat and one in our corporate or finance areas.

Working closely with partners and associates on high-quality work from the outset, you'll get regular support and feedback every step of the way to align your career to the growth and needs of the firm and our clients. There are also secondment opportunities to our clients.

Vacation schemes

Our vacation schemes are designed for you to experience life as a trainee solicitor in a uniquely innovative City law firm. You'll spend two weeks in two different practice groups gaining first-hand experience under the supervision of associates and partners.

Places: 40. Duration: 2 weeks. Remuneration: £250 per week. Closing date: 31 January 2014.

Sponsorship

GDL and LPC fees at BPP London sponsored. A maintenance grant is provided.

TaylorWessing

Thomas Cooper

Ibex House, 42-47 Minories, London EC3N 1HA
Tel: (020) 7481 8851 Fax: (020) 7480 6097
Email: recruitment@thomascooperlaw.com
Website: www.thomascooperlaw.com

Firm profile

Thomas Cooper is an international law firm which was founded in 1825.

Thomas Cooper has experience of dealing with the law in key jurisdictions around the world, with offices in London, Athens, Madrid, Paris, Sao Paulo and Singapore. The firm takes a pragmatic approach, providing clear advice that helps clients navigate through the complexity of international commerce.

The firm is recommended by and recognised by the major legal directories for its expertise.

The firm's clients operate globally and range from shipowners to charterers and traders, from banks and other financial institutions to underwriters and P&I clubs, from blue chip companies to small businesses and private individuals.

The firm gives insightful and pragmatic advice to clients and allows them to manage their exposure to risk more effectively.

Main areas of work

The firm's core practice areas are maritime, trade, finance, company and commercial, international arbitration, insurance, oil and gas.

Trainee profile

As a trainee with the firm you will be exposed to clients and fee earning work from your first seat. Thomas Cooper works for a wide variety of clients and as such, you can expect to find yourself dealing with finance, personal injury, wet or dry shipping claims.

Thomas Cooper values its trainees because they are vital for the future of the business. If you are bright, confident and a self starter who has a keen interest in maritime then the firm would encourage you to apply to its trainee programme.

Thomas Cooper recruits a maximum of 4 trainees per year.

Training environment

Thomas Cooper has a four-seat trainee programme over two years: two seats in shipping, one in defence and personal injury; and one in finance and international trade. There is also opportunity to do a seat in one of the firm's international offices, this is dependent upon language skills and team workload.

Benefits

Private medical insurance; permanent health insurance; life assurance; 25 days holiday; pension scheme; loan for dental insurance; season ticket loan; loan for gym membership. LPC course fees are paid by the firm.

Partners 27	
Assistant solicitors 28	
Total trainees 7/8	

Contact
Karan Tapley - Human
Resources Manager
Tel: (020) 7481 8851

Method of application
Online application form

Selection procedure
Interviews and assessments

Closing date for 2016
31 July 2014

Application
Required degree grade
2:1

Training
Salary
Starting salary for trainees is:
Year 1 £33,000
Year 2 £36,500 (based on 2013 salaries)
25 days holiday

Overseas/ regional offices
Athens, Madrid, Paris, Sao Paulo and Singapore

TLT LLP

One Redcliff St, Bristol BS1 6TP
Tel: (0117) 917 8905 Fax: (0117) 917 7649
Email: graduate@TLTsolicitors.com
Website: www.TLTcareers.com/trainee

Firm profile
Here, the firm is open. Open to connected working, open plan and open minded. It has reshaped the traditional law firm model into a fresh, bright, inclusive and creative place to work. TLT LLP, TLT Scotland Ltd and TLT NI LLP all operate under the TLT brand and between them have offices in Bristol, London, Manchester, Glasgow, Edinburgh, Belfast and Piraeus (Greece). Named by the Financial Times as one of Europe's most innovative law firms for four consecutive years and voted by clients as the best UK law firm for client service (Legal Week Client Satisfaction Report 2012), TLT is confident its way works. TLT continues to win business from FTSE-listed, national and international companies including Punch Taverns, Merlin Entertainments, Dyson, WHSmith, Barclays Bank, Canal & River Trust and EDF Energy, and is forecast to turnover £49 million in 2013/2014. So the firm is going places – and quickly. If you want to make your mark in law and work progressively, then this is where your career really begins.

Main areas of work
The firm's full service legal offering spans the financial services, leisure, retail and consumer goods, technology and media, renewables, housing and public sectors, and its core legal specialisms are real estate, banking and finance, commercial, corporate, employment, dispute resolution and litigation, but it believes there's more to legal work than being a lawyer – you need to embrace management, technology and business skills too.

Trainee profile
Genuinely ambitious, talented and technically impressive, you don't just tick all the boxes – you open them up, reshape them and connect them all together. You'll stand out, stand up for what's right, and stand shoulder to shoulder with your colleagues – you must embrace team working and share a passion for exceptional client service. And while academic achievement is important, your personal qualities also count for a lot here.

Training environment
Whether you join us for your training contract or a one week vacation scheme placement, you'll work on live cases for real clients, get input from a partner and develop a broad range of skills across the full legal and business spectrum. Our training contracts are designed to have more in them so you get more out of them, something recognised by The Lex 100 who awarded us Recommended Firm status in 2012/13. Here you'll gain invaluable technical knowledge and professional skills, all backed up by a one-to-one mentor, expert guidance and unlimited support throughout.

Benefits
The firm offers a full and flexible benefits plan, which means you can design your benefits package to meet your lifestyle needs, picking and choosing from a selection of rewards and benefits. As part of the firm's commitment to giving something back, you'll also be encouraged to get involved in community support work, pro bono legal advice, fundraising activities and environmental initiatives.

Vacation placements
Spend a week with TLT and you'll pick up unparalleled experience and a real taste of life at a leading law firm - especially when you consider the amount of partner contact you'll enjoy, and we've built assessments into the week, which means you won't have to make a separate training contract application or attend an assessment day.

Sponsorship & awards
We will sponsor the completion of GDL and LPC for individuals who have not already undertaken them.

Partners 83
Solicitors 171
Total Trainees 21

Contact
Gemma Cowley, HR
Recruitment Officer - Trainees
Tel 0117 917 8905

Method of application
Online application form at
www.TLTcareers.com/trainee

Selection procedure
Application form, telephone screening, verbal reasoning testing, assessment centre

Closing date
31 July each year

Application
Training contracts up to 15 p.a.
Applications circa 700 p.a.
% interviewed 12% p.a.
Required degree grade
2:1 or above in any discipline at degree level and a minimum of 300/24 UCAS points at A level

Training
Salary See website for details
Holiday entitlement 25 days

Post-qualification
Salary
See website for details
% trainees offered job on qualification 80-100%

Offices
Bristol, London, Manchester, Glasgow, Edinburgh, Belfast, Piraeus (Greece)

A-Z of Solicitors

Travers Smith LLP

10 Snow Hill, London EC1A 2AL
Tel: (020) 7295 3000 Fax: (020) 7295 3500
Email: graduate.recruitment@traverssmith.com
Website: www.traverssmith.com

Firm profile
A leading independent City firm with a major corporate and commercial practice, and a reputation for excellence in its chosen fields. Less than a quarter of the size of the largest firms, Travers Smith handles high profile and top quality work, much of which has an international dimension.

Main areas of work
Corporate law, commercial law, intellectual property and technology, litigation, investment funds, financial services and markets, banking, corporate recovery, competition, tax, employment, pensions and real estate.

Trainee profile
The firm looks for people who combine academic excellence with common sense; who are determined and articulate, who can think on their feet, and who take their work but not themselves seriously.

Applications are welcome from law and non-law undergraduates and graduates.

Training environment
Travers Smith has earned a phenomenal reputation in relation to its size. The work the firm undertakes is complex, exciting, and intellectually demanding, involving blue-chip clients and big numbers.

The firm has a comprehensive training programme which ensures that trainees experience a broad range of work. All trainee solicitors sit in rooms with partners and associates, which leads to a refreshing lack of hierarchy. It also means that trainees receive an individual and extensive training from experienced lawyers, enjoying client contact, and the responsibility that goes with it, from day one.

During the two year training contract, trainees spend six months in the corporate department and, six months in either the litigation or employment departments. The other two six month seats are spent in two of the other specialist departments. Trainees may also have the opportunity to spend six months in the firm's Paris office.

Benefits
Private health insurance, permanent health insurance, life insurance, health screening, 25 days' holiday, Ride2Work and Cyclescheme, subsidised bistro, childcare vouchers, season ticket loan.

Vacation placements
Summer 2014: 3 schemes with 15 places on each; Duration: two weeks; Remuneration: £275; closing date: 31 January 2014. The firm also offers a two week Christmas scheme for 15 students.

Sponsorship & awards
GDL and LPC paid in full plus maintenance of £7,000 per annum to those in London and £6,500 per annum to those outside of London.

Partners 64	
Associates 190	
Total Trainees 41	
Contact	
Germaine VanGeyzel	
Method of application	
Online	
Selection procedure	
Interviews (2 stage process)	
Closing date for 2016	
31 July 2014	
Application	
Training contracts p.a. 25	
Applications p.a. 2,000	
% interviewed p.a. 15%	
Required degree grade 2:1	
Training	
Salary	
1st year (2013) £39,000	
2nd year (2013) £44,000	
Holiday entitlement 25 days	
Post-qualification	
Salary (2013) £63,000	
% of trainees offered job	
on qualification (2013) 95%	

TRAVERS SMITH

Trethowans LLP

London Road, Salisbury, Wiltshire, SP1 3HP
The Director General's House, 15 Rockstone Place, Southampton SO15 2EP
Tel: 0845 302 4695 Fax: 01722 333 011
Email: recruitment@trethowans.com
Web: www.trethowans.com

Firm profile
Trethowans is a premier law firm based in the South with a team of 141 including 24 partners and 47 lawyers. The firm has a diverse and expanding client base. Our continued success is due to the quality of our people and the growing strength and reputation of our brand. With offices in Salisbury and Southampton our partners and staff enjoy the benefit of living close to the south coast whilst having the quality of work and clients often associated with a city firm. Many of our clients are household name clients. Service excellence is a priority – clients value the firm's ability to deliver top-quality, expert advice, on time, in a very personable manner and at a competitive price.

Main areas of work
On the commercial side, we represent international and national household brand names, owner-managed businesses, entrepreneurs and major regional employers across the UK. When acting for individuals, we represent landowners, entrepreneurs, local families, property developers and trustees amongst others.

Legal advice to businesses include: corporate, commercial, commercial property, commercial litigation, insurance litigation, employment and licensing. Legal advice to individuals includes: personal injury, private client (wills, trusts and tax; wealth structuring and inheritance planning), agriculture and rural property, family and residential property.

Many of our teams and individuals are rated in both the Chambers Guide to the Legal Profession and Legal 500, the two independent guides to the legal profession in the UK.

Trainee profile
Trainees should possess sound academic abilities and be able to demonstrate commercial acumen. Flexibility, ambition and enthusiasm are valued. Candidates should be good communicators and adopt a problem solving approach to client work.

Training environment
Trainee solicitors usually undertake four separate specialist seats, each lasting six months. The firm offers a flexible approach in deciding trainees' seats to suit individual needs, while providing a broad training programme in accordance with the Solicitors Regulation Authority guidelines. Trainees work closely with the supervising lawyer/partner to whom they are responsible. They are considered an important part of each team and become closely involved in the team's work to obtain first-hand legal experience. Each trainee's performance is reviewed regularly by their supervisor and Training Partner and regular feedback is provided. This enables the trainee scheme to be continually evaluated and also ensures that the highest possible standards are maintained. Prospects for trainees are excellent. Most trainees are offered a position as solicitors at the end of their training contract. Trainees are an integral part of the firm from day one. They are responsible for the firm's staff newsletter, participate in business development, and actively communicate via twitter about their work and progress as a trainee (www.twitter.com/trethtrainees).

Benefits
Incremental holiday entitlement up to 28 days, contributory pension scheme, death in service benefit, PHI scheme, performance-related bonus scheme, car parking, new staff recruitment bonus, childcare voucher scheme and employee assistance programme.

Sponsorship & awards
None.

Partners 24	
Solicitors 47	
Total Trainees 8	

Contact
Nicola Richards
01722 426947

Method of application
Applications by online application form and covering letter

Selection procedure
Two stage process; interview and assessment day

Closing date for 2015
31 July 2014

Application
Training contracts p.a. 3-4
Applications p.a. 100+
% interviewed p.a. 25-30%
Required degree grade 2:1

Training
Salary Competitive market rate with regular reviews
Holiday entitlement 23 days

Post-qualification
Salary Competitive market rate with regular reviews
% of trainees offered position on qualification 100% (Nov 2009), 67% (Nov 2010), 75% (Nov 2011), 67% (Nov 2012)
Holiday entitlement 25 days

Regional offices
Salisbury, Southampton

A-Z of Solicitors

TRETHOWANS
SOLICITORS

Trowers & Hamlins LLP

3 Bunhill Row, London, EC1Y 8YZ
Tel: (020) 7423 8312 Fax: (020) 7423 8001
Email: avithlani@trowers.com   Website: www.trowers.com/careers/students

Firm profile

Trowers & Hamlins is a City, national and international full-service firm with a unique mixture of practice areas. We are the number one firm in the UK for Housing and Public Sector work, and we are consistently ranked as one of the leading firms in the Middle East. We pride ourselves on providing down-to-earth and commercially savvy advice to our clients, and no matter where our clients are, they have access to a connected network of lawyers across jurisdictions, sectors and disciplines.

Main areas of work

Banking and finance, commercial property, corporate, dispute resolution and litigation, employment and pensions, housing and regeneration, international (based in the UK, Middle East and Far East), projects and construction, public sector (commercial), tax and private wealth.

Trainee profile

We usually recruit around 20 trainees each year, split between September and March intakes. The majority of our trainees will be recruited for our London office, with a small number of trainees taken on in our Exeter and Manchester offices respectively. However, we expect our trainees to be ready to undertake seats in any of our UK or overseas offices.

Excellent academics are essential. However, we also look for other attributes in our potential trainees, including enthusiasm and a drive to succeed, teamworking skills, good humour, an analytical and logical mind, excellent communication skills, good commercial awareness, and a genuine passion for the law and the firm.

Training environment

The training contract itself is divided into four six-month seats and you can expect to experience a broad range of departments over the course of the two-year period. You will be allocated a supervisor and will be appraised every three months (with a mid-seat and end-of-seat appraisal). This gives you a great opportunity to receive detailed feedback on your performance and allows us to see that you are developing at an appropriate pace.

We believe in learning by experience. Throughout your training contract, you will be given responsibility and you will be challenged.

However, you will benefit from a strong network of support around you in addition to that which is provided departmentally. Our Graduate Recruitment & Development Manager is always on hand, along with the Training Principal and the Trainee Solicitors' Committee. The Committee meets regularly to discuss training, selection and trainee events, and includes four trainee solicitor representatives (one from each intake).

Vacation placements

The firm runs two fortnight long summer vacation schemes that are open to candidates looking to secure a training contract commencing in 2016. We only consider applications submitted to us through our online application system, which can be accessed via our dedicated graduate recruitment webpages on the firm's website.

Sponsorship & awards

If you join us and have yet to complete the Graduate Diploma in Law (GDL) and / or the Legal Practice Course (LPC), we will cover your course fees in full and will provide you with a maintenance grant. All future trainees intending to study the LPC in London are required to attend Kaplan Law School. For those wishing to study outside of London, we are flexible with your choice of institution.

Partners 129
Assistant Solicitors 186
Total Trainees 35

Contact
Anup Vithlani, Graduate
Recruitment & Development
Manager

Method of application
Online application form

Selection procedure
Assessment centre, interviews,
psychometric tests & practical
test

Closing date for 2016
1 August 2014

Application
Applications pa
circa 1,500
% interviewed pa 4%
Required grades
minimum of 320 UCAS points
(ABB) and 2.1 degree or above

Training
London Salary
1st year £36,000
2nd year £39,000
Holiday entitlement 25 days
% of trainees with a
non-law degree p.a. 50% / 50%
No. of seats available
abroad pa 14

Post-qualification
Salary £58,000
% of trainees offered job on
qualification (March 2013)
100%

Offices
London, Birmingham, Exeter,
Manchester, Abu Dhabi,
Bahrain, Cairo, Dubai, Malaysia
and Oman

Veale Wasbrough Vizards

Orchard Court, Orchard Lane, Bristol BS1 5WS
Tel: (0117) 925 2020 Fax: (0117) 925 2025
Barnards Inn, 86 Fetter Lane, London EC4A 1AD
Tel: (020) 7405 1234 Fax: (020) 7405 4171
Email: careers@vwv.co.uk Website: www.vwv.co.uk Twitter: @VWVCareers

Firm profile

Veale Wasbrough Vizards acts nationally for clients in the education and charities, healthcare, private wealth, family owned business and public sectors. The firm also offers a dedicated service to individuals.

Our combination of specialist expertise, genuine teamwork and client commitment sets us apart. That's why we're confident we can deliver the best and most effective legal solutions to help our clients succeed. Our staff of 300 are based at our offices in the heart of two cities; Bristol and London.

As part of our commitment to staff and clients, the firm has three core values which span all work groups and business plans. These are teamwork and collaboration, putting the client at the centre of the firm and commercial approach.

VWV is also a founder member of the Association of European Lawyers and has strong connections with law firms in Southern China.

Main areas of work

The firm is recognised for excellence in specific sectors and for its established commitment to training, teamwork and approachability. Our goal is to help our clients succeed, through high standards, technical expertise, a creative approach and commitment to our people.

As well as offering a wide range of services expected from a commercial law firm, including commercial litigation, construction, family and matrimonial, corporate and real estate, we also deal with residential conveyancing through our dedicated division Convey Direct and personal injury claims through Augustines Injury Law.

Trainee profile

The firm recruits 8-10 trainees annually. It is looking for graduates who will become dynamic lawyers, who will make the most of the training opportunities and positively contribute to the future of the firm. Applicants should have proven academic ability, be good team players, with strong communication skills and commercial awareness.

Training environment

The firm offers its trainees early responsibility. It provides four seats of six months each in a variety of teams, including charities, commercial, commercial litigation, corporate, employment, personal injury, private client and real estate (including construction and property litigation). Trainees also benefit from experience in the five sectors as mentioned above. Many of the firm's partners and senior lawyers trained with the firm and are now widely respected experts in their chosen field.

Sponsorship & awards

Successful candidates may be eligible for sponsorship for the Diploma in Law and/or Legal Practice Course, consisting of a grant for LPC fees and an interest-free loan.

Vacation scheme

The firm's summer vacation scheme offers a week's unpaid work experience, providing an insight into the day to day workings of a large firm of commercial lawyers, as students spend time in different legal teams.

Partners 47	
Assistant Solicitors 82	
Total Trainees 16	
Contact	
Ellen Marsh, HR Advisor	
Method of application	
Application form on website	
Selection procedure	
Interview	
Closing date for September 2016	
30 June 2014	
Application	
Training contracts p.a. 8-10	
% interviewed (2012) 10%	
Required degree grade	
Preferably 2:1	
Training	
1st year £23,000	
2nd year £25,000	
Holiday entitlement 25 days plus bank holidays	
Post-qualification	
Salary £35,000	
% of trainees offered job on qualification (2012) 75%	

A-Z of Solicitors

Vinson & Elkins

CityPoint, 33rd Floor, One Ropemaker Street, London EC2Y 9UE
Tel: (020) 7065 6000 Fax: (020) 7065 6001

Firm profile
Vinson & Elkins RLLP is one of the largest international law firms and has been repeatedly ranked as the world's leading energy law firm. Founded in Houston in 1917 (and with an office in London for over 40 years), Vinson & Elkins currently has over 700 lawyers with offices in Abu Dhabi, Austin, Beijing, Dallas, Dubai, Hong Kong, Houston, London, Moscow, New York, Palo Alto, Riyadh, San Francisco, Shanghai, Tokyo and Washington, DC.

Main areas of work
Cross-border M&A, private equity, corporate finance and securities advice (including London Main Market and AIM listings and international equity and debt capital markets), banking and finance, international energy transactions, construction, project development and finance transactions, litigation and arbitration and tax.

Trainee profile
The firm is looking for ambitious individuals with strong academic results, sound commercial awareness and rounded personalities. The ability to think laterally and creatively is essential, as is a need for common-sense and a willingness to take the initiative.

Training environment
The firm currently offers three to four training contracts commencing each September. These are not run on a rigid seat system, but instead a trainee will gain wide experience in many different areas, working with a wide variety of associates and partners from across the firm. V&E is proud of the fact it has twice won LawCareers.Net awards for the quality of its training with a further five nominations.

Whilst the trainees are based in London, the firm is currently regularly seconding its trainees to other offices (particularly its offices in Abu Dhabi, Dubai, Hong Kong and Houston).

Benefits
Private medical and dental, pension, season ticket loan, life assurance.

Vacation placements
We view vacation placements as a key part of its recruitment process. For summer 2014 apply by 28 February 2014, by way of online application form.

Sponsorship & awards
The firm pays all GDL and LPC course fees and a discretionary stipend (of up to £7,500) to assist with the LPC year.

Partners 17
Assistant Solicitors 22
Total Trainees 8

Contact
Natalie Perkin (020) 7065 6048

Method of application
Online application form

Selection procedure
Interview

Closing date for 2016
31 July 2014

Application
Training contracts p.a. 3-4
Applications p.a. 450
% interviewed p.a. 10%
Required degree grade 2:1

Training
Salary
1st year £40,000
2nd year £42,000
Holiday entitlement 25 days
% of trainees with a
non-law degree p.a. 62.5%
No. of seats available
abroad p.a. 4

Post-qualification
Salary £80,000
% of trainees offered job
on qualification 87.5%

Overseas / Regional offices
Abu Dhabi, Austin, Beijing, Dallas, Dubai, Hong Kong, Houston, London, Moscow, New York, Palo Alto, Riyadh, San Francisco, Shanghai, Tokyo and Washington DC.

Vinson&Elkins RLLP

Walker Morris

Kings Court, 12 King Street, Leeds LS1 2HL
Tel: (0113) 283 2500 Fax: (0113) 245 9412
Email: hellograduates@walkermorris.co.uk
Website: www.walkermorris.co.uk

Firm profile
Based in Leeds, Walker Morris is one of the largest commercial law firms in the North, with over 500 people, providing a full range of legal services to commercial and private clients both nationally and internationally.

Main areas of work
CDR, commercial, commercial property, construction, corporate, employment, finance, intellectual property, insolvency, PFI/ public sector, planning and environmental, regulatory, sports, tax.

Trainee profile
Bright, articulate, highly motivated individuals who will thrive on early responsibility in a demanding yet friendly environment.

Training environment
Trainees commence with an induction programme, before spending four months in each main department (commercial property, corporate and commercial litigation). Trainees can choose in which departments they wish to spend their second year. Formal training will include lectures, interactive workshops, seminars and e-learning. The PSC covers the compulsory elements and the electives consist of a variety of specially tailored skills programmes. Individual IT training is provided. Opportunities can also arise for secondments to some of the firm's major clients. Emphasis is placed on teamwork, inside and outside the office. The firm's social and sporting activities are an important part of its culture and are organised by a committee drawn from all levels of the firm. A trainee solicitors' committee represents the trainees in the firm but also organises events and liaises with the Leeds Trainee Solicitors Group.

Vacation placements
Places for 2014: 48 over 3 weeks; Duration: 1 week; Remuneration: £175 p.w.; Closing date: 31 January 2014.

Sponsorship & awards
LPC & PGDL fees plus maintenance of £5,000.

Partners 51
Assistant Solicitors 150
Total Trainees 29

Contact
Nick Cannon

Method of application
Online application form

Selection procedure
Assessment centre & face-to-face interviews

Closing date for 2016
31 July 2014

Application
Training contracts p.a. 15
Applications p.a.
Approx. 800
% interviewed p.a.
Face to face 5%
Required degree grade 2:1

Training
Salary
1st year (2013) £24,000
2nd year (2013) £26,000
Holiday entitlement 24 days
% of trainees with a
non-law degree p.a.
30% on average

Post-qualification
Salary £36,000
% of trainees offered job
on qualification 75%
% of assistants who joined as
trainees 55%
% of partners who joined as
trainees 50%

Ward Hadaway

Sandgate House, 102 Quayside, Newcastle upon Tyne NE1 3DX
Tel: (0191) 204 4000 Fax: (0191) 204 4098
Email: recruitment@wardhadaway.com
Website: www.wardhadaway.com

Firm profile

Ward Hadaway is one of the most progressive law firms in the North of England and is firmly established as one of the region's legal heavyweights. Operating from offices in Newcastle, Leeds and Manchester, the firm attracts some of the most ambitious businesses in the region and has a substantial client base of regional, national and international clients from the private and public sectors.

As a business founded and located in the North, the firm has grown rapidly, investing heavily in developing its existing people and recruiting further outstanding individuals from inside and outside of the region. The firm is listed in the top 100 UK law firms.

Main areas of work

The firm is divided into five main departments; litigation, property, corporate, commercial and private client, with a number of cross departmental teams. The firm is commercially based, satisfying the needs of the business community in both business and private life. Clients vary from international plcs to local, private clients. The firm is on a number of panels including; the Arts Council, NHS (four panels), English Heritage, Department of Education and the General Teaching Council.

Trainee profile

The usual academic and professional qualifications are sought. Sound commercial and business awareness are essential as is the need to demonstrate strong communication skills, enthusiasm and flexibility. Candidates will be able to demonstrate excellent interpersonal and analytical skills.

Training environment

The training contract is structured around four seats, each of six months duration. At regular intervals, and each time you are due to change seat, you will have the opportunity to discuss the experience you would like to gain during your training contract. The firm will give high priority to your preferences. You will work closely with a Partner or associate who will supervise and encourage you as you become involved in more complex work. Your practical experience will also be complemented by an extensive programme of seminars and lectures. All trainees are allocated a 'buddy', usually a second year trainee or newly qualified solicitor, who can provide as much practical advice and guidance as possible during your training. The firm has an active social committee and offers a full range of sporting and social events.

Benefits

25 days holiday (27 after five years service), death in service insurance, contributory pension, flexible benefits package, travel scheme.

Vacation placements

Vacation placements run spring/summer between June and July and are of 1 week's duration. Applications should be received by 28 February 2014.

Sponsorship & awards

CPE/GDL and LPC fees paid and maintenance grants in accordance with the terms of the firm's offer.

Partners 80
Total Trainees 18

Contact
Graduate recruitment team

Method of application
Firm's application form

Selection procedure
Assessment Centre and interview

Closing date for 2016
31 July 2014

Application
Training contracts p.a. 10
Applications p.a. 600+
% interviewed p.a. 10%
Required degree grade 2:1

Training
Salary 2012
Newcastle
1st year £20,000
2nd year £20,500
Leeds
1st year £23,000
2nd year £23,500
Holiday entitlement 25 days
% of trainees with a non-law degree p.a. Varies

Post-qualification
Salary (2012)
£32,000

Watson, Farley & Williams LLP

15 Appold Street, London EC2A 2HB
Tel: (020) 7814 8000 Fax: (020) 7814 8017
Email: graduates@wfw.com
Website: www.wfw.com/trainee

Firm Profile
WFW was founded in 1982 in the City of London. It has since grown rapidly to over 120 partners and a total staff of over 700. The firm has offices in London, New York, Paris, Frankfurt, Hamburg, Munich, Rome, Milan, Madrid, Athens, Piraeus, Singapore, Bangkok and Hong Kong.

Main areas of work
WFW is a distinctive law firm with a leading market position in international finance and investment, maritime and energy.

In our chosen sectors we compete successfully with some of the best law firms in the world. Building on our origins in ship finance, demand for our maritime work remains as strong as ever. At the same time we have seized opportunities to excel in related areas where our finance expertise has most relevance, such as energy, natural resources, transport, real estate and technology.

Trainee profile
Although there is no typical WFW trainee, there are certain attributes that we look for. You will need a 2:1 or above and at least 320 UCAS points (ABB) – from A-level results, or their equivalent. We also particularly value applicants with initiative, drive and commercial awareness.

Training
At WFW we deal with training and ongoing development in an individual way. During each seat we discuss with you plans for the next one to ensure you gain valuable insight from the six seat programme, including one seat in either Paris, Singapore, Piraeus or Bangkok.

Your training contract will be hands-on, with as much experience of clients and real, high-profile work as possible. You'll also benefit from plenty of exposure to senior lawyers, many acknowledged leaders in their field.

The firm has a reputation for challenging work. Yours will be no exception as we believe that only total immersion can provide you with the experience you require.

Benefits
Various benefits are available to trainees after a qualifying period of service e.g. 25 days holiday, bank holidays, income protection scheme, life assurance, employee assistance scheme, pension scheme, interest-free season ticket loan, £250 contribution towards a sports club and healthcare membership.

Vacation placements
Our vacation scheme is the best way to really familiarise yourself with WFW. The two-week placements are at our London office, throughout the year. To appreciate first-hand the kind of work trainees undertake day to day, you will work with solicitors in one of our practice groups for the whole period. To complement this focus on one area, you will also participate in a variety of training and social events designed to give you a general overview of the firm. Deadline to apply: 31 January 2014.

Sponsorship & awards
GDL and LPC fees are paid depending on point of offer plus a maintenance grant of £6,500/£5,500 dependant on location.

Partners 126
Total fee-earners 400+
Total Trainees 26

Contact
Graduate Recruitment Manager

Method of application
Online application

Selection procedure
Assessment centre and interview

Closing date for 2016
31 July 2014

Application
Training contracts p.a. 12-14
Applications p.a. 700
% interviewed p.a. 20-30%
Required degree grade
Minimum 2:1 and 320 UCAS points (ABB)

Training
Salary
1st year (2012) £35,000
2nd year (2012) £40,000
Holiday entitlement 25 days
% of trainees with a non-law degree p.a. 50%
No. of seats available abroad p.a. 12-14

Post-qualification
Salary (2013)
£60,000
% of trainees offered job on qualification (2013) 85%
% of assistants who joined as trainees 60%
% of partners who joined as trainees 10%

Overseas offices
New York, Paris, Frankfurt, Hamburg, Munich, Rome, Milan, Madrid, Athens, Piraeus, Singapore, Bangkok, Hong Kong

A-Z of Solicitors

Watson, Farley & Williams
www.wfw.com

Wedlake Bell

52 Bedford Row, London, WC1R 4LR
Tel: (020) 7395 3000 Fax: (020) 7395 3100
Email: recruitment@wedlakebell.com
Website: www.wedlakebell.com

Partners 52
Assistant Solicitors 78
Total Trainees 12

Contact
The Graduate Recruitment Department

Method of application
Application form

Selection procedure
Two interviews & open day

Closing date for 2016
End of July 2014

Application
Training contracts p.a. 6
Required degree grade 2:1

Training
Holiday entitlement
25 days
% of trainees with a
non-law degree p.a. 50%

Firm profile
Wedlake Bell LLP is a medium-sized law firm providing legal advice to businesses and high net worth individuals from around the world. The firm's services are based on a high degree of partner involvement, extensive business and commercial experience and strong technical expertise. The firm has approximately 130 lawyers in central London and affiliations with law firms throughout Europe and in the United States.

Main areas of work
For the firm's business clients: banking and asset finance; corporate; corporate tax; business recoveries; commercial; intellectual property; information technology; media; commercial property; construction; residential property.

For private individuals: family, tax, trusts and wealth protection; offshore services; residential property.

Trainee profile
In addition to academic excellence, Wedlake Bell LLP looks for commercial aptitude, flexibility, enthusiasm, a personable nature, confidence, mental agility and computer literacy in its candidates. Languages are not crucial.

Training environment
Trainees have four seats of six months across the following areas: business recoveries, commercial property, construction, corporate, employment, family, IP and commercial, private client, pensions, property litigation and residential property. As a trainee, the firm encourages you to have direct contact and involvement with clients from an early stage. Trainees will work within highly specialised teams and have a high degree of responsibility. Trainees will be closely supervised by a partner or senior solicitor and become involved in high quality and varied work. The firm is committed to the training and career development of its lawyers and many of its trainees continue their careers with the firm, often through to partnership. Wedlake Bell LLP has an informal, creative and co-operative culture with a balanced approach to life.

Sponsorship & benefits
LPC funding available subject to the terms and conditions of any offer. During the training contract: pension, travel loans, gym membership, private medical insurance, life assurance, permanent health insurance, cycle to work scheme, employee assistance scheme.

Vacation placements
Places for 2014: 8; Duration: 3 weeks in July; Closing date: End of February, 2014.

Wedlake Bell

Weil, Gotshal & Manges

110 Fetter Lane, London EC4A 1AY
Tel: (020) 7903 1000 Fax: (020) 7903 0990
Email: graduate.recruitment@weil.com
Website: www.weil.com

Firm profile

International law firm Weil, Gotshal & Manges has approximately 1,300 lawyers, including 340 partners, in 21 cities throughout the US, Europe and Asia.

The London office was established in 1996 and has grown to become the second largest of the firm's worldwide offices, with over 130 lawyers, at least 90% of which are UK-qualified. Approximately 80% of the work completed in London is home grown and many of our European cross-border activities are coordinated from the London office. We pride ourselves on providing our clients with unmatched legal services, which is why the world's most sophisticated clients call upon Weil to provide counsel on their most complex and important issues.

Main areas of work

Private equity is the cornerstone of the London office, with the firm ranked in the top tier of Chambers UK for buyouts with more partners ranked at the top of the individual rankings than any other firm. The establishment of our London funds practice, linking in with our well-established US and Asian teams, provides clients with full coverage for both raising and investing funds.

Our restructuring practice is widely recognised as one of the leading practices in its field, referred to as "the gold standard of bankruptcy bar" (The American Lawyer). The firm has been at the forefront of the credit crisis, advising global financial institutions such as Lehman Brothers, AIG, General Motors and Kaupthing, as well as providing integrated crisis management advice. Our restructuring expertise in the US and Europe has also enabled us to provide corporate and private equity clients with cutting-edge advice on the current markets, how best to weather the current storms and prepare for opportunities in the distressed M&A markets.

We advise on all aspects of domestic and cross-border transactional and general corporate issues, including acquisitions and disposals, corporate governance, demergers and re-organisations, equity capital markets, joint ventures, public and private mergers and strategic alliances.

Full-service transactional support is provided by specialists in the fields of commercial contracts, competition, employment/employee benefits, environment, IP/IT, pensions, real estate and tax.

We have an international finance practice which continues to be among the very best practices in London, and spans asset finance, acquisition finance (including bank / bond financing structures), bank and institutional lending, debt capital markets (including high yield), derivatives, lease financings, refinancings and recapitalisations and structured finance.

Few firms can match the quality and depth of Weil's experience in litigation, arbitration and other forms of dispute resolution. The London dispute resolution team advises upon, manages and conducts all aspects of domestic and international litigation, from strategic advice during the early stages of negotiations to courtroom advocacy.

The London office also works closely with cross-disciplinary teams across the firm on a wide range of industry specialisms, including energy, healthcare, infrastructure and TMT.

Vacation placements

We have up to 30 places for spring and summer. Please refer to the website for further information.

Partners 29
Solicitors 90
Total Trainees 21

Contact
Victoria Wisson

Method of application
Online application form

Closing date for 2016
31 July 2014

Application
Training contracts p.a. up to 14
Required degree grade 2:1

Training
Salary
1st year (2013) £41,000
Holiday entitlement 23 days

Overseas offices
Beijing, Boston, Budapest, Dallas, Dubai, Frankfurt, Hong Kong, Houston, London, Miami, Munich, New York, Paris, Prague, Princeton, Providence, Shanghai, Silicon Valley, Warsaw, Washington DC and Wilmington

A-Z of Solicitors

White & Case LLP

5 Old Broad Street, London EC2N 1DW
Tel: (020) 7532 1000 Fax: (020) 7532 1001
Email: trainee@whitecase.com
Website: www.whitecasetrainee.com

Firm profile
White & Case LLP is a global law firm with more than 2,200 lawyers worldwide. The firm has a network of 39 offices, providing the full range of legal services of the highest quality in virtually every major commercial centre and emerging market. They work with international businesses, financial institutions and governments worldwide on corporate and financial transactions and dispute resolution proceedings. Their clients range from some of the world's longest established and most respected names to many start-up visionaries. The firm's lawyers work on a variety of sophisticated, high-value transactions, many of which feature in the legal press worldwide as the firm's clients achieve firsts in privatisation, cross-border business deals, or major development projects.

Main areas of work
Banking and capital markets; construction and engineering; corporate (including M&A and private equity); dispute resolution (including arbitration and mediation); employment and benefits; energy, infrastructure, project and asset finance; IP, PPP/PFI; real estate; tax; and telecommunications.

Trainee profile
Trainees should be ambitious, creative and work well in teams. They should have an understanding of international commercial issues and have a desire to be involved in high profile, cross-border legal matters.

Training environment
Trainees undertake four seats, each of six months in duration. The firm guarantees that one of these seats can be spent overseas. Regardless of where they work, trainees get a high level of partner and senior associate contact from day one, ensuring they receive high quality, stimulating and rewarding work. Trainees are encouraged to take early responsibility and there is a strong emphasis on practical hands-on training, together with plenty of support and feedback. The firm recruits and develops trainee solicitors with the aim of retaining them on qualification.

Benefits
The firm operates a flexible benefits scheme, through which you can select the benefits you wish to receive. Currently, the benefits include private medical insurance, dental insurance, life assurance, pension, critical illness insurance, travel insurance, retail vouchers, gym membership, season ticket loan and green bikes.

Vacation placements
Places for 2014: 15 places available on one two-week Easter placement and 60 places available on four two-week summer placements. Remuneration: £350 per week; Closing Date: 31 January 2014.

Sponsorship & awards
GDL and LPC fees and maintenance paid p.a. Awards for commendation and distinction for LPC.

Partners 72
Assistant Solicitors 226
Total Trainees 55

Contact
Shahnaz Begum

Method of application
Online application via firm website

Selection procedure
Interview
Closing date for August 2016/February 2017
31 July 2014

Application
Training contracts p.a. 30
Applications p.a. 1,500
Required degree grade 2:1

Training
Salary
Year 1 £42,000
Year 2 £45,000
Plus welcome payment of £2,000
Holiday entitlement 25 days
All trainees are guaranteed to spend a seat overseas

Post-qualification
Salary £72,500

Overseas offices
Abu Dhabi, Almaty, Ankara, Beijing, Berlin, Bratislava, Brussels, Bucharest, Budapest, Doha, Düsseldorf, Frankfurt, Geneva, Hamburg, Helsinki, Hong Kong, Istanbul, Johannesburg, London, Los Angeles, Madrid, Mexico City, Miami, Milan, Monterrey, Moscow, Munich, New York, Paris, Prague, Riyadh, São Paulo, Silicon Valley, Singapore, Shanghai, Stockholm, Tokyo, Warsaw, Washington DC

WHITE & CASE

Wilsons Solicitors LLP

Alexandra House, St Johns Street, Salisbury, Wiltshire SP1 2SB
Tel: (01722) 412 412 Fax: (01722) 427 610
Email: jo.ratcliffe@wilsonslaw.com
Website: www.wilsonslaw.com

Firm profile
Ranked as one of the top private client and charity law firms in the country, our 280-year heritage, combined with lawyers who are recognised leaders in their fields, enables Wilsons to provide a unique combination of skills and experience to our clients. Our lawyers are dedicated to ensuring a detailed understanding of their clients' interests and a seamless working relationship across the different specialities of the practice.

Main areas of work
Private Client: We act for clients with business interests, landed and inherited wealth, foreign domiciliaries, UK and offshore trustees and non-resident individuals with links to the UK. Services including tax planning, estate and succession planning, asset structuring, UK and offshore trust formation and advice, wills and trusts and estate administration and probates and intestacies valued at up to £50m.

The family team's expertise ranges from pre-nuptial agreements and civil partnerships to divorce and children's arrangements.

Charity: Wilsons has one of the most highly ranked teams in the UK. We advise on the complete range of legal needs and have a particular specialism in contentious and noncontentious legacy work. The constitutional and governance team has considerable expertise in advising military charities and the charitable care sector.

Agriculture: Wilsons' rural team has developed a practice centred on the needs of rural business and landowners. These include complex sales and purchases, development options for landowners, grants and diversification advice and property litigation, including landlord and tenant, partnership matters, boundary, title and rights of way disputes.

Commercial: The commercial team specialises in employment, commercial property and corporate work. Corporate work focuses on commercial tax and asset planning, transactions and refinancing. The team deals with an unusual breadth of work requiring high-quality, bespoke commercial advice.

Property: Our clients have substantial commercial, agricultural and residential property interests and the firm advises on purchasing, letting and sales, and has a reputation for gaining excellent results in the options over and sales of development land.

Litigation and dispute resolution: Wilsons has one of the largest teams outside London. We advise clients on a wide range of contentious matters to provide an efficient and effective means of dispute resolution. In addition to its expertise in agricultural and probate disputes, the firm has specialists who can advise on all aspects of commercial dispute claims.

Trainee profile
We aim to employ the highest quality people; our reputation relies upon this. We place considerable emphasis on teamwork and look for applicants who are clear team players.

Training environment
The firm has attracted several senior City lawyers and an enviable client base and being based in Salisbury ensures an exceptional quality of work within beautiful surroundings.

Benefits
Pension, life assurance, choice of optional benefits and private medical insurance.

Work experience placements
One week available in July at our head office in Salisbury.

Partners 33	
Trainees 8	
Total Staff 150	
Contact	
Mrs J Ratcliffe	
jo.ratcliffe@wilsonslaw.com	
Method of application	
Application via website	
Selection procedure	
Interview and assessment day	
Closing dates for training scheme	
31 July 2014 for training contract to commence in September 2016	
Application	
Training contracts p.a. 4	
Salary	
Above market rate	
Holiday entitlement 22 days	
Offices	
Salisbury, London	

WILSONS

Winckworth Sherwood

Minerva House, 5 Montague Close, London SE1 9BB
Tel: (020) 7593 5000   Fax: (020) 7593 5099
Email: trainees@wslaw.co.uk
Website: www.wslaw.co.uk

Firm profile

Winckworth Sherwood is a highly individual law firm, committed to delivering a relevant, competitive and professional service. Our lawyers include leaders in their fields, many with deep personal investment in our clients' sectors. We are at the forefront of the private and public sector interface and our modern and collaborative approach enables us to adapt to our clients' diverse activities.

Main areas of work

Administrative law, banking and finance, charity law, company and commercial, construction, data protection, disciplinary proceedings, ecclesiastical, education, employment, environmental, estate planning and wills, family, licensing, litigation and dispute resolution, parliamentary, PFI/projects, planning, property (commercial and institutional), property dispute resolution, public private partnerships, outsourcing, public law, private client, procurement, real estate, regeneration, residential conveyancing, social housing, trusts, probate and tax.

Trainee profile

We require a strong academic record both at school and university, but we also look for attributes which demonstrate the potential for making a positive contribution to the firm. It is important to be able to empathise with clients whilst at the same time keeping a clear business head; we look for evidence of these qualities at the outset.

Training environment

Trainees will be placed in four departments in six month placements. We encourage substantial client interaction and you will be involved in all phases of a matter. You will usually sit with a partner or associate and may be given the opportunity to manage your own files, subject to suitable supervision.

We have a well developed in-house CPD programme which draws upon the expertise of partners, associates and guest professionals, in which trainees are encouraged to participate.

Sponsorship & awards

Under certain conditions the firm provides financial assistance for course fees to trainees attending the Legal Practice Course (LPC) or in exceptional circumstances studying for a Graduate Diploma in Law (GDL).

Partners 43	
Assistant Solicitors 77	
Total Trainees 12	
Contact	
Heather Cornish	
020 7593 5077	
Method of application	
Online application form (https://www.apply4law.com/winckworths/)	
Selection procedure	
Summer Vacation Scheme, Trainee Assessment Day and Panel Interviews	
Closing date for August 2016	
30 June 2014	
Application	
No. of training contracts p.a. 6	
Applications p.a. 300	
% interviewed 15%	
Required degree grade 2.1	
Training	
Starting salary £32K	
Holiday entitlement 24 days plus Bank Holidays and one extra day at Christmas	
Post-qualification	
% trainees offered job on qualification 80% (2012)	
Overseas/regional offices	
London	

A-Z of Solicitors

Withers LLP

16 Old Bailey, London EC4M 7EG
Tel: (020) 7597 6000 Fax: (020) 7329 2534
Email: jaya.louvre@withersworldwide.com
Website: www.withersworldwide.com

Firm profile

Withers LLP is a leading international law firm dedicated to the business, personal and philanthropic interests of successful people, their families, their businesses and their advisers.

The firm's mission is to offer a truly integrated legal service to people with sophisticated global wealth, management and business needs. Withers' reputation in commercial law along with its status as the largest Private Client Team in Europe and leading Family Team sets it apart from other City firms. The firm has been recognised for its great working environment having been listed in both The Sunday Times 100 Best Companies to work for and in receiving Legal Week's Best Legal Employer Award for the past two years. The firm also won the Financial Mail's 2013 Breaking the Mould Award for its work promoting and supporting women.

Main areas of work

The wealth of today's private client has increased considerably and many are institutions in their own right. Withers has been able to respond to these changing legal needs and offers integrated solutions to the international legal and tax needs of its clients. The firm has unparalleled expertise in commercial and tax law, trusts, estate planning, litigation, charities, employment, family law and other legal issues facing high net worth individuals. Work is often international due to the complexity of our client base which includes some of the wealthiest global citizens. Currently we act for around a quarter of the UK Sunday Times 'Rich List' and a significant number from the US 'Forbes' and Asian 'Huran' rich lists. Trainees who speak a relevant language may have the opportunity to complete a seat in one of our offices abroad.

Trainee profile

Each year the firm looks for a diverse mix of trainees who are excited by the prospect of working with leaders in their field. Trainees must have an excellent academic background and great attention to detail. Team players with leadership potential are of interest to the firm, as is an international outlook and foreign language skills.

Training environment

Trainees spend six months in four different departments. Working in a team with a partner and an assistant solicitor provides autonomy, responsibility and fast development. Buddy and mentor systems as well as on the job training ensure trainees are fully supported from the outset.

Application

Apply online by 31 July 2014 to begin training in August 2016. Interviews take place between May and September.

Vacation scheme

The firm runs two-week long placements at Easter and over the summer in London. Apply online by 31 January 2014 for places in 2014. Interviews take place between January and March.

Sponsorship

Fees plus £5,000 maintenance for both the GDL and/or LPC are paid.

Partners 105
Total Staff 747
Trainees 38

Contact
Jaya Louvre
Recruitment Manager

Method of application
Application form (available online)

Selection procedure
2 interviews incl. written exercise and presentation

Closing dates for 2016
Training scheme
31 July 2014
2014 vacation placements
31 January 2014

Application
Training contracts p.a. 11
Applications p.a. 900
% interviewed p.a. 20%
Required grades 2:1, AAB at A-Level

Training
Salary
1st year (2012) £34,000
2nd year (2012) £36,000
Holiday entitlement 23 days
% of trainees with a non-law degree p.a. 50%

Post-qualification
Salary (2012) £56,000

Offices
London, Milan, Geneva, Zurich, New York, New Haven (Connecticut), Greenwich (USA), Hong Kong, Singapore, BVI

A-Z of Solicitors

	Lincoln's Inn	Inner Temple	Middle Temple	Gray's Inn
Contact	Tel: 020 7405 1393 www.lincolnsinn.org.uk	Tel: 020 7787 8250 www.innertemple.org.uk	Tel: 020 7427 4800 www.middletemple.org.uk	Tel: 020 7458 7800 www.graysinn.info
Architecture	The Old Hall was build in 1490 and the larger Great Hall in 1845, the same year as the library. The Stone Buildings are Regency. The largest Inn, it covers 11 acres.	12th-century Temple Church stands opposite the modern Hall, which was built after the original was destroyed in WWII and stands on the site of an ancient hall of the Knights of the Temple.	Grand style includes smoking rooms decked out in oak, Van Dyck paintings and a large private collection of silver. The splendid Elizabethan Hall has ornate carvings and is tucked down an intricate maze of alleys and narrow streets.	Its ancient Hall and Chapel are still intact, despite suffering serious war damage. The rest is largely a 1950s red-brick creation. One of the smaller Inns.
Gardens	Always open and especially popular at lunchtimes.	Well kept and stretch down to the Thames. Croquet, chess and giant Connect Four can be played.	Small and award-winning, with a handy bar.	Famous 'Walks' good for nearby City Law School students. Restaurant during the summer.
Style	Friendly, international and large.	Sociable, progressive and switched on.	Musical, arty and very sociable. Christmas revels are notorious.	Traditional and cosy with a personal touch.
Gastronomy	Meals in Hall are subsidised for students.	Lunch served every day. 15% discount for students.	Good-quality lunch served daily.	Lunch served in Hall every day, with subsidised rates for students.
Accommodation	14 flats available for students and 3 are let to pupils. All on-site.	Not for students.	Not for students.	Not for students.
Bar	The stylish Members' Common Room has a restaurant and a terrace bar.	The Pegasus Bar has a terraced open-air area. Good for people-watching but not a place to go incognito.	St. Clement's Bar closed recently and is looking for new digs.	The Bridge Bar is above the gateway between South and Gray's Inn Squares.
Old Members	John Donne, Lord Hailsham LC, Lord Denning MR, Muhammad Ali Jinnah, H. Rider Haggard, Wilkie Collins, some 16 British Prime Ministers.	Dr Ivy Williams (first woman called to the Bar), Bram Stoker, Judge Jeffreys of 'Bloody Assizes', M K Gandhi, Lord Falconer of Thoroton.	Sir Walter Raleigh, William Blackstone, Charles Dickens, William Makepeace Thackeray.	Sir Francis Bacon, Thomas Cromwell, Dame Rose Heilbron (the first female QC, first female Old Bailey judge and first female treasurer at an Inn).
Points of Interest	Together with the Royal Navy, Lincoln's Inn takes the Loyal Toast seated, which commemorates a meal with King Charles II during which the entire company got too drunk to stand. Inn offers subsidised trips to The Hague, Luxembourg & Strasbourg.	Temple Church includes part of the Knights Templar's round church, which was modelled on the Church of the Holy Sepulchre in Jerusalem and used as a film set in The Da Vinci Code.	Shakespeare's Twelfth Night enjoyed its first performance here. Hall has a table from the Golden Hind. Every new barrister signs their name in a book on this table.	The first performance of Shakespeare's Comedy of Errors took place here. Law has been taught on the site of Gray's Inn since the reign of Edward III. The ornate carved screen in the Hall is made from an Armada ship.
Scholarship Interview Process	Panel interview with no set question beforehand. Expect chat about preferred areas of practice and items of legal interest in the news. Scholarship awarded solely on merit, then weighted according to financial means.	Panel interview with set question. GDL scholars entitled to automatic funding for BPTC, but can apply for higher award. Merit and academic excellence prioritised, but all awards (save for the top ones) are means tested.	Every applicant interviewed in a 15 minute panel interview that tests a range of skills. Awards based on merit and then weighted according to financial means.	Shortlisted applicants interviewed by a three-person panel prioritising an ability to think on one's feet over legal knowledge. Extra-curricular achievements taken into consideration – eg music, sport or overcoming adversity.
Scholarship Money	A total of nearly £1.5m available each year through over 130 scholarships. GDL: up to 32 scholarships of between £2k and £7k. BPTC: up to 70 scholarships of between £6k and £18k, plus up to 40 bursaries of up to £3k each.	A total of £1.43m available. GDL: 2 major scholarships plus various awards totalling £173k. BPTC: 7 major grants (of between £17k and £22k), and further awards totalling over £1m.	A total of around £1m available. A fund of £900,000 for BPTC scholarships and awards. A fund of £90,000 for GDL scholarships and awards. Overseas scholarships totalling at least up to £15,000.	A total of over £830k available. GDL: around 23 awards of between c.£2k and £9k. BPTC: around 44 awards of between £13k and £20,000 each. Various overseas scholarships and miscellaneous awards – eg £10k Hebe Plunkett award for disabled.

Practice areas at the Bar

The Chancery Bar

In a nutshell

The Chancery Bar is tricky to define. The High Court has three divisions: Family, Queen's Bench (QBD) and Chancery, with cases allocated to and heard by the most appropriate division based on their subject matter. But what makes a case suitable for the Chancery Division? Historically it has been the venue for cases with an emphasis on legal principles, foremost among them the concept of equity (fairness). Cases are generally categorised as either 'traditional' Chancery (trusts, probate, real property, charities and mortgages) or 'commercial' Chancery (company law, shareholder cases, partnership, banking, pensions, financial services, insolvency, professional negligence, tax, media and IP). Most Chancery sets undertake both types of work, albeit with varying emphases. In practice, there is an overlap between Chancery practice and the work of the Commercial Bar (historically dealt with in the QBD). Barristers at commercial sets can frequently be found on Chancery cases and vice versa, though some areas, such as tax and IP, require specialisation.

The realities of the job

- This is an area of law for those who love to grapple with its most complex aspects. It's all about the application of long-standing legal principles to modern-day situations.
- Barristers must be very practical in the legal solutions they offer to clients. Complex and puzzling cases take significant unravelling and the legal arguments/principles must be explained coherently to the solicitor and the lay client. Suave and sophisticated presentation when before a judge is also vital.
- Advocacy is important, but the majority of time is spent in chambers perusing papers, considering arguments, drafting pleadings, skeletons and advices, or conducting settlement negotiations.
- Some instructions fly into chambers, need immediate attention and then disappear just as quickly. Others can rumble on for years.
- Variety is a key attraction. Traditional work can involve human interest: wills and inheritance can cause all sorts of ructions among families. Commercial Chancery practitioners deal with blood-on-the-boardroom-table disputes or bust-ups between co-writers of million-selling songs.

- Schedules aren't set by last-minute briefs for next-day court appearances, so barristers need self-discipline and good time management skills.
- The early years of practice feature low-value cases like straightforward possession proceedings in the County Court, winding-up applications in the Companies Court and appearances before the bankruptcy registrars. More prominent sets will involve baby barristers as second or third junior on larger, more complex cases.

Current issues

- The Chancery Bar attracts high-value, complex domestic cases and offshore and cross-border instructions. They might involve Russian and Eastern European business affairs or massive offshore trusts in the Cayman Islands, the British Virgin Islands, Bermuda and the Channel Islands.
- The scope of the Chancery Division means that practitioners get involved in some enormous commercial and public law matters.

Some tips

- Most pupils at leading Chancery sets have a first-class degree. You should enjoy the analytical process involved in constructing arguments and evaluating the answers to problems. If you're not a natural essay writer, you're unlikely to be a natural-born Chancery practitioner.
- Don't wander into this area by accident. Are you actually interested in equity, trusts, company law, insolvency, IP or tax?
- Though not an accurate portrayal of modern practice, Dickens' novel *Bleak House* is the ultimate Chancery saga.

Read our Chambers Reports on...

Maitland Chambers	South Square
XXIV Old Buildings	Wilberforce Chambers
Serle Court	

The Bar

The Commercial Bar

In a nutshell

The Commercial Bar handles a variety of business disputes. Commercial cases are classically defined as those heard by the Commercial Court – a subsection of the Queen's Bench Division of the High Court. But cases can also be heard in county courts, by the Chancery Divisions or by the Technology and Construction Court (TCC). The Commercial Bar deals with disputes in all manner of industries from construction, shipping and insurance to banking, entertainment and manufacturing. Almost all disputes are contract and/or tort claims, and the Commercial Bar remains rooted in common law. That said, domestic and European legislation is increasingly important and commercial barristers' incomes now reflect the popularity of the English courts with overseas litigants. Cross-border issues including competition law, international public and trade law and conflicts of law are all growing in prominence. Alternative methods of dispute resolution – usually arbitration or mediation – are also popular because of the increased likelihood of preserving commercial relationships that would otherwise be destroyed by the litigation process.

The realities of the job

- Barristers steer solicitors and lay clients through the litigation process and advise on strategy, such as how clients can position themselves through witness statements, pleadings and pre-trial 'interlocutory' skirmishes.
- Advocacy is key, but as much of it is paper-based, written skills are just as important as oral skills.
- Commercial cases can be very fact-heavy and the evidence for a winning argument can be buried in a room full of papers. Barristers have to work closely with instructing solicitors to manage documentation.
- Not all commercial pupils will take on their own caseload in the second six. At first, new juniors commonly handle small cases including common law matters like personal injury, employment cases, possession proceedings and winding-up or bankruptcy applications.
- New juniors gain exposure to larger cases by assisting senior colleagues. As a 'second junior' they assist the 'first junior' and QC leading the case. They use this as an opportunity to pick up tips on cross-examining witnesses and how best to present arguments.
- In time, a junior's caseload increases in value and complexity. Most commercial barristers specialise by building up expertise on cases within a particular industry sector, eg shipping, insurance or entertainment.
- Developing a practice means working long hours, often under pressure. Your service standards must be impeccable and your style user-friendly, no matter how late or disorganised the solicitor's instruction. In a good set you can make an exceedingly good living.

Current issues

- The Commercial Bar is booming with cases involving ever larger sums of money, ever greater levels of complexity and ever larger teams of lawyers. One recent mega-case saw a Norwegian-owned investment firm bring an $8bn breach of contract claim against Deutsche Bank over purported trading losses in October 2008.
- As the above case shows, the fallout from the credit crunch continues to be felt in the courts. Financial, insurance and professional negligence disputes are all the rage in 2013 and this trend will continue into 2014. The number of cases brought to the High Court spiked in 2009, and has remained steady at pre-crunch levels since.
- With more claims being settled through mediation, only the big, multi-issue cases tend to reach court, as there are so many other opportunities for dealing with smaller, less complex cases.
- Third-party funding of litigation and costs risk-sharing arrangements are becoming more prevalent.

Some tips

- Competition for pupillage at the Commercial Bar is fierce. A first-class degree is commonplace and you'll need impressive references.
- Don't underestimate the value of non-legal work experience; commercial exposure of any kind is going to help you understand the client's perspective and motivations.
- Go to our website to read more about **Shipping** and **Construction** at the Bar.

Read our Chambers Reports on...

Atkin Chambers	4 New Square
Blackstone Chambers	XXIV Old Buildings
Crown Office Chambers	Pump Court Tax Chambers
One Essex Court	Quadrant Chambers
Henderson Chambers	Serle Court
Keating Chambers	South Square
7 King's Bench Walk	3 Verulam Buildings
Maitland Chambers	Wilberforce Chambers
Monckton Chambers	

The Common Law Bar

In a nutshell

English common law derives from the precedents set by judicial decisions rather than the contents of statutes. Most common law cases turn on principles of tort and contract and are dealt with in the Queen's Bench Division (QBD) of the High Court and the county courts. At the edges, common law practice blurs into both Chancery and commercial practice, yet the work undertaken in common law sets is broader still, and one of the most appealing things about a career at one of these sets is the variety of instructions available.

Employment and personal injury are the bread and butter at the junior end, and such matters are interspersed with licensing, clinical negligence, landlord and tenant issues, the winding-up of companies and bankruptcy applications, as well as small commercial and contractual disputes. Some sets will even extend their remit to inquests and criminal cases.

The realities of the job

- Although you can express an interest in receiving certain work from the clerks, most sets expect their juniors to be common law generalists. There is an opportunity to begin to specialise at between five and ten years' call.
- Advocacy is plentiful. Juniors can expect to be in court three days a week and second-six pupils often have their own cases. Small beginnings such as 'noting briefs' (where you attend court simply in order to report back on the proceedings) and masters' and district judges' appointments lead to lower-value 'fast-track' personal injury trials then longer, higher-value, 'multi-track' trials and employment tribunals.
- Outside court, the job involves research, an assessment of the merits of a case and meetings with solicitors and lay clients. The barrister will also be asked to draft statements of claim, defences and opinions.
- Dealing with the volume and variety of cases requires a good grasp of the law and the procedural rules of the court, as well as an easy facility for assimilating the facts of each case.
- Interpersonal skills are important. A client who has never been to court before will be very nervous and needs to be put at ease.
- At the junior end, work comes in at short notice, so having to digest a file of documents quickly is commonplace.
- Acting as a junior on more complex cases allows a younger barrister to observe senior lawyers in court.

Current issues

- The trend for mediation and arbitration of disputes, and the trend for solicitors to undertake more advocacy themselves, has reduced the amount of court work somewhat. Barristers remain involved with alternative dispute resolution, however.
- Britons have become increasingly litigious over the past few decades. Personal injury and clinical negligence claims (often against the NHS) are now an established part of the legal landscape, as individuals have become aware of the expanded protections afforded by health and safety regulation and professional codes of conduct.
- Since legal aid was cut from common law areas like PI in the 1990s, conditional fee agreements (aka 'no-win no-fee') and third-party funding of cases have helped sustain barristers' work volume.
- The Jackson reforms of civil litigation costs came into effect on 1 April 2013. The biggest change is that conditional fees and certain insurance premiums are no longer recoverable from the losing party. This lays a greater financial burden on claimants and is expected to result in less litigation and affect fees.
- Other proposed changes – an increase in the small claims limit, changes to whiplash-related cases and restrictions on workplace-injury claims – could affect work at both the junior and senior end.

Some tips

- Though there are a lot of common law sets, pupillages and tenancies don't grow on trees. You'll have to impress to get a foot in the door and then make your mark to secure your next set of instructions. Personality and oral advocacy skills often matter a lot.
- If you want to specialise, thoroughly research the sets you apply to – many want their juniors to retain a broad practice many years into tenancy, while others do allow some space to carve out a niche.

Read our Chambers Reports on...

Atkin Chambers	Maitland Chambers
Blackstone Chambers	Matrix Chambers
1 Chancery Lane	4 New Square
Cloisters	XXIV Old Buildings
Crown Office Chambers	Old Square Chambers
One Essex Court	Serle Court
Henderson Chambers	South Square
11KBW	2 Temple Gardens
7 King's Bench Walk	3 Verulam Buildings
Littleton Chambers	Wilberforce Chambers

The Bar

The Criminal Bar

In a nutshell

Barristers are instructed by solicitors to provide advocacy or advice for individuals being prosecuted in cases brought before the UK's criminal courts. Lesser offences like driving charges, possession of drugs or benefit fraud are listed in the Magistrates' Courts, where solicitor advocates are increasingly active. More serious charges such as fraud, supplying drugs or murder go to the Crown Courts, which are essentially still the domain of barristers. Complex cases may reach the Court of Appeal or Supreme Court. A criminal set's caseload incorporates everything from theft, fraud, drugs and driving offences to assaults of varying degree of severity and murder.

The realities of the job

- Criminal barristers need a sense of theatre and dramatic timing, but good oratory skills are only half the story. Tactical sense, a level head and great time management skills are important.
- The barrister must be able to inspire confidence in clients from any kind of background.
- Some clients can be tricky, unpleasant or scary. Some will have pretty unfortunate lives, others will be addicted to alcohol or drugs, or have poor housing and little education.
- Barristers often handle several cases a day, frequently at different courts. Some of them will be poorly prepared by instructing solicitors. It is common to take on additional cases at short notice and to have to cope with missing defendants and witnesses. Stamina and adaptability are consequently a must.
- Sustained success rests on effective case preparation and an awareness of evolving law and sentencing policies.
- Pupils cut their teeth on motoring offences, committals and directions hearings in the magistrates' courts. By the end of pupillage they should expect to be instructed in their own right and make it into the Crown Court.
- Juniors quickly see the full gamut of cases. Trials start small – offences such as common assault – and move onto ABH, robbery and possession of drugs with intent to supply.
- It may be sexy work, but baby barrister pay on publicly-funded cases can be abysmal. Increasingly, barristers earn as little as £10,000 annually for their first few years in practice.

Current issues

- To save costs, the Crown Prosecution Service is trying to bring more advocacy in-house. The CPS wants many of its lawyers to develop to become Senior Crown Advocates and handle contested trials in the Crown Court. The move has reduced the work available at the Bar's junior end, and has caused concern about the quality of CPS advocacy.
- Legal aid cuts and reforms are hitting the number of available criminal instructions and remuneration. This problem is fast becoming a crisis, especially at the junior end. Justice Secretary Chris Grayling has said he wants to cut an additional £220m a year from the criminal legal aid budget. A fair chunk of that will come out of barristers' fees.
- Partially as a consequence of legal aid cutbacks, many top-end criminal sets (and barristers themselves) are branching out into fraud, bribery, regulatory, VAT tribunal and professional discipline work.
- Private paying criminal practice is as healthy as ever.

Some tips

- Mini-pupillage experience and plenty of mooting and debating is required before you can look like a serious applicant.
- The Criminal Bar tends to provide more pupillages than other areas, but these don't necessarily translate into tenancies. Third and fourth sixes are not uncommon.
- There are many ways of getting that all-important exposure to the criminal justice system. See our website for tips on useful voluntary opportunities.

Read our Chambers Reports on...

2 Bedford Row

Matrix Chambers

The Employment Bar

In a nutshell

The Employment Bar deals with any and every sort of claim arising from the relations or breakdown of relations between employees and employers. Disputes relating to individuals and small groups of employees are generally resolved at or before reaching an Employment Tribunal. Such 'statutory' claims may relate to redundancy; unfair dismissal; discrimination on the grounds of gender, sexual orientation, race, religion or age; workplace harassment; breach of contract; and whistle-blowing. Sometimes a tribunal will consist of an Employment Judge sitting with two 'wing members' (one from a trades union and one from a business background). In other tribunal cases – including unfair dismissals – the Employment Judge sits alone. Appeals are heard by the Employment Appeal Tribunal (EAT).

Accessibility is a key aim of the employment tribunal system, legal representation is not required, and many more cases proceed to a full hearing than in other areas of civil law. Such is the emphasis on user-friendliness that employment claims can even be issued online. Claimants often represent themselves, though in complex, high-value cases both parties usually seek specialist legal representation from solicitors and barristers.

Employees and employers may also bring claims in civil court. High-value claims, applications for injunctions to prevent the breach of restrictive covenants, and disputes over team moves or use of trade secrets are usually dealt with in the county courts or the High Court.

The realities of the job

- For pupils and juniors, most advocacy takes place in employment tribunals or the EAT. Hearings are conducted with everyone sitting down and barristers do not wear wigs. The emphasis is on oral advocacy, with witness statements generally read aloud.
- A corporate respondent might pay for a QC, while the applicant's pocket may only stretch to a junior. Solicitor advocates feature prominently in tribunals.
- Tribunals follow the basic pattern of examination in chief, cross-examination and closing submissions; however barristers have to modify their style, especially when appearing against someone who is unrepresented.
- Employment specialists need great people skills. Clients frequently become emotional or stressed, and the trend for respondent companies to name an individual (say a manager) as co-respondent means there may be several individuals in the room with complex personal, emotional and professional issues at stake.
- Few juniors act only for applicants or only for respondents. Most also undertake civil or commercial cases, some criminal matters.
- UK employment legislation mirrors EU law and changes with great rapidity. Cases are regularly stayed while others with similar points are heard on appeal.

Current issues

- The number of claims brought to employment tribunals was 332,859 in 2012/13, much higher than before the recession. This means there is ample work for juniors on 'fixed fee' arrangements for insurers or large employers.
- Layoffs, bonus disputes and team moves resulting from the economic downturn are all key sources of claims.
- Ongoing redundancies in the public and private sector mean that strike disputes continue to pop up, though the number of days lost to strikes fell dramatically in 2012.
- The changes to legal aid introduced in April 2013 have removed public funding from all employment cases except discrimination claims. This may adversely affect the volume of tribunal claims and increase the number of claimants representing themselves.
- The Equality Act 2010 has brought discrimination and human rights cases to the fore.
- A number of cost-saving measures were introduced to employment tribunals in April 2012. These include the removal of 'wing members' in some cases (as mentioned above), the doubling of deposit and other costs imposed on claimants and witness statements being taken as read to save time.

Some tips

- Get involved with the Free Representation Unit. No pupillage application will look complete without some involvement of this kind.
- Practically any kind of job will give you first-hand experience of being an employee – an experience that is not to be underestimated.
- High-profile cases are regularly reported in the press, so there's no excuse for not keeping abreast of the area.

Read our Chambers Reports on...

Blackstone Chambers	Littleton Chambers
Cloisters	Matrix Chambers
11KBW	Old Square Chambers

The Family Bar

In a nutshell

Family law barristers deal with an array of cases arising from marital, civil union or cohabitation breakdown and related issues concerning children. Simple cases are heard in the county courts, while complex or high-value cases are listed in the Family Division of the High Court. Around half of divorcing couples have at least one child aged under 16, and together divorces affect nearly 160,000 children a year. Consequently, a huge amount of court time is allotted to divorce, separation, adoption, child residence and contact orders, financial provision and domestic violence.

The realities of the job

- Financial cases and public and private law children's work each offer their own unique challenges.
- Emotional resilience is required, as is a capacity for empathy, as the work involves asking clients for intimate details of their private life, and breaking devastating news to the emotionally fragile. Private law children's cases can sometimes involve serious allegations between parents and require the input of child psychologists. The public law counterpart (care proceedings between local authorities and parents) invariably includes detailed and potentially distressing medical evidence.
- For many clients, involvement with the courts is out of the ordinary and they will rely heavily on their counsel to guide them through the process. The law can never fix emotional problems relating to marital breakdown or child issues, but it can pacify a situation.
- The job calls for communication, tact and maturity. Cases have a significant impact on the lives they involve, so finding the most appropriate course of action for each client is important. The best advocates are those who can differentiate between a case and client requiring a bullish approach and those crying out for settlement and concessions to be made.
- Where possible, mediation is used to resolve disputes in a more efficient and less unsettling fashion.
- Teamwork is crucial. As the barrister is the link between the client, the judge, solicitors and social workers, it is important to win the trust and confidence of all parties.
- The legislation affecting this area is comprehensive, and there's a large body of case law. Keeping abreast of developments is necessary because the job is more about negotiating general principles than adhering strictly to precedents.
- Finance-oriented barristers need an understanding of pensions and shares and a good grounding in the basics of trusts and property.
- The early years of practice involve a lot of private law children work (disputes between parents), small financial cases and injunctions in situations of domestic violence.

Current issues

- The number of divorces fell slightly in 2011 – part of a general decade-long decline – while the volume of litigation over the division of assets after divorce continues to rise.
- Compulsory mediation for divorcing couples was introduced in 2011, but has so far failed to bring down the number of cases going through the courts.
- Legal aid cuts are hitting the Family Bar hard, with funding removed from a majority of cases. An estimated 200,000 people a year are affected. Perversely, the result has been a massive increase in cases with more and more individuals representing themselves without consulting a lawyer.
- Big divorces involving wealthy couples are often big news and are often accompanied by strategic use of the media.
- A 2012 Law Commission report urged reform of the rules governing the division of assets on divorce, even going so far as to suggest a statutory formula could be introduced to determine how wealth is divided.
- The Marriage (Same Sex Couples) Act 2013 and further efforts to equalise marriage rights could affect divorce laws and civil partnerships.
- Since *Radmacher v Granatino*, prenuptial agreements are now part of the English legal landscape. Barristers are often involved in drafting the agreements too.

Some tips

- The Family Bar is quite small and competition for pupillage is intense. Think about how you can evidence your interest in family law. See our **Pro Bono and Volunteering** section.
- Younger pupils might find it daunting to advise on mortgages, marriages and children when they've never experienced any of these things personally. Those embarking on a second career, or who have delayed a year or two and acquired other life experiences, have a distinct advantage.

Read our Chambers Reports on...

Public Law at the Bar

In a nutshell

Centred on the Administrative Court, public law relates to the principles governing the exercise of power by public bodies. Those which most often appear as respondents in the High Court include government departments, local authorities, the prison service and NHS trusts. Often the headline cases are challenges to central government policies, like terror suspect control orders, the extradition of failed asylum seekers and the anonymity of giving evidence. Other big-ticket work comes from public inquires: the Chilcot, Leveson and Francis inquiries are all illustrative examples. However, for all the (in)famous cases reported in the media, there are hundreds of public bodies taking daily decisions that affect just about everybody in the country. It is decisions like these – on immigration, welfare, planning applications or a child's school allocation – which provide most work for private practitioners. The most important process in public practice is judicial review: the Administrative Court may order that any decision made unlawfully be overturned or reconsidered. Decisions are often reviewed on the basis of the Human Rights Act 1998. Many barristers also have practices in areas that dovetail with their public law practice. Criminal barristers will, for example, frequently handle issues relating to prisoners or breaches of procedure by police, whereas commercial barristers may handle judicial review of decisions made by the Department for Business, Innovation and Skills.

The realities of the job

- The Administrative Court is extremely busy, so an efficient style of advocacy is vital.
- Barristers need to cut straight to the chase and succinctly deliver pertinent information, case law or statutory regulations. Barristers need a genuine interest in the legislative process and the fundamental laws by which we live.
- A real interest in academic law is a prerequisite. Complex arguments are more common than precise answers.
- While legal intellect is vital, public law's real world issues demand a practical outlook and an ability to stand back from the issue in question.
- Junior barristers often hone their nascent advocacy skills at the permissions stage of judicial review in short 30-minute hearings.

Current issues

- The Health and Social Care Act 2012 is expected to lead to more disputes and more litigation in the health sector.
- The Legal Aid, Sentencing and Punishment of Offenders Act 2012 and other reforms to public funding of the Bar are affecting public law cases and the livelihoods of barristers.
- In 2011, the Freedom of Information Act was extended to cover UCAS, the Association of Chief Police Officers and the Financial Ombudsman Service, continuing a trend which is seeing the ever closer scrutiny of public bodies by pressure groups, the media and individuals.
- The Justice and Security Act 2013 expanded the use of closed material procedures (aka 'secret courts') in the civil courts, a move which has been widely criticised by public law practitioners.
- There are an increasing number of disputes related to welfare benefits, other public spending cuts (eg library closures) and government cock-ups.

Some tips

- The competition for public law pupillages is exceptionally fierce. Having the highest possible academic credentials is key when applying to a public law set but most successful candidates will also have impressive hands-on experience in the public or voluntary sectors.
- Public international law is popular, but it's an incredibly small field with few openings. Moreover, it's dominated by sitting or ex-professors at top universities, alongside Foreign Office veterans and the occasional senior barrister.
- If administrative and constitutional law were not your favourite subjects you should reconsider your decision before choosing public law.
- As a rewarding alternative, there are opportunities available within the Government Legal Service.
- An interest in current affairs is essential.

Read our Chambers Reports on...

Blackstone Chambers	11KBW
Government Legal Service	Matrix Chambers
Henderson Chambers	Monckton Chambers
Keating Chambers	

Chambers Reports: Introduction

Making an informed choice about where to apply for pupillage isn't easy. Once you establish your desired area of practice, you have to select a balanced collection of up to 12 Pupillage Gateway sets and figure out how many sets to apply to outside the scheme. But how do you know just where you'll fit in and who's interested in your particular working style?

These days the majority of chambers' websites display all the essential information – not just details about their size, nature of work and location, but also specifics on what to expect from their pupillage schemes. Still, internet surfing can only take you so far; there's no real substitute for the insights you'll gain into the inner workings of a set through a mini-pupillage. Of course, it's impossible to do minis at every set, so lucky for you we've done some digging.

For the last decade we've called in on various chambers regularly, taking time to speak with pupils, juniors, pupil supervisors, QCs, clerks and chief execs about life at their set. This is no small task, so we divvy up our approach, visiting each of our chosen sets every other year and refreshing the existing Chambers Report in the intervening year. This year's roll call of 29 sets includes 16 new features and 13 refreshed from our 2013 edition. We've tried to visit as many different types of sets as possible to paint a picture of the variety of practices available. Our visits took us from the grandeur of the Chancery Bar to the more modest surroundings of sets conducting significant amounts of publicly funded worked. Our selection strives to include something to suit most tastes, from commercial and common law to criminal, IP and tax. The wild card in our pack is the Government Legal Service, which admittedly isn't a chambers proper but still offers what we regard as a cracking pupillage.

All of the sets covered this year are located in London, where the majority of chambers and pupillages are based, but don't forget there are some excellent sets in the regions, mostly in larger cities like Leeds, Liverpool, Manchester, Birmingham and Bristol. Bear in mind our selected sets are not the only ones in the Premier League of each practice area; believe us when we say we'd visit many others if we had the time. We should also add that the on-the-record nature of our research at the Bar means we can't – and don't pretend to – give the same warts-and-all, anonymously sourced True Picture treatment to the following sets as we do to solicitors' firms. You'll have to find out about any warts yourself...

Whichever chambers you target, rest assured they're not expecting ready-formed barristers to turn up at their door. If you've done well academically and can prove your commitment to the relevant areas of practice through your extracurricular pursuits, most chambers will gladly make allowances for a lack of knowledge or experience on specific legal issues. Much has been said and written about how awful pupillage interviews can be, and from what we can tell that holds true in so far as interviews are a trying and disheartening process that can span anywhere from one to five years. However, the profession is increasingly business-oriented, with management taking greater notice of what constitutes good HR practice and acting more thoughtfully towards Bar hopefuls these days. You might also come across the occasional claims that pupillage itself amounts to little more than a year of pain and humiliation. We'd be remiss not to counter such claims. Sets don't try to push pupils to the edge of sanity – at least not on purpose; rather, their aim is to mentor and challenge pupils so as to gauge their compatibility with the set and overall potential at the Bar. Of course, that doesn't mean pupillage is a walk in the park by any means, though we can say with some conviction that any misery accompanying the year is likely driven by the demanding work at hand rather than any malevolence on behalf of chambers themselves.

The aim of our research for our Chambers Reports is not merely to get the low-down on pupillage at each set, but also to get a feel for each chambers' culture and to pick up tips for applicants. To this end we selflessly drank copious cups of tea, munched our way through kilos of biscuits and enjoyed numerous guided tours, checking out some crazy artwork and truly dishevelled libraries along the way. Now it's over to you to make your choices.

Set	Location	Head of Chambers	QCs/Juniors
Atkin Chambers*	London	Andrew White QC	16/25
2 Bedford Row	London	William Clegg QC	16/56
Blackstone Chambers*	London	Carss-Frisk QC/Peto QC	38/54
1 Chancery Lane*	London	John Ross QC	5/39
Cloisters*	London	Robin Allen QC	9/43
Crown Office Chambers*	London	Richard Lynagh QC	13/77
One Essex Court*	London	Lord Grabiner QC	30/55
Government Legal Service	London	N/A	400
1 Hare Court	London	Nicholas Cusworth QC	12/30
Henderson Chambers	London	Charles Gibson QC	9/36
11KBW*	London	Cavanagh QC/Goudie QC	16/40
Keating Chambers	London	Paul Darling QC	26/31
1 King's Bench Walk*	London	Eaton QC/Marshall QC	12/40
7 Kings Bench Walk	London	Gavin Kealey QC	25/28
Littleton Chambers	London	Clarke QC/Freedman QC	13/40
Maitland Chambers*	London	Christopher Pymont QC	25/42
Matrix Chambers	London	Thomas Linden QC	27/47
Monckton Chambers*	London	Paul Lasok QC	14/41
4 New Square	London	Ben Hubble QC	19/55
XXIV Old Buildings*	London, Geneva	Mann QC/Steinfeld QC	11/29
Old Square Chambers	London, Bristol	Cooksley QC/McNeill QC	14/73
Pump Court Tax Chambers	London	Andrew Thornhill QC	10/23
Quadrant Chambers	London	Luke Parsons QC	16/39
Queen Elizabeth Building*	London	Lewis Marks QC	6/27
Serle Court*	London	Alan Boyle QC	20/33
South Square	London	William Trower QC	21/20
2 Temple Gardens	London	Benjamin Browne QC	12/42
3 Verulam Buildings*	London	Ali Malek QC	22/45
Wilberforce Chambers*	London	John Martin QC	22/31

The Bar

*Sets visited in 2013

Atkin Chambers

The facts

Location: Gray's Inn, London
Number of QCs/juniors: 16/25 (10 women)
Apply though Pupillage Gateway
Pupils per year: 2
Seats: 2x3 and 1x6 months
Pupillage award: £60,000 (can advance £10,000 for BPTC)

In the past year, this set's case-load has spanned the world, from a power station on Teesside to cases relating to over a dozen overseas jurisdictions.

One of London's top two construction sets, Atkin is currently enjoying a wealth of interesting work, notably in the IT and international arbitration fields.

Build me up Buttercup

Although best known for its construction work, there's a lot more to Atkin than just bricks and mortar. Its practice extends into fields like renewable energy, engineering and IT. *"We've actually just completed one of the largest IT disputes ever,"* senior clerk Justin Wilson tells us. *"It was an 85-day arbitration worked on by eight of our barristers."* Much of the work centres around contracts and tort, and an interest in these areas is a must if you want to do a pupillage here. *"You don't have to come to your interview raving about construction law,"* one interviewee said. *"In fact, when we arrived most people here had never done any construction work – but you do need to be interested in contracts and tort."* Another source added: *"If you are interested in dealing with important questions of principle that arise in the law – for example, the approach to remedies in contract law or economic loss in tort law – then look at construction as a possible field to practice in. The tangible project-based nature of our work always makes getting your head around everything easier."*

Pupils at Atkin are exposed to a range of work, although there's no set programme. *"They'll encounter a lot of energy cases,"* pupillage committee member Fiona Parkin QC says, *"but what we're trying to ensure is that they develop the skillset to feel comfortable in any of our specialisms, be it pure construction or the computer/tech work that we're seeing more of."* Pupils themselves commented on the increasing amount of international work, as well as telling us that *"clients range from massive businesses to the privileged few who are still building swimming pools in their Mayfair homes."*

Justin Wilson confirms the set *"isn't looking to diversify from its construction core, but is always looking to adapt its skills to relevant sectors. The Bar is changing and there is a recognition that the status quo can't continue. We are still a referral profession and this set understands the importance of collaboration and building relationships."* Although the set retains certain traditional elements, such as afternoon tea and its classic Gray's Inn location, one member pointed out: *"We are modernising and always looking to approach the law with a strong commercial sense."* Another barrister added: *"We enjoy good relations with the biggest solicitors' firms in London, but we remain one of the smallest commercial sets at the Bar. We haven't undergone the same massive expansion which has made some sets more like law firms."* Perhaps it's this which gives Atkin its friendly atmosphere. *"Everyone is genuinely welcoming and deals with you on equal terms."* There's a *"super"* Christmas party, which in 2012 saw junior members belting out hits in a karaoke bar until the wee hours of the morn.

To err is human, to forgive divine

Pupillage is divided into three stages. In the first three months, until Christmas, pupils sit with their first supervisor. *"That's the period when mistakes are allowed,"* a pupil explained. *"They're happy for you to ask plenty of questions, and your supervisor understands that you will err. The general message is: just don't make the same mistake twice."* The second 'seat' lasts from January through to March. Pupils work on larger pleadings and advices, and research complex facts. *"Your lever arch files definitely get bigger as you go along..."* laughed one pupil.

Chambers UK rankings

Construction	Information Technology
Energy & Natural Resources	International Arbitration
	Professional Negligence

Throughout, *"you're always doing live work, rather than something your supervisor has dusted off for you to take a look at. This means you can learn more and get better feedback."* Pupils are also expected to complete set pieces of work for the pupillage committee throughout the period up to March. It's important to note that pupils do not spend any time on their feet. *"That's the nature of the commercial bar. If your main passion is oral advocacy then don't approach this set."* Pupils did assure us that they often attend court to observe members in action, and felt immersed in the process.

In April, pupils begin the assessment process for tenancy. *"We have a very structured programme,"* pupillage committee member Fiona Parkin says. A panel is made up, and all pupils have to submit five pieces of work to be assessed. *"You have three weeks to finish all five pieces,"* a pupil informed us. *"The exercises are really difficult and there is a lot of time pressure, but they do test your organisational skills and how you cope under pressure."* The panel looks at all five, alongside a sixth piece the pupils have previously completed, and produces a report for the pupillage committee. Alongside the written pieces comes an advocacy exercise. *"You get two practice runs, then it's the real deal,"* a baby junior recalled. *"It's quite scary as it's actually assessed by a High Court judge."* That would be Sir Robert Akenhead, head of the Technology and Construction Court. *"He used to be head of chambers and comes back to Atkin as a favour."* Last but not least, pupils are given a week to complete a test paper – normally an advice on a set of pleadings. *"Everything, including reports from the first two supervisors, is put together, marked and discussed. Then the tenancy decision is made."* Although it sounds tough (and in fact no pupils were taken on in 2013) junior members and pupils applauded the assessment process. *"The formalised system is very clear and distinct,"* one said. *"You know going in that if you meet the standard required, you will be kept on. It's as simple as that."* Another said: *"It never comes down to a choice between pupils. We always have the*

work and capacity to take on new tenants, they just have to meet our standards."

Hours, you'll be happy to hear, *"are better then expected,"* pupils and juniors agreed. Typical days range from 8:30am to 6pm during pupillage, with no weekend work. Naturally this increases dramatically during the assessment process. *"In that period you work round the clock, but that gives you a good sense of what junior practice is like."*

The third degree

Applications are made through the Pupillage Gateway, and the subsequent interview process consists of a single round split into three stages. In the first part, candidates have the opportunity to ask questions about pupillage and the set. The second part consists of a legal question designed to be accessible to both law and non-law graduates. Interviewees are given 20 minutes prior to the entire interview to prepare. Fiona Parkin tells us: *"The question allows us to see how candidates structure their response to an issue, but also how they respond to persistent questioning from several barristers. Can they think on their feet, or do they dry up?"* The final part is a discussion of a topical ethical issue like organ donation or prenuptial agreements. 2013's question was about whether or not security forces based overseas should be subject to judicial oversight. *"Again, this tests a candidate's ability to structure an argument, and is normally the most important part of the interview for those who haven't done a law degree,"* says Fiona Parkin. *"The interview as a whole isn't designed to find out how many cases you know or whether you've read the most recent Lawtel decisions. Instead we're looking for an ability to approach problems logically and apply that logic to areas not encountered before."*

Applicants are required to have at least a 2:1, although one member admits that *"realistically, with the quality of applications we get most pupils now have a First. However, if you have a 2:1 and are able to speak passionately about matters at hand during your interview, that will put you in a strong position to compete with candidates with Firsts."* We spoke to some juniors with 2:1s, albeit ones with Masters degrees, additional Firsts and 'Outstandings' in their BPTC in the bag too.

And finally...

Atkin's tough pupillage assessments mean it is not for the fainthearted, but its stellar reputation makes it a great prospect for those with the right skills and interests.

2 Bedford Row

The facts

Location: Bedford Row, London
Number of QCs/Juniors: 16/56 (19 women)
Applications: 457
Apply through Pupillage Gateway
Pupils per year: Up to 4
Seats: 3x6 months
Pupillage award: £12,000 grant + £10,000 guaranteed earnings

"We get more exposure to trials in the Mags' than anyone else I've heard of."

The crime-heavy pupillage here is *"an amazing thing to be part of,"* providing you are prepared to be on your feet...

Murder and lies

"You often see our QCs on the front of the Metro," one source told us in our visit to chambers this year. The many headline-hitting cases that go through 2 Bedford Row hint at why it has won top-tier rankings for both crime and criminal fraud in *Chambers UK*. The set is home to the mighty William Clegg QC, who made the news this year defending Sergeant Danny Nightingale. The set's line-up of raw talent – and youthful QCs – is a key driver in its success. Outside of the crime and fraud world, 2BR has made a very big footprint thanks to some first-class names: Jim Sturman QC for sports, Ian Stern QC for professional discipline, and Richard Matthews QC for health and safety, to name a few.

In recent years, this defence-focused set has added practices in finance and regulatory work. As such, it has broadened its client base, which now encompasses major City firms and institutions, local councils, high street solicitors, offshore clients, Premier League football teams and public and international bodies. 2BR's latest assignments have seen it working with the European Court of Human Rights, acting for the General Medical Council, and taking cases before the Court of Arbitration for Sport.

Gone in 70 seconds

2 Bedford Row does everything with a no-nonsense attitude, and that includes the hiring process. If all the stuffy tradition and old boys' club stereotypes about the Bar put you off applying, then 2 Bedford Row may be your answer. Head of pupillage Stephen Vullo echoed this: *"I honestly don't know what uni the current pupils went to. They have to be bright, of course, but what we are really*

looking for is someone who is a good advocate on their feet." All interviewees stressed this point, so take note. Two-Bedfordronians spend much more time in court than most, so the interview is built around judging advocacy potential.

Of the 457 applicants, the set aims to interview between 70 and 80. The first interview goes like this: the panel gives the applicant a topic to argue, with very brief preparation time. *"We tell candidates to talk for no more than 70 seconds,"* says Vullo. *"We are looking for brevity: half of them talk far too long and that weeds out a lot."* Don't be surprised if the panel gives you a different topic to argue seconds before the interview. *"That throws them a bit, the point being that they read, understand and react quickly."* That said, our interviewees did claim that the interview process is *"more straightforward than most places I applied to. There was no 'bad cop' on the panel."* In 2012, the set put 22 interviewees through to the second round, and four are usually awarded pupillage. The second round lasts a little longer and applicants are sent the exercise in advance. *"This year we are sending them a sentencing guidelines exercise and they will be expected to give five to ten minutes on their feet. They will respond to our questions on it."*

"If you can't stand up and talk, don't apply," said one interviewee. Vullo elaborated: *"If we feel nervous for the person, they are not right for us. We look for poise and confidence. And we don't cross them off for getting minor legal points wrong."* A pupil also offered: *"Be as succinct as possible. They are looking for spontaneity."* Pupils also strongly recommended equipping yourself with prior experience, which will go some way to boosting your confidence in this advocacy-focused process.

Chambers UK rankings

Crime	Professional Discipline
Fraud	Sports Law
Health & Safety	

Sin City

In one of 2BR's swanky conference rooms, the pupils opened up to us about their lot. During the first six, senior clerk John Grimmer *"has us in court every day from the get-go."* During this time, pupils work for two supervisors simultaneously, but aren't allowed to represent clients themselves. *"During the second six you'll be in court from day one,"* though. *"Most of my work has been in the Mags' Courts defending cases like theft, assault and harassment,"* remarked one interviewee. The cases tend to be on the lighter end of the criminal scale during pupillage, but one interviewee was starting to get involved in *"cases like violent crime, rape, murder,"* while another mentioned weighty cases like *"child grooming, kidnap and fraud."*

"This isn't a glamorous job," thought one pupil, and speaking to those who had done pupillage here it becomes clear a hardy constitution is a must. Pupils agreed that they often worked *"four out of five evenings a week, sometimes until midnight if you include travel."* One confided: *"When people ask me out for a beer I tell them this is like having two jobs."* The up-side, claimed one source, is that *"we get more exposure to trials in the Mags' than anyone else I've heard of."* In a similar vein, 2BR also starts its pupillage in the spring, with the aim that *"by the end of the year pupils are streets ahead of the competition."*

This lifestyle evidently suits a certain type of person, and pupils recommended *"doing a mini-pupillage – it's the best way to work out if it's for you."* All agreed that the lifestyle was a price worth paying: *"The pupillage here is an amazing thing to be part of."* Vullo tells us: *"We are conscious not to crush people in pupillage. We always think pupils are worth investing in. Members here are expected to give up time to pupils."* And they really do invest the time; a snapshot of this might include *"Bill Clegg QC giving talks on tactics, Jim Sturman QC on closing speeches and Mark Milliken-Smith QC on cross-examination."* One junior enthused: *"This place is a breeding ground for success. You learn from class acts."*

Call of Duty: Blackfriars Ops

"Pupillage feels like a year-long interview," admitted a source. Pupils are judged on their performance throughout the year. *"You've got to do well on your feet,"* said one, but added, *"they put more emphasis on the second six."* The year culminates in a mock trial in Blackfriars Crown Court, which 2BR hires out for the purpose. A panel of silks and other members is there to judge the Blackfriars gig, and they give their verdict on tenancy towards the end of September, drawing upon performance throughout the year, too. Aside from the obvious advocacy points, the panel also looks for *"decent written work and recommendations from solicitors."*

So what's the magic formula to gaining tenancy? Awkwardly, the message seems to be: *"Keep a low profile, but impress everyone."* A junior added: *"It's not a popularity contest but you've got to fit with chambers: be respectful, work hard."* John Grimmer shed more light: *"We need to see clearly that in five years' time they will have a practice of their own."*

As we were shown through the doors of the grand Bloomsbury townhouse at no. 2 Bedford Row, it struck us that fitting in here isn't in fact the greatest challenge. Guided though a dark maze of corridors and a cavernous basement, we saw a set comfortable with its own disarray. Down there amid the piles of files we were greeted by a welcoming bunch ready to make friendly chat. Pupils confirmed this: *"The atmosphere is open, collegial and quite different to many sets."* Pupils are *"always included in things,"* and this set has no truck with ceremony or needless hierarchy; all interviewees threw around the phrase *"down to earth"* with abandon. The set puts on the usual welcome drinks, Christmas knees-ups and summer parties. Otherwise the hub of chambers' social life is at The Old Nick just round the corner. Friday drinks here are pretty common, unless you're one of the pupils, it seems, who *"genuinely don't have the time for much socialising."* Stephen Vullo adds: *"Part of the test for pupils is striking the right balance with socialising."* Chambers is also rumoured to take part in white-collar boxing – find out more if you get here...

The recruitment team wanted to stress to ethnic minority applicants that although its current line-up is hardly a beacon of diversity, it is striving to address this with future hiring. This doesn't mean the set is making exceptions. *"It's a level playing field once you're in the interview,"* said a pupil. In 2013, two out of four pupils were offered tenancy.

And finally...

There is no secret to the rewards of a 2BR pupillage *"just make sure you're committed to the Criminal Bar and prepared to be in court."*

The Bar

Blackstone Chambers

The facts

Location: Temple, London
Number of QCs/juniors: 38/54 (23 women)
Applications: 400+
Apply through Pupillage Gateway
Pupils per year: 4 – 5
Seats: 4x3 months
Pupillage Award: £60,000 (can advance £17,000 for BPTC)

On chambersstudent.co.uk...

Details of Blackstone's application process
An interview with star of the Bar, Dinah Rose QC

This leading set marries a standard of excellence with a laid-back environment. It's none too shabby on the social front, either...

Smooth operator

Blackstone runs a slick operation. From its swish reception and glorious roof terrace to its swanky meeting rooms and frankly delightful biscuit selection, this set scores big points in the aesthetics department. Its practice is nothing to whine about, either: home to public law superstars like Dinah Rose QC, chambers boasts a sky-high reputation in the field and is up there with the best in many others. Along with its administrative and public law and its civil liberties and human rights practices, Blackstone scores top-tier *Chambers UK* rankings for its employment, financial services, fraud, sport, telecoms and media and entertainment work. A number of other areas – among them competition, environment and immigration – follow closely behind in the charts.

According to deputy chambers director Mat Swallow, commercial, public and employment law "*are at the heart of Blackstone, but so much of chambers' expertise falls under the broader regulatory banner, across the full spectrum of our practice areas including, for example, competition, financial services, energy and sport. We act for many of the regulators and our junior tenants regularly go on secondment to Ofgem, Ofcom and the FCA (formerly FSA), among others.*" While general commercial instructions technically account for the biggest spread of work – clocking in somewhere around 45% – it's Blackstone's public law undertakings that dominate the headlines. The BBC recently appointed Rose to spearhead its sexual harassment investigation following the Jimmy Savile scandal, while James Eadie QC acted for the government during the Leveson Inquiry and recently represented the Secretary of State for Health in the Francis Inquiry, the infamous probe into the disconcertingly high mortality rates at Stafford Hospital. Given Blackstone's commercial origins, it comes as little surprise that many of its public law cases bear a commercial tinge. "*A good example is the litigation surrounding tobacco advertising and calls for plain packaging legislation,*" Swallow says. "*In that kind of matter – which raises a blend of EU, competition, public law and human rights issues – we're likely to work with City firms or directly with the tobacco companies themselves.*"

Of course, pure commercial work definitely makes its mark at Blackstone. Sports-related cases – for example, Pakistani cricketer Danish Kaneria's much publicised appeal against his lifetime ban for corruption – have gained the set a good deal of attention in recent years, as have crossover matters like Client Earth's Supreme Court appeal to reduce nitrogen dioxide levels, which combines elements of environmental, public, commercial and EU law. At the time of our visit, lawyers were grappling with the kick-off of the Madoff trial, "*one of the highest-profile pieces of commercial litigation to come to trial this year,*" according to Swallow. Pushpinder Saini QC is leading the way on multiple bankruptcy and insolvency disputes that have arisen out of the notorious Ponzi scheme. "*We're really driving our commercial work and are striving for more recognition on both the international and arbitration front,*" Swallow says, mentioning Blackstone's participation in one of India's biggest domestic arbitrations to date, a claim regarding cyclone damage to an oil refinery.

Learning from the best

Pupils rotate through four supervisors throughout their year, working exclusively for each. "*There's always some-*

Chambers UK rankings

Administrative & Public Law	Fraud
	Immigration
Civil Liberties & Human Rights	Insurance
	Media & Entertainment
Commercial Dispute Resolution	Professional Discipline
	Public International Law
Competition/European Law	Public Procurement
Employment	Sports Law
Environment	Telecommunications
Financial Services	

one who primarily practices commercial, and the same goes for public and employment law – they want to ensure everybody sees our three main areas." Members of the current cohort praised this set-up for "*allowing you to see how four different people operate*" and "*offering the chance to impress a good number of people by the end of pupillage.*" Under this system, our sources had encountered everything from telecoms and media cases to sports, fraud, regulatory and competition matters. "*I wouldn't recommend coming here if you're set on a particular type of law because the point is to expose you to a breadth of practice areas,*" advised one. That said, there was a warning to prospective applicants, particularly those keen on public law, that "*the bulk of your work as a pupil will quite likely fall under the general commercial and employment umbrellas. I've found pupillage to be less public law-oriented than Blackstone's reputation suggests.*"

Pupils undertake six written assessments and a handful of advocacy exercises throughout their year. The former entails "*picking up a live piece of work, such as a legal note or opinion, at 8am on Monday and returning them by 6pm on Tuesday. These are marked and then a while later you sit down with somebody and get quizzed about what you wrote.*" Only two of the seven or so advocacy assignments are assessed, with each videotaped. "*It's the worst watching them back! You notice how rumpled your tie was or how much hair you had in your face. But the upside is that you end up righting a lot of wrongs. Also, knowing everyone is doing the same exercise keeps the assessment process fair and measured.*" Additional feedback comes in the form of a sit-down between pupils and supervisors at the end of each seat.

Tenancy decisions are made in early July, and everyone in chambers gets a vote. "*At the meeting, the pupil super-*

visors are very influential of course, but everyone contributes to the decision,*" Mulcahy assures us. "*We chat about our experiences with each pupil and where their strengths lie, and if they're good enough we'll take them all.*" Our sources credited this attitude with eliminating a sense of competition among the intake. "*Knowing they have enough accommodation for everyone makes it possible to be friends and support each other.*" In 2013 four of five stayed on as tenants.

Welcome to the family

It was clear right off the bat during our visit that Blackstone doesn't have a particularly formal environment. For starters, we encountered more than one tenant dressed "*like a student*" (their words), and one source actually guffawed when we asked about afternoon tea. "*I think because we've got so many fantastic people, nobody's pretending to try to be better or more professional by obsessing over sharp suits and outdated traditions,*" thought a junior. Indeed, a "*relaxed and co-operative*" vibe prevails, and several likened the set to "*a family*" in that "*people genuinely seem to like each other and many are deeply involved with one another's personal lives – they go on holiday together and socialise regularly outside of work.*" As Mulcahy added: "*All of my daughters' godparents work in this building!*" A big factor is this genial atmosphere is an egalitarian attitude "*wielded from the top down – there's a big focus on fairness and equality, and everyone's opinion is valued. People naturally respect the work of their senior colleagues, but no one is asked to bow down to anyone else.*" As such, even the relationship between barristers and clerks is "*relatively flat – we go out together for drinks all the time; they're not hidden away like you see at some sets.*"

Pupils told of a "*civilised*" work/life balance in which they're "*rarely*" beholden to hours beyond the core 8.30am to 6.30pm. "*Supervisors do their best to make sure no one's overworked or too stressed out.*" For junior members, this leaves plenty of time for socialising, which often takes place at the nearby Edgar Wallace or in the form of occasional dinners out. Chambers' roof terrace gets a good workout come summer, when there are Friday drinks outside, and various marketing events – such as football games and ping pong competitions with City firms – keep tenants busy during the rest of the year. There's a family-friendly Christmas do – last year's was James Bond-themed – plus a cracking summer shindig, which we can confirm is just peachy, having attended ourselves.

And finally...

We've no space here to talk about the application process, but our website provides plenty of detail on how to get into Blackstone.

The Bar

1 Chancery Lane

The facts

Location: Chancery Lane, London
Number of QCs/juniors: 5/39 (10 women)
Applications: 200-250
Outside Pupillage Gateway
Pupils per year: 2 every other year
Seats: 3x4 months
Pupillage award: £40,000 (will consider advancing some for BPTC)

This successful set mixes tradition with a progressive outlook.

Personal injury work forms the backbone of this civil set, although pupils will *"turn their hand"* to a comprehensive range of matters.

Bustin' out of Templetown

Nestled between a legal bookshop and a dry cleaners, this set is in a convenient spot for the well-turned-out and well-versed barrister. The building is a contemporary granite-clad affair, but the set hasn't always been located in such modern premises. *"Chambers was formed in the 1950s,"* explains Clark Chessis, 1 Chancery Lane's aptly-named senior clerk. *"Back then we were a traditional broad set in the Temple doing crime, family, civil and property work. In 1991 we moved out of Temple – a statement of intent that we wanted to become more specialised. By the mid-1990s we were almost exclusively a civil set specialising in personal injury, professional negligence and local authority work. Over the past ten years that has evolved to include property. In 2006 we moved here."* Nowadays the set has 44 members, and is content with its moderate size. *"We're not looking to become a 70 or 80-strong set,"* says Chessis, *"we like to grow from the bottom. up"*

The set takes on a mix of claimant and defendant work, and receives a lot of instructions from major insurance-focused law firms. Personal injury forms the biggest chunk of chambers' undertakings – around 50% – followed by clinical negligence, travel and property. The set is also ranked by *Chambers UK* for police law and professional negligence. On the PI side, recent cases have included that of a former police officer suffering from post-traumatic stress who claimed that his suicide attempt and detention under the Mental Health Act resulted from a negligent decision to return him to work without proper supervision. Lord Faulks QC (brother of novelist Sebastian) successfully acted for the defendant, the Chief Constable of Sussex Police. Another silk, Andrew Warnock, is acting for the BBC in the civil claim brought by Jimmy Savile's sex abuse victims. Travel work includes a lot of overseas accident litigation on behalf of both claimants and defendants and their insurers. One member recently defended Virgin Holidays in a case involving a holidaymaker claimant who collided with a glass door which then shattered and caused significant injuries.

Existential questions

1 Chancery Lane eschews the Pupillage Gateway in favour of its own tailor-made application form. *"It allows us to ask the questions that are most relevant to us,"* says Andrew Warnock, head of the admissions committee. *"This way we know people really want to apply."* Recent recruits remember tackling some fairly unconventional questions on the form. *"It said, 'What are you doing right now?' I wasn't quite sure how to answer it. I think I made a joke out of it,"* laughed one baby junior. Chambers receives around 200 to 250 applications, which are sifted down to 50 and then again down to 20. These applicants are invited in for an interview, during which they face a panel of barristers and are asked to demonstrate their reasoning skills by talking the panel through a legal problem.

1 Chancery Lane offers two pupillages every other year. (There were no pupils with the set in 2012/13.) *"Recruitment is focused not so much on what you know but how you think,"* reported one newly-minted tenant. What else does the set look for? *"We want people who want to work hard,"* Andrew Warnock informs us. *"This isn't a nine-to-five job. I'm often getting up at the crack of dawn. There's also a lot of oral advocacy, so it's important that a pupil is articulate. As well as this, we look for those who can work in a team and get on with people. You need to be person-*

Chambers UK rankings

Clinical Negligence	Professional Negligence
Personal Injury	Travel
Police Law	

able." The baby juniors we spoke to also emphasised that a willingness to get stuck into a wide range of work is paramount. *"It's all civil common law but there's a great breadth – that means you need to be able to take risks and just give it a go. Some people would hate that – they'd rather be a specialist and get very good at one thing."* Another interviewee pointed out that *"as we are all active litigators, you need to hit the ground running and have a certain amount of confidence in the first place. We tend to take on people who are capable of taking on that hostile challenge."* So: tireless energy, a talent for advocacy, an easy social manner, all-embracing legal antennae and a certain chutzpah... combine these ingredients and you might just create a 1 Chancery Lane pupil. What about background? Well, being an Oxbridge don doesn't seem to be a prerequisite here. We spoke to members who'd attended state school and graduated from a range of universities including Durham, Bristol and UCL.

I will survive!

Pupillage comprises three seats of four months each; all three supervisors have a different specialism. A typical pupillage might be spent with *"a first supervisor whose focus is clinical negligence, police law, human rights and inquests, then a second who does property and a third who does personal injury."* At the start *"you're pretty much doing the same work as your supervisor. They give your paperwork that they're doing, let you have a crack at it and then compare it to how they did it. As you move on, from about the middle of your second seat, you're up on your feet, so the work from your supervisor decreases."* If errors are made, so be it. *"You realise that mistakes are part and parcel of pupillage,"* recalled one junior. *"I spent my first day fretting about whether I'd broken my pupilmaster's ring binder."* In their second six, pupils find they're in court two to three times a week on their own cases. *"We don't like it to be more than that because they're still being trained,"* says Andrew Warnock. Baby juniors concurred that *"they keep it a happy medium between being in court and doing your supervisor's work."*

Four months in, pupils will start tackling pieces of assessed written work. *"These could be particulars of claims or written advice."* They'll complete six in total – one for each member of the admissions committee. Each supervisor also produces a written appraisal for perusal by the admissions committee. Then the tenancy decision is made. *"Our hope and aim is to take pupils on,"* asserts Warnock.

1 Chancery Lane retains elements of tradition within its modern premises. Clark Chessis had this to say: *"We're old-fashioned. We don't have regular management meetings, but for the most part we have a relaxed style of management. I discuss issues with the head of chambers."* Former pupils agreed that *"in some respects we're formal – we have a dress code."* However, *"there's not much of a hierarchy – I can walk into virtually any member of chambers' room and ask a question."* Andrew Warnock added that *"we're a friendly set and perceived as such by the outside world."* For the most part, clerks and members are on first-name terms, although Chessis laughs: *"I'm a bit of a dinosaur: I quite like the 'mister' and 'miss' business."* He also says that the clerks' relationship with pupils *"is a good one – we're sympathetic, we know it's a difficult time for them. We will never add to their problems."* Happily, juniors agreed: *"The clerks here aren't pushy."*

A *"relatively low-key"* afternoon tea is held daily in the library. *"Everyone just grabs a mug, grabs a biscuit and chats about whatever. As a pupil, you're encouraged to go along to get to know people informally."* On the social side, there's a family-orientated Christmas party in which Clark Chessis plays a significant role: *"I dress up as Father Christmas every year. And I go to Toys R Us with my wife beforehand to buy presents."* There's also a junior practitioners group that organises social excursions. *"We've done urban golf and gone bowling together,"* reported one interviewee. Of course, different gatherings will occur over the year: *"There was a karaoke party a while ago at Lord Faulks' house in Notting Hill. You wouldn't have thought members of chambers would be into karaoke, but they really were!"* Well, it's nice to know that even lordly silks like to crank up the Gloria Gaynor every once in a while.

And finally...

Pupils were realistic about the feel of chambers given their position: *"You can't get away from the fact that it's the people who you are working with who will eventually decide whether to take you on. But people are as friendly as can be given the circumstances."*

The Bar

Cloisters

The facts

Location: Temple, London
Number of QCs/juniors: 9/43 (24 women)
Applications: 350-450
Apply through Pupillage Gateway
Pupils per year: 2
Seats: 3x4 months
Pupillage award: £40,000 (can advance £6,000 for BPTC)

"Everyone here believes strongly in equality and social justice and we are generally pro-union as well"

Splitting its work between employment, clinical negligence and personal injury, Cloisters is a leader in all these areas.

Big guys, little guys, good guys, bad guys

"Helping the little guy," is how one member summed up the ethos and outlook of this set. Its clin neg and PI practice is entirely claimant-side, and while employment is split between claimant and respondent work *"there is a slant towards discrimination and human rights focused cases."* In all, 60% of the set's practice is devoted to employment, 20% to PI and 20% to clin neg.

Cloisters works on some big, interesting cases defending the underprivileged. Back in 2010 two members represented the Nepalese Gurkhas in their Court of Appeal pensions battle with the MoD. Another member recently won £40,000 in compensation for a Co-op cashier after she was verbally harassed by her manager, while another defended former Travers Smith trainee Katie Tantum in her case claiming she was not offered an NQ job because she was pregnant.

Meanwhile, head of chambers Robin Allen QC (who was *Chambers UK*'s 2012 employment silk of the year) worked on *O'Brien v Ministry of Justice* establishing the right of part-time judges to receive a public pension. There are respondent cases too, which see barristers *"acting for the big guy."* One member recently represented Peter Stringfellow in the Employment Appeal Tribunal case over whether stripper Nadine Quashie was self-employed or not.

Being respondent counsel *"doesn't always mean acting for the bad guy"* and Cloisters is a set with a clear moral compass. *"Everyone here believes strongly in equality and social justice and we are generally pro-union as*

well," one member told us. The set has a *"lefty"* feel but it's *"not rammed down your throat"* and members are *"not uniformly of the same party-political persuasion."*

The bare bones

All pupillage applications are marked out of 20 by two members of chambers. Ten of those points are for academic achievement, while the other ten are for advocacy (worth 3), communication skills (2), initiative and independence (2), commitment to the law (2) and suitability to Cloisters' areas of work (1). This gives each applicant a score out of 40 – in recent years a tally of 34 has been needed to get through to the first interview round. That first interview – to which around 80 are invited – consists of a non-legal problem question designed to assess presentation skills, analytical ability, common sense and time management. In 2012 the hypothetical question was about what action a head girl should take after discovering her school's model Santa Claus had had all of its clothes removed by a prankster.

Fifteen to 20 individuals make it through to a second interview – *"a fiendishly difficult legal problem"* based around a PI, clin neg or employment case. Applicants have one or two weeks to prepare and tons of legal research is required. *"The interview moves very quickly and you have to give every answer your best shot,"* a pupil recalled. At the end of the interview, applications are asked to argue for or against a political or moral question. In 2012, the question was 'Are lawful tax avoidance schemes morally wrong?'

Should aspiring pupils share the set's moral ethos? Pupillage committee head Lisa Sullivan told us that there are

The Bar

Chambers UK rankings

Clinical Negligence	Personal Injury
Employment	

no specific marks for this in the recruitment process, but: *"Activities undertaken by people who share our ethos are likely to be one way of evidencing the competencies we do look for."* Sullivan also encourages applicants to ask themselves whether they *"really want pupillage or tenancy in a set where they don't share, at least to some extent, the ethos of that chambers."*

A summer in the heat

Pupils spend four three-month periods with four different supervisions, two practising in PI/clin neg and two in employment. During their first six, pupils shadow their supervisors, frequently attending court and taking on tasks like legal research for closing submission and first drafts of advices. *"There is also the opportunity to work for other members, although you are not required to do work for anyone in particular,"* a pupil said. *"They ease you in quite nicely,"* a baby junior recalled. *"I had little experience of employment law and I was given the time I needed to understand everything."* Also *"if you are here beyond 6.30 or 7pm people will usually pop in to ask what you are still doing at your desk. They'll tell you to save your energy for the second six!"*

And energy is what's required for the second half of pupillage. As well as continuing to shadow their supervisors pupils take on their own caseload, which eventually ramps up to court appearances several times a week. *"My first assignment was a two-day unfair dismissal case,"* a baby junior recalled, *"and by the end of my second six I was running a five-day discrimination trial."* Employment work gets pupils on their feet a lot and they'll also be running case management discussions and telephone hearings. A lot is expected of pupils here and we weren't surprised to hear one of our interviewees *"had gained some FRU advocacy experience before joining chambers."* Oral talents are highly valued for employment barristers, while drafting is the main skill for PI and clin neg specialists.

During the summer, from May onwards, pupils undergo four rigorous assessments. These constitute 90% of the basis of the tenancy decision (10% is based on supervisor feedback). The first assessment is a drafting exercise (worth 20%), the second is advocacy (also worth 20%), and the third is a piece of legal research (again worth 20%), usually a lengthy note of advice. Finally, a weight of 30% is given to an interview based around a legal problem question. Each exercise is assessed by different members of chambers, and a score of over 70% is required to be considered for tenancy, while a pupil getting 80% or above is unlikely to be turned away. It may seem harsh to judge someone based primarily on four exercises rather than their day-to-day work, but the pupil we spoke to saw the system's merits: *"It is fair and transparent and avoids the tendency for a set to pick members based on a personality match."* Pupils receive a lot of support in preparing for the exercises as well as time off to research and draft the written assessments. In 2013, one of the two pupils took up tenancy with the set.

Doing good

We mustn't forget to mention that pro bono is a big thing at Cloisters. Its tenants are expected to do at least five days of unpaid work a year, *"but people do it because they want to and because it is interesting work,"* a baby junior said. Members can get involved with projects through FRU, the Bar Human Rights Committee, the Bar Pro Bono Unit and charities like Reprieve.

Sniffing the air at Cloisters, we found there was more than a whiff of egalitarianism about the place. *"It's not stuffy,"* a baby barrister said. *"All my friends are always disappointed that I can't dish the dirt on any Silk-style intrigues!"* That same baby barrister shared an office with a QC and a mid-ranking junior. We also noted that all members are listed on the website in alphabetical order rather than by seniority, and Cloisters is home to a higher proportion of female barristers than any other set in this year's *Student Guide*.

Furthermore, *"when you are new, people make an effort to talk to you at chambers drinks,"* the current pupil told us. Speaking of drinks, apparently *"some of the set's previous big drinkers have now had kids,"* so inebriation is not an obligatory part of life at Cloisters and *"there is no culture of presenteeism for pupils at social events."* But sometimes *"drinks are held for no particular reason"* and there's a *"fun Christmas party."*

And finally...
Shared interests among its members help make this set a strong one. *"Come to Cloisters "it's great,"* a junior said when we concluded our interview with them, giving the set a literal thumbs up.

"It's good to be the type of person who can stand up for themselves, but that's not about brash self-confidence. That won't get you anywhere. It's about being calm and clear."

Pupil barrister

Crown Office Chambers

The facts

Location: Inner Temple, London
Number of QCs/juniors: 13/77 (20 women)
Applications: 150-200
Outside Pupillage Gateway
Pupils per year: 2-3
Seats: 2x3 and 1x6 months
Pupillage award: £50,000 + £10,000 guaranteed earnings (can advance £15,000 for BPTC)

COC puts its pupils through an intense regime of assessments before they are considered for tenancy.

Pupils at the Bar's biggest common law set need to be the cat's pyjamas when it comes to advocacy – court appearances are customary in the second six.

It's health and safety gone mad

Overlooking the floral splendour of Inner Temple Gardens, Crown Office Chambers is *"going from strength to strength,"* according to senior managing clerk Andy Flanagan. COC was formed in 2000 by the merger of Two Crown Office Row and One Paper Buildings, *"both of which had quite a broad practice."* The result is the Bar's biggest common law set, a mighty prospect with 90 members.

The main areas of work are personal injury, health and safety, insurance, professional negligence, construction, product liability and clinical negligence. *"In 2011 we restructured our clerking team into groups that look after different practice areas,"* Andy Flanagan told us. *"This means we can align ourselves with our clients and it allows clerks to talk the talk as well as walk the walk."* Around 75% of instructions are on the defendant side. *"Another recent development has been that there is more commercial construction work coming into chambers,"* says Andy Flanagan.

The set is top ranked by *Chambers UK* for personal injury, health & safety and property damage work. Members are frequently involved in cases like *R v Lion Steel Equipment*, defending a director charged with gross negligence manslaughter after a factory worker fell to his death. And one senior junior recently represented Siemens after an employee at Harwich International Port was killed by a falling wind turbine blade during an attempt to move it from quayside to vessel. On the insurance side, members were involved in *AXN v Worboys*, which asked whether insurers were liable for damages because the crimes of 'black cab rapist' John Worboys were committed in his insured taxi. *"The lion's share of work comes from insurers' subrogation claims but that doesn't mean you're not representing a range of people or working on a variety of issues,"* explained a pupil. *"You could have to deal with a road traffic accident one day and property damage from a tree root the next. You can get insurance for just about everything – and if it's insurable you can argue about it in court!"*

Smooth talking

COC recruits two to three pupils every year. It operates outside the Pupillage Gateway and has its own online application form. *"The questions are pretty standard,"* recalled a current pupil. *"They ask about public speaking and work experience. You have to convey yourself in a succinct and clear way."* Stellar advocacy ability is crucial. *"We focus very much on advocacy during pupillage,"* says Patrick Blakesley, chair of the pupillage committee. *"Our pupils go to court a good deal in the second six, so they really do have to be fairly polished and mature performers from an early stage."* Another interviewee adds: *"The way we judge that from someone's CV is by looking for FRU or pro bono work, mooting, debating, or anything that's either client-facing or involves presenting something to a tribunal or judge of some description."*

The initial applications are filtered down to a first interview list of around forty. *"During my first interview, I was asked to explain a parliamentary system to a five-year-old,"* one pupil told us. *"It caught me off guard at first, but it's actually a good interview question because it allows*

The Bar

655

Chambers UK rankings

Clinical Negligence	International Arbitration
Construction	Personal Injury
Health & Safety	Product Liability
Insurance	Professional Negligence

you to demonstrate the skills needed to be a barrister, even if you haven't done a law degree." Approximately 12 to 14 candidates make it through to a second round of interviews, overseen by a panel of five barristers. Interviewees are given half an hour to prepare their views on a problem question such as an insurance issue.

On your toes

Pupils spend time with three supervisors. The first two seats last three months and the remaining six months are overseen by a final supervisor. *"You don't spend an even span of time with each supervisor because by the second six you're meant to be more independent and starting to become a self-employed practitioner,"* explained a pupil. There's an initial grace period of two months in which pupils aren't assessed. *"They appreciate that it's a baptism of fire and that you'll make mistakes. That's how you learn."*

Fledgling pupils often take on work that their supervisor has just completed. *"You have the opportunity to give it a try and then you'll get feedback straight afterwards – supervisors compare your work with theirs and tell you how to improve next time. It's very natural and not high-pressured. You don't get marks – they'll just sit with you and go through it."* Supervisors often have a roommate who'll also give work to a pupil, becoming *"like a quasi-supervisor."* The set makes sure that pupils see a broad spread of work. *"My first supervisor's practice was PI-orientated but his roommate was a construction specialist so I got a range of work from both,"* reported one interviewee.

From the start of the second six, pupils are on their feet in small claims trials and the like. *"Going to court so often absolutely distinguishes pupillage here,"* said one pupil. *"You have the opportunity to be in court all the time and so hopefully you'll be a confident advocate by the time you start tenancy. I've been up against people who are two or three years' call and they have been very complimentary of the pupils here, purely because we get*

so much experience in the second six." Natural talent for advocacy doesn't stop the first trial from being *"petrifying – I prepared the case within an inch of its life and then my appearance lasted all of two minutes. I thought, 'I've prepared for four days! What's wrong with you?! Let me show you my submissions!' Often as a pupil you'll be a lot younger than your lay client and the witnesses. You have to convince them that you're competent. It's nerve-racking because you want to do the job well."* In the second six especially, pupils are also encouraged to do written work for as many members as possible.

Shaken or stirred?

Starting two months in, pupils complete oral and written assessments which will inform the tenancy decision. First up are the advocacy assessments, in which pupils *"do things like applications before a panel. Afterwards they give you feedback on everything: whether you gesticulate too much, on the law – the whole nine yards."* Over time, these tests *"get more serious and harder. I had one before a High Court judge."* However, pupils remain sanguine about the process: *"It's a bit daunting but excellent practice for court."* As well as this, there are two to three written assessments which are blind marked. Pupils undertake these alongside their 'normal' duties. When it comes to the tenancy crunch, the pupillage committee *"only involves people in the decision-making process if they've had direct experience of pupils."* In 2013 neither pupils was kept on as a tenant, although the firm did recruit two third sixers.

Stepping into COC, we were impressed by the welcoming ambience, tasteful lithographs, soft coral carpet and suede tissue boxes (although we were disappointed not to spot Hunter the Inner Temple Garden cat on patrol outside). What do members and pupils have to say about the atmosphere? *"It's not particularly old-fashioned and definitely not stuffy,"* reported one. Instead of afternoon tea there are Friday drinks, which is *"basically a chambers cocktail night."* Pupils attested to the idea of COC's supportive atmosphere. *"The Bar can be off-putting for someone who is from a non-traditional background and is an ethnic minority like me,"* one pupil told us. *"I'd done mini-pupillages at more traditional sets where I perceived that it would be challenging to undertake pupillage. But here it's very friendly and open, and that's very important to me."*

And finally...

As well as good academics and talent as an advocate, this set is *"looking for people with extremely good interpersonal skills who will inspire confidence in their clients."*

The Bar

One Essex Court

The facts

Location: Middle Temple, London
Number of QCs/juniors: 30/55 (17 women)
Applications: c.200
Apply through Pupillage Gateway
Pupils per year: 5
Seats: 2x3 + 1x6 months
Pupillage award: £60,000 (can advance £20,000 for BPTC)

This top commercial set now offers a specialist IP pupillage too.

Top-of-the-tree commercial set One Essex Court is praised for its *"very good pupil supervision."* Only the very best get a chance to sample its qualities.

In black and white

Founded in 1966, One Essex Court has spent the past half-century building up an extraordinarily strong reputation for high-end commercial work. One of the Bar's magic circle sets, it has grown membership by 25% in the past five years alone. The set's advocates remain a very popular choice for banks, businesses and investors of all kinds when resolving disputes.

Browse OEC's website and it's soon clear what its main areas of practice are. Low-angle shots of Canary Wharf, a share index and a wind farm loom large. Banking and finance, arbitration, civil fraud and energy are all key breadwinners, while the set also has a stash of specialists dealing with tax, competition, IP and insolvency disputes. Barristers often work with top City firms and *"direct instruction by in-house teams is increasingly prevalent,"* according to senior clerk Darren Burrows. *"In addition, the emergence of boutique litigation firms and international arbitration practices has provided a variety of new opportunities."*

Burrows also told us that 2012 was a record year for the set in revenue terms: *"We saw sustained periods of full engagement for all our members."* Or, as one member put it, *"everyone's been really busy making pots of money!"* The set's reputation and breadth of practice no doubt help a lot here. *"When your core practice is commercial disputes, you benefit from the broad umbrella of areas you can cover,"* says Burrows. OEC is also capitalising on London's increasing importance as an international disputes hub. To boost its international credentials, the set opened a representative office in Singapore in 2012. *"We*

do a huge amount of international work," one member observed.

One international dispute saw the set combine its expertise in energy and tax law: members acted for a subsidiary of Chiswick-based Tullow Oil on a $313m claim against Heritage Oil over unpaid tax liabilities in Uganda. The set has also been active on a large number of energy-related arbitrations. For example, three members acted for a Kuwaiti oil company in arbitration with Dow Chemical over whether Dow was entitled to claim damages after a failed merger between the two.

OEC's members act on a ton of disputes between banks and investors every year. A more unusual example saw Laurence Rabinowitz QC represent the Sisters of Charity of Jesus and Mary and other investors in a commercial case against Morgan Stanley over the loss of a $20m investment in a defunct German bank. Some clients are less saintly: one member is acting for newspaper proprietor Richard Desmond, who is suing Credit Suisse over a complex insurance swap investment contract. Members also frequently advise regulators like the FCA and Ofgem, sometimes going on secondments there too. And head of chambers Lord Grabiner was recently tapped by News Corporation to lead a £53m internal investigation in the wake of the phone-hacking scandal.

Purple prose

After an initial CV sift, 35 to 40 applicants are invited to face a single interview. They are given a set of facts on a case, an analytical question and a copy of Chitty on

The Bar

Chambers UK rankings

Banking & Finance	Energy & Natural
Commercial Dispute	Resources
Resolution	Fraud
Competition/European Law	Intellectual Property
	International Arbitration

Contracts, and get 90 minutes prep time. *"You are then asked to present your answer to the interview panel, who challenge and cross-examine you,"* a pupil told us. The panel also asks some CV-based questions.

By our count, around half of the present juniors under five years' call were Oxbridge undergraduates. To give you a further idea of their backgrounds, around one in three has a BCL, while a similar number studied overseas or worked (briefly) in academia. *"But we're not looking for a brain on a stick,"* a pupil supervisor said. *"We want persuasive advocates who can perform well in court and give focused commercial advice."* Another member added: *"If an applicant has a business background and it's relevant to the type of work we do, that could be advantageous. But if someone's background is not relevant to the job that doesn't count against them."*

Pupils sample all areas of practice during their year with the set. They spend time with three supervisors: two in the first six and one in the second. Each supervisor usually has a broad commercial practice, so pupils see a variety of cases during each seat. At present, pupils also have the option of completing a distinct IP seat. From 2014/15 onwards, OEC is offering a specialist IP pupillage alongside its four regular commercial slots. Applicants are given a different interview question and, although science or industry experience is not required, *"an interest and aptitude for IP"* is a must. It sounds like an interesting gig to us: the set's IP lawyers recently acted for M&S in its dispute with Interflora about Google search terms, and represented Cadbury in a case about the trade marking of its distinctive purple packaging.

Grabiner chance

From their first day, pupils work solely on active cases. *"They expect a lot of you from the start,"* a pupil said, *"but supervisors spend a lot of time getting you up to speed on their cases and they give good feedback."* Typical tasks in the first six include research, attending court and drafting skeleton arguments. From the off, pupils work for other members too. *"I met Lord Grabiner in my first week and was given the opportunity to shadow him in court,"* one pupil beamed. *"It was impressive to see him in action – being able to work with people like that is one of the reasons I came to this set."* Are working hours as long as the set's busy commercial vibe suggests? *"It varies,"* a pupil said. *"You're always going to be working from 9am to 6pm and that lengthens into the evening later in pupillage. And every hour you spend here is going to be quite intense and require a lot of brainpower."*

After six months, pupils are given an official review on their progress. There's no definite indication of whether tenancy is on the cards, but underperforming pupils are given a heads-up. In their second six, pupils get to spend time on their feet, appearing in small claims cases. *"We make a concerted effort to provide a steady stream of advocacy opportunities suitable for pupils and very junior members,"* says senior clerk Darren Burrows. Such cases may come from smaller provincial firms and are often RTAs or debt claims. *"My first case was an application to have a claim form extended,"* a pupil told us. *"It was in the High Court and in front of a judge, which I hadn't expected!"*

There are no advocacy or other exercises during pupillage. The tenancy decision is made by all members of chambers based on the three pupil supervisors' reports and score cards marking each piece of work done by a pupil for another member of chambers. In 2013 the set made tenants out of all three of its pupils.

As OEC is a fairly sizeable set, *"it's not the sort of place where members all rent a chalet and go on a skiing holiday together."* That said, on Fridays members often club together for lunch in halls and there are drinks in chambers at the end of the day. *"I usually go along as it's a good way to meet people,"* a pupil said, and there will often be *"cameo appearances"* from the top silks. A pupil told us that chambers *"isn't formal"* and *"you don't really notice the hierarchy,"* adding that *"at lunch in Halls we'll have social conversations more than we have legal ones."* Members aren't required to buy into any prescriptive culture or traditions. *"I want to feel like I'm a member of a barristers chambers not a rugby club!"* said one.

The Bar

And finally...

"Launching new junior tenants into practice is relatively straightforward when you have a strong position in the market, a high quality product and a reputation for providing a first class service," says OEC's senior clerk Darren Burrows.

Government Legal Service (GLS)

The facts

Location: London

Number of barristers: 400

Applications (solicitor and barrister route): 3,000

Outside Pupillage Gateway

Pupils per year: Varies: around 10-15

Seats: 2x6 or 3x4

Pupillage award: 1st year: £23,900-£25,000; 2nd year: £25,300-£27,000. Plus BPTC fees and a maintenance grant of £5,400-£7,600

With a varied pupillage and the chance to work on *"really big cases,"* the GLS is an impressive alternative to the independent Bar

Should you favour stability over independence, generalism over specialism and the chance to draft legislation over the glamour of advocacy, the GLS's unique pupillage could be for you.

Our country's good

Fancy working on issues as varied as prisoners' rights, the Pensions Bill or the cost of drugs to the NHS? Over 30 government departments – from Her Majesty's Revenue & Customs (HMRC) to the Ministry of Justice (MoJ) employ lawyers. People here tend to be attracted by public service's altruism: *"It all seems a bit more real and everything you work on has a direct effect on someone you know."* Another said: *"I like the political side of the law."* However, an interest in politics isn't a prerequisite, as such (*"though people who apply often are"*): *"It's more about your skills and interests generally."*

At the time of our calls there were six pupil barristers at the GLS: three in the Treasury Solicitor's Department (TSol), one in HMRC, and two in Business, Innovation & Skills (BIS). TSol just got bigger: thanks to the Coalition's cost-saving initiatives, legal teams at various government departments have merged with TSol and now come under its banner, including those at the Department for Work and Pensions (DWP), the Ministry of Justice (MoJ) and the Department for Environment, Food and Rural Affairs (Defra). To the envy of their trainee counterparts, pupils here qualify after one year and spend two years as 'legal officers' before they notch up the pay scale again to become Grade 7 lawyers. *"As far as the Bar is concerned you're qualified after a year – a good way of looking at it is you spend a year learning to be a barrister and a year learning to be a civil servant. The second year is when you really get to grips with how Whitehall works. The first teaches you about the courts, but you don't understand how policy gets turned into your second year."*

Wannabe barristers apply in the same way the GLS's trainee solicitors do, merely specifying their preferred path on the application form. There's not actually that much to distinguish between the two routes after qualification, so why choose pupillage as opposed to traineeship? *"The skills taught on the BPTC were far more relevant to what we do at the GLS,"* was one person's answer. There's *"still a lot of drafting and opinion-writing,"* though not offering the advocacy opportunities of the private Bar. HMRC still does some of its own though, *"but it's the kind of thing a solicitor advocate would do – people shouldn't come here thinking they'll do vast amounts of advocacy, as it's just not the kind of place where you get to perform in court."*

Ch-ch-ch-ch-chambers

One seat will be spent away from Whitehall at a leading barristers' chambers. *"Taking a GLS pupil is seen as a sign that you're a top set, as the GLS only sends people places where they also send a lot of work."* Time spent in chambers has a dual purpose: GLS employees spend a lot of time instructing barristers, so *"it's great to understand how the other side works, get an idea of issues and build contacts."* Equally, *"there's some training that the GLS just can't give – it's a recognition that should you want to leave the employed Bar, it'd be a bit odd if you'd never had experience in chambers."* Another found: *"At chambers you don't do so much of your own work – it's more focused on your development. I did all the advocacy training alongside the set's pupils. Whereas in my department at the GLS I felt more valuable – if I don't do the cases no-one will!"*

The Bar

TSol offers *"all kinds of legal services within government departments, but mainly litigation."* The department is divided between public and private work: *"You deal with a lot of different ministries and go into a lot of detail on the specifics of other people's working lives."* Pupils should receive *"work from one really big case, which should give interesting, headline work."* There's also the opportunity to deal with smaller files: *"I had a sideline in revoking people's driving licences due to fraud at the testing centre,"* revealed one pupil. There's a lot of breach of contract and inquest work too. In public law and planning *"you can see work that spans trials about tuition fees to arguments about solar panel subsidies."* The latter involved the government's fight to cut solar panel incentives to 21p per kWh of energy generated from the previous 43p. Proceedings were successfully brought by Friends of the Earth to prevent this. Pupils also help draft new legislation. BIS *"is different, as you're expected to be in court once a week and do advocacy."* Generally speaking, though, *"there isn't a great deal of advocacy on offer"* at the GLS.

The other key strand of work for trainee barristers is policy advice. *"A minister will come up with a great idea; we have to look at it and say they can't do it or they'll get sued. It's all about the ability to communicate."*

The Daily Mail test

If you've read our True Picture feature on the GLS's training contract, you won't need telling twice about the benefits of public service. Stability, regular hours and immediate responsibility are only three. *"If you're going to have a monthly salary, holidays and a pension, it seems fair that the government is occasionally entitled to have a say in what you do with your life,"* thought one. Remaining generalists and forgoing the sky-high earnings of those at the private Bar – in addition to forgoing advocacy – is a

choice, but one it's easier to make when *"you can walk in at 10am and leave at 7pm."*

But publicly employed barristers didn't get where they are today just because of an aversion to corporate hours. It helps to be extremely into *"the convergence between law and politics. To some extent they're both sides of the same coin, as it's about vital decision-making, albeit in different ways."* Many see the civil servants' impartiality as an extension of the barristers' cab-rank rule. *"One of the things about government work is you sometimes have to defend things that aren't that nice, but you can't criticise it because you're defending something called a democratically elected parliament. I'm happy defending positions I wouldn't necessarily agree with myself as you're not defending the policy, you're defending the capacity to make it. To work for the GLS you must ultimately believe that politics works, though."*

Most departments are *"quite family oriented,"* though there's *"a good amount of drinking on Fridays."* TSol's slightly more corporate vibe shouldn't be mistaken for anything hard-nosed. *"Management makes a huge effort to involve staff with the department's plans, and we're encouraged to solve problems collaboratively by e-mailing round."* If there are grumbles, they come down to the *"irritations"* of a life in the Civil Service. *"We have to bring in our own tea bags otherwise an MP would end up asking a question in Parliament about staff spending, or if I see a first-class train ticket that's cheaper than second-class I still can't buy it. It's a recognition that politics isn't commercially logical, but part of our training is to understand and manage this."*

One current pupil gives the following decent advice to students: *"Focus on how good you are as an individual AND whether you're a good fit with the GLS."*

And finally...
Life in the GLS is *"not just about being very smart, it's about communicating effectively with ministers."*

1 Hare Court

The facts

Location: Temple, London
Number of QCs/juniors: 12/30 (19 women)
Applications: 100
Outside Pupillage Gateway
Pupils per year: 2
Seats: 3x4 months
Pupillage award: £35,000 (can advance £10,000 for BPTC)

This set is looking for pupils with a passion for the field of family law.

This top family set encourages pupils *"to spend time with the silks going to court and getting to grips with some high net worth divorces, which throw up really complex issues."*

All that jazz

"Family law melds commercial concerns with the 'people' side of law," enthused pupils at this specialist set. A member added: *"I like it because it blends the social with the practical and the intellectual."* All of 1 Hare Court's barristers are family law specialists, and over half are ranked in *Chambers UK*. The set's work is dominated by ancillary relief (or 'matrimonial finance') – the division of a couple's spoils as part of a divorce. *"Those who instruct us know our specialism is ancillary relief – that is why we have so much of that type of work,"* explains senior clerk Steve McCrone. In all, about 85 to 90% of the set's work falls into this category. The rest includes children's cases and advice on drafting pre-nups.

In the past few years 1HC has been involved in many high-profile family cases. In 2010, silks Richard Todd and Nicholas Mostyn (now a High Court judge) were instructed on both sides of the Supreme Court case which determined that pre-nup agreements are binding under English law. Mostyn also represented Paul McCartney during his divorce proceedings and more recently members acted on the divorce case of Russian oligarch Boris Berezovsky, which saw his ex-wife walk away with a tidy £200m – the largest-ever UK divorce payout. In 2013 Richard Todd and Stephen Trowell won a victory for Mrs Prest in the headline-grabbing *Petrodel v Prest* case. The Supreme Court ordered Mr Prest to transfer to his ex-wife properties held by companies owned and controlled by him as part of a £17.5m divorce award widely heralded as a ray of light through the corporate veil. It's increasingly common for cases at 1HC to have an international flavour: quite a few clients hail from overseas or own assets abroad.

"Family law is more rigorous than it used to be," one member told us. *"You need more skills in areas like finance and other disciplines: from forensics to child psychology."* And don't imagine divorce law is about endlessly haranguing opposing counsel either. An increasing number of cases settle out of court. *"The Family Bar is undergoing a big shake up as lots of areas are losing legal aid,"* we were told. *"The government is putting an increasing emphasis on alternative dispute resolution."* 1HC has really been pushing the use of mediation and arbitration and now has three accredited arbitrators and 16 accredited mediators. Emotions do still run high in divorce cases, of course. But: *"We're lawyers, not therapists. We have to be commercial about how we deal with difficult family problems. We have to explain to clients – who might have thought family law was all about sitting on beanbags talking about your problems – what remedies the law offers."*

Follow my lead

Pupils sit with three different supervisors for four months each. They are also encouraged to do work for other members of chambers. *"In my first four months my supervisor would ring around and ask if anyone had suitable work for me. My second supervisor made it clear they wanted me to take the initiative making contact. I often went along to court with other members."* Pupils get stuck in to a range of written work. *"I was asked to do some quite big tasks,"* one told us. *"I have drafted skeleton arguments and one legal opinion as well as doing discrete research*

The Bar

Chambers UK rankings

Family/Matrimonial

tasks. I have also put together schedules of assets and chronologies of events." One interviewee said they split their time 50/50 between working in chambers and shadowing members in court. Pupils often accompany silks and get a taste of the action in some of 1HC's most high-value cases. These aren't necessarily the most complex or interesting ones though: *"The lower the value of the divorce case, the more intense it often is, as the parties have less to divide up."*

There are *"not that many differences"* between the first and second six, other than pupils' increasing experience level. Towards the end of the pupillage they usually get the opportunity to be on their feet two or three times. One we spoke to had done a first appointment in a financial remedies proceeding. *"I was quite pleased to be in a set where I didn't get on my feet too early, as the cases are fairly complex,"* one pupil told us. Pupils do get to practise their advocacy during two non-assessed exercises in the second six.

Keeping it in the family

1HC makes some tough demands of its recruits. Good academics are a given and, as *"nearly all our applicants look really impressive on paper,"* it's vital to show you have a clear interest in family law. *"You have to show a really spirited interest – or, dare I say it, a passion – for family law,"* a member told us. *"When I interview someone, I want to have the impression that they have read the Family Law Journal that week, or know about major issues at the Family Bar."* The set also likes to see family law mini-pupillages on CVs and it could help if, for example, you did your dissertation on divorce law or shadowed a judge in the Family Division. In addition, the financial nature of ancillary relief means applicants need an interest in, or knowledge of, tax and personal finance. *"I am looking for someone who is either good with numbers or has the capacity to be good with numbers,"* says Ann Hussey, head of the pupillage committee.

1HC operates outside the Pupillage Gateway, and applicants first have to impress with a CV and hand-written cover letter. In 2012, 29 candidates were invited to a ten-minute first-round interview. *"It was a CV chat focusing on what I did at university and why I wanted to work here,"* recalled one pupil. As well as questions like 'What makes a good family barrister?' candidates may be asked their views on developments at the Family Bar or, for example, the effects of legal aid cuts. The second-round interview – reached by 11 candidates in 2012 – is more structured. *"I was given three cases plus the judgments and a mock legal question beforehand,"* recalled one pupil. *"In the interview I was asked to analyse the problem, compare the cases and talk about what parts of the judgments were most relevant."*

1HC has traditionally only taken on one of its three pupils a year and did so again in 2013. It also advertises its tenancy position externally, though the last time it took on a new member this way was in 2005. As of autumn 2013, the set recruits two pupils with the aim of offering tenancy to one. At the end of pupillage there is an interview for tenancy, consisting of two parts: a general interview and a 15-minute advocacy exercise. *"My impression is that the tenancy decision is predominantly based on that interview,"* a pupil told us. *"But of course our supervisors do give us references which are taken into account by the tenancy committee, along with feedback from other members."*

The well tempered workplace

"I think we are a progressive set, but we are still run on a successful traditional basis," says senior clerk Steven McCrone. Apparently some of the junior clerks still prefer to call the members Sir and Ma'am, and inside chambers you'll find some traditional fixtures and fittings – we understand the head of chambers even has a harpsichord in his office. That traditional outlook includes a non-expansive approach to the set's membership. *"As we lose people at the top, we recruit new people at the bottom,"* says McCrone. *"We don't usually advertise for new members other than those we take on after pupillage."*

We don't want to make this set sound like a stuffy place, though. It has *"a strong group of young juniors,"* a youthful head of chambers and a high proportion of female tenants. *"And people often pop into each other's rooms for tea, coffee and a natter."* The Pegasus Bar in the Inner Temple is popular for a drink and there are also chambers dinners and an annual networking seminar.

And finally...

Take note that a huge chunk of 1HC's work is ancillary relief for divorces, so besides people skills, you'll need a love of numbers, tax and things financial to work here.

Henderson Chambers

The facts

Location: Temple, London

Number of QCs/juniors: 9/39 (10 women)

Applications: 180

Apply through Pupillage Gateway

Pupils per year: 2

Seats: 4x3 months

Pupillage award: £50,000 (can advance a sum for BPTC)

This top common law set is not afraid to seek out new practice with potential

From the outside, it has the look and feel of the traditional Bar, but in fact Henderson and its cheery tenants have a thoroughly modern approach to their product liability, consumer, and health and safety work.

Crash, bang, wallop

Train crash? Salmonella outbreak? Nasty injury? Defective drugs? Mis-sold PPI? Henderson Chambers is your set. Its expertise lies in health and safety, product liability and consumer credit law, or, as one junior put it, *"things that have broken or gone wrong."* Enthusiastic senior clerk John White gave us a more corporate-style summary: *"We are a recognised leader in a number of specialist fields, like product liability and health and safety. But we have noticed an increase in regulatory and compliance issues."* In addition to these three core areas, Henderson also works on personal injury and disease claims, employment, property, commercial and local government disputes.

Chambers' traditional strength in health and safety has seen its members involved with litigation over the Buncefield oil depot explosion and the Hatfield, Potters Bar, Ladbroke Grove and Grayrigg rail disasters. The atomic veterans litigation was another big case – Henderson acted for the MoD in this high-profile injury claim by about 1,000 servicemen involved in atomic tests in the 1950s. On the product liability side, members have acted as counsel for Clover Leaf, the UK distributor of the allegedly defective French PIP breast implants. Members also defended drug maker Sanofi against a group action over the anti-epileptic drug Sabril. Meanwhile, barristers in the *"burgeoning"* consumer finance practice were active on *Sternlight v Barclays Bank* over the interest rates charged on credit cards. Members have also recently been very busy on cases related to the mis-selling of PPI (payment protection insurance).

This broad range of practices certainly appealed to our interviewees when they applied to Henderson. And things could become broader still; the set seems constantly to be seeking out new practice areas with potential. In 2011 it launched a consumer law practice, topping up its consumer finance expertise with the arrival of William Hibbert and Julia Smith from Gough Chambers (Hibbert is a big noise in the world of consumer credit and OFT matters). John White also mentions environmental health and safety actions, insurance, economic torts and technology as growth areas. Speaking of technology, in late 2011 one Henderson barrister was responsible for the first anti-harassment injunction sent to an unknown party via text message.

PI to four significant figures

Pupils spend three months with four different supervisors. Each supervisor usually practises in more than one field, so a seat might combine employment with PI work or property with consumer finance. In their first seat, pupils work primarily for their supervisor doing things like preparing skeleton arguments, pleadings, research notes and notes for conference. *"All the work I did was on ongoing cases,"* one pupil told us. *"My very first task was drafting a skeleton argument for a county court debt action."* One supervisor asks pupils to *"plan and draft an outline – a roadmap – of the cross-examination of the defendant in one of his current cases."* After three months pupils also take on work from other members of chambers: *"There is an informal list of other people you should do work with, including all the members of the recruitment committee and the head of chambers."* Midway through the

The Bar

Chambers UK rankings

Consumer Law	Professional Discipline
Health & Safety	Public Procurement
Information Technology	Real Estate Litigation
Product Liability	

year, pupils spend a month seconded to the competition department of US law firm McDermott Will & Emery's Brussels office, picking up commercial experience working with solicitors.

Advocacy comes hard and fast in the second six, when there is *"a big change of pace."* By the end of this period pupils are on their feet two or three times a week. *"The advocacy is wonderful,"* one pupil cooed. *"I have really had to argue complex points."* Pupils cut their teeth on RTAs and possession hearings in the Magistrates' and Crown Court, and might eventually even end up in the High Court. Sources we spoke to had gained advocacy experience in a five-day employment tribunal case, a half-hour costs application, and a *"possession hearing where the defendant hadn't paid his rent... because he's in prison."* Pupils also do three or four mock advocacy exercises, the final one in front of a Master at the RCJ.

Easy rider?

In line with Henderson's *"friendly and warm"* ethos, this set isn't intent on beasting its pupils. *"I was told that in the first three months nobody expects you to be marvellously amazing,"* one pupil said, *"but you do push yourself and it's important to show willingness to assist and work with other people."* A lever-arch file is kept on each pupil containing *"each supervisor's written report and feedback on every piece of written work you have done for other members."* This file is the main basis for the tenancy decision taken by the recruitment committee. In addition, *"the other members are informally canvassed for their opinions,"* and the clerks weigh in too. Chief clerk John White says the first thing he looks for in a pupil is personality – first and foremost as they need to be attractive prospects for solicitor clients. In 2013, Henderson took on both of its pupils as tenants.

One reason personality matters when it comes to tenancy is that the pupillage application process has already weeded out anyone who isn't an excellent barrister. All

pupillage applications are marked out of 100, with most weight given to academics followed by non-academic achievements, commitment to the Bar and your interest in Henderson. The highest scorers go through to a first-round interview, based around a *"fairly nebulous"* problem question (in 2013 applicants were asked about third-party funding of litigation). There is also a brief CV chat: *"They looked at what I had done and said 'That's interesting!' and we talked a bit about it."* The second interview is more *"alarming."* A seven-member panel grills candidates on a more legalistic question, for example about a piece of case law. In addition to its twelve-month pupils, the set takes on a third-six pupil almost every year.

Big bash and the Hendersons

A recent renovation (we could still smell the fresh paint when visiting in summer 2012) has seen Henderson replace its wood panelling and shelves stocked with old law reports with white-painted walls and video-conferencing facilities. In 2013, the set launched a specific pupillage website and Twitter account. It might be embracing social media, but the set retains a cosy – almost homely – feel which fits its location right at the heart of Inner Temple. Sources agreed that this cosy atmosphere is reflected in familial relations among the tenants: *"People are very ready to help you, which means it's easy to keep learning."* We sense this culture strongly contributes to Henderson's market standing and the quality of the instructions it receives.

We can give you more of a feel of the Henderson 'type' by telling you that one pupil we spoke to used to be a radio DJ for BBC Oxford, while a baby junior previously worked in sales for Channel Four. More senior members don't shy away from non-law activities either: head of chambers Charlie Gibson moonlights as an amateur boxer in the East End (honestly!) and has an electric drum kit in his office. Junior James Purnell is apparently a dab hand at the piano: *"He leads the carol singing at the Christmas party and everyone is 'forced' to join in."* For more frequent fun there are the *"well-attended"* 5pm Friday drinks: *"What I like about them is that the talk tends not to be about law. At most, people might tell you about funny things that happened in court. It's a nice way to wind down – suddenly all your week's hardships become hilarious anecdotes."*

And finally...
Stuffed full of bright, charming and diligent barristers and interesting work, Henderson offers pupils great advocacy opportunities and quality feedback on their work – we can't recommend it highly enough.

11KBW

The facts

Location: Inner Temple, London
Number of QCs/juniors: 16/40 (17 women)
Applications: 150
Pupils per year: 2-4
Seats: 2x3 and 1x6 months
Pupillage award: £55,000 (can advance £15,000 for BPTC)

"As a pupil, your work is a really interesting balance of long-running, intellectually tough matters and fairly straightforward assignments."

Public law is a strong suit at 11KBW, which handles education, local government and employment work.

Public frenemy

With just 32 years under its belt, 11KBW is still young in the grand scheme of things. But what this set lacks in age it more than makes up for in eminent alumni – former tenants include political power couple Tony and Cherie Blair and Alexander 'Derry' Irvine QC, founding member turned Lord Chancellor. Another distinguished figure is 11KBW's original senior clerk Philip Monham, a *"steady hand"* who rang in his 2012 retirement with a Chambers & Partners Lifetime Achievement Award. The basic cornerstones of this set are public law, employment, commercial/business and information law work, each of which encompasses a number of sub-sectors – *"for example, community care, education, local government and mental health work all fall under the first bracket,"* joint senior clerk Lucy Barbet tells us. She estimates some 40% of instructions involve public law matters, while information law work accounts for 20% and employment and commercial issues together comprise the remaining 40%.

This spread of undertakings lends itself to *"an incredibly broad"* client base, from universities, investment banks and professional services firms to local authorities, central government bodies and trade unions. On the education front, 11KBW barristers represented both claimants and respondent examination boards in the headline-grabbing GCSE marking challenge of 2012 and acted for a Birmingham girls' school in a landmark appeal against the Secretary of State for Education's decision to remove it from the Register of Independent Schools. The set's education and local government practices are both top-ranked in *Chambers UK* and between them represent the likes of the Department of Education, the University of Oxford, Surrey County Council and the London Borough of Brent.

11 KBW is also recognised as a top employment set, regularly handling discrimination, unfair dismissal, equal pay and trade law cases, often in the Employment Appeals Tribunal. Recent court appearances include acting on behalf of News International during an indemnity claim related to the infamous *News of the World* phone-hacking scandal and winning a female client's sex discrimination case against German financial giant Commerzbank. The set's also known for its human rights expertise, working across the immigration, mental health and social care sectors, and is upping its reputation on the informational law side, contending with a growing number of hot-button issues like late-term abortions and MPs' expenses.

The ailing economy has prompted 11KBW to expand its private sector capabilities in recent years. *"We've had to reconsider the level at which we pitch ourselves,"* Barbet says. *"The aim is to continue increasing turnover on the private side and add to our international offerings as well."* Much of the set's commercial work of late has involved the financial services sector, with members enjoying a growing involvement in high-profile City cases like the conspiracy wars between brokers Tullett Prebon and BGC Brokers and ContiCap's long-running claim under the Swiss Unfair Competition Act.

Checks and balances

Pupillage is split into two three-month seats followed by a six-month one. *"Over the year, pupils tend to spend three months with somebody who works at the commercial/employment end, then another three months with someone*

Chambers UK rankings

Administrative & Public Law	Data Protection
	Education
Civil Liberties & Human Rights	Employment
	Local Government
Competition/European Law	Public Procurement

who predominately practises public law. After that, who they sit with depends on which areas of work they have yet to observe," chair of the pupillage committee Daniel Stilitz QC tells us. "It's all about providing a balanced legal education and making sure they see as wide a range of chambers' work as possible." According to pupils, the first seat is "a settling-in period – you're not expected to do a whole lot other than observe the work your supervisor is doing and absorb how that works." Indeed, "it's only after a few months that you assume a management function and start working for other people in chambers."

"As a pupil, your work is a really interesting balance of long-running, intellectually tough matters and fairly straightforward assignments," said one source. "I've worked on a big judicial review exploring the extraterritorial application of the Human Rights Act with respect to drone strikes in Pakistan; equally, I've been asked to draft grounds for an individual's small employment claim." While the public law arena often supplies the more "prestigious" cases, the employment side of things is hardly humdrum: "The junior end involves a lot of claims made against big organisations, which tend to be pretty exciting because you've got to have a good case to take it to court." Working styles vary among supervisors, but "all take the education aspect of pupillage very seriously by making sure we're not overworked and getting us involved as much as they can; pupils aren't just the lackeys walking two steps behind with the papers." One source estimated "around a fifth" of the year is spent in the courtroom.

Devil's advocate

Virtually all pupils are recruited via assessed mini-pupillages, which are obtained through written applications and offer "an accurate insight into how chambers operates day-to-day." Stints normally last a week and "function essentially as a first interview. There's a lot of focus on your written work and ability to argue and express yourself orally." According to Stilitz, plans are in place to make the interview stage – "wherein we gather the ten or twelve who've impressed us during their mini-pupillage"– more assessment-based. "This year we'll judge candidates on a legal problem they're given in advance plus a short advocacy exercise. These exercises give us a much better idea of what a candidate will be like in practice than anything on his or her CV."

Between our interviewees, one had two undergrad degrees and a Master's in law, while another spent time as a philosopher and human rights volunteer abroad before opting for the Bar. Easy enough, right? Beyond pure academic success, advocacy experience is "a definite plus" in applicants, Stilitz says. "Advocacy skills are as important as analytical. Experience that shows your interest in and aptitude for being a strong advocate." Competition for spots is undeniably tough, but insiders assured us "once you're in, you're only up against yourself. We're told we'll all be kept on if we're good enough." In keeping with its stellar retention record of years past, chambers welcomed both of its two pupils to its junior tenant ranks in 2013.

A "sincere interest" in pro bono work prevails at 11KBW. Recent activity includes representing anti-poverty charity Z2K in a challenge to the 2012 housing benefit freeze and spearheading a disability discrimination claim made by a law student suffering from multiple sclerosis. "There's loads of scope to get involved, and just about everybody in chambers does."

Despite chambers' "rigorous academic approach," the day-to-day atmosphere is "relaxed," sources agreed. "Everyone has a friendly attitude and is supportive, even the silks with rock star practices. Nobody's ever told me off for taking up their time with a really basic question!" Likewise, the relationship between tenants and clerks is "pretty informal – you won't hear anyone addressed as 'mister' or 'ma'am' around here." Pupils are "fully incorporated" into chambers' social scene, which includes holiday parties, regular networking events and a weekly tea one source characterised as "kind of ironic – we all flock to it to grab some food and catch up; it's not like we're sitting silently around a table waiting for the senior clerk to speak." Another weekly tradition is Friday night drinks at The Witness Box, though we heard this might change following the famous dive's decision to go down the trendy wine bar route. "I'm just not sure how much longer our loyalty will last now they're charging us more," an interviewee grumbled.

And finally...

Our interviewees urged applicants to *"bear in mind how crucial it is to display clear, logical and concise writing skills in your application form and mini-pupillage assessments. We're a place that believes written advocacy is as important as oral advocacy, so you will be judged harshly."*

The Bar

Keating Chambers

The facts
Location: Essex Street, London
Number of QCs/juniors: 26/31 (15 women)
Applications: 130
Apply through Pupillage Gateway
Pupils per year: Up to 3
Seats: 4x3 months
Pupillage award: £50,000 (can advance £15,000 for BPTC)

A background in construction is not a necessity to work at Keating; an interest in commercial law is.

As experts in the field for over three decades, Keating Chambers literally wrote the book on construction law.

The house that Keating built

Indisputably one of London's top two construction sets, Keating has been honing its specialism ever since Donald Keating QC was head of chambers in the 1980s. He first penned the seminal construction tome *Keating on Construction Contracts* in 1955 – the ninth edition was published in February 2012, still authored by members of this chambers.

Keating's members have been instructed in disputes over landmark construction projects like Wembley Stadium, the London Eye, the Gherkin, the Millennium Stadium, Portcullis House and the Lowry Centre. The set works on construction cases of all shapes and sizes – its reputation means members are often to be found on both sides of a dispute. For example, members recently advised both Cambridge City Council and engineering firm BAM in a bust-up over the construction of a guided busway.

"Right now we have no real need to go outside our chosen disciplines. We concentrate on those things we are really good at," senior clerk Nick Child tells us. But he doesn't just mean construction contracts disputes. Keating's work extends into squabbles over energy infrastructure projects; professional negligence claims related to engineers, architects and surveyors; and international construction arbitration. Chambers is also expanding its existing presence in technology, procurement and shipbuilding disputes, all areas where the law involved – contract and tort – is closely linked to construction law. On the shipping side, members recently acted for Serco in a $30m dispute over the termination of an Abu Dhabi shipbuilding contract. A recent procurement case saw the set represent train manufacturer Alstom in its appeal against Eurostar's

decision to have Siemens build its new Channel Tunnel trains. International disputes – often dealt with through ADR – are a lucrative market at the moment, while the UK construction market remains relatively depressed. So, in the name of marketing Keating overseas, Nick Child has joined the jet-set: Russia, the Middle East and East Asia are all hot sources of work at the moment.

Building your CV

A pupillage at Keating is a hard-won thing. Around 30 applicants are invited to a first-round interview. Candidates have just 15 minutes to impress the four-lawyer interview panel with their legal knowledge, confidence, speaking skills, motivation and interest in construction law. There's room for *"topical"* questions – one example we heard was: *"Do you favour compulsory mediation?"* while another was: *"Should policemen be allowed to serve on juries?"* A second-round 30-minute interview includes a presentation on a (preferably non-legal) topic of the applicant's choice. Past candidates have spoken about the Elgin Marbles and hang-gliding. Applicants are also presented with a legal problem and complete a written test. *"They wanted me to show myself at my best,"* recalled a current pupil. *"I was pushed by the interviewers, who took a purposefully different viewpoint to mine to challenge me."*

"In the interviews we don't usually ask anything about construction," says pupillage committee head Alexander Nissen QC. *"We don't expect any specialist knowledge from applicants; 90% of our barristers do not have any technical background at all. In practice we get assistance from technical experts instructed by the clients and that is sufficient. So do you need to be an engineer? Definitely*

Chambers UK rankings

Construction	International Arbitration
Energy & Natural Resources	Professional Negligence
	Public Procurement

not. But do you need an interest in commercial law? Yes, absolutely." A junior tenant told us: "I was interested in the language and complexity of contract and tort law. The fact it was complicated is what attracted me." If an applicant does have an engineering or construction background this can count as a plus at the initial application stage.

Size matters

Pupils spend time with four supervisors. In the past we've written that supervisors often have a similar practice remit, but vary in seniority and style. We're told this has changed in that "some individuals focus more on a certain area – like energy or procurement," making each seat more distinct. Nonetheless, you will need a strong interest in the contractual principles that underlie construction law. You must also have the ability to combine handling stacks of documentation (construction cases are often huge and lengthy) with easy banter among contractor clients. "Construction is an industry where personality matters a lot." says one source. "You have to be able to relate to the man in the street who put his shovel through a cable digging up the road, and to the CEO of the corporation that owned the digger that dug the hole for the cable in the first place."

Shadowing is at the core of the first six. "I did work my supervisor was currently on or had just done, drafting memos, written advice and skeleton arguments. I also attended conferences with clients." In contrast to some other commercial sets, pupils have the chance to be on their feet once a week or more in their second six. Not on any construction cases, though. The clerks intentionally seek out lower-value work – direction hearings, infant settlements – for pupils to cut their teeth on. "The opportunity to do advocacy in our second six is great," one pupil said. "You get used to the feeling of a courtroom and learn about the type of questions judges ask, which helps when you're preparing briefs." Drafting and shadowing continues in this period, and pupils do more live work, such as "drafting particulars of claim which are sent to the solicitors."

Pupils also are put through their paces in three advocacy assessments. "They are quite tricky and excellent prep for the real thing," said one. "You're given a huge bundle,

and managing that is a real test." Cases are always mocks of recent large matters the set has worked on. Pupils go head-to-head as opposing counsel, and a senior QC sits in judgment.

The tenancy decision is based on a variety of factors, including the quality of the pupils' work, their performance in the advocacy exercises and the extent to which the pupils are "likely to gel well with the clients." Alexander Nissen QC says: "Feedback from supervisors is probably the most reliable source of information upon which to base the decision. The tenancy committee places much store by what they say." The decision of the committee is ultimately reviewed by the whole of chambers, but the committee's recommendations carry great weight. One out of the two pupils was offered tenancy in both 2012 and 2013.

Keating Rocks

Spurning a traditional chambers tea, Keating has a chambers lunch. It's only for members, and pupils are not invited, but rather than a snub we're told this is to "take the pressure off" and stop lunch becoming a hob-nobbing affair. Pupils are always invited to other events, such as the Christmas party, drinks and celebrations. "There's always a Keating table in halls too which you can join," a pupil told us. "And Daly's Wine Bar is a frequent haunt on Fridays, and as a pupil they never let you pay for your own drinks."

Pupils usually work 9am to 6pm, but there are exceptions. "You do put the pressure on yourself sometimes and urgent things can come up. I got a call from the clerks once at 7pm on a Friday, saying some papers had come in and did I want to take a look at them. It was up to me to say whether I felt I could. In the end I did and worked over the weekend, but I wasn't judged on it. The supervisors are good at applying just the right amount of pressure."

Unusually, Keating is now split 50/50 between silks and juniors. Perhaps this contributes to what one source called the "collegiate" atmosphere: "There are plenty of interesting characters, but not a singular chambers personality. Everyone is different, so you do treat everyone differently." This doesn't seem to be a set stuffed with eccentrics, although one pupil recalled once hearing the strum of an electric guitar from one silk's office. That would be Marcus Taverner QC. He plays lead guitar in Keating's entry for the Law Rocks 'Battle of the Bands' fund-raiser. The charity – set up by Keating's own senior clerk Nick Child – raised £11,000 at one event in November 2011. Well, rock on, we say.

And finally...

A great set, not just for those interested in construction law, but for anyone who relishes the complexities of contracts law.

1 King's Bench Walk

The facts

Location: Inner Temple, London
Number of QCs/juniors: 12/40 (24 women)
Applications: 150
Outside Pupillage Gateway
Pupils per year: 2x3 and 1x6 months
Pupillage award: £22,500

This is one of London's best family law sets. Keep up to date on this area by regularly checking familylaw.co.uk.

1 King's Bench Walk is the only set in London which can claim to have top-table expertise in all areas of family law.

Family fortunes

This set has been a fixture in the Inner Temple for over 40 years and has spent that time building up an excellent reputation at the family Bar. 1KBW has been listed as a top family set by *Chambers UK* since the first edition of that guide in 1990. *"Historically we did start out as a general common law set, but we have always done a lot of family work,"* long-serving senior clerk David Dear recalls. Recently, the set has formally confirmed its specialist status. *"Over the past year we have chosen to identify ourselves exclusively as specialists in family law,"* says head of pupillage Richard Harrison QC. The two pupillages on offer here, then, are both specialist family law ones.

1KBW is the only set which *Chambers UK* ranks in the top two bands for both children's disputes and matrimonial finance ('ancillary relief'). Instructions in the latter category include all the usual financial wranglings involved in marriage break-ups, as well as foreign and jurisdictional issues, prenuptial agreements, civil partnership break-ups, TOLATA disputes (over the division of property between cohabiting couples), inheritance issues and the freezing of assets. One silk was recently involved in a big money divorce case related to funds in the Cayman Islands which hinged on the different definitions of 'matrimonial assets' in the Caymans and the UK. Unsurprisingly these disputes are known internally as 'money cases'.

Divorce disputes can also involve haggling to reach a settlement because a client is too emotionally distraught to go ahead with court proceedings, or working out how to divvy up a divorcing couple's assets if one party earns very little, but has a huge potential income because of

a previous high-flying career. Back in 2010, member of chambers Deepak Nagpal was also involved in the case between German heiress Katrin Radmacher and her ex-husband Nicolas Granatino which established the circumstances under which prenuptial agreements are legally valid. The set's children's work divides into 'private law children' – covering issues of residency, contact and international relocation – and 'public law children'. The latter covers cases in which the state intervenes, and sees barristers represent local authorities and charities as well as parents and children in care order, adoption and guardianship cases. The most serious work of this set comes in the form of cases related to child abduction by family members. *"In the children's cases you often feel like you've made a real difference,"* reflected one pupil. *"But it's really interesting to do the big-money divorce cases for oligarchs too."* A junior added: *"Family law is fascinating because you're always dealing with people and their lives, helping them with their biggest concerns – their children and their marriage."*

A quick side-note: 1KBW's website makes a mention of criminal work too, but senior clerk David Dear told us this type of work is done full-time by just two of the set's most senior members, and it's not an area that pupils are likely to have any involvement in.

The kids are alright

Pupils have two supervisors for three months each during their first six, and then a single supervisor for their second six. The two pupils spend time with the same three supervisors, all fairly senior and all fairly specialised: one who does public/private children's work, one from matrimonial finance, and one child abduction practitioner. *"If*

Chambers UK rankings

Family/Matrimonial

I do work for other members it always goes through my supervisor – 95% of the work I did in my first six was for my supervisor," reported one pupil. *"For example, I was given the bundles for a big finance case the next week and told to take my time drafting a position statement and chronology as if I were conducting the case myself. My supervisor took the time to go through my draft line by line and offer constructive criticism."*

Initially, supervisors are lenient with mistakes, but they quickly start expecting more and *"parts of your work might be lifted out and used by your supervisor."* First-sixers also attend court, shadowing both their supervisors and more junior tenants heading off to Magistrates' Courts. *"There have been times when I have spoken to clients on my own,"* a pupil said, *"and my opinion does get asked during meetings."*

"I got given my first case in the first week of my second six," one pupil told us. *"I acted for a mother who wanted access to her child in a case at Southend County Court."* Other cases pupils take on include direction hearings, injunctions, custody disputes, public care work and non-molestation orders. One *"appeared in Staines County Court acting for a woman with a small child who had been very badly treated by her ex-boyfriend, and we got him kicked out of the flat."* Having just one supervisor through this period *"works well and helps you to build a close relationship with one person while you are on your feet – you know you can always call them from court to ask advice."* Senior clerk David Dear stresses that the clerks don't push pupils into work before they are ready. We visited 1KBW two months into pupils' second six and one had been on his feet four times – the caseload increases as pupillage goes on.

Pupils undertake monthly advocacy training exercises. *"It is set up like a real-life situation,"* a pupil said. *"You are given the case papers a few days in advance, introduced to a 'client' and argue in front of one of the senior members playing a judge."* Other on-the-job training is provided by 'end-of-seat' feedback reports from supervisors. There are no formal assessments for tenancy. Richard Harrison tells us: *"The tenancy decision is made by a committee which prepares a detailed report based primarily upon written evidence from the pupil supervisors and other members of chambers who have come into contact with the pupils. The committee also interviews the pupils before preparing its report."* 1KBW has a strong track record of retaining youngsters, telling us that it offered tenancy to 17 out of 20 pupils between 2002 and 2012. In 2013 both pupils were kept on. The set does not offer third sixes.

Wedding march

So you fancy tying the knot with 1KBW? Initial applications are marked based on academic achievement, extra-curricular and work experience, commitment to the set's areas of work, and the presentation of the application form itself. At the very least, applicants need to express a strong interest in family law. The two pupils we spoke with had done this through a Master's specialisation and personal experiences respectively. And we reckon something along the lines of hands-on experience working with children, couples or vulnerable individuals would stand an applicant in good stead.

There are two rounds of interviews for pupillage – around 45 applicants are invited to the first and around 15 to the second. Neither tests specific knowledge of family law. *"I remember being asked what attracted me to the set and ending up talking about myself for ages!"* a current pupil recalled. *"I was also given a one-and-a-half page outline of a family law case 20 minutes before the interview and then asked to argue for and against certain viewpoints."* Richard Harrison told us: *"We are looking for evidence of intellectual ability, the ability to advance a reasoned argument, emotional intelligence, the ability to relate to people's concerns and good advocacy."*

Once at 1KBW, pupils don't have to sweat it out being challenged to intellectual duels in the corridors by senior members. *"This is a very social set,"* said one junior, *"and there's never that feeling that pupils mustn't speak when they're around the silks – there are friendships across the hierarchy."* A pupil added: *"There are plenty of occasions when I speak to senior people. On Friday we often all go for lunch at a pizzeria nearby. Recently I was sitting opposite a very senior silk and I remember talking about who was going to win Wimbledon – because I'm really into tennis."* We don't know if that silk is the same member of chambers who is *"a fantastic organist and plays at all our weddings!"*

And finally...

Many of this set's members have a *"strong social conscience"* and engage in pro bono – for example, for the National Centre for Domestic Violence.

The Bar

7 King's Bench Walk

The facts

Location: Inner Temple, London
Number of QCs/juniors: 25/28 (12 women)
Applications: 150
Apply through Pupillage Gateway
Pupils per year: Up to 4
Seats: Usually 4 in the first 9 months
Pupillage award: £60,000 (can advance up to £15,000 for BPTC)

"We are a little bit more informal and slightly less corporate than other commercial sets."

7KBW has a sterling reputation for all things insurance and shipping, but there's more to discover at this top commercial set.

Knights of the round table

7KBW's premises have been home to a number of illustrious figures over the years. Former occupant William Tidd's 18th-century common-law tome *Practice of the Court of King's Bench* is mentioned in *David Copperfield*. Future Lord Chancellor Lord Halsbury practised here too before penning *Halsbury's Laws of England*, which is still in print today. More recently, many ex-tenants have joined the Bench including Supreme Court Justice Mance and Lord Justices of Appeal Sir Andrew Longmore and Sir Stephen Tomlinson.

The set is top-ranked by *Chambers UK* for insurance litigation, which *"constitutes at least 50% of the practice."* But insurance isn't just one thing: it can be marine insurance for shipping firms or professional negligence insurance for accountants... *"There are many different bents to it!"* We mentioned marine insurance there as shipping is an area which *"90-something per cent"* of members spend at least some of their time on. Maritime law is paper-heavy and suffused with its own language and customs, so we were pleased to hear pupils refer to it lightly as *"contract law with boats"* and say that *"it's about things your granny would understand, like a ship hitting a rock."* True. In one recent case members were called in to represent the operator of a berth at a harbour in Ecuador after the 'CCNI Antártico' struck the quayside there. Other cases have involved vessels suddenly splitting in two, catching fire, or grounding in ecologically sensitive areas.

Other areas of expertise include professional negligence, banking and finance, trade and commodities, fraud, construction, media and communications, EU and competition law, and oil and gas. The last one of these is really on the up. Five members worked on one of the largest commercial cases of the year, *Excalibur Ventures v Texas Keystone*, which centred on oil exploration concessions in Kurdistan. Arbitration is another area in which the set is well regarded and it adds an international dimension to the work, with members frequently sailing off to places like Singapore, the Bahamas and Hong Kong.

Exercise books

Pupils have four supervisors. They usually sit with the first until Christmas. This period *"focuses on learning and you work mostly for your supervisor."* Subsequent seats usually last two or three months. Supervisors are usually senior juniors, though junior silks occasionally fulfil the role too.

Each supervisor's practice usually includes insurance, shipping and other work. A pupil we spoke to had come across reinsurance, professional negligence and energy cases, as well as what he termed *"general commercial matters – those cases which don't fit neatly into any one category but help keep everything more varied."* Pupils worked on the Excalibur case too, which offered *"the fantastic opportunity to watch a senior silk do some cross-examination – there's no better way to learn than that."*

Opinions, skeleton arguments, pieces of advice, pleadings and defences are standard drafting fare for pupils. The work is overwhelmingly on live cases, although *"sometimes your supervisor will give you the brief for one of his past cases and have you draft the relevant documents, so you can learn about a particular point."* Supervisors' cases *"can last anywhere from two days to two weeks, which means that you get to see a lot of what goes on."* Lengthy

The Bar

671

Chambers UK rankings

Commercial Dispute Resolution	International Arbitration
	Professional Negligence
Insurance	Shipping

cases can be real head-scratchers and hinge on verbose precedents and statute. Shipping, insurance and commercial law are known as fairly academic fields. *"People here spend a lot of time doing serious, challenging work and are often buried under difficult papers for days on end."* Our interviewees didn't feel they were forced to do book-heavy drudgework though. *"I haven't been sent off to the library for six months to go and read 50 million books to figure out the meaning of one word!"*

Pupils don't spend any time on their feet during the second six, but do complete two formal advocacy exercises. The first is an application for summary judgment while the second is more meaty – an appeal to the Supreme Court. *"They're fun and scary at the same time"* a pupil told us, but luckily *"there's plenty of time to prepare."* Pupils draft a skeleton argument beforehand, which they submit to the panel of silks and juniors conducting the exercise.

During pupillage you're also asked to complete eight to ten written pieces of work for several named pupil assessors. These can be *"quite difficult,"* but then the aim is to allow members other than the four supervisors to test the mettle of the pupils. The tenancy decision is made based on feedback from supervisors, pupil assessors and those who oversaw the advocacy exercises. In 2013, one of two pupils gained tenancy with the set.

Brain trust

Despite the tough intellectual demands of being a pupil and tenant at this set, recruiters told us that you needn't be put off from applying if you don't have an encyclopaedic knowledge of shipping or insurance. *"The learning curve is going to be very steep whatever your background, so we're looking for people with an ability to pick things up quickly."* We were told that *"a substantial number of people come here after doing the GDL"* – a quick snoop

on the firm's website revealed that a third of the members under five years' call didn't do law at undergrad. But we would be lying if we didn't admit that we were very impressed by the academic calibre of 7KBW's baby barristers. Between them the five youngest members have a double First in Japanese and jurisprudence, a PhD in mathematics, a ten-year career at the Bar in Australia, an LLM from Harvard and a year's lecturing experience at Oxford, as well as at least 25 prizes and scholarships.

If you think you live up to these high standards and want to win a pupillage here, then you'll have to pick 7KBW as one of your 12 Pupillage Gateway sets. Around 25 individuals make it through the initial application sift. The interview process consists of an advocacy exercise (which candidates are given a couple of weeks to prepare) and *"a more traditional interview with all the normal CV-related questions."* A current pupil told us that *"the interview panel wants to see how you respond to difficult, off-the-cuff questions and whether you can think on your feet and demonstrate the lively intellect required to work here."*

7KBW's tenants don't specialise in just one area, which means that *"all members will end up working with one another at some point, so you get to know everyone."* Perhaps as a consequence this is *"not a fusty, unfriendly place – quite the opposite."* Members also admitted that *"because of the work we do there is an academic atmosphere, but that doesn't mean people are weird and don't talk to each other!"* Another source added: *"We are less into the idea of developing a brand than some other sets, and our organisation is more in line with the traditional idea of how a barristers' chambers should work, but we're certainly not traditional in the sense of being stuffy."*

There's chambers tea every day, and *"at least six to ten members usually come along to have a chat."* One of our interviewees was keen to dispel the myth that teas are crusty and old fashioned. *"Some people seem to be allergic to the idea of chambers tea, but I think it should be rehabilitated at the Bar: it's just like having a drink with your mates really, except that you go back to work afterwards..."* There are also frequent lunches in halls, drinks in the clerks' room on Friday evenings, and a Christmas party which usually brings everybody together each year.

The Bar

And finally...
You need both a strong dose of academic intellect and a head for business law to work at this busy commercial set.

Littleton Chambers

The facts

Location: Inner Temple, London
Number of QCs/juniors: 13/40 (9 women)
Applications: 200
Outside Pupillage Gateway
Pupils per year: 2
Seats: 3x4 months
Pupillage award: £45,000 (can advance £10,000 for BPTC)

Since 2006, only two of Littleton's pupils have not been offered tenancy.

"Proactive in pushing business development," Littleton is known for top-drawer employment, commercial litigation and professional negligence work.

Citius, altius, fortius

"What attracted me to this set is that it is forward-looking, keen at marketing and progressive," one pupil told us. Littleton has indeed 'progressed' of late, increasing in size by a quarter since 2007, from 44 members to 53. It was also one of the first sets to appoint a CEO. That position is now split into administrator and commercial director roles. The latter is currently fulfilled by Nigel McEwen, a solicitor who was previously managing partner of a small City firm. *"It is unusual for a set to hire a solicitor into the role I have,"* he tells us, *"but one of my responsibilities is to go out, meet solicitors and give feedback to members and clerks on what our clients are looking for and what our perceived strengths and weaknesses are."* A business development manager – also a former solicitor – has been hired to help McEwen in his role. As well as revamping management and marketing, Littleton recently renovated its offices to give them a more modern look and is investing in bringing in more work from overseas, with a particular focus on the CIS region.

Employment law is Littleton's forte and makes up 60% of its work. *"The great thing about this area of law is that it is commercial, but there is a people perspective too,"* one pupil reflected. *"You also get the opportunity for advocacy at an early stage."* Chambers UK ranks Littleton as one of the three best employment sets in London and it has one of the biggest stables of specialist employment barristers anywhere. There are also five Chambers-ranked commercial litigation barristers, and this area makes up around 25% of the set's work, with the remaining 15% being professional negligence and one or two smaller specialisms (sports is one of these, and two Littleton bar-

risters were among the 15 selected to resolve disputes between athletes, coaches and participating nations during the 2012 Olympics).

Employment work breaks down into two broad types (most of Littleton's tenants do both). There's 'statutory' work – unfair dismissal claims, tribunal work and so on. For example, one member defended law firm Clyde & Co in the Employment Appeals Tribunal against a whistle-blowing claim by a former partner. Then there are 'civil' or common law employment cases: contractual disputes, bonus claims, breach of fiduciary duty claims, team move cases and the like. These tend to be bigger and hinge around commercial contracts. For instance, Littleton barristers acted on both sides of a High Court case between QBE Insurance and a rival over breach of fiduciary duty and misuse of confidential information by a departing team. The set has also represented Savile Row tailors Ede & Ravenscroft, disgraced police commander Ali Dizaei, Gordon Ramsay's father-in-law and the governor of the Tower of London in employment scraps. Industrial disputes are another breadwinner, and could be on the up given the current state of the economy. Commercial litigation is conducted by a distinct 'practice group' of barristers, and Nigel McEwen tells us Littleton aims to expand this practice until it makes up around half of chambers' work.

Pupil people

"Our barristers deal with people, so they have very high levels of interpersonal and emotional skills as well as very strong academic credentials," says Nigel McEwen. But don't think you'll get pupillage at Littleton just by being

Chambers UK rankings

Employment

a people-person. *"There is no substitute for a strong academic background: getting a good degree from a good university,"* says pupillage committee chair Dale Martin. We'd add that a good degree usually means a First, and a good university often means Oxford or Cambridge (although the set's 2011/12 pupil was a King's graduate). Martin adds that *"the difference between a good and a brilliant CV is being able to show you have strong advocacy and communication skills."* The set doesn't expect applicants to have any prior experience of employment law.

Around 20 of the 200 or so applicants make it to a first interview, lasting 30 minutes. Candidates are given documentation about a case study and then asked for their legal opinion on it. Fifteen make it through to the next round, a three-day assessed mini-pupillage. *"It gives us a real chance to observe their interpersonal skills, ability to master information and even things like punctuality. It also allows the applicants to obtain a good feeling for what practicing in our chambers is really like,"* says Dale Martin. Mini-pupils are also judged on three pieces of advisory drafting work and an assessed legal exercise. Twelve candidates get through to a final interview, which covers a pre-set legal problem question. *"Our process is fairly intense,"* Martin admits. *"In interviews we look for people able to make points clearly and succinctly and hold out well under fire. Our interviews are culture-free and not based on personality."*

Employment advocates

Pupillage consists of four three-month seats with four supervisors. Most are employment barristers, although as of 2012 there is also one commercial supervisor and *"you do get to work on purely commercial cases for other members."* Pupillage starts with a grace period during which *"your supervisor makes sure you don't have too much on your plate and you always finish at 6pm."* Pupils draft opinions, skeleton arguments, research notes and bits of pleadings. After four months things stop being so *"laid back"* and pupils start to take on work from other members of chambers and shadow them in court. *"Your supervisor is the gatekeeper of that work,"* a pupil tells us. *"If another member wants you to do work for them they put in a request with your supervisor, who also seeks out interesting pieces of work for you."*

In addition, second-six pupils have their own caseload and are up on their feet perhaps once a week. *"Oral advocacy is what it is all about. If you don't want to do that don't come here,"* says Dale Martin. *"My first advocacy was on a race discrimination unfair dismissal case,"* recalled one junior tenant. *"I also worked on quite a few multi-day cases and appeared in front of a registrar in Companies Court."* Pupils also do enforcement applications, case management hearings, pre-hearing reviews and pick up judgments.

As if all this doesn't make pupils busy enough, there are four *"tough"* advocacy assessments and two written assessments to contend with. Furthermore, each supervisor produces a report, while every piece of written work pupils complete for other members of chambers is reviewed and given a mark out of ten. Pupils have full access to these reviews. The tenancy decision is taken *"democratically"* by an all-member meeting. *"There is no official recommendation from the pupillage committee,"* a junior tells us. *"Each supervisor makes a presentation and says whether they are supporting the pupil."* Our sources agreed that the views of supervisors – and by extension the quality of work – are key to the decision, with lesser weight given to feedback on your live advocacy and the assessed exercises. Two out of three pupils were offered tenancy in 2013.

Some sets leave marketing and business development to the clerks; at Littleton, barristers are closely involved too. *"I am on the business development committee,"* a junior told us. *"We organise a lot of talks and social events, often designed to get young barristers and solicitors together."* Pupils attend these events and are expected to network their socks off as *"ambassadors for chambers."*

The slick corporate look of Littleton's offices and its renewed business focus make us suspect that in future the commercial side of chambers will increasingly come to dominate life here. Nevertheless, *"it is a very sociable set – lots of people are friends."* There's no chambers tea or weekly drinks as apparently *"there is no need to set it up as people naturally get together."* The set houses *"a variety of personalities and perspectives, from those who want to wear a suit every day to those in T-shirts and shorts."* Speaking of shorts, one junior was proud to tell us of a recent *"Caribbean-flavoured leaving do"* which saw shorts-wearing tenants *"limbo dancing surrounded by fake palm trees and flower garlands."*

And finally...
The quality of training Littleton offers in this interesting area of law means we fully understand why winning a pupillage here is a very competitive business.

Maitland Chambers

The facts

Location: Lincoln's Inn, London
Number of QCs/juniors: 25/42 (11 women)
Applications: 170+
Outside Pupillage Gateway
Pupils per year: Up to 3
Seats: 1x3 months and 4x2 months
Pupillage Award: £60,000 (can advance £20,000 for BPTC)

"Maitland does all things commercial chancery – you're not signing up to go down a narrow path."

This leading commercial chancery set continues to thrive and is seeking out multi-jurisdictional opportunities.

Venn diagrams and international plans

Breaking down Maitland's practice areas is a potentially difficult task – *"you need a Venn diagram not a pie chart!"* joked one interviewee. *"Roughly 50 to 60% of what we do is commercial chancery while the rest is property, charity, private client, trusts, company law and insolvency."* Other areas of expertise include charities, fraud, offshore finance, partnership disputes and professional negligence. Most members *"span two to four of these areas"* but there are single-area specialists too. *Chambers UK* ranks the set in 11 distinct areas and has recognised Maitland as a top-tier commercial chancery set for ten years running.

Recent high-profile instructions have come on cases like that of Mukhtar Ablyazov, the former director of Kazakhstan's BTA Bank who's been accused of embezzling funds worth billions of dollars. Another case saw a member represent the British Phonographic Society in its successful bid to get the UK's six-biggest ISPs to block illegal peer-to-peer websites. And the set is also acting for Rangers in the wake of the club's much-publicised financial difficulties.

Maitland has an internal business development committee, which – as part of an ongoing drive to draw in more international work – is scrutinising global geographical regions with a cautious eye. *"We are looking quite thoroughly at East Asia,"* says senior clerk John Wiggs, who queries whether the market there *"will take off in the same way as many people think it will."* Maitland definitely is interested in strengthening its hand in more established jurisdictions like the British Virgin Islands and the Cay-

man Islands. And while the recession has seen areas like property and private client dip slightly *"the beauty of Maitland is that as one area goes down another goes up."* Work from the financial sector has definitely picked up. Members have recently been working on disputes relating to the collapse of Lehman and the Madoff fraud. Wiggs anticipates that more lender claims, derivatives actions and hedge fund disputes will be coming Maitland's way.

Headaches and BVI breaks

Maitland recruits outside of the Pupillage Gateway, and maintains an early deadline: applications for pupillage in 2015/16 have to be in by February 2014. Pupils described the short application form as *"an advocacy exercise in itself"* and recommend giving *"punchy"* responses – *"avoid any rambling statements."* The set whittles down 150 paper applications to 30 for the first round of interviews. These are 20-minute affairs and *"an opportunity for the set to get to know the candidate and test some basic non-legal skills."* There's also a logical reasoning problem to contend with, and those on the panel will *"try to catch interviewees off guard by putting forward a contrary position, just to see if they can hold the line or judge appropriately when to back off from it."* Between ten and 12 candidates make it through to a second interview, which consists of a *"fuller legal problem."* The panel are *"not interested in testing legal knowledge,"* so *"don't get het up because you didn't revise this bit of law or that before the interview."* Interviewers are interested in candidates' ability to assimilate information quickly and *"distil a problem down to the actual issues."*

Chambers UK rankings

Agriculture & Rural Affairs	Offshore
Chancery	Partnership
Charities	Pensions
Commercial Dispute	Professional Negligence
Resolution	Real Estate Litigation
Company	Restructuring/Insolvency
Fraud	

Four supervisors – usually between seven and 15 years' call – are chosen each year, and all pupils spend time with each one of them. *"We pick the supervisors so that they are representative of the spread of work in chambers: one might do commercial work, another property, and yet another traditional chancery."*

Pupils work alongside their supervisor *"doing everything they do."* They'll be given the papers on a case as it's ongoing and asked to draft an opinion or other documents while their supervisor is doing the same. A comparison between the two is then made and feedback provided. *"My supervisors give me their version so I can build up a dossier of good-quality work to look back at later on,"* a pupil told us. If a supervisor is *"stuck on a very big case"* pupils are given older work to do. One told us: *"Supervisors build up a bag of work which they think might be useful for a pupil to undertake. I enjoy being able to observe the litigation process on live cases and work on my own projects at the same time."* Another source added: *"Some of the work we do is unbelievably hard – I frequently leave chambers with a headache and I have to think about problems which are far more difficult than anything I ever encountered during my studies."*

The range of work experienced is *"quite something"* and pupils have to make *"rapid mental adjustments."* One told us: *"One week you might be drafting a skeleton argument for a possession hearing and the next you could be writing an opinion for a huge commercial fraud case."* The breadth of work experienced by pupils continues into the first year of tenancy. A baby junior told us they had recently been working on a bankruptcy case, a land possession hearing and a contractual contract dispute as well as *"winging off to the BVI."* Awesome! Well, *"it was a disclosure exercise so it was slightly less glamorous than it sounds...."*

Terror stakes and biscuit breaks

Pupils do not get to spend time on their feet, as the complexity of the set's work means *"it's not fair on pupils to give them their own cases during the second six."* That doesn't mean there's no advocacy though: an in-house programme consisting of six oral exercises fills the gap instead. *"Each one is based on a real set of papers and pupils will hand in a skeleton argument before conducting a hearing in front of members."* Pupils described the exercises as *"hard work"* and *"one of those terrifying experiences that you enjoy nonetheless."* Luckily, supervisors set aside preparation time and to ensure fairness the same members evaluate each exercise for all pupils. Interviewees also appreciated the *"quality and detail"* of the feedback provided afterwards.

Throughout their year with Maitland, pupils' progress is monitored by both their supervisors and the advocacy assessors. After each seat supervisors fill out an assessment form and twice during pupillage there's a sit-down chat to discuss the comments. Nine months in, supervisors and advocacy assessors get together to decide whether to recommend a pupil for tenancy. *"People who have seen your work have the most input into the ultimate tenancy decision."* In 2013, two out of the three pupils were kept on as tenants.

Despite its slick interior furnishings, Maitland is a *"relaxed set"* according to our interviewees. *"It's not the type of place where the most senior person gets the best choice of biscuits,"* but there's *"a respect and deference to senior people where it's due."* Pupils said that *"everyone is keen to make you feel as much a part of things as possible,"* while members called the set *"very democratic."* How so? *"There have been a number of occasions when decisions have effectively been dictated by the needs of the junior end rather than the senior one."*

Maitland's 'pubco' organises regular pub-based socials. *"Every Thursday someone will ping around an e-mail inviting people out for a drink. It's usually the juniors who attend, and it's good to have the opportunity to catch up with people who you usually only see fleetingly."* There's chambers tea every day, which is *"a little more formal: some people use it as a place to discuss legal problems, but it's a social gathering too and people enjoy gossiping about judges and funny things that have happened in court."*

And finally...

Some of the work may be so complicated it's headache-inducing, but pupils certainly enjoy the challenge and the breadth of work available at this set.

The Bar

Matrix Chambers

The facts

Location: Gray's Inn, London
Number of QCs/juniors: 27/47 (30 women)
Applications: 250
Outside Pupillage Gateway
Seats: 4x3 months
Pupillage award: £50,000 (can advance £10,000 for BPTC)

"Some sets may put ethics first; some put commerce first: we try to mix the two."

Its pioneering human rights work and a star cast of QCs has made Matrix one of the most famous businesses in the legal profession.

Dodging bullets

"Founded to do things differently to how they are done at the traditional Bar," Matrix caused quite a stir when 22 barristers from seven different sets created it in April 2000. With swish modern premises and a businesslike brand-focused strategy, not to mention pet fish, it was an outlier in an often staid world. Today, more and more chambers have CEOs, business strategies and contemporary offices, and *"Matrix may be less 'different' to other sets than it used to be."* But its brand and practice have been a roaring success: its casework litters the pages of the mainstream press. *"It is important we have a recognisable brand,"* says chief executive Lindsay Scott. That brand includes everything from work quality to job titles: Matrix dubs its clerks 'practice managers' and pupils 'trainees', as *"changing the vocabulary gets rid of the upstairs-downstairs mentality of 'members' and 'clerks'."*

Matrix clocks up ten Chambers rankings and – although best known for its human rights work – trainees said: *"There is so much to choose from in terms of practice."* The *"cool"* areas of crime and public law (including human rights, education and immigration) make up about a quarter of the set's work, with the rest split between media, employment, tax/competition, commercial and public international law.

Cool shades

Matrix was founded just after the Human Rights Act came into force, and its barristers have been involved in some of the most famous matters of the past decade. Terrorism-related cases – from the Jean Charles de Menezes shooting to the detention of Iraqi civilians – continue to be a large area of work. Members also worked on a European Court of Human Rights case on the legality of the police use of 'kettling'.

Immigration barristers were recently active on *HJ (Iran) & Another v Secretary of State for the Home Department* – concerning an Iranian national using his right to a gay lifestyle as a base for an asylum claim. Other members won the deportation appeal for alleged Russian spy Ekaterina Zatuliveter (who had been working for Lib Dem MP Mike Hancock in Parliament).

"Crime work is quite confronting," a trainee told us. *"In my first week I attended an inquest about a man who had been killed outside a nightclub by a gang of people ten years ago. We actually got an admission during evidence revealing who had done it. It was hugely emotional for the family."* Admittedly crime is overwhelmingly of the privately funded kind, meaning *"there is not so much blood and gore."* Fraud is a mainstay. Barristers recently defended property tycoons Robert and Victor Tchenguiz in a multibillion-pound investigation related to the collapse of Icelandic bank Kaupthing.

"Media has been a growth area for us over the past year," says Lindsay Scott: super-injunctions, phone hacking, the Leveson Inquiry, the extradition of Julian Assange – Matrix has been all over it. *"Media law guru"* Hugh Tomlinson QC has been heading up the group claim against News International brought by more than 50 victims of phone hacking. *"I was thrown straight into the world of phone hacking and super-injunctions,"* one trainee beamed. *"I also worked with Lorna Skinner and Anthony White QC preparing submissions and closing documents for Module 2 of the Leveson Inquiry."* Unsurprisingly, *"you have to be careful not to be drawn into the glamour of it all. But it is fascinating to be part of such a topical issue."*

The Bar

Chambers UK rankings

Administrative & Public Law	Employment
	Environment
Civil Liberties & Human Rights	Fraud
	Immigration
Competition/European Law	POCA Work & Asset Forfeiture
Crime	
Defamation/Privacy	Police Law
Education	Public International Law

Competition and employment are two other major areas of practice we should mention. Rhodri Thompson QC recently acted for MasterCard in a dispute with the European Commission on whether its international credit and debit card fees breached EU competition laws. When it comes to employment, members were active on the much-publicised *Eweida v British Airways* case about the rights of BA staff to wear religious jewellery in the workplace. The set also has a line in representing individuals, employer and trade unions – notably UNISON – in employment tribunals.

Long black coats

Trainees spend time with four different supervisors, often sampling four different areas of Matrix's work. *"I felt like a kid in a candy shop with all the different areas to choose from,"* one told us. One interviewee had completed seats in prison law, education, immigration and competition, while another had done immigration, media, crime and education. Unusually, *"you get genuine input into who you sit with. Half way through my first seat I had coffee with Lindsay Scott and we talked about who I might want to work with next."*

"I was never given an old piece of work to practise on," one trainee told us. *"Mostly my supervisor would give me their work to do first. For example, I drafted grounds for a judicial review in a prison and police law case. Most of the time he would end up using some of it, but in a significantly amended state."* With all these big silk-led cases around you'd think there would be few cases for trainees to take on themselves. You'd be wrong. All our interviewees had had their own cases as a trainee, most gaining advocacy experience too. Employment Tribunal work is a common first starter, but Magistrates' and Crown Court work are up for grabs too. Through choice, some trainees do more advocacy than others. *"I was on my feet a couple of times during my second six,"* one trainee told us. *"It can be quite a roller coaster. One of my first cases was a bail application*

hearing. I acted for a man with learning difficulties who had been detained for two years pending deportation."*

You'll need some pretty impressive credentials to get a look-in here. The four trainees the set took on between 2010 and 2012 had respectively worked: in Afghanistan; for the ECHR in Strasbourg; for the Yugoslavia Tribunal in The Hague; and for the Lord Chief Justice. *"After a Masters degree and two years' work experience I felt more prepared for pupillage,"* one told us. So if you've graduated and want to work at Matrix, go and do something interesting for a year or two and then apply. *"We don't penalise people for not having saved the world three times over,"* joked Tom Linden QC, head of Matrix's management committee, *"but having done voluntary or other work which they have really put their heart and soul into is important."* Matrix offered membership to its one trainee.

Taking the red pill

With its record representing individuals against the government in human rights and public law cases, you may wonder whether Matrix is on a mission. Well, in part. *"We want to pursue the ethical side of legal practice, as well as being commercial,"* says Tom Linden. *"Some sets may put ethics first; some put commerce first: we try to mix the two. We represent banks and big businesses as well as individuals."* Matrix is committed to pro bono work, which makes up about 10% of its practice. *"We're pushed to take some on,"* a trainee told us. *"I have a special education needs case coming up soon."* Members have in the past worked with the charity Reprieve on death row cases and one tenant even spent a year in the Gaza Strip working with the Palestinians.

Matrix is one of the few sets that does do corporate culture. *"Our brand and strong identity mean everyone buys into the idea of a sense of community,"* one trainee said. *"It is a really sociable place. We have a weekly Thursday lunch in our 'chill-out area'. Nobody talks about law. We're more likely to talk about the quality of that week's food."* Maletti's pizzeria apparently provides the best Thursday lunches. It's just across the road, opposite the Yorkshire Grey which is *"Matrix's default pub – we have Matrix drinks there every few weeks. There is always a good mix of barristers and staff, and the Matrix credit card will be put behind the bar."* We were also told about the *"Matrix"* Christmas and summer parties. And yes, our interviewees did use the word 'Matrix' that often – it seems even going to the pub can't escape the branding exercise.

And finally...

No, it's not named after the 1999 Keanu Reeves movie. Matrix also means an environment of substance in which a thing is developed'.

"Going to my first interview I was frightened because I hadn't been to Bar School and didn't know about procedures or rules in the profession. But my interview wasn't a technical one testing me on areas of law – it was about how I reacted and behaved when I didn't know the precise answer to a question."

Pupil barrister

The Bar

Monckton Chambers

The facts

Location: Gray's Inn, London
Number of QCs/Juniors: 14/41 (15 women)
Applications: 150-200
Apply through Pupillage Gateway
Pupils per year: 2
Seats: 4x3 months
Pupillage award: £60,000 (can advance **£20,000** for the BPTC)

On chambersstudent.co.uk... Read an extended version of this feature

Monckton barristers *"work hard on brain-aching problems"* related to EU, competition and public law.

Monckey business

Monckton Chambers has been enjoying a boom period. According to a recent article in *The Lawyer*, its revenue swelled by 59% between 2007 and 2012 (to £21m) and it's the fastest growing set in the UK top 30. That same *Lawyer* spread featured a photoshoot of some of chambers' up-and-coming young QCs sitting awkwardly on a branch, highlighting the crop of excellent juniors that have come though the ranks in recent years.

"There's a sense that there's plenty of work in this area," says a member. Monckton's forte is EU and competition law, and with more and more cases going to the European courts it's hard to argue with that. The other *"core areas" "* in which chambers excels are public law and regulatory, procurement, telecoms and VAT – all recognised with top-tier *Chambers UK* rankings.

Furthermore, *"we're looking to develop areas that complement our core practices,"* says clerk John Keegan, *"so, for example, we're putting efforts into the financial services area, where there's a clear synergy with our regulatory experience."* Monckton was recently involved in the Icesave dispute, which resulted from the 2008 collapse of Landsbanki. The governments of the UK and the Netherlands sought to compensate those who had invested in the bank and went after Iceland for the money. Chambers will use its work on high-profile cases such as this as a *"springboard"* to win more work in that area. Among many other headline matters that members have worked on is *R (Shoesmith) v Ofsted & Others*, which arose out of the death of Baby P.

In competition for competition

A Master's in competition law isn't required to get in here, though an interest in the field would obviously help. If you don't know much about the areas and are wondering what the appeal might be, here's how a junior summed it up: *"The reason I love it is that it's a wonderful eclectic mix of work on big commercial cases which have public law points. You find yourself advising on public law while at the same time being stretched to think in a commercial way."* It is *"cerebral"* work, and there's no point pretending that anything other than the highest academic qualifications are necessary. Examine members' profiles on the set's website and you'll see what we mean.

Something more is needed, though, and if you can demonstrate *"ambition"* and *"dynamism"* through your extracurriculars, your application may be one of the 40 or so that gets through to the first interview stage. This is *"as relaxed as an interview can be"* – a *"getting-to- know you session"* with two or three juniors, covering mainly CV-related topics. After this stage, promising candidates who haven't yet done a mini-pupillage with Monckton are invited to do one. This isn't assessed but it's a chance for both chambers and applicant to get a closer look at each other.

The second-round interview is the tough one. About 20 applicants get through to this, and have half an hour to look at a problem which they'll then be quizzed on by silks and juniors acting the part of difficult clients. *"Our head of chambers always starts by saying we're going to be horrible, but we are trying to see what you're capable of. It's an insight into what people are like and how they do under pressure."* One member of the pupillage committee gave the example of a recent successful candidate:

Chambers UK rankings

Administrative & Public Law	Public Procurement
	Tax
Competition/European Law	Telecommunications
Environment	

"What swung the decision in their favour was that despite having got something very silly wrong, they held their own. Barristers are always under pressure and do make mistakes, and you have to be professional about it, acknowledge it and yet remain in control of a meeting. Some candidates are like a rabbit caught in headlights. This person handled his mistake beautifully and you could imagine putting him in front of a judge or a client and him handling that situation."

Just say no

Pupillage takes the form of four three-month seats, and there's an effort to ensure pupils see the whole spread of chambers' work, *"so in my first seat I was sitting with a competition lawyer, my second supervisor did a mix of EU and commercial law, and my third did a mix of competition and human rights,"* recalled one source. The tenancy decision comes at the end of the third seat, so the final one is *"almost a handover seat"* to ease pupils into full practice.

Sources recalled starting by taking on discrete pieces of work mainly for their supervisor – *"typically they'll say, 'I've got a write an opinion on this by next week, why don't you try the first draft?'"* Gradually, other members of chambers will start to send over work: *"You'll tend to get asked to do the first draft of a skeleton or a research note so that they can see how you present things."* To ensure pupils are *"never put in a situation where you are killing yourself for too many people,"* all other barristers have to come through the supervisor to give pupils work, *"and if the supervisor says no, it means no."* Nor are pupils expected to regularly work longer than standard office hours.

Pupils receive oral feedback on every piece of work they do for barristers who aren't their supervisor, and written feedback, which pupils don't see, is sent to the tenancy committee. *"You also get quite a detailed report at the end of each seat."* There are no formal assessments (two advocacy exercises are pitched as *"practice sessions."*) Instead, everything is assessed and pupils' performance in totality is taken into account at the final reckoning. One source joked that *"everyone is entitled to one complete screw-up! It's expected that you will get something*

wrong at some point, and that you're not going to have a pile of reports with everyone saying you are phenomenal." What pupils should have amassed, however, is *"something that looks representative of a good body of work."* Anyway, Monckton has a really good record when it comes to keeping people on, and has offered tenancy to 15 out of 17 pupils since 2002, with one of its two pupils kept on in 2013.

"I enjoy written advocacy as much as oral – I didn't have dreams of wearing the wig and doing the Rumpole act," said one baby, and the nature of chambers' work does mean that *"there are fewer opportunities for second-sixers to get into court"* than in some sets. Monckton takes on a lot of very large cases which don't require rookies to get on their feet, *"but the good side to that,"* points out Tim Ward QC, *"is that pupils get to see some very heavy litigation, so they might end up as a de facto junior on a very big case worth tens of millions of pounds."* Clerks make an effort to get new tenants their own smaller cases, doing things like freedom of information and immigration tribunals which allow more opportunities for advocacy.

Smells like team spirit. Also anchovies

One junior described Monckton as *"horizontal"* in terms of hierarchy, while another cited its defining feature as *"team spirit"* – perhaps due to the fact that members are so often *"sitting on the floor together at midnight eating pizza from a box"* when working on those very big cases. We mentioned those branch-perching young QCs earlier – there aren't many silks who could pass as the lead singer of an indie band but Daniel Beard is probably one of them. Barristers like him and Tim Ward, senior figures who can still remember the days when their own wigs were pristine, are clearly appreciated by juniors.

Not that the older generation are unapproachable: one source recalled the only time they'd ever been reprimanded, on entering the office of a senior QC: *"He's the nicest man you'll ever meet, and he has this open-door policy where he says, 'Don't knock, just come in and if I'm on the phone I'll ask you to wait a minute.' I couldn't bring myself to enter without knocking, so I kept on doing it, and that's the only thing I've ever been told off for – not just walking straight in to someone's room!"* All in all, we left Monckton with the impression that it's a fairly level-headed place with a sensible attitude to life at the Bar and members who keep calm even at stressful times.

The Bar

And finally...
Monckton is a set in good shape with a lot to offer super-bright applicants.

4 New Square

The facts

Location: Lincoln's Inn, London

Number of QCs/juniors: 19/55 (16 women)

Applications: 160

Outside Pupillage Gateway

Pupils per year: 2-3

Seats: 2x3 + 1x6 months

Pupillage award: £60,000 (can advance £15,000 for BPTC)

"If you achieve the appropriate standard, you will be kept on. It's not rocket science at this set."

Located in leafy Lincoln's Inn, this dynamic commercial set has a particular penchant for professional liability work.

Common people

"Our roots are in general common law, but over the years we've developed into a diverse commercial offering," senior clerk Lizzy Stewart told us. Having moved to 4 New Square in 2000, *"we took the opportunity to focus on becoming more modern and businesslike."* 12 years on, the set is physically expanding into newly refurbished 2 New Square.

From construction and insurance to public and sports law, this set undertakes a variety of work. *"We are maintaining a focus in professional liability, however,"* Lizzy Stewart explains. *"The area still generates around 50% of our revenue."* Top-ranked by *Chambers UK* for its professional negligence work, the set was involved in 2012's most complex litigation in the Caribbean, the $2-3bn civil fraud claim arising from the collapse of Trinidad and Tobago's largest insurance company. Members also acted for Barclays Private Lending in a claim for fraud and negligence against a number of property professionals and mortgage introducers, and represented Bank of Scotland in its £10m claim against law firm Dundas & Wilson for failure to detect a potential fraud.

4NS's barristers were busy during the 2012 Olympic year, among other things representing the Montenegrin Olympic Committee in relation to the selection and participation of boxers, and working for GB Rhythmic Gymnastics in its Olympic selection dispute against the British Amateur Gymnastics Association.

Practice, practice, practice

All pupils sit with supervisors who are about nine to 15 years' call. Alex Hall Taylor, head of pupillage recruitment at the time of our interviews, said: *"We feel by that point supervisors will have developed enough of an experienced and varied practice to give pupils a broad seat. We also make a point to regularly mix in new supervisors every year, to ensure variety."* Pupils said: *"All of the supervisors do some sort of professional liability, but make sure you experience different kinds of work."* One added: *"I did the full range, from sports and Chancery to public law."* For the first six, pupils are often doing 'dead' work, but stressed how *"seriously"* feedback is taken throughout: *"Every piece of work is thoroughly discussed, and supervisors always sit down and give you a detailed assessment of how you're doing. We also have both mid and end-of-seat reviews, so you're very aware of what you need to improve on."*

Make no mistake, feedback is taken so seriously because *"every single piece of work here is assessed."* Obviously, *"for the first couple of weeks your standard of work is going be lower, but the expectation understandably rises and rises. Everything you do is marked."* Alongside work for supervisors, there are also written and advocacy assessments. One junior explained: *"Throughout pupillage you're assessed on your intellect, advocacy, temperament and motivation, and written work,"* We're told the latter carries the most weight, though *"you really need to meet an excellent standard on each."* Alex Hall Taylor says: *"Pupils also need to display that 'can-do' attitude."*

Gaining tenancy *"is the objective here. If you achieve the appropriate standard, you will be kept on. It's not rocket*

Chambers UK rankings

Construction	Product Liability
Costs Litigation	Professional Discipline
Insurance	Sports Law

science at this set," juniors said. Alex Hall Taylor added: *"All reports are reviewed and the decision is taken by chambers as a whole. The intention is to create two tenants a year. We have the work, so as long as the standard is reached we are looking to take the pupils on."* Senior clerk Lizzy Stewart said: *"We have a very structured program here and it's very strictly regulated. There are no hidden bars to reach."*

Toy cars

Advocacy plays a big part of the 4 New Square pupillage. Juniors said: *"You're not in court every day, but we're much more involved in advocacy than some peers at other commercial sets."* In the second six, pupils are expected to pick up 'real work' and get on their feet. *"You're not going to the Court of Appeal, mind you,"* pupils said. *"It's more on the Bow County Court level, and you're always supported by your supervisors."*

Pupils are also supported by a thorough advocacy training programme called 'First Days on Your Feet.' *"It's training in all major areas you're likely to be in court for. You'll have one hour on mortgages, one on motor accidents, one for small claims, and so on. It's practical exercises all the way through and is incredibly helpful."* One junior added: *"As a tradition, whoever gives the road traffic accident session gives a set of toy model cars to the pupil. They're actually a very useful tool in court, but it's also something you can keep and remind you of your learning days."* Take in all the training you can, because pupils are required to take part in an assessed moot in their first six. Run by a former member, and now High Court judge, this experience forms a good part of the tenancy decision.

Strong characters

4 New Square isn't part of the Pupillage Gateway. The set has its own application form, which you can download off the website. *"In every application we're looking for intellect, motivation, personal qualities, evidence of leadership and advocacy potential,"* says Alex Hall Taylor. *"This assessment process will cut numbers by 70 to 80%."* Out of all applicants, about 40 to 50 people are invited for a short CV-focused interview, which reduces the numbers further to between ten and 20. A second-round,

"much longer and more formal" interview follows. *"This is focused on both legal and ethical questions. There's also an advocacy exercise,"* says Hall Taylor. *"Often you're asked to argue a certain point and then argue the complete opposite,"* junior members disclosed, *"to assess how you formulate your arguments."* Finally, candidates attend a non-interview based meeting with members of the set, after which offers are made. Increasingly, previous candidates are re-applying and several people have been successful at the second time of asking.

"Realistically, not everyone has a Masters from Harvard and a First from Oxford, but those people are out there," says Hall Taylor, so strong academics are a must if you're going to compete. Otherwise, 4 New Square expects a *"degree of self-confidence without the arrogance."* A junior said: *"We are quite an outgoing set and applicants should be excited to be a part of that."* As this chambers has a proud advocacy history, *"we would also expect our applicants to have a hunger for getting on their feet. That is a vital quality in coming here,"* says Alex Hall Taylor.

Stars of the Bar in the bar at the Stars

"I wouldn't say this was a fussy, old traditional place by any stretch," pupils reflected. *"We're genuinely a lot more informal than other sets and, it sounds like a cliché, but we really are very friendly."* Although still residing in beautiful, traditional settings, it's clear there's a bright spark to this set. Our interviewees were dynamic and straightforward, and only one was in a suit – *"because I've been in court,"* we were assured. Clerks and barristers are all on a first-name basis, with juniors adding: *"It would be odd any other way, as we all get on so well."* Special commendation goes to the female presence in this set. Although there are ultimately fewer women at a senior level, Lizzy Stewart is senior clerk and the set can boast three female QCs. Juniors said: *"There are still plenty of chambers where you'll hardly see any women on a senior level, but we have very balanced numbers here. Lizzy is amazing and instils an attitude of genuine equality."*

In keeping with their non-trad vibe, there isn't afternoon tea, *"but chambers does regularly get together for breakfasts,"* juniors said. *"Everyone just chats and the QCs are always particularly keen to hear about your early court experiences."* There are also drinks *"once a fortnight"* and all are treated to a summer party. Otherwise *"there's a big junior quota and we're all very sociable."* On a Friday night, 4 New Squarers can be found at traditional barristers' hangout the Seven Stars.

The Bar

And finally...

One of the set's two pupils was awarded tenancy in 2013.

Pump Court Tax Chambers   www.chambersstudent.co.uk

Pump Court Tax Chambers

The facts

Location: Bedford Row, London
Number of QCs/juniors: 10/23 (8 women)
Applications: 80
Outside Pupillage Gateway
Pupils per year: 2
Seats: 3 core supervisors
Pupillage award: £50,000 (can advance £12,000 for BPTC)

If you're looking for an intellectual challenge, or just get a kick out of taxes, PCTC could be the perfect set.

We don't need to tell you what this chambers specialises in, but we should tell you its reputation in that field is second to none.

Getting Pump-ed up

The variety and complexity of the work done by Pump Court Tax Chambers is impressive and much greater than the three-letter word in the set's name implies. And it's not just about doing sums. In fact, they don't even really come into the equation. This set deals with some of the most interesting contentious tax issues in the country, many of which relate to fundamental principles of law. PCTC handles disputes involving elements of politics, current affairs, international business, media regulation, offshore finance and family matters.

Tax is a challenging and academically rigorous field – barristers have to get their heads around a heap of complex precedents with names like the 'Ramsay principle', the 'Redrow principle' and 'Francovich damages'. And legislation changes every year with each new Budget. *"It is interesting because it is complicated and very structured,"* says tax silk and Pump Court's pupillage committee secretary, Giles Goodfellow, *"and because taxation affects everybody, the facts of the case and the industries you work with are very diverse."*

Pump Court Tax Chambers is the only set to be top-ranked in all three categories of tax law by *Chambers UK*. Its revenue comes in equal measure from these three areas. They are: direct tax (income tax, capital gains and so on); indirect tax (including VAT and customs duties) and personal tax or private client (including trusts, inheritance tax and estates). *"It is interesting just how many areas you get involved with as a tax lawyer,"* Giles Goodfellow reflects. *"You might work on anything from a dispute over the tax deductibility of travel expenses to a corporate restructuring resulting from a divorce."* PCTC's standing is

such that in 2011 one silk was even asked by the Treasury to produce an independent study into anti-tax avoidance rules.

Around 20% of PCTC's work is advisory, but the set is increasingly litigation-heavy. Most of that consists of disputes between 'the taxpayer' (corporations, companies and individuals) and HMRC (usually dubbed 'the Revenue'). Most instructions come from the taxpayer, but PCTC is also increasingly a go-to set for HMRC. Its market standing means members frequently appear on both sides of the same dispute – for example, acting for both Marks & Spencer and HMRC in a dispute over EU law and tax relief on losses made by M&S subsidiaries in Belgium and Germany. Chambers also represented the British Film Institute in a case against HMRC, claiming that an EU cultural exemption applied to VAT on cinema tickets. As these two cases indicate, disputes often arise over perceived clashes between EU and UK law. Tax avoidance – now under increasing scrutiny by the government – also brings in a lot of business. For example, chambers acted for Ocean Finance in a dispute over the offshoring of its advertising business to Jersey for tax purposes.

Money matters

Pupils spend their first three months with one supervisor, followed by two months each with two others. *"I drafted opinions for my supervisor, attended meetings and went to court with them and produced notes,"* said one pupil. *"I also did the skeleton argument for a trusts issue."* Live work is mixed with some on cases supervisors have already completed. After this first six, pupils spend one or two weeks each with eight to ten other members of chambers. Some are silks, which means *"there is quite*

Chambers UK rankings

Tax

a bit of pressure," but *"you are usually just given one or two pieces of work and left to get on with it. And the more you draft and research, the more you know what you are doing."*

"Different areas of tax require different skills," one source told us. For example, issues of VAT and indirect tax often have an EU dimension. They can also be quite political. *"What appeals to me is that public law can play a big part in our cases,"* said one pupil. *"A case may be about a small £100 fine which HMRC imposes on people who pay their taxes late. But if that policy isn't implemented properly it can be a breach of the obligation to treat people fairly, which links to the core of the relationship between the citizen and the state."* Private client issues can be *"very personal"* and involve *"understanding family dynamics and the fact that some things are more important than money."* One pupil recalled working on a case regarding taxation on someone's redundancy payments after they lost their job.

The size and nature of PCTC's cases means pupils don't get on their feet in their second six, but they do sharpen their advocacy skills in three assessed moots involving *"a fictional set of facts, but based on a real problem."* Each moot is more complex than the last, and the final one – which comes just before the tenancy decision – is attended by around 20 members of chambers. The moots are taken into account as part of the tenancy decision, but *"the most important element of that decision is the recommendations from supervisors,"* says Giles Goodfellow. The set's single pupil did not gain tenancy in 2013, although both did in 2012.

The tax haven

Applications to PCTC begin with a CV and covering letter. First-round interviews last 30 minutes, with 20 of those dedicated to a problem question related to interpretation of a statute which candidates are presented with half an hour before the interview. *"The question is self-contained and we make the facts simple to understand. You don't need to be a tax lawyer or even a lawyer to answer them. A few years ago we asked about tax exemptions for principal private residences."* Up to eight candidates get through to a second round: a piece of written work, which candidates have eight hours to complete and can be up to 2,000 words long. Recently candidates were asked to analyse a Court of Appeals judgment.

A cosy-sized set with just over 30 tenants, PCTC is still managed fairly traditionally as a 'co-operative' of the clerks and members. Change comes at a leisurely pace: membership has increased from 24 to 33 since 2002. In the place of the usual chambers tea, members enjoy 11am morning coffee. *"It can be just social chit-chat, but usually people discuss legal issues or the cases they are working on. It can get pretty heavy sometimes, and if the top silks are there the discussion can be pretty entertaining."* Younger members tend to do more listening than talking. *"As a pupil you don't speak much, but that is because you don't know very much yet, not because they don't want to hear from you. You usually sit back and soak things up."*

"This set is small and feels like a bit of a family," said one source. Indeed, a few days before we visited, it had organised drinks to celebrate a junior member's engagement. Members enjoy occasional lunches and the odd pint together and there's a *"Christmas jolly"* to which spouses are invited. Mostly, though, members go home at the end of the day as *"everyone has a life outside chambers."* Asking for examples, we were told that Andrew Thornhill QC collects boats, fellow silk Julian Ghosh QC fences and Chambers-ranked junior Elizabeth Wilson dances the flamenco.

And finally...

PCTC is a real gem and we're surprised more students who love the academic and complex side of law haven't cottoned onto it.

Quadrant Chambers

The facts

Location: Fleet Street, London
Number of QCs/juniors: 16/39 (9 women)
Applications: 150-200
Outside Pupillage Gateway
Pupils per year: 3
Seats: 2x3 months and 1x6 months
Pupillage award: £60,000 (part of which can be drawn during the BPTC)

Quadrant operates from swanky modernised historic premises, reflecting its up-to-date and fresh approach to an ancient area of law.

Top of the game in shipping, aviation and general commercial work, Quadrant Chambers continues to be a leader at the modern Bar.

Infinity chambers

"I think we're a very modern set," juniors reflected. *"Quadrant has moved more in the direction of a business, rather than just lots of individuals. We have a CEO and are marketed as a team."* One added: *"It's all about embracing change and in many ways this is reflected in the building."* Ah yes, the building. Quadrant Chambers definitely has one of the most impressive offices we've ever set foot in. Aptly described last year as *"a bit like an M.C. Escher painting,"* Victorian stucco and grandeur complement open space and light. *"The building is almost like a firm, but its intricacies of rooms are reminiscent of the old Bar. It's a symbol of balance really,"* interviewees thought. Head of pupillage Tom Macey-Dare added: *"We do have a corporate ethos, but it only goes so far. We intend to provide the best commercial service, but there is no intention to change business model and we intend to stay an independent chambers."*

Already top-ranked by *Chambers UK* in aviation, shipping/commodities and travel, Quadrant is also looking to increase its offshore energy practice, said Macey-Dare. Members have also developed practices in areas such as insurance and reinsurance, international arbitration, insolvency and banking. Chambers has acted for the now-deceased Russian tycoon Boris Berezovsky in his successful appeal for the commission paid on the sale of his $240m super-yacht; represented Coakley (an air speed sensor manufacturer) in its case against Air France in relation to a fatal crash of June 2009; and represented JPMorgan in a $1.3bn dispute regarding oil prospecting licences in Nigeria.

The need for focus

Quadrant runs a pupillage system of two three-month seats followed by a six-month one, with a change of supervisor each time. Supervisors are chosen in regards to the different types of work they have on. Typically, each will do some form of shipping work, but the pupils *"are exposed to a variety of work, in particular the stuff you'll do upon gaining tenancy,"* juniors explained. *"Certainly when you arrive your first three months are a grace period. You take that time to become accustomed to how we do things and mistakes are almost expected."* From the second three onwards, pupils regularly get involved in real work and become a *"support for their supervisors."*

As we're talking about the Commercial Bar, pupils don't get on their feet until after the tenancy decision. Quadrant *"takes the sensible view that you need to have mastered the theory before being sent to court. By the end of the nine months, you're prepared enough with the knowledge, so can simply concentrate on the traditions of advocacy."* Once the tenancy decision is made, *"you're in court quite a bit. That's actually only three months later than your peers."* Juniors focus on a variety of general commercial work in their first couple of years.

Beyond work for their supervisor, pupils undergo written and advocacy assessments. Otherwise pupils are reliant on their supervisors to assess and teach them. *"Your supervisors are protective of you. You don't get ad hoc pieces of work from other members of chambers, so your supervisors fully assess you as a whole."*

Chambers UK rankings

Aviation	International Arbitration
Commercial Dispute Resolution	Shipping
	Travel

The process of gaining tenancy is quite straightforward. *"It's definitely not a popularity contest,"* juniors agreed. *"Ultimately it's about your work and competency levels – at every level. Even if it's photocopying or bringing documents to court, your work needs to have been consistent. A lot of pupillage is about being reliable and organised."* The emphasis *"is on learning and enjoying the work itself. If you're meeting a high standard, the expectation is that you will be taken on and they're preparing you for that."* Quadrant didn't take on either of its two pupils in 2013, but all three stayed on as tenants in 2012.

Thoughts and thinkers

"I think we have one of the most thorough application processes around, actually," says Tom Macey-Dare. Quadrant isn't part of the Pupillage Gateway, instead opting for an application form you can download off its website. *"We sift down the numbers to about 50 people. Those are sent out a set of papers, from which they need to write an opinion to be returned to the set."* Don't worry if you haven't written an opinion before. *"I hadn't done anything of the like,"* a junior said. *"Mine wasn't laid out perfectly, but then chambers isn't looking for that. They want to see that you can write well, have analysed the papers and thought of some potential solutions."* The opinion is marked blindly. *"It's one of the best things about the application – because it doesn't matter if you have a starred First from Cambridge: the assessor won't know. Decisions are made totally on the merit of your paper."*

The best 16 are called for a panel interview, where they're given two sets of papers to discuss. *"One is a passage from a judgment and the other's an ethical issue."* The interview is a chat about their opinion and the documents, with questions increasing in difficulty. *"It's not about getting the right answer, but about how you develop and present your arguments. At no stage do you require specific*

legal knowledge and all those from halfway through the GDL should be completely comfortable with the level."*

Quadrant is looking for people who *"think clearly and rationally and can thoroughly express themselves under pressure,"* says Macey-Dare. Showing interest in the Commercial Bar is clearly easier if you've done a law degree, but if you haven't, *"assess which method of learning you enjoy and which GDL subjects you like best. If you enjoy those with more factual detail and intellectual, yet practical issues, then the Commercial Bar is suited to you. Applicants need to show that they enjoy the analytical dissecting of problems on a practical scale, rather than an encyclopaedic knowledge of the business world."* Juniors stressed the importance of doing mini-pupillages although it's not a prerequisite to have done one at Quadrant. As for the firm's shipping specialism, *"you definitely don't have to be an avid sailor to want to come here,"* juniors reassured us.

We saw three shipping lawyers...

"We're pretty relaxed within chambers," juniors said. *"Everyone is very close-knit and friendly."* One source had *"even been on holiday with people from Quadrant – that closeness is encouraged here."* Interviewees thought this was partly by virtue of never being directly compared throughout your pupillage. *"I don't think I ever did the same piece of work as my fellow pupils, and ultimately if they want to, Quadrant can take everyone on. It means you can all support each other and actually become friends."* There is a certain amount of hierarchy between juniors and QCs, and pupils are still expected to wear formal dress, but we were assured *"pupils always feel integrated. Part of the suit thing is that you never know when you'll be off to court to help or observe, so it's really more common sense than anything."*

There's no official tea at the set, but *"we have both a summer and Christmas party. The Crimbo do is particularly special."* Well-known (if you listen to Classic FM) choir The Sixteen are partly sponsored by chambers. *"In return they line the balcony of our library for Christmas and sing, while we enjoy mince pies and mulled wine. It's a phenomenal occasion."* Otherwise, *"there's always a fairly consistent trickle of people going down to Daly's Wine Bar on a Friday evening."*

And finally...

"You need to be comfortable with the fact that you're going to predominantly be at your desk, undertaking research and analysis. It's less about the theatrics and more about those interested in minute detail." If that's the sort of barrister you'd like to be, look up Quadrant.

The Bar

Queen Elizabeth Building (QEB)

The facts

Location: Temple, London
Number of QCs/juniors: 6/27 (15 women)
Apply through Pupillage Gateway
Pupils per year: Up to 3
Seats: 3x4 months
Pupillage award: £25,000 minimum

This top-quality family law set can also boast a caring and supportive *"family atmosphere."*

"To keep a set at the top you have to bring the best people from the bottom and that means you have to train them properly. We take pupillage really seriously and spend a lot of time improving it, structuring it, teaching, assessing and feeding back. It's not a process of following the pupil supervisor around, being ignored, and grabbing a cup of tea every now and again."

Family history

Queen Elizabeth Building has been a big name on the family law circuit for over 100 years and *Chambers UK* consistently top-ranks the set for its work in this field. What's been the secret behind such prolonged success? *"Excellence,"* Tim Amos QC responded with absolute conviction. *"People don't care if lawyers are this, that or the other; it's all about the service that's delivered. Not only in terms of the academic argument, but also the client feeling as though they were looked after. We provide excellence in the law and in interpersonal relations."*

QEB is particularly known for dealing with the financial consequences of relationship breakdowns but has vast experience in all aspects of family law including: jurisdictional disputes, foreign divorces, premarital agreements, civil partnerships, injunctions, forced marriage, Inheritance Act claims and an important line of child work. In addition, some members practise general common law, with personal injury and professional negligence work being the focus of their attention. Many members also continue into high judicial office and at present five Family Division judges are former QEB-ers while another, Lord Wilson of Culworth, sits in the Supreme Court. Legal Aid – despite the cuts – still accounts for a portion of the set's work, *"especially at the junior end,"* but chambers handles cases for an *"absolutely huge"* range of clients. One junior explained: *"Everybody has family problems and the most difficult of those go to court no matter who you are. We look after the whole spread – the* rich and famous, all the way down to people who literally have nothing."

Family ties

The set receives around 180 applications through the Pupillage Gateway each year, with up to three individuals then taken on as pupils. Tim Amos says: *"We've always been on the smaller side, even if it's bigger now than when I started [in 1988]. That enables us to keep a family atmosphere among the members of chambers."* However, pupils should feel no undue pressure to outdo their cohorts, as space can always be found for the right candidate. *"Because we don't deal in quotas, it's not a question of the pupils being in competition with each other. It's more subtle than that: it's a competition with themselves and a standard of excellence."* In 2013 the set took one of its three pupils on. QEB also swings the pendulum in favour of its pupils by not externally recruiting any new tenants.

Pupils are assigned three supervisors across the year, spending four months with the first, three-and-a-half months with the second, and a four-and-a-half-month stint with the third to allow pupils a longer period to show off their potential in the build up to the tenancy decision. *"The most important thing is that they get a breadth of experience with different supervisors so they can get the best out of the training system,"* says pupil supervisor Katie Cowton. Member of the pupillage committee Amy Kisser

Chambers UK rankings

Family/Matrimonial

adds: *"Your day-to-day is spent with your supervisor and you do the work they're doing and receive feedback on it. It's not like you're not left in the pupils' room by yourself. You have to create a rapport, as you end up sharing your life with them for four months."* Formal assessments kick in after the Christmas break and *"it's fair to say you're being informally assessed the rest of the time."* QEB follows the mantra of *"there's no such thing as a stupid question during your first three months. Nobody is perfect and it's very much a learning process. However, from Christmas onwards we expect pupils to know what they're doing."* A junior contact, usually a baby tenant, is also on hand *"to offer personal support or act as a go-to point for any issues you don't want to discuss with your supervisor."*

The second six provides ample opportunities to get into court. *"When you're first on your feet, you'll go once or twice a week to children hearings or simple money cases,"* says Amy Kisser. *"As a rule of thumb, you'll be in court three or four times a week by the end."* Making the transition from first to second six isn't always straightforward, though. A pupil commented: *"It's quite an adjustment to make as when you're with your supervisor you'll be doing quite high-end stuff, but when you go to court you'll come across a lot of run-of-the-mill legal aid cases. It can be difficult going from a family law injunction application in Southend to a multimillion-pound divorce the same afternoon – it's hard to make that jump in the mind."*

Family dinner

For the lucky few who secure themselves an interview, there's no need to fear an incessant grilling from people determined to catch you out. In fact you can expect a much more affable atmosphere. *"Our interview is designed to be fun,"* concludes Tim Amos. *"It's clearly challenging, but some people have likened it to a dinner party. That may sound flippant but it has this characteristic in common: it's a group of people talking as equals."* Katie Cowton concurs: *"We don't want to scare people or make them nervous because it doesn't work. We don't think we've done a good interview unless we've given the candidate the opportunity to show us what they've got."* What is QEB looking for in its potential recruits? *"Because of our specialism we're looking for a good analytical brain,"*

continues Cowton. *"We need a rounded person who can relate to a wide range of different people because it's a people-facing area. We need people who are empathetic but able to be clear in their advice. We also look for a certain self-confidence and presence, because within six months they'll take on their own clients and have to be able to convince them they know what they're doing."*

Tim Amos described the structure of the set as follows: *"When I arrived it was a benevolent dictatorship. It moved more into an oligarchy, and is now pretty close to mass democracy in the sense that we have a head of chambers [Lewis Marks QC] who is important, but he is assisted by a management committee drawn from all levels and sectors. That committee takes all the decisions."* However, there is one exception: when it comes to tenancy decisions the full set will converge for deliberations that Katie Cowton insists *"rarely take less than a few hours."*

Modern family

There's no denying a sense of the traditional remains at this family law stalwart. Afternoon tea runs like clockwork at 4pm every day and *"as a pupil it's a great way of hearing what cases are going on and to generally pick up what's happening in chambers."* Clerks will address members mister or missus, but this formality masks a much closer relationship between these two factions within the set. Amy Kisser told us: *"I was talking to my dad the other day and was adamant I'd told him something, but it turned out it was [senior clerk] Ivor [Treherne] that I'd spoken with. That was worrying. The clerks run your life for you and they really look after us. They treat you with the utmost respect regardless of whether you're the head of chambers or the bottom baby."*

QEB is more progressive than it may initially seem, though. *"Lots of people think we're really traditional – shooting, hunting, fishing types,"* says Kisser. *"That's not true at all. From the bottom end and now up, we're very modern. We may have traditional values in that we support and care for each other, but equally we have a wide array of members too. Nobody would ever feel like they don't fit the mould here, because there just isn't one."* Tim Amos also believes the set has progressed significantly since he joined: *"Definitely it's changed, and definitely for the better. At the time I arrived QEB was said to be rather stuck-up. There may have been some truth in that but I don't think people would say it about us now. We're all pretty outgoing and available to other people."*

And finally...

"You feel safe and secure here," a pupil told us. *"You will have a nice year, and if you're successful you'll have a nice practice. If you're not, then you can guarantee you'll be taken on somewhere else."*

The Bar

Serle Court

The facts

Location: Lincoln's Inn, London
Number of QCs/juniors: 20/33 (6 women)
Applications: Around 150
Outside Pupillage Gateway
Pupils per year: 2
Seats: 4 x 3 months
Pupillage award: £60,000 (can advance £20,000 for BPTC)

"People might think that we just look at trust deeds all day, but that's not true. It's tough to convey the breadth of practice this set offers."

Inclusive and innovative, this leading commercial chancery set continues to cultivate a diverse practice.

The times they are a-changin'

Serle Court has its roots in a 2000 merger between a chancery and a commercial set. An innovative move at the time, but as one member points out: *"It's interesting that other chancery sets have now moved into commercial work too, and vice-versa."* That may be the case, but Serle Court has gone on to become one of the largest in its field, and it brandishes 11 practice area rankings in *Chambers UK. "There's a lot of fraud, offshore, probate and contentious trusts work, some straightforward commercial work, quite a lot of partnership disputes and company cases,"* one member informed us. *"But our practice varies from one year to the next. If you had said ten years ago that in 2013 we would be working on lots of Russia-related litigation everybody would have laughed!"* Members were recently embroiled in one the largest group of fraud actions ever brought to the High Court, while other fraud cases have revolved around a Russian oil company, a goldmine in Kazakhstan and the privatization of state property in Azerbaijan. Other commercial chancery work has plunged members into disputes over Liverpool Football Club and a Chinese accountancy firm.

Interviewees told us that one legacy of the 2000 merger is that this set *"continues to move forward and be open to people with new areas of expertise – cross-fertilisation of ideas can be really helpful."* A number of 'lateral hires' have joined Serle to do work which didn't exactly fall within its traditional remit. For example, Michael Edenborough QC joined the set in 2008 to do IP law, while Conor Quigley QC arrived in 2010 as an expert on all things EU law. *"These are both practice areas which we didn't have before these arrivals, but still these individuals came to us."*

Serle receives around 150 applications each year. Recruiters are on the lookout for advocacy ability, even at the paper stage. However, *"students often think it's all about oral advocacy,"* one member told us, *"but written advocacy is very important in this area of the law – we want people who can be persuasive and concise on paper."* In order to be in with a shot at starting a pupillage in October 2015, applications must be submitted by noon on February 3rd, 2014.

Between 30 and 45 candidates make it through to a first-round interview, which is *"fairly friendly but quite probing."* There's a *"part-legal"* problem question to mull over, but interviewees shouldn't expect to get bogged down by the finer points of the law at this stage. Around ten are invited back for a second interview – *"a role-play conference scenario which includes more legal reasoning."* One baby junior recounted that *"in retrospect the interview was hilarious – my interviewers had a bit of competition to see who could come up with the most fun problem."*

Liar liar

Each pupil has four supervisors throughout the year, and spends three months with each. "We like to have a mixture of new supervisors and people who have done it before," said one source, and although *"very few people cover our entire spectrum of work,"* an effort is made to pick supervisors who work in several areas, rather than specialists.

The current set of pupils had experienced a wide variety of work, including offshore cases, company disputes and *"large commercial cases involving Russian oligarchs."*

Chambers UK rankings

Banking & Finance	Offshore
Chancery	Partnership
Commercial Dispute	Professional Negligence
Resolution	Real Estate Litigation
Company	Restructuring/Insolvency
Fraud	

Supervisors *"get you involved in their current cases, which makes everything more exciting."* One pupil had experienced *"a three-week trial all the way through,"* and was surprised to see a strong human element in this large Russia-related fraud case: *"It had all the commercial complexity that you'd expect, but underlying it all was the question of whether these blokes had lied at some point. You can imagine that the characters involved were quite eccentric..."*

By the third seat, it's not uncommon to be doing work for other members too, *"partly so that your work gets seen by them, but also to give you a broader experience."* Work in given to pupils via their supervisors so *"you don't have that awkward situation of being asked to do work that you don't have time for."* Beyond drafting skeleton arguments, research notes, particulars of claim and defences, pupils spend a lot of time *"preparing for conferences, and trying to set down the ways in which we'll try to convince the client to do what's in their own best interest – that involves commercial as much as legal knowledge."*

Bridging the gap

Mock advocacy sessions take place once every two to three months: *"We do different types of exercises and put pupils in front of different members of chambers with different judging styles."* Exercises may involve *"straightforward applications"* or *"more intensive applications with skeleton arguments."* There's also a mock client conference. *"It's one of those things which you'd think would be quite easy, but in practice it's quite intimidating."* Pupils get plenty of time to prepare, and said that *"you get constructive feedback about what might happen in practice."*

Halfway through their time with the set, pupils are given feedback on their performance. If weaknesses are identified, then the conversation gives pupils a snap-shot of *"where you are now compared to where you should be. If someone is so far off that tenancy looks unlikely then we may advise them that the Bar isn't for them."* Any member who has seen a pupil's work *"gets some sort of input"* in the tenancy decision, but supervisors have the most influence. Pupils are told of the decision in either May or June each year.

Pupils were struck by the fact that *"the atmosphere in chambers doesn't fit the stereotypical image of what a chancery set is like – we are far more laid back."* The most junior members occupy rooms *"right next to the head of chambers, and he'll pop in and say hello, meaning any potential gap in the hierarchy is bridged."* It's a *"very live and let live environment, and everybody is able to fashion the practice that they want. If you want to be working 20 hours a day then that's fine, and if you want a more varied practice that's fine too. There's a sense of collectivity, but that comes from recognising individual aspirations and not making value judgements about them."*

In this *"inclusive"* culture, future pupils are included from the outset: *"As soon as you accept the offer of pupillage, you are invited to celebratory drinks and chambers lunches to ensure you meet the members and current pupils."* This trend continues into pupillage, when pupils are invited to client events, including a client party which occurs every 18 months and was most recently held at the Museum of London. There's also a Christmas party each year and Friday drinks in the clerks' room. For caffeine lovers, there's daily morning coffee and afternoon tea, and pupils told us they *"feel comfortable making conversation – tea is quite far removed from the , 'let a silk hold court' model and we're positively encouraged to speak!"* Informal drinks are also organised *"every now and again,"* and although the night *"often starts in the Members' Common Room in Lincoln's Inn,"* members have a free-spirited approach to how their evening will progress...

The Bar

And finally...

Offering a *"combination of incredible intellect and intense niceness,"* Serle Court remains a great choice for ambitious barristers. In 2013, two out of three pupils were offered tenancy.

South Square

The facts

Location: Gray's Inn, London
Number of QCs/juniors: 21/20 (7 women)
Applications: 150
Outside Pupillage Gateway
Pupils per year: 2
Seats: 6x6 weeks
Pupillage award: £60,000 (some can be drawn down for BPTC)

A sleek modern set with a hint of the City about it

South Square does some of the best insolvency and restructuring work in London.

Top billing

Insolvency has always been this set's top focus. *"We have several financial, commercial and business practices here, but insolvency and restructuring is at our core and we intend to stay at the top of our specialism,"* says pupillage director Martin Pascoe QC. Top-ranked by *Chambers UK* for insolvency, South Square is also highly rated for its banking/finance and offshore expertise. About one-quarter of the set's work now involves offshore disputes. *"There's also been an increase in our sport and shipping work this year,"* Pascoe says. Located in picturesque Gray's Inn, chambers has recently undergone renovation. *"You have to move with the times,"* says senior practice manager Michael Killick.

"We've basically been involved in every large insolvency that's been," says Michael Killick. Judging from the case list, this is a pretty accurate statement. From Lloyds, Enron, Woolworths, Madoff Securities to Lehman and Swissair, the list of big names brought low is almost endless, and in these troubled times business is good. Interviewees were drawn to the set for its *"excellent reputation"* and market focus, but stressed the set's focus on heads-down research and complex analysis. As one explained: *"Insolvency covers a range of legal disciplines, so requires a wealth of legal knowledge. This in turn needs to be intertwined with a full understanding of the business world."*

Southern Exposure

South Square pupils sit with a different supervisor every six weeks (which usually works out at about six to eight supervisors across the course of pupillage). *"It's really one of the best things about doing a pupillage here,"* said one source. *"It not only gives you exposure to the different practices we have, but also allows you to get to know more members of chambers. Six weeks is just the right amount of time to observe and immerse yourself in the work."* Another said: *"It also exposes you to a variety of working styles, helping you develop your own."* Pupillage director Martin Pascoe added: *"From our point of view we think it's better for a greater number of members to assess the pupils on an extended basis. We don't think it's enough, or indeed fair, for them simply to be assessed on the odd piece of work here and there."* Around April, pupils return to their first supervisor, *"so chambers can evaluate your progression,"* Pascoe said. One pupil added: *"It's evidence of how carefully orchestrated the system is, and how seriously training is taken here."*

As with any system, there are downsides. *"It'd be a lie not to say you're thrown into the deep end every six weeks. It isn't a huge length of time, so there is slightly less grace period in which to make mistakes. It also makes it doubly important to make a good personal impression from the offset."* Sources did add: *"Although not always easy, it's very reflective of practice and real life. You're given excellent work from day one, and although nerve-wracking, it's the best way to learn."* Each supervisor has an informal review with the pupil at the end of the six weeks, followed by a formalised appraisal after the first six months. *"You know how you're doing throughout."*

Pupils won't get on their feet until after the tenancy decision. *"The sort of work we do is of labyrinthine complexity, remember,"* sources said. *"There's a huge amount of documentation and research, and the emphasis of the pupillage needs to be on how to conduct the appropriate analysis."* Martin Pascoe added: *"That's the nature*

The Bar

Chambers UK rankings

Banking & Finance	Offshore
Chancery	Restructuring/Insolvency
Company	

of the commercial Bar. Cases are larger and there will inevitably be more paperwork." Interviewees agreed they *"would rather be working at a high level of law"* than getting into advocacy earlier. Once they gain tenancy, juniors are in court on average twice a week. New tenants are paired with both a junior of two to three years' call and a senior member of chambers to help them learn the ropes of advocacy.

The tenancy decision is made by the executive committee. *"Ultimately it's working hard and getting on with people,"* one junior said. As obvious as that sounds, *"you have to show that your standard of work has improved throughout and that you have deployed good personal skills. A premium really is placed on your diplomacy and client-facing abilities."* The set stresses that it never takes on more pupils than it could potentially retain. *"If you're achieving a high enough standard, you will be kept on,"* Pascoe confirmed, and the pupil taken on in 2012 was offered tenancy in 2013.

Analyse This

South Square usually takes on two (sometimes three *"if they're good enough"*) pupils a year. The set is not on the Pupillage Portal, and applications should be made using the application form (available to download from the website) and sent to the pupillage administrator at South Square by post or email. *"We review all applications and then take about 30 to 40 candidates on to the next stage,"*

says Pascoe. *"The first interview is conducted by two members and aims to test candidates' analytical abilities and ability to identify and discuss important issues."* 16 to 20 applicants are taken on to a second interview with the entire pupillage committee. *"We tend to ask each candidate a set of standardised questions, in order to give each an equal chance. We often ask them to discuss or argue an ethical issue."* On occasion, candidates are invited for a third interview, *"but normally after two we know enough."*

Sources advised: *"The most important thing is to do your research on the set. Beyond the internet, we have a chambers magazine with updates of work and cases, so reading that is a good way to get a sense of what's going on."* Additionally, *"you need to have an interest, or be prepared to develop an interest, in the financial and business world,"* they continued. *"We're in a service industry and the commercial Bar is all about the needs of clients."*

The specified academic baseline is a 2:1, but it's important to remember *"of the people applying, the level is very high across the board."* If you poke around the member bios on South Square's website, you'll find plenty of Oxbridge alumni and those with post-graduate qualifications. *"We are looking for good academics, but a good transcript isn't enough,"* says Pascoe. *"We're looking for those who can flourish in a commercially demanding environment and perform to an excellent standard under pressure."*

Chambers doesn't do tea and we get the impression there are more sociable sets out there, but the overall atmosphere of the chambers was praised for being *"measured and amiable."* *"There is a genuine emphasis on personability."* In our experience, the set is one of calm and sophistication.

And finally...

Pupils are required to wear suits. *"There's some notion of hierarchy I suppose,"* one source said, *"but it's by no means oppressive; everyone is very willing to help you."* By not being in direct competition for places, juniors said, *"the set allows you to foster wonderful and supportive relationships with fellow pupils."*

2 Temple Gardens

The facts

Location: Temple, London
Number of QCs/Juniors: 12/42 (21 women)
Applications: 259
Apply through Pupillage Gateway
Pupils per year: 1-3
Seats: 2x3 and 1x6 months
Pupillage award: £60,000 (can advance up to £22,500 for BPTC)

With an increasingly well-rounded practice, 2TG is *"forward-thinking"* but with *"the best elements of the traditional Bar."*

With well-regarded personal injury, clinical negligence, professional negligence and insurance practices, 2 Temple Gardens mixes the old with the new.

A Room with a View

2 Temple Gardens' Grade I-listed building – replete with Edwardian fireplaces and stuccoed ceilings – sits at the southern end of the Temple, with panoramic views of Inner Temple Gardens and the River Thames. Some of the antiquity of the building rubs off on its members. *"We retain the best elements of the traditional Bar,"* they say: *"We're not stuffy, but we are quite a mixed bunch and everyone is willing to help each other out."* But this is a *"forward-looking"* set, too: its building was recently renovated to give it a contemporary edge, and it puts on a large number of seminars for solicitors *"for us as barristers to sell ourselves."*

Chambers' strengths lie in personal injury and clin neg on the civil side, and in professional discipline, professional negligence and insurance disputes on the commercial side. There are also a few smaller areas of practice, such as banking and finance, property, contract disputes and employment. *"In the last two years the commercial side of this set has grown,"* says senior clerk Lee Tyler. *"We rightly have a strong reputation as a defendant insurance claims set, but our commercial practices are rapidly growing."*

Call for Poirot

Personal injury and clin neg make up 30 to 40% of the practice. Most of this is work for defendants, but there is a growing claimant practice too. NHS trusts and strategic health authorities are frequent clients in clin neg cases. Recent cases have centred on the misuse of forceps and the suicide of a mental health patient. On the PI side, members frequently represent insurers in workplace stress and harassment, asbestos disease and RTA claims. Head of chambers Benjamin Browne QC recently worked on an RTA claim worth £20m, and has represented claimants in the atomic test veterans litigation. Other claims have involved a horse startled by pigs, an escaped cow, an arm cut off by a circular saw, a schoolgirl falling out of a window and – we kid you not – an accident on the Orient Express. Appropriately, *"we sometimes have to act like detectives, as there are always new factual details which need to be investigated."*

Ranked in *Chambers UK* for both professional negligence and professional discipline work, 2TG is often instructed by professional indemnity insurers, and has built a strong reputation for acting on cases against engineers and insurance brokers as well as lawyers and financiers. In one recent case, members defended a refrigeration business against a claim brought by a pharma company over the loss of £1m worth of drugs due to a malfunctioning fridge. The set's barristers have also worked on several insurer-on-insurer disputes recently, including Municipal Mutual Insurance (MMI) v Zurich – a £70m spat over the structuring of insurance policies between 1948 and 1992 in relation to the asbestos disease mesothelioma.

Academic results – including A-levels – are most important to recruiters, followed by advocacy experience, extracurricular activities (especially leadership and teamwork), any prizes won, and interest in the set's practices. 45 applicants are invited to an assessment day, which starts with a group exercise: eight candidates at a time debate a non-legal topic. *"We were told we represented small start-up businesses and asked to argue why we should receive funding,"* one pupil recalled. Following this, applicants are given ten minutes' notice of an *"inde-*

Chambers UK rankings

Clinical Negligence	Personal Injury
Insurance	Professional Negligence

fensible" topic of which they are asked to argue in favour. Chambers also *"sets out its stall"* with presentations on each practice group and a chance to meet some of the maybe 15 tenants present. 15 candidates progress to a second interview, which includes a legal problem case study and standardised competency and CV questions.

Bingo!

Pupils sit with three supervisors over the course of the year, each usually offering experience in a different field. One source had done commercial banking and prof neg work, followed by employment and PI, and then clin neg. *"When you start, you often have a first go at your supervisor's drafting work while they are doing it too. Then they will go through it and explain what you have done right and wrong. It is gratifying if a few of your words are inserted into the final version. As you progress through pupillage more of your work gets used."* Documents to be drafted include particulars of claim, advice to clients, skeleton arguments and pleadings. *"The drafting work is factually complicated and there are a lot of precedents involved. At the end of the first six you've seen all the major bits of paperwork come by."* Pupils also receive work from other members of chambers and shadow them in court. *"I did maybe ten or 12 large pieces of work for others during my first six."*

Oral advocacy dominates the second half of pupillage. *"As soon as the second six starts you are available to be sent off to court."* Pupils often begin with infant approval hearings, moving on to small claims, fast-track trials and case management on RTA cases. *"Because of the volume and the low value of the cases, the insurers are happy for pupils to take them on. You get experience dealing with everything, from shouting judges to missing clients."* Eventually pupils are on their feet two or three times a week. *"It can be very entertaining: I once had to go to Chelmsford to represent a lorry driver called Johnny Bingo. You meet people you would never meet otherwise and for a few hours you get really obsessed by their case."*

Assessment at 2TG is a *"cumulative process"* – pupils are given appraisals after three and six months. When it comes to the tenancy decision, *"the supervisors' reports are most important, followed by oral and written feedback from other members."* Feedback from the clerks and two assessment exercises have weight too, but when it comes to the latter a baby junior says: *"I don't think the exercises impact on the tenancy decision unless you were entirely hapless."* One of the two pupils gained tenancy in 2013, a successful continuation of a strong retention rate: 2TG has taken on all but two of its eleven pupils since 2008.

Cycling PI

"This is a sociable set. There is a Christmas do, and we also recently had a party with drinks and fish and chips to celebrate part of the building being redecorated." Chambers tea is held weekly on Wednesdays: *"There is a rota and a different member hosts and brings a cake each week."* The chat is *"mostly about law. Members use it as an opportunity to talk about their recent work, but anyone can talk and there is no strict etiquette. And when you've just started your second six, everyone takes an interest and gets all nostalgic about their first time on their feet."* Weekly Friday drinks also take place and members frequently go for lunch in Middle Temple Hall. *"It is important to meet members during pupillage,"* a junior reflected, *"but it doesn't have to be during tea or the social events."*

"You come to know the varying styles and personalities of your supervisors and the other members," one pupil said. *"They are all quite different. There is never one chambers view on things."* For example, Chambers UK-ranked silk Martin Porter QC is something of a road safety campaigner. A keen cyclist, he writes a personal blog (www.thecyclingsilk.blogspot.com) about cycling (obviously) and about the PI cases he's bringing against dangerous drivers.

2TG's marketing strategy revolves around its seminar programme. Held three or four times a month, the seminars are given by members of chambers and are designed to show off practice areas to prospective solicitor clients. Pupils attend too, and *"learn new things, pass around drinks and chat to the solicitors."* The set also recently hosted a *"fabulous"* 'thank you' marketing event for its clients at the top of The Gherkin.

And finally...

Two top tips: firstly, when applying to this set, showcasing your logical reasoning and advocacy skills matters more than past experiences. Secondly, doing a mini-pupillage is viewed as a big plus.

3 Verulam Buildings

The facts

Location: Gray's Inn, London
Number of QCs/juniors: 22/45 (13 women)
Applications: Around 125
Apply through Pupillage Gateway
Pupils per year: Up to 3
Seats: 4x3 months
Pupillage award: £60,000 (can advance £20,000 for BPTC)

"We're relatively future-proof, we're very solid and we're not going anywhere."
Richard Ansell, practice manager

3VB offers pupils top-end banking experience and a rare opportunity *"for a commercial set to gain advocacy experience."*

Feathers in the cap

"We now have far greater recognition in the marketplace and the directories than we did five years ago," said one 3VB member: *"It's much more generally accepted that we're a big-hitting commercial set of the first tier."* Top-ranked practices in *Chambers UK* include banking and finance, commercial dispute resolution and civil fraud, while the set's professional negligence, international arbitration and media and entertainment expertise is also ranked highly.

3VB's *"core work"* is in the banking and finance arena, and *"mis-selling work is high on the list, on both the claimant and the defendant side."* There's also a good flow of regulatory cases coming in, *"both on the government side – the regulators – and for the people who fall foul of the regulators."* According to practice manager Richard Ansell, *"regulation is something that's only on the increase."* Members have recently been involved in *"the Parliamentary Commission into banking standards – it's a pat on the back for the banking work we do."* There's also a broader mix of commercial work on the table, covering areas such as insurance, company, IT and telecoms, as well as a lot of arbitration.

One recent high-profile banking case saw the set act for Deutsche Bank during its dispute with Sebastian Holdings over unpaid margin calls equating to an estimated £150m. Sebastian Holdings responded with a counterclaim worth a staggering $7bn. Meanwhile, 3VB member Paul Lowenstein QC advised steel magnate Lakshmi Mittal on a multimillion-pound claim brought by 'rice king' Manmohan Varma over allegations that Mittal backtracked on a verbal agreement to pay Varma fees in relation to an oil deal.

Ansell says that *"chambers is increasingly seeing international work,"* and the set has been casting an eye eastward, developing links with Singapore, the Middle East, India and Hong Kong. The set laterally hires *"when the right opportunity presents itself,"* but there's a strong commitment to *"looking to recruit from the stock of pupils that we have."*

All n my grill

3VB receives around 125 paper applications each year. *"We've discerned a trend,"* said one member, who relayed that *"applicants are getting older and more experienced – they tend to come with two degrees, and very often have a bit of real world experience in law or something else."* The current pupil had spent seven years working for a bank, while the current baby junior had started out as a solicitor, and had worked at a magic circle firm. However, 3VB is *"keen to recruit both more mature and earlier stage applicants."* 40-ish applicants make it through to the first round. Each interviewee faces a panel of three, who discuss the candidate's CV, and ask *"a set topical question: it's normally not a legal question, and it forms the basis for a discussion."*

The *"top 15"* or so make it to the second round, which is a *"much more structured and lengthy affair."* Candidates are set a problem in advance, and usually have a week to prepare. *"This time it was an advice in conference on a point of contractual interpretation. They had to write a very short advice. The panel of six take on the role of the client – a slightly demanding client it has to be said! – and we grill the candidates."* We were assured that members are *"careful when dealing with people of wildly different levels of experience,"* so legal content is *"set to a low level"* and what recruiters are judging is a candidate's

Chambers UK rankings

Banking & Finance	Insurance
Commercial Dispute	International Arbitration
Resolution	Media & Entertainment
Financial Services	Professional Negligence
Fraud	Restructuring/Insolvency
Information Technology	Telecommunications

"persuasiveness, intellectual ability and flexibility." A baby junior, recalling the experience, said that *"the process is designed to favour people who are quick on their feet, and who are willing to turn an objection around and work it to their benefit."* The golden piece of advice: *"recognise structure, so, for example, set out three headline points and deliver them one by one – don't ramble."*

Litigating all the way to the bank

Pupils will sit with four supervisors for three months at a time. Efforts are made to sit pupils with *"a range of seniorities,"* especially with a *"fairly junior pupil supervisor"* so they can *"see the more junior style of work that they'll graduate onto."* The pupillage committee also *"does its best to match a pupil to a supervisor if there's a particular preference for a practice area."*

It's highly likely that pupils will see a range of banking work, touching on insolvency, professional negligence and fraud – *"all the types of cases that crop up regularly in the banking context."* Some of it comes down to *"pot luck,"* so *"one person might happen to be seeing a judicial review based on a decision by the financial ombudsman, whereas another might happen to be seeing a big fraud case."* The stakes in these cases are *"often quite high"* and involve *"fiddly bits of the law which you need to get right, so you need to be on your toes."* It's not all banking though, and pupils get a taste of *"neighbouring areas"* like insurance. There are also *"some things that you don't expect my last supervisor gave me a case about water pollution, which was very interesting."*

The work itself involves *"shadowing your supervisor and pretending that his work is your work – which is nice except for the fact that you can't hope to do it is nearly as well!"* This means that pupils get to experience a *"whole range of things,"* such as producing statements of case, particulars of claim defences, skeleton arguments and notes for cross-examinations.

On your own two feet

By the second six, pupils start receiving their own work, which is *"unusual for a commercial set."* The current pupil had worked on *"about half a dozen cases so far, and only one of them was paperwork – the rest were in front of a judge."* Usually there are three to four advocacy exercises throughout pupillage as well, which involve preparing a *"standard application, like a summary judgment, or an application to amend,"* but *"they make it difficult because that is what the training is intended to be like – they're useful exercises."* However, one member stated that although there's *"a certain amount of advocacy in the second six, it's not something that we push particularly hard – the pupillage year is important for learning, and the crucial part is spending time with your supervisor."* After nine months, a tenancy decision is made. The pupillage committee *"receives reports from all the people who have seen the pupil's work throughout the year."* In 2013, 3VB's only pupil was kept on.

"The sheer volume of work never seems to dry up, and chambers is very busy at the moment," said the current baby junior. *"As a junior here a large component of your work is retail banking – that's the steady diet of chambers and that's what gets you into court. If you're doing led work or devilling for more senior members then it could be absolutely anything – I did some research in relation to an academic plagiarism case!"*

"We're not a place where there are daggers drawn," said one member, much to our relief: *"We want to cultivate friendliness, humanity and diversity."* What 3VB definitely doesn't want is a *"chambers type – some of the people we recruit are formal and more old-fashioned, while others are progressive and so forth. We see it as a source of our strength, and we have people of different political persuasions and backgrounds."*

One interviewee picked up on the collaborative nature of the set: *"We're all in it together, under the 3VB umbrella, doing the best we can to build up the reputation of the set – everyone has a part to play."* Some had come to 3VB expecting it to be *"one of the more conservative sets because you associate banking and finance work with that, and although people are very serious about their work, the culture is informal and you do socialise."* Pupils are welcomed to the set via a drinks party, and they also get to revel in the annual summer party. Junior tenants are *"good at going out for drinks on a Friday evening,"* and there are also *"once-a-term drinks between junior members and the clerking team."*

And finally...

If commercial and banking are on your radar, then 3VB should be on your list, but remember to bring the *"zest and energy"* that recruiters expect to see.

The Bar

Wilberforce Chambers

The facts

Location: Lincoln's Inn, London
Number of QCs/juniors: 22/31 (9 women)
Applications: Around 150
Outside Pupillage Gateway
Pupils per year: 2
Seats: 6x2 months
Pupillage Award: £65,000 (can advance £20,000 for BTPC)

"Supreme intellectual ability - that's what we're about."
Martin Hutchings QC, chairman of the pupillage committee

Chancery law: for types who like a thorny legal problem. So where better to look than Wilberforce? Just be sure you bring your A-game.

Smart People

"Barristers here are frighteningly good at their jobs," reflected one pupil during our visit to Wilberforce Chambers. Sprawling across two sides of the handsome 17th-century New Square, this Lincoln's Inn set impresses in every respect. Its true forte is neatly summed up in a trio of top-tier *Chambers UK* rankings for chancery, offshore and pensions. The set amasses rafts of other rankings besides – commercial, fraud, professional negligence, real estate – but this is at its heart a *"traditional chancery set,"* albeit *"one of the first to overlap to cover chancery and commercial,"* says Declan Redmond, senior clerk.

So what about the Wilberforce name – was this the famed 19th-century abolitionist's own set? It turns out his great-grandson, who was a dab hand at chancery, founded the set. The early-'90s name change came about partly because *"the old 3 New Square address was confusing,"* Redmond explains, but it also heralded a new, more commercially savvy operation that set out to be the best at what it does. And it achieved it, if its recent accomplishments are any indication. Recent cases include Rybolovleva v Rybolovlev, the highest-value divorce ever ($12bn), and 11 of its barristers representing various parties in the £2bn Nortel pension deficit case.

"Supreme intellectual ability – that's what we're about," Martin Hutchings QC, chairman of the pupillage committee declares. Wilberforce people are pretty brainy – every interviewee stressed this. Scanning through its members online, *"you could be forgiven for thinking we're all Oxbridge males with firsts,"* admits Hutchings, but in fact *"the university you went to is irrelevant,"* he stressed. The set is concerned about the *"image issue with top chancery sets,"* asserting that it's *"not something we have deliberately engineered, and we're keen to de-engineer it."* Hutchings adds: *"We would love to have more women in chambers,"* and the set's bid to boost its diversity profile is *"something we need to do professionally, because our practice is becoming fantastically international."* This also means linguists should apply.

No bullshitters, please

That Wilberforce is *"looking for people of high intellectual calibre"* should not come as a shock, then, and there are more key qualities listed on the set's website. To get your application noticed (outside of the Pupillage Gateway) *"there's no substitute for clarity of expression,"* hinted one pupil. The 30-ish candidates invited to the long-list interview face a short test of their legal reasoning ability. *"We've just changed the system,"* Hutchings tells us. The old interview format of a non-legal problem *"played to the strengths of the debaters – the public school boys – who were more confident at bullshitting,"* explains Tiffany Scott, pupillage committee member. Women, being *"less prone to bullshit,"* now fare more equally with the men, now that they're tested on *"legal analysis and a logical application of your legal knowledge."*

About half make it to the shortlist interview. This 45-minute panel-facing session focuses on a legal problem *"designed to test legal reasoning skills, not legal knowledge."* Non-law undergrads can breathe a sigh of relief, as Hutchings emphasises: *"We make allowances for what we expect from non-law candidates,"* echoing one junior who had *"only looked at a law book in earnest a few months earlier."* One pupil explained: *"It tests whether you're able to cope with pressure, and able to come to

Chambers UK rankings

Chancery	Fraud
Charities	Offshore
Commercial Dispute	Pensions
Resolution	Professional Negligence
Company	Real Estate Litigation

uting to skeleton arguments and pleadings." 'Dead' work "*enables them to spend time giving you feedback,*" and pupils truly valued "*getting feedback from some of the best practitioners in their fields,*" although some would have appreciated more emphasis on this. All agreed, however, that the true buzz comes from the 'live' work, taking the barristers-to-be into their natural habitat: "*Outside of my comfort zone.*"

a definitive view and then defend that view." Hutchings expands on this: "*At this stage we're looking for an ability to reason, to sustain an argument, to switch a view, to appreciate the consequences of what they're arguing.*" Scott stresses that the aim is "*to look beyond the terms of the contract and towards the commercial purpose of the agreement.*" While the panel will rate your potential to "*engage with clients, your commercial nous*" and whether you're a "*forceful personality,*" one source did reassure us: "*I felt kind of bad because getting pupillage is meant to be a great self-flagellation process, but it was actually pretty simple.*" The breezy riposte of the man who got the job? Perhaps, but in relative terms it appears true: "*They're just not looking to catch you out.*"

Life in the shadows

Every year chambers takes on two pupils, who are each assigned to a supervisor to shadow for two months. They then rotate after every two-month period until the year is up. Scott elaborates: "*we tend to give them to the person they get the best experience from,*" with the plan being to expose them to "*all the main bases of our work here: property, commercial, pensions and trust/private client work.*" Pupils tend to start with a very senior QC for the first seat, and diversify thereafter, shadowing those offering the most interesting cases in chambers. And there is no real distinction between the first and second six, incidentally. All juniors reported happily that "*none of them treated me like a subspecies,*" and that "*pupillage was a very, very positive experience!*"

A taster of a pupil's assignments might be: "*Big commercial breach of contracts, breach of confidence trials, or trusts and pensions disputes.*" One pupil raved about "*seeing five trials during pupillage – I've been to the Supreme Court twice and the Court of Appeal twice.*" Supervisors will either give pupils 'dead' work (old cases) or 'live' work (current). Both scenarios presented "*a lot of paperwork,*" agreed sources, but also saw them "*contrib-*

Wilberforce bans slavery

"*There's no expectation of hours,*" Scott confirms, and pupils appreciate this: "*The best thing was that no one screws you over, you didn't get unreasonable requests - everyone gave me enough time to do all the work.*" Thankfully, this leaves pupils with enough time to devote to the new advocacy training coming in this year, culminating in a "*mock courtroom test.*" Another big plus is that "*you're not in competition with your fellow pupil,*" one told us. While the set certainly doesn't go soft on pupils, there is "*an understanding that you're learning as well as being assessed, and you're allowed to make mistakes - but the key thing is learning from that,*" one pupil reflected. The tenancy decision is made in June – relatively early on – a bonus on the occasion that you'd have to find a third six. The decision is based principally on the views of the four supervisors who mentored the pupils until June, assessing them on broadly the same criteria that got them the job in the first place. In 2013, Wilberforce kept on one out of two pupils. The unsuccessful pupil was offered a third six very soon after, and at another top set.

How does life change after tenancy? Aside from the obvious, "*you get your own room on the top floor, which I like a lot.*" We detected a no-nonsense, businesslike vibe on our visit. Tenants, pupils and clerks work pragmatically together, everyone does their job but respects down time: "*You control your own time; I took a three-week holiday after a big case and they didn't bat an eyelid,*" said a junior. Be it supervisor lunches, fortnightly chambers lunches, cocktail parties with clients, karaoke, fireworks or pétanque, Wilberforce does enough to ensure no end of pastoral support and social hoopla. "*I was made to feel very welcome,*" one pupil told us – no more so than down the Seven Stars, where you'll find a Wilberforce crowd "*pretty much any night of the week.*" "*There's no set type of person here,*" one source commented. "*It's as normal an existence as much as being a barrister can be.*"

The Bar

And finally...

All our interviewees did something non-legal before joining Wilberforce. *"Some knowledge of the world does help,"* says Hutchings.

"The statistics are terrible. Trying to get a pupillage is horrendous, and every year you've got a backlog of students from previous years who are still trying to get one... [To win a pupillage] you've got to be robust and prepared to be the person that takes the flak, and also highly articulate – these are the core skills. There's no point in saying, 'I want to be a barrister' if you don't have them."

Dinah Rose QC, Blackstone Chambers.

Read the full interview on chambersstudent.co.uk

A-Z of Barristers

Atkin Chambers

1 Atkin Building, Gray's Inn, London, WC1R 5AT
Tel: (020) 7404 0102 Fax: (020) 7405 7456
Email: clerks@atkinchambers.com
Website: www.atkinchambers.com

No of Silks 16	
No of Juniors 25	
No of Pupils 2	
Contact	
Andrew Burrows	
(pupillage@atkinchambers.com)	
Method of application	
Pupillage Gateway	
Pupillages (p.a.)	
2 - 12 month pupillages	
Income	
£60,000	
Tenancies	
4 in the last three years	

Chambers profile

Atkin Chambers is a leading commercial set specialising in construction, energy and technology disputes and related professional negligence claims. As well as leading in the domestic field, its barristers have a significant international practice spanning Europe, the Middle East, Asia, Africa and the Caribbean.

Type of work undertaken

Atkin Chambers is a leader in the fields of construction and engineering law. This specialism means that members of chambers are often instructed in related commercial disputes such as those pertaining to energy, information technology, shipbuilding (including repair and conversion) and general commercial law matters arising from such commercial projects. Members of Chambers are recommended as leaders in their field in the areas of construction, energy and natural resources, information technology, international arbitration (construction/engineering) and professional negligence (technology and construction). Members of Atkin Chambers regularly appear at international arbitrations seated in the Gulf States, Hong Kong and Singapore.

Pupil profile

Chambers is committed to recruiting pupils and tenants (generally from its own pupils) that will participate in its continued success in international and domestic practice. Chambers looks for pupils who are well motivated and have an interest in practising in the areas of law in which chambers specialises.

Applicants for pupillage should have a first-class degree or a good upper second-class degree. Postgraduate qualifications are viewed favourably but are not essential. Applications from non-law graduates are welcomed. Pre-existing knowledge of construction law is not required, although candidates should have a strong grounding in contract and tort law.

Mini pupillage

Although a mini-pupillage is not a pre-requisite to applying for a pupillage, prospective pupils are encouraged to apply for a mini-pupillage so as to gain some knowledge of the areas of law in which Atkin Chambers specialises. Six mini-pupillages are offered each year. Applicants are invited to apply by letter with CV during March 2014 (pupillage@atkinchambers.com).

Pupillage

Atkin Chambers takes recruitment to pupillage and tenancy extremely seriously. The pupillage year is structured to provide all of the Bar Council's minimum training requirements and the additional training chambers considers is necessary for successful entry into the high-quality commercial work of its practice. Atkin Chambers provides its own advocacy training and assessment in addition to that provided by the Inns of Court.

Full and up-to-date details of the structure and goals of Atkin Chambers' pupillage training programme may be reviewed on our website.

Funding

Chambers offers up to two 12-month pupillages, all of which are funded. The pupillage award is £60,000 for pupils starting in 2015-2016. A proportion of this award may be drawn down in advance to assist pupils during their BVC year.

In their first years of practice, new members may expect earning potential equivalent to peers at the largest commercial sets.

AtkinChambers Barristers

2 Bedford Row (William Clegg QC)

2 Bedford Row, London WC1R 4BU
Tel: (020) 7440 8888 Fax: (020) 7242 1738
Email: clerks@2bedfordrow.co.uk
Website: www.2bedfordrow.co.uk

No of Silks 16
No of Juniors 54
No of Pupils 4
Graduate recruitment contact Stephen Vullo 020 7440 8888
Method of application Pupillage Gateway
Pupillages (p.a.) 4 x 18 months Tenancies offered according to ability

Chambers profile

Widely regarded as one of the leading crime sets in the UK, 2 Bedford Row continues to excel in the fields of crime, fraud and regulatory law. Chambers has been described by 'Chambers UK' 2012 as 'one of the strongest sets in fraud', 'packed with extremely talented barristers', and 2011 as 'indubitably one of the best criminal sets in the country'.

Type of work undertaken

Chambers has a broad-based criminal practice and its members have appeared in some of the most high-profile criminal cases of recent years (Sgt Danny Nightingale R v Barry George, R v Levi Bellfield, R v Mark Dixie). In addition, members of chambers have particular experience in the fields of confiscation/restraint, health and safety, financial services law, sports law, professional regulation/discipline and inquests. Members are frequently instructed to appear before regulatory bodies such as the GMC, the FA, the VAT tribunal and the Police Disciplinary Tribunal.

Pupil profile

Chambers recruits candidates from all backgrounds who display the highest intellectual ability, excellent advocacy skills, sound judgement and a real commitment to criminal law and its related fields. Candidates will also be well-rounded individuals who are able to communicate effectively with a wide variety of people.

Pupillage

Chambers offers up to four 18-month pupillages each year. Each pupil will have one pupil supervisor in their first six and a different one in their second six. This ensures that pupils are provided with a thorough grounding in all aspects of chambers' practice. Chambers also provides structured advocacy training throughout the pupillage year and will pay for pupils to attend the 'Advice to Counsel' and 'Forensic Accountancy' courses. Applications for tenancy are usually made after the completion of a 3rd six.

Mini-pupillages

Chambers welcomes applications for mini-pupillage. Please see the website for details.

Funding

Chambers provides a grant of £12,000 to each pupil, paid monthly throughout the year and, in addition, guaranteed earnings of £10,000 in second six. All earnings retained in 3rd six.

Blackstone Chambers (Monica Carss-Frisk QC and Anthony Peto QC)

Blackstone House, Temple, London EC4Y 9BW   DX: 281 Chancery Lane
Tel: (020) 7583 1770   Fax: (020) 7822 7350
Email: pupillage@blackstonechambers.com
Website: www.blackstonechambers.com

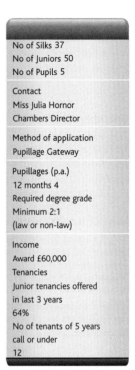

No of Silks 37
No of Juniors 50
No of Pupils 5
Contact
Miss Julia Hornor
Chambers Director
Method of application
Pupillage Gateway
Pupillages (p.a.)
12 months 4
Required degree grade
Minimum 2:1
(law or non-law)
Income
Award £60,000
Tenancies
Junior tenancies offered
in last 3 years
64%
No of tenants of 5 years
call or under
12

Chambers profile

Blackstone Chambers occupies large and modern premises in the Temple.

Type of work undertaken

Chambers' formidable strengths lie in its principal areas of practice: commercial, employment and EU, public law, human rights and public international law. Commercial law includes financial/business law, international trade, conflicts, sport, media and entertainment, intellectual property and professional negligence. All aspects of employment law, including discrimination, are covered by chambers' extensive employment law practice. Public law incorporates judicial review, acting both for and against central and local government agencies and other regulatory authorities, all areas affected by the impact of human rights and other aspects of administrative law. EU permeates practices across the board. Chambers recognises the increasingly important role which mediation has to play in dispute resolution. Seven members are CEDR accredited mediators.

Pupil profile

Chambers looks for articulate and intelligent applicants who are able to work well under pressure and demonstrate high intellectual ability. Successful candidates usually have at least a 2:1 honours degree, although not necessarily in law.

Pupillage

Chambers offers four 12-month pupillages to those wishing to practise full-time at the Bar, normally commencing in October each year. Pupillage is normally divided into four sections and every effort is made to ensure that pupils receive a broad training. The environment is a friendly one; pupils attend an induction week introducing them to chambers' working environment. Chambers prefers to recruit new tenants from pupils wherever possible. Chambers subscribes to Pupillage Gateway.

Mini-pupillages

Assessed mini-pupillages are an essential part of the pupillage procedure and no pupillage will be offered at Blackstone Chambers unless the applicant has undertaken an assessed mini-pupillage. Applications for mini-pupillages must be made by 1 April 2014; earlier applications are strongly advised and are preferred in the year before pupillage commences.

Funding

Awards of £60,000 per annum are available. The pupillage committee has a discretion to consider applications for up to £17,000 of the pupillage award to be advanced during the BTPC year. Since chambers insists on an assessed mini-pupillage as part of the overall application procedure, financial assistance is offered either in respect of out of pocket travelling or accommodation expenses incurred in attending the mini-pupillage, up to a maximum of £250 per pupil.

Blackstone
CHAMBERS

The Bar

1 Chancery Lane (John Ross QC)

1 Chancery Lane, London WC2A 1LF
Tel: 0845 634 6666   Fax: 0845 634 6667
Email: jfensham@1chancerylane.com
Website: www.1chancerylane.com

No of Silks 5
No of Juniors 39
No of Pupils 2
Contact
Jenny Fensham, Practice Administrator
jfensham@1chancerylane.com
Method of application
Application form on Chambers website
Pupillages (p.a.)
2 every other year (next pupillage intake October 2015)

Chambers profile

A leading civil common law set, specialising in professional and clinical negligence litigation, personal injury actions, claims for and against public authorities (including the police), disciplinary and regulatory work, property and travel claims.

Reputation: an unstuffy and approachable chambers. Atmosphere: collegiate and supportive. Our pupil and tenant retention rate is very good. We focus on providing a full client service.

Type of work undertaken

We are involved in a wide range of high profile work including education negligence, novel duty of care claims against public authorities, human rights claims, stress related claims, discrimination, social welfare, undue influence claims and judicial review. Members of Chambers have appeared in the Supreme Court in the leading case on duties owed by doctors and social workers investigating child abuse; the leading case on limitation in child abuse claims; and the leading case on police protection and the Human Rights Act. Chambers is listed as a leading set in several practice areas in the Legal 500 and Chambers & Partners and individual members of Chambers are recommended as leading practitioners in additional areas.

Pupil profile

Strong academics are only a small (if essential) part of what we're looking for. Motivation is important; communication skills are absolutely vital; common sense and commerciality are also useful. The desire to excel and a commitment to the profession are important attributes.

Pupillage

Three seats of four months, each with a different pupil supervisor. Pupils are exposed to a variety of paperwork, court work, alternative dispute resolution and conferences and can expect to be in court on average several times each week. There is a mutual feedback and appraisal system in place.

Mini-pupillages

Eight mini-pupillages of a week's duration, four in June and four in July. Please see the recruitment section of our website for further details.

Funding

Pupillages are funded (not less than £40,000 for pupils commencing in 2015).

Cloisters

Cloisters, 1 Pump Court, Temple, London, EC4Y 7AA
Tel: (020) 7827 4000 Fax: (020) 7827 4100
Email: clerks@cloisters.com
Website: www.cloisters.com

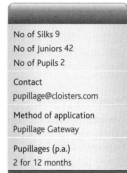

No of Silks 9	
No of Juniors 42	
No of Pupils 2	
Contact	
pupillage@cloisters.com	
Method of application	
Pupillage Gateway	
Pupillages (p.a.)	
2 for 12 months	

Chambers profile

Cloisters is a leading set advising in employment, discrimination and equality, personal injury, clinical negligence, sports and commercial law with a reputation for delivering exceptional results. It provides responsive first-class client service combined with technical excellence and commercial perspective to resolve the most complex legal problems for individuals and organisations of all sizes.

Type of work undertaken

Employment; discrimination and equality: Cloisters is at the forefront of all aspects of employment law and has unrivalled expertise in discrimination and equality issues. Recent landmark cases include Employees v Birmingham City Council the largest equal pay claim brought against a local authority; Heyday, a case bringing about the end of the default retirement age; Homer v West Yorkshire Police and Seldon v Clarkson Wright & Jakes, two of the first age discrimination cases to go to the Supreme Court and X v Mid-Sussex Citizens Advice Bureau in which the Court of Appeal ruled that volunteers are not covered by the Disability Discrimination Act.

Personal Injury and Clinical Negligence: Cloisters is consistently rated as a top-ranked clinical negligence set in Chambers & Partners and is highly regarded for personal injury. Cloisters continues to be at the forefront of high value litigation involving catastrophic brain and spinal injury, including: Pankhurst v White, Houghton, Mohamed, Iqbal v Whipps Cross University Hospitals, and A v Powys. Chambers also continues to be at the forefront of PI litigation. Recent Court of Appeal case include Crofton v NHSLA (local authority payments and double recovery), Connor v Surrey County Council (psychiatric injury at work/breach of statutory duty), Stanton v Collinson (seatbelts and contributory negligence), Noble v Owens (video surveillance), and Grevil v Redruth Rugby Club (vicarious liability for employed sportsman). Members of chambers have consistently appeared in the leading stress at work cases including: Barber v Somerset County Council, Majrowski v Guys and St Thomas's, and Hartman v South East Essex Mental Health and Community Care NHS Trust. Members of chambers are currently instructed in the Godstone farm ecoli group litigation.

Sport: Cloisters' sport practitioners act for football clubs and players up to Premier League as well as a diverse range of sports bodies and personalities. They handle disciplinary regulations, consultative work, litigation, non-professional sporting activity cases and matters arising from sports and entertainment cases such as employment or contractual issues.

Pupil profile

Chambers welcomes applications from outstanding candidates from all backgrounds and academic disciplines including lawyers coming late to the Bar.

Pupillage

Chambers offers two 12 month pupillages for those wishing to practise full-time at the Bar, normally commencing in October each year. Each pupil is supervised and the supervisor changes every three months to show the pupil different areas of practice. Second six pupils will be allocated work by clerks subject to availability of work and pupil ability.

Mini-Pupillages

Cloisters offers up to ten three day mini-pupillages each year. All applicants must have completed at least their first year at university in any subject. The mini-pupillage is not assessed and is not a requirement for applications for pupillage.

Funding

Cloisters offers two funded pupillages each year. Each pupil will receive an award (currently £40,000 per year). Pupils can also ask for an advance.

The Bar

Crown Office Chambers

Head of Chambers: Richard Lynagh QC
2 Crown Office Row, Temple, London, EC4Y 7HJ
Tel: (020) 7797 8100 Fax: (020) 7797 8101
Email: mail@crownofficechambers.com
Website: www.crownofficechambers.com

No of Silks 13
No of Juniors 77
No of Pupils up to 3
Contact
Carlo Taczalski
Method of application
Chambers' application form, downloadable from chambers' website
Pupillages (p.a.)
Up to three per year, 12 months £60,000, comprising £50,000 award plus £10,000 guaranteed earnings
Tenancies
No of tenancies offered in last 3 years 6

Chambers profile

Crown Office Chambers is one of the leading sets of chambers specialising in civil common law work. Chambers has an established reputation in the fields of construction, health and safety, insurance and reinsurance, personal injury, product liability, professional negligence and property damage. It is not a 'pure commercial' set, and pupils will see a range of work during pupillage.

Junior tenants also undertake a range of work with an emphasis on developing advocacy skills; in addition to working on their own paperwork and accepting junior briefs, junior tenants in their first years of practice are generally in court several times per week. Tenants have the opportunity to specialise as their practices develop, by which time chambers considers that their blend of early advocacy and advisory experience gives them the edge over their contemporaries at many 'pure commercial', and indeed 'pure' common law / personal injury sets. It also keeps work varied and gives allows members to make a more informed decisions to specialise in a given field or fields.

Pupil profile

Members pride themselves on their professionalism, an astute and business-orientated awareness of the practical needs of solicitors and lay clients, combined with an approachable and unstuffy attitude to their work. Chambers looks for the same in its pupils, all of whom are regarded as having strong tenancy potential. Pupils are expected to display the motivation, dedication and intelligence which are the hallmarks of a first-class barrister. Academically, they should have a first or upper second-class honours degree (not necessarily in law), a flair for oral and written advocacy, and a strong and committed work ethic.

Pupillage

Pupils rotate through three pupil supervisors during the course of the year. In their second six, pupils are briefed to attend County Court hearings on their own, probably at least two or three times per week. Generally these will be small personal injury cases. Pupils receive regular feedback on their work from pupil supervisors and other members of chambers. They also undertake a series of advocacy exercises in front of a panel of four members of chambers and receive extensive feedback after each exercise. There are also two to three assessed written exercises during the course of pupillage. Tenancy decisions are made in early July to enable any pupils who are not taken on to apply for third sixes.

Mini-pupillage

Limited number of mini-pupillages in selected weeks throughout the year. Online application form downloadable from chambers' website.

The Bar

One Essex Court

Chambers of Lord Grabiner QC, One Essex Court, Temple, London EC4Y 9AR
Tel: (020) 7583 2000 Fax: (020) 7583 0118
Email: clerks@oeclaw.co.uk Website: www.oeclaw.co.uk

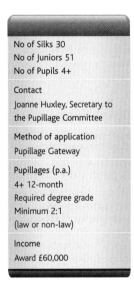

No of Silks 30
No of Juniors 51
No of Pupils 4+

Contact
Joanne Huxley, Secretary to
the Pupillage Committee

Method of application
Pupillage Gateway

Pupillages (p.a.)
4+ 12-month
Required degree grade
Minimum 2:1
(law or non-law)

Income
Award £60,000

Chambers profile

One Essex Court is a pre-eminent set of barristers' chambers, specialising in commercial litigation. Members provide specialist advice and advocacy services worldwide, which include all areas of dispute resolution, litigation and arbitration.

Type of work undertaken

Chambers' work embraces all aspects of domestic and international trade, commerce and finance. Members of chambers are recognised specialists in the many diverse fields characterised as commercial disputes, also regularly accepting nominations as arbitrators, mediators and experts. Chambers' work includes, but is not limited to: arbitration, banking and finance, civil fraud, commercial litigation, company and insolvency, competition and EU, energy (oil, gas and utilities), financial services, insurance, IP, professional negligence and revenue law.

Pupil profile

Chambers has for many years maintained a policy of active recruitment and expansion and only offers pupillage to those who are thought capable of becoming tenants. Provided a candidate is proven to have the requisite ability, no distinction is drawn between candidates who do and those who do not have a law degree. Pupils at One Essex Court do not compete against one another for a predetermined maximum intake.

Pupillage

At least four guaranteed 12-month pupillages are offered per year, each with substantial funding. From the beginning, pupils assist pupil supervisors with their papers, do legal research, draft opinions, pleadings and skeleton arguments. There are substantial opportunities for advocacy in the second six months of pupillage. Chambers subscribes to Pupillage Gateway.

Mini-pupillage

Mini-pupillages last for either one or two days. They are not assessed. A mini-pupillage is not a pre-requisite for pupillage although it is encouraged as it can provide a good opportunity both to see how chambers works and to meet members of chambers. Please visit chambers' website for the application process and deadlines.

Funding

Chambers offers each pupil £60,000, supplemented by earnings in the second six. It is understood that this is amongst the highest, if not the highest, remuneration package available to pupils. An advance of the Award is available, upon request, during a prospective pupil's Bar Professional Training Course ("BPTC") year.

ONE ESSEX COURT

The Bar

1 Hare Court

1 Hare Court, Temple, London EC4Y 7BE
Tel: (020) 7797 7070 Fax: (020) 797 7435
Email: clerks@1hc.com
Website: www.1hc.com

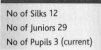

No of Silks 12
No of Juniors 29
No of Pupils 3 (current)

Contact
Sarah Hardwicke (Chambers
Administrator)

Method of Application
Curriculum Vitae with
handwritten covering letter

Pupillages (pa)
Two 12 month pupillages

Tenancies offered
7 in the last 5 years

Chambers profile

Chambers is proud to be consistently identified as a market leader in family and matrimonial law, at the forefront of high-end financial remedy work.

Type of work undertaken

Chambers work involves the resolution of a broad range of disputes arising out of the breakdown of family relationships, including the dissolution of civil partnerships. Our reputation has been built upon our high net worth financial remedy work, increasingly with an international element. Members of chambers are also regularly instructed in property disputes arising from unmarried parties' cohabitation, Inheritance Act claims, Child Support Act appeals and private law children cases, including child abduction. We have a burgeoning reputation in the area of nuptial agreements.

Our work is undertaken predominantly in and around London, but can be as far a field as Hong Kong and the Cayman Islands. We represent clients at every level of Court and Tribunal, from the Family Proceedings and Magistrates Court to the Supreme Court and Privy Council.

In addition to advocacy and advice, 1 Hare Court provides a comprehensive dispute resolution service, including mediation, arbitration and collaborative law.

Pupil profile

Chambers looks to recruit pupils with ability, application and the potential to be first-rate advocates. Candidates should have excellent communication skills, sound judgement, a confident grasp of financial concepts and issues and good academic qualifications (at least a 2:1 honours degree).

Pupillage

Chambers offer two 12 months pupillages, commencing in October each year. Each pupil will have three different supervisors over the year and will be introduced to all aspects of chambers' work. We run in-house advocacy training and pupils will undertake a broad range of written work and research. We have a strong preference for recruiting tenants from our pupils.

Mini Pupillage

Mini-pupillages are available: for further details please consult our website at www.1hc.com/pupillages

Funding

Each pupil will receive an award of £35,000, of which £10,000 may be drawn down in the BTPC year.

1 HARE COURT

Henderson Chambers

2 Harcourt Buildings, Temple, London EC4Y 9DB
Tel: (020) 7583 9020 Fax: (020) 7583 2686
Email: clerks@hendersonchambers.co.uk
Website: www.hendersonchambers.co.uk

No of Silks 9
No of Juniors 36
No of Pupils 2

Contact
pupillages@hendersonchambers
.co.uk

Method of application
Pupillage Gateway

Pupillages (p.a.)
2 12 month pupillages offered
Remuneration for pupillage
£50,000 for 12 months
(£42,500 award, £7,500
guaranteed earnings)

Tenancies
5 in the last 3 years

Chambers profile

Henderson Chambers is a leading commercial/common law chambers with acknowledged expertise in all of its principal areas of practice. Members and pupils are frequently involved in high-profile commercial and common law litigation.

Type of work undertaken

Henderson Chambers has unrivalled expertise in product liability (which covers a wide range of commercial work including sale of goods and insurance disputes, multi-party pharmaceutical and medical device claims and regulatory and enforcement proceedings) and is consistently rated as the leading set in this area. Chambers is also widely recognised for the excellence of its health and safety work.

In addition, members are noted for their expertise and experience in areas including: employment law, regulatory and disciplinary proceedings, public law and judicial review, personal injury, property law, and technology and construction.

Pupil profile

Chambers looks for individuals who can demonstrate a first-class intellect whether via the traditional route of an outstanding higher education record or via proof of success in other professions, in business or in employment. It is a friendly and sociable set, and expects candidates to be able to show how they have both worked hard and played hard.

Pupillage

Pupillages are for 12 months, usually with four different pupil supervisors for three months each. Pupils have the opportunity to spend four weeks in Brussels at McDermott Will & Emery in order to experience European practice at first hand. Pupils will attend court regularly during their second six months.

Mini-pupillage

Chambers offers unassessed mini-pupillages. Applications can be made online at www.hendersonpupillage.co.uk

Funding

Chambers offers two funded 12-month pupillages with minimum remuneration of £50,000 each. This consists of an award of £42,500 and guaranteed earnings of £7,500 during the second six months.

HENDERSON CHAMBERS

The Bar

11KBW

11 King's Bench Walk, London EC4Y 7EQ
Tel: 020 7632 8500 Fax: 020 7583 9123
Email: clerksteam@11kbw.com Web: www.11kbw.com

No. of Silks 20
No of Juniors 34
No. of Pupils 2 (current)
Contact
Ms Claire Halas – Operations Manager
Method of application
Pupillage Gateway
Pupillages (pa)
12 months – 2-3
Required degree: first or upper second class (in any academic field)
Income
£55,000pa
Tenancies
No of tenancies offered in last 3 years: 5

Chambers profile

We are a specialist civil law set providing high quality advice and advocacy to a wide range of private and public sector clients, both claimants and defendants. Current members of chambers include First Treasury Counsel.

Types of work undertaken

Pupils can expect to gain a range of experience across the following areas; public law and human rights; employment and discrimination law; business law; European community law; information law and sports law.

Pupillage

The great majority of tenants are recruited from those who have done a 12 month pupillage here. We offer pupillages only to those who we believe have the potential to become tenants and our policy is to offer tenancy to all pupils who meet the required standard during their pupillage. We place a high premium on outstanding intellectual ability, but we are also looking for the strong advocacy skills, determination and practical common sense that will lead to a successful practice.

11KBW is a member of the Pupillage Gateway. Applications for pupillage commencing October 2015 should be made in the Pupillage Gateway summer round in 2014 (although we accept deferred applications). Interviews will be held in mid-July 2014 and offers of pupillage made in accordance with the Pupillage Gateway timetable. We require applicants for pupillage to do an assessed mini-pupillage in chambers. When we make pupillage selection decisions we take into account performance in assessed mini-pupillages, together with Pupillage Gateway application forms and performance at interview. Applicants must have a first or good upper second class degree (in any academic field).

Mini-pupillages

Chambers requires applicants for pupillage through Pupillage Gateway to do a one week assessed mini-pupillage in chambers. The deadline for applications for mini-pupillage is 1 March 2014 for those applying through Pupillage Gateway for pupillage commencing in October 2015. We will invite candidates for assessed mini-pupillages to a short interview in chambers in March 2014. If that causes particular difficulties, we will consider applications for alternative arrangements, such as interview by video conference. Assessed mini-pupillages will take place between April and June 2014. In exceptional circumstances, applicants for pupillage may ask to submit a written answer to a mini-pupillage problem instead of doing an assessed mini-pupillage in chambers. Any such application should also be made by 1 March 2014 for those applying for pupillage commencing in October 2015.

We also offer some unassessed mini pupillages for those who are at an earlier stage of their legal studies and who wish to consider practising as a barrister within our areas of expertise.

Awards

We offer a Pupillage Award of £55,000 (up to £15,000 of the pupillage award may be paid to prospective pupils as an advance in their BPTC year).

The Bar

Keating Chambers

15 Essex Street, London, WC2R 3AA
Tel: (020) 7544 2600
Fax: (020) 7544 2700

No of Silks 26	
No of Juniors 30	
No of Pupils up to 3	
Contact	
ebrowne@keatingchambers.com	
Method of application	
Pupillage Portal	
Pupillages (p.a.)	
Pupillages (p.a.) 3x12-month pupillages available	
Tenancies	
3 offered in last 3 years	

Chambers profile

Keating Chambers is a leading commercial set specialising in construction, technology and related professional negligence disputes. These disputes often relate to high-profile projects in the UK and overseas and typically involve complex issues in the law of tort, contract and restitution. Chambers is based in modern premises outside the Temple. In their first years of practice, tenants can expect earnings equivalent to those in other top sets of commercial chambers.

Type of work undertaken

Our members are involved in disputes of all shapes and sizes: from residential building works to multi-million pound projects for the construction of airports, dams, power stations and bridges. Members of chambers have been instructed on projects such as the Olympic venues, Wembley Stadium, the "Pinnacle", the "Shard", the "Gherkin", the Millennium Bridge, the London Eye and the Channel Tunnel. Work now also includes rapidly developing areas such as information technology, telecommunications, energy and EU law. Members of chambers act as advocates in litigation and arbitration throughout the UK.

We are often instructed to act in international hearings elsewhere in Europe and throughout Asia, Africa and the Caribbean. A number of our members specialise in international arbitration. New and alternative methods of dispute resolution are often used and several of our members are frequently appointed as mediators, arbitrators and adjudicators.

Chambers' area of practice is dynamic and challenging. The relevant principles of law are constantly developing and the technical complexity of disputes requires thorough analytical skills.

Members of Keating Chambers regularly publish books, articles and journals. Keating on Construction Contracts, the leading textbook in its field, is written and researched by current members of chambers, along with the Construction Law Reports. We also contribute to Halsbury's Laws of England and Chitty on Contracts.

Pupil profile

It must be emphasised that no specialist or technical knowledge of construction or engineering is required or assumed. However, a sound understanding of the principles of contract and tort law is essential. Save in exceptional cases, we expect applicants to have an upper second or first class degree, whether in law or not. Chambers assesses all applications using its own selection criteria.

Pupillage

Pupils are normally allocated four supervisors in the course of their 12 month pupillage. This ensures that each pupil sees a variety of work of differing levels of complexity within chambers.

Comprehensive training in the core skills required for practice in our field. To this end, pupils are encouraged to prepare drafts of pleadings, advices, letters and other documents that their supervisor or another member of chambers is instructed to prepare. Pupils are also asked to prepare skeleton arguments for hearings. They attend conferences with clients, both in and out of chambers and, of course, hearings in court, arbitration, adjudication and mediation.

Mini-pupillages

For details please see our website www.keatingchambers.com.

Funding

We offer up to three 12 month pupillages with an award for 2014 of up to £55,000. Of this, an advance of £17,500 is available in respect of BVC/BPTC fees (incurred or to be incurred).

1 King's Bench Walk

Temple, London EC4Y 7DB DX: 20 LDE
Tel: (020) 7936 1500 Fax: (020) 7936 1590
Email: pupillage@1kbw.co.uk
Website: www.1kbw.co.uk

No of Silks 12
No of Juniors 41
No of Pupils 2 (current)

Contact
Sue Gray
Chambers Director

Method of application
Application form and details on
1kbw website

Pupillages p.a.
12 months 2
Required degree grade
Minimum 2:1
(law or non law)

Tenancies
Junior tenancies offered in the
last 3 years 6

Chambers profile

1 King's Bench Walk is a leading barristers' chambers in London, specialising in family law, with a pre-eminent reputation both nationally and internationally. We are consistently ranked by the legal directories in the top tier of leading sets for family law. Our barristers have been in most of the groundbreaking cases over the last two decades.

1kbw are market leaders for both matrimonial finance and children. We have a reputation for recruiting the most talented pupils and then providing training and support that is second to none. We proactively try to recruit our tenants from our pupils. In the last decade 17 of the 20 pupils in chambers have been offered tenancy. For that reason, our selection procedure is rigorous.

Pupil profile

We are looking for outstanding candidates who are confident, articulate and have the right aptitude for life at the bar. They will be interesting, intelligent and enthusiastic individuals with an interest in the particular specialisms of chambers.

Pupillage

1KBW offers two specialist family law pupillages each year. Each pupillage is full time and for twelve months. The first six months (non-practising) are divided between two pupil supervisors, and the second six months (practising period) is spent with a third, each of whom will be a specialist family law practitioner. Chambers also provides 'in-house' advocacy training.

We offer each pupil a (tax free) grant of £22,500 which is paid during the first 6 months. In addition, pupils may retain any income which they earn in the second six months. The reputation of 1KBW is such that our pupils are regularly briefed from the outset.

Mini pupillages

We consider applications three times a year (in April, September and December), made using the online application form that can be found on our website. There is no interview; mini-pupils are chosen on the strength of their paper applications.

1 King's Bench Walk has a firm commitment to equality and diversity.

7 King's Bench Walk

7 King's Bench Walk, Temple, London, EC4Y 7DS
Tel: (020) 7910 8300 Fax: (020) 7910 8400
Website: www.7kbw.co.uk

Chambers profile

7 King's Bench Walk is a leading commercial set of chambers, with a reputation for excellence and intellectual rigour. The Legal 500 describes it as "One of the Bar's true elite".

Type of work undertaken

Chambers is at the forefront of commercial litigation, specialising in particular in the fields of insurance and reinsurance, shipping, international trade, professional negligence and private international law. Most of its work has an international dimension. Members regularly appear in the High Court (particularly the Commercial Court), the Court of Appeal and the Supreme Court, as well as in arbitrations in London and overseas.

Pupil profile

Applicants must have at least a good 2:1, coupled with lively intelligence and strong advocacy skills (both oral and in writing). Chambers encourages applications from all outstanding candidates no matter what their background or academic discipline.

Pupillage

Chambers offers up to four (but typically two or three) 12 month pupillages each year (with a review after 6 months). Pupils will sit with four pupillage supervisors prior to the tenancy decision in July. Pupils will assist their pupil supervisors with their work, and accompany them to hearings. Pupils will, particularly after completion of the first three months of pupillage, also do work for other members of chambers.

Mini-pupillage

Funded and non-funded mini-pupillages offered. Up to 12 funded mini-pupillages with an award of £250 together with a guaranteed pupillage interview upon subsequent application through Pupillage Gateway. Applications for funded mini-pupillages must be received by 30 November and will be scheduled in the period 1 February to 31 May. Applicants may be invited to a short interview.

Non-funded mini-pupillages are available in 2 periods during the year. Applications for the period from 1 June to 30 September (excluding August) must be received by 31 March; applications for mini-pupillages in the period 1 October to 31 January must be received by 31 July.

All applications are to be in the form of a covering letter and must be made to the mini-pupillage secretary by email to mini-pupillage@7kbw.co.uk.

The CV should give a breakdown of all university examination results achieved to date.

Funding

A pupillage award of at least £60,000 will be available for the 2015/16 and 2016/2017 years, of which up to £15,000 may be drawn down during the BPTC.

.

No of Silks 25
No of Juniors 27
No of Pupils at least 2 and up to 4
Contact
Emma Hilliard (pupillage secretary)
Pupillage@7kbw.co.uk
Method of application
Pupillage Gateway
Pupillages (p.a.)
Up to 4 12-month pupillages offered
Required degree grade
Minimum 2:1 (law or non-law)
Remuneration for pupillage at least £60,000
Tenancies
Junior tenancies offered in last 3 years 4
No of tenants of 5 years call or under 7

7KBW
BARRISTERS

The Bar

Littleton Chambers

3 King's Bench Walk North, Temple, London EC4Y 7HR
Tel: (020) 7797 8600 Fax: (020) 7797 8699
Email: fschneider@littletonchambers.co.uk
Website: www.littletonchambers.co.uk

No of Silks 13
No of Juniors 38
No of Pupils currently 3
Contact   Felicity Schneider,   Administration Director
Method of application   Pupillage Gateway
Pupillages (p.a.)   12 month 2   Required degree level 2:1 (law or non-law)
Income   £55,000 award.   Earnings not included.

Chambers profile

Littleton Chambers is acknowledged as being a top class set in each of its main practice areas. Its success is based upon both the desire to maintain high professional standards and a willingness to embrace change. It prides itself on the skills of its tenants, not only as advocates and advisers on the law, but also for their analytical and practical skills.

Type of work undertaken

Littleton Chambers specialises in commercial litigation, employment law, professional negligence, sports law, mediation and arbitration.

Pupil profile

Chambers takes a considerable amount of care in choosing its pupils and prefers to recruit its tenants from persons who have completed a full 12 months of pupillage with chambers. Chambers endeavours to take on pupils who not only have good academic skills, but who also show flair for advocacy and the ability to understand practical commercial issues.

Pupillage

Chambers generally offers pupillage to two people each year.

During your 12 month pupillage you will have the benefit of three pupil supervisors in succession. Your pupil supervisors will provide support and guidance to you throughout your pupillage, ensuring that you understand not only the nuts and bolts of a barrister's work, but also the ethical constraints which are such a distinctive feature of chambers' professional life.

After six months pupillage, you will be entitled to take on your own work. Typically, pupils in Littleton Chambers have been briefed once or twice a week. Your pupil supervisor will provide assistance in the preparation of these briefs to ensure that your client receives the best possible service from you.

Mini-pupillage

Assessed mini-pupillage forms part of the pupillage application process. Mini-pupillages are NOT offered outside of this process.

Funding

Each pupillage is funded (currently £55,000 per year) and, if necessary, it is possible to draw down some of this funding during the year of Bar Finals.

LITTLETON

Maitland Chambers

7 Stone Buildings, Lincoln's Inn, London WC2A 3SZ
Tel: (020) 7406 1200 Fax: (020) 7406 1300
Email: clerks@maitlandchambers.com
Website: www.maitlandchambers.com

Chambers profile
Chambers UK has rated Maitland in the top rank of commercial chancery sets every year since 2001.

Type of work undertaken
Maitland is instructed on a wide range of business and property related cases – from major international commercial litigation to disputes over the family home. Its core areas of practice include commercial litigation, banking, financial services and regulation, civil fraud, insolvency and restructuring, media law, pensions, professional negligence, real property, charity law, trusts and tax. Much of the set's work is done in London (as well as in other parts of England and Wales), although instructions often have an international aspect, involving acting for clients and appearing in court abroad. Chambers' work is predominantly concerned with dispute resolution; but it also does non-contentious work in the private client field.

Pupil profile
Academically, Maitland looks for a first or upper second class degree. Pupils must have a sense of commercial practicality, be stimulated by the challenge of written and oral advocacy and have an aptitude for and general enjoyment of complex legal argument.

Pupillage
Maitland offers up to three pupillages, all of which are funded. All pupils in chambers are regarded as potential tenants.

Pupils spend their first three months in chambers with one pupil supervisor in order that the pupil can find his or her feet and establish a point of contact. For the balance of the pupillage year each pupil will sit with different pupil supervisors, usually for two months at a time. The set believes that it is important for pupils to see all of the different kinds of work done in chambers.

Chambers believes that oral advocacy remains a core skill of the commercial chancery barrister. The set provides in-house advocacy exercises for pupils during their pupillage. These take the form of mock hearings, prepared in advance from adapted sets of papers, with senior members of chambers acting as the tribunal. They provide detailed feedback after each exercise. These exercises are part of the assessment process and help develop essential court skills.

Mini-pupillages
Applications are considered three times a year; please see chambers' website for current deadlines. Applications should be made with a covering letter and CV specifying degree classification obtained (or if you are still doing a law degree listing marks obtained in university examinations to date) and sent clearly marked 'Mini-pupillage' to the Pupillage Secretary.

Funding
Chambers offers up to three 12-month pupillages, all of which are funded (£60,000 for pupils starting in October 2015). Up to £20,000 of the award may be drawn down in advance during the BPTC year or to pay BPTC fees. There is also a cashflow assistance scheme available at the start of practice as a tenant.

No of Silks 25
No of Juniors 40
No of Pupils up to 3

Contact
Valerie Piper
(Pupillage Secretary)
pupillage
@maitlandchambers.com

Method of application
See Chambers' website from January 2014. Application deadline for pupillage in 2015-16 is 4 February 2014

Pupillages (p.a.)
Up to 3 funded

Income
£60,000 p.a.

Tenancies
5 in last 3 years

maitland
CHAMBERS

The Bar

Matrix Chambers

Griffin Building, Gray's Inn, London WC1R 5LN
Tel: (020) 7404 3447 Fax: (020) 7404 3448
Email: matrix@matrixlaw.co.uk
Website: www.matrixlaw.co.uk
Twitter: @matrixchambers

No of Silks 25	
No of Juniors 46	
No of Pupils 1	

Contact
Lindsay Clarke
Tel: (020) 7404 3447

Method of application
Our application form can be found on our website. We are not a member of the Pupillage Gateway.

Pupillages (p.a.)
Up to 2 per year - 12 months

Tenancies
4 in the last 3 years

Chambers profile

Matrix was founded in 2000 with the aim of innovating the way legal services are delivered, and to move beyond traditional divisions at the Bar. Described as "one of the most recognisable sets at the UK Bar" and "home to many leaders in their field" (Chambers & Partners 2013), it is the people, approach and attitude that make the atmosphere at Matrix different. The bright and contemporary offices, the commitment to quality of service, the friendly professionalism of the staff and the lack of old fashioned language, hierarchies and attitudes demonstrated by the members are all core values that make Matrix a unique and great place to train.

Type of work undertaken

Although renowned for its high profile international and human rights work, Matrix also specialises in a unique crossover of practice areas including public, crime, EU/competition and commercial law. For the complete range of 25 international and domestic areas of law we cover, please visit the 'Areas of Practice' page on our website.

Pupil profile

Matrix welcomes applications from exceptional candidates from all backgrounds. For further details, please see our traineeship brochure on the 'Opportunities' page of our website.

Pupillage

Matrix offers up to two traineeships, both starting 1 October for 12 months. Traineeships are organised into four periods of three months each. Trainees' preferences are taken into account in assigning them supervisors. In each three month period, trainees will be assigned to a different supervisor with the objective of providing experience of a full range of legal practice. In their second two seats, trainees are encouraged to take on their own cases, in a supervised and well mentored way. Trainees will also be invited to attend internal and external continuing education seminars.

Mini-pupillages

Matrix do not offer mini-pupilages. Instead, we run a Student Open Day in April for those considering applying for traineeship. For more details, please visit our website.

Funding

£50,000 (£10,000 to be drawn down during the BPTC).

Monckton Chambers

1&2 Raymond Buildings, Gray's Inn, London WC1R 5NR
Tel: (020) 7405 7211 Fax: (020) 7405 2084
Email: pupillage@monckton.com
Website: www.monckton.com

| No of Silks 14 |
| No of Juniors 41 |
| No of pupils 1 |
| Contact |
| Claire Alderman |
| 020 7468 6345 |
| Method of application |
| Pupillage Gateway |
| Pupillages (p.a.) |
| Two 12 month pupillages |

Chambers profile

Monckton Chambers is recognised by both Chambers UK and The Legal 500 as a leading set in our core areas of EU/competition, indirect tax and public and administrative law. We provide specialist advocacy services in courts and tribunals across many jurisdictions. Our members have a vast range of experience and an unrivalled knowledge of European and domestic law. We are renowned for our intellectual rigour and commercial focus.

Pupil profile

Monckton recruits pupils with the expectation of making an offer of tenancy, should they meet the required standard. Most candidates successful in their application for pupillage will have a First Class Honours degree (although it need not be in law) or a graduate degree in law.

Monckton is looking for candidates who have the ability, personal skills, and willingness to learn which will enable them to get the most out of our pupillage training programme and to go on to enjoy successful careers as tenants in our chambers. Successful candidates will therefore need to demonstrate: academic excellence, an ability and appetite for intellectually challenging legal work, excellent communication skills (both oral and written), an ability to reason and argue persuasively, and the spirit and personality needed to succeed at the self-employed Bar.

Pupillage

Monckton provides training of the highest quality delivered by, and through the opportunity of working with, barristers who are leaders in their fields and who fight cases and advise clients in the context of rapidly developing areas of law. Training is an interactive process in which we seek to accommodate the pupil's individual ambitions and interests, and help them to develop the legal knowledge, practical skills and sure judgement that will enable them to enjoy a lifetime of professional success.

Mini-pupillages

Please refer to www.monckton.com for further information on Monckton's mini pupillage scheme.

Funding

Monckton offer a pupillage award of £60,000.

4 New Square

4 New Square, Lincoln's Inn, London WC2A 3RJ
Tel: (020) 7822 2000 Fax: (020) 7822 2001
Website: www.4newsquare.com

No of Silks 19
No of Juniors 56
No of Pupils 2
Contact
Georgie Ruane
Tel (020) 7822 2000
Email
pupillage@4newsquare.com
Method of application
Online www.4newsquare.com
Pupillages (p.a.)
Up to 2

Chambers profile

4 New Square is a leading commercial and civil set of barristers comprising 75 members, of whom 19 are Queen's Counsel, with particular expertise and a high reputation in the areas of insurance work and claims against professionals. 4 New Square enjoys a formidable reputation in its principle areas of work: commercial litigation and arbitration, insurance and reinsurance, professional liability and construction and engineering. Its members are also recognised as leading practitioners in the fields of chancery litigation, consumer law, costs litigation, financial services, pensions, product liability, professional discipline, public law and sports law.

Members of 4 New Square appear in a wide range of tribunals (court and arbitral) and are regularly instructed to take landmark cases to the Court of Appeal and the Supreme Court. Recent examples include, the 'Trigger' Litigation (Supreme Court), the Atomic Veterans Litigation (Supreme Court), Jones v Kaney (Supreme Court) and Motto v Trafigura (Court of Appeal). Jackson & Powell on Professional Negligence (the main text in this area) is written and edited by current members of chambers. Chambers attracts a large amount of junior advocacy work which reflects the emphasis on developing pupils and junior tenants into experienced advocates to equip them for a successful career at the Bar.

Type of work undertaken

Professional liability, product liability, chancery, commercial dispute resolution, construction and engineering, costs, international arbitration, insurance and reinsurance, financial services and banking, offsure, human rights, administrative and public law and sports law.

Pupil profile

Chambers does not stream its pupils. Each has an equal prospect of securing a tenancy. Selection criteria: evidence of intellectual ability; potential as an advocate; personal qualities such as self-reliance, integrity, reliability and the ability to work effectively with colleagues and clients; motivation. Equal opportunities: Chambers observes a policy of equal opportunities in accordance with the Bar Code of Conduct. All applicants are required to complete the Bar Council Equality Code questionnaire. This is used for monitoring purposes only.

Pupillage

The first six months: You will go to court and attend conferences with your pupil supervisor. You will also assist your pupil supervisor with their written work: carrying out written advisory and drafting work on their current papers and undertaking detailed research on the law. The second six months: During your second six months, as well as continuing with work for your pupil supervisor, you will take on an increasing amount of your own court work. Chambers places a strong emphasis on advocacy and supports its pupils in gaining valuable practical experience. You can expect to be in court on your own about once a week up to the tenancy decision and potentially on a more regular basis thereafter. You will be expected to complete three assessed pieces of work for members of chambers who are not your pupil supervisors. Advocacy: You will also take part in an assessed moot. Workshop training sessions are run to help you prepare for the moots. Environment: Chambers aims to provide a friendly and sociable atmosphere. Pupils are included in chambers' social events throughout the year.

Mini-pupillages

Mini-pupillages generally last for two days and take place in specific weeks in May, July, November and December of each year. Chambers will pay travelling expenses of £50. Applications must be made on chambers' own mini-pupillage application form, which is available to download from our website.

NEW SQUARE

The Bar

XXIV Old Buildings

XXIV Old Buildings, 24 Old Buildings, Lincoln's Inn, London, WC2A 3UP
Tel: (020) 7691 2424 Fax: (0870) 460 2178
Website: xxiv.co.uk

No of Silks 9	
No of Juniors 29	
No of Pupils 2	
Contact	
Steven Thompson	
Method of application	
Letter and CV. Please see	
www.xxiv.co.uk for guidance	
Pupillages (p.a.)	
2	
Tenancies	
Usually 1-2 per year	
Other offices	
Geneva	

Chambers profile

XXIV Old Buildings is a commercial Chancery chambers of 38 barristers based in Lincoln's Inn. Its members provide specialist legal advice and advocacy services in the UK and worldwide on a range of contentious, advisory and transactional matters to the financial, commercial and professional community and to private individuals. Our expertise covers all areas of dispute resolution, litigation and arbitration.

Type of work undertaken

The barristers at XXIV Old Buildings specialise in a variety of commercial Chancery areas with a particular emphasis on trusts and estates and commercial litigation. Areas in which members regularly take instructions include arbitration; aviation; charities; civil fraud, asset tracing and recovery; company; construction and projects; financial services; insolvency; international and offshore; partnership; pensions; professional negligence; real estate litigation and trusts, probate and estates.

XXIV Old Buildings is known for its pre-eminence in international and offshore work, both contentious and advisory. With offices in both London and Geneva, the barristers at XXIV Old Buildings regularly appear in courts and tribunals in offshore centres including the British Virgin Islands, the Cayman Islands, Bermuda, Jersey, the Isle of Man, the DIFC, the Bahamas, Gibraltar, Hong Kong and Malaysia.

Pupillage

The set likes to recruit its junior members from those who have undertaken pupillage with the set. Chambers are therefore careful that its pupils acquire all the skills necessary to make them successful commercial Chancery barristers. During a 12 month pupillage, a pupil will have, on average, four pupil supervisors with whom they will spend the majority of their time. Each year the set is looking for pupils with a first or 2:1 degree, though not necessarily in law, who have an enthusiasm for the type of work the set does, sound judgment and the application required to succeed in a very competitive and intellectually demanding environment. Application is by CV and covering letter.

The closing date for applications for pupillages commencing in October 2014 is 9am on 1 February 2013.

Mini pupillages

Chambers accepts applications for mini-pupillages throughout the year. Application should be made by CV and covering letter. Please see our website www.xxiv.co.uk for details of how to apply.

Funding

Up to £65,000 per pupil.

Old Square Chambers

10-11 Bedford Row, London, WC1R 4BU DX: 1046 Chancery Lane
Tel: (020) 7269 0300 Fax: (020) 7405 1384
Email: clerks@oldsquare.co.uk
Website: www.oldsquare.co.uk

No of Silks 15	
No of Juniors 58	
No of Pupils 2	
Contact	
Betsan Criddle	
Gudula Crawford	
Method of application	
Pupillage Portal	
Pupillages (p.a.)	
2 12-month pupillages	
Income	
£40,000 (£30,000 award plus £10,000 guaranteed earnings)	
Plus additional earnings	
Tenancies	
6 in last 3 years	
Annexes	
Bristol	

Chambers profile

Old Square Chambers is recognised as a premier set in its core specialist areas of employment and discrimination, personal injury and environmental law. Chambers' defining quality is excellence, both in the specialist legal expertise it has to offer and in the customer service which it provides. Members and staff have a reputation for being approachable and unstuffy. Many members hold part-time judicial positions, sit on specialist panels, act as mediators and edit or contribute to leading practitioner texts.

Type of work undertaken

Chambers' strength lies in the depth of experience and expertise in its core practice areas. The Employment and Discrimination Group is widely regarded as one of the foremost in the UK. Work is in all aspects of employment and discrimination law. Clients range from individual employees and directors to major trade unions, private and public sector organisations. Personal injury work covers all aspects of this wide-ranging and complex field, from employers' liability and road traffic claims to high-value head, brain and spinal injury cases, with particular expertise in disaster litigation and multi-party actions. In environmental law, chambers has been at the forefront of developing litigation in the area of toxic torts. Members appear in high-profile multi-party claims arising from pollution of various kinds. Alongside its core areas chambers also has expertise in professional discipline, clinical negligence, product liability, public inquiries, health and safety and ADR.

Pupil profile

Chambers assesses candidates on intellectual ability (usually a first or upper second degree will be required), potential as an advocate, interest in chambers' fields of practice, ability to cope with hard work and pressure and interpersonal skills.

Mini-pupillages

Chambers runs a programme of mini-pupillages during the summer. Applications should be made through chambers' website.

Funding

The current award is £40,000 (£30,000 award plus £10,000 guaranteed earnings). Pupils keep additional earnings from their second six.

OLD SQUARE
CHAMBERS

Pump Court Tax Chambers

16 Bedford Row, London WC1R 4EF
Tel: (0207) 414 8080 Fax: (0207) 414 8099
Email: clerks@pumptax.com
Website: www.pumptax.com

Chambers profile

Pump Court Tax Chambers is the largest specialist tax set.

Type of work undertaken

All areas of tax work (both contentious and non-contentious) are covered. On the corporate side, clients typically include the 'Big 4' accountants and 'magic circle' solicitors sending a wide variety of work such as M&A, reconstructions and demergers and structured finance. Chambers' private client work comes from a broad range of sources – city solicitors, accountants, regional firms, chartered tax advisers and IFAs, who act for private individuals, trustees and landed estates. Much of chambers' work concerns large scale litigation (especially in the field of VAT) and members of chambers regularly appear in the Tax Tribunals, the High Court, the Court of Appeal, the Supreme Court and the CJEU.

Pupil profile

Chambers looks for applicants who are intelligent, articulate and well-motivated. Successful candidates will have at least a 2:1 honours degree (although not necessarily in law). Prior experience of studying tax law is not required.

Pupillage

Chambers offers up to two 12-month pupillages (terminable after six months by either party) to those wishing to practise full-time at the Bar. Pupillage normally commences in October each year. Pupils will have at least three pupil supervisors and will also sit with other members of chambers so as to receive a broad training in all aspects of the work of chambers.

Mini-pupillages

The programme runs throughout the year. Applications should be made via email to pupils@pumptax.com with accompanying CV and marked for the attention of the Pupillage Secretary.

Funding

Awards of up to £50,000 are available. The pupillage committee has discretion to consider applications for up to £12,000 of the pupillage award to be advanced during the BPTC year.

No of Silks 11
No of Juniors 23
No of Pupils 1 to 2 in any given year

Contact
Thomas Chacko
pupils@pumptax.com

Method of application
CV and covering letter (non-Pupillage Gateway) by 3 February 2014

Pupillages (p.a.)
Up to 2 funded

Tenancies
4 in the last 3 years

PUMP COURT TAX CHAMBERS

Quadrant Chambers (Lionel Persey QC & Simon Rainey QC)

Quadrant House, 10 Fleet Street, London EC4Y 1AU
Tel: (020) 7583 4444 Fax: (020) 7583 4455
Email: pupillage@quadrantchambers.com
Website: www.quadrantchambers.com

No of Silks 16
No of Juniors 39
Contact
Pupillage Secretrary
Method of application
Chambers' application form
Pupillages (p.a.)
1st 6 months 3
2nd 6 months 3
12 months
Required degree
1st or high 2:1
Income
1st 6 months
£30,000
2nd 6 months
£30,000
Earnings not included
Tenancies
Current tenants who served pupillage in chambers 34
Junior tenancies offered in last 3 years 5
No of tenants of 5 years call or under 9

Chambers profile

Quadrant Chambers is a leading set of barristers specialising in commercial law. We act as advocates in courts, arbitrations and inquiries, and provide specialist legal advice to clients from around the world in a wide range of industry areas. Many of us are qualified to practice in other jurisdictions, including Australia, the BVI, California, Germany, Hong Kong, New York and South Africa. Distinguished former members of chambers have gone on to chair public enquiries and to sit as judges in the High Court (QBD, Commercial, Administrative and Admiralty Court), European General Court, Court of Appeal, House of Lords, Privy Council and UK Supreme Court.

Type of work undertaken

We undertake all types of commercial law. We are market leaders in shipping and aviation, and have an excellent reputation in banking and finance, energy, commercial Chancery, insurance and reinsurance, insolvency and restructuring commodities and international trade, commercial litigation and arbitration, and sport and media. Our work has a strongly international flavour, and much of it involves international clients.

Pupil profile

We look for candidates with a very strong academic background. Successful applicants will generally have (or be predicted) a first class degree, and they must have / be predicted at least a high 2:1 to apply. They must have excellent analytical abilities, outstanding written and oral communication skills and the ability to perform under pressure. They must also be able to demonstrate that they have the commitment, energy and robustness to succeed at the Commercial Bar.

Successful candidates often read law for their first degree, and an increasing number also have postgraduate law degrees, but these are not pre-requisites, and we welcome applications from candidates who have studied any serious academic subject at university.

Pupillage

We offer up to three pupillages of 12 months' duration each year. We aim to develop in our pupils the skills, knowledge and judgment they will need to become successful commercial barristers. During their first six months, pupils sit with two pupil supervisors for three months each, and are exposed to a wide range of commercial work. Tenancy decisions are made at the end of June.

We hold an open day each December for those in the second year of university or above. This is an opportunity to meet the barristers and clerks, and learn about life at the Commercial Bar. Places are limited. See our website for details.

We do not use the Pupillage Gateway to manage our pupillage applications. There are three stages to our application process: (i) our own online application form, (ii) test set, and (iii) interview. See our website for details.

Mini pupillages

Mini-pupillages are available in March / April, July and September of each year. Places are limited. See our website for details.

Funding

Pupils receive awards of £60,000, part of which may be advanced during the BPTC year. They also have the opportunity to do fee-earning work during their 2nd 6.

quadrant chambers

The Bar

Queen Elizabeth Buildings (QEB)

Chambers of
Lewis Marks QC

Queen Elizabeth Building, Temple, London EC4Y 9BS
Tel: (020) 7797 7837 Fax: (020) 7353 5422
Email: clerks@qeb.co.uk
Website: www.qeb.co.uk

Number of Silks 6
Number of Juniors 26
Number of Pupils up to 3
Contact
Miss Amy Kisser, Secretary to
the Pupillage Committee
Method of Application
Pupilage Gateway
Pupillages
Up to three 12-month
pupillages
Award
£25,000 minimum pa +
earnings in second six and from
devilling
Tenancies
Five tenancies offered in the
last three years
Annexes
None

Chambers profile

QEB is a leading set of family law chambers, particularly well-known for dealing with the financial consequences of divorce, but with immense experience in all aspects of family law including: jurisdictional disputes, foreign divorces, pre-marital agreements, civil partnerships, injunctions both financial and domestic, private law child work, child abduction, Inheritance Act claims and disputes between former cohabitees. In addition some members practise in general common law, particularly personal injury and professional negligence work.

QEB has been established for well over 100 years and is consistently rated as one of the top-ranking sets for family law. Members of QEB have been involved in many of the most important cases of legal principle, including: White, Sorrell, Miller, Spencer, Marano, Robson, Schofield, Jones and Prest.

Many members of chambers have continued into high judicial office. At present, our former members include: Lord Wilson in the Supreme Court and five out of 19 Family Division judges.

Pupil profile

The practice of family law is infinitely varied and clients come from all walks of life. International and conflict of laws issues arise increasingly often. An ability to deal not only with complex financial disputes, often involving commercial issues, but also with child-related or other emotionally fraught and sensitive situations, is essential. We are looking for applicants with a strong academic record (minimum 2:1 law or non-law degree save in exceptional circumstances), good legal and analytical skills, and an ability to communicate sensitively with a wide range of people at a critical time in their lives.

Pupillage

QEB offers up to three pupillages each year. A 12-month pupillage at QEB offers top-quality training and very good financial support in a busy, friendly environment. Pupils have three pupil supervisors, but are also encouraged to work with other tenants at all levels to gain a broad experience of our work. Pupils are automatically considered for tenancy, and our new tenants are only recruited from our pupils. QEB's reputation is such that where a pupil is not taken on, he/she is usually well placed elsewhere.

Chambers is a part of the Pupillage Gateway system. Applicants should apply in the summer 2014 season for a pupillage beginning in October 2015. Please consult the Pupillage Gateway website for details of the timetable.

Mini-pupillages

Applications for mini-pupillages are made by CV and covering letter to the Mini-Pupillage Secretary. Please consult our website at www.qeb.co.uk for full details.

Funding

Chambers offers a pupillage award of £25,000 pa minimum, plus earnings in the second six and from devilling. Pupils do not pay chambers' expenses or clerks' fees. Chambers also funds the compulsory Inn Advocacy and Practice Management Training Courses.

The Bar

Serle Court

Serle Court, 6 New Square, Lincoln's Inn, London WC2A 3QS
Tel: (020) 7242 6105 Fax: (020) 7405 4004
Email: pupillage@serlecourt.co.uk
Website: www.serlecourt.co.uk

No of Silks 20	
No of Juniors 34	
No of Pupils 2	

Contact
Kathryn Barry
Tel (020) 7242 6105

Method of application
Chambers application form,
available from website or
chambers. Not a member
of Pupillage Gateway.

Pupillages
Two 12-month pupillages

Tenancies
Up to 2 per annum

Chambers profile

Serle Court has "a phenomenally good reputation that is really well deserved" with "staggeringly fine commercial ability and a marvellous business-like approach". It has an "outstandingly welcoming attitude, charming informality" and "no other set boasts quite so unstuffy an attitude" (*Chambers UK*). Serle Court is one of the leading commercial chancery sets with 54 barristers including 20 silks. Widely recognised as a leading set, Chambers is recommended in 21 different areas of practice by the legal directories. Chambers has a stimulating and inclusive work environment and a forward looking approach.

Type of work undertaken

Litigation, arbitration, mediation and advisory services across the full range of chancery and commercial practice areas including: administrative and public law, banking, civil fraud, commercial litigation, company, financial services, human rights, insolvency, insurance and reinsurance, intellectual property, partnership and LLP, professional negligence, property, sports, entertainment and media and trusts and probate.

Pupil profile

Candidates are well-rounded people, from any background. Chambers looks for highly motivated individuals with outstanding intellectual ability, combined with a practical approach, sound judgement, an ability to develop good client relationships and the potential to become excellent advocates. Serle Court has a reputation for "consistent high quality" and for having "responsive and able team members" and seeks the same qualities in pupils. Chambers generally requires a degree classification of a good 2:1 as a minimum. Serle Court is committed to equality and diversity and encourages and welcomes applications from women, people of minority ethnic origin and people with disabilities, as well as candidates from other groups which are under represented in the legal sector.

Pupillage

Pupils sit with four pupil supervisors in order to experience a broad range of work. Two pupils are recruited each year and Chambers offers: an excellent preparation for successful practice; a genuinely friendly and supportive environment; the opportunity to learn from some of the leading barristers in their field; a good prospect of tenancy.

Mini-pupillages

About 30 available each year. Apply online at www.serlecourt.co.uk.

Funding

Serle Court offers awards of £60,000 for 12 months, of which up to £20,000 can be drawn down during the BPTC year. It also provides an income guarantee worth up to £120,000 over the first two years of practice.

serle court

The Bar

South Square

3-4 South Square, Gray's Inn, London WC1R 5HP
Tel: (020) 7696 9900 Fax: (020) 7696 9911
Email: pupillage@southsquare.com
Website: www.southsquare.com

No of Silks 21	
No of Juniors 20	
No of Pupils 2	
Contact Pupillage Administrator Tel (020) 7696 9900	
Method of application Mini-Pupillage - CV with covering letter Pupillage - application form (available to download from the website)	
Pupillages (p.a.) Up to two 12-month pupillages offered each year	

Chambers profile

Chambers is an established successful commercial set, involved in high-profile international and domestic commercial litigation. Members of chambers have been centrally involved in some of the most important commercial cases of the last decade including Lehman Brothers, Kaupthing, Landsbanki, Woolworths, Madoff Securities and Stanford International.

Type of work undertaken

South Square has a pre-eminent reputation in insolvency and restructuring law and specialist expertise in related areas including banking, financial services, company law, trusts and asset tracing and general commercial litigation. A significant proportion of our work involves international elements: members are called for specific cases in Hong Kong, the Cayman Islands, the British Virgin Islands and Bermuda, and other recent cases have had links to Poland, Russia, Slovakia, Switzerland, Germany, Jersey, Singapore and Dubai.

Pupil profile

Chambers seeks to recruit the highest calibre of candidates who must be prepared to commit themselves to establishing a successful practice and maintaining chambers' position at the forefront of the modern Commercial Bar. The minimum academic qualification is a 2:1 degree. A number of members have degrees in law, and some have BCL or other postgraduate qualifications. Others have non-law degrees and have gone on to take the Graduate Diploma in Law.

Pupillage

Pupils are welcomed into all areas of chambers' life and are provided with an organised programme designed to train and equip them for practice in a dynamic and challenging environment. Pupils sit with a number of pupil supervisors for periods of six to eight weeks and the set looks to recruit at least one tenant every year from its pupils.

Mini-pupillages

Chambers also offers funded and unfunded mini-pupillages – please see the set's website for further details.

SOUTH SQUARE

Sponsorship & awards

Currently £60,000 per annum (reviewable annually). A proportion of the pupillage award may be paid for living expenses during the BPTC.

The Bar

2 Temple Gardens (Chambers of Benjamin Browne QC)

2 Temple Gardens, London EC4Y 9AY DX: 134 Chancery Lane
Tel: (020) 7822 1200 Fax: (020) 7822 1300
Email: clerks@2tg.co.uk
Website: www.2tg.co.uk

No of Silks 12	
No of Juniors 40	
No of Pupils 3	
Contact	
Katie Seingier	
Pupillage Administrator	
Method of application	
Pupillage Gateway (Summer)	
Pupillages (p.a.)	
Up to three 12-month pupillages	
Award 2014 £60,000	

Chambers profile

2tg is regarded as one of the leading commercial and civil law barristers' chambers. The firm specialises in professional negligence, insurance and personal injury and also has significant practices in banking, employment, technology, construction and clinical negligence, alongside strength in private international law.

Pupil profile

Academically, you will need at least a good 2:1 degree to be considered. Chambers look for applicants who work well in teams and have the ability to get on with solicitors, clients and other members of chambers.

Pupillage

Chambers offers one of the most generously funded, well-structured and enjoyable pupillages at the Bar. It takes pupillage very seriously and aims to recruit the best applicants, and to ensure that its pupils have an excellent foundation from which to start a successful career at the Bar. Pupils have three different pupil supervisors during pupillage, and will also do work for other members of chambers. The aim is for pupils to experience as much of chambers' work as possible during their pupillage year.

Mini-pupillages

Chambers welcomes 'mini-pupils'. Generally applicants will only be considered after their first year of a law degree or during CPE. Mini-pupillages are a good way to experience life at 2tg first hand. Most mini-pupillages are 2-3 days long. We aim to show you a wide range of barristers' work during your mini-pupillage. It offers an assessment at the completion of your mini-pupillage and encourages you to give feedback too. Chambers also offers help with reasonable expenses (up to £50).

Mini-pupillages are usually unfunded but a few funded mini-pupillages (maximum £250 per person) are also available.

Funding

Chambers offers up to three 12-month pupillages, all of which are funded. Its pupillage award for 2014 is £60,000. Please see our website www.2tg.co.uk for details of the award for 2014.

The Bar

3 Verulam Buildings (Ali Malek QC)

3 Verulam Buildings, Gray's Inn, London WC1R 5NT   DX: LDE 331
Tel: (020) 7831 8441 Fax: (020) 7831 8479
Email: chambers@3vb.com
Website: www.3vb.com

Chambers profile

Sitting comfortably and spaciously in a newly refurbished and expanded row of buildings in Gray's Inn, 3VB is one of the largest and most highly regarded commercial sets, its members being involved in many of the leading cases. Recent examples include the Beresovsky/Abramovitch dispute, Belmont Park Investments v BNY Corporate Trustees, The Rangers Football Club plc v Collyer Bristow LLP and Tom Hicks/George Gillett litigation.

Type of work undertaken

3VB's 22 silks and 44 juniors lead the field in banking and financial services, and are also among the top practitioners in the fields of professional negligence, civil fraud, insurance, arbitration, and company and insolvency. Chambers also has significant expertise in IT and telecommunications, energy, construction, and media and entertainment.

Pupil profile

Commercial practice is intellectually demanding and 3VB seeks the brightest and the best. The typical successful applicant will have a first or upper second class degree (not necessarily in law) from a good university, with good mooting experience and proven experience of the commercial bar (generally through mini-pupillages with us or elsewhere). Many have a Master's degree or other legal or commercial experience.

Pupillage

Chambers seeks to recruit up to three 12-month pupils each year through the Pupillage Gateway. Chambers is committed to recruiting new tenants from its pupils whenever it can. Although tenancy is offered to all pupils who make the grade, on average two out of three pupils are successful in any one year.

Mini-pupillages

Two-day mini-pupillages are an important part of chambers' selection procedure and it is strongly encouraged that prospective applicants for pupillage apply for a mini-pupillage (e-mail Christopher Bond at minipupillage@3vb.com, attaching a detailed CV).

Funding

For the year 2015/2016, the annual award will be at least £60,000, up to £20,000 of which may be drawn during the BPTC year.

No of Silks 22
No of Juniors 44
No of Pupils 1

Contact
Miss Charlotte Eborall
(Pupillage)
Christopher Bond and Anne Jeavons
(Mini-Pupillage)

Method of application
Gateway (Pupillage); CV with detailed breakdown of examination results and covering letter explaining why 3VB (Mini-pupillage)

Pupillages (p.a.)
12 months up to 3
Required degree grade
High 2:1/First

Income
In excess of £60,000 plus any earnings

Tenancies
Current tenants who served pupillage in Chambers approx 41
Junior tenancies offered in last 3 years 9
No of tenants of 5 years call or under 12

Wilberforce Chambers

8 New Square, Lincoln's Inn, London WC2A 3QP
Tel: (020) 7306 0102 Fax: (020) 7306 0095
Email: pupillage@wilberforce.co.uk
Website: www.wilberforce.co.uk

No of Silks 22
No of Juniors 32
Method of application
Chambers application form available from website
Pupillages (p.a.)
2 x 12 months
Mini-pupillages
Total of 28 places
Award
£65,000
Minimum qualification
2:1 degree
Tenancies in last 3 years
5

Chambers profile

Wilberforce Chambers is a leading commercial chancery set of chambers and is involved in some of the most commercially important and cutting-edge litigation and advisory work undertaken by the Bar today. Members are recognised by the key legal directories as leaders in their fields. Instructions come from top UK and international law firms, providing a complex and rewarding range of work for international companies, financial institutions, well-known names, sports and media organisations, pension funds, commercial landlords and tenants, and private individuals. Clients demand high intellectual performance and client-care standards but in return the reward is a successful and fulfilling career at the Bar. Chambers has grown in size in recent years but retains a united and friendly 'family' atmosphere.

Type of work undertaken

All aspects of traditional and modern chancery work including property, pensions, private client, trust and taxation, professional negligence, general commercial litigation, banking, company, financial services, intellectual property and information technology, sports and media and charities.

Pupil profile

Chambers looks to offer two 12-month pupillages. You should possess high intellectual ability, excellent communication skills and a strong motivation to do commercial chancery work. You need to be mature and confident, have the ability to work with others and analyse legal problems clearly, demonstrating commercial and practical good sense. Chambers looks for people who have real potential to join as tenants at the end of their pupillage. Wilberforce takes great care in its selection process and puts effort into providing an excellent pupillage. There is a minimum requirement of a 2:1 degree in law or another subject, and Wilberforce has a track record of taking on GDL students.

Pupillage

Chambers operates a well-structured pupillage programme aimed at providing you with a broad experience of commercial chancery practice under several pupil supervisors with whom you will be able to develop your skills. Wilberforce aims to reach a decision about tenancy after approximately 9-10 months, but all pupils are entitled to stay for the remainder of their pupillage on a full pupillage award.

Mini-pupillages

Wilberforce encourages potential candidates for pupillage to undertake a mini-pupillage in order to learn how chambers operates, to meet its members and to see the type of work that they do - but a mini-pupillage is not a prerequisite for pupillage. Wilberforce runs four separate mini-pupillage weeks (two in December, one at Easter and one in July). Please visit the website for an application form and further information.

Funding

Wilberforce offers a generous and competitive pupillage award which is reviewed annually with the intention that it should be in line with the highest awards available. The award for 2015 is £65,000 for 12 months and is paid in monthly instalments. A proportion of the award (up to £20,000) can be drawn down during the BPTC year.

WILBERFORCE CHAMBERS

Contacts

The Law Society
113 Chancery Lane,
London WC2A 1PL
Tel: 020 7242 1222
www.lawsociety.org.uk

Solicitors Regulation Authority
Ipsley Court,
Berrington Close,
Redditch B98 0DT
Tel: 0870 606 2555
E-mail: contactcentre@sra.org.uk
www.sra.org.uk

Junior Lawyers Division
The Law Society,
113 Chancery Lane,
London WC2 A 1PL
Helpline: 0800 328 4203
E-mail: juniorlawyers@lawsociety.org.uk
www.juniorlawyers.lawsociety.org.uk

The Bar Council
289-293 High Holborn,
London WC1V 7HZ
Tel: 020 7242 0082
www.barcouncil.org.uk

Bar Standards Board
289-293 High Holborn
London WC1V 7HZ
Tel: 020 7611 1444
www.barstandardsboard.org.uk

Gray's Inn, Education Department
8 South Square, Gray's Inn,
London WC1R 5ET
Tel: 020 7458 7900
E-mail: quinn.clarke@graysinn.org.uk
www.graysinn.info

Inner Temple, Education & Training Department
Treasury Office, Inner Temple,
London EC4Y 7HL
Tel: 020 7797 8208
E-mail: ffulton@innertemple.org.uk
www.innertemple.org.uk

Lincoln's Inn, Students' Department
Treasury Office, Lincoln's Inn,
London WC2A 3TL
Tel: 020 7405 1393
www.lincolnsinn.org.uk

Middle Temple, Students' Department
Treasury Office, Middle Temple Lane,
London EC4Y 9AT
Tel: 020 7427 4800
E-mail: members@middle-temple.co.uk
www.middletemple.org.uk

Chartered Institute of Legal Executives
Kempston Manor,
Kempston,
Bedfordshire MK42 7AB
Tel: 01234 841000
E-mail: info@ilex.org.uk
www.ilex.org.uk

National Association of Licensed Paralegals
Canterbury Court,
Kennington Business Park,
1-3 Brixton Road,
London SW9 6DE
Tel: 0845 8627000
E-mail: info@nationalparalegals.co.uk
www.nationalparalegals.com

Crown Prosecution Service
Rose Court,
2 Southwark Bridge,
London SE1 9HS
Tel: 020 3357 0000
E-mail: recruitment@cps.gsi.gov.uk
www.cps.gov.uk

Citizens Advice Bureau
Head Office, Myddelton House,
115-123 Pentonville Road,
London N1 9LZ
Tel: 020 7833 2181
Get Advice: 08444 111444
www.citizensadvice.org.uk

Law Centres Federation
64 Great Eastern Street,
London, EC2A 3QR
E-mail: info@lawcentres.org.uk
www.lawcentres.org.uk
Tel: 020 77499120

Free Representation Unit
Ground Floor, 60 Gray's Inn Road,
London, WC1X 8LU
Tel: 020 7611 9555
www.thefru.org.uk

The Bar Lesbian & Gay Group
E-mail: contactus@blagg.org
www.blagg.org

Lesbian & Gay Lawyers Association
c/o Alternative Family Law,
3 Southwark Street,
London SE1 1RQ
Tel: 020 7407 4007
E-mail: andrea@lagla.org
www.lagla.org.uk

Interlaw Diversity Forum (LGBT)
www.interlawdiversityforum.org

LawWorks
National Pro Bono Centre,
48 Chancery Lane,
London WCA2 1JF
Tel: 020 7092 3940
www.lawworks.org.uk

MLAW (The Association for Muslim Lawyers)
Meridien House,
42 Upper Berkeley Street,
London, W1H 5QJ
E-mail: info@muslimlawyer.co.uk
Tel: 020 75350798
www.muslimlawyer.co.uk

The Society of Asian Lawyers
Mr Sailesh Mehta,
18 Red Lion Court,
London, EC4A 3EB

E-mail: nick@sethi.co.uk
www.societyofasianlawyers.org

Society of Black Lawyers
www.blacklawyer.org
The Association of Muslim Lawyers
E-mail: info@aml.org.uk
www.aml.org.uk

The Association of Women Barristers
E-mail: fj@33cllaw.com
www.womenbarristers.co.uk

The Group for Solicitors with Disabilities
113 Chancery Lane,
London WC2A 1PL
Tel: 020 7320 5793
E-mail: Judith.McDermott@lawsociety.org.uk
www.gsdnet.org.uk

LPC/CPE Central Applications Board
PO Box 84, Guildford,
Surrey GU3 1YX
Tel: 01483 301282
E-mail: lpc@lawcabs.ac.uk
www.lawcabs.ac.uk/gdl

Pupillage Portal
E-mail: enquiries@Pupillage-portal.com
www.pupillages.com

c/o The General Council of the Bar,
289-293 High Holborn,
London WC1V 7HZ
Tel: 020 7242 0082
Career Development Loans
Tel: (freephone) 0800 585505
www.direct.gov.uk

The Bar

Notes